LINCOLN CHRISTIAN COLLEGE

P9-CCS-262

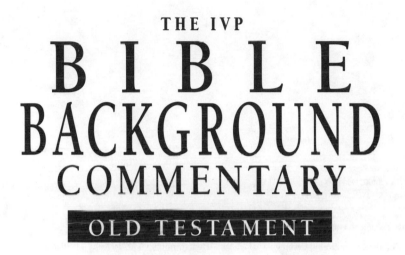

THE IVP

BIBLE
BACKGROUND
COMMENTARY

OLD TESTAMENT

John H. Walton
Victor H. Matthews &
Mark W. Chavalas

ivp

InterVarsity Press
Downers Grove, Illinois

InterVarsity Press
P.O. Box 1400, Downers Grove, IL 60515
World Wide Web: www.ivpress.com
E-mail: mail@ivpress.com

©2000 by John H. Walton, Victor H. Matthews and Mark W. Chavalas

The IVP Bible Background Commentary Genesis—Deuteronomy ©1997 by John H. Walton and Victor H. Matthews

All rights reserved. No part of this book may be reproduced in any form without written permission from InterVarsity Press.

InterVarsity Press® is the book-publishing division of InterVarsity Christian Fellowship/USA®, a student movement active on campus at hundreds of universities, colleges and schools of nursing in the United States of America, and a member movement of the International Fellowship of Evangelical Students. For information about local and regional activities, write Public Relations Dept., InterVarsity Christian Fellowship/USA, 6400 Schroeder Rd., P.O. Box 7895, Madison, WI 53707-7895.

All Scripture quotations, unless otherwise indicated, are taken from the Holy Bible, New International Version®. NIV®. Copyright ©1973, 1978, 1984 by International Bible Society. Used by permission of Zondervan Publishing House. All rights reserved.

Charts on pages 821-22 taken from Chronological & Background Charts of the Old Testament by John H. Walton. Copyright ©1978 by The Zondervan Corporation. Used by permission of Zondervan Publishing House.

Cover photograph: ©Daniel Blatt

ISBN 0-8308-1419-1

Printed in the United States of America ∞

Library of Congress Cataloging-in-Publication Data

Walton, John H., 1952-
  The IVP background Bible commentary : Old Testament / John H. Walton, Victor H.
Matthews, & Mark W. Chavalas.
    p. cm.
  Includes bibliographical references and index.
  ISBN 0-8308-1419-1 (cloth : alk. paper)
    1. Bible. O.T.—Commentaries. I. Matthews, Victor Harold. II. Chavalas, Mark W.
  (Mark William), 1954- III. Title.

BS1151.2 .W35 2000
221.7—dc21

                                                                                      00-057545

20	19	18	17	16	15	14	13	12	11	10	9	8	7	6	5	4	3	2	1
17	16	15	14	13	12	11	10	09	08	07	06	05	04	03	02	01	00		

Contents

15.60 *

99799

Preface

This book is an attempt to fill a particular niche in the vast field of one volume commentaries on the Bible. Rather than addressing all the varied elements of theology, literary structure, word meanings, history of scholarship, and so on, we have focused on the task of providing background information to the text.

Some might wonder what significance background information has for the interpretation of the text. What is it that we might expect to gain from knowing what this commentary seeks to make available? It has been rightly observed that the theological message of the Bible is not dependent on knowing where the places are or what the cultural background was. It is also correct to observe that one could gather all the proof from history and archaeology that, for instance, there actually was an Israelite exodus from Egypt, but that would still not prove that God orchestrated it—and it is God's involvement that is the most important point of the biblical author. So why should we spend so much time and effort trying to understand the background of Israelite culture, history, geography and archaeology?

The purpose of this book is not apologetics, though certainly some of the information we present could find use in apologetic discussions. Nevertheless, it was not an apologetic agenda that dictated our selection or presentation of the data. Instead, we are trying to shed light on the Israelite culture and worldview. Why? When we read the Bible as a community of faith, we want to draw as much theological content out of the text as possible. As a result people tend to read theological significance into the details. There is an inclination to read our own cultural biases and our own perspectives and worldview into the text as a basis for understanding theological significance if we are not alerted to the differences that existed in the Israelite way of thinking. The larger ancient Near Eastern world becomes significant in that many times it can serve as a window to the Israelite culture. In many cases, by offering insight into the Israelite or ancient Near Eastern way of thinking, this book can help the interpreter avoid erroneous conclusions. So, for instance, the theological significance of the pillar of fire, the scapegoat or the Urim and Thummim can be understood in new ways once we make connections to the general culture of the ancient Near East.

We have not limited our identification of similarities to precisely delineated time periods. We fully recognize that the occurrence of some cultural element in the town of Ugarit in the mid-second millennium may not have any relationship to the way Israelites of the mid-first millennium thought. Nevertheless, often our interest has been in merely indicating that certain ideas or concepts existed in the ancient Near Eastern cultures. It is not impossible that such ideas could have represented aspects of the general cultural matrix of the ancient world. We bring them up merely as examples of the kind of thinking that existed in the ancient world. Such information must be used with caution, however, because we cannot assume a flat homogeneity across the eras, regions or ethnic groups of the ancient Near East. In our own day, for instance, it would be foolhardy to speak of "European culture" given our awareness of the significant differences between, for example, the Italians and the Swiss. We have attempted to show some sensitivity to these issues but have not imposed strict limitations on the information we offer.

The issue at hand is not a question of whether the Israelites "borrowed" from their neighbors or not. We are not seeking to discover a literary path and feel no need to establish that Israelites would have been familiar with this or that piece of literature in order to employ similar motifs. We have avoided terms like "influence" or "impact" to describe how information was shared. That is because we are trying to look at those elements that may simply be part of the cultural heritage of the ancient Near East. That heritage may be reflected in various pieces of literature, but the Israelites need not have had knowledge of, or been influenced by, those pieces of literature. They simply are a part of the common cultural matrix. God's process of revelation required that he condescend to us, that he accommodate our humanity, that he express himself in familiar language and metaphors. It should be no surprise then that many of the common elements of the culture of the day were adopted, at times adapted, at times totally converted or transformed, but nevertheless used to accomplish God's purposes. Indeed, we would be surprised if this were not the case. Communication requires a shared circle of common conventions and understandings. When we speak of "daylight-saving time" we assume the person we are speaking to understands this strictly cultural convention, and we do not explain it. Someone from a different era or culture that had no such practice of adjusting clocks would be absolutely clueless as to what was meant by the phrase. They would have to become familiar with our culture in order to understand. The same holds true as we try to penetrate Israelite literature. Therefore, if circumcision is to be understood in Israel's context, it is helpful to understand its ancient Near Eastern form. If sacrifice is to be appreciated for what it represented in Israel, it is helpful to compare and contrast what it represented in the ancient world. While sometimes this search for knowledge can result in problems that are difficult to resolve, maintaining ignorance of those problems would not mean they did not exist. And more often than not, our new knowledge has positive results.

Sometimes the information we provide is simply to satisfy curiosity. As teachers, however, we have found that much of our task is taken up with developing in our students a curiosity about the text and then attempting to satisfy, in some degree, that curiosity. In the process it is often possible to bring the biblical world to life—to help us become alert and informed readers. When information is presented in an entry, it is not necessarily being offered to help interpret the passage but perhaps only to provide data that may be pertinent to interpreting the passage. So information in Job 38 about mythological images of creation in the ancient Near East does not serve as a suggestion that the thinking in Job should be thought of in the same terms. The data are simply being provided for comparison.

This book is intended to serve a nonprofessional market rather than the academic and scholarly communities. If we were to footnote every piece of information here so that our colleagues could find the resources and check out the original publications, we would end up with a multivolume work too detailed to be of any use to the lay people for whom we are seeking to provide a service. Though we often found it excruciating to omit references to journals and books, we here acknowledge our debt to our colleagues and hopefully the few bibliographic references we provide can lead the interested reader to them. We have additionally tried to be very careful with proprietary information and ideas so that a standard of integrity could be maintained. Another consequence of targeting the nonprofessional market is that our references to the primary literature have of necessity been somewhat vague. Rather than citing text reference and publication resource, we have had to be content to say, "Babylonian laws contain . . ." or "Hittite regulations include . . ." or "Egyptian reliefs show . . ." Knowing that the typical layperson would not have the opportunity or the inclination to go look up the text and that many of the citations would be obscure and inaccessible to nonspecialists, we concentrated our efforts on giving the pertinent information rather than on offering a research trail. We recognize that this will create some frustrations for those who would like to track the reference for further information. We can only recommend going back to some of the bibliography we have listed and tracing the information from there. As an aid to readers unfamiliar with certain terms that arise repeatedly, we have provided a glossary at the back of the book. Asterisks (*) in the text point readers to terms that can be found there.

For the lay reader, it is possible that the information will occasion some confusion. It was our objective to provide information, not to go into detail to show how that information should be used or what it proves or does not prove. The reader may well often ask, What am I to do with that information? In many cases there may not be anything that can be done with the information, but having that information may prevent one from doing something with the text that should not be done. For instance, information given concerning the "circle of the earth" in Isaiah 40:22 may not solve the readers quandaries concerning how to account theologically for Scripture's use of old-world ideas about the shape of the earth, but it will give the reader sufficient information to avoid the misconception that the text incorporated modern scientific ideas between its lines. More generally, it is hoped that even when the specific information may not be usable in one's context, there will be a greater appreciation developed for the many ways in which Israel and the Old Testament reflect the cultural heritage of the ancient Near East.

Other Resources for the Cultural Context of the Old Testament

This list provides the reader with some of the significant sources we found useful in developing the information we present. It is not a "beginning bibliography" in that some of the sources listed are fairly technical or advanced in nature. Neither is it a comprehensive bibliography—many fine works, even standard works, have been omitted. However, these would be the key works to refer to if the reader wants to find more information or discussion on the topics presented.

General Reference

Biblical Archaeologist. Now *Near Eastern Archaeology*.

Biblical Archaeology Review.

Boardman, John, et al., eds. *The Cambridge Ancient History*. Cambridge: Cambridge University Press, 1970.

Botterweck, G. Johannes, and Helmer Ringgren, eds. *Theological Dictionary of the Old Testament*. Grand Rapids: Eerdmans, 1975-.

Bromiley, Geoffrey, ed. *The International Standard Bible Encyclopedia*. Grand Rapids: Eerdmans, 1988.

Douglas, J. D., ed. *The Illustrated Bible Dictionary*. Wheaton: Tyndale House, 1980.

Freedman, D. N., ed. *The Anchor Bible Dictionary*. New York: Doubleday, 1992.

Hallo, W. W., and K. L. Younger, eds. *Context of Scripture*. Leiden: Brill, 1997.

Mazar, Benjamin, ed. *Views of the Biblical World*. Jerusalem: International Publications, 1959.

————, ed. *World History of the Jewish People*. Jerusalem: Masada, 1963-1979.

Meyers, Eric, ed. *The Oxford Encyclopedia of Archaeology in the Near East*. New York: Oxford University Press, 1997.

Pritchard, James, ed. *Ancient Near East in Pictures*. Princeton, N.J.: Princeton University Press, 1954.

————. *Ancient Near Eastern Texts*. Princeton, N.J.: Princeton University Press, 1969.

Reiner, Erica, et al., eds. *Chicago Assyrian Dictionary*. Chicago: University of Chicago Press, 1956-.

Ryken, Leland, et al., eds. *Dictionary of Biblical Imagery*. Downers Grove, Ill.: InterVarsity Press, 1998.

Sasson, Jack. *Civilizations of the Ancient Near East*. New York: Scribner's, 1995.

Stern, Ephraim, ed. *The New Encyclopedia of Archaeological Excavations in the Holy Land*. New York: Simon & Schuster, 1993.

Van der Toorn, Karel, et al., eds. *Dictionary of Deities and Demons in the Bible*. Leiden: Brill, 1995.

VanGemeren, Willem, ed. *New International Dictionary of Old Testament Theology and Exegesis*. Grand Rapids: Zondervan, 1997.

Books on Particular Aspects of Bible Background

Aberbach, Moshe. *Labor, Crafts and Commerce in Ancient Israel.* Jerusalem: Magnes, 1994.

Ackerman, Susan. *Under Every Green Tree: Popular Religion in Sixth-Century Judah.* Harvard Semitic Monographs 46. Atlanta: Scholars, 1992.

Aharoni, Yohanan. *The Land of the Bible.* Philadelphia: Westminster Press, 1979.

Amiet, Pierre. *Art of the Ancient Near East.* New York: Abrams, 1980.

Anderson, B. W. *Gemstones for Everyman.* New York: Van Nostrand Reinhold, 1976.

Baines, John, and Jaromír Málek. *Atlas of Ancient Egypt.* New York: Facts on File, 1980.

Beckman, Gary. *Hittite Diplomatic Texts.* Atlanta: Scholars, 1996.

Beitzel, Barry. *The Moody Atlas of Bible Lands.* Chicago: Moody Press, 1985.

Berquist, Jon. *Judaism in Persia's Shadow.* Minneapolis: Fortress, 1995.

Borowski, Oded. *Agriculture in Iron Age Israel.* Winona Lake, Ind.: Eisenbrauns, 1987.

———. *Every Living Thing.* Walnut Creek, Calif.: Alta Mira, 1998.

Bottéro, Jean. *Mesopotamia.* Chicago: University of Chicago Press, 1992.

Cansdale, George. *All the Animals of the Bible Lands.* Grand Rapids: Zondervan, 1970.

Chirichigno, Gregory. *Debt-Slavery in Israel and the Ancient Near East.* Sheffield, U.K.: JSOT, 1993.

Clifford, R. J. *Creation Accounts in the Ancient Near East and the Bible.* Washington, D.C.: Catholic Biblical Association, 1994.

Cook, J. M. *The Persian Empire.* New York: Schocken, 1983.

Crenshaw, James C. *Education in Ancient Israel.* New York: Doubleday, 1998.

Cross, F. M. *Canaanite Myth and Hebrew Epic.* Cambridge, Mass.: Harvard University Press, 1971.

Cryer, Frederick H. *Divination in Ancient Israel and Its Near Eastern Environment.* Sheffield, U.K.: JSOT, 1994.

Currid, John. *Ancient Egypt and the Old Testament.* Grand Rapids: Baker, 1997.

Dalley, Stephanie. *Myths of Mesopotamia.* New York: Oxford University Press, 1991.

Davies, W. D., et al. *The Cambridge History of Judaism.* Vol. 1, *The Persian Period.* Cambridge: Cambridge University Press, 1984.

Dearman, Andrew. *Religion and Culture in Ancient Israel.* Peabody, Mass.: Hendrickson, 1992.

Eshkenazi, Tamara, and Kent Richards, eds. *Second Temple Studies.* Sheffield, U.K.: Sheffield Academic Press, 1994.

Fisher, Loren R., ed. *Ras Shamra Parallels* 2. Rome: Pontifical Biblical Institute, 1975.

Forbes, R. J. *Studies in Ancient Technology.* 9 vols. Leiden: Brill, 1964-.

Foster, Benjamin. *From Distant Days.* Bethesda, Md.: CDL, 1995.

Frankfort, Henri. *Before Philosophy.* Baltimore: Penguin, 1946.

Fritz, Volkmar. *The City in Ancient Israel.* Sheffield, U.K.: Sheffield Academic Press, 1995.

Gammie, John, and L. G. Perdue, eds. *The Sage in Israel and the Ancient Near East.*

Winona Lake, Ind.: Eisenbrauns, 1990.

Gershevitch, Ilya, ed. *The Cambridge History of Iran*. Vol. 2, *The Median and Achaemenid Periods* Cambridge: Cambridge University Press, 1985.

Gower, Ralph. *The New Manners and Customs of Bible Times*. Chicago: Moody Press, 1987.

Grabbe, Lester. *Judaism from Cyrus to Hadrian*. Minneapolis: Fortress, 1992.

Haran, Menahem. *Temples and Temple Service in Ancient Israel*. Winona Lake, Ind.: Eisenbrauns, 1985.

Hepper, F. Nigel. *Baker Encyclopedia of Bible Plants*. Grand Rapids: Baker, 1992.

Hill, Andrew. *Enter His Courts with Praise*. Grand Rapids: Baker, 1993.

Hillers, D. R. *Covenant: The History of a Biblical Idea*. Baltimore: Johns Hopkins University Press, 1969.

Hoerth, Alfred. *Archaeology and the Old Testament*. Grand Rapids: Baker, 1998.

Hoerth, Alfred, Gerald Mattingly, and Edwin Yamauchi. *Peoples of the Old Testament World*. Grand Rapids: Baker, 1994.

Horowitz, Wayne. *Mesopotamian Cosmic Geography*. Winona Lake, Ind.: Eisenbrauns, 1998.

Jacobsen, Thorkild. *The Harps That Once . . .* New Haven, Conn.: Yale University Press, 1987.

———. *Treasures of Darkness*. New Haven, Conn.: Yale University Press, 1976.

Keel, Othmar. *The Symbolism of the Biblical World*. New York: Seabury Press, 1978.

Keel, Othmar, and Christoph Uehlinger. *Gods, Goddesses and Images of God in Ancient Israel*. Minneapolis: Fortress, 1998.

King, Philip. *Hosea, Amos, Hosea, Micah: An Archaeological Commentary*. Philadelphia: Westminster Press, 1988.

Kitchen, Kenneth A. *The Third Intermediate Period in Egypt*. Warminster, U.K.: Aris & Phillips, 1986.

Kloos, Carola. *Yhwh's Combat with the Sea*. Leiden: Brill, 1986.

Kuhrt, Amélie. *The Ancient Near East: 3000-330 B.C.* London: Routledge, 1997.

Lambert, W. G. *Babylonian Wisdom Literature*. Oxford: Clarendon Press, 1960.

Lichtheim, Miriam. *Ancient Egyptian Literature*. Berkeley: University of California Press, 1980.

Matthews, Victor. *Manners and Customs in the Bible*. Peabody, Mass.: Hendrickson, 1988.

Matthews, Victor, and Donald Benjamin. *The Social World of Ancient Israel, 1250-587 B.C.E.* Peabody, Mass.: Hendrickson, 1993.

———. *Old Testament Parallels: Laws and Stories from the Ancient Near East*, 2d ed. New York: Paulist, 1997.

Mazar, Amihai. *Archaeology of the Land of the Bible*. New York: Doubleday, 1990.

McNutt, P. M. *The Forging of Israel: Iron Technology, Symbolism and Tradition in Ancient Society*. Sheffield, U.K.: Almond, 1990.

Millard, Alan. *Treasures from Bible Times*. Tring, U.K.: Lion, 1985.

Miller, J. Maxwell, and John Hayes. *A History of Ancient Israel and Judah*. Philadelphia: Westminster Press, 1986.

Miller, Patrick D. *They Cried to the Lord*. Louisville: Fortress, 1994.

Moore, Carey. *Studies in the Book of Esther*. New York: Ktav, 1982.

Moran, William L. *The Amarna Letters*. Baltimore: Johns Hopkins University Press, 1992.

Morenz, Siegfried. *Egyptian Religion*. Ithaca, N.Y.: Cornell University Press, 1973.

Nemet-Nejat, Karen Rhea. *Daily Life in Ancient Mesopotamia*. Westport, Conn.: Greenwood, 1998.

Oppenheim, A. L. *Ancient Mesopotamia: Portrait of a Dead Civilization*. Chicago: University of Chicago Press, 1964.

————. *Interpretation of Dreams in the Ancient Near East*. TAPS 46, no. 3. Philadelphia: American Philosophical Society, 1956.

Parker, Simon. *Ugaritic Narrative Poetry*. Atlanta: Scholars, 1997.

Paul, Shalom, and William Dever. *Biblical Archaeology*. Jerusalem: Keter, 1973.

Perdue, Leo G., et al., eds. *Families in Ancient Israel*. Louisville: Westminster John Knox, 1997.

Pitard, Wayne. *Ancient Damascus*. Winona Lake, Ind.: Eisenbrauns, 1987.

Rasmussen, Carl. *NIV Atlas of the Bible*. Grand Rapids: Zondervan, 1989.

Redford, D. B. *Egypt, Canaan, and Israel in Ancient Times*. Princeton, N.J.: Princeton University Press, 1992.

Reiner, Erica. *Astral Magic in Babylonia*. Philadelphia: American Philosophical Society, 1995.

Reviv, Hanoch. *The Elders in Ancient Israel*. Jerusalem: Magnes, 1989.

Roaf, Michael. *Cultural Atlas of Mesopotamia and the Ancient Near East*. New York: Facts on File, 1990.

Rogerson, John. *Atlas of the Bible*. New York: Facts on File, 1985.

Roth, Martha. *Law Collections from Mesopotamia and Asia Minor*. Atlanta: Scholars, 1995.

Saggs, H. W. F. *Encounter with the Divine in Mesopotamia and Israel*. London: Athlone, 1978.

————. *The Greatness That Was Babylon*. New York: Mentor, 1962.

————. *The Might That Was Assyria*. London: Sidgwick & Jackson, 1984.

Selms, Adrianus van. *Marriage and Family Life in Ugaritic Literature*. London: Luzac, 1954.

Shafer, Byron E., ed. *Religion in Ancient Egypt*. Ithaca, N.Y.: Cornell University Press, 1991.

Snell, Daniel. *Life in the Ancient Near East*. New Haven, Conn.: Yale University Press, 1997.

Stadelmann, Luis. *The Hebrew Conception of the World*. Rome: Biblical Institute, 1970.

Stillman, Nigel, and Nigel Tallis. *Armies of the Ancient Near East*. Sussex, U.K.: War Games Research, 1984.

Thiele, Edwin. *The Mysterious Numbers of the Hebrew Kings*. Grand Rapids: Zondervan, 1983.

Thompson, J. A. *Handbook of Life in Bible Times*. Downers Grove, Ill.: InterVarsity Press, 1986.

Tromp, Nicholas. *Primitive Conceptions of Death and the Nether World in the Old Testament*. Rome: Pontifical Biblical Institute, 1969.

Van der Toorn, Karel. *From Her Cradle to Her Grave*. Sheffield, U.K.: JSOT, 1994.

————. *Sin and Sanction in Israel and Mesopotamia.* Assen, Neth.: Van Gorcum, 1985.

Vaux, Roland de. *Ancient Israel.* New York: McGraw-Hill, 1961.

Walton, John H. *Ancient Israelite Literature in Its Cultural Context.* Grand Rapids: Zondervan, 1989.

Weinfeld, Moshe. *Social Justice in Ancient Israel.* Minneapolis: Fortress, 1995.

Wiseman, D. J. *Nebuchadrezzar and Babylon.* New York: Oxford University Press, 1985.

Wright, Christopher J. H. *God's People in God's Land.* Grand Rapids: Eerdmans, 1990.

Wright, David. *The Disposal of Impurity.* Atlanta: Scholars, 1987.

Yadin, Yigael. *The Art of Warfare in Biblical Lands.* London: Weidenfeld & Nicolson, 1963.

Yamauchi, Edwin. *Persia and the Bible.* Grand Rapids: Baker, 1990.

Younger, Lawson. *Ancient Conquest Accounts.* Sheffield, U.K.: JSOT, 1990.

Zohary, Michael. *Plants of the Bible.* Cambridge: Cambridge University Press, 1982.

Commentaries and Other References

Genesis

Hamilton, Victor. *The Book of Genesis.* 2 vols. New International Commentary on the Old Testament. Grand Rapids: Eerdmans, 1990, 1995.

Sarna, Nahum. *JPS Torah Commentary: Genesis.* Philadelphia: Jewish Publication Society, 1989.

Wenham, Gordon. *Genesis.* 2 vols. Word Biblical Commentary. Dallas: Word, 1987, 1994.

Exodus

Beegle, Dewey. *Moses: The Servant of Yahweh.* Grand Rapids: Eerdmans, 1972.

Davis, John. *Moses and the Gods of Egypt.* Grand Rapids: Baker, 1971.

Durham, John. *Exodus.* Word Biblical Commentary. Dallas: Word, 1987.

Kelm, George. *Escape to Conflict.* Ft. Worth, Tex.: IAR, 1991.

Sarna, Nahum. *Exploring Exodus.* New York: Schocken, 1986.

————. *JPS Torah Commentary: Exodus.* Philadelphia: Jewish Publication Society, 1991.

Leviticus

Grabbe, Lester. *Leviticus.* Old Testament Guides. Sheffield, U.K.: JSOT, 1993.

Hartley, John. *Leviticus.* Word Biblical Commentaries. Dallas: Word, 1992.

Levine, Baruch. *JPS Torah Commentary: Leviticus.* Jewish Publication Society, 1989.

Milgrom, Jacob. *Leviticus 1—16.* Anchor Bible. New York: Doubleday, 1991.

Wenham, Gordon. *The Book of Leviticus.* New International Commentary on the Old Testament. Grand Rapids: Eerdmans, 1979.

Numbers

Ashley, Timothy. *The Book of Numbers.* New International Commentary on the Old Testament. Grand Rapids: Eerdmans, 1993.

Levine, Baruch. *Numbers 1—20*. Anchor Bible. New York: Doubleday, 1993.

Milgrom, Jacob. *JPS Torah Commentary: Numbers*. Philadelphia: Jewish Publication Society, 1990.

Wenham, Gordon. *Numbers*. Tyndale Old Testament Commentaries. Downers Grove, Ill.: InterVarsity Press, 1981.

Deuteronomy

Tigay, Jeffrey. *JPS Torah Commentary: Deuteronomy*. Philadelphia: Jewish Publication Society, 1996.

Weinfeld, Moshe. *Deuteronomy 1—11*. Anchor Bible. New York: Doubleday, 1991.

Joshua

Boling, Robert G. *Joshua*. Anchor Bible. New York: Doubleday, 1982.

Hess, Richard. *Joshua*. Tyndale Old Testament Commentaries. Downers Grove, Ill.: InterVarsity Press, 1996.

Judges

Block, Daniel I. *Judges/Ruth*. New American Commentary. Nashville: Broadman & Holman, 1999.

Boling, Robert G. *Judges*. New York: Doubleday, 1975.

Ruth

Bush, Frederic. *Ruth/Esther*. Word Biblical Commentary. Dallas: Word, 1996.

Campbell, Edward F. *Ruth*. Anchor Bible. New York: Doubleday, 1975

Hubbard, Robert. *The Book of Ruth*. New International Commentary on the Old Testament. Grand Rapids: Eerdmans, 1988.

1-2 Samuel

Bergen, Robert. *1 & 2 Samuel*. New American Commentary. Nashville: Broadman & Holman, 1996.

McCarter, P. Kyle. *Samuel*. 2 vols. Anchor Bible. New York: Doubleday, 1980, 1984.

1-2 Kings

Cogan, Mordecai, and Hayim Tadmor. *2 Kings*. Anchor Bible. New York: Doubleday, 1988.

Gray, John. *1 & 2 Kings*. Old Testament Library. Louisville: Westminster John Knox, 1970.

Jones, G. H. *1 & 2 Kings*. New Century Bible. Grand Rapids: Eerdmans, 1984.

Wiseman, D. J. *1 & 2 Kings*. Tyndale Old Testament Commentaries. Downers Grove, Ill.: InterVarsity Press, 1993.

1-2 Chronicles

Braun, Roddy. *1 Chronicles*. Word Biblical Commentary. Dallas: Word, 1986.

Dillard, Raymond. *2 Chronicles*. Word Biblical Commentary. Dallas: Word, 1986.

Japhet, Sara. *1 & 2 Chronicles*. Old Testament Library. Louisville: Westminster John Knox, 1993.

Selman, M. J. *1 & 2 Chronicles*. 2 vols. Tyndale Old Testament Commentaries. Downers Grove, Ill.: InterVarsity Press, 1994.

Williamson, H. G. M. *1 & 2 Chronicles*. New Century Bible. Grand Rapids: Eerdmans, 1982.

Ezra, Nehemiah, Esther

Bush, Frederic. *Ruth/Esther*. Word Biblical Commentary. Dallas: Word, 1996.

Clines, D. J. A. *Ezra, Nehemiah, Esther*. New Century Bible. Grand Rapids: Eerdmans, 1984.

Fensham, Charles. *The Books of Ezra and Nehemiah*. New International Commentary on the Old Testament. Grand Rapids: Eerdmans, 1982.

Fox, Michael V. *Character and Ideology in the Book of Esther*. Columbia: University of South Carolina Press, 1991.

Williamson, H. G. M. *Ezra and Nehemiah*. Word Biblical Commentary. Dallas: Word, 1985.

Yamauchi, Edwin. *Ezra and Nehemiah*. Expositors Bible Commentary 4. Edited by F. Gaebelein. Grand Rapids: Zondervan, 1988.

Job

Clines, D. J. A. *Job 1—20*. Word Biblical Commentary. Dallas: Word, 1989.

Habel, Norman. *Job*. Old Testament Library. Louisville: Westminster John Knox, 1985.

Hartley, John. *The Book of Job*. New International Commentary on the Old Testament. Grand Rapids: Eerdmans, 1988.

Pope, Marvin. *Job*. Anchor Bible. New York: Doubleday, 1965.

Psalms

Allen, Leslie. *Psalms 101—150*. Word Biblical Commentary. Dallas: Word, 1983.

Anderson, A. A. *Psalms*. 2 vols. New Century Bible. Grand Rapids: Eerdmans, 1972.

Avishur, Yitzhak. *Studies in Hebrew and Ugaritic Psalms*. Jerusalem: Magnes, 1994.

Craigie, Peter C. *Psalms 1—50*. Word Biblical Commentary. Dallas: Word, 1983.

Dalglish, E. R. *Psalm 51 in the Light of Ancient Near Eastern Patternism*. Leiden: Brill, 1962.

Goulder, M. D. *The Psalms of the Sons of Korah*. Sheffield, U.K.: JSOT, 1982.

Kraus, H.-J. *Psalms 1—59*. Continental Commentaries. Minneapolis: Augsburg, 1988.

Sarna, Nahum. "Psalms, Book of." In *Encyclopaedia Judaica*. Edited by Cecil Roth, cols. 1316-22. Jerusalem: Keter, 1973.

Tate, Marvin. *Psalms 51—100*. Word Biblical Commentary. Dallas: Word, 1990.

Weiser, Artur. *The Psalms*. Old Testament Library. Louisville: Westminster John Knox, 1962.

Proverbs

Clifford, R. J. *Proverbs*. Old Testament Library. Louisville: Westminster John Knox, 1999.

McKane, William. *Proverbs: A New Approach*. Louisville: Westminster John Knox, 1970.

Murphy, R. E. *Proverbs*. Word Biblical Commentary. Dallas: Word, 1998.

Whybray, Norman. *Proverbs*. New Century Bible. Grand Rapids: Eerdmans, 1994.

Ecclesiastes

Crenshaw, James. *Ecclesiastes*. Old Testament Library. Louisville: Westminster John Knox, 1987.

Longman, Tremper. *The Book of Ecclesiastes*. New International Commentary on the Old Testament. Grand Rapids: Eerdmans, 1997.

Murphy, R. E. *Ecclesiastes*. Word Biblical Commentary. Dallas: Word, 1992.

Seow, C. L. *Ecclesiastes*. Anchor Bible. New York: Doubleday, 1997.

Whybray, Norman. *Ecclesiastes*. New Century Bible. Grand Rapids: Eerdmans, 1989.

Song of Songs

Carr, G. Lloyd. *The Song of Solomon*. Tyndale Old Testament Commentaries. Downers Grove, Ill.: InterVarsity Press, 1984.

Fox, M. V. *The Song of Songs and the Ancient Egyptian Love Songs*. Madison: University of Wisconsin Press, 1985.

Keel, Othmar. *The Song of Songs*. Continental Commentaries. Minneapolis: Fortress, 1994.

Murphy, R. E. *The Song of Songs*. Hermeneia. Minneapolis: Fortress, 1990.

Pope, M. H. *Song of Songs*. Anchor Bible. New York: Doubleday, 1977.

Isaiah

Oswalt, John. *The Book of Isaiah*. 2 vols. New International Commentary on the Old Testament. Grand Rapids: Eerdmans, 1986, 1997.

Wildberger, Hans. *Isaiah 1—12*. Continental Commentaries. Minneapolis: Fortress, 1991.

————. *Isaiah 13—27*. Continental Commentaries. Minneapolis: Fortress, 1998.

Jeremiah

Holladay, William. *Jeremiah*. 2 vols. Hermeneia. Minneapolis: Fortress, 1986, 1989.

Thompson, J. A. *The Book of Jeremiah*. New International Commentary on the Old Testament. Grand Rapids: Eerdmans, 1980.

Lamentations

Provan, Iain. *Lamentations*. New Century Bible. Grand Rapids: Eerdmans, 1991.

Ezekiel

Allen, Leslie. *Ezekiel*. 2 vols. Dallas: Word, 1990, 1994.

Block, Daniel I. *The Book of Ezekiel*. 2 vols. New International Commentary on the Old Testament. Grand Rapids: Eerdmans, 1997, 1998.

Bodi, Daniel. *The Book of Ezekiel and the Poem of Erra*. Freiburg, Switz.: Vandenhoeck & Ruprecht, 1991.

Garfinkel, Stephen. *Studies in Akkadian Influences in the Book of Ezekiel*. Ann Arbor:

University of Michigan Microfilms, 1983.

Greenberg, Moshe. *Ezekiel 1—20.* Anchor Bible. New York: Doubleday, 1983.

————. *Ezekiel 21—37.* Anchor Bible. New York: Doubleday, 1997.

Zimmerli, Walther. *Ezekiel.* Vol. 1. Hermeneia. Minneapolis: Fortress, 1979, 1983.

Daniel

Baldwin, Joyce. *Daniel.* Tyndale Old Testament Commentaries. Downers Grove, Ill.: InterVarsity Press, 1978.

Collins, John J. *Daniel.* Hermeneia. Minneapolis: Fortress, 1993.

Goldingay, John. *Daniel.* Word Biblical Commentary. Dallas: Word, 1989.

Hosea

Andersen, F. I., and D. N. Freedman. *Hosea.* Anchor Bible. New York: Doubleday, 1980.

MacIntosh, A. A. *A Critical and Exegetical Commentary on Hosea.* International Critical Commentary. Edinburgh: T & T Clark, 1997.

Stuart, Douglas. *Hosea—Jonah.* Word Biblical Commentary. Dallas: Word, 1987.

Wolff, H. W. *A Commentary on the Book of the Prophet Hosea.* Hermeneia. Minneapolis: Fortress, 1974.

Joel

Allen, Leslie. *The Books of Joel, Obadiah, Jonah and Micah.* New International Commentary on the Old Testament. Grand Rapids: Eerdmans, 1976.

Crenshaw, James. *Joel.* Anchor Bible. New York: Doubleday, 1995.

Dillard, Raymond. "Joel." In *The Minor Prophets* 1. Edited by T. E. McComiskey, pp. 239-313. Grand Rapids: Baker, 1990.

Finley, Thomas. *Joel, Amos, Obadiah.* Chicago, Moody Press, 1990.

Hubbard, David. *Joel, Amos.* Tyndale Old Testament Commentaries. Downers Grove, Ill.: InterVarsity Press, 1989.

Stuart, Douglas. *Hosea—Jonah.* Word Biblical Commentary. Dallas: Word, 1987.

Wolff, Hans Walter. *Joel and Amos.* Hermeneia. Minneapolis: Fortress, 1977.

Amos

Andersen, F. I., and D. N. Freedman. *Amos.* Anchor Bible. New York: Doubleday, 1989.

Paul, Shalom. *A Commentary on the Book of Amos.* Hermeneia. Minneapolis: Fortress, 1991.

Wolff, Hans Walter. *A Commentary on the Books of the Prophets Joel and Amos.* Hermeneia. Minneapolis: Fortress, 1977.

Obadiah

Raabe, Paul R. *Obadiah.* Anchor Bible. New York: Doubleday, 1996.

Wolff, Hans Walter. *Obadiah and Jonah.* Continental Commentaries. Minneapolis: Fortress, 1986.

Jonah

Sasson, Jack. *Jonah*. Anchor Bible. New York: Doubleday, 1990.

Walton, John. *Jonah*. Grand Rapids: Zondervan, 1982.

Wolff, Hans Walter. *Obadiah and Jonah*. Continental Commentaries. Minneapolis: Fortress, 1986.

Micah

Hillers, Delbert. *Micah*. Hermeneia. Minneapolis: Fortress, 1983.

Waltke, Bruce. "Micah." In *The Minor Prophets* 2. Edited by T. E. McComiskey, pp. 591-764. Grand Rapids: Baker, 1993.

Nahum

Baker, David. *Nahum, Habakkuk, Zephaniah*. Tyndale Old Testament Commentaries. Downers Grove: InterVarsity Press, 1988.

Longman, Tremper. "Nahum." In *The Minor Prophets* 2. Edited by T. E. McComiskey, pp. 765-829. Grand Rapids: Baker, 1993.

Roberts, J. J. M. *Nahum, Habakkuk and Zephaniah: A Commentary*. Old Testament Library. Louisville: Westminster John Knox, 1991.

Habakkuk

Roberts, J. J. M. *Nahum, Habakkuk and Zephaniah: A Commentary*. Old Testament Library. Louisville: Westminster John Knox, 1991.

Smith, R. L. *Micah—Malachi*. Word Biblical Commentary. Dallas: Word, 1984.

Zephaniah

Berlin, Adele. *Zephaniah*. Anchor Bible. New York: Doubleday, 1994.

Roberts, J. J. M. *Nahum, Habakkuk and Zephaniah: A Commentary*. Old Testament Library. Louisville: Westminster John Knox, 1991.

Smith, R. L. *Micah—Malachi*. Word Biblical Commentary. Dallas: Word, 1984.

Haggai

Meyers, Eric, and Carol Meyers. *Haggai and Zechariah 1—8*. Anchor Bible. New York: Doubleday, 1987.

Verhoef, Peter A. *The Books of Haggai and Malachi*. New International Commentary on the Old Testament. Grand Rapids: Eerdmans, 1986.

Wolff, Hans Walter. *Haggai*. Continental Commentaries. Minneapolis: Fortress, 1988.

Zechariah

Ellis, Richard S. *Foundation Deposits in Ancient Mesopotamia*. New Haven, Conn.: Yale University Press, 1968.

Halpern, Baruch. "The Ritual Background of Zechariah's Temple Song," *Catholic Biblical Quarterly* 40 (1978): 167-90.

Meyers, Eric, and Carol Meyers. *Zechariah 9—14*. Anchor Bible. New York: Doubleday, 1993.

Malachi

Glazier-McDonald, Beth. *The Divine Messenger.* Atlanta: Scholars, 1987.

Hill, Andrew. *Malachi.* Anchor Bible. New York: Doubleday, 1998.

PENTATEUCH

Introduction

T hough there are many reasons to consider the Pentateuch as a single, unitary piece of literature, the background materials pertinent to the study of each book are vastly different. As a result, we offer here an introduction to each of the five books individually.

Genesis

Genesis is typically divided into two main sections (1—11, 12—50). The background material most helpful for understanding the first section is the mythological literature of the ancient Near East. Both Mesopotamian and Egyptian mythology provide a wealth of materials concerning contemporary perspectives on the creation of the world and of human beings. These works include the *Enuma Elish* and the Atrahasis Epic, as well as a number of *Sumerian myths from the region of Mesopotamia. From Egypt there are three main creation texts, one each from Memphis, Heliopolis (in the Pyramid Texts) and Hermopolis (in the Coffin Texts). Additionally, there are several flood stories available from the region of Mesopotamia, found in the Gilgamesh Epic and in the Atrahasis Epic. Examination of this literature helps us to observe many similarities and differences between ancient Near Eastern and Israelite concepts. Similarities will make us aware of the common ground that existed between Israel and her neighbors. Sometimes the similarity will be in the details of the narrative (such as sending out birds from the ark) or in aspects of the text we might not have noticed before (such as the naming of things in conjunction with their creation). Some similarities might lead us to question whether we have read too much theological signifi-

---

*The asterisk (*) here and others throughout the text are designed to point readers to terms explained in the glossary. Not all terms will be found in exactly the same form; for example, the asterisk here points to the term *Sumer* in the glossary.

cance into certain elements in the text (e.g., the creation of woman from a rib), while in other cases we might find that we have not seen enough of the theological significance (e.g., God's coming to the garden in the "cool of the day"). In general such similarities help us to understand the biblical accounts in broader perspective.

The differences between the ancient Near Eastern and biblical literatures will help us to appreciate some of the distinctives of both the Israelite culture and the biblical faith. These will again include specific details (shape of the ark, length of the flood) as well as foundational concepts (the contrast between the biblical view of creation by the spoken word of God and the Mesopotamian view that the creation of the world was associated with the birth of the cosmic deities). In many cases the differences are related (either directly or indirectly) to the unique monotheistic faith of Israel.

It is not unusual for the similarities and the differences to come together in a single element. The concepts of humankind's being created (1) from clay and (2) in the image of deity are both familiar in the ancient Near East, but Israel puts a unique twist on the idea that moves it into an altogether different sphere.

We cannot always account for the similarities and the differences as clearly or as conclusively as we might wish. Different scholars will have varying opinions of the implications based on some of their own presuppositions. The issues are often complex, and any individual scholar's conclusions may be highly interpretive. For this reason it is easier to offer information than it is to offer satisfying answers.

Finally, the comparative literature not only provides parallel accounts to some of those found in Genesis 1—11 but also provides a parallel to the overall structure of this section. The Mesopotamian Atrahasis Epic, like Genesis 1—11, contains a summary of creation, three threats and a resolution. Such observations can help us to understand the literary aspects to how this portion of the Bible is pieced together. Additionally, if this parallel is legitimate, it can help us see the genealogies in a different light, because when the biblical text has genealogies it reflects the Genesis blessing of being fruitful and multiplying, while in the comparable sections of Atrahasis the gods are distressed by the growth of human population and try to curb it.

Finding literary parallels to Genesis 12—50 presents more of a challenge. Though scholars have attempted to attach various descriptive terms to the patriarchal narratives (such as "sagas" or "legends"), any modern terminology is inadequate to encompass the nature of the ancient literature and is bound to mislead as much as it helps. There is nothing in the literature of the ancient Near East to parallels the stories about the patriarchs. The closest material is found in Egypt in works such as the *Story of *Sinuhe*, but that account covers only the lifetime of one man, rather than following several generations, and has nothing to do with resettlement or relationship with God. Even the Joseph story, considered on its own, is difficult to classify and compare. Again comparisons could be made to the stories of Sinuhe, *Wenamon or *Ahiqar (all dealing with the life and times of royal courtiers), but the similarities are quite superficial.

The background information for understanding these narratives comes from a different set of materials. These chapters concern the lives of the patriarchs and their families as they move from Mesopotamia to Canaan to Egypt in the process of the formation of the covenant. A number of archives (*Nuzi, *Mari, *Emar, *Alalakh) that have been discovered in Syria and Mesopotamia have provided information about the history, culture and customs of the ancient Near East in the second millennium. Often these materials can shed light on the political events or settlement history of the region. They can also help us to see how families lived and why they did some of the things that appear odd to us. In the process we gain important information that can help us process the biblical materials. For instance, we commonly seek ethical guidance in the behavior of biblical characters (though this is not always a productive procedure). In order to understand why people do what they do and to understand the decisions they make, it is important to become familiar with the norms of culture. We may find, then, that some of the behavior of the patriarchs is driven by norms that we have misunderstood or that we could easily misconstrue. Corrective information can often be provided by the archives.

One of the interesting conclusions that can be drawn from this kind of analysis is the understanding that there was not much in the worldview of the patriarchs and their families that differentiated them from the common ancient Near Eastern culture of the day. Again, then, an understanding of the general culture may help us to sort out what elements in the text have theological significance and what elements do not. For instance, an understanding of the practice of *circumcision in the ancient Near East may provide helpful guidelines to our assessment of it in the Bible. Observations about the use of the torch and censer in ancient Near Eastern *rituals may open up the meaning of Genesis 15. Even Abraham's understanding of God can be illuminated by information from the ancient Near Eastern documents.

As we encounter all of this information, we must be impressed with how often God uses the familiar to build bridges to his people. As what was familiar to them becomes more familiar to us, we can understand more of the text. On the other hand it is important to realize that the purposes of the book of Genesis go far beyond any of the literature available in the ancient Near East. The presence of similarities does not suggest in any way that the Bible is simply a secondhand, second-class repackaging of ancient Near Eastern literature. Rather, the background material helps us understand Genesis as a unique theological product linked to people and events embedded in a specific cultural and historical context.

Exodus

The book of Exodus contains a virtual cornucopia of types of literature, from narrative to law to architectural instructions. All are skillfully woven together to narrate the sequence of events that led a people from feeling that God had abandoned them to understanding themselves to be God's elect people with his presence in their midst. As a result there are many different primary sources that may offer assistance.

As might be expected, Exodus has more connections to Egyptian sources than any other book. Unfortunately the uncertainty concerning the date of the events and the sparsity of materials from some of the related periods of Egyptian history leave many questions unanswered. As a result it is not so much the historical literature of Egypt that we depend on but all the sources that give information about geography or culture. Locating the cities and places mentioned in the biblical text is very difficult and many uncertainties remain, yet one by one some of the gaps are being closed as archaeology continues to investigate significant sites.

The legal passages of Exodus are comparable to a wide range of law collections from Mesopotamia. These include *Sumerian legal texts such as the reform of Uruinimgina (or Urukagina), the laws of *Ur-Nammu and the laws of *Lipit-Ishtar. These are fragmentary texts that date from the late third millennium and early second millennium B.C. The more extensive texts are the laws of *Eshnunna and *Hammurabi (from the *Old Babylonian period, eighteenth century B.C.), the *Hittite laws from the seventeenth century and the Middle Assyrian laws from the twelfth century. These law collections, as indicated by the paragraphs that surround them, are intended to testify to the gods how successful the king has been at establishing and maintaining justice in his kingdom. As such, the laws are designed to reflect the wisest and fairest decisions the king could imagine. Like the candidate making a campaign speech who seeks to find every possible piece of legislation that he can claim responsibility for, the king wanted to show himself in the best possible light.

These laws help us to see that the actual legislation that determined the shape of Israelite society was not all that different on the surface from the laws that would have characterized Assyrian or Babylonian society. What was different was that for Israel the law was part of God's revelation of what he was like. The Babylonians had just as strong prohibitions of murder as the Israelites had. But the Babylonians would have refrained from murder because murder was disruptive to the smooth ordering of society and the principles of civilization. Israelites would have refrained from murder because of who God was. The laws may look the same, but the foundation of the legal system was remarkably different. For the Israelites, *Yahweh their God was the source of all law and the foundation of all societal norms. In Mesopotamia the king was entrusted with the authority to perceive what the law ought to be and to establish the law. The gods were not moral, nor did they require moral behavior, but they did expect humans to preserve the values of civilization and therefore to act in orderly and civilized ways.

The point is, then, that the law given at Sinai does not necessarily prescribe new laws. Its actual legislation may be very much like the laws that Israel had been living under in Egypt and is clearly similar to the laws that governed other societies of the ancient Near East. What is new is the revelation of God that is accomplished through the institutionalization of the law as part of the *covenant between God and Israel. Comparing the law of the Bible to the ancient Near Eastern law collections can help us to understand both the concept of law and order as well as the philosophical and theological underpinnings of the law.

When we get to the section of Exodus that has to do with the construction of the tabernacle, we may be well served by understanding the use and construction of shrines (portable and otherwise) in the ancient Near East. The detailed description of the materials that were used in the construction of the tabernacle, can be understood as we become aware of the value that culture attached to those materials. For example, consider the value that our society places on a mink coat, an oak desk, a leather chair or a stone house. Alongside of materials, we also attach value to positioning, as in the penthouse apartment, the corner office or the house at the top of the hill. So as we become acquainted with the materials and positions that the ancient Israelites attached value to, we can appreciate the rationale behind certain details. Again, we will often find that the rationale is cultural rather than theological. Once we understand the cultural elements, we can avoid attaching a foreign theological significance to some of the features.

Leviticus

The book of Leviticus is filled with instructions concerning how to maintain the holy space that was set apart for God's presence. This includes details of the sacrificial system, instructions for the priests and laws concerning *purity. In the ancient world *impurity was believed to create an environment for the demonic, so *purity needed to be maintained. This generally involved *rituals as well as incantations. For Israel *purity was a positive value that included rules of ethical behavior as well as issues of etiquette.

The ancient Near Eastern material that is most helpful for understanding the book of Leviticus is that which gives information about sacrifices, rituals and instructions for priests and dealing with *impurity. This information usually must be gleaned in bits and pieces from many different sources. There are, however, a few major ritual texts available that serve as significant sources of information. While *Hittite literature contains many sorts of ritual texts, among the most helpful is the *Instructions for the Temple Officials* from the mid-second millennium. This text details the means that should be used to protect the sanctuary from sacrilege and trespass. Mesopotamian sources are also plentiful.

The *maqlu* texts contain eight tablets of incantations as well as one tablet of rituals connected to the incantations. Most of these incantations are attempts to counter the powers of witchcraft. Other important series would include the *shurpu* texts, which concerned purification, the *bit rimki* texts concerning royal ablutions and the *namburbu* rituals of undoing.

Most of these texts assume a background of magic and divination where witchcraft, demonic forces and incantations represented powerful threats in society. Israelite beliefs ideally did not accept this worldview, and their concepts of *purity and *impurity had noticeable differences. Nevertheless, studying this material can expose many facets of the ancient worldview that the Israelites shared. Even though the biblical literature purged the rituals of the magical element, the institutionalized practices and the terminology describing them at times still contained the trappings or vestiges of the broader culture.

Certainly Israelite beliefs and practices were closer to the ancient Near East than they are to our own concepts of ritual, magic and *purity. Since we understand so little concerning these aspects of their worldview, we are often inclined to read very foreign theological concepts or symbolism into some of the practices and rules. This often creates an erroneous view of the nature and teaching of the book. By acquainting ourselves with the ancient Near Eastern worldview, we can avoid this type of error and understand the text a little more in the way that the Israelites would have understood it.

Numbers

The book of Numbers contains instructions for travel and setting up the camp, as well as records of the events that took place during the nearly forty years the Israelites spent in the wilderness. It also includes a number of ritual and legal passages. Many of the sources that contribute to an understanding of the books of Exodus and Leviticus also provide background for the book of Numbers. In addition, itineraries from Egyptian sources can help in locating various places listed in the Israelites' travels. These itineraries come from a number of different sources, including the *Execration Texts (where the names of certain cities were written on bowls and then shattered in connection with cursing rituals; Twelfth Dynasty, *Middle Bronze period) and the topographical lists carved on the walls of temples such as those at Karnak and Medinet Habu (*Late Bronze period). They preserve maps in a list form as they name each of the cities that would be encountered traveling along certain routes. It is interesting that some biblical sites, which archaeologists have considered suspect because no remains from a given period have been found there, are attested in the Egyptian itineraries for the same period.

Numbers, like several of the other books of the Pentateuch, contains information concerning Israel's ritual calendar. Information about feast days and ritual calendars is abundant in the ancient Near East because calendars were generally regulated by the priesthood. Nevertheless, it is difficult to ferret out many of the critical details of observances and especially to discover what is behind the formation of the traditions that are institutionalized in these calendars. It is a treacherous path that seeks to identify the links between the festivals of differing cultures even though there may be evidence of many areas of cultural exchange or dependence.

Deuteronomy

The book of Deuteronomy follows the format of agreements between nations, as described in the sidebar "The Covenant and Ancient Near Eastern Treaties." In these ancient covenants, the largest section was usually the stipulations section, which detailed the obligations of the vassal. These would include general expectations, such as loyalty, as well as specifics, such as paying tribute and housing garrison troops. There would also be prohibitions against harboring fugitives and making alliances with other nations. There were obligations to contribute to the defense of the suzerain nation and to treat envoys with respect.

In Deuteronomy the stipulations are in the form of laws that detail expectations and prohibitions. Some interpreters believe that the laws in chapters 6-26 (or 12-26) are arranged according to the Ten Commandments. Just as the ancient law collections have a prologue and an epilogue to give them a literary framework (see the introduction to Exodus), it is the covenant that provides the literary framework for the law. The literary framework of *Hammurabi's laws helps us to understand that the collection of laws was not for framing legislation but for demonstrating how just Hammurabi's reign was. Likewise the literary framework of

Deuteronomy gives us an idea of why these laws were collected. Deuteronomy is framing these laws not as legislation but as *covenant.

When the people of the ancient Near East agreed to a treaty and its stipulations, they were obliged to abide by the terms of the treaty. It is the same level of obligation that would be connected to the laws of the land, but it operates differently, not within a legal system. For example, in today's world each country has its own laws, enacted by its legislative bodies, that are binding on its citizens. But there is also international law, which in part has been established by multinational bodies, often by treaty-type agreements. This international law is binding on all of the parties involved in the agreement. The binding nature of Deuteronomy is tied to treaty rather than to law (that is, to the covenant rather than to legislation). What that means is that Israel's obligations were connected to sustaining the relationship outlined in the covenant. If they were to be God's people (covenant), they were expected to conduct themselves in the described ways (stipulations). We should therefore not look at the laws as laws of the land (though they may well have been). The Israelites were not supposed to keep the law because it was the law; they were to keep the law because it reflected something of the nature of God and of what he wanted them to be like in order to remain in relationship with him.

An additional characteristic of Deuteronomy is that it is presented as the exhortations of Moses to the people. In this way Moses is seen as the mediator of the covenant because as God's messenger or envoy he is establishing the terms of the treaty. The *Hittite treaties preserve only the treaties themselves and offer no insight into the envoy who delivered the treaty. Other texts, however, allow us to gain some insight into the role of the envoy. He often presented his message verbally but had a written copy for the documentation and for the records. The words of Moses admonishing the people to be loyal to the terms of the covenant are very much in line with what any royal envoy would have been expected to say. The vassal would have been reminded that it was a privilege to be brought into this agreement and that it would be prudent to refrain from any action that would jeopardize those privileges.

1:1—2:3

Creation

1:1. In the beginning. An Egyptian creation text from Thebes speaks of the god Amun who evolved in the beginning, or "on the first occasion." Egyptologists interpret this not as an abstract idea but as a reference to a first-time event. In the same manner, the Hebrew word translated "beginning" usually refers not to a point in time but to an initial period. This suggests that the beginning period is the seven days of chapter one.

1:2. formless and empty. In Egyptian views of origins there is the concept of the "nonexist-ent" that may be very close to what is expressed here in Genesis. It is viewed as that which has not yet been differentiated and assigned function. No boundaries or definitions have been established. The Egyptian concept, however, also carries with it the idea of potentiality and a quality of being absolute.

1:2. Spirit of God. Some interpreters have translated this as a supernatural or mighty wind (the Hebrew word translated "Spirit" is sometimes translated "wind" in other passages), which has a parallel in the Babylonian *Enuma Elish*. There the sky god, Anu, creates the four winds that stir up the deep and its goddess, Tiamat. There it is a disruptive wind bringing unrest. The same phenomena can be seen in Daniel's vision of the four beasts where "the four winds of heaven were churning up the great sea" (7:2), a situation that disturbs the beasts there. If this is correct, then the wind would be part of the negative description of verse 2, paralleled by the darkness.

1:1-5. evening and morning. The account of creation does not intend to give a modern scientific explanation of the origin of all natural phenomena, but rather to address the more practical aspects of creation that surround our experiences of living and surviving. In the course of this chapter the author relates how God set up alternating periods of light and darkness—the basis for time. The narrative speaks of evening first because the first time period of light is just coming to a close. The author does not attempt an analysis of the physical properties of light, nor is he concerned about its source or generation. Light is the regulator of time.

1:3-5. light. The people of the ancient world did not believe that all light came from the sun. There was no knowledge that the moon simply reflected the light of the sun. Moreover, there is no hint in the text that "daylight" was caused by sunlight. The sun, moon and stars were all seen as bearers of light, but daylight was present even when the sun was behind a cloud or eclipsed. It made its appearance before the sun rose, and remained after the sun set.

1:6-8. firmament. In a similar way the expanse (sometimes called "the firmament") set up in day two is the regulator of climate. The ancient Near Eastern cultures viewed the cosmos as featuring a three-tiered structure consisting of the heavens, the earth and the underworld. Climate originated from the heavens, and the expanse was seen as the mechanism that regulated moisture and sunlight. Though in the ancient world the expanse was generally viewed as more solid than we would understand it today, it is not the physical composition that is important but the function. In the Babylonian creation epic, *Enuma Elish*, the goddess representing this cosmic ocean, Tiamat, is divided in half by Marduk to make the waters above and the waters below.

1:9-19. function of the cosmos. Just as God is the One who set time in motion and set up the climate, he is likewise responsible for setting up all the other aspects of human existence. The availability of water and the ability of the land to grow vegetation; the laws of agriculture and the seasonal cycles; each of God's creatures, created with a role to play—all of this was ordered by God and was good, not tyrannical or threatening. This reflects the ancient understanding that the gods were responsible for setting up a system of operations. The functioning of the cosmos was much more important to the people of the ancient world than was its physical makeup or chemical composition. They described what they saw and, more important, what they experienced of the world as having been created by God. That it was all "good" reflects God's wisdom and justice. At the same time the text shows subtle ways of disagreeing with the perspective of the ancient Near East. Most notable is the fact that it avoids using names for the sun and moon, which to the neighbors of the Israelites were also the names of the corresponding deities, and refers instead to the greater light and the lesser light.

1:14. signs and seasons. In a prologue to a Sumerian astrological treatise, the major gods, An, Enlil and Enki, put the moon and stars in place to regulate days, months and omens. In the famous Babylonian Hymn to Shamash, the sun god, reference is also made to his role in regulating the seasons and the calendar in general. It is intriguing that he is also the patron of divination. The Hebrew word used for "sign" has a cognate in Akkadian that is used for omens. The Hebrew word, however, has a more neutral sense, and again the author has emptied the elements of the cosmos of their more personal traits.

1:20. great creatures of the sea. In the Babylonian Hymn to Shamash, the sun god is said to receive praise and reverence even from the worst groups. Included in the list are the fearsome monsters of the sea. The hymn thus suggests that there is a total submission of all creatures to Shamash, just as the Genesis creation texts shows all creatures created by, and therefore submitted to, Yahweh. The Labbu Myth records the creation of the sea viper, whose length was sixty leagues.

1:20-25. zoological categories. The zoological categories include various species of (1) sea creatures, (2) birds, (3) land-based creatures, which are divided into domestic and wild animals and "creatures that move along the ground" (perhaps the reptiles and/or amphibians), and (4) humans. Insects and the microscopic world of creatures are not mentioned, but the categories are broad enough to include them.

1:26-31. function of people. While the organizational or functional focus of the account may have similarities with the ancient Near Eastern perspective, the reason for it all is quite different. In the ancient Near East, the gods created for themselves—the world was their environment for their enjoyment and existence. People were created only as an afterthought, when the gods needed slave labor to help provide the conveniences of life (such as irrigation trenches). In the Bible the cosmos was created and organized to function on behalf of the people that God planned as the centerpiece of his creation.

1:26-31. creation of people in ancient Near Eastern myths. In creation accounts from Mesopotamia an entire population of people is created, already civilized, using a mixture of clay and the blood of a slain rebel god. This creation comes about as the result of conflict among the gods, and the god organizing the cosmos had to overcome the forces of chaos to bring order to his created world. The Genesis account portrays God's creation not as part of a conflict with opposing forces but as a serene and controlled process.

1:26-27. image of God. When God created people, he put them in charge of all of his creation. He endowed them with his own image. In the ancient world an image was believed to carry the essence of that which it represented. An idol image of deity, the same terminology as used here, would be used in the worship of that deity because it contained the deity's essence. This would not suggest that the image could do what the deity could do, nor that it looked the same as the deity. Rather, the deity's work was thought to be accomplished through the idol. In similar ways the governing work of God was seen to be accomplished by people. But that is not all there is to the image of God. Genesis 5:1-3 likens the image of God in Adam to the image of Adam in Seth. This goes beyond the comment about plants and animals reproducing after their own kind, though certainly children share physical characteristics and basic nature (genetically) with their parents. What draws the idol imagery and the child imagery together is the concept that the image provides the capacity not only to serve in the place of God (his representative containing his essence) but also to be and act like him. The tools he provided so that we may accomplish that task include conscience, self-awareness and spiritual discernment. Mesopotamian traditions speak of sons being in the image of their fathers (*Enuma Elish*) but do not speak of humans created in the image of God; but the Egyptian *Instructions of Merikare* identifies humankind as the god's images who came from his body. In Mesopotamia a significance of the image can be seen in the practice of kings setting up images of themselves in places where they want to establish their authority. Other than that, it is only other gods who are made in the image of gods. (See comment on 5:3.)

2:1-3. seventh-day rest. In the Egyptian creation account from Memphis, the creator god Ptah rests after the completion of his work. Likewise the creation of humans is followed by rest for the Mesopotamian gods. In Mesopotamia, however, the rest is a result of the fact that people have been created to do the work that the gods were tired of doing. Nonetheless, the desire for rest is one of the motivating elements driving these creation narratives. The containment or destruction of chaotic cosmic forces that is often a central part of ancient creation narratives leads to rest, peace or repose for the gods. Likewise it is the gods' inability to find rest from the noise and disturbance of humankind that leads to the flood. In all it is clear that ancient ideologies considered rest to be one of the principal objectives of the gods. In Israelite theology, God does not require rest *from* either cosmic or human disturbances but seeks rest *in* a dwelling place (see especially Ps 132:7-8, 13-14).

2:1. sabbath divisions. Dividing time into seven-day periods was a practice that is so far unattested in the other cultures of the ancient Near East, though there were particular days of the month in Mesopotamia that were considered unlucky, and they were often seven days apart (that is, the seventh day of the month, the fourteenth day of the month, etc.). Israel's sabbath was not celebrated on certain days of the month and was not linked to the cycles of the moon or to any other cycle of nature; it was simply observed every seventh day.

2:4-25

Man and Woman in the Garden

2:5. botanical categories. Only the most general descriptions of plants are found. Trees, shrubs and plants are listed, but no specific species. We know, however, that the principal trees found in the Near East were acacia, cedar, Cypress, fig, oak, olive, date palm, pomegranate, tamarisk and willow. Shrubs included the oleander and juniper. The principal cultivated grains were wheat, barley and lentils. The description in this verse differs from day three in that it refers to domesticated or cultivated plants. The reference then is not to a time before day three but to the fact that agriculture was not taking place.

2:5. description of condition. A creation text from Nippur sets the scene for creation by saying that waters did not yet flow through the opening in the earth and that nothing was growing and no furrow had been made.

2:6. watering system. The word used to describe the watering system in verse 6 (NIV: "streams") is difficult to translate. It occurs elsewhere only in Job 36:27. A similar word occurs in *Babylonian vocabulary drawn from early *Sumerian in reference to the system of subterranean waters, the primordial underground river. The Sumerian myth of *Enki and Ninhursag likewise mentions such a watering system.

2:7. man from dust. The creation of the first man out of the dust of the earth is similar to what is found in ancient Near Eastern mythology. The Atrahasis Epic portrays the creation of humankind out of the blood of a slain deity mixed with clay. Just as dust in the Bible represents what the body becomes at death (Gen 3:19), so clay was what the body returned to in *Babylonian thinking. The blood of deity represented the divine essence in mankind, a similar concept to God's bringing Adam into being with the breath of life. In Egyptian thinking it is the tears of the god that are mixed with clay to form man, though the *Instructions of Merikare* also speak of the god's making breath for their noses.

2:8-14. location of Eden. Based on the proximity of the Tigris and Euphrates Rivers and the *Sumerian legend of the mystical, utopian land of *Dilmun, most scholars would identify Eden as a place in or near the northern end of the Persian Gulf. *Dilmun has been identified with the island of Bahrain. The direction that it is "in the east" merely points to the gen-

---

ANCIENT NEAR EASTERN MYTHOLOGY AND THE OLD TESTAMENT

Mythology in the ancient world was like science in our modern world—it was their explanation of how the world came into being and how it worked. The mythological approach attempted to identify function as a consequence of purpose. The gods had purposes, and their activiteis were the causes of what humans experienced as effects. In contrast, our modern scientific approach identifies function as a consequence of sturcture and attempts to understand cause and effect based on natural laws thaat are linked to the structure, the composite parts, of a phenomenon. Beccause our scientific worldview is keenly interested in structure, we often go to the biblical account looking for information on structure. In this area, however, the biblical worldview is much more like its ancient Near Eastern counterparts in that it views function as a consequence of purpose. That is what Genesis 1 is all about—it has very little interest in structures. This is only one of many areas where understanding ancient Near Eastern culture, literature and worldview can help us understand the Bible.

Many parallels can be identified between ancient Near Eastern mythology and Old Testament passages and concepts. This is not to suggest that the Old Testament is to be considered simply as another example of ancient mythology or as being dependent on that literature. Mythology is a window to culture. It reflects the worldview and values of the culture that forged it. Many of the writings we find in

eral area of Mesopotamia and is fairly typical of primordial narratives. This, plus the direction of flow of the rivers (the location of the Pishon and Gihon being uncertain), has caused some to look in the Armenia region, near the sources of the Tigris and Euphrates. However, the characteristics of a well-watered garden in which humans do little or no work and in which life springs up without cultivation fits the marshy areas at the base of the Gulf and may even be an area now covered by the waters of the region.

2:8. The "garden of Eden." The word *Eden* refers to a well-watered place, suggesting a luxuriant park. The word translated "garden" does not typically refer to vegetable plots but to orchards or parks containing trees.

2:9. tree of life. The tree of life is portrayed elsewhere in the Bible as offering extension of life (Prov 3:16-18), which sometimes can be viewed as having rejuvenating qualities. Various plants with such qualities are known from the ancient Near East. In the *Gilgamesh Epic* there is a plant called "old man becomes young" that grows at the bottom of the cosmic river. Trees often figure prominently in ancient Near Eastern art and on cylinder seals. These have often been interpreted as depicting a tree of life, but more support from the literature would be necessary to confirm such an interpretation.

2:11. Pishon. Analysis of sand patterns in Saudi Arabia and satellite photography have helped identify an old riverbed running northeast through Saudi Arabia from the Hijaz Mountains near Medina to the Persian Gulf in Kuwait near the mouth of the Tigris and Euphrates. This would be a good candidate for the Pishon River.

2:11. Havilah. Perhaps because gold is mentioned in relation to Havilah, it is named in several other passages (Gen 10:7; 25:18; 1 Sam

15:7; 1 Chron 1:9). It has most often been placed in western Saudi Arabia near Medina along the Red Sea, an area that does produce gold, bdellium and onyx. Genesis 10:7 describes Havilah as the "brother" of Ophir, a region also known for its wealth in gold.

2:21-22. rib. The use of Adam's rib for the creation of Eve may find illumination in the *Sumerian language. The Sumerian word for rib is *ti*. Of interest is the fact that *ti* means "life," just as *Eve* does (3:20). Others have suggested that a connection should be seen with the Egyptian word *imw*, which can mean either clay (out of which man was made) or rib.

2:24. man leaving father and mother. This statement is a narrative aside, which provides a comment on the social world of the people in later times. It uses the story of Eve's creation as the basis for the legal principle of separate households. When a marriage was contracted, the wife left her parents' home and joined the household of her husband. New loyalties were established in this way. Furthermore, the consummation of the marriage is associated here with the idea of the couple becoming one flesh again, just as Adam and Eve come from one body. The statement here that the *man* will leave his family does not necessarily refer to a particular sociology, but to the fact that in this chapter it is the man who has been seeking a companion. It also may reflect the fact that wedding ceremonies, including the wedding night, often took place in the house of the bride's parents.

3:1-24

The Fall and the Pronouncement

3:1. significance of serpents in ancient world. From the very earliest evidence in ancient Near Eastern art and literature, the serpent is presented as a significant character. Perhaps

the Old Testament performed the same function for ancient Israelite culture that mythology did for other cultures—they provided a literary mechanism for preserving and transmitting their worldview and values. Israel was part of a larger cultural complex that existed across the ancient Near East. There are many aspects of that cultural complex that it shared with its neighbors, though each individual culture had its distinguishing features. When we seek to understand the culture and literature of Israel, we rightly expect to find help in the larger cultural arena, from mythology, wisdom writings, legal documents and royal inscriptions.

The community of faith need not fear the use of such methods to inform us of the common cultural heritage of the Near East. Neither the theological message of the text nor its status as God's Word is jeopardized by these comparative studies. In fact, since revelation involves effective communication, we would expect that whenever possible God would use known and familiar elements to communicate to his people. Identification of similarities as well as differences can provide important background for a proper understanding of the text. This book has only the task of giving information and cannot engage in detailed discussion of how each individual similarity or difference can be explained. Some of that type of discussion can be found in John Walton, *Ancient Israelite Literature in Its Cultural Context* (Grand Rapids: Zondervan, 1987).

because its poison was a threat to life and its lidless eyes provided an enigmatic image, the serpent has been associated with both death and wisdom. The Genesis account evokes both aspects in the wisdom dialogue between the serpent and Eve and with the introduction of death after the expulsion from Eden. Similarly, *Gilgamesh is cheated out of perpetual youth when a serpent consumes a magical plant the hero had retrieved from the sea bottom. The sinister image of the serpent is graphically displayed by the intertwining coils of a snake encompassing a *cult stand found at Beth-Shean. Whether as a representative of primeval chaos (*Tiamat or *Leviathan) or a symbol of sexuality, the serpent harbors mystery for humans. Of particular interest is the *Sumerian god Ningishzida, who was portrayed in serpent shape and whose name means "Lord of the Productive/Steadfast Tree." He was considered a ruler in the nether world and "throne-bearer of the earth." He was one of the deities that offered the bread of life to *Adapa (see next comment). Even when not related to a god, the serpent represented wisdom (occult), *fertility, health, chaos and immortality, and was often worshiped.

3:2-5. temptation to be like God. Aspiration to deity and lost opportunities to become like the gods figure prominently in a few ancient myths. In the tale of *Adapa an offer of the "food of life" is inadvertently refused. Adapa, the first of the seven sages before the flood, is attempting to bring the arts of civilization to the first city, Eridu. As a fisherman, he had an unfortunate escapade with the south wind one day that eventuated in an audience with the chief god, Anu. Under the advice of the god *Ea, when Anu offered him food he refused it, only to discover that it was food that would bring immortality. Eternal life also eludes *Gilgamesh. In the famous epic about him, the death of his friend Enkidu leads him in a search for immortality, which he discovers is unattainable. In both of these accounts, being like the gods is viewed in terms of achieving immortality, whereas in the biblical account it is understood in terms of wisdom.

3:7. fig leaf significance. Fig leaves are the largest found in Canaan and could provide limited covering for the shamed couple. The significance of the fig's use may lie in its symbolism of fertility. By eating the forbidden fruit, the couple have set in motion their future role as parents and as cultivators of fruit trees and grain.

3:8. cool of the day. *Akkadian terminology

has demonstrated that the word translated "day" also has the meaning "storm." This meaning can be seen also for the Hebrew word in Zephaniah 2:2. It is often connected to the deity coming in a storm of judgment. If this is the correct rendering of the word in this passage, they heard the thunder (the word translated "sound" is often connected to thunder) of the Lord moving about in the garden in the wind of the storm. In this case it is quite understandable why they are hiding.

3:14. eating dust. The depiction of dust or dirt for food is typical of descriptions of the netherworld in ancient literature. In the Gilgamesh Epic, Enkidu on his deathbed dreams of the netherworld and describes it as a place with no light and where "dust is their food, clay their bread," a description also known from the *Descent of Ishtar*. These are most likely considered characteristic of the netherworld because they describe the grave. Dust fills the mouth of the corpse, but dust will also fill the mouth of the serpent as it crawls along the ground.

3:14-15. curses on serpents. The Egyptian Pyramid Texts (second half of third millennium) contain a number of spells against serpents, but likewise include spells against other creatures considered dangers or pests who threaten the dead. Some of these spells enjoin the serpent to crawl on its belly (keep its face on the path). This is in contrast to raising its head up to strike. The serpent on its belly is nonthreatening, while the one reared up is protecting or attacking. Treading on the serpent is used in these texts as a means of overcoming or defeating it.

3:14-15. all snakes poisonous. While it would have been observable that not all snakes were poisonous, the threat provided by some would, in the haste to protect oneself, attach itself to all. Of thirty-six species of snake known to the area, the viper *(Vipera palaestinae)* is the only poisonous snake in northern and central Israel. Snakes are associated occasionally with fertility and life (bronze serpent in the wilderness). However, they most often are tied to the struggle for life and the inevitability of death. The poisonous snakes would be the most aggressive, so an attack by a snake would always be viewed as a potentially mortal blow.

3:16. labor pains. Perhaps displaying the dual character of life, the joy of motherhood can be gained only through labor pain. Without modern medicine, these pains are described as the worst possible agony for humans (see Is 13:8; 21:3) and gods (note the *Babylonian goddess *Ishtar's cry in the *Gilgamesh flood epic when she sees the horror of the flood unleashed). *Babylonians associated demons such as Lamashtu with the pain of childbirth and the tenuous condition of life for both mother and child in the birth process.

3:16. husband-wife relationship. Arranged marriages downplayed the role of romantic love in ancient Israelite society. However, in this labor-poor society men and women had to work together as a team. While pregnancy and child care periodically restricted the woman's work in the fields or the shop, a couple's survival was largely based on shared labor and the number of children they produced. Domination of the wife by her husband, while evident in some marriages, was not the ideal in ancient relationships. Both had their roles, although the legal rights with regard to making contracts, owning property and inheritance rights were primarily controlled by males. It is also a fact that concern over female chastity led to restrictions on associations by females and male control of the legal process.

3:17. toil. In Mesopotamian thinking people were created to be slaves and to do the work that the gods had tired of doing for themselves, much of it concerned with the agricultural process. In *Enuma Elish* the entire purpose for creating people was to relieve the gods of their toil, unlike the biblical account, in which people were created to rule and became burdened with toil only as a result of the Fall.

3:18. thorns and thistles. In the Gilgamesh Epic, a paradiselike place is described as featuring plants and trees that grow gems and precious stones instead of thorns and thistles.

3:20. significance of naming. Adam earlier had named the animals, which was a demonstration of his authority over them. Here his naming of Eve suggests Adam's position of rule, as referred to in verse 16. In the ancient world when one king placed a vassal king on the throne, a new name would often be given to demonstrate the overlord's dominion. Likewise, when God enters *covenant relationships with Abram and Jacob, he changes their names. A final example occurs in the *Babylonian account of creation, *Enuma Elish*, which opens with the situation before heaven and earth were named. The account proceeds to give names, just as God names the things he creates in Genesis 1.

3:21. skin garments. The long outer tunic is still the basic garment for many people in the Middle East. This replaces the inadequate fig leaf covering made by Adam and Eve. God provides them with these garments as the type of gift given by a patron to a client. Gifts of clothing are among the most common presents mentioned in the Bible (see Joseph in Gen 41:42) and other ancient texts. It also prepares them for the rigors of weather and work which await them. In the *Tale of Adapa* (see comment on 3:2-5), after *Adapa loses the opportunity to eat from the bread and water of life, he is given clothing by the god Anu before being sent from his presence.

3:24. cherubim. The cherubim are supernatural creatures referred to over ninety times in the Old Testament, where they usually function in the capacity of guardians of God's presence. From the guardian of the tree of life, to the ornamental representation over the mercy seat on the ark of the covenant, to the accompaniment of the chariot/throne in Ezekiel's visions, the cherubim are always closely associated with the person or property of deity. Biblical descriptions (Ezek 1, 10) agree with archaeological finds that suggest they are composite creatures (like griffins or sphinxes). Representations of these creatures are often found flanking the throne of the king. Here in Genesis the cherubim guard the way to the tree of life, now forbidden property of God. An interesting Neo-Assyrian seal depicts what appears to be a fruit tree flanked by two such creatures with deities standing on their backs supporting a winged sun disk.

4:1-16
Cain and Abel

4:1-7. sacrifices of Cain and Abel. The sacrifices of Cain and Abel are not depicted as addressing sin or seeking atonement. The word used designates them very generally as "gifts"—a word that is most closely associated with the grain offering later in Leviticus 2. They appear to be intended to express gratitude to God for his bounty. Therefore it is appropriate that Cain should bring an offering from the produce that he grew, for blood would not be mandatory in such an offering. It should be noted that Genesis does not preserve any record of God requesting such offerings, though he approved of it as a means of expressing thanks. Gratitude is not expressed, however, when the gift is grudgingly given, as is likely the case with Cain.

4:11-12. nomadic lifestyle. The wandering nomadic lifestyle to which Cain is doomed represents one of the principal economic/social divisions in ancient society. Once animals had been domesticated, around 8000 B.C., herding and pastoral nomadism became a major economic pursuit for tribes and villages. Genera` ly, herding was part of a mixed village economy, including agriculture and trade. However, some groups concentrated more of their efforts on taking sheep and goats to new pasture as the seasons changed. These semi-nomadic herdsmen followed particular migration routes which provided adequate water for their animals as well as grazing. Contracts were sometimes made with villages along the route for grazing in harvested fields. These herdsmen occasionally clashed with settled communities over water rights or because of raiding. Governments tried to control nomadic groups within their area, but these attempts were not usually successful over long periods of time. The result is the composition of stories which describe the conflict between herders and farmers as they compete for use of the land.

4:14-15. blood vengeance. In areas where the central government had not gained full control, blood feuds between families were common. They were based on the simple principle of "an eye for an eye," which demanded the death of a murderer or the death of a member of his family as restitution. There was also an assumption that kinship ties included the obligation to defend the honor of the household. No hurt could be ignored, or the household would be considered too weak to defend itself and other groups would take advantage of them. Cain's comment assumes that there is a more extensive family in existence and that some from Abel's line would seek revenge.

4:15. mark of Cain. The Hebrew word used here does not denote a tatoo or mutilation inflicted on a felon or slave (referred to in the Laws of *Eshnunna and the Code of *Hammurabi). It best compares to the mark of divine protection placed on the foreheads of the innocents in Jerusalem in Ezekiel 9:4-6. It may be an external marking that would cause others to treat him with respect or caution. However, it may represent a sign from God to Cain that he would not be harmed and people would not attack him.

4:17-26

The Line of Cain

4:17. city building. Because the founding of a city is tied so intimately to the founding of a nation or people in the ancient world, stories about the founder and the circumstances surrounding its founding are a part of the basic heritage of the inhabitants. These stories generally include a description of the natural resources which attracted the builder (water supply, grazing and crop land, natural defens-

es), the special attributes of the builder (unusual strength and/or wisdom) and the guidance of the patron god. Cities were constructed along or near rivers or springs. They served as focal points for trade, culture and religious activity for a much larger region and thus eventually became political centers or city states. The organization required to build them and then to keep their mud-brick and stone walls in repair helped generate the development of assemblies of elders and monarchies to rule them.

4:19. polygamy. The practice of a man marrying more than one wife is known as polygamy. This custom was based on several factors: (1) an imbalance in the number of males and females, (2) the need to produce large numbers of children to work herds and/or fields, (3) the desire to increase the prestige and wealth of a household through multiple marriage contracts and (4) the high rate of death of females in childbirth. Polygamy was most common among pastoral nomadic groups and in rural farming communities, where it was important that every female be attached to a household and be productive. Monarchs also practiced polygamy, primarily as a means of making alliances with powerful families or other nations. In such situations the wives might also end up as hostages if the political relationship soured.

4:20. animal domestication. Raising livestock is the first stage in animal domestication, which involves human control of breeding, food supply and territory. Sheep and goats were the first livestock to be domesticated, with the evidence extending back to the ninth millennium B.C. Larger cattle came a bit later, and evidence for pig domestication begins in the seventh millennium.

4:21. musical instruments. Musical instruments were among the first inventions of early humans. In Egypt the earliest end-blown flutes date to the fourth millennium B.C. A number of harps and lyres as well as a pair of silver flutes were found in the royal cemetery at *Ur dating to the early part of the third millennium. Flutes made of bone or pottery date back at least to the fourth millennium. Musical instruments provided entertainment as well as background rhythm for dances and *ritual performances, such as processions or *cultic dramas. Other than simple percussion instruments (drums and rattles), the most common instruments used in the ancient Near East were harps and lyres. Examples have been found in excavated tombs and painted on the walls of temples and palaces. They are described in literature as a means of soothing the spirit, invoking the gods to speak and providing the cadence for a marching army. Musicians had their own guilds and were highly respected.

4:22. ancient metal technology. As part of the account of the emergence of crafts and technology in the genealogy of Cain, it is appropriate that the origin of metalworking would be mentioned. *Assyrian texts mention Tabal and Musku as the early metalworking regions in the Taurus Mountains (of eastern Turkey). Copper tools, weapons and implements began to be smelted and forged in the fourth millennium B.C. Subsequently, alloys of copper, principally bronze, were introduced in the early third millennium as sources of tin were discovered outside the Near East and trade routes expanded to bring them to Egypt and Mesopotamia. Iron, a metal which requires much higher temperatures and skin bellows (portrayed in the Egyptian Beni Hasan tomb paintings) to refine and work, was the last to be introduced, toward the end of the second millennium B.C. *Hittite smiths seem to have been the first to exploit it, and then the technology spread east and south. Meteorite iron was cold-forged for centuries prior to its smelting. That would not represent as large an industry as the forging of terrestrial deposits, but it would explain some of the early references to iron prior to the *Iron Age.

5:1-32

The Line of Seth

5:1. the account of (toledoth). This chapter begins by introducing "the written account of Adam's line"—just as 2:4 had referred to the account of the heavens and earth. Genesis uses this label eleven times throughout the book. Earlier translations used the word "generations" in place of "account." In other places in the Bible this word is most often associated with genealogies. Some believe that in Genesis they indicate written sources that the author used in compiling the book. Alternatively, they could simply be understood as introducing the people and events that "eventuated" from the named individual. In any case they serve as convenient division markers between the sections of the book.

5:1-32. importance of genealogies. Genealogies represent continuity and relationship. Often in the ancient Near East they are used for purposes of power and prestige. Linear genealogies start at point A (the creation of Adam and Eve, for example) and end at point B (Noah and the flood). Their intention is to bridge a gap between major events. Alterna-

tively they can be vertical, tracing the descendants of a single family (Esau in Gen 36:1-5, 9-43). In the case of linear genealogies, the actual amount of time represented by these successive generations does not seem to be as important as the sense of completion or adherence to a purpose (such as the charge to be fertile and fill the earth). Vertical genealogies focus on establishing legitimacy for membership in the family or tribe (as in the case of the Levitical genealogies in Ezra 2). Mesopotamian sources do not offer many genealogies, but most of those that are known are linear in nature. Most of these are either of royal or scribal families, and most are only three generations, with none more than twelve. Egyptian genealogies are mostly of priestly families and are likewise linear. They extend to as many as seventeen generations but are not common until the first millennium B.C. Genealogies are often formatted to suit a literary purpose. So, for instance, the genealogies between Adam and Noah, and Noah and Abraham, are each set up to contain ten members, with the last having three sons. Comparing biblical genealogies to one another shows that there are often several generations skipped in any particular presentation. This type of telescoping also occurs in *Assyrian genealogical records. Thus we need not think that the genealogy's purpose is to represent every generation, as our modern family trees attempt to do.

5:3. Adam's son in his likeness and image. This same type of comparison is made in *Enuma Elish between the generations of the gods. Anshar begets Anu like himself, and Anu begets Nudimmud (Enki) in his likeness.

5:3-32. long lives. Although there is no satisfactory explanation of the long life spans before the flood, there are *Sumerian lists of kings who purportedly reigned before the flood with reigns as long as 43,200 years. The Sumerians used the sexagesimal number system (a combination of base six and base ten), and when the numbers of the Sumerian king list are converted to decimal, they are very much in the range of the age spans of the preflood genealogies of Genesis. The Hebrews, like most other Semitic peoples, used a base-ten decimal system as far back as writing extends.

5:21-24. God took Enoch. Seventh in the line, Enoch was the most outstanding individual in the line of Seth. As a result of walking with God (a phrase expressing piety) he was "taken"—an alternative to dying, the stated fate of all the others in the genealogy. The text does not say *where* he was taken, a possible indication that the author did not profess to know.

We can properly assume that he was believed to have been taken to a better place, for this fate was seen as a reward for his close relationship to God, but the text stops short of saying he went to heaven or to be with God. In the Mesopotamian lists of preflood sages, the seventh in the list, Utuabzu, is said to have ascended to heaven. In the Egyptian Pyramid Texts, Shu, the god of the air, is instructed to take the king to heaven so he does not die on earth. This simply represents the transition from mortality to immortality. Jewish writings after the time of the Old Testament offer extensive speculation about Enoch and portray him as an ancient source of revelation and apocalyptic visions (*1, 2* and *3 Enoch*).

5:29. comfort us. The name Noah means "rest," bringing out again the importance of this motif in the ancient Near East (see comment on 2:1-3). The Mesopotamian gods sent the flood because the disturbances of the human world were preventing them from getting rest. So in that case, the flood provided rest for the gods. Here Noah is rather associated with bringing rest for people from the curse of the gods.

6:1-4
The Sons of God and the Daughters of Men

6:2. sons of God. The term "sons of God" is used elsewhere in the Old Testament to refer to angels, but the idea of sonship to God is also portrayed corporately for the Israelites and individually for kings. In the ancient Near East kings were commonly understood as having a filial relationship to deity and were often considered to have been engendered by deity.

6:2. marrying whom they chose. The practice of marrying "any of them they chose" has been interpreted by some to be a reference to polygamy. While it is not to be doubted that polygamy was practiced, it is difficult to imagine why that would be worthy of note, since polygamy was an acceptable practice even in Israel in Old Testament times. It is more likely that this is a reference to the "right of the first night," cited as one of the oppressive practices of kings in the *Gilgamesh Epic. The king could exercise his right, as representative of the gods, to spend the wedding night with any woman who was being given in marriage. This presumably was construed as a *fertility rite. If this is the practice referred to here, it would offer an explanation of the nature of the offense.

6:3. 120 years. The limitation of 120 years most

likely refers to a reduction of the life span of humans, since it is in the context of a statement about mortality. While the verse is notoriously difficult to translate, modern consensus is moving toward translating it "My spirit will not remain in man forever," thus affirming mortality. Just as the offense can be understood in light of information from the Gilgamesh Epic, so this statement may refer to the never-ending quest for immortality; a quest such as is at the core of the Gilgamesh Epic. Though Gilgamesh lived after the flood, these elements of the narrative resonate with universal human experience. A wisdom text from the town of Emar cites 120 years as the most years given to humans by the gods.

6:4. Nephilim. *Nephilim* is not an ethnic designation but a description of a particular type of individual. In Numbers 13:33 they are identified, along with the descendants of Anak, as some of the inhabitants of the land of Canaan. The latter are described as giants, but there is no reason to consider the Nephilim to be giants. It is more likely that the term describes heroic warriors, perhaps the ancient equivalent of knights errant.

6:5—8:22
The Flood

6:13. violence as cause of flood. In the Atrahasis Epic's account of the flood the reason that the gods decide to send the flood is the "noise" of mankind. This is not necessarily different from the biblical reason in that "noise" can be the result of violence. Abel's blood cries out from the ground (4:10) and the outcry against Sodom and Gomorrah is great (Gen 18:20). The noise could be generated either by the number of petitions being made to the gods to respond to the violence and bloodshed or by the victims who cry out in their distress.

6:14. gopher wood. *Gopher* is the Hebrew word translated "cypress wood" in the NIV. This is an unknown type of material, although it undoubtedly refers to some sort of coniferous tree thought to possess great strength and durability. Cypress was often used by shipbuilders in the ancient Near East. Similarly, the cedars of Lebanon were prized by the Egyptians for the construction of their barques for transport on the Nile, for instance in the eleventh century B.C. *Diary of *Wenamon*.

6:14. boats in the ancient world. Prior to the invention of seaworthy vessels that could carry sailors and cargo through the heavy seas of the Mediterranean, most boats were made of skin or reeds and were designed to sail through marshes or along the river bank. They were used for fishing or hunting and would not have been more than ten feet in length. True sailing ships, with a length of 170 feet, are first depicted in Old Kingdom Egyptian art (c. 2500 B.C.) and are described in *Ugaritic (1600-1200 B.C.) and Phoenician (1000-500 B.C.) texts. Remains of shipwrecks from the mid-second millennium (*Late Bronze Age) have also been found in the Mediterranean. They still generally navigated within sight of land, with trips to Crete and Cyprus as well as the ports along the coasts of Egypt, the Persian Gulf and Asia Minor.

6:14-16. size of the ark. Based on a measurement of one cubit equaling eighteen inches or forty-five centimeters, the ark Noah constructs is approximately 450 feet (135 meters) long, 75 feet (22 meters) wide, and 45 feet (13 meters) deep. If it had a flat bottom, the total surface capacity would be about three times that of the tabernacle (100 by 50 cubits in Ex 27:9-13), with a displacement of 43,000 tons. In comparison, the ark constructed by *Utnapishtim in the *Babylonian version of the *Gilgamesh Epic is either a cube or ziggurat-shaped (120 by 120 by 120 cubits), with a displacement of three or four times that of the Genesis ark. Noah's ark was not designed to be navigated—no rudder or sail is mentioned. Thus the fate of the company aboard was left in the hands of God. Although *Utnapishtim does employ a navigator, the shape of his ark may be magical, since he could not depend on the gods to preserve him.

6:15-16. length measurements. The standard measurement unit for length was the cubit, which was eighteen inches (forty-five centimeters). This was based on the length of a man's forearm, from his fingertips to his elbow. Other units include the span, the hand-breadth/palm and the finger. Use of a "four-finger equals one palm" and of a "twenty-four-finger equals one cubit" measure is common throughout the ancient Near East. Some variations do occur, such as seven palms equals one cubit in Egypt and thirty fingers equals one cubit in *Babylonia until the *Chaldean period (perhaps based on their use of a sexagesimal mathematics system).

6:17. archaeological evidences of flood. There is presently no convincing archaeological evidence of the biblical flood. The examination of silt levels at the *Sumerian cities of *Ur, Kish, Shuruppak, *Lagash and *Uruk (all of which have occupation levels at least as early as 2800 B.C.) are from different periods and do not reflect a single massive flood that inundated them all at the same time. Similarly, the city of Jericho, which has been continuously occupied since 7000 B.C., has no flood deposits whatsoever. Climatological studies have indicated that the period from 4500 to 3500 B.C. was significantly wetter in this region, but that offers little to go on. The search for the remains of Noah's ark have centered on the Turkish peak of Agri Dagh (17,000 feet) near Lake Van. However, no one mountain within the Ararat range is mentioned in the biblical account, and fragments of wood that have been carbon-14 dated from this mountain have proven to come from no earlier than the fifth century A.D.

7:2-4. seven of every kind. Though Noah

ANCIENT NEAR EASTERN FLOOD ACCOUNTS
The most significant ancient Near Eastern flood accounts are found in the Atrahasis Epic and the Gilgamesh Epic. In these accounts the chief god, Enlil, becomes angry at mankind (the Atrahasis Epic portrays him as disturbed over the "noise" of mankind, see next comment) and, after trying unsuccessfully to remedy the situation by reducing the population through things like drought and disease, persuades the divine assembly to approve a flood for the total elimination of mankind. The god Ea manages to forewarn one loyal worshipper, a king who is instructed to build a boat that will preserve not only him and his family, but representatives skilled in the various arts of civilization. The other people of the city are told that the gods are angry with the king and he must leave them. The pitch-covered boat has seven stories shaped either as a cube or, more likely, a ziggurat (see comment on 11:4). The storm lasts seven days and nights after which the boat comes to rest on Mt. Nisir. Birds are sent out to determine the time of leaving the ark. Sacrifices are made for which the gods are very thankful since they have been deprived of food (sacrifices) since the flood began.

The Atrahasis Epic is dated to the early second millennium B.C. The Gilgamesh Epic came into its present form during the second half of the second millennium, but used materials that were already in circulation at the end of the third millennium. From the short summary above one can detect a number of similarities as well as a number of differences. There is no reason to doubt that the ancient Near Eastern accounts and Genesis refer to the same flood. This would certainly account for the similarities. The differences exist because each culture is viewing the flood through its own theology and worldview.

takes two each of most animals into the ark, he is instructed in verse 2 to take seven pairs of every clean animal and of every bird. Additional clean animals would be needed both for the sacrifice after the flood and for quicker repopulation for human use. In some sacrificial *rituals seven of each class of designated animal are offered (cf. 2 Chron 29:21), but, of course, Noah is not going to sacrifice all of them.

7:2. clean and unclean before Moses. The distinction between clean and unclean animals was not an innovation established at Sinai but is seen as early as Noah. Evidence from Egypt and Mesopotamia offer no system equivalent to the Israelite system of classification. While there are dietary restrictions in those cultures, they tend to be much more limited, that is, certain animals restricted only to certain classes of people or on certain days of the month. Even here one cannot assume that the classification has implications for their diet. Up to this time no permission had been granted to eat meat (see 1:29). When meat was granted to them as food after the flood (9:2-3), there were no restrictions along the lines of clean and unclean. As a result it appears that the classification concerned sacrifice, not diet, in this period.

7:11. floodgates opened. The text uses the poetic phrase "windows of heaven" to describe the openings through which the rain came down. This is not scientific language but reflects the perspective of the observer, much as we would speak of the sun "setting." The only other occurrence of such a term in ancient Near Eastern literature is in the Canaanite myth of *Baal building his house, where the "window" of his house is described as a rift in the clouds. But even here it is not associated with rain. Alternate terminology occurs in the Mesopotamian texts, where gates of heaven are in the east and west for the sun to use in its rising and setting. Clouds and winds, however, also enter by these gates.

7:11—8:5. time periods of flood. The total elapse of time in the flood narrative can be viewed in different ways depending on how the given information is merged. From the information given in 7:11 and 8:14 it can be determined that Noah and his family were in the ark for twelve months and eleven days. The exact number of days would depend on how many days were counted in a month and whether any adjustments were being made between lunar and solar reckonings. The eleven days has been found interesting by some, since the lunar year of 354 days is eleven days shorter than the solar year.

8:4. Ararat. The mountains of Ararat are located in the Lake Van region of eastern Turkey in the area of Armenia (known as Urartu in *Assyrian inscriptions). This range of mountains (the highest peak reaching 17,000 feet) is also mentioned in 2 Kings 19:37, Isaiah 37:38 and Jeremiah 51:27. The *Gilgamesh epic, however, describes the flood hero's ark coming to rest on a specific mountaintop, Mount Nisir in southern Kurdistan.

8:6-12. use of birds in ancient Near East. One of the enduring pictures of the Noah account is that of Noah sending out the birds to gain information about the conditions outside the ark. The flood stories in the *Gilgamesh Epic and the Atrahasis Epic feature a similar use of birds. Rather than a raven and three missions for the dove, we find a dove, swallow and raven sent out. The dove and swallow return without finding a place, while the raven is pictured, as in 8:7, as flying about cawing and not returning (Gilg. 11.146-54). Ancient navigators were known to use birds to find land, but Noah is not navigating, and he is on land. His use of the birds is not for purposes of finding direction. It is also known that the flight patterns of birds sometimes served as omens, but neither Genesis nor Gilgamesh make observations from the flight of the birds sent out.

8:7. habits of ravens. Unlike pigeons or doves, which will return after being released, a raven's use to seamen is based on its line of flight. By noting the direction it chooses, a sailor may determine where land is located. The most sensible strategy is to release a raven first and then use other birds to determine the depth of the water and the likelihood of a place to land. A raven, by habit, lives on carrion and would therefore have sufficient food available.

8:9. habits of doves. The dove and the pigeon have a limited ability for sustained flight. Thus navigators use them to determine the location of landing sites. As long as they return, no landing is in close range. The dove lives at lower elevations and requires plants for food.

8:11. olive leaf significance. The olive leaf retrieved by the dove suggests the amount of time it would take for an olive tree to leaf out after being submerged—a clue to the current depth of the flood waters. It is also symbolic of new life and fertility to come after the flood. The olive is a difficult tree to kill, even if cut down. This freshly plucked shoot shows Noah that recovery has begun.

8:20-22. use of altars. Altars are a common element in many religions, ancient and modern. In the Bible altars were usually constructed of stone (hewn or unhewn), but in certain cir-

cumstances even a large rock would suffice
(Judg 13:19-20; 1 Sam 14:33-34). Many believe
that the altar would have been understood as
the table for the deity, since sacrifices were
popularly understood as providing a meal for
the god, though that imagery is not easily recognized in the Old Testament.

8:20. purpose of Noah's sacrifice. The purpose of Noah's sacrifice is not stated. The text
calls them "burnt offerings," which served a
broad function in the sacrificial system. It may
be more important to note what the text does
not call the sacrifice. It is not a sin offering, nor
specifically designated a thank offering. The
burnt offerings are usually associated with petitions or entreaties set before God. In contrast, the sacrifice offered after the flood in the
*Gilgamesh Epic and in the earlier *Sumerian
version of the flood story feature libations and
grain offerings as well as meat sacrifices in order to provide a feast for the gods. The general purpose for sacrifice in the ancient world
was to appease the anger of the gods by gifts
of food and drink, and that is probably the intention of the flood hero in the Mesopotamian
accounts.

8:21. pleasing aroma. Sacrifice here, as well as
throughout the Pentateuch, is said to produce
a pleasing aroma—terminology that was retained from the ancient contexts in which sacrifice was viewed as food for deity. This
account falls far short of the graphic description in the *Gilgamesh Epic, where the famished gods (deprived of food for the duration
of the flood) gather around the sacrifice "like
flies," glad to find reprieve from starvation.

9:1-17
The Covenant with Noah

9:2-4. meat eating in ancient world. Meat was
not a common dish on ancient dinner tables.
Animals were kept for their milk, hair and
wool, not specifically for their meat. Thus
meat was only available when an animal died
or was killed as a sacrifice. While meat is now
put on the list of acceptable foods, there is still
a restriction on eating meat with the blood. In
ancient times blood was considered a life force
(Deut 12:23). The prohibition does not require
that no blood at all be consumed, but only that
the blood must be drained. The draining of
the blood before eating the meat was a way of
returning the life force of the animal to the
God who gave it life. This offers recognition
that they have taken the life with permission
and are partaking of God's bounty as his
guests. Its function is not unlike that of the
blessing said before a meal in modern prac-

tice. No comparable prohibition is known in
the ancient world.

9:5-6. capital punishment. Human life, because of the image of God, remains under the
protection of God. The accountability to God
for preserving human life is put into humanity's hands, thus instituting blood vengeance
in the ancient world and capital punishment
in modern societies. In Israelite society blood
vengeance was in the hands of the family of
the victim.

9:8-17. covenant. A *covenant is a formal
agreement between two parties. The principal
section of a covenant is the stipulations section, which may include requirements for either party or both. In this covenant God takes
stipulations upon himself, rather than imposing them on Noah and his family. Unlike the
later covenant with Abraham, and those that
build on the covenant with Abraham, this
covenant does not entail election or a new
phase of revelation. It is also made with every
living creature, not just people.

9:13. rainbow significance. The designation
of the rainbow as a sign of the *covenant
does not suggest that this was the first rainbow ever seen. The function of a sign is connected to the significance attached to it. In
like manner, *circumcision is designated as a
sign of the covenant with Abraham, yet that
was an ancient practice, not new with Abraham and his family. In the *Gilgamesh Epic
the goddess *Ishtar identified the lapis lazuli
(deep blue semiprecious stones with traces of
gold-colored pyrite) of her necklace as the
basis of an oath by which she would never
forget the days of the flood. An eleventh-century *Assyrian relief shows two hands reaching out of the clouds, one hand offering
blessing, the other holding a bow. Since the
word for rainbow is the same word as that
used for the weapon, this is an interesting
image.

9:18-28
Noah's Pronouncement Concerning His Sons

9:21. drinking wine. The earliest evidence of
winemaking comes from neolithic Iran (Zagros region), where archaeologists discovered
a jar dated to the second half of the sixth millennium with a residue of wine in the bottom.

9:24-27. patriarchal pronouncements. When
Noah discovered that Ham had been indiscreet, he uttered a curse on Canaan and a
blessing on Shem and Japheth. In the biblical
material the patriarchal pronouncement generally concerns the destiny of the sons with re-

gard to the fertility of the ground, the fertility of the family and relationships between family members. Other examples in Genesis can be seen in 24:60; 27:27-29, 39-40; 48:15-16; 49:1-28. From this practice we can draw several conclusions concerning this passage. First of all, Ham's indiscreet action need not be seen as the "cause" for the curse, only the occasion that evoked it. Compare, for example, when Isaac asked Esau to prepare a meal so that he could bless him; the meal was not the cause of blessing, it only created a suitable environment for it. Second, we need not be concerned that Canaan appears to be singled out without cause. We could well assume that the pronouncement was much more comprehensive, including some unfavorable statements about Ham. The biblical writer has no need to preserve the whole—he merely chooses those sections that are pertinent to his point and relevant to his readers, since the Canaanites were the Hamites with whom Israel was most familiar. Third, we need not understand these as prophecies originating from God. There is no "Thus says the Lord . . ." They are the patriarch's pronouncement, not God's (cf. the use of the first person in 27:37). Even so, they were taken very seriously and considered to have influence in the unfolding of history and personal destiny.

10:1-32
The Table of Nations

10:1. criteria of division. The genealogy of Noah's family provides information on the future history and geographical distribution of peoples in the ancient Near East. Clues are given about the settlement of the coastal areas, northern Africa, Syria-Palestine and Mesopotamia. All of the major regions are thus represented, as well as most of the nations who will in some way interact with the Israelites, among them Egypt, Canaan, the Philistines, the Jebusites, *Elam and Asshur. This suggests the political division of the "world" at the time this list was written and provides a definite indication that the roots of the Israelites are in Mesopotamia. There is no attempt, however, to link these peoples to racial divisions. Ancient peoples were more concerned with distinctions based on nationality, linguistics and ethnicity.

10:2-29. names: personal, patronymic, political. The names of Noah's descendants listed in the "Table of Nations" are designed to reflect the totality of humanity and to give at least a partial sense of their geopolitical divisions and affiliations. A total of seventy peoples are listed, a number found elsewhere in the text for the number of Jacob's family to enter Egypt (Gen 46:27) and as the representatives of the nation (seventy elders, Ex 24:9; Ezek 8:11). Other examples of seventy representing totality are found in the number of gods in the *Ugaritic pantheon and the number of sons of Gideon (Judg 8:30) and of Ahab (2 Kings 10:1). The kinship ties established in the list of peoples have been considered by some to reflect political affiliation (lord-vassal relationships) rather than blood tie. Kinship language is sometimes used in the Bible to reflect political associations (1 Kings 9:13). Some of the names in the list appear to be the names of tribes or nations rather than of individuals. In *Hammurabi's genealogy a number of the names are tribal or geographical names, so this would not be unusual in an ancient document. As a vertical genealogy, this list is simply trying to establish relationships of various sorts.

10:2-5. Japhethites. Although not all of the descendants of Japheth are tied to contiguous regions, they could all be defined from an Israelite perspective as coming from across the sea (NIV: "maritime peoples" in v. 5). A *Babylonian world map from the seventh or eighth century illustrates the geographical worldview that there were many peoples considered on the outskirts of civilization beyond the sea. Many named here can be identified with sections or peoples in Asia Minor (Magog, Tubal, Meshek, Tyras, Togarmah) or the Ionian islands (Dodanim), as well as Cyprus (Elisha and Kittim). There are also several that seem, based on *Assyrian and *Babylonian records, to originate in the area to the east of the Black Sea and in the Iranian plateau— Cimmerians (Gomer), Scythians (Ashkenaz), Medes (Madai), Paphlagonians (Riphat). Tarshish presents the most problems, since it has generally been identified with Spain and that takes it out of the geographic sphere of the others. However, the theme of Greek or Indo-European peoples for these "nations" would make a tie to Sardinia or perhaps Carthage possible.

10:6-20. Hamites. The common theme in the genealogy of the Hamites is their close geographical, political and economic importance to the people of Israel. These nations serve as major rivals and literally surround Israel (Egypt, Arabia, Mesopotamia, Syro-Palestine). Most important here is the political placement of groups within the Egyptian sphere (Cush, Put, Mizraim and his descendants) and the Canaanite sphere (various peoples like the Jebusites and Hivites), and, interestingly, several are classified ethnically as Semitic peoples (Canaanites, Phoenicians, *Amorites). The list is also marked by brief narratives (Nimrod and Canaan) which break up the stereotypical genealogical framework and tie in areas (*Babylon, *Nineveh, Sidon, Sodom and Gomorrah) which will be significant in later periods of Israelite history.

10:8-12. Nimrod. Interpreters over the years have attempted to identify Nimrod with known historical figures such as Tukulti-Ninurta I (an *Assyrian king during the period of the biblical judges), or with Mesopotamian deities such as Ninurta, a warrior god and patron of the hunt, who in one myth hunts down a number of fantastic creatures and defeats or kills them. In Genesis, however, Nimrod is clearly a human hero rather than divine or even semidivine. Late Jewish tradition picked up occasionally by church fathers envisioned him as the builder of the Tower of Babel and the originator of idolatry, but these ideas have no basis in the text. The extension of his kingdom from southern Mesopotamia (v. 10) to northern Mesopotamia (v. 11) corresponds to the growth of the first known empire in history, the dynasty of Agade ruled by Sargon and Naram-Sin (about 2300 B.C.), among the greatest of the heroic kings of old Nimrod's kingdom included Erech (=*Uruk), the city where *Gilgamesh reigned and one of the oldest and greatest centers of *Sumerian culture.

10:21-31. Semites. Even though Shem is the oldest son of Noah, his genealogy appears last, as is typical in Genesis for the son the text seeks to follow most closely. There is a mixture of Semitic and non-Semitic nations (by our ethnic criteria) in this list. For instance, *Elam (east of the Tigris) and Lud (Lydia in southern Asia Minor) are considered non-Semitic, but there are close historical ties to both areas in later periods. Sheba, Ophir and Havilah are all part of the Arabian region, and *Aram originated east of the Tigris and north of Elam but came to be associated with the Aramaeans, who dominated Syria and northwest Mesopotamia at the end of the second millennium B.C.

10:25. dividing of the earth. While this has traditionally been taken to refer to the division of the nations after the Tower of Babel incident (Gen 11:1-9), other possibilities exist. It could, for instance, refer to a division of human communities into sedentary farmers and pastoral nomads; or, possibly a migration of peoples is documented here that drastically transformed the culture of the ancient Near East—perhaps one represented in a break-off

group traveling southeast in Genesis 11:2.

11:1-9
The Tower of Babel

11:1. common language tradition. The account of a time when all mankind spoke a single language is preserved in *Sumerian in the epic entitled *Enmerkar and the Lord of Aratta.* It speaks of a time when there were no wild beasts and only harmony among people: "The whole universe in unison spoke to *Enlil in one tongue." It then reports that speech was changed and "contention" was brought into it. There is nothing else in this account that parallels the Tower of Babel, but confusion of language by deity can be seen as an ancient theme.

11:2. Shinar. Shinar is one of the biblical designations for the lower region of the Tigris-Euphrates basin. It has long been identified as linguistically equivalent to "Sumer," the designation for the same region that witnessed the earliest development of civilization. The principal cities of the region in earliest times were *Ur, Eridu, *Uruk and Nippur.

11:3. brick technology. The passage speaks of using kiln-baked bricks in place of stone. In Palestine readily available stone was used for the foundations of important buildings and sun-dried brick for the superstructure. Kiln-fired brick was unnecessary and is not attested in this region. In the southern plains of Mesopotamia, however, stone would have to be quarried some distance away and transported. The technology of baking brick was developed toward the end of the fourth millennium, and the resulting product, using bitumen as a mastic, proved waterproof and as sturdy as stone. Since it was an expensive process, it was used only for important public buildings.

11:4. urbanization. Urbanization in southern Mesopotamia was pioneered by the *Sumerians in the early centuries of the third millennium B.C. The "cities" of this period were not designed for people to live in. They housed the public sector, for the most part religious buildings and storage facilities enclosed by a wall. Since the government of these early cities was made up of elders connected to the temple, there would not even have been separate government buildings, though there may have been residences for these public officials. The determination to build a city suggests a move toward urbanization, which can easily be understood as a course of action that would prevent scattering. The cooperative living available through urbanization would allow more people to live together in a defined region, as it would allow for large-scale irrigation and excess grain production. The need for nonurbanized peoples to scatter is well demonstrated in the story of Abraham and Lot in Genesis 13.

11:4. tower. The central feature of these early cities in southern Mesopotamia was the temple complex. Often, the temple complex *was* the city. The temple complex in this period would have been comprised of the temple itself, where the patron deity was worshiped, and, most prominently, by the ziggurat. Ziggurats were structures designed to provide stairways from the heavens (the gate of the gods) to earth so that the gods could come down into their temple and into the town and bring blessing. It was a convenience provided for the deity and his messengers. These stairways were featured in the mythology of the *Sumerians and also are portrayed in Jacob's dream (Gen 28:12). The ziggurats were constructed of a sun-dried brick frame filled with dirt and rubble and finished off with a shell of kiln-baked brick. There were no rooms, chambers or passageways of any sort inside. The structure itself was simply made to hold up the stairway. At the top was a small room for the deity, equipped with a bed and a table supplied regularly with food. In this way the deity could refresh himself during his descent. None of the festivals or *ritual acts suggest that *people* used the ziggurat for any purpose. It was for the gods. The priests certainly would have to go up to provide fresh supplies, but it was holy ground. The ziggurat served as the architectural representation of the pagan religious developments of this period, when deity was transformed into the image of man.

11:4. head in the heavens. This phrase is reserved almost exclusively for the description of ziggurats in Akkadian usage. Additionally, there are some intriguing omens in the series entitled *Summa Alu* ("If a city . . .") that indicate an impending doom that hangs over cities or towers built high. If a city lifts its head to the heaven, it will be abandoned, or there will be a change on the throne. A city that rises like a mountain peak will become a ruin, and if it goes up like a cloud to heaven there will be calamity.

11:4. making a name. The people were interested in making a name for themselves. This is a desire that God recognized as legitimate in other contexts, saying that he will make a name for Abraham and David. Having descendants was one way of making a name.

While there need not be anything evil or sinful about wanting to make a name for oneself, we must also acknowledge that this desire may become obsessive or lead one to pursue wicked schemes.

11:4. avoiding scattering. Likewise, it is logical that the people would want to avoid scattering. Though God had blessed them with the privilege of multiplying so much that they would fill the earth, that did not obligate them to scatter. The filling was to be accomplished by multiplying, not by spreading out. Economic conditions would have eventually forced the breakup of any group of people, which was why they embarked on the course of urbanization. God scattered them not because he did not want them to be together, but because their united efforts were causing mischief (as we separate children who misbehave).

11:5. came down to see. The ziggurat would have been built so that God could come down into their midst to be worshiped and bring blessing with him. God indeed "came down" to see. But rather than being pleased at their provision of this convenience, he was distressed by the threshold of paganism that had been crossed in the concepts represented by the ziggurat.

11:8. settlement patterns of *Uruk phase. Many of the features of this account point to the end of the fourth millennium as the setting of the narrative. This is the period when receding water allowed settlement of the southern Tigris-Euphrates basin. Many settlements on native soil show that the occupants brought the northern Mesopotamian culture with them. It is likewise in the period known as the Late *Uruk phase (toward the end of the fourth millennium) that the culture and technology known from these settlements in southern Mesopotamia suddenly starts showing up in settlements throughout the ancient Near East. Thus both the migration referred to in verse 2 and the dispersion of verse 9 find points of contact in the settlement pattern identified by archaeologists for the end of the fourth millennium. Urbanization, ziggurat prototypes and experimentation with kiln-baked brick also fit this time period.

11:9. ancient Babylon. The ancient history of *Babylon is difficult to recover. Excavations at the site cannot go back further than the beginning of the second millennium because the water table of the Euphrates has shifted over time and destroyed the lower levels. In the literature of Mesopotamia there is no significant mention of Babylon until it is made the capital of the *Old Babylonian empire in the eighteenth century B.C.

11:10-32
The Line of Shem, the Family of Abraham

11:28. Ur of the Chaldees. Abraham's family is from *Ur of the Chaldees. For many generations the only *Ur that has been known to modern scholars is the famous *Sumerian city on the southern Euphrates. It has been somewhat of a mystery why this southern city would be referred to as *Ur of the Chaldees—since at this time the Chaldeans were settled primarily in the northern section of Mesopotamia. An alternative was provided when textual evidence from Mesopotamia began to produce evidence of a smaller town by the name of *Ur in the northern region, not far from Haran (where Terah moves his family). This town could logically be referred to as *Ur of the Chaldees to differentiate it from the well-known *Ur in the south. This would also explain why Abraham's family is always seen as having its homeland in "Paddan *Aram" or "Aram Naharaim" (24:10; 28:2, descriptions of northern Mesopotamia between the Tigris and Euphrates).

11:30. barrenness in the ancient Near East. Failure to produce an heir was a major calamity for a family in the ancient world because it meant a disruption in the generational inheritance pattern and left no one to care for the couple in their old age. Thus legal remedies were developed which allowed a man whose wife had failed to provide him with a son to impregnate a slave girl (Code of *Hammurabi; *Nuzi texts) or a prostitute (Lipit-Ishtar Code). The children from this relationship could then be acknowledged by the father as his heirs (Code of Hammurabi). Abram and Sarai employ the same strategy when they use the slave girl Hagar as a legal surrogate to produce an heir for the aged couple (see comments on Gen 16:1-4).

11:31. Haran. The city of Haran was located 550 miles northwest of the southern *Ur, on the left bank of the Balikh River (a tributary of the upper Euphrates). Today it is in modern Turkey about ten miles from the Syrian-Turkish border. It is mentioned prominently in the *Mari texts (eighteenth century B.C.) as a center of *Amorite population in northern Mesopotamia and an important crossroads. It was known to feature a temple to the moon god, Sin. There has been very limited excavation at the site due to continuing occupation.

12:1-9
Abraham Travels to Canaan

12:1. father's household. A man was identified in the ancient world as a member of his father's household. When the head of the household died, his heir assumed that title and its responsibilities. It is also identified with ancestral lands and property. By leaving his father's household, Abram was thus giving up his inheritance and his right to family property.

12:1. The *covenant promises. Land, family and inheritance were among the most significant elements in ancient society. For farmers and herdsmen land was their livelihood. For city dwellers land represented their political identity. Descendants represented the future. Children provided for their parents in old age and enabled the family line to extend another generation. They gave proper burial to their parents and honored the names of their ancestors. In some of the ancient Near Eastern cultures these were considered essential to maintaining a comfortable existence in the afterlife. When Abram gave up his place in his father's household, he forfeited his security. He was putting his survival, his identity, his future and his security in the hands of the Lord.

12:6. tree of Moreh. Most likely this was a great Tabor oak (*Quercus ithaburensis*), which served as a landmark at Shechem and perhaps could have functioned as a point where a teacher (the literal meaning of *Moreh*) or judge would come to hear legal cases or provide instruction (such as Deborah's palm tree in Judg 4:5 and Danil's judgment tree in the *Ugaritic epic of *Aqhat). Besides being valued for their shade, such trees also served as evidences of *fertility and were therefore often adopted as places of worship (not often as objects of worship).

12:6. Shechem. The site of Shechem has been identified with Tell Balatah, east of modern Nablus and thirty-five miles north of Jerusalem. Perhaps because of its proximity to two nearby peaks, Mount Gerizim and Mount Ebal, it has had a long history as a sacred site. The strategic position of Shechem, at the east entrance to the pass between these mountains, also made it an important trading center. As early as the *Middle Bronze I period, Shechem is mentioned in the Egyptian texts of Pharaoh Sesostris III (1880-1840 B.C.). Excavations have revealed an apparently unwalled settlement in *Middle Bronze IIA (about 1900 B.C.) with the development of fortifications in Middle Bronze IIB (about 1750).

12:6-9. significance of altars. Altars function as sacrificial platforms. Their construction can also mark the introduction of the worship of a particular god in a new land. Abram's setting up of altars in each place where he camped defines areas to be occupied in the "Promised Land" and establishes these places as religious centers in later periods.

12:10-20
Abraham in Egypt

12:10. famine in the land. Syria-Palestine has a fragile ecology that is based on the rains which come in the winter and spring months. If these rains fail to come at the appropriate time, are less or more than is expected, or fail to come at all, then planting and harvests are negatively affected. It was not uncommon for drought and resulting famine to occur in this region. Egyptian Papyrus Anastasi VI reports of an entire clan going down into Egypt during a drought. Modern archaeologists and geologists have found evidence of a massive three-hundred-year drought cycle that occurred during the end of the third millennium and the beginning of the second millennium—one of the time periods to which Abraham is dated.

12:11-12. wife as sister. The wife/sister theme appears three times in Genesis. It functions as (1) a protective strategy by migrants against local authorities, (2) a contest between God and the god-king Pharaoh in Genesis 12 and (3) a literary motif designed to heighten tension in the story when the promise of an heir to the *covenant is threatened. The logic is possibly that if an individual in power desired to take a woman into his harem he might be inclined to negotiate with a brother, but he would be more likely to eliminate a husband. In each case, the ancestral couple are reunited and enriched and the local ruler is shamed. On a personal level this does not speak well of Abram, but it does make him appear more human than in other stories.

12:11. the beauty of aged Sarah. Sarah is described as a beautiful woman, though by this time she is between sixty-five and seventy years of age. The phrase used to describe Sarah here is sometimes used to describe a woman's beauty (2 Sam 14:27), but it does not necessarily refer strictly to feminine allure or attractiveness. It is sometimes used to describe male good looks (1 Sam 17:42), but it may be important to note that the phrase is also used to describe a fine specimen of cow (Gen 41:2). We need not therefore assume that Sarah has miraculously retained the stunning

beauty of youth. Her dignity, her bearing, her countenance, her outfitting could all contribute to the impression that she is a striking woman.

12:10-20. Beni Hasan tomb painting. The Twelfth Dynasty (nineteenth century B.C.) tomb painting of Khnumhotep III at Beni Hasan (near Minya in Middle Egypt) depicts one of many caravans of "Asiatics" that brought raw materials and exotic items (frankincense, lapis lazuli). These traders wear multicolored robes, bring their families with them and travel with their weapons and donkeys laden with "ox-hide," ingots of bronze and other trade goods. Their garb and the ease with which they were able to travel to Egypt may well reflect the look of Abram's household. Egypt served as both a market as well as a source of food and temporary employment for many groups driven by war or famine from the rest of the Near East.

12:17. nature of disease. The assumption in the ancient world is that all disease is a reflection of the displeasure of a god or gods. Infectious disease could be coped with through purification and sacrifice and might be treated with herbal medicines, but the root cause was viewed as divine, not physical. Thus disease was considered the direct result of sin or some violation of custom, so the ancients would seek to determine which god might be responsible and how he might be appeased. Medicinal remedies would be augmented by magical remedies and incantations.

13:1-18
Abraham and Lot

13:1-4. Abram's itinerary. Since the household is depicted as pastoral nomads, they would have had to stop periodically to find pasture and water for the herds and flocks. The Negev was more heavily populated in the early second millennium and might have provided specific staging points for this journey (see Ex 17:1). The return to the vicinity of Bethel marks the resumption of the *covenantal narrative and sets the stage for the separation from Lot. From the border of Egypt to the area of Bethel/Ai would be a journey of about two hundred miles.

13:5-7. herding needs and lifestyle. The primary requirements for a successful herding group are pasturage and water sources. The hot, dry months from April through September require movement of herds to higher elevations where grass remains and streams and springs can be found. In the colder, wet months of October through March, the animals will be brought back to the plains for grazing. This seasonal movement necessitates long separations of herders from their villages or the establishment of an unconnected, semi-nomadic lifestyle in which whole families travel with the herds. The knowledge of natural resources along their routes of travel would be their primary lore. Disputes over grazing land and water rights would be the most frequent cause of quarrels between herdsmen.

13:7. Canaanites and Perizzites. See comment on Exodus 3:7-10.

13:10. the plain of the Jordan. It would be possible to get a good view of the Jordan Valley and the northern area of the Dead Sea from the hills around Bethel. While the area around the Dead Sea is not a particularly hospitable region today, this verse makes it clear that prior to the Lord's judgment the area had a far different quality. It should be noted that there are extensive areas along the Jordan Plateau that do provide ample grazing, and this may also be represented in this narrative.

13:12. the boundaries of Canaan. The eastern boundary of Canaan is everywhere identified as the Jordan River (see especially Num 34:1-12 and the comments on it). Thus it becomes clear that by moving to the vicinity of the cities of the plain Lot has gone outside the land of Canaan, leaving it entirely to Abram.

13:18. Hebron. The city of Hebron is located in the Judean hill country (c. 3,300 feet above sea level) approximately nineteen miles southeast of Jerusalem and twenty-three miles east of Beersheba. Ancient roadways converge on this site coming east from Lachish and connecting with the road north to Jerusalem, indicating its importance and continuous settlement. Its springs and wells provide ample water for olive and grape production and would have supported a mixed agricultural-pastoral economy such as that described in Genesis 23. Hebron is said to have been founded "seven years before Zoan" (Avaris in Egypt), dating it to the seventeenth century B.C. (see comment on Num 13:22). The construction of an altar here, as at Bethel, transforms this into an important religious site, and its subsequent use as a burial place for the ancestors established its political importance (reflected in the Davidic narrative—2 Sam 2:1-7; 15:7-12).

14:1-16

Abraham Rescues Lot

14:1-4. the kings of the East. The kings of the East have remained stubbornly obscure despite numerous attempts to link them to historically known figures, though the geographical areas they represent can be identified with some confidence. Shinar refers elsewhere in the Bible to the southern Mesopotamian plains known in earliest times as *Sumer and later connected to *Babylonia. Ellasar corresponds to an ancient way of referring to *Assyria (a.la₅.sar). *Elam is the usual name for the region, which in this period comprised the whole of the land east of Mesopotamia from the Caspian Sea to the Persian Gulf (modern Iran). Goiim is the most vague, but it is generally associated with the *Hittites (who were located in the eastern section of present-day Turkey), mostly because the king's name, Tidal, is easily associated with the common Hittite royal name, Tudhaliyas. As a reference to a group of people, Goiim would most likely refer to a coalition of "barbaric" peoples (like the *Akkadian designation, *Umman Manda*). In *Mari it is a designation used to refer to the Haneans. While there were many periods in the first half of the second millennium when the Elamites were closely associated with powers in Mesopotamia, it is more difficult to bring the Hittites into the picture. We do know that *Assyrian merchants had a trading colony in the Hittite region, but there is no indication of joint military ventures. Early Hittite history is very sketchy, and we have little information concerning where the Hittites came from or precisely when they moved into Anatolia. The names of the kings of the East are authentic enough, but none of them have been identified or linked to the kings of these respective regions at this period. So, for instance, there is an Arioch who was prince of Mari in the eighteenth century. We certainly have no information of Elamite control of sections of Palestine as suggested in verse 4, but it must be admitted that there are many gaps in our knowledge of the history of this period. None of the five kings of Canaan are known outside the Bible, for even these cities are yet unattested in other ancient records, despite occasional claims of possible references to Sodom.

14:5-7. the itinerary and conquests of the kings of the East. The itinerary of conquest is given as is common in chronographic texts. The route goes from north to south along what is known as the King's Highway, the major north-south artery in Transjordan, just east of the Jordan Valley. Ashtaroth, neighboring the capital later called Karnaim, was the capital of the region just east of the Sea of Galilee inhabited by the Rephaim. Virtually nothing is known of these peoples, or of the Zuzites and Emites, though all of them are identified with the giants of the land at the time of the conquest under Joshua (cf. Deut 2). The next stop was Ham in northern Gilead. Shaveh, also known as Kiriathaim, was in Reubenite territory when the land was divided among the tribes and bordered on the Moabite region. The Horites were the people living in the region later known as Edom, the next region south. After reaching the area of the gulf of Aqaba (the town of El Paran= Elath?), the invaders turn northwest to confront the Amalekites in the region of Kadesh Barnea (at that time called En Mishpat) and the *Amorites in the southern hill country. This route then brings them around to the cities of the plain in the region south and east of the Dead Sea. The towns of Sodom and Gomorrah have not been located with any certainty, though some think that their remains are beneath part of the Dead Sea (see comments on Gen 19). After the battle in the Valley of Siddim, the four kings traveled along the west side of the Jordan and got as far as Dan, in the very north of the land of Canaan, before being overtaken by Abraham and his men.

14:10. tar pits. Tar pits are common in this area that is so rich in bitumen that large amounts bubble to the surface and even float on the Dead Sea. The word translated "pits" is the same word used for wells of water throughout the Old Testament and therefore generally refers to a spot that has been dug out. The Valley of Siddim, then, had many pits that had been dug to extract bitumen, and these provided refuge for the kings (they "lowered themselves into them" rather than "they fell into them").

14:13. "the Hebrew." Abram is referred to as "Abram the Hebrew." Typically the designation "Hebrew" in early times was used only as a point of reference for foreigners. Besides the use here, it is used to identify Joseph in Egypt (e.g., 39:14-17), the Israelite slaves in reference to the Egyptian masters (Ex 2:11), Jonah to the sailors (Jon 1:9), the Israelites to the Philistines (1 Sam 4:6), and other such situations. Some have thought that "Hebrew" is not in these cases an ethnic reference but a designation of a social class of people known as the "Habiru" in many ancient texts, where they are typically dispossessed peoples.

14:14-16. 318 trained men. Here we discover that Abram has a household of significant size (318 recruits or retainers). The word used to describe these men occurs nowhere else in the Old Testament, but does occur in an *Akkadian letter of the fifteenth century B.C. Whether Abram is placed within the early part of the *Middle Bronze Age, when the area was predominantly occupied by herdsmen and villagers, or within the later *Middle Bronze Age when there were more fortified settlements, this army would have been a match for any other armed force in the region. Even as late as the *Amarna period the armies of any particular city state would not have been much larger.

14:15. battle tactics. Abram caught up to the eastern army at the northern border of the land, Dan. Abram uses the strategy of nighttime ambush, which is attested in texts as

THE RELIGION OF ABRAHAM

It is important to notice that Abraham comes from a family that is not monotheistic (see Josh 24:2,14). They would have shared the polytheistic beliefs of the ancient world at that time. In this type of system the gods were connected to the forces of nature and showed themselves through natural phenomena. These gods did not reveal their natures or give any idea of what would bring their favor or wrath. They were worshipped by being flattered, cajoled, humored and appeased. Manipulation is the operative term. They were gods made in the image of man. One of the main reasons that God made a covenant with Abraham was in order to reveal what he was really like—to correct the false view of deity that people had developed. But this was projected to take place in stages, not all at once.

The Lord, Yahweh, is not portrayed as a God that Abraham already worshiped. When he appears to Abraham he does not give him a doctrinal statement or require rituals or issue demands; he makes an offer. Yahweh does not tell Abraham that he is the only God there is, and he does not ask him to stop worshiping whatever gods his family was worshiping. He does not tell him to get rid of his idols nor does he proclaim a coming Messiah or salvation. Instead, he says that he has something to give Abraham if Abraham is willing to give up some things first.

In the massive polytheistic systems of the ancient Near East the great cosmic deities, while respected and worshiped in national and royal contexts, had little personal contact with the common people. Individuals were more inclined to focus their personal or family worship on local or family deities. We can best understand this through an analogy to politics. Though we respect and recognize the

early as the Judges period in Egyptian as well as in *Hittite documents.

14:17-24
Abraham and Melchizedek

14:17-20. Melchizedek. Melchizedek is introduced as the king of Salem and is portrayed as the principal king of the region in that he receives a portion of the booty. Salem is generally considered to be Jerusalem, though early Christian evidence and the Madeba map associate it with Shechem. (The Madeba map is the earliest map of Palestine. It is a mosaic on the floor of a sixth-century A.D. church.) Often one city-state would gain predominance over the others in the region, as is seen in the book of Joshua where kings of Jerusalem and Hazor put the southern and northern coalitions together. Whether Melchizedek is Canaanite, *Amorite or Jebusite cannot be easily determined. The name of God that he uses to bless Abram, *El Elyon* ("God Most High"), is well known as a way of referring to the chief Canaanite god, *El, in Canaanite literature.
14:18-19. meeting of Abraham and Melchizedek. Their meeting takes place in the Valley of Shaveh. The designation of it as the King's Valley connects it to the valley just south of Jerusalem, most likely where the Kidron and Hinnom valleys come together. In a later period, Absalom built a monument here (2 Sam 18:18). The communal meal that they share would typically indicate a peaceful agreement between them. *Hittite treaties refer to the provision of food in wartime by allies. Melchizedek is anxious to make peace with such a proven military force, and Abram submits by paying the tithe, thereby acknowledging Melchizedek's status.

14:21-24. agreement between Abraham and kings of Sodom. The king of Sodom acknowledged that Abram had a right to the booty, but asks that the people be returned to him. Abram refuses the booty with the explanation that he is under oath to *El Elyon (whom he identifies as *Yahweh) not to profit from his military action. It is possible that this agreement would have occasioned the formulation of a document to formalize the terms. Such a document could easily have taken the form that this chapter takes and may have even served as a source for this chapter.

15:1-21
Ratification of the Covenant

15:1. visions. Visions were a means used by God to communicate to people. All of the other visions of this category in the Old Testament were given to prophets (the writing prophets as well as Balaam) and often resulted in prophetic *oracles which were then delivered to the people. Visions may be experienced in dreams but are not the same as dreams. They may be either visual or auditory. They may involve natural or supernatural settings, and the individual having the vision may be either an observer or a participant. Visions are likewise part of the prophetic institution in other cultures in the ancient Near East.
15:2-3. inheritance by servant. In those instances where the head of a household had no male heir, it was possible for a servant to be legally adopted as the heir, as particularly demonstrated in an *Old Babylonian text from *Larsa. This would most likely be a course of last resort, since it would mean transference of property to a person (and his line) who was (1) originally a servant or

---

authority of our national leaders, if we have a problem in our community we would pursue it with our local government rather than write a letter to the president. In Mesopotamia in the first part of the second millennium an important religious development can be observed that parallels this common sense approach to politics. The people began to relate to "personal gods" who were often then adopted as family gods from generation to generation. This was usually the function of minor deities and was at times no more than a personification of luck. The personal god was one that was believed to have taken special interest in the family or an individual and became a source of blessing and good fortune in return for worship and obedience. While the personal god was not worshipped exclusively, most of the worship by the individual and his family would be focused on him.

It is possible that Abraham's first responses to Yahweh may have been along these lines—that Abraham may have viewed Yahweh as a personal god that was willing to become his "divine sponsor." Though we are given no indication that Yahweh explained or demanded a monotheistic belief, nor that Abraham responded with one, it is clear that the worship of Yahweh dominated Abraham's religious experience. By making a break with his land, his family and his inheritance, Abraham is also breaking all of his religious ties, because deities would be associated with geographical, political and ethnic divisions. In his new land Abraham would have no territorial gods; as a new people he would have brought no family gods; having left his country he would have no national or city gods; and it was Yahweh who filled this void becoming the "God of Abraham, Isaac and Jacob."

bondsman, and (2) not a blood relative. It signals the frustration of the childless Abram that he tells God that he has designated Eliezer of Damascus as his heir, though it is not clear whether he has actually adopted Eliezer or is simply referring to that as the only remaining course of action.

15:9-10. the ritual of dividing animals. As in the case in Jeremiah 34:18, where a *covenant *ritual is represented by passage between the severed body of a sacrificial animal, here Abram is given the "sign" of the covenant promise for which he asked. Each "three-year old" animal (calf, goat, ram, dove, pigeon, the same animals featured in the sacrificial system described in Leviticus) is cut in half, although the body sections of the birds are not separated. Second-millennium *Hittite texts use a similar procedure for purification, while some first-millennium *Aramaic treaties use such a ritual for placing a curse on any violation of the treaty. Texts from *Mari and *Alalakh feature the killing of animals as part of the ceremony of making a treaty. Walking through this sacrificial pathway could be seen as a symbolic action enacting both the covenant's promise of land and a curse on the one who violates the promise, though interpreters have wondered what significance a self-curse could possibly have for God. Abram's driving away the birds of prey further symbolizes the future protection from their enemies when they take possession of the land.

15:17. smoking firepot and blazing torch. The firepot is made of earthenware and could be of various sizes. It functioned as an oven principally for baking, including the baking of grain offerings (Lev 2:4). The torch could certainly be used to provide light, but it is also used in military contexts or to speak of God's judgment (Zech 12:6). Mesopotamian *rituals of this period usually featured a sacred torch and censer in the initiation of rites, particularly nocturnal rites of purification. Purification would be accomplished by the torch and censer being moved alongside of someone or something. While in Mesopotamia the torch and oven represented particular deities, here they represent *Yahweh, perhaps as the purifier. This would be one of many instances where the Lord used familiar concepts and motifs to reveal himself.

15:18. river of Egypt. The usual designation of Israel's southwestern border is the "brook [wadi] of Egypt," identified with Wadi el 'Arish in the northeastern Sinai (Num 34:5). It is unlikely that it refers to the Nile River. Another possibility is that it refers to the eastern-most delta tributary that emptied into Lake Sirbonis.

15:19-21. occupants of Canaan. This is the longest (including ten groups) of seventeen such lists of Canaan's pre-Israelite peoples (see Deut 7:1; Josh 3:10; 1 Kings 9:20). Each of these lists, which usually comprise six or seven names, ends with the Jebusites (perhaps tied to David's conquest of Jerusalem), but the list in Genesis 15 is the only one to exclude the Hivites. For the *Hittites, Perizzites, *Amorites, Canaanites and Jebusites, see the comments on Exodus 3:7-10 and Numbers 13. The Kenites are often associated with the Midianites and appear as a seminomadic people from the Sinai and Negev region. The name suggests that they were metalworkers, tinkerers or smiths. The Kenizzites, Kadmonites and Girgashites are little known, though the latter is also attested in the *Ugaritic texts. The Rephaim are considered to be Anakites in Deuteronomy 2:11, who in turn appear as giants in Numbers 13:33. Aside from these associations, nothing is known of this ethnic group.

16:1-16
The Birth of Ishmael

16:1-4. maidservants. Slave women or bondswomen were considered both property and legal extensions of their mistress. As a result it would be possible for Sarai to have Hagar perform a variety of household tasks as well as to use her as a surrogate for her own barren womb.

16:2. contractual arrangements for barrenness. *Concubines did not have the full status of wives but were girls who came to the marriage with no dowry and whose role included childbearing. As a result concubinage would not be viewed as polygamy. In Israel, as in most of the ancient world, monogamy was generally practiced. Polygamy was not contrary to the law or contemporary moral standards but was usually not economically feasible. The main reason for polygamy would be that the first wife was barren. In the Bible most cases of polygamy among commoners occur prior to the period of the monarchy.

16:3-4. surrogate mothers. Surrogate mothers appear only in the ancestral narratives: Hagar and the two maidservants of Rachel and Leah (Gen 30). There is no contract mentioned here, since these women were all legal extensions of their mistress and any children they bore could be designated as the children of their mistress. The eighteenth century B.C. *Babylonian Code of *Hammurabi does contain surrogate contracts for priestesses who were not allowed to conceive children. As in the biblical examples, these surrogates had a lower legal standing than the wife.

16:5-6. relationship of Sarah and Hagar. Women in the ancient world obtained honor through marriage and children. Although Hagar was a servant, the fact that she had conceived a child and Sarai had not gave her cause to hold her mistress in contempt. Sarai's reaction in abusing Hagar may be based on both jealousy and class difference.

16:7-10. angel as messenger. The word translated "angel" simply means "messenger" in Hebrew and can be used for either human or supernatural messengers. Since these messengers represent God, they do not speak for themselves, but only for God. It is therefore not unusual for them to use the first person, "I." Messengers were granted the authority to speak for the one they represented and were treated as if they were the one they represented.

16:13-14. "seeing God." Hagar affirms a supernatural identity for the messenger and may well believe that the messenger was indeed a deity, but the fact that she expresses incredulity about the likelihood of having seen a deity does not mean that she actually has seen one (additionally the text is very difficult to translate and may not even suggest this much). Most likely Hagar is expressing surprise that she has encountered a deity who is inclined to show favor to her in such an unlikely place.

16:13. naming God. The text identifies the deity as the LORD (*Yahweh) but gives no indication that Hagar knew it was Yahweh. This is the only example in the Old Testament of someone assigning a name to deity. Usually naming someone or something is a way of affirming authority over the one named. Here it is more likely that since she does not know the name of the deity that has shown her favor, she assigns a name to him as an identification of his nature and so that she might invoke him in the future.

16:14. Kadesh and Bered. The location of the well of Beer Lahai Roi, where Hagar experienced a *theophany and was told of her son's future, is most likely in the Negev between Kadesh Barnea and Bered. The oasis of Kadesh Barnea is in the northeast section of the Sinai, on the southern border of the Wilderness of Zin (see comment on Num 13). Since Bered does not appear elsewhere in the text, its location is uncertain, though Jebel umm el-Bared to the southeast is as good a guess as any.

17:1-27

Circumcision, the Sign of the Covenant

17:1-2. El Shaddai. *El Shaddai ("God Almighty") in verse 1 is a relatively common name used for the Lord in the Old Testament (48 times), though the conventional translations are little more than guesses. It appears only once outside the Old Testament in the name "Shaddai-Ammi" on an Egyptian statue from the Judges period, though there may be a reference to Shaddai-beings in the Deir Allah inscription. One of the most frequent suggestions understands Shaddai as related to the *Babylonian *sadu*, "steppe, mountain," but evidence is sparse.

17:3-8. name changing. Names had power in the ancient world. By naming the animals, Adam demonstrated his mastery over them. In a similar way, God's changing Abram's name to Abraham and Sarai's name to Sarah signifies both a reiteration of the *covenant promise and the designation of these people as God's chosen servants.

17:4. covenanting with God. There are no parallels in the ancient world to *covenants between deity and mortal, though certainly gods are known to make demands and promise favorable treatment. In most of these cases kings report their care of the sanctuaries of the god and then tell how the deity responded with blessing. But these fall far short of a covenant relationship initiated by deity for his own purposes.

17:9-14. circumcision. *Circumcision was practiced widely in the ancient Near East as a rite of puberty, fertility or marriage. Although the Israelites were not the only people to circumcise their sons, this sign was used to mark them as members of the *covenantal community. When used in relation to marriage, terminology suggests it was performed by the new male in-laws, indicating that the groom was coming under the protection of their family in this new relationship. Performed on infants, it is more a ritual scarring than something done for health reasons. The fact that blood is shed also signifies that this is a sacrificial *ritual and may function as a substitution for human sacrifice, which was practiced by other people. Waiting until the eighth day to perform this ritual may reflect the high infant mortality rate and the desire to determine if the child was viable. The *Hittites also had a ritual for the seventh day of the newborn's life. Circumcision can be seen as one of many cases where God transforms a common practice to a new (though not necessarily unrelated) purpose in revealing himself and relating to his people.

17:15-22. divine announcement of sons. The divine announcement of a son to be born is a common motif found throughout ancient Near Eastern literature. Perhaps most notable is the announcement by the Canaanite deity *El to King Danil that he would finally have a son in his old age, in the *Ugaritic story of *Aqhat. Additional examples are found in the *Hittite tale where the sun god tells Appu he will have a son, and in Mesopotamian literature where the god Shamash advises *Etana, king of Kish, how to procure a son. Also notable in this text is the statement that Sarah will be the mother of kings. This would be an indication of long survival of the line and great success for the line.

18:1-15
Abraham's Visitors

18:1. entrance to tent at heat of day. The goatskin tents of pastoral nomadic people were designed to hold in heat at night with the flaps down and to allow a breeze to pass through during the day, when the flaps were up. Sitting at the entrance during the heat of the day would provide needed shade while a person enjoyed the breeze and guarded the tent's contents.

18:2-5. hospitality (meals). Hospitality customs required that all strangers who approached a dwelling were to be offered the opportunity to rest, refresh themselves and eat a meal. This was done to transform potential enemies into at least temporary friends. Protocol required that the meal served to the guest exceed what was first offered. Thus Abraham simply offers a meal, but what he orders prepared is freshly baked bread, a calf and a mixture of milk and yogurt. What is particularly generous here is the fresh meat, an item not usually found in their daily diet. This meal is similar to that offered by Danil to the representative of the gods, Kathar-wa-Hasis (when he comes traveling through town), in the Ugaritic epic of Aqhat.

18:4. foot washing. Washing the feet of guests was a standard act of hospitality in the dry, dusty climate that characterized much of the ancient Near East. Open leather sandals were common, as were enclosed soft leather boots. Neither style succeeded in keeping out the dirt of the road.

18:6-8. flour and baking. The three seahs of flour (c. twenty quarts) used to make bread again reflects Abraham's generosity to his guests. The method of baking, since nomadic people lacked ovens, would be placing the dough on the sides of a heated pot or dutch oven. This produced a slightly raised, circular loaf of bread. Curds (yogurt) and milk are served along with the meal as customary side dishes and normal byproducts of the herd. The fact that Sarah remains in the tent may reflect a custom of women not eating with men.

18:16-33
Discussion of God's Justice and Mercy

18:20-21. judge collecting evidence. There is a combination of anthropomorphism (God being given humanlike qualities) and theodicy (explanation of divine action) in this story and in the Tower of Babel episode (Gen 11). In both cases, to demonstrate divine justice and fairness, God "comes down" to investigate a situation before taking action.

18:22-33. Abraham's bargaining. Haggling is a part of all Middle Eastern business transactions. In this case, however, Abraham's determination of the exact number of righteous persons needed to prevent the destruction of Sodom and Gomorrah provides a repeated demonstration of God's just actions. A just God will not destroy the righteous without warning or investigation. Even the unrighteous, in this early period, can be spared for the sake of the righteous. On the other hand, however, justice is not served by overlooking wickedness. The discussion of the number of righteous people may concern not whether they can balance the wickedness of the rest but whether, given time, they might be able to exert a reforming influence.

19:1-29
The Destruction of Sodom and Gomorrah

19:1, 24. Sodom and Gomorrah. The "cities of the plain" along the eastern shore of the Dead Sea have not been positively located. Their association with Zoar (Zoara on the sixth-century A.D. Madaba map) and the bitumen pits "in the Valley of Siddim" (Gen 14:10) both point to the southern end of the Dead Sea. Arguments for their identification with the north end are based on the distance to travel from Hebron (eighteen miles versus forty miles to the southern location) and the mention of the "plain of the Jordan" in Genesis 13:10-12. Cities located in this arid region survived and prospered on the salt, bitumen and potash deposits around the Dead Sea and as trading centers for caravans traveling the road north and south. There are five sites of *Early Bronze Age cities on the southeast plain of the Dead Sea, demonstrating that fairly large populations once existed here (occupied from 3300 to 2100 B.C.): Bab-edh Dhra' (Sodom?), Safi (Zoar), Numeira (Gomorrah?), Feifa and Khanazir. Only Bab-edh Dhra and Numeira have been excavated, and the destruction of these cities has been set by archaeologists at about 2350 B.C., too early for Abraham (though chronological reckoning of this period is difficult).

19:1-3. sitting at the gate. In ancient cities the gate area functioned as a public square. Its constant flow of people made it the ideal place for businessmen to set up their booths and for judges to hear cases. The fact that Lot is sitting in the gate suggests he was doing business there and had been accepted in the community of Sodom.

19:1. bowing to the ground. One way to show respect to superiors and to demonstrate peaceful intentions was to bow to the ground. Some Egyptian texts from *El Amarna (fourteenth century B.C.) exaggerate this gesture by multiplying it seven times.

19:2. hospitality (lodging). When a host offered a guest the opportunity to spend the night, he was also accepting responsibility for the safety and well-being of his guest. The offer generally extended for a total of three days.

19:3. bread without yeast. As in the case of the unleavened bread eaten on Passover prior to the exodus (Ex 12) from Egypt, Lot's "bread without yeast" was made quickly. It was evening when his guests arrived, and he did not have time to let his bread rise before baking it.

19:4-10. behavior of men at Sodom. The angels' visit to Sodom was to determine if there were ten righteous men there. The legal formula in verse 4 makes it clear that all of the men of the city confronted Lot about his guests. In addition to the fact that homosexuality was considered a capital offense, their refusal to listen to reason and their unanimous insistence on violence as they rushed toward his house confirmed the fate of the city.

19:8. Lot's offer of his daughters. When Lot offers his virgin daughters to the men of Sodom as a substitute for his guests, he is playing the consummate host. He is willing to sacrifice his most precious possessions to uphold his honor by protecting his guests. He was saved from making this sacrifice by the refusal of the mob and the actions of the angels.

19:11. blindness. The word for blindness here is used elsewhere only for the Aramean army

at Dothan (2 Kings 6:18). It is a term related to an Akkadian word for day-blindness (pertinent to 2 Kings 6) and also serves in Hebrew (as in Aramaic) to refer to night-blindness. Both of these conditions are seen in Akkadian texts as requiring magical remedies. Day-blindness and night-blindness have vitamin A deficiency as their principal cause, and vitamin B deficiency may contribute to the sense of confusion evident in both passages. It is therefore of interest that liver (rich in vitamin A) figures prominently in the magical procedures to correct the condition.

19:24. burning sulfur. The scene is one of divine retribution. Brimstone appears here and elsewhere as an agent of purification and divine wrath upon the wicked (Ps 11:6; Ezek 38:22). The natural deposits of bitumen and the sulfurous smell attached to some areas around the Dead Sea combine to provide a lasting memory of Sodom and Gomorrah's destruction. One can only speculate about the actual manner of this destruction, but perhaps the combustion of natural tars and sulfur deposits and the release of noxious gases during an earthquake are a part of the story (Deut 29:23).

19:26. pillar of salt. The story of the punishment of Lot's wife is often illustrated by some grotesquely humanlike, salt-encrusted objects that have become landmarks in the Dead Sea area (alluded to in the apocryphal Wisdom of Solomon 10:4). This phenomenon is a result of the salt spray that blows off the Dead Sea. Huge salt nodules still appear in the shallow sections of the lake. The mineral salts of the region include sodium, potash, magnesium, calcium chlorides and bromide. An earthquake in the area could easily have ignited these chemicals, causing them to rain down on the victims of the destruction.

19:30-38. origins of Moabites and Ammonites. One primary intent of the ancestral narrative is to demonstrate the origin of all of the peoples that inhabited Canaan and Transjordan. Archaeological survey of the area indicates a resettlement between the fourteenth and twelfth centuries B.C., and the language of both the Moabites and Ammonites is similar to Hebrew. Although both are considered enemy nations for most of their history, it is unlikely that their "birth" as a result of the incestuous union between Lot and his daughters (see Deut 2:9; Ps 83:5-8) is simply a political or ethnic slur. The initiative taken by Lot's daughters in the face of likely childlessness and the extinction of Lot's household may have appeared to them as the only feasible option in their desperate plight.

20:1-18

Abraham and Abimelech

20:1. Kadesh and Shur. Again a story begins with the itinerary of Abraham's travels, this time taking him south on a line between Kadesh (an oasis forty-six miles south of Beersheba in the northeastern Sinai) and Shur. The latter site probably refers to the "wall" (*shur*) of Egyptian fortresses in the eastern Delta region. The Egyptian story of *Sinuhe (twentieth century B.C.) mentions this "Wall of the Ruler" as a barrier to the incursions of Asiatics into Egypt.

20:1. Gerar. Although it is not within the range of the Kadesh-Shur line, Gerar may not have been too far of a journey for pastoral nomads such as Abraham's household. Its exact location, beyond the general area of the western Negev, is uncertain (Gen 10:19), and it may in fact be the name for a territory rather than a city. Most archaeologists, noting strong Egyptian influence in this region between 1550 and 1200 B.C., point to Tell Haror (Tell Abu Hureireh), fifteen miles northwest of Beersheba, as its probable location.

20:3. God speaking to non-Israelite in dream. There are few instances of messages being given in dreams by the Lord to Israelites, but dreams are one of the most common forms divine revelation was believed to take for the uninitiated. In the *Mari texts it is usually those who are not among the professional temple personnel who receive messages by means of dreams. In most places in the Bible where significant dreams are given to individuals the text does not explicitly state that God spoke to the individual in the dream (Pharaoh, Nebuchadnezzar).

20:7. prophet's intercession. Abraham is identified by God as a prophet who is capable of intercession on Abimelech's behalf. The role of prophet was well understood in the ancient Near East, as evidenced by over fifty texts found in the town of *Mari that report messages given by various prophets. Generally the prophet offered a message from deity, but here Abraham is praying for healing (cf. v. 17). This reflects the broader view of a prophet as one who has powerful connections to deity such that he can initiate curses or remove them. A similar prophetic role can be seen in Scripture in 1 Kings 13:6. In the ancient Near East this role would typically be played by an incantation priest.

20:11-13. relationship of Abraham and Sarah. In this repetition of the wife/sister motif, Abraham reveals that Sarah is actually his half sister. There was no incest taboo against such marriages in the ancestral period, and it was a way of insuring that female children from sec-

ond marriages were cared for by a household. Abraham's deception of Abimelech is reinforced by Sarah's willingness to repeat the half-truth.

20:16. 1000 shekels. A thousand shekels of silver is a sizable sum. In *Ugaritic literature it is the amount of the bride price paid among the gods. In weight it would equal about twenty-five pounds of silver. In value it would be more than a worker could expect to make in a lifetime. The king's generosity should be understood as his guarantee that Sarah had been untouched, but also as appeasing the deity who had virtually cut off all fertility in his family.

20:17. plague on Abimelech's house. The plague of barrenness or sexual dysfunction is placed on Abimelech's house until he returns Sarah to Abraham. Abraham's intercession causes God to open their wombs. The irony is that Abimelech is denied children as long as Abraham is denied his wife (for information on barrenness in the ancient Near East see comment on 11:30).

21:1-21

The Birth of Isaac and the Expulsion of Ishmael

21:4. 8 days. Initially the eight-day waiting period distinguishes Isaac from Ishmael, who was *circumcised at age thirteen. Subsequently, it serves as a determination of the infant's viability and may be tied to the period of uncleanness after the birth (Lev 12:1-3).

21:14. desert of Beersheba. The southern Negev region around Beersheba, Tell es-Seba', is steppe land and would have been inhospitable enough to be described as a desert. Hagar's wanderings after being expelled from Abraham's camp took her southeast through a relatively flat portion of the Negev toward northern Arabia.

21:8-21. expulsion of wife. There is a contract in the *Nuzi documents that contains a clause prohibiting the expulsion of the children of the secondary wife by the primary wife. The situation in Genesis is different on two counts: first, it is Abraham who sends them away; and second, Hagar is given her freedom, which, according to one ancient law code (Lipit-Ishtar) would mean that her children would forfeit any inheritance rights.

21:20. archer. The expulsion of Hagar and Ishmael and their subsequent life in the desert of Paran would require them to acquire survival skills. As a skilled archer, Ishmael could provide food for his family and perhaps could find occupation as a mercenary (see Is 21:17

for reference to the bowmen of Kedar, Ishmael's son).

21:21. desert of Paran. The arid wilderness of the northeastern Sinai desert was given the name of Paran. Situated west of Edom, it figures prominently in the wilderness period (Num 13:3, 26; Deut 1:1) and is the area where Kadesh is located. Its associations with Egypt are probably based on caravan trade and Egypt's military interest in the Sinai.

21:22-33

Abraham and His Neighbors

21:25-31. wells and water rights. In the semiarid region around Beersheba, water would have been a precious resource. Disputes between herdsmen and farmers over wells and springs would have arisen. To prevent this, treaties like that between Abraham and Abimelech would have established firm ownership or right of usage to wells. Note that Abraham's payment of seven ewe lambs provides the basis for the name Beersheba (well of seven) and serves as a gesture of goodwill toward the people of Gerar.

21:32. land of the Philistines. The first known mention of the Philistines outside the Bible is in the records of Pharaoh Rameses III (1182-1151 B.C.). As part of the invading *Sea Peoples, they settled in five city-states along the southern coast of Canaan and were employed by the Egyptians as mercenaries and trading partners. The picture of Abimelech (a Semitic name) as "king of Gerar" in the land of the Philistines does not match the known history of this people. This story may thus represent contact with an earlier group of Philistines who settled the area prior to the Sea Peoples' invasion, or this may simply be the *anachronistic use of the name Philistines for the area rather than the people Abraham encountered.

21:33. tamarisk tree. The tamarisk grows in sandy soil. It is deciduous and may reach over twenty feet in height, with small leaves that excrete salt. Its bark is used for tanning and its wood for building and making charcoal. Bedouin commonly plant this hearty tree for its shade and the branches which provide grazing for animals. Abraham's action probably signifies the sealing of the treaty with Abimelech—a life-giving plant symbolizing a fertile and prosperous future.

22:1-24

Abraham Requested to Sacrifice Isaac

22:2. region of Moriah. The only indication of Moriah's location given here is that it is three days' journey from Beersheba. That may simply be a conventional number of a completed journey, but in any case no direction is provided. The only other reference to Moriah is in 2 Chronicles 3:1, which refers to the site of the temple in Jerusalem but makes no mention of Abraham or this incident. Since the wooded hills around Jerusalem would not have required the transport of firewood for the sacrifice, it is most likely a coincidence of the same name rather than a reference to the same place.

22:1-2. child sacrifice. In the ancient Near East, the god that provides *fertility (*El) is also entitled to demand a portion of what has been produced. This is expressed in the sacrifice of animals, grain and children. Texts from Phoenician and Punic colonies, like Carthage in North Africa, describe the *ritual of child sacrifice as a means of insuring continued fertility. The biblical prophets and the laws in Deuteronomy and Leviticus expressly forbid this practice, but that also implies that it continued to occur. In fact, the story of Abraham's "sacrifice" of Isaac suggests that Abraham was familiar with human sacrifice and was not surprised by *Yahweh's demand. However, the story also provides a model for the substitute of an animal for a human sacrifice that clearly draws a distinction between Israelite practice and that of other cultures.

22:3. donkey domestication. The wild ass was domesticated about 3500 B.C. Its primary function from the beginning was as a pack animal because of its ability to tolerate heavy loads and to survive for long periods on little water. As a result it was often relied upon for long-distance travel and transport.

22:13-19. sacrifice as replacement. In this section the ram is offered as a sacrifice in the place of Isaac. The concept of substitution in sacrifice is not as common as we might think. In the ancient Near East the sympathetic magic of incantation *rituals would often include substitution of an animal that would be killed to remove a threat to the human subject. But the concept behind the regular institution of sacrifice was generally either to offer a gift to deity or to establish communion with deity. Even in Israel there is little to suggest that the sacrificial institution was understood to have a principally vicarious or substitutionary element. Redemption of the firstborn and Passover would be notable exceptions on the fringe of the sacrificial institution.

22:19. Beersheba. This important city, often identified as the southern limit of Israel's territory (Judg 20:1; 1 Sam 3:20), is traditionally located in the northern Negev at Tell es-Seba' (three miles east of the modern city). Its name derives from its association with the wells dug to provide water for the people and flocks in this area (see Gen 26:23-33). Archaeological evidence has been found of occupation during the monarchy through the Persian periods. The lack of archaeological evidence for the patriarchal period may suggest that the city by this name changed location, but more important is the observation that there is no suggestion here in the text that there was a walled settlement at Beersheba. There are evidences of early settlement under the modern town (Bir es-Saba') about two miles from the *tell, where some now suspect the ancient city of Beersheba was located.

23:1-20
Sarah's Death and Burial

23:2. variant place names. Place names change as new people enter a region or events occur which provide the reason to memorialize them with a name change (see Jebus and Jerusalem, 1 Chron 11:4; Luz and Bethel, Gen 28:19). Hebron's association with the name Kiriath Arba ("village of four") is unclear, but it may be related to either the joining of four villages into a single settlement or the convergence of roads at the site.

23:3-20. Hittites in Palestine. The origin of the *Hittite presence in Canaan is uncertain, although Genesis 10:15 identifies them as descendants of Canaan through their eponymous ancestor Heth. The use of Semitic names and the ease with which Abraham deals with them in Genesis 23 suggest that this particular group of Hittites was either part of the indigenous population or a trading colony that had partially assimilated to the Canaanite culture (see Gen 26:34). The Hittite empire of Asia Minor (Anatolia, modern Turkey) was destroyed during the invasion of the *Sea Peoples around 1200 B.C. A successor kingdom of Neo-Hittites continued to exist in Syria until the seventh century B.C. and is mentioned in *Assyrian and *Babylonian records. These records often refer to Palestine as the "Land of Hatti," confirming an association with these people. The groups known as Hittites occupying sections of Syria and Canaan may or may not be related to these well-known Hittites. The Hittites in Canaan have Semitic names, while the Hittites of Anatolia were Indo-European.

23:4-5. burial practices. Burial practices vary in the ancient Near East. Nomadic groups often practiced secondary burial—transporting the skeletal remains to a traditional site long

after death. Burial chambers were used by village cultures. These could be natural or hand-carved caves, or subterranean, multichambered tombs. Most often these tombs were used by several generations. A body would be laid in a prepared shelf, along with grave goods (food, pottery, weapons, tools), and then the skeletal remains were removed and placed in another chamber or an ossuary box or simply swept to the rear of the tomb to accommodate the next burial.

23:7-20. ownership of land. Arable land was so precious a possession that it was not supposed to be sold to anyone outside the kinship group. The lack of a buyer within the family and/or the practicalities of business sometimes required a sale to an unrelated person. This could be legally sidestepped through the adoption of the buyer or the intercession of village elders on his behalf with the owner. The designation of Abraham as "a prince" suggests he would be a desirable neighbor. The offer to receive the land as a gift was refused by Abraham because that would have enabled Ephron's heirs to reclaim the land after Ephron's death.

23:14. 400 shekels of silver. Four hundred shekels of silver was a substantial price. It would be equal to about seven and a quarter pounds of silver. In comparison, Omri bought the site of Samaria for six thousand shekels (1 Kings 16:24), and David bought the site of the temple for six hundred gold shekels (1 Chron 21:25), with the threshing floor itself fetching fifty shekels (2 Sam 24:24). Jeremiah bought property, at greatly deflated prices, for seventeen shekels (Jer 32:7). Abraham's payment would be more likely viewed as exorbitant rather than discounted, for rather than negotiating, he paid the inflated initial quote. It is likely that he was anxious to pay full price because a discounted price could be later connected to family debt problems that would allow the heirs of Ephron to reclaim the land. A laborer or artisan at ten shekels per year would not expect to make this much in a lifetime.

23:5-16. bargaining procedures. Haggling and staged bargaining are typical business procedures in the Middle East. They are both entertaining and competitive. However, when it is clear that the potential buyer is in a situation where a purchase is necessary or highly desired, the seller will use the bargaining to his advantage.

23:16. weight current among merchants. Terminology from roughly contemporary Old Assyrian trade letters suggests that this phrase concerns conformity to the standard for silver that was used in overland trade.

24:1-67

A Wife for Isaac

24:1-9. swearing oaths. An oath is always sworn in the name of a god. This places a heavy responsibility on the one who swears such an oath to carry out its stipulations, since he would be liable to divine as well as human retribution if he did not. Sometimes, as in this case, a gesture is added to the oath. The gesture usually is symbolic of the task to be performed by the oath taker. For instance, by placing his hand inside Abraham's thigh (in the vicinity of or on the genitals), the servant ties his oath of obedience to the acquisition of a wife for Isaac and thus the perpetuation of Abraham's line.

24:4. marrying from same tribe. The practice of marrying within one's own tribe or family is called endogamy. Endogamy could be the result of religious, social or ethnic concerns. In this text it appears to be ethnic in that there are no suggestions that the family of Laban, Rebekah and Rachel shares the religious beliefs of Abraham and his family. Likewise social standing is usually an issue only when nobility and commoners are involved or certain classes of urban society are seen as necessarily distinct. Ethnic concerns usually center around clan traditions or family land holdings. At times they represent long-established hostilities between two groups. In this text the endogamy seems motivated by the *covenant that seeks to prevent Abraham and his family from simply being assimilated into the ethnic melting pot in Canaan.

24:10-11. camel domestication. Although camel remains in Arabia date back to 2600 B.C., domesticated camels were not common in Palestine until 1200 B.C. The occasional references to them in Genesis are authenticated by evidence of domestication in an *Old Babylonian text from *Ugarit from the early second millennium. Evidence that the camel was used as a beast of burden in Arabia dates to the end of the third millennium. The stages of domestication may be traced by the development of the saddles. Camels were extremely valuable animals capable of carrying heavy loads through hostile desert terrains. Thus they were seldom used for food and would have been a sign of wealth.

24:10. Aram Naharaim. *Aram Naharaim (Aram of the two rivers), containing Haran on the Balikh River, includes the general area between the Euphrates River and the Habur River triangle in northern Mesopotamia. The name also appears in Deuteronomy 23:4, in the superscription of Psalm 60 and in 1 Chron-

icles 19:6. It may be the same as *Nahrima* in the fourteenth-century B.C. *El Amarna letters between the Egyptian Pharaoh and the rulers of Canaanite city-states.

24:11. well at evening time outside of town. The cool of the early morning and evening would have been the best times for women to go to the village well for water. Since the well was often outside the town to accommodate watering of animals, women would normally travel in groups for protection. Strangers could be expected to use the well, but it may be assumed that they would ask permission of the villagers. Hospitality custom would have necessitated offering them a drink.

24:12-21. mechanistic oracle. Abraham's servant is using an *oracular approach to identifying Isaac's bride-to-be. In an oracle a yes-no question is posed to deity, and a mechanism of some binary nature is used so that deity can provide the answer. In post-Sinai Israel the priest carried the Urim and Thummim to use in oracular situations. Abraham's servant must be more creative and uses a natural mechanism for the oracle. His yes-no question is whether the girl that he is about to approach is the right wife for Isaac. His oracular mechanism is based on a question that he will pose to the girl. When asking for a drink, one would normally expect that a drink would be offered. That would be normal behavior in the context of etiquette and hospitality. In this case such a response would indicate a "no" answer to his oracular question. For the alternative the servant chooses something far out of the range of expectation: that prompted by such a common, unimposing request, the girl would volunteer to water all his camels. This unbelievable offer would indicate a "yes" answer to his oracular question. The thought behind this process is that if deity is providing the answer, he can alter normal behavior and override natural instinct in order to communicate his answer. For similar mechanistic oracles, see Judges 6:36-40 and 1 Samuel 6:7-12. The prophets occasionally approach this type of oracular situation from the other side when they provide signs to verify that they represent God, as in Numbers 16:28-30 or 1 Samuel 12:16-17.

24:11, 13. spring versus well. The difference in terminology between verse 11 ("well") and verse 13 ("spring") may reflect a variety of water sources available. There are examples where a water source originated from a spring but as the water table shrank it became necessary to dig down, thereby forming a well. This is the case at Arad, where a deep well now replaces the original spring.

24:19-20. how much camels drink. Camels drink only as much water as they have lost and do not store it in the hump. The concentration of fat and the coat of hair allows dissipation of heat, less sweating and a wider range of body temperature during the day and night. The camel also is able to maintain a constant amount of water in its blood plasma and thus sustain higher water loss than most animals. A camel that has gone a few days without water could drink as much as twenty-five gallons. In contrast, the jars that were used for water would usually hold no more than three gallons.

24:22. nose rings. Nose rings were especially popular during the *Iron Age (1200-600 B.C.), though there are examples from earlier periods. Made of silver, bronze and gold, and often tubular in design, they were round with two ends for insertion and sometimes included a tiny pendant. The beka is the half-shekel measure of weight, equal to one-fifth of an ounce.

24:22. jewelry. The bracelets would have been bands worn around the wrist as bangles. They were very popular items and are often found on the arms and wrist of females in tombs. By placing them on her arms, the servant may be symbolizing the marriage contract. A ten-shekel bracelet would weigh about four ounces. Legal materials from the first half of the second millennium suggest a worker might expect to make at most ten shekels per year and often less. These would typically be shekels of silver—gold would be more valuable.

24:28. mother's household. It would be natural for a young, unmarried woman to refer to her home as her mother's house until she was wed (see Song 3:4).

24:50-59. presents of betrothal. For a marriage to be arranged, the groom's family must provide a bride price, while the bride's family provided a dowry. The silver and gold objects and the garments presented to Rebekah are part of her transformation into a member of Abraham's household. The word used in the text denotes metal worked into useful items, whether jewelry or plates and other utensils. The presents given to her brother Laban and her mother demonstrate Abraham's wealth and the desirability of the marriage.

24:57-58. Rebekah making decision. It was unusual in the ancient world for the woman to have any part in major decisions. Rebekah was not consulted with regard to the marriage (vv. 50-51), but when the servant asked to leave right away the men looked to Rebekah for consent. Marriage contracts of this general period show a great concern for maintaining

the woman's security within her husband's family. The presence of her family was one of the guarantees that she would be cared for and treated properly. The ten days that Rebekah's family requested (v. 55) would have given them a little more opportunity to make sure that everything was as it appeared to be. It is likely that she was consulted because of the substantial risk that was involved in leaving the family protection under such unusual circumstances.

24:59. accompanying nurse. It would have been suitable for a woman betrothed to a wealthy man to have an entourage of servants. The nurse, however, would have higher status as the nurturer of the child who would now remain as part of her new household and serve as a chaperon on the return journey.

24:62. Beer Lahai Roi. The place name means "well of the living who sees me" and is first associated with Hagar's *theophany in Genesis 16:14. It would have been southwest of Hebron in the Negev. Either Isaac and Abraham have moved their encampment south or Isaac is now living separately.

24:62-66. use of veil. Since she had gone unveiled during the journey, Rebekah's veiling herself once Isaac is identified to her suggests that this is her way of demonstrating to him that she is his bride. Brides were veiled during the wedding but went unveiled as married women. Veil customs differed in various locations and times. Asiatic women on the Beni Hasan tomb painting (early second millennium) are not veiled, but in the Middle *Assyrian laws (late second millennium) all respectable ladies went about veiled in public.

24:67. tent of his mother. Sarah's tent, due to her status of mistress of the household, would have been empty since her death. By taking Rebekah into his mother's tent, Isaac demonstrates that she is now the mistress of the household. This is similar to the importance placed on entering the house of the bridegroom in *Ugaritic texts.

25:1-11

The Death of Abraham

25:1-4. descendants of Abraham from Keturah. Not all of these sixteen names can be identified, although most are associated with the Syro-Arabian desert to the east of the Jordan and may represent a confederation of tribes involved in the lucrative spice trade. Of the six sons born to Abraham and Keturah, the name of Midian is the most prominent in later narrative as a people living on the fringe of Israelite territory in the Negev and Sinai region. Some of the names appear in the *Assyrian annals (Medan is Badana, south of Tema; Ishbak is the northern Syrian tribe of Iasbuq; Sheba is in the southwestern part of Arabia). Shuah also appears in *cuneiform texts as a site on the middle Euphrates near the mouth of the Habur River (see Job 2:11).

25:1-4. concubines. The *concubines, or secondary wives, of Abraham were Hagar and Keturah. Concubines were usually women who did not possess a dowry, and thus their children did not have primary rights to inheritance. The father may choose to designate one of them as his heir if his primary wife has not produced a son. However, if he does not do so, then any claims they may have on his property would be based on the stipulations of the marriage contracts.

25:2, 4. Midianite origins. Midian is one of the children born to Abraham and Keturah, and the reference to him shows the writer's continued interest in establishing links between Abraham and all of the peoples of Palestine, Transjordan and Arabia. The Midianites are most frequently mentioned as a pastoral nomadic group of tribes living in the Negev and the Sinai deserts. Midianite traders carry Joseph to Egypt (Gen 37:28). Moses marries the daughter of Jethro, the priest of Midian, after fleeing Egypt (Ex 2:16-21). During the conquest narrative, Midianites are allied with Moab and are targeted as enemies of the Israelites (Num 25:6-18). There is no extrabiblical information about their history or origins.

25:5-6. giving gifts. It is the prerogative of the father to designate his heir. However, he must also provide for his other children. Thus by giving his other sons gifts and sending them away he shares his wealth with them but also protects Isaac's position as heir of the household.

25:6. land of the east. The Hebrew *qedem* in this unique phrase may indicate a direction, "east," or an actual place name. The twentieth-century B.C. Egyptian story of the political exile *Sinuhe mentions the land of Qedem as lying near Byblos. In other biblical texts it refers to the peoples who inhabit the desert region on the eastern edges of Israel (Judg 6:3; 7:12; Is 11:14).

25:8. gathered to his people. In the worldview of ancient peoples the past was less like a train moving toward them and more like a village spread out in the valley. They saw themselves as facing the past (rather than the future). Being gathered to their ancestors not only expressed the idea of being buried in the family tomb but of joining the ranks of the ancestors in the "ancestral village" that comprised the

past. This is more a view of history than of the afterlife per se.

25:12-18

Ishmael's Line

25:12-16. Ishmael's descendants. Continuing the listing of those descendants of Abraham who inhabited neighboring regions are the sons of Ishmael. The term son sometimes represents political affiliation rather than blood ties, but whatever the case, this list comprises a confederation of tribes living in the Syro-Arabian desert. The occurrence of these names in *Assyrian records, intermixed with names from the Keturah list, suggests both shifts in tribal affiliation and allegiance. Most prominent among the names are Nebaioth, probably the Nabaiati of Ashurbanipal's campaigns against the Arab tribes and possibly to be associated with the later Nabateans of Petra; Tema, an oasis northeast of Dedan on the caravan route between southern Arabia and Mesopotamia; and Kedar, a people mentioned elsewhere as pastoral nomads (Ps 120:5; Is 42:11, 60:7).

25:18. area of Ishmael's descendants. The region from Havilah (see Gen 2:11; 10:7) to Shur (see Gen 16:7) probably represents migration and caravan routes for the descendants of Ishmael. This area is not suitable for large, sedentary populations, but it could support pastoral nomadic groups, and it was the center of the spice trade from southern Arabia traveling west to Egypt and east to Mesopotamia and Syria. Asshur, in this context, would not be the Mesopotamian kingdom of the upper Tigris region, but rather one of the northern Arabian areas (see Gen 10:22; 25:3).

25:19-26

The Birth of Jacob and Esau

25:21. barrenness. Barrenness is used in the ancestral narratives to heighten tension, as the element of the *covenantal promise of descendants (12:2) is thereby endangered. It also marks the son who is eventually born as special, because only God could relieve this infertility.

25:22-23. oracular response. Rebekah's concern about her pregnancy leads her to ask for an *oracle. The text gives no indication of what means Rebekah uses to inquire of the Lord. She is not using a mechanistic oracular device, for that only provides yes/no answers. There is no mention of a prophet, oracular priest, or angel delivering the oracle. In Egypt and Mesopotamia oracles such as this were almost always provided by a priest. Another alternative is that the oracle could be sought in a dream. This usually involved sleeping in a holy place. The text is less interested in the means and more concerned about the content of the oracle. The oracle does not concern the children themselves as much as it addresses the ultimate destiny of the family lines that each will establish. Such an oracle would not have suggested any particular treatment of the children by the parents.

25:24-26. naming children. The giving of names in the ancient world was a significant act. A name was believed to affect a person's destiny; so the person giving the name was exercising some degree of control over the person's future. Often names expressed hopes or blessings. At other times they preserved some detail of the occasion of the birth, especially if the occasion appeared significant. Here Esau is named by a physical characteristic, whereas Jacob is named for his peculiar behavior during birth. The names need not mean the word associated with them, but are often linked by wordplay. So the Hebrew word Jacob does not mean "heel"—it only sounds like the word for heel. The name was expected to play a role in the unfolding destiny of the individual and to take on additional significance and appropriateness throughout his life, though the direction of that appropriateness was impossible to foresee.

25:27-34
Esau Trades His Birthright

25:28. mother's role in inheritance decisions. A Canaanite contract from *Ugarit contains a situation in which the father allows the mother to choose which son receives preferential treatment in the inheritance.

25:29-30. Jacob cooking stew. The incident with the stew appears to take place away from home, otherwise Esau could have appealed to his parents. Jacob is not the hunting type, so it would be unusual for him to be out in the countryside alone. He has been described as a man "staying among the tents," which may indicate he was more closely associated with the shepherding business. The shepherds moved their camps over a broad area of land in order to find water and grazing for the flocks. It is most likely that Jacob would be out supervising some of the shepherds at such a camp when Esau stumbled upon them. Jacob would be the one in charge at the camp, so the decision would be his, and there would therefore be witnesses to the agreement made between Jacob and Esau.

25:31-34. birthright. The birthright concerned only the material inheritance from the parents. The inheritance was divided into the number of sons plus one. The eldest son then received a double share. This was a customary practice throughout the ancient Near East. The stew buys from Esau that additional share (probably not his entire inheritance). There are no examples in the known literature from the ancient Near East of such a deal being made. The closest is in the legal materials from *Nuzi, where one brother sells some already inherited property to one of his brothers.

26:1-16
Isaac and Abimelech

26:1-6. recurrent famine. The uncertainties of rainfall in season and in the proper amount made drought and famine fairly common occurrences in ancient Palestine. The writer here notes this frequent disaster and differentiates between the famine in Abraham's day (Gen 12) and that of Isaac.

26:1. Philistines in Palestine. Large numbers of Philistines entered Canaan after the invasion of the *Sea Peoples (1200 B.C.) broke Egyptian control over the area. In this context they are mentioned in the records of Ramses III (1182-1151 B.C.). They established a pentapolis of five major city-states (Gaza, Gath, Ashdod, Ekron, Ashkelon) along the southern coastal plain and quickly gained political control over nearby regions as well (Judg 15:11). Their mention in Genesis may reflect an earlier group that settled in Canaan prior to 1200 B.C., or it may be an *anachronism based on their presence in the Gerar region in later periods (see Gen 21:32), earlier people of the vicinity being referred to by the name known to later readers. Archaeological evidence of their presence is found in the introduction of new pottery types, grave goods (such as the sarcophagi with human features) and new architectural designs.

26:7-11. wife as sister. The wife/sister theme is used three times in the ancestral narratives (see also chaps. 12 and 20). Here Abimelech (either a throne name or a dynastic name meaning "My father is king") is tricked by Isaac and Rebekah. The result is their obtaining royal protection and the right to farm and to graze his herds in Gerar.

26:12-16. planting crops. It is not unusual for pastoral nomadic tribes to plant a crop or to harvest date palms along their usual line of march. This may be a step toward settling into a village life, but that is not necessarily the case. Generally sedentarism (settling of nomads) is more directly related to the actions of governments or changes in the political boundaries through which they drive their herds. Wealth may also cause them to settle down, but this is not a major factor.

26:17-35

Isaac's Wells

26:17-22. well rights and disputes. Wells are generally dug and protected by villages. The likelihood that they will silt up or collapse requires at least occasional oversight. The labor involved and the necessity of water for humans, crops and animals makes it likely that disputes will arise between villages and/or herdsmen who also wish to claim and use the wells.

26:20. naming wells. One way to designate ownership of a well or other natural resource is to give it a name. Once this has become its traditional name, title is not difficult to establish. It thus prevents later disputes or settles any that may arise. Naming is also part of the traditional lore of a tribe which is passed on to later generations.

26:23-25. build altar, call, pitch tent, dig well. The three acts of verse 25 are all related to possession of the land and are therefore a suitable response to the *covenant promise of verse 24. The altar gave recognition to the holiness of the place where the Lord spoke to him. Pitching a tent and digging a well are generally accepted means by which to establish a right to unclaimed land.

26:26-33. peace treaty. The peace treaty of verses 28-30 would constitute recognition by Isaac's neighbors that his presence in that area was acceptable. The agreement was validated by the sharing of a meal and by the swearing of oaths. Just as Abraham had built altars (chap. 12) and established recognized rights to land (chap. 23), so Isaac is now doing the same.

26:33. folk etymology of town names. Beersheba was named earlier by Abraham (in 21:31). The designation of significance to a name is not necessarily a suggestion that the name originated at that time. Just as people's names can be reinterpreted (for instance, Jacob in 27:36), so a place name can be reinterpreted. The ancients were less concerned with the origin of a name than they were with the significance the name acquired. This town at the southern extreme of the land becomes the home base for Isaac. The site identified by archaeologists as Beersheba has no remains prior to the Judges period (*Iron Age, 1200), but there is no suggestion in the story of Isaac that

there was a town on the site in his day, so this is not a problem.

27:1-40

Isaac's Pronouncement on His Sons

27:1-4. deathbed blessings. Blessings or curses pronounced by the patriarch of the family were always taken seriously and considered binding. Such pronouncements from a patriarch's deathbed would be even more momentous. In this text, however, Isaac is not portrayed as being on his deathbed, merely aged enough that he wants to put his house in order by providing the traditional blessing.

27:4. proper atmosphere for blessings. While the feast that Esau is to prepare may provide a pleasant atmosphere and appropriate mood for the blessing, it also provides the context of celebration that would accompany significant events, much as we might go out to dinner at a fancy restaurant.

27:11-13. curse appropriation. Rebekah responds to Jacob's fears of bringing a a curse on himself by appropriating to herself any curse that may result. Can she do that? As this chapter demonstrates, a blessing is not transferable, and neither is the pronouncement of a curse. But in this case Rebekah is most likely referring to the consequences of the curse rather than the curse itself. Since deity is the enforcer of the curse, this acknowledgment that she has forced Jacob to deceive his father would target her if a curse was to result.

27:14. food preparation. Food preparation was done by both men and women. One way to provide variation of taste to meals (which were often monotonous and meatless) was to hunt wild game. This meat might be tough and gamey-tasting, and thus it would be stewed to tenderize it and mixed with herbs to improve the flavor.

27:27-29. nature of blessing. The blessing that Isaac bestows on Jacob (whom he mistakes for Esau) grants him fertility of the ground, dominion over other nations, including those descended from siblings, and a boomerang effect for curses and blessings. These are typical elements for the patriarchal blessing and have no relationship to either material inheritance or to the *covenant, though some of these features are also present in the covenant benefits that the Lord promises to Israel. They constitute the foundational elements of survival and prosperity.

27:34-40. no negation of blessing. The power of the spoken word was such that it could not be "unsaid"—this is true even outside the realm of superstition in that many words spoken do the benefit or damage they intend regardless of any second thoughts the speaker may have. The pronouncement regarding Esau's destiny thus reflects the realities of the previously uttered blessing on Jacob. It would not be considered a curse because it assumes continuing existence and eventual freedom.

27:37. "I have made." Isaac explains to Esau, "I have made him lord . . . I have sustained him." The first-person forms show that Isaac is not suggesting that this blessing is a prophetic proclamation from deity. Neither does Isaac call on deity to perform it. Similar formulas in Mesopotamia regularly invoke deity in such blessings and curses.

27:41-46
The Outcome of the Deception

27:45. lose both in one day. Rebekah expresses the concern that she might lose both in one day. This could either refer to losing both Isaac and Jacob, that is, Isaac dies and Jacob is killed by Esau; or losing both Jacob and Esau, that is, Jacob would be killed and Esau, as his murderer, would either have to flee or end up the victim of blood vengeance.

27:46. Hittite women. The *Hittite women that Esau married were part of the indigenous culture of Canaan at this time. While it is possible that this group is related to the well-known Hittites of Anatolia, our knowledge of the culture and history of the Canaanite Hittites in the patriarchal period is insufficient to allow informed conclusions. There is a well-established Anatolian Hittite presence in Canaan during the monarchy period, and even as early as the middle of the second millennium the *Amarna texts contain Hittite and *Hurrian personal names.

28:1-22
Jacob's Dream and Vow

28:2. Paddan Aram. This place name only appears in Genesis. It is either a designation for the general area of northern Mesopotamia (= *Aram Naharaim in 24:10) or perhaps another name for Haran. In *Akkadian, both *padanu* and *harranu* mean "path" or "road." In either case, Jacob is instructed to return to his ancestors' homeland to seek a bride as part of their practice of endogamy (marrying within a select group).

28:5. Aramean. The origin of the *Arameans is problematic. They do not actually appear in Mesopotamian records until the end of the second-millennium *Assyrian annals of Tiglath-Pileser I (1114-1076 B.C.). In the ninth century Shalmaneser III mentions kings of Aram in Damascus (including Hazael and Ben-Hadad III). However, this is many centuries after the setting of the ancestor narratives. The mention of Arameans in relation to Abraham and Jacob is likely a reference to scattered tribes of peoples in upper Mesopotamia who had not yet coalesced in the nation of Aram, which appears in later texts. Based on other examples from *cuneiform literature, the name Aram may in fact have originally been that of a region (cf. Sippar-Amnantum of the *Old Babylonian period) and was later applied to people living there. Current evidence suggests that the Arameans inhabited the upper Euphrates throughout the second millennium, first as villagers and pastoralists, then as a political, national coalition.

28:10-12. Jacob's itinerary. Jacob takes the central ridge road that goes through the hill country from Beersheba through Hebron, Bethel and Shechem to join the main artery, the Great Trunk road, in Beth Shan. It would have taken a couple of days to get from Beersheba to Bethel (about 60 miles), and the trip to Haran would have taken over a month (about 550 miles).

28:13-15. stairway. The ladder or stairway that Jacob sees in his dream is the passageway between heaven and earth. The comparable word in *Akkadian is used in Mesopotamian mythology to describe what the messenger of the gods uses when he wants to pass from one realm to another. It is this mythological stairway that the *Babylonians sought to represent in the architecture of the ziggurats. These had been built to provide a way for the deity to descend to the temple and the town. Jacob's background would have given him familiarity with this concept, and thus he would conclude that he was in a sacred spot where there was a portal opened between worlds. Though he sees the stairway in his dream, and the messengers (angels) are using it to pass between realms (embarking on and returning from missions, not a procession or parade), the Lord is not portrayed as having used it, but as standing beside it (this is the proper translation of the Hebrew idiom).

28:16-17. house of God, gate of heaven. When Jacob awakes he identifies the sacred place as the house of God *(beth-el)* and the gate of heaven. In *Akkadian mythology the stairway used by the messengers went up to the gate of the gods, while the temple of the deity was located at the bottom. In this way the patron deity could leave the assembly of the gods and descend to the place of worship.

28:18-19. pillars and anointing. The sacred pillars or standing stones are well known in the religious practice of the ancient Near East predating the fourth millennium B.C. They are featured prominently in Canaanite *cultic installations such as the high place at Gezer and were also used in the Israelite temple at Arad. Other standing stones were simply set up as memorials. From basins sometimes found near the foot of such pillars, it is inferred that libations (liquid offerings) were poured over them, as we see Jacob doing in 35:14. The anointing of the pillar would constitute the dedication of it.

28:19. Bethel/Luz. As noted in Genesis 23:2, place names change based on the appearance of new peoples or significant events. Bethel was an important town located in the central hill country just north of Jerusalem. An important east-west road lay just south of the town, making it a crossroads for travelers and a likely place for the establishment of a *cultic site. There is some speculation that Luz was the original city site and that Bethel (literally "house of God") was a separate cultic site located outside the town. Once the Israelites had established themselves in the region, however, the site's association with Abraham (12:8) and Jacob would have caused the older name to be superseded.

28:20-22. vows. Vows are promises with conditions attached, almost always made to God. In the ancient world the most common context for a vow was when a request was being made to deity. The condition would typically involve God's provision or protection, while that which was vowed was usually a gift to deity. This would most commonly take the form of a sacrifice but could refer to other types of gifts to the sanctuary or priests. Fulfillment of a vow could usually be accomplished at the sanctuary and was a public act. In Jacob's vow the conditions actually extend through the end of verse 21. Jacob promises a tithe upon the fulfillment of the conditions.

28:22. tithe. In the ancient world tithing was often a means of taxation. There were tithes paid to the temple as well as those paid to the king. Since income and personal wealth was often not primarily in money, all goods were included in the calculations of the tithe, as indicated here by Jacob in the phrase "all that you give me." Jacob's tithe is clearly voluntary rather than imposed and therefore would not be associated with taxation of any sort. There is no temple or priesthood at Bethel, so to whom would Jacob give his tithe? It is likely that Jacob anticipates that any wealth coming to him would be in the form of flocks and herds. In such a case the tithe would be represented in sacrifices at Bethel.

29:1-14

Jacob Finds Laban and His Family

29:2, 3, 10. stone over well mouth. The stone served a double function, as a guard against contamination or poisoning of the well and as a social control mechanism, preventing any of the herdsmen in the area from drawing more water than was their right. Apparently water was scarce in this "open country" and thus the right to use the well was a jealously guarded one. Bedouin herders seldom wish to even divulge the location of wells within their territory, so this degree of security is not out of place. The stone may even have served to disguise the location of the well from the casual passerby. Wells of this time were not surrounded by protective walls, so the stone would also have prevented animals (or people) from inadvertently stumbling into it.

29:3. watering agreements. In regions where water sources were scarce, it would have been necessary to make agreements between herdsmen for use of the local well or spring. A lack of trust, however, could result in a scene like the one in the text, where all of the herds had to be assembled before any could drink.

29:6. female shepherd. While it is not uncommon today for women and small children to herd Bedouin flocks, in antiquity women would have done so only when the household had no sons. It was a dangerous practice since they might be molested, but it was also a way of attracting a husband.

29:11. kiss of greeting. The traditional form of greeting for friends and relatives in the Middle East is a warm hug and a kiss on each cheek. This is done with both male and female relatives.

29:15-30

Jacob Works for His Wives

29:17. Leah's eyes. In the comparative description of Rachel and Leah, the only comment about Leah concerns her eyes. The term used is generally considered positive and speaks of fragility, vulnerability, tenderness or a delicate quality (NIV note). Although eyes were a principal component of beauty in the ancient world, Leah's positive features paled in comparison to Rachel's loveliness.

29:18-20. seven years' labor. Typical marriage customs would have included a payment made to the bride's family by the groom or his family. This could provide a sort of trust fund to provide for the wife should the husband die, desert her or divorce her. Alternatively it was at times used by the family to pay the bride price for the bride's brothers. In some cases it was even returned to the bride in the form of an indirect dowry. In the *Nuzi texts a typical bride price is thirty or forty shekels of silver. Since ten shekels of silver is a typical annual wage for a shepherd, Jacob is paying a higher price. That can be understood, however, given the circumstances: Jacob is in no position to negotiate, and the payment is being made in labor.

29:21-24. wedding feast. Since a wedding is based on a contract between two families, it is similar to treaties and to business transactions. Like them, the marriage would have been consummated with a *ritual meal (a sign of peace between the parties). There would also be a procession to a designated "first home" (usually within the house or tent of the groom's father, although not in Gen 29) and sexual intercourse between the couple. The bride would be veiled during these public festivities, and it may be assumed that the high spirits would have led to drunkenness, both factors in Jacob's inability to recognize the substitution of Leah for Rachel at the feast.

29:24. gift of maidservant. It was quite common for the bride to receive a gift of a maidservant on the occasion of her marriage. In this way she obtained her own personal household or entourage, providing her with both greater prestige and help in performing her duties.

29:26-30. custom of older married first. It is the practice of people of the ancient Near East, and still a tradition today in that area, for the oldest daughter to be married first. This prevents a younger sibling from shaming a sister who may not be as beautiful and also prevents the financial drain on the family caused by spinsters. Females were used, through marriage contracts, to obtain wealth and prestige for the family. If an older sister was bypassed and then never married, her family would be left with the responsibility to support her.

29:27. bridal week. The relationship between the seven-day story of creation and the idea of creating new life through marriage may be the origin of the bridal week. Diverting the bride and groom from other tasks was also designed to insure a pregnancy early in the marriage.

29:31—30:24
Jacob's Children

29:33. naming of children. The naming of children was a significant act and typically represented some circumstance or sentiment at the time of birth. It rarely addressed the supposed fate or destiny of the child directly and was not thought to determine the child's destiny, but it was believed that the name was directly related to a person's essential self and therefore could be expected to find significant associations with the person's nature and experiences.

30:3-13. maidservant as surrogate wife. Just as Sarah gave Abraham her maid Hagar as a surrogate wife (16:1-4), so too the wives of Jacob give him their maids. The object is for a barren (or unloved) wife to have children by means of this legal surrogacy. Provision for this custom is also found in the *Lipit-Ishtar Code and in the Code of *Hammurabi from Mesopotamia.

30:14-15. mandrake plants. *Mandragora officinarum* is a stemless, perennial root in the potato family found growing in stony ground. It resembles the human figure and has narcotic and purgative properties, which explain its medicinal use. Its shape and pungent fragrance may be the origin of its use in *fertility rites and as an aphrodisiac (see Song 7:13-14). It has dark green, wrinkled leaves from which rise a violet, bell-shaped flower. Its fruit is a yellowish berry, approximately the size of a small tomato, which can be consumed. The mandrake is native to the Mediterranean region but is not common in Mesopotamia.

30:25-43
Jacob Employed by Laban

30:22-25. Jacob's request. A woman's status in the family would be very tenuous if she had not borne children. A barren woman could be and often was discarded, ostracized or given a lower status and would find protection in her relatives. Now that Rachel's status in Jacob's family is established, Jacob feels free to request permission to leave.

30:27. divination of Laban. An Israelite reader would have been struck by Laban's suggestion that *Yahweh has given information by means of *divination. There is no mention of what type of divination Laban used, but all divination was later forbidden under the law. Divination assumed that there was knowledge to be gained about the activities and motives of the gods through the use of various indicators (such as entrails of sacrificed animals). It operated in a worldview that was contrary to that promoted in the Bible. Nevertheless, God occasionally chooses to use such methods, as the Bethlehem star attests.

30:32-33. sheep breeding. The coloring chosen by Jacob (dark lambs and variegated goats) generally made up a very small proportion of the herd. Jacob seems to be settling for a share that was far smaller than usual, in that contracts of the day designated sometimes as much as 20 percent of new births for the shepherd (Bedouin studies today suggest that 10 percent is common). Byproducts (wool, milk products) are not mentioned here, but a percentage of those were also often part of the shepherd's compensation.

30:37-43. use of rods. Jacob's solution to Laban's treachery contains elements of scientific breeding and folklore tradition. Clearly, shepherds would have been aware of the estrus cycle of their sheep (which runs from June to September), and observation would have demonstrated that breeding healthy animals would produce vigorous lambs. What is not scientific, however, is the principle that certain characteristics (coloration in this case) can be bred for through visual aids. The stripped rods which Jacob places before the troughs of the sheep cannot genetically affect the sheep. This type of sympathetic magic is found in many folk traditions (including modern tales of colors worn by a mother determining the sex of her child). It plays a part in the trickster theme of this narrative and is reflective of a culture which depended on a mixture of magical and commonsense methods to produce results.

31:1-21
Jacob's Flight

31:1. Laban's sons' complaint. Jacob's success in Laban's employ would naturally result in the reduction of Laban's assets and therefore the depletion of the inheritance his sons could expect to receive. It is no wonder then that they nurse a grudge against their brother-in-law.

31:13. God of Bethel. By identifying himself as the God of Bethel, the Lord has reminded Jacob of the vow of Jacob in 28:20-22. Though it is true that Canaanites would have viewed sacred sites as each having their own separate deities, there is no suggestion in the text that Jacob considers the God of Bethel to be distinct from *Yahweh, and certainly the author of the Pentateuch sees them as one (compare vv. 3 and 13).

31:14-16. Rachel and Leah's complaint. Rachel and Leah express willingness to leave with Jacob because of the way Laban has treated them in his financial dealings. It has been suggested that they are referring to assets that were generally held in escrow for the care of the woman should her husband die or divorce her. Such assets would have been part of the bride price, which, in this case, Jacob had paid in labor rather than tangible assets. If Laban never put aside the value of Jacob's fourteen years of labor, there would be nothing in reserve to provide for the women. As a result they would not enjoy any additional protection in economic terms by staying in the vicinity of their family. They identify this as treating them as foreigners, because Laban had gained from Jacob's labor but had not passed the gain on to them—it is therefore just as if he had sold them.

31:18. Paddan Aram. Paddan Aram seems to refer to the region of northern Mesopotamia and northeast Syria (see comment on 28:2). The inclusion of *Aram suggests connections with the Arameans (see comment on 28:5).

31:19-20. sheep shearing. Shearing domestic sheep of their woolly fleece occurs in the spring a few weeks prior to lambing. This allows wool to grow back during the summer to help protect against extreme temperatures. Shepherds would bring their animals to a central location where the wool was also processed, dyed and woven into cloth. Archaeological excavations at Timnah (see 38:12) have produced large numbers of loom weights, suggesting that this was a center for shearing and weaving. Because this involved a journey, provisions would have had to be made to protect the villagers left behind. There would also be a celebration associated with the event after the hard work of shearing was completed.

31:19. household gods. The *teraphim* or "household gods" were associated with luck and prosperity of the family. One suggestion is that, like the *lares* and *penates* of Roman tradition, these small images guarded the threshold and hearth. They were passed from one generation to the next as part of the inheritance. The fact that Rachel was able to hide them under a saddle suggests their tiny size, though some were larger (see 1 Sam 19:13). Many of these small figurines have been found in Mesopotamia and Syro-Palestine. They were a part of the popular or local religion, not associated with temples or national *cults for the major deities. One recent study has suggested they were figurines of the ancestors, but others see them as more generally related to the family's patron deity. Laban's frantic desire to retrieve these images suggests their importance to his family, in contrast to Jacob's disposal of them before he departs for Canaan.

31:21. hill country of Gilead. Jacob's departure from the area of Haran takes him south and west across the Euphrates River and into the Transjordanian region known as Gilead.

This area comprises most of the Jordanian plateau between the Yarmuk River near the Sea of Galilee and the northern end of the Dead Sea.

31:22-55
The Settlement of Jacob and Laban
31:27. musical instruments. Tambourines and harps were the common musical instruments associated with celebrations in the village culture. They were used to mark major events, such as military victories (Ex 15:20), celebratory and religious dances (1 Sam 10:5), and, as in this case, feasts of departure.

31:35. Rachel's excuse. Rachel's excuse that she had her period would have been sufficient to warn off Laban, for in the ancient world a woman in menstruation was considered a danger because menstrual blood was widely believed to be a habitat for demons.

31:38-42. shepherd's responsibility. Herding contracts have been discovered in excavations in Mesopotamia which spell out the responsibilities and the wages of herdsmen. They describe activities in much the same way as in this passage: taking animals to proper grazing areas and water sources, birthing of lambs, treatment of sick and injured animals, protection from wild predators and retrieval of lost sheep. It was expected that losses through neglect or failure to protect the flock would be deducted from the shepherds' wages. Plus, only animals that had been killed or died of natural causes could be eaten by the shepherds.

31:42. ancestral Deity. Jacob's use of the terms the "God of my father, the God of Abraham" and the "Fear of Isaac" provide a sense of kinship based on the worship of an ancestral deity by these tribal people (see 28:12; Ex 3:6; 4:5). "The Fear of Isaac" appears only in Genesis and may represent a cognomen (nickname) for the patron God as well as an implied threat against any violence by Laban (see 31:29). The reference to divine patrons, "Ashur, the god of your fathers," is also found in Old *Assyrian texts (early second millennium B.C.).

31:45-53. pillar as witness. The use of a heap of stones as a boundary marker or a memorial to an event or to bear witness to a *covenant appears several places in the biblical text (see 28:18; 35:20; Josh 24:27). In Canaanite religion, the massebah, or standing stone, was erected and considered as a guardian or a dwelling place of a god (see Deut 16:21-22; 1 Kings 14:23). The fact that two are erected here and each is given a name is suggestive of an invoking *ritual in which the god(s) of each party are called to witness the treaty-making ceremony and to enforce its stipulations. One possible parallel to this may be the twin pillars, Jachin and Boaz, placed in front of Solomon's temple in Jerusalem (1 Kings 7:15-22).

31:48-53. nature of agreement. Like other treaty documents in the ancient Near East (such as the seventh-century B.C. *Assyrian vassal treaties of Esarhaddon and the thirteenth-century B.C. treaty between Rameses II and Hattusilis III), the gods of each party are invoked as witnesses, a set of exact stipulations is spelled out and a sacrifice and *ritual meal conclude the agreement. While the only explicit charge here is that Jacob not take any more wives, it is suggested by the setting up of the pillars that this is also a boundary agreement and territory is now marked. Parallels to this restriction on taking another wife are found in *Nuzi legal documents (fifteenth century B.C.). The stipulation is intended to protect the rights and status of the current wife/wives, especially in this context where the wives' family would not be there to assure fair and equitable treatment.

31:54. sacrificial meal. It was apparently standard procedure to use a meal to seal an agreement (see 14:18; 26:30; Ex 24:5-11). Just as food is a part of the hospitality *ritual (18:2-5), here it functions as a means of drawing each party into a familial, nonhostile relationship. By adding the element of sacrifice, it also insures the participation of the gods and heightens the solemnity of the occasion.

32:1-21
Jacob's Return to Canaan
32:1. met by angels. Just as Jacob experienced an angelic *theophany as he left the Promised Land (28:12), so too he is met by angels on his return. This forms an *inclusio* (a literary device in which the same events or lines occur at the beginning and the end of a literary segment) in the narrative and signals both divine sanction for the treaty just concluded and a reestablishment of direct contact with the *covenantal heir.

32:2. naming places. Applying names to sites where specific events occur, especially *theophanies, is fairly common in the ancestral narratives (see 16:14; 21:31; 26:20, 33; 28:19). In this way the presence of the deity is established at that site. For instance, Bethel, the location of one of Abraham's altars and the place where Jacob experienced a theophany, later became a major religious site. The name of the place in this passage, Mahanaim, means "two camps," but the reference is obscure. Although it has not been located, this is a fairly important city in the tribal territory of Gad (see Josh 13:26; 21:38; 2 Sam 2:8-9).

32:3. Seir. The land of Seir is generally considered to be the mountainous central region of Edom (elevations generally over 5,000 feet) between Wadi al-Ghuwayr on the north and Ras en-Naqb on the south.

32:3-5. Jacob's communication. Jacob's communication to Esau is intended to make several points. First, he has not been in hiding or sneaking around the land behind Esau's back. Second, and more importantly, he has not come to lay claim to inheritance rights. By describing his success and wealth, he insinuates that he has not returned because he is broke and looking to demand what is due him.

32:13-21. gifts for Esau. The generosity of Jacob's gifts can be understood when compared to tribute paid by one nation to another. So, for instance, in the ninth century B.C. the town of Hindanu paid to *Assyrian king Tukulti-Ninurta II some silver, bread, beer, thirty camels, fifty oxen and thirty donkeys. This gift would be sufficient for Esau to get a good start on a herding operation of his own or, alternatively, to reward any mercenaries in his employ who may have been anticipating booty.

32:13-21. Jacob's strategy. Jacob's gifts to Esau demonstrate that he is as shrewd as ever. Besides being an attempt to gain Esau's favor through generosity, the continuous arrival of the herds of animals will wear out any schemes for ambush and deflate any degree of military readiness that Esau might be planning in his encounter with Jacob. Additionally, traveling with the animals will slow Esau down and make his company much noisier. Finally, the plan adds Jacob's servants to Esau's retinue—a decided advantage if there is to be fighting.

32:22. river fords. River crossings or fords function in much the same way as gates. Both are entranceways giving access in and out of territory. Both have strategic value for armies (see Judg 3:28; 12:5; Jer 51:32). As such, they are tied to power, both physical and supernatural. Thus it is not difficult to imagine a link between Jacob's entrance into the Promised Land and a struggle with a supernatural being beside the fast flowing waters at the ford of the Jabbok River.

32:24-26. detaining for blessing. A *Hittite *ritual text envisions a struggle between the goddess Khebat and the king in which the goddess is detained and there is discussion of who will prevail over whom, leading to a request for blessing by the king.

32:24. leaving at daybreak. The reference to time indicates both the length of the struggle between Jacob and the divine being and serves as an indicator of Jacob's lack of perception during the fight. Daybreak or "cock's crow" are often found in folklore as the moment when powers and creatures of the dark lose their power to affect humans, though this is not a familiar element in ancient Near Eastern literature. In this case the issue is not one of potency, but one of supremacy (as indicated by the naming) and discernment (see v. 29).

32:28-30. name changing. There is, of course, an etiological (explaining how things came to be) aspect to name changes (e. g., Abram to Abraham in 17:5, which reenforces the *covenantal promise of fathering many nations). When the angel asks Jacob his name, this provides the opportunity to highlight the change to Israel. Thus the change serves both an etiological purpose (memorializing this event at Peniel), but it also marks the Jacob/Israel shift from an outcast and usurper to the heir of the covenant and the chosen leader of God's people. Name changing was also a way to exercise authority over an individual. When a suzerain put a vassal on the throne, he sometimes gave him a new name, demonstrating his power over that vassal.

32:31-32. etiological comments. An etiological comment is one that provides an origin for a name, characteristic or practice. In folklore etiological comments are often fanciful (how the camel got its hump), while in ethnic or national traditions they tend to be legendary. While such fanciful or legendary accounts can often be entirely fabricated, etiological comments need not be only the consequence of a creative imagination but may preserve an accurate story of a tradition. The naming of the place where Jacob/Israel wrestled with God draws its name from his exclamation of surprise at "seeing God face to face" (a clear parallel to his earlier encounter at Bethel, 28:16-19). The final notation in this episode provides an explanation for a unique dietary law, which does not appear elsewhere in Jewish law. However, the legal value in forbidding the consumption of the "tendon attached to the socket of the hip" (possibly the sciatic nerve) is found in its memorializing of Jacob/Israel's struggle at the Jabbok—in that sense comparable to the institution of *circumcision (17:9-14)—marking a significant *covenantal reaffirmation.

33:1-20

Jacob's Reunion with Esau

33:1-3. bowing seven times. One way that

person showed respect for a superior in the ancient world was by bowing to the ground. To magnify the honor being given and the subservience of the person who bowed, this gesture could be repeated seven times. Some Egyptian texts from El Amarna (fourteenth century B.C.) portray vassals bowing seven times to Pharaoh.

33:16. Seir. This region comprises the hill country stretching to the southeast of the Arabah, between the Dead Sea and the Gulf of Aqabah, in territory later inhabited by the Edomites (see 36:20; Judg 5:4). Because of its relatively high annual rainfall and elevation, the area has sufficient water and snow melt to support scrub forests and brushes. This may be the origin of the name Seir, which means "hairy."

33:17. Succoth. A town situated east of the Jordan River near its confluence with the Jabbok River (Judg 8:5). A number of archaeologists have identified it with the site of Tell Deir 'Alla, based on Egyptian records (the stele of Shishak) and cultural remains which date from the *Chalcolithic to *Iron Age II. The name, which means "booths," would be appropriate for the temporary housing of this region's mixed population of pastoral nomads and miners (evidence of smelting has been found in Iron I levels).

33:18-19. Shechem. Identified with Tell Balata in the central highlands, about thirty-five miles north of Jerusalem, Shechem is known from many ancient sources, including the Egyptian records of Sen-Usert III (nineteenth century B.C.) and the *El Amarna tablets (fourteenth century B.C.). Nearly continuous occupation is evidenced through the second and first millennia, demonstrating the importance of this strategic city on the highway network running north from Egypt through Beersheba, Jerusalem and on to Damascus. It was Abram's first stop in Canaan (see comment on 12:6). The fertile soil in this area promoted agriculture as well as good grazing.

33:19. purchase of land. As in the case in Genesis 23, this land transaction includes an exact price (one hundred pieces of silver), thereby marking this as a deeded sale rather than a fee for usage of the property. Since he is settling within the landed territory of the town, Jacob must purchase the property he settles on. The amount he pays is uncertain because the value of the unit of money referred to here is unknown. As in Genesis 23 the eventual use of this land is for burial (see Josh 24:32).

33:20. altar significance. Altars function as sacrificial platforms. Their construction can also mark the introduction of the worship of a particular god in a new land. One tie between the generations of *covenantal leaders is their construction of altars in order to worship *Yahweh in the Promised Land (12:7-8; 13:18; 26:25). The name given to Jacob/Israel's altar, "El Elohe Israel," is an acknowledgment of his own name change and his acceptance of the role of covenantal heir that had been promised at Bethel (28:13-15). For another example of naming an altar, see Exodus 17:15.

34:1-31
Dinah and Shechem

34:2. Hivites. Based on their appearance in various narratives, the Hivites apparently inhabited an area in the central hill country of Canaan, ranging from Gibeon, near Jerusalem (Josh 9:1-7), to Shechem and on north to Mount Hermon (Josh 11:3; Judg 3:3). The origin of the Hivites is unknown (descendant of Ham in Gen 10:17), but it is possible that they are related to either *Hurrian or *Hittite peoples settling in Canaan during the period from the mid-second to early first millennium B.C.

34:2. ravishing women. Rape as a means of obtaining a marriage contract was apparently one stratagem used in the ancient Near East. Laws regulating this practice are found in Exodus 22:16-17, Deuteronomy 22:28-29, the Middle *Assyrian Laws and the *Hittite laws. These often require the rapist to pay an especially high bride price and sometimes forbid any possibility of divorce. *Sumerian Law 7, like Genesis 34, deals with a case where a young, unbetrothed woman leaves her parents' home without permission and is raped. The result is an option by the parents to marry her to the rapist without her consent.

34:7. concept of universal law. Ancient Near Eastern literature contains law collections of this time and earlier that make it clear that prohibitions concerning illicit and violent sexual behavior were not innovations at Sinai. The codes of conduct by which people lived in this time show great similarity to the laws enshrined at Sinai and demonstrate a common universal sense of morality and justice. Laws and less formal standards often sought to protect the honor and integrity of the family, the dignity of the individual and security within society.

34:11-12. bride price and gift. The bride price and gift paid by the groom's family was often dependent on the desirability of the marriage. A higher price could be expected if the bride's family was socially superior to that of the groom or there were other factors (such as the bride's beauty) which made her value rise. In the *Nuzi texts a typical bride price is thirty to forty shekels of silver.

34;13-17. circumcision. At the time that *circumcision was introduced (Gen 17), adult males as well as infants underwent this procedure as a mark of their membership in the community. Circumcision was practiced widely in the ancient Near East as a rite of puberty, fertility or marriage, but was not practiced by all peoples. The men of Shechem agree to submit to this in order to become acceptable as husbands to Jacob's daughters. The procedure performed on adults is quite painful and would have virtually debilitated the adult male population for several days.

34:20. gate of the city. The city gate was a place of assembly for legal and business transactions. It could also be used for public meetings that affected all of the city's citizens. In the small towns that were the ancient cities the houses were close together and the streets were narrow. The only open areas would be the market place (if the town had one) and the area of the gate. The former would have been unsuitable for matters of public business.

34:25-29. plundering the city. The negotiation between the parties had concerned appropriate recompense (bride price) for Dinah in the circumstances of her having been taken forcibly. As it turns out, the compensation that Dinah's brothers considered appropriate was the forfeiture of the life and goods of the entire city. Such was also attempted by the Greeks in the *Iliad* as they laid siege to Troy to recover Helen.

35:1-15

Jacob's Return to Bethel

35:1. building an altar. When Abram built altars during his journeys (12:6-8), it was not for the purpose of sacrifice but for calling on the name of the Lord. This also seems to be the case with Jacob, since no reference is made to offering sacrifices on the altar. Some have suggested that the altars served to mark the territory of the deity. Alternatively they were memorials to the name of the Lord.

35:2-5. ridding of foreign gods. The call to rid themselves of foreign gods is a call to commit themselves exclusively to *Yahweh. This does not mean that they understood or accepted philosophical monotheism, but that they accepted Yahweh as their family patron deity. The belief in a personal god who gave protection and provision to the family was common in early second-millennium Mesopotamia. This deity was not understood to replace the great cosmic gods but was the principal object

of worship and religious devotion for the individual.

35:2. purification. Purification would have accompanied *ritual procedures but also may be a response to the bloodshed of chapter 34. It typically involved bathing and changing garments. Preparation for worship and *ritual also includes the disposal of any signs of loyalty to other gods. All of this took place at Shechem, where the events of chapter 34 took place, some twenty miles north of Bethel. The worship act is portrayed as a pilgrimage, as indicated by the terminology of verse 1. The relationship of earrings to worship of other gods is unclear. While the use of earrings to fashion idols is attested (Ex 32:2; Judg 8:24), and they are often part of the plunder of looted cities, neither of these appear to offer an explanation. It has been suggested that perhaps the earrings were *amulets of some sort, even stamped with an image of deity, though there is no evidence of earrings serving such a purpose. There is, however, an earring with an inscription of dedication to a goddess from the *Ur III period (about 2000 B.C.).

35:4. buried under the oak. The objects were buried under a special tree in Shechem, which possibly figures also in 12:6, Joshua 24.23-27 and Judges 9:6, 37. Sacred trees played a significant role in popular religion of the day, which would have viewed stone and tree as potential divine dwellings. In Canaanite religion they are believed to be symbols of *fertility (see Deut 12:2; Jer 3:9; Hos 4:13), though there is very little in the archaeological or literary remains of the Canaanites that would clarify the role of sacred trees.

35:14. anointed pillar. Just as Jacob had set up a stone at Bethel and anointed it in 28:18, so now another is set up and a libation (liquid offering) performed to commemorate the *theophany (God's appearance). It would not be unusual to have several standing stones erected in the same vicinity.

35:16-29

The Deaths of Rachel and Isaac

35:16-18. midwifing. Midwives, who were generally older women, served as resources to teach young women about sexual activity and to aid in the birth of children. They were also a part of the naming *ritual and may have helped teach new mothers about nursing and child care.

35:16-18. death in childbirth. Death in childbirth was not an uncommon occurrence in ancient world. The incantation literature *Babylon contains a number of exam spells to protect the mother and child in the birthing process; particularly incantations against Lamashtu, the demon who was believed to attack women and children.

35:18. naming children. Rachel names her child as she dies, giving a name that reflects her misery. It was customary for circumstances surrounding the birth to serve as the occasion for the name. In this case Jacob changes the name, as was the father's right. *Benjamin* can mean either son of the right (hand), signifying a place of protection, or son of the south (since Israelites oriented themselves toward the east, the south was on their right).

35:19-20. Rachel's tomb. Rachel's death in childbirth is placed on the way to Ephrath, north of Bethlehem, on the border of the later tribal territories of Judah and Benjamin (see 1 Sam 10:2), some twelve miles north of Bethlehem. Another example of raising a memorial pillar for the dead is found in 2 Samuel 18:18. The late mention of Rachel's tomb in Jeremiah 31 suggests that it was a well-known pilgrimage site down to the end of the monarchy period. More recent traditions demonstrate some confusion between a site for Rachel's tomb in Bethlehem and another north of Jerusalem.

35:21. Migdal Eder. The name of this place means "herding tower," a installation used by pastoralists to protect their animals from predators. Based on Jacob's itinerary, journeying south after burying Rachel, Migdal Eder would be near Jerusalem. This identification may be strengthened by mention in Micah 4:8 of "watchtower of the flock." Later traditions, however, place it closer to Bethlehem.

35:21-22. son with father's concubine. *Concubines are women without dowry who include among their duties providing children to the family. Childbearing was an important function in the ancient world, where survival of the family, and often survival at all, was tenuous at best. Since a concubine has been a sexual partner, a son who used his father's concubine was seen not only as incestuous but as attempting to usurp the authority of the family patriarch.

36:1-30
The Line of Esau

36:1-43. Esau's descendants. The genealogy of Esau unfolds in stages, beginning with his first three wives (two *Hittite and one the daughter of Ishmael). In the subsequent levels the list twelve tribal names are identified 9-14, excluding Amalek, who is the son of cubine), which matches the genealogical Nahor (22:20-24), Ishmael (25:13-16)

and Israel. A third tier of descendants (vv. 15-19) appear to be clan names, with some repetition from the previous level. The final grouping contains the names of eight kings who reigned in Edom prior to the establishment of the Israelite monarchy (vv. 31-39). Among the best known of the names in the entire genealogy are Teman, identified with the southern region of Edom, and Uz, named as the homeland of Job.

36:12. Amalekite origins. The Amalekites wandered through vast stretches of land in the Negev, Transjordan and Sinai peninsula. They are unattested outside the Bible, and no archaeological remains can be positively linked to them. However, archaeological surveys of the region have turned up ample evidence of nomadic and seminomadic groups like the Amalekites during this period.

36:15-30. chiefs. The inclusion of many chiefs of different regions makes this list as much a king list as a genealogy in that these Bedouin groups had a chieftain form of government. The *Sumerian king list similarly features brief lines of kings connected to various geographical regions.

36:24. hot springs. One way of distinguishing persons with the same name in a genealogy is to provide a brief comment based on their career (see Lamech in 4:19-24; 5:25-31). Here Anah is distinguished from his uncle by the additional information that he discovered a "hot springs"—a natural phenomenon that could have benefited the clan. The translation here is based solely on the Vulgate. Jewish tradition translates it as "mules" and gives Anah credit for learning to crossbreed horses and donkeys.

37:1-11
Joseph's Dreams

37:3. Joseph's coat. The special coat provided to Joseph by his father signified a position of authority and favor. Though such coats may have been colorful, they were often distinguished by material, weave or length (of either hem or sleeve). Since the Hebrew word describing it is used only here, it is difficult to be certain which type of quality characterizes the coat. Egyptian paintings of this period depict well-dressed Canaanites as wearing long-sleeved, embroidered garments with a fringed scarf wrapped diagonally from waist to knee.

37:5-11. importance of dreams. Dreams in the ancient world were thought to offer information from the divine realm and were therefore taken very seriously. Some dreams, given to prophets and kings, were considered a means of divine revelation. Most dreams, however, even the ordinary dreams of common people, were believed to contain omens that communicated information about what the gods were doing. Those that were revelation usually identified the deity and often involved the deity. The dreams that were omens usually made no reference to deity. Dreams were often filled with symbolism necessitating an interpreter, though at times the symbols were reasonably self-evident. The information that came through dreams was not believed to be irreversible. Dreams of a rise to power like the ones Joseph had are known in the ancient Near East, notably one concerning Sargon, king of Akkad, half a millennium earlier than Joseph.

37:12-36
Joseph Sold into Slavery

37:12-13. shepherds grazing. The lush vegetation produced by the winter rains would have allowed shepherds to remain in pastures near their villages and camps. Once the rains ended, the herds would graze in harvested fields and then would be taken into the hill country, where vegetation remained through the summer months.

37:17. Dothan. Located at Tell Dothan, this is an imposing site covering twenty-five acres. It is situated fourteen miles north of Shechem, on the main route used by merchants and herdsmen going north to the Jezreel Valley. It developed into a major city site in the *Early Bronze Age (3200-2400 B.C.) and would have served as a natural landmark for travelers. The area around the city provided choice pasture land, thus explaining the presence of Joseph's brothers.

37:19-24. cisterns. Cisterns were hollowed out of the limestone bedrock or were dug and then lined with plaster to store rain water. They provided water for humans and animals through most of the dry months. When they were empty, they sometimes served as temporary cells for prisoners (see Jer 38:6).

37:25-28. slave trade. The slave trade existed from earliest times in the ancient Near East. Slaves were generally war captives or persons taken in raids. Traders often accepted slaves, whom they transported to new areas and sold. These persons seldom obtained their freedom.

37:25. spice trade and caravan routes. Caravans brought incense from south Arabia to Gaza on the Palestinian coast and to Egypt, using various routes through the Sinai Peninsula. It would have been along one of these

northern Sinai routes that the Midianites met Joseph's brothers and purchased him for resale in Egypt along with the rest of their trade goods.

37:25-36. Midianite/Ishmaelite. The interchange of these two names in the story probably reflects a close affinity between the two groups. Some suggest that the Ishmaelites were considered a subtribe of the Midianites. Others suggest the Midianites simply purchased Joseph from the Ishmaelites. However, based on the intermingling of the names in Judges 8:24, it would appear that the biblical writer either assumed they were related or is reflecting a known kin tie between them.

37:28. twenty shekels. The twenty shekels paid for Joseph was about normal for a slave in this time period, as attested in other literature of this time (for instance, the laws of *Hammurabi). It would constitute approximately two years of wages.

37:34-35. mourning practices. Mourning practices generally included tearing one's robe, weeping, putting dust and ashes in the hair and wearing sackcloth. Sackcloth was made of goat or camel hair and was coarse and uncomfortable. In many cases the sackcloth was only a loin covering. The official period of mourning was thirty days but could continue for as long as the mourner chose to continue to grieve.

38:1-30
Judah's Sons

38:1. Adullam. Located in the Shephelah, Adullam has been identified with Tell esh Sheikh Madhkur northwest of Hebron (see 1 Sam 22:1; Mic 1:15). It would have been at a lower elevation than Hebron (3,040 feet above sea level), and thus the statement that Judah "went down" is appropriate.

38:6-26. levirate marriage. One remedy for the disruption of inheritance caused by the premature death of a man before he had produced an heir was the custom of levirate marriage. As outlined in Genesis 38, the dead man's brother was required to impregnate the widow so that his brother's name (his inheritance share) would be passed on to the child born of this obligatory act. A similar statute is found in *Hittite Law 193 and some form of it may be represented in Ruth 4. The law is detailed in Deuteronomy 25:5-10, where the levir is allowed to refuse his obligation by participating in a public ceremony in which the widow shames him. This was probably made necessary by situations like the one Judah faces here, in which a greedy brother (Onan) refuses to impregnate Tamar because it would decrease his eventual inheritance share.

38:11. widows. In a society that is subject to disease and warfare, it is not uncommon to find widows. Ancient Israel dealt with this problem through levirate marriage (to insure an heir for the deceased husband) and remarriage of young widows as soon as possible after the mourning period. They wore special garments which designated them as widows. Since a widow had no inheritance rights, special provisions were made for widows under the law allowing them to glean in harvested fields (Ruth 2) and protecting them from being oppressed (Deut 14:29; Ps 94:1-7). Only the widowed daughter of a priest could honorably return to her father's house (Lev 22:13).

38:13. Timnah. The exact location of the town in this narrative is uncertain. It is a fairly common place name in the allotment list and in the Samson epic (see Josh 15:10, 56; Judg 14:1-2; 2 Chron 28:18), with connections to the tribal territory of Judah in the southern hill country (possibly Tell el-Batashi, three and a half miles east of Tel Miqne-Ekron).

38:13-14. widow's clothes. A widow, like a married woman, did not wear a veil. She did wear a special garment which set her apart as a widow. These clothes entitled her to the privileges provided for widows in the law, such as gleaning and a portion of the tithe.

38:14, 21. Enaim. The two references to this place in the narrative argue for a place name rather than the more traditional translations of "an open place" (KJV) or "a fork in the road" (Vulgate, Targums). It may be the same as Enam (Josh 15:34) and may take its name from local springs. However, other than a general reference to the territory of Judah, its exact location is unknown.

38:15-23. prostitution. The Canaanite culture utilized *cult prostitution as a way of promoting *fertility. Devotees of the mother goddess *Ishtar or *Anat would reside at or near shrines and would dress in a veil, as the symbolic bride of the god *Baal or *El. Men would visit the shrine and use the services of the cult prostitutes prior to planting their fields or during other important seasons such as shearing or the period of lambing. In this way they gave honor to the gods and reenacted the divine marriage in an attempt to insure fertility and prosperity for their fields and herds.

38:18, 25. seal, cord and staff. One distinctive means of signing a document in the ancient Near East was to use a cylinder seal, which contained a mirror-image incision that could be rolled onto a clay tablet or pressed into sealing wax or clay bullae. Cylinder seals, many carved from precious and semiprecious stones, have been discovered from nearly every period post-*Early Bronze by archaeologists. The seal was often threaded onto a leather cord and worn around the neck of the owner. In Palestine it is more common to find stamp seals engraved on the flat side. Another form of identification mentioned here is the staff, an aid to walking as well as an animal goad and weapon. Since this was a personal item, it may well have been carved and polished, and thus known to belong to a particular person.

38:24. prostitution as capital crime. Prostitution or harlotry was generally punished by stoning to death (Deut 22:23-24). Tamar's sentence of death by fire is exceptional. This sentence is prescribed elsewhere only in cases

---

MAJOR TRADE ROUTES IN THE ANCIENT NEAR EAST

Trade was the lifeblood of the major cultures of the ancient Near East. As early as 5000 B.C. there is evidence of trade in obsidian from northern Anatolia throughout the Near East. Although land travel was time consuming (fifteen to twenty miles a day) and dangerous, the desire for exotic as well as functional products was so great that merchants and governments were willing to take the risk in order to obtain the very high profits involved (a minimum of 100 percent). For instance, business documents from the Old Assyrian period (2100-1900 B.C.) and from the Mari archive (1800-1700 B.C.) mention commercial caravans of as many as 200-300 donkeys traveling in Asia Minor and northern Syria. They followed the trade route from the Assyrian capital at Asshur on the Tigris River west to Habur region to the Taurus mountains and on to the commercial center of Kanish in west central Asia Minor. The route then continued west through Cilicia to Antioch in Pisidia, Philadelphia, Sardis, Pergamum and Troy on the Ionian coast. Each city provided shelter, supplies, and a ready market for these enterprising merchants.

The actual routes taken were dictated by the topography of the various regions (avoiding disease-infected swamps, uneven and deeply cut hill country) as well as political situations and potential markets. They radiated out from major population centers. Thus from Egypt the major trade route, known as the Great Trunk Road, started in Memphis on the Nile, crossed the northern Sinai Peninsula, turned north up the coastal plain of Canaan, the jogged east through the Valley ofJezreel at Megiddo and

where a daughter of a priest engages in harlotry and in cases of incest (Lev 20:14).

39:1-23
Joseph in Potiphar's House

39:1-20. Egyptian tale of two brothers. The Nineteenth Dynasty (c. 1225 B.C.) Egyptian tale of Anubis and Bata has many similarities to the story of Joseph and Potiphar's wife. In both cases a younger man is seduced by his master's wife and then falsely accused of rape when he refuses to give in to her desires. What may have made this Egyptian story so popular (the surviving papyrus is written in a cursive style [hieratic] rather than the more formal *hieroglyphic characters) is the common tale of rivalry between brothers (like Jacob and Esau), the high suspense and the use of folklore techniques (talking animals, intervention of the gods). Aside from the common general setting, the Joseph story has little else in common with this Egyptian tale.

39:16. keeping the cloak. Besides the interesting parallel to Joseph's brothers' taking his cloak, it should be noted that here again the cloak is to serve to identify Joseph. Garments often contained indications of status, rank or office and therefore could be used in such ways.

39:20. imprisoned with the king's prisoners. One indication of Potiphar's understanding of the affair between Joseph and his wife may be in the choice of prison. Rather than being executed for rape (as dictated in, for instance, the Middle *Assyrian laws), Joseph was put into a royal prison holding political prisoners. This may have been a bit more comfortable (as prisons go), but more importantly it will put him in contact with members of Pharaoh's court (Gen 40:1-23).

40:1-23
Pharaoh's Cupbearer and Baker

40:1-4. cupbearer's role. The cupbearer was a high-ranking member of a monarch's court (see Neh 1:11). He would have to be a trusted individual, since his primary responsibility was to taste all of his lord's food and drink and thus prevent his lord from being poisoned.

40:1-2. offenses against Pharaoh. Offenses against Pharaoh certainly could have taken many forms. Whether these officials were suspected of involvement in a conspiracy or just guilty of displeasing Pharaoh in the disposition of their duties is impossible to tell. It may be that they are under house arrest awaiting the investigation of charges against them.

40:5-18. interpretation of dreams. Dream interpretations were usually carried out by experts who had been trained in the available dream literature. More information is available from Mesopotamia than from Egypt. Both the Egyptians and the *Babylonians compiled what we call dream books, which contain sample dreams along with the key to their interpretation. Since dreams often depended on symbolism, the interpreter would have to have access to these documents preserving the empirical data concerning past dreams and interpretations. It was believed that the gods communicated through dreams but not that they revealed the meanings of dreams. If they were going to reveal the meaning, why use a dream in the first place? But Joseph held a different view. He did not consult any "scientific" literature, but consulted God. Nevertheless, he interprets along the same lines as some of the dream literature would have suggested. As in Mesopotamian literature he draws a time indication from a number that

---

then north to Hazor. From there the route went northeast to Damasca passed Ebla and Aleppo in Syria and then came to the northwestern spur of the Euphrates River, which then served as a guide southward into the major cities of Mesopotamia. The other major route, known as the King's Highway, joined by the caravans coming north through Arabia, traversed the Transjordanian region from the Red Sea port of Ezion-geber north through Edom, Moab, and Ammon and joining the Trunk Road at Damascus.

Since the northern and central deserts of Arabia were so inhospitable, trade routes skirted them to the north, traveling up the Tigris and Euphrates river valleys, west to Palmyra and Damascus, and then south along either the coastal highway through Palestine or down the King's Highway in Transjordan. Caravans transporting spices (myrrh, frankincense) and indigo traced the western coast of Arabia, transshipped to Ethiopia and further north to Egypt and traveled up the Nile. Eventually these merchants reached deep water sea ports (various ports used between 2500-100 B.C.: Byblos, Tyre, Sidon, Acco, Ugarit, Aqaba, Alexandria), which gave them access to markets and sources of natural resources (such as the copper mines of Cyprus) in the Mediterranean (Crete, Cyprus, the Aegean and Ionian Islands, the coast of Turkey and North Africa) as well as along the Arabian Peninsula and East Africa. The carrying trade was dominated by Ugarit (1600-1200 B.C.) and by the Phoenicians (1100-600). The fleets would have hugged the coasts or navigated between islands in the Mediterranean or Red Sea, traveling about forty miles a day.

features in the dream. The symbols in these dreams are similar to some of those found in the dream books. A full goblet, for instance, is indicative of having a name and offspring. Carrying fruit on one's head is indicative of sorrow.

40:22. execution. Hanging was a way of dishonoring the corpse of an executed person (see Josh 8:29; 2 Sam 4:12). It may involve suspension from a rope by the neck or impalement on a stake. The actual form of execution may be stoning or beheading.

41:1-32
Joseph Interprets Pharaoh's Dreams

41:1-55. the identity of Pharaoh. The name of the Pharaoh of the Joseph story is unknown. Elements of the story have suggested to some a setting in either the *Hyksos period (1750-1550 B.C.) or the *Amarna Age (fourteenth century B.C.), when large numbers of Semites were either settled in Egypt or mentioned in Egyptian sources as serving in government positions. Our current knowledge of Egyptian history and practice would support this as the most logical and feasible choice. Biblical chronological information, however, suggests to some an earlier time in the Middle Kingdom Twelfth Dynasty (1963-1786). Without specific, historical references in the story it is impossible to associate the narrative with a particular reigning king. It is the practice of the author(s) of the book of Genesis to not mention any Pharaoh by name. This may have been intentional, since the Pharaoh was considered by his people to be a god and the Israelites did not wish to invoke that name.

41:1-7. double dreams. In the ancient Near East, dreams were generally assumed to be communications from the gods. Some were quite simple and straightforward (see Jacob's dream at Bethel, 28:10-22), but in cases where the king or Pharaoh was involved special emphasis was sometimes added through the experience of a double dream. Thus here Pharaoh has two visions that warn of the coming famine in Egypt. Similarly, the *Sumerian king Gudea is said to have had a double dream in which he was instructed to build a temple. In both cases their dreams were interpreted by magicians or representatives of a god. In a Mari text the same dream on consecutive nights added weight to the message of the dream. In both the Gilgamesh Epic and a poem about a righteous sufferer, a threefold repetition of a dream confirms its reliability.

41:8-16. magicians and wise men. Egypt, as well as the Mesopotamian and *Hittite kingdoms, developed guilds of magicians whose task was to interpret signs and dreams and to concoct remedies for various types of medical problems through magical means. These specialists used *exorcism to frighten away demons and gods and incantations and curses to transmit evil into some one or some place (seen in the Egyptian *execration texts and Jer 19:10-13). Thousands of texts have been discovered throughout the ancient Near East which contain protection spells as well as recipes for the manufacture of *amulets to ward off evil and for the construction of dolls, incantation bowls and miniature figures designed to bring destruction on one's enemies. Mesopotamian magic distinguished between black and white magic, and thus practitioners were divided into sorcerers and magicians or wise men. Egypt, however, did not draw this distinction among its guild of magicians. Although their major task was medical, Egyptian magicians seemed to have employed a less respectful manner toward the gods, including providing spells for souls to escape punishment in the underworld (Book of the Dead). It is very unusual in Egypt for the Pharaoh to be in need of an interpreter of his dreams. Since the Pharaoh was considered divine, the gods would communicate to him through dreams, and the meaning was typically presented as transparent to him. The Hebrew word used to describe the specialists Pharaoh sends for is from a technical Egyptian term sometimes thought to describe dream interpreters. It is used to describe the famous official Imhotep in a late inscription (second century B.C.) where he is portrayed giving advice to Pharaoh concerning a seven-year famine.

41:14. shaved. As a way of making himself more presentable to the Pharaoh, Joseph shaves. This may have involved shaving the head (Num 6:9) as well as the face (Jer 41:5). He would have thereby changed his appearance to look more like an Egyptian. Egyptian wall paintings demonstrate that the Egyptians were typically clean-shaven.

41:27-32. famine in Egypt. Although Egypt was one of the most consistent grain-producing areas in the ancient Near East because of the regularity of the Nile floods, it was occasionally plagued with famine. Such a disaster is mentioned in *Visions of Neferti*, an Egyptian document dating to the reign of Amenemhet I (1991-1962 B.C.). Here, as in Joseph's narration, a vision is interpreted and a national calamity predicted.

41:33-57

Joseph's Advice and Elevation

41:33-40. food rationing. In the face of the coming famine, Joseph's advice is to store one-fifth of the grain from each of the years of good harvest, which can then be distributed to the people when it becomes necessary. The building of storehouses accompanies this sensible advice (see Ex 1:11; 1 Kings 9:19).

41:35. storage cities. Egypt's management of the Nile River and its predictability made that land a breadbasket for the rest of the ancient Near East. Storage cities were a hallmark of a prosperous people who thought in terms of the long run and realized that famine was always a possibility that needed to be planned for. There would typically be storage cities centrally located in each geographical region.

41:40. second to Pharaoh. Many Egyptian nobles could make the claim of being second only to Pharaoh, and several different titles imply this position: "Great Favorite of the Lord of the Two Lands," and "Foremost among his Courtiers" are two that have been identified from inscriptions.

41:41-45. Joseph's position. The job description and investiture ceremony detailed here give Joseph a position in Egyptian government comparable to "Grand Vizier" or "Overseer of the Royal Estates," both of which appear in Egyptian documents (see 1 Kings 16:9; Is 22:15, 19-21, for use of this latter title in Israel's bureaucracy). Such a position is detailed in Egyptian tomb paintings, showing the entire sequence of events from the granting of the title to the placing of robes and rings on the appointee by the Pharaoh. Joseph functions much the same as the "Overseer of the Granaries of Upper and Lower Egypt" would have done. Such a position for a non-Egyptian is uncommon prior to the *Hyksos period (1750-1550 B.C.), when a greater number of Semites served in Egypt. From the *El Amarna reign of Akhenaten comes a tomb of the Semitic official Tutu, who was appointed "highest mouth in the whole country," a position with powers comparable to Joseph's. Biographies in Egyptian tombs and literature from Egypt such as the *Story of *Sinuhe* give us ample information about the details of the life of officials of Pharaoh. It is not unusual to find accounts of officials who were elevated from lowly status to high positions of authority. In Sinuhe's story he fled the royal court and lived in exile for many years, finally returning and being honored. As a result the description of Joseph's elevation and honors can be seen as typical against the Egyptian background of the time.

41:42. signet ring. Kings and royal administrators used a signet ring to seal official documents. This ring would have been distinctive and would have contained the name (cartouche in Egypt) of the king. Anyone using it thus acted in the name of the king (see Num 31:50; Esther 3:10; Tobit 1:20; 1 Maccabees 6:15). The chains and linen garment are given in a ceremony of investiture providing him with the accessories that will signify his status, rank and office.

41:43-44. Joseph's perquisites. Riding in a chariot with a set of guardsmen to clear his path and proclaim his position as "second in command" gave Joseph extremely high status (see 2 Sam 15:1; Esther 6:7-9). The title of second only to Pharaoh, or viceroy (*Akkadian *terdennu*; Is 20:1 *tartan*), gave Joseph extraordinary powers and would have required all but the king to bow to him. Furthermore, since Joseph had been given the king's favor or protection, no one was permitted to "raise a hand or foot" against him or oppose his orders (compare the powers granted in Ezra 7:21-26).

41:45. Egyptian name. The intent of giving Joseph an Egyptian name is to complete the transformation process of the investiture ceremony. Egyptianized, he is more likely to be accepted at court and by the Egyptian people (see the Egyptian tale of *Sinuhe's return to Egypt and his consignment of his barbarian clothing to the "sand crawlers"). This practice of renaming a Semite official is also found in the reign of Pharaoh Merenptah (1224-1208 B.C.). The meaning of Joseph's Egyptian name is uncertain, but may be "the God has spoken and he will live" or "the one who knows."

41:45. priest of On. The marriage arranged for Joseph allied him with one of the most powerful priestly families in Egypt. During the period from 1600 to 1100 B.C., only the priests of Ptah of Memphis were more influential. The priest of On officiated at all major festivals and supervised lesser priests who served the sun god Re in the temple city of Heliopolis (ten miles northeast of Cairo).

42:1-38

The Brothers' First Encounter with Joseph

42:6-17. spying. Just as the Israelites later send out spies to reconnoiter the land of Canaan, so

Joseph's brothers are accused of working on behalf of another country. Traders and merchants would have been commonly employed for such business, as they could move around the country unnoticed or unsuspected. Some governments are naturally suspicious of foreigners, and the charge of spying is always difficult to disprove.

42:25-28. trading of silver. Coined money was not invented and put into common use until the sixth century B.C. Thus precious metals, gems, spices, incense and other luxury items were bartered by weight. Their relative value would also depend on scarcity. Silver was used throughout antiquity as a common item of exchange. Since Egypt lacked native silver deposits, this metal was particularly desirable as a standard for business transactions

43:1-34
The Brothers' Second Encounter with Joseph

43:11. products of the land. The gifts that were sent by Jacob to Joseph represent the costliest and thus the most pleasing items available. Only the balm, honey/syrup and nuts would have been actual products of Canaan. The spices and myrrh were imported and thus were precious gifts intended to buy favorable treatment from Pharaoh's representative.

43:16. steward of the house. A high status and large household, such as Joseph's, would have required a staff of servants headed by a chief butler or steward. This person would have been in charge of the maintenance of the house, kept track of financial obligations and supervised the other servants. Joseph's use of this man as his confidant (see Gen 44:1, 4) suggests it was a position of high trust. Apparently, he was also a person to whom supplicants could go to intercede with his master (see Gen 43:19-23).

43:26. bowing to honor. The standard method of demonstrating obeisance in the ancient Near East was to bow to the ground. Egyptian tomb art is filled with examples of servants and royal officials prostrating themselves before the Pharaoh. In the *El Amarna tablets (fourteenth century B.C.), the format of each letter contains a greeting, followed by a set formula of honoring the Pharaoh by bowing seven times forward and backwards.

43:32. eating procedures. The Egyptians considered all other peoples barbarians. Thus they would not associate with them directly by eating at the same table. Joseph's meal was also separated from both the Egyptians and the sons of Jacob because of his high rank.

44:1-34
Joseph's Plot Is Hatched

44:5. divination cup. The cup that Joseph plants in Benjamin's sack is identified as being used for *divination. Just as tea leaves are read today, the ancients read omens by means of liquid in cups. One mechanism involved the pouring of oil onto water to see what shapes it would take (called lecanomancy). More popular methods of divination used everyday occurrences, configurations of the entrails of sacrificed animals or the movements of the heavenly bodies. Lecanomancy was used in the time of Joseph, as is attested by several *Old Babylonian omen texts concerned with the various possible configurations of the oil and their interpretations. Another technique, hydromancy, made its observations from the reflections in the water itself. Not enough is known about Egyptian divination techniques to offer more specific information, but in these early periods typically only people of status had access to divination procedures.

45:1-28
Joseph Reveals His Identity

45:8. titles of Joseph. The use of the title "father of Pharaoh" most likely is related to the Egyptian title *it-ntr*, "father of the god," used to refer to a variety of officials and priests who serve in the Pharaoh's court. "Father" represents an advisory relationship, perhaps to be equated with the role of the priest hired by Micah in Judges 17:10 or the role of Elisha as the king of Israel's counselor in 2 Kings 6:21.

45:10. Goshen. This Semitic place name most likely refers to the delta region of Lower Egypt in the area of the Wadi Tumeilat (from the eastern arm of the Nile River to the Great Bitter Lake). Egyptian texts from *Hyksos period make reference to Semites in this region, and it is an area which provides excellent pasturage for herds. Also arguing in favor of its location in Egypt proper is the use of the phrase "in the district of Rameses" (47:11) as an equation for Goshen.

45:19. carts. The provision of carts does not contrast Egyptian carts to Canaanite carts but is simply a thoughtful gesture so that the women and children will not have to walk, for seminomadic people would not usually keep carts.

45:22. provision for Benjamin. Joseph's role as administrator of Egypt was to ration out food and clothing to the people (a common feature in ancient Near Eastern texts from

*Babylon and *Mari). He does this with his family as well (an ironic turn of events, since his story begins with his receiving a piece of clothing, 37:3). Just as Jacob has singled out Joseph for special favor, now Joseph shows his favor to his full brother Benjamin by giving him five times the amount as his other half brothers, as well as a large quantity of silver.

46:1-34
Jacob and His Family Travel to Egypt
46:1. sacrifice at Beersheba. Though the patriarchs build many altars, there is little reference to their offering sacrifices. The only previous one mentioned was connected to Jacob's agreement with Laban (31:54). Isaac had built an altar at Beersheba (26:25), but no record is made of his offering of sacrifices on that altar. Jacob is taking advantage of this trip to the south to make a pilgrimage to the place where he grew up and the shrine where his father worshiped.

46:29. chariots. Chariots in Egypt during this period were light, constructed of wooden frames and leather with two spoked wheels. The ornamental chariots of pharaohs (and undoubtedly their high officials) are often depicted in the art of the New Kingdom period.

46:34. shepherds in Egypt. It is unlikely that native Egyptian herdsmen would be detested by other Egyptians. Joseph's advice to his father is both a warning about Egyptian attitudes toward strangers and a piece of diplomacy in that they would claim independent status (they had their own herds to support them) and show they were not an ambitious group who wished to rise above their occupation as shepherds.

47:1-12
Jacob's Family Settles in Egypt
47:11. district of Rameses. An equation is made here between the "district of Rameses" and the land of Goshen (see 45:10). This northeastern section of the Delta region was known to be inhabited by Semites and it is the center of *Hyksos activity during the eighteenth to sixteenth centuries B.C. It will also be equated with the Tanis district, where the storehouse cities of Pithom and Rameses were said to be constructed by the Hebrew slaves (Ex 1:11). Pharaoh Rameses II, who did build and expand cities in this region during the mid-thirteenth century B.C., may be *anachronistically referred to in this phrase.

47:13-31
Joseph's Economic and Agrarian Strategies
47:16-17. bartering. Bartering has been a means of exchange from earliest times. The mutually beneficial exchange of property, goods or manufactured items was the basis of the ancient nonmonetary economy. In this case, livestock is used as payment for grain during the famine.

47:20-26. government ownership of land. Government acquires land through forfeiture of debt, through failure to pay taxes and because a family lacks an heir. With nothing else to pay for grain during the famine, the Egyptians must sell their land to the government and become tenant farmers for Pharaoh.

47:21-25. debt slavery. Debt slavery was fairly common throughout the ancient Near East. Peasants who had lost their land and would sell themselves into short-term servitude to support themselves and their families. This might be for a day (Ex 22:26-27) or a period of years. In Israel the term of debt servitude could not exceed six years (Ex 21:2). The Egyptian example in this text, however, suggests perpetual servitude as tenant farmers for Pharaoh. Their rent was paid with one-fifth of the harvest.

47:22. priests' exemption. The observation that the priests had an allotment of food from Pharaoh and therefore did not have to sell their land reflects a common situation of priestly privileges in Egypt. The priesthood often accumulated significant political power to itself and used its sometimes extensive economic resources to wield that power. Many pharaohs found it advantageous to curry favor with them. In contrast, the Israelite system granted no land holdings to the tribe of Levi.

47:24. 20 percent to Pharaoh. Taxation of 20 percent would not be unusual in the ancient world, but too little is known of taxation in Egypt to shed specific light on the levy imposed by Joseph.

47:28-31. burials of ancestors. Once a family tomb was established, it would have become traditional for each family member to be entombed with all of the others. This tied the generations together and further strengthened a family's claim to the land where the tomb was located.

48:1-22
Jacob's Blessing on Ephraim and Manasseh
48:5-6. Ephraim and Manasseh as firstborn. While Jacob does not disinherit Reuben and

Simeon, he adopts Joseph's sons, Ephraim and Manasseh, and gives them prioritized standing in inheritance. The adoption practice and formula here are very similar to those attested in the Code of *Hammurabi. Additionally, one *Ugaritic text features a grandfather adopting his grandson. In one sense this adoption could be seen as the means by which Joseph is given the double portion of the inheritance due to the firstborn, since two of his sons receive shares from Jacob's inheritance.

48:7. Rachel's tomb. Jacob's reminiscence about the death of his wife Rachel places her tomb in the vicinity of Bethlehem and Ephrath (see the discussion of this in 35:19-20).

48:12-19. reversed blessing. The younger son has received privileged treatment in each generation of the patriarchal narratives. Isaac received inheritance over Ishmael, and Jacob over Esau; Joseph was favored over his brothers, and now Ephraim is favored over Manasseh. In most ancient civilizations the firstborn had certain privileges in the division of the inheritance, and Israel was no different. Nevertheless, exceptions could be made for various reasons. For comments about deathbed pronouncements see 27:1-4.

48:22. the land of the Amorites. It appears that *Amorite* is being used here as a generic term for all of the peoples of presettlement Canaan (see 15:19-21) and specifically those in the vicinity of Shechem where Jacob had purchased a piece of land (33:18-19). Although this does not detail the ethnic diversity of that region, certainly the Amorites, whose primary area of influence was in northern Mesopotamia and Syria, had a profound effect on the customs and religious practices of Canaan.

49:1-33
Jacob's Pronouncement Concerning His Sons

49:1. patriarchal blessing. In the biblical material the patriarchal pronouncement generally concerns the destiny of the sons with regard to fertility of the ground, fertility of the family and relationships between family members. Blessings or curses pronounced by the patriarch of the family were always taken seriously and considered binding, even though they were not presented as prophetic messages from God.

49:8-12. hand on the neck. Jacob's blessing of his son Judah is reflective of the great importance attached to the tribe of Judah in later history. One sign of its power is found in the phrase "your hand will be on the neck of your enemies," which signifies control or subjugation of Judah's foes. The difficult term *Shiloh* in the third line of verse 10 (NIV: "to whom it belongs") has been most plausibly explained as reference to a gift offering (Hebrew *shay*) paid in tribute, thus "until one brings him tribute."

49:11. washing robes in wine. In this blessing of Judah, the future prosperity of that tribe is symbolized by abundant fertility. Wine will be so plentiful that they will be able to wash their clothes in it. It is also possible this is a reference to the dyeing industry, but that would figure into future economic prosperity.

49:13. haven for ships. As the coastline was lacking natural harbors, the sea was generally little more than a boundary to Israelites. Only in the northern coastal regions would there have been any inclination to develop seafaring skills.

49:14-15. donkey habits. The blessing of Issachar contains this characterization of a strong animal, which is sometimes stubborn and lazy and may sit down unexpectedly in an inconvenient place. The idea may also be suggestive of a tribe that allies itself with outsiders or is forced to serve others (contra Judg 5:15).

49:17. horse domestication. Reference to a rider on the horse assumes an advanced level of domestication of the horse. This was achieved in the third millennium. In Mesopotamia horseback riders are depicted in the middle of the third millennium, but in Egyptian materials not until a millennium later. Horses were usually used for pulling chariots, and horseback riding was not common.

50:1-14
Jacob's Burial

50:1-3. embalming. Although it was the usual practice in Egypt for everyone who could afford it, embalming of Israelites is found only in this passage. This was an elaborate and *ritual-filled procedure performed by a trained group of mortuary priests. It involved removing the internal organs and placing of the body in embalming fluids for forty days. The idea behind this is based on the Egyptian belief that the body had to be preserved as a repository for the soul after death. The bodies of Jacob and Joseph are embalmed, and while this may have been done to soothe the feelings of the Egyptians, it also served the purpose of preserving their bodies for later burial in Canaan.

50:3. mourning period. This period of mourning may include the forty days required to embalm the body plus the traditional thirty-day mourning period (see Deut

34:8). Since the Egyptians are also described as mourning Jacob's death, it would appear he was accorded royal honors as a visiting dignitary.

50:10-11. threshing floor of Atad. No exact location has been identified for this site, said to be east of the Jordan. It is strange that Jacob's remains would be taken east through Transjordan instead of on a more direct route to Hebron. Having the seven-day mourning ceremony on a threshing floor is quite appropriate. This is a place associated with business, law and life and thus suitable as a place for memorializing a tribal leader (see Num 15:20; Ruth 3; 2 Sam 24:16-24).

50:11. Abel-mizraim. The renaming of the threshing floor of Atad provides a lasting memorial to Jacob and the remarkable seven-day mourning ceremony conducted there. The name itself contains a familiar element: abel means "stream" and appears in several other place names (Num 33:49— Abel Shittim; Judg 11:33—Abel Keramim). Here, however, there is a pun on the Hebrew word ebel, "mourning."

50:15-26
The Last Years of Joseph
50:26. Joseph's age. Joseph dies at the age of 110, considered the ideal age for an Egyptian. Examination of mummies has demonstrated that the average life expectancy in Egypt was between forty and fifty years. The use of the coffin or sarcophagus in mummification was an Egyptian, not an Israelite, practice.

EXODUS

1:1-22
Israelite Slavery in Egypt
1:8-14. king who didn't know Joseph. The book of Exodus maintains the anonymity of the Pharaohs who have dealings with the Israelites. Since Egyptian records have preserved no accounts of the Israelite presence, enslavement or exodus, identifying these Pharaohs can only be attempted by using the vague hints contained in the narrative. In the sixteenth and seventeenth centuries B.C. a group known as the Hyksos, who were not native Egyptians, ruled the land. It is usually thought that the Pharaoh referred to in this verse represents either the first of the *Hyksos rulers or the first of the native Egyptian rulers after the *Hyksos were driven out. The difference would be at least one hundred years (c. 1650 or 1550 B.C.), or up to two hundred years if some of the early *Hyksos rulers with only partial control subjected the Israelites to slavery.

1:10. reason for enslaving Israel. The argument for enslaving the Israelites is that if they are not enslaved they will join the enemy and leave the country. This would suggest the period when the *Hyksos are being driven from the land. The Egyptians would have wanted to keep the Israelite presence for economic reasons.

1:11. forced labor. The sheer number of manhours needed for the massive engineering and construction projects undertaken in the ancient world made the use of forced labor not infrequent. It was used as a form of taxation (for instance, the common people might work one month out of the year without pay on government building projects). When the government projects proved too ambitious to staff with native people and prisoners of war, and too expensive to hire labor for, vulnerable groups of people would be targeted for forced labor.

1:11. Pithom. Pithom has been identified as the Egyptian Pi(r)-Atum, "real-estate of Atum," currently known as Tell el-Rataba, along the Ismalia Canal, approximately sixty miles northeast of Cairo. The text's identification of the building projects as store cities does not suggest they were only for storage of grain. The store cities were centrally located hubs in the region and could be capital cities.

1:11. Rameses. The location of the city of Rameses, disputed for many years, has now been positively identified as Tell ed-Dab'a, about twenty miles north of Pithom. The site has been extensively excavated by M. Bietak. It served as the *Hyksos capital, Avaris, and was rebuilt by Rameses II as his capital, Pi-Ramesse, in the thirteenth century. It was dismantled to build Tanis (about twelve miles to the north) as the Delta capital in the Twentieth Dynasty during the twelfth century B.C. (Judges period). Rameses II used various peoples as slave labor for building the city, including the

Apiru (a term used in the second millennium to describe dispossessed peoples), a designation that would have been applied to the Hebrews as well as to other people.

1:14. brick making. The ancient records agree that brick makers had a filthy job. A work known as the *Satire on the Trades* attests to an existence that is perpetually muddy and miserable. Houses, public buildings, walls around cities and even pyramids were at times constructed of brick. Literally millions of bricks were needed, and daily individual quotas would vary depending on how many were assigned to a crew. Crews operated by division of labor, with tasks such as fetching and breaking up straw, hauling mud and water, shaping the bricks by hand or using molds, setting the bricks to dry in the sun and several days later hauling them to the building site. The bricks for a large building would be over a foot long and half as wide, and perhaps six inches thick.

1:15-22. delivery stools. In the ancient world women normally gave birth in a crouching or kneeling position. Small stools, stones or bricks could be used to support the mother's weight as she gave birth. Midwives did not just aid in parturition but were advisers through the whole process of conception, pregnancy, birth and child care.

2:1-10
The Birth of Moses

2:1-10. heroes spared at birth. In the ancient world there are other accounts of heroes being miraculously spared at birth or being raised in unlikely circumstances. The most intriguing such literary work is the *Legend of Sargon's Birth* (probably eighth century B.C.). Rather than sacrificing her child (as priestesses were supposed to do), Sargon's mother hid him in a reed basket by the bank of the Euphrates. After being carried down the river, he was found and raised by the royal gardener. He grew up to become the founder of the dynasty of *Akkad in the twenty-fourth century B.C. But there are important differences. Most of these stories feature a royal personage discarded to his fate and raised by commoners, while Moses, under careful supervision, is rescued by royalty and raised in privileged circumstances. There is no reason to assume that this daughter of Pharaoh would have been in a position of power or influence. Harem children by the score existed in every court, and daughters were considered less highly than sons.

2:3. reed basket coated with tar. The Hebrew word used for Moses' basket is the same as that used for Noah's ark. The papyrus used to make the floating cradle was also used in the construction of light boats in Egypt and Mesopotamia, a practice the biblical writers were aware of (Is 18:2). The reed bundles overlapped in three layers, and the pitch would make it watertight (Gen 6:14 uses a different word but shows the same concept). In a Hittite myth titled *A Tale of Two Cities: Kanesh and Zalpa*, the queen of Kanesh is said to have given birth to thirty sons in a single year and placed them in caulked baskets and sent them down the river. The myth reports that the gods took them out of the sea and raised them.

2:8. wet nurse. Procurement of a wet nurse to nurse and care for the child until it was weaned was a normal procedure in wealthy or aristocratic households. Though Egyptian literature has provided little information, Mesopotamian legal texts speak of the adoption procedures for an abandoned child who has been found. The wet nurse serves as the paid legal guardian, with adoption taking place after weaning.

2:10. the name Moses. The name Moses is from the Egyptian *ms(w)*, meaning "to beget." It is a common element in names, often connected to a god's name, so Thutmosis ("Thoth begets" or "Thoth is born") or Rameses ("Ra begets" or "Ra is born"). Alternatively, since *ms* in Egyptian means "boy," Moses may simply have been called by a generic name. Wordplay occurs in that the closest Hebrew root means "to draw out."

2:10. growing up in Pharaoh's court. Growing up in the household of Pharaoh would have involved certain privileges in terms of education and training. This would have included training in literature and scribal arts as well as in warfare. Foreign languages would have been important for any work in diplomacy and probably were included. One of the qualities that Egyptians prized most was rhetoric (eloquence in speech and argumentation). Literary works such as *The Eloquent Peasant* show how impressed they were with someone who could speak well. Though Moses would have been trained in rhetoric, he did not consider himself skilled in this area (4:10-12).

2:11-25
Moses' Flight from Egypt to Midian

2:12-15. Moses' crime. Egyptians maintained a substantial sense of ethnic pride that caused them to consider foreigners inferior. For a foreigner to kill an Egyptian was a great crime.

2:15. flight from Egypt: Sinuhe. In one of the most well-known Egyptian tales, *The Story of *Sinuhe,* the main character fears disfavor from a new pharaoh early in the second millennium B.C. and flees through Canaan to Syria. There he marries the daughter of a Bedouin chieftain and becomes a powerful leader among those people.

2:15. Midian. The Midianites were a seminomadic people who are located in various regions in different stories and sources, from the Transjordan and the Negev in the region of Palestine to the northern Sinai. But the region east of the Gulf of Aqaba in northwest Arabia has the strongest claim to being the central location of the Midianite people.

2:16-19. shepherdesses. Normally women would have been shepherdesses only when there were no sons in the family. The disadvantages of this situation are highlighted in this account, where the other shepherds bully the girls.

2:23. Pharaoh's identity. Again the identity of this Pharaoh is not given. Most conclude that he is either Thutmose III or Rameses II.

3:1—4:17
The Burning Bush and the Call of Moses

3:1. name differences: Reuel (2:18); Jethro (3:1). In the previous chapter Moses' father-in-law was called Reuel, while here he is referred to as Jethro and in Numbers 10:29 as Hobab (see Judg 4:11). The difficulty can be resolved once the ambiguity of the terminology is recognized. The term designating male in-laws is nonspecific. The term referred to a woman's male relatives and could be used for her father, brother or even grandfather. Most solutions take account of this. Perhaps Reuel is the grandfather head of the clan, Jethro is the father of Zipporah and technically the father-in-law of Moses, and Hobab is the brother-in-law of Moses, Jethro's son. Alternatively, Jethro and Hobab could both be brothers-in-law, and Reuel the father.

3:1. mountain of God. The mountain of God is here designated Horeb and elsewhere Sinai, though either one of those names could refer to the general area, a particular range or a single peak. Moses most likely calls it the mountain of God in recognition of the status it is going to achieve in the following chapters rather than because of any prior occurrences or superstitions. In the ancient and classical world deities normally were believed to have their dwelling places on mountains.

3:2-4. burning bush. Natural explanations for the burning bush have been plentiful, from bushes that exude flammable gas to those covered with brightly colored leaves or berries. In the late Egyptian Horus texts at the temple of Edfu the sky god is envisioned as a flame manifest in a particular type of bush, but this is a full millennium after Moses.

3:2-7. Yahweh, God of your father. God's identification of himself with the "God of your father" suggests that the concept of patron deity may still provide the most accurate understanding of how the Israelites thought about *Yahweh. This title ceases to be used once Yahweh becomes the national deity at Sinai. It also serves to identify him as the God of the *covenant.

3:5-6. taking off sandals. It was common practice for priests to enter temples barefoot to prevent bringing in dust or impurities of any sort.

3:7-10. land of milk and honey. The land of Canaan is described as a land "flowing with milk and honey." This refers to the bounty of the land for a pastoral lifestyle, but not necessarily in terms of agriculture. Milk is the product of herds, while honey represents a natural resource, probably the syrup of the date rather than bees' honey. A similar expression to this is found in the *Ugaritic epic of *Baal and Mot that describes the return of fertility to the land in terms of the wadis flowing with honey. Egyptian texts as early as the *Story of *Sinuhe* describe the land of Canaan as rich in natural resources as well as in cultivated produce.

3:8. peoples of Canaan. In the list of the six people groups that inhabited Canaan, the first three are well known while the latter three are barely known at all. Canaan is mentioned as early as the Ebla tablets (twenty-fourth century B.C.), and the Canaanite people were the principal inhabitants of the fortified cities of the land, though they do not seem to have been native to the land. The *Hittites were from Anatolia, modern Turkey, but groups had migrated south and occupied sections of Syria and Canaan. *Amorites (known in Mesopotamia as *Amurru* or *Martu*) are known from written documents as early as the middle third millennium B.C. Most scholars think that they occupied many areas in the Near East from their roots in Syria. There is still debate as to whether the term *Perizzites* is ethnic or sociological (those living in unwalled settlements). The Hivites are sometimes connected to the Horites, in which case they may be *Hurrians. The Jebusites occupied the region later associated with the tribe of Benjamin, notably the city of Jerusalem, and are often related to the Perizzites who were located in the same region. There is no mention of the Per- izzites, Hivites or Jebusites outside the Bible.

3:11. Moses' objection. Moses' objection carried little persuasiveness, given the training provided for him in the household of Pharaoh (see comment on 2:10).

3:13. revelation of divine name. Names in the ancient world were believed to be intimately connected to the essence of the individual. Knowledge of a person's name gave knowledge of their nature and, potentially, power over them. As a result, the names of gods were at times carefully guarded. For instance, Egypt's sun god, Re, had a secret, hidden name that only Isis, his daughter, knew. See comment on 20:7.

3:13-15. I AM. The personal name of Israel's God, *Yahweh (usually rendered LORD, v. 15), is built from the Hebrew verb "to be." Verse 14 uses an alternate form of the verb in the first person, "I am." The name Yahweh for the Israelite God is attested outside the Old Testament in the Mesha Inscription, the Arad Ostraca, the Lachish letters and inscriptions from Khirbet el-Qom and Kuntillat Ajrud, to name a few of the more prominent places. There are a number of possible occurrences of Yahweh or Yah as a deity's name outside of Israel, though all are debatable. One of the most intriguing is the reference to "*Yhw* in the land of the Shasu," mentioned in some Egyptian inscriptions in Nubia (modern Sudan) from the mid-second millennium. The Shasu are Bedouins related in the same inscriptions to the area of Seir (see Deut 33:2; Judg 5:4). This might find confirmation in the biblical indication that Jethro the Midianite was a worshiper of Yahweh (chap. 18). We must remember, however, that Midian was also a descendant of Abraham (Gen 25:2-4), so this may not be unrelated to the Israelite God.

3:16-17. elders. The elders here are the clan leaders of Israel. Elders typically served as a ruling assembly overseeing the leadership of a village or community. The people would look for the endorsement of Moses by the elders before they would accept his leadership.

3:18-20. God of the Hebrews. "God of the Hebrews" is a title that is used only in the context of the exodus. Since the Israelites generally only refer to themselves as Hebrews to foreigners, some have related the term *Hebrew* to the Apiru/*Habiru known from ancient texts from this period. Apiru/Habiru is not an ethnic designation but a sociological one, referring to displaced peoples.

3:18. three-day journey to sacrifice. The request to Pharaoh is for a three-day religious pilgrimage into the wilderness. This would generally consist of one day for travel each way and one full day for the religious ceremonies. The refusal adds religious oppression to the crimes of Pharaoh.

3:19-20. mighty hand of God. The image of an outstretched or mighty hand or arm is common in Egyptian inscriptions to describe the power of Pharaoh. It is used throughout the exodus narratives to describe God's power over Pharaoh. See comment on Deuteronomy 26:8.

4:1-9. the three signs of Moses. The three signs the Lord gave to Moses each most likely had symbolic significance. The rod was the symbol of authority in Egypt, and Pharaoh was represented by the serpent figure, the uraeus, featured prominently on his crown. The first sign then suggests that Pharaoh and his authority are completely in the power of God. The second sign inflicts a skin disease, often translated "leprosy," on Moses' hand. In fact, however, the Hebrew term used describes many dermatological conditions, most far less severe than Hansen's disease (leprosy; see comment on Lev 13). Nonetheless, when inflicted in the Bible it is consistently a punishment for hubris—when an individual in pride presumptuously assumes a divinely appointed role (Num 12:1-12; 2 Kings 5:22-27; 2 Chron 26:16-21), thus demonstrating God's intention to punish Pharaoh. Its result is to drive the individual from God's presence, since it rendered the afflicted unclean. The third, turning water to blood, shows God's control of the prosperity of Egypt, which was entirely dependent on the waters of the Nile. It also anticipates the plagues that God will send.

4:17. Moses' staff. Moses' staff becomes the symbol of God's power and presence with Moses. It is carefully distinguished from instruments of magic in that Moses never uses it in connection with incantations or words of power. It is not used to manipulate God so, except in one unfortunate incident (Num 20), Moses does not wield it but only employs it as instructed.

4:18-26

Moses' Bloodguilt

4:19. Moses' standing. The fact that Egyptians are no longer seeking to kill Moses for his act of murder does not mean that he has been absolved of all guilt in the matter.

4:20-23. hardening Pharaoh's heart. This section contains the first reference to the hardening of Pharaoh's heart—a motif that occurs twenty times over the next ten chapters (during the plagues and up to the crossing of the sea). Several different verbs are used, and Pharaoh sometimes hardens his own heart, while other times it is hardened by the Lord. The concept has parallels to similar Egyptian expressions that convey perseverance, stubbornness, persistence and an unyielding nature. These can be good qualities or bad, depending on what type of behavior or attitude one is persisting in.

4:22. Israel, the firstborn of God. The passage artfully develops the issue of jeopardy to the firstborn: God's first-born, Israel; Pharaoh's firstborn; and Moses' firstborn. Israel is God's first-born in the sense that they are the first nation to enter into a relationship with him.

4:24-26. the Lord was about to kill him. The text has told us that there was no one in Egypt seeking to kill Moses (v. 19), but Moses still stood guilty of bloodshed before God. Later, cities of refuge were established to provide shelter for someone who felt there were mitigating circumstances in a homicide, but Moses had sought refuge in Midian. By leaving his place of refuge, Moses became vulnerable to being called to account for his crime. Others in the Old Testament whom the Lord called on to go somewhere but then accosted on the way include Jacob (Gen 31—32) and Balaam (Num 22). In each instance God did indeed want the individual to make the journey but had an issue to settle before he could proceed.

4:25. flint knife. A flint flake was used for to perform *circumcision in Israel and Egypt even after metal tools and weapons were readily available. They were very sharp, easily accessible and the traditional instrument for age-old *rituals.

4:25. bridegroom of blood. One recent study has plausibly suggested that *circumcision in many cultures was done by the man's in-laws and extended the protection of the family over the man and his children. If such was the Midianite practice, this could serve as an extension of the refuge that Moses had in Midian. From the Israelite side, the dabbing of the blood (v. 25) is seen also in the Passover *ritual (12:7) and offers protection from the slaughtering angel (12:44-48). Zipporah's comment that Moses was a bridegroom of bloodshed would indicate both his need for protection by the family and his need for expiating blood.

4:27-31
Moses' Return to Egypt

4:29. elders. The elders here are the clan leaders of Israel. Elders typically served as a ruling assembly overseeing the leadership of a village or community. The elders here accept the legitimacy of Moses' role and mission and acknowledge that he carries the authority of God.

5:1-21
Moses Confronts Pharaoh

5:1-5. festival in the desert. Festivals in the ancient world centered around cycles of nature (new year's or *fertility festivals), mythological events (enthronement or deity conquering chaos), agricultural events (harvest), or historical memorials (dedications or deliverances). They celebrate what deity has done and seek to perpetuate deity's action on their behalf. Often these elements were combined. They usually are celebrated at a holy place and therefore often require pilgrimage.

5:6-14. straw for bricks. Straw serves as a bonding agent in the brick as it is heated. Without sufficient straw or with poor-quality stubble, the bricks would not form as easily and a higher proportion would fall apart, thus making the quota harder to achieve. Quotas found in Egyptian literature often do not clarify the number in the crew or the time period involved, but we do know that the quotas were often not met.

5:22—6:12
God's Determination to Deliver

6:3-8. LORD. A casual reading of verse 3 might lead one to conclude that the name *Yahweh (LORD) was unfamiliar to the patriarchs, though Genesis 15:7 and 28:13 clearly suggest otherwise. It is true that El-Shaddai (God Almighty) was known to the patriarchs, and in Genesis 17:1 and 35:11 it is El-Shaddai who is connected to the aspects of the *covenant that were realized during the lifetimes of the patriarchs. In contrast, "Yahweh" is connected to the long-term promises, particularly that of the land, so it can rightfully be said that the patriarchs did not experience him (that is, he did not make himself known in that way). The patriarchs probably did not worship God by the name Yahweh, but the text does not require the conclusion that the name was foreign to them.

6:6. outstretched arm. The Egyptians were used to hearing of the outstretched arm of Pharaoh accomplishing mighty deeds. Now Yahweh's outstretched arm is going to overwhelm Pharaoh. He is confirming this in fulfillment of the oath he made to Abraham, represented by the gesture of raising a hand (toward heaven). Here we can see that naming the gesture is simply another way of referring to the oath, for there is no higher power for God to swear by. See comment on Deuteronomy 26:8.

6:28—7:13
Moses and Aaron Before Pharaoh
7:9. serpent. The serpent was considered a wise and magical creature in Egypt. Wadjet, the patron goddess of lower Egypt, is represented as a snake (uraeus) on Pharaoh's crown. This came to symbolize the power of Pharaoh. But additionally Apopis, the enemy of the gods, in the form of a snake, represented the forces of chaos. It is therefore not arbitrary that the sign featured a serpent (whether cobra or crocodile, see below), for in Egyptian thinking there was no other creature so ominous.

7:11-13. magicians of Pharaoh. Pharaoh's magicians would have been specialists in spells and incantations as well as being familiar with the literature for omens and dreams. They would have practiced sympathetic magic (based on the idea that there is an association between an object and that which it symbolizes; for example, that what is done to a person's picture will happen to the person) and would have used their arts to command the gods and spirits. Magic was the thread that held creation together, and it was used both defensively and offensively by its practitioners, human or divine.

7:11-12. staffs turning into serpents. Some have reported that there is a type of cobra that can be immobilized in rigid form if pressure is applied in a certain way to the neck, perhaps allowing the Egyptian magicians to appear to have rods that turned into snakes. This procedure is portrayed on Egyptian scarab *amulets and is practiced even today. It must be noted, though, that the word translated "serpent" in this section is not the same as the one used in 4:3-4. The creature referred to here is usually considered a sizable monster (see Gen 1:21), though it is used parallel to "cobra" in two places (Deut 32:33; Ps 91:13). This same creature is equated to Pharaoh in Ezekiel 29:3 and is thought by some to be a crocodile. There is no need to attribute a mere sleight of hand to Pharaoh's magicians—these were masters of the occult.

7:12. Aaron's staff swallowing magicians' staffs. When Aaron's serpent swallowed the magicians' serpents, the symbolism would clearly imply an Israelite triumph over Egypt. So, for instance, an Old Kingdom Pyramid Text uses the portrayal of one crown swallowing another to tell of Upper Egypt's conquest of Lower Egypt. In Egyptian Coffin Texts swallowing is a magical act that signifies absorption of the magical powers of that which was swallowed. Thus the Egyptian magicians would have concluded that the power of their rods had been absorbed into the rod of Moses.

7:13. hardening of heart. This second mention of Pharaoh's hardened heart (see comment on 4:20-23) reflects his resolve to pursue the course he has chosen.

7:14—11:10
The Ten Plagues
7:14—11:10. plagues as attack on Egypt's gods and as natural occurrences. The plagues have been viewed by many as specific attacks on the gods of Egypt (see 12:12). This is certainly true in the sense that the Egyptians' gods were unable to protect them and that areas supposedly under the jurisdiction of their gods were used to attack them. Whether individual gods were being singled out is difficult to confirm. In another vein, some have suggested that a sequence of natural occurrences can explain the plagues from a scientific point of view, all originating from an overflooding in the summer months and proceeding through a cause-and-effect process into March. Those who maintain such a position will still sometimes admit to the miraculous nature of the plagues in terms of timing, discrimination between Egyptians and Israelites, prior announcement and severity. For each plague we will cite the natural explanations that have been offered as well as indicating which gods have been considered targets of the plague. It will be for the reader to decide what role either of these explanations should play in the understanding of the text.

7:14-24. water to blood. The Nile was the lifeblood of Egypt. Agriculture and ultimately survival were dependent on the periodic flooding that deposited fertile soils along the river's 4,132 miles. The obese Hapi, one of the children of Horus, was technically not the god of the Nile but the personification of the inundation of the Nile. The blood-red coloring has been attributed to an excess of both red earth and the bright red algae and its bacteria, both of which accompany a heavier than usual flooding. Rather than the abundant life usually brought by the river, this brought death to the fish and detriment to the soil. Such an occurrence is paralleled in an observation in the *Admonitions of Ipuwer* (a few centuries before Moses) that the Nile had turned to blood and was undrinkable. The biblical comment about the Egyptians digging down (v. 24) would be explained as an attempt to reach water that had been filtered through the soil.

7:19. buckets and jars. In verse 19 most translations make reference to wood and stone vessels, suggesting that water in such vessels was also changed. The Hebrew text says nothing of vessels. The combination of "sticks and stones" is used in *Ugaritic literature to refer to outlying, barren regions. The text also includes canals, which suggests the artificial channels used for irrigation.

8:1-15. frog plague. It is natural that the frogs would desert the waters and banks clogged with decomposing fish. The goddess Heqet was envisioned as a frog and assisted with childbirth, but it is difficult to imagine how this was seen as a victory over her. The Egyptian magicians could not remove the plague, only make it worse.

8:11. hardening heart. Here a different verb is used than in the previous references (see comments on 4:20-23; 7:13). This verb means "to make heavy" and therefore is associated with very familiar Egyptian imagery. In the judgment scene from the Book of the Dead, the heart of the deceased is weighed in the balance against a feather (representing Maat, truth and justice) to determine whether the individual will be ushered into an afterlife of happiness or be devoured. Increasing the weight of Pharaoh's heart is a way of expressing that his afterlife doom is being sealed. The expression is most similar to the English cliche "driving another nail into his coffin." It represents simply accelerating the inevitable.

8:16-19. gnat plague. The type of insect (NIV: "gnats") involved in this plague is not clear, since the Hebrew word is used only in this context. Most studies have favored either the mosquito or the tick as the likeliest identification. The former would breed in all the stagnant pools of water left from the flooding. "Finger of God" may be an Egyptian expression referring to Aaron's rod. The failure of the magicians and their admission that God is at work begins to fulfill the Lord's purpose: They will know that I am *Yahweh.

8:20-32. land ruined by flies. The insect featured in the fourth plague is not named. Instead the text speaks of swarms, using a word known only in relation to this context. Flies are logical both to the climate and to the conditions that exist with rotting fish and frogs and decaying vegetation. Because it is a carrier of skin anthrax (associated with later plagues), the species *Stomoxys calcitrans* has been the most popular identification. As both pests and carriers, these insects brought ruin-

ation on the land.

8:22. Goshen. This is the first plague that does not afflict the Israelites living in Goshen. The precise location of Goshen is still unknown, though it is certainly in the eastern part of the Delta region of the Nile.

8:26. sacrifice detestable to Egyptians. When Pharaoh offers to let them make their sacrifices in the land, Moses does not claim the need to conduct the *rituals at a holy site but objects that their rituals are unacceptable because they sacrifice that which is detestable to the Egyptians. Slaughter of animals to provide food for the gods was prevalent in Egyptian religious practice, as many reliefs portray, but blood sacrifices of animals played little role in the sun worship, king worship and *funerary observances that constituted much of Egyptian religion. Often the animal being slaughtered was considered to represent an enemy of the god.

9:1-7. livestock plague. The plague on the cattle is regularly identified as anthrax that was contracted from the bacteria that had come down the Nile and infected the fish, the frogs and the flies. The Egyptian goddess of love, Hathor, took the form of a cow, and the sacred Apis bull was so highly venerated that it was embalmed and buried in a necropolis with its own sarcophagus at death.

9:8-12. handful of soot. While some have concluded the ashes are taken from a brick kiln (symbolizing the labor of the Israelites), the Egyptians generally used sun-dried brick rather than kiln-fired. The furnace spoken of here is sizable and alternatively could be viewed as the place where the carcasses of the dead animals have been burned. The scattering of ashes is sometimes used as a magical *ritual in Egypt to bring an end to pestilence. Here it may bring an end to the cattle plague, but it translates into human misery.

9:10-12. boils plague. Skin anthrax would be carried by the bites of the flies which had had contact with the frogs and cattle, and would produce sores, particularly on the hands and feet.

9:13-35. effects of hail. Hail is destructive to crops as well as to humans and animals. The text's designation of which crops were affected (vv. 31-32) indicates that it was January or February.

10:1-20. locust plague. Locusts were all too common in the ancient Near East and were notorious for the devastation and havoc they brought. The locusts breed in the region of the Sudan and would have been more plentiful than usual in the wet climate that initiated the entire sequence. Their migration would strike in February or March and would follow the prevailing winds to either Egypt or Palestine. The east wind (v. 13) would bring them into Egypt. A locust will consume its own weight each day. Locust swarms have been known to cover as many as four hundred square miles, and even one square mile could teem with over one hundred million insects. Certainly anything that had survived the hail was now destroyed, and if they laid their eggs before being blown out to sea, the problem would recur in cycles. The economy in Egypt was destroyed, but the principal gods had yet to be humiliated.

10:19. west wind. The plague was ended by a "wind from the sea." In Israel this is a west wind, but in Egypt it would come from the north or northwest and therefore drive the locusts back to the sea.

10:21-29. darkness plague (that can be felt). The comment that it was darkness that could be felt (v. 21) suggests that the darkness was caused by something airborne, namely, the *khamsin* dust storms known in the region. There would be excessive dust from all of the red earth that had been brought down and deposited by the Nile, as well as from the barren earth left behind in the wake of the hail and locusts. The three-day duration is typical for this type of storm, which is most likely to occur between March and May. The fact that the text emphasizes the darkness rather than the dust storm may indicate that the sun god, Amon-Re, the national god of Egypt, the divine father of Pharaoh, is being specifically targeted.

11:1-10. tenth plague and Pharaoh. In Egypt Pharaoh was also considered a deity, and this last plague is directed at him. In the ninth plague his "father," the sun god, was defeated, and now his son, presumably the heir to the throne, will be slaughtered. This is a blow to Pharaoh's person, his kingship and his divinity.

11:2. ask for gold and silver. The instructions for the Israelites to ask for gold and silver articles and clothing (mentioned in other passages) from the Egyptians would most likely have correlated with the idea that the Israelites were going to have a feast for their God. Finery would be natural for such occasions, and it would not be odd to think that the Israelite slaves would not possess such luxuries. By now the people of Egypt would have been in despair from the plagues, and the thought that Israel's God might be appeased by a feast would make them very cooperative.

11:4. the Lord going throughout Egypt. In Egypt the most notable and anticipated event of the major festivals was the god coming forth among the people. Here, however, the going forth of Israel's God throughout the land will be for the purposes of judgment.

11:4. hand mill. The slave girl at her hand mill is portrayed as the lowest on the social ladder. The hand mill, or saddle-quern, was made up of two stones: a lower stone with a concave surface and a loaf-shaped upper stone. The daily chore of grinding grain into flour involved sliding the upper stone over the grain spread on the lower stone.

11:7. not a dog will bark. Dogs were not kept as pets but were considered undesirable and a general nuisance, perhaps as a rat would be viewed today. The statement that no dog would bark suggests unusual calm, for these roaming curs were easily antagonized by the slightest irregularity.

12:1-28

Passover

12:1-28. roots of Passover. According to the biblical account the Feast of Passover is instituted in association with the tenth plague, but that does not mean that its institution did not build on a previously existing festival of some sort. We should recall that God instituted *circumcision as a sign of the *covenant using a practice that previously existed with other purposes. Many elements of the Passover *ritual suggest that it may be adapted from a nomadic *ritual that sought to protect herdsmen from demonic attack and insure the *fertility of the herd. Even if this is so, each of the elements is suitably "converted" to the new context of the tenth plague and the exodus from Egypt. If such a conversion of a nomadic festival took place, it would be similar to the early western European Christians' superimposing Christmas on their pagan winter solstice festivals, with tokens such as holly, mistletoe and evergreen trees carried over.

12:1-11. calendar. This event established Abib (later called Nisan) as the first month in the religious calendar of Israel. By the civil calendar, Tishri, six months later, was the first month, and thus the month that "New Year's Day" was celebrated. The Israelite calendar was a lunar calendar with periodic adjustments to the solar year. Abib began with the first new moon after the spring equinox, generally mid-March, and went through mid-April.

12:5. year-old males without defect. As a yearling, the male would have survived the vulnerable period of early life (mortality rates were between 20 and 50 percent) and would be preparing to take on its role as a productive member of the flock. A flock needs fewer male members, however, and particularly among goats many of the males were slaughtered as yearlings for their coats and their meat. The females were kept until about age eight for bearing young and producing milk.

12:6. slaughtered at twilight. In Egypt's civil calendar each month was thirty days in length and divided into three periods of ten days each. The Egyptian religious calendar, including festivals, remained in a lunar sequence. The occurrence of the feast and the plague corresponded to the eve of what Egyptians called "half-month day." More importantly, since the month in lunar reckoning began at the new moon, the feast occurred at the time of the full moon, always the first after the spring equinox. The slaughter would take place at twilight, when the first full moon of the Israelite year rose.

12:7. function of blood. In primitive religions blood is often used to ward off evil powers, whereas in Israelite *ritual the blood served as a purifying element. While the former could certainly have been superstitiously believed by Israelites who retained these primitive elements in their religious thought and practice, the latter was the intended function. Door frames of Mesopotamian houses were often painted red because the color was believed to ward off demons.

12:8. menu. The menu for the Passover meal is one that would have been common in nomadic herding communities. The prohibition of yeast may additionally carry symbolic value. In later rabbinic literature and the New Testament it is associated with *impurity or *pollution. It is difficult to discern whether it carried such a connotation this early. The bitter herbs are identified in later rabbinic literature as lettuce, chicory, eryngo, horseradish and sow thistle, all easily prepared. It is uncertain, however, whether these are the ones included in the biblical terminology. Lettuce is known to have been cultivated in Egypt, and the Hebrew word translated "bitter herbs" corresponds to an *Akkadian (Babylonian) word for lettuce. The command to roast avoids two other possibilities. On the one hand, it has been thought to contrast to pagan spring feasts that sometimes included raw meat. On the other hand, those in haste would not boil the meat, for that would necessitate greater preparation time to butcher, gut and dress the meat. Since this is a sacral meal, the meat, may not be eaten at any other time and must be properly disposed of.

12:11. Passover. The English translation "Passover" does not do justice to the Hebrew terminology *(pesah)*. That the verb has to do with

protection can be seen in Isaiah 31:5, where it is parallel to shielding and delivering. The Lord is not portrayed as "passing over" the door but as protecting the entrance from the slaughtering angel (see 12:23). The blood on the doorposts and lintel can now be seen as purifying the doorway in preparation for the Lord's presence.

12:12-30
The Tenth Plague

12:12-13. Egyptian kingship festival. There may be some echo here of the famous Egyptian Sed festival, which represented a renewal of royal authority. Its celebration was intended for all the gods to affirm the kingship of Pharaoh, while here, as a result of the plagues, all the gods must acknowledge the kingship of *Yahweh—not a new enthronement, but a recognition of his ongoing power. In the Sed festival the king asserted his dominance of the land by going throughout the land (symbolically) as he desired. Pharaoh's kingship is being mocked even as Yahweh's is being asserted, for God goes throughout the land to establish his dominance by the plague.

12:14-20. Feast of Unleavened Bread. The Feast of Unleavened Bread is celebrated during the seven days after Passover. As a commemoration of the exodus from Egypt, it conveys that in their haste the Israelites were not able to bring any leaven and therefore had to bake their bread without it. Leaven was produced from the barley content of the dough that fermented and served as yeast. Small amounts would be kept from one batch, allowed to ferment, then used in another. With no "starter" set aside to ferment, the process would have to begin again, taking seven to twelve days to reach the necessary level of fermentation.

12:16. sacred assembly. Sacred assemblies or proclamations were an important part of most religious practice in the ancient world. They were local or national gatherings for public, corporate worship. The people were summoned together away from their normal occupations.

12:19. unleavened bread and barley harvest. The Feast of Unleavened Bread also coincided with the barley harvest and is the beginning of the harvest season. In this context the significance of the unleavened bread is that a new beginning is being made, and the first fruits of the barley harvest are eaten without waiting for fermentation.

12:22. use of hyssop. The blood is spread on the door frame with hyssop, a marjoram plant that came to be associated with purification, probably because of its use in *rituals such as these. Its consistency made it very adaptable for brushes and brooms.

12:23. the destroyer. The blood on the door frame would signal the Lord to protect those in that house from the destroyer. In Mesopotamia the demon Lamashtu (female) was seen as responsible for the death of children, while Namtaru (male) was responsible for plague. Egyptians likewise believed in a host of demons who threatened life and health at every level. In this passage, however, this is no demon operating independently of the gods, but a messenger of God's judgment. In Jeremiah the same term is used for a destroyer and plunderer of the nations (Jer 4:7).

12:29-30. firstborn. In Israel the dedication of the firstborn was a means of acknowledging the Lord as the provider of life, fertility and prosperity. By taking the firstborn of both man and beast, Yahweh is again asserting his rights to be viewed as the deity responsible for life in Egypt—a role usually attributed to Pharaoh.

12:31-42

Leaving Egypt

12:34. kneading troughs. The easiest way to transport the dough already mixed for the next day's bread was, as described, in the troughs used for kneading, covered with a cloth to keep the dust out.

12:37. route of journey. Rameses is Tell el-Dab'a in the eastern Delta (see comment on 1:8-14), where the Israelites were working to build a city for Pharaoh. Succoth has been identified as Tell el-Maskhuta toward the eastern end of the Wadi Tumilat. This would be a normal route to take to leave Egypt going east, as several Egyptian documents demonstrate. It is approximately one day's journey from Rameses to Succoth. (For the route of "The Exodus," see map 1 on p. 87.)

12:37. number of Israelites. The size of the Israelite population has been considered problematic for several reasons. If there were six hundred thousand men, the total group would have numbered over two million. It is contended that the Delta region of Egypt could not have supported a population of that size (estimates suggest the entire population of Egypt at this time was only four or five million). The modern population of the area of the Wadi Tumilat is under twenty thousand. Egyptian armies of this time period comprised under twenty thousand. Indeed, for the battle of Qadesh (thirteenth century) the *Hittites amassed an army of thirty-seven thou-

---

THE DATE OF THE EXODUS

Assigning a date to the exodus has proven to be a difficult task over the years. Since neither of the Pharaohs in the account are named, scholars have had to seek out other more circumstantial pieces of data in order to make a case. These pieces of data can be divided into *internal* data (from the biblical text) and *external data* (pieced together from archaeological and historical research).

The internal evidence, comprised primarily of genealogical or chronological time spans given in the text (e.g., 1 Kings 6:1), suggests a date in the middle of the fifteenth century B.C. If this date is adopted as having the support of the biblical text, it can be defended in historical/archaeological terms, but has to assume that a number of the conclusions that archaeologists have reached are either suffering from lack of data or are the result of misinterpretation of the data. For instance, if the Exodus took place around 1450, the conquest would be assigned to the Late Bronze Age in Canaan. Unfortunately, archaeologists excavating the sites of the Israelite conquest have found no remains of walled cities in Late Bronze Age Canaan. Many of the sites show no evidence of occupation at all in the Late Bronze Age. In response it has been suggested that the destruction of the great fortified cities of Middle Bronze Age Canaan should be associated with the Conquest. However, archaeologists have usually dated the end of the Middle Bronze to about 1550, and it is quite complex to try to shift the whole system of dating one hundred years.

The external evidence is usually considered to be more supportive of a thirteenth century date, during the time of Rameses the Great. This view has to assume that some of the numbers given in the biblical text need to be read differently. For instance, the 480 years of 1 Kings 6:1 would have to be viewed as suggesting twelve generations (12x40) which may be significantly less than 480 years. Additionally, while it has been claimed that the historical/archaeological data of the thirteenth century fits better with the Exodus, there are a number of difficulties that remain. Among them is the inscription of Pharaoh Merenptah toward the end of the thirteenth century that mentions Israel as a people group in Canaan.

Both dates have their difficulties and it is likely that there are still certain presuppositions that are being held that prevent us from seeing how all the pieces fit together. It is likely that historical and archaeological research will eventually be able to bring greater clarity to the issue. Until that time we will have to be content with our uncertainty.

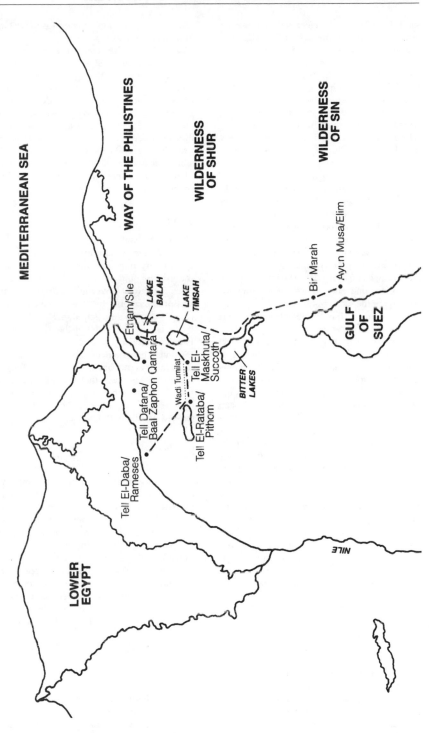

Map 1. The Exodus
This map traces the possible route of the exodus from Egypt.

sand (thought to be exaggerated) that was believed to be one of the largest fighting forces ever assembled. Shamshi-Adad (1800 B.C. Assyria) claimed to have amassed an army of sixty thousand for the siege of Nurrugum. If Israel had a fighting force of six hundred thousand, what would they have to fear?

As it traveled, the line of people would stretch for over two hundred miles. Even without animals, children and the elderly, travelers would not expect to make twenty miles a day (though caravans could make twenty to twenty-three). When families and animals move camp, the average would be only six miles per day. Whatever the case, the back of the line would be at least a couple of weeks behind the front of the line. This would create some difficulties in the crossing of the sea which seems to have been accomplished overnight, though certainly some have calculated how it could be done. The line, however, would be long enough to stretch from the crossing of the sea to Mount Sinai.

Furthermore, if a couple of million people lived in the wilderness for forty years and half of them died there, archaeologists expect they would find more traces of them—especially in places like Kadesh Barnea where they stayed for some time. When we turn our attention to their arrival in Canaan, the situation is no better. The population of Canaan during this period was far less than this Israelite force, and all archaeological evidence suggests there was a sharp decline in the population of the region in the *Late Bronze Age, when the Israelites took possession. Some estimates for the eighth century B.C. suggest there were still not a million people in the entire land of Israel even by that time. The modern population of Israel, even given the extensive metropolitan regions, is only about twice what the exodus population would have been. Yet the text is consistent in its reports of the size of the group (see Num 1:32; 11:21; 26:51). Many solutions have been offered, but all have problems. All of the above suggests that it is unlikely the numbers should be read the way that they traditionally have been. Studies of the use of numbers in Assyrian inscriptions have suggested the possibility that numbers were understood and used within an ideological framework rather than to offer a strict accounting. But it is very difficult to step out of our own cultural expectations. The most promising approach comes through a recognition that the Hebrew word translated "thousand" can also be translated "military troop," in which case there would be six hundred military troops. For more information see comments on Joshua 8:3 and Numbers 2:3-32.

12:40. 430 years. The chronology of this period is very difficult. First Kings 6:1 reports that 480 years separated the exodus from the dedication of the temple in 966. This would place the exodus in the mid-1400s. Adding the 430 years of this verse would suggest that the Israelites came to Egypt in the first half of the nineteenth century B.C. All sorts of variations exist, and several different options are defensible from both biblical and archaeological evidence. For a longer discussion see "The Date of the Exodus," p. 86.

12:43-51
Passover Regulations

12:43. Passover regulations. Verse 38 mentions many non-Israelites who have joined the exodus, and so three additional regulations for the Passover are addressed in this section. First, only those who have been circumcised may participate. This indicates that it is a festival only for the community of Israel. Second is the command that none of the meat be taken outside the house, and third is that no bones be broken. Both of these concern ways that the meal might be shared with other noncommunity members, which is disallowed. The lamb must be cooked whole, in the house.

13:1-16
The Firstborn

13:1-3. consecration. The first male offspring born to any mother is considered as belonging to deity. In the ancient Near East this concept sometimes led to child sacrifice to insure *fertility. Alternatively, in ancestor worship the firstborn would have inherited the priestly function for the family. In Israel it leads to consecration—transferring the firstborn to the domain of deity for cultic service or to the temple for holy use. From that status the son may be redeemed, and Israelite law sees his place being taken by the Levites (Num 3:11-13).

13:4. Abib. The month of Abib spans our March and April. It is the ancient name for what was later called Nisan in the Israelite calendar.

13:5. peoples of Canaan and land of milk and honey. For the peoples of Canaan and the land flowing with milk and honey, see comments on 3:7-10 and 3:8.

13:6-10. Feast of Unleavened Bread. See comment on 12:14-20.

13:9. amulets. *Amulets were often worn in the ancient Near East as protection to ward off evil spirits. Precious metals and gems were considered particularly effective. At times amulets would include magical words or spells. Israelite practice disapproved of amulets, but the concept was converted to reminders of the law (such as this feast served), or at other places (see Deut 6:8) consisted of physical reminders that contained prayers or blessings such as the small silver scrolls that were found in a preexilic tomb just outside Jerusalem in 1979. These contain the blessing of Numbers 6:24-26 and represent the oldest copy of any biblical text now extant.

13:11-16. sacrifice of firstborn. First-born livestock were sacrificed in thanks to the Lord, but donkeys were not approved for sacrifice. In Canaanite practice donkeys were occasionally sacrificed and a covenant confirmation ceremony in the *Mari texts also features the sacrifice of a donkey. The importance of the donkey as a pack animal is probably responsible for this exclusion. Therefore donkeys, like sons, were to be redeemed—that is, another offering given in their place.

13:17—14:31

The Crossing of the Sea

13:17. road to the Philistines. The road through the Philistine country is a reference to the major route that ran through the Fertile Crescent from Egypt to Babylonia and is known as the Great Trunk road. It went along the coast of the Mediterranean, which took it through Philistine territory in southern Palestine before moving inland through the valley of Jezreel just south of the Carmel range. Along the north of the Sinai peninsula the Egyptians referred to it as the Way of Horus, and it was heavily defended since it was the route used by armies as well as trade caravans.

13:18. Red Sea. The body of water referred to in translations as the "Red Sea" is termed in Hebrew the "Reed Sea"—a term that can be used for a number of different bodies of water. The reeds it refers to are probably papyrus, which used to proliferate along the marshy section that extended from the Gulf of Suez to the Mediterranean, now largely obliterated by the Suez Canal. Such reeds grow only in fresh water. Proceeding north from the Gulf of Suez, one would have encountered the Bitter Lakes, Lake Timsah, Lake Balah and finally, right by the Mediterranean, Lake Menzaleh. The Wadi Tumilat through which Israel is traveling would have led to Lake Timsah, so

that is often identified as the Sea of Reeds in this context, though each of the other lakes has its supporters. If the Israelites originally headed northwest, they may have turned back and found themselves by Lake Balah. If they were heading toward the region of Sinai, they certainly would not have gone down the west side of the Gulf of Suez, and, in any case, that is further away than the narrative suggests (about 120 miles from Succoth). So though the translation "Red Sea" has led to that being the popular identification, it is the least likely. An alternative to "Reed Sea" as a geographical distinction is the suggestion that the translation should be "Sea of Extinction." In this case the waters that are being parted are identified by imagery referring to a common ancient Near Eastern creation motif of the waters of chaos being harnessed and the enemies of God being overthrown.

13:20. Succoth. Succoth is generally identified as Tell el-Maskhuta toward the eastern end of the Wadi Tumilat. In Egyptian literature this is the area known as *Tjeku*, the Egyptian equivalent of Hebrew *succoth*. Etham is the equivalent of Egyptian *htm*, "fort," and could refer to any number of fortresses in this area. Since God turns them back in 14:2, they may still be following the way of the Philistines on this first leg. If so, Etham would most likely be Sile, modern Tell Abu Sefa, where the first fortress guarding the passage onto the frontier was located in ancient times. It was the normal point of departure for expeditions to Canaan. In this case, 13:17-18 is described in detail in 14:1-3. The problem is that this is some fifty miles from Succoth and would have taken several days to reach. There is also a fortress of Pharaoh Merenptah (end of thirteenth century) mentioned near Tjeku in Papyrus Anastasi VI. (For a possible route of the exodus, see map 1 on p. 87.)

13:21-22. pillar of cloud/fire. Some have thought the pillar of cloud and fire is best explained as the result of volcanic activity. An eruption on the Island of Thera (six hundred miles northwest) in 1628 B.C. brought an end to Minoan civilization, and it is possible that its effects could have been seen in the delta. But the date is far too early (see "The Date of the Exodus," p. 86), and this theory would offer no explanation of the movements of the pillar nor of the location described for it in the biblical account (they are moving southeast). The text does not suggest that the pillar was supernaturally generated, only that it was the means of supernatural guidance. For this reason some have suggested that it was the result of a brazier of some sort carried on a pole that would be used by the vanguard scouts. This was a method often used by caravans. On the other hand, the pillar is always portrayed as acting (coming down, moving) rather than being operated (no human is ever said to move it), so the vanguard theory is difficult to support. In the ancient world a bright or flaming aura surrounding deity is the norm. In Egyptian literature it is depicted as the winged sun disk accompanied by storm clouds. *Akkadian uses the term *melammu* to describe this visible representation of the glory of deity, which in turn is enshrouded in smoke or cloud. In Canaanite mythology it has been suggested the *melammu* concept is expressed by the word *anan*, the same Hebrew word here translated "cloud," but the occurrences are too few and obscure for confidence. In any case, the pillar here would then be one: smoke being visible in the daytime, while the inner flame it covered would glow through at night.

14:1-4. Pi Hahiroth. Pi Hahiroth is not otherwise known, but many interpret it as meaning "mouth of the diggings," possibly referring to canal work. It is known that a north-south canal was being constructed during this period (Seti I) and that it passed through the region near Qantara, a few miles west of Sile.

14:2. Migdol. *Migdol* means "tower" or "fort" in Hebrew and was a term borrowed from Semitic languages into Egyptian. There were several locations so designated, and one is known near Succoth in this period.

14:2. Baal Zephon. Baal Zephon is connected to Tahpanhes in Jeremiah 44:1; 46:14, in turn identified as Tell Dafana, about twenty miles west of Sile. If they camped near here, Lake Balah would be the closest sea.

14:5-9. Egypt's army. Most chariot units of this period range between 10 and 150, so 600 is a large muster, and this represents only Pharaoh's unit. When Rameses II fought the *Hittites at the battle of Qadesh, his enemy boasted 2,500 chariots.

14:19-20. hidden by cloud. Annals from the *Hittite king Murshili report that the storm god provided a cloud to hide them from their enemy, a claim also made by Priam, king of Troy, as well as others in Homer's *Iliad*.

14:21-22. sea driven back with east wind. Any sea shallow enough to be dried up by an east wind and shifting tides would not be sufficient to drown the Egyptians or to make walls of water. It is therefore difficult to devise any natural scenario to account for the facts reported by the text. This wind would not be the same as the *khamsin* (sirocco) that we associated with the ninth plague. That is a phe-

nomenon drawn by a strong low-pressure system in North Africa, usually accompanied by thermal inversion. The east wind referred to here drives out of a high-pressure system over Mesopotamia and—opposite to a tornado, which rotates around a low-pressure system—features a sharp rise in barometric pressure.

14:23-25. the morning watch. The morning watch was from two to six a.m. The image of deity as flaming brilliance in the midst of a cloud is common throughout the Near East as well as in Greek mythology as early as Homer's *Iliad*, where Zeus sends forth lightning and causes horses to stumble and chariots to break. The Mesopotamian warrior god, Nergal, and the Canaanite *Baal each asserts his superiority in combat by means of his dazzling brilliance and fire.

15:1-21
The Song of Moses and Miriam

15:3. the Lord as warrior. The book of Exodus has been developing the idea of *Yahweh fighting for the Israelites against the Egyptians and their gods, so here the Lord is praised as a warrior. This is a concept that remains significant throughout the Old Testament and even into the New Testament. It is especially prominent in the books of Samuel, where the title "Yahweh of Armies" (Lord of Hosts) is common. Yahweh is the king and champion of the Israelites and will lead them forth victoriously in battle. Ancient mythologies often portrayed gods in battle, but these depictions generally concerned the harnessing and organizing of the cosmos. Both *Marduk (Babylonian) and *Baal (Canaanite) subdue the sea, which is personified in their divine foe (*Tiamat and Yamm respectively). In contrast, this hymn recognizes how Yahweh harnessed the natural sea (not representing a supernatural being) to overcome his historical, human foes. Nevertheless, bringing secure order out of conflict, being proclaimed king and establishing a dwelling are common themes both here and in the ancient Near Eastern literatures concerning cosmic battle.

15:4. Red Sea. Here the reference to the Reed Sea does not suggest further discussion of its identity (see comment on 13:18) but may well include a pun. The Hebrew word *suph* not only means "reed" but also means "end" as a noun and "swept away" as a verb (see Ps 73:19).

15:6-12. right hand. The right hand is the one that holds the weapon, so that it is the one that brings victory. In verse 12 the right hand is not seen as literally causing the earth to open up. In Hebrew the term for earth can occasionally also mean "netherworld," and that seems likely here. To say that the netherworld swallowed them is to say that they were sent to their graves. It should also be remembered that in Egyptian concepts of afterlife the wicked are devoured by the "Swallower" when they fail to convince the judges of their goodness.

15:13-16. terrified peoples. The terror of the peoples becomes a standard theme in the account of the conquest. While the peoples of Canaan may have previously been terrified of the Egyptians (as the *Amarna correspondence from this period suggest some were), it is now not the arm of Pharaoh, but the arm of Yahweh, who has defeated Pharaoh, that poses a threat to them.

15:17-18. mountain of your inheritance. The combination of mountain, inheritance, dwelling and sanctuary suggests that Mount Zion (Jerusalem) is being referred to.

15:18. Yahweh as king. Yahweh is not portrayed as a mythological king, a king of the gods who has subdued the cosmos and reigns over the subordinate gods of the pantheon. Rather he rules in the historical realm over his people, whom he has delivered by means of the forces of nature that he controls. This hymn does not exalt his defeat of other gods or of chaotic cosmic forces but his power over historical peoples.

15:20-21. prophetess. Miriam, here hailed as a prophetess and sister of Aaron (no mention of Moses), takes up the song. This is the only mention of Miriam by name in the book, and the only place she is referred to as a prophetess. The only other account that she is named in is the challenge to Moses' authority in Numbers 12. Other prominent prophetesses in the Old Testament include Deborah (Judg 4) and Huldah (2 Kings 22). There is no reason to think that it was odd for women to be found in this role. In fact, the prophetic texts from *Mari feature women in this role as often as men. It was also common for musical troupes to feature women. Music and prophecy also were associated, since music was commonly used to induce the trances from which prophetic utterances proceeded (1 Sam 10:5; 2 Kings 3:15).

15:22—17:7
God's Provision in the Wilderness

15:22-27. Desert of Shur. The wilderness of Shur is located in the northwest region of the Sinai peninsula. An east-west route runs through the region that connects Egypt to the King's Highway in Transjordan at Bozrah, or leads up into Palestine through Beersheba, but the Israelites did not take this route. Shur means "wall" in Hebrew, so it is possible that this term refers to the well-known Egyptian line of fortresses in this region. This is supported by Numbers 33:8, where it is called the wilderness of Etham (*etham* means "fort"). Built a few centuries earlier to protect the northeastern frontiers of Egypt, this series of garrisons was known as the Wall of the Ruler. This marked *Sinuhe's point of departure as he fled from Egypt in the *Story of Sinuhe*.

15:22. archaeological evidence in the Sinai. Although archaeological remains from the Bedouin population that has inhabited Sinai for ten thousand years have been found throughout the peninsula, archaeology has produced no evidence of the Israelites' passage through this region.

15:23. Marah. They traveled for three days before reaching Marah ("bitter"). If they crossed at Lake Balah, this would place them by what are well known today as the Bitter Lakes. If they crossed further south, Marah could be identified with an oasis called Bir Marah, where the water is saline with heavy mineral content.

15:25. wood turning water sweet. It is not uncommon for commentators to cite local traditions about a type of thorn bush native to the region that will absorb salinity, but no scientific investigation has provided identification or confirmed the existence of such a bush. In a later period Pliny reported that there was a type of barley that could neutralize saline content.

15:27. Elim oasis. The oasis at Elim with twelve springs and seventy palm trees is often identified as Wadi Gharandal, about sixty miles down the coast of the Gulf of Suez. It features tamarisks (*elim*) as well as palms and springs. It remains a major resting place for modern Bedouin. Closer to Marah is the site of Ayun Musa, just a few miles south of the tip of the Gulf of Suez. Besides having the appropriate groves of tamarisks and palms, it also features twelve springs and is probably to be preferred.

16:1-3. Desert of Sin. The Desert of Sin is an area in the west-central region of the peninsula. Here the main route moves inland five to ten miles for about the next seventy-five miles until it rejoins the coast at Abu Zenimah and the El Markha plain. This may be where they camped by the sea (Num 33:10-11). From there they moved east and northeast across the wilderness of Sin by way of the Wadi Ba'ba and

Rod el 'Air to the region of Serabit el-Khadim, which is likely where Dophkah was (Num 33:11).

16:1. time of journey. Thus far the journey has taken about a month (the Israelites came out the fifteenth day of the first month).

16:3. pots of meat. In their exaggerated recollection of the situation in Egypt they refer to large pots filled with meat—we might say "meat by the bucketload."

16:4-9. bread from heaven/manna. The bread from heaven was called "manna" in verse 31, where it is described (see also Num 11:7). The fact that it came with the dew (v. 4) suggests that God's miraculous provision used a natural process. The most frequent identification is with the secretion of small aphids that feed on the sap of tamarisk trees. When it hardens and falls to the ground, it can be collected and used for a sweetener. The problem is that this occurs only during certain seasons (May to July) and only where there are tamarisk trees. A full season would normally produce only about five hundred pounds, in contrast to the biblical account that has the people gathering about half a pound per person per day. Alternatively, some would favor the sweet liquid of the hammada plant, common in southern Sinai, which is used to sweeten cakes. As with the plagues, it is not necessarily the occurrence of this phenomenon that is unnatural but the timing and magnitude. Nevertheless, these natural explanations seem to fall far short of the biblical data. The comparison to what most translations identify as the seed of the coriander (rarely found in the desert) is more likely to refer to a wider generic category of desert plants with white seeds.

16:10-11. glory of the Lord in the cloud. "The glory of the LORD" refers to the brightness that was evidence of his presence. The concept of deity appearing in this way was not limited to Israelite theology, for in Mesopotamia the gods displayed their power through their *melammu,* their divine brilliance.

16:13. quail. Small, plump migratory quail often come through the Sinai on their way north from the Sudan to Europe, generally in the months of March and April. They generally fly with the wind and are driven to ground (or water) if caught in a crosswind. In their exhaustion it is not unusual for them to fly so low that they can be easily caught. Quail looking for a place to land and rest have been known to sink small boats, and in the Sinai they have been noted to cover the ground so densely that some landed on the tops of others.

16:14-36. omer. An omer is a daily ration of bread or grain and represents about two quarts.

16:20. spoilage. If manna is the secretion of aphids (see above on 16:4-9), ants are responsible for carrying it off each day once the temperature rises. They would also be the bugs that got into any additional manna the people tried to collect and save. The Hebrew word translated "maggots" can refer to any number of scale insects, but there is a different word for ants. Furthermore, the insect secretions are not subject to spoilage.

16:34. in front of the testimony. The testimony in verse 34 can only refer to the ark of the covenant, which has not been built at this point in the narrative. This appendix (vv. 31-36) is from the end of the wilderness wanderings (see v. 35), and therefore the manna sample was put in the ark later in the wilderness experience.

17:1. Rephidim. If the theory that Mount Sinai is toward the south of the peninsula is accepted, the journey to Rephidim begins the move inland to follow the most attractive route to the mountain. Wadi Refayid intersects Wadi Feiran a few miles north of the mountain and has been often identified as the site of Rephidim.

17:5-7. rock at Horeb. The location of this provision of water is identified with the rock at Horeb, but Horeb most likely refers to the region in the vicinity of Mount Sinai (Mount Horeb) rather than to a specific location.

17:6. water from rock. Sedimentary rock is known to feature pockets where water can collect just below the surface. If there is some seepage, one can see where these pockets exist and by breaking through the surface can release the collected water. Again, however, we are dealing with a quantity of water beyond what this explanation affords.

17:7. Massah and Meribah. Massah and Meribah do not represent new places but refer to this particular site at Rephidim.

17:8-15

The Attack of the Amalekites

17:8. Amalekites. The Amalekites, who were descended from Abraham through Esau (Gen 36:15), were a nomadic or seminomadic people who inhabited the general region of the Negev and the Sinai during the second half of the second millennium B.C.

17:11-12. battle signals. Signals were often used to deploy the various divisions in battle. It is possible that Moses used the staff in just such a way. When he was unable to relay divine guidance through the signals, the Israelites were not able to succeed. Alternatively, it has been noticed that Egyptian texts speak of the uplifted arms of Pharaoh to bring protection as well as to signal the attack.

17:15. altar: "Lord my banner." The altar Moses builds is one of commemoration of the victory. The name given it, "Yahweh is my standard," reflects the theology of Yahweh as the leader of the armies of Israel. In the Egyptian army the divisions were named for various gods (e.g., the division of Amun, division of Seth) and the standards would identify the division by means of some representation of the god.

18:1-27
Jethro and Moses

18:1-2. priest of what god? Jethro is identified as a priest of Midian rather than as a priest of a particular deity. Little is known of which god or gods the Midianites of this period worshiped. Priests were not necessarily affiliated to only one god, and therefore Jethro's recognition of *Yahweh's superiority does not suggest he was a priest or worshiper of Yahweh. Priests serving a sanctuary would be viewed as servants of the god of that sanctuary, but even these individuals were not monotheistic, so they would acknowledge the power of other deities when manifested.

18:5. mountain of God. "Mountain of God" is used to describe Mount Sinai. At Rephidim they are in the general vicinity of Sinai, but this chapter probably records events that took place after they had set up camp at the foot of the mountain itself.

18:7. respectful greeting. Moses' greeting of Jethro follows standard practice. Bowing down is a greeting to one who is of higher social standing and is an act of respect. The kiss on the cheek is the greeting of friendship. This is the only recorded incident where both are performed.

18:9-12. Yahweh and the gods. Jethro's acknowledgment of the superiority of *Yahweh does not suggest that he was a worshiper of Yahweh or that he became a worshiper of Yahweh. The polytheism of the ancient world allowed for the recognition of the relative strengths of various deities and would expect each deity to be praised in superlative terms when there was evidence of his activity or displays of his power. Regardless of Jethro's religious persuasions, Yahweh was accomplishing his purpose that through his mighty acts "all the world will know that I am Yahweh."

18:12. sacrificial meal. Sacrifices in the ancient world were often opportunities for communal meals. Though communal meals were used to ratify formal agreements, they were also a part of offerings of thanksgiving, more suitable to this context. This is like a banquet with *Yahweh as the guest of honor.

18:13-27. Moses' seat. The seat of the judge is a designated seat of authority when the judge's "court" was "in session." In cities this seat was usually at the entrance to the gate. Jethro advises Moses to establish a hierarchical judiciary with Moses at the top, as a king would have been in a monarchy, and as a priest or family patriarch would have been in tribal societies. In this structure it is recognized that some disputes can be settled on point of law or by objective discretion (for information concerning the judiciary system in the ancient Near East, see comment on Deut 1:9-18). Such cases can be settled in the lower levels. In the absence of sufficient evidence in complex or serious cases, the matter was handled "prophetically"—that is, it was brought before God. This was where Moses' involvement was essential. It separates the "civil" aspects of the judiciary, in which Moses did not have to be involved, from the "religious" aspects. This system is not unlike that found in Egypt, where Pharaoh guaranteed justice but set up a system headed by the vizier, who was the "Prophet of Ma'at" (Ma'at is the goddess of truth and justice) and occupied the judgment chair. The establishment of this system formalized a sociological, if not political, role for Moses that moved Israel beyond being a purely tribal society to being a quasi-centralized government.

19:1-25
The Israelites at Mount Sinai

19:1-2. desert of Sinai. The Israelites reach the wilderness surrounding Sinai three months after leaving Egypt, though it is unclear whether "to the day" refers to the new moon or the full moon. Nevertheless, it is in the month of June. The location of Mount Sinai is far from certain, and at least a dozen different alternatives have been suggested. The three strongest contenders are Jebel Musa and Jebel Serbal in the south, and Jebel Sin Bishar in the north. Jebel Musa (7,486 feet) is in the cluster of mountains in central southern Sinai. As one of the highest peaks in the range it has enjoyed traditional support as far back as the fourth century A.D. It also features the er-Raha plain to its north that would have been suitable for the Israelite camp (providing about four hundred acres), though it lacks ready access to water. Jebel Serbal (6,791 feet) is about twenty miles northwest of Jebel Musa and separated from the range so that it rises isolated above the Wadi Feiran. Its location near an oasis and on the main road passing through the region makes it an attractive choice, though the area available for the camp is much smaller than that at Jebel Musa. Some have favored a northern location, assuming that Moses' initial request of Pharaoh for a three-day pilgrimage (5:3) would take them to Mount Sinai. They also point out that a northern route is more directly linked to Kadesh Barnea and the vicinity of Moses' time in Midian.

19:4. carried on eagles' wings. Though the eagle cannot be ruled out, the bird named here is more usually taken to be the griffin vulture, with a wingspan of eight to ten feet. While Bible reference books often report how the eagle carries its young on its wings when they grow weary of flying, or catches them on their wings when they are fluttering in failure (see Deut 32:11), this behavior has been difficult for naturalists to confirm through observation. In fact most eagles and vultures do not take their first flight until they are three or four months old, at which time they are nearly full grown. Furthermore, observations by naturalists have consistently confirmed that the first flight is usually taken while the parents are away from the nest. Alternatively, if the metaphor here concerns a vulture, it may be political in nature. In Egypt the goddess Nekhbet is the vulture goddess who represented Upper Egypt and served as a protecting deity for Pharaoh and the land. Israel was protected in Egypt until Yahweh brought them to himself.

19:5-6. kingdom of priests. The phrase "treasured possession" uses a word common in other languages of the ancient Near East to describe accumulated assets, whether through division of spoils or inheritance from estate. That people can be so described is evident in a royal seal from *Alalakh, where the king identifies himself as the "treasured possession" of the god Hadad. Likewise in a *Ugaritic text the king of Ugarit's favored status as a vassal is noted by naming him a "treasured possession" of his *Hittite overlord. Additionally, the Israelites are identified as a "kingdom of priests," which identifies the nation as serving a priestly role among the nations, as intermediary between the peoples and God. Additionally there is a well-attested concept in the ancient Near East that a city or group of people may be freed from being subject to a king and placed in direct subjection to a deity. So Israel, freed from Egypt, is now given sacred status (see Is 61:5).

19:7. elders. The elders here are the clan leaders of Israel. Elders typically served as a ruling assembly overseeing the leadership of a village or community. They represent the people in accepting a *covenant arrangement, now a national agreement with commitment expected beyond the family covenant made with Abraham centuries earlier.

19:10-15. consecration. Consecration consisted of steps taken to make oneself ritually pure. This process primarily entailed washing and avoiding contact with objects that would render one unclean. The mountain was designated holy ground, so much so that even touching it would constitute desecration punishable by death. Stoning was the most common means of execution. In this way the entire community took responsibility for the penalty, though no single individual could be considered to have brought about the death of the criminal.

19:13. ram's horn. The ram's horn in verse 13 is referred to by a different word from that used for the shofar (trumpet) in verse 16, though it may be used for the same instrument. The shofar is capable of a variety of tones but cannot play a tune, so it is used primarily for signals either in worship or in warfare. The ram's horn was softened in hot water, bent and flattened to produce its distinctive shape.

20:1-17
The Ten Commandments

20:1-17. apodictic law. A number of collections of legal material have been found from ancient times, including *Sumerian, *Babylonian, *Hittite and *Assyrian collections. The most famous is the Code of *Hammurabi, dating from several hundred years earlier than Moses. These collections consist primarily of sample rulings in particular types of cases. As case law they present what penalties were assigned to a wide range of offenses, rather than indicating certain behavior to be right or wrong or telling people what they should or should not do. The type of law found in the Ten Commandments that prohibits or requires certain types of behavior is called *apodictic law and is rarely found in the legal collections of the ancient Near East.

20:1-17. Decalogue as covenant (not law). The Ten Commandments not only are connected to law but are also a part of the *covenant. The literary formulation of the covenant is quite similar to the formulations of international treaties in the ancient Near East. In the stipulations of these treaties, one often finds certain behavior either required or prohibited. In this sense it could be understood that the *apodictic form of the Ten Commandments puts them more in the category of covenant than in the category of law.

20:3. first commandment. When the text says that there should be no other god "before me," it does not refer to others having a higher position than *Yahweh. The introduction in verse 2 has already indicated as a preexisting assumption that *Yahweh is their God. The phrase "before me" means "in my presence" and therefore prohibits other gods from being considered to be in the presence of Yahweh. This prohibits several concepts that were a standard part of ancient beliefs. Most religions of that day had a pantheon, a divine assembly that ruled the realm of the gods, the supernatural, and, ultimately, the human world. There would typically be a deity who was designated head of the pantheon, and he, like the other gods, would have at least one consort (female partner). This commandment forbids Israel to think in these terms. Yahweh is not the head of a pantheon, and he does not have a consort—there are no gods in his presence. The only divine assembly that is legitimate for their thinking is made up of angels (as in 1 Kings 22:19-20), not gods. This commandment also then effectively bans much mythology that deals with the interactions of the gods with one another.

20:4. second commandment. The second commandment concerns how *Yahweh is to be worshiped, for the idols that it prohibits are idols of him (the previous commandment already dismissed the thought of other gods). The commandment has nothing to do with art, though the graven images of the ancient world were indeed works of art. They were typically carved of wood and overlaid with hammered sheets of silver or gold, then clothed in the finest attire. But the prohibition is more concerned with how they are employed, and here the issue is power. Images of deity in the ancient Near East were where the deity became present in a special way, to the extent that the *cult statue became the god (when the god so favored his worshipers), even though it was not the only manifestation of the god. As a result of this linkage, spells, incantations and other magical acts could be performed on the image in order to threaten, bind or compel the deity. In contrast, other rites related to the image were intended to aid the deity or care for the deity. The images then represent a worldview, a concept of deity that was not consistent with how Yahweh had re-

vealed himself. The commandment also prohibits images of anything in heaven, earth or under the earth. In contrast to Egypt, it was not the practice in Syria-Palestine to worship animals or to have gods in the form of animals. Nevertheless, there were animals that were believed to represent the attributes of deity, such as bulls and horses, that would be portrayed in art and sculpture to stand in the place of deity.

20:5-6. punishing third and fourth generations. Punishment to the third or fourth generation is not granted to human judges but to God. It expresses the fact that *covenant violation brings guilt on the entire family. The third and fourth generation is then a way to refer to all living members of the family. But there is also a contrast here in the loyalty that extends over thousands of generations as over against the punishment that extends only three or four.

20:6. corporate solidarity. In the ancient Near East a person found his or her identity within a group such as the clan or family. Integration and interdependence were important values, and the group was bound together as a unit. As a result, individual behavior would not be viewed in isolation from the group. When there was sin in a family, all members shared the responsibility. This concept is known as *corporate identity.

20:7. third commandment. As the second commandment concerned the issue of exercising power over God, the third turns its attention to exercising God's power over others. This commandment does not refer to blasphemy or foul language. Rather it is intended to prevent the exploitation of the name of Yahweh for magical purposes in hexing. It also continues the concerns of the second commandment in that someone's name was believed to be intimately connected to that person's being and essence. The giving of one's name was an act of favor, trust and, in human terms, vulnerability. Israel was not to attempt to use Yahweh's name in magical ways to manipulate him. The commandment was also intended to insure that the use of Yahweh's name in oaths, vows and treaties was taken seriously.

20:8-11. fourth commandment. Sabbath observation has no known parallel in any of the cultures of the ancient Near East and is distinctive in that it is independent of any of the patterns or rhythms of nature. A similar term was used in *Babylonian texts as a full moon day when the king officiated at rites of reconciliation with deity, but it was not a work-free day and has little in common with the Israelite sabbath. The legislation does not require rest as much as it stipulates cessation, interrupting the normal activities of one's occupation.

20:12. fifth commandment. Honoring and respecting parents consists of respecting their instruction in the *covenant. This assumes that a religious heritage is being passed on. The home was seen as an important and necessary link for the covenant instruction of each successive generation. Honor is given to them as representatives of God's authority for the sake of covenant preservation. If parents are not heeded or their authority is repudiated, the covenant is in jeopardy. In this connection, notice that this commandment comes with covenant promise: living long in the land. In the ancient Near East it is not the religious heritage but the fabric of society that is threatened when there is no respect for parental authority and filial obligations are neglected. Violations would include striking parents, cursing parents, neglecting the care of elderly parents and failing to provide adequate burial.

20:12-17. commandments and community. Commandments five to nine all deal with issues of *covenant in community. They affect the transmission of the covenant in the community and the standing of individuals within the covenant community. Injunctions concern those things that would jeopardize the covenant's continuity from generation to generation or that would jeopardize the family line or reputation. The covenant must be passed on in the family, and the family must be preserved. In the ancient Near East the concerns were similar, but the focus on preservation of the community was viewed more in social and civil terms. Lists of ethical violations are found in Egypt in the Book of the Dead, where the individual denies that he has committed any of a long list of crimes. In Mesopotamia the incantation series known as *Shurpu* contains a list of crimes the individual confesses to in order to absolve himself of unknown offenses and thus appease an angry deity. But in neither of these works are these actions prohibited. They also include a wide range of other types of offenses.

20:13. sixth commandment. The word used here is not technically restricted to murder, but it does assume a person as both subject and object. It has been observed that it is used only in the context of homicide (whether accidental or intentional, premeditated or not, judicial, political or otherwise) within the *covenant community. Because of the nature of the term used, this verse cannot easily be brought into discussions of pacifism, capital

punishments or vegetarianism. Some law collections of the ancient Near East do not treat murder, while in others the punishment only entails monetary compensation. Nevertheless the murderer still ran the risk of being targeted for execution by the victim's family in a blood feud.

20:14. seventh commandment. The purpose of the legislation was to protect the husband's name by assuring him that his children would be his own. The law does not insure marital fidelity; its focus is paternity, not sexual ethics. The integrity of the family is protected rather than the integrity of the marriage. If a married man had an affair with an unmarried woman, it was not considered adultery. The offender had to pay damages to the father (22:16-17). This is a natural result of a polygamous society. Promiscuous behavior is not acceptable (Deut 22:21; 23:2), but it is not called adultery if the woman is not married. In the Bible the wife is an extension of the husband, and his name is damaged through adultery. In other cultures the wife was considered property, and this would merely have been a case of damaged goods. Nonetheless, in Egypt (marriage contracts), Mesopotamia (hymns to Ninurta and Shamash) and Canaan (king of *Ugarit extradites and executes his wife), adultery was regularly referred to as "the great sin" and was considered extremely detrimental to society in that it was characteristic of anarchy. *Hittite laws, Middle *Assyrian laws and the Code of *Hammurabi all contain legislation against adultery. The protection of the integrity of the family unit was important because the family was the foundation of society. Compromise or collapse of the family meant compromise or collapse of society.

20:15. eighth commandment. Property theft is prevented by the tenth commandment one step before the act. Though the verb used here in the eighth commandment can be used of stealing property, the command is much broader in its focus. Issues such as kidnapping (cf. Deut 24:7) as well as stealing intangibles (dignity, self-respect, freedom, rights) are all important. The word is also used for stealing in the sense of cheating—by cheating someone out of something, you are stealing from him.

20:16. ninth commandment. The terminology indicates the main focus is on formal slander and libel and is concerned primarily with the legal setting. The maintenance of justice was dependent on the reliability of the witness. Nevertheless, character assassination in any of its forms, legal or casual, would constitute false witness and would be a violation of this commandment.

20:17. tenth commandment. In the ancient Near East the concept of coveting occurs in expressions such as "to lift the eyes"—but it is a crime that can be detected and punished only when the desire is translated into action. Ancient Near Eastern literature shows that offenses such as theft and adultery can be described generally in terms of the desire that triggered the chain of events. Whatever action it spawns, this illegitimate desire for something that belongs to someone else is the core of the problem and a threat to the community; any action taken to fulfil such a desire is sin.

20:18. thunder and lightning. Thunder and lightning were considered to regularly accompany the presence of a deity in the ancient Near East, though that is often in a battle setting, not a revelation setting, since the gods of the ancient Near East were not accustomed to revealing themselves.

20:24-26

Altars

20:24. altar of earth. Some altars of this period were made of mud bricks, and that is perhaps what the text refers to when it speaks of altars of earth. Another possibility is that it refers to altars that had outer walls of stone but were filled with earth. No altars in the Bible are said to have been built of earth, and no altars of earth have been found by archaeologists.

20:25. altar of stones. Stones, if used, were not to be hewn. Unhewn stone was used for the Israelite altar uncovered by archaeologists at Arad, though altars at sites such as Dan and Beersheba feature ashlar masonry (a type of worked stone).

20:26. priestly modesty. Ritual nudity was widespread in the ancient Near East, whereas here every precaution is taken to assure modesty. Early Canaanite altars with steps are known from sites such as Megiddo. Israelite law also preserved modesty by legislating longer tunics and prescribing undergarments for the priests.

21:1—23:19

The Book of the Covenant

21:1—23:19. casuistic law. The principal form of law found throughout the ancient Near East was case or *casuistic law. It is characterized by an "if . . . then" clause, which is based on the idea of cause and effect. In the Israelite law codes, case law assumes the equality of all citizens, and thus punishment for crime is not hindered or magnified by class or wealth. This is not the case, however, in ancient Mesopotamia, where in *Hammurabi's code (c. 1750 B.C.) different degrees of punishments (from fines to execution) were prescribed for slaves, citizens and members of the nobility. Case law can be traced in its origins to *apodictic (command) laws, such as those found in the Ten Commandments. As persons committed crimes under varying circumstances, it became necessary to go beyond the simple statute "Do not steal" to take into account such things as time of day and the value of what had been stolen.

21:1—23:19. nature of the book of the covenant. The law code found in Exodus 21—23 is referred to as the "book of the *covenant" and is probably the oldest example of *casuistic law in the Bible. It deals with a wide variety of legal situations (slavery, theft, adultery) and tends to impose fairly harsh sentences (nine require execution), many of which are based on the principle of lex talionis, "an eye for an eye." The laws anticipate the range of life situations that would be faced in the village culture of the settlement and early monarchy period. They regulate business, marriage practice and personal responsibility. Their tone is less theological than the law collections in Leviticus and Deuteronomy.

21:2. Hebrew. The term *Hebrew* is used to designate an Israelite who has become landless and destitute. Although this person may be forced to sell himself or his family into debt slavery, he retains his rights as a member of the community and cannot be held in perpetual servitude. He is to be released, debt-free, after six years of labor.

21:2-6. debt slavery. Because of the fragile nature of the environment in much of the ancient Near East, farmers and small landowners often found themselves in debt. Their problems could magnify if a drought and resulting poor harvests continued over more than one year, and they could be forced to sell their land and property and eventually even their family and themselves. Israelite law takes this situation into account by providing a fair period of labor service to the creditor as well as a time limit on servitude for the debt slave. No one could serve more than six years, and when they were freed they went out debt-free. This would have been a good solution for some, but without their land to return to, many may have chosen to remain in the service of their creditor or to move to the cities to find jobs or join the military.

21:2-6. slave laws compared to ancient Near East. Israelite slave laws tend to be more humane than those found elsewhere in the ancient Near East. For instance, no slave could be kept in perpetual servitude without the permission of the slave. Escaped slaves did not have to be returned to their masters. In Mesopotamia a slave (generally obtained through warfare) could be freed by his master or he could purchase his freedom. Hammurabi's laws set a time limit of three years on a debt slave, compared to six years in Exodus 21:2. Slaves were not given equal rights, and their punishment for injuring a free man was much more severe than if a free man injured him.

21:5-6. ear pierced on doorpost. Entrance ways are sacred and legally significant spots. When a slave chose to remain in slavery in order to preserve a family that he had established while in servitude, it would be appropriate to bring him to his master's doorway and then symbolically attach the slave to that place by driving an awl through his earlobe into the doorpost. It is possible that a ring was then placed on the ear to mark him as a perpetual slave.

21:7-11. sale of daughter into slavery. When a daughter was sold into slavery by her father, this was intended both as a payment of debt and as a way of obtaining a husband for her without a dowry. She has more rights than a male in the sense that she can be freed from slavery if her master does not provide her with food, clothing and marital rights. Selling children into slavery is attested across Mesopotamia in nearly every time period.

21:10. minimum provision. Since perpetual slavery was generally reserved for foreigners and prisoners of war, those persons who sold themselves into slavery because of debt were protected by law from being abused by their creditors. The law determines that six years is sufficient to pay off any debts and that the debt slave is to be released in the seventh year (a clear parallel with the seven-day creation cycle). *Hammurabi's law requires that a debt slave be released after three years of service, thus providing a Mesopotamian precedent for this procedure.

21:10-11. wife's provisions. Provision for a woman in one's charge throughout the ancient Near East consisted of food, clothing and oil. The third in the series here (NIV: "marital rights") is an attempt to translate a word that occurs only here in the Old Testament. The frequent occurrence of "oil" in that position in numerous ancient Near Eastern documents has led some to suspect that the word in the Hebrew text might also be an obscure term for oil (compare Hos 2:7; Eccles 9:7-9).

21:12. capital punishment. Capital punishment is required in those cases where the culprit is a threat to the well-being and the safety of the community. Thus murder, disrespect for parents (abuse), adultery and false worship are capital crimes, because they injure persons and corrupt the fabric of society. The principle involved assumes that leniency would encourage others to commit these crimes. Stoning is the usual form of execution. In this way no one person is responsible for the culprit's death, but the entire community has participated in the elimination of evil.

21:13. place of sanctuary. In those instances where unintentional homicide is committed, the person involved is given a chance to claim sanctuary in an appointed place, usually an altar or a shrine (see Num 35:12; Deut 4:41-43; 19:1-13; Josh 20). This protects him from the deceased's family and gives the authorities time to hear witnesses and make a judgment. The continued grant of sanctuary would then depend on whether the killing was judged a murder or an accidental death. Eventually, the number of places of sanctuary had to be increased as the size of the nation grew.

21:15, 17. cursing parents. Contrary to the NIV translation, studies have demonstrated that the infraction here is not cursing but treating with contempt. This is a more general category and would certainly include the prohibition of 21:15 that forbids striking a parent and would be the opposite of the fifth commandment to "honor your father and your mother" (20:12). Each injunction is designed to protect the cohesion of the family unit as well as insure that each subsequent generation provide their parents with the respect, food and protection they deserve (see Deut 21:18-21). Mesopotamian law codes and legal documents are also clear on the issue of treating parents with contempt. The *Sumerian laws allow a son who disowns his parents to be sold as a slave. *Hammurabi requires the amputation of the hand of a man who strikes his father. A will from *Ugarit describes a son's behavior using the same verb used in this verse and stipulates disinheritance.

21:16. kidnapping (slave trade). Kidnapping occasionally occurred because of the failure to pay a debt, but more often it was simply a part of the illicit slave trade. Mesopotamian and biblical law both require the death penalty for this crime. Such a harsh penalty reflects concern for individual freedom as well as protection against the raiding of weak households.

21:18-19. personal injury laws compared to ancient Near East. Liability for personal injury done as a result of a quarrel and not due to premeditated action is similar in the Bible and the codes of the ancient Near East. In both cases the injured party is entitled to compensation for medical expenses. There are some additions to this provision in each of the codes. The Exodus passage hinges on whether the injured person recovers enough to walk without a staff. *Hammurabi deals with the subsequent death of the injured person and the fine to be paid, based on social status. The *Hittite code requires that a man be sent to manage the injured person's house until he recovers.

21:20-21. human rights (slave as property). The basic human right to life means that no death can go unpunished. Thus when a slave's owner beats him to death, an unspecified penalty is imposed. Such an assurance of punishment is designed to prevent such extreme abuse. However, there is no penalty if the slave recovers from his beating. The assumption is that the owner has the right to discipline his slaves, since they are his property. Their human rights are restricted, in this respect, because of their status.

21:22. miscarriage. Several ancient law codes include this statute penalizing a man for causing a woman to have a miscarriage. The variation between them generally depends on the status of the woman (*Hammurabi's laws indicate a small fine for injuring a slave woman; *Middle Assyrian laws specify a large fine, fifty lashes and a month's labor service for injuring a citizen's daughter), or the intent behind the injury (*Sumerian laws prescribe a fine for accidental injury and impose a much larger fine for deliberate injury). The Exodus law hinges on whether there is any further harm to the mother beyond the loss of the fetus and imposes a fine based on the claim of the husband and the pronouncement of the judges. The object of the fine is to compensate for the injury to the mother rather than the death of the fetus. However, Middle Assyrian law demands compensation for the death of the fetus with another life.

21:23-25. lex talionis. The legal principle of lex talionis, "an eye for an eye," is based on the idea of reciprocity and appropriate retaliation (see Lev 24:10-20). Ideally, when an injury is done to another person, the way to provide true justice is to cause an equal injury to the culprit. Although this may seem extreme, it in fact limits the punishment which can be inflicted on the person accused of the injury. It cannot exceed the damage done. Since most personal liability laws involve the payment of a fine rather than a retaliatory body injury, it is most likely that the talion statement is a desig-

nated limit on compensation, with a value assigned to each item injured (see the laws of *Eshnunna, which set fines for the nose, finger, hand and foot). The talion is also found in its basic form in *Hammurabi's code 196-97, but the laws following that section contain variations based on the social status (free or slave or member of nobility) of the persons involved. In most cases the talion is applied when there is premeditated intent to do harm.

21:22-36. personal liability. There is a great emphasis placed on personal liability in the ancient Near East. In order to protect the person and that person's ability to work, very detailed statutes are written to deal with every conceivable injury done by human hand or by a person's property. The classic example is the case of the goring ox. In addition to Exodus, it is found in the laws of *Eshnunna and *Hammurabi, where the penalty for allowing a known gorer to run loose is a fine. The biblical example, however, requires that both the ox and his owner be stoned to death. Similar laws involving failure of an owner to deal with a known danger, include vicious dogs (Eshnunna), building code violations (Eshnunna; Ex 21:33-34), and injury to valuable animals by another animal or a human (*Lipit-Ishtar; Hammurabi—veterinary malpractice). Generally, these crimes are punishable by fines based on the degree of injury and the value of person or animal injured.

21:26-36. penalties for personal liability. The penalties imposed in cases of personal liability generally depend on who or what was injured. If a slave owner abuses his slaves to the point that he mutilates them—destroying an eye or knocking out a tooth—then the slave is freed in compensation. In cases where a death occurs, the circumstances decide the punishment. If an owner is aware of a dangerous situation and fails to do anything, then his life is forfeited if someone is killed due to his negligence. Similarly, if valuable animals are harmed or destroyed, then the owner who is responsible must provide equal compensation. There is latitude in the law, however, in cases where an owner is unaware of a potential danger and is thus not fully responsible for loss or injury.

22:1-4. theft in the ancient Near East. Theft can be defined as appropriation of goods or real property without legal consent. The number and specificity of the laws regarding theft in the ancient Near East suggest that it was a real problem. There are cases of burglary (22:2-3; *Hammurabi), robbery (Hammurabi), looting during a fire (Hammurabi), and use of property or natural resources without permission (e.g., illegal grazing in 22:5 and Hammurabi). The "paperwork-oriented" Mesopotamian culture placed a great deal of importance on contracts, bills of sale and the corroboration of witnesses to the sale (Hammurabi). These business practices, which were designed to prevent fraud, are also mentioned in the biblical text, but more often in narrative (Gen 23:16; Jer 32:8-15) than in the law codes. There are also instances where an oath is taken in cases where physical evidence is unavailable or responsibility for loss is uncertain (22:10-13; Hammurabi). In this way, God is solicited as a witness and the person taking the oath is laying himself open to divine justice.

22:1-4. penalties for theft. Prescribed punishments for theft vary based on the identity of the owner and the value of the property stolen. In *Hammurabi's laws the death penalty is required for persons who steal from the temple or the palace. However, this is reduced to a fine of thirty times the value of the property stolen if the victim is a government or temple official and ten times the value for property of a citizen. This same law imposes the death penalty for a thief who fails to pay the fine. Exodus 22:3 tempers this by having the thief sold as a slave to compensate for the loss. These penalties, with their heavy fines or death sentences, suggest how seriously the society took this crime.

22:2-3. burglary. It is assumed that people have a right to defend themselves and their property from theft. Thus when a burglar enters a house at night and is killed by the homeowner, this is considered a case of self-defense (for instance in *Ur-Nammu's laws). That changes, however, if the break-in occurs during the day, because the homeowner could more clearly see the degree of threat and could call for help. *Hammurabi's laws add a symbolic deterrent to its burglary injunction by having the body of an executed burglar walled up in the hole he had dug in the mud-brick wall of his intended victim.

22:5-15. property liability. In most cases, liability for property damage or loss was based on circumstances or contracts. Restitution was generally based on the loss of real property (animals, grain, fruit) or the loss of productivity, if fields or orchards were damaged or taken out of production. There was also a clear sense of responsibility in cases based on negligence. Examples include the unchecked spread of fire, rampaging animals or the failure to maintain dams or irrigation systems. In each of these cases the person who allowed dangerous defects to persist or who did not keep a rein on the movement of his animals was re-

quired to pay restitution for any loses incurred (as in *Hammurabi and *Ur-Nammu). Not all loss was covered, however. In some cases, claims for loss were dismissed due to unforeseeable events or because they were included in rental agreements (22:13, 15).

22:5-15. penalties for property liability. Since loss of or damage to property can be computed in real terms, penalties in cases involving property liability were designed to provide just restitution of monetary value. According to the biblical statutes, this would sometimes be left up to the judges to determine. In other cases a set amount of double the value of the lost item is imposed. There is more specificity in the Mesopotamian codes, where the exact nature of the damage to a rental animal is listed with the appropriate compensation (as in *Lipit-Ishtar) and the exact amount of grain per acre in a flooded field is prescribed (*Hammurabi).

22:16. marriage pledge. Families negotiated marriage contracts that provided a bride price from the groom's family and a dowry from the bride's household. Once the couple was betrothed or pledged to each other, they were considered legally bound to the contract. Thus the penalty for rape depended on whether the woman was (1) a virgin and (2) pledged to be married.

22:16-17. bride price. The groom's household paid the bride price as part of the marriage agreement. This price would vary based on whether the woman was a virgin or had been married before. In this case the price for a virgin is required even though she has been raped.

22:16-17. premarital sex perspective. Premarital sex was discouraged for several reasons: (1) it usurped the authority of the father to arrange the marriage contract, (2) it diminished the potential value of the bride price, and (3) it prevented the husband from being assured that his first child was indeed his offspring. This law regulated illicit premarital sex by imposing a forced marriage on the culprit and/or a fine equal to the bride price for a virgin. In this way the father would be spared the embarrassment and loss of revenue when negotiating a contract for a daughter who is no longer a virgin.

22:18. sorceress. Practitioners of magic were outlawed on pain of death within the Israelite community (see Lev 19:31; 20:27). Each law concerning them is in *apodictic or command form. This total intolerance may be due to their association with Canaanite religion or simply because their arts represented a challenge to God's supremacy over creation.

22:19. bestiality. Also written in command form are the laws forbidding sexual relations with animals (see Lev 21:15-16; Deut 17:21). Bestiality, like homosexuality, violates the basic injunction to be fruitful and multiply (Gen 1:28; 9:1). It also blurs the categories of creation by intermixing species. Such acts are also forbidden in the *Hittite laws.

22:21. vulnerability of aliens. The injunction to protect the "alien" is always based on the remembrance of the exodus and the alien status of the Israelites before they settled in Palestine (see Deut 24:17-22). It is also based on the image of God as the ultimate protector of the weak—whether that be the entire nation or the most vulnerable members of society. Humane treatment of aliens follows the spirit of the hospitality code, but it also recognizes a class of persons who are not citizens and who could be subject to discrimination or abuse if special provision were not made for them.

22:22-24. vulnerability of orphans. Orphans, aliens and widows formed the three classes of powerless persons in ancient society. God took special care of these people because of their basic vulnerability, requiring that they not be oppressed and cursing those who did oppress with the threat of becoming orphans themselves. The frequency of war, famine and disease insured that there would always be a large number of orphans. Although they could contribute to the general work force, they would have had to be adopted for them to inherit property or to learn a skill as an apprentice (as in *Hammurabi's laws).

22:22-24. vulnerability of widows. Like aliens and orphans, widows were often dependent on charity for survival. All three groups needed protection under the law because they were powerless to protect themselves. They were allowed to glean in fields, orchards and vineyards (Deut 24:19-21), and they retained their dignity as a protected class through divine statute. They could not inherit their husband's property, and their dowry would have been used to support their children (as in *Hammurabi's laws). In some cases they were owed levirate obligation by their deceased husband's family (see Deut 25:5-10; *Hittite laws), but otherwise they would be forced to seek employment or attempt to arrange a new marriage (see Ruth).

22:22-24. treatment of vulnerable classes. Based on the statements in the prologues of the *Ur-Nammu code and the Code of *Hammurabi, it is clear that kings considered it part of their role as "wise rulers" to protect the rights of the poor, the widow and the orphan. Similarly, in the Egyptian *Tale of the Eloquent Peasant,* the plaintiff begins by identifying his judge as "the father of the orphan, the husband of the widow." Individual statutes (seen in several Middle *Assyrian laws) protect a widow's right to remarry and provide for her when her husband is taken prisoner and presumed dead. In this way the vulnerable classes are provided for throughout the ancient Near East. Only the "alien" is not specifically mentioned outside the Bible. This is not to say that hospitality codes did not apply elsewhere, but this category is tied in the Bible to the unique exodus experience.

22:25. charging interest. Two principles are evident in the restriction on charging interest on loans: (1) a village-based, agricultural people realize they must depend on each other to survive, and (2) interest payments are a phenomenon of the city-based merchants with whom farmers sometimes had to deal and who were not concerned with the village community (see Hos 12:7-8). Thus to maintain their sense of the equality of all Israelites and to prevent growing antagonism between rural and urban citizens (see Neh 5:7, 10-11 and Ezek 22:12 for violations of the law), charging interest of Israelites had to be outlawed (see Lev 25:35-38; Deut 23:19). Only loans to non-Israelites could accrue interest (Deut 23:20). This stands in contrast to the more familiar business practices employed elsewhere and to the systematic listing of interest that can be charged on loans in the laws of *Eshnunna and *Hammurabi.

22:25. moneylending practices. Just as is the case today, farmers, craftsmen and businessmen borrowed amounts from moneylenders to finance the next year's planting, an expanded working area or a new business venture. All of these loans were made at interest, and, if the law codes are to be taken as community standards, the interest rates were set by law. The laws of *Eshnunna provide technical details on the rate of exchange on interest payments in either barley or silver. The produce of a field could be given as collateral on a loan (*Hammurabi), but if a natural disaster occurred, provision was made to cancel interest payments (Hammurabi). To prevent fraudulent practices, moneylenders were not allowed to harvest fields or orchards to claim what was owed to them. Instead the owner did the harvesting and thus insured that only the proper amount was paid; interest could not exceed 20 percent (Hammurabi).

22:26-27. cloak as pledge. Day laborers regularly pledged their garment as collateral against a full day's work. In many cases it was their only extra covering besides their loincloth. Thus the law requires it to be returned at the end of the day so that they are not left without protection against the night's chill (see Deut 24:12-13; Amos 2:8). If it were not returned to them, they would have to give up their free status and sell themselves as slaves. A late-seventh-century B.C. Hebrew inscription from Yavneh-Yam contains a plea by a field worker that his garment had been unjustly taken. He asks that his rights and his free status be returned to him along with the robe.

22:28. blasphemy of God or ruler. The Hebrew here allows for a translation of either "God" or "the judges," neither of whom should be ignored or slighted. Both judges and rulers (a chieftain was elected by the elders and certified in the position by God prior to the monarchy) were to be respected. Failure to do so cast doubt on the authority of the elders and God to chose a ruler and thus was punishable by death (see 2 Sam 19:9; 1 Kings 21:10). Blasphemy, the rejection of God's divine presence and power, is also a capital offense (Lev 24:15-16).

22:29. offerings from granaries. Cities stored the harvest in huge, stone-lined granary pits, and villagers had smaller versions cut out of the native limestone near their houses. A portion of every harvest was to be set aside as an offering to God. This injunction reminds the people to provide that offering before they filled and sealed their storage containers.

22:29. sacrifice of firstborn. The common belief was that fertility could be assured only if the firstborn of the flock and of every family was sacrificed to God (see 13:2; Lev 27:26). Israelite religion forbade human sacrifice, substituting an animal in place of the child (see Gen 22), and the service of the Levites in place of the dedicated firstborn (Num 3:12-13).

22:30. eighth day. The requirement that animals not be taken from their mothers and sacrificed until the eighth day after birth (see Lev 22:27) may be (1) a parallel with the *circumcision of sons on the eighth day (Gen 17:12), (2) a sign of humane treatment of animals or (3) an attempt to key sacrifice to the completion of a seven-day creation cycle.

22:31. meat from dead animal. As a sign that they are "set apart" as a people of God, the Israelites are restricted from eating food which may ritually contaminate them. Thus an animal that has been killed by other beasts may not be eaten because of the contact of the flesh with predators, which may be impure, and the uncertainty that its blood has been completely drained (see Lev 17:15).

22:31. dogs. Packs of feral dogs are often associated with eating carrion (Ps 59:6; 1 Kings 14:11). They scavenged in the streets and in the refuge piles on the outskirts of towns and villages. Dogs are often identified as impure, and the word is used in taunting an enemy or taking an oath (1 Sam 17:43; 2 Sam 16:9).

23:1-9. preserving integrity in justice system. Any justice system is subject to abuse when its officials are corrupt. To preserve the integrity of the legal process in Israel, judges are admonished to provide equal justice to all, not execute judgment on the guiltless and not take bribes. Witnesses are warned against giving false testimony and thus contributing to the conviction of the innocent. All Israelites are reminded of their responsibility to help their neighbor and to treat the alien with hospitality and fairness. In this way persons will feel confident in speaking to judges and can be assured of getting a fair hearing. Additionally everyone can rest easier knowing that their person and their property are the concern of all citizens.

23:1-9. vulnerability of the poor in ancient Near East. Because most cultures of the ancient Near East were class conscious, the poor were not always treated with the same equity as the rich and powerful. *Hammurabi did describe himself as a "devout, god-fearing prince" who brought justice to the land and protected the weak, but there are sufficient suggestions of abuse in the law codes and in wisdom literature to suggest that all was not well. The Egyptian *Teachings of Amenemope* includes admonitions against stealing from the poor, cheating the cripple and poaching on a widow's field. The speech of the "eloquent peasant" (Middle Kingdom Egypt, 2134-1786 B.C.) reminds a magistrate that he is to be a father to the orphan and a husband to the widow.

23:8. bribes in ancient world. Bribes include any income which is acquired by government officials and judges through illegal means. They are generally received in support of a legal claim and are designed to influence the decision on that claim. Because this is a subversion of justice, this practice is universally and officially condemned in the ancient world. The Code of *Hammurabi disbars a judge who changes a sealed judgment, and Hammurabi's royal correspondence refers to the punishment of an official who received a bribe. The biblical text includes legal prohibitions (23:8; Deut 16:19), and bribery of judges is condemned in the prophets (Is 1:23; Mic 3:11).

23:10-11. fallow year. Leaving the land fallow in the seventh year follows the pattern of the creation story and God's rest on the seventh day. It is likely that Israelite farmers set aside as fallow one-seventh of their fields each year rather than leaving all of their land fallow for an entire year. In Mesopotamia fields were left fallow even more frequently to limit the impact of the salt in the water used for irrigation. The practice also helps to prevent exhaustion of the nutrients in the soil. The social welfare aspect of the law (more directly explained in Lev 25:1-7, 18-22; see comments there) provides one more expression of concern for the poor.

23:13. invoking the names of other gods. In making sacrifices and participating in everyday activities like plowing or building a house, it was common practice in the ancient Near East to invoke the name of a god to bless their actions. To prevent the Israelites from practicing polytheism, it was necessary to ban the use of the names of other gods or to acknowledge their existence (see 20:3). Only Yahweh could be called upon for help and blessing.

23:15. Feast of Unleavened Bread. The Feast of Unleavened Bread signals the beginning of the barley harvest (March-April). Unleavened bread was made from the newly harvested grain and celebrated as the first sign of coming harvests that year. What was probably originally a Canaanite agricultural celebration was associated with the exodus and the Passover festival by the Israelites.

23:16. Feast of Harvest. This second of the three harvest festivals comes seven weeks after the harvest of the early grain (34:22; Deut 16:9-12) and is better known as the Feast of Weeks or Pentecost. In the agricultural cycle it marks the end of the wheat harvest season, and by tradition it is tied to the giving of the law on Mount Sinai. It is also associated with *covenant renewal and pilgrimage. Celebration includes the bringing of a "wave offering" of two loaves of bread and a basket of ripe fruit in thanksgiving for a good harvest.

23:16. Feast of Ingathering. The final harvest of the year occurred in the autumn prior to the onset of the rainy season and marked the beginning of a new agricultural year. At this time the last of the ripening grain and fruits were gathered and stored. The seven-day event is also known as the Feast of Tabernacles and is symbolized by the construction of booths for the harvesters. The festival was tied into Israelite tradition as a commemoration of the wilderness wanderings. It was also the occasion for the dedication of Solomon's temple in Jerusalem (1 Kings 8:65).

23:17. pilgrimage obligation. The require-

ment that all Israelite families (see Deut 16:11, 14) appear before God at the temple three times a year is tied to the agricultural calendar and the three major harvest festivals: Feast of Unleavened Bread, Feast of Harvest and Feast of Ingathering. This religious obligation would have been the occasion for fairs, the adjudication of legal disputes, the contracting of marriages and the rites of purification for those who had been physically or spiritually contaminated.

23:18. no yeast mixed in blood sacrifice. Yeast and leavened dough were strictly prohibited from use in animal sacrifice. This is based on the association of yeast with the process of corruption. Sacrificial blood, associated with life, might therefore be debased or corrupted if brought into contact with leaven.

23:18. handling of fat. The fatty portions of the animal sacrifice which were attached to the stomach and intestines were reserved for God's portion (29:12-13; Lev 3:16-17). They were not to be saved or put aside for the night, because they, like blood, contained the essence of life.

23:19. first fruits. The first produce of the harvest, associated with the Feast of Harvest, was to be brought to God as a sacrifice. This represented both thanksgiving as well as a symbolic portion of what was to come in the autumnal harvest (see Deut 26:2-11).

23:19. goat in mother's milk. The prohibition against cooking a young goat (perhaps symbolic of all young animals) in its mother's milk has been interpreted as a reaction against Canaanite or other foreign religious practices (see 34:26 and Deut 14:21). The regular birth of goats near the Feast of Ingathering and their inclusion in celebratory meals may be the basis of this law. It may also be based on an injunction to treat animals humanely, since an animal still nursing may have mother's milk in its stomach. There is also the consideration that mother's milk contains blood and would therefore corrupt either sacrificial meat or meals.

23:20-33
Bringing Israel to the Land

23:20. angel preparing way. The promise of an angel preparing the way for the people follows the narrative pattern of divine presence and guidance that is first set by the pillar of cloud and the pillar of fire in the exodus event (13:21-22).

23:21. my Name is in him. The "messenger" or angel sent by God is an extension of God himself, representing a continuous presence with the people of Israel. Since names and naming (see Gen 2:19; 17:5) were considered powerful in the ancient world (see 9:16; Lev 19:12), to say that Yahweh has invested his Name in this angel is to say that it is to be obeyed just as God is to be obeyed. All of God's presence and power is to be found in this messenger. He is to be trusted to do what God has promised.

23:23. peoples of Canaan. The list of peoples who inhabit Canaan is representative of the diverse ethnic character of that area. Because Canaan serves as a land bridge between Mesopotamia and Egypt, it has always attracted settlers from many different groups.

23:24. sacred stones. Among the objects that were erected at cultic sites in Canaan were altars, sacred poles and sacred stones. The latter were huge standing stones that represented the power of a local god. They occur alone as well as in groups.

23:28. hornet. The term which is translated "hornet" (see Deut 7:20; Josh 24:12) may be a form of divine "terror" like the plagues in Egypt. Egyptian and *Assyrian texts and reliefs portray the god as a winged disk terrifying the enemy before the arrival of their own armies. It may also be a pun based on its similarity to the word for Egypt (*zirah* and *mizraim*) and thus reflect Yahweh's use of Egyptian military campaigns in Canaan that weakened the area and made the Israelite settlement possible.

23:31. borders of the land. The limits of the Promised Land are set at the Red Sea (Gulf of Aqaba) or the border of Egypt to the southwest, the coast of the Mediterranean Sea on the west, and the Euphrates River and Mesopotamia on the east. At no time, even during Solomon's reign, did the nation actually include this much territory. However, given an ideal image, which includes all of the land between the two superpowers of the time, these borders are logical.

24:1-18

Ratification of Covenant

24:1. seventy elders. These men are the appointed representatives of the tribes. Their place here with Moses, Aaron and Aaron's sons is as *covenantal representatives. Their voice, like their number (seventy), stands for the nation as a whole accepting the covenant.

24:4. writing. Evidence of writing systems does not appear until about 3100 B.C. in the ancient Near East. Both Egyptian hieroglyphic and Mesopotamian *cuneiform scripts were

syllabic and complex, thus creating the need for professional scribes who would read and write for the illiterate majority. The earliest examples of alphabetic script in the world are found in the region of Sinai (Serabit el-Khadim) during the mid-second millennium (these inscriptions are designated proto-Sinaitic; the Canaanite counterparts are called proto-Canaanite). Every alphabet in the world derives from this early script. The invention of alphabetic writing dramatically increased the literacy rate. Writing was used from its inception for business documents, treaties, histories, literature and religious works. The medium for writing was baked clay tablets in Mesopotamia and papyrus scrolls in Egypt. Monumental inscriptions were carved into stone in both areas. Unfortunately most of the documents written on papyrus or animal skins have decayed or been destroyed over the centuries. Writing something down was not only a way of preserving the memory of a transaction but also represented the conclusion of a treaty or *covenant (as in the case of this verse), and the act itself initiated the terms of the agreement.

24:4. altar and twelve pillars. The erection of an altar and pillars is part of the *covenant-making ceremony. They represent the presence of God and the twelve Israelite tribes who have come together to solemnly pledge their allegiance to each other through written treaty and sacrificial act (see Gen 31:45-54 and Josh 24:27 for similar commemorative pillars).

24:5. fellowship offering. This type of offering fits well into a *covenant ceremony, since it is designed to be shared with the participants. Only a portion was completely burned on the altar while the rest served as a meal consummating the treaty agreement between the people and God.

24:6. sprinkling blood on the altar. Blood, as the essence of the life force, belongs to God the Creator. Thus the blood drained from sacrificial animals was nearly always poured back on the altar. In this way the people were reminded of the sanctity of life and the giver of life.

24:7. book of the covenant. A public reading of the terms of the *covenant was a part of every covenant-renewal ceremony (see Josh 24:25-27; 2 Kings 23:2; Neh 8:5-9). In this way the law which had been given to them was recited, acknowledged and put into effect from that point on for the people of Israel. A number of *Hittite treaties from this time also stipulate that the agreement should be read aloud periodically.

24:8. sprinkling blood on the people. The use

of sacrificial blood to sprinkle the people is unusual and occurs elsewhere only in the ordination ceremony of Aaron and his sons (Lev 8). A special bond is established through these symbolic acts marking the people as God's own. It may be that the twelve standing stones actually received the shower of blood, since they represented the people and could all be sprinkled at once.

24:10. saw the God of Israel. Seeing God face to face (a *theophany) is always described as dangerous (Gen 16:7-13; 28:16-17; 32:24-30; Judg 6:22-23). Here the representatives of the Israelites conclude the *covenant ceremony with a meal. God's presence, in this instance, however, raises no danger to them. They are there at God's bidding and under divine protection.

24:10. sapphire pavement. Since the blue gemstone sapphire was unknown in the ancient Near East, this richly decorated pavement was most likely made of lapis lazuli (brought by traders from Afghanistan) It was used to trim royal audience chambers and thrones (see Ezek 1:26). Some first-millennium Mesopotamian texts whose traditions are thought to go back to the Kassite period speak of three heavens. Each level of heaven is described as having a particular type of stone as its pavement. The middle heavens are said to be paved with *saggilmud*-stone, which has the appearance of lapis lazuli. This was believed to give the sky its blue color. The middle heavens were where most of the gods had their residence.

24:12. tablets of stone. It was common practice in the ancient Near East to record important documents, law codes and the heroic military campaign annals of kings on stone (see comment on 32:15-16 for more on stone tablets). The stone tablets given to Moses by God on Mount Sinai follow this pattern. Unfortunately, there is no certainty about what was written on them, although the tradition that it is the Ten Commandments is very old. The original tablets are destroyed (32:19) and then replaced by God (34:1). The second set were housed in the ark of the *covenant (Deut 10:5).

24:18. 40 as approximation? The number forty appears many times as a number of completion, signifying the passage of the appropriate amount of time: a generation (Gen 25:20), the age of a mature man (2:11), the period in the wilderness (16:35; Num 14:33), the rule of a judge or chief (Judg 3:11; 13:1). The regularity with which this symbolic number is used suggests it has both cultural and literary significance and is therefore not to be taken precisely in most instances.

25:1—27:21

The Tabernacle and Its Furniture

25:3. precious metals. Gold, silver and bronze represent the most important metals and alloys available to the Israelites in the premonarchic period. They were commodities of exchange and were used to fashion jewelry, cultic objects and incense altars. In this instance they represent the willingness of the people to contribute their most precious items to the construction and furnishing of the tabernacle.

25:4. colored yarns. Only the most precious items were to be used to decorate the tabernacle. Dyes, some made from the glandular fluid of sea mollusks and certain plants, were extremely expensive and were generally imported. The colors listed here are in descending order of expense and desirability: blue, purple, scarlet.

25:4. linen. Like other fabrics, the linen made from beaten flax was produced in various grades of fineness. Coarser linen was used for sailcloth, headgear and tunics. The term used here is for the "finest linen," which was used to garb Egyptian officials (Joseph in Gen 41:42) and in this case is to be used to furnish the tabernacle (see 26:31, 36; 38:9).

25:5. red dye. The tanning process is not often mentioned in the biblical text. It involved the use of lime, tree bark and plant juices, and required a ready water supply. In this case, it is possible that the ram skins were either tanned or dyed red or both through the manufacturing process.

25:5. sea cows (dolphins?). Both sea cows (a herbivorous mammal—dugong) and dolphins are found in the Red Sea, and their hides could have been tanned and used for decoration. These creatures had been hunted for their hides along the Arabian Gulf for millennia. This word may also be compared to an *Akkadian word which refers to a semiprecious yellow or orange stone and thus to the color of dye used.

25:5. acacia wood. A variety of desert tree found in the Sinai with extremely hard wood, suitable for use in the construction of the tabernacle and its furnishings. The word used here may be an Egyptian loan word, since acacia was widely used in Egypt.

25:6. anointing oil. The spices which were to be used for anointing purposes were myrrh, cinnamon, cane and cassia (see recipe in 30:23-25). Their purpose was to remove all trace of secular odors and to transform the interior of the tabernacle into a sanctuary suitable for worship and God's presence.

25:7. onyx stones. Although translated "onyx" here, the exact identity of this precious gemstone is unknown. It is also mentioned in Genesis 2:12 as native to the land of Havilah near or in the Garden of Eden. Among the possibilities for this engravable stone are lapis lazuli and onyx, a chalcedony with milky-white bands alternating with black.

25:7. ephod. A priestly vestment reserved for the high priest (see chap. 28). It is constructed of gold and elaborately decorated with gemstones and is attached to the breastplate and one of the priest's outer garments (28:25, 31). It is associated with both the authority of the high priest and the presence of Yahweh.

25:8. temple ideology. The temple was not a structure for corporate worship but a place for God to dwell in the midst of the people. It had to be maintained in holiness and purity so that God's continuing presence could be vouchsafed. The priests existed to maintain that purity and to control access. The temple idea was not invented so that there would be a place to offer sacrifices. Rather, several of the sacrifices existed as a means of maintaining the temple. God's presence was the most important element to preserve. The sacrifices such as the purification offering (see comment on Lev 4:1-3) and the reparation offering (see comment on Lev 5:14-16) were designed for that purpose.

25:10-22. the ark (size, design, function). The ark was a wooden box, open at the top, approximately 3 feet in length and 2 feet in both width and height based on eighteen inches to the cubit. It was overlaid inside and out with sheets of the finest gold and had four rings (also gold-covered) attached to the sides for the insertion of two gold-encrusted poles, which were used to carry the ark and to protect it from the touch of all but the high priest. A golden cover, decorated with two winged cherubim, sealed the ark, securing the tablets of the law within it. Its primary function was to store the tablets and to serve as a "footstool" for God's throne, thereby providing an earthly link between God and the Israelites. In Egypt it was common for important documents that were confirmed by oath (e.g., international treaties) to be deposited beneath the feet of the deity. The Book of the Dead even speaks of a formula written on a metal brick by the hand of the god being deposited beneath the feet of the god. Therefore the footstool/receptacle combination follows known Egyptian practice. In Egyptian festivals the images of the gods were often carried in procession on portable barques. Paintings portray these as boxes about the size of the ark carried on poles and decorated with or flanked by guardian creatures. A similar-sized chest with rings (for carrying with poles) was found in Tutankhamen's tomb.

25:10. cubit. The standard dimension for the Israelite cubit was measured from the elbow to the tip of the middle finger. Using the measure of the Siloam tunnel, which is described as 1,200 cubits, and its actual length of 1,732.6 feet, this places the length of the cubit as between 17.5 and 18 inches. Since no cubit markers have been discovered by archaeologists, the actual length of a cubit is still uncertain.

25:16. the testimony. This term refers to the tablets of the law which were given to Moses. It was common practice in the ancient Near East to house law codes in specially constructed containers to represent their presentation before deity.

25:17. the kapporet (size, design, function). The kapporet, "atonement cover," is a sheet of solid gold which served as the lid of the ark (with the same dimensions specified in the text), but because it appears as a separate item from the ark, it has special significance. Decorating the kapporet were two facing cherubim, whose uplifted wings nearly met above the ark and served to symbolically uphold the invisible throne of God. Thus with the ark as the "footstool" and the kapporet as the support for the throne, God's presence is demonstrated to the people.

25:18-20. cherubim. Biblical descriptions as well as archaeological discoveries (including some fine ivory pieces from Nimrud in Mesopotamia, Arslan Tash in Syria and Samaria in Israel) suggest the cherubim are composite creatures (having features of a number of different creatures, like the Egyptian sphinx), often four-legged animal-bodies with wings. The cherubim appear in ancient art with some regularity flanking the thrones of kings and deities. The combination of cherubim as throne guardians, chests as footstools and statements in the Old Testament concerning Yahweh being enthroned on the cherubim (e.g., 1 Sam 4:4) supports the concept of the ark as representing the invisible throne of Yahweh. The use of empty thrones was widespread in the ancient world. They were provided for use by deities or royal personages when they were present.

25:23-30. table of bread of the Presence. The table of the Presence was a gold-encrusted, four-legged table, also carried by poles slipped through rings on each side. It held the twelve loaves of "show bread" (see Lev 24:5-9), which were perpetually displayed and replaced at the end of each week.

25:31-40. lampstand. The seven-branched golden menorah, or lampstand, stood in the outer sanctum of the tabernacle opposite the table of the Presence. Although its dimensions are not given, the lampstand was to be hammered from a single block of gold. Its function was to illumine the sacred precinct, and only Aaron and his sons were allowed to tend it. Numerous reliefs and even mosaics of menorahs have been found from New Testament times, when it had come to be used as a symbol for Judaism and for eternal life, but it is generally believed that these do not take the same form as the menorah of the Old Testament period. The earliest representation of the menorah is on a coin from the first century B.C., which depicts a very plain-looking seven-branched lampstand with a sloping base. Some believe that the lampstand represented the Tree of Life—a popular symbol in artistic work.

26:1-6. linen curtains with cherub design. Of the four layers which cover the tabernacle, this is the innermost. It consists of ten multicolored sheets of fine linen, decorated with a cherubim design. Each sheet measures twenty-eight cubits by four cubits (42 feet by 6 feet). They are sewn together in paired sets of five, producing two longer sheets, which are in turn clipped together with blue loops and gold clasps (total measurement, 60 feet by 42 feet).

26:7-13. goat-hair curtains. The layer of goat-hair curtains served as a protective covering over the linen curtains that cover the tabernacle. Like the linen curtains, they consisted of eleven separate sheets sewn together and then connected with loops and bronze clasps (measuring 66 feet by 45 feet).

26:14. ram-skin covering. No measurement is given for this third layer covering the top of the tabernacle, which was made of tanned ram's skin. These two middle layers may serve the dual purpose of protecting the tabernacle and of symbolizing the two animals most important to the economy (sheep and goats).

26:14. sea cow covering. The progression of coverings over the tabernacle is from finest fabric to strongest leather, thus providing an impermeable seal to the sacred precinct within. No measurements are given for the fourth layer of "sea cow" or dolphin hide (this would have served best as waterproofing; see 25:5).

26:15-30. the frame. The skeletal structure which held up the drapes screening the tabernacle was made of acacia wood. It consisted of three walls of upright planks connected by tenons and crossbars, which were inserted into gold or silver-lined slots. The entire structure measured thirty cubits (45 feet) in length and ten cubits (15 feet) in height and width.

26:31-35. the veil. The veil curtained off a cube-shaped section of the tabernacle, creating an inner sanctum known as the Holy of Holies where the ark of the covenant was housed. It measured ten cubits (15 feet) on each side, was hung from four gold-inlaid posts standing in silver bases and was made of multicolored yarns and fine linen. A cherubim design was stitched into it, as on the innermost hanging over the tabernacle.

26:1-36. design, size and layout of tabernacle. The tabernacle was a rectangular structure (50 cubits wide and 100 cubits long, or 75 feet by 150 feet) divided into two equal, sacred squares (75 feet by 75 feet), comprising three separate zones of holiness: the holy of holies containing the ark; the holy place, outside the veil, which housed the lampstand, the altar of incense and the table of the bread of presence; and the outer court, where the sacrificial altar was placed. Both the ark and the sacrificial altar were located at the exact center of their respective sacred squares. The entrance to the outer court was located at the eastern end and was 20 cubits (35 feet) wide. The most sacred zones of the tabernacle (oriented on an east-west axis) could only be reached through the outer court. Portable structures of similar design (curtains hung over gold-gilded beams or poles) are found in Egypt as early as the mid-third millennium in both sacred and secular use. Egyptian royal tents of the nineteenth dynasty were a two-roomed tent with the outer chamber twice the length of the inner.

26:1-36. portable sanctuaries in ancient Near East. Although there is no evidence of a portable sanctuary quite as elaborate as the tabernacle, it is clear that Bedouin groups (both ancient and modern) do carry sacred objects and portable altars with them from one encampment to another. Ancient Near Eastern texts also describe the itineraries of priestly processions that took the images of gods, along with their various divine accoutrements, from one town to another within a kingdom. This allowed the god to visit shrines, make inspection tours of facilities owned by the principal temple community and participate in annual festivals outside the capital. Canaanite religious texts also speak of pavilions used for the dwelling of the gods. Archaeologists have found the remains of a Midianite tent shrine at Timnah that dates to the twelfth century B.C. It too was composed of curtains draped over poles, though it was not portable.

26:1-36. direct axis design of sanctuaries. The architectural symmetry of ancient sanctuaries suggests the importance placed in antiquity on the geometry of sacred space. The divine being was considered the center of power in the universe. Therefore the sanctuary, at least symbolically, should reflect this central role by mapping the sacred precinct into zones of progressive holiness and placing both the altar and the object associated with the god's presence at the exact center of the most holy spot within the sanctuary. In this way a nexus of power and majesty was created that made the prayers, sacrifices and invocations to the god more effective. Temples are typically classified by archaeologists on the basis of the arrangement of the chambers through which one gains access to the inner recesses and by the orientation of the main chamber, where the presence of the god is represented. "Direct axis" architecture allowed one to walk in a straight line from the altar to the inner shrine (cella). "Bent axis" required a ninety-degree turn between the altar and the place where the image stood. The door through which one entered the rectangular cella in the direct access arrangement could either be on the short wall ("long room") or the long wall ("broad room"). The tabernacle was of the "direct axis" style, but it was neither long room nor broad room because the holy of holies (cella) was square, not rectangular.

27:1-8. altar. The altar was the place for the burning of sacrifices. Because it had to be portable, it was constructed as a hollow square (5 cubits by 5 cubits; 3 cubits high) made from acacia logs, with horns at each corner, and overlaid with a bronze sheath and a bronze grate. A variety of utensils (firepans, shovels, meat forks and sprinkling bowls) were used in dealing with sacrificial meat and ash. Like the ark it had attached rings and poles for easy transport. Although not as sacred as the ark, the altar also served as a touch point with God, placed at the I-axis of the outer court of the tabernacle. Its service was restricted to Aaron's priestly family, and its function tied the people to the *covenant promise of fertility and the Promised Land. Through sacrifice the people acknowledged the bounty provided by God. Thus the altar brought them into communion with the power that protected and blessed them.

27:9-19. courtyard. Temple architecture demands that the most sacred precincts be separated from the profane world of everyday life by an area of enclosed space—in the case of the tabernacle, by the courtyard. This area was marked off by linen screen walls (7 feet high),

enclosing an area of approximately 11,250 square feet (100 cubits by 50 cubits). Since the inner portion of the tabernacle was fifteen feet high, these walls only screened the view from ground level and left the symbol of God's presence clearly visible. The draperies of the courtyard were held up by fifty-six columns placed in copper sockets. The use of these less valuable materials is reflective of the progression from precious to commonplace in the construction of the tabernacle.

27:21. the tent of meeting. Aaron and his sons are to place olive oil lamps before the "tent of meeting," which was the "holy place" immediately outside the veil separating that area from the Holy of Holies. Here God's presence was to be made manifest to Moses, and instruction was to be given to the people through these oracular messages (see 39:32; 40:2, 6, 29). The function of this space is therefore symbolic as well as utilitarian. The presence of God is acknowledged with the perpetually burning lamps. Aaron's servicing of the lamps provides a role for the priestly community here, and the assumption of guidance, first promised to Moses and thus to the people, is implicit in its name.

27:20-21. continually burning lamps. The clearest refined olive oil was to be used to provide a perpetual light before the entrance to the Holy of Holies. These lamps, serviced by Aaron and his sons, symbolized the presence of God. The continuation of this priestly function is seen in 1 Samuel 3:3.

28:1-43
The Priests' Garments

28:1. priesthood. The creation of a professional priesthood is a mark of a maturing religious system. By singling out Aaron and his sons, God designates who is worthy to serve in the tabernacle and establishes a hereditary succession for future generations of high priests in Israel. Their lineage derives from the tribe of Levi and specifically through Aaron. Because their task will be to perform sacrifices for the people and officiate at major religious festivals, the priests have certain rights and responsibilities that no other Israelite will have. Special garments are worn only by priests. A portion of the sacrifice is set aside for them. They are not allowed to own land or to perform nonpriestly functions. They are held to a higher standard of obedience and are subject to swift punishment for failure to perform their duties or to provide the proper example to the people.

28:1. priests in ancient Near East. Every culture in the ancient Near East developed a priesthood. Only the Bedouin tribes did not set these individuals aside to perform priestly duties exclusively. Their role was to function as a part of a priestly community, serving temples, performing sacrifices, conducting religious services and staging festivals. Priests would have been educated within the temple from an early age, and their position in the priestly class was hereditary in some cases. They would have been among the few literate persons in their society and thus were relied upon to keep records of major events and tie them to the will of the gods. This process was known as *divination, and it, along with *ritual sacrifice, was the chief source of priestly power and authority. There was a distinctive hierarchy among priests—ranging from a chief priest, who sometimes rivaled the king in power, to midlevel individuals who performed daily *rituals and sacrifices, to musicians, and on down to temple servants, who performed the mundane housekeeping and custodial tasks necessary in any large community.

28:6-14. ephod. The most important of Aaron's priestly garments is the ephod, which was either a linen robe covering the upper body or a frontal piece attached to the shoulders and sashed at the waist. The use of all five colored yarns indicates its importance, as does the use of gold filigree and engraved stones. Placing the names of six tribes on each stone provided a continual reminder to all that he was representing the nation before God. The fact that the ephod is related to idols and false worship in later passages (Judg 17:5 and 8:24-27) suggests that it was a garment borrowed from Mesopotamian society—perhaps worn by priests or used to clothe idols. The breastpiece (28:15), the Urim and Thummim (28:30), and the ephod are used in *divination (1 Sam 23:9-11). Thus the high priest is clothed in garments that aid in the discernment of God's will.

28:15-30. breastpiece. Using a piece of the same multicolored linen as in the ephod, a nine-inch square pouch is created by doubling it over. This breastpiece is then securely attached to the ephod by means of gold braid and blue cords which attach to the rings on the breastpiece, the shoulder pieces of the ephod and the sash of the ephod. Embedded in gold settings on the breastpiece are twelve semiprecious stones in four rows of three stones (compare the list of precious stones in Ezek 28:13). Each stone is engraved with the name of one of the tribes of Israel and thus provides an additional reminder to all (in-

cluding God) of the priest's responsibility as the people's representative. In the pouch, lying against the priest's heart, are placed the Urim and Thummim. Both these objects and the breastpiece itself are to be used as oracular devices to discern God's will. In the ancient Near East stones (including gemstones of various sorts) were believed to have *apotropaic value (offering protection from spirit forces). A seventh-century B.C. *Assyrian handbook preserves a list of various stones and what they "do"—possibilities range from appeasing divine anger to preventing migraine headaches. One ritual text lists twelve precious and semiprecious stones that are to be used to make a phylactery to be worn as a necklace.

28:30. Urim and Thummim. Unlike most of the other objects in this passage, there is no mention of "making" the Urim and Thummim. This suggests that they were already in use prior to this time and now were to be housed in the breastpiece and used by the high priest (see Lev 8:8 and Deut 33:8). No description of these objects is found in Scripture, although traditions from the Hellenistic and later periods suggest they were markers whose appearance and presentation when cast like lots would determine God's will (see Num 27:21; 1 Sam 14:37-41 and 28:6). There is no negative character attached to the Urim and Thummim as there are to other divinatory practices, and they are never mentioned in passages describing non-Israelite worship or *ritual. Nevertheless the practice of posing yes-no questions to the gods (asking *oracles) is known throughout the ancient Near East. Particularly of interest are the *Babylonian *tamitu* texts, which preserve the answers to many oracular questions. Positive and negative stones (thought to be bright stones and dark stones) were also used widely in Mesopotamia in a procedure called psephomancy. In one *Assyrian text alabaster and hematite are specifically mentioned. The yes-no question would be posed and then a stone drawn out. The same color stone would have to be drawn out three times consecutively for the answer to be confirmed. *Urim* is the Hebrew word for "lights" and therefore would logically be associated with bright or white stones. One recent study has pointed out that hematite, because of its use for weights and seals, was termed the "truth stone" in *Sumerian. The Hebrew word Thummim could have a similar meaning.

28:31-35. robe. Under the ephod, the high priest was to wear a loose-fitting, pullover blue robe that fell almost to the ankles. The collar was reinforced to prevent tearing, and there were only armholes, no sleeves. The hem was richly decorated with embroidered pomegranates, and bells were attached between the pomegranates.

28:33-34. pomegranates. Pomegranates were embroidered around the hem of the priest's robe in blue, purple and scarlet thread. This fruit is commonly mentioned in narrative and songs (Num 13:23, 20:5; Song 4:3, 6:7) and was used in decorating Solomon's temple (1 Kings 7:18). They generally are symbolic of the fertility of the Promised Land. Pomegranates were also used for decoration of ritual accessories in *Ugarit.

28:33-35. gold bells. Tiny gold bells were attached to the priest's robe between the embroidered pomegranates. Their function was to signal the high priest's movements within the Holy of Holies. They reminded the priest to perform his duties exactly according to the law and indicated to the people that he was within the holy precinct.

28:36-38. engraved plate. As a continuous reminder of his special role as priest, an engraved golden plate with the words "Holy to the LORD" is attached to his turban. It would parallel the diadem in the king's crown as symbolizing his authority. The plate of office also placed responsibility for infractions on the person in charge of all *rituals.

28:38. bearing guilt. As the person in charge of all religious *rituals, it was important that the high priest took his office seriously. Thus an engraved plate was attached to his turban as a sign of his authority and as a signal to him that he would bear the blame and the punishment for any failure to obey the laws of *ritual and sacrifice.

28:39-41. tunic. The standard garment worn by both men and women in the biblical period was a linen tunic. Worn next to the skin, ankle length, with long sleeves, it provided protection from the sun and sometimes was embroidered or given a fancy hem by the wealthy (Gen 37:3 and 2 Sam 13:18-19) or by priests.

28:39. turban. The turban was made of linen and, according to Josephus, was nonconical in shape (*Antiquities of the Jews* 3.7.6). It may be assumed that the turban of the high priest would have been more elaborate then that of ordinary priests (28:40). It had the engraved plate attached to it and would have been more colorful.

28:42-43. linen undergarments. Unlike the common people, the priests were required to wear linen undergarments beneath their tunics in order to cover their genitals. Thus they would not expose their nakedness when climbing the altar stairs or cleaning around it.

Nudity, although common among Mesopotamian priests, was prohibited in Israelite practice.

29:1-46

Ordination Instructions

29:1-46. consecration ceremony. Having ordered the manufacture of the tabernacle, the ark, the altar and all the associated utensils and decorations, Moses now gives instruction about their consecration, and that of the priesthood, to the service of God. Moses functions as priest in orchestrating and performing the rituals of consecration, which will hereafter be handled by Aaron and his descendants. This is a seven-day *ritual designed to set precedents for the use of tabernacle and altar, the types of sacrifices that are to be made in these sacred precincts, and the role and privileges attached to the priests. One of the most significant items in the ritual is blood, which is the symbol of life and is sprinkled both on the altar and on the garments of the priests. Sacrificial items (wheat, cakes and oil) as well as animals are presented and burnt on the altar. In this way the tabernacle and altar are purified, preparing them for use. Some pieces of the meat are used for a wave offering and then set aside as the portion reserved for the priests. Throughout the ceremony the sense of continuity is drawn between the first consecration and all future priestly action.

29:2-3. fine wheat flour. The items used to consecrate the tabernacle, altar and priests are representative of the fertility of the land, the gifts of God to the people. The wheat flour used to make unleavened bread and cakes would be of finest quality and thus a fitting sacrifice by a people who were dependent on farming for most of their food.

29:2-3. cakes with oil. Wheat and olive oil were the chief cash crops of ancient Israel. By mixing them into a sacrificial cake, the people recognized the role of God in providing them with fertility each year. The sequence of offerings also signifies the seasonal events of planting and harvest and the agricultural festivals.

29:2-3. wafers spread with oil. The presentation of grain and meat offerings together signify the people's acceptance of the *covenant and the acknowledgment of God's role as the provider of fertility. While the significance of providing unleavened bread, cakes and wafers is not clear, it may represent either the standard baked goods of the time or items set aside for *ritual use.

29:4. wash with water. It would not be appropriate for the new priests to clothe themselves in their new sacral garments without first taking a ritual bath. They were to be fully immersed as a part of the consecration ceremony. After this only their hands and feet had to be washed before performing their duties (30:17-21).

29:5. waistband. Only the high priest has a specially designed and woven waistband to sash his garments. The lesser priests use ordinary sashes (29:9). This would be a mark of rank and would also serve the utilitarian function of keeping his robes bound when he had to bow or make sacrifices.

29:7. anointing. In this passage and in Leviticus 8:12, only the high priest was consecrated in his office by having his head anointed with oil. However, both Aaron and his sons are anointed in Exodus 30:30 and 40:15. Anointing their heads with oil would compare with the anointing of kings in later periods (1 Sam 10:1; 16:13). In both cases the oil would symbolize the gifts of God to the people and the responsibilities now laid on their leaders through this ceremony. In Israelite practice anointing was a sign of election and was often closely related to endowment by the Spirit. See the comment on Leviticus 8:1-9.

29:8-9. tunics, headbands, sashes. Aaron's sons, who will serve as lesser priests under their father, have less elaborate priestly garments. They have distinctive clothing which sets them aside from other Israelites, but their consecration does not involve as much ceremony, just as their duties will be less important than those of the high priest.

29:10, 15, 19. laying hands on animals. As each sacrificial animal is brought to the altar, it is necessary for the priests to examine it to make sure it is suitable. Once that is done, a symbolic certification *ritual is performed in which the priests lay their hands on the animal, taking responsibility for its death and the purpose for which it is sacrificed. Some would also suggest that this constitutes an affirmation of ownership. See comment on Leviticus 1:3-4 for discussion of various possibilities.

29:12. blood on the horns of the altar. The horns of the altar are specifically symbolic of the presence of God in any sacrificial act. By placing the blood of the sacrificed bull on the horns, the priests are acknowledging that presence, the power of the God who gives life, and purifying themselves of their sin (see comment on Lev 4:7).

29:12. blood at the base of the altar. The altar is the focal point of animal sacrifice. It is the platform associated with giving God his due. For it to be fully consecrated to this service its very roots (base) must be purified with the blood of the sin offering (v. 14).

29:13. fat parts burned. No portion of the bull was to be saved, since this was a sin offering. Thus the fatty parts as well as the kidneys and liver, which might have been used for *divination (as was the practice in Mesopotamia) or given to the participants, were instead to be burned on the altar.

29:14. other parts outside the camp. Impurities and waste were to be disposed of outside of the camp (see Deut 23:12-14). Since this bull had been used for a sin offering, its meat, hide and offal had become contaminated and thus could not be consumed or used in any way (see Lev 4:12).

29:14. sin offering. There are various kinds of sacrifices and offerings performed by the Israelites: generally for thanksgiving or expiation. A sin offering was designed to purify a person who had become unclean through contact with *impurity (physical or spiritual) or because of some event (nocturnal emission in Deut 23:10). It was also used in consecrating priests, since they were required to maintain an even higher standard of *purity than ordinary Israelites. The animals which were used in these *rituals received the sin and *impurity of the persons for whom they were sacrificed. Thus their entire substance was contaminated and could not be consumed or used to produce anything. Every portion of the sacrificed animal must be disposed of, with the organs and fat burnt on the altar and the flesh, hide and bones burned to ash outside the camp. This latter act prevented the people's habitation from becoming polluted. For more information see comment on Leviticus 4:1-3.

29:15-18. ram as a burnt offering. The first ram sacrificed in the *ritual of consecration is to be completely consumed by fire on the altar. Its carcass is cut up and washed so that it fits on top of the altar and retains no contaminating offal. Meat was precious to these pastoral people, but the ram and the bull, both symbols of fertility, must be totally destroyed so that the sacrificial offering to God is complete. There can be no holding back when the sacrifice is made in honor of God's power.

29:18. pleasing aroma. The gods of Mesopotamia could also be attracted to the smell of sacrifices (as in the *Gilgamesh flood story). However, additionally they had to consume the sacrifice to sustain themselves. In Israelite tradition, a "pleasing aroma" signified a proper sacrifice that would please God (see Gen 8:21). It becomes a technical term for a sacrifice acceptable to and accepted by God (compare Lev 26:31), not something he eats.

29:20. blood on earlobe, thumb, big toe. Just

as blood is used to make the altar fit for service, so too it is used to designate the faculties of the priest: to hear the word of God, perform sacrifices with his hands and lead the people to worship with his feet. There is also an element of purification of each of these abilities through the blood of expiation (compare Lev 14:14).

29:20. blood on sides of altar. The blood of the three sacrificial animals is used to care for the sins of the newly consecrated priests. By sprinkling the first ram's blood on the altar, they also acknowledge God's power to grant life and the significance attached to their service as well as their commitment as God's servants (compare 24:5-6).

29:21. sprinkling priests with blood and oil. Blood and oil are the chief elements of the sacrificial process. By sprinkling the priests and their garments with these items, the ordination ceremony is completed, and the priests are physically marked for service (compare the marking of the people as guarantors of the *covenant in 24:8) as well as purified.

29:22-25. wave offering. In the third stage of sacrificial *ritual, portions from the basket of cereal offerings and the ram of ordination are to be elevated as a "wave offering." It is more likely that the ungainly pile of sacrificial gifts was elevated rather than actually waved, since that act would be less likely to unbalance and/or drop the sacred items. The terminology used in the text is more appropriately rendered "elevation offering" and such treatment of offerings is likewise depicted in Egyptian reliefs. This gesture physically signifies that all sacrificial items derive from and belong to God. In this case the cakes and wafers are elevated and then burnt on the altar. However, the meat from the ram will be used as the basis for a *covenantal feast that Aaron and his sons will consume, unlike the first ram, which was totally burned. A precedent is also set here regarding which portions of the sacrifice belong to the priests (note that Moses takes his share since he serves as the officiating priest—v. 26).

29:26-28. parts of sacrifice as food for priests. Since the priests were restricted entirely to religious duties and they did not own land, they were sustained through a portion of the sacrifices brought to the altar. Certain portions, the breast and the leg of the ram, were set aside specifically for the priests. Because this food had been presented for sacrifice and offered up to God, only the priests were allowed to consume it. What they did not consume was for the same reason to be destroyed.

29:29-30. priestly garments hereditary. In this section, which interrupts the discussion of sacrificial meat, provision is made for the ordination of future generations of priests. The original high priestly vestments created for Aaron were to be passed on to his successor at Aaron's death. Thus when Aaron dies Moses strips his body of all of his sacral garments and in a seven-day *ritual invests them on Aaron's son Eleazer (Num 20:22-29).

29:31. cooked in a sacred place. Since the meat of the wave offering and presentation offering was now sacred, it could not be prepared in ordinary precincts. Thus it is taken into the courtyard of the tabernacle to be cooked. In this way sacred items retain their power and authority by only being used or dealt with in similarly sacred areas.

29:34. burning leftovers. Because of its sacred nature, the sacrificial meat which has been set aside for the nourishment of priests cannot be used for any other purpose or consumed by ordinary individuals. Thus the portion which is not immediately consumed must be destroyed by fire to prevent any misuse of sacred substance.

29:36-37. making atonement. Basic to the transformation process that the sacrificial altar undergoes is the idea of purification. No item made by humans can, by definition, be pure enough to be used for God's service. Only through a lengthy (twice a day for seven days) and prescribed *ritual of daily sacrifices of valuable animals (bulls) can the altar be sufficiently purified to become holy and sacred itself. Through this process the inherent sin of the men who built the altar and the contaminated materials (in the sense that they are not holy) of which it is constructed become usable for God's service. Hereafter everything that comes in contact with the altar must be pure (both priests and sacrifices). If the level of *purity is maintained, then the sacrifices will be accepted and the people will benefit from their service. See comment on Leviticus 1:4.

29:37. whatever touches it will be holy. Because of the superior quality of the sacrificial altar's level of holiness (second only to the Holy of Holies in the tabernacle), anything that touches it becomes holy. Similarly, it is important that the altar be guarded from those persons or things which are impure so that the holiness is not lost or corrupted.

29:38. daily offerings. Caring for sin and the giving of thank offerings by the people are required daily, not just on special occasions (such as ordination). Thus the priests are to sacrifice two year-old lambs each day (known as the tamid, "perpetual" offering), one in the morning and the other in the evening. This daily *ritual signals to the people the continual presence of God among them as well as their constant obligation to obey the *covenant. The constant flow of movement to the sacrificial altar also maintains its holiness and reinforces the role of the priests as religious professionals.

29:40. tenth of an ephah. The principal dry measure in Israel was the homer, which equaled the load carried by a donkey. This weight varies in the sources from 3.8 bushels to 6.5 bushels. The ephah (an Egyptian loan word) equaled one-tenth of a homer (Ezek 45:11), or three-eighths to two-thirds of a bushel. One-tenth of an ephah (about 1.6 quarts) of fine flour was part of the daily sacrificial offering.

29:40. fourth of a hin. The hin (an Egyptian loan word) was a liquid measure equal to about a gallon. One-fourth of a hin (one quart) of olive oil was to be mixed with the flour as part of the daily sacrificial offering. In addition, a drink offering of a quart of wine was to be given daily.

29:40-41. drink offering. A libation or drink offering was part of the daily sacrifices in the tabernacle. They were presented with the lamb and the mixture of flour and oil in the morning and in the evening to signify God's protection and favor throughout the day. The pouring out of libations was a common household practice before meals, and that *ritual is carried over in the daily sacrifices as part of a communal, *covenant meal between God and the people.

30:1-38

Incense, Oil and Water

30:1-10. incense altar. Once the tabernacle was furnished and cleansed and the priesthood was ordained, the Presence of God entered the Holy of Holies to meet regularly with Moses (29:42-43). An additional object was therefore needed that would both represent the Presence and protect humans by veiling the Presence from their eyes. This was the incense altar, a small table (18 inches square and 3 feet high) constructed of acacia wood, with horns like the sacrificial altar, and covered with gold. It was placed in the area immediately outside the veil closing off the Holy of Holies. Like the ark, this inner altar had rings for carrying it with poles. A special blend of incense was burned on this altar every morning and evening. On the Day of Atonement blood from the sacrifice was to be daubed on each of its horns as a yearly repurification process.

30:7-8. burning of incense. The use of incense has been attested archaeologically from the earliest periods in Israelite history, although few incense altars have yet been excavated *in situ in Israelite shrines (Arad is the exception). The incense used probably consisted of a mixture of frankincense and other aromatic gums. The practice of burning incense has both practical and religious purposes. The smell of burning flesh from the sacrificial altar would have been unpleasant, and incense would have helped to mask that odor. The smoke from incense was also used to fumigate sacred precincts and to cast a veil of mystery within them to represent the presence of God or to mask God's presence from human eyes. It is also possible that the billowing of incense smoke signified the prayers of the people rising to God.

30:10. yearly atonement. The Day of Atonement was a special day set aside each year to remove the contamination from the sins of the past year. According to Leviticus 23:27-32 it fell ten days after the opening of the new year. On that day the high priest was to enter the inner precincts of the tabernacle and burn incense on the golden incense altar. Blood from the special sacrifice of the day was also to be daubed on the horns of the incense altar to tie this holiest of altars and its flow of incense to the need for cleansing of the nation's sins. A more elaborate description of this yearly *ritual, including the casting of the people's sins on the scapegoat, is found in Leviticus 16.

30:11-16. census temple tax. Every male aged twenty years and older was to pay a per capita tax of one-half shekel to help support the tabernacle. There is a sense of equality in this that no distinction is made between rich and poor—all pay the same amount. However, there is also a darker image here based on the threat of a plague and divine displeasure if they do not all submit to this census. Comparison with other such countings (Num 1 and 2 Sam 24) suggest that there is a real fear of taking a census because of its use for drafting men into the military and in the levying of taxes. However, in this case, at least, the "passing over" of the men as they paid their fee and were counted seemed to signify their acceptance of their responsibility to provide support for the construction and maintenance of the tabernacle.

30:11-16. census superstition. Taking a census was a practical measure utilized by governments in the ancient Near East as early as the Ebla tablets of around 2500 B.C. The benefits derived from this practice were not necessarily appreciated by the people since they led to increased tax levies as well as military or forced labor service. Viewed in this light, it is not surprising that popular notions existed that the census was a source of bad luck or the basis of divine displeasure. *Mari texts (eighteenth century B.C.) from Mesopotamia describe men fleeing to the mountains to avoid being counted. In 2 Samuel 24 God punishes David and Israel with a plague after a census is taken. The explanation for such a calamity could be that the census was motivated by human pride.

30:13. shekels. The half-shekel payment made by each Israelite male as temple tax, at least until the sixth century B.C., would have been made in a measure of precious metal, not coined money. The average shekel weighed 11.4 grams, but this text refers to a "sanctuary shekel," which is believed to be a smaller fraction of the common shekel. Weights discovered in archaeological finds evidence a shekel weighing 9.3-10.5 grams. The sanctuary weight listed here may also refer to a shekel of more standard value and weight than the "marketplace" shekel.

30:13. gerah. The gerah (an *Akkadian loan word) is the smallest of the Israelite measures of weight. It weighed approximately half a gram and was equivalent to one-twentieth of a shekel.

30:17-21. bronze basin. A water-filled bronze basin was to be placed near the entrance to the courtyard between the sacrificial altar and the tabernacle proper. It was to be used by the priests to wash their hands and feet each time they entered this holy precinct, in preparation for their holy service. In this way they washed the impurities of the outside world from their hands before making sacrifices and cleaned their feet so that they did not track in the dust and grime of the street. This item is added to the list of tabernacle utensils after the ordination and consecration since it was to be used daily, not just on special occasions.

30:22-33. anointing oil. A special formula is prescribed for the mixture of precious spices (myrrh, cinnamon, cane, cassia) with olive oil into a substance for anointing the tabernacle and all of its furnishing as well as the priests. The process involved soaking the spices in water, boiling the water, then aging the concoction with the oil until the fragrance permeated the whole. To insure its exclusivity, the anointing oil is to be concocted by a professional perfumer and is designed to mark the sacred precincts and priests as holy.

30:23-24. spices. Since all of the spices listed in the anointing oil are imported products, they would have been expensive and extremely precious. They came from southern Arabia

(myrrh), India or Sri Lanka (cinnamon), and other distant lands (see Jer 6:20 for fragrant cane) by sea and by way of the established caravan routes. They were mixed into aromatic oils by guilds of professional perfumers and were used for personal enhancement as well as to anoint priests and sacred places.

30:30-33. sacred recipe. The recipe for the anointing oil was reserved for sacred use. The special fragrance of the holy substance was only for the tabernacle and its personnel and was not to be used for secular purposes.

30:34-38. incense recipe. The incense burned on the golden incense altar in the tabernacle was mixed according to a special recipe that was not to be duplicated or used for other purposes. The recipe includes four specific items: gum or resin, perhaps from balsam trees; onycha from the glands of mollusks; galbanum, a resin native to Persia which adds pungency to other scents; and frankincense from southern Arabia.

31:1-18
Preparation for Construction of the Tabernacle and Its Furnishings

31:1-11. wood and metal craftsmanship. Having given instructions on how to construct the tabernacle and its furnishings, Moses now singles out craftsmen to carry out the task. They are said to have been given by God great skill in metalworking, engraving and carpentry. The idea of a deity lending expertise to the craftsmen involved in a sacred task is also attested in the god Ea guiding the skills of the experts who produced the cult statue of Sippar (ninth century). These two will then supervise the team of trained workers who will shape the various pieces of the tabernacle; cover many of its sacred objects with bronze and gold, stitch the fabrics used for the canopy, veil, and vestments of the priests; and engrave the stones for the ephah and breastplate.

31:12-17. sabbath as a sign of the covenant. While the individual's sign of participation in the *covenant is *circumcision, the sign of Israel's corporate participation in the covenant is the keeping of the sabbath. Like circumcision, the keeping of the sabbath is a continuous obligation required of each generation. Unlike circumcision, it is not a single act but an attitude to be consistently maintained and periodically expressed in action. With instruction given for construction of the tabernacle and workmen chosen to perform the task, it is now necessary to tie even this sacred work to the law of sabbath. Even this work must cease every seventh day as a sign of respect for God's role as the Creator and in acceptance of the covenantal promise to obey God's command (see 20:8-11). Although refraining from work may be an economic burden, this is counterbalanced by the rejuvenation of the spirit and the body through rest. The commandment to rest on the sabbath is so important that the death penalty is imposed on all violators.

31:14-15. work as criterion (profane vs. holy). The sign of obedience to the *covenant is the willingness to cease work on the sabbath. Neither profane nor holy work may be done on this day of total rest. No specific examples are given here, but the text cites both exclusion from the community and execution as punishment for violators. This may mean that each individual case would have to be examined to determine if the act performed was to be defined as "work" (see examples in Num 15:32-26 and Jer 17:21).

31:18. two tablets of the testimony. This statement in which God gives Moses the two stone tablets returns the narrative to the point where it was broken off at 24:18. It also provides the narrative indicator that the parenthetical material on the construction of the tabernacle and the consecration of the priesthood is at an end and that the storyteller is about to resume the narrative of the events on Mount Sinai. The term "tablets of the testimony" also appears in 32:15 and is the basis for the name "ark of the testimony" (25:16-22).

32:1-35

The Golden Calf

32:1. make us gods who will go before. Moses was the Israelites' sole contact with Yahweh and was the mediator of Yahweh's power and guidance, and, for all the people knew, he might be dead. With him gone it was believed that contact with Yahweh was lost and that they therefore needed a replacement mediator to serve the role of "going before them." This role is filled by an angel in 33:2. The calf is formed to likewise fill the role of Yahweh's representative.

32:2-4. calf idol. Bull or calf figurines, made either of bronze or of a combination of metals, have been found in several archaeological excavations (Mount Gilboa, Hazor and Ashkelon), but they are only three to seven inches long. The calf symbol was well known in the Canaanite context of the second millennium and represented fertility and strength. The gods were typically not depicted in the form of bulls or calves but portrayed standing on the back of the animal. Nevertheless worship of the animal image was not unknown, and there is little in the biblical text to suggest the Israelites understood the figure merely as a pedestal (not unlike the ark). The fact that the calf is worshiped in the context of a feast to Yahweh suggests that this may be a violation of the second commandment rather than the first.

32:4. manufacture of calf. When the heated gold was pliable enough, Aaron began to shape it, probably around a carved wooden figure.

32:4. these are your gods. The proclamation "These are your gods" implies that the calf is in some way representative of Yahweh—history is not being rewritten to suggest that a different deity was responsible for the deliverance.

32:5-6. altar for festival to Yahweh. Since the altar was built for the celebration of a sacred feast, it may be concluded that the altar was for sacrificial use, as verse 6 states. But just as the worship of Yahweh had been corrupted by introducing an image to represent him, so it was also corrupted in the conduct of the Israelites in worship. Their coarse and excessive carousing was a typical feature of pagan *fertility festivals.

32:9-14. anger of God. In ancient Near Eastern religions it was believed that gods habitually became angry with their worshipers (for both unknown and unknowable reasons) and lashed out at them. Moses' plea is thus focused on preserving the distinctiveness of Yahweh's reputation.

32:15-16. inscribed front and back. The use of two tablets probably indicates that Moses was given two copies, not that some of the commandments were on one tablet and some on the other. The fact that they were stone suggests a larger size than clay tablets would have been, though inscribed stone tablets such as the Gezer calendar were small enough to fit in the palm of the hand. The Egyptian practice of this period was to use flakes of stone chipped from rocks. Inscription on front and back was not unusual. When the writing reached the bottom of one side, the scribe would often continue around the bottom edge and move onto the second side. Even flakes that fit in the palm of the hand could contain fifteen to twenty lines.

32:19-20. dancing. Dancing was often connected with cultic festivals in the ancient world and, especially in *fertility contexts, was often sensual in nature, though not necessarily so. Dancing is also known in the context of celebration of military victories, which would fit with this being a celebration of the deity who brought them out of Egypt.

32:19. breaking of tablets. The breaking of the tablets, though a result of Moses' anger, is not a fit of temper. The severance of a *covenant was typically symbolized by the breaking of the tablets on which the terms of the agreement were inscribed.

32:20. drinking idol-dust brew. The sequence of burn-grind-scatter-eat is also found in a *Ugaritic text to indicate total destruction of a deity. That gold does not burn is insignificant (the gold was probably shaped around a wooden figure; see comment on 32:4)—a very destructive action is being carried out. The forced drinking by the Israelites is not specified as punishment against them but represents the final, irreversible destruction of the calf.

32:30-35. the book. The concept of divine ledgers is well known from Mesopotamia, where the ledgers concern both the decrees of one's destiny and one's rewards and punishments. For further information see comment on Psalm 69:28.

32:35. the plague. Epidemic disease is known from numerous sources throughout the ancient Near East, but specific identification is impossible in the absence of symptoms.

33:1-6
Preparing to Leave Sinai
33:2. peoples of the land, flowing with milk and honey. For the peoples of the land see the comment on 3:8, and for the description of Canaan as "flowing with milk and honey" see the comment on 3:7-10.

33:7-23
Moses' Meeting with the Lord
33:7-10. tent of meeting. The system prescribed in the law (chaps. 25-30) was for a sanctuary to be built so that the Lord could dwell in their midst. Given the present situation, however, the Lord is not going to dwell in their midst, but the tent of meeting was to be set up outside the camp where Moses would receive guidance. Nothing is said to take place inside this tent, but the Lord meets with Moses at the door of the tent when the pillar of cloud descends. There are no sacrifices offered there, and it contains no altar. It is a place for prophetic, not priestly, activity. Once the tabernacle is constructed and takes its place in the middle of the camp, it also serves as a tent of meeting.

33:11. speaking face to face. Speaking face to

face is an idiom suggesting an honest and open relationship. It does not contradict 33:20-23. Numbers 12:8 uses a different expression with the same meaning, "mouth to mouth."

33:18-23. God's glory, God's back, God's face. Moses' request to see the glory of God is not a request for God to do what he has never done before. In 16:7 the people were told they would see God's glory (see also Lev 9:23). Moses has negotiated for God's presence to accompany them (actually, to precede them). Moses requests that he might see the presence/glory of God taking his place in the lead. God agrees but warns that his face may not be seen. The concept of deity having an awesome, unapproachable appearance was not limited to Israelite theology, for in Mesopotamia the gods displayed their power through their *melammu*, their divine brilliance.

34:1-35
New Tablets and More Laws
34:6-7. God's attributes and willingness to punish to third and fourth generation. Moses had asked to "know" God's ways (33:13), and this list of the thirteen attributes of God (according to Jewish tradition) serve as his answer. It is not unusual in the ancient world to find lists of various deities' attributes. While mercy and justice figure prominently among them, many lists are more interested in attributes of power, while this one focuses on the benevolent graciousness of God. This list is quoted many times in the Scriptures (Num 14:18; Neh 9:17; Ps 86:15; 103:8; 145:8; Joel 2:13; Jonah 4:2; Nah 1:3) and forms a sort of confessional statement. The litany of God's characteristics is still used in Jewish liturgy today and was probably an established part of the temple worship prior to the exile. Although compassion, constancy and the reliability of God's love are stressed, the conse-quences of failure to obey God's command are made perfectly clear by the magnification of punishment on future generations (see Deut 5:9). Punishment to the third or fourth generation expresses the fact that *covenant violation brings guilt on the entire family. "The third and fourth generation" thus refers to all living members of the family. This is a stark reminder of communal guilt after the incident of the golden calf (32:19-35).

34:12-13. destruction of pagan worship objects. In this section, which reiterates the importance of obedience to the commandments, special attention is given to the destruction of all forms of pagan worship, especially *cult objects and idols. This may be another response to the golden calf incident (32:19-35). It is clear that the inhabitants of the Promised Land will have other gods and other ways of worshiping them. The Israelites are warned not to be enticed into alliance with these people or into worshiping their gods. Thus they are not to leave any sign of foreign worship intact. Carrying out this command would be evidence of great faith, for the destruction of sacred objects was considered a grave offense to a deity and was believed to result in the severest of punishments. The obedience of the Israelites would be tangible expression of their confidence that God could protect them from reprisals.

34:13. Asherah poles. The goddess *Asherah (under various related names) appears to be the divine consort of the principal male deity in a number of Mesopotamian and Syro-Palestinian pantheons: the *Babylonian storm god Amurru; the *Ugaritic god *El; and perhaps even the Canaanite god *Baal. She was often represented in the Bible by sacred poles erected near an altar. Her popularity among Israelites still tainted by a polytheistic worldview may be suggested by the inscription from Kuntillet 'Ajrud in the northwest part of the Sinai, "Yahweh and his Asherah." The order to cut down these cultic poles signified the need to purify the nation of foreign influence. It also follows the theme in this section of obedience to the commandments of a "jealous God" who would not countenance the worship or the symbols of rival deities (20:4-5).

34:16. sacred prostitution. One can distinguish between several different categories. In "sacred" prostitution, the proceeds go to the temple. In "cultic" prostitution, the intent is to insure *fertility through sexual *ritual. We must also differentiate between occasional sacred/cultic prostitution (as in Gen 38) and professional sacred/cultic prostitution (as in 2 Kings 23:7). The evidence for cultic prostitution in ancient Israel or elsewhere in the ancient Near East is not conclusive. Canaanite texts list prostitutes among the temple personnel, and *Akkadian literature attests those who were dedicated for life to serve the temple in this way. Although the Hebrew word used here is related to an Akkadian word for prostitute, this does not prove that any religious ritual or cultic practice is involved. It is quite possible for prostitutes to be employed by temples as a means of raising funds without their having any official status as priestesses. Furthermore, since women often did not have personal assets, sometimes the only way of earning money by which to pay a vow appeared to be prostitution. The injunction

against bringing the wages of a prostitute to the temple may, however, be a reaction against practices like that of the *Ishtar temple servants in the Neo-Babylonian period, who hired out female members of their community as prostitutes. Their wages would have been placed in the temple treasury. All of this demonstrates the existence of sacred prostitution, both occasional and professional, in Israel and the ancient Near East. But the existence of cultic prostitution on either level is more difficult to prove. Cultic prostitution is not easily confirmed in Mesopotamia, unless one includes the annual sacred marriage ritual. But it is hard to imagine that prostitutes serving at the temple of Ishtar (who personified sexual force) were not viewed as playing a sacred role in the fertility cult.

34:17. cast idols. It was a fairly common practice (attested by archaeological data) to mass produce images of many of the gods of the ancient Near East using cast molds. They could thus be manufactured in a variety of metals or clay and sold to individuals, who would in turn establish private shrines in their homes (see Judg 17:4-5). The prohibition here is a specific example further clarifying the commandment in 20.4 and speaks to the case of the casting of the golden calf in 32:2-4.

34:18. Feast of Unleavened Bread. This is a reiteration of the commandment in 23:15. It gains greater authority here by being included in the ritual version of the Ten Commandments (see 34:28).

34:19-20. first-born offerings. This commandment in the ritual version of the Ten Commandments is a repetition of the injunction given during the exodus narrative to redeem the first-born sons and the first-born of their livestock (13:11-13).

34:21. sabbath. This command to rest on the sabbath is a repetition of 20:9 (see comment there).

34:22. Feast of Weeks. This is the same wheat-harvest festival that is described as the Feast of Harvest in 23:16, one of the three major festivals of the agricultural year. It gains extra authority from its inclusion in the ritual version of the Ten Commandments.

34:22. Feast of Ingathering. This is the same spring-harvest festival that is described in 23:17. These major agricultural festivals are also mentioned in Deuteronomy 16:9-17. The additional promise to protect the harvesters from attack by neighboring peoples is a further incentive to the people to comply with the commandment to bring their harvest offerings three times a year.

34:23-24. pilgrimages. This is the same command to come with their harvest offerings that is set out in 23:17 and Deuteronomy 16:11, 14. Every male is required to appear before the Lord three times a year with the fruits of his labor in order to insure the future fertility of the land and to demonstrate compliance with the *covenant.

34:25. no blood with yeast. This command in the ritual version of the Ten Commandments is a repetition of the law in 23:18. Yeast allows bread to rise but is also associated with the corruption or spoiling of food and so must not be mixed with the blood, a symbol of life.

34:25. Passover leftovers. This command regarding the Passover meal first appears in 12:8-10 and is reiterated in 23:18. Its inclusion here follows the sequence established of laws concerning the major agricultural festivals and reinforces the tie between this group of laws and the exodus event. The prohibition of keeping leftovers is a sign of the sacred character of the feast.

34:26 first fruits. This command is a repetition of the law in 23:19. Just as the first-born son is redeemed through sacrifice, so too is the cereal and fruit harvest redeemed for the people's use by bringing the first of the harvest to God as a sacrifice.

34:26. kid in mother's milk. This command is a repetition of the law in 23:19. It is the basis for the prohibition against the mixture of milk and meat in cooking and in sacrifice. It may also reflect a reaction against such practices in Canaanite worship.

34:28. Ten Commandments, ritual version. The first set of Ten Commandments, which were written on two stone tablets by God, was destroyed by Moses in his disgust over the unfaithfulness of the people in the golden calf incident (32:19). Thus a second set of tablets is inscribed in 34:28, but the laws do not exactly correspond to those found in Exodus 20 and Deuteronomy 5. There is a greater emphasis on the exodus event in the laws included in this second list. It is also much more heavily balanced toward proper worship practices (including nearly verbatim sections from chap. 23) than the first set of the commandments.

34:29. Moses' "horns." The radiance of God is reflected in the shining texture of Moses' face when he returns with the tablets of the law. Although he is at first unaware of this phenomenon, Moses and the people recognize it as evidence that Moses has had direct contact with God. Subsequently, he wears a veil over his face to hide the radiance of his skin from the people. Jerome used the word *cornuta*, "horns," in translating Hebrew *qaran*, "radiant," in the Vulgate (c. A.D. 400) because the

Hebrew term often refers to horns. Consequently tradition held that Moses grew horns as a result of this experience. The mistake is graphically portrayed in the horned statue of Moses sculpted by Michelangelo in the sixteenth century. The relatedness of horns and radiance can be seen in the ancient Near Eastern iconography that depicts rays or horns as symbols of power on the crowns of deities. These are related to the divine glory (Akkadian *melammu*) that emanated from the gods, especially from their heads or crowns. So, for instance, the goddess Inanna in a *Sumerian hymn is portrayed as having a terrible countenance that glows radiantly and intimidates all those around her. A closer parallel may be found in the instance of Samsuiluna (son of *Hammurabi), who receives messengers from the god *Enlil whose faces are radiant. One text makes reference to the god Enlil "whose horns gleam like the rays of the sun."

35:1-4
Sabbath

35:2-3. lighting a fire on the sabbath. This command repeats the injunction against any form of sabbath labor found in 31:15, with the additional statement prohibiting the lighting of a fire on the sabbath. It is another expansion on the theme of those types of work that could not be performed on the sabbath (see 34:21). Later rabbinic pronouncement required the kindling of a light prior to the sabbath so that the house would not be left in darkness. However, no further fueling of the fire was allowed on the sabbath.

35:4—39:31
Carrying Out the Instructions

These chapters discuss the actual construction of the tabernacle. They include the gathering of the materials (35:4-29) and the introduction of Bezalel and Oholiab as the chief craftsmen and the selection of their crew (35:30—36:7; cf. 31:1-10). Exodus 36:8-38 describes the building of the tabernacle to the exact dimensions outlined in 26:1-36. This is followed by the construction of the ark (37:1-9; see 25:10-22), the lampstand (37:17-24; see 25:31-40), the altar of incense (37:25-29; see 30:1-10), the altar of burnt offering (38:1-8; see 27:1-8) and the courtyard (38:9-20; see 27:9-19), and a summary of the materials used by the craftsmen (38:21-31). The final section describes the creation of the vestments for the priests: the ephod (39:2-7; see 28:6-14), the breastpiece (39:8-21; see 28:15-30) and the other priestly garments (39:22-31; see 28:31-43).

Moses then inspects everything, certifies it is correct and according to God's command, and gives it his blessing (39:32-43).

38:8. women who served at the entrance. In the ancient Near East there are many examples of women serving temples in various capacities. From menial tasks to priestly duties, from celibacy to prostitution, from short-term vows to lifelong dedication, examples of all sorts are available. It is therefore difficult to identify the nature of the service that the women mentioned here are performing. In 1 Samuel 2:22 the indictment of the sexual misconduct of Eli's sons suggests that the women either were involved in some duty of piety or were virgins. It must be noted, however, that there is no evidence of religiously motivated celibacy in Israel, and the text does not describe the women as virgins.

38:24. gold from the wave offering. The metals used in the construction of the tabernacle are listed in descending order of their value. As was done with the sacrificial meat set aside for the use of the priests (29:27), these materials were first presented as a wave offering to God as a way of consecrating them to their purpose.

38:24. 29 talents, 730 shekels of gold. The total amount of gold used in the decoration of the tabernacle's furnishings is described in talents (the largest unit of Israelite weight measure, equaling 3,000 shekels). The talent weighed 75.6 pounds, while the shekel weighed 0.4 ounces. Thus the total weight of gold used was 2,210.65 pounds.

38:25. 100 talents, 1775 shekels of silver. The total amount of silver given and used for the embellishment of the tabernacle's furnishings was 7,601 pounds (based on 3,000 shekels at 0.4 ounces equaling one talent and weighing

75.6 pounds). This amount is also linked to the total atonement tax (30:11-16) collected from each Israelite male.

38:26. beka. The beka is a weight of measure equal to one half of a shekel, that is, 0.2 ounces. This was the amount of the atonement tax exacted from every man twenty years old and above to provide funds for the construction and maintenance of the tabernacle (see 30:11-16).

38:26. number of Israelites. The number of men counted in the census and paying the atonement tax (see 30:11-16) of one-half shekel of silver is 603,550. This is the same number listed in the census in Numbers 1:46, which was used to determine the number of males who were twenty years old and thus able to serve in the military.

38:29-31. 70 talents, 2,400 shekels of bronze. With the equation of 3,000 shekels (0.4 ounces) per talent (75.6 pounds), the total amount of bronze presented as a wave offering and used in the construction of the tabernacle was 5,350 pounds. This more durable metal was used for the bases of the entranceway, the bronze altar and its grating, and the altar utensils, as well as the bases for each of the poles supporting the tent and the tent pegs.

39:32—40:38
Completion of the Tabernacle

40:17. timing. The tabernacle was erected on New Year's Day, two weeks short of the anniversary of the exodus event and exactly nine months after the people arrived at Mount Sinai. The construction process had been carried out with no deviation from the instructions given by God. It was only appropriate that a new era in the manner of worship should begin on New Year's Day.

L E V I T I C U S

1:1-17
The Burnt Offering

1:1-2. tent of meeting. Prior to the construction of the tabernacle in Exodus the tent of meeting was outside the camp and served as a place of revelation (see the comment on Ex 33:7-10). However, now that the tabernacle is in operation, it also is referred to as the tent of meeting.

1:1-2. revelation of rituals. In the ancient Near East the priests undoubtedly claimed deity to

be the source of the ritual procedures they used, though documents preserving such rituals do not present themselves as divine revelation as here. Some ritual procedures were prescribed through divination or by prophetic oracle, but they were not permanently established by those mechanisms. Early Sumerian literature portrays the mother goddess giving instructions for purification, petition and appeasement.

1:2. animal sacrifice. There have been many

theories about what thinking was represented in the sacrificial system. In some cultures sacrifice was viewed as a means of caring for the deity by providing food. Others saw the sacrifice as a gift to please the god and request his aid. In other contexts the sacrifices have been viewed as a means of entering into relationship with deity or maintaining that relationship. These are only a few of over a dozen possibilities. The history of animal sacrifice is difficult to trace. Earliest *Sumerian literature, specifically the Lugalbanda Epic, attests that sacrifices (better considered "ritual slaughter") originated as a means of permitting meat consumption. Sharing the meat with the deity allowed people to slaughter the animal for their food. Earliest archaeological evidence for sacrifice comes from the altars of the Ubaid period in fourth millennium B.C. Mesopotamia. Through most of *Assyrian and *Babylonian history, *ritual slaughter was carried out in order to obtain the entrails, believed to provide omens.

1:3-4. burnt offering. The burnt offering is always a male animal that is completely burned on the altar, except for the skin. This is the type of sacrifice that was offered by Noah and the type that Isaac was supposed to be. Other peoples are portrayed in the Bible as making burnt offerings (e.g., Num 23:14-15), and texts from Syria (*Ugarit and *Alalakh) and Anatolia (the *Hittites) testify to the practice in Syro-Palestine. In contrast there is not yet any evidence of this type of sacrifice in Egypt or Mesopotamia. The burnt offering serves as a means to approach the Lord with a plea. The plea could concern victory, mercy, forgiveness, purification, favor or any number of other things. The purpose of the offering is to entreat the deity's response. At least one each day was offered up on behalf of the people of Israel. Special ceremonies and festival days also generally featured burnt offerings.

1:3. male. Male animals were both more valuable and more expendable. A herd could be sustained with only a few males in proportion to the many females needed to bear the young. This would mean that a large percentage of the males that were born could be used for food or sacrifice. On the other hand, the good strong males were desirable because their genetic traits would be reflected in a large portion of the herd.

1:4. laying hand on the head. The laying on of the hand is an important part of the sacrificial *ritual. It is not designed to transfer sin, for it is used in sacrifices that do not deal with sin. Other possibilities are that the offerer in some way identifies with the animal, perhaps as his substitute, or identifies the animal as belonging to him. Most occurrences of the ritual confirm that either transferring or designating is taking place (or both), but it is not always clear what is being transferred or designated, and it may vary from one situation to another.

1:4. atonement. The function of this sacrifice as well as others is "to make atonement" (NIV). Many scholars now agree, however, that "atonement" is not the best translation for the concept on either the *ritual or the theological level. Perhaps most convincing is the fact that in the ritual texts the object of "atonement" is neither the sin nor the person, but a holy object connected with God's presence, such as the ark or the altar. A second important observation is that in a number of cases this "atonement" is necessary even though no sin has been committed (for instance, the ritual *impurity of women each month). For these and other reasons recent scholars have preferred "purification" or, more technically, "purgation," as the translation. So the altar would be purged on behalf of the offerer whose sin or *impurity had ritually tarnished it. The purpose was to maintain the sanctity of God's presence in their midst. The ritual, like a disinfectant, is normally remedial, but it can be preventative. The agent is usually blood, but not always. This decontamination of the sanctuary renders the offerer clean and paves the way for his reconciliation with God. The purging of objects (including cities, houses, temples and persons) from ritual contamination or evil influence by wiping or rubbing on a substance is also known in ancient Near Eastern practice, though these are mainly magical rites.

1:5-9. role of priests. Some aspects of the *ritual were performed by the priests, because only the priests had access to the altar and the holy place. (See comment on Exodus 28:1 for general information.) The priests of the ancient Near East were involved not only in sacrificial rituals but also in *divination and other magical rites. Incantations and general advice concerning appeasement of the gods were also under the jurisdiction of the priests. Priests were expected to be skilled in the knowledge of which rituals were to be used for any desired results and in the appropriate performance of the rituals.

1:5. importance of blood. Blood serves as the mechanism for ritual cleansing in Israel—a concept not shared by its ancient Near Eastern neighbors. The blood represented the life or life force of the animal, so the animal had to be killed for the blood to have efficacy. See the comment on 17:11 for more information.

1:5. sprinkling on the altar. The sprinkling of the blood on all sides of the altar is the symbolic means of applying the death of the animal to the purging of any contamination that might interfere with the entreaty that is being made on the occasion of the sacrifice. The blood represents the life/death of the animal, and the altar represents the sanctuary (God's presence) and is specifically the place where a request before God would be made.

1:8-9. parts. The pieces include the head as well as the suet (the fat that surrounds the internal organs). The only parts washed are the entrails (intestines) and the legs, both so that no dung is present on the altar.

1:9. pleasing aroma. It is typical for sacrifices to yield what is identified as the pleasing aroma of roasting meat. While it is certainly anthropomorphic (picturing God in human terms) to phrase it this way, cooked meat would have generally been used only for communal meals and special occasions, so important concepts of community were associated with the scent (like the smell of a Thanksgiving meal). It would be no different from God's being pleased by a sight or sound. In surrounding ancient Near Eastern thought the anthropomorphism is much stronger, for there the gods need and receive sustenance from food, and the smell is associated with their anticipation of a meal.

1:10-13. north side of altar. The north side of the altar is indicated, most likely because that is where there was the most room for this work to be done.

1:14-17. birds as offering. Birds, mainly domesticated doves, were the offering used by those who were too poor to own or to give up one of the larger herd animals. Texts from *Alalakh and Anatolia show that birds were also suitable sacrifices in surrounding cultures. Recent study has suggested it is not the crop that was removed but the crissum, including the tail, anus and intestines. Again, then, this is a matter of cleaning the animal in preparation for sacrifice.

1:16. east side where the ashes are. As early as the rabbis, it was suggested that the ash heap was on the east side because that was farthest away from the sanctuary, but the text never offers a reason.

2:1-16

The Grain Offering

2:1-3. grain offering. The rabbis considered the grain offering to be a substitute for the burnt offering for poor people. Mesopotamian practice is known to have made similar provision for the poor. The word used to describe this offering means "gift" or tribute. The offering is used in situations where respect or honor are intended. The same term is used the same way in *Ugaritic and *Akkadian (Canaan and Mesopotamia). It is typically found on occasions of celebration rather than the context of sadness or mourning. Generally a small portion was burned on the altar as a token of the gift to the Lord, while the remainder was given to the officiating priest. Sometimes it was offered in conjunction with other offerings.

2:1. fine flour with oil and incense. The ingredients of this offering were grain, oil and incense. The grain was the grits or semolina left in the sieve after wheat was ground into flour. The oil was olive oil. The best-quality oil was extracted by crushing the olives. But for the grain offerings the lower quality was acceptable; this was extracted through pressing and grinding. Oil was used as shortening in cooking and was easily combustible. The incense was frankincense, which was made from the gum resin of a type of tree found only in southern Arabia and Somaliland, on either side of the Gulf of Aden. This *Boswellia* tree will grow only where there is a very particular combination of rainfall, temperature and soil condition. Its fragrant aroma made the demand for frankincense high throughout the Near East, where it was used widely in both Mesopotamia and Egypt (some was found in Tutankhamen's tomb). This demand, along with its rarity, made it very expensive and one of the staples of the camel caravan trade. The grain offerings used a small amount that was entirely burned in a slow smolder.

2:3. the portion of the priests. As was the case with many offerings, the priest received a portion of the grain offering to eat. This was a means of providing for the needs of the priesthood. For fuller discussion of this practice, see comment on 6:14-18.

2:4-10. baked grain offering; cakes, no yeast, with oil. The grain offering that is for the priests' consumption can be prepared in oven, griddle or pan. The same oil and semolina are used, but no incense. Here it is specified that no yeast is to be used. Sacred use typically prohibited yeast of any sort, perhaps because it introduced a principle of spoilage (fermentation).

2:11-13. honey. Honey represents a natural resource, probably the syrup of the date rather than bees' honey. There is no evidence of bee domestication in Israel, though the *Hittites had accomplished that and used bee honey in their sacrifices (as did the Canaanites). In the

Bible honey occurs in lists with other agricultural products (see 2 Chron 31:5).

2:13. salt. Salt was used widely as symbolic of preservation. When treaties or alliances were made, salt was employed to symbolize that the terms would be preserved for a long time. *Babylonian, Persian, Arabic and Greek contexts all testify to this symbolic usage. In the Bible, likewise, the *covenant between the Lord and Israel is identified as a covenant of salt—a long-preserved covenant. Allies entering into such an agreement would generally share a communal meal where salted meat was featured. Thus the use of salt in the sacrifices was an appropriate reminder of the covenant relationship. Additionally, salt impedes the action of yeast (leaven), and since leaven was a symbol of rebellion, salt could easily represent that which inhibited rebellion. Finally, salt is symbolic for that which is infertile and therefore is used in curse pronouncements in treaties. In a Hittite treaty, the testator pronounces a curse: if the treaty is broken may he and his family and his lands, like salt that has no seed, likewise have no progeny.

2:14-16. first-fruits grain offering. Besides the grain offerings that substituted for burnt offerings and those that accompanied other sacrifices, some grain offerings were made in connection with the first fruits of the harvest. This grain has not undergone any processing but involves roasting from the sheaf in the green stage of ripening. It is likely that this offering used barley rather than wheat.

3:1-17
The Fellowship Offering

3:1-5. fellowship offering. The fellowship offering often accompanies the burnt offering and also involves an animal sacrifice. It is often present in conjunction with shared *covenantal meals (Ex 24:5; Josh 8:31) and, once kingship is instituted, often recognizes the role of the king in relation to either God or the people. A similar word referring to a gift between dignitaries also occurs in conjunction with festive meals from *Ugarit and *El Amarna (Canaanite). The three types of sacrifices in this category are the freewill offering, the vow offering and the thanksgiving offering. The common ground between them is that they provide the occasion for a meal with the offerer and his family and friends. The suet was burned on the altar, but all the meat became part of the meal.

3:4. fat covering the inner parts. The suet is the layer of fat around the internal organs, mainly the intestines, liver and kidneys. This can easily be peeled off and is inedible. Mesopotamians did not include the suet in their sacrifices, but many other cultures of the ancient Near East did. The description in the text is quite technical. J. Milgrom translates it in his commentary as follows: "The suet that covers the entrails and all the suet that is around the entrails; the two kidneys and the suet that is around them, that is on the sinews [not "loins" as in NIV]; and the caudate lobe of the liver, which he shall remove with the kidneys."

3:6-11. fat tail. When a flock animal is offered, the "fat tail" is included in the sacrifice. The sheep of this region had long tails, as long as four or five feet, weighing up to fifty pounds.

3:11. burned "as food." The language here again shows that the sacrificial terms used in Israel were influenced by non-Israelite notions of sacrifice. It is clear from passages such as Psalm 50:12-13 that the Israelites were not to consider sacrifices as food needed by God. Since the terminology is used only in this particular offering, perhaps it represents God's inclusion in the communal meal more than the meeting of any need for nourishment.

3:12-17. fat is the Lord's. The suet is grouped with the blood as the portion belonging to the Lord. Just as the blood is a token of the life of the animal, the suet is a token of the meat of the sacrifice.

4:1—5:13
The Purification Offering

4:1-3. sin offering. The purification offering has traditionally been called the "sin offering." The terminology has shifted as it has been recognized that the offering did not deal just with moral offenses but also with purification in cases of significant ritual uncleanness. In personal circumstances as well as in public services of consecration and in connection with certain festivals, the offering purified or purged the sanctuary (not the offerer) from the effects of the offense or condition. In the ancient Near East the purification of temples was a constant need, because the people felt that *impurity made the temple vulnerable to destructive demons. In Israel the preservation of the *purity of the sanctuary had to do with the holiness of God. If the Lord was to remain in their midst, the holiness of his sanctuary must be maintained.

4:4-12. laying on of the hands. The laying on of the hand is an important part of the sacrificial *ritual. It is not designed to transfer sin, for it is used in sacrifices that do not deal with sin. Other possibilities are that the offerer in some way identifies with the animal, perhaps as his substitute, or identifies the animal as belonging to him. Most occurrences of the ritual confirm that either transferring or designating is taking place (or both), but it is not always clear what is being transferred or designated, and it may vary from one situation to another.

4:6. sprinkling seven times. The sevenfold sprinkling is a means of purifying all the parts of the sanctuary without going to each one individually. The sprinkling is directed toward the veil that separated the outer sanctuary from the Holy of Holies.

4:7. horns of the altar. The horns at the four corners of the altar were part of altar design throughout the ancient Near East. Research has suggested that they are emblems of the gods, though their function is unknown. Both the incense altar inside the sanctuary and the altar for sacrifice outside the sanctuary had horns.

4:7. incense altar. In this sacrifice the blood is spread on the horns of the incense altar. Incense altars were a typical piece of furniture in both Israelite and Canaanite sanctuaries. The incense offered on these altars was a mixture of spices featuring most prominently frankincense, but also gum resin, onycha and galbanum. Later Jewish tradition included a dozen spices in the mixture. The smoke of the incense represented the prayers of the people going up to God.

4:12. burning of extra parts outside the camp. Once the blood and fat are offered, the rest of the animal (including the meat) is burned outside the camp, so that none of it benefits the human offerers. There is no meal connected to this sacrifice. The ash pile from the second-temple period was just north of the wall in Jerusalem. Analysis of its contents has confirmed that it contained animal remains.

4:13-32. forgiveness. Forgiveness is the intended result of the purification and reparation offerings. The verb *forgive* has only God as the subject, never humans, and does not rule out punishment (see Num 14:19-24). We must therefore conclude that the concept concerns relationship rather than the judicial issue of punishment. The one who is offering these sacrifices seeks reconciliation with God, not pardon from punishment.

5:1-4. public charge to testify. The first case concerns one who does not respond to a public proclamation requesting information concerning a court case. It was common in the ancient Near East for such public requests to be made. The second and third cases concern contact with *impurity. The fourth concerns an impulsive oath. *Hittite texts also connect oath breaking with *impurity.

5:5-10. actions classified as "sins." These cases constitute a separate category because they are neither inadvertent nor defiant. Whether through carelessness or weakness an offense has been committed, and time has passed either because of a memory lapse or perhaps unwillingness to pay the price. This offering is unlike that of chapter 4 in that it required confession but resembles it in that it results in purification of the sanctuary and reconciliation to God.

5:11-13. no oil or incense. The offering to be brought was determined by the means one had. Even a grain offering could be used by the very poor. Oil and incense are omitted because they were associated with celebration, and this was not a festive occasion.

5:14—6:7
The Reparation Offering

5:14-16. reparation offering. The reparation offering was traditionally termed the guilt offering. Though the term that is used is often appropriately translated as guilt, the term serves a more technical function within the sacrificial system. This offering is designed to address a particular category of offense—understood to represent a breach of faith or an act of sacrilege. "Breach of faith" would appropriately describe the violation of a *covenant, while "sacrilege" refers generally to desecration of sacred areas or objects. Both of these crimes were well known in the ancient Near East, and examples can be found from the *Assyrians, *Babylonians, Egyptians, *Hittites and *Aramaeans. The Hittite *Instructions for Temple Officials* is particularly helpful in its identification of a number of categories of sacrilege, including (1) priests taking portions of sacrifices that do not belong to them, or taking valuables given to the temple for their families' use, and (2) laypeople failing to deliver offerings that belong to deity in a timely manner. The crime addressed by the purification offering (previous chapter) was contaminating the holy place with that which was unholy. The crime addressed by the reparation offering was appropriating that which was holy into the realm of that which was profane. Neither of these offerings existed in the other sacrificial systems of the ancient Near East.

5:18. ram, one fifth surcharge, sanctuary shekel. While the purification offering for a leader of Israel required a male goat, the male sheep (ram) of the reparation offering distinguishes this sacrifice from any that could be brought for purification. In addition to the ram, the offender had to pay in silver the value of what he had desecrated and add one-fifth of the value for restitution. The sanctuary shekel used for the valuation is generally considered to be a fraction of the regular shekel, but precise information is not available. Archaeological finds do attest shekel pieces weighing 9.3-10.5 grams.

6:1-7. comparison of crimes. In the cases listed here the innocence or guilt of the supposed offender can be determined only by resort to an oath, because in most cases the evidence is not available or identifiable. While the previous section of the text concerned sacrilege with regard to sacred objects, this section refers to the sacrilege committed by swearing falsely. Fines are imposed here to deal with the offense on the civil level, where it would be classified as a misdemeanor rather than as a felony. In many of the ancient law collections, however, monetary reimbursement was used even in felony cases.

6:8-13

The Burnt Offering

6:9. burnt offering kept burning through the night. This section begins the instructions to the priests concerning the sacrifices that have been described in the previous chapters. The burnt offering was the last sacrifice to be offered for the day, and the regulations here specify that it should burn all night, with cleaning of the altar to take place in the morning. In this way petition on behalf of Israel can continue throughout the nighttime hours.

6:10. linen garments. The linen for the clothing worn by the priests was imported from Egypt, where it was also distinctively used for priests' garments. Angels, too, are said to be dressed in linen (for example, Dan 10:5).

6:14-23

The Grain Offering

6:16. provision for the priests. Whether or not the worshiper ate a portion of the sacrifice, a number of the sacrifices provided an opportunity for the priests to eat. This was also true in *Babylonian practice, where the king, the priest and other temple personnel received portions of the sacrifices. As early as the *Sumerian period, texts show that it was considered a grievous crime to eat that which had been set apart as holy.

6:16. courtyard of the tent of meeting. The Israelite temple that was discovered at Arad has the courtyard divided into two, the area closer to the sanctuary being more private. Ezekiel's description of the temple features special rooms adjoining the temple for the priests to eat their portions. It is likely, then, that the courtyard mentioned here, whether a partitioned open-air section or adjoining rooms in an area still considered the courtyard, would have been a private area.

6:18. holiness by touch. There was a contagion to various of the sacred objects that could be transmitted directly, but not secondarily (Hag 2:12). Tortuous analysis has led some experts to conclude that only objects, not persons, became holy by contact with something holy, but not all are convinced that such a distinction existed. Mesopotamian regulations likewise forbade the touching of sacred objects, but there is no discussion of contagion. An object that "contracted" holiness was confiscated by the priests and thereafter restricted to sacred use.

6:20. tenth of an ephah. This is about five cups of flour for two offerings, each one making a flat cake of eight to ten inches in diameter.

6:24-30

The Purification Offering

6:27. laundering a blood-spattered garment. Since the blood in this sacrifice has absorbed *impurity, the garment is now rendered impure and must be washed.

6:28. treatment of pottery vessels and metal vessels. Earthenware vessels retain their porosity and therefore absorb the *impurity of what they contain. Bronze or copper containers, in contrast, can easily be rinsed and thereby be purified for further use.

7:1-10

The Reparation Offering

7:2. blood sprinkled on all sides. The sprinkling of the blood on all sides of the altar is the symbolic means of applying the death of the animal to the purging of any contamination that might interfere with the entreaty that is being made. The blood represents the life and death of the animal, and the altar represents the sanctuary (God's presence).

7:3. fat parts. The suet is the layer of fat around the internal organs, mainly the intestines, liver and kidneys. This can easily be peeled off and is inedible. See 3:1-5 for more information.

7:6. eaten in a holy place. There were areas in the tabernacle compound provided for such occasions. See 6:14-23.

7:6. priestly shares. The concept of priestly

portions was discussed above in 6:14-23. Here the hide also belongs to the priest, a practice attested in *Babylon as well as in the larger Mediterranean context.

7:11-21
The Fellowship Offerings

7:12. preparation of thanksgiving offering. One each of four different breads are presented to the priest. The "cakes" are probably braided ring-bread perforated in the baking process, while the "wafers" are the thin disk-shaped variety, perhaps half an inch thick.

7:14. contribution. This term is traditionally rendered "heave offering" and refers to a dedicated gift. Cognate terms are attested in *Akkadian (Babylonian) and *Ugaritic. Being put in this category transfers ownership from the individual to the deity using informal procedures, generally not within the confines of the sanctuary.

7:15. difference between thanksgiving offering and other fellowship offerings. Unlike the other fellowship offerings, the thanksgiving offering was often made in places other than the sanctuary. As a result there is a stricter rule about eating it the day of the sacrifice, perhaps to avoid situations where *impurity could be contracted. This would not be as big a problem in the sanctuary precincts.

7:19-21. cutting off of those eating unclean food. The penalty cited here is not something that people carry out but refers to the action of God. Such a penalty is generally reserved for those encroaching on that which is sacred.

7:22-27
Eating of Fat (Suet) and Blood

7:22-27. prohibition against eating fat or blood. The suet is grouped with the blood as the portion belonging to the Lord. Just as the blood is a token of the life of the animal, the suet is a token of the meat of the sacrifice. The suet of nonsacrificial animals may be eaten, but the blood of any animal may not.

7:28-36
Priestly Portions

7:30-34. wave offering. Close textual analysis has demonstrated that nothing is "waved" in these offerings, though it is possible that the offering is lifted up before God in dedication (a practice attested in Egyptian "elevation offerings"). It is different from the "contribution" (v. 14) in that it is always in the presence of the Lord, that is, at the sanctuary. Most

agree that it represents a special dedication ceremony. There are waving ceremonies attested in Mesopotamian and *Hittite rituals, but these are in quite different contexts from this Israelite ritual.

7:31-34. use of the breast and thigh. Since there is no mention of which breast, it is assumed that the animal is not quartered lengthwise but across the middle below the ribs, leaving the whole breast intact, a large piece of choice meat to be shared among the priests. The thigh is the choice individual portion and is reserved for the officiating priest.

8:1-36
The Consecration of Aaron and His Sons

8:1-9. anointing and anointing oil. The spices which were to be used for anointing purposes were myrrh, cinnamon, cane and cassia (see recipe in Ex 30:23-25). Oil symbolizes the gifts of God to the people and the responsibilities now laid on their leaders through this ceremony. In Israelite practice anointing was a sign of election and was often closely related to endowment by the Spirit, though that is never implied concerning the priests. Among the Egyptians and *Hittites, anointing was believed to protect a person from the power of netherworld deities. They anointed both kings and priests. In the *Amarna texts there is reference to a king of Nuhasse being anointed by the Pharaoh, and at Emar the priestess of Baal is anointed. There is no evidence that kings in Mesopotamia were anointed, but some priests were. Additionally, throughout the ancient world anointing symbolized an advance of a person's legal status. Both concepts of protection and change of status may correlate to the priest's anointing, for it would offer him protection in handling sacred things and identify him with the divine realm.

8:5-30. consecration ceremony. Investiture and anointing would have been normal procedures for social occasions. In Mesopotamian literature examples would include preparing Enkidu for entrance into society in the *Gilgamesh Epic and the hospitality offered *Adapa when he is called before the high god Anu in the *Myth of Adapa*. In the Israelite consecration ceremony, preparation for entering the serving circle of deity simply accentuates the normal procedures by using the very finest clothing and the most expensive oil. Installation of priests in Egypt also included clothing and anointing rituals.

8:1-7. priests in the ancient world. Every culture in the ancient Near East developed a priesthood. Only the Bedouin tribes did not set these individuals aside to perform priestly duties exclusively. Their role was to function as a part of a priestly community, serving temples, performing sacrifices, conducting religious services and staging festivals. Priests would have been educated within the temple from an early age, and their position in the priestly class was hereditary in some cases. They would have been among the few literate persons in their society and thus were relied upon to keep records of major events and tie them to the will of the gods. This process was known as *divination, and it, along with *ritual sacrifice, was the chief source of priestly power and authority. There was a distinctive hierarchy among priests—ranging from a chief priest, who sometimes rivaled the king in power, to midlevel individuals who performed daily *rituals and sacrifices, to musicians, and on down to temple servants, who performed the mundane housekeeping and custodial tasks necessary in any large community.

8:7. ephod. The most important of Aaron's priestly garments is the ephod, which was either a linen robe covering the upper body or a frontal piece attached to the shoulders and sashed at the waist. The fact that the ephod is related to idols and false worship in later passages (Judg 17:5 and 8:24-27) suggests that it was a garment borrowed from Mesopotamian society—perhaps worn by priests or used to clothe idols. The breastpiece (Ex 28:15), the Urim and Thummim (Ex 28:30), and the ephod are used in *divination (1 Sam 23:9-11). Thus the high priest is clothed in garments which aid in the discernment of God's will. Discussion of the other items of the priests' garments can be found in the comments on Exodus 28.

8:8. Urim and Thummim. No description of these objects is found in Scripture, although traditions from the Hellenistic and later periods suggest they were markers whose appearance and presentation when cast like lots would determine God's will (see Num 27:21; 1 Sam 14:37-41; 28:6). There is no negative character attached to the Urim and Thummim as there are to other divinatory practices, and they are never mentioned in passages describing non-Israelite worship or *ritual. Nevertheless, the practice of posing yes-no questions to the gods (asking *oracles) is known throughout the ancient Near East. Particularly of interest are the *Babylonian *tamitu* texts, which preserve the answers to many oracular questions. Positive and negative stones (thought to be light stones and dark stones) were also

used widely in Mesopotamia in a procedure called psephomancy. In one *Assyrian text, alabaster and hematite are specifically mentioned. The yes-no question would be posed and then a stone drawn out. The same color stone would have to be drawn out three times consecutively for the answer to be confirmed. *Urim* is the Hebrew word for "lights" and therefore would logically be associated with bright or white stones. One recent study has pointed out that hematite, because of its use for weights and seals, was termed the "truth stone" in *Sumerian. The Hebrew word *Thummim* could have a similar meaning.

8:9. the diadem. This refers to a symbol of authority worn on the forehead or on the front of a headpiece. Perhaps the best-known example of this in the ancient world is the serpent (uraeus) on the front of Pharaoh's crown, which was believed to be a protective device. In the descriptions of the high priest's garments the diadem is generally associated with a "gold plate" (NIV). Since the word translated "plate" here is also the word for flower, it is possible that the insignia was flower-shaped.

8:10-21. anointing the sancta. This is done to consecrate the tabernacle and its parts for sacred use. Egyptians regularly anointed the images of the gods, but this was part of the care procedures, not a consecration.

8:14. laying on the hand. See comment on 4:4-12.

8:22-30. ram for ordination. The idiom used here for ordination, the "filling of the hand," is known from *Akkadian contexts for both priests and kings. For *Assyrian king Adad-Nirari II it is specifically a scepter that is placed into his hand signifying the authority of his office. The idiom has wider use, however, and does not require an insignia. Here it is a sacrifice of a ram in addition to the purification offering (vv. 14-17) and the burnt offering (vv. 18-21) that provides the authorization for their office.

8:23. right ear, right thumb, right big toe. It is uncertain which part of the ear is intended (lobe and antihelix are the most often suggested). The blood functions both to cleanse from *impurity and protect from "sacred contagion." Smearing or daubing *rituals in the ancient Near East generally focus on edges and entrances.

8:29. wave offering. See comment on 7:30-34. Discussion of the details of verses 25-29 can be found in comments on chapter 1.

8:30. sprinkling of oil and blood. Aaron has already been anointed with oil and daubed with blood, but the sprinkling here serves a different purpose, that of consecration.

8:31-36. atonement. The concept of "purification" is closer to the mark than "atonement." See the comment on 1:4.

8:35. staying for seven days. The high priest may not leave for any reason because this would expose him to uncleanness. In his duties he absorbs *impurity but remains immune to its effects as long as he is in the sanctuary complex. Leaving would make him vulnerable to the lethal jeopardy such *impurity creates. *Sumerian texts attest to the same concerns for *entu*-priestesses, who must not venture out of the temple while *Dumuzi, still in the realm of the dead, roams the streets (Dumuzi is a dying and rising god connected to the fertility cycle of the seasons). Seven-day dedication ceremonies were common, as in Gudea's dedication of the temple in *Lagash.

9:1-22
The Beginning of Priestly Service

9:1. eighth-day ceremony. Information concerning the details of this section may be found in the previous comments. With the seven-day initiation and dedication ceremony completed, the eighth day marks the inauguration of the system. This ceremony is to be punctuated with the appearance of the Lord (vv. 4-6, 23-24). A similar initiation ceremony occurs when Solomon's temple is initiated (1 Kings 8:62-64), where the term *hanok* ("initiation") is used (cf. Hanukkah, though the present-day Jewish holiday is not related to this event but rather to the reinitiation of the altar and temple by the Maccabees after they had been desecrated by Antiochus Epiphanes in the second century B.C.).

9:23—10:20
The Appearance of the Glory of the Lord and the Response

9:23. the glory of the Lord. Most temple dedications in the ancient Near East featured the deity being officially installed in the temple (generally by means of the image of the deity being taken in). Here there is no installation of *Yahweh, but his glory appears to emerge from the newly dedicated tabernacle, most likely in the form of the pillar of cloud and fire (see comment on Ex 13:21-22) that has represented the Lord's presence throughout the wilderness experience. Here the fire erupts from the pillar to consume the offerings.

10:1. censers. These are most likely long-handled pans that could also shovel up the hot coals. They served as portable altars because the incense was actually burned in them. Censers are also used for burning of incense in Egypt when people wanted to protect themselves from demonic forces. For a close parallel in the Bible, see Numbers 16:46-50.

10:1. unauthorized fire. Since access to the main altar (where coals for incense offerings were supposed to be obtained) was difficult given the consuming fire, and since Aaron's sons decided that incense was needed to shield the people from viewing the glory of the Lord (see 16:13), coals from another source (unauthorized fire) were used.

10:3. Aaron's silence. Aaron's silence is in contrast to the loud wailing that usually accompanied mourning. Rather than a stunned silence, it represents a determination to follow the procedure that officiating priests should not be in mourning.

10:4. relatives caring for the dead. One of the important roles for a family is to care for their dead. In this situation the brothers of the dead were not available in that they were still involved in officiating at the sacrifice. Therefore the cousins were instructed to perform the necessary duties.

10:6-7. mourning rites and anointing oil. Disheveled hair and torn clothing are two of the principal signs of mourning. Other signs would include shaving hair or beard, putting dust on the head, and even slashing oneself. The mourning period generally lasted seven days. Aaron was warned against doing this because it contradicted the priestly condition that he was required to maintain for the ceremony. It would cheapen the holiness of the sanctuary and God's presence to interrupt that which the anointing oil had put in motion. See 21:10-12.

10:8. wine and fermented drink. Dates, honey and grain products all could be fermented and used as beverages, but barley beer was probably the most common alcoholic beverage. There is some evidence of ritual intoxication in ancient Near Eastern literature and the Bible also attests the practice (Is 28:7).

10:10. the sacred compass. Verse 10 establishes several categories. Everything that was holy (consecrated to deity) was clean (ritually purified). That which was not holy (therefore profane or common) could be either clean or unclean. It was the duty of the priests to maintain the distinctions between these categories, and they did so by maintaining what is called the sacred compass. In this concept the center of sacred space was the Most Holy Place, where the ark was. Radiating from that point out were concentric zones of holiness, each with its requirements of levels of *purity. The priests enforced the rules that would maintain the appropriate level of holiness and *purity for each zone.

10:11. priestly instruction. Instruction by the priests would have included ethical as well as *ritual matters, though here the emphasis is likely on the latter. Deuteronomy 24:8 offers an example of such priestly instruction. Priests in the ancient world were considered experts in ritual matters of the performance of the *cult and were regularly consulted about often complex procedures.

10:12-15. priestly portions. The details of verses 12-15 have been considered in comments on chapters 6 and 7.

10:16. the importance of eating the purification offering. The purification offering was believed to absorb the impurities that it was presented to remedy. This concept of ritual absorption is common in the ancient Near East. When a great amount is absorbed (as on the Day of Atonement), the entire offering is burned so as to dispose of the *impurity. But on most occasions the priest's eating of the prescribed parts plays a role in the purification process. Milgrom suggests that it symbolized holiness swallowing up *impurity. If this is so, Milgrom is right in understanding Aaron's explanation to Moses here as reflecting his fearful caution. The presence of his sons' corpses in the sanctuary area may have greatly increased the amount of *impurity absorbed by the purification offering, making it lethal to the priest.

11:1-46
Clean and Unclean Food

11:2. dietary restrictions. In Mesopotamia there were numerous occasions on which certain foods were prohibited for a short period. There is also evidence in *Babylonia that there were certain restrictions concerning animals that particular gods would accept for sacrifice. But there is no overriding system such as that found here. Yet though there is no known parallel in the ancient world to anything like the Israelite system of dietary restrictions, the permitted animals generally conform to the diet common in the ancient Near East.

11:3-7. criteria for classification of animals. The main criteria are (1) means of locomotion and (2) physical characteristics. Nothing is mentioned of their eating habits or the conditions of their habitat. Anthropologists have suggested that animals were considered clean or unclean depending on whether they possessed all the features that made them "normal" in their category. Other suggestions have concerned health and hygiene. The weakness of each of these is that there are too many ex-

amples that do not fit the explanation. A popular traditional explanation suggested that the animals prohibited had some connection to non-Israelite *rituals. In fact, however, the sacrificial practices of Israel's neighbors appear strikingly similar to Israel's. A recent promising suggestion is that the Israelite diet is modeled after God's "diet"—that is, if it could not be offered in sacrifice to God, then it was not suitable for human consumption either.

11:7. pigs. *Assyrian wisdom literature calls the pig unholy, unfit for the temple and an abomination to the gods. There is also one dream text in which eating pork is a bad omen. Yet it is clear that pork was a regular part of the diet in Mesopotamia. Some *Hittite *rituals require the sacrifice of a pig. Milgrom observes, however, that in such rituals the pig is not put on the altar as food for the god but absorbs *impurity and then is burned or buried as an offering to underworld deities. Likewise in Mesopotamia it was offered as a sacrifice to demons. There is evidence in Egypt of pigs used for food, and Herodotus claims they were used for sacrifice there as well. Egyptian sources speak of herds of swine being kept on temple property, and they were often included in donations to the temples. The pig was especially sacred to the god Seth. Most evidence for the sacrifice of pigs, however, comes from Greece and Rome, there also mostly to gods of the underworld. In urban settings pigs along with dogs often scavenged in the streets, making them additionally repulsive. The attitude toward the pig in Israel is very clear in Isaiah 65:4; 66:3, 17, the former showing close connection to worship of the dead. It is very possible then that sacrificing a pig was synonymous with sacrificing to demons or the dead.

11:8. transfer of *impurity. Objects that come into contact with a carcass absorb the uncleanness of the carcass unless they are imbedded in the ground. Springs and wells are therefore exempt, as is seed that is to be planted. The wet seed of verse 38 is being prepared to be used as food, and so it does become unclean. Any contact with a carcass made the individual unclean as well and required purification. Most eating of meat would have involved animals that had been ritually slaughtered and therefore would not transfer uncleanness.

12:1-8
Purification After Childbirth

12:2. ceremonial uncleanness. Not all uncleanness was avoidable, and the cause of uncleanness was often something that would in no way be considered sinful. There are several categories of uncleanness that could not be easily avoided, including sexual impurities, disease-related impurities and the uncleanness that came from contact with a corpse or carcass. Though it was a matter of etiquette rather than ethics, the sacred compass needed to be protected from that which was inappropriate. Additionally it was a common belief that demons inhabited menstrual blood. In Israel bodily emissions such as menstrual blood and semen were closely associated with life. When the potential for life that they represented went unfulfilled, they would represent death and therefore uncleanness. That the uncleanness from childbirth should be seen as similar to monthly uncleanness from the menstrual cycle was common in ancient cultures, including Egypt, *Babylonia and Persia.

12:3. circumcision. See comment on Genesis 17:9-14.

12:4-5. purification for 33/66 days. The initial seven-day period plus the thirty-three additional days brings the total to forty—the normal number for estimations. Postpartum blood flow can last anywhere from two to six weeks, so this would be a suitable approximation. Persians and Greeks had similar forty-day restrictions concerning entering sacred areas after giving birth, and many cultures require a longer purification time for girls. *Hittites considered the child unclean for three months (male) or four (female). There is no sure rationale for why the purification time differs depending on the gender of the child.

12:7. atonement. Cases like this make it clear that what has been called a "sin offering" is actually a purification offering (see the comments on chap. 4). There is no sin here that needs "atonement." Rather the *impurity is cleansed from the altar (see the comment on 1:4).

13:1-46
Skin Disease

13:2. varieties of skin disease. Those studying the language have concluded that the term often translated "leprosy" (NIV: "infectious skin disease") is more accurately rendered "lesion" or, less technical, "scaly skin." Such patches could be swollen or weeping, as well as flaking. Similar broad terminology also exists in *Akkadian, where the *Babylonians likewise considered it an unclean condition and the punishment of the gods. Clinical leprosy (Hansen's disease) has not been attested in the ancient Near East prior to the time of Alexander the Great. None of the most prominent characteristics of Hansen's disease are listed

in the text, and the symptoms that are listed argue against a relationship to Hansen's disease. The condition discussed in the text is not presented as contagious. Descriptions suggest that modern diagnoses would include psoriasis, eczema, favus and seborrheic dermatitis as well as a number of fungal-type infections. Comparison to "snow" most likely concerns the flakiness rather than the color ("white" is added in the translations that contain it). The great cultural aversion to skin diseases may be that in appearance (and sometimes odor) they resemble the rotting skin of the corpse and are therefore associated with death. This natural revulsion adds considerably to the victim's outcast status when combined with the quarantine that is ritually rather than medically motivated. A reflection of this can be seen in an Old Babylonian omen that interprets white areas of skin as an indication that that person has been rejected by his god and should therefore be rejected by people as well.

13:45. behavior of victim. The disheveled hair, torn clothing and covered face characterize the victim as a mourner. In the superstitions of the day the mourner would thus disguise himself from the evil forces hovering in the places of the dead. His cry would prevent someone from coming near, for popular belief held that even his breath could contaminate.

13:46. living outside the camp. Though the camp did not need to maintain the same level of *purity as the temple compound, there were restrictions. This restriction is also found in *Babylonian literature for victims of skin diseases forced to live in isolation. It is likely that they would have lived in the vicinity of the tombs.

13:47-59. contaminated cloth. This is a reference to various fungi and molds that can infect cloth or wood. Mesopotamian literature considers these growths to be associated with evil or the demonic, but they are not so personified in biblical text.

14:1-57
Purification of Scale Contamination

14:2. cleansing ritual. These *rituals are not concerned with dirt or bacteria but with ritual *impurity. Wild birds are used because the freed (contaminated) bird must never be inadvertently used for sacrifice. In Mesopotamian and *Hittite purification rituals birds are used because they are believed to carry the *impurity back to its source in the heavens. Cedar is apparently used for its red color, along with the yarn and the blood. This is not used magically by the Israelites (curing had already taken place) but symbolically. Many interpreters consider the red to represent life.

14:8. significance of shaving. Hair sometimes represents a person's life or identity, but here it has no symbolic value. It is shaved off so all may see the restored condition of the skin and so no residual *impurity could be harbored there.

14:10. three-tenths of an ephah. Three-tenths of an ephah is about six quarts, the equivalent of offering a grain offering for each of the three sheep offered.

14:10. log of oil. A log is a small amount, less than a pint, but it is difficult to be precise. The Bible uses the term only in this chapter, and the occurrences in other languages are equally vague.

14:12. guilt offering. This offering, better translated "reparation offering," is described in chapter 5. It is generally offered when the sanctuary has somehow suffered loss. It may be part of this *ritual to make amends for any offerings that had to be omitted by the individual during his quarantine. Another suggestion is that since skin affliction could at times be a punishment from God for an act of sacrilege, the reparation offering is made just in case there was some such offense that the victim was unaware of.

14:12. the wave offering. See comment on 7:30-34. This context is the only one in which the entire animal in included in the ceremony (see chaps. 7—8).

14:14. right ear, right thumb, right big toe. See comment on 8:23.

14:15. the use of the oil. Oil is used in the ancient Near East as a protective substance. Though that function may well have disappeared in Israel, oil was retained as an important ritual element (like mistletoe in homes today being no longer considered protection from demons but associated with the season). An Egyptian *ritual for preparing an idol for the day includes a similar procedure to that described here in verse 18.

14:18. atonement. The oil (or, more likely, the entire reparation *ritual), the purification offering, the burnt offering and the grain offering are each said to make atonement for the individual. For atonement as purgation see comments on chapter 1. Here it is used to describe the complex ritual process that provides the individual with a clean slate for being reinstated into full participation in the ritual system.

14:34. mildew. The reference here is to fungal infections, which were considered to be evil

omens in the ancient world. Mesopotamian *rituals target fungus growths in a number of different contexts. The wall containing the fungus was believed to be the indicator of which member of the family would die. The fungus was an omen of the coming of demons and their troubles. There is no such element here, and only the house needs the ritual procedures, not the inhabitants.

14:48. purification ritual. This *rite shows some similarity to the fungus purification rites known from the rest of the ancient Near East. The *Hurrian ritual uses birds (two sacrificed, one released) and burns cedar just as the Israelites did. *Babylonians used a raven and a hawk. The latter was released into the wilderness. For the other details of this ritual, see the comment on the beginning of this chapter.

15:1-33
Discharges

15:1-15. discharges caused by disease. Described here is the discharge of mucus that is most frequently caused by gonorrhea (though only the more benign varieties were present in the ancient world). Alternatively it has been identified as infectious urinary bilharzia, a known scourge of the ancient world. This disease was caused by the parasite *Schistosoma* related to snails in the water system that have been detected in excavations. Such discharges were believed to be evidence of demonic presence in the person in the larger ancient Near East, but in Israel they required only washing of the individual and purification of the sanctuary, not *exorcism as in Mesopotamia.

15:16-18. seminal emissions. Among the *Hittites nocturnal emissions were considered to result from sexual intercourse with spirits. There is no such stigma here, and the purification requires only washing, not sacrifice. Any sexual activity would prevent one from entering the temple compound until evening. This was also true in Egyptian practice, though it is not in evidence in many other ancient Near Eastern cultures, presumably due to the prevalence of ritualized prostitution. In these cultures, illustrated by *Hittite practice, sexual intercourse required washing prior to participation in rituals but required no waiting period and was not explicitly prohibited on temple grounds.

15:19-24. menstruation. Menstrual flow was considered a source of *impurity throughout the ancient world and in a few cultures represented danger of demonic influence. Again Israel treats it only as requiring washing, not sacrifice, and offers no protective rituals. A royal *Assyrian decree toward the end of the second millennium prohibited a menstruating woman from coming into the king's presence when sacrifices were being made.

15:25-33. irregular discharges. Menostaxis is the name for the principal cause of continued blood flow beyond the regular monthly period. This could result in nearly perpetual uncleanness and make it nearly impossible to have children, for sexual intercourse is prohibited when such a blood flow exists.

16:1-34
Day of Atonement (Purgation)

16:2. limited access to holy places. Temples in the ancient world were typically not houses of public worship. Access to sacred precincts was heavily restricted because they were considered holy ground. The more sacred the area, the more restricted the access, both to protect the human beings who would be taking their lives in their hands to trespass on sacred ground and to prevent desecration of the dwelling place of deity.

16:2. appearing in a cloud. *Akkadian uses the term *melammu* to describe the glowing, visible representation of the glory of deity, which in turn is enshrouded in smoke or cloud. In Canaanite mythology it has been suggested the *melammu* concept is expressed by the word *anan*, the same Hebrew word here translated "cloud," but the occurrences are too few and obscure for confidence.

16:2. atonement cover. Traditionally translated "mercy seat," though all translations are speculative. The term refers to the solid gold rectangular plate or sheet (made of one piece with the cherubim) that sat on top of the ark (see comment on Ex 25:17). One suggestion is that the word comes from Egyptian, where a similar-sounding word refers to a place to rest one's feet. Since the ark is at times viewed as a footstool for God, this would fit well.

16:4. Aaron's garments. See the comments on Exodus 28 for the description of the high priest's garments. Here he is not dressed in full regalia but, as an act of humility, in more simple linen clothing. The linen for the clothing worn by the priests was imported from Egypt, where it was also distinctively used for priests' garments. Angels, too, are said to be dressed in linen (for example, Dan 10:5). Later in the ceremony the high priest will change into the regular uniform (vv. 23-24).

16:6-10. purpose of the day. Though other cultures of the ancient Near East have *rituals to dispose of evil, in all of those the evil is of a ritual or demonic nature, while in Israel all of the sins of the people are included. The ceremony begins with purification offerings so that the priest can enter the holy place. Once inside, the blood ritual cleanses all the parts of the sanctuary from the impurities accumulated throughout the year. It works from the inside out until the sins are placed on the head of the "scapegoat," which carries them away. The goal of the regular purification offerings was forgiveness (see comment on 4:13-32). In contrast, this annual ritual is intended to dispose of the sins of the people.

16:8. Azazel. The Hebrew word translated "scapegoat" is *azazel*. This translation results in dividing the Hebrew word into two words—an unlikely solution. Since verse 8 identifies one goat as "for *Yahweh" and the other goat as "for Azazel," it is most consistent to consider Azazel a proper name, probably of a demon. Early Jewish interpreters had this understanding, as is demonstrated in the book of Enoch (second century B.C.). This goat is not sacrificed to Azazel (consistent with 17:7) but released "to Azazel" (v. 26). *Babylonians believed in *alu*-demons that lived in deserted wasteland, and this may be a similar concept. In Ebla tablets there is a purification rite for a mausoleum using a goat which is then released into the steppe country.

16:8. scapegoat concept in the ancient Near East. A number of *Hittite *rituals feature the transfer of evil to an animal that is then sent away. In some cases the animal is considered a gift to appease the gods or a type of sacrifice to the gods, but in others it is simply a means of disposing of the evil. Mesopotamian rituals that transfer *impurity often see the animal as a substitute for an individual—a substitute that will now become the object of demonic attack instead of the person. In the *Asukki Marsuti* ritual for fever, the goat that is the substitute for the sick man is sent out into the wilderness. All of these differ significantly from Israelite practice in that they are enacted by means of incantations (reciting words of power)—a concept totally absent in Israelite ritual. Additionally the Israelite practice shows no intention to appease the anger of deity or demon, whereas this is the most common motivation of the ancient Near Eastern rituals.

16:8. casting lots. Casting lots gives the Lord the opportunity to choose the goat for sacrifice.

16:12. function of the incense. Incense altars were typical of both Israelite and Canaanite sanctuaries. The incense offered on these altars was a mixture of spices featuring most prominently frankincense but also including

gum resin, onycha and galbanum (see the comment on Ex 30:34-38). Later Jewish tradition included a dozen spices in the mixture. The smoke of the incense represented the prayers of the people going up to God.
16:29. tenth day of the seventh month. This would be in the fall, ten days after New Year's Day. In our calendar it falls toward the end of September.
16:34. atonement once a year. In the *Babylonian new year *ritual the priest slaughtered a ram to be used in purging the sanctuary. Incantations to exorcise demons were recited. The king declared himself free of a number of crimes concerning his office, and the body of the ram was thrown into the river.

17:1-18
Meat Consumption and Blood

17:4. guilty of bloodshed. Domestic animals suitable for sacrifice could not be ritually slaughtered for fellowship offerings except at the tabernacle/temple. This prohibition would help prevent the offering of these sacrifices to other gods or at unapproved shrines. It would also hinder the concept that the blood of an animal slaughtered away from the sanctuary could be considered as appeasing netherworld deities. It was this spilling of blood in illicit rituals that the individual would be guilty of.
17:7. goat idols. The term most likely refers to satyrlike demons who were believed to haunt the open fields and uninhabitable places.
17:9. cut off from his people. This terminology is generally accepted as reflecting a belief that God would carry out the appropriate punishment. It does not suggest any judicial or societal action against that person but awaits the action of God.
17:11. life in the blood. The idea that blood contained the essence of life is evident in the Mesopotamian belief that the first people were created from the blood of a slain deity. But there were no dietary restrictions regarding blood and nothing to suggest a ritual use of blood, either in terms of what was offered to deity or in purification rituals, anywhere else in the ancient Near East.
17:11. blood as atonement. It is because the blood was believed to contain the essence of life that it could serve as a purifying agent in the *rituals of the sacrificial system. For more discussion about the word translated "atonement," see the comment on 1:4.
17:12. prohibition against eating blood. Eating the blood could easily be viewed as one way of absorbing the life force of another crea-

ture. This type of thinking is forbidden, as is the idea that by ingesting it the individual has destroyed the life force by dissipation. Instead, the life is to be offered back to God, whence it came.

18:1-30
Sexual Prohibitions

18:1-29. sexual taboos. Every society develops sexual taboos to regulate marriage practices, adultery and unacceptable sexual practices. These restrictions vary from one culture to another, but they are all designed to reflect the economic and moral values of their society. The laws in chapter 18 are *apodictic (command) laws, which note only that these practices defile the people. The word used in verses 22-29 (NIV: "detestable") identifies the behavior as contrary to the character of God. A parallel term in *Sumerian and *Akkadian designates conduct as being despicable to deity. In the case of incest (vv. 6-18), the primary concern is over relations with immediate blood kin (father, mother, sister, brother, son, daughter) and affinal relations (wife, husband, uncle, aunt). The only exception is in the case of levirate obligation (Deut 25:5-10), when a man's brother is required to have sexual relations with his sister-in-law. Incest was equally abhorrent in most other societies (e.g., the prohibitions in *Hittite laws). A Hittite treaty prohibits sexual relationships with sisters-in-law or cousins on pain of death. The exception is Egypt, where incest was a common practice in the royal family (but little attested elsewhere) as a means to strengthen or consolidate royal authority. This concept is also seen among *Elamite kings. Adultery (v. 20) violates the sanctity of the family and contaminates the inheritance process (see the comment on Ex 20:14).
18:21. children passed through the fire to Molech. Evidence of child sacrifice has been recovered from Phoenician sites in North Africa (Carthage) and Sardinia, and it was also practiced in Syria and Mesopotamia during the *Assyrian period (eighth and seventh centuries B.C.). Dedicating children to a god as a form of sacrifice is found in several biblical narratives. It can be explained as a means of promoting *fertility (Mic 6:6-7) or as a way of obtaining a military victory (Judg 11:30-40; 2 Kings 3:27). In no case, however, is this considered acceptable as a sacrifice to *Yahweh under biblical law (Deut 18:10). Many consider Molech to be a netherworld deity whose worship featured *rituals with Canaanite origins focusing on dead ancestors. An eighth-

century B.C. Phoenician inscription speaks of sacrifices made to Molech before battle by the Cilicians and their enemies.

18:22-23. homosexuality and bestiality. Homosexuality (v. 22) and bestiality (v. 23) were both practiced in the context of *ritual or magic in the ancient Near East. The latter particularly occurs in the mythology of *Ugarit and is banned in legal materials (especially the *Hittite laws). The mixing of realms was contrary to concepts of *purity.

18:24-28. Canaanite sexual perversions. These perversions should not be considered simply the result of human depravity. Sex had been ritually incorporated into worship in order to procure *fertility of the land, the herds and flocks, and the people. While the fertility aspect of Canaanite religion is well attested, little is known of specific details of ritualized sex. Temple personnel included male and female prostitutes, but their ritual role is still obscure. The implication of these verses is also that violation of the sexual code pollutes both the people and the land, requiring a cleansing process that will drive them out and allow resettlement by the Israelites. There is thus an understanding of an intimate relationship between land and people that would have been natural to a people who based their lives on agriculture and herding. Despite the assurance that the land would ultimately belong to them, however, caution is expressed that the Israelites not follow this same course of personal defilement and be exiled in turn.

19:1-37
Miscellaneous Laws

19:9-10. intentionally inefficient harvesting. In *fertility *cults, the portion left in the field would have served as an offering to the deities of the ground. Here it becomes a means to care for the poor. While no examples of this legislation survive in ancient Near Eastern law, texts from the town of *Nuzi suggest a similar practice.

19:11-19. social contract. This is another set of *apodictic (command) decrees similar to the Decalogue (Ten Commandments) of Exodus 20:1-17. It provides an even fuller concept of the social contract between God and the Israelites, as well as the rights and obligations of the Israelites among themselves. There are no other examples of such social contracts between people and their deity. However the ancient Near Eastern gods were believed to be concerned about justice in society, and people considered themselves accountable to the gods, either to their personal/family gods or

to Shamash, the god of justice. The gods were believed to judge people's conduct and were called upon to witness behavior in the human realm. Thus the social contracts that governed human behavior among Israel's neighbors were made between the human parties with the gods invoked by oath as protectors.

19:19. mixing animals, seeds, materials. Some mixtures were considered to be reserved for sacred use. The parallel passage in Deuteronomy 22:9-11 makes it clear that this is the issue in Israel as well. The mixture of wool and linen was used in the tabernacle and in the high priest's outer garments, and it was thus reserved for sacred use. This interpretation is also current in the Dead Sea Scrolls (4QMMT). Sowing of two types of seed is also prohibited in the *Hittite laws, with a death threat to violators.

19:20-22. status of slave girl. Standards of conduct and penalties vary for slaves. Ancient Near Eastern law contains several examples of punishment for the rape of a female slave. Both the Neo-Sumerian laws of *Ur-Nammu and the *Babylonian laws of *Eshnunna (both c. 2000 B.C.) prescribe fines for rape of a female slave. The Eshnunna law adds the further provision that the woman remains the property of her original owner, so that rape cannot become a predatory means of obtaining a slave. In the biblical example, the case is not considered adultery and therefore does not end in execution (see Deut 22:23-24), since she is still technically a slave, not a free woman (see Ex 22:16-17).

19:23-25. fruit tree husbandry. Orchards of fruit trees were of such great value that the law forbade cutting them during times of war (Deut 20:19). They usually contained more than one variety of tree (see Amos 9:14). Among the most common fruit trees were fig, olive, date and sycamore fig. Some orchards were irrigated (Num 24:6), but most appear to have been planted on terraced hillsides (Jer 31:5). Careful cultivation and pruning was necessary during the first three years in order to insure eventual good harvests and proper maturing of the trees. The fruit during this period could not be eaten and was declared unclean (literally, "uncircumcised"). In the fourth year the entire harvest was to be dedicated to God as an offering, and from the fifth year on the owner could eat the fruit.

19:26. divination. *Divination involves a variety of methods used by prophets (Mic 3:11), soothsayers, mediums and sorcerers to determine the will of the gods and to predict the future. These included the examination of the entrails of sacrificial animals, the analysis of omens of various types and the reading of the future in natural and unnatural phenomena (see Gen 44:5). The prohibition against eating meat with the "blood still in it" in this verse is tied to the injunction against participating in any form of divination or sorcery. Thus, rather than being a dietary law, this decree involves the practice of draining blood from a sacrificial animal into the ground or a sacred pit, which was designed to attract the spirits of the dead (see 1 Sam 28:7-19) or chthonic (underworld) deities in order to consult them about the future. Such practices are found in several *Hittite ritual texts and in Odysseus' visit to the underworld (*Odyssey* 11.23-29, 34-43). These practices were condemned (Deut 18:10-11) because they infringed on the idea of *Yahweh as an all-powerful God who was not controlled by fate.

19:27. significance of hair trimming. For men hair has symbolic value as a sign of manhood or virility (see 2 Sam 10:4). Women decorate their hair and groom it carefully as a sign of beauty. The prohibition against trimming the "sides of your head" or the "edges of your beard" uses the same terminology as in 19:9-10, which deals with the harvesting of fields. In both cases an offering is involved—one to the poor and the other to God. The law's placement here immediately after the prohibition against *divination suggests that the restriction on cutting the hair is based on the Canaanite practice of making an offering of hair to propitiate the spirits of the dead (see Deut 14:1). *Hammurabi's code penalizes false witnesses by having half the person's hair cut off. The Middle Assyrian code allows a debt-slave's master to pull out his or her hair as punishment (see Neh 13:25). Both laws suggest that shame is attached to the loss of hair. There is a Phoenician inscription from the ninth century B.C. reporting the dedication of shaven hair by an individual in fulfillment of a vow made to the goddess *Astarte. In ancient thinking hair (along with blood) was one of the main representatives of a person's life essence. As such it was often an ingredient in sympathetic magic. This is evident, for instance, in the practice of sending along a lock of a presumed prophet's hair when his prophecies were sent to the king of *Mari. The hair would be used in divination to determine whether the prophet's message would be accepted as valid.

19:28. cutting body for dead. Mourning and *cultic practices sometimes included lacerating oneself (see 1 Kings 18:28; Jer 16:6, 41:5). This may have been done to attract a god's attention, ward off the spirits of the dead or

demonstrate greater grief then simply wailing. The prohibition may be due to its association with Canaanite religion. For instance, the *Ugaritic cycle of stories about the god *Baal (c. 1600-1200 B.C.) includes an example of mourning by the chief god *El over the death of Baal. His grief takes the ritual form of filling his hair with dirt, wearing sackcloth and cutting himself with a razor. The text reads that "he plowed his chest like a garden."

19:28. tattoo marks. The prohibition against marking the skin may involve either tattooing or painting the body as part of a religious *ritual. Such markings may have been designed to protect a person from the spirits of the dead or to demonstrate membership in a group. Some evidence for this has been found in the examination of human remains in Scythian tombs dating to the sixth century B.C. The Israelite law may prohibit this practice since it involves a self-imposed alteration of God's creation, unlike *circumcision, which is commanded by God.

19:29. prostitution. In line with the surrounding laws, which prohibit defiling either the people or the produce of the land, this law against selling a daughter into prostitution is designed to prevent defiling both her honor and that of the family. Financial problems might tempt a father to do this, but it is considered a moral pollution of both the people and of the land itself. As in 18:24-28, such a practice could result in eventual expulsion from the land. The extreme nature of this penalty may be based on the loss of honor of both the household and the community. However, it is also possible that this refers to *cultic prostitution and thus would mean the worship of gods other than *Yahweh.

19:31. mediums and spiritualists. The practitioners of spiritism and sorcery are condemned (Deut 18:10-11) because of their association with Canaanite religion and because their "art" attempted to circumvent *Yahweh by seeking knowledge and power from spirits. They represented a form of "popular religion" that was closer to the folk practices of the common people and served as a form of "shadow religion" for many. Sometimes, because of its association with *divination, their *rituals and methods stood in direct opposition to "official religion" or as an alternative to be used in times of desperation (see Saul's use of the outlawed witch of Endor in 1 Sam 28). Sorcery and potions used in the practice of magic were also banned in *Hammurabi's code and the Middle Assyrian law, suggesting that the prohibition and fear of these practices was not unique to Israel.

19:35-36. honest measurements. The injunction to deal in honest weights and measures when doing business is directly related to the laws in 19:11-18, which require fair dealing and an internalized sense that your neighbor is to be treated as you would want to be treated. Standardization of weights and measures was required in *Hammurabi's code with regard to repayment of debts in grain or silver, and involving the measuring out of grain to pay for wine. Penalties for violators ranged from forfeiture of property to execution.

20:1-27

Defiling Conduct

20:2-5. children of Molech. One of the major themes in this book equates idolatry with prostituting oneself after other gods. This in turn pollutes *Yahweh's sanctuary, the Israelites themselves and the land. The practice of sacrificing children to Molech (see comment on 18:21) is condemned, and the perpetrators are to be stoned (a form of communal execution which draws everyone into the act of purification). No violation of this command will be tolerated, even if God must mete out the punishment when the community chooses to turn a blind eye to sin. The idea of "cutting off" the sinner implies complete banishment from God and the community and was generally a punishment that was seen as being carried out by God.

20:9. cursing parents. Contrary to the NIV translation, studies have demonstrated that the infraction here is not cursing but treating with contempt. This is a more general category and would certainly include the prohibition of Exodus 21:15, which forbids striking a parent, and would be the opposite of the fifth commandment to "honor your father and your mother" (Ex 20:12). Each injunction is designed to protect the cohesion of the family unit as well as insure that each subsequent generation provide their parents with the respect, food and protection they deserve (see Deut 21:18-21). Mesopotamian law codes and legal documents are also clear on the issue of treating parents with contempt. The *Sumerian laws allow a son who disowns his parents to be sold as a slave. *Hammurabi requires the amputation of the hand of a man who strikes his father. A will from *Ugarit describes a son's behavior using the same verb used in this verse and stipulates disinheritance.

20:10-16. capital punishment for sexual crimes. The violation of sexual codes (adultery, incest, homosexuality, bestiality) is placed on a par with idolatry in this law code and thus requires the sentence of death. Both defile persons and the land and cannot be tolerated. Crimes of this nature are also punishable in *Hammurabi's code (adultery requires trial by ordeal in laws 129 and 132; rape is a capital crime in law 130; incest is punished by exile in law 154), the *Middle Assyrian laws (homosexuality punished by castration in law 20) and the *Hittite laws (bestiality with pigs or dogs punished by death in law 199). In the Hittite treaty between Shuppiluliuma and Huqqana, the latter is charged not to take his sister or cousin sexually because among the Hittites people are put to death for such behavior. Such inhibitions, however, were certainly not universal. In the Persian period, for instance, men were encouraged to marry their sisters, daughters or mother as acts of piety. In Israelite practice, however, these were all believed to undermine the family, the foundational element of Israelite society. To undermine the family was to undermine the *covenant.

20:20-21. penalty of childlessness. Having children meant having someone to care for you in old age and give proper burial and the extension of the family into the next generation. Being childless represented the cutting off of the family and the risk of being neglected in old age and death.

20:27. medium or spiritist. See comment on 19:31.

21:1—22:32

Regulations for Priests

21:5. shaving practices of priests. Priests have the special injunction to keep themselves pure and holy because it is their responsibility to bring offerings to God. As a result, their skin and hair must remain intact, free of blemish or injury, as a testimony to that holiness. Thus they are prohibited from engaging in the mourning practices common in Canaan of gashing themselves, tearing their hair or shaving their beard. In fact it would be shameful for them to present themselves in any condition that was not holy (see Satan's accusation against the high priest Joshua in Zech 3:3).

21:7. marriage regulations for priests. There was a special regulation for priests against marrying a woman who was known to have engaged repeatedly in prostituting herself ("defiled by prostitution" implies flagrant abuse). Furthermore, he was also denied the right to marry a woman who was divorced. This is probably due to the fact that the principal charge made against a woman by her husband in a divorce proceeding was infidelity (see Num 5:11-31; Deut 22:13-14; 24:1).

21:10-14. special regulations for high priest.
Even a higher standard of *purity was required for the high priest. He must avoid contaminating his person by coming into contact with the dead, even if this means absenting himself from his parents' funeral, and he cannot engage in the usual forms of mourning (see purification rituals for corpse contamination in Num 19). This restriction may also be an attempt to disassociate the priesthood from *cults of the dead. Furthermore, the priest's wife must be a virgin. She cannot have been married before, nor can she be either a divorcee or a prostitute. The high priest was anointed to represent the *purity of the nation in its dealings with God. Therefore he must avoid all contact with persons or objects that might defile him and through him the Holy of Holies.

21:16-23. prohibiting priests with defects.
Just as animals with physical defects or blemishes may not be offered for sacrifice (22:19-22), priests who have a physical defect may not serve before the altar. Ritual *purity is required for the sacred precincts of the altar, the sacrifice and the religious practitioner officiating at the altar in every religion in the ancient Near East. Priests must therefore be in perfect health and in full command of their bodies and senses. Thus anyone who is "blind [even in one eye], lame, disfigured or deformed," is restricted from priestly service. The list is quite graphic and includes defects caused by accidents (broken bones, crushed testicles), birth defects (dwarfism, lameness, hunchback) or disease (skin afflictions, sores). Even though he may not approach the altar, the disabled priest is still entitled to his share of the priestly portion of the sacrifice.

21:21. food of his God. A portion of most sacrificial offerings was reserved for the nourishment of the priests (see 2:3, 10; 7:6, 31-34; 24:8-9; Num 18:12-13, 15, 26, for a description of the sacrifices and the priestly portion). Even if a priest is disqualified from taking part in the sacrificial *ritual, due to physical defect, he still has the right to eat from this divine meal, for he is still a priest. The sharing of the sacrificial repast by the deity and attending priests is also found in Egyptian and Mesopotamian texts, creating a special bond between servitor and deity. See comments on 1:1-2 and 3:6-11.

22:3-9. prohibiting priests with uncleanness.
The altar and those who officiated at it were required to maintain strict *purity and cleanliness. This was the case among the Israelites as well as other peoples of the ancient Near East. Egyptian priests were required to undergo lengthy purification rites before approaching the altar. One *Hittite text contains a long list of instructions on maintaining the ritual *purity of priest and temple as well as the means to cleanse them in case of contamination, which is very similar to that found in chapter 22. Any source of contamination (improper or defective sacrifice or a defiled person or priest) would defile them and require lengthy purification rites before they could once again fulfill their function. The list in 22:4-5 provides a guide to persons who must be kept away from the sacred precincts and the priests, including those who have come in contact with the dead or an unclean animal or person or have eaten unclean food. *Hittite law, which prohibits persons who have had sexual relations with a horse or mule from becoming priests, provides another type of uncleanness which is not commensurate with serving as a priest.

22:8. carcasses. All animals found dead were unclean, so only those that had been ritually slaughtered with the blood properly drained were available for the priests.

22:10-16. eligibility for priestly portions.
There are foods which are only to be consumed by their god(s) and their priests. A graphic example of this is found in the oath of a *Hittite prince, "Prayers of Kantuzilis," which certifies that he has never eaten "that which is holy to my god." At least in the Israelite law, the portion set aside for the priest may also be shared with members of his household, although not with guests or hired workers. The restrictions are based on the fact that this is sacred food, and it must not be given to persons outside his extended family (including his slaves). Even daughters who marry outside the priestly community are prohibited from eating this food. There is provision for her return to her father's household after the death of her husband, and in that case she will once again be allowed to eat from the sacrificial offering.

22:17-28. classes of unacceptable sacrifices.
Just as the altar and the priests must be without defect and ritually pure, so too must the items brought for sacrifice. However, there are categories of acceptable offerings based on the type of sacrifice. For instance, when an animal is presented as a freewill offering or to fulfill a vow, it must be male and without defect. No beast which is blind, injured or maimed or which has skin disorders (warts or sores) will be accepted. But for lesser freewill offerings, a cow or sheep which is deformed or stunted will be accepted, although not one whose testicles are damaged. Similarly, in *Hittite *ritual, dogs, which were normally considered

unclean, could be sacrificed to the gods of the underworld.

22:28. prohibition concerning slaughter of mother and young. The regulation that a mother and her young should not be offered the same day provided some protection to those with just a few animals who might otherwise have found themselves with ritual requirements that would decimate their small herd. There is nothing known of foreign *cultic practice that this would combat, though some have defended the alternative that the regulation had humanitarian concerns.

23:1-44
Religious Calendar

23:1-44. Israel's religious calendar. Versions of Israel's festal calendar are found in Exodus 23:12-19; 34:18-26; Leviticus 23; Deuteronomy 16:1-17; and Numbers 28—29. Each has its own characteristics and emphases. In Leviticus a list of the sacrifices required throughout the year is intertwined with the festivals of sabbath, Passover, the Feast of Unleavened Bread, the Feast of Weeks, the Feast of Trumpets, the Day of Atonement and the Feast of Tabernacles. These feasts mark the various stages in the agricultural year, celebrate harvests and give both credit and a sacrificial portion back to God, who has provided their bounty. Several also became related to historical events. Although the sabbath is not technically a feast day, it is appended here to mark its importance, and it provides a sense of how the ancients calculated time. Much of the rest of the ancient Near East had calendars more cognizant of the sun and moon, since these were manifestations of principal deities. While Israel's calendar did not neglect lunar and solar cycles, less attention was paid to equinoxes and solstices (sometimes viewed as times of conflict between sun and moon gods). Since the agricultural seasons ultimately link to the solar cycles, the lunar month/year system used throughout the ancient Near East had to be periodically adjusted to the solar cycle. This was done by adding a thirteenth month a few days in length when priests determined that an adjustment was called for.

23:3. sacred assembly on the sabbath. Sacred assemblies or proclamations were an important part of most religious practice in the ancient world. They refer to local or national gatherings for public, corporate worship. The people were summoned together away from their occupational work. Aside from performance of corporate *rituals, it is unclear what took place at these gatherings. In later times they were used for public readings, but evidence for this on all such occasions in the early periods is lacking (see Deut 31:10-13). This passage is the only reference to these gatherings in association with the sabbath.

23:5. Passover. This celebration refers to the Passover sacrifice commemorating the departure from Egypt (detailed in Ex 12—13). It is to begin at twilight on the fourteenth day of the first month (March-April). Since the sacrifice is to be a year-old lamb, some speculate that the origin of this event is found among the pastoral nomadic groups of the land and was at this time appended to the agriculturally based Feast of Unleavened Bread. Eventually, Passover became a pilgrimage festival when worship was centralized in Jerusalem, but it returned to home celebration after the destruction of the temple in A.D. 70.

23:6-8. Feast of Unleavened Bread. The Feast of Unleavened Bread signals the beginning of the barley harvest (March-April). Unleavened bread was made from the newly harvested grain without adding yeast and was celebrated as the first sign of coming harvests that year. The seven days of celebration and burnt offering are enclosed by days at the beginning and the end when no work is allowed (see comment on Ex 12:14-20).

23:10-14. wave offering for harvest. As a part of the harvest festival, the "first fruits" are brought to the priest. He in turn waves the sheaf of grain or elevates it before the altar of the Lord. This gesture physically draws God's attention to the sacrifice and signifies that all gifts and sacrificial items derive from and belong to God. It also releases the remainder of the harvest for the people's use (see comment on 7:28-38).

23:12-13. burnt, grain and drink offering. The burnt offering of the year-old lamb, a quantity twice the usual amount of grain, and a libation of wine constituted the three major products of Israel (sometimes with olive oil replacing or supplementing wine—see 2:1; Num 15:4-7). By combining them, the fertility provided by God will be directed toward all of their efforts in animal husbandry and farming. The pleasing odor draws *Yahweh's attention to the sacrifice (see Noah's sacrifice in Gen 8:20-21) and marks it as the properly prescribed thanksgiving *ritual—not the feeding of a god as in Mesopotamian and Egyptian religions.

23:15-22. Feast of Weeks. This second of the three major harvest festivals comes seven weeks after the harvest of the early grain (Ex 34:22; Deut 16:9-12) and is also known as the

Feast of Harvest or Pentecost (Ex 23:16). In the agricultural cycle it marks the end of the wheat harvest season, and by tradition it is tied to the giving of the law on Mount Sinai. It is also associated with *covenant renewal and pilgrimage. Celebration includes the bringing of a "wave offering" of two loaves of bread, animal sacrifices (seven year-old lambs, one bull and two rams) and a drink offering in thanksgiving for a good harvest. A goat is also to be sacrificed as a sin offering for the people. **23:16-20. offerings.** The Feast of Weeks requires a variety of offerings from the people. The "new grain" offering is distinct from the regular grain offering (see 2:13). The two loaves are made with yeast, but they will not actually be taken up on the altar (see regulations in 7:13). The animals that serve as burnt offerings (seven year-old lambs, a young bull and two rams) demonstrate the mixed character of the Israelite economy. The reason for the inclusion of a sin offering of a goat is unclear beyond the idea that the people must be restored to *cultic *purity prior to consuming their harvest.

23:23-25. Feast of Trumpets. The first day of the seventh month (the most sacred month in the Israelite calendar) was to be marked with the blowing of ram's horn (shofar), commemorating the *covenantal agreement and gifts of God to the people. No work is allowed, and burnt offerings are presented (see Num 29:2-6 for items sacrificed). The festival would continue until the tenth day of the month when the Day of Atonement would be observed (see 16:29-34 for details). In later times the Feast of Trumpets would become the New Year's festival, but that occurred in late postexilic times.

23:26-32. Day of Atonement. For information on the Day of Atonement, see the comments on chapter 16.

23:33-43. Feast of Tabernacles. The final harvest of the year occurred in the autumn prior to the onset of the rainy season and marked the beginning of a new agricultural year (fifteenth day of the seventh month). At this time the last of the ripening grain and fruits were gathered and stored. The seven-day event was also known as the Feast of Ingathering (Ex 23:16) and was symbolized by the construction of booths decorated with greenery for the harvesters. The festival was tied into Israelite tradition as a commemoration of the wilderness wanderings. It was also the occasion for the dedication of Solomon's temple in Jerusalem (1 Kings 8:65).

23:40. fruit, leaves and branches. To represent the abundance and lushness of the land, Israelites were instructed to celebrate, decorating their booths with fruit (citron) as well as leaves and branches from willow and palm trees. The festal occasion probably included dancing and processions carrying bundles of the leafy branches. In this way, the people acknowledge the abundance provided by God and communally celebrate the visible fulfillment of the *covenant.

23:42-43. live in booths. As a way of commemorating their life in the wilderness, the Israelites are told to construct booths and live in them during the seven days of the Feast of Tabernacles. The more practical application of these temporary shelters would be to serve as housing for workers who would protect the harvest until its distribution after the festival.

24:1-9
Maintaining the Holy Place

24:2-4. oil lamps. Only the highest quality olive oil was to be used in the sacred oil lamps that illuminated the sacred precincts of the tabernacle. They were placed on golden lampstands (see Ex 25:31-39), which stood just outside the curtain of the testimony in the tent of meeting (see Ex 27:20-21). They were to burn from evening until morning, and Aaron and his descendants were given a sacred trust to keep them lit for all time to come. Like many of the *cultic items associated with the tent of meeting, the oil lamps symbolized the presence and protection of *Yahweh as well as the perpetual service of the priests.

24:4. significance of the menorah. The familiar image of the menorah, with its six branches and center lamp, comes from the description in Exodus 25:31-40 and may be symbolic of the tree of life in the Garden of Eden. However, the description of the lampstand in 24:4 only includes the fact that it is made of gold. The number of lamps is also not specified here.

24:5-9. setting out of the bread and incense. The twelve loaves of the bread of the Presence (Ex 25:23-30) represented the twelve tribes of Israel. These loaves were consumed by the priests every sabbath, and new loaves were put in their place. The burning of frankincense provided the "sacrificial aroma," substituted for burning the flour on the altar. Because the loaves were sacred, they were reserved for the priests (although see 1 Sam 21:4-6).

24:10-23
The Case of the Blasphemer

24:10-16. nature of blasphemy. The name of God is holy. Just as the people are warned not

to misuse the name of God (Ex 20:7), to pronounce a curse using God's name without authorization or to curse God by name (Ex 22:28)
is considered blasphemy. This is a capital offense, punishable by stoning. The *Assyrian
texts condemn blasphemers to having their
tongues cut out and to being skinned alive.

24:14-16. stoning as means of execution.
Stoning is a communal form of execution and
the most commonly mentioned form of execution in the Bible. It is used to punish crimes
against the entire community (apostasy in
20:2; sorcery in 20:27), and it requires all those
persons who have been offended to participate. Because it cannot be determined whose
individual stone caused the death of the condemned, no one person need bear the guilt for
the death. Mesopotamian texts do not mention stoning, but employ drowning, impalement, beheading and burning as forms of
execution.

24:17-22. lex talionis. The legal concept of
equal retribution or "an eye for an eye," is
found in biblical (Ex 21:23-25; Deut 19:21) and
Mesopotamian law codes. It has variations in
*Hammurabi's code (eighteenth-century B.C.
*Babylonia) based on the social status (nobili-
ty, citizen, slave) of the accused and the person harmed. It is possible that a price was set
to redeem a life in capital cases or to replace
the necessity of inflicting matching harm (broken arm, gouged eye, etc.). The basis for such
laws was to insure legal restitution and thereby avoid the culturally disruptive necessity of
seeking private revenge. Ideally, when an injury is done to another person, the way to provide true justice is to cause an equal injury to
the culprit. Although this may seem extreme,
it in fact limits the punishment that can be inflicted on the person accused of the injury.

25:1-55
Sabbatical Year and Jubilee

25:2-7. sabbatical rest for land. This set of
laws requiring that the land lie fallow every
seventh year parallels that found in Exodus
23:10-11. However only here is the term sabbatical applied to the seventh year. The benefit
derived from resting the land is to retard the
rate of salinization (sodium content in the soil)
caused by irrigation. Large areas in Mesopotamia were actually left abandoned due to exhaustion of the soil and a disastrously high
salt content. During the seventh year no cultivation of the soil is allowed. *Ugaritic texts
likewise feature seven-year agricultural cycles, and some would contend that a fallow-
year concept is also included. However, all of

the people, as well as hired laborers and the
farm animals, are allowed to eat the produce
of the land that grows on its own. Such a policy may actually have been enforced on portions of each field every year, so that
eventually it was all allowed to rest.

25:8-55. Jubilee year. Every fiftieth year (sev-
en sabbaths of years plus one year) was
marked by a general release from debt, servitude and a return of all land that had been
mortgaged or sold to the rightful owner. Such
concerns for the perpetual ownership of the
land are also evident in *Ugaritic real estate
documents. Declarations that returned land to
its original owners and freed debt slaves were
periodically made among the *Hittites and in
Mesopotamia (often in the first year of a new
king's reign) and are attested in proclamations
by early kings such as Uruinimgina and Ammisaduqa. At the heart of the Israelite laws is
the idea of the inalienable right of the people
to their land. The land could be used to redeem a debt but must be released at the Jubilee in much the same way that debt slaves
were to be released in the seventh year of their
servitude (Ex 23:10-11; Deut 15:1-11). This
could, of course, serve as the basis for the returned exiles' claim to their former lands, but
this does not exclude the practice from previous historical periods.

**25:23. God as owner of land compared to
temple economy.** All of the land occupied by
the Israelites was the property of *Yahweh. It
was granted to them as tenants, and as such
they could not sell it outright to anyone. In the
Jubilee year (every fiftieth year), all land that
had been consigned for payment of debts was
to be returned to its owners. If a man died, it
was the responsibility of his nearest kin to redeem the land so that it would remain in the
family (25:24-25; Jer 32:6-15). This concept is
similar to that found in Egypt, where the "divine" Pharaoh owned the land and granted it
to his subjects. However, it stands in contrast
with the temple economy that existed in Mesopotamia. There land was owned by individual citizens, the king and the temples of the
various gods. The laws of *Hammurabi speak
of the king's land grants, which could revert
to him upon the death of the vassal. The land
owned by the temples was granted to tenants,
who paid a portion of their harvest for the
right to work the land. This patchwork of
ownership, while depending in many cases on
tenants who could not sell the land, did not
provide the sense of unity implied in the biblical concept.

25:24-25. kinsman redeemer. Since *Yahweh
has granted the land to the Israelites as ten-

ants, they cannot sell it, and if they mortgage a portion of it to pay debts, it is the obligation of their kinsman to "redeem" the land by paying off the mortgage. This demonstrates both the sense of obligation and the solidarity that are the hallmarks of ancient Israel's communally based society. Evidence of this legislation's being put into practice is found in Jeremiah's redeeming of his kinsman's land during the siege of Jerusalem (Jer 32:6-15) and in the legal background to Ruth 4:1-12. In this way the land remained within the extended family as a sign of their membership in the *covenantal community. The importance of this inalienable right to land can be seen in Naboth's refusal to relinquish the "inheritance of my fathers" when King Ahab offers to buy his vineyard (1 Kings 21:2-3). In Mesopotamia (especially the earlier periods) land was often privately owned by families rather than individuals.

25:29-31. difference between houses in walled cities and houses in villages. There is a different legal classification for dwellings in walled towns and those in unwalled villages. In the towns, inhabited by Levites, artisans and government officials, a house could only be redeemed from its buyer within one year. After that the sale was final. Similarly, the Law of *Eshnunna allows a debtor who has sold his house first claim to repurchase it when it comes up for sale again. However, Israelite village dwellings (literally, "encampments") adjacent to fields and pasture lands fell within the same legal category as arable land and could not be sold in perpetuity and were to be released in the Jubilee year. Such legislation is based on the different social conditions in these two settings and indicates an awareness that property in urban centers produced no harvest. It merely provided shelter and business space.

25:38. prohibition against taking interest. Like the other prohibitions against charging interest on loans to fellow Israelites (Ex 22:25; Deut 23:19, see comments there), this legislation is designed to help a person to escape his insolvent condition and to prevent him from falling into debt servitude due to default on a loan. This applies to loans of money as well as grain, which would ordinarily be paid back at the end of the harvest. These laws are also a way to allow the debtor to retain a measure of personal dignity and honor by being treated on a level higher than a slave or a foreigner (see Deut 23:20). Both the laws of *Eshnunna and *Hammurabi's code contain set rates of interest on loans (20 percent to 33.3 percent was not uncommon and was considered fair).

However, it was understood that "acts of god," such as a flood, require compassion on the debtor and a cancellation of interest payments.

25:39-55. slavery in Israel. Ancient Israel considered permanent slavery the most inhumane condition possible. The laws dealing with slavery reflect an understanding of the reasons for poverty and try to deal with its victims nonviolently. They also do not account for the principal cause of slavery in Mesopotamia—warfare. One sign of Israelite concern may be seen in the practice of allowing a household to pledge the work of its members as collateral when it borrowed goods or services from another household. To avoid confiscation of their land and children, the members of a household in default would work off their debt one day at a time. As a state, Israel tried to prevent debt from accumulating to the point where slavery was the only option. Thus the laws against charging interest on loans worked in most cases to aid the poor (Ex 22:24; Deut 23:19-20; Lev 25:35-37; Ezek 18:3). In these cases a household could become destitute and at the insistence of its creditors sell members of the household into slavery to pay debts (2 Kings 4:1; Neh 5:1-5). Slavery in this case is defined as temporary debt slavery, since the law restricts the number of years a man may be held to six (Ex 21:2-11; Deut 15:12-18). Regulations also restrict the sale or the enslavement of Israelites by other Israelites (Lev 25:35-42). In this case the Israelite who is in financial difficulties would be reduced to the status of a hired hand or indentured servant rather than a slave, even if his owner is a non-Israelite (25:47-55). Verse 48 refers to the redemption of slaves, a practice also attested in a number of Mesopotamian sources.

26:1-46
Obedience and Disobedience

26:1. carved stone. This term occurs only here (though it is probably referred to again in Num 33:52) and is quite obscure. A. Hurowitz (on the basis of an Assyrian inscription) has suggested that it may refer to a decorated or engraved threshold slab in the temple area that the king prostrated himself on when making a petition for a favorable sign. For a potentially similar situation see comment on Ezekiel 44:3.

26:1. sacred stone. Like idols (19:4), sacred standing stones are also prohibited as foreign *cult objects. They may have been huge monoliths representing a god or a set of pillars arranged around an altar or shrine. Some of those found in excavations at Gezer and Hazor were decorated with carvings such as raised hands or symbols associated with a particular deity.

26:1. nature and forms of idols. Idols came in a variety of shapes and sizes in the ancient Near East. They were carved from stone and wood and were cast in molds using gold, silver and bronze (see Is 40:19-20). Basically human in appearance (except those from Egypt, which combined human and animal characteristics), they had distinctive, even formalized, poises, clothing and hairstyles. The image was not the deity, but the deity was thought to inhabit the image and manifest its presence and will through the image. Archaeologists have found very few life-sized images that the texts describe, but there are renderings of them that allow accurate knowledge of details.

26:3-45. blessings and curses in treaty formulae. It is typical of ancient Near Eastern legal codes and treaties to append a section of divine blessings and curses (see Deut 28; Code of *Hammurabi [eighteenth century B.C.]; Esarhaddon Treaty [680-669 B.C.]; thirteenth-century B.C. treaty between Rameses II of Egypt and *Hittite king Hattusilis III). Characteristically, the curses far outweigh the blessings and, as in this case, are generally arranged in order of increasing severity. The principle behind these statements is the need to insure compliance with law or with treaties by bringing in divine goodwill and sanction. In this way the parties will feel more obligated than if they were to simply depend on the conscientiousness of their people or neighbors.

26:4-5. importance of fertility. Without continuous yield from the land, the people could not survive. Thus fertility, in the form of regular rainfall and abundant harvest from fields and vines, was a constant concern. As a result many of the gods of the ancient Near East were concerned with rain and storm, *fertility and the growing seasons. The inclusion of fertility in the set of blessings here is a reiteration of *Yahweh's *covenant promise to give the people land and children (i.e., a country of their own and fertility to insure life to each successive generation).

26:5. agricultural calendar. As noted in the Gezer calendar, a tenth-century B.C. schoolboy exercise on a fragment of limestone, the Israelite year was divided into agricultural seasons. Thus the "rain in season" would come in the fall (October-November) to moisten the newly planted fields and in early spring (March-

April) to complete the ripening process before harvest (Deut 11:14).

26:8. five will chase a hundred. A sign of the promised blessing of peace is that *Yahweh, the "Divine Warrior," will fight for them and give them the victory over their enemies, no matter how great the odds against them. Thus five can rout a hundred. This underdog-turned-conqueror theme is also found in Deuteronomy 32:30, Joshua 23:10 and Isaiah 30:17. Similar assurance of the aid of a "Divine Warrior" is found in the Moabite inscription of King Mesha (c. 830 B.C.).

26:13. bars of the yoke. Yokes, usually made of wood, consisted of a bar across the nape of the animals' necks. The bar had pegs placed down through it on either side of each animal's head. The pegs were then tied together under the chin. As slaves in Egypt, the people were burdened with work like oxen bound to a yoke (see Jer 28:10-14). God has broken this yoke of bondage, freeing them of their heavy burdens and allowing them to stand upright like free men and women. Their freedom and their human dignity have thus been restored.

26:16. nature of the illnesses. The diseases promised in this curse include a "wasting disease," a fever, an illness that damages the sufferer's eyesight and causes loss of appetite. These may all be explained by the "terror"— depression and anxiety caused by God's wrath and the incursions of their enemies. Although there have been clinical diagnostic texts discovered from Mesopotamia, it is impossible to attach a specific diagnosis to the diseases mentioned here.

26:19. iron sky, bronze ground. The sense of this metaphoric curse is also found in the execration (curse) of Deuteronomy 28 and in the Treaty of Esarhaddon (seventh century B.C.). It implies that the land itself will turn against the people, becoming hard as bronze because the iron gates of heaven will have closed and no rain will fall on it.

26:26. ten women baking with one oven. The picture of so little grain that numerous women can all bake their bread in the same oven is also found on the *Aramaic statue found at Tell Fekherye, where one hundred women cannot fill up an oven with their bread.

26:29. cannibalism in ancient Near East. Only ultimate desperation and immanent starvation would cause the people of the ancient Near East to resort to cannibalism (see 2 Kings 6:24-30). It is included as part of the curses section here and in Deuteronomy 28:53-57 and in the *Assyrian treaties of the seventh century B.C. to demonstrate just how horrible God's punishment will be on the disobedient.

27:1-34

Vows

27:2-13. nature of vows. Information concerning vows can be found in most of the cultures of the ancient Near East, including *Hittite, *Ugaritic, Mesopotamian and, less often, Egyptian. Vows are voluntary agreements made with deity. In this case the vow involves pledging the value of a person dedicated to temple service (see 1 Sam 1:11). This may relate back to the redemption of the firstborn in Exodus 13:13; 34:20 and Numbers 18:15-16, but it does not involve human sacrifice. The table of equivalences defines the value of the person to be redeemed based on gender, age and ability to work. In this way the temple received sufficient funds to make needed repairs and purchase equipment (see 2 Kings 12:5-6). As is the case in all vows, God is invoked (note the seriousness of this act in Ex 20:7), and both parties are expected to act according to the terms of the vow. The vows would typically be conditional and accompany a petition made to deity. The items that are given to redeem the person become sacred and cannot be redeemed themselves unless, by their nature, they are unacceptable for dedication (i.e., unclean or unfit). The huge amounts involved (up to fifty shekels) make it unlikely this vow was common.

27:2-8. dedication of persons. The concept of dedicating a person to temple service may be based on the idea that a family must sacrifice (i.e., give up their labor) to God's service. Thus Samuel was dedicated to the shrine at Shiloh by Hannah prior to his birth (1 Sam 1:11). However, in the labor-poor region of Israel, this would have been impractical. Thus a system was created whereby the obligation was fulfilled by redemption of the person through a set table of equivalencies based on age, gender, ability to work and ability to pay. This might be compared to the laws of bodily injury in the *Ur-Nammu code, the Laws of *Eshnunna and the laws of *Hammurabi, which set a specific monetary fine based on the type of injury, age, social status and gender of the victim.

27:3-8. relative values. The set of relative values established for redemption of persons dedicated to temple service is based on four criteria: age, gender, ability to work and ability to pay. The assumption is that the value of the labor service of an adult male between age twenty and sixty is fifty silver shekels. Even though they may serve longer than an adult, the value set for children is only a fraction of this amount (based on gender). However, for persons over sixty, the amount, understandably, is less than for those of standard working age. The amount set for the poor is based on a priest's determination of their ability to pay. Although these amounts may reflect the value of slaves, this amount fluctuates too much over time to be a reliable indicator.

27:3-7. amounts of money. The amounts of money specified for redemption of persons dedicated to temple service are all in silver. The largest, fifty shekels, based on the silver content of twenty gerahs/shekels (27:25), was many times the annual wage for a laborer. This makes it unlikely that many persons would have made this type of vow, knowing it must be paid once the vow is made. They simply could not have paid this sum and therefore the redemption of a dedicated person may have been a rare occasion.

27:3. sanctuary shekel. The price in silver to be paid was based on the sanctuary shekel as opposed to a common shekel weight, which was generally 11.4 grams. The sanctuary shekel used for the valuation is generally considered to be a fraction of the regular shekel, but precise information is not available. Archaeological finds do attest shekel pieces weighing 9.3-10.5 grams.

27:9-13. redeeming animals. If a person wished to use an animal as payment of the vow, then the determination of its value and its acceptability would be based on priestly inspection for blemish or other imperfection, and on whether the animal was clean (i.e., acceptable for sacrifice). If an animal was ceremonially unclean, it could still be offered, but it in turn would be redeemed with an extra payment of one-fifth of its value. If it was the intent of the donor to give the animal up for sacrifice, it could not under any circumstances be redeemed (see 22:21-25). Such care over the ritual *purity of sacrificial animals was also common in *Hittite and Mesopotamian rituals.

27:14-25. dedication of house or land. The consecration of a dwelling or of fields, whether owned by a person or held as collateral for a debt, may be made, but they must be inspected and valued by the priest. This allows for a set amount should the owner wish to redeem them, plus one-fifth of their value. It also could involve a purification *ritual of the property, as is also evident in *Hittite texts. The basis for this practice might involve a vow to make special provision, beyond normal sacrifices or tithes, for God's sanctuary or priesthood, and it may result from the lack of an heir. Thus the produce of land or the use of the house (for storage or rents) would belong to God. The Year of Jubilee is also a factor which must be taken into account in this valuation and assignment of property. Only land which was owned and not redeemed may ultimately become the permanent property of the priests (27:20-21).

27:21. priest property. We know from *Hittite, Egyptian and Mesopotamian texts that temple communities owned land and benefited from its produce. Although the practice of deeding over property to the temple is not mentioned outside the Bible, it seems likely that the priestly community throughout the ancient Near East could acquire ownership of land that was consecrated to the use of the god(s). This is made possible if the owner of the land fails to redeem it. At that point, the land becomes "holy" and like sacrificial animals may not be redeemed in the future. Thus in the Israelite Jubilee year celebration, instead of the land reverting to its original owner, it becomes the permanent property of the priests.

27:25. twenty gerahs to the shekel. The sanctuary shekel (weighing 11-13 grams) was to have a silver content of twenty gerahs (0.571 grams or 8.71 grains). This established the weight as acceptable payment for dedicated persons or property.

27:29. person dedicated to destruction. There are some acts which cannot be expiated through sacrifice or redemption. Persons who have been condemned for false worship (Ex 22:19) or for violating the ban (Josh 7:13-26) or for murder (Num 35:31-34) or willful violations of ritual *purity (as in the *Hittite texts) may not be redeemed. In some cases their families and their property were also destroyed in a general purging of evil. They have committed acts that violate God's holiness and contaminate the community. Therefore their sentence must be carried out without exception. Only in this way can God's name be restored to its proper sanctity and the people be cleansed of their *impurity.

27:31-33. redeeming the tithe. Since all of the produce of the land (grain and fruit) belongs to God, a tithe must be made on it (Deut 14:22-26). Those items set aside for the tithe could not be considered part of the "freewill" offerings, since the tithe is considered the unrestricted property of *Yahweh. The amount of the tithe may be redeemed by a payment of its value plus one-fifth of that value. Note that this payment can be made only for farm produce (compare Num 18:14-19). Animals not only cannot be redeemed, but any attempt to do so results in the loss of both the animal originally chosen for the tithe and the one substituted.

NUMBERS

1:1-46

Census

1:1. Desert of Sinai. "Desert of Sinai" refers to the wilderness area surrounding the mountain where the Israelites were camped (see comment on Ex 19:1-2).

1:1. chronology. By comparing this to Exodus 40:17 it can be seen that the tabernacle has now been set up for one month and the people have been camped at Sinai for nearly a year.

1:2. purpose of census. Censuses in the ancient world were used as a means of conscripting men for either military service or government building projects. They also were often accompanied or even motivated by the collection of a head tax. This census is for conscription into the army, but it cannot easily be separated from the one in Exodus 30:11-16 (see comment) where a temple tax is collected.

1:46. size of the population. For some of the problems see the comment on Exodus 12:37.

1:47—2:34

The Arrangement of the Camp

1:52. grouping of the tribes. The camp of the priests and Levites surrounded the sanctuary, while the other tribal camps formed an outer rectangle with three camps on each side. Rectangular military encampments were the norm in Egyptian practice of this time and are portrayed in ninth-century *Assyrian art with the king protected in the center. Judah leads the prominent eastern camp (the tabernacle entrance faced east) as the leader among the tribes. Reuben, the tribe of the eldest son, leads the southern group, while Dan, the tribe of the eldest of the *concubines' sons, leads the northern group. The tribes from Rachel's sons are on the west side, led by Ephraim, the son of Joseph with firstborn rights.

1:52. standards. In Egypt each army division was named after a deity, and the standard for that division bore a representation of that deity. It would therefore be reasonable to assume that the standard of each tribe displayed a symbol of the tribe. On the other hand, some interpreters have interpreted this word to refer to a military unit rather than a standard.

2:3-32. numbers of the census. As discussed in the comment on Exodus 12:37, there is a problem with the numbers. The most probable solution at this point is to understand that the numbers given here are mixtures. Since the Hebrew word translated "thousand" (*'lp*) looks the same as the word translated "military division," a number like 74,600 (v. 4) may be read as 74 military divisions, (totaling) 600 men. The total in verse 32 would originally have been written 598 military divisions (*'lp*), 5 thousand (*'lp*) and 5 hundred men. But at some point in the transmission of the text the two words were confused and added together to make 603 thousand. If this solution is correct, the size of the Israelite group that left Egypt would have been about 20,000.

3:1—4:49
The Levite Clans

3:7-10. Levites as sanctuary guards. Encamped around the sanctuary and instructed to put to death any trespasser, the Levites restricted the access to the tabernacle. Ancient sanctuaries were not public places for gathering but were the divine residences. The priests are seen as guards in *Hittite texts as well as in texts from *Mari on the upper Euphrates. In *Babylonian beliefs there were also demons or protective spirits who guarded temple entrances.

3:12-13. Levites in the place of the first-born. In the ancient world many cultures featured an ancestor *cult in which libations were poured out on behalf of the dead ancestors, whose spirits would then offer protection and help to those still living. In *Babylon the disembodied spirit (*utukki*) or the ghost (*etemmu*) could become very dangerous if not cared for and often were the objects of incantations. Care for the dead would begin with proper burial and would continue with ongoing gifts and honor of the memory and name of the deceased. The firstborn was responsible for maintaining this ancestor worship and therefore inherited the family gods (often images of deceased ancestors). While ancestor worship or *funerary cult was not approved for Israelites, the indictments of the prophets make it

clear that it was one of the deviant practices of the common people. The transfer of the status of the firstborn to the Levites therefore implies that rather than a family-level ancestor worship maintained by the firstborn, Israel would have a national-level religious practice maintained and regulated by the Levites (see also the comments at Ex 13:1-3; Deut 14:1-2; 26:14). For legal background see comment on 8:24-26.

3:47-51. redemption money. The concept of ransom or redemption money occurs both in *Akkadian (Babylonian) and *Ugaritic (Canaanite) texts, though not in this same function. The nation here bought back its firstborn from God by "trading" the Levites, and the remainder of the firstborn had to be bought back with money according to the value set in Leviticus 27:6. The average shekel weighed 11.4 grams, although there are also references to a "heavy shekel," which may have weighed more. The sanctuary weight listed here may refer to a shekel that has a more standard value and weight than the standard "marketplace" shekel. It is generally considered a lighter shekel (see comment on Ex 30:13). Five shekels would have represented about half a year's wages.

4:6. hide of sea cows. Both sea cows (a herbivorous mammal, the dugong) and dolphins are found in the Red Sea, and their hides could have been tanned and used for decoration. These creatures had been hunted for their hides along the Arabian Gulf for millennia. Alternatively, this word may be compared to an *Akkadian word which refers to a semiprecious yellow or orange stone, and thus to the color of dye used rather than to an animal.

4:6. blue cloth. This has more recently been interpreted as a blue-purple or violet color. The dye for this color was one of the major exports of Phoenicia, where it was extracted from the murex snail (*Murex trunculus*), which inhabited shallow coastal waters of the Mediterranean. An ancient refinery has also been found at Dor along the northern coast of Israel. One chemist estimated that a quarter of a million snails would be needed to produce one ounce of pure dye. This dye was used in the manufacture of the most sacred objects such as the veil of the Holy of Holies and the high priestly garments.

4:46-48. number of the Levites. Here the number of Levite men aged thirty to fifty is 8,580, while in 3:30 the total number of males over a month old was 22,000. This would imply that there were 13,420 males younger than thirty and older than fifty. This is a reasonable distribution and argues that the numbers are in right proportion. It is still likely that there has been confusion concerning the word *thousand,* as described in the comment on 2:3-32.

5:1-4
Persons Sent Outside the Camp
5:2. infectious skin diseases. For the nature of these diseases see comment on Leviticus 13:2.
5:2. discharges. For discussion of the various classes of discharges, see the comments on Leviticus 15.
5:2. ceremonial uncleanness. Not all uncleanness was avoidable, and the cause of uncleanness was often something that would in no way be considered sinful. There are several categories of uncleanness that could not be easily avoided, including sexual impurities, disease-related impurities and the uncleanness that came from contact with corpse or carcass. Though it was a matter of etiquette rather than ethics, the sacred compass needed to be protected from that which was inappropriate. Additionally it was a common belief that demons inhabited menstrual blood. That the uncleanness from childbirth should be seen as similar to monthly uncleanness is common in ancient cultures, including Egypt, *Babylonia and Persia.
5:3. living outside the camp. Though the camp did not need to maintain the same level of *purity as the temple compound, there were restrictions. This restriction is also found in *Babylonian literature for victims of skin diseases forced to live in isolation. It is likely that they would have lived in the vicinity of the tombs.

5:5-10
Restitution in Fraud Cases
5:6-7. nature of the legislation. This section concerns a case where someone has used a formal oath to defraud someone else in court and later feels guilty about having done so. Giving restitution plus 20 percent to the defrauded individual, his next of kin or to the priest, plus the appropriate reparation offering, is commanded. In *Hammurabi's laws one-sixth is typically added to restitution amounts in the form of interest payments.

5:11-31
The Case of the Jealous Husband
5:14. basis for legal action. The only basis for this action is the jealousy of the woman's husband. The word used to describe the nature of the crime in verse 12 usually refers to a breach of faith or an act of sacrilege (see the comment

on Lev 5:14-16). It is therefore likely that the woman has previously been asked to swear an oath to her innocence and is now being accused of swearing falsely. Such an accusation may come about if the woman is now found to be pregnant and the husband contends that the child is not his.
5:15. the husband's actions. It is unclear why the husband brings the particular offering that he does. Unlike the regular meal offering, it is barley (as offered by the poor) instead of wheat, and it omits the oil and incense as meal offerings associated with potential offenses do. Generally oil and incense were associated with celebration, and this was not a festive occasion.
5:16-17. the priest's actions. A text from *Mari (northwest Mesopotamia) speaks of a trial by ordeal where the gods are asked to drink water which contains dirt taken from the city gate. This bound the gods to their oath to protect the city. Here the ingredients are sacred (water from the laver, dirt from the sanctuary floor) and mixed with the inscribed curses that concern the woman's obligation to preserve the *purity of the sanctuary.
5:18. loosening the hair. This is elsewhere connected to mourning and may suggest that the woman is to adopt a posture of mourning until the Lord's verdict is clarified.
5:23-24. trial by ordeal in the ancient Near East. "Ordeal" describes a judicial situation in which the accused is placed in the hand of God using some mechanism, generally one that will put the accused in jeopardy. If the deity intervenes to protect the accused from harm, the verdict is innocent. Most trials by ordeal in the ancient Near East involved dangers such as water, fire or poison. The accused who is exposed to these threats is in effect being assumed guilty until the deity declares otherwise by action on her behalf. In contrast, the procedure in this text invokes neither magic nor danger but simply creates a situation for God to respond to. Thus the woman here is presumed innocent until circumstances (directed by the Lord) show otherwise. *Hammurabi's laws contain similar cases in which the woman undergoes a river ordeal to determine her guilt or innocence.
5:27. the negative potential results. Suggestions have ranged from a flooded uterus to false pregnancy to pelvic prolapse to atrophied genitalia. Whatever the actual physical manifestations might be, the text clearly indicates that the result is sterility. If the woman has been brought into this process because of pregnancy, it may be that the potion would be expected to induce a miscarriage in the case

that the pregnancy came about through illicit behavior.

6:1-21

The Nazirite Vow

6:3. abstinence from drinks. There are a number of different words used to describe fermented drinks made from grapes used here. While some of the terms could at times refer to intoxicants made from other ingredients (e.g., grain), only those that can refer to grape products are used here. That suggests that only grape intoxicants are prohibited to the *Nazirite. It is not drunkenness that is the issue here, but grape drinks of any sort.

6:3-4. abstinence from grape products. Prohibition of grape products has suggested to some interpreters that a nomadic lifestyle is being elevated, but it is very difficult to see that as a biblical or priestly agenda. Alternatively one must notice that the grape is one of the principal, one could say characteristic, staples of Canaan and therefore symbolically connected to the issue of fertility (note that the spies bring back a huge cluster of grapes [13:24] as evidence of the fertility of the land). The use of raisins in raisin cakes for the *fertility *cult can be seen in Hosea 3:1.

6:5. significance of hair. There is a Phoenician inscription from the ninth century B.C. reporting the dedication of shaven hair by an individual in fulfillment of a vow made to the goddess *Astarte. It is of importance that in the biblical text there is no discussion of what should be done with the hair that is cut. It is neither dedicated as in the above inscription, nor is it deposited in the temple as in some cultures. The dedicated hair is uncut (v. 9), not cut. For men hair has symbolic value as a sign of manhood or virility (see 2 Sam 10:4). Women decorate their hair and groom it carefully as a sign of beauty. The prohibition against trimming the "sides of your head" or the "edges of your beard" uses the same terminology as in Leviticus 19:9-10, which deals with the harvesting of fields. In both cases an offering is involved—one to the poor and the other to God. *Hammurabi's code penalizes false witnesses by having half the person's hair cut off. The Middle Assyrian code allows a debt-slave's master to pull out his or her hair as punishment (see Neh 13:25). Both laws suggest that shame is attached to the loss of hair. In ancient thinking hair (along with blood) was one of the main representatives of a person's life essence. As such it was often an ingredient in sympathetic

magic. This is evident, for instance, in the practice of sending along a lock of a presumed prophet's hair when his prophecies were sent to the king of *Mari. The hair would be used in divination to determine whether the prophet's message would be accepted as valid. (See Lev 19:27.) Studies have shown that hair cutting was used in the ancient world as an act of distinguishing oneself from those around (as in mourning), or of reentering society (as seems to be the case with the Nazirites).

6:6-7. corpse prohibition. Corpse contamination was one of the most common and unavoidable causes of ritual uncleanness (see comment on 19:11). Some have further speculated that ritual uncleanness from corpse contamination may also represent a statement against the always prevalent *cult of the dead (see comment on 3:1, Levites in the place of the first-born).

6:8. Nazirite background. It may be no coincidence that the three prohibited areas for the *Nazirite represent fertility (grape products), sympathetic magic (hair) and the *cult of the dead (corpse contamination). These are the three principal popular religious practices that *Yahweh worship sought to eliminate. It is difficult to reconstruct, however, why these elements were chosen, or what the original thinking behind the vow was.

6:9-12. ritual procedure in case of violation. Ritual violation of the vow required the purging of the altar but only included the least expensive offerings (pigeons). It was also necessary to offer a lamb for a reparation offering because the violation involved a breach of faith (see comment on Lev 5:14-16).

6:13-20. conclusion of the vow. A whole series of offerings (see the comments on the early chapters of Leviticus for more information on each) concludes the vow, followed by the cutting and burning of the hair. Most vows in the ancient Near East were conditional vows attached to some past or present entreaty (see comment on Lev 27), and there is no reason to assume that the *Nazirite vow is any different. It is not surprising, then, that the vow culminates in offertory gifts. What is unusual, against the background of ancient Near Eastern vows, is the ritualized period of abstinence that precedes the offerings.

6:22-27

The Priestly Blessing

6:24-26. ancient Near Eastern blessings. In the ancient world blessings and curses were believed to have a power all their own that would result in their fulfillment. This blessing is probably one that the priests were to give to someone leaving the sanctuary after participating in some *ritual. Two small silver scrolls (about one inch long) have been found in the area known as Keteph Hinnom in Jerusalem. They were *amulets in a burial cave from the sixth or seventh century B.C., and they contained this benediction. At present they represent the oldest example of any text of Scripture. The concept of the shining face of the deity resulting in mercy is found in Mesopotamian documents and inscriptions from as early as the twelfth century B.C. as well as in a letter from *Ugarit. Additionally a phrase invoking the gods to grant watch-care and well-being is used regularly in *Ugaritic and *Akkadian salutations. Finally, the phrase "the Lord bless you and keep you" is also included in the words (Hebrew) painted on a large storage jar from the ninth century B.C. found at Kuntillet Ajrud in the northern Sinai.

7:1-89

Offerings for the Tabernacle

7:1. function of anointing sacred objects. Anointing is an act of dedication. It is unclear whether here the anointing is with oil or blood—the former is usually deemed more likely.

7:13. silver plate. The two silver objects named here are more bowl-shaped, the former almost twice the size of the latter and probably deeper. They weigh about three pounds and one and a half pounds respectively.

7:13. fine flour. The flour here was the grits or semolina left in the sieve after wheat was ground into flour. It is the same as was used for the grain offerings (see comment on Lev 2:1).

7:14. gold ladle. These ladles weighed about four ounces. The word translated "ladle" is simply the word for "hand." There are tongs found at *Amarna whose ends are shaped like hands, but the fact that these implements could be filled with incense suggests ladles rather than tongs. Though they were relatively small, the incense they held was valuable so even this small amount was a substantial gift, in addition to the value of the gold.

7:84-88. function of the offerings brought. The text does not speak of the animals actually being sacrificed, and the word translated "offerings" does not refer to sacrifices. The animals were dedicated for tabernacle use for particular offerings (as indicated in the lists),

but they became part of the sanctuary livestock to be used as the need arose. In providing basic supplies for operation, this resembled a housewarming party.

8:1-4

The Lampstand

8:2. lampstand. The design of three branches on either side of a central axis is common in the *Late Bronze Age cultures of the Mediterranean. See comment on Exodus 25:31-40.

8:5-26

The Levites

8:7. shaving the body for purification. Egyptian priests were also required to shave their heads and bodies as part of their purification process. Razors were often bronze, either knife-shaped with rounded handles or blades with a thin handle attached perpendicular to the flat.

8:10. laying on of hands. This is the same procedure that the Israelites used when presenting a sacrifice (see comment below). It is symbolic of designating the Levites to serve on behalf of the Israelites.

8:11. Levites as a wave offering. The wave offering (better: elevation offering) is a rite of dedication (see comment on Lev 8:27).

8:12. Levites laying hands on the bulls. See comment on Leviticus 1:4.

8:12. making "atonement" for Levites. For the word here translated "atonement" as a purifying consequence of sacrifice, see comment on Leviticus 1:3-4. But there is no sacrifice being offered here, only sacrificial symbolism being used. The Levites do not perform purification rites on behalf of the Israelites— that is the task of the priests. Instead the Levites protect against divine wrath by providing a ransom. Such attempts are commonplace in *Babylonian and *Hittite appeasement *rituals.

8:24-26. role of the Levites. In the ancient Near East there was a legal transaction by which a creditor would receive the service of a person in the family of the individual to whom he had extended a loan or commodity. The person on loan is assigned a specific area of work over a predetermined length of time. This service took the place of interest on a loan. The person on loan became part of the household of the creditor and received support and sustenance from him. In the same way, the Levites do specified service at the house of the creditor (God) and receive support and sustenance from him. That which is received by the Israelites in exchange is their firstborn.

9:1-14

The Passover

9:1. Desert of Sinai. This is the wilderness area around Mount Sinai (see comment on 1:1).

9:2. Passover. This is the first celebration of Passover since its inception a year earlier in Egypt. For the meaning of the Hebrew term see comment on Exodus 12:11. For further discussion about Passover see the comments on Exodus 12:1-23.

9:15-23

The Guidance of the Cloud

9:15. the function and nature of the cloud. Some have thought the pillar of cloud and fire could be best explained as the result of volcanic activity. An eruption on the Island of Thera (six hundred miles northwest) in 1628 B.C. brought an end to Minoan civilization, and it is possible that its effects could have been seen in the Delta. But the date is far too early (see "The Date of the Exodus," pp.96-97, and this theory would offer no explanation of the movements of the pillar, nor of the location described for it in the biblical account (they are moving southeast). The text does not suggest that the pillar was supernaturally generated, only that it was the means of supernatural guidance. For this reason some have suggested that it was the result of a brazier of some sort carried on a pole that would be used by the vanguard scouts. This was a method often used by caravans. On the other hand, the pillar is always portrayed as acting (coming down, moving) rather than being operated (no human is ever said to move it), so the vanguard theory is difficult to support. In the ancient world a bright or flaming aura surrounding deity is the norm. In Egyptian literature it is depicted as the winged sun disk accompanied by storm clouds. *Akkadian uses the term *melammu* to describe this visible representation of the glory of deity, which in turn is enshrouded in smoke or cloud. In Canaanite mythology it has been suggested the *melammu* concept is expressed by the word *anan*, the same Hebrew word here translated "cloud," but the occurrences are too few and obscure for confidence. In any case, the pillar here would then be one; smoke being visible in the daytime, while the inner flame it covered would glow through at night. (See Ex 13:21-22.)

10:1-10

The Trumpets

10:2. silver trumpets. As is obvious from the materials they are made of, these are not the ram's horn trumpets that are referred to in other contexts. Tubular flared trumpets were used in this period in military as well as ritual contexts. This is depicted on Egyptian reliefs as well as evidenced by actual instruments found, for example, in the tomb of King Tut (a silver trumpet nearly two feet long).

10:2. silver work. The techniques of silver mining were known as early as the mid-third millennium. A process called cupellation using a crucible was used to extract silver from lead and refine it through several stages of purification. In *Ur silversmith artisans were producing musical instruments as well as jewelry and other items in the third millennium.

10:3-7. trumpet signaling. In warfare signaling was done in various ways. Fire signals were common both along garrison lines as well as in the open field. Basic commands were at times communicated by upraised staff or javelin. Trumpet signals are attested in Egypt in the *Late Bronze Age (this time period) in both military and religious contexts. A preset code would include some combination of long and short blasts.

10:11-36

Leaving Sinai

10:11. chronology. At this point the Israelites are still at Sinai having left Egypt only thirteen months earlier. In our calendar it would be early May.

10:12. itinerary. If the Wilderness of Sinai is in the southern section of the Sinai peninsula, as we have suggested, this is a march toward the northeast. The Wilderness of Paran includes Kadesh Barnea and is generally located in the northeast corner of the Sinai peninsula. Several of the sites they stop at on the way are mentioned at the end of chapter 11. The Israelites spend the bulk of their forty years of wandering in the Wilderness of Paran.

10:29. Hobab, son of Reuel. In Exodus 2 Moses' father-in-law was called Reuel, in Exodus 3 he is referred to as Jethro, and here he appears to be named Hobab (see Judg 4:11). The difficulty can be resolved once the ambiguity of the terminology is recognized. The term designating male in-laws is nonspecific. Referring to a male near-relative of the bride, the term could be used for her father, brother, or even grandfather. Most solutions take account of this. Perhaps Reuel is the grandfather head of the clan, Jethro is the father of Zipporah and technically the father-in-law of Moses, and Hobab is the brother-in-law of Moses, Jethro's son. Alternatively, Jethro and Hobab could both be brothers-in-law, and Reuel the father. (See Ex 3:1.)

11:1—12:16
A Rebellious and Quarrelsome People

11:3. Taberah. There is good reason to associate Taberah with Kibroth Hattaavah (v. 34), since there is no record of travel between these two accounts. Each name reflects an incident that occurred there. No firm identification of these sites is possible.

11:4. meat. The meat they are craving is not beef, lamb or venison. The Israelites had livestock with them but would have been reluctant to slaughter them and thus deplete their herds and flocks. Furthermore, these meats were not part of their normal diet but were eaten only on special occasions. Life by the river in Egypt had accustomed them to a regular diet of fish, however, and the next verse clarifies that this is the meat referred to.

11:5. diet in Egypt. Five types of produce are mentioned here as staples of the Israelite diet in Egypt. Several of them are known from Egyptian texts and wall paintings. The melons are either watermelons or muskmelons.

11:7-9. manna. The bread from heaven was called manna in Exodus 16:31, where it is described. The fact that it came with the dew (Ex 16:4) suggests that God's miraculous provision used a natural process. The most frequent identification is with the secretion of small aphids that feed on the sap of tamarisk trees. When it hardens and falls to the ground, it can be collected and used for a sweetener. The problem is that this only occurs during certain seasons (May to July) and only where there are tamarisk trees. A full season would normally produce only about five hundred pounds, in contrast to the biblical account that has the people gathering about half a pound per person per day. Alternatively, some would favor the sweet liquid of the hammada plant, common in southern Sinai, that is used to sweeten cakes. As with the plagues, it is not necessarily the occurrence of this phenomenon that is unnatural but the timing and magnitude. Nevertheless, these natural explanations seem to fall far short of the biblical data. The comparison to what most translations identify as the seed of the coriander (rarely found in the desert) is more likely to refer to a wider generic category of desert plants with white seeds. (See Ex 16:4-9.)

11:25. the Spirit and prophesying. Ecstatic prophecy, or prophecy that appears to proceed from someone in a "possessed" or trancelike state, is known in Israel as well as in the ancient Near East. In Mesopotamia the ecstatic prophet's title was *muhhu*, and in Israel the ecstasies often resulted in the prophets being thought of as madmen (see, for example, 1 Sam 19:19-24; Jer 29:26). Here the phenomenon does not result in prophetic messages from the Lord but serves as a sign of the power of God on the elders. In that sense it could be compared to the tongues of fire in the upper room in Acts 2.

11:31. quail. Small, plump migratory quail often come through the Sinai on their way north from the Sudan to Europe, usually in the months of March and April. They generally fly with the wind and are driven to ground (or water) if caught in a crosswind. In their exhaustion it is not unusual for them to fly so low that they can be easily caught. Quail looking for a place to land and rest have been known to sink small boats, and in the Sinai they have been noted to cover the ground so densely that some landed on the tops of others. (See Ex 16:13.)

11:32. 10 homers A homer is a donkey load. It certainly became a more precise dry measure in time, but it is not always used with precision. Estimates of ten homers would run anywhere from forty to sixty bushels. By any estimate the Israelites were overcome with greed. Normally the quails would have been preserved with salt before being laid out to dry. Since this step is not mentioned by the text, it may have been omitted. This suggests that the plague was food poisoning.

11:34. Kibroth Hattaavah. This location cannot be identified with any degree of confidence.

11:35. Hazeroth. Tentatively identified by some as Ain el-Khadra.

12:1. Cushite wife of Moses. Cush can refer to several different places in the Old Testament, though it is most frequently the designation for the area translations usually render "Ethiopia." This is misleading, for the area Cush refers to is not modern Ethiopia (Abyssinia) but the area along the Nile just south of Egypt, ancient Nubia (in modern Sudan). The boundary between Egypt and Nubia in ancient times was usually either at the first or second cataract of the Nile. It is unlikely that Nubia ever extended much beyond the sixth cataract at Khartoum. Another possibility connects Cush here with Cushan, identified in Habakkuk 3:7 with Midian. This has been attractive to some because of Moses' known marriage to a Midianite woman, Zipporah (see Ex 2—4). While the objection of Miriam and Aaron appears to have been ethnic, there is insufficient evidence to clarify what her ethnic background was. Nubians are depicted with dark skin pigmentation in Egyptian paintings but are sometimes lacking other features designated "negroid."

12:5. pillar of cloud. For a general discussion of the pillar of cloud, see the comment on Exodus 13:21-22. For the pillar as a means of God meeting with Moses, see comment on Exodus 33:10. Here they come to the tent of meeting for judgment of a case. In Canaanite literature the chief deity *El also dwells in a tent and from that tent (where the divine assembly is thought to meet) come forth decrees and judgments. For another example of judgment proceeding from the tent in terms of punishment, see the comment on Leviticus 9:23.

12:6. prophets. By this date there was already a well-established prophetic institution in the ancient Near East. As this text indicates, the usual modes of revelation were dreams and visions. In over fifty texts from the town of *Mari (several centuries earlier than Moses) local officials report prophetic utterances to the king of Mari, Zimri-Lim. Yahweh could choose to speak through anyone, but Moses' status and experience go beyond that of other prophets. Both dreams and visions often used symbolism that required interpretation (often through use of *divination or by an expert in the dream books; see comment on Gen 40:5-18), but there were no such riddles to solve in order to understand God's revelation to Moses.

12:10. Miriam's disease. Hansen's disease (the modern term for leprosy) is unattested in the ancient Near East prior to the time of Alexander the Great (see comment on Lev 13:1-46). The skin diseases described here and elsewhere in the Old Testament are more along the line of psoriasis and eczema. The analogy to a stillborn in verse 12 further confirms this type of diagnosis in that it describes exfoliation (peeling of the skin, not associated with Hansen's disease), not necrosis (destruction of body tissue, including bones and nerves). A stillborn progresses from reddish coloring to a brownish gray and then begins to lose its skin.

12:16. Desert of Paran. See comment on 10:12.

13:1-33

The Reconnaissance of the Land

13:21-22. scope of the exploration. The Wilderness of Zin is the area going south from an imaginary line drawn between the southern tip of the Dead Sea and the Mediterranean, an area also referred to as the Negev. It constitutes the southern border of Canaan. Rehob has often been identified with Tell el-Balat Beth-rehob, almost halfway from the Mediterranean to Hazor. Lebo Hamath is most likely modern Lebweh on one of the sources of the Orontes. This was the southern border of the land of Hamath and therefore the northern border of Canaan. These reference points suggest the scouts explored the land between the Jordan River and the Mediterranean up and down its full 350-mile length.

13:22. Anakites. The descendants of Anak are specifically mentioned in verses 22 and 28. When names are given, they are *Hurrian (biblical Horites; see comment on Deut 2). The descendants of Anak are generally considered "giants" (v. 33; Deut 2:10-11; 2 Sam 21:18-22), though the description "gigantic" may be more appropriate. There is no mention of the Anakites in other sources, but the Egyptian letter on Papyrus Anastasi I (thirteenth century B.C.) describes fierce warriors in Canaan that are seven to nine feet tall. Two female skeletons about seven feet tall from the twelfth century have been found at Tell es-Sa'ideyeh in Transjordan.

13:22. the building of Hebron. Hebron was built seven years before Zoan. Zoan refers to the Egyptian city of Dja'net, which the Greeks called Tanis. It became the capital city of the Delta region in the Twenty-first Dynasty (twelfth century B.C.). The earliest major builder identified by the archaeological finds is Psusennes I in the middle of the eleventh century. The archaeology of Hebron is very complex. The site was occupied in the *Early Bronze Age (third millennium), and there was a fortified city on the site in the Middle Bronze Age II (up to the middle of the second millennium). There is evidence of a tribal population during the period of the conquest and then a permanent settlement again in the *Iron Age (from 1200 on). It is difficult to be certain which building of Hebron this verse refers to.

13:24. the Valley of Eshcol. There are many wadis in this general area, and there is no way of telling which one may have been referred to here. Around Hebron today, Ramet el-'Amleh is known for its grape produce and is near a wadi.

13:26. Kadesh. Kadesh Barnea is usually identified as 'Ain el-Qudeirat, about fifty miles south of Beersheba, which has the most plentiful water supply in the region. There are no archaeological remains on this site from this period, but the site has long been a stopping place for nomads and Bedouin, and the abundance of "Negev" ware (pottery dated to this period) suggests that was true during the time of the Israelite wanderings as well.

13:27. land flowing with milk and honey. The land of Canaan is described as a land "flowing with milk and honey." This refers to the bounty of the land for a pastoral lifestyle, but not necessarily in terms of agriculture. Milk is the product of herds, while honey represents a natural resource, probably the syrup of the date rather than bees' honey. A similar expression to this is found in the *Ugaritic epic of *Baal and Mot, which describes the return of fertility to the land in terms of the wadis flowing with honey. Egyptian texts as early as the *Story of *Sinuhe* describe the land of Canaan as rich in natural resources as well as in cultivated produce. (See Ex 3:7-10.)

13:29. inhabitants of the land. The people groups inhabiting the land are identified in verse 29 as the Amalekites, *Hittites, Jebusites, *Amorites and Canaanites. The Amalekites, who were descended from Abraham through Esau (Gen 36:15), were a nomadic or seminomadic people who inhabited the general region of the Negev and the Sinai during the second half of the second millennium B.C. The well-known Hittites were from Anatolia, modern Turkey, but groups occupying sections of Syria and Canaan were also called Hittites and may or may not be related. The Hittites in Canaan have Semitic names, while the Hittites of Anatolia were Indo-European. Jebusites inhabited the area around Jerusalem and are known only from the Old Testament, which tells us very little about them. *Amorites (known in Mesopotamia as *Amurru* or *Martu*) are known from written documents as early as the middle third millennium B.C. Most scholars think that their roots were in Syria but that they came to occupy many areas in the Near East. The term can be used to refer to a geographical area ("westerners") or to an ethnic group. Some Amorites were nomadic, but there were Amorite city-states in Syria as early as the end of the third millennium. The Canaanites were the principle inhabitants of the fortified cities of the land, though they do not seem to have been native to the land. The kings of this area refer to themselves in the *Amarna letters (mid-second millennium) as *Kinanu*, a term also used in Egyptian inscriptions of this period. There are also records from Egypt concerning the population of Canaan. A prisoner list from a campaign of Amenhotep II (fifteenth century) lists numbers of Canaanites, *Apiru* (unlanded or dispossessed peoples), *Shasu* (nomadic peoples sometimes connected with biblical groups like the Midianites or Amalekites) and *Hurru* (Hurrians).

13:33. like grasshoppers. It is not unusual to use an animal metaphor to describe relative size in exaggerated comparison (cf. English "shrimp"). Grasshoppers were edible, so this invites the additional frightening prospect that "we wouldn't have even made a mouthful to them." In the *Ugaritic Epic of *Keret an army is compared to grasshoppers to indicate the vast number of soldiers.

13:33. Nephilim. The only other sure reference to the Nephilim is in Genesis 6:4, which offers little information in terms of identification. Some have also seen the word in Ezekiel 32:27 (with a slight text variation), where it would refer to warriors. Earliest interpretation (intertestamental) is divided between considering them giants, heroes and fallen angels.

14:1-45
The People Decide Not to Enter the Land

14:6. tearing clothes. Along with placing ashes in the hair, the tearing of clothing was a common form of mourning in the ancient Near East. One example outside the Bible is found in the *Ugaritic Epic of *Aqhat (c. 1600 B.C.) in which the sister of the hero tears her father's garment as she foretells a coming drought. Such an act often implied grief over the death of a relative, friend or prominent individual (2 Sam 3:31). However, it also was a sign of shame (as in this case) or loss of honor or status (2 Sam 13:19).

14:8. flowing with milk and honey. See comment on 13:27.

14:13-16. divine sponsorship and its implications. All of the peoples of the ancient Near East believed in the patronage of the gods. Each city had a patron deity (e.g., *Marduk in *Babylon), and many professions also had particular gods to whom they looked for special aid. Such associations, however, meant that when a city or a group of people warred with another, their gods also joined in the battle. The god/gods of the losing side were discredited and often abandoned by their worshipers. Thus Moses' prayer to Yahweh involves the knowledge of God's sponsorship of the Israelites and the promise of land and children. If Yahweh should destroy the Israelites in the wilderness for their disobedience, it could be construed as failure on God's part to fulfill these promises.

14:25. geographical information. These instructions require the Israelites, who fear moving directly north into Canaan, to proceed south from Kadesh in the Wilderness of Paran to the area of Elath on the Gulf of Aqaba. *Yam Suph* in this verse is therefore not the Red Sea but, as in Numbers 21:4 and Deuteronomy 1:40; 2:1, refers to the Gulf of Aqaba on the eastern coast of the Sinai peninsula.

14:36-38. fate of the spies. Initially God was so angry at the Israelites' grumbling that they were all condemned to die of a plague (v. 12). However, after Moses asked Yahweh to have mercy, this sentence is changed to the death of all these unfaithful people in the wilderness without seeing the Promised Land. Only the spies who had brought a report questioning God's power died immediately of a plague. The term translated "plague" is too vague to identify a particular disease, although some consider it to represent bubonic plague. In the Old Testament it is generally a punishment from God for serious desecration or blasphemy.

14:45. Hormah. "Hormah" has a double meaning here. In the Hebrew it means "destruction," and this is what happened to the invading Israelites. It is also a geographic term for a site seven and a half miles east of Beersheba, tentatively identified with Tell Masos (Khirbet el-Meshash).

15:1-31
Sacrifice Regulations in the Land

15:1-31. general elements of the sacrificial system. Within the Israelite sacrificial system there were both obligatory and voluntary offerings, and they applied to the entire Israelite community as well as to resident aliens. The obligatory sacrifices, brought to a shrine or temple and burnt on the altar by priests, included portions of the harvest (grain, fruits, oil, wine) as well as from the flocks and herds. A portion of each offering was then designated for the use and maintenance of the priestly community. Some sacrifices were expiatory and designed to mitigate specific sins or infractions of the law as well as to serve as part of the *ritual of purification after a person came in contact with unclean items (corpses, diseased persons, body fluids). Voluntary sacrifices were offered as evidence of generosity or in thanksgiving for a particular joy (marriage, birth of a son, a particularly good harvest). Unlike sacrificial offerings in the rest of the ancient Near East, however, those to *Yahweh were not designed to nourish the god (see the famished gods at the end of the flood story in the *Babylonian *Gilgamesh Epic). They only were presented in a ritually correct manner ("an aroma pleasing to the Lord") in order to obtain God's blessing or forgiveness. For further information see the comments on the early part of Leviticus.

15:22-26. community culpability. Inadvertent violations of the law also require purification. For example, in *Hammurabi's code, an unknowing violator of the slave laws must take an oath before the god to clear himself. In the Israelite context, the entire community is held responsible for sins committed unknowingly and for sins of omission (usually involving *ritual or matters of law). The community is defined as both Israelites and resident aliens. The infraction may involve commission of an act without knowledge that it is a violation of the law or confusion over the consumption of some portion of the sacrificial meat or fat. Unlike in Leviticus 4:13-21, however, the expiatory sacrifice of a young bull is not called a "sin" (purification) offering. Instead it is referred to here as a "burnt offering," and a male goat is also to be sacrificed as the purification offering (see comment on Lev 4:1-3).

15:30. defiant sin. Providing contrast to inadvertent sin, this offense is committed with full knowledge of one's actions and premeditated defiance of God and community. For instance, in *Sumerian law a son who publicly denounces his father is disinherited and can be sold as a slave. Similarly, according to Israelite law deliberate criminal acts cannot be allowed to go unpunished, since they violate not only God's laws but the community's collective *covenant to obey these statutes. The sentence "to be cut off from his people," implies punishment by both human and divine agencies—perhaps capital punishment by the authorities and extinction of his family line by God.

15:30. blasphemy. The verb "to blaspheme" is used only here in the Old Testament and means to taunt or revile God so as to deny the authority of God. Such an act demonstrates total defiance of the law, and, because of its danger to the community, the violator must be "cut off from his people." This may involve capital punishment, but it also probably implies punishment by God through the elimination of the person's entire family line. One example of the extreme nature of this offense can be found in the Cyrus Cylinder (c. 540 B.C.), which charges the *Babylonian king Nabonidus with failing to recognize *Marduk's authority as the city god and explains that the god has abandoned him and allowed the Persians to capture the city unmolested.

15:32-36
The Sabbath Breaker

15:32-36. gathering wood on the sabbath. This story provides a legal *etiology explaining the seriousness of violating the sabbath (gathering wood, presumably to cook with, violates Ex 35:3) and provides a precedent for future violations of the sabbath (see Nehemiah's civil reforms in Neh 13:15-22). Detention of the culprit is only until God provides the proper form of punishment, which in this case is stoning. Communal and other forms of execution must be performed outside the camp in order to prevent contamination from contact with the corpse.

15:37-41

Tassel Regulation

15:37-41. tassels on the garments. All adult male Israelites were commanded to sew blue cords into the four quarters of the hem of their robes as a perpetual reminder of God's commandments. The blue dye was extracted from the gland of the *Murex trunculus* snail and was very costly (see comment on 4:6). Decorative hems are common in ancient Near Eastern fashion as many reliefs, paintings and texts attest. Hem design was often an indication of a person's status or office. The tassels are symbolic and are designed to promote right action, not to serve as an *amulet to ward off danger or temptation. The blue cord may signify the status of each Israelite as a member of a kingdom of priests (see comment on Ex 19:5-6).

16:1—17:13

Korah's Revolt and Aaron's Rod

16:1-3. clan and tribal political structure. Each person within the Israelite community was identified as a member of a particular household, clan and tribe. This not only set them into particular kinship groups (the Reubenites claiming ascendancy here over Moses) but also served as the basis on which they could be appointed elders and members of council—so many from each tribe and clan to aid in maintaining order and assisting Moses in the administration of justice. Rivalries between the kinship groups are typical of tribal confederations. In this type of loose political structure, loyalties to the smaller kin affiliations often supersede ties of loyalty to the overall group. Even during the monarchy period, the kings will be faced with this type of mixed loyalty (2 Sam 20:1-2; 1 Kings 12:16-17). **16:6-7. the function of incense censers.** The censers are most likely long-handled pans that could also shovel up the hot coals. They served as portable altars, because the incense was actually burned in them. Censers were

also used for burning of incense in Egypt when people wanted to protect themselves from demonic forces. Burning incense purifies the area of the altar and signifies God's presence (see comments on Ex 30:7-8, 34-38). Moses proposes a test, ordering the followers of the rebellious Korah to offer incense in a censer before God. This was the exclusive prerogative of priests and could be very dangerous for anyone, priest or nonpriests, who might do it incorrectly (Lev 10:1-2).

16:10. distinction between Levites and priests. The Levites were given custody of the tabernacle and the sacred precincts around the altar. It was their responsibility to monitor Israelites who brought their offerings to be sacrificed and prevent them from violating any statute or encroaching on sacred areas reserved for the priests. Priests actually performed the *ritual and the sacrifices on the altar. Although both groups belonged to the priestly community and received a share of the sacrificial offerings, priests had the greatest responsibility and power over *ritual acts. Differentiation of task and authority were also common in Mesopotamian temple communities.

16:13-14. land flowing with milk and honey. The phrase "flowing with milk and honey" becomes synonymous with the Promised Land. It occurs as part of the *covenant promise and is used here in contrast to the harshness of life in the wilderness. This would also relate the lush grazing that would insure good milk production in sheep, goats and cattle. See also comment on Exodus 3:7-10.

16:14. gouging out the eyes. This is an idiom meaning to trick or "pull the wool over one's eyes." Korah's followers refuse to participate in any test suggested by Moses, calling him a charlatan who has already hoodwinked the people into following him.

16:28-30. curse pronouncement. To demonstrate his authority from God, Moses calls for a demonstration of power similar to the plagues in Egypt. The rebel leaders Dathan and Abiram stand in defiance, along with their households, and Moses must curse them so thoroughly that no doubt is left about God's choice of leader. Therefore he asks God to open the earth and take these men and their families down to Sheol alive. The underworld in ancient Near Eastern tradition (Ugaritic and Mesopotamian epics) is often portrayed as a gaping mouth. Thus no one can claim a natural event like an earthquake killed them. Their fate was predicted, and Moses proves to be a true prophet when it occurs.

16:31-35. earthquake and fire as judgment.

Both earthquake and fire cause the death of many people. However in this case the men opposing Moses and Aaron are consumed, along with their households, by the earth and by a divine fire (God's *kabod*, "glory"). The entire community witnesses the event, which demonstrates God's choice of Moses as leader. The *Lament for the Destruction of Ur* in Mesopotamian literature provides a similar manifestation of divine wrath through firestorm and earthquake. Additionally, in an Assyrian text of Ashurbanipal, divine intervention resulted in fire falling from heaven and consuming the enemy.

16:47. incense as atonement. In this instance, God's wrath over the people's rebellion against Moses had "broken out" in the form of a plague. Moses has Aaron burn incense as a type of *apotropaic remedy (similar to the blood painted on their door frames during the Passover in Ex 12:7). The burning of the incense by an authorized priest was designed to provide expiation for the people's sins and guard them from God's anger. However, the more common means of expiation was blood sacrifice (see Lev 17:11). Egyptian use of incense to ward off hostile supernatural powers is well attested. To that end censers were carried in cultic processions. They are depicted in the *rituals performed when a city was under siege.

16:47-50. nature of the plague. The plague, which kills 14,700 people, takes the form of the "Angel Destroyer" who had cut down the firstborn in Egypt. So devastating is its power that Moses orders Aaron to carry a burning censer in among the dead and dying in order to ward off any further destruction. This is extraordinary, since priests normally were not to come in contact with the dead. Apparently this was the only way to hold the plague in check. An exact diagnosis of the plague is not possible from the text (see comment on 25:8).

17:2-7. staff as insignia of tribal leadership. The staff was used by shepherds to guide their flocks. In the hands of an elder or tribal leader, the staff (probably distinctively carved and known to belong to that man) symbolized his authority (see Gen 38:18). By writing the name of each of the twelve tribal leaders on the staffs and placing them before the tent of meeting, there would be no question whose flowered at God's command and who was therefore the designated priest. This public pattern of discernment is also found in Joshua 7:14-15 and 1 Samuel 10:20-21.

17:4-11. divination by wooden objects. The method of determining who is God's chosen priestly leader involves a form of *divination

(using objects to ascertain God's will). This method is not to be confused with the divination practices condemned in Hosea 4:12, which involve either a wooden idol or an *Asherah pole. Here each tribal leader, plus Aaron, is commanded to place his staff in the tent of meeting. The text contains a pun on the word for staff, which also means "tribe" in Hebrew, signifying God's intention to differentiate between the leaders of the tribes. This event is never repeated and thus is not a part of a cultic *ritual. When Aaron's blooms, his authority is certified and no further argument is allowed on this matter. Association of divination practices in proximity to a tree may be found in the references to the soothsayer's tree in Judges 9:37 and to Deborah's palm tree in Judges 4:4-5. *Ugaritic texts also mention the use of trees in ritual contexts.

17:8. significance of almonds. Aaron's staff sprouts, blossoms and flowers as an almond branch. This whole creative process signifies God's power over creation, the fruitfulness of the Promised Land (see Gen 43:11) and the "diligence" (Hebrew meaning for *saqed* "almond") expected of Aaron's priesthood. In Jeremiah 1:11-12 the sprouting almond branch symbolizes God's watching over Israel. The almond was recognized as the earliest of the blossoming plants of the region (e.g., in the Egyptian Wisdom of *Ahiqar) and may therefore also signify the priority of Aaron's office.

18:1-32
Priestly Duties and Prerogatives

18:1-7. concept and care of the sacred compass. The center of the sacred space was the Most Holy Place where the ark was. Radiating from that point out were concentric zones of holiness, each with its requirements of levels of *purity. One of the principal tasks of the priests was to enforce the rules that would maintain the appropriate level of holiness for each zone. Since the entire tribe of Levi had been singled out to serve as priests, it was necessary to assign duties and responsibilities and to create a hierarchy within the group headed by Aaron and his sons. All of the Levites were put in the charge of Aaron's household. They were to perform the mundane tasks necessary to maintain the tent of meeting, guard its precincts and assist worshipers who brought offerings for sacrifice. However, no one other than Aaron and his sons and their descendants was to be allowed to actually perform the sacrifices or to minister before the ark of the testimony. Any violation by a Levite of these restrictions would result in the death of both the Levite and Aaron. Any non-Levite who entered the forbidden precincts of the sanctuary was condemned to death. Through these restrictions on the community and the placing of such heavy responsibilities on Aaron's family, the mystery and power associated with God's service and the items tied to it are magnified and protected.

18:8-10. sacrificial portions. The most sacred sacrificial portions are designated to be consumed by Aaron and his sons as a reward for their heavy responsibilities. This consists of those items which are brought into the most sacred precincts of the tent of meeting (see Lev 6:1-7:10). They may not be shared, as are other portions, with their families but must be eaten by priests who are ritually pure and therefore holy enough to consume sacred gifts. This includes grain, sin and guilt offerings, some of which is to be burnt on the altar while the remainder becomes the holy food of the priests. Hittite sacred texts also express concern over the consumption of the "god's food" by princes and other secular officials. The seriousness of sacred property is also found in Mesopotamian law, where strict penalties (heavy fines or capital punishment) are prescribed for theft of temple property.

18:11. wave offerings. Continuing the list of sacrificial portions set aside for the priests and their families are the wave offerings. These consist of items brought to the sanctuary and given a special distinction through an elevation *ritual before the altar (see comment on Lev 8:22-30). This does not include all wave offerings, since some are totally consumed by fire (Ex 29:22-25) and some are reserved solely for male priests (Lev 14:12-14).

18:12-19. priestly prerogatives. Completing the list of items perpetually set aside for the priests and their families (excluding daughters-in-law and laborers) are the first fruits of the harvest (grain, oil and wine) and the meat of first-born animals. Some regulations are imposed. Unclean animals may be redeemed for a set price by their owners, and human babies must be redeemed by their parents (see Ex 13:12-13; 34:19-20). All blood, fat and certain internal organs are to be burnt on the altar as a well-being offering (see Lev 3:9; 7:3). Since these animal products contain the symbolic essence of life, it is proper that they be given entirely to God rather than set aside for priestly consumption.

18:16. sanctuary shekel. The shekel weight used for the redemption of children and unclean animals is equivalent to 20 gerahs of silver (11.5 grams). It will not be in the form of coined money until the fourth century B.C. For weight considerations see comment on Exodus 30:13.

18:19. covenant of salt. Salt was used widely as symbolic of preservation. When treaties or alliances were made, salt was employed to symbolize that the terms would be preserved for a long time. *Babylonian, Persian, Arabic and Greek contexts all testify to this symbolic usage. In the Bible, likewise, the *covenant between the Lord and Israel is identified as a covenant of salt—a long-preserved covenant. Allies entering into such an agreement would generally share a communal meal where salted meat was featured. Thus the use of salt in the sacrifices was an appropriate reminder of the covenant relationship. Additionally, salt impedes the action of yeast (leaven), and since leaven was a symbol of rebellion, salt could easily represent that which inhibited rebellion. (See Lev 2:13.)

18:21-32. tithing as priests' wages in the ancient Near East. Apparently, the practice of designating one-tenth of all produce (cereal, fruit and animal) as wages for the priesthood was unique to the Israelites. Although Mesopotamian temples did exact rents from tenant farmers on their lands, they were not able to tax the entire population. As a result, the revenues needed to maintain the temple and the priesthood came from their own lands and from gifts from individuals and royalty. Kings also had lands from which they derived revenue in Egypt and Mesopotamia, but this did not have the same significance as a tithe. In Canaanite culture the tithe was very similar to that in Israel but went to the king and his administration rather than to the priesthood, though priests were sometimes included among the administrative personnel. Since the Levites were not given land in the distribution after the conquest, they were to be supported by all of the people through the tithe. It should be noted, however, that the Levites also paid a tithe of what they received to Aaron and his family, thereby providing a clear distinction between Levites and priests.

19:1-22

The Ceremony of the Red Heifer

19:2-10. significance of the red heifer. The animal designated for sacrifice and whose blood will be mixed with ashes to serve as a means of purifying persons who have come in contact with the dead is a young cow. The color red may symbolize blood, but that is uncertain. The exact age of the animal is not made clear by the Hebrew, but the fact that it was not to be allowed to pull the plow or do any other type of work suggests it may have just reached maturity. One example of this may be the cows hitched to the wagon bearing the ark by the Philistines in 1 Samuel 6:7. They were suitable for sacrifice and thus could be used in this test of divine intention. The case of an unknown homicide in Deuteronomy 21:1-9 also requires the sacrifice of a heifer and the use of its blood for a purification *ritual. The blood and the innocence of the animal are the keys to purification.

19:2-10. ritual of the red heifer. In order to create the mixture needed to cleanse a person who has become contaminated through contact with a corpse, the law requires that a red heifer without blemish that has never been yoked for labor be taken outside the camp and slaughtered by Eleazar, Aaron's son. Eleazar does this because Aaron, the high priest, would have been contaminated by the carcass of the animal. Eleazar sprinkles some of its blood seven times on the tent of meeting and then supervises the burning of the carcass, while throwing cedar wood, hyssop and scarlet wool on the fire. The ashes are kept outside the camp for later use in purification *rituals. These actions cause participants in the sacrifice to become unclean until evening, even though they bathe and wash their clothes. Comparison with *Hittite ritual corroborates that it is the ritual act, plus the ingredients concocted to purify persons, that causes a temporary *impurity by the priest.

19:11. ritual contamination from a corpse. There was a widespread *cult of the dead in the ancient Near East. Although there was no well-defined concept of afterlife in Mesopotamia or ancient Israel, it was still believed that the spirits of the dead could effect the living. For instance, in Hittite texts the terror of the dead seems to come from the fear of being "unclean before" the spirits of the dead, just as one would be before a god. Thus offerings were made in tombs to the ancestors, but actual contamination by corpses does not appear to be a concern for the *Hittites. In contrast the Mesopotamian *namburbi* *ritual evidences a significant fear of corpse contamination. What may have been of concern was a mixing of the two spheres of existence, the living and the dead. When a person came in contact with the dead, whether human or animal, contamination occurred. Purification was necessary so that that person did not infect others or the entire community with his *impurity. The biblical purification rituals are perhaps the most detailed of any developed in the ancient Near East, although those employed by the Hittites also involved bathing,

sacrifices and a period of exclusion.

19:17-19. cleansing ritual. To cleanse a person contaminated by a corpse, a ceremonially clean man takes the ashes of the red heifer, mixes them with water from a spring or running stream, and sprinkles the unclean person using a hyssop branch. The hyssop is used because its hairy branches can absorb liquid. Sprinkling takes place on the third and seventh days (both of these prime numbers are often used in *rituals and stories). Then, on the seventh day, the unclean person purifies him- or herself by bathing and washing clothing. That evening he or she will be ritually pure again. In this way there is no mixing of clean and unclean within the community itself, and the ideal is maintained of a community worthy to serve their God.

19:20-21. water of cleansing. The mixture of ashes from the sacrificed heifer and water from a spring or running stream is called the "water of cleansing." It is sprinkled on an unclean person as part of the cleansing *ritual. Hittite ritual texts also include water as a means of removing actual or suspected *impurity. However, the mixture described in Numbers also makes the person who sprinkles the water unclean until evening. This is based on association with the mixture's purpose and the assumed contamination created by the sacrificial ingredients themselves.

20:1-13
Water from the Rock

20:1. chronological note. At this point the forty years of wandering in the wilderness are coming to an end, and the remaining survivors of the exodus must leave the scene, since they are not allowed to enter the Promised Land. Thus in the first month of the fortieth year Miriam, Moses' sister, dies, marking the transition of leadership that will culminate in Aaron's death in the fifth month (Num 33:38).

20:1. Wilderness of Zin. The Wilderness of Zin lies north of the Wilderness of Paran. Although its exact location is unknown, it is referred to as the southern boundary of the Promised Land (Num 34:3-4; Josh 15:1, 3). Kadesh, the oasis where the Israelites spend a considerable time, is in the Desert of Zin (see chaps. 13—14).

20:6. appearance of the glory of the Lord. During times of crisis Moses and Aaron turn to God for guidance and assistance. They go to the entrance of the tent of meeting and as supplicants they bow to the ground. Because of their humble submission of their plea,

God's "glory" (kabod) appears and provides a solution (see similar instances in Num 14:5-12; 16:19-22). A physical manifestation of a god's aura or power is common in Mesopotamian epics, where it is referred to as the god's melammu, and it can be used as a means of defeating an enemy (as in *Marduk's struggle with *Tiamat in the *Enuma Elish).

20:1-13. water from the rock. Sedimentary rock is known to feature pockets where water can collect just below the surface. If there is some seepage, one can see where these pockets exist and by breaking through the surface can release the collected water. Again, however, we are dealing with a quantity of water beyond what this explanation affords.

20:13. waters of Meribah. The location of the waters of Meribah in Exodus 17 had been in the vicinity of Sinai, specifically at Rephidim. Now they are at Kadesh, about 150 air miles north-northeast of Rephidim. Nevertheless, these are waters of quarreling (meribah), just as those had been.

20:14-21
Request to the Edomites

20:14-21. Late Bronze Age Edom. Edom was the territory ranging south from the Dead Sea to the Gulf of Aqaba. Recently archaeologists have found small amounts of pottery from the *Late Bronze period at a number of settlements in this region, but no architectural remains or written records. The Egyptians referred to the nomadic population there as the Shosu, though that term may refer to social class rather than to ethnic origin.

20:22-29
The Death of Aaron

20:22-26. Mount Hor. The death site for Aaron (although Deut 10:6 identifies his death with Moseroth). The traditional location is near Petra at Jebal Nabi Harun, but this is not "on the border of Edom." Another possibility is Jebal Madrah, west of Kadesh and near the Edomite border, but it lacks sufficient water sources.

20:29. 30 days of mourning. The normal mourning period is seven days (Gen 50:10; 1 Sam 31:13). However, to demonstrate their importance, both Moses (Deut 34:8) and Aaron are mourned for thirty days. The occasion is also marked by transition of leadership, with Eleazar succeeding his father as high priest and wearing his vestments (Num 20:26). Similarly, Joshua succeeds Moses (Deut 34:9).

21:1-3
The Destruction of Arad

21:1-3. Arad. The site identified as Arad was a walled city in the *Early Bronze period (first half of the third millennium), well before the time of Abraham. It had a major role in the copper industry that thrived in the Sinai peninsula. The next occupation detected by archaeologists is connected with the Early *Iron Age (Judges period), and there was a series of citadels and even a temple on the site about the time of Solomon. Since there is no sign of occupation during the period of the exodus and conquest, some archaeologists have suggested that the Arad of the Canaanite period is the site now identified as Tell Malhata, about seven or eight miles southwest of the site now known as Arad. Egyptian inscriptions of the tenth century identify two Arads.

21:1. Atharim. This word is obscure and may be either a place name or a profession (KJV and LXX translate it "spies"). Most likely it is to be identified with the area just south of the Dead Sea, possibly with the site of Tamar. Here the Israelites were attacked by the army of the king of Arad.

21:3. Hormah. The Hebrew word means "destruction." It is applied as a place name here to commemorate the Israelite victory. They had vowed to totally destroy the cities of the Canaanites in that area and dedicate the spoil to the sanctuary if God gave them the victory. This is similar to the *herem, "holy war," declared against Jericho (Josh 6:17-19, 24). As a geographical name it refers to a site seven and a half miles east of Beersheba tentatively identified with Tell Masos (Khirbet el-Meshash).

21:4-9
The Bronze Serpent

21:4. itinerary. The Israelites marched south from Mount Hor on the border of Edom toward Elath at the northern end of the Gulf of Aqabah. Archaeological survey of the area suggests that the Edomites did not extend this far until the time of Solomon (tenth century B.C.).

21:6-7. snakes. The snakes are not clearly identified but may be a species of desert viper. Their "fiery" or "winged" character may have to do with their association with the cobra or their quick spring as they strike (Deut 8:15). For general information see the comment on Genesis 3:1.

21:8-9. bronze snake on a pole. The Hebrew here is actually "copper" snake. Bronze, an alloy of copper and tin, was smelted in the Timnah region where this event occurred, and thus the translation here has a physical background. Excavations in that area have unearthed an Egyptian temple to the god Hathor. During the period of the Judges this temple was adopted by Midianites in the area, who made it into a shrine draped with curtains. In the inner chamber of this shrine was found a five-inch long copper image of a snake. It was common in the ancient Near East to believe that the image of something could protect against the thing itself. As a result Egyptians (living as well as dead) sometimes wore snake-shaped *amulets to protect them from serpents. Finally it is of interest that a well-known bronze bowl from *Nineveh with Hebrew names on it depicts a winged snake on a pole of some sort.

21:10-20
Journey Through Moab

21:10-20. itinerary. A fuller list of stops on this journey is given in Numbers 33:41-48. A number of the towns are unknown, making it difficult to offer archaeological evidence. Nevertheless, a number of the stops also occur on Egyptian maps and itineraries from this period. The Zered Valley is today the Wadi el-Hesa, and the Arnon River flows through the Wadi el-Mojib. Both flow from east to west, the former into the southern end of the Dead Sea and the latter into a midpoint on the east side.

21:14. book of the wars of the Lord. In compiling the history and traditions of the conquest, the biblical writers drew on a variety of sources, both written and oral. Among the written sources was the Book of Jashar (see Josh 10:13; 2 Sam 1:18) and the Book of the Wars of the Lord. Based on the three fragments of these documents that appear in the Bible, they were composed primarily of victory songs and tales of the mighty acts of God and the leaders of the Israelites during this formative period. Unfortunately, neither book has survived, but their mention in the biblical text indicates that the narrative was based, at least in part, on cultural memories.

21:21-35
Sihon and Og

21:21. Amorites. The *Amurru or Amorites of Mesopotamia formed a significant ethnic group after 2000 B.C. and are mentioned in the *Mari texts and the administrative documents of *Hammurabi of *Babylon during the eighteenth century B.C. Egyptian records list them

as one of several kingdoms during the fourteenth century B.C. in the area south of the Orontes River and into Transjordan. Their effective control of Transjordan may be associated with the conflict between Egypt and the Hittite Empire. The indecisive battle of Kadesh (c. 1290 B.C.) between these two powers opened a temporary political opportunity for Amorite control, but the coming of the *Sea Peoples in 1200 B.C. further disrupted the region. In the Bible, *Amorites* is used as an ethnic term for the kingdoms of Sihon and Og (Num 21:21, 33) as well as for the inhabitants of Canaan (Gen 15:16; Deut 1:7).

21:23. Jahaz. The site of the battle with the forces of the *Amorite king Sihon is given as Jahaz. Its probable location, based on the church historian Eusebius (fourth century A.D.) and the Mesha inscription (ninth century B.C.), is between the territories of Madaba and Dibon, at Khirbet Medeiniyeh at the eastern edge of Moab by the Wadi al-Themed. The battle is also mentioned in Deuteronomy 2:33 and Judges 11:20.

21:24-30. captured land. The area of central Transjordan which is here described as the kingdoms of Sihon and Og stretches from the Arnon River valley in the south to the Jabbok River in the north. It would include Moab but not Ammon. It seems likely that these "kingdoms" were not organized states in this period and that their conquest provided passage for the Israelites without the tribes actually taking control of and settling this region.

21:25-28. Heshbon. The modern site of Tell-Heshban is located nearly fifty miles directly east of Jerusalem. However, archaeologists have not been able to detect any evidence that this site was settled prior to 1200 B.C. Some have suspected that the *Late Bronze city of Heshbon may have been at a different site, with Tell Jalul named as one possibility. Recent surveys and excavations in this region have turned up more and more *Late Bronze pottery, but it remains difficult to assess the nature of the occupation during this period.

21:29. Chemosh. The Moabite god *Chemosh, mentioned here in Israel's "taunt song" marking their victory over the Transjordanian kingdoms of Sihon and Og, is also mentioned in the ninth-century B.C. Moabite inscription of King Mesha (see also Judg 11:24; 1 Kings 11:7). As the national god of Moab, Chemosh stood in opposition to *Yahweh, just as Moab did to Israel. His *cult has similarities to Yahweh worship, and his attributes (giving of land to his people and victory in battle) are also similar. This may simply be an indication that the expectations placed on their gods by the people of the ancient Near East were very much the same from one nation to another. Chemosh first appears in the list of gods from ancient Ebla in northern Syria (c. 2600-2250 B.C.) and may have also been worshiped in Mesopotamia and *Ugarit as an elemental deity associated with clay or mud bricks.

21:30. area of destruction. Heshbon and Dibon are the major cities in the north and south respectively in the northern section of Moab (north of the Arnon). For Heshbon see the comment earlier in this chapter. Dibon is modern Dhiban, just a mile or two north of the Arnon (Wadi al-Mujib). In the ninth century B.C. it served as one of Mesha's royal cities and is prominent in the Mesha inscription that was found there. The lack of *Late Bronze finds at the site raises questions about whether the ancient city was at Dhiban or somewhere else nearby. The fact that Rameses II also lists Dibon on his itinerary shows that there was a Late Bronze city of that name. Nophah has not been identified, and even the reading of the name is uncertain. Medeba is the principal city in the central region of north Moab and is identified with the modern city of the same name. There has been limited excavation on the site because of the modern town.

21:32. Jazer. This geographical name is associated with both a city as well as the surrounding region, including small villages or "daughters." Although its location is disputed, the most likely site is Khirbet Jazzir, twelve miles south of the Jabbok River. It served as an outpost on the border with Ammon and represented the eastward thrust of the Israelite forces.

21:33. Bashan. After defeating Sihon, the Israelites travel northward to the region of Bashan in the area (known today as the Golan Heights) bordered by Mount Hermon to the north, Jebel Druze to the east and the Sea of Galilee to the west where they defeated King Og at Edrei (modern Der'a, thirty miles east of the Sea of Galilee). It is a broad, fertile plateau region noted for its grazing (Ps 22:12; Amos 4:1-3). See the comment on Deuteronomy 3 for more detail.

21:33. Edrei. The Israelites defeat the *Amorite king Og at Edrei on the southeastern border of Bashan. The site is identified as modern Der'a in Syria about sixty miles south of Damascus and thirty miles east of the Sea of Galilee near the Yarmuk River. Though no excavations have been conducted there, the town is also mentioned in ancient texts from Egypt and *Ugarit.

21:33. Og. The *Amorite king of Bashan, Og, is mentioned as the last of the Rephaim or gi-

ants, whose "bed was made of iron and was more than thirteen feet long and six feet wide" (see comment on Deut 3:11). There is no historical information that sheds light on this individual. The victory was celebrated many times in Israelite tradition and is recorded in Deuteronomy 1:4; 3:1-13; 4:47; 29:7; 31:4; Joshua 2:10; 9:10; and 1 Kings 4:19.

22:1—24:25
Balaam and Balak

22:1. plains of Moab. This is the broad plain or steppe region immediately north of the Dead Sea and east of the Jordan River, just opposite the "plains of Jericho" (Josh 4:13). Its location serves as the jumping-off point for entrance into Canaan.

22:2. Balak of Moab. Balak, the king of Moab, is unknown in other historical sources. In fact, there is very little of Moab's history that has been recovered aside from the information given in the Mesha Inscription concerning the ninth century. It must be remembered that the title *king* could be used for rulers of vast empires or, as most likely in this case, petty rulers or tribal leaders.

22:4-7. Midianites. The Midianites are a people living in the southern portions of the Transjordan region. They are described as the descendants of Abraham and Keturah (Gen 25:106) and operate as traders and caravaneers in the Joseph narrative (Gen 37:25-36). Moses joins the Midianite clan of Jethro after fleeing Egypt (see comment on Ex 2:15), but the Midianites do not join the Israelites in the conquest of Canaan. In the Balaam narrative, the Midianite elders are allied with the Moabites and participate in the hiring of the prophet to curse Israel.

22:4-20. Balaam at Deir Allah. In 1967 a Dutch archaeological expedition led by H. J. Franken discovered some inscribed pieces of plaster at a site in Jordan known as Deir 'Allah. The fragments are apparently written in *Aramaic and date to about 850 B.C. They mention Balaam son of Beor, the same figure described as a "seer" in Numbers 22—24. Although the text is very fragmentary, with many breaks and uncertain words, it can be established that Balaam was a seer who received a divine message during the night and that his message was not what his neighbors expected to hear. Whether this text refers to the events described in the Bible is questionable, but it does establish a nonbiblical tradition current in the ninth century of a prophet named Balaam. It may be that Balaam's notoriety was such that he remained an important prophetic figure for centuries and could thus be identified with the earlier Israelite narratives of the conquest.

22:5. Pethor. This is probably to be identified with Pitru on the Sajur River, a tributary of the upper Euphrates, located about twelve miles from Carchemish in northern Syria. Since Balaam is said to have been brought from *Aram in Numbers 23:7, this identification seems appropriate. However, the distance involved (about four hundred miles) has caused some to look closer to Moab for the site of Pethor.

22:6. prophetic status of Balaam. In Joshua 13:22, Balaam is described as a "soothsayer," while in Numbers 22:6 he is said to be a man whose blessings and curses are effective. He is from the region of upper Mesopotamia, near Carchemish, and has an international reputation as a true prophet. Throughout the narrative in Numbers 22—24, Balaam continually reminds Balak that he can speak only the words which God gives him to speak (Num 22:18, 38; 23:12, 26; 24:13). Although Balaam uses sacrificial rituals to obtain God's answer, he is not to be considered simply a diviner. *Divination, while sometimes used by Mesopotamian prophets, is more often associated with *cultic personnel who examine sacrificial animals or natural conditions (flights of birds, etc.). In each case, Balaam seems to have direct communication with God and then speaks God's word in the form of *oracles to Balak. This is the typical form of prophetic address found in the books of Isaiah, Jeremiah and other Israelite prophets. Spoken oracles are also recorded in over fifty *Mari texts (a few centuries earlier than Balaam, about 250 miles downstream from Carchemish). Through either lay people or temple personnel, various messages are offered to Zimri-Lim, king of Mari, from various deities. Therefore it is clear that prophetic activity in the ancient Near East during this general time period was not uncommon.

22:6. power of a curse. Curses draw the wrath of the deity on persons, groups, cities or places. They may be composed and spoken by anyone, with an intent to bring death, destruction, disease and defeat. Ritual performance was also employed, as in a Hittite text that requires water to be poured and a curse spoken against anyone who gave the king "polluted" water to drink. Curses often accompanied *covenant or treaty agreements to involve the power of the gods as cosigners and to put treaty breakers on notice of their peril. However, cursing can have negative effects on the one who curses as well. The death penalty was imposed on those who curse their parents (Ex 21:17) or God (Lev 24:11-24). In the Israel-

ite tradition expressed in the Balaam narrative, Yahweh alone was capable of carrying out a curse, and no prophet acting, on his own could effectively curse anyone. Yet Balak describes Balaam as one so attuned to the gods that both his blessings and his curses are always effective. In effect, the prophet, as a god's intermediary or representative, is believed to be capable of interceding for good or ill with the god(s). Balaam discounts this, however, saying he can only speak what God gives him to speak.

22:7. fee for *divination. It is to be expected that a fee or reward would be paid for vital information (see 2 Sam 4:10). Diviners, as religious practitioners, would be paid for their services (1 Sam 9:8). However, Balaam is not to be paid until after he curses the Israelites (Num 24:11). Thus this may simply be an offer rather than a retainer for services.

22:18. Balaam and Yahweh. If Balaam is truly a Mesopotamian prophet who has spoken in the name of many gods, it seems unusual that he would refer to *Yahweh as "the LORD my God." It is perfectly possible that Balaam was familiar with the Israelite God, at least by reputation (see Rahab's speech in Josh 2:9-11). Or he may always refer to each god he is dealing with in these intimate terms to demonstrate his prophetic authority. Balak's interest in Balaam seems to be based on his ability to invoke blessings or curses—no matter which god he calls upon. There is little reason to maintain that Balaam served Yahweh exclusively.

22:21-35. God opposing after sending. There are times when there seems to be a strange change of mind by God. The Lord called on Jacob (Gen 31—32) and Moses to go somewhere but then accosted each on the way. In each instance God did indeed want the individual to make the journey but had an issue to settle first.

22:22-35. angel of the Lord. In the ancient world direct communication between heads of state was a rarity. Diplomatic and political exchange normally required the use of an intermediary. The messenger who served as the intermediary was a fully vested representative of the party he represented. He spoke for that party and with the authority of that party. He was accorded the same treatment as that party would enjoy were he there in person. While this was standard protocol, there was no confusion about the person's identity. All of this treatment simply served as appropriate recognition of the individual that he represented. Gifts given were understood to belong to the represented party, not the representative. Words spoken to the representative were expected to be reported back in accurate detail and were understood as having been spoken directly to the represented individual. When official words were spoken by the representative, everyone understood that he was not speaking for himself but was merely conveying the words, opinions, policies and decisions of his liege. In the same way the Angel of the Lord serves as the messenger, the royal envoy endowed with the authority of the sender of the message. The word in Hebrew describing what the angel of the Lord does here is *satan*. This being is not the personified "accuser" or "adversary" found in Job 1—2 and Zechariah 3:1. The term is used only to explain the adversarial role played by the angel.

22:28-30. speaking animals. The only other instance in the Bible of a talking animal is the dialogue between Eve and the serpent in Genesis 3:1-5. In that case the serpent is described as the most cunning of the animals, and it is possible that it was the only animal that could speak. In the Balaam narrative the donkey is able to speak only after God gives it that ability. Such stories are commonly identified as fables, and they are quite popular in ancient as well as more recent literature. They generally have a wisdom theme and are designed to establish or question basic truths. Among the ancient Near Eastern examples are the talking cattle in the Egyptian *Tale of Two Brothers* and the dialogue between the leopard and the gazelle in the *Assyrian Teachings of *Ahiqar*. The effect of the speaking animal in this story is to make it clear to Balaam that God can speak through any creature he chooses, with no credit to the creature.

22:36-41. geography. From the city of Ar-Moab (NIV: "the Moabite town") near the northern border of Moab, the two proceed north to Kiriath Huzoth and Bamoth Baal. Ar-Moab (see 21:15) has not been identified with certainty, but is usually connected with modern Balu'a along the southern tributary that the King's Highway followed to the Arnon. The location of Kiriath Huzoth is unknown, as is Bamoth Baal. Some place the latter some twenty-five to thirty miles north of Ar along the King's Highway, though some would place it farther north, in closer proximity to where the Israelites were camped.

23:1. seven altars. The number seven is often attested in the Bible and may be associated with the days of creation or the fact that it is a prime number (see 1 Kings 18:43; 2 Kings 5:10). Nowhere else in the Bible are seven altars constructed for sacrifice. This may relate to a non-Israelite *ritual in which each of the

altars is dedicated to a different god. It is conceivable that when an international treaty was concluded and the gods were called to witness the agreement (as in the treaty between the *Assyrian king Esarhaddon and Baal of Tyre, which calls on the "seven gods"), altars to each god would be erected and sacrifices made before them (see Gen 31:44-54). But non-treaty contexts in Mesopotamia also attest the practice of using seven altars in order to offer seven sacrifices simultaneously before the high gods.

23:1. sacrifice of bulls and rams. These were the most prized and valuable stock animals in the ancient Near East, and thus their sacrifice would have signified a supreme effort on the part of the worshipers to please the god(s) and gain their aid. The sacrifice of seven of these animals is also found in Job's sin offering for his three friends (Job 42:8).

23:3. barren height for revelation. The translation "barren height" is contested, and the meaning of the Hebrew word questionable. It seems clear from the context that Balaam separated himself from the Moabites to practice his *divination alone. This may have been required by the *ritual or perhaps by God's desire to only communicate directly with Balaam. In any case, high places are often associated with gods and their revelations (Mounts Sinai, Zaphon, Olympus).

23:4. meeting with *Elohim. In the ancient world messages from deity were generally conveyed through dreams, communications from the dead or temple personnel in prophetic trances. The language here suggests none of those options, though the nature of Balaam's encounter with God is not described.

23:14. Zophim/Pisgah. *Zophim* means "watchmen" or "lookout." Used in relation to Pisgah, the generic term for the promontories of the Moabite plateau looking west toward Canaan (see Num 21:20), *Zophim* simply means that Balaam went to a known observation point to watch for a sign from God. It is possible that he intended to observe the flight of birds in order to receive an omen. This is not only a common *divination practice in Mesopotamia but one that the Deir Allah inscription (see comment on 22:4) appears to relate to Balaam.

24:1-2. difference in Balaam's method and role of the Spirit of God. As a Mesopotamian prophet, Balaam's usual procedures when invoking a god or seeking an omen would have been to engage in some form of *divination. Having now perceived that Yahweh's intent is to bless the Israelites, Balaam dispenses with these mechanical methods and leaves himself open to direct revelation from God. At that point he turns toward the Israelites and is empowered by God's Spirit. He speaks the divine blessing, probably in a trance. It is his willingness to become vulnerable in the sight of the Moabite king that demonstrates the truth of his message and provides an example of ecstatic prophecy (see 1 Sam 10:5-6, 10-11).

24:5-7. metaphors. Balaam's *oracle contains a promise of abundance and prosperity for Israel. Looking down on their tents, he likens them to a forest containing aromatic aloe and cedars. Aloes are not native to Canaan, but the metaphor may refer to the immigrant Israelites "planted" in the Promised Land by God. Cedars do not grow near streams, and this may simply refer to any coniferous tree. The image of abundant waters and seed refer to the richness of the land of Canaan and the *covenantal promise of children. By referring to a king, the author speaks of the future nation's triumph over its enemies, the Amalekites, whose king, Agag, will be defeated by Saul (1 Sam 15:7-8).

24:7. Agag. Agag was the mighty king of the Amalekites in the time of Saul (1 Sam 15:7-8). Although Saul defeats them, the Amalekites continue to be a thorn in Israel's side (1 Sam 27:8; 30:1; 2 Sam 1:1). Agag's name appears again in the book of Esther as the ethnic name for the villain Haman the Agagite. Some have suggested that Agag should be understood as a title (like Pharaoh), but evidence is unavailable.

24:17. star and scepter metaphors. While a star is a common metaphor for kings in the ancient Near East, it is seldom used in the Bible (Is 14:12; Ezek 32:7). Its association here with a scepter, the symbol of royal power (Ps 45:6), however, makes this identification more certain. Balaam's *oracle thus predicts the rise of the monarchy in Israel and the extension of its power (like the waving of the scepter) over the lands of Transjordan. As in the Egyptian inscription of Tuthmoses III (c. 1504-1450 B.C.), the scepter is also used as a mace to crush the heads of enemy nations.

24:20. Amalekites. The Amalekites were a confederation of tribes living primarily in the steppe area southeast of Canaan (Ex 17; Judg 6—7). There may have also been groups of Amalekites in the hill country west of Samaria. They are always portrayed as Israel's rival for territory. The title of "first among the nations" may refer to what they called themselves or perhaps to their distinction as the first people to challenge the Israelites (Ex 17:8-15).

24:21-22. Kenites. Although the Kenites are described as friendly prior to this *oracle

(Moses' father-in-law, Ex 2:16-22), they are condemned here with the Amalekites. They were nomadic tribes living around Kadesh in the northern Sinai peninsula and in the region of Galilee and may have been itinerant metalworkers (there were copper mines nearby in Sinai) as well as shepherds. Balaam mocks their mountain settlements, saying that they cannot prevent their eventual fall to Asshur.

24:22-24. Asshur. It is unlikely that this reference is to the Neo-Assyrian empire, which dominated the entire ancient Near East during the eighth and seventh centuries B.C. That would place the focus (and, some would say, composition) of this *oracle very late. However, the Asshurim, a tribe descended from Abraham and Keturah (Gen 25:3) does not seem significant enough to defeat the Kenites. The *Assyrians of the fourteenth century were sufficiently militaristic to contribute to the fall of the *Hurrian kingdom of Mitanni, but there is no evidence of military activity further west. This most likely should be identified as the Asshur mentioned in connection with the Ishmaelites in Genesis 25:18.

24:24. Kittim. This is the ancient name for the island of Cyprus (Gen 10:4) and derives from the name of the city Kition. In later texts (Qumran), Kittim is used as a generic for maritime nations (Dan 11:30) or for the Romans. Here some have suggested that it may refer to the "Sea Peoples"—the amalgamation of tribes (including the Philistines) that invaded the Near East around 1200 B.C.

24:24. Eber. Eber is identified as the ancestor of the Hebrews in Genesis 10:21 and 11:14. That cannot fit the context of this *oracle, however, since it would be a curse on Israel. Possible solutions may be a reference to an attack by the Kittim on "Heber," either one of the clans of the Kenites or of the Israelite tribe of Asher. No really satisfactory explanation has been put forward for this name.

25:1-18

The Incident at Baal-Peor

25:1. Shittim. The full name of this site was Abel-shittim (Num 33:49), and it is the jumping-off point for Joshua's spies and for the Israelite's entrance into Canaan (Josh 2:1; 3:1; Mic 6:5). Josephus places it seven miles from the Jordan River. Its actual location is uncertain, but it may be Tell el-Hammam on the Wadi Kefrein.

25:3. Baal of Peor. It is not uncommon for the god *Baal to be identified with different mountains (Zaphon) or city sites in the region of Canaan (see Num 32:38; 33:7; 2 Kings 1:2).

In this case, the Israelites are influenced by the Moabite women to worship the city god of Peor (see Deut 3:29 for Beth Peor). This is apparently their first contact with Baal, the Canaanite god of *fertility and rain, since the name does not appear in Genesis. The result is disastrous and sets a precedent for God's reaction to idolatry.

25:4. corpse exposure. Although the form of execution is unclear here (see 2 Sam 21:9 for a similar use of words), there is a purpose in placing the bodies of these unfaithful leaders on public display. It may be an attempt to propitiate God's anger or a warning to others that idolatry will not be tolerated. Legal tradition forbade leaving bodies exposed or impaled overnight (Deut 21:22-23). Impalement and public display of corpses was common punishment by the *Assyrians (referred to in the annals of Sennacherib and Ashurbanipal).

25:6. brought to his family. The unnamed Israelite may simply be introducing this Midianite woman to his family as his wife. But many have believed that the cause of distress here is the practice of ritual intercourse. By bringing a Midianite woman to his family, this man was encouraging all of his male kin to participate in this forbidden *ritual—even though the people were supposed to be repenting for their previous idolatry. The "chamber" (v. 8) into which they enter appears to be in the sacred enclosure and therefore suggests ritual intercourse. Though the ritual may have been *fertility-oriented, the Israelites are not engaging in agriculture, so it is difficult to imagine what connection that might have here. Alternatively, Psalm 106:28 links Baal-Peor to sacrifices for the dead (NIV: "lifeless gods"). The plague of verse 3 may have been attributed to ancestral spirits who could be appeased by ritual intercourse. In this case the "family" the woman was brought to may be the ancestral spirits.

25:8. the plague. Since no symptoms are given, the nature of the plague afflicting the Israelites is unclear. Diagnostic texts from Mesopotamia often sought to identify a causal relationship between certain symptoms or illnesses and the presumed sins that caused them. Israel had no such hierarchy of diseases, but they would interpret major or sudden outbreak of serious disease as punishment from God. Endemic and epidemic diseases in the ancient world included typhoid, malaria, cholera, tuberculosis, anthrax, bubonic plague, diphtheria and more. Yahweh's use of plague is similar to that associated with plague deities in the ancient Near East. In Mesopotamian mythology, Nergal (or, Erra) is the god of plague and king of the netherworld. The comparable Canaanite deity is Resheph, and the Hittite, Irshappa. Murshilish, a Hittite king of this general period, complains in one prayer about a plague that has lasted twenty years. He sees it as a punishment for his father's sins.

25:13. covenant of priesthood. Like the *covenant made with David (2 Sam 7:8-16; Ps 89:29), this is an "everlasting" covenant. Again, this language and the concept of a perpetual treaty agreement is not unique. It is common in Mesopotamian treaty texts (see the *Assyrian Vassal Treaties of Esarhaddon). In this instance, Phineas's act of piety is the basis for marking his particular branch of Aaron's family as the group with the sole right to officiate in the temple (see the genealogy in 1 Chron 6:3-14, which traces Phineas's lineage and not that of his brothers).

26:1-65

The Second Census

26:55. distribution by lot. By employing lots to determine the distribution of the land, the decision is left to God's judgment. This process was also employed at *Mari in Mesopotamia to allocate fiefs by the king to vassals and military retirees.

27:1-11

The Case of Zelophehad's Daughters

27:1-11. daughters' inheritance rights. Land is generally redeemed by a male relative if a man dies without a male heir (for the levirate obligation see comment on Deut 25:5-10; for the Jubilee year see comment on Lev 25:8-55; for the relative's claim see Lev 25:25-28). The separate question of a daughter's right to inherit requires, in this case, an *oracle and a divine decision, since it cannot be dealt with under existing legislation. Levirate rights (Deut 25:5-10) apparently do not apply here, since no male heirs (sons or paternal brothers) are mentioned. In this situation, therefore, the decision is made and laws are enacted giving daughters the right to inherit in the absence of any male heirs, as well as establishing a law of procedure in cases of inheritance. Some precedent seems to exist for this in Mesopotamian legal documents (Sumerian text Gudea statute B [c. 2150 B.C.]; *Alalakh [eighteenth century B.C.]; *Nuzi; and *Emar). The law in Numbers 27, however, has to be modified later due to the problem of the potential loss of a family's land if the daughter marries out of her tribe. Thus Numbers 36:6-9 adds the further stipulation that daughters who inherit land from their father must marry within their own tribal clans.

27:12-23
Joshua Commissioned

27:12. Abarim range. This is a range of mountains extending east of the mouth of the Jordan River and on around the northern end of the Dead Sea (see Deut 32:49). It forms the northwestern rim of the Moabite plateau. The specific peak in this range from which Moses will view the Promised Land is Mount Nebo, 2,740 feet in height.

27:14. geography. The parenthetical note that retells the story of Moses' and Aaron's sin at Meribah is based on the version in Numbers 20:1-13. This places the events near the oasis of Kadesh Barnea, probably 'Ein Qudeirat in the wadi el'Ain, the largest oasis in the northern Sinai. The Wilderness of Zin is the barren region in the Negev south of Canaan that extends toward the Sinai.

27:18. the spirit. As Moses' chosen successor, Joshua's qualification for this position is based on the authority of God with which he has been endowed. He has shown this trait in military campaigns (Ex 17:9-13) as well as in his courage in standing up to the people and the elders (Num 14:6-10; 26:65). Eventually he will be invested with the spirit of wisdom (Deut 34:9), but here it is his God-given skills as a leader that stand out as the basis of his elevation to command. There is no established political authority over all the tribes except that designated by the Lord. The recognition of the empowerment by the spirit of God becomes the criterion by which political authority is granted by the tribes.

27:18. laying on of hands. Part of the process of investing a person with authority and signifying the transferral of power from one leader to another involves the laying on of hands (see Num 8:10; Lev 16:21). For instance, the paintings found in the *El Amarna rock tombs (c. 1400-1350 B.C.) portray the investiture of officials by Pharaoh. They are given special garments, and Pharaoh is pictured extending his arms over them as a sign of their new authority.

27:21. priest and the Urim. One sign of Joshua's new leadership role as Moses' successor is his use of the oracular office of the High Priest. By using the Urim and Thummim, the high priest could consult God and obtain a yes or no answer to questions (see this practice by David and Abiathar in 1 Sam 23:9-12; 30:7-8). While it is uncertain what the Urim and Thummim actually looked like, their use is similar to the oracular questions and answers found in *Babylonian omen texts. They were kept in a pocket inside the high priest's "breastplate" and next to his heart (Ex 28:16; Lev 8:8). For further information, see the comment on Exodus 28:30.

28:1-15
Offerings

28:1-30. festivals and holy days. The major religious festivals and holy days celebrated throughout the ancient Near East were for the most part agriculturally based. While daily offerings were made to the gods, there were "patron days" in specific towns and villages for locally honored deities, as well as occasions when the national god(s) were paraded from one town to another, "visiting" shrines and promoting the general *fertility and well-being of the land. The single most important of the Mesopotamian festivals was the Akitu or new year's celebration. The monarch assumed the role of the chief god, while the high priestess served as his consort and represented the chief goddess. Their performance of a series of intricate sacred *rituals and sacrifices was designed to please the gods and thus insure a prosperous and fertile year ahead. During the year, based on a lunar calendar, "new moon" festivals were celebrated, as were the events of the agricultural calendar (the coming of the rains or annual flood waters, plowing and harvesting). Some rituals grew out of the changing of the seasons, such as the mourning for the "dying god" Tammuz (or *Dumuzi), who could be released from the underworld only through the tears of devotees (see Ezek 8:14).

28:1-8. daily offerings: who makes them and why. The heart of the sacrificial system in ancient Israel was the daily offering made for the people by the priests. This was a communal offering made on behalf of the people rather than an offering that each person made. Although the actual content of the sacrifice apparently differed from one time period to another (compare morning and evening animal sacrifice here with a morning animal sacrifice and an evening grain offering in 2 Kings 16:15), its intent was to provide continuous thanksgiving to God and signify daily compliance with the *covenant (see the comment on burnt offerings at Lev 1:1). The belief is quite clear that any interruption in this pattern would have resulted in dire consequences for the people (see Dan 8:11-14).

28:9-10. sabbath offering: who and why. The injunction to observe the sabbath each seventh day by ceasing work and by offering an additional burnt offering marks the weekly commemoration of the release from Egyptian bondage (Ex 20:11). Every Israelite, as well as their animals, servants and visitors, is required by this statute to observe the sabbath (Ex 31:12-17). This offering is not made by each family or clan but is made on behalf of the people as a whole. There is little evidence that the sabbath was used as a time for worship gatherings in ancient Israel. The sabbath is not tied to any other calendar event during the year and only has parallels in the celebration of the sabbatical and Jubilee years (Lev 25). Because the exodus event is unique to the Israelites, no similar, weekly holy day is observed by the peoples of the ancient Near East.

28:11-15. new moon offering: who and why. The lunar calendar was used throughout the ancient Near East and the worship of the moon god Sin was quite common, especially in northern Mesopotamia. Each new month began the first day of the new moon and signified the moon god's continuing dominion. The inclusion of a new moon offering in the liturgical calendar only appears in Numbers 28, although its celebration is known elsewhere (1 Sam 20:5; 2 Kings 4:23). Like the sabbath offering, the sacrifice marking the new moon is in addition to the daily offering. It is placed on a par with other major festivals with its sacrifice of a larger number of valuable animals (two bulls, a ram and seven sheep) and the addition of a sacrificial goat as a sin offering.

28:16—29:40
The Festival Calendar

28:16-25. Feast of Unleavened Bread. The Feast of Unleavened Bread signals the beginning of the barley harvest (March-April). Unleavened bread was made from the newly harvested grain without adding yeast and was eaten with joy as the first sign of coming harvests that year. For further information see the comments on Exodus 12:14-20.

28:26-31. Feast of Weeks. This second of the three major harvest festivals comes seven weeks after the harvest of the early grain (Ex 34:22; Deut 16:9-12) and is also known as the Feast of Harvest or Pentecost (Ex 23:16). Like the sabbath celebration, the Feast of Weeks is not tied to the lunar calendar (in this case because of the inaccuracy of a calendar based solely on the phases of the moon). In the agricultural cycle it marks the end of the wheat harvest season, and by tradition it is tied to the giving of the law on Mount Sinai. It is also

associated with *covenant renewal and pilgrimage. Celebration includes the bringing of a "wave offering" (see comment on Lev 8:27) of two loaves of bread, animal sacrifices (seven year-old lambs, one bull and two rams) and a drink offering in thanksgiving for a good harvest (see Lev 23:15-22). Like the other major feasts, a goat is also to be sacrificed as a sin offering for the people (Num 28:30).

29:1-6. Feast of Trumpets. The first day of the seventh month (the most sacred month in the Israelite calendar) was to be marked with the blowing of ram's horns (shofar) by the priests, commemorating the *covenantal agreement and gifts of God to the people. Its significance may partially derive from its being the seventh new moon of the seventh month of the year (compare this to the sabbatical cycle). No work is allowed, and burnt offerings are presented in addition to the daily offerings. The festival would continue until the tenth day of the month when the Day of Atonement would be observed (see Lev 16:29-34 for details). In later times the Feast of Trumpets would become the new year's festival, but that occurs in late postexilic times (see Lev 23:23-25).

29:7-11. Day of Atonement. The Day of Atonement was a special day set aside each year to deal with the people's sins. The seriousness of this occasion is demonstrated by the fact that all of the *rituals had to be performed inside the sanctuary by the high priest. According to Leviticus 23:27-32 the Day of Atonement fell ten days after the opening of the civil new year (during the seventh month). On that day the people remained home in prayer and fasting while the high priest entered the inner precincts of the tabernacle and burned incense on the golden incense altar. Blood from this special sacrifice was also to be daubed on the horns of the incense altar to tie this holiest of altars and its flow of incense to the need for getting rid of the nation's sins. A more elaborate description of this yearly ritual, including the casting of the people's sins on the scapegoat, is found in Leviticus 16. See comments there for further information.

29:12-39. Feast of Tabernacles. The final harvest of the year occurred in the autumn prior to the onset of the rainy season and marked the beginning of a new agricultural year (fifteenth day of the seventh month). At this time the last of the ripening grain and fruits were gathered and stored, allowing time afterwards for pilgrimage to Jerusalem. The seven-day event is also known as the Feast of Ingathering (Ex 23:16) and is symbolized by the construction of booths decorated with greenery for the harvesters. The festival was tied into Israelite tradition as a commemoration of the wilderness wanderings (see Lev 23:33-43). It was also the occasion for the dedication of Solomon's temple in Jerusalem (1 Kings 8:65) and was such a popular festival that the prophet Zechariah described it as the eschatological feast celebrated by the nations following Yahweh's ultimate triumph (Zech 14:16).

29:13-38. number of animals. There are more animals sacrificed during the eight days of the Feast of Tabernacles than any other annual festival. A total of 71 bulls, 15 rams, 105 lambs and 8 goats are sacrificed, with accompanying cereal and drink offerings (compare the much smaller number prescribed in Ezek 45:13-25 for holy days). The number of bulls offered diminishes during the days of the festival, perhaps as a way of denoting the passage of time or possibly as a means of sparing the nation some of its most valuable livestock. The very large number of animals involved, however, speaks both to the joy associated with the harvest (a sign of the *covenant's fulfillment) and to the need to feed the large number of persons who have made the pilgrimage to Jerusalem.

30:1-16
Regulations Concerning Vows

30:2-15. importance and role of vows. The taking of a vow magnifies the devotion of an individual in performing a specific task (sacrifice—see Lev 27; transport of the ark to Jerusalem by David—Ps 132:2-5) or serves as a form of bargaining with the deity to obtain a goal (Jephthah's vow to gain a victory—Judg 11:30-31). Thus a vow differs from an oath in that it is generally conditional rather than just promissory. It can also be used to initiate a special dedicatory period, as was the case with the *Nazirite vows (Num 6), or, during war, as a form of abstinence sacrifice, which devotes all of the spoils to God (Num 21:1-3; Josh 6:18-19). Since this is a religious act, drawing the deity into a pact with the worshiper, it may not be broken under penalty of God's displeasure (see Ex 20:7 and the injunction not to "misuse" God's name). For more information, see the comment on Leviticus 27:2-13.

30:3-15. women and vows. According to the injunction in this passage, young women and wives may not pledge themselves to a vow without the consent of their father or husband. The father or husband, as head of a household, has the right to annul any such vow. However, if he first approves of the vow and later attempts to obstruct a woman from

carrying it out, he bears the punishment for its nonfulfillment (vv. 14-15). In the first case (vv. 3-5) unmarried women are considered wards of their father and thus do not own property and may not, without prior consent, obstruct their father's ability to arrange their marriage or to utilize their person to benefit the family. Married women are similarly bound to their husband's household and may not make decisions without consulting their husband that might affect the functioning or economic viability of the household (vv. 6-8, 10-13). Only in the case of Hannah (1 Sam 1) does a wife on her own initiative make a vow, dedicating her child to temple service at Shiloh.

30:3-15. the subordinate role of women. Although women often had great influence over their husbands (especially royal women), only widows and elderly women appear to have been able to act on their own in Israelite society. Young women still living with their parents and wives were under the legal control of their fathers and husbands. They could not own property, start a business, initiate a lawsuit or arrange their own marriage. All of these acts were reserved for the male. There do seem to have been instances in which married women functioned more freely in the community (as in Prov 31), but the implication is always that this was done with the consent of their husbands. Their primary responsibility, in the biblical context as well as in the wider ancient Near Eastern context, was to maintain the home, provide heirs for their husbands and, when possible, assist with the economic assets of the household (farming, herding, manufacturing). In *Hammurabi's laws a woman who neglected her household duties in preferring business pursuits could be divorced by her husband. Older women beyond childbearing years may have moved into a different social category, functioning as female elders (see Deborah [Judg 4—5] and the wise women of Tekoa and Abel [2 Sam 14:2-20; 20:15-22]).

31:1-54
Battle with the Midianites

31:1-12. Midianites. Midianite territory centered in the region east of the Gulf of Aqaba in northwest Arabia, but the Midianites ranged west into the Sinai peninsula as well as north into Transjordan in various periods. Though their early history appears to be seminomadic or Bedouin in nature, archaeological study has revealed villages, walled cities and extensive irrigation in this region, beginning as early as the *Late Bronze period (the time of the exodus and early judges). There is, so far, no reference to the Midianites in ancient texts.

31:6. articles from the sanctuary. Nearly every army in the ancient Near East included priests and diviners (as seen in the *Mari texts), prophets (2 Kings 3) and portable sacred objects (Assyrian Annals of Shalmaneser III [858-824 B.C.]). In this way, the god(s) could be consulted on the battlefield or invoked to lead the soldiers to victory. Phineas, Aaron's son and a high-ranking priest himself, thus helps build the confidence of the army with his presence. Exactly which items are included here is uncertain but may have included the ark of the covenant, the breastplate of the priest and the Urim and Thummim (see the carrying of the ark into battle elsewhere—Josh 6:4-7; 1 Sam 4:3-8).

31:6. trumpets for signaling. When large numbers of troops are deployed over a fairly wide area, the piercing notes of the trumpets could serve a dual purpose, symbolizing the voice of God to frighten the enemy (see Judg 7:17-22) and giving signals to the various detachments of the army (see 2 Chron 13:2). While the shofar or horn trumpet is used elsewhere as a signaling device (Judg 3:27; 6:34; Neh 4:18-20), the Hebrew word here is for a metal trumpet, probably made of bronze or silver and capable of producing four or five tones. Tubular flared trumpets were used in this period in military as well as ritual contexts. This is depicted on Egyptian reliefs as well as evidenced by actual instruments found, for example, in the tomb of King Tut (a silver trumpet nearly two feet long). Trumpet signals are attested in Egypt in the *Late Bronze Age (this time period) in both military and religious contexts. A preset code would include some combination of long and short blasts.

31:17-18. rationale for who is put to death. The criteria used to determine who would be executed were two: (1) all the boys must be killed to prevent them from presenting a military threat in the future, and (2) all nonvirgins must die since they have already been contaminated by sexual contact with a proscribed people. Virgins represent an "unplowed field" and may be adopted through marriage into the Israelite tribes (see Judg 21:11-12). It is also possible that they were enslaved or used as *concubines. These young women were presumably innocent of the seduction of the Israelites by Midianite women at Baal-Peor (Num 25).

31:19-24. purification. The soldiers required purification because of their contact with the dead. The seven-day purification *ritual for the soldiers and for the plunder taken in war had to be performed outside the camp (compare Deut 23:10-15) in order to prevent contamination of the rest of the people (see Num 19:11-13, 16-22). Purification included bathing (Num 19:18-19) and laundering by the soldiers (see Lev 11:25, 28 and the *War Scroll* from Qumran for similar injunctions). The spoils are purified by means of fire and water. Bathing metals in fire is also found in *Hittite birth rituals.

31:25-50. conventions for distribution of plunder. Soldiers until very recently were paid in plunder. This became a sacred right in the ancient Near East. In the *Mari texts officers took oaths that they would not infringe on the booty due to their men. Normally, the god(s) also received a share, which was collected on the battlefield by the accompanying priests. In this case the convention set for distribution provides the soldiers with a share ten times that of the civilians, while one-five-hundredth of the army's share was set aside for Eleazar (and the maintenance of the sanctuary) and one-fiftieth of the civilians' share was given to support the Levites. This could be compared to the tithe given by Abraham to Melchizedek of Salem in Genesis 14:20 and David's equal distribution to soldiers and civilians in 1 Samuel 30:24-25.

31:50. gold for ransom. Counting people in the ancient world was particularly unpopular (see comment on Ex 30:11-16) and could be subject to divine displeasure, since it might suggest distrust of the god(s) as well as a concern with personal power (see the plague which results from David's census in 2 Sam 24:1-17). According to the law in Exodus 30:12, whenever a census is taken a ransom must be paid for the life of each man counted. Thus after counting the army of Israel and determining that not a single casualty had been inflicted by the Midianites, the officers paid this ransom with the golden objects they had stripped from the bodies of the dead. This ransom (NIV: "atonement") is made to prevent a plague (see Num 8:19), and the golden jewelry is melted into sacred vessels that will serve the needs of the sanctuary as an eternal memorial to the victory and the people's willingness to submit to God's law. The amount of gold given is about six hundred pounds.

32:1-42

The Tribes Who Inherited Transjordan

32:1. Jazer and Gilead. The Transjordanian region in the area of the Jabbok River provided suitable grazing and was an attractive place for the tribes of Reuben and Gad to settle. Jazer is probably Khirbet Jazzir, twelve miles south of the Jabbok, on the border with Ammon (see Num 21:32). The region of Gilead (mentioned in *Ugaritic texts) extends from the Arnon River in the south to Bashan and the Transjordanian side of the Galilee in the north.

32:3. cities list. This same list of cities also appears in Numbers 32:34-38. Ataroth is identified with Khirbet 'Attarus, eight miles northwest of Dibon and eight miles east of the Dead Sea. It is also mentioned in the Mesha stele inscription (c. 830 B.C.) as a site built by the Israelites and inhabited by the tribe of Gad. Dibon (=Diban), the Moabite capital, is approximately four miles north of the Arnon River and twelve miles east of the Dead Sea. Nimrah, near modern Tell Nimrin, is in the northern sector of Transjordan along with Jazer. Heshbon (=Hesban), on the northwest corner of the Madaba plain (three miles northeast of Mount Nebo), is said to be the capital of the *Amorite king Sihon, but there is no archaeological evidence for permanent occupation prior to 1200 B.C. (see comment on Num 21:25-28). Elealeh (= el-'Al) is located northeast of Heshbon (see Is 15:4; 16:9; Jer 48:34). Sebam is an unknown site. Nebo has also not been located, but it is mentioned in the Mesha stele. Beon (=Ma'in, Baal Meon in Num 32:38) is ten miles southwest of Heshbon. In his victory stele Mesha (ninth-century king of Moab) claims to have built it.

32:1-37. Transjordan topography. A wide range of topography characterizes Transjordan, which included the areas of Bashan, Gilead, Ammon, Moab and Edom. In the north this includes the Mount Hermon range (highest peak at 9,230 feet above sea level) and a portion of the rift valley between the Huleh basin (230 feet above sea level) and the Sea of Galilee (695 feet below sea level). The southern limit of the region is at the Gulf of Aqaba. The rift valley extends south following the Jordan River to the Dead Sea (2,550 feet below sea level at its deepest point). East of the Jordan, the hills of Gilead rise to 3,500 feet above sea level and in the south the mountains of Edom stand 5,700 feet near the region of Petra. Most north-south travel followed the "King's Highway," starting at Damascus, cutting across the major wadis and skirting the desert to the east. East-west travel followed the Yabis, Jabbok, Nimrin and Abu Gharaba wadis. The generally dry climate necessitates irrigation farming but supplies sufficient pasturage for pastoral nomadic groups.

32:34-42. geography of tribal settlements in

Transjordan. Based on the locations of the cities in this list (see Num 32:3 for locations of most of them), the tribe of Gad built cities in the southern, northern and northwestern sectors of the region of Transjordan (principally Gilead and Bashan). The Reubenites focused on the city of Heshbon, along with its surrounding villages. Joshua 13:15-31 presents the final distribution of cities, which yields to Reuben certain of the cities that the Gadites had built. Locations which can be posited for cities not discussed in Numbers 32:3 include Aroer, three miles south of Diban on the Arnon River; Jogbehah (=Jubeihat), five miles northwest of Rabbah; Beth Haran (=either Tell er-Rame or Tell Iktanu), south of Tell Nimrim; Kiriathaim (=Khirbet el-Qureiyat), six miles northwest of Diban. Archaeological attention to this area has increased in the last couple of decades, but many of these sites have yet to be excavated.

33:1-56
The Wilderness Itinerary

33:1-49. the itinerary of the journey. The itinerary form is common in ancient Near Eastern annals, including those of the ninth century B.C. *Assyrian kings, who described their campaigns in terms of stopping points and cities conquered. Closer to this period are the Egyptian itineraries preserved in the records of their various excursions into the Syro-Palestine region. This list provides a fairly complete chronicle of the journey from Rameses in Egypt to the Jordan crossing prior to the conquest. However, the omission of some important sites (Massah, Meribah) suggests that it is not comprehensive. The stages of the journey include (1) Egypt to the wilderness of Sinai (vv. 5-15; many of these sites are discussed specifically in the comments on Ex 13—17); (2) from the wilderness to Ezion Geber (vv. 16-35); (3) Ezion Geber to Kadesh in the wilderness of Zin (v. 36); and (4) Kadesh to Moab (vv. 37-49). Many of the names are obscure, occurring only here in the biblical record and unknown from ancient records or modern geographical and archaeological studies. Among those place names that can be at least tentatively identified are Rameses (=Tell el-Dab'a, see comment on Ex 1:8-14); Ezion Geber, a port city located at the head of the Gulf of Aqaba (1 Kings 9:26), either Tell el-Kheleifeh or on the island of Jezirat Far'on (the only site in the region with evidence of a substantial harbor area); Punon (=Khirbet Feinan), thirty miles south of the Dead Sea; mountains of Abarim, near Mount Nebo, just east of the Dead Sea (see comment on Num 27:12); and Abel-shittim (Shittim, see comment on Num 25:1), which is either Tell el-Hammam on the Wadi Kefrein (runs east-west into the Jordan across from Jericho) or just east of that site at Tell Kefrein.

34:1-29
The Land to Be Assigned

34:1-12. trace the boundaries. The boundaries of the Promised Land are laid out here as a logical sequel to the order to displace the present inhabitants of the area (Num 33:50-56). Although these are not the actual borders of the nation of Israel at any point in its history, they are a close approximation of the territory claimed by Egypt in Canaan during the fifteenth to thirteenth centuries B.C. (see 2 Sam 3:10 for the realized dimensions: "from Dan to Beersheba") and are also approached by the description of the territory controlled by David and Solomon. The boundaries are outlined, using a set of then-known border points (see Josh 15—19 for the tribal divisions). The most obvious limits are those to the east and west—the Jordan River and the Mediterranean Sea respectively. The northern border reaches to the mountains of Lebanon as far as Mount Hor (unknown peak, probably in the Lebanese range) and Lebo (=Lebo Hamath, most likely modern Lebweh on one of the sources of the Orontes). This was the southern border of the land of Hamath and therefore the northern border of Canaan, including the Damascus area and Bashan (roughly equated to the modern Golan Heights). Zedad is likely modern Sedad, about thirty-five miles northeast of Lebweh, while Ziphron and Hazar Enan are commonly identified as the two oases to the southeast of Zedad. Moving south, the territory passes through the Galilee to the Yarmuk valley (the sites mentioned in v. 11 are unknown) where it moves west to the Jordan valley and from there south to Kadesh Barnea (see the comment on Num 13) in the Wilderness of Zin (see comment on Num 20:1) before swinging west to the Mediterranean at El-'Arish. It is common to identify Hazar Addar and Azmon with two of the other springs in the vicinity of Kadesh, namely, 'Ain Qedeis and 'Ain Muweilih. The location of Scorpion Pass (akrabim) is unknown, though it is usually identified with a narrow passage along the Wadi Marra headed northeast toward the south end of the Dead Sea.

35:1-34
Cities of Refuge

35:1-5. Levitical cities. Since their primary responsibility is as sacrificial priests and reli-

gious officials, the Levites are not given a portion of the Promised Land to farm (see Num 18:23-24). However, they do receive forty-eight towns, with their surrounding area as pasturage for their flocks and herds (see Lev 25:32-34 for their property rights in these towns). The precedent of assigning towns to priestly control can be seen in the practice of Egypt's rule in Canaan (and also in Hittite practice), where some cities were set aside as royal estates and placed in the hands of the priesthood, which administered that territory. These Egyptian administrative centers were typically fortified and collected the tribute or tax money from that region. Likewise in Mesopotamian and Syrian practice, designated cities had royal pasturelands connected to them. While a secular administrative role is not evident for the Levitical cities, they may well have been centers for religious instruction and collection of sanctuary revenues. Since pastureland is specified, it may also be that livestock collected for ritual use was provided for in this way.

35:6-34. cities of refuge and the judicial system. Six of the Levitical cities were to serve as places of refuge for persons who had committed an unintentional homicide (see also Deut 4:41-43). This solution, which provides asylum to the accused and prevents the "blood avenger" from killing him, may be an extension or alternative to the use of asylum altars mentioned in Exodus 21:12-14. The priestly community would have been concerned about polluting the altar and the sanctuary when a lawbreaker grasped the horns of the altar. Thus by extending the asylum zone to the entire city of refuge, this *pollution would not happen, and the person accused would also have better accommodations until the trial was completed. Sacred cities or royal cities with privileged status are evidenced throughout the ancient Near East, but the protection they offer is often in terms of freedom from certain government imposed obligations, though one text speaks of a prohibition against shedding the blood of anyone under such protection. The concept of asylum is also found in classical sources and suggests an attempt on the part of the government to tighten control over the judicial system, removing the rights of revenge from families, and insuring due process.

35:9-34. family responsibility for vengeance. While the biblical law clearly indicates the responsibility of the "blood avenger" to avenge the death of a kinsman, this practice of blood feud could be disruptive to the administration of justice, and thus the six cities of refuge were established to provide a "cooling off" phase as well as due process for the accused. Two witnesses were necessary to convict (Num 35:30), and then it became the responsibility of the "blood avenger" to execute the felon (Num 35:19-21; Deut 19:12). No ransom for the convicted murderer was possible (Num 35:31-32). This contrasts with laws formulated elsewhere in the ancient Near East. Both the Hittite laws and the Middle *Assyrian laws provide for the payment of a ransom to buy back the life of the murderer. The Assyrian law reflects a middle ground, giving the deceased's next-of-kin the option of executing the murderer or accepting a ransom.

35:25, 28. death of the high priest. It is not the period of exile within the city of refuge that absolves a person of unintentional homicide (see Josh 20:2-6). The blood of the slain can only be expiated by another death, for bloodguilt accompanies every human slaying. However, since the accused has not been judged a murderer, he must remain in refuge until the death of the high priest. It is thus the high priest's death that eliminates the bloodguilt attached to the homicide. In this way even the death of the high priest continues his *cultic service to the people by removing bloodguilt and disposing of their sins (see Ex 28:36-38; Lev 16:16).

35:33. bloodshed polluting the land. The Promised Land, as a gift of the *covenant, is sacred and can be polluted by bloodshed and idolatry (see Ezek 36:17-18). Since blood is the source of life and a gift of God, the *pollution caused by shedding blood can be wiped away only by the shedding of blood. Thus even the

blood of animals must be poured on the altar as a ransom for the person who slaughtered them (see Lev 17:11). That is why the convicted murderer must be executed and why the death of the high priest wipes away the pollution of the unintentional homicide. Failure to obey this command corrupts the land. If the land and its people become polluted, God can no longer dwell in their midst. And if he abandons the land, it will no longer yield its covenantal bounty (see Gen 4:10-12).

36:1-13
Case of Inheritance Law

36:1-13. tribal retention of land inherited by daughters. In the law established in Numbers 27:1-11, Zelophehad's daughters were given the right to inherit land since there was no male heir (the apocryphal book Tobit [6:13] shows an application of the law). A loophole was inadvertently created here which would have allowed for the transference of property to another tribe through marriage. Thus this codicil was added, restricting women who had inherited land from marrying outside their tribe so that the original tribal allotment would remain intact. Here it becomes clear that the preservation of family property holdings was one of the highest values in Israelite society. That is because the land was the gift of the *covenant, so each family's allotment was its share in the covenant. While land ownership was important in the rest of the ancient Near East, no other country had such strong religious overtones connected to the land.

DEUTERONOMY

1:1-8
Introduction

1:1-2. geography. The Arabah is the area of the Jordan rift, sometimes limited to the section between the Dead Sea and the Gulf of Aqaba. The list of locations looks more like an itinerary than a description of the Israelites' present location (thus the comment concerning the trip along the Mount Seir road). The sites are difficult to identify with any certainty. Mount Seir is another name for Edom, and the Mount Seir road takes one from the Sinai peninsula into Edom. For details on Kadesh Barnea see the comment on Numbers 13:26, and the for

location of Sinai/Horeb see the comment on Exodus 19:1-2. The eleven-day journey (140 miles) mentioned here is consistent with a southern location for Mount Sinai.

1:3. chronology. The eleventh month is Tebet, and it spans our December-January. In Israel it is the middle of the rainy season, but in the southern region where the Israelites still are there is very little rainfall (an average of two inches per year), and though it is winter, the average daytime temperature would still be about sixty-five degrees Fahrenheit. It is difficult to assign a number to this fortieth year since the text has offered us no anchor to absolute chronology. In the ancient world chronology was only noted in relative terms ("the fifth year of king X"), and the biblical text does the same (here, the fortieth year since the exodus). There was no absolute chronology system ("the year 1385"). See "The Date of the Exodus," p. 86.

1:4. history. The account of these battles is found in Numbers 21:21-35. Of the three sites mentioned here, only Heshbon has been excavated, and it has been controversial (see comment on Num 21:25-28). Ashtaroth is identified here as the capital city of Bashan. It is mentioned in Egyptian and *Assyrian texts and the *Amarna letters, and some think it occurs in a text from *Ugarit as a place where the god *El reigns. It is known today as Tell 'Ashtarah and is located on the Yarmuk River about twenty-five miles east of the Sea of Galilee. Neither Sihon nor Og is known from any extrabiblical records.

1:6. Horeb. Horeb is another name for Mount Sinai, most likely located in the southern section of the Sinai peninsula. For more detailed discussion see the comment on Exodus 19:1-2.

1:7. geography. The description in this verse is largely by topographical areas. The hill country of the *Amorites may refer to the entire southern region, in contrast to the land of the Canaanites, which would be the northern region. The Arabah refers to the Jordan rift valley from the Gulf of Aqaba north, while the hill country extends north and south along the west side of the Jordan River, interrupted by the valley of Jezreel. The Shephelah (NIV: "western foothills") descend from the mountains to the coast in the southern section. The Negev is the wilderness in the triangle formed by the Dead Sea, the Mediterranean Sea and the Gulf of Aqaba. The Lebanon is the northern mountain range, and the northwestern spur of the Euphrates marks the northeastern border.

1:9-18
Judiciary System

1:16. judicial structures in the ancient Near East. Egyptian and *Hittite records of this general period likewise evidence a judicial system set up in tiers, and the Hittite *Instructions to Officers and Commanders* even has military leaders in the position of judge, as verse 13 here does. This suggests the close relationship between military activity and the activity of judging that the book of Judges implies. In most other systems difficult cases were referred to the king, whereas here Moses serves as the final adjudicator. Thus in the ancient Near East, leaders, whether tribal, military,

city, provincial or national, had the obligation of judging the cases under their jurisdiction. There was no trial by jury, though at times a group of elders may have been involved in judging a case together. When only one individual judge was involved, the danger of favoring the powerful or the wealthy was very real. In both ancient Near Eastern documents and the Bible impartiality is valued, along with discernment. There were no lawyers, so most people represented themselves in court. Witnesses could be called, and oaths played a very significant role since most of our scientific means of gathering evidence were not available.

1:19-25
The Commission and Report of the Spies

1:19. Amorites. The *Amorites were also known as the Amurru (in *Akkadian) and the Martu (in *Sumerian). The term *Amorites* ("westerners"), like the term *Canaanites*, can be used to describe the general population of the land of Canaan. As an ethnic group, Amorites are known from written sources as early as the middle third millennium B.C. Most scholars think that their homeland was in Syria, from where they came to occupy many areas in the Near East.

1:24. the valley of Eshcol. There are many wadis in this general area, and there is no way of telling which one may be referred to here. Around Hebron today, Ramet el-'Amleh is known for its grape production and is near a wadi.

1:26-46
The Rebellion of the People

1:28. Anakites. The descendants of Anak are specifically mentioned in Numbers 13:22, 28. When names are given, they are *Hurrian (biblical Horites; see comment on Deut 2). The descendants of Anak are generally considered "giants" (Num 13:33; Deut 2:10-11; 2 Sam 21:19-22), though the description "gigantic" may be more appropriate. There is no mention of the Anakites in other sources, but the Egyptian letter on Papyrus Anastasi I (thirteenth century B.C.) describes fierce warriors in Canaan that are seven to nine feet tall. Two female skeletons about seven feet tall from the twelfth century have been found at Tell es-Sa'ideyeh in Transjordan.

1:44. Seir to Hormah. Seir is generally considered the mountainous central region of Edom (with elevations generally over five thousand feet) between Wadi al-Ghuwayr on the north and Ras en-Naqb on the south. Hormah is a site seven and a half miles east of Beersheba, tentatively identified with Tell Masos (Khirbet el-Meshash). Seir to Hormah is about fifty miles along a route to the northwest.

1:46. Kadesh Barnea. Kadesh Barnea is usually identified as 'Ain el-Qudeirat, about fifty miles south of Beersheba, which has the most plentiful water supply in the region. There are no archaeological remains on this site from this period, but the site has long been a stopping place for nomads and Bedouin, and the abundance of "Negev" ware (pottery dated to this period) suggests that was true during the time of the Israelite wanderings as well.

2:1-25
Wandering in the Wilderness

2:1. geography. Traveling the road to the Red Sea took the Israelites south along the Arabah, but probably not as far south as Elath at the tip of the Gulf of Aqaba. Instead it appears they turned north at one of the east-west wadis in the southern region of Seir to arrive at the route north that would take them to the plains of Moab.

2:8. Arabah road. The Arabah road runs north-south from the Gulf of Aqaba to the Dead Sea through the rift valley.

2:8. Elath and Ezion Geber. Elath is near the modern city of Aqaba at the tip of the Gulf of Aqaba. Ezion Geber was a port city located at the head of the Gulf of Aqaba (1 Kings 9:26) and may be either Tell el-Kheleifeh (which some identify as Elath) or on the is-land of Jezirat Far'on (the only site in the region with evidence of a substantial harbor area).

2:9. Ar. "Ar" is sometimes seen as a variant of Aroer. While some consider it a regional name, others have suggested it be identified with Khirbet Balu along one of the tributaries of the Arnon on the King's Highway, the major north-south route running on the east side of the Jordan.

2:10. Emites. These people are also referred to in Genesis 14:6, but nothing else is known of them.

2:10. Anakites. See comment on 1:26-46.

2:11. Rephaites. The Rephaites are mentioned as one of the ethnic groups inhabiting the land of Canaan in Genesis 15:20, but nothing else is known of them either inside or outside the Bible. The *Ugaritic texts speak of the Rephaim, whom some scholars consider to be the shades of dead heroes and kings. There is no cause, however, to think of this biblical group in those terms, though the Rephaim referred to in poetic texts such as Isaiah 14:9 (as well as in Job and Psalms) may be spirits.

2:12. Horites. The Horites are known throughout ancient Near Eastern literature as the *Hurrians. They were an Indo-European ethnic group centered along the Euphrates River in the third and second millennia. They established a political empire known as *Mitanni in the mid-second millennium, but it was breaking up around the time of the events of this book. Many Hurrian groups therefore ended up as displaced people and wandered into Syria and Palestine. The Hurrians were the dominant ethnic group in *Nuzi, and Hurrian

---

THE COVENANT AND ANCIENT NEAR EASTERN TREATIES
Archaeologists have recovered many treaties from the second and first millennia between nations and their vassals. The second millennium treaties are mostly made between the Hittites and others, while the first millennium examples come during the time of Assyrian kings Esarhaddon and Ashurbanipal of the seventh century B.C. The format followed in these treaties shows striking similarity to the format of a number of covenant documents in the Bible, most notably, Deuteronomy. These treaties begin with a preamble that identifies the suzerain who is making the treaty. Besides giving his titles and attributes it emphasizes his greatness and his right to proclaim the treaty. In Deuteronomy this occupies the first five verses of ch. 1. Next the treaties offer a historical prologue in which the relationship between the parties is reviewed. Priority is given to the kindness and power of the suzerain. In Deuteronomy this section comprises 1:6—3:29 (and some would extend it through the end of ch. 11). The core of the treaty is the stipulations section which details the obligations of each party. Deuteronomy accomplishes the same thing by its presentation of the law in chaps. 4-26. The treaties are concluded by three sections of legal material including instructions concerning the document, witnesses to the agreement and blessings and curses that will result from either honoring or violating the treaty. Deuteronomy addresses such issues in chaps. 28 and 31.

As a result of the recognition of this format, it becomes evident that the Lord used a very familiar literary form to communicate his covenant to Israel. Israelites would have realized that the Lord was putting himself in the place of the suzerain and that they should respond as a vassal would. It is a relationship bringing support and protection to the vassal as he is loyal to the suzerain.

groups are known from *Alalakh, *Mari, *Ugarit and the *Amarna texts as well. The Egyptians often referred to Canaan as Khurri land.

2:13. Zered Valley. The Zered Valley is the border between Edom and Moab. It is probably the wadi known today as Wadi al-Hesa, which runs east from the southern tip of the Dead Sea for about thirty miles.

2:19. Ammonites. The Ammonites lived north of the Moabites in the region around the Jabbok River. They are known from *Assyrian records as Bit-Ammon and as the land of Benammanu. They were settling this territory just around the time of the Israelite wanderings.

2:20. Zamzummites. The Zamzummites are known as the Zuzim in Genesis 14:5, but aside from their association with the Rephaites, nothing more is known about them.

2:22. Edomites and Horites. Nothing is known of this historic warfare between Esau's descendants and the *Hurrians. There have so far been no positive archaeological evidences of a Hurrian presence in Edom.

2:23. Avvites and Caphtorites. Caphtor is identified as Crete and is often associated with the homeland of the Philistines (Gen 10:14; Amos 9:7). Gaza was one of the five cities of the Philistines in the coastal plain. The Avvites are unknown outside the few obscure references to them in the Bible.

2:24. Arnon Gorge. The Arnon is today identified as the Wadi al-Mawjib, which flows about thirty miles northwest and west through Transjordan before emptying into the Dead Sea at its midpoint. The Arnon was often the northern border of Moab, though at times the Moabites extended their control north to Heshbon.

2:25. divine terror. The dread of a deity as a divine warrior was often believed to precede a powerful, successful army into battle. Egyptian texts attribute this terror to Amun-Re in the inscriptions of Thutmose III, and *Hittite, *Assyrian and *Babylonian texts all have their divine warriors who strike terror into the hearts of the enemy.

2:26-37

Battle Against Sihon the Amorite

2:26. Sihon the *Amorite. This battle is initially recorded in Numbers 21. Sihon is known only from the biblical records, and archaeology has little information to offer regarding his capital city or his kingdom.

2:26. Heshbon. The modern site of Tell-Heshban is located nearly fifty miles directly east of

Jerusalem. However, archaeologists have not been able to detect any evidence that this site was settled prior to 1200 B.C. Some have suspected that the *Late Bronze city of Heshbon that was Sihon's capital was at a different site, with Tell Jalul named as one possibility. Recent surveys and excavations in this region have turned up more and more Late Bronze pottery, but it remains difficult to assess the nature of the occupation during this period.

2:26. Desert of Kedemoth. This refers to the wilderness region beyond the eastern border of Moab. The city of Kedemoth is identified tentatively as Saliya at the southern corner.

2:32. Jahaz. The site of the battle with the forces of the *Amorite king Sihon is given as Jahaz. Its probable location, based on the church historian Eusebius (fourth century A.D.) and the Mesha inscription (ninth century B.C.), is between the territories of Madaba and Dibon, at Khirbet Medeiniyeh at the eastern edge of Moab by the Wadi al-Themed. The battle is also mentioned in Deuteronomy 2:33 and Judges 11:20.

2:24-30. captured land. The area of central Transjordan, which is here described as the kingdoms of Sihon and Og, stretches from the Arnon River valley in the south to the Jabbok River in the north. It would include Moab but not Ammon. It seems likely that these "kingdoms" were not organized states in this period and that their conquest provided passage for the Israelites without the tribes' actually taking control of and settling this region.

2:34. complete destruction. See comment on the "ban" in 7:2.

2:36-37. geography. Aroer was a border fortress, identified as modern 'Ara'ir just north of the Arnon gorge, where it turns south. *Late Bronze remains have been found at the site. The Israelites are victorious throughout the Transjordan territories from the Arnon (north boundary of Moab) up to the Jabbok (the territory of the Ammonites), about fifty miles north to south and twenty to twenty-five miles east to west.

3:1-11

The Battle Against Og of Bashan

3:1. Bashan. After defeating Sihon, the Israelites traveled northward to Og's kingdom in the area known today as the Golan Heights. It was bordered by Mount Hermon to the north, Jebel Druze (Mount Hauran) to the east, the Sea of Galilee to the west and the Yarmuk region to the south. They defeated King Og at Edrei (modern Der'a, thirty miles east of the Sea of Galilee). Bashan proper, more limited to the region of the (upper?) Yarmuk, is a broad, fertile plateau region noted for its grazing (Ps 22:12; Amos 4:1-3).

3:1. Og. There is no extrabiblical information either from historical sources or from archaeology to shed light on Og.

3:4. Argob. From the description here it is obvious that the region of Argob is heavily populated. It is sometimes equated with Bashan, and one possibility is that it refers to the area just south of the Yarmuk and half encircled by it. The *Assyrian kings of the ninth century also found and conquered many cities in this region in the vicinity of Mount Hauran.

3:5. fortified cities in Transjordan. There has been little excavation in this region, but sites such as Tel Soreg may be characteristic of the unwalled farming communities in the area. Seven cities in the area east of the Sea of Galilee are mentioned in the *Amarna texts of the fourteenth century in an area they identify as Garu (=Geshur?). Archaeological surveys in the Golan Heights have located twenty-seven cities occupied at the end of the *Middle Bronze period and eight in the *Late Bronze.

3:5. gates and bars. Gateways were often multichambered (featuring inner and outer gates) and sometimes included a turn of some sort within the gateway. The *Iron Age outer gate at Tell en-Nasebeh has slots in the stone beside the gate where bars would have been placed. The inhabitants would lock the gates by sliding the bars into sockets in the wall.

3:9. Hermon/Sirion/Senir. Hermon is in the Anti-Lebanon range. Its highest peak, Jabal ash-Shaykh, has an elevation of 9,232 feet and is usually snowcapped. The term *Sirion* is used in Egyptian, *Hittite and *Ugaritic materials. *Assyrian records of the ninth century refer to it as Saniru.

3:10. Salecah and Edrei. Edrei is identified as modern Der'a in Syria, about sixty miles south of Damascus and thirty miles east of the Sea of Galilee near the Yarmuk River. No excavations have been conducted here. The town is also mentioned in ancient texts from Egypt and *Ugarit. Salecah, modern Salhad, is another twenty-five miles east of Edrei.

3:11. Og's iron bed. Though many commentators and even some translations have identified this as a basalt sarcophagus, the language is clear enough and "iron bed" should be retained. Just as many objects described as gold, silver or ivory are not made of those but are decorated, overlaid or gilded with them, so we need not imagine a bed of solid iron. This account is still in the *Bronze Age, when iron was considered precious, so it would not be strange for this to be noted as a remarkable

piece. The bed is about thirteen feet long and six feet wide. This is the same size as Marduk's bed in the temple Esagila in Babylon. Beds were not just for sleeping but were often used for reclining on during feasts and celebrations. Some reliefs picture kings reclining on magnificent couches.

3:11. Rephaim. See comment on 2:11.

3:12-20
The Division of Transjordan

3:12-17. geography. Gilead is the hilly section of Transjordan between the Jabbok on the south almost to the Yarmuk on the north. The southern half of this, as well as the territory taken from Sihon south to the Arnon (northern border of Moab), was given to the tribes of Reuben and Gad. The section of Gilead that extends into the curve of the Yarmuk (the region of Argob?) as well as some territory north of the Yarmuk (all taken from Og) was assigned to Manasseh. Geshur and Maacah are excepted, though apparently part of Og's kingdom. Geshur is a small area just east of the Sea of Galilee. Maacah is just north of Geshur and stretches to Hermon. It is referred to in the Egyptian *Execration Texts.

3:17. Pisgah. Pisgah is the designation of one of the peaks of the Abarim range (Num 27:12) paired with Mount Nebo, which is slightly higher. They are identified as the two peaks of Jebel Shayhan, about five miles northwest of Medeba and about a mile and a half apart. They stand about ten miles from the Jordan River.

3:21-29
Moses Views the Land

3:27. view from Pisgah. Though Pisgah is about four hundred feet lower than Nebo in elevation, it is farther north and west and affords a better view of the Jordan Valley and the land opposite. At this point the Mediterranean is about sixty miles west, but it cannot be seen because the hills on the west side of the Jordan obscure the view. On a clear day one can see Mount Hermon, about a hundred miles to the north, the mountains to the northwest that flank the Jezreel Valley (Tabor and Gilboa), the mountains of the central hill country (Ebal and Gerizim) and to the southwest as far as Engedi.

3:29. valley near Beth Peor. The Wadi Ayun Musa at the foot of Mount Nebo is generally considered to be the Valley of Beth Peor, with the site Khirbet Ayun Musa as probably the town.

4:1-40

Call to Obedience to the Law

4:3. Baal Peor. *Baal Peor is the god who was worshiped at Beth Peor. This refers back to the incident in Numbers 25, when the Israelites were drawn into idolatrous worship by the Moabite women. It was perhaps their first exposure to the *fertility worship of Canaan. Fertility *cults are common in agrarian societies where the populace is dependent on rainfall and the fertility of the soil for survival. These cults often featured a "dying and rising" god in the pattern of the change of the seasons. The association of human fertility with the earth's fertility led to the development of sexual elements in the religious *rituals.

4:6-8. result of the laws. The laws are presented here as an evidence of wisdom and righteousness that will distinguish Israel from the other nations. In a number of the collections of laws known from the ancient Near East there is a prologue and epilogue explaining that the collection of laws will demonstrate how wise and just the king is. Likewise Solomon's wisdom was evidenced by how he was able to make just decrees and rulings. The kings of the ancient Near East usually counted on their collections of laws to convince the gods that they were wise and just rulers. Here the Lord is revealing his own wisdom and justice to his people and the world.

4:7. nearness of god. In Mesopotamia the laws were presented to the god of justice (Shamash) by the king as evidence that he was a just king. The king had been given the authority to make laws by the gods, the guardians of cosmic law. Law was seen as something inherent in the universe, and laws were supposed to somehow reflect that impersonal cosmic law. In Israelite thinking, however, law emanated from the character of God and he was seen as the source of the laws. Moses was not the lawmaker, *Yahweh was. By proclaiming laws, the Lord is therefore revealing himself in an act that distinguished him from the other gods of the ancient world. This is the "nearness" that the text remarks on.

4:10. Horeb. Horeb is another name for Mount Sinai, most likely located in the southern section of the Sinai peninsula. See the comment on Exodus 19:1-2.

4:13. two stone tablets. See the comments on Exodus 24:12; 32:15-16.

4:15-18. prohibition of images. The second commandment concerns how *Yahweh is to be worshiped, for the idols that it prohibits are idols of him (the previous commandment already dismissed the thought of other gods). The commandment has nothing to do with art, though the graven images of the ancient world were indeed works of art. They were typically carved of wood and overlaid with hammered sheets of silver or gold, then clothed in the finest attire. But the prohibition is more concerned with how they are employed, and here the issue is power. Images of deity in the ancient Near East were where the deity became present in a special way, to the extent that the *cult statue became the god (when the god so favored his worshipers), even though it was not the only manifestation of the god. As a result of this linkage, spells, incantations and other magical acts could be performed on the image in order to threaten, bind or compel the deity. In contrast, other rites related to the image were intended to aid the deity or care for the deity. The images then represent a worldview, a concept of deity that was not consistent with how Yahweh had revealed himself.

4:19. astral worship in the ancient Near East. The celestial gods (sun god, moon god and Venus particularly; in *Babylonia, Shamash, Sin and *Ishtar respectively) were primary in most ancient religions. Controlling calendar and time, seasons and weather, they were viewed as the most powerful of the gods. They provided signs by which omens were read, and they looked down on all. *Yahweh has now warned the Israelites against *fertility worship (v. 3), magic and manipulation (idolatry, vv. 16-18), and omens and linking deities to cosmic phenomena (v. 19), all the major characteristics of the pagan polytheism of the ancient world.

4:20. iron-smelting furnace. The ancient world did not have the blast furnace, which is used today to produce cast iron. Iron has a melting point of 1,537 degrees C., a temperature that could not be consistently achieved with ancient technology. But once the iron is heated beyond 1,100 degrees C., it takes a spongy, semisolid form that can be forged. The furnace was usually fueled by charcoal to provide the carbon necessary for the chemical process. The strength of the steel is dependent on the amount of carbon it is able to absorb. The lower the temperature, the more often the process has to be repeated in order to get rid of enough slag to achieve a usable product. While a furnace can certainly be a metaphor of oppression, the fire of the smelting furnace is not destructive but constructive. It is the furnace that transforms the malleable ore to the durable iron product. The exodus experience transformed Israel into the *covenant people of God.

4:26. heaven and earth as witnesses. In ancient Near Eastern treaties the gods are typically called to witness as ones who would be able to adjudicate any failures to adhere to the terms. Here heaven and earth are not understood as deified, but, representing the entire created universe, they signify that the agreement is intended to endure long beyond human life spans. A clearer indication of the implications can be seen in the fuller wording of Psalm 89:28-29, 34-37 (see also Jer 33:20-21).

4:28. view of idols. Other passages that articulate this view are Isaiah 44; Jeremiah 10; and Psalm 115:4-8. On the beliefs about idols in ancient Near Eastern religious practice, see the comment on 4:15-18. It has long been of interest to scholars that the text does not refute mythology or the existence of the pagan gods but attacks their understanding of idols. In the end, however, it is very difficult to prove to someone that his gods do not exist. But it can be shown that the gods do not operate in the way they are believed to. To the biblical authors the "idol as fetish" aspect of pagan belief was the most vulnerable and the most ridiculous. If the gods were not manifest in their images, then many of the other aspects of the common worldview were also in jeopardy.

4:32-34. Israel's unique experience with deity. The two aspects the text highlights as unique are the two major features of the *covenant: election (vv. 34, 37) and revelation (vv. 33, 35). *Yahweh distinguished himself from the gods of the ancient Near East by these actions. The gods of the ancient Near East were sometimes believed to have chosen an individual or a family to favor with their blessing. Usually this would be a king who claimed a particular deity as his sponsor. But without revelation, such "election" is only inference or propaganda. The gods of the ancient Near East did not reveal their long-term plans and were not necessarily considered to have any. They did not reveal what they were like or what pleased or displeased them. All of this had to be inferred or deduced by those who worshiped them. But *Yahweh has chosen to reveal himself both through the law ("I am holy, so you are to be holy") and through his actions (covenant with forefathers, plagues, exodus, bringing them to the land, etc.).

4:41-43
Cities of Refuge
4:42. cities of refuge. For more information on the cities of refuge, see the comments on Numbers 35. Bezer is in the region around Medeba. It is known from the Mesha inscrip-

tion (ninth century B.C.), but its archaeological identification is uncertain. The principal candidates are Umm al-Amad (about seven miles northeast of Medeba) and Tell Jalul (three or four miles directly east of Medeba). Ramoth Gilead is generally identified as Tell er-Rumeith near modern Ramtha south of Edrei along the King's Highway. Excavations at the site, however, have turned up nothing earlier than Solomon. Golan, the modern Sahm al-Joulan, is at the eastern boundary of the Golan Heights on the east side of the river el-Allan.

4:44-49
Territorial Description
4:48. borders. Finally the whole Transjordan territory is circumscribed, from the Arnon River in the south (the north border of Moab proper) to Mount Hermon in the north. The Jordan rift valley is included and the Dead Sea (Sea of Arabah).

5:1-33
The Ten Commandments
5:2. Horeb. Horeb is another name for Mount Sinai, most likely located in the southern section of the Sinai peninsula. For more detailed discussion see the comment on Exodus 19:1-2.

5:6-21. the Ten Commandments. See the comments on Exodus 20.

5:22. two stone tablets. The use of two tablets probably indicates that Moses was given two copies, not that some of the commandments were on one tablet and some on the other. The fact that they were stone suggests a larger size than clay tablets would have been, though inscribed stone tablets such as the Gezer calendar were small enough to fit in the palm of the hand. The Egyptian practice of this period was to use flakes of stone chipped from rocks. Inscription on front and back was not unusual. When the writing reached the bottom of one side, the scribe would often continue around the bottom edge and move onto the second side. Even flakes that fit in the palm of the hand could contain fifteen to twenty lines.

6:1-25
The Importance of the Law
6:3. milk and honey. The land of Canaan is described as a land "flowing with milk and honey." This refers to the bounty of the land for a pastoral lifestyle, but not necessarily in terms of agriculture. Milk is the product of herds, while honey represents a natural resource, probably the syrup of the date rather

than bees' honey. A similar expression to this is found in the *Ugaritic epic of *Baal and Mot that describes the return of fertility to the land in terms of the wadis flowing with honey. Egyptian texts as early as the *Story of *Sinuhe* describe the land of Canaan as rich in natural resources as well as in cultivated produce.

6:4. categories of monotheism. There are several levels of monotheism that can be identified and that may have characterized the beliefs of various Israelites in various periods. The ultimate monotheism could be called *philosophical monotheism:* there has only ever been one God in existence. *Henotheism* acknowledges the existence of other gods but often insists on the supremacy of one's own god. Similarly, *monolatry* describes a situation where a person or group has determined to worship only one God, regardless of whether other gods, exist or not. Finally, a *practical monotheist* may acknowledge a number of gods, but most of his religious and worship activity is focused on one particular deity. The material in Deuteronomy does not allow for practical monotheism but does allow for henotheism and monolatry at the very least.

6:4. Yahweh is one. The claim that a deity is one, or alone, in other ancient Near Eastern texts (made, for instance, by *Enlil [Sumerian] and *Baal [Canaanite]) generally relates to the supremacy of their rule. Another possibility is that the statement insists on a unified view of *Yahweh. Since a major god in the ancient Near East may have a number of different shrines, each shrine would come to emphasize a different perspective on the god. In Mesopotamia they may consider *Ishtar of Arbela quite differently from Ishtar of *Uruk. Inscriptions in Palestine do in fact indicate that this was true in Israel as well, as reference is made to Yahweh of Samaria and Yahweh of Teman.

6:4. monotheism in the ancient Near East. There were two movements interpreted as monotheistic in the ancient Near East of the Old Testament period. The first was by the Egyptian pharaoh Akhenaten in the general time period of the Pentateuch; the second by the *Babylonian king Nabonidus in the years just before the fall of Babylon to the Persian king Cyrus. Neither movement lasted more than twenty years. Akhenaten attempted to establish the sole worship of the sun disk, Aten, a god with no mythology, portrayed with no human form. It was a worship without image and had little use for temple or *ritual. Every attempt was made to eradicate the worship of Amun-Re, previously the major deity of the land, and the sun disk was proclaimed the sole god (though there was no apparent

attempt to eradicate many other gods). Though Akhenaten may have intended this to be philosophical monotheism (some have even tried to identify it as trinitarian), it does not appear that many of his subjects adopted his beliefs. Nabonidus embarked on an official sponsorship of the moon god Sin by restoring his temple in Harran. For ten years he then stayed in Teima in northwest Arabia, apparently (according to some interpretations) devoted to establishing the *cult of Sin. There is little evidence, however, that this was done to the exclusion of other deities. Though he favored Sin, he continued to make requisite appearances at and donations to other temples. His time in Teima may have been the result of a falling out with the priestly powers in Babylon, or may have had trade policies or other political ends motivating it, but there is no reason to attribute monotheistic reform to it. Whether Israelite belief at this stage is labeled monotheism or henotheism, there is thus little to compare it with in the rest of the ancient world.

6:6. anatomical metaphors. Like English, Hebrew used parts of the body metaphorically to refer to different aspects of the person. "Hand" can refer to power or authority; "arm" to strength; "head" to leadership, and so on. Many of these metaphors have carried into English either because of their inherent logic or because of the role of the Bible in the English-speaking world. Not all anatomical metaphors, however, carry the same significance in the two languages. For instance, the kidneys were considered the seat of the conscience in Hebrew, and the throat was connected with life and essence of personhood. In English, "heart" is used metaphorically for the seat of emotions, in contrast to logic and reason. Hebrew uses it as the center of both emotions and reason/intellect. This usage is also true of the related Semitic languages, such as *Ugaritic, *Aramaic and *Akkadian.

6:8. symbols on hands and forehead. Headbands and armbands were common accessories in Syro-Palestine, though there is no graphic evidence proving Israelites wore them. *Amulets were often worn in the ancient Near East as protection from evil spirits. Precious metals and gems were considered particularly effective. At times amulets would include magical words or spells. Israelite practice disapproved of amulets, but if used here they are converted to reminders of the law or, in other places, may contain prayers or blessings, such as the small silver scrolls that were found in a preexilic tomb just outside Jerusalem in 1979. These miniature scrolls contain the blessing of Numbers 6:24-26 and represent the oldest extant copy of any biblical text. There is also evidence that symbols worn on the forehead or arm were used as indicators of loyalty to a particular deity.

6:9. inscription on door frames and gates. Aside from doorways as entrances representing the house itself and needing special protection, there is evidence from Egypt of sacred inscriptions on doorposts. Requirements of this sort could function either to *preserve* the continuity of life in positive ways and a mutually beneficial relationship with deity; or to *prevent* negative consequences of dangerous situations. While Passover blood on the doorposts functioned in the latter way, the law on the doorposts is an example of the former. The idea that written texts provided protection is found in the Mesopotamian *Erra Epic,* where the invasion by the god of plague can be prevented as long as a copy of the text of this work is kept in the house.

6:10-11. cities of Canaan in the Late Bronze Age. *Late Bronze Age Canaan (1550-1200 B.C.) was characterized by declining population and fewer fortified cities than the *Middle Bronze period. Even the villages and rural settlements show significant decline. In the *Amarna letters (fourteenth-century correspondence between Canaan and Egypt), Hazor and Megiddo were two of the most important and powerful city states in the north, Shechem in the central region, and Jerusalem and Gezer in the south. Archaeology has found that the cities' wealthier inhabitants had comfortable houses, usually with center courtyards. Most cities were surrounded by arable land farmed by the majority of the population. The work of digging wells and hewing out stone cisterns, preparing the soil and setting up irrigation had all been part of the agricultural lifestyle in Canaan. Groves and vineyards usually took many years to develop and be productive, but all of this groundwork was already done.

6:13. oaths in Yahweh's name. Since oaths were considered powerful and effective, the utterance of oaths would demonstrate which deity was truly considered powerful. Though inheriting the cities, homes and farms of the Canaanites, the Israelites are not to inherit the gods that had been associated with protecting these cities and providing fertility to this land. One of the ways to demonstrate their rejection of those gods is to refuse to attribute power to them through oaths.

6:16. Massah. Massah is the name given to the place at Rephidim near Sinai where water came out of the rock (see Ex 17:7).

7:1-26
Promises and Policies Concerning the Nations

7:1. peoples of Canaan. The *Hittites were from Anatolia, modern Turkey, but groups occupying sections of Syria and Canaan were also called Hittites and may or may not have been related. The Hittites in Canaan have Semitic names, while the Hittites of Anatolia were Indo-European. Girgashites are little known, though they are attested in the *Ugaritic texts. *Amorites (known in Mesopotamia as Amurru or Martu) are known from written documents as early as the middle third millennium B.C.. Most scholars think that they came to occupy many areas in the Near East from their roots in Syria. The term can be used to refer to a geographical area ("westerners") or to an ethnic group. Some Amorites were nomadic, but there were Amorite city-states in Syria as early as the end of the third millennium. Canaan is mentioned as early as the Ebla tablets (twenty-fourth century B.C.), and the Canaanite people were the principal inhabitants of the fortified cities of the land, though they do not seem to have been native to the land. The kings of this area refer to themselves in the *Amarna letters (mid-second millennium) as *Kinanu,* a term also used in Egyptian inscriptions of this period. There is still debate as to whether the term *Perizzites* is ethnic or sociological (those living in unwalled settlements). The Hivites are sometimes connected to the Horites, in which case they may be *Hurrians. The Jebusites occupied the region later associated with the tribe of Benjamin, notably the city of Jerusalem, and are often related to the Perizzites who were located in the same region. There is no mention of the Perizzites, Hivites or Jebusites outside the Bible.

7:2. the ban *(herem). *Ban* is sometimes chosen as the English word to represent the concept of total destruction that is commanded here in verse 2 and elaborated in verses 5-6. Just as there were some types of sacrifices that belonged entirely to the Lord, while others were shared by priest and offerer, so some plunder was set aside as belonging solely to the Lord. Just as the whole burnt offering was entirely consumed on the altar, so the ban mandated total destruction. Since the warfare was commanded by Yahweh and represented his judgment on the Canaanites, the Israelites were on a divine mission with Yahweh as their commander. Since it was his war, not theirs, and he was the victor, the spoil belonged to him. Although the divine warrior motif occurs throughout the ancient Near East, the *herem* concept is more limited—the only other occurrence of the term is in the Moabite Mesha inscription, but the idea of total destruction is also in the *Hittite material. Some sites, such as Gezer, feature a distinct burn layer in association with the *Late Bronze period. Under siege conditions sanitation is at its worst and disease is often rampant. The practice of burning everything after the defeat of a city thus had an element of health connected to it.

7:3. command not to intermarry. In *Hittite documents of this period certain cities are designated temple cities and accorded special privileges. In order to protect those privileges, the inhabitants are prohibited from marrying outside the community. In a similar way the entire land of Israel has been designated "God's land," and the Israelites are a kingdom of priests. The prohibition against intermarriage therefore protects the privileges of the *covenant as well as the "purity of their religious ideals.

7:5. sacred stones. Standing stones or *masseboth* were apparently a common feature of Canaanite religion and also appear as memorials in a number of Israelite *covenantal contexts (see Ex 24:3-8; Josh 24:25-27). Their association with *Asherah, *Baal and other Canaanite deities is the basis for their being condemned as rivals and a threat to *Yahweh worship. Archaeologists have discovered sacred stones at Gezer, Shechem, Hazor and Arad. In the latter three cases, they are clearly within a sacred precinct and part of the *cultic practices at these sites. The Hazor stones include incised representations of upraised arms and a sun disk.

7:5. Asherah poles. *Asherah can be either the name of a *fertility goddess or the name of a *cult object (as here). The goddess was popular in the pagan deviations in Israel and was sometimes considered to be a mediator of *Yahweh's blessings. An indication of this belief is found in the inscriptions from Kuntillet Ajrud and Khirbet el-Qom. In Canaanite mythology she was the consort of the chief god, *El. She appears in Mesopotamian literature as early as the eighteenth century, where she is the consort of the *Amorite god Amurru. The *cult symbol may or may not have borne a representation of the deity on it. The pole may represent an artificial tree, since Asherah is often associated with sacred groves. Sometimes the cult object can be made or built, while on other occasions it is planted. We have little information on the function of these poles in *ritual practice.

7:6-11. the *covenant relationship. The terminology used here of love, loyalty and obedience are common to the international treaties of this time. *Hittite, *Akkadian, *Ugaritic and *Aramaic examples all show that the positive action of the suzerain toward the vassal is expressed as love, kindness and graciousness, and in return the vassal is expected to respond with obedience and loyalty.

7:15. diseases of Egypt. Some consider this to be a reference to the plagues, while others associate it with diseases indigenous to Egypt. If the latter is intended, it is difficult to be more specific, though examination of mummies has suggested the prevalence of smallpox, malaria and polio. Emphysema and tuberculosis are also evidenced. Egyptian medicine was well known for its treatment of eye diseases and diseases of the digestive and excretory/urinary systems. This might suggest that that was where persistent disease was encountered. All of these were worsened by the very primitive sanitation conditions archaeologists have identified even around the estates of the wealthy. The dry season in Egypt is known for its proliferation of diseases, usually brought to an end by the annual flooding of the Nile.

7:20. the hornet. Insects are often used as metaphors for armies, for instance, bees and flies (Is 7:18-19) and locusts (Joel 1—2). However, some interpreters see this as a wordplay on *Egypt* (see comment on Ex 23:28) or a reference to Egypt by means of an insect that was used to symbolize Lower Egypt. Other interpreters have translated the word as "plague" or "terror."

8:1-19

Remembering What God Had Done

8:3. manna. The food that nourished the Israelites in the wilderness is not easily identified. For possibilities see the comment on Exodus 16:4-9.

8:4. clothes not wearing out. In the Gilgamesh Epic, *Utnapishtim instructs that *Gilgamesh be clothed with garments that do not wear out for his return journey. Job 13:28 describes the "wearing out" of clothes as being "moth-eaten" or perhaps moldy. This verse suggests a supernatural protection from decay.

8:7. water sources. The text mentions streams, pools and springs. The first is the result of runoff from precipitation at high elevations, and the other two represent subterranean water sources. In a land where rainfall is seasonal and, in some areas, limited, irrigation is necessary to sustain agriculture, and water sources are important both for animal herds and for human settlements. While there are few streams west of the Jordan, there are many springs that were used to sustain cities and villages.

8:8. staples of agriculture. Seven agricultural products are mentioned here that are the staple products of the region. The Egyptian *Story of *Sinuhe* describes the land of Canaan and lists six of the seven named here (pomegranates are omitted). Wine and olive oil were two of the principal exports of the region, while the other products provided a significant portion of their diet. The honey referred to here is the product of the date palm, not bees' honey.

8:9. iron and copper. The text also identifies the natural resources of the land from the mining perspective. There are numerous deposits of poor-quality iron ore in Palestine, but few of high quality. The only major deposits of iron ore known in Palestine today are at Mughar-at el-Wardeh in the Ajlun hills by the Jabbok River. Copper mining sites are mostly in Transjordan. While iron can be mined on the surface, copper mining requires shafts.

9:1-6
Conquest as Punishment

9:1. walled cities. City defenses were of most concern in troubled, insecure times. The latter part of the *Middle Bronze Age in Canaan (eighteenth-sixteenth centuries) was one such time, and many fortified cities were built. The end of that period brought the destruction of many of these cities, and many were not rebuilt during the *Late Bronze Age (1550-1200). It is generally assumed that this was because Egypt controlled the region and offered security to it. There were, however, still a number of fortified cities that served as administrative centers for Egyptian control. The fortification techniques developed in the Middle Bronze period included steep earthen slopes (some reaching fifty feet) at the foundation of the walls and a ditch around the outside dug to bedrock. These features would both hamper the approach of siege machines and prevent tunneling. The stone walls were twenty-five to thirty feet wide and perhaps thirty feet high.

9:2. Anakites. See comment on 1:28.

9:7—10:11
Remembering the Events at Sinai

9:8. Horeb. Horeb is another name for Mount Sinai, most likely located in the southern section of the Sinai peninsula. See comment on Exodus 19:1-2.

9:9. stone tablets. See comment on 5:22.

9:16. golden calf. Bull or calf figurines, made either of bronze or a combination of metals, have been found in several archaeological excavations (Mount Gilboa, Hazor and Ashkelon), but they are only three to seven inches long. The calf symbol was well known in the Canaanite context of the second millennium and represented fertility and strength. The gods were typically not depicted in the form of bulls or calves, but portrayed standing on the back of the animal. Nevertheless worship of the animal image was not unknown, and there is little in the biblical text to suggest the Israelites understood the figure merely as a pedestal (not unlike the ark). The fact that the calf is worshiped in the context of a feast to Yahweh suggests that this may be a violation of the second commandment rather than the first.

9:22. Taberah, Massah, Kibroth Hattaavah. These are all places where the Israelites experienced God's judgment. Taberah and Kibroth Hattaavah are in Numbers 11 in connection with the plague from eating quail, and Massah is associated with the incident in Exodus 16 where the people challenged the Lord to provide water.

9:23. Kadesh Barnea. Kadesh Barnea was the main camping place during the wilderness wandering. See comment on 1:46.

9:28. belligerent deities. Though the claim made in verse 28 might seem a preposterous way to think, it would not have been an unusual view in the religious world of the ancient Near East. In a polytheistic system gods could not be omnipotent, so they might fail to accomplish something they set out to do. Additionally they were not considered to be friendly, forthright or predictable. Examples would include the Mesopotamian god *Ea telling his "favorite" *Adapa that the food he would be offered was "bread of death" when in reality it would have procured eternal life for him. In the *Gilgamesh Epic, Ea advises deceiving the people into thinking that blessings cannot rain down on them unless *Utnapishtim leaves in his boat. After they send him off, they are rained on in a totally unexpected way when the flood comes and destroys them. Around 1200 B.C. the Libyans complain that the gods gave them initial success against Egypt with the intent to eventually destroy them. In Egypt the mortuary texts (Pyramid Texts and Coffin Texts) are targeted against hostile deities.

10:6. wells of the Jaakanites, Moserah, Gudgodah, Jotbathah. These sites are also in the itinerary of Numbers 33:30-34. Most of them are unidentified, but Jotbathah has been associated with Tabeh, an oasis along the western shore of the Gulf of Aqaba.

10:12—11:32

Covenant Response to Yahweh

10:17. divine titles. The enumeration of divine names and attributes is a common form of praise in the ancient Near East. Perhaps most notable is the *Babylonian creation epic, *Enuma Elish*, that proclaims the fifty names of *Marduk, chief god of Babylon.

10:17. gods accepting bribes. In the religious beliefs of the ancient Near East the gods could be manipulated because they were believed to have needs. Sacrifice and temple upkeep were part of a program of taking care of them and feeding them. By providing the food, clothing and shelter that the gods needed, an individual could win the favor of the deity. This text makes it clear that *Yahweh is not to be thought of in the same way as the gods of Israel's neighbors. This also reflects the picture of Yahweh as a just judge who refuses to distort justice for personal gain.

11:1. loving deity in ancient Near East. In the *Amarna letters (from vassal kings of Canaan to their Egyptian overlord) "love" is used as a characterization of friendly and loyal international relationships. It expresses the vassal's intentions to be loyal and to honor the terms of the treaty agreement between the parties. The biblical text shows a clear example of this usage in 1 Kings 5:15. There are rare instances in Mesopotamian literature where an individual is admonished to love a deity, but in general the gods of the ancient Near East neither sought love from their worshipers nor entered into *covenant relationships with them.

11:2. outstretched arm. The "outstretched arm" is a metaphor that was used by the Egyptian Pharaohs for the extension of their power and authority. It was *Yahweh's outstretched arm that extended his power over Egypt to bring deliverance to his people. See comment on Deuteronomy 26:8.

11:4. Red Sea/Reed Sea. There have been many different suggestions concerning the identification of this body of water. Lake Balah or Lake Timsah are the most common. See comment on Exodus 13:18.

11:9. land of milk and honey. See comment on 6:3.

11:10. irrigation methods in Egypt. The contrast here does not favor rainfall over irrigation, for everyone recognized the value and success of irrigation methods and technology. Furthermore, it is not suggested that the often-sparse rainfall of Palestine is superior to the regular abundant annual flooding of the Nile. There is no known irrigation method

that would be identified as "watering by foot," but that phrase is used as a euphemism for urinating in the reading preserved in some manuscripts of 2 Kings 18:27. If that is the meaning here, the contrast would have to do not with technologies of irrigation or abundance of water supply but with the purity of the water used to grow food.

11:11-15. seasons in Israel. Israel has a rainy season (winter months) and a dry season (summer months). The rainy season begins with the autumn rains ("early rains," October-November) and ends with the spring rains ("latter rains," early April). These are important for what they contribute to the overall moisture levels in the earth and for softening the ground for plowing. Grain is harvested in the spring (barley in May, wheat in June), and the summer months (July and August) are for threshing and winnowing. Grapes are harvested in the fall, while the olive harvest stretches into the winter.

11:18. symbols on hands, foreheads and doorframes. See comment on 6:8-9.

11:24. Lebanon to the Euphrates. For the general boundaries of the land, see the comment on 1:7.

11:29. Gerizim and Ebal. Gerizim and Ebal are the mountains that flank the town of Shechem in the central hill country, Gerizim (elevation 2,849 feet) to the south, Ebal (elevation 3,077 feet) to the north. This site was chosen for the ceremony because it was believed to represent the center of the land (Judg 9:37) and because from here a large portion of the land could be seen. The valley that runs between the two mountains, Wadi Nablus, was one of the only passageways through the region. The valley at its southeastern end is quite narrow (the lower flanks of the hills are separated by little over a quarter of a mile) and would easily accommodate the antiphonal ceremony anticipated here.

11:29. blessings and curses. The international treaties of this time featured blessings and curses on the parties responsible for keeping the terms of the *covenant. The blessings and curses typically were seen as to be carried out by the deities in whose name the agreement had been made. The blessing formulas are rarer and the curse formulas grow longer between the second and first millennia.

11:30. Gilgal. This is not the same Gilgal that the Israelites use as a base in the book of Joshua but is farther north in the vicinity of Shechem. One possibility is the site of El-Unuk, about four miles east of Shechem along the Wadi Far'ah.

12:1-32

Central Place of Worship

12:2-3. outdoor shrines. Apparently the use of outdoor shrines was common among the Canaanites. These local *cult sites were considered abhorrent to the writer because they promoted a "popular" brand of religion that contained elements of Canaanite worship that deviated from the established *Yahweh-only doctrine. Thus local altars, sacred poles dedicated to *Asherah, sacred groves and any place associated with a Canaanite god (*Baal, *El, etc.) and the worship of God outside of Jerusalem, "the place the Lord your God will choose" (Deut 12:5), were forbidden. There is a difference between these outdoor *cultic places and the "high place" *(bamah)* often mentioned as a religious center in the local towns and cities (1 Kings 11:7; Jer 7:31; Ezek 16:16; 2 Chron 21:11; Mesha's inscription). The "high place" was apparently an indoor facility, built to house sacred furniture, an altar and precincts large enough to accommodate a priesthood. A clear differentiation is drawn between these two types of religious sites in 2 Kings 17:9-11.

12:3. sacred stones. See comment on 7:5.

12:3. Asherah poles. One common feature of Canaanite worship and of *syncretized Israelite worship on "high places" and in city shrines is the erection of *Asherah poles (Judg 3:7; 1 Kings 14:15; 15:13; 2 Kings 13:6). There is some uncertainty about whether these were simply wooden poles erected to symbolize trees, perhaps containing a carved image of the *fertility goddess, or part of a sacred grove. The reference in 2 Kings 17:10, which refers to Asherah poles beside "every spreading tree," seems to indicate that these were poles erected for *cultic purposes rather than planted trees. As the consort of *El, Asherah was clearly a popular goddess (see 2 Kings 18:19), and her worship is mentioned in *Ugaritic texts (1600-1200 B.C.). Her prominent appearance in the biblical narrative indicates that her *cult was a major rival to *Yahweh worship (see the prohibition in Ex 34:13; Deut 16:21). This explains the number of examples in which Asherah poles are erected and venerated, the strong condemnations of this practice and the depictions of these poles being cut down and burned (Judg 6:25-30; 2 Kings 23:4-7). For more information see the comment on Deuteronomy 7:5.

12:4, 30-31. their way of worshiping. The prohibited aspects of Canaanite religion would have included the use of idols to manipulate the deity, *fertility practices (perhaps including *ritual sex with temple prostitutes, but see comment on 23:17-18), child sacrifice, *divination and appeasement rituals.

12:3-5. wipe out their names, the Lord establishing his name. The potency and power associated with names and name giving are clearly demonstrated in the biblical narrative (see Gen 17:5; 41:45; Ex 3:13-15; Deut 5:11). One sign of this is found in the practice of erasing the names of discredited officials and even pharaohs from their monuments in ancient Egypt. Names were also used in *execration formulas throughout the Near East to curse enemies and to call down divinely inspired disaster (Num 22:6; Jer 19:3-15). *Execration texts are known in Egypt throughout the second millennium and consist of names of rulers or cities written on objects that were then smashed. When the Israelites are called on to wipe out the names of the Canaanites and their gods, the command is to wipe them from the pages of history. Utter destruction, in a world tied to the service of named persons and gods, could only come if all memory of these names was obliterated. Once that was done, only one name would remain, and there would be no reason or desire to worship another (see Is 42:8).

12:5-7. sacrifices in the presence of deity. Throughout the ancient Near East it was a common understanding that deities had their own realms of influence and thus were tied to particular sites (e.g., *Marduk of *Babylon or Baalzebub of Ekron). It was expected that devotees of these gods would come to the principal shrines, where they could offer sacrifices, take vows, formalize contracts or treaties, or provide legal testimony within the sacred precinct of the god (as in the Code of *Hammurabi and the *Middle Assyrian laws). By doing this, the supplicant could draw on the god as a witness and thus add force to the act being performed. It also provided validity to the shrine, marking it as the place where God's presence was made manifest.

12:11. vows. See comment on Leviticus 27:2-13.

12:16. pouring out blood before eating meat. Sacred literature from *Ugarit and Mesopotamia identified blood as the life force of any animal. In Israelite tradition, blood as the life force belonged to the life-giver, the Creator God *Yahweh. Therefore, the Israelites were prohibited from consuming meat which still contained blood. This sacred fluid had to be drained from the meat and "poured on the ground like water" so that it returned to the earth. In sacrificial contexts, the blood was to be poured on the altar (see Lev 17:11-12).

12:20. eating meat. The promise that the Israelites would be able to eat their fill of meat is tied to the *covenantal promise of land and fertility. This society, however, was generally never so rich in animals that they could be slaughtered indiscriminately. Animal sacrifice was therefore both a sacred and a solemn occasion. The meat of the sacrifice might be the only meat eaten for weeks at a time.

13:1-18
Those Who Encourage the Worship of Other Gods

13:1-18. sources of rebellion. In this passage prophets, close relatives and a localized subversive population are viewed as potential breeding grounds for rebellion. In Assyrian king Esarhaddon's instructions to his vassals, he requires that they report any improper or negative statements that may be made by enemy or ally, by relatives, prophets, ecstatics or dream interpreters.

13:1-3. prophet urging worship of other gods. In its effort to delineate a *Yahweh-only religion, Deuteronomy had to discredit and disavow the teachings and pronouncements of all other gods and their prophets. Prophets, diviners and priests for these other gods were present among the Canaanites and other neighboring groups (mentioned in *Mari texts, the account of Balaam in Numbers 22—24 and the Deir 'Alla inscriptions). However, what seems most heinous here are Israelites who speak in the name of other gods. This type of internal proselytizing was particularly frightening since it had a stronger degree of credibility and could therefore be most effective (see Num 25:5-11). Should the words or the predictions of prophets come true (a sign of their validity as prophets, Deut 18:22), the Israelites were to be alert to whether they attributed the signs to Yahweh. If not, it was a test of their faithfulness, and they must reject the prophet and condemn him to death as a corrupting influence.

13:1-5. foretelling by dreams in ancient Near East. Dreams were one of the standard means for receiving messages from a god in the ancient Near East (see Jacob in Gen 28:12; Joseph in Gen 37:5-11; Nebuchadnezzar in Dan 2, 4). They appear in *Old Babylonian omen texts, along with reports of the examination of sheep livers, anomalies in the weather and birth of animals, and other presumed signs of divine will. Among the most famous is the dream of Gudea of *Lagash (c. 2150 B.C.), who was commanded in a dream to build a temple by a figure reminiscent of the apocalyptic figures in Daniel's dreams and Ezekiel's call narrative (Dan 7; Ezek 1:25-28). The royal correspondence from *Mari (c. 1750 B.C.) contains around twenty prophetic utterances involving dreams, always from nonprofessional personnel. These portents were taken quite seriously and studied. The professional priesthood in both Mesopotamia and Egypt included instruction in the interpretation of dreams and other omens (see the appearance of wise men, mediums and astrologers in Gen 41:8 and Dan 2:4-11).

13:10. stoning as capital punishment. Aside from the ready availability of stones in Israel, stoning was chosen as a form of execution because it was communal. No one person was responsible for the death of the condemned criminal, but in the case of public offenses (apostasy, blasphemy, sorcery, stealing from the *herem) every citizen was required to take a hand in purging the community of evil (see Deut 17:5; Lev 20:27; 24:14; Josh 7:25). Familial offenses such as adultery and recurrent disobedience also were punishable by stoning, and again the entire community was involved (Deut 21:21; 22:21). Stoning is not mentioned as a form of capital punishment outside the Bible. Ancient Near Eastern law codes list only drowning, burning, impalement and beheading, and in each case it is an official body, not the community at large, that is charged with carrying out the punishment.

13:16. plunder as burnt offering. There are two types of plunder reckoned as belonging solely to God: that taken in a *herem (holy war, Josh 6:18-19) and that gathered from a village condemned for its apostasy. To keep any of these objects corrupts the one who takes them and brings down God's wrath on the people (Josh 7).

13:16. ruin. The Hebrew word that the NIV translates as "ruin" is *tel*, and it has come into English as *"tell," referring to a mound made up of the layers of the accumulated ruins of ancient settlements.

14:1-21
Clean and Unclean Food

14:1-2. ritual for the dead. Ancestor worship and *rituals associated with mourning and memorializing the dead were common in ancient Israel. The assumption behind them was that the dead, although having a rather shadowy existence, could for a time have some effect on the living (see 1 Sam 28:13-14). Thus libations were poured out during meals, and special garments were worn by the mourner. Unlike public worship, however, the rituals for the dead were private and thus more difficult to control. These practices were specifically targeted in the late monarchy period as efforts were made to nationalize *Yahweh worship and move toward strict monotheism in the reigns of Hezekiah and Josiah (2 Kings 23:24). The specific practices (such as lacerating the skin) prohibited in Deuteronomy are also mentioned in the *Baal cycle of stories and in the *Aqhat epic from *Ugarit (c. 1600-1200 B.C.). Their association with magic and with polytheistic cultures would have made them prime targets for the Israelite writers. See comments on Numbers 3:12-13 and Deuteronomy 26:14.

14:2. treasured possession. The phrase "treasured possession" uses a word common in other languages of the ancient Near East to describe accumulated assets, whether through division of spoils or inheritance from estate. That people can be so described is evident in a royal seal from *Alalakh, where the king identifies himself as the "treasured possession" of the god Hadad. Likewise in a *Ugaritic text the king of Ugarit's favored status as a vassal is noted by naming him a "treasured possession" of his *Hittite overlord. Additionally, the Israelites are identified as a "kingdom of priests," which identifies the nation as serving a priestly role among the nations as intermediary between the peoples and God. Additionally there is a well-attested concept in the ancient Near East that a city or group of people may be freed from being subject to a king and placed in direct subjection to a deity. So Israel, freed from Egypt, is now given sacred status.

14:3-21. dietary restrictions. In Mesopotamia there were numerous occasions on which certain foods were prohibited for a short period. There is also evidence in *Babylonia that there were certain restrictions concerning animals that particular gods would accept for sacrifice. But there is no overriding system such as that found here. Yet though there is no known parallel in the ancient world to anything like the Israelite system of dietary restrictions, the permitted animals generally conform to the diet common in the ancient Near East.

14:6-10. criteria for classification of animals. The main criteria are (1) means of locomotion and (2) physical characteristics. Nothing is mentioned of their eating habits or the conditions of their habitat. Anthropologists have suggested that animals were considered clean or unclean depending on whether they possessed all the features that made them "normal" in their category. Other suggestions have concerned health and hygiene. The weakness

of each of these is that there are too many examples that do not fit the explanation. A popular traditional explanation suggested that the animals prohibited had some connection to non-Israelite *rituals. In fact, however, the sacrificial practices of Israel's neighbors appear strikingly similar to Israel's. A recent promising suggestion is that the Israelite diet is modeled after God's "diet"—that is, if it could not be offered in sacrifice to God, then it was not suitable for human consumption either.

14:8. pigs. *Assyrian wisdom literature calls the pig unholy, unfit for the temple and an abomination to the gods. There is also one dream text in which eating pork is a bad omen. Yet it is clear that pork was a regular part of the diet in Mesopotamia. Some *Hittite *rituals require the sacrifice of a pig. Milgrom observes, however, that in such rituals the pig is not put on the altar as food for the god but absorbs *impurity and then is burned or buried as an offering to underworld deities. Likewise in Mesopotamia it was offered as a sacrifice to demons. There is evidence in Egypt of pigs being used for food, and Herodotus claims they were used for sacrifice there as well. Egyptian sources speak of herds of swine being kept on temple property, and pigs were often included in donations to the temples. The pig was especially sacred to the god Seth. Most evidence for the sacrifice of pigs, however, comes from Greece and Rome, there also mostly to gods of the underworld. In urban settings pigs, along with dogs, often scavenged in the streets, making them additionally repulsive. The attitude toward the pig in Israel is very clear in Isaiah 65:4; 66:3,17, the former showing close connection to worship of the dead. It is very possible then that sacrificing a pig was synonymous with sacrificing to demons or the dead.

14:21. disposal of roadkill. In a protein-starved area such as ancient Israel, it would have been almost criminal to let good meat go to waste. However, since the carcass would not have been drained of its blood, Israelites might not eat it (see Deut 12:16; Lev 11:40; 17:50). The meat could be distributed as charity to resident aliens (one of the protected classes, Deut 1:16; 16:11; 26:11). It could also be sold to foreigners who were not settlers in Israel.

14:21. goat in its mother's milk. See comment on Exodus 23:19.

14:22-29

Tithes

14:22-29. tithes and taxes. In the ancient Near

East there was little difference between tithes and taxes. Both were exacted from villages as payment to the government and usually stored in temple complexes, from which the grain, oil and wine were then redistributed to maintain royal and religious officials. In collecting and redistributing the tithe, the distinction between sacred and secular was blurred. The kings were considered divinely chosen, and the storage centers were religious centers. The services that were provided in exchange for the tithe/tax included both administrative and sacred tasks. The process is well laid out in 1 Samuel 8:10-17, a text describing how the king will "take a tenth . . . and give it to his officials and attendants." This is precisely the same procedure outlined in *Ugaritic economic texts and royal correspondence. There too specialists (artisans, bureaucrats, temple personnel) are listed, along with their ration. State building throughout the ancient Near East required assessing the annual production of their lands and villages. The harvesting of the tithe is a reflection of that type of state planning. See comment on Numbers 18:21-32 for further information.

14:23. eating the tithe. It is unlikely that the one who is tithing is expected to eat the entire tithe. That would frustrate its purpose of providing for the priestly community and serving as a reserve for the destitute. The injunction probably has more to do with bringing the tithe (or its value in silver) to God's sanctuary in Jerusalem and thereby demonstrating devotion (see Deut 14:24-26). What is eaten would serve as a *covenantal meal, similar to that eaten in Exodus 24:9-11.

14:27-29. provision for the Levites. As spelled out more completely in 18:1-8, the Levites were to receive a portion of the sacrificial tithe because they were not apportioned any section of the land after the conquest. As religious specialists, they would be allotted a ration from the land's produce in much the same way that bureaucrats and artisans are assigned specific grain and wine rations in the *Ugaritic economic documents (see comment on 14:22-29). It is therefore to be expected that the Levites would be paid for services rendered.

14:29. provision for the vulnerable. A major aspect of Israelite legal tradition involves making provision for groups classified as weak or poor: widows, orphans and the resident alien (see Ex 22:22; Deut 10:18-19; 24:17-21). Thus the tithe from the third year (not an additional tithe in that year) is to be set aside and used to support the vulnerable of society. Concern for the needy is evident in Mesopota-

mian legal collections as early as the mid-third millennium, but this generally addresses protection of rights and guarantee of justice in the courts rather than financial provision.

15:1-18
Cancellation of Slavery and Debts
15:1-11. financial systems in the ancient Near East. Since the wealth of the nations of the ancient Near East was based on the dual economic foundations of natural resources (mines and agriculture) and trade, an intricate financial system had to be developed to support these ventures. For instance, risk capital (in the form of gold, silver, precious stones, spices, etc.) was provided by kings and entrepreneurs in Egypt and Mesopotamia to mariners plying the Mediterranean routes to Cyprus and Crete and the trade routes south along the Red Sea to Arabia, Africa and India. Loans were also made to merchants leading caravans throughout the Near East (with an expected yield on investment of at least 100 percent) and to farmers to provide seed and equipment for the growing season. These loans were generally made at interest (although there was an interest-free category of loan within a set payment period). *Hammurabi's code contains numerous examples governing the rate of interest and even prescribing forfeiture of investment if the creditor charged more than 20 percent. Individual farmers who experienced a bad harvest would often have to incur debt in order to provide food for the coming year and supplies for the next year's planting. Continuing bad harvests would lead to the indenturing of the land or the sale of his family and eventually himself into debt slavery.

15:2-3. debt remission. In granting an absolute remission of all debt at the end of the seventh year, the Deuteronomic law expands on the original sabbatical year legislation (Ex 23:10-11), which related to the fallowing of the land. As the economy expanded, this required broadening the law to include debt as well as the return of property that had been given as collateral for debt (see the Jubilee law in Lev 25). The likelihood that this is total remission of debt rather than a suspension of debt for the year is confirmed by the *misharum* decree of the *Old Babylonian king Ammisaduqa (1646-1626 B.C.). This document prohibits creditors from pursuing the payment of debt after the decree has been issued, on pain of death. However, as in Deuteronomic law, merchants, who were often foreign nationals or new settlers (foreigners in 15:3), are still required to repay investors, since this is a transaction rather than a debt.

15:1-6. sabbatical year. The fallowing of the land in the seventh year, as an acknowledgment of the Creator's work and an example of good husbandry, is first found in Exodus 23:10-11. An expansion of that law is later found in Leviticus 25:2-7, providing more specificity about how it affects the land and the people. The Deuteronomic legislation is more concerned with debt remission, manumission of slaves (15:12-18) and the educational process of reading the law publicly (31:10-13) during the sabbatical year. Although there is no direct parallel to either sabbath or sabbatical-year legislation outside the Bible, the *Ugaritic epic of *Baal contains a seven-year agricultural cycle that may be related. In *Hammurabi's laws women and children sold into slavery would be freed after three years.

15:12. Hebrew. It may well be that originally *Hebrew,* like *Habiru* in *Akkadian texts, was a generic term for landless, stateless persons who contracted themselves as mercenaries, laborers and servants. This is not necessarily a pejorative designation. There are some negative connotations present, since persons in the ancient world tended to identify themselves with a group or place. But considering the fact that the first "Hebrew," Abram, was a landless immigrant, something like "gypsy" might give a general idea of meaning. Israelite villagers considered themselves to be free landowners. *Hebrew,* therefore, would refer to an Israelite who had become destitute (compare Jer 34:9) or was living in foreign lands (Judg 19:16). The Hebrew had to work his full six-year term in order to regain his mortgaged land and landowner status. Thus the Hebrew in Exodus 21:2, Deuteronomy 15:12 and Jeremiah 34:9 would be an Israelite, who, unlike the non-Israelite, could not be sold into permanent slavery. It was his right to release that distinguished him from the non-Israelite.

15:16-17. ear-piercing ceremony. See the comment on Exodus 21:5-6. The only difference in the description of the ceremony is that Deuteronomy has added the phrase "Do the same for your maidservant" in verse 6, since this version of the manumission law deals more fully with both male and female slaves.

15:19-23
Firstborn Animals

15:19-23. treatment of firstborn animals. Dedication of firstborn animals to deity is without firm attestation in the other cultures of the ancient Near East, though some claim to have found such a practice in the *Ugaritic texts. If it is there, the texts give us little information to understand the reasoning behind the practice.

15:23. eating blood. See the comments on Leviticus 17:11 and Deuteronomy 12:16, 20, regarding the prohibition against consuming the blood of animals along with their meat.

16:1-17
The Three Major Festivals

16:1-17. Israel's sacred calendar. Other versions of the calendar are found in Exodus 23:12-19; 34:18-26; Leviticus 23; and Numbers 28—29 (see the comments there).

16:1. Abib. The month of Abib (March-April) is considered the first month in the Israelite calendar and is tied to the exodus event (see Ex 13:4; 23:15). It is one of the month names that is often thought to have been brought over from the Canaanite month names. The first month later came to be known as the month of Nisan when the names were adopted from the *Babylonian calendar. In Exodus 23:15, Abib is tied to the Feast of Unleavened Bread, while in the Deuteronomic law it is keyed to the Passover.

16:1-8. Passover. Compare the comment on the Passover in Exodus 12. This Deuteronomic legislation makes allowance for the changes in Israelite society that have taken place since the exodus and centralizes the celebration of the Passover in "the place [God] will eventually choose as a dwelling for his Name" (v. 5), that is, Jerusalem.

16:8. sacred assembly. Sacred assemblies or proclamations were an important part of most religious practice in the ancient world. They refer to local or national gatherings for public, corporate worship. The people were summoned together away from their occupational work.

16:9. standing grain. The Feast of Weeks (see Ex 23:16) is tied to the wheat harvest of March-April. The Gezer calendar notes this as the month to "reap and feast." Since the grain would have matured at different times in the various locales of the country, the harvest of "standing grain" would have required the prescribed seven-week period to complete.

16:9-12. Feast of Weeks. This second of the three major harvest festivals comes seven weeks after the harvest of the early grain (Ex 34:22) and is also known as the Feast of Harvest or Pentecost (Ex 23:16). In the agricultural cycle it marks the end of the wheat harvest season, and by tradition it is tied to the giving of the law on Mount Sinai. It is also associated with *covenant renewal and pilgrimage. Celebration includes the bringing of a "wave offering" of two loaves of bread, animal sacrifices (seven year-old lambs, one bull and two rams) and a drink offering in thanksgiving for a good harvest. A goat is also to be sacrificed as a sin offering for the people.

16:13-17. Feast of Tabernacles. The final harvest of the year occurred in the autumn prior to the onset of the rainy season and marked the beginning of a new agricultural year (fifteenth day of the seventh month). At this time the last of the ripening grain and fruits were gathered and stored. The seven-day event is also known as the Feast of Ingathering (Ex 23:16) and is symbolized by the construction of booths decorated with greenery for the harvesters. The use of the term *booths* for this festival appears first in Deuteronomy and is probably a reflection of the practice of harvesters of setting up shelters in the fields so that they could work throughout the day without returning to their homes (see Lev 23:42). The festival was tied into Israelite tradition as a commemoration of the wilderness wanderings. It was also the occasion for the dedication of Solomon's temple in Jerusalem (1 Kings 8:65).

16:16. pilgrimage feasts. See the comment on Exodus 23:17 regarding the obligation imposed on the Israelites to come before the Lord as pilgrims three times a year. In the rest of the ancient world each town had its patron deities and its local temples. Festivals and other worship activities would therefore not require lengthy pilgrimage. Nevertheless festivals such as the great Akitu (new year's) festival of *Marduk in *Babylon would undoubtedly have drawn pilgrims from near and far. One of the primary aspects of the ancient Near Eastern festivals was procession, where the image of the God was carried through various symbolic stages. Instead of finding its parallels in other religions' festivals, the pilgrimage aspect of Israel's festivals finds similarity to the *Hittite treaty documents that require the vassal king to travel periodically to the suzerain in order to reaffirm his loyalty (and pay the annual tribute).

16:18—17:13
Establishing Justice

16:18-20. judiciary institutions in ancient Near East. As evidenced by the preface to the Code of *Hammurabi (c. 1750 B.C.) and the statements made by the "eloquent peasant" in Egyptian wisdom literature (c. 2100 B.C.), those in authority were expected to protect the rights of the poor and weak in society. "True justice" (see Lev 19:15) was required of kings, officials and local magistrates. In fact, the "world turned upside down" theme found in the book of Judges and in prophetic literature (Is 1:23) describes a society in which "laws are enacted, but ignored" (for example in the Egyptian *Visions of Neferti* [c. 1900 B.C.]). An efficiently administered state in the ancient Near East depended on the reliability of the law and its enforcement. To this end, every organized state created a bureaucracy of judges and local officials to deal with civil and criminal cases. It was their task to hear testimony, investigate charges made and evaluate evidence, and then execute judgment (detailed in the *Middle Assyrian laws and the Code of Hammurabi). There were some cases, however, that required the attention of the king (see 2 Sam 15:2-4), and appeals were occasionally forwarded to that highest magistrate (as in the *Mari texts).

16:19. bribes in the ancient world. The temptation for judges and government officials to accept bribes is found in every time and place (see Prov 6:35; Mic 7:3). Taking bribes becomes almost institutionally accepted in bureaucratic situations as competing parties attempt to outmaneuver each other (see Mic 3:11; Ezra 4:4-5). However, at least on the ideal level, arguments and penalties are imposed to eliminate or at least lessen this problem. Thus *Hammurabi's code places harsh penalties on any judge who alters one of his decisions (presumably because of a bribe), including stiff fines and permanent removal from the bench. Exodus 23:8 forbids the taking of bribes and the perversion of justice as an offense against God, the weak and innocent, and the entire community (see Is 5:23; Amos 5:12).

16:21. Asherah poles. See the comments on Exodus 34:13 and Deuteronomy 7:5; 12:3.

16:22. sacred stones. See the comments on Exodus 23:24 and Deuteronomy 12:3.

17:3. astral worship. The worship of the celestial bodies (sun, moon, planets, stars) was common throughout the ancient Near East. One of the principal gods of *Assyria and *Babylonia was a sun god (Shamash), and a moon god (Thoth in Egypt; Sin in Mesopotamia; Yarah in Canaanite religion) was widely worshiped. During most of their history the Israelites would have been familiar with and heavily influenced by Assyrian culture and religion (see Deut 4:19; 2 Kings 21:1-7; 23:4-5). These forbidden practices continued to be a source of condemnation during the Neo-Babylonian period, as Israelites burned incense on altars placed on the roofs of their houses to the "starry hosts" (Jer 19:13). Because worship of the elements of nature diminished *Yahweh's position as the sole power in creation, they were outlawed. However, the popular nature of this type of worship continues to appear in prophetic literature and in Job (see Job 31:26-28; 38:7). For additional information see comment on Deuteronomy 4.

17:5. stoning as capital punishment. See the comment on 13:10.

17:6-7. witnesses in the ancient court system. The task of serving as a witness occurs in a variety of legal contexts and is a solemn duty which is not to be abused (Ex 20:16; Num 35:30; Deut 19:16-19). It can involve hearing testimony, signing commercial or civil documents, or testifying on a legal matter (laws of *Ur-Nammu, Code of *Hammurabi and the *Middle Assyrian laws). Witnesses serve an essential purpose in verifying business transactions (Jer 32:44; Hammurabi), such as the sale of property, marriages and changes in social status (*Middle Assyrian laws). Occasionally, they function as representatives of the people in matters brought before a god (Ex 24:9-11; Hammurabi).

17:8-13. verdict by omen in ancient Near East. In situations where physical evidence was not present or was insufficient, a verdict could be determined by the reading of omens. This meant that plaintiffs had to consult religious professionals (Levitical priests in 17:9), whose service included seeking divine verdicts. Among the *divination methods used in the ancient Near East were the examination of a sheep's liver (hepatoscopy), the interpretation of dreams (specific *Babylonian texts contain lists of dreams and what they portend—accidents, deaths, military defeats or victories; see Dan 2:9), the noting of freak occurrences in nature and the use of astrological charting (especially during the period of the *Assyrian empire in the tenth to seventh centuries B.C.). In the biblical text, the Urim and Thummim (Ex 28:30; Num 27:21) were used to help divine God's will, and a number of the prophets point to famines, droughts and other natural calamities as a sign of God's judgment on an unfaithful people (Amos 4:10-12; Hag 1:5-11).

17:14-20

The King

17:14-20. king chosen by deity. The *Sumerian King List, which purports to contain the names of kings from before the flood until the end of the *Ur III dynasty (c. 2000 B.C.), begins with the line, "When the kingship was lowered from heaven." The assumption through-

out Mesopotamian history is that every ruler received his certification to reign from the gods. Thus *Hammurabi (1792-1750 B.C.) speaks in the prologue to his law code of the gods' establishment of "an enduring kingship" in *Babylon and how the gods Anum and *Enlil specifically chose him to rule on behalf of the people. The result is an obligation imposed on the king to rule wisely and with justice, never abusing his power and being responsible to the commands and requirements of the gods. The situation is slightly different in Egypt, where each pharaoh was considered to be a god.

17:16. proliferation of horses. Since horses were used primarily to draw chariots and carry horsemen into battle, the acquisition of large numbers of these animals implies either an aggressive foreign policy or a monarch who wishes to impress his people and his neighbors with his wealth and power. The reference to Egypt is suggestive of dependence on that nation as an ally and a supplier of horses for war (Is 36:6-9). Such alliances in the late monarchy period proved disastrous for Israel and Judah and were roundly condemned by the prophets (Is 31:1-3; Mic 5:10).

17:17. royal marriage as alliance. Marriage was a tool of diplomacy throughout the ancient Near East. For instance, Zimri-Lim, the king of *Mari (eighteenth century B.C.), used his daughters to cement alliances and establish treaties with his neighboring kingdoms. Similarly, Pharaoh Thutmose IV (1425-1412 B.C.) arranged a marriage with a daughter of the *Mitannian king to demonstrate good relations and end a series of wars with that middle Euphrates kingdom. Solomon's seven hundred wives and three hundred *concubines (1 Kings 11:3) were a measure of his power and wealth (just as horses are in Deut 17:16), especially his marriage to the daughter of the pharaoh (1 Kings 3:1). While the political advantages were quite evident, the danger of such marriages is demonstrated in the introduction of the worship of other gods by Solomon's wives (1 Kings 11:4-8).

17:17. royal treasuries. The theme of excessive acquisition of royal symbols of power (horses, wives, gold and silver) continues in this admonition against overtaxing the people simply to fill the royal treasury. All of the categories of wealth are said to lead to excessive pride, apostasy and a rejection or diminution of *Yahweh's role (compare 8:11-14). The vanity of kings who amass wealth without purpose other than pride is found in Ecclesiastes 2:8-11 and Jeremiah 48:7. The treasuries typically contained the precious metal assets of temple and state, including contributions as well as plunder. Though coinage or bullion may have been included, much of it would be in the form of jewelry, vessels for *ritual use, religious objects or the various accessories of royal or wealthy households. Payment of tribute at times required drawing from or even emptying the treasuries (see 1 Kings 14:26; 2 Kings 18:15). Excavations or descriptions of temples and palaces often indicate rooms as treasuries, and royal officers included keepers of the treasuries.

17:18-20. king subject to the law. In Egypt and Mesopotamia the king was the fountainhead of law. It was his task to perceive and maintain the order that was built into the universe (Egyptian *ma'at;* Mesopotamian *me*). The king could not be "brought to justice," except by the gods. He was not above the law, but there was no mechanism by which he could be tried in a human court. Judicially this may have been no different in Israel, though the prophets, as spokesmen for the deity, could call the king to account.

18:1-13
Priests and Levites

18:1-5. provision for Levites. Whether or not the worshiper ate a portion of the sacrifice, a number of the sacrifices provided an opportunity for the priests to eat. This was also true in *Babylonian practice, where the king, the priest and other temple personnel received portions of the sacrifices. As early as *Sumerian texts it was considered a grievous crime to eat that which had been set apart as holy. See also the comment on Numbers 18:12-19 for tithes paid to the priests.

18:6-8. function of the Levites in the towns. During the early settlement period, Levites officiated at local shrines and altars. It would have been their role to serve as religious professionals, performing sacrifices and instructing the people on the law. While some Levites may have been tied to these places for generations (1 Sam 1:3), there is also evidence of itinerant Levites, who traveled about the country and were hired to serve for a time at a local shrine or high place (Judg 17:7-13). Without an inheritance of their own (Josh 14:3-4), the Levites stood out within a society that was territorial. The Levites were supposed to instruct the people in proper worship, though the book of Judges makes it clear that sometimes they were a major part of the problem rather than the solution. They were supposed to be preservers of tradition and law and would have often served as judges.

18:9-22
Receiving Information from Deity

18:10. divination. See the comment on Leviticus 19:26. *Divination involves a variety of methods used by prophets (Mic 3:11), soothsayers, mediums and sorcerers to determine the will of the gods and to predict the future. These included the examination of the entrails of sacrificial animals, the analysis of omens of various types and the reading of the future in natural and unnatural phenomena (see Gen 44:5). While there were acceptable divination practices among the Israelites (use of the Urim and Thummim), what is being condemned here is a group of practitioners, who served as professional fortunetellers.

18:10. sorcery. Since magic in the ancient world was a means of contacting the supernatural realm, it was considered to have two facets: good magic and evil. In Mesopotamia and among the *Hittites harmful magic was practiced by sorcerers and was punishable by death. It involved the use of potions, figurines and curses designed to bring death, disease or bad luck to the victim. This was distinguished from the practical and helpful magic of professional exorcists and "old women," whose role included the rites involved in temple construction and dedication, as well as medical aid. Only in Egypt was there no distinction between white and black magic. There the practitioners' job involved intimidating demons and other divine powers to perform required tasks or to remove curses. The Israelite law totally rejected all these practices because of their polytheistic character and the diminishing of *Yahweh's role as lord of creation (see Ex 22:18).

18:10. omens. One of the priestly classes mentioned in Mesopotamian texts is the *baru*-diviners. It was their task to perform extispicy (generally on lambs), examining the liver and interpreting this omen for the person who has asked for a reading of the future. The *baru* might be consulted by a king who wished to go to war (compare 1 Kings 22:6), a merchant about to send out a caravan or a person who had become ill. Government officials often included the report of omens in their letters (*Mari texts). However, since omens were not always clear, several groups of diviners might be used before action was taken. An entire body of omen texts (with descriptions of past events and predictions) were archived in temples and palaces for consultation by staff diviners. Even clay models of livers were used in schooling apprentices in the trade.

18:10. witchcraft. Like sorcery, witchcraft was

generally classed as an illegitimate use of magic. Its practitioners might serve in royal courts or temples or as local herbalists and itinerant diviners, who would, for a price, provide the means to harm or destroy an enemy (see Lev 19:26; 20:6; 2 Kings 21:6). The Mesopotamian distinction between good and evil magic is lost in Israelite law, where the female witch is condemned (Ex 22:18) and the words of sorcerers are declared to be unreliable (Jer 27:9; Mal 3:5).

18:11. spells, medium, spiritist. The practitioners of spiritism and sorcery are condemned because of their association with Canaanite religion and because their "art" attempted to circumvent *Yahweh by seeking knowledge and power from spirits. They represented a form of popular religion that was closer to the folk practices of the common people and served as a form of "shadow religion" for many. Sometimes, because of its association with *divination, their *rituals and methods stood in direct opposition to official religion or as an alternative to be used in times of desperation (see Saul's use of the outlawed witch of Endor in 1 Sam 28). Sorcery and potions used in the practice of magic were also banned in the Code of *Hammurabi and the *Middle Assyrian laws, suggesting that the prohibition and fear of these practices were not unique to Israel.

18:11. consulting the dead. Although there was no clear sense of an afterlife in ancient Mesopotamia, no envisioning of a place of reward or punishment, ancestor worship did exist, and offerings were made to the spirits of the dead. A group of magical practitioners created a means for consulting the spirits of the dead to find out about the future (see the witch of Endor in 1 Sam 28:7-14). This was called necromancy and could involve consulting a particular or "familiar" spirit, or it could be the raising of any ghost attracted by the spells of the medium. Ritual pits, stuffed with bread and blood, were commonly used in *Hittite ritual by diviners, and the Greek hero Odysseus used a pit filled with blood to attract the shades of his dead companions. It was believed that if libations were poured out to them, the spirits of dead ancestors could offer protection and help to those still living. In *Babylon the disembodied spirit (*utukki*) or the ghost (*etemmu*) could become very dangerous if not cared for, and such spirits were often the objects of incantations. Proper care for the dead would begin with proper burial and would continue with ongoing gifts and honor of the memory and name of the deceased. The firstborn was responsible for maintaining this

ancestor worship and therefore inherited the family gods (often images of deceased ancestors).

18:10-13. worldview basis for prohibiting divination. The worldview promulgated in the Old Testament maintains that *Yahweh is the sole God and is the ultimate power and authority in the universe. In stark contrast, the polytheistic religions of the ancient Near East did not consider their gods (even as a group) to represent the ultimate power in the universe. Instead they believed in an impersonal primordial realm that was the source of knowledge and power. *Divination attempted to tap into that realm for the purposes of gaining knowledge; incantations tried to utilize its power. Both *divination and incantation can therefore be seen to assume a worldview that was contradictory to Yahweh's revealed position.

18:14-22. function of the prophet. These individuals were more than simple religious practitioners. While some of them were members of the priestly community, they stood outside that institution. Their role was to challenge the establishment and the social order, to remind the leadership and the people of their obligation to the *covenant with *Yahweh and to provide warning of the punishment that went with violation of the covenantal agreement. The prophet is invested with special powers, a message and a mission, and there is a special compulsion associated with being called as a prophet. It can be denied for a time (see Jonah's flight) but ultimately must be answered. It should also be noted that prophets may be reluctant to speak harsh words or condemnations of their own people. When this occurs, the prophet will experience a compulsion to speak that cannot be resisted (Jer 20:9). Since they speak a message that comes from God, they separate themselves from the words and thus cannot be charged with treason, sedition or doomsaying. The message is thus the most important thing about the prophet, not the prophet himself or herself. Certainly, there were some prophets like Balaam and Elijah who acquired a personal reputation, but this was based on their message or their ability to speak for God. For a prophet to gain credibility with the people, the message must come true. Although sometimes the prophets are mentioned as part of the *cult community (Isaiah and Ezekiel) and as court prophets (Nathan), they always seem to be able to stand apart from these institutions to criticize them and to point out where they have broken the *covenant with God. In the early periods of the monarchy, the prophets primarily addressed the king and his court, much like their ancient Near Eastern counterparts did (they have been termed "preclassical" prophets). Beginning in the eighth century, however, they turned their attention increasingly to the people and became the social/spiritual commentators whom we most readily identify with the prophetic institution (the "classical" prophets and the "writing" prophets). Their role was not to predict as much as it was to advise of God's policies and plans.

18:20-22. false prophecy. Like Deuteronomy 13:1-3 and its discussion of persons urging the worship of other gods, false prophets are generally those who speak in the name of other gods. Deuteronomy discounts the existence of these other gods and thus the veracity of their prophets. In cases where prophets presume to speak in *Yahweh's name without permission, the test of true prophecy is whether what they say actually occurs. There are a number of examples of false prophecy cited in the biblical text. Jeremiah rails against it in his accusation against Hananiah (Jer 28:12-17) and in his warning against other prophets who predicted a quick end to the exile (29:20-23). In some cases, the potential for confusion involved is such that events must take their course before the true prophet is revealed (see 1 Kings 22). The Israelites were not alone in their caution concerning false prophecy. In other cultures, however, they generally used *divination to try to confirm the message of the prophet, but this was not permissible for Israel.

18:14-22. prophecy in the ancient Near East. Texts from Mesopotamia, Syria and Anatolia contain a large number of prophetic utterances, demonstrating the existence of prophets throughout much of ancient Near Eastern history. While some of these texts may actually fall into the realm of wisdom literature or omen reports, many involve individuals who claim to have received a message from a god. Most famous among these texts are about fifty texts from *Mari (eighteenth century B.C.) that contain reports from both male and female prophets: warnings about plots against the king, admonitions from a god to build a temple or to provide a *funerary offering, and assurances of military victory. These prophets present divine messages received in dreams or through omens. Others are said to fall into a trance state and speak as ecstatic prophets. This type of prophecy is also found in the eleventh-century B.C. Egyptian tale of *Wenamon and in 1 Samuel 10:5-11 and 2 Kings 3:15.

19:1-21

Capital Punishment Cases

19:1. Late Bronze Canaanite cities. Most of what is known about *Late Bronze Canaanite cities comes from archaeological excavations and surveys and the inscriptions of the Egyptian Pharaohs who ruled that region. Evidence suggests that the major cities of this period (Jerusalem, Shechem, Megiddo) were walled, but settlements were spaced fairly far apart. The central hill country was sparsely inhabited prior to 1200 B.C. The population was mixed, containing peoples who had come from the *Hittite kingdom, Syria, Mesopotamia and the desert areas of Arabia. The Egyptians apparently had some difficulty governing the area and were required on numerous occasions to send military expeditions to quell revolts and end brigandage (reported in the fourteenth-century B.C. *Amarna letters as well as in the victory inscriptions of Amenophis II [c. 1450-1425 B.C.] and of Merenptah [c. 1208 B.C.]).

19:2-3. refuge cities in ancient Near East. See the comment on Numbers 35:6-34 for a discussion of the cities of refuge in Israel. The concept of asylum and refuge is quite old. *Babylonian and *Hittite texts both speak of sacred space where all are to be protected. The inhabitants of the great temple cities of Nippur, Sippar and Babylon were granted special status because of the protection afforded by patron deities of these places. The principle was that only the god could withdraw protection from persons here, and thus no one could shed their blood without an omen or sign from the god (Herodotus has an example from the classical period). Egyptian tradition regarding asylum appears to apply only to the temple precinct rather than to the entire city. This would parallel the biblical examples in which a fugitive takes refuge at the altar (1 Kings 1:50-53; 2:28-34).

19:6. avenger of blood and the justice system. See the comment on Numbers 35:9-34 for a discussion of the responsibility of the family to avenge a death. It is possible that the title "avenger of blood" evolved out of the family obligation to engage in blood revenge when one of their clan members was slain. Such a process, while typical of tribal society, is extremely disruptive to the maintenance of order within an organized state. As a result, the "avenger of blood" (a term which appears only in the context of the cities of refuge) may have been appointed by the government to serve the needs of both the family and the state by apprehending the accused and then carrying out the sentence if the verdict was murder.

19:11-13. capital punishment. In the Bible capital punishment is the sentence imposed for apostasy (Lev 20:2), blasphemy (Lev 24:14), sorcery (Lev 20:27), violation of the sabbath (Num 15:35-36), stealing from the *herem* (Josh 7:25), gross disobedience to parents (Deut 21:21), adultery (Deut 22:21), incest (Lev 20:14) and deliberate homicide (Num 35:9). While stoning is the most common form of capital punishment, some offenses require burning or stabbing with a sword. In every case the purpose is to eliminate contaminating elements from society and thereby purge the evil that threatened to draw the people away from the *covenant.

19:14. moving boundary stones. Since the land had been given to the people by God and apportioned according to a God-given formula, to move boundary stones and thus appropriate territory unlawfully was a crime of theft against God. The antiquity of laws concerning property rights is affirmed by inscriptions on sixteenth-century B.C. Kassite *kudurru* boundary stones, admonitions in eleventh-century B.C. Egyptian wisdom literature against relocating a surveyor's stone *(Teachings of Amenemope)* and in the curse in Hosea 5:10. Each example calls on the gods to protect the owner's rights against encroachment.

19:15-20. the role of witnesses in the ancient judicial system. Witnesses were an essential part of the judicial system in the ancient world. One sign of this is that Israelite law required two witnesses to convict a person of a crime (Num 35:30; Deut 17:6; 1 Kings 21:13). Both *Hammurabi's code and the *Middle Assyrian laws rely heavily on the presence of witnesses to certify business transactions and to testify in civil and criminal cases.

19:21. lex talionis. The legal principle of "an eye for an eye" or *lex talionis* ("law of retaliation") is found in both the biblical law codes and the codes of Mesopotamia. Biblical examples (Ex 21:24; Lev 24:20) express the desire to eliminate a corrupting or unclean element in society. The admonition is to have "no mercy" on the culprit. Mesopotamian law contains both the idealized version of *lex talionis* and an amelioration to set limits of compensation. For instance, the law collection of *Eshnunna sets a fine of one mina of silver for the loss of an eye. In the personal liability laws found in *Hammurabi's code, reciprocity for injury may be an exactly equivalent injury, a fine or mutilation, depending on the social status of the injured party and the accused. Even in the cases where exact reciprocity is required by

Mesopotamian law, it is quite possible that a monetary equivalent was taken in compensation (if not explicitly included in the law), rather than an eye or a tooth being actually removed.

20:1-20
Rules for Warfare

20:2. priest addressing the army. Since warfare was considered a religious enterprise, it was expected that priests and other religious functionaries would accompany the army. *Assyrian texts and reliefs depict the roles performed by priests accompanying the troops. They carried or attended the images and emblems of the gods (see Josh 6:4-5; 1 Sam 4:4), performed religious *rituals and sacrifices, and undoubtedly addressed the army in the name of the gods. This latter task may have involved interpreting of omens, assuring the aid of the gods and exhorting the troops to fight for the god's chosen king (as in the annals of Tukulti-Ninurta I [1244-1208 B.C.] and Ashurnasirpal II [883-859 B.C.]).

20:5-9. exemptions from military duty. While every able-bodied free man was expected to serve in the military, in practice exemptions were allowed for special categories, such as priests (in the *Mari texts), newlyweds (Deut 24:5) and those who have religious duties to perform (see Lev 19:23-25). Conscription of troops was necessary to fulfill feudal obligations to kings and took various forms, including census taking and coercion (at Mari). The biblical injunction to allow the "frightened" to leave the army may have had its basis in maintaining discipline in the ranks, but it is also an assurance that those who fight are certain of Yahweh's aid in battle (see Judg 7:1-3). The law codes are at times contradictory on the matter of hiring substitutes for service in the military. The *Hittite code allows this practice, but it is outlawed in the Code of *Hammurabi. This latter case is based on a direct order to join the king's campaign. It is possible that arrangements could be made for members of the nobility that would preempt any awkward legal problems. In the Canaanite *Keret Epic the king raises an army in a cause so important that normal exemptions (newlywed among them) are abandoned.

20:10-15. normal warfare practices. In the ancient world, the standard procedure was not to pay soldiers a wage. Instead they were given a portion of the loot taken in the capture of villages and towns. Because warfare was also seen as a divine mission, ordered by the god(s) and facilitated by divine intervention, all plunder taken in battle was technically the sacred property of the god(s). As a result strict procedures had to be followed in its division in order to prevent a violation of sacred taboos. For instance, in the *Mari texts officers took an oath not to "eat the *asakkum*" (i.e., infringe on the rights) of their peers or of lesser ranks. Violators were punished with heavy fines. Following this pattern, Mesopotamian as well as Israelite armies commonly took women and children as spoils, along with animals and moveable property, while the men were killed (see Gen 34:25-29; *Assyrian Annals of Sennacherib). In this way the efforts of the victorious were rewarded, and the psychological effect of the sight of devastated cities served the purpose of enhancing the reputation of the conquering nation and its god(s).

20:16-18. holy war procedures. In unusual circumstances, an army chose to forego taking prisoners or spoils and dedicated it entirely to the god who had given them the victory. This practice is known as *herem* in Hebrew and is used very sparingly as a method of warfare. Only in a few instances is the total destruction of a city called for: Jericho in Joshua 6:17-24, Hazor in Joshua 11:10-11, Zephath in Judges 1:17 and the Amalekites in 1 Samuel 15:3. There are several instances where some variation on utter destruction is allowed, as in Deuteronomy 2:34-35 and 3:6-7 (people killed, livestock taken as spoil). Outside the Bible, this perspective on war is attested as early as the ninth century B.C. in the war against the tribe of Gad by the Moabite king Mesha. A similar concept may be reflected in the annals of several of the *Assyrian kings, who used total destruction as a psychological ploy to make revolting nations submissive.

20:20. siege works. To capture a walled city, it was necessary to employ a variety of siege works, including ramps (2 Sam 20:15; 2 Kings 19:32), towers (Is 23:13; Ezek 21:22) or perimeter walls to prevent escape (Ezek 26:8; Mic 5:1). Battering rams (Ezek 26:9) as well as supports for tunnels undermining the walls also required the use of timbers. This explains the dispensation allowed in Deuteronomy for the cutting of trees during a siege. The *Assyrian reliefs of Ashurnasirpal II (883-859 B.C.) at Nimrud portray many of these siege engines and simultaneous methods of warfare.

21:1-9

Unsolved Murder

21:1-9. innocent blood procedures and concepts. See the comments on Numbers 19 dealing with the significance of the purification *ritual and the use of the red heifer. These comments also deal with the importance of expiation for the shedding of "innocent blood." In *Hittite law if a body was found out in the open country, the person's heir was entitled to some property from the town nearest the place where the body was found, up to three leagues' distance. This legislation is more concerned with the rights of the heir than with the issue of innocent bloodshed.

21:10-14

Rights of Captive Women

21:10-14. treatment of captive women. Part of warfare is the disposition of prisoners. Some female captives could expect to serve as slaves (2 Kings 5:2-3), but many would also be taken as wives by the soldiers. The Deuteronomic law deals with the transformation process as these women were adopted into Israelite society. This included the shaving of the head, a change of clothing and a period of mourning marking the death of the woman's old life and the beginning of a new one (compare Joseph's transformation in Gen 41:41-45). The *Mari texts also provide clothing and a job to captive women. The rights extended to the former captive after she has married are similar to those of Israelite women and are designed to demonstrate that there is no reduction of her status if a divorce occurs. Similar concerns are reflected in the *Middle Assyrian laws, which require former captives who are now married to dress like all Assyrian women of that class.

21:15-21

Treatment of Sons

21:15-17. right of the firstborn. Inheritance rights are based on the law of primogeniture. This stipulates that the firstborn son is to receive a double share of his father's property. That this was the normal situation in the ancient Near East can be seen in Middle Assyrian texts, *Larsa, *Mari and *Nuzi documents, just to name a few. The intent of such laws is to insure orderly transmission of property from one generation to the next. *Hammurabi's law gives the father the right to favor whichever son he chooses. In the Nuzi texts the father had the option of altering the firstborn rights. In the ancient Near East the closest legislation to that found here is the stipulation in Hammurabi's law that says the children of the slave wife, if acknowledged as children during the father's lifetime, have an equal share in the inheritance with the full wife's children.

21:18-21. execution of a rebellious son. When a breakdown of family coherence occurred and a son refused to give his parents the obedience and support they were entitled to, it became a threat to the community as a whole. The language used here makes it clear that a repudiation of the *covenant is involved. The references to gluttony and drunkenness are considered indications that the son is beyond reform. Due process includes parental witness of the offense, and then a communal form of execution is prescribed (see comment on Deut 13:10). This offense is as grave a threat to the covenant as worshiping other gods. Mesopotamian law also defends the rights of parents, but only extending to disinheritance or mutilation. See the comment on Exodus 21:17. The legislation limits the authority of the parents in that they have to bring such a matter before the elders rather than having the freedom to act independently.

21:22-23

Treatment of Executed Criminals

21:22-23. exposure of executed criminals. Since the Deuteronomic laws are seldom concerned with matters of ritual *purity and polluting elements (see Lev 13—17 and comments on Lev 20:10-16; 22:3-9), it may be that the sense of "desecrating" the land is based on either the sight or the smell of an exposed and decaying body. The corpse was considered a defiling object (Lev 22:8; Num 5:2) and thus a danger to the living. Very few narratives describe the practice of exposing a body (Josh 8:29; 10:26-7; 2 Sam 4:12; 21:8-13). It is unlikely that hanging was the form of execution used here. Rather, a tree or pole was used to impale the bodies for public display. *Assyrian reliefs from the palace of Sennacherib in *Nineveh (704-681 B.C.) depict soldiers erecting stakes holding the impaled bodies of men of Lachish. It is possible that the horror of this form of shameful display is the basis for the Israelite law requiring the body to be removed and buried at sunset rather than leaving it to be devoured by birds and other animals (Gen 40:19; 2 Sam 21:10).

22:1-12

Miscellaneous Laws

22:1-3. lost property. Just as in Exodus 23:4, it is expected that an Israelite will either return lost property (animals, clothing, etc.) or keep it safe until the owner reclaims it. Taking the two laws together, this maxim applies to fellow Israelites as well as enemies. The laws of *Eshnunna and *Hammurabi also deal with lost property, but they broaden the legislation to include both the responsibilities of the finder and the legal rights of the owner when property is resold.

22:5. transvestism in the ancient Near East. Just as clothing served as a status marker in the ancient world, it also distinguished gender. In classical contexts, cross-dressing occurred in the theater, where women were not allowed to perform, and was also an aspect of homosexual practice. Most instances in which cross-dressing or transvestism are mentioned in ancient Near Eastern texts are *cultic or legal in nature. For instance, when the *Ugaritic hero *Aqhat is murdered, his sister Paghat puts on a male garment under her female robes in order to assume the role of blood avenger in the absence of a male relative. An *Assyrian wisdom text contains a dialogue between husband and wife who propose to exchange their clothing and thus assume each other's gender roles. This may be a *fertility rite or perhaps a part of a religious drama honoring a goddess. It may be this association with other religions that made transvestism an "abomination" in Deuteronomy, but the issue may also be the blurring of gender distinctions. *Hittite texts use gender-related objects as well as clothing in a number of magical rites used to influence one's sexual status or diminish or alter the gender status of an adversary. The objects of the female were mirror and distaff; those of the male, various weapons.

22:6-7. treatment of bird's nest. Aside from the apparent humanitarian concern for the welfare of the creatures involved here, conservation of nature is found in leaving the mature bird to breed again. One might compare this with the prohibition against cutting down fruit trees in Deuteronomy 20:19-20. In both instances, future sources of food are preserved while an alternative is suggested for immediate needs.

22:8. parapet on house. Since roofs were considered living space (see 2 Sam 11:2; 2 Kings 4:10), a parapet would have been an appropriate safety measure. This law deals with the liability of a homeowner for injury to a visitor in the case of negligent building practices. *Hammurabi's code (laws 229-33) cautions builders against doing a substandard or unsafe job that could lead to injury or death. Penalties ranged from fines to capital punishment.

22:9-11. mixing. Some mixtures were considered to be reserved for sacred use. The mixture of wool and linen was used in the tabernacle and in the high priest's outer garments, and was reserved for those uses. This interpretation is offered in the Dead Sea Scrolls (4QMMT). Sowing of two types of seed is also prohibited in the *Hittite laws with a death threat to violators. While it is not entirely clear why these mixtures are prohibited, it is possible that their origin is based on either religious or cultural taboos. The fact that the crop is "defiled" or forfeited to the priesthood suggests religious implications and perhaps a reaction to a Canaanite *fertility *ritual or practice. In Leviticus 19:19 the prohibition is against mating two kinds of animals, while here it concerns plowing with them together. Experiments with hybridization and crossbreeding are attested as early as the third millennium B.C.

22:12. tassels. All adult male Israelites were commanded to sew blue cords into the four quarters of the hem of their robes as a perpetual reminder of God's commandments (Num 15:37-41). Decorative hems are common in ancient Near Eastern fashion as many reliefs, paintings and texts attest. Hem design was often an indication of a person's status or office. The tassels are symbolic and are designed to promote right action, not to serve as an *amulet to ward off danger or temptation.

22:13-30
Laws Concerning Marriage

22:13-21. proof of virginity. Virginity prior to marriage was prized as a means of insuring that one's children and heirs were actually one's own. The integrity of the woman's household was based on her being able to show proof of her virginity. The physical evidence demanded in this case could be either the sheets from the initial consummation (bloodied by the breaking of the hymen) or possibly rags used during the woman's last menstrual period, showing that she was not pregnant prior to the marriage.

22:19. one hundred shekels of silver. The fine imposed here for false accusation amounts to about two and one-half pounds of silver. *Hammurabi's laws include cases of false accusation of sexual misconduct, but these do not concern the wedding context, and monetary fines are not set. Based on the bride price paid in Deuteronomy 22:29 of fifty shekels, this penalty amounts to twice the bride price and thus would be a real deterrent to such accusations. It would be the equivalent of about ten years of normal wages.

22:22. adultery. Having sexual relations with another man's wife was punishable by death in both the biblical and ancient Near Eastern codes. The Egyptian *Tale of Two Brothers* calls it a "great crime" that no honest man or woman would consider. This was an attack on a man's household, stealing his rights to procreate and endangering the orderly transmission of his estate to his heirs (see comment on Ex 20:14). The act itself defiles both participants (Lev 18:20; Num 13:5). Since it is not only an attack on the sanctity of the household but also a source of general contamination, adultery serves as a reason for God to expel the people from the land (Lev 18:24-25).

22:23-24. "in town" criterion. The rape of a virgin within a town brings an automatic death penalty because the woman had the opportunity to cry out and could expect to receive assistance. This is based on implied consent on her part. Mesopotamian codes also include locale as part of the rape law. However, in the *Sumerian laws, the focus is more on whether her parents were aware that she was out of the household and whether the rapist knew whether she was slave or free (laws of *Ur-Nammu and *Eshnunna impose fines for raping a virgin slave woman). *Hammurabi's law most closely resembles the Deuteronomic law. In this case the rapist is to be executed if he attacks a woman in the street and witnesses testify that she defended herself. *Middle Assyrian laws allow the parents of the victim to take the rapist's wife and have her raped. There is also provision for the rapist to marry the victim, if the family chooses, for a premium bride price.

22:23, 25. "pledged" status. A marriage contract was a sacred compact, comparable to the *covenant agreement made with Yahweh (see Ezek 16:0). The "pledge" agreement (1) set a bride price as well as the amount of the dowry, (2) guaranteed that the bride would be a virgin at the time of marriage and (3) required complete fidelity of the parties. Marriage was such an important economic and social factor in the ancient Near East that it was the basis of a huge amount of legislation. For instance, the laws of *Eshnunna and *Hammurabi explain the importance of having an official marriage contract. Hammurabi's laws also provide guidance on payment of the bride price and instances when one party or the other wishes to break the contract (see 2 Sam 3:14). Once an agreement is in place, it is expected that other persons will respect the betrothed status of the woman as technically already married (see Gen 20:3). Thus the laws of adultery are in full force even before the actual ceremony and consummation of the marriage.

22:25-27. "in the country" criterion. In this case, Israelite law adds another criterion by specifying the guiltlessness of the woman who is raped in the countryside, where her screams were unlikely to attract assistance. The assumption of her innocence is based on implied resistance to the rape in this circumstance. It is likely that the law applied to married as well as to betrothed women, even though only the latter are mentioned. A similar statement appears in *Hittite law, which condemns the man only if he seizes a woman "in the mountains" and condemns the woman only if the crime occurs "in (her) house" (see the adulterous woman in Prov 5:3-14).

22:29. fifty shekels. The bride price probably varied depending on the status and wealth of the bride-to-be's family. Fifty shekels of silver may have been a standard amount (equivalent to the value of the bride's virginity, according to *Middle Assyrian laws), but there were probably other items exchanged as well (compare Ex 22:16-17). To provide one measure of these transactions, in the *Ugaritic religious texts the moon god Yarih offers one thousand shekels of silver as a bride price for the moon goddess Nikkal. These amounts should be measured against the fact that the standard annual wage in the ancient world was ten shekels.

22:29. divorce in ancient Near East. The most straightforward statement on divorce in the ancient Near Eastern law codes is Middle Assyrian law 37, which simply says that it is a man's right to divorce his wife and that he may choose whether or not to provide her with a settlement. Other legal clauses, however, at least provide grounds for divorce: wife neglects household duties to go into business (Hammurabi); wife's desertion of her husband (*Middle Assyrian laws); failure to produce children (Hammurabi). General indications are that men in both Egypt and Mesopotamia could divorce their wives on almost any grounds. There are also a number of sources that prescribe a fixed settlement: one mina of silver to a primary wife and one-half mina of silver to a former widow (Ur-Nammu); one mina of silver if no bride price was paid (Hammurabi). It should be noted that women did have some rights in divorce proceedings: to keep the bride price (*Middle Assyrian laws); to have dowry returned (Hammurabi); to receive a share of the inheritance as a dowry (Hammurabi). There is also one case in which a woman was able to leave an unsatisfactory marriage, taking her dowry with her (Hammurabi). However, this was based on an examination of her character, which could lead to her execution if she was found to be at fault (Hammurabi).

22:30. incest. Incest was equally abhorrent in most other societies (e.g., the prohibitions in *Hittite laws). The most well-known exception is Egypt, where it was a common practice in the royal family (but little attested elsewhere) as a means to strengthen or consolidate royal authority. This concept is also seen among *Elamite kings. *Hammurabi's laws call for the execution of a son who has intercourse with his mother after the death of his father.

23:1-14
Defiling the Assembly and the Camp

23:1-8. exclusions from the assembly. "Assembly of the LORD," like the more common "assembly of Israel," is a technical term for all those adult males who are enfranchised to make decisions, participate in *cultic activities and serve in the military of Israel (Mic 2:5). Because they were a chosen people, who were required to maintain their *ritual purity as part of the *covenant (Ex 19:6), the unclean and the stranger were excluded from the activities of the assembly. The examples listed include persons who were sexually impaired (probably eunuchs) and thus incapable of procreation, men of illegitimate birth (including incest and intermarriage) and certain national groups who were excluded from ever being adopted into the assembly.

23:4. Balaam's home. The exact location of Balaam's home is unknown. Numbers 22:5, 23:7 and Deuteronomy 23:4 seem to indicate the area of the upper Euphrates, perhaps the site of Pitru, twelve miles south of Carchemish, mentioned in the monolith inscription of the *Assyrian king Shalmaneser III (858-824 B.C.). However, the journey of Balaam described in Numbers 22:21-35 suggests a shorter distance, possibly a journey from Ammon.

23:9-14. sanitation in the camp. Since the army is engaged in a holy war, they must maintain themselves in a state of ritual purity consistent with God's holiness. Thus matters of personal hygiene are elevated to reinforce the need to keep both person (see Lev 15:16-17) and place clean. Obviously, there would be health value in digging latrines outside the camp, but such mundane activities here are keyed to preventing the ritual *impurity that would cause God to abandon them (see Deut 8:11-20).

23:15-25
Miscellaneous Laws

23:15-16. slavery. Although debt slavery occurred in ancient Israel, it had a term limit of six years and then the slave was freed. Perpetual slavery did exist as well, but that involved foreign captives and Israelites who had made the decision to accept that condition (Ex 21:2-11; Deut 15:12-18). It is most likely this latter class of persons that is mentioned in this law, since debt slaves could expect to be released eventually. Israel's fugitive slave law is unusual in the context of ancient Near Eastern law. However it is tied to Israel's former condition as slaves in Egypt and thus is based on a national hatred of the institution (see Ex 22:21). The Code of *Hammurabi makes hiding a runaway slave a capital crime and sets a bounty of two shekels of silver for the return of a slave. Similarly, the international treaty between Pharaoh Rameses II and the *Hittite king Hattusilis III (c. 1280 B.C.) includes an extradition clause requiring the return of fugitive slaves.

23:17-18. cultic *prostitution. One can distinguish between several different categories. In "sacred" prostitution, the proceeds go to the temple. In "cultic" prostitution, the intent is to insure *fertility through sexual *ritual. We must also differentiate between occasional sacred/cultic prostitution (as in Gen 38) and professional sacred/cultic prostitution (as in 2 Kings 23:7). The evidence for cultic prostitution in ancient Israel or elsewhere in the ancient Near East is not conclusive. Canaanite texts list prostitutes among the temple personnel, and *Akkadian literature attests those who were dedicated for life to serve the temple in this way. Although the Hebrew word used here is related to an Akkadian word for prostitute, this does not prove that any religious ritual or cultic practice is involved. It is quite possible for prostitutes to be employed by temples as a means of raising funds without their having any official status as priestesses. Furthermore, since women often did not have personal assets, sometimes the only way of earning money by which to pay a vow appeared to be prostitution. The injunction against bringing the wages of a prostitute to the temple may, however, be a reaction against practices like that of the *Ishtar temple servants in the Neo-Babylonian period, who hired out female members of their community as prostitutes. Their wages would have been placed in the temple treasury. All of this demonstrates the existence of sacred prostitution, both occasional and professional, in Israel and the ancient Near East. But the existence of cultic prostitution on either level is more difficult to prove. Cultic prostitution is not easily confirmed in Mesopotamia, unless one includes the annual sacred marriage ritual. But it is hard to imagine that prostitutes serving at the temple of Ishtar (who personified sexual force) were not viewed as playing a sacred role in the fertility cult. The translation "male prostitute" in Deuteronomy 23:18 is based on the use of the Hebrew word that usually means "dog." In the fourth-century B.C. Kition inscription, this term is used to describe a group that receives temple rations. It is possible, but not certain, that this refers to a temple official or priest. Recent study has shown that, at least by the Persian period (sixth-fifth century), dogs had some significant role in Phoenician *cultic practice. *Kalbu* (dog) has a more positive meaning of "faithful one," as can be seen in its use in personal names (like the biblical Caleb). (See Ex 34:16.)

23:19-20. charging interest. See the comment on Exodus 22:25. In Deuteronomy, though not in Exodus, it is explicitly stated that interest may be charged on loans to non-Israelites.

23:21-23. vows. In the Decalogue is the commandment that no one should "misuse the name of the Lord" (Ex 20:7). When a vow using God's name is spoken, it brings God into contract with that person. Thus any failure to carry out the stipulations of the vow breaks the contract and subjects that person to divine wrath (see Judg 11:35-36). The instruction about vows contained in Deuteronomy is a wisdom statement similar in form to Ecclesiastes 5:4-7. It is designed as a caution against unwise speech and has many parallels in ancient Near Eastern wisdom literature. For instance, the seventh century B.C. *Assyrian *Instructions of *Ahiqar* notes that "a human word is a bird; once released it can never be recaptured." Similarly, the Egyptian *Admonitions of Amenemope* state that "to stop and think before you speak . . . is a quality pleasing to the gods" (c. 1100 B.C.). For more information on vows, see comments on Leviticus 27 and Numbers 30.

23:24-25. hand gleaning. Just as widows may glean in a ripe field or orchard to sustain themselves from the harvest provided by God, it is permissible for a traveler to refresh himself with a handful of fruit or grain, taken in passing from a field (see Deut 24:19-21). However, it is theft if a person purposefully harvests from a neighbor's field. The hospitality rights of travelers are also discussed in the Egyptian *Tale of the Eloquent Peasant* (c. 2100 B.C.).

24:1-22

Protection of Dignity

24:1-4. divorce. The basis for divorce in the

biblical text is the dissatisfaction of the husband with his wife (as in the *Middle Assyrian Laws). In that sense there must be clear grounds for the divorce (as in *Hammurabi and the *Middle Assyrian Laws). A "bill of divorcement" is drawn up specifying these particulars (see Jer 3:8), which, if it follows the manner of other legal proceedings, would be reviewed by a body of elders, and testimony would be given (as in Hammurabi's laws). For further information see the comment on Deuteronomy 22:29.

24:4. defilement. The very unusual form of the Hebrew verb used in verse 4 makes it clear that the woman in this case is the victim, not the guilty party. She has been forced to declare her uncleanness by the uncharitable actions of the first husband, and the second marriage demonstrates that another husband has been capable of accommodating whatever *impurity she was plagued with. The prohibition is aimed at preventing the first husband from marrying the woman again (in which case he might be able to realize some financial gain), whereas if the woman were impure the prohibition would be against her and would preclude a marriage relationship with anyone.

24:5. newlywed rule. This humanitarian law could be compared to the recruitment law in Deuteronomy 20:7. The latter exempts men who are betrothed from service, while this one specifically exempts the newly married man. In both cases the object is to give him time to father an heir and establish a household. However, the law in chapter 24 also concerns itself with the right of the individual to take pleasure in the joys of life before going to war.

24:6. millstone as necessary for survival. The millstone was made up of two stones, usually basalt. The lower millstone was heavy (sometimes nearly one hundred pounds), a flat or slightly curved stone upon which the grain was laid and then ground into flour with the upper, lighter stone (weighing four or five pounds), which was shaped to the hand of the worker. The poor, who could not buy processed grain from others, had to grind it themselves each day. If they were forced to give their millstone in pledge for a day's labor, they could be left without the means to feed themselves.

24:7. slave trade in ancient Near East. While slaves were bought and sold throughout the ancient Near East (see Gen 37:28-36), it was forbidden by law for persons to kidnap free citizens and sell them as slaves (compare Ex 21:16). Both the Deuteronomic law and *Hammurabi's laws condemned the kidnapper to death. In this way some restraint was placed

on slave traders adding to their stock by simply taking stray children or unlucky adults. The vast majority of persons who did end up on the slave block either were sold to the slavers by their own families or were prisoners of war.

24:8-9. leprosy. See the comments on the diagnosis of skin diseases by the priests in Leviticus 13:1-46. The Deuteronomic injunction simply reinforces the prerogatives and authority of the priests to determine whether a person had the skin condition (probably psoriasis or other skin disease, since Hansen's disease was unknown in the Near East until the Hellenistic period) and, when it was cured, to perform a purification *ritual.

24:10-15. regulations concerning a pledge. It was a common business practice in the ancient Near East for a person to "make a pledge" (i.e., offer as collateral) a portion of his property as a guarantee of paying off a debt or other financial obligation. For instance, the Code of *Hammurabi and *Hittite laws stipulate the pledging of land or planted fields. Hammurabi and *Middle Assyrian laws both deal with the legal rights of persons who have been taken in pledge for a debt. What is distinctive about the Deuteronomic law, as compared to the older version in the *covenant code (Ex 22:26-27), is its emphasis on protecting both the humanitarian rights and the personal honor of the debtor. Thus the creditor may not enter the debtor's house to take an object in pledge. Instead, the debtor's dignity is preserved by maintaining the sanctity of his personal dwelling and by giving him the opportunity to choose what will be offered. In this way the poor are treated on a par with all other Israelites.

24:16. family culpability. This legal concept of personal responsibility is cited in 2 Kings 14:6 as the basis for sparing the sons of condemned men. What is unclear is this principle's relationship to the concept of *corporate responsibility, evidenced in Deuteronomy 13:12-17 and 21:1-9. In the latter cases, the entire nation was expected to maintain their ritual purity by eliminating contaminating elements. If individual and corporate responsibility were coexisting legal ideas, then the instances where entire families were slain because of the sin of the father (Josh 7:24-26; 2 Sam 21:1-9; 2 Kings 9:26) would be viewed as cases of divine punishment rather than the actions of the civil legal system.

24:17-18. justice for the vulnerable. Once again the legal rights of the "protected classes" of society (widows, orphans, resident aliens) are listed (see Ex 22:21-24; Deut 26:12).

The basis for protecting and providing for these persons is God's compassion during the exodus event, as well as the *covenant promise of a fertile land. The theme of legal protection for the vulnerable is quite common in the ancient Near East (Ex 23:6), especially in wisdom literature. For example, in the Egyptian *Teachings of Amenemope* appears the admonition not to "steal from the poor, nor cheat the cripple . . . nor poach on the widow's field." Among the titles that the "Eloquent Peasant" of Egyptian literature uses for the local governor is "father of the orphan" and "husband of the widow," reminding him of his responsibilities to uphold the rights of the weak in society.

24:19-22. provision for the needy. Since the bounty of the harvest is a reflection of God's *covenant promise, it is only just that the owners of fields and orchards share a portion of their harvest (see comments on Ex 22:22-24 and Deut 23:24-25). Such a provision served several purposes. It insured that the entire community participated in the humanitarian efforts to sustain the poor (see Lev 23:22). The practice of leaving a portion of a field unharvested may also be tied into the regular fallowing of fields (Ex 23:10-11), which allowed the land to rest and regain its fertility. In the ancient Near East in general it is likely that what was left in the fields was originally associated with sacrificial offerings to local *fertility gods. By designating this produce for the poor, rather than local deities, the biblical writer both removes the taint of false worship and establishes a practical welfare system.

25:1-19
Individual Rights

25:1-3. punishments meted out by courts. In complex societies, when a legal dispute arises, it is necessary to take it to the judicial system. This system must include judges and a place for the hearing of testimony. On the village level this simply means drawing together the "elders" at the gate or threshing floor (see Deut 21:18-21; Ruth 4:1-12). In towns and cities, the judges were officials appointed by the government, who could hear appeals from village courts (Deut 17:9-10) or try cases within their own jurisdiction (2 Sam 15:3; Jer 26:10-19). Their responsibility included hearing testimony, making a judgment based on the law and officiating to insure that punishment was meted out exactly as the law decreed (in the *Middle Assyrian laws the judges are expected to observe the punishment).

25:2-3. limitation on number of lashes. Ancient Near Eastern law (*Middle Assyrian laws and *Hammurabi) stipulate that both men and women be flogged for various crimes. The number of lashes ranges from twenty to sixty. In Deuteronomy, however, forty lashes serves as the upper limit. This limit may be based on either the symbolic value of forty or the degree of mutilation and personal humiliation permissible for an Israelite to bear without being permanently excluded from social and religious activities.

25:4. role of oxen in grain processing. Oxen were used to plow fields and to pull threshing sleds to crush the stocks of grain once they were harvested. At the threshing floor, the grain would be laid in such a way that a heavy sled could be driven over it. The hooves of the oxen would also aid in the processing of the grain. The injunction that the ox not be muzzled follows the humanitarian pattern of previous laws and allows the animal to eat a portion of the grain as its wage. Since few farmers owned their own team of oxen, they were provided by government officials (observed in *Mari texts) or hired from wealthier farmers or even other villages (as in *Lipit-Ishtar laws and *Hammurabi, which include statutes regarding the hire and liability for oxen).

25:5-10. levirate marriage. For additional information on this practice, see the comment on Genesis 38:6-26. *Hittite law 193 and *Middle Assyrian law 33 have very similar legislation, though neither offers an explanation in terms of providing a family heir or of passing on property in an orderly fashion. Both of these concerns are referred to in Deuteronomy. Thus the law, although it is also designed to provide the widow with the security attendant upon marriage and having a son, is primarily focused on the rights of the deceased husband. The obligation owed to the deceased by his brother (defined best as nearest male kin) can be an economic hardship (see Ruth 4). Thus the second part of this law allows the levir to renounce his obligation publicly and thus, judging by the example in Ruth, presumably allow the widow to marry whomever she wishes. Even though the levir must submit to public humiliation and be labeled uncooperative, the financial factors involved might make it justifiable.

25:7-8. elders at town gate. Because of the constant traffic at the gate as people went to and from the fields, it became the place of judgment and business transaction in ancient Near Eastern towns. Merchants would set up collapsible booths or simply sit under an umbrella while their customers came to them (see Lot in Gen 19:1). When a legal matter came up, a group of the town elders either could be found sitting in the gate (Prov 31:23) or could be gathered from those passing by (Ruth 4:1-2).

25:9. removing sandal. Sandals were the ordinary footwear in the ancient Near East, but they were also a symbolic item of clothing, especially in the relationship between the widow and her legal guardian or levir. This is due to the fact that land was purchased based on whatever size triangle of land one could walk off in an hour, a day, a week or a month (1 Kings 21:16-17). Land was surveyed in triangles, and a benchmark was constructed of fieldstones to serve as a boundary marker (Deut 19:14). Since they walked on the land in sandals, the sandals became the movable title to that land. By removing the sandals of her guardian (Ruth 4:7), a widow removed his authorization to administer the land of her household.

25:11-12. law. There is a very close parallel to this law in the *Middle Assyrian code, in which the degree of physical punishment on the woman is dependent on whether one or both testicles are damaged. It would appear that punishment in the Deuteronomic law is based not on the degree of injury inflicted on the man's genitals but on the act of immodesty displayed by the woman. Her hand is severed because it is the offending appendage (see the comment on the laws of talion in Deuteronomy 19:21). Although she is attempting to help her husband, by grasping another man's genitals she has committed a sexual act that disonors her and her husband.

25:13-16. weights and measures standards. Commerce in a society without coined money is dependent on standard weights and measures. Examples of stone and metal weights, marked with specific symbols designating weight values, have been found in Egyptian tombs as well as at several sites in Israel and Mesopotamia (stylized lion-weights were found in eighth-century B.C. levels of Nimrud in *Assyria). The merchant who used a heavier weight to buy than to sell defrauded his suppliers and customers (see Prov 11:1; 20:23; Amos 8:5). Although this was condemned as an abhorrent practice, it was common enough in the ancient world. A good example is in the Egyptian *Tale of the Eloquent Peasant*, which accuses government officials and grain distributors of "shorting" the people.

25:17-19. Amalekites. See the comment on Numbers 24:20. The Amalekites wandered through vast stretches of land in the Negev, Transjordan and Sinai peninsula. They are unattested outside the Bible, and no archaeological remains can be positively linked to them. However, archaeological surveys of the region have turned up ample evidence of nomadic and seminomadic groups like the Amalekites during this period. Despite several attempts to eliminate the Amalekites (Ex 17:8-13; 1 Sam 15:2-3), they reappear as enemies of Israel on an alarming number of occasions (Judg 6:3; 1 Sam 30:1; 2 Sam 8:12; 1 Chron 4:43). Their refusal to aid the Israelites as they crossed Sinai functions, as it does here, as the basis for the original enmity, but subsequent disputes are probably based on territorial clashes and raiding of each others' villages.

26:1-18
First Fruits

26:1-15. first-fruit offering in ancient Near East. The religious principle involved in offering the "first fruits" (animal, vegetable or human) to the gods is based on the promotion of fertility. From earliest times the assumption was made that the gods created life in its various forms and that they expected to receive as their due offering the first of the harvest or the first fruit of the womb. Israelite religion tempered this by allowing for the redemption of some animals and all human firstborn males (Ex 13:11-13; Num 18:14-15). The giving of the first fruits could also take on a political character. The *Assyrian annals of Sennacherib (705-681 B.C.) contain his command that conquered peoples pay their first-fruit offerings of sheep, wine and dates to the gods of Assyria.

26:5. wandering Aramean. The creedal statement contained here emphasizes the nomadic character of Israel's ancestors. The original homeland of Abraham and his family is generally identified as Paddan Aram or Aram Naharaim (see comment on Gen 11:28). The mention of Arameans in relation to Abraham and Jacob is likely a reference to scattered tribes of peoples in upper Mesopotamia who had not yet coalesced into the nation of *Aram that appears in later texts. Based on other examples from *cuneiform literature, the name Aram may in fact have originally been that of a region (cf. Sippar-Amnantum of the *Old Babylonian period) that was later applied to people living there. For more on the Arameans see comment on Genesis 28:5.

26:8. mighty hand and outstretched arm as Egyptian metaphors. These two attributes of God also appear together in 4:34; 5:15; 7:19; 11:2; and 26:8, and in the prophetic literature (Jer 32:21; Ezek 20:33). Its origin may be found in Egyptian royal hymns and official correspondence. For example, in the fourteenth-century B.C. *Amarna letters, Abdi-Heba, the governor of Jerusalem, refers to "the strong arm of the king" as the basis for his government appointment. Similarly, the Eighteenth-Dynasty "Hymn to *Osiris" equates Osiris's growing to majority with the phrase "when his arm was strong," and Haremhab's "Hymn to *Thoth" describes the moon god as guiding the divine bark through the sky with "arms outstretched."

26:9. milk and honey. See comment on 6:3.

26:11. sharing with Levites and aliens. Once again the "protected classes" are listed, and the command is made to share a portion of the sacrificial offering with them. In the case of Levites and aliens, neither group is allowed to own land, and thus both are economically impaired (see 1:16; 12:18; 14:29; 16:11). Their receipt of aid is balanced in the case of the Levites by their service as priests and in the case of aliens by their itinerant labor service.

26:12-15. tithing in ancient Near East. See the comments on tithing in 14:22-29 and Numbers 18:31-32.

26:12. third year, year of the tithe. See comment on 14:29.

26:12-13. provision for the needy. The four categories of needy persons are the Levites, aliens, widows and orphans. Because they lack either land or the protection of a household, it becomes the obligation of the nation to provide food and legal protection to these vulnerable people (see 1:16). In this case, the form of support which they are to receive is the tithe in the third year. However, it may be presumed that additional provision was made throughout the year, every year, for them (see Ruth 2:2-18).

26:14. eating while mourning or unclean. This threefold litany of ritual purity and obedience, similar in form to Job's "oath of clearance" (Job 31), maintains that the offerer has not contaminated the sacred meal by being in an impure state. For example, persons who had come in contact with the dead were considered unclean (Lev 5:2). *Hittite *ritual for the preparation of the king's food and meal offerings for the gods included meticulous attention to physical cleanliness as well as the exclusion of ritually impure animals (dogs and pigs) and ritually unclean persons. The Deuteronomic statute may also be tied to ritual meals associated with the ancestor *cult or with Canaanite or Mesopotamian *fertility rituals (see women mourning for *Dumuzi/Tammuz in Ezek 8:14).

26:14. offerings for the dead. See the comments on Numbers 3 and Deuteronomy 14:1-2 on *rituals associated with the ancestor *cult.

In this case the assurance is given that the sacrificial meal has not been contaminated by unclean persons or polluting actions, such as giving a portion as an offering to the dead. This might include food provided for the spirit of a dead person, to strengthen it for its journey to Sheol (as seen in Tobit 4:17) or to learn something of the future (Deut 18:11). In addition, an association between eating "sacrifices offered to the dead" and the worship of the Canaanite god *Baal is made in Psalm 106:28. Either purpose would place reliance on powers other than *Yahweh, and both were therefore condemned by the biblical writer as polluting and leading to destruction.

27:1-8
Setting Up the Altar on Mount Ebal

27:2. monuments on stones coated with plaster. Ancient writing techniques included ink on papyrus (Egypt), a stylus on clay tablets (Mesopotamia), an inscribing tool on stone and a stick on wax-coated wooden boards. Engraving in stone could be very time-consuming, so one variation for longer inscriptions was to coat the stone surface with plaster and then write in the soft plaster. Inscriptions of this type have been found in the Palestine region at Deir Allah (see comment on Num 22:4-20) and Kuntillet Ajrud (see the comment on Asherah poles in 7:5).

27:4. Mount Ebal. Gerizim and Ebal are the mountains that flank the town of Shechem in the central hill country, Gerizim (elevation 2,849 feet) to the south, Ebal (3,077 feet) to the north. The altar spoken of here is actually constructed in Joshua 8. Some archaeologists believe that the remains of this altar have been found. It is a structure on one of the peaks of Mount Ebal about twenty-five by thirty feet with walls about five feet thick and nine feet high made of fieldstones. The fill is dirt and ashes, and what appears to be a ramp leads up to the top. The structure is surrounded by a courtyard, and animal bones litter the site. Pottery on the site goes back to 1200 B.C.

27:5. altar built with fieldstones; no iron tool. These instructions parallel those found in Exodus 20:25. Iron tools were used for dressing the stone—shaping it to make a sturdier structure. Altars of dressed stone have been found in Judah (the best example is at Beersheba). This altar was not supposed to be attached to a sanctuary, and perhaps the use of unhewn stone helped keep that distinction. There is a fieldstone altar in the court of the Arad fortress sanctuary dating from the monarchy period.

27:6-7. purpose of the altar. It appears that

this altar was not intended to be a permanent installation (another reason to use field-stones), but was set up for the purpose of the celebration ceremonies of this occasion. It is specifically fellowship offerings (see comment on Lev 3) that are offered here—no purification or reparation offerings.

27:8. law on monumental stones. *Hammurabi's laws were inscribed on a diorite stele eight feet tall and displayed publicly for all to see and consult. Royal inscriptions often were placed in prominent locations. Memorial inscriptions in our culture are used on tombstones, cornerstones of buildings and at various historical sites. The purpose in these cases is for people to see, take note and remember. Treaty documents in the Near East, in contrast, were often stationed in holy places that were not accessible to the public. Here the purpose was to put the agreement in writing before the gods in whose name the agreement had been sworn.

27:9-26
The Recitation of Covenant Curses

27:12. Mounts Gerizim and Ebal. See comment on 11:29.

27:15-26. curse recitation. The curses here are not statements of what will happen to the one breaking the *covenant but statements calling down unspecified curses on particular types of covenant-breaking conduct. This section constitutes a solemn oath entered into by the people concerning secret violations. Such oath-taking ceremonies regularly accompanied international treaties.

27:15. use of idols. See comment on 4:15-18.

27:16. dishonoring parents. Honoring and respecting parents consists of respecting their instruction in the *covenant. This assumes that a religious heritage is being passed on. The home is seen as an important and necessary link for the covenant instruction of each successive generation. Honor is given to parents as representatives of God's authority and is for the sake of covenant preservation. If parents are not heeded or their authority is repudiated, the covenant is in jeopardy. In this connection, notice that this commandment comes with covenant promise: living long in the land. In the ancient Near East it is not the religious heritage but the fabric of society that is threatened when there is no respect for parental authority and filial obligations are neglected. Violations would include striking parents, cursing parents, neglecting the care of elderly parents and failing to provide adequate burial. (See Ex 20:12.)

27:17. importance of boundary stones. See comment on 19:14.

27:19. justice for vulnerable classes. A major aspect of Israelite legal tradition involves making provision for groups classified as weak or poor: widows, orphans and the resident alien (see Ex 22:22; Deut 10:18-19; 24:17-21). Concern for the needy is evident in Mesopotamian legal collections as early as the mid-third millennium and generally addresses protection of rights and guarantee of justice in the courts.

27:20-23. incest and bestiality. Incest was abhorrent in most other societies as well (see, for example, the prohibitions in *Hittite laws). The exception is Egypt, where it was a common practice in the royal family (but little attested elsewhere) as a means to strengthen or consolidate royal authority. This concept is also seen among *Elamite kings. Bestiality was practiced in the context of *ritual or magic in the ancient Near East. It occurs in the mythology of *Ugarit (and was probably ritually imitated by the priests) and is banned in legal materials (especially the Hittite laws).

27:25. taking bribe to kill innocent. What is uncertain in this context is whether the curse concerns a payment made to an assassin (thus giving a variation on the previous verse) or a bribe made to a judge or witness in order to condemn an innocent man of a capital crime and thus have him executed (cf. 1 Kings 21:8-14). The temptation for judges and government officials to accept bribes is found in every time and place (see Prov 6:35; Mic 7:3). Taking bribes becomes almost institutionally accepted in bureaucratic situations as competing parties attempted to outmaneuver each other (see Mic 3:11; Ezra 4:4-5). However, at least on the ideal level, arguments and penalties are imposed to eliminate or at least lessen this problem. Thus *Hammurabi's code (law 5) places harsh penalties on any judge who alters one of his decisions (presumably because of a bribe), including stiff fines and permanent removal from the bench. Exodus 23:8 forbids the taking of bribes and the perversion of justice as an offense against God, the weak and innocent, and the entire community (see Is 5:23; Amos 5:12).

28:1-14
Covenant Blessings

28:2-11. ancient Near Eastern treaty curses and blessings. Curses and blessings are standard elements of the ancient treaties of the third, second and first millennia B.C., though they vary in specificity and proportion from one period to another. Since the treaty documents were confirmed by oath in the names of deities, the curses and blessings were usually those that were to be brought by the deities rather than by the parties to the treaty. Here that is of little difference because God is a party to the *covenant rather than simply the enforcer of it. Many of the curses found here are found in similar wording in the *Assyrian treaties of the seventh century B.C. Similarities can also be seen in the Atrahasis Epic, where, prior to sending the flood, the gods send various plagues on the land. These include the categories of disease, drought and famine, sale of family members into slavery, and cannibalism.

28:15-68

Covenant Curses

28:22. pathology in the ancient Near East. Affliction by various diseases is one of the curses found in *Assyrian treaty texts. Pathology in the ancient Near East was always considered in the light of supernatural cause and effect. Generally either hostile demons or gods angry at the violation of some taboo were considered responsible. "Wasting disease" probably included tuberculosis (rare in ancient Israel) as well as other diseases characterized by the same outward symptoms; verse 22 also includes categories of diseases characterized by fevers and inflammation; verse 27 describes a variety of skin diseases; and the symptoms of verse 28 are common with syphilis (in the ancient Near East generally the nonvenereal type). The categories of pathology can therefore be seen to be symptom related.

28:23. bronze sky, iron ground. An *Assyrian treaty curse from the seventh century B.C. (Esarhaddon) is very similar to this, not only using the analogies of bronze and iron but elaborating that there is no fertility in iron ground and no rain or dew comes from bronze skies.

28:25-29. devoured, infected, insane, plundered. Esarhaddon's treaties likewise include a series very similar to this and in nearly the same order. These, then, were typical ingredients of a curse section of a document such as this.

28:27. boils. Boils again represent a symptom, not a disease. The symptoms are not given in enough detail for specific diagnosis (guesses have included smallpox, chronic eczema, skin ulcers, syphilis and scurvy), but it is the symptom more than the disease that is the curse. This same symptom is the sixth plague in Egypt (Ex 9:8-11) and the affliction that tor-

mented Job (Job 2:7-8), as well as being named among the skin diseases in Leviticus 13 (vv. 18-23).

28:40. olives dropping off. The oil of the olive is derived only from the black, ripe fruit. Olive trees normally lose a large percentage of the potential fruit due to the blossoms or the green olives dropping off the tree. The small proportion left can be further depleted by drought or disease, causing heavier dropping off. This curse is not found in *Assyrian texts because sesame seed oil was used in Mesopotamia.

28:42. locusts. The Aramaic Sefire treaty has a seven-year locust curse included in its list. Locusts were all too common in the ancient Near East and were notorious for the devastation and havoc they brought. The locusts breed in the region of the Sudan. Their migration would strike in February or March and would follow the prevailing winds either to Egypt or Palestine. A locust will consume its own weight each day. Locust swarms have been known to cover as many as four hundred square miles, and even one square mile can teem with over one hundred million insects.

28:48. iron yoke. Yokes, usually made of wood, consisted of a bar across the nape of the animals' necks. The bar had pegs placed down through it on either side of each animal's head. The pegs were then tied together under the chin. The iron yoke would likely be one that featured iron pegs, the part most liable to break.

28:51. grain, new wine, oil as staple products. Besides being the three most significant staple products of the region, grain, new wine and oil represent the main produce of the three major harvesting seasons (grain in the spring-summer, grapes in the fall and olives in the winter). The oil referred to here is olive oil. It was also one of the principal exports of the region, since olives were not grown in either Egypt or Mesopotamia.

28:53. cannibalism. Cannibalism is a standard element of curses in *Assyrian treaties of the seventh century B.C. It was the last resort in times of impending starvation. This level of desperation could occur in times of severe famine (as illustrated in the Atrahasis Epic) or could be the result of siege, when the food supply had become depleted, as mentioned in this text and anticipated in the treaty texts. Siege warfare was common in the ancient world, so this was not as rare an occasion as might be presumed. An example of this drastic measure can be seen in the biblical record in 2 Kings 6:28-29.

28:56. touch the ground with the sole of her foot. The author is showing that the most genteel, refined woman imaginable, one who would not even dream of walking around barefoot, would be so desperate that she would begin cannibalizing her family.

28:58. book. We tend to think of a book as having pages, a binding and a cover. Books of that sort did not exist in the ancient world. The term used here can refer to any document from inscription to scroll, from papyrus to clay tablet to stone.

28:68. returning to Egypt in ships. *Assyrian kings of the seventh century coerced their vassals into supplying troops for their military campaigns. One way then for Israelites to return to Egypt in ships would be in the Assyrian campaigns launched from the Phoenician coast in which they were obliged to take part. This represents continued oppression by foreign enemies, as the curses have detailed. Another possibility would include falling victim to Egypt's slave trade in Syro-Palestine, where the slaves were often transported by ship.

29:1-29
Covenant Renewal

29:5. clothes and sandals not wearing out. See comment on 8:4.

29:6. no bread or wine. The Lord's provision for them instead of bread and wine was manna and water. The inclusion of strong drink here is unusual—the only individuals restricted from this were serving priests (Lev 10:9) and those under a *Nazirite vow (Num 6:3).

29:7. Sihon and Og. These battles are initially recorded in Numbers 21. Sihon is known only from the biblical records, and archaeology has little information to offer regarding his capital city or his kingdom. There is also no extrabiblical information from historical sources or archaeology to shed light on Og. For information about Heshbon and Bashan, see comments on Numbers 21:25-28, 33 and Deuteronomy 3:1.

29:19-21 the secret violator. The concept that one who keeps a violation secret will nevertheless be vulnerable to the curses is found in Aramaic (Sefire) and *Hittite treaties, where the curse includes the destruction of the violator's name (family).

29:23. land of salt and sulfur. Salt and Sulfur (sometimes translated "brimstone"; see Gen 19) are both minerals that are detrimental to the soil. They are the two most evident in the Dead Sea region known for its infertility and associated with the destruction of Sodom and Gomorrah.

29:24-25. reason identified for punishment. This same question and similar answer are found in an *Assyrian text of the seventh cen-

tury where the Assyrian king Assurbanipal describes his reasons for putting down an Arab revolt that had violated the terms of a treaty. The Arabs had broken the oaths they made before the Assyrian gods.

29:29. secret things. In the ancient world there were areas of knowledge that were believed to belong only to the gods. In a hymn to Gula, the craft of a physician is identified as a secret of the gods.

30:1-20
Response to Curses and Blessings

30:2-5. forgiveness clause. Unlike the treaties of the ancient Near East, the *covenant as represented in Deuteronomy has a forgiveness clause that offers second chances when the covenant has been violated. Repentance and recommitment to the terms of the covenant would result in restoration. Such mercy was not impossible with ancient treaties, but there is no example of such a possibility being explicitly included in the written document.

30:6. circumcise the heart. This is of course not asking for a physical surgical procedure. *Circumcision had been adopted as a sign of commitment to the *covenant and acceptance of its terms. As such it could be applied to the heart as a reflection that the outer *ritual had permeated the inner being.

30:19. heaven and earth as witness. See comment on 4:26.

31:1-8
Commissioning of Joshua as Moses' Successor

31:2. life expectancy in ancient Near East. In Egypt the ideal length of life was 110 years; in a wisdom text from *Emar in Syria it was 120. Examination of mummies has demonstrated that the average life expectancy in Egypt in this general period was between 40 and 50, though texts speak of some reaching 70 and 80. Mesopotamian texts of several different periods mention individuals who lived into their seventies and eighties, and the mother of the *Babylonian king Nabonidus was reported to have lived 104 years.

31:4. Sihon and Og. For details on these two kings and the battles against them, see comments on Numbers 21.

31:9-13
Instructions for the Reading of the Law

31:9. writing down laws. From the laws of

*Ur-Nammu (probably compiled in actuality by his son Shulgi) around 2000 B.C. through the laws of *Lipit-Ishtar, *Eshnunna and *Hammurabi and the *Hittite laws in the first half of the second millennium, to the *Middle Assyrian Laws toward the end of the second millennium, rulers made it a practice to compile laws and write them down as evidence that they were fulfilling their duty of maintaining justice.

31:10. reading the law every seven years. Several *Hittite treaties contain clauses requiring periodic public reading of the document—one stipulates three times a year, while others are less specific, saying "always and constantly."

31:10. year of canceling debts. The sabbatical year featured remission of debts. See comment on 15:1-6.

31:10. Feast of Tabernacles. The Feast of Tabernacles is the fall harvest feast that commemorates the wandering in the wilderness. See comment on 16:13-17.

31:14-29
Future Rebellion

31:15. pillar at the entrance of the tent of meeting. Prior to the construction of the tabernacle in Exodus, the tent of meeting was outside the camp and served as a place of revelation (see the comment on Ex 33:7-10). However, now that the tabernacle is in operation, it also is referred to as the tent of meeting. The Lord again appears in a pillar of cloud. In the ancient world a bright or flaming aura surrounding deity is the norm. In Egyptian literature it is depicted as the winged sun disk accompanied by storm clouds. *Akkadian uses the term *melammu* to describe this visible representation of the glory of deity, which in turn is enshrouded in smoke or cloud. It has been suggested that in Canaanite mythology the *melammu* concept is expressed by the word *anan*, the same Hebrew word here translated "cloud," but the occurrences are too few and obscure for confidence. See comment on Exodus 13:21-22.

31:22. covenant song. Songs of all sorts are known throughout the ancient Near East from the first half of the third millennium. One *Assyrian list of songs about a century before David includes titles of about 360 songs in dozens of different categories. Songs concerning the *covenant are also present in the book of Psalms (e.g., Ps 89).

31:26. contents of the ark. The only objects placed inside the ark were the tablets with the law on them (10:2, 5). In Egypt it was common for important documents that were confirmed

by oath (e.g., international treaties) to be deposited beneath the feet of the deity. The Book of the Dead even speaks of a formula written on a metal brick by the hand of the god being deposited beneath the feet of the god. There were a number of objects placed *before* the ark, including a jar of manna (Ex 16:33-34) and Aaron's rod that budded (Num 17:10). Here the book of the law is added to them.

32:1-43
The Covenant Song of Moses

31:30. covenant song. See comment on 31:22.

32:4. rock metaphor. Used in 2 Samuel 22:3 as a divine epithet, *rock* could also carry the meaning "mountain" or "fortress." It is used in Israelite names both as a metaphor for God (Zuriel, Num 3:35, "God is my Rock") and as a divine name (Pedahzur, Num 2:20, "Rock is my redeemer"). It is used of other deities in *Aramaic and *Amorite personal names, and its application to other gods is hinted at here in verses 31 and 37. As a metaphor it speaks of safety and deliverance.

32:8. Most High (Elyon). In the Old Testament the term *Elyon* is usually used as an epithet for *Yahweh (see comments on Gen 14:17-24). There is no convincing evidence thus far of *Elyon* as the name of a deity in the ancient Near East, but it is fairly common as an epithet for various gods, particularly *El and *Baal, the principal gods in the Canaanite pantheon.

32:8. deity granting nations inheritance. In Israelite theology *Yahweh had assigned each nation its inheritance (5:2, 9, 19; Amos 9:7), though there is also some accommodation to the concept that each god gave territory to his people (Judg 11:24). It was not uncommon for kings in the ancient Near East seeking expansion of territories to claim that deity had assigned or delivered land to them. In Israel the territorial assignment was uniquely based on a *covenantal bond with *Yahweh.

32:10. apple of the eye metaphor. "Apple" is the English idiom, not the Hebrew one. The pupil is referred to here as a sensitive, protected and significant part of the body.

32:11. eagle behavior. Though the eagle cannot be ruled out, the bird named here is more usually taken to be the griffin vulture, with a wingspan of eight to ten feet. While Bible reference books often report how the eagle carries its young on its wings when they grow weary of flying, or catches them on their wings when they are fluttering in failure, this behavior has been difficult for naturalists to confirm through observation. In fact most eagles and vultures do not take their first flight until three or four months of age, at which time they are nearly full grown. Furthermore, observations by naturalists have consistently confirmed that the first flight is usually taken while the parents are away from the nest. Alternatively, if the metaphor here concerns a vulture, it may be political in nature. In Egypt, Nekhbet was the vulture goddess who represented Upper Egypt and served as a protecting deity for Pharaoh and the land. Israel was protected in Egypt until Yahweh brought them to himself. Nekhbet was depicted as particularly maternal and was believed to assist at royal and divine births. Significant building of her temple in el-Kab (capital of third nome in Upper Egypt) took place in the Eighteenth Dynasty toward the end of the Israelite stay in Egypt, so we know that she was a popular goddess at that time. It is conceivable that the imagery of this verse was not drawn from actual observation of the behavior of vultures but from elements in the depiction of the vulture goddess, Nekhbet, whose characteristics are here transferred to *Yahweh (see v. 12, "no foreign god was with him"). The first half of the verse would then introduce the metaphor of the vulture that cares for and protects its young. The second half of the verse speaks of the Lord's care and protection of his people using the imagery that was familiar from Egyptian metaphors of care and protection. Additionally, in Mesopotamia the *Tale of Etana* includes an eagle that carries *Etana and then repeatedly lets him go and catches him on its wings. (See Ex 19:4.)

32:13. heights of the land metaphor. Cities were typically built on hills because of their natural defensibility, and armies chose hills as strategic points of control. The metaphor of treading on the heights therefore is one that speaks of victory and security.

32:13. source of honey and oil. While most honey spoken of in the Old Testament is the syrup from the date palm, mention of the rock here suggests bees' honey from honeycombs in the rocks. Olive trees, which were the main source of oil, were able to grow in rocky soil because they could thrive with minimal amounts of water.

32:14. rams of Bashan. The region of Bashan (see comment on Deut 3:1) was well known for its choice livestock. The prime grazing land of the area provided a natural diet that produced animals of the highest quality.

32:15. Jeshurun. The word *Jeshurun* is built from a root related to the one used in the name Israel, and it is a poetic way to refer to Israel.

32:17. sacrifice to demons. This word for demon is used elsewhere in the Old Testament only in Psalm 106:37, but it is a well-known type of spirit/demon *(shedu)* in Mesopotamia, where it describes a protective guardian mostly concerned with the individual's health and welfare. It is not the name of a deity, but a category of being (like *cherub* would be in the Old Testament). A *shedu* could destroy one's health just as easily as it could protect it, so sacrifices to keep it placated were advisable. They are depicted as winged creatures (similar to the cherub; see comments on Gen 3:24 and Ex 25:18-20), but they do not have idols (as the gods have idols) by which they are worshiped (see comment on Deut 4:28 for how this worked).

32:22. foundations of the mountains. In the ancient worldview the netherworld, the realm of the dead, was down beneath the earth where one found the foundations of the mountains, especially those mountains that were believed to support the dome of the heavens. Though the Israelites clearly use the language of this conceptual worldview, it is difficult to distinguish between beliefs and poetic usage.

32:23-25. divine punishment in the ancient Near East. Famine, disease, wild beasts, war —these are the tools of the gods when they desire to punish their human subjects. Throughout history and literature the apparent randomness of these "acts of God" led them to be considered signs of divine displeasure. Atrahasis and the *Gilgamesh Epic both contain accounts of the gods trying to reduce human population through these means prior to the flood. In contrast to the Old Testament, where the offenses are identified that would lead to these judgments, in the ancient Near East the judgments would indicate only that some deity was angry about something, leaving the people to figure out what offense might have been committed. Examples include the *Hittite prayer of Mursilis, where he prays that a plague might be abated, several *Sumerian and *Akkadian texts of lamentations over the fall of a major city, and Egyptian Wisdom Admonitions (Ipuwer). These all view various national calamities as the punishment of the gods. Perhaps the most striking example is the Erra Epic, in which civilization itself is threatened by the anarchy and havoc wreaked by the violence of Erra (the *Babylonian deity Nergal). The text of Deuteronomy 32, however, must also be understood in the context of its treaty form, where the punishments are not random, arbitrary or unexplained. Rather, they are commensurate with the violation of the terms of the agreement.

32:33. poisonous serpents. The allusions in the second half of verse 24 are generic, speaking of carnivorous or ferocious beasts on the one hand and creatures with poisonous bites or stings on the other. The latter are not limited to snakes, of which there were a few poisonous species around, but could also include scorpions.

32:38. food and drink of the gods. A common view of sacrifices in the ancient Near East was that they served as food and drink for the gods, who needed their sustenance (see comments on Lev 1:2). This view was rejected in the ideal Israelite worldview (see Ps 50:7-15), though many Israelites would have probably accepted the concept. This text is mocking the idea that gods who have needs would be adequate for deliverance.

32:39. no pantheon. Most religions of that day had a pantheon, a divine assembly that ruled the realm of the gods, the supernatural and, ultimately, the human world. There would typically be a deity who was designated head of the pantheon, and he, like the other gods, would have at least one consort (female partner). The first commandment forbids Israel to think in these terms. *Yahweh is not the head of a pantheon, and he does not have a consort—there are no gods in his presence. This verse goes further to insist that there is no other god exercising power or competing for jurisdiction and authority. Just as blessing and prosperity is not the result of a benevolent deity's managing to hold back demonic forces and chaos, so punishment is not the surge of malevolent power to overwhelm the protector. All happens within Yahweh's plan—an impossible concept in the pagan polytheism of the rest of the world.

32:44-52
Conclusion and Instructions to Moses

32:49. Abarim range and Mount Nebo. The Abarim range extends east of the mouth of the Jordan River and on around the northern end of the Dead Sea (see Deut 32:49). It forms the northwestern rim of the Moabite plateau. The specific peak in this range from which Moses will view the Promised Land is Mount Nebo, 2,740 feet in height. Pisgah and Nebo are identified as the two peaks of Jebel Shayhan, about five miles northwest of Medeba and about a mile and a half apart. They stand about ten miles from the Jordan River.

32:50. Mount Hor. The death site for Aaron (although 10:6 identifies his death with Mose-

roth). The traditional location is near Petra at Jebal Nabi Harun, but this is not "on the border of Edom." Another possibility is Jebal Madrah, west of Kadesh and near the Edomite border, but it lacks sufficient water sources.

32:51. Meribah Kadesh in the Desert of Zin. Kadesh Barnea is in the wilderness of Zin (see comment on Num 13:26). This is where the incident in Numbers 20 occurred when Moses struck the rock for water. Meribah means "quarreling," and it is a name applied to both instances when water was brought from the rock.

33:1-29
The Blessing on the Tribes

33:1. patriarchal pronouncements. In the biblical material the patriarchal pronouncement generally concerns the destiny of the sons with regard to fertility of the ground, fertility of the family and relationships between family members. Blessings or curses pronounced by the patriarch of the family were always taken seriously and considered binding, even though they were not presented as prophetic messages from God. They were usually given when the patriarch was on his deathbed. This chapter is most reminiscent of Genesis 49, when Jacob blessed his sons, the forefathers of the tribes Moses now blesses.

33:2. Seir. Seir is generally considered the mountainous central region of Edom (elevations generally over 5,000 feet) between Wadi al-Ghuwayr on the north and Ras en-Naqb on the south.

33:2. Mount Paran. Mount Paran is considered by most a poetic variation for Mount Sinai/Horeb.

33:5. Jeshurun. See comment on 32:15.

33:8. Thummim and Urim. These were devices used by the priests to give *oracular messages. See the comment on Exodus 28:30.

33:17. bull/ox metaphor. The bull and ox are symbols of fertility and strength. As such, the latter term is used as a title of *El, the head of the Canaanite pantheon. Both elements are included in this blessing on the Joseph tribes, Manasseh and Ephraim. One *Ugaritic text describes the gods *Baal and Mot as strong, goring like wild bulls, and the *Babylonian king *Hammurabi describes his own military might in terms of an ox goring the foe.

33:22. Bashan. The region of Bashan is centered in the area of the upper Yarmuk River, east of the Sea of Galilee. Its northern border is Mount Hermon. Dan's territory was originally in the south by the Philistine coast, but the

Danites moved north to the region of the city called Dan north of the Sea of Galilee and contiguous to Bashan.

33:24. bathing feet in oil. Washing feet was a constant need and an act of hospitality in the dusty terrain. Only the wealthy and genteel, however, would regularly make use of (olive) oil for the washing. Compare John 12:3. This metaphor speaks of prosperity.

33:25. bolts of the gates. The locking system on gates and doors usually included a bar (wood or metal) that slid into openings in the posts. Brackets that held the bar firmly to the doors are probably what is referred to by the "bolts" of this passage. The gate could be breached by applying a battering ram to the center where the doors met in order to break the bar. Brackets would make the bar much harder to break, but they in turn could break. Brackets of bronze or iron could make a gate much harder to break through.

34:1-12
The Death of Moses

34:1. Nebo and Pisgah. See comment on 32:49.
34:1-3. view from Mount Nebo. At this point the Mediterranean Sea is about sixty miles west, but it cannot be seen because the hills on the west side of the Jordan obscure the view. On a clear day one can see Mount Hermon, about a hundred miles to the north, the mountains to the northwest that flank the Jezreel Valley (Tabor and Gilboa), the mountains of the central hill country (Ebal and Gerizim)

and to the southwest as far as Engedi.

34:1-3. the boundaries of the land. Even though the land has not been distributed yet, this viewing of the land is described partially by tribal territories, to be distinguished from the geographical descriptions given in Deuteronomy 1:7. The description moves from Moses' point toward the north and then counterclockwise through the land.

34:6. Baal Peor. The Wadi Ayun Musa at the foot of Mount Nebo is generally considered to be the Valley of Beth Peor, with the site Khirbet Ayun Musa as probably the town.

34:7. apocryphal literature concerning the death of Moses. Jude 9 speaks of a dispute over the body of Moses, and apocryphal and rabbinic literature speculated about it in a number of places, particularly in *The Assumption of Moses* (of which manuscripts are no longer known) and *The Testament of Moses* (known from one Latin manuscript from the sixth century A.D.). The former speaks of Moses ascending directly to heaven, while in the latter it is implied that he dies a natural death. Deuteronomy makes it very clear that he died, and there is nothing remarkable in the account. The text leaves it somewhat ambiguous who buried Moses, but it is clear that the grave site is unmarked and unknown.

34:8. plains of Moab. This is the broad plain or steppe region immediately north of the Dead Sea and east of the Jordan River, just opposite the "plains of Jericho" (Josh 4:13). Its location serves as the jumping-off point for entrance into Canaan. (See Num 22:1.)

HISTORICAL LITERATURE

Introduction

We find a wealth of ancient Near Eastern material to illuminate the historical literature of the Old Testament—far more than for other genres of Old Testament literature. Among these ancient resources are items we may classify as royal inscriptions, chronographic texts and historical literary texts. *Royal inscriptions* preserve an account of the achievements of kings, particularly their military exploits and their building projects. *Chronographic texts* delineate a sequence of historical events ranging from simple lists of kings to court chronicles or military annals. *Historical literary texts* are mostly poetic, epic narratives that recount the experiences of kings. These texts are occasionally carved in stone (on cliff faces or on stone reliefs or statues) but are more often inscribed on clay tablets. Some chroniclers kept records on small rectangular shaped tablets, while others used large slabs or even barrel, cylinder or brick-shaped clay polygons.

If a record of events is to be preserved for future generations, it must at some point become part of a text. But writing that record as a text requires the compiler, whether consciously or subconsciously, to work under a set of guiding principles. We call this set of guiding principles *historiography*, and it will vary from culture to culture, even from historian to historian. How history writers feel about the appropriate form, content and structure for preserving a record of events contributes to this historiography, but these are only surface issues. What is important about the events of the past? Why is the account being compiled? How do events come to pass? What causes or forces drive history? Are there patterns in history? Is there design in history? The answers to these questions play a significant role in determining how history is written. It goes without saying that different individuals, different *cultures*, will answer such questions in different ways. Thus any given historical record represents a particular perspective about the events of the past. The shape of any given historiography is determined by the questions the compiler seeks to answer. We cannot legitimately speak of "right" perspectives or "wrong" perspectives concerning history. To do so would assume a commonly accepted absolute criterion. Perspectives, perceptions and feelings exist or do not exist. It is rarely a simple matter to label them right or wrong. In this light *any* historiography should be referred to as "perspectives on history." Any historiography must in some sense be viewed as an editorial column.

When we study historiography, we must discover what purposes authors have in writing their documents. Otherwise we will not know how to use their work as we reconstruct the history of a period. It is important not to assume that their ideas of writing history were the same as current western ideas. When history is written in Western culture, it is often understood to be history for history's sake (even though that is sometimes not the case). One of the values of contemporary society is the belief that it is essential to record, evaluate and thereby preserve the events of the past—just for the record. Along with that comes a desire to reconstruct "what really happened" and to identify cause and effect.

In most ancient historiography "what really happened" appears to be far less important. A large majority of the documents that supply us with historical information are generated through the sponsorship of the royal house. These documents are designed to serve the king, not the objective interests of the historian. Royal reputation is a far greater value than reliability. Our modern terminology calls this propaganda. The historiography of the ancient Near East, whether represented in royal inscriptions or chronicles, king lists or annals, has by all accounts a propagandistic agenda. As with campaign speeches of our day, truth can be useful to the royal house, but it is not its prime objective. Propaganda is greatly enhanced when it has truth in its favor; but if it only has statistics or other random "facts" it will make do. The perspective on truth that these texts take will present the king in the best light. The recorder is trying to provide answers to the question "Why should the king be considered good and successful?" In most cases it cannot be determined whether concealment or disinformation are part of the strategy, but negative information is uniformly lacking. When accounts of a particular battle are available from both sides, it is not odd for each to claim victory. It was common practice for a king to alter inscriptions by putting his own name in place of his predecessor's (even if it was his father). An ancient king would rarely admit to a defeat, and negative assessments of a reign come rather from later kings who may be seeking only to legitimate their own rule. Historiography among ancient cultures was largely a self-serving enterprise.

Israel's historical literature has features similar to chronographic texts and contains a few isolated examples that can be compared to royal inscriptions or historical literary texts. But the purpose of Israel's literature is theological. It is selective, as all historical writing must be, and it has an agenda. It is not interested in preserving events for history's sake. Its purpose is to document Yahweh's action in history and his control of the flow of events. In these documents the nation is more important than the king, and God is the main focus. Israel's identity and function as Yahweh's covenant people is the backbone of the entire historical corpus. Thus we could say that whereas the objective of much of ancient historiography is to offer the desired understanding of the accomplishments of the king, the objective of Israelite historiography is to offer the desired understanding of the accomplishments of God.

It is also important to realize that the ancient world had a different view of deity's role in history than is common in Western culture. Until the Enlightenment it was common for a person's worldview to be thoroughly supernaturalistic. The role of deity was admitted, and the belief in occurrences that defied natural explanation was commonplace. With the Enlightenment a significant shift occurred. The resulting historical-critical method suggested that we should accept as true only that which can be empirically proven. The new historiography was concerned only with natural cause and effect in history. This is largely the view adopted by our contemporary Western culture.

The worldview of society around us thus differs dramatically from the worldview of the ancient historians. The way in which history is written today would seem quite foreign to ancient authors. The simple recital of facts and events would be meaningless to them unless the information was put to some use. While the ancients would not deny the existence of natural cause and effect in history, they were much more interested in the divine role in history. A modern historian's response to Israelite historiography might be "it has not provided information that is reliable"; the Israelite historian's response to modern historiography might be "it has not provided information that is worthwhile."

When we study the historiography of a pre-Enlightenment culture, then, it is important to recognize the worldview that drives that historiography and to respect the integrity of it. The worldview represented in Israel's historiography is one in which the directive activity of God is of primary importance. This view extends far beyond the recognition of occasional supernatural interventions to see God's activity in natural occurrences as well. In fact, it insists that all events are woven into the plan of God, which is the driving force of history.

Israel's historiography holds much in common with neighboring ancient cultures. Historical records in Mesopotamia, while not claiming to be revelation from deity, nonetheless show great interest in discerning the activities of the gods. The polytheistic nature of Mesopotamian religion, however, impedes the development of any concept of a singular divine plan encompassing all of history. At best the reigning dynasty may identify a divine plan in establishing and sustaining that dynasty. Some documents look back into the distant past to see a pattern that led to the present (e.g., the Weidner and the Akitu Chronicles). These typically concern not what the deity has done but what has been done to the deity. In Mesopotamia it is assumed that deity plays an active part in the cause and effect process that makes up history. The gods are capable of intervention and are expected to intervene. The causation of the gods and the intervention of the gods are understood to be ad hoc rather than in accordance with any overarching plan or grand design. As in the Mesopotamian view, Israel counted God as the cause of every effect and as actively intervening to shape events. Israel's record of history was not intended to be a record of events but a record of the ways in which God had acted in history. There is no secular Israelite historiography.

In the supernaturalistic view of the ancient world, events were revelation, the result of divine activity. Unfortunately, those events required interpretation to discern why the gods were doing what they did. Such interpretation was not provided in the polytheistic cultures surrounding Israel. Mesopotamians were left to their own devices to discern what the gods were up to. In Israel's view, not only events but historiography was revelation. That is, God took it upon himself not only to act but to provide an interpretation of his acts, communicating why they were done and what purposes they served. In this way Yahweh was both the cause of the events and the source of the interpretation of the events. In theological terms we would say that the general revelation of history was supplemented by the special revelation of historiography.

In summary then, Israel shared with the ancient world the idea that events are revelation—the evidence that the gods were at work. This approach stands in contrast to Western historiography. But Israel distinctively believed that its historiography was also revelation, a novel view in contrast to both modern and other ancient historiography.

JOSHUA

1:1-18

Joshua's Commission

1:4. territory of the promised land. The "wilderness" circumscribes the southern and eastern boundaries of the land. The Lebanon and the Euphrates are the northern boundaries on both east and west. The Euphrates in similar descriptions of the boundaries of the land (see comment on Deut 1:7) refers to the area where the river turns north in the region of Emar. The Great Sea, the Mediterranean, marks the western boundary. The Hittite country most likely refers to Syria, where many Hittite groups settled after the fall of the Hittite empire about 1200 B.C.

1:8. Book of the Law. We tend to think of a book as having pages, a binding and a cover. Books of that sort did not exist in the ancient world. The term used here can refer to any document: from inscription to scroll, from papyrus to clay tablet to stone. The Book of the Law is the copy of instructions given to Moses in Deuteronomy and put in front of the ark (see comment on Deut 31:26).

1:16-18. pledge of loyalty. In international relations as they are known from the documents of the ancient Near East, when a new king came to the throne, vassals of the previous king were asked to subscribe to loyalty oaths professing their allegiance to the new king. This practice is attested between the pharaohs of Egypt and the city-state kings of Palestine during this period.

2:1-24

Spies in Jericho

2:1. Shittim. The full name of this site was Abel Shittim (Num 33:49), and it was the jumping-off point for Joshua's spies and for the Israelites' entrance into Canaan (Josh 2:1; 3:1; Mic 6:5). Josephus places it seven miles from the Jordan River. Its actual location is uncertain, but it may be Tell el-Hammam on the Wadi Kefrein.

2:1. Jericho. Jericho is located by an oasis (er-Riha) about five miles west of the Jordan River along the Wadi Kelt and six miles north of the Dead Sea. It guards the strategic passageway between the Jordan valley and the central hill country to the west (including Jerusalem, about fifteen miles west-southwest, and Bethel, about the same distance

west-northwest), as well as the major ford between the Jabbok and the Dead Sea. Though it averages only four to six inches of rain per year, Jericho is supplied with ample water from the spring system today called Ain es Sultan. The tell of the ancient city is Tell es Sultan. It is 825 feet below sea level, the lowest city in the world. The oblong-shaped mound covers an area of about ten acres, with a circumference of about half a mile. A city of that size would have housed perhaps as many as two thousand people, though more would have lived in surrounding farms and villages. See comment on 6:1 for archaeological information.

2:2. spies in the ancient Near East. Spies in the ancient Near East regularly collected information about enemy movements and troop sizes. It would not be unusual for spies to infiltrate the enemy forces by posing as deserters or refugees. In reconnoitering a city they would be interested in defenses, food and water supply, number of fighting men and general preparedness for attack or siege. Most important was to find out what they could about the source of the water supply. If that could be cut off or compromised, a siege would have a much better chance of success.

2:3. city-state kings. Canaan at this time was not a unified political entity. Instead it was made up of many small "kingdoms"—city-states, usually including a major fortified city plus the small villages and farms in the region. Each such city-state would have its own king and its own army. The Amarna letters from the fourteenth century are the correspondence between many such Canaanite city-states and the Egyptian pharaoh of whom they were vassals.

2:5. closing city gate at dusk. Closing the city gate at dusk was not an unusual practice for walled towns, but it was much more rigorously observed when an enemy was at hand. Hittite records speak of the diligence with which this was undertaken. The highest ranking officials in the town personally supervised the locking and sealing of the gate. Since the gates were massive structures with chambers between the several entrances, watchmen and even officers slept right by the gate.

2:6. house architecture. The typical Israelite house known mostly from 1200 on is called a four-room house. It was a rough stone or baked brick structure about thirty feet square.

It had an open courtyard surrounded by rooms (sometimes two stories) with a flat roof. Less is known about the earlier Canaanite houses, though they still featured an open courtyard with rooms arranged around it. Outside walls would be made of larger stones piled up (sometimes only one row thick, other times several feet thick) with smaller stones stuck in the cracks. The wall was usually coated on the outside with mud and on the inside with plaster. Doors were wooden and turned on a stone socket beneath the ground. There were often no windows. The rooms were usually separated from the courtyard by a row of wooden or stone pillars, perhaps with curtains hung as dividers. The roof would be made of wooden beams laid across the walls, covered with twigs and straw and coated with clay. The dirt floors were sometimes coated with plaster, though stone slabs would be put down in the kitchen area.

2:6. stalks of flax. Flax is a plant used for making linen. Young plants are used for high quality cloth and ripe, tougher plants for sturdy material such as rope. Although there is reference to the cultivating of flax in the Gezer calendar, much of it was imported from Egypt. The harvested plants need to be laid out to dry before "retting," a process involving soaking in stagnant water to separate the usable fibers. The stalks must then be laid out to dry thoroughly before the process can continue. The smell and the sogginess would have made hiding here a distinctly unpleasant experience, perhaps equivalent to burying oneself in a pile of pig slops.

2:7. fords of the Jordan. Without bridges, the places where a river could be forded served as strategic locations. From the southern end of the Sea of Galilee to the Yarmuk River, the Jordan is not easily fordable. From the Yarmuk south to the Wadi Jalud (Herod Stream) are a number of fording places, especially from the region of Beth Shan coming out of the Jezreel Valley across into Gilead. South of this area the mountains come up closer to the rift valley until the confluence with the Jabbok, with the fords at Adam just below it. The terrain then becomes difficult on either side of the Jordan until one reaches the fords by Jericho nearly twenty miles further south.

2:10. Sihon and Og. There is no historical information on Sihon and Og outside the Bible. They are the two Amorite kings who were defeated by the Israelites in Transjordan. For more information see the comments on Numbers 21:21-35.

2:11. Rahab's Confession. Rahab expresses fear of Israel's God, Yahweh, and acknowl-edges him as God in heaven and on earth. In the context of ancient Near Eastern religious thought, this places Yahweh in the category of cosmic deity and recognizes him as a powerful national patron god. The report the Canaanites have heard suggests that he can influence the weather as well as bodies of water, disease and the animal world. Though her confession expresses how impressed they all are with the range of Yahweh's authority and power, it is far from an expression of monotheism. She has neither renounced her gods nor offered to dispose of them. She has not affirmed any loyalty to Yahweh but has requested his help. She shows no knowledge of the obligations of the law, and we have no reason to think she is aware of the revolutionary religious system that was developing in Israel. In short, her speech does not suggest that she has risen much above her polytheistic perspective—but she knows power when she sees it. The dread of a deity as a divine warrior was often believed to precede a powerful, successful army into battle. Egyptian texts attribute this terror to Amun-Re in the inscriptions of Thutmose III, and Hittite, Assyrian and Babylonian texts all have their divine warriors who strike terror into the hearts of the enemy.

2:15. houses on the wall. Houses built into the side of the city wall were common to this period. This benefited the city by adding extra width and support for the wall and benefited the resident by providing a firm wall to support the house. Excavations at Jericho have discovered houses built on the plaster rampart between the two walls with their backs up against the inside of the outer wall (see comment on 6:1).

3:1—4:24

Crossing Jordan

3:1. Shittim. See comment on 2:1.

3:4. two thousand cubits. Two thousand cubits is a little over half a mile.

3:10. the inhabitants of the land. The list here is similar to that occurring frequently in the Pentateuch. In the list of the seven people groups that inhabited Canaan three are well known, while the other four are barely known at all. Canaan may be mentioned as early as the Ebla tablets (twenty-fourth century), but the earliest certain reference is in the material from Mari (eighteenth century). The *Canaanite* people were the principal inhabitants of the fortified cities of the land, though they do not seem to have been native to the land. The kings of this area refer to themselves in the Amarna Letters (mid-second millennium) as

Kinahhu, equivalent to a term *(Kinanu)* also used in Egyptian inscriptions of this period. The well-known *Hittites* were from Anatolia, modern Turkey, but groups occupying sections of Syria and Canaan were also called Hittites and may or may not be related. The Hittites in Canaan have Semitic names, while the Hittites of Anatolia were Indo-European. The *Hivites* are sometimes connected to the Horites, in which case they may be Hurrians. There is still debate as to whether the term *Perizzites* is ethnic or sociological (those living in unwalled settlements). *Girgashites* are little known, though they are attested in the Ugaritic texts. *Amorites* (known in Mesopotamia as *Amurru* or *Martu)* are known from written documents as early as the middle third millennium. Most scholars think that they had roots in Syria and came to occupy many areas in the Near East. The term can be used to refer to a geographical area ("westerners") or to ethnic groups, though not necessarily related to one another. Some Amorites were nomadic, but there were Amorite city states in Syria as early as the end of the third millennium. The *Jebusites* occupied the region later associated with the tribe of Benjamin, notably the city of Jerusalem, and are often related to the Perizzites, who were located in the same region. There is no mention of the Perizzites, Hivites or Jebusites outside the Bible.

3:16 parting of the Jordan. This is springtime (see 4:19), and the melting snow from the Anti-Lebanon mountains often creates a flood stage for the Jordan. Mudslides as a result of flood waters undercutting the cliffs or from seismic activity occasionally interfere with the flow of the Jordan at the very place mentioned here in the text (once as recently as 1927). Those recorded have generally blocked the Jordan for a couple of days.

3:16. Adam in Zarethan. Adam is modern Damiya on the east side of the Jordan just south of where the Jabbok River flows, eighteen miles north of the fords at Jericho. The steep banks of the Jordan are particularly susceptible to mudslides because of the large amount of water flowing together here from the two rivers. Zarethan is often identified either with Tell es-Sa'idiyeh, about twelve miles further north, or with Tell Umm Hamad on the north side of the Jabbok.

3:17. on dry ground. There is an interesting inscription of Sargon II of Assyria (eighth century) where he claims that he led his army across the Tigris and Euphrates at flood stage as on dry ground.

3:17. the role of the ark. In the divine warrior motif, the deity is fighting the battles and defeating the deities of the enemy. In Assyria Nergal is the king of battle and Ishtar is viewed as a war goddess. The Canaanite Baal and the Babylonian Marduk are divine warriors. This is not to be viewed as "holy war," because in the ancient Near East there was no other kind of war. In most situations prayers would be made and omens asked to assure the god's presence. Standards or statues of the deity were usually carried to symbolize their presence. The ark, as Yahweh's standard, represents the Lord as clearing the way before the Israelites and leading the armies into Canaan. This concept is not very different from the Assyrian belief that the gods empowered the weapons of the king and fought before him or at his side.

4:13. forty thousand men. The word translated "thousand" can sometimes refer to a military division. The latter may be intended here, though it is a complex issue. For more information see the comment on Exodus 12:37. Compare this number to the estimated population of Jericho, fifteen hundred or two thousand.

4:13. the plains of Jericho. Jericho is about five miles from the Jordan, and there is a broad flat area across the entire region between.

4:18. return to flood stage. If the stoppage was caused by a mudslide up river, a tremendous amount of water would have backed up, and when the blockage was broken up by the force of the water, the renewed flow would have been considerable.

4:19. tenth day of first month. The last chronological notation we had was in Deuteronomy 1:3, the first day of the eleventh month of the fortieth year. After that address Moses went up to the mount and died (Deut 32:48), and then the people mourned for thirty days (Deut 34:8). We would assume that it is now the first month of the forty-first year, just two months after the death of Moses. The first month is Nisan (spanning March-April), time for the Passover celebration. It is a good time for military activity because the invading troops can be sustained from crops in the field. If the early date for the exodus is accepted (see date of the exodus sidebar in Exodus 12), the date is right around 1400 B.C. If the later date of the exodus is correct, it is around 1240.

4:19. Gilgal. The site of Gilgal is currently unidentified. Some guesses put it to the northeast of Jericho near Khirbet Mefjir, where there is a decent water supply, a significant outcrop of flint (see 5:2) and remains from ancient times (but only after 1200). Another biblical Gilgal has been identified with Khirbet ed-Dawwara, located in the middle of a circle circumscribed around Jericho, Ai, Gibeon and Jerusalem, no more than six miles from any of them. But this is not considered a likely site for this Gilgal.

5:1-12
Circumcision and Passover

5:1. Amorite and Canaanite Kings. The region at this time was comprised of many small city-states, each with their own king, army and territory. Amorites occupied the hill country, while Canaanites were in the coastal plains. The Canaanite cities were more strategically located, since the major trade route from Egypt came up the coast (for more information on the trade routes see sidebar on page 69). The Israelites were much more successful gaining control of the hill country than they were the plains. The Amarna letters give us a good deal of information about the city-states of Canaan in the fourteenth century. In many of these letters the kings are appealing to Egypt to send more troops to help them against the Apiru/Habiru who are stirring up trouble. *Habiru* is a term used to describe dispossessed peoples in over 250 texts spanning the second millennium and ranging from Egypt to Anatolia to east of the Tigris. Certainly the Israelites (Hebrews) would have been counted among the Habiru. The most prominent kings in the region of Palestine from the Amarna archives are Milkilu (Gezer), Abdi-Heba (Jerusalem), Lab'ayu (Shechem) and Abdi-Tirshi (Hazor). The Egyptians had a number of administrative cities, including Gaza and Joppa on the coast and Beth Shan where the Valley of Jezreel (and the trade

route) goes to the Jordan.

5:2. flint knives. The earliest tools and weapons known from the Stone Age were flakes of stone produced by striking flint at the proper angles. The edges of these flakes were extremely sharp, easily accessible and reasonably durable. A flint flake was used for the process of circumcision in Israel and Egypt even after metal tools and weapons were readily available. The use of stone blades may reflect either a long tradition that precedes the ready availability of metal blades or simply the need for many blades at once. It has been suggested that the text refers to obsidian, which was valued for the smooth sharp edges it afforded.

5:2. circumcision. Circumcision was practiced widely in the ancient Near East as a rite of puberty, fertility or marriage. Egyptian reliefs from as early as the third millennium depict the circumcision of adolescents by priests using flint knives. Although the Israelites are not the only people in the ancient Near East to circumcise their sons, it is used to mark them as members of the covenantal community. When used in relation to marriage, terminology suggests it was performed by the new male in-laws, indicating that the groom was coming under the protection of their family in this new relationship. Performed on infants it is more a ritual scarring than something done for health reasons. The fact that blood is shed also signifies that this is a sacrificial ritual and may function as a substitution for the human sacrifice that was practiced by other people. Circumcision can be seen as one of many cases where God transforms a common practice to a new (though not necessarily unrelated) purpose in

---

EGYPTIAN INFORMATION ABOUT CANAAN AND ISRAEL

From the rise of the eighteenth dynasty in the mid-sixteenth century B.C., the Egyptians established a foothold in Canaan that waxed and waned over four centuries. Military expeditions were common, and in some periods Egyptian presence was established in terms of garrisons at critical points along the trade routes. During the reign of Thutmose III (fifteenth century), Syria-Palestine became an Egyptian province. After a period of decline in the Amarna period (fourteenth century), the early part of the nineteenth dynasty (early thirteenth century) brought renewed military activity, with Canaan secured as a base of operations against the Hittites in a struggle for the control of Syria. Aside from the Amarna texts, which provide invaluable information about the political situation in Canaan and the significant role of Egypt in the region, Egyptian records have provided other pieces of information that contribute to this period. (1) Itineraries from Egyptian campaigns often make reference to cities that the Bible also mentions. Thutmose III lists over one hundred cities of Canaan. Sometimes these itineraries can help locate a city because it will identify the cities on either side of it. In addition, there are some cities for which excavations show no occupation for this period, but the Egyptian itineraries name them so we know they were occupied. (2) Egyptian reliefs from the thirteenth century depict Canaanite fortresses and fortified cities of the same sort that must have been encountered by Joshua. (3) The famous victory stele of Merenptah (second half of thirteenth century B.C.) is the earliest reference to Israel in extrabiblical sources. Discovered in 1896, the black granite monument, standing seven and a half feet tall, details the campaigns of the pharaoh against the Libyans and Sea Peoples. It then mentions victories over Ashkelon, Gezer, Yanoam and Israel as part of the plundering of Canaan. One Egyptologist (F. Yurco) has suggested that these campaigns of Merneptah are also engraved on the walls at Karnak. If he is correct, this would constitute the earliest depiction of Israelites.

revealing himself and relating to his people.

5:2. "again." One might well wonder how an individual could be circumcised again. This could refer to initiating the rite of circumcision a second time (see v. 5) or to a more radical surgical procedure. Egyptian circumcision involved only a dorsal incision rather than a total removal of the foreskin. Verses 5-8 argue against this latter explanation.

5:3. Gibeath Haaraloth. Gibeath Haaroloth means "hill of foreskins." If this is meant to refer to a place name, its location is unknown.

5:6. milk and honey. The land of Canaan is described as a land "flowing with milk and honey." This refers to the bounty of the land for a pastoral lifestyle but not necessarily for agriculture. Milk is the product of goat herds, while honey represents a natural resource, probably the syrup of the date rather than bees' honey. A similar expression to this is found in the Ugaritic epic of Ba'al and Mot, which describes the return of fertility to the land in terms of the wadis flowing with honey. Egyptian texts as early as the Story of Sinuhe describe the land of Canaan as rich in natural resources as well as in cultivated produce.

5:10. Passover. Passover celebrated the deliverance from Egypt and also may have represented a purification ceremony in preparation for the conquest. See comments on Exodus 12:1-11.

5:12. manna. For a full discussion of Manna see comment on Exodus 16:4-9. The fact that manna has been provided through all the different terrains that Israel has passed through suggests something far different from what the various natural explanations can provide.

5:13—6:27
The Conquest of Jericho

5:13. commander. The supernatural commander that Joshua encounters is another indication that Yahweh has taken charge and is going to be responsible for their military success. Just as Moses had an encounter at the burning bush that communicated God's plan for the exodus, so Joshua's encounter is providing God's plan for the conquest. The message brought by the commander includes the strategy for Jericho (reported beginning in 6:2). In the ancient Near East war was usually presented as originating from divine instructions and following a divine plan. Divine visitations on the eve of battle are not common in ancient Near Eastern literature. The divine word commanding the battle comes instead in the form of an oracle, while the divine presence is seen in the battle itself. In the Ugaritic Epic of Keret, however, the god El comes to

King Keret in a dream with instructions for battle. Another closer parallel is when the Babylonian king Samsuiluna (eighteenth century B.C.) receives supernatural messengers from Enlil giving him instructions for a number of campaigns against Larsa and Eshnunna. Neither of these, however, are on the eve of battle—the armies have yet to be mustered.

6:1. Jericho. Settlement at Jericho goes back to the ninth millennium B.C., giving it the designation of the oldest city in the world. The site has occasioned much controversy, and archaeological interpretation has been complicated by significant amounts of erosion, which tends to confuse the layers that archaeologists depend on and totally obliterate large amounts of evidence. Excavations by Kenyon in the 1950s concluded that city 4 was violently destroyed (signs of earthquake and fire) about 1550 (at the end of the Middle Bronze period) and was then only sparsely and occasionally occupied until the ninth century. This poses a problem for both the late and the early date of the exodus and conquest. Most significant was the absence of Late Bronze imported Cypriote pottery. It has been argued, however, that there are many pottery samples of local ware from the Late Bronze period (1550-1200). There are still many unanswered questions about the archaeology of the site. City 4 was surrounded by a stone revetment wall (about fifteen feet high and topped by a mudbrick wall at least another eight feet high) supporting a plastered rampart that sloped up about fifteen feet to a second, upper wall also made of mudbrick. If city 4 is not the city overthrown at the time of Joshua, it is nonetheless likely that the walls of city 4 were still being used. There were houses built on top of the plaster rampart between the two walls. The city is not mentioned in the Amarna texts or in the Egyptian itineraries of the period. See comment on 2:1 for geographical information.

6:3-4. seven days marching in silence. In the Ugaritic Epic of Keret (which would likely have been known to the people of Jericho) Keret's army arrives at the city of Udm and is instructed by the god El to stay quiet for six days and to shoot no weapons, and on the seventh day the city would send out messengers and offer tribute if they would leave.

6:4. the role of the priests. The priests are necessary in order to maintain the sanctity of the ark. The importance of their lead role is to offer one more reminder that this is Yahweh's battle, not the Israelites'. For the ark's symbolism see the comment on 3:17.

6:4-5. trumpet signals. The trumpet referred to here is the rams' horn (*shofar*). The *shofar* is capable of a variety of tones but cannot play a tune, so it is used primarily for signals in worship or warfare. The ram's horn was softened in hot water, then bent and flattened to produce its distinctive shape. In warfare signaling was done in various ways. Fire signals were common both along garrison lines as well as in the open field. Basic commands were at times communicated by upraised staff or javelin. Trumpet signals are attested in Egypt in the Late Bronze Age (this time period) in both military and religious contexts. A preset code would include some combination of long and short blasts.

6:20. city walls. The fortification techniques developed in the Middle Bronze period and continuing in use in the Late Bronze included steep earthen slopes (some reaching fifty feet) at the foundation of the walls and a ditch around the outside dug to bedrock. These features would both hamper the approach of siege machines and prevent tunneling. The walls, made of mudbrick on stone foundations, were ten to twenty-five feet wide and perhaps thirty feet high. Hittite texts preserve an account where in similar fashion a deity carried out retributive justice by causing walls (wooden in this case) to fall down.

6:21-24. devoted to the Lord (ḥerem). The "ban" is sometimes chosen as the English word to represent the concept of total destruction that is commanded here in verse 2 and elaborated in verses 5-6. Just as there were some types of sacrifices that belonged entirely to the Lord while others were shared by priest and offerer, so some plunder was set aside as belonging solely to the Lord. Just as the whole burnt offering was entirely consumed on the altar, so the ban mandated total destruction. Since the warfare was commanded by Yahweh and represented his judgment on the Canaanites, the Israelites were on a divine mission with Yahweh as their commander. Since it was his war, not theirs, and he was the victor, the spoil belonged to him. Although the divine warrior motif occurs throughout the ancient Near East, the ḥerem concept is more limited—the only other occurrence of the term is in the Moabite Mesha inscription, but the idea of total destruction is also in the Hittite material. Some sites, such as Gezer, feature a distinct burn layer in association with the Late Bronze period. Under siege conditions sanitation is at its worst and disease is often rampant. The practice of burning everything after the defeat of a city thus also had an element of health connected to it. The best analogy for us to understand ḥerem is to think in terms of radiation. A nuclear explosion would destroy many things and irradiate much more. The abhorrence and caution with which we would respond to that which has been irradiated is similar to what is expected of the Israelites regarding things under the ban. If radiation were personified, one could understand that once something was given over to it, it was irredeemable. It was this condition that Achan exposed himself to by taking things under the ban.

6:21. the edge of the sword. The expression used in the Bible referring to the "mouth" or "edge" of the sword reflects the fact that at this time period swords were not straight with two edges. The blade was straight coming out of the haft, but the sharp edge was along the outer side of a curved, sickle-shaped section. This was not a stabbing but a striking weapon.

6:26. curse on rebuilding. Assyrian inscriptions commonly express an intention that a destroyed city never be rebuilt, but not accompanied with an oath as here. In a Hittite document concerning the conquest of Hattusha early in the second millennium, Anitta pronounces a curse on any king who would rebuild the city.

6:26. connection of building and losing children. See 1 Kings 16:34. It used to be thought that the dedication of a house would feature human sacrifice of a child from the family. This was used to explain the incidence of skeletal remains of children buried under the thresholds of houses. This interpretation has been largely abandoned, and some researchers now see a connection between the curse and the disease schistosomiasis (bilharzia). This disease is caused by a blood fluke carried by snails of the type found in abundance at Jericho. It infects the urinary tract and affects fertility and child mortality.

7:1-26
The Results of Achan's Sin

7:1. devoted things. See comment on 6:21-24.

7:1. corporate responsibility. In the ancient Near East a person found his or her identity within the group. Integration and interdependence were important values, and the group was bound together as a unit. As a result, individual behavior would not be viewed in isolation from the group. When one Israelite sinned, the group shared the responsibility. In addition to reflecting the perspective of society, this corporate responsibility was also a result of the covenant relationship that Israel had with the Lord. The law included many guidelines for individual behavior and when individual violations occurred the benefits of the covenant were in jeopardy for all Israel.

7:2. Ai. The city of Ai is usually identified with the site et-Tell, a twenty-seven-acre tell located nine miles west-northwest of Jericho, about ten miles north of Jerusalem. The major occupation of the site was during the third millennium (Early Bronze), and it was destroyed well before the time of the patriarchs. This site shows no further sign of occupation until a very small village (covering about six acres) was established there sometime after 1200 B.C., using what remained of the Early Bronze walls for defense. There is therefore no indication that this site was occupied during any of the potential periods of the conquest. This archaeological record has made some doubt the authenticity of the biblical record, while others doubt whether this is truly the city of Ai. Over the last century many alternative sites have been and continue to be considered, but no strong candidates have yet emerged.

7:2. Beth Aven. The town of Beth Aven has not been identified with any certainty. The way it is introduced in the texts suggests it was more prominent than Ai. Tell Maryam is often considered the prime candidate. It has not been excavated, but surveys have turned up Iron Age remains. Hosea is thought to use Beth Aven as an alternate name for Bethel (4:15; 5:8; 10:5).

7:2. Bethel. See comment on 8:9.

7:5. stone quarries. Some translations have the Israelites fleeing to the stone quarries (NIV; the word means "breaks"; others render it a place name, Sheharim). Stone quarries were common in the area, but this is not the usual word for quarries. One archaeologist (Z. Zevit) has suggested that the word should be translated "ruins," referring to the ruins of the Early Bronze city wall that lay further down the slope from this smaller Late Bronze settlement. The text does not say the men of Ai chased the Israelites *from* in front of the gate (though many translations do); they chased them "past the gate to the ruins." In this case, the gate may also be the Wadi gate from the Early Bronze city.

7:6. mourning. Mourning practices generally included tearing one's robe, weeping, putting dust and ashes in one's hair, and wearing sackcloth. Sackcloth is made of goat or camel hair and was coarse and uncomfortable. In many cases the sackcloth was only a loin covering. The official period of mourning was thirty days, but it could continue as long as the mourner chose to continue to grieve.

7:7-8. Amorites and Canaanites. The Amorites and Canaanites are the main inhabitants of the land. For ethnic background see the comment on 3:10; for political background,

see comment on 5:1.

7:13. consecration. Consecration consisted of steps taken to make oneself ritually pure. This process primarily entailed washing and avoiding contact with objects that would render one unclean. It typically preceded ritual action. For Israel this included sacrifices, festivals or procedures in which Yahweh was involved, such as war and oracular procedures.

7:14-18. oracular selection procedure. The text does not mention the mechanism by which groups or individuals are singled out, though some translations supply "by lot." In Israel, however, lots were typically used when a random quality was desired. Here, in contrast, they are seeking an oracle in which a question is put to God in order to receive divine guidance or information (see comment on Gen 24:12-21). The presentation of a tribe or clan before the Lord would pose the question, "Is the guilty party in this group?" If a process is used similar to the Urim and Thummim (see comment on Ex 28:30), an answer would only be given divine standing if it defied the odds (for instance, if the same results were repeated several times). In the ancient Near East lots were sometimes used to receive oracles, though in most cases oracles were pursued through divination (such as examining the entrails of a sacrificed animal for favorable or unfavorable indications). In light of the consecration that precedes the process, it is possible that there is no mechanism but rather direct communication from Yahweh.

7:21. Achan's plunder. The precious metals from the Canaanite cities had been assigned to the sanctuary, so Achan was taking what properly belonged to the Lord. There are five or six pounds of silver and about a pound and a half ingot of gold in Achan's treasure trove. That represents what it would take the average worker a lifetime to earn. The Babylonian robe of this period was fringed and draped over one shoulder, with the edge carried over the arm.

7:25. stoning as execution. Stoning is a communal form of execution and the most commonly mentioned form of execution in the Bible. It is used to punish crimes against the entire community that constitute violations of the covenant (apostasy, Lev 20:2; sorcery, Lev 20:27) and requires all those persons who have been offended to participate. Because it cannot be determined which individual's stone caused the death of the condemned, no one person must bear the guilt for that death. Mesopotamian texts do not mention stoning but employ drowning, impalement, beheading and burning as forms of execution.

7:25. entire family executed. The punishment

for violation of the ban was to be put under the ban. The ban required the obliteration of the family line. The law had forbidden children to be punished for the sins of their parents (Deut 24:16), but that was intended to curtail some very specific practices. For instance, in Hammurabi's laws if a man brought about the death of another man's son, the penalty would be that the perpetrator's son would be put to death. Another example would be where blood vengeance would extend its range to the family of a murderer. The law was intended to put restrictions on the civil law system. This incident is an entirely different category in that God is personally judging the case. Obliteration of the family line was a punishment only God could dole out.

7:26. Valley of Achor. The identification of the Valley of Achor is uncertain. One suggestion is el-Buqeia in the Judean desert about ten miles southeast of Jerusalem, running north-south just west of Qumran. Unfortunately this seems too far from Jericho in the wrong direction to suit. The other occurrences of Achor locate it on the border between Judah and Benjamin (see 15:7). El-Buqeia is too far south for that, but something in the vicinity of Jericho/Ai/Gilgal (such as Wadi Nu'eima) would be too far north.

8:1-29

Defeat of Ai

8:1. Ai. See comment on 7:2.

8:2. ambush. The strategies employed by Israel often fall into the category of indirect warfare, characterized by ambush, pretend retreats, decoys, infiltration and the like, rather than lengthy siege or pitched battle. Such tactics are known from the ancient Near East in the Mari texts (eighteenth century), the Egyptian Papyrus Anastasi (thirteenth century) and a Middle Assyrian text (tenth century).

8:3. thirty thousand fighting men. Thirty thousand appears an exorbitant number to send against a town that would probably not have more than a few hundred soldiers. It certainly is impractical for a successful ambush. Verse 25 translates that twelve thousand people of Ai were killed. Ai is presented as a small town with few men (7:3). If it was smaller than Jericho, its entire population would be less than a thousand. All of this suggests that the word translated "thousand" in these passages should be rendered by its alternate meaning, "companies" or "divisions." Rather than a specified number, it has been suggested that each clan supplied a division with the number

varying dependent on the size of the clan. Later in history these companies were standardized as having a thousand, but here there may be as few as ten in a division. In the first attack on Ai in 7:4-5 there were three "thousand" sent and they treated it as a massacre when thirty-six were killed. In the Amarna letters the kings of the city states would beg Egypt for ten or twelve soldiers to reinforce their armies. For difficulties with the number of the Israelites see comment on Exodus 12:37. For further discussion of large numbers see comments on 2 Chronicles 11:1; 13:2-20.

8:9. Bethel. Bethel is just listed as a location nearby until verse 17, when the men of Bethel become involved in the chase. There is no mention of destroying the city of Bethel, though the king is mentioned as defeated in 12:16. In Judges 1 it comes under specific attack by the tribes of Joseph. Bethel is usually identified with Beitin just over 10 miles north of Jerusalem, about a mile and a half west of et-Tell, the traditional site of Ai. There was a major fortified city on the site during the Middle Bronze Age that was destroyed in the mid-sixteenth century. It was grandly rebuilt in the Late Bronze age, and there is evidence of two destructions during that period (1550-1200). Some have contested whether Beitin is Bethel, because it has been difficult to find a satisfactory adjoining site for Ai (see comment on 7:2). The main alternative is Bireh, a mile or two south of Beitin.

8:9-13. battle positions. The ten-mile march by the ambush contingent was done under the cover of darkness. They secured a position on the far side of the city (the west; Jericho and Gilgal were east of Ai). The main army marched west the next morning through the Wadi el-Asas that led them to a camp in the valley or on the slope of the hill to the north of Ai. When the soldiers of Ai came out, the Israelite army fled east, back toward their base, allowing the ambush to unfold.

8:18. javelin. Javelins of Joshua's time had a metal head attached to a short wooden shaft. Later javelins were thrown with the aid of a loop to make them spin, giving greater distance and accuracy, but these are unknown in this period. Many have suggested that the weapon described in this text is not a javelin but the well-known sickle sword (for description see the comment on 6:21).

8:25. twelve thousand killed. Probably referring to twelve divisions. See note at 8:3.

8:28. burning the city. The site of et-Tell shows no indication of destruction by fire in the Late Bronze period, nor was the Iron Age settlement destroyed by fire. See discussion of the archaeological problems with Ai at 7:2.

8:29. hanging the king. In 10:26 the kings were executed first, then hung, suggesting that this was not a manner of execution but a treatment of the corpse (see 2 Sam 21:12 compared with 1 Sam 31:10). Many believe it refers to impalement on a gibbet, as was known to be practiced later by the Assyrians and Persians. Exposing the corpse was also occasionally practiced by the Egyptians. It represented a final humiliation and a desecration (see Is 14:19-20; Jer 7:33; 8:1-3), for most ancient peoples believed that proper, timely burial affected the quality of the afterlife. See comment on 1 Kings 16:4. In the Gilgamesh Epic Enkidu, returned from the netherworld, reports to Gilgamesh that the one who died unburied has no rest and that the one who has no living relatives to take care of him can only eat what is thrown into the street. A Babylonian curse relates burial to the uniting of the spirit of the dead with loved ones. We know that even Israelites believed that proper burial affected one's afterlife because they, like their neighbors, buried their loved ones with the provisions that would serve them in the afterlife; most often pottery vessels (filled with food) and jewelry (to ward off evil), with tools and personal items sometimes added.

8:29. raising a cairn. Cairn burials were common in Palestine around 2000 B.C., mostly in the southern areas of the Negev and the Sinai, which are dry and rocky. Canaanite burials of this period featured multiple-use tombs in which whole families would be buried together in rock-cut chambers at the foot of vertical shafts. The tombs would typically be provided with all of the accessories of daily life.

8:30-35
Covenant Renewal at Ebal

8:30. function of altar. It appears that this altar was not intended to be a permanent installation (another reason to use fieldstones) but was set up for the purposes of the celebration ceremonies of this occasion. It is specifically burnt offerings and fellowship offerings (see comment on Lev 3) that are offered here—no purification or reparation offerings.

8:30-31. modern find on Ebal. Some archaeologists believe that the remains of the altar on Mount Ebal have been found. It is a structure on one of the peaks of the mountain about twenty-five by thirty-five feet, with walls about five feet thick and nine feet high made of fieldstones. The fill is dirt and ashes, and a ramp leads up to the top. The structure is surrounded by a courtyard, and animal bones were found at the site. Pottery on the site goes back

to 1200 B.C.

8:31. altar built with fieldstones; no iron tool. These instructions parallel those found in Exodus 20:25. Iron tools were used for dressing the stone—shaping it to make a sturdier structure. Altars of dressed stone have been found in Judah (the best example at Beersheba). This altar was not supposed to be attached to a sanctuary, and perhaps the use of unhewn stone helped keep that distinction.

8:32. law on monumental stones. Hammurabi's laws were inscribed on a diorite stele eight feet tall and displayed publicly for all to see and consult. Royal inscriptions often were placed in prominent locations. Memorial inscriptions in our culture are used on tombstones, cornerstones of buildings and at various historical sites. The purpose in these cases is for people to see, take note and remember. Treaty documents in the Near East, in contrast, were often stationed in holy places that were not accessible to the public. Here the purpose was to put the agreement in writing before the gods in whose name the agreement had been sworn. For information regarding stones serving as boundary markers and land grant documents, see comment on 1 Samuel 7:12.

8:34. public reading. In cultures where many people were illiterate and where virtually no one would have possessed written materials (other than basic family documents) in their homes, the public reading of documents that were of religious, cultural or political significance was important. Several Hittite treaties contain clauses requiring periodic public reading of the document—one stipulates three times a year, while others are less specific, "always and constantly."

9:1-27
The Gibeonite Agreement

9:1. the political situation in the Late Bronze Age (1550-1200 B.C.). The Late Bronze Age was a period of political stalemate among major international powers. Egypt exercised control over Palestine for most of the period and often desired to extend its control into Syria, where important land and sea trade routes merged. A second major power in the region was the Hurrian coalition known as Mitanni that occupied a broad arc of the northern region between the Tigris and the Mediterranean. As Mitanni slid into decline and eventually broke up (around 1350), it was replaced by a growing Assyrian power along the upper Tigris, extending eventually to the Euphrates. The Hittite Empire took advantage of the decline of Mitanni to extend its control south from Anatolia and competed with Egypt for control of the important corridor between the seaports of Phoenicia and the river trade of the Euphrates. All during this time southern Babylonia was under the control of the Kassites. These major power struggles all left the petty city-states of Palestine little hope of achieving political significance. The region was nevertheless strategically important, providing administrative and supply garrisons for Egypt and continuing as the only option for overland trade routes into and out of Egypt.

9:1. the Amarna letters. The Amarna letters archive contains nearly four hundred letters written primarily from Canaanite city-state kings to Egyptian pharaohs Amenhotep III and Akhenaten during the first half of the fourteenth century B.C. They were discovered at Tell el-Amarna, the site of Akhenaten's capital city along the upper Nile, almost two hundred miles south of Cairo. The letters offer the best insight available into the political situation of the time. The petty kings of Canaan are little worried by all of the international struggles described in the previous comment. They are much more concerned with the threat posed by the Habiru (see next comment), against whom they seek Egyptian aid. In these texts they show their anxiety that various of the leading kings in the area may defect and align themselves with the Habiru. Such realignment would be a great temptation in light of the neglect that characterized Egypt in this period. This same concern can be understood in the context of the Israelite conquest. The city-state kings would have been very distraught at the thought of this enemy gaining control of a fortified city.

9:1. Habiru. *Habiru/Apiru* is a term used to describe dispossessed peoples in over 250 texts spanning the second millennium and ranging from Egypt to Anatolia to east of the Tigris. In many of the Amarna letters the kings of Canaan are appealing to Egypt to send more troops to help them against the Habiru, who are stirring up trouble. Certainly the Israelites would have been counted among the Habiru, and it is possible that the term *Hebrew,* in some of its uses, developed from the term *Habiru* (see comments on Gen 14:13 and Ex 21:2). The wide geographical region in which the Habiru occur in the first half of the second millennium, when Israel is in Egypt, makes it impossible to associate the Habiru exclusively with the Israelites.

9:3. Gibeon. The city of Gibeon is usually identified with the modern el-Jib, located six miles northwest of Jerusalem and about seven miles southwest of Ai. The excavations there have discovered a double water system constructed as early as the Judges period. The earlier of the two systems involved cutting straight down through the limestone some thirty-five feet (descended by a stairway spiraling down the wall) to a tunnel, allowing the inhabitants of the city to have access to spring waters at the base of the mound. A second, later system provided a stepped tunnel leading to another (more reliable) spring. This water system is strong evidence that the site is Gibeon, because of the well-known "pool of Gibeon" (see 2 Sam 2:13). The identification is further confirmed by jar handles found at the site with the city's name inscribed on them (although it should be noted that jar handles with other cities' names stamped on them were found as well, explained by the city's major industry: wine export). Little has been found that can be dated to the period of the conquest, but the excavations (done in the late fifties) covered a very limited area on the site. The city of Gibeon is noted in few extrabiblical sources. Pharaoh Sheshonk I (late tenth century B.C.) added Gibeon to a list of captured (or visited) towns during a successful military campaign into Palestine.

9:3. strategy of a ruse. Though there are no examples of a ruse of this exact nature, the literature contains numerous examples of dishonesty and deception in the course of treaty making in the ancient world.

9:7. Hivites. The Hivites are often confused or interchanged with the Horites, and together they are both identified as Hurrians. The Hurrians were Indo-European tribes that had united in the political kingdom of Mitanni from about 1500-1350 B.C. (see comment on 9:1 on the political situation). Some of the correspondence between the Hurrians of Mitanni and the Egyptians is preserved in the Amarna archives. The Hurrians were one of the principal ethnic groups in the Hittite Empire as well as the major ethnic group in the town of Nuzi. In Egyptian documents of this period, Canaan is often referred to as the land of Hurru.

9:10. Sihon and Og. There is no historical information on Sihon and Og outside of the Bible. They are the two Amorite kings who were defeated by the Israelites in Transjordan. For more information see the comments on Numbers 21:21-35.

9:10. Ashtaroth. Ashtaroth is identified here as the capital city of Bashan. It is mentioned prominently in Egyptian texts of this period, the Amarna letters (as ruled by Ayyab) and later Assyrian texts, and some think it occurs in a text from Ugarit as a place where the god El reigns. Known today as Tell 'Ashtarah, it is located on the Yarmuk River about twenty-five miles east of the Sea of Galilee.

9:14. inquiring of the Lord. Inquiring of the Lord was done through the use of oracles, which, in Israel, usually used a mechanism such as the Urim and Thummim. See comment on 7:14-18.

9:17. cities of Gibeon. Two of the three cities of Gibeon can be identified with some confidence. Kephirah is modern Khirbet el-Kefireh, five or six miles west and a bit south of Gibeon. Kiriath-Jearim, a few miles south of Kephireh, is Tell el-Azhar. Beeroth is generally looked for north of Kephireh toward the Bethel/Ai area, perhaps at el-Bireh or Nebi Samwil.

9:18. the binding nature of oaths. In a culture where the gods were considered active and powerful and were feared, oaths took on a very serious nature. Vows could be mitigated (Lev 27; Num 30), but oaths bound those who had sworn them with the threat of divine vengeance. If an oath was not kept, the invoked deity's name was being held as worthless and powerless. The fourteenth-century Hittite king Murshili saw war and plague as the result of broken treaties that had been sealed by oaths. That Joshua was right to treat this oath as sacred is clear from 2 Samuel 21, where this same oath was broken with dire consequences.

9:26. woodcutters and watercarriers. For the sacrificial fires to be maintained and the purifying waters to be constantly replenished, much labor was involved. This task of providing wood and water was delegated to the Gibeonites. The menial nature of the work gave them permanent lowerclass status in the servitude they had chosen.

10:1-43
The Defeat of the Southern Coalition

10:1. Adoni-Zedek. This name is quite similar to the king of Jerusalem in Genesis 14, Melchizedek (Melchi = "my king"; adoni = "my lord"). There are no extrabiblical texts that offer information about him.

10:1. Jerusalem in the Amarna texts. There are six letters in the Amarna texts (see comment on 9:1) from Abdi-Heba, king of Jerusalem, to the pharaoh requesting military support. He warns that Egyptian control in the area is in jeopardy, both from the Habiru as well as from the other city-state kings, who are less than loyal and are taking advantage of Egypt's unresponsiveness. Jerusalem is one of the key cities in the region and is competing with Shechem for control of the hill country.

10:1. Late Bronze Age remains in Jerusalem. The city of Jerusalem in this period occupied only the north-south ridge covering about ten acres that runs south of the modern city walls. The population would not have exceeded one thousand. The top of the ridge is only about four hundred feet wide and about fifteen hundred feet long. Remains from the Late Bronze period are sparse and confined to area G at the northeastern rim of the ridge. The finds there include the foundations of an identified structure and a massive stone terrace.

10:2. strategic location of Gibeon. One of the major passes from the hill country to the plains, from the Beth Horon pass into the Valley of Aijalon, was in the area controlled by Gibeon. With Jericho, Ai and Bethel already defeated, that gave Israel control of the primary lateral route across Palestine (from the Jordan rift to the coast).

10:2 royal cities. Royal cities would be the administrative centers of larger districts. The Egyptians had a number of cities during the Amarna period where their governors were housed, such as Gaza and Beth Shan. Cities like Shechem and Hazor could also have been considered royal cities because of the large areas they controlled. Gibeon's strategic location and fortifications give it the potential to be such a city.

10:3. the allies: Hoham, Piram, Japhia and Debir. None of these are known from contemporary sources, but all are the types of names well documented in this period. Compare, for instance, the name Japhia to the king of Beirut in the Amarna texts, Yapa'-Hadda. Names often made a statement about deity; Yapa'-Hadda means (the god) Hadda has appeared. Such names were often shortened by dropping the god's name. Even closer is the name of the king of Gezer in the Amarna texts, Yapahu.

10:3. Hebron. Tell Hebron is the site of a twelve-acre ancient city about twenty miles south of Jerusalem. Excavators have found no evidence of Late Bronze Age occupation, and it is not named in the Amarna texts but Egyptian itineraries of Rameses II (thirteenth century) list Hebron among the cities of the region. For more information see comments on Genesis 13:18 and Numbers 13:22.

10:3. Jarmuth. Jarmuth is identified with Khirbet el-Yarmuk, about fifteen miles southwest of Jerusalem. The four-acre acropolis was occupied by a Late Bronze Age city strategically located between the Elah and Sorek valleys, the two passageways from the Shephelah (low hills between the hill country and the coastal

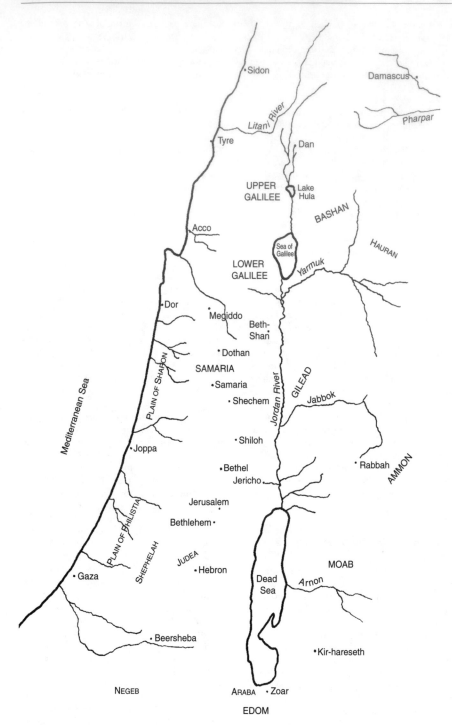

Map 2. Map of Major Cities and Regions of Palestine

plains) to the cities of the coast.

10:3. Lachish. Located about thirty miles southwest of Jerusalem, Lachish (Tell ed-Duweir) is one of the major cities of the Shephelah, covering some thirty acres. Along with Hebron it guarded the passage into the hill country. In the Amarna texts Abdi-Heba of Jerusalem claims that Lachish, along with Gezer and Ashkelon, had delivered provisions to the Habiru (tribute or alliance?). Another letter indicates that the Habiru had killed the king of Lachish, Zimredda. Other kings mentioned in the texts are Shipti-Balu and Yabni-Ilu. There are five letters in the archive from the kings of Lachish. Excavations at the site have uncovered a Middle Bronze Age city with impressive fortifications destroyed by fire at the end of that period (middle 1500s). The Late Bronze occupation of the Amarna period established a sizable though probably unfortified city. There is no evidence of destruction during this period (and the biblical text suggests none). There was a large temple on the site throughout this period.

10:3. Eglon. Tell Aitun, about seven miles southeast of Lachish between Lachish and Hebron, is most likely the site of Eglon. There is no mention of this city in extrabiblical sources, and the site has not been excavated.

10:5. Amorites. See comment on 5:1.

10:6. Gilgal. Location is unknown; see comment on 4:19.

10:9. march from Gilgal to Gibeon. Since the location of Gilgal is unknown, it is difficult to judge the length of the Israelites' march. Jericho to Gibeon is about fifteen miles, so the march certainly would not exceed twenty miles and may be as short as five miles.

10:10. Beth Horon, Azekah, Makkedah. The Beth Horon pass is guarded by the twin cities of Beth Horon: Upper Beth Horon, Beit Ur el-Foqa (about two miles northwest of Gibeon), and Lower Beth Horon, Beit Ur et-Tahta (about a mile and a half further to the northwest, and about a thousand feet lower in elevation). It has been suggested that this is the city referred to as Bit Ninurta in the Amarna letters. The pass leads into the Aijalon Valley (referred to in the Amarna texts as Ayyaluna), the major route from the hill country to the coastal plains. Once in the Aijalon Valley the Amorites turned south, crossing the Sorek Valley heading southeast about twelve miles to Azekah (about a mile west of Jarmuth) overlooking the Elah Valley. From there they continued south about fourteen more miles to Makkedah. This route runs along the flanks between the hill country and the Shephelah. Makkedah is identified as Khirbet el-Qom, about halfway between Lachish and Hebron and only about three miles northeast of Eglon, so this is centrally located to several of the cities of the coalition. Limited excavation has been done at the site, with no Late Bronze finds reported. Azekah is Tell Zakariya, where there is evidence of a Canaanite settlement but little light shed on that level from archaeology.

10:11. hailstones. The occurrence of hailstones as divine judgment in conquest accounts is not unique. In a letter to his god (Assur), Sargon II of Assyria reports that in his campaign against Urartu (714 B.C.) the god Adad stormed against his enemies with "stones from heaven" and so annihilated them. This battle included a coalition that fled through the passes and valleys pursued by Sargon, with the enemy king hiding at last in the clefts of his mountain.

10:12. Gibeon and Aijalon. The relative positions of the sun and moon are important to the interpretation of this passage. Gibeon is east and Aijalon is west, suggesting that the sun is rising and the moon is setting. During the phase of the full moon, the moon sets in the west shortly after the sun rises in the east.

10:12-13. sun and moon as omens. In the ancient Near East the months were not standardized in length but varied according to the phases of the moon. This lunar calendar was then periodically adjusted to the solar year so as to retain the relationship of months with the seasons. The beginning of a month was calculated by the first appearance of the new moon. The full moon came in the middle of the month and was identified by the fact that the moon set just minutes after the sun rose. The day of the month on which the full moon occurred served as an indicator of how many days the month would have. It was considered a good omen if the full moon came on the fourteenth day of the month, because then the new crescent would be seen on the thirtieth day and the month would be the "right" length and all would be in harmony. If "opposition" (moon and sun simultaneously on opposite horizons) occurred on the fourteenth, it was considered to be a "full-length" month made up of full-length days. Thus days were viewed as longer or shorter based on the way the month was going. Verse 13 reports that the sun and moon did not behave as they would have on a full-length day. As a result of these beliefs, the horizon was observed very carefully in the middle section of the month, hoping for this opposition of sun and moon to come on the propitious day (fourteenth). Opposition on the wrong day was believed to be an omen of all sorts of disaster, including military defeat and overthrow of cities. In this way the movements of the sun and the moon became monthly omens of good fortune or ill. In the ancient Near East great significance was attached to these omens and they were often used to determine whether battle should be done on a particular day or not. As noted in the above comment on Gibeon and Aijalon, the positions reported in Joshua for the sun and moon suggest that it is near sunrise in the full moon phase.

10:12-13. terminology in the celestial omens. The Mesopotamian celestial omens use verbs like *wait, stand* and *stop* to record the relative movements and positions of the celestial bodies. When the moon or sun do not wait, the moon sinks over the horizon before the sun rises and no opposition occurs. When the moon and sun wait or stand, it indicates that the opposition does occur for the determination of the full moon day. The omens in the series known as Enuma Anu Enlil often speak of changing velocities of the moon in its course to effect or avoid opposition with the sun. Likewise in verse 13 the text here reports that the sun did not hurry but instead stood in its section of the sky. It should be noted that the text does not suggest the astronomical phenomena were unique, but instead, verse 14 says plainly that what was unique was the Lord accepting a battle strategy from a man ("the Lord listened to a man"). A Mesopotamian lamentation (first millennium) shows this same type of terminology for divine judgment when it speaks of the heavens rumbling, the earth shaking, the sun lying at the horizon, the moon stopping in the sky and evil storms sweeping through the land. Joshua's knowledge of the Amorites' dependence on omens may have led him to ask the Lord for one that he knew would deflate their morale—for the opposition to occur on an unpropitious day.

10:13. Book of Jashar. It is inferred that the Book of Jashar contained ancient poetic accounts of heroic deeds (the only other reference to it is in 2 Sam 1:18). The title Jashar could be the adjective *upright* or a form of the Hebrew verb *sing.* It has not been preserved.

10:16-43. conquest narratives in the ancient Near East. Egyptian war diaries (day books) record military campaigns in much the same way that Joshua does. The combination of longer narratives with short reports using standard, repeated phrases is attested in the records of Thutmose III. Studies of Hittite and Assyrian campaign reports also demonstrate much stylistic similarity. The claims that deity has commissioned the campaign and inter-

vened to bring victory, as well as the reports of pursuing, subduing and conquering to bring about complete and utter defeat of the enemy are all common elements. This suggests that the biblical author was well aware of ancient Near Eastern scribal style and practice.

10:19. prevent reaching cities. Makkedah is only a few miles from each of the cities of Lachish, Eglon and Hebron. Joshua would rather prevent the kings from reaching their cities, where they could rally a defense. Without leadership the cities would be easier to conquer.

10:24. foot on the neck symbolism. The Assyrian king Tukulti-Ninurta I (thirteenth century) "puts his foot on the neck of" individual conquered kings as well as (symbolically) on that of conquered lands, clarifying that they have thus become his footstool. As a result the symbolism of making one's enemies their footstool (Ps 110:1) can be related to the action here.

10:26. exposure of the corpses. The kings were executed first, then hung, suggesting that this was not a manner of execution but a treatment of the corpse (see 2 Sam 21:12 compared with 1 Sam 31:10). Many believe it refers to impalement on a gibbet as was known to be practiced later by the Assyrians and Persians. Exposing the corpse was also occasionally practiced by the Egyptians. It represented a final humiliation and a desecration (see Is 14:19-20; Jer 7:33; 8:1-3), for most ancient peoples believed that proper, timely burial affected the quality of the afterlife (see comment on 8:29).

10:29. Libnah. The town of Libnah, on the way from Makkedah to Lachish, is usually identified with Tell Bornat, strategically located by the Wadi Zeita guarding the best route to Hebron from the coast. There have been no excavations there, but surveys have turned up both Late Bronze and Iron Age evidence on the site. Others identify it with a site five miles further east, Khirbet Tell el-Beida (nine miles northeast of Lachish).

10:33. Gezer. Gezer, modern Tell Jezer, is a thirty-three-acre mound at the west end of the Valley of Aijalon, some twenty-five or thirty miles north of the area of concentration. Its army is defeated, but the city is not conquered in this campaign (see 16:10). It is one of the cities listed as conquered by Pharaoh Merenptah and was one of the most important cities in Canaan in the Amarna texts, where there are ten letters to the pharaoh from its king, Yapahu. Extensive excavations have been carried out at the site. A heavily fortified Middle

Bronze city was destroyed by fire at the end of that period (perhaps the destruction claimed by Thutmose III, fifteenth century). The Late Bronze city was surrounded by a wall that was twelve or fourteen feet wide and over fifteen feet high.

10:33. Horam. Horam, king of Gezer, is not known from any other texts of the period, though it is a typical West Semitic name.

10:36. destruction of Hebron. For general information about Hebron see comment on 10:3. Since there has been no occupation level from the Late Bronze Age uncovered at Hebron, archaeology can shed little light on the destruction by Joshua and the Israelites. Since Hebron is the site of a modern town, there are many areas that are not available for excavation.

10:38. Debir. Debir is Khirbet Rabud, a fifteen-acre site about eight miles southwest of Hebron. A fortified Canaanite city in the Late Bronze Age, it has a commanding location along the Wadi Hebron that goes from Beersheba to Hebron. Excavation has been limited to two trenches, so there is not much information concerning the destruction by Joshua.

10:40. region and extent of conquest. The cities that have been described in this passage are all in the southern hill country and the southern Shephelah. Cities such as Gezer and Jerusalem are not mentioned as being attacked. The description given in the verse circumscribes this region. Since the kings who controlled the region had been defeated, the territory was now considered to belong to the Israelites. The use of hyperbole in describing the total nature of the destruction is common in conquest accounts. The text itself demonstrates that it is hyperbole in Joshua 15:13-16, where inhabitants of Hebron and Debir are mentioned. This type of hyperbole is used in reference to Israel in the Merenptah Inscription, where it is claimed that there are no descendants of Israel remaining, and in the Mesha Inscription, where Israel is described as utterly perished forever. Such statements are the rhetoric indicative of military victory and can be found in Hittite, Egyptian and Assyrian accounts of campaigns. This does not suggest the account is inaccurate, deceptive or misleading, for any reader would have recognized this well-known rhetorical style for reporting the results of battle.

10:41. Kadesh-barnea to Gaza. Kadesh-barnea represents the border between the Negev section of the promised land and the Sinai wilderness. Gaza (about sixty miles directly north) represents the border between Palestine and Egyptian territories in the Sinai along the coast of the Mediterranean. Together these serve as the southwestern border of the land.

10:41. Goshen to Gibeon. Goshen does not refer to the territory by the same name in the delta region of Egypt but to an area in the hill country of Judah, as indicated by 11:16 and 15:51, where it stands with the southernmost sites in the hill country. Gibeon represents the northernmost acquisitions of the southern campaign. Together these serve as the eastern border of the territories conquered in this campaign.

11:1-15
The Defeat of the Northern Coalition

11:1. Jabin. This may be another name that has been shortened by dropping the god's name (see comment on 10:3 on the allies). A similar name is found in the Amarna texts for the king of Lachish, whose name is Yabni-Ilu ("[the god] Il created"). In the Mari texts (eighteenth century B.C.) the king of Hazor is named Yabni-Addu ("[the god] Adad created"). The name may also be referred to on an itinerary list from Rameses II, where Ibni is named as the king of Qishon. Qishon is possibly the same as Qedesh, where Deborah and Barak fight against a king named Jabin also connected to Hazor (Judg 4:1-13).

11:1. Hazor. Hazor (Tell el-Qedah) is located about ten miles north of the Sea of Galilee along the major trade routes of the region. The upper city on top of the tell was about 25 acres, while the lower city covered another 175 acres, making it one of the largest cities in the fertile crescent. The tell was about 140 feet high. The Middle Bronze wall around the upper city was of mudbrick and was 23 feet wide. Parts of the lower city were defended by a rampart wall and fosse (dry moat). Hazor is the most important city in the region in the Amarna texts. Hazor's king in the Amarna texts, Abdi-Tirshi, claims loyalty to Egypt, though he is named as one of those siding with the Habiru. He is also accused of taking cities from Ayyab, king of Ashtaroth (see comment on Deut 1).

11:1. Madon. Because of textual variations most have accepted that Madon is the same as Merom, mentioned here in verse 5 as the site of the coalition camp. The currently favored location for Merom is Tell Qarnei Hittin, about five miles west of Tiberias and the Sea of Galilee. Excavations at the site have discovered a Late Bronze fortress that was destroyed in the thirteenth century. Both Thutmose III of Egypt (fifteenth century) and Tiglath-Pileser III of Assyria (eighth century) claim to have taken

Merom. The king, Jobab, is not known from any other sources.

11:1. Shimron. Shimron (Shamhuna of the Amarna texts, also in the itinerary of Thutmose III) is Khirbet Sammuniya at the western end of the Jezreel Valley, five miles west of Nazareth and seventeen miles southwest of Qarnei Hittin. There have been Late Bronze Age remains found at the site.

11:1. Acshaph. Acshaph (Akshapa of the Amarna texts, also in the itinerary of Thutmose III) has been tentatively identified as Tell Keisan, about twelve miles north-northwest of Shimron, about three miles from the Mediterranean coast on the plain of Acco. Papyrus Anastasi I (thirteenth century) confirms a location on the plain of Acco, though it leads one to expect a site a bit further south than Keisan. There have been Late Bronze Age remains found at the site.

11:2. regions. The description of the region in verse 2 is very uncertain, but it appears to cut a swath from Hazor and the Sea of Galilee on the east angling southwest through the Galilee region to the coast at Naphoth Dor. The latter is probably one of the names of the town of Dor (Khirbet el-Burj), which was an important seaport in the Late Bronze period. Kinnereth could refer either to the town on the northwest shore of the lake or to the lake itself. The Arabah is the Jordan rift valley.

11:3. people groups. For discussion of these people groups see the comment on 3:10.

11:3. Hivites in Mizpah. The region of Mizpah is the valley that comes south through the Huleh basin flanked on the east by Mount Hermon. The Hivites that lived in there were most likely Hurrians resettled from the Mitanni region. See comment on 9:7.

11:4. chariots in the Late Bronze Age. Canaanite chariots of the Late Bronze Age were light vehicles with almost no armor and wheels with four spokes. They were drawn by two horses. These are in contrast to the iron chariots of the next period, which were armored and featured six-spoke wheels to carry the extra weight.

11:5. Waters of Merom. If Merom is properly located at Qarnei Hittin (see comment on Madon at 11:1), then the Waters of Merom would be either a spring near the site or a river nearby. There is a wadi that runs through the valley north of the site.

11:6. hamstringing horses. Horses could not be mercifully shot as they are today, and the Israelites had no use for them and no means of caring for them; they certainly did not want their enemies to have continued use of them. Hamstringing involves cutting through the

rear tarsal tendon in the hock joint (the equivalent of the human Achilles tendon).

11:8. path of pursuit. The path of pursuit appears to circumscribe the area known as Upper Galilee going west to the coast through the Turan Valley and the Valley of Iphtahel (the valleys north of Nazareth), then up the coast to the territory of Sidon, whose southern border is the east-west section of the Litani River (Misrephoth Maim?), east to where the Litani River swings from north-south into the Huleh Valley (the Valley of Mizpah, Marj 'Ayyun), then south again to Hazor to lay claim to the cities of the defeated kings.

11:11. destruction of Hazor. Hazor's upper and lower city were destroyed by fire in the thirteenth century B.C., and the lower city was never reoccupied. Solomon's building at the site was limited to the upper city.

11:12. royal cities. Royal cities would be the administrative centers of larger districts. The Egyptians had a number of such cities during the Amarna period where their governors lived, such as Gaza and Beth Shan. Cities like Shechem and Hazor could also have been considered royal cities because of the large areas they controlled. Gibeon's strategic location and fortifications give it the potential to be such a city.

11:13. built on their mounds. The mounds referred to here are the tells that characterize many ancient sites. A city was more defensible if it was built on elevated ground, but in addition to the natural mound, as each successive occupation level was destroyed or abandoned, the rubble was flattened for the reconstruction of the city. As one layer piled on top of another century after century, an artificial mound, or tell, rose higher and higher. Some sites have more than twenty occupation levels, and the task of the archaeologist is to peel through these layers to reconstruct the history of the site.

11:16—12:24
Summary of the Conquest

11:16-17. extent of the conquest. Verse 16 names the geographical areas of the land that covers all but the coast from Galilee in the north to the Negev in the south. Verse 17 uses two landmarks to designate the conquered territory. Mount Halak is near the Edomite border on the south and is generally identified as Jebel Halaq, along the Wadi Marra between Beersheba and the wilderness of Zin. Baal Gad is the northern boundary in the vicinity of Dan/Laish north of Hazor, sometimes identified as Banias, just east of Dan. The Valley of

Lebanon is often considered the same as the Valley of Mizpah (see comment on 11:8), joining the Litani Valley to the Huleh Valley. For the totality of the language see the comment on 10:40.

11:21. Anakites. The descendants of Anak are generally considered "giants" (see Num 13:21-33; Deut 2:10-11; 2 Sam 21:18-22), though the description "gigantic" may be a more appropriate line of thinking. There is no sure mention of the Anakites in other sources, though a possibility exists in the Egyptian execration texts. Additionally, the Egyptian letter on Papyrus Anastasi I (thirteenth century B.C.) describes fierce warriors in Canaan that are seven to nine feet tall. Two female skeletons about seven feet tall from the twelfth century have been found at Tell es-Sa'ideyeh in Transjordan.

11:21. Hebron, Debir, Anab. Hebron and Debir were identified in the comments on 10:3 and 10:38 respectively. Anab is also in the hill country of Judah and is probably Khirbet Unnab es-Seghir (Tell Rekhesh) about fifteen miles southwest of Hebron. It is referred to in Egyptian texts of the period, and surveys have identified Iron Age remains.

11:22. Gaza, Gath, Ashdod. Gaza, Gath and Ashdod become three of the five capital cities of the Philistine rulers along the southern coastal plains. Ashdod is about three miles from the coast, directly west of Jerusalem. It is mentioned in the Ugaritic texts, and excavations have demonstrated a large Late Bronze settlement on the site. Gaza is two miles from the coast, about twenty miles southwest of Ashdod. The modern city prevents significant excavation, but the site is well known in extrabiblical sources of the biblical period. Gath, Tell es-Safi, is further inland by the Elah Valley where it enters the Shephelah, five or six miles west of Azekah. There has been little modern excavation on the site.

12:1-24
List of Defeated Kings

12:1. Arnon to Hermon. The Transjordanian area said to be conquered stretched from the Arnon River (border between Moab and the kingdom of Sihon) in the south to Mount Hermon in the north (see Deut 3:8), a distance of about 130 air miles. This type of geographic range would be similar to the Dan to Beersheba designation in Palestine.

12:2-3. geographical area. Since the exact location of biblical Heshbon is still un-known (Tell Hesban does not contain materials related to the Conquest period), it can only be said to lie near the northern end of the Dead Sea in Moabite territory (see comment on Num 21:25-28). The eastern region of Sihon's rule ranges from Aroer, a border city located on the lip of the Arnon Valley and controlling that area, through the portion of Gilead south of the Jabbok River. Along the eastern side of the Jordan Valley, Sihon is said to rule north of the Jabbok as far as the Sea of Chinnereth (Sea of Galilee), and south as far as the northeastern shores of the Dead Sea, within the slopes of the Pisgah range, directly across from Jericho.

12:4. Rephaim. The Rephaim appear in the biblical text as either the spirits of the dead (Ps 88:10-12; Is 26:14) or, as in this text, as one of the original peoples in the Transjordanian area of Bashan (Gen 14:5; Deut 3:13). They were known for their tall stature (Num 13:33; 2 Sam 21:16) and, like the Anakim and Emim of Moab, were displaced by the invading Israelites. King Og, with his huge iron bed, is designated as the last of these people, another indicator of their demise during the Israelite conquest. The origin of the Rephaim's association with the dead may be found in the Ugaritic legends of ancient kings and heroes (see Is 14:9). Their ties to Transjordanian peoples may be remnants of Ugaritic lore about that area and may also be tied to the god or eponymous ancestor Rapah (see Deut 3:11, 13 for parenthetical information on the Rephaites).

12:4-5. geographical area. The compass of Og's territory stretches from the Mount Hermon range and Bashan in the northern section of the Transjordan to the Yarmuk River in the south. He reigns in Ashtaroth (Tell Ashtarah, twenty-five miles northeast of the Sea of Galilee) and Edrei (which is mentioned in the annals of the Egyptian pharaoh Thutmose III, lies on one of the Yarmuk tributaries and is located at Der'a, in modern Jordan). The eastern border of Og's domain is Salecah, possibly modern Salkhad (see comment on Deut 3:1-11).

12:7-8. geographical area. This list of conquered territory west of the Jordan River is a repetition of Joshua 11:16-17. Such repetition further strengthens the Israelite claim on the land, based on the covenant of Genesis 15:19-21, and provides the basis for its distribution to the tribes. The southern boundary is Mount Halak (modern Jebel Halaq) near the region of Edom, and the northern border is Baal-gad near the base of Mount Hermon on the border of Lebanon. Some additions are made in terms of geographical features, such as "the mountain slopes" (see Josh 10:40; possibly the decline toward the Shephelah or in the Judean desert angling toward the Dead Sea) and "the desert," an area later occupied by the tribe of Judah (see Josh 15:61).

12:9-12. list of kings. The list of conquered kings roughly follows the sequence of the Israelite conquest in Joshua 6—11. Thus Jericho and Ai (beside Bethel, see Josh 7:2) appear in Joshua 6—8. The kings of the southern Canaanite coalition are listed in verses 10-12 and are found in Joshua 10:3, 23. Assyrian inscriptions occasionally list the lands and kings conquered by a particular king in the course of his campaign. Tiglath-Pileser I, for instance, tells of forty-two lands conquered over a period of five years. Shalmaneser I reports that he destroyed fifty-one cities.

12:13. Debir. See the comment describing Debir in Joshua 10:38.

12:13. Geder. The site of Geder is unknown. Some suggest that this is a scribal error for Gerar, a Canaanite city in the western Negev region. However, one of Solomon's officials is identified as a Gederite in 1 Chronicles 27:28, indicating that it is the actual name of a city. One suggestion is Khirbet Jedur about seven miles north of Hebron.

12:14. Hormah. With its name meaning "destruction," it is possible that this site name has been applied to several places. It appears to be located in the southern Negev region of Judah, but its exact location is still in dispute (among the suggestions are Tell el-Milh, seven miles northeast of Beersheba, and Tell Masos, seven miles east of Beersheba). The name is associated with Israel's initial defeat in Numbers 14:45 as well as a victory over Arad (Num 21:1-3).

12:14. Arad. The site of Tell 'Arad is eighteen miles east northeast of Beer-sheba in the southern Negev region. There are a number of small sites associated with this settlement, and it is possible that the Arad of Joshua was actually Tell Malhata, four miles east of Tell 'Arad, or possibly Tel Masos (Khirbet el-Meshash), about seven miles east of Beersheba. Ceramic evidence or its absence from these sites, however, has led to a variety of opinions. It can be noted that Tell 'Arad was virtually abandoned at the end of the Early Bronze Age after being a major, fortified site with significant Egyptian influence. There is also evidence of the appearance of an unfortified village during the Iron Age (eleventh century B.C.), which might correspond to the settlement of the Kenites mentioned in Judges 1:16.

12:15. Libnah. See the comment describing Libnah in Joshua 10:29.

12:15. Adullam. Located in the Shephelah in southern Judah, about sixteen miles south-

west of Jerusalem, Adullam has been identified as Tell esh Sheikh Madhkur. Although it only appears here as part of the list of conquered kings, the site is associated with David (1 Sam 22:1) and is among the list of the fortified cities of Solomon (2 Chron 11:7). In prophetic tradition, Micah mourns its destruction during the Assyrian invasion (Mic 1:15).

12:16. Makkedah and Bethel. See the comments on 10:10 for Makkedah and on 8:9 for Bethel.

12:17. Tappuah. Identified with the hilltop site of Tell Sheikh Abu Zarad, nine miles southeast of Nablus, Tappuah was a border town between the tribal areas of Ephraim and Manasseh (see 16:8; 17:7-8). Another town by that name is also mentioned in 15:34 in Judah, but it has not been positively identified.

12:17. Hepher. Although the city-state of Hepher has not been positively identified, it was most likely within the northeast segment of the tribal allotment of Manasseh, perhaps as far north as the Dothan valley and the Gilboa range. Recent archaeological survey in that region suggests Tell el-Muhaffar as a possible site for Hepher (see 17:2-3 for ties between Hepher and the allotment of Zelophehad).

12:18. Aphek. Mentioned in the annals of the Egyptian pharaohs Thutmose III (c. 1490-1436) and Amen-hotep II (c. 1447-1421), this Aphek was located on the Sharon Plain and is identified with Tell Ras el-'Ain, at the source of the Yarmuk River near modern Tel Aviv. It is also the site of at least two major battles between the Israelites and the Philistines (1 Sam 4:1; 29:1).

12:18. Lasharon. It is possible, based on the Septuagint reading, that Lasharon is simply a geographic indicator for Aphek, since that site name is used elsewhere for other cities (see Josh 13:4; 1 Kings 20:26-30). If it is a separate site, it is most likely to be located near Philistine territory.

12:19. Madon and Hazor. See the comment on 11:1 dealing with these conquered cities.

12:20. Shimron, Meron and Acshaph. See the comment on 11:1 dealing with these conquered cities.

12:21. Taanach. Although founded about 2700 B.C. at Tell Ti'innik, about four miles northwest of Megiddo on a crest above the Jezreel Valley, Taanach does not appear in extrabiblical records until the fifteenth-century annals of Pharaoh Thutmose III in his account of the Battle of Megiddo (c. 1468 B.C.). It is one of several Jezreel sites that are regularly included in the lists of conquered cities in this rich, disputed area. Its inclusion in Joshua's conquest list thus follows that pattern. Although it was originally a part of the tribal allotment of Asher, later references describe it as part of Manasseh (Josh 17:12; Judg 5:19). Based on excavation reports, Taanach experienced its greatest period of importance during the mid-third millennium and between the seventeenth and fourteenth centuries B.C. It was only sparsely settled during the twelfth century B.C., following the collapse of Egyptian control of the area and the incursion of the Sea Peoples. However, a new defense system was constructed in the tenth century, indicating a resurgence of population during the monarchy period.

12:21. Megiddo. Since Megiddo commanded the western entrance to the strategic Valley of Jezreel, the Plain of Sharon and the coastal international trade route between Egypt and Mesopotamia, it claimed the attention of many ancient rulers. Founded around 3300 B.C. near two springs, Megiddo was destroyed and rebuilt twenty times as Egyptian (annals of Thutmose III, Seti, Rameses II; El Amarna letters), Hittite and Mesopotamian armies contended to control it and the economic link through Syro-Palestine. The destruction of the Late Bronze city (stratum VIIA) of the twelfth century probably coincides with the break in Egyptian suzerainty following the incursion of the Sea Peoples (based on the discovery of Philistine pottery). Other than in this list of conquered kings, Megiddo is not mentioned in the conquest narrative. It was assigned to Manasseh (Josh 17:11) but was not captured by the Israelites (Judg 1:27) until the monarchy period (1 Kings 4:12; 9:15).

12:22. Kedesh. This place name appears in several geographic contexts, including within Galilee (Tell Qades) and Naphtali near Megiddo (Judg 4:11, 5:19; Tel Abu Kudeis). Its appearance at this point in the list suggests a site in the Jezreel Valley, but it is not possible to make an exact determination.

12:22. Jokneam. Identified with Tel Yoq-neam, this site is located just northwest of Megiddo at the exit of the Wadi Milh in the Jezreel Valley on the border of Zebulun (Josh 19:11; 21:34). It was founded in the Early Bronze period and continued to be occupied until the Ottoman era. Its strategic importance is documented by its inclusion in the conquest list of Thutmose III. The city was destroyed in the thirteenth-century upheaval and again at the end of the eleventh century, perhaps as part of the Israelite expansion to the north.

12:23. Dor. The coastal city of Dor was most likely founded during the thirteenth century B.C. as part of Rameses II's attempt to increase trade between Syro-Palestine and the Aegean.

The Philistines subsequently settled here (evident in the Egyptian story of Wen-Amon's journey), and then it was taken by Solomon and served as one of his administrative centers (1 Kings 4:11). It was in the tribal territory of Manasseh but not conquered until the monarchy period (Josh 11:2; Judg 1:27).

12:23. Goyim/Gilgal. There are several cities identified as Gilgal, and they are found throughout ancient Canaan. The identifier Goyim, "Gentiles," is not particularly helpful, although some, using the LXX reading, tie the name to Harosheth Haggoyim in Judges 4:2. Since it appears between Dor and Tirzah on the list in Joshua, this may indicate a location in the eastern quadrant of the Sharon Plain.

12:24. Tirzah. Generally identified with Tell el-Far'ah (seven miles northeast of Nablus in the central highlands), Tirzah's only biblical appearance prior to the monarchy period is in Joshua's list of conquered kings. Its association with Manasseh is based on a woman named Tirzah in the genealogy (Num 26:33; Josh 17:3). Settlement began in the Neolithic period with the largest city dated to about 1700, with thick walls and a citadel. Its Iron Age heights were reached when it served as Israel's capital (1 Kings 15:21), but the shift to Samaria left it a minor post.

13:1-33
Division of Transjordan

13:1. boundary lists in the ancient Near East. There are several Hittite treaties that offer similarities to the boundary lists found in Joshua 13—19. In the treaties the boundary lists indicate the frontiers of the land that is entrusted to the vassal by the suzerain. Even though the land technically belongs to the suzerain, he offers local control to the vassal and delineates the boundaries of the land that defines this legal relationship. It is land that is designated as territory to be protected in loyalty to the suzerain. The most extensive boundary list is found in the treaty between the Hittites and their vassal district Tarhuntassa (in south-central Anatolia). The purpose of the lists in these two treaties is to specify which territory belongs to Tarhuntassa and which territory belongs to its neighbors, the other vassal districts. This would be similar to the purpose of Joshua 13—19, to distinguish which territory belongs to which tribe. It is the role of the suzerain to define the frontiers in this way, and it demonstrates the suzerain's control of the vassals and their land.

13:2-5. the land that remained. The summary statement of territories that remained to be conquered is divided into three regions: (1) Philistia, including the five major Philistine city-states, and the area to the south that borders on Egypt at the Wadi el-'Arish (see Josh 15:4); (2) the Phoenician coastal zone; and (3) Byblos and the Lebanon mountain zone east of Syria. This final area was never conquered by the Israelites, although commercial and diplomatic ties did exist (1 Kings 9:19). The Phoenician city-states of Tyre and Sidon in the second region were assigned to Asher but never conquered (Judg 1:31). However, they were certainly allied with the governments of David and Solomon (1 Kings 5:1; 9:11-13). Within Philistia are the settlements of a segment of the Sea Peoples. Excavations at several of these sites (most recently at Tel Miqne/Ekron) demonstrate destruction levels consistent with their incursion and the displacement of Canaanite inhabitants (for the Avvim, see Deut 2:23). Of these cities, only Gath has not been positively identified (Tell esh-Sheri'ah and Tell es-Safi have been proposed, with the latter being most likely).

13:6. geography of. This statement reiterates the geographic region of Phoenicia, although it refers to it entirely as Sidonian. It is possible to see this verse as part of the geographic summary in Joshua 13:5, but it may also be a summary statement. In any case, it proves a northern border to the region actually said to be conquered by Joshua (for Misraphoth Mayim see Josh 11:8).

13:9-13. geography of. For discussion of this geographic description of Transjordan, see the comments on Joshua 12:2-6 and Deuteronomy 3:8-17.

13:9. Medeba plateau. This fertile tableland, within the Mishor (northern Moab), lies about twenty-five miles south of Amman, Jordan. It was assigned to Reuben and was the scene of numerous battles between Israelites and Moabites for control of this area (Judg 3:12-30; 1 Sam 14:47; 2 Sam 8:2; 1 Chron 19:7).

13:10. Heshbon. See the comments on Numbers 21:26-30 dealing with the Amorite kingdom of Sihon in this region of Moab.

13:17-20. locations in. The list of captured cities within the kingdom of Sihon (Heshbon, Jahaz, Edrei, Dibon, Medeba) also appears in Numbers 21:21-35. Numbers 32:33-41 also lays claim to cities within this region for Reuben, Gad and Manasseh. Bamoth Baal is also found within the Balaam cycle of stories (Num 22:41), and several of these sites appear in the list of Levitical cities (Josh 21). Location for sites not discussed elsewhere include Beth Baal Meon with Ma'in (four miles southwest of Medeba); Kedemoth with Khirbet er Remeil

or 'Aleiyan (fifteen miles southeast of Medeba); Mephaath with Khirbet Nef'a (four miles south of Amman), Tell Jawah (five miles south of Amman) or, most likely, Umm er-Rasas (almost twenty miles southeast of Medeba); Sibmah with Khirbet qurn el-Kibs; Zereth Shahar with Khirbet ez-Zarat (near the shore of the Dead Sea); and Beth Peor with Khirbet 'Uyun Musa.

13:21. Midianite chiefs. The list of defeated Midianite chiefs or princes is also found in Numbers 31:8, where they are referred to as kings. Evi and Reba only appear in these identical lists, while Zur is referred to as a tribal chief in Numbers 25:15 (1 Chron 8:30), and Hur is the name of an Israelite chief in Exodus 17:10. Rekem is a fairly common personal name (1 Chron 2:43-44; 7:16) as well as a place name (Josh 18:27). The names may also be associated with specific places ranging from southern Transjordan to northern Arabia, thereby tracing control of the trade routes of that region.

13:22. Balaam. See the comments on Balaam in Numbers 22 and the comment on Numbers 25:3, which discusses the incident at Baal-Peor and may be the basis for the account of Balaam's death here in Joshua 13.

13:24-29. geography of Gad. The territory assigned to the tribe of Gad includes most of Gilead. This region is located to the south of the Jabbok River as far as the hill country near Amman. The Aroer listed here is near Amman (Rabbah), not the southern site mentioned in Joshua 13:16. Jezer is probably to be identified with Khirbet es-Sar (about eight miles from Hesbon), and Betonim is located at Khirbet el-Batne about three miles southeast of es-Salt. Mahanaim is most often identified with Tell Heggag in the Jabbok valley just south of Penuel, and Lo-Debar (NIV: Debir) may be a little north of there, but its exact site is unknown (see Amos 6:13). Of the other sites listed, Beth Haram is either Tell er-Rameh or Tell Iktanu at the confluence of the Wadi Hesban; Beth Nimrah is either Tell el-Blebil or Tell Nimrin; Succoth is probably Tell Deir 'Alla on the Jabbok; and Zaphon is Tell es-Sa'idiye on the Wadi Kafrinji.

13:30-31. geography of Manasseh. The description of the territory assigned to the eastern half of the tribe of Manasseh is not as detailed as that for Gad. It has parallels in Numbers 32:39-42 and Deuteronomy 3:13-14. In general the area extended from Mahanaim, also a northern boundary point for Gad, northward through much of Bashan (see Josh 12:4 and 13:11-12) as far as Mount Hermon. The "settlements of Jair" cannot be identified since they would have been tent encampments (see Num 32:41; Deut 3:14; 1 Chron 2:22), but they would have been scattered throughout Bashan. For Machir as a descendant of Manasseh, see Genesis 50:23 and Numbers 26:29. This tribal segment would have been associated with northern Gilead (see Num 32:39-40; Judg 5:14).

14:1—19:51
The Distribution of the Land

14:6. Kenizzite. The Kenizzites were a non-Israelite tribal group, geographically and ethnically tied to the Kenites, Calebites and Othnielites (see Gen 15:19; Num 32:12; Judg 1:13). Their territory included the region southwest of Hebron and reaching south of the Dead Sea in the vicinity of Edom. These smaller tribal groups were eventually absorbed into the tribe of Judah after the establishment of the monarchy.

14:15. Anakites. See the comment on 11:21.

14:15. Hebron. See the comment on 10:3.

15:2-4. geography of Judah's southern boundary. Judah's southern border is the same as that of the nation in Numbers 34:3-5. It extends from the southern end of the Dead Sea, on the border with Edom, to the Desert of Zin (see Num 13:21; 20:1) and eventually west to the Mediterranean Sea. "Scorpion Pass" may be identified with Naqb es-Safa (see Num 34:4). Kadesh-barnea was the staging point from which the Israelites traversed the wilderness and from which they began the conquest (see Num 13:26; Deut 1:19, 46). It is most likely located at 'Ain el-Qudeirat on the Wadi el-'Ain in the northern Sinai. The villages of Hezron, Addar and Karka have not been located, although they may be associated with wells or springs near Kadesh-barnea, and the site of Azmon is also uncertain, though it has been identified with Ain Muweilih, another of the springs in the area. For the Wadi (or Brook) of Egypt, the Wadi el-'Arish, see Joshua 13:3. The various directional qualifiers in the list of place names are very general and give only an approximation of direction and exact location.

15:5a. Judah eastern border. The eastern border of the tribal territory of Judah is the Dead Sea. It extended from its southern end bordering on Edom, northwest to Jericho and the Wadi Qelt, and on to the hill country of Bethel. The reference to the "mouth" implies the confluence of the Jordan River into the Dead Sea at a point 1285 feet below sea level. Like many ancient nations, Judah utilized a natural barrier to mark its border.

15:5b-11. Judah northern border. The northern border begins at the "mouth of the Jordan" and extends northwest to Jericho and the Wadi Qelt. It passes just to the south of Jerusalem (Jebus) and then on to Kiriath Jearim (Deir el-Azhar) by way of the Judean hills to Beth Shemesh (Tell el-Rumeileh) on to the border of Philistia on the "northern slope of Ekron" (Tel Miqne). It then passes through the Sorek Valley westward to Jabneel (2 Chron 26:6; later Jamnia) and the Mediterranean Sea. Reference to Gilgal is problematic since this site is generally thought to lie north of Judah's territory (Josh 5:9). The Pass of Adummim, literally "ascent of blood," is Tal'at ed-Damm. En Shemesh refers to a well south of Jerusalem and has been identified with 'Ain el-Hod to the east of the Mount of Olives. En Rogel is found at the meeting of the Kidron and Hinnom Valleys east of Jerusalem. Nephtoah is identified with Lifta, two miles northwest of Jerusalem.

15:7. Debir. See the comment on this name in Joshua 10:3. There Debir is identified as the king of Eglon and part of a Canaanite coalition defeated by Joshua. It is also noted as a city name in Joshua 10:38. In this case Debir is a place name but is not to be identified with the city in Joshua 10:38. It may be identified with Thogret ed-Debr, northeast of Jerusalem.

15:15. Kiriath Sepher. This is the Canaanite name for the site later known as Debir (see Judg 1:11-12). The name means "city of the book" or "town of the treaty," and may thus reflect either a local scribal school or possibly the site of a treaty. The biblical references indicate that the city was located southwest of Hebron in the southern portion of the Judean hill country. Recent excavation indicates its likely site is Khirbet Rabud.

15:13-19. land grant. Caleb's grant of land to Othniel and his daughter Acsah is typical of feudatory grants in the ancient Near East. Very often kings or princes would offer land grants to military officers as a reward for services rendered as well as a means of bringing uncultivated land into production and increasing the tax base (evident in some of Hammurabi's laws). This practice was also used by governments to facilitate the settlement of tribal peoples who might otherwise become a problem to the peace and economic activity of the kingdom (a practice seen in the Mari texts). The fact that this land grant is coupled with an offer of a marriage (see 1 Sam 17:25; 18:17) simply adds weight to the importance of the task of conquering the Anakim. Since the assigned land is quite arid, Acsah's request for water sources (see Gen 26:17-33) is not out of line and holds her father to a more honest position than was originally the case.

15:21-32. southern towns of Judah. These southern towns center on Beersheba and stretch from the Edomite border to Sharuhen (see Josh 19:6) on the Mediterranean coast. Of those that have been identified, Kabzeel (2 Sam 23:20; Neh 11:25) may be Tell Gharreh between Beersheba and Arad; Jagur may be Khirbet el-Gharrah, nine miles east of Beersheba; Kinah is identified with Horvat 'Uza, three miles southwest of Arad; Kerioth Hezron may be Khirbet el-Qaryatein, four miles north of Arad; Amam may be Be'er Navatim near Beersheba; Moladah may be Khirbet el-Waten, six miles east of Beersheba; Baalah may be Tulul el-Medbah near Tel Masos; Madmannah is tentatively identified as Khirbet Tatrit; Sansannah may be Khirbet esh-Shamsaniyat in the Negeb plains; and Rimmon may be Tel Halif, eight miles northeast of Beersheba (see Neh 11:29; Zech 14:10).

15:33-47. western towns of Judah. The list of Judah's western towns and villages in the Shephelah is arranged in four groups, with a north-south orientation centering on Lachish. The last group, which includes Philistia and its major city-states (Ekron, Ashdod, Gaza), was assigned to Judah in name only since it was not forced into submission until the monarchy. Of those that can at least tentatively be identified, Jarmuth (see Josh 10:3) is Khirbet Yarmuk, sixteen miles west of Jerusalem; Zenan may be 'Araq el-Kharba near Lachish; Lachish is Tell ed-Duweir (Josh 10:3) and was massively fortified during the monarchy period; Eglon remains unknown (its traditional identification with Tell el-Hesi is unfounded); Libnah may be Tell es-Safi or Tell Bornat; Ether is Khirbet el-'Ater; Ashnah is Idhnah; Nezib is at Khirbet Beit Nesib, eight miles northwest of Hebron; and Keilah is Khirbet Qila in the eastern portion of the Shephelah (Amarna Tablets: *Qiltu?*).

15:48-60. hill country towns. The Judean hill country, which lies in a narrow, north-south strip between the Judean wilderness on the east and the Shephelah tableland on the west, contained five (six in the LXX) districts with their towns and villages assigned to the tribe of Judah. Of those that have been tentatively identified, Shamir is el-Bireh; Jattir is Khirbet 'Attir (see 1 Sam 30:27); Anab is Khirbet 'Anab; Anim may be Khirbet Ghuwein et-Tahta, seven miles southwest of Hebron; Holon is at Khirbet 'Illin; Arab is located at er-Rabiyeh; Dumah may be at Deir ed-Domeh (possibly Udumu in EA #256); Beth Tappuah is at Taffuh, three miles west of Hebron; Zior is at Si'ir,

five miles northeast of Hebron; Maon may be Tell Ma'in, just south of Hebron (see 1 Sam 25:2); Carmel is at Khirbet el-Kermel; Juttah is at Yatta; Gibeah may be el-Jeba' southwest of Jerusalem; Beth Zur is Khirbet et-Tubeiqah, four miles north of Hebron; Gedor may be Khirbet Jedur; and Rabbah may be the Rubutu mentioned in Egyptian conquest lists and Amarna texts.

15:61-62. wilderness towns. The arid band of land along the eastern shore of the Dead Sea comprised the Judean Wilderness (see Ps 63:1). High cliffs and deep-cut valleys mark the area immediately along the shore. Further inland the eastern slopes of the hill country descend over three thousand feet in a space of about ten miles. This drastically effects the climate and effectively cuts off annual rainfall amounts needed to support farming or large permanent settlements. Life here was only possible near springs and wells and thus there are only six towns mentioned. Of these Beth Arabah (possibly 'Ain el-Gharabeh on the north bank of the Wadi Qelt, three miles southeast of Jericho) and En Gedi have been located with any confidence. The latter is identified with the oasis with hot springs at Tell ej-Jurn on the western shore of the Dead Sea. Some have identified Secacah with Khirbet Qumran.

16:1-4. Joseph tribes' boundaries. Touching on the northern boundary of Judah at the Jordan River, near the Dead Sea and Jericho, and on the border of Benjamin, which included the city of Jericho, this territory extended north of that city. Its border then continued on toward the hill country and Bethel through the arid region known as the desert of Beth Aven (see 18:12). The boundary extended westward to Gezer (see 10:33) and eventually to the Mediterranean Sea. This latter section would have been only nominally within Israelite territory.

16:2. Bethel/Luz. The connection between Luz and Bethel involves more than a name change (see Gen 28:19; Josh 18:13; Judg 1:23). They may have been originally two sites, but the importance of cultic site of Bethel in later history eclipsed Luz and combined them. Both would have been at or near the site of Beitin (see comment on 8:9).

16:5-9. Ephraim's boundaries. With its southern boundary already delineated in verses 1-4, Ephraim's border extended as far north as the area around Shechem and then swung east and south toward Tanaath Shiloh (Khirbet Ta'nah el-Foqa) and Janoah (Khirbet Yanun). Sites identified in this region include Ataroth (possibly Tell Sheikh ed-Diab or Tell-Mazar) and Naarah (Tell el-Jisr near Jericho or Khirbet

Mifgir). The western end of their territory included Tappuah (possibly Sheikh Abu Zarad; see Josh 17:7-8).

16:10. forced labor. It was a common practice to employ subject people as work gangs or menial laborers (see Josh 9:27). Forced labor is also one of the abuses of power attributed to kings and tyrants, who conscript men to do corvee labor, building roads, bridges and city walls (see 1 Kings 5:13-14; 12:4; charge against Babylonian king Nabonidus in the Cyrus Cylinder, sixth century B.C.). In this period the practice is seen in the Amarna texts employed by the king of Megiddo.

17:3-4. Zelophehad's daughters. See the comment on Numbers 36:1-13, which deals with the inheritance by daughters.

17:7-11. territory of Manasseh. The dimensions of this tribal territory are rather vague, speaking of the territory immediately north of Ephraim, in the vicinity of Shechem, and extending to a point contiguous with Asher. There is some overlap of territory, at least in the sense that the city of Tappuah (see Josh 12:17) belonged to Ephraim while the surrounding region was assigned to Manasseh (see Josh 16:9). The western boundary was the Mediterranean Sea, and the eastern border touched the region of Issachar. Again cities or their inhabitants in other tribal territories are assigned to Manasseh, all but Dor in the Plain of Esdraelon (see Josh 12:21). They are Beth Shan (Tell el-Husn), Megiddo (Tell el-Mutesellim), Ibleam near Nablus, Dor on the coast south of Mount Carmel, Endor (seven miles southeast of Nazareth), and Taanach (Tell Ti'innik, four miles northwest of Megiddo)

17:16. iron chariots. As in Judges 1:19, the use of iron chariots by the enemy is given as the reason for the Israelites' failure to completely conquer areas of Canaan. Iron technology was introduced by the Hittites and the Sea Peoples in the twelfth century B.C. However, it did not become widespread in Syro-Palestinian culture until the tenth century. References to iron chariots in the conquest narrative most likely refer to the use of iron fittings to strengthen the chariot basket or iron-shod wheels. It is possible that studs or projectile points were added to make this engine of warfare heavier and more of a factor when rammed into lines of infantry. However, maneuverability and the strength and size of the horses pulling the chariots would have limited the actual amount of iron employed.

17:16. Beth Shan. The site of Beth Shan stands at the eastern end of the Jezreel Valley and guards that important trade route's entrance into the Jordan Valley. It was assigned to Manasseh but was not captured during Joshua's time because of the inhabitants' use of iron chariots. It continued as an independent Canaanite enclave into the monarchy period (1 Sam 31:10-12) but was incorporated into Solomon's administrative districts (1 Kings 4:12). This is a double site, with a Roman-Byzantine city (Scythopolis) built at the base of the tell. Archaeological investigations have shown almost continuous occupation of the site since Chalcolithic times (4500-3300), and the water supply (Wadi Jalud), arable land and strategic location have insured that its population prospered, generally under Egyptian rule (starting with Thutmose III in the sixteenth century) and later under the Sea Peoples and Israelites.

18:1. Shiloh as cultic center. Shiloh (Khirbet Seilun), in a fertile valley within the Ephraimite hills between Bethel and Shechem, was occupied throughout the Iron Age and at several points in its history had significant architectural features. These included a gate complex and what may have been a temple complex. A destruction level in the mid-eleventh century may coincide with the capture of the ark in 1 Samuel 4:1-10 by the Philistines. Indications of premonarchic religious activity at this site come from Judges 21:19-23, and later traditions (Ps 78:60; Jer 7:12-15) suggest that it had served as a cultic center prior to the construction of the temple in Jerusalem.

18:4-8. ancient mapmaking. Mapmaking goes back at least into the third millennium B.C. Clay tablets have been found with maps etched onto their surfaces. Most notable are the maps of the Mesopotamian city of Nippur (from about 1500 B.C.), and a Babylonian map of the "world" (middle of the first millennium B.C.). From Egypt there is a mining map that dates to the time of Rameses II (thirteenth century B.C.).

18:6-10. casting lots. The practice of casting lots to determine God's will is a form of divination. See the comments on "Urim and Thummim" in Exodus 28:30 and on the use of lots in Numbers 26:55. Since the tribes are listed in their logical order of priority, it can be inferred that lots were not used to choose which tribe got to pick first. Instead the tribes sent their representatives in prescribed order, and the lot was cast to see which parcel of land that tribe received. In the ancient Near East, division of a father's property among his heirs was customarily accomplished by the eldest choosing his parcel and the rest being divided by lot.

18:11-20. Benjamin's allotment. Benjamin's territory lay between that of Judah and Joseph, with Judah's northern boundary being roughly the same as Benjamin's southern border. The northern boundary follows that of Ephraim until it reaches Kiriath Jearim instead of extending on to the Mediterranean. In this way space is reserved for the tribal territory of Dan. The description runs east to west (from the Jordan River's entrance into the Dead Sea). It extended from just north of Jericho, through the hill country and then south toward the mountain slope of Luz (Bethel) and on to Beth Horon and Kiriath Baal (also known as Kiriath Jearim), which was the terminus point for the western boundary. The fact that its boundary ran through the valley of Hinnom means that Jerusalem was in Benjaminite territory.

18:14. Beth Horon. This is a twin city (upper and lower): Upper Beth Horon, Beit Ur el-Foqa (about two miles northwest of Gibeon), and Lower Beth Horon, Beit Ur et-Tahta (about a mile and a half further to the northwest and about a thousand feet lower in elevation). It has been suggested that this is the city referred to as Bit Ninurta in the Amarna letters. The Beth Horon pass leads into the Aijalon Valley (referred to in the Amarna texts as Ayyaluna), the major route from the hill country to the coastal plains. Although it is unclear whether the Beth Horon mentioned in Joshua 16 and 18 is the upper or lower, it is possible that their dual importance in guarding the trade route made them of equal importance and thus undifferentiated in the mind of the biblical writer.

18:15. Kiriath Jearim. Located eight miles north of Jerusalem at Deir el-Azhar, Kiriath Jearim, or "city of woods," lay at the point of intersection for the tribal territories of Benjamin and Judah. It is referred to as Baalah in Joshua 15:9 and as Kiriath Baal in Joshua 15:60 and 18:14. The city figures in the conquest narrative (Josh 9—10) and in the story of the ark's temporary retirement (1 Sam 6:19—7:2).

18:21-28. Benjaminite cities. Although several of the cities are unknown, others have been identified: Parah is Khirbet el-Farah, northeast of Anathoth; Ophrah is et-Taiyibeh, four miles northeast of Bethel; Geba may be Khirbet et-Tell, seven miles north of Bethel; Gibeon is generally identified with el-Jib, four miles northwest of Jerusalem (see Josh 9:3-5); Ramah is er-Ram, five miles north of Jerusalem; Beeroth may be el-Bireh; Mizpah may be Tell en-Nasbeh; Kephirah is Khirbet Kefirah, southwest of el-Jib; Mozah may be Khirbet Beit Mizze, west of Jerusalem; and Gibeath-Kiriath may be a high place known as the "hill of Kiriath Jearim" (see 1 Sam 7:1-2).

19:1-9. Simeon's allotment. Since the territory of Simeon is said to be "within the territory of Judah," this tribe may have been destroyed or assimilated very early, leaving only the memory of its original holdings. Most of its cities are in the Negev and two (Ether and Ashan) are in the Shephelah (see comments on Josh 15:21-32). Of those not mentioned earlier, Beth Marcaboth, "house of chariots," and Hazor Susah, "village of horses," may be functional titles rather than place names and may be equated with Madmannah and Sansannah (Josh 15:31).

19:8. Baalath Beer. This site may be the same as Bealoth in 15:24 (see Baal in 1 Chron 4:33) and was probably located just east of Beersheba. The reference to "Ramah in the Negev" suggests a "high place" or cultic site (see 1 Sam 30:27).

19:10-16. Zebulun's allotment. Although not listed, the primary orientation point for this territory is Nazareth. The boundaries and most of the cities radiate from this city both east and west. The northern boundary is about twelve miles west of Tiberias and six miles northeast of Nazareth at Rimmon (modern Rummaneh). Sarid, probably Tell Shadud (five miles southeast of Nazareth) is another orientation point looking west. From there the boundary extends along the Kishon to Jokneam (see Josh 12:22). The eastern limit stretches as far as the territory of Issachar, about two miles southeast of Nazareth. Sites mentioned in this area are Dobrath (Daburiyeh near Mount Tabor) and Japhia (Yafa, southeast of Nazareth). The only connection Zebulun has with the coast (despite Gen 49:13 and Deut 33:18-19) is by way of trade with Acre, perhaps through the nearby city of Nahalal (Tell en-Nahl). Its territory did not stretch to the Mediterranean.

19:15. Bethlehem. This site, northwest of Nahalal in Zebulun, is not to be confused with the southern site of Bethlehem in Judah. The judge Ibzan was buried here (Judg 12:9-10). A modern Arab village in the vicinity still retains the name Beit-Lahm.

19:17-23. Issachar's allotment. This territory lay primarily in the valley of Jezreel, north of Manasseh, east of Asher and south of Naphtali. Its northern border extended from Mount Tabor to the Jordan River, just south of the Sea of Galilee. The strategic and volatile nature of this area is shown by its mention in the Egyptian annals of pharaohs Thutmose III (Anaharath and Kishion) and Seti I (Remeth = Jarmuth, perhaps the same as Mount Yarmuta, six miles north of Beth Shan). Other sites which have been identified are Jezreel, which is Zer'in northwest of Mount Gilboa; Chesulloth = Chisloth-Tabor (see Josh 19:12) is modern Iksal, two miles southeast of Nazareth; Shunem is Solem, three miles northeast of Jezreel.

19:24-31. Asher's allotment. Situated on the Plain of Acre, Asher lay west of Zebulun and Naphtali and extended as far north as the Phoenician ports of Tyre and Sidon. Again this is an area that figures prominently in Egyptian royal annals. Thutmose III lists Helkath (possibly Tell el-Harbaj or Tell el-Qassis), Acshaph (see Josh 11:1), Mishal (near Mount Carmel) and Allammelech, and Rameses II lists Kanah (seven miles southeast of Tyre) among captured Canaanite towns. Identified sites include Cabul (Kabul); Ebron (Khirbet 'Abdeh, ten miles northeast of Acco); Ummah may be Acco; this Rehob (not the same site as in Josh 19:28) may be Tell el-Gharbi, seven miles east of Acco. Mention of Tyre and Sidon do not necessitate actual control. More likely the border was more theoretical than real, although it is possible that villages associated with these city-states may have been controlled by Israel at various times.

19:29. Aczib. Located north of Acco, Aczib was allotted to Asher but was never captured (Judg 1:31). Excavations at the site demonstrate it to be a flourishing commercial center from the Middle Bronze I through the Roman period. It was sacked and rebuilt a number of times, and reached its largest extent in the eighth century B.C. before being destroyed by Sennacherib in 701. This site is not to be confused with the city mentioned in 15:44 as allotted to Judah in the Shephelah.

19:32-39. allotment for Naphtali. Mount Tabor is the principal reference point for this tribal territory. The southern boundary of Naphtali follows the Wadi Fajjas as far east as the Jordan River. There is some dispute over this based on the location of the "large tree" in Zaanannim (see Judg 4:11), but a southern perspective is most likely. Sites along this line which have been identified are Heleph (Khirbet 'Arbathath near Mount Tabor); Adami Nekeb (Khirbet et-Tell); Jabneel (Tell en Na'am), and Lakkum (Khirbet el-Mansurah). The exact location of Hukkok is disputed but most identify it with Yaquq, just west of the Sea of Galilee. Other identified sites include Adamah (possibly Hajar ed-Damm, two and one-half miles northwest of the confluence of the Jordan and the Sea of Galilee); Iron (Yarun, on the Lebanese border); for Hazor see the comment on 11:1; Kedesh is north of the now drained Lake Huleh.

19:40-48. allotment for Dan. Although Dan has a fairly large territory to the west of Benjamin, taking in the coastal region from the Brook Sorek to the Yarkon River near Joppa, it is unlikely that the tribe occupied more than a fraction of the land. Most of this area was controlled by the Philistines and later by the Assyrians. During Solomon's time it comprised his southwest district and was annexed to Judah. An example of this is their city of Beth Shemesh (Tell er-Rumeileh), which was later listed as a Levitical city in Judah (21:16). Other Danite sites located include Shaalabbin (east of Gezer, possibly Selbit; see Judg 1:35); Aijalon is probably Yalo, five miles east of Gezer (mentioned in the Amarna texts); Timnah (Tell el-Batashi, five miles northwest of Beth Shemesh); Gibbethon (possibly Tell el-Melat; mentioned in the campaign list of Thutmose III); Bene-Berak appears in Sennacherib's annals and is located near the Arab village el-Kheiriyah near Joppa; Rakkon may be either a river or possibly Tell er-Reqqeit near Joppa.

19:47. Leshem. The tribe of Dan probably migrated under pressure from the Philistines (see Judges 18). They went north to Leshem (Laish), which was renamed Dan and subsequently became a major cultic center under King Jeroboam. The city site (largest in that region at about fifty acres) was located north of the Huleh basin on the road north to Damascus and has the benefit of a spring which is one of the sources of the Jordan River. Its importance is found in its listing in the Egyptian execration texts and in the Mari letters.

19:50. Timnath Serah. Also known as Timnath Heres (Judg 2:9), this is the portion allotted to Joshua after all of the tribal territories had been apportioned. The variation in name may be the result of this process, since *serah* means "leftover," and popular etymology might have transformed an original place name. It is located within Ephraim, but it was a political enclave belonging solely to Joshua and his household. It has been identified with Khirbet Tibnah, about twelve miles southwest of Shechem. Excavation has shown a fairly large settlement that was rebuilt in the Iron I period (see Josh 19:50).

20:1-9 Cities of Refuge. See comment on Numbers 35.

21:1-45
Levites' Cities

21:1-2. Levitical cities concept. See the comment on Numbers 35:1-5.

21:3-40. distribution of towns through territory. The legislation in Numbers 35:1-5 that sets aside the revenue from towns and pasturelands for the support of the Levites is implemented here by the casting of lots—a means of divine determination. However, there is an uneven distribution of towns among the tribes, and it is not based on the population size of the tribes. One possibility is that the distribution has more to do with the size of the clans of the Levites.

21:3-40. Levitical cities. While some of the Levitical cities are well known as cultic centers (Hebron, Shechem) and some, like Anathoth, have connections with later Levitical groups (the descendants of Abiathar), many of the cities are in frontier or border areas and thus may be "colonies" or outposts. Thus in verses 11-15, the sites are along the Philistine border, and verses 28-35 contain cities along the northern and coastal boundaries of Israel, which were controlled by powerful Canaanite city-states like Megiddo, and verses 36-39 describe the area east of the Jordan that was lost to Israelite control after the reign of Solomon. Among the cities in this list, which do not appear earlier and have been identified, are Jattir (Khirbet 'Attir, thirteen miles southwest of Hebron); Eshtemoa (es- Samu', eight miles southwest of Hebron), whose excavation has shown Iron Age deposits; 'Ashan (Khirbet 'Asan, just over a mile northwest of Beersheba; rather than Ain, 1 Chron 6:59); Juttah (Yatta, five miles southwest of Hebron); Geba (Jeba, six miles northeast of Jerusalem); Almon (Khirbet Almit, a mile northeast of Anathoth); Eltekeh (Tell el-Melat, northwest of Gezer) is mentioned in Sennacherib's annals of the year 701; Aijalon (Yalo, twelve miles northwest of Jerusalem); Abdon (possibly Khirbet 'Abdeh, four miles east of Achzib); Kedesh (Tell Qedes, six miles north of Hazor, with occupation levels more marked in Early Bronze and sporadic in the Iron Age); Dimnah (possibly Rummaneh, six miles northeast of Nazareth).

21:16. Beth Shemesh. This town was located on the Philistine border in the Valley of Sorek in the northeastern section of the Shephelah. It is identified with Tell er-Rumeilah, and excavation has shown nearly continuous occupation from Middle Bronze I to the Roman period. Its most prominent role in the biblical narrative occurs in 1 Samuel 6:9-15 in the story of the capture of the ark. An eleventh-century destruction preceded its occupation as an Israelite administrative post during the United Monarchy (not fortified by Rehoboam and perhaps unoccupied during part of the ninth century). The appearance of Egyptian scarabs of Amenhotep III and Rameses II, as well as a Ugaritic tablet, attests to the trading contacts of this strategically placed city.

21:18. Anathoth. Located at Ras el-Kharubeh, about three miles northeast of Jerusalem, Anathoth was a Levitical city within Benjaminite territory. It is the site of exile for Abiathar and his clan (1 Kings 2:26) and the home of the prophet Jeremiah (Jer 1:1). Survey excavations show occupation from Iron I to the Byzantine period.

21:21. Shechem. See the comments on Genesis 12:6, Joshua 24:1 and Judges 9:1.

21:21. Gezer. The site of Gezer, which guarded the strategic road from the coast to Jerusalem, is identified with Tell Jezer, five miles southeast of Ramleh. Earliest occupation at the site was in the Chalcolithic period (3400-3300 B.C.), but there was a long period of abandonment between 2400-2000 B.C. In the Middle Bronze period, Gezer was rebuilt and after 1800 became a major fortified site. A "high place" was constructed some time after 1650, with ten standing stones or monoliths erected in a north-south line. The destruction of this occupation level may be associated with the campaign of Thutmose III (c. 1482). Another high period occurred during the Amarna age, when Gezer served as one of the principal centers of Egyptian control in Canaan. The Philistines controlled the site during the Iron I period of the twelfth-eleventh centuries. The first Israelite occupation took place during Solomon's reign (1 Kings 9:15-17), and excavations have identified the typical Solomonic casemate walls and multichambered gate, which were also found at Megiddo and Hazor.

21:24. Gath Rimmon. This city has been identified with two nearby sites, Tell Abu Zeitun and Tell Jerishe. Both are within a couple of miles of the Mediterranean near modern Tel Aviv and close to the Yarkon River. It is possible that both are correct, since many times one site will be abandoned for a time and the city relocated nearby with the same name. This site may be the Gath mentioned in Thutmose III's city list as *knt,* and it may have also been mentioned in the El Amarna tablets as Giti-rimuni.

21:38. Ramoth in Gilead. Originally allotted to Gad, Ramoth in Gilead was also designated as a city of refuge (Deut 4:43) and in the Joshua list as a Levitical city. Its exact location is unknown since the text is not explicit and there are a number of tells along the Syrian border that could match its description. The most likely choice is Tell Ramith, three miles south of Ramtha on the modern border between Syria and Jordan, which has produced Iron Age deposits.

21:43-45. universal statements in conquest accounts of the ancient Near East. Summary statements which proclaim total conquest and complete subjugation of an area according to divine plan and the valiant efforts of the god's ruler are fairly common in the royal annals of the ancient Near East. For instance, the Assyrian king Sennacherib's recording of his third campaign (which included the siege of Jerusalem in 701 B.C.) contains not only a list of cities conquered (the type of list also found in the Merneptah Stele, the Moabite Stone and many other inscriptions), but also a concluding statement which indicates the magnitude of his accomplishment. Similarly, the Armant Stele (1468 B.C.) of Pharaoh Thutmose III contains a summary "of the deeds of valor and victory which this good god performed on every excellent occasion." Such statements were one of the common literary features included as part of the code of conquest annals in the ancient Near East (for further discussion see comment on 10:40).

22:1-34

Misunderstanding with the Transjordan Tribes

22:8. nature of plunder. A successful conquest resulted in a large and varied plunder taken from defeated cities and peoples. The list of items here is fairly typical of the ancient economy and objects of value. The injunction to share the loot signifies the unity of the tribes in their common effort and was conducive to later cooperation (see 1 Sam 30:16-25).

22:9. Shiloh. See the comment on 18:1 for its role as a meeting place and cultic center for the Israelites.

22:10. Geliloth. There is an interchange of names between Geliloth and Gilgal in 18:17, and it is possible that that is also the case here (Codex Vaticanus does replace Geliloth with Gilgal). However, the concern here seems to be with the erection of an unauthorized altar on the very edge of Canaan by tribes who live east of the Jordan. Nearly all identifications for the site of Gilgal place it a little northeast of Jericho on the Jordan River.

22:9-34. the ambiguity of the altar (dual functions). The building of an altar by the tribes of Gad and Reuben raises a concern on the part of the other tribes, who lived west of the Jordan River, that these Transjordanian groups were seeking to establish a rival cultic site to Shiloh. What is unusual about the dispute is that the priest Phineas is the principal character rather than Joshua, and that further emphasizes the ritual concerns of the story. However, the Gileadite tribes are quick to note that they have not built an altar for sacrifice but only as a monument to their covenantal alliance with Yahweh and the other tribes (see 4:19-24). Its "imposing" size is thus explained as a monumental signal of unity rather than religious rivalry. In this way, Gilgal retains its role as rallying point for treaty-making (9:6-15), but Shiloh, and later Jerusalem, claims the role of sacrificial center.

22:11-20. covenant violation as cause for war. It was standard to include a stipulation in treaty documents that violation of any of the terms or covenants of the agreement was grounds for war. For instance, in the treaty between Pharaoh Rameses II and the Hittite king Hattusilis III (c. 1280 B.C.), the kings place a curse on the violator of their alliance and call on a list of gods as witnesses. The charges made against the Reubenites and Gadites suggest a tie to the covenant which requires not only military allegiance during and after the conquest but also recognition of the cult center at Shiloh. The emphasis placed on this site may reflect priestly rather than political concerns. Here the rivalry between tribes was apparently based on a misunderstanding of intentions or perhaps a concern for free passage across the Jordan River (see Judg 12:1-6).

22:17. sin of Peor. The reference made here is to the sin of idolatry committed by the Israelites in worshiping the Baal of Peor (see the comments on Num 25:3, 4, 6, 8). The assumption being made is that the unauthorized altar built by the Reubenites and Gadites was a potential influence that would lead to false worship and a resumption of God's wrath (a plague results in Num 25).

22:34. naming of altars. The naming of places and monuments to commemorate important events is quite common in the Bible. For instance, Hagar's theophany in Genesis 16:7-14 results in the name Beer Lahai Roi ("well of the Living One who sees me") for a nearby well. Similarly, in Judges 6:24 Gideon names a newly rebuilt altar "The LORD is Peace."

23:1-16

Joshua's Charge to the Leaders

23:1. chronology. There is no real indication in the text whether Joshua's "final sermon" to the leaders of the people occurred immediately after the incidents in Joshua 22 or even whether this is the precursor to the covenant renewal ritual in Joshua 24 (note also the lack of a geographical designation). Most important, perhaps, is the tie between the end of the conquest (God's promised "rest") and the end of Joshua's leadership.

23:2. categories of leaders. Moses had appointed a group of officials to serve as judges in Exodus 18:21-22 to relieve some of the burden of leadership. During the conquest the various leaders of the tribes and clans are mentioned on several occasions: elders (Josh 7:6; 8:33), judges (8:33), officials (1:10; 3:2; 8:33). These individuals provided counsel to Joshua on administrative and military issues, carried out his orders in organizing and keeping order in the camp, but their appearance in the text is also ceremonial. Elsewhere in the text, the leaders serve as representatives of the people on important ritual and covenant-making occasions (see Ex 24:1; Num 11:16). In addition, their legal role is mentioned frequently (Deut 16:18; 19:16-18; 21:1-4, 20).

23:13. oppression metaphors. The lure of other cultures and their gods are metaphorically compared to traps, the sting of a slaver's whip and tearing thorns that can blind the traveler. This is an often repeated warning against succumbing to syncretism (Ex 23:33; 34:12; Num 33:55; Deut 7:16). While this metaphor has the ring of a local wisdom saying (see Ps 69:22; Prov 29:6), it has been tied to the covenant relationship and the consequences of disobedience.

24:1-27
Covenant Renewal

24:1. Shechem. Located thirty-five miles north of Jerusalem in the Ephraimite hill country, Shechem (Tell Balatah) dominated a pass and trade route between Mount Ebal and Mount Gerizim. Its archaeological history contains twenty-four strata of occupation reaching from the Chalcolithic to the Hellenistic period. During the Middle Bronze Age, the Hyksos apparently administered or controlled the city, building huge ramparts and a temple. Egyptian resurgence in the area in the sixteenth century B.C. totally destroyed the Middle Bronze III city. However, it was rebuilt in the Late Bronze, when it is mentioned in the El Amarna texts as the base for the local king Lab'ayu, who professed allegiance to Egypt but created a mini-empire in northern Canaan (c. 1400 B.C.). There are no destruction levels leading into the Iron Age and thus the city may have come under Israelite control without major conflict (it is absent from Joshua's list of conquered cities—12:7-23). Its choice as the site of Joshua's covenant renewal ceremony may be the result of previous associations with the ancestors (Abram's altar in Gen 12:6; Jacob's land purchase in Gen 33:18-20, and the rape of Dinah in Gen 34). It is also possible that the ceremony took place in or near the Canaanite sanctuary on the city acropolis as

the Israelites proclaimed the supremacy of their God over Canaanite deities (for additional information see comment on Judg 9:1).

24:1. categories of leaders. See the comment on 23:2.

24:2-27. covenant-treaty format. This covenant renewal ceremony follows the same format as that used for treaties in the ancient world and for the book of Deuteronomy. For discussion see the sidebar on ancient Near Eastern treaties and covenants at the beginning of Deuteronomy (p. 172).

24:2. pagan roots of Israel. The original home of the ancestors was in Mesopotamia, a land with polytheistic religious traditions. It is indicated here that Abram and his family worshiped many gods, including the patron gods of their city as well as ancestral deities and individual gods whose properties were to cure illness or provide fertility. They were only weaned of these practices by the covenantal promise made to Yahweh (see the sidebar on the religion of Abraham in Gen 12). This is important evidence to demonstrate that Abram was not the heir to a long, unbroken tradition of ancient monotheism.

24:2. land beyond the river. This designation is a technical term applied to the region west of the Euphrates River. For example, Haran, the city to which Terah migrated in Genesis 11:31, was west of the Euphrates. Technically, so was the city of Ur, but the province, as suggested by the campaign annals of Mesopotamian kings and later Persian administrative documents (see Ezra 7:21) implied the northern stretches of the Euphrates and west into Syria and Phoenicia-Palestine.

24:5-7. the Red Sea. See comments on Exodus 13—14 for further information.

24:8. the land of the Amorites. For more information see comments on Numbers 21:21-35.

24:9-11. Balaam and the Moabites. For more information see comments on Numbers 22—24.

24:11. hornet. The exact meaning of the word translated "hornet" is uncertain. The Septuagint (the oldest Greek translation of the Old Testament) reads "hornet" or "wasp," and many commentators accept this as a symbol of divine intervention, which helped prepare the way for the Israelite conquest. Insects are often used as metaphors for armies, for instance, bees and flies (Is 7:18-19) and locusts (Joel 1—2). However, some interpreters see this word as a wordplay on Egypt (see comment on Ex 23:28) or a reference to Egypt by means of an insect that was used to symbolize lower Egypt. This would suggest a previous invasion of Palestine by the Egyptians that aided the Israelite cause. Other interpreters have translated the word as "plague" or "terror."

24:1-27. covenant renewal ceremonies. There are four identifiable covenant renewal ceremonies in the biblical text, and each represents not only a reaffirmation of the stipulations of the covenant but also the inauguration of a new phase in Israelite history (see Ex 24:1-8; 2 Kings 23:1-3, 21-22; Neh 8:5-9). Each contains an assembling of the people, either a recitation of the mighty acts of God or a reading of the law, a reaffirmation of the people's allegiance to the covenant and a sacrifice or festival celebration. Joshua's actions at Shechem place a final stamp on the past (the exodus and conquest) and signal a future in which the people will settle in the Promised Land.

24:26. stone and oak. Standing stones and sacred trees or groves are a part of Canaanite (see the Ugaritic Epic of Aqhat) and early Israelite cultic sites (see for stones Gen 28:18-22; Ex 24:4; 2 Sam 18:18; for trees Gen 12:6; Deut 11:30; Judg 6:11; 9:6; 1 Sam 10:3). Although both will be condemned in later traditions (Ex 23:24; Lev 26:1; Deut 12:2; 2 Kings 16:4), their use here is quite natural. It is also possible that they serve as monumental reminders of major events (as do the twelve stones noting the crossing of the Jordan River in Josh 4:2-9). They also separate the covenant renewal ceremony from the Baal temple at Shechem.

24:28-33
Death and Burial of Joshua

24:30. Mount Gaash. Although its exact loca-

tion is unknown, Mount Gaash would have been in the hill country of Ephraim, south of Timnath Serah (Khirbet Tibneh). That would place it about twenty miles southwest of Shechem.

24:32. Israelite ancestor burial tracts in Canaan. The original burial tracts used by the ancestors were both purchased from the local inhabitants. The first was the cave of Machpelah, purchased by Abraham from Ephron the Hittite near Hebron. This served as the burial place for Abraham, Sarah, Isaac, Rebekah and Jacob. Only Rachel was not buried here because of her sudden death during childbirth near Bethlehem (Gen 35:19). The pillar Jacob raised over her tomb is typical of the tumulus burials of nomadic peoples in that area. The account in Joshua notes the burial of Joseph on the plot of land near Shechem that Jacob had purchased from Hamor as a grazing area. As immigrants, the ancestors would not have been able to simply bury their dead in family tracts. They had to buy the land first and thus gain title in perpetuity; otherwise their graves might be disturbed or become inaccessible. The burial of Joshua and Eleazar, however, stand in contrast to this practice, since they were buried in land claimed through conquest and allotted to them and their descendants.

24:33. Gibeah. The burial site of Aaron's son Eleazar was in the Ephraimite allotment. Eusebius placed it about five miles north of Gophna. However, there are a number of sites named Gibeah, and what the text refers to may simply be the "hill of Phineas," a local name which is presently unidentifiable.

JUDGES

1:1—2:5
Attempt to Possess the Land

1:1-2. oracular information. Prior to military engagements, it was common practice for ancient Near Eastern army commanders to seek divine aid and information through oracles and omens (see 20:18). For instance, the assumption in the Assyrian royal inscription is that war occurred "by the command of the god Ashur." However, in order to learn the nature and urgency of this call, a variety of divination practices were utilized: the examination of an animal's organs, the casting of

lots or the observation of natural phenomena such as the flight of birds or cloud formations. The oracle or response would often determine (1) whether they would fight that day and (2) what tactics to employ.

1:3. territory of Simeon and Judah. The allotment assigned to Simeon in Joshua 19:1-9 was in the southern area of Palestine and "within that of Judah." The pairing of these two neighboring tribes in this episode makes logical sense. However, Simeon is eventually absorbed by the more prominent tribe of Judah. Thus Judah's offer to aid them to conquer their allotment became, in effect, an invitation to tribal oblivion for Simeon.

1:4. Bezek. This is the site of a battle with the Canaanites and Perezzites in which Judah and Simeon defeat their leader Adoni-Bezek. Although no geographical information appears in Judges, the place name also appears in the Saul narrative (1 Sam 11:8-11). This text indicates an open plain suitable for a military muster, no more than twelve or fifteen miles southwest of Jabesh Gilead (El Maklub), just east of the Jordan River. Survey of the hill country between Shechem and the Jordan Valley indicates Khirbet Salhab as a likely location (with Iron Age deposits evidenced) for ancient Bezek.

1:6. cutting off thumbs and big toes. Like the blinding of the right eye in 1 Samuel 11:2, this act of mutilation was designed both to humiliate prisoners and to insure they could never serve as warriors again. Unsteady on their feet and unable to grasp a sword, spear or bow, these men could only beg to survive. Assyrian reliefs from the time of Shalmaneser III (ninth century) depict prisoners being mutilated and dismembered.

1:7. picking up scraps under the table. These mutilated and helpless prisoners had no resort but to beg at their captor's table. They were kept on display as a sign of the power of their conqueror, eating scraps like dogs under the table (Ugaritic parallels include the god El treating enemy gods in this manner). The irony in this passage is that Adoni-Bezek was reduced to the same condition as the seventy kings he had previously mutilated.

1:7-8. Jerusalem. Despite the description of the sacking and burning of Jerusalem in this passage, all other references to that city and its Jebusite inhabitants during the settlement period indicate a failure to occupy the site by either Judah (Josh 15:63) or the tribe of Benjamin (Judg 1:21). In Judges 19:10-12 it is still considered a foreign city. The lack of archaeological evidence for this period (post-El Amarna breakup and post-Sea Peoples disruption) leaves the question unanswered. Some commentators suggest an unfortified area of the city was attacked and burned, but there is no way to prove this assertion. It will remain for David to finally conquer the city and transform it into the Israelite capital (2 Sam 5:6-10).

1:9. geography. The orientation of this verse suggests a generally southern movement, including the southern range of the hill country of Judah in the direction of Hebron and the northern range of the Negev desert westward toward the Shephelah and the Philistine coastal area. What is implied is an attempt to cap-

ture as much as possible of the area allotted to Judah (Josh 15:1-12, 21-63) and to Caleb (Josh 15:13-19).

1:10. Hebron. Located at Jebel er-Rumeidah, twenty-three miles northeast of Beersheba and nineteen miles southeast of Jerusalem, Hebron sat at the conjunction of roads from the Shephelah, the western Negev and Jerusalem. The text mentions an earlier name, Kiriath Arba (see Gen 23:2; Neh 11:25), possibly a clan center of the Anakites (Josh 14:15, 15:13). For additional information on this site, see the comment on Joshua 10:3-5.

1:11. Debir. Located southwest of Hebron in the southernmost part of the Judean hill country, Debir in the early Iron Age may have been an outpost of the invading Sea Peoples (if the Anakim of Josh 11:21 were not Canaanites). It is most likely situated at the Khiriath Rabud. See the comments on Joshua 10:3, 38-39 and 11:21.

1:12. daughter as reward. While this is not a frequent occurrence, the idea of "status-elevation" through an otherwise unavailable marriage arrangement would be appealing to some ambitious men. For instance, David is able to marry into Saul's royal household as a result of Saul's offer of a daughter and David's eventual conquest of Goliath (1 Sam 17:25). The feat involved here and in the Goliath incident is considered both difficult and dangerous. Thus the extraordinary offer of a valuable marriage contract is made to entice a hero to step forward. Othniel already has a high status in his relationship to Calelo, but there was still greater prestige to be gained.

1:14. request for a field. Having obtained a wife through the conquest of Kiriath Sepher, Othniel is now urged by his wife Acsah to ask for a piece of land with which to support his household. This could be considered a dowry since it is not mentioned earlier in the narrative. Daughters, however, did not generally obtain land as part of their dowry or as an inheritance (see, however, Num 36:1-13). Thus the request for land had to be made by a male kinsman. Additionally, Othniel is a prized vassal who has previously done exemplary military service and could be in line for a land grant (similar cases are found in Mari texts). There is a Babylonian boundary marker from this period that depicts a father transferring land rights to a daughter.

1:14. getting off donkey. Interpretation of this action is varied. Some believe Acsah made a noise (clapped her hands) to both draw her father's attention and as a sign of derision at the land grant made to her husband. Another suggestion is that by alighting from her donkey she became a supplicant, once again her father's daughter asking for a favor. Certainly, unwatered land was worthless; Acsah's embassy is to insure her household's survival.

1:15. upper and lower springs. This may refer to water sources that may be tapped by shallow excavations in wadi beds or by drilling deep well shafts in places where the water table is much lower. It is also possible that specific geographical locations are being refer-enced in the Negev region, but no current location can be discerned for this.

1:16. Kenites. The Kenites were one of several tribes or clans which inhabited the deserts of the Sinai peninsula and the area south and east of the Negev as far as the Gulf of Aqabah (Gen 15:19; 1 Sam 27:10; 30:29; 1 Chron 2:55). It is also possible, based on the placement of Heber's camp in Judges 4:11, that the Kenites ranged as far north as the Jezreel Valley. Their connection to Moses and Jethro (Hobab) goes back to Exodus 3:1. They are portrayed as herders (Judg 5:24-27), caravaneers and itinerant metalworkers. This latter skill is deduced from the etymology of their name, which can mean "to forge." See the comment on Numbers 24:21-22.

1:16. City of Palms. Based on the description in the text and its association elsewhere (Judg 3:13), this is most likely Jericho, the ancient oasis city just eight miles northwest of the Dead Sea (Tell es-Sultan). Its existence and fertility (boasting many palm trees as well as cultivated fields) is based on the continual flow of the springs of 'Ain es-Sultan and 'Ain Duq. Earliest occupation of the site began in the Mesolithic period (c. 9000-8700 B.C.), and eventually the population and importance of the city grew to such an extent that a complete mudbrick wall system was constructed during Early Bronze III (c. 2700 B.C.). There are some breaks in occupation due to invasion and conquest (as at the end of the Early Bronze III, c. 2500 B.C., and again during the early part of Late Bronze IIb, c. 1350 B.C.). At the time of the judges, the site was sparsely occupied and may have only served as an outpost or perhaps a caravan stop. It will not be rebuilt as a city site until the ninth century B.C. (see 1 Kings 16:34).

1:16. Arad. Located at Tell 'Arad in the Beersheba Valley, twenty miles south of Hebron, this site was first occupied in the Chalcolithic period, and the lower city (situated around a natural depression that functioned as a cistern/well combination) expanded during the Early Bronze Age due to extensive economic contacts with Egypt. An unfortified settlement was constructed on the upper tell during the

Iron Age. Its occurrence and the remains of a cultic area or courtyard in addition to housing may be signs of the Kenite occupation of this area mentioned in Judges and in 1 Samuel 27:10. The upper tell of Arad contains a total of seven strata during the Iron Age, with a fortress and temple complex constructed in the tenth century B.C.

1:17. Zephath (Hormah). This is one of the Negev villages captured by Judah and Simeon in the Judges account of the conquest. It was renamed Hormah, "destruction," by the Israelites (see also Num 21:3, which places it near Arad). It has been identified with Tel Masos and Tel Ira, both in the region between Arad and Beersheba.

1:18. Gaza. Located in the southwest section of Canaan's coastal plain and on the important international highway ("Way of the Philistines" or Via Maris), Gaza (Tell Harube) functioned as Egypt's provincial capital in Canaan from 1550-1150 B.C. It is mentioned in the annals of Pharaoh Thutmose III and the El Amarna texts. After the invasion of the Sea Peoples, it became the most important of the five Philistine cities and figures in a number of the conflicts between these people and the Israelites (6:3-4; 16:1-4). The text concerning its capture by Judah is uncertain. The Septuagint states that they did not capture Gaza, Ashkelon and Ekron, and this seems to be confirmed by 1:19, which says the Israelites were unable to conquer the cities of the plain.

1:18. Ashkelon. One of the main cities of the Philistine Pentapolis, Ashkelon is located about ten miles north of Gaza and functioned as a seaport for much of its existence. Its strategic location brought it to the attention of the Egyptians, who wished to control Canaan and the highways north, beginning in the Middle Bronze Age (c. 2000-1800 B.C.), when the city appears in the Execration texts. During the El Amarna period (fourteenth century B.C.), Ashkelon's ruler was a vassal of Akhenaton and wrote several letters to that pharaoh. Merenptah also lists the city among his conquests in his victory stele (c. 1208 B.C.) and depicts its capture on the walls of the great temple at Karnak. Although it was allotted to Judah, this city and the other Philistine cities of the plain were not con-quered by the Israelites.

1:18. Ekron. Assigned in the lists to both Judah (Josh 15:11) and Dan (Josh 19:43), Ekron lay on the border between the Shephelah and the Central Hill Country. It is identified with Tel Miqne, about twenty miles southwest of Jerusalem in the frontier area separating Philistia from Judah. Although there are traces of occupation as far back as the Chalcolithic, excavations have shown the first major city site appears in the Late Bronze Age, when contact with Egypt and Cyprus are indicated by ceramic and scarab (Nineteenth Dynasty) remains. The abrupt shift in the material culture resulting from the Sea Peoples invasion of the twelfth century B.C. led to expansion of the city and a new population group. During the first millennium, under Assyrian and Babylonian domination, Ekron became a major industrial city, producing huge quantities of olive oil in its refineries. Its appearance in the list in Judges indicates its place as a major Philistine city and one not captured by Judah (Judg 3:1-4).

1:19. iron chariots. The use of iron chariots is ascribed to Israel's enemies in Canaan, especially the cities of the plain, throughout the conquest period (see the comments on Josh 17:16 and Judg 4:3). They reflect a higher level of technology and greater wealth than that of the Israelites (see 1 Sam 13:19-21) and as such a major threat to the success of the conquest. The actual amount of iron used may have been very small, but its appearance as decoration, reinforcements or as wheel sheaths may have been enough to strike terror in their enemies. In this passage, the mention of iron chariots suggests a realistic appraisal of the military situation which kept the Israelites bottled up in the hill country where chariots would be of less use. Certainly, there are assurances that the tribal forces, with the help of God as the Divine Warrior, would be able to overcome this obstacle (Josh 17:18; Judg 4:7). However, the archaeological record as well as the admission here that some areas were never conquered indicates a rationalization for failure based on the physical reality of the situation. It will only be when Israel acquires iron technology and military parity with the Philistines that this dreaded weapon will lose its ability to frighten them.

1:20. sons of Anak. These were among the inhabitants of Canaan at the time of the conquest. Their territory centered on Hebron (Josh 21:11), and they were said to be men of great size (Deut 2:10; 9:2) and greatly feared by the Israelites (Num 13:28, 33). Their expulsion from Hebron by Caleb may have marked at least one success in displacing a native people from the area of Judah. Subsequently, the surviving Anakim may have taken refuge in the Philistine cities of Gaza, Gath and Ashdod. See the comment on Joshua 11:21.

1:21. Jebusites. First mentioned as descendants of Canaan (Gen 10:16), the Jebusites were probably non-Semitic peoples, related to

Hittites or Hurrians, who moved into this region during the early second millennium. They inhabited the hill country along the southern border with Benjamin (Josh 15:8) and the city of Jebus (Josh 15:63; 2 Sam 5:6). Jerusalem, but not Jebus, is mentioned in the El Amarna texts, and Jebus also does not appear in the Execration texts. The statement that the Benjaminites could not conquer the city is reinforced by the Levite's refusal to stop in an "alien city" of non-Israelites in Judges 19:10-12. After David captured Jerusalem, the Jebusites apparently were either assimilated or eventually lost their ethnic identity as an enslaved people (2 Sam 5:6-9).

1:22-23. Bethel. The strategic location of Bethel (modern Beitin), on a crossroads that bisected the central hill country just north of Jerusalem, made it a natural target for the Israelites and later conquerors as well (Joseph's [i.e., Ephraim's] mention here may reflect later tribal alliances subsequent to its allotment to Benjamin; see Josh 18:22). Its role as a sanctuary site has long standing in the biblical narrative (see the comment on Gen 28:19), and excavations have revealed a Middle Bronze cultic installation at the site. It will eventually become one of the two major cultic centers during the divided monarchy (1 Kings 12:29-33). The description of its capture, which is not mentioned in Joshua, may be based on the use of a postern gate (a minor passage used when the city gates were closed for the night) such as that found in the excavations at Ramat Rahel (just south of Jerusalem). Excavations indicate a massive destruction level at Bethel dating to the late thirteenth century B.C.

1:26. Luz in the land of the Hittites. The reference to the Hittites has generally been equated with Syria or the area of Lebanon, two regions that were a part of the Hittite empire prior to the Sea Peoples' invasion in 1200 B.C. It is also possible that the new city of Luz was simply established further north within Palestine and west of Bethel (see Num 13:29; Josh 16:2).

1:27. Beth Shan. Identified with Tell el-Husn, Beth Shan is located at the eastern end of the Jezreel Valley in northern Canaan. Like Megiddo on the western end, it serves as a guardian of the important Via Maris highway. Settlement began in the Chalcolithic period and was nearly continuous up until the present. A second city lies at the base of the tell, built during the Hellenistic period as one of the Decapolis cities and greatly expanded during Roman and Byzantine times (Scythopolis). Excavations seem to indicate that, unlike many Late Bronze sites, Beth Shan was not destroyed by the Sea Peoples, and Rameses III continued to maintain control of this important commercial center during the first half of the twelfth century B.C. The biblical text notes that Saul did not conquer this city (1 Sam 31:10-12), and it is only in Solomonic times that it is added to Israelite territory (1 Kings 4:12).

1:27. Taanach. See the comment on Joshua 12:21 for discussion of this northern Canaanite city.

1:27. Dor. See the comment on Joshua 12:23 for discussion of this coastal city in northern Canaan.

1:27. Ibleam. This fortress site (Khirbet Bel'ameh) is situated at the eastern end of the Jezreel Valley and functioned as one of a group of cities guarding that important transportation link. It is listed as one of the cities that the tribe of Manasseh was unable to conquer (Josh 17:11-12), but it does have some significance as an Israelite outpost during the divided monarchy (2 Kings 9:27). Its strategic importance is confirmed by its mention in the conquest list of Thutmose III (c. 1504-1450 B.C.).

1:27. Megiddo. See the comment on Joshua 12:21 for discussion of this major city located at the western entrance to the Jezreel Valley.

1:29. Gezer. See the comment on Joshua 12:21 for discussion of this major city, which linked the coastal plain and Philistia with the central hill country and Jerusalem.

1:30. Kitron. Assigned to Zebulun, the most likely location for this site is in the northwestern portion of the Jezreel Valley. Other suggestions, which place it more in the Acco Plain (Tell Qurdaneh and Tell el-Far) simply because this would have been a factor favoring Canaanite military tactics, are less likely based on current information.

1:30. Nahalol. Although its exact location is uncertain, a case has been made to equate this city of Zebulun's allotment with Tell en-Nahl, five miles east of the Mediterranean Sea near Haifa. Etymological similarities in the name and the appearance of artifactual remains covering the Early Bronze to the Arabic periods favor this identification, but its placement in Asher's territory creates a geographic problem that has not been resolved.

1:31-32. territory of Asher. See the comment on Joshua 19:24-31 for a discussion of Asher's tribal allotment.

1:33. Beth Shemesh. See the comment on Joshua 21:16 for discussion of this city located in the northeastern section of the Shephelah as it borders on Philistia.

1:33. Beth Anath. The precise location of this site is still unknown. The most likely claimant at this point is Safed el-Battikh in the upper Galilee region. The city was apparently mentioned in Egyptian records from the time of Thutmose III, Seti I and Rameses II, and appears to lie on the route between Hazor and Tyre.

1:34-36. Amorites. See the comment on Numbers 21:21 for discussion of this ethnic group which existed in Canaan prior to the formation of Israel. Their cultural and linguistic influence on Mesopotamia and Syro-Palestine is perhaps the most pervasive of any people, creating the high civilization of Hammurabi's Babylon and maintaining their cultural identity, at least in some regions, until the beginning of the Iron Age.

1:35. Mount Heres. The "mountain of the sun" has often been equated with Beth Shemesh (see Josh 21:16) or Ir Shemesh (Josh 19:41). That is, however, not certain, and the site itself may be one of several villages identified just southeast of Yalo (five miles east of Gezer). As part of Dan's tribal allotment, it would have been located in the southeastern area of the Valley of Aijalon.

1:35. Aijalon. This site, assigned to Dan (Josh 19:42), is probably to be equated with Yalo, situated five miles east of Gezer at the western end of the Valley of Aijalon. Its strategic importance, lying on a major road leading into the hill country, is confirmed by its mention in the El Amarna texts and its appearance in Saul's campaigns (1 Sam 14:31).

1:35. Shaalbim. This city in the territory of Dan (Josh 19:42) has been identified with Selbit, three miles northwest of Aijalon. It was later incorporated into Solomon's second administrative district (1 Kings 4.9) and may have served, like Aijalon, as a fortress guarding the passage through the Valley of Aijalon.

1:36. Scorpion Pass. This refers to a pass southwest of the Dead Sea, the Neqb es-Safa, which may have first been used by the Egyptians as they traveled to the copper-mining area near the Arabah and Eilat (see Num 34:4; Josh 15:3).

1:36. Sela. Although its identification is uncertain, its placement in association with the Scorpion Pass suggests a location to the southwest of the Dead Sea. Because its name means "the rock," some commentators equate it with either Petra, the Nabatean rock city, or with modern Sela', two miles northwest of Buseira. Excavations, however, have not revealed deposits earlier than the ninth century B.C. for these sites.

2:1-5. Bokim. This site is named for the weeping of the Israelites after they were rebuked by

God's angel for failing to obey the covenant and failing to wage total war against the Canaanites. Its location is unknown, although the text suggests placement just west of the Jordan River near Gilgal.

2:6—3:6
The Cycles of the Judges

2:9. Timnah Heres. See the comment on Joshua 19:50 (Timnah Serah) for this place name, which is associated with Joshua's portion of the land within the boundaries of Ephraim. It is identified with Khirbet Tibnah, fifteen miles southwest of Shechem, which contains extensive evidence of a village site during Iron I and II.

2:9. Mount Gaash. Associated with Timnah Heres and Joshua's allotment of the land, this mountain has not been identified. It should, however, be located within a range of fifteen to twenty miles southwest of Shechem in the territory of Ephraim. The hilly terrain in that region makes exact identification difficult (see 2 Sam 23:30).

2:11-13. Baals. The use of a plural form here does not indicate a large number of different Canaanite gods. Rather it refers to various local manifestations of the same storm and fertility god Baal. Gods were generally tied to local sites (high places, shrines, cities). This also seems to be the case with Yahweh (Bethel, Jerusalem and Shiloh are all associated with God's name or presence). Baal, which means "lord," occurs as a divine name as early as the eighteenth century B.C. in Amorite personal names from Mari. Some would offer examples as early as the late third millennium. By the fourteenth century it was used by Egyptians to refer to the storm god. The name is also evident in texts from Alalakh, Amarna and Ugarit as the personal name of the storm god, Adad. Baal was a fertility deity and was a dying (winter) and rising (spring) god. In the mythology of Ugarit he is pictured in combat with Yamm (the sea) and Mot (death). His consorts are Anat and Astarte.

2:13. Ashtoreths. The plural form of Astarte, the consort of Baal within the Canaanite pantheon, is indicative of her appearance in various local manifestations. She was both a fertility goddess and a goddess of war. The singular form of the name only appears in 1 Kings 11:5 and 2 Kings 23:13, where it refers to the chief goddess of the Phoenician city of Sidon. In fact there are several female deities who are mentioned as Baal's consort (Anath, Ashtoreth, Asherah) in Ugaritic and Phoenician texts. Astarte's popularity among the Canaanites may reflect a merging of these other goddesses into her person or simply a local preference. The cult of Astarte also appears in Egypt during the New Kingdom (perhaps due to greater contact with Canaan) and in Mesopotamia.

2:11-19. relationship cycle. The idea of a cycle of relationship with deity is a common pattern in the ancient Near East. The sequence of certain types of behavior alienating deity, making him angry and leading to devastation of the country, followed by the land recovering divine favor, bringing restoration, is offered as a common explanation of rise and fall. It can be observed, for instance, in Assyrian king Esarhaddon's account of the destruction of Babylon (carried out by his father, Sennacherib, in the seventh century). Differences would include (1) that the offenses in the Esarhaddon text were ritual offenses, and (2) that there is no raising up of a deliverer, though it is clear that Esarhaddon fashions himself in that role.

2:16-19. judges. In English the term *judge* is used to describe an official who maintains justice within the established court system. The Hebrew term used in the context of this book describes an individual who maintains justice for the tribes of Israel. This justice comes in bringing protection from foreign oppressors. Maintaining international justice was often the role of the king. What made these judges unlike kings was that there was no formal process for assuming the office, nor could it be passed on to one's heirs. There was no supporting administration, no standing army and no taxation to underwrite expenses. So while the actual function of the judge may have had much in common with the king, the judge did not enjoy most of the royal prerogatives. Just as a king also judged civil cases, the judges may have had some of that responsibility (see 4:5), but this would have been a minor role. The judges did not serve as heads of government in general but did have the authority to call out the armies of the tribes. Prior to the monarchy, no one from any one tribe would have been able to exercise such authority over another tribe. God was the only central authority. Therefore, when a judge successfully rallied the armies of several tribes, it was seen as the work of the Lord through that judge (see 6:34-35). Only the establishment of kingship assigned a permanent human central authority over the tribes.

3:3. five rulers of the Philistines. After the invasion of the Sea Peoples (c. 1200 B.C.), a group known as the Philistines settled along the Coastal Plain and in the Shephelah region of Canaan. Eventually five major city-states emerged: Gaza, Ashkelon, Ashdod, Gath and Ekron (Josh 13:2-3). Destruction levels found in excavations at Ashdod and Ashkelon indicate the overthrow of Egyptian garrisons about 1150 B.C. and the resettlement of the area by the Philistines. While their city-states and attendant villages were independent politically, they often functioned as a coalition in their dealings with Israel and other states (see 1 Sam 6:16; 29:1-5). At their height, the Philistine coalition expanded northward to Tell Qasile (on the coast at the Yarkon River) and east through the Jezreel Valley to Beth Shan. It is only the emergence of a strong monarchy under David and Solomon that eventually holds Philistine hegemony in check in the rest of Palestine.

3:3. Canaanites. See the comment on Genesis 15:19-21 for discussion of these inhabitants of Canaan prior to the conquest. In the Judges context, *Canaanites* is used as a generic ethnic term to designate one of four groups of people who are neighbors of the invading Israelites (Philistines, Hivites, Phoenicians [Sidonians]). This is a much reduced list from that found in Genesis 10:15-18 and 15:19-21, and is probably more reflective of the major political groups with which the Israelites had to deal.

3:3. Sidonians. The Sidonians are listed in Genesis 10:15 as descendants of Canaan. However, in the context of the Judges period, they represent the people of Lebanon and Phoenicia, which bordered on the northern edge of the Israelite tribal allotments. The city-state of Sidon was a major seaport on the Mediterranean coast, twenty-five miles north of the other important Phoenician seaport, Tyre. It is mentioned in the Ugaritic Epic of Keret (c. 1400 B.C.) as well as in the El Amarna texts and the campaign lists of Pharaoh Thutmose III. Its later associations with Israel are diplomatic (Jer 27:3) and commercial (Is 23:2).

3:3. Hivites. See the comment on Genesis 34:2 for a discussion of these people of Canaan and their possible relation to either Hurrian or Hittite settlers.

3:3. Lebanon Mountains. These heights extend for over one hundred miles north-south and rise to an elevation of over ten thousand feet. The western slopes of these mountains receive as much as sixty inches of rain and snow a year and thus provide fertile ground for agricultural pursuits. The extensive cedar forests that also existed in antiquity were the direct result of this pattern of Mediterranean climate. Although the eastern slopes do not receive as much rainfall, there are a number of rivers and springs that make their more gentle slopes fertile in the Beqa' Valley region.

3:5. peoples of Canaan. The list of nations with which the Israelites had to contend in Canaan is found in several other places, with some variations (see Gen 15:19-21; Deut 7:1 lists seven nations, including the Girgashites, which are excluded in Judges). For discussion of the individual groups, see the comments on Judges 3:3 (Canaanites); Genesis 23:3-20 (Hittites); Judges 1:34-36 and Numbers 21:21 (Amorites); Genesis 15:20 (Perizzites); Genesis 34:2 (Hivites); and Judges 1:21 (Jebusites).

3:7-11
Othniel

3:7. Baals and Asherahs. These Canaanite fertility deities often appear together. They represent the bounty of rain and the growth of crops in the fields. See the comments on Judges 2:11-13 for discussion of them as a danger to the Israelites' adherence to the covenant.

3:8. Aram Naharaim. The region identified with Aram Naharaim is the northern portion of the Euphrates in eastern Syria and the Habur triangle region within which Nahor and Haran are located (see Gen 24:10). This is the area where the Hurrian empire of Mitanni was located from 1500-1350. The Hittites had begun action against Mitanni as early as 1365, and the middle of the fourteenth century brought the breakup of the Hurrian kingdom, creating refugees and displaced tribes from the region. Cushan-Rishathaim's name, though admittedly hebraized, shows similarities to common Hurrian names of the period (Kuzzari-rishti). It is possible, then, that this first threat comes from a displaced tribe trying to find a new homeland rather than from a foreign conqueror trying to enlarge his empire.

3:12-30
Ehud

3:12-13. Moabites, Ammonites, Amalekites. Moab and Ammon were Transjordanian kingdoms that had genealogical ties to the Israelites (see the comment on Gen 19:30-38). Their appearance here as rival states probably reflects the growing border tensions resulting from the expansion of the Israelite tribes. The Amalekites are always portrayed as sworn enemies of Israel (see Num 24:20; Deut 25:17-19). Although tied to the Sinai peninsula and Midian in some narratives, they seem to have also ranged into the southeastern portion of Canaan and into the hill country of Samaria. As such, they would be a useful ally for any encroaching enemy such as Eglon's Moabite force.

3:13. City of Palms. The reference once again, as in Judges 1:16, is to the oasis site of Jericho, just north of the Dead Sea. It was a natural stronghold for any force attempting to control the Judean wilderness and the roads leading into the central hill country.

3:15. left-handed. The appearance here and in Judges 20:16 of left-handed Benjaminites suggests a practice of teaching ambidextrous use of weapons by that tribe. However, being left-handed was sufficiently unusual that it could be used as a strategic factor, allowing Ehud to enter Eglon's presence with a concealed weapon.

3:15. tribute. When one state or other political entity conquered another or extended hegemony over its affairs, the result was the exaction of tribute payments from the subject people (see 2 Sam 8:2; 1 Kings 4:21; 2 Kings 17:3-4). This could take the form of precious metals (by weight or as jewelry or implements), farm produce (a significant portion of the harvest), or labor service. Not surprisingly, this draining of the economy was unpopular and was generally the reason for revolt or warfare. Extrabiblical documentation for this practice is widespread. For instance, the annals of the Assyrian kings often include lists of items received as tribute: the "Black Obelisk" inscription of Shalmaneser III (859-824 B.C.) contains Jehu's tribute to Assyria of silver, gold, lead and hard woods; Tiglath-Pileser III (744-727 B.C.) received elephant hide, ivory, linen garments and other luxury items from his vassals in Damascus, Samaria, Tyre and elsewhere.

3:16. Ehud's sword. The dagger fashioned by Ehud was probably made of bronze. At only eighteen inches in length and straight, it was less likely to be detected by Eglon's Moabite guards. This also allowed it to be doubled-edged, unlike the more common "sickle-swords" of that era, which were designed for chopping, not thrusting. Since the blade was made to be punched into its victim, it would not have had a cross piece, only a grip or wrapped surface for the wielder to hold. Thus it could be forced completely into the body of Eglon, killing him quickly, and very little blood would result from what was in essence a corked wound. Like so many other factors in this narrative, this was an unusual weapon, used by a left-handed man, and designed for a single purpose: assassination.

3:16. strapped to right thigh. Since Ehud was left-handed, it would be natural for him to strap his dagger on his right thigh. Thrusting weapons must be drawn across the body in order to be placed on guard immediately.

However, since most people are right-handed, Eglon's guards would be less careful about checking what to them would be an awkward placement for a weapon.

3:19. the idols near Gilgal. These images (perhaps either standing stones or carved idols) may mark the boundary between Israelite (Ephraim/Benjamin) territory and that held by Eglon at Jericho. It is possible that a Canaanite sanctuary existed at Gilgal and that the tribute brought by Ehud would have had to be brought here in order that the gods could witness this show of submission. However, subsequent action (and its second mention in Judg 3:26) suggests that this is just Ehud's turning-back point prior to returning to Eglon's court.

3:19. secret message. Eglon's reaction to Ehud's proffered secret message (sending his attendants away), suggests that this is considered an important and prized piece of information. It is unlikely he was expecting to receive the report of a spy but rather an oracle from a god. Otherwise he would have wanted his advisors to hear the news. Ehud had singled him out with the title "O king" and then confirmed his desire by stating that the message was from Yahweh (v. 20). Just as Ehud's people had submitted to him, Eglon now expected divine word of future conquests and favor (in a prophecy text from Mari the king is given a secretive warning of a revolt). In this way Eglon's ambition led to his demise.

3:20. king rising from seat. This statement has been included in the translation based on the reading from the Septuagint. It provides an extra piece of narrative action. Certainly, by rising to a standing position, Eglon made himself a better target for Ehud's stabbing thrust in 3:21.

3:23. architecture. The architectural features of Eglon's audience chamber are predicated on a term which does not appear elsewhere but may be translated "the upper chamber over the beams." This implies a raised platform, reached by a staircase, within a larger audience chamber. There were apparently doors which separated this private room from the larger area and since it was the king's private meeting area it probably contained a toilet facility, which was at times a display of pride. Thus when Eglon drew Ehud up the stairs and into this room, closing and locking the door behind them, Ehud was able to dispatch him in private. He was then able to escape by removing the toilet seat and descending through the floor into the latrine below (the NIV translates it "porch") and out through the "janitor's door" into the larger audience room. His departure through the portico would not have aroused the guards waiting there, and they would have been slow to investigate the king's absence due to the fecal smell emanating from his inner chamber.

3:24. smell. At the point when Ehud stabbed Eglon, the murdered man's anal sphincter exploded, creating a smell similar to that associated with a bowel movement. Eglon's guards hesitated to interrupt the king while he was relieving himself (see similar euphemistic reference in 1 Sam 24:3) and thus gave Ehud time to escape and rally his troops.

3:26. Seirah. This site or geographic features has not been positively identified. Its proximity to the "idols near Gilgal" (see Judg 3:19) suggests the area just north of Jericho in the Jordan Valley. Such a spot would have been sufficiently close to rally the Israelites to attack the Moabite garrison at Jericho.

3:28. fords. To hold the fords (shallow crossing) of the Jordan River was to effectively control passage of armies from Canaan into Transjordan and vice versa (see comment on Josh 2:7). Ehud's strategy was to prevent the evacuation of Eglon's garrison and to hold off any reinforcements that might come from the direction of Moab. Similar strategic use of the fords is also found in Judges 12:5-6 when Jephthah held them against the Ephraimites and in Rameses II's depiction of the Battle of Kadesh against the Hittites (c. 1285 B.C.).

3:31
Shamgar

3:31. Shamgar. There is no reason to think of Shamgar as an Israelite or as a judge. The Philistines were moving from the north toward Egypt at the end of the thirteenth century, and the Egyptians undoubtedly would have used mercenary bands to engage them. Shamgar could well have been the leader of such a band (perhaps Apiru, see comment on Josh 5:1). His military intervention would have benefited Israel as much as Egypt. Nevertheless, he was used by the Lord as an instrument of salvation.

3:31. son of Anath. This designation or title for Shamgar may indicate his dedication to or association with the Canaanite goddess Anath, who was a patron of warriors. Shamgar's name may well be Hurrian (although some suggest it is West Semitic and therefore Canaanite). Thus he may be a mercenary, like Jephthah or David's thirty mighty men (2 Sam 23:8-39). The title has been compared to the Haneans in the Mari texts, who are warlike mercenaries from the shrine of Hanat (=Anat).

There is additionally an Egyptian warrior in the thirteenth century who is identified as son of Anat, and also an arrowhead from Late Bronze Age Palestine engraved with Ben Anat. All of these suggest a military class designated by this title.

3:31. Philistines. As the Sea Peoples began to settle in Syro-Palestine after their successful invasion of all of the Near Eastern coastal areas (except for Egypt, where Rameses III barely drives them off), they had to contest the area with its local inhabitants (see Judg 3:3). The Philistines, one of these Sea People contingents, must have faced a variety of opponents, including the Israelites. In this case, a unit of six hundred Philistines is attacked by Shamgar. The story could be read to suggest that he alone slew them all with an oxgoad. However, it does not rule out the possibility that he was a local Canaanite or Hurrian mercenary leader (well-known enough to also appear in the Deborah narrative in Judg 5:6) whose exploits at least indirectly aided the Israelites by destroying a common enemy.

3:31. oxgoad. The term *malmad* appears only in this story. It could refer to the goad or cattle guide used by herdsmen to direct their animals. If it had a fire-hardened or metal point, it could also serve its wielder as a short spear or pike when no formal weapon was available. Like many of the makeshift weapons used in Judges, it reflects a less technologically advanced culture.

4:1-24
Deborah and Barak

4:2. Hazor. Mentioned as an important city in both the eighteenth-century Mari texts and the fourteenth-century El Amarna letters, Hazor (Tell el-Qedah) stood at a strategic point in northern Galilee (ten miles north of the Sea of Galilee) on the road between Damascus to Megiddo. The Joshua account describes it as "the head of all those kingdoms" (Josh 11:10), and in both Joshua and in Judges, its king Jabin is defeated (Josh 11:13; Judg 4:24; see also 1 Sam 12:9). Archaeological investigations do show a major destruction level in the thirteenth century, which could be the result of attacks by either the Sea Peoples, the Israelites or some other group. Subsequently the city was refortified by Solomon (1 Kings 9:15) and remained a major center of commerce and a key to Israel's northern border until the Assyrian conquest (2 Kings 15:29). See the comment on Joshua 11:1 for additional information.

4:2. Harosheth Haggoyim. It is uncertain

whether this place name, translated "forests of the nations" in the Septuagint, is a city site or a forested region in Galilee. Attempts have been made to identify it with various sites (Tel el-Harbaj and Tell Amr), but the archaeological evidence is not conclusive. Similarly, there is no definitive reason to equate it with Muhrashti of the El Amarna letters. From the description in the text, it appears to either be a staging area or rallying point within the Jezreel Valley, perhaps within a zone under the control of Philistines (Sisera's name is non-Semitic). It may simply refer to that area of the Galilee region under the control of Sisera, who appears to be a military governor allied with Jabin of Hazor.

4:3. nine hundred iron chariots. The number of chariots involved in this engagement is so substantial that some have considered it exaggerated. Exaggerated figures were sometimes used in the ancient Near East to magnify the strength of an opponent and serve as a means to add greater glory to the commander or deity when the victory is won. Other examples of suspected hyperbole in the annalistic style of writing occur in the Assyrian Annals of Shalmaneser III (858-824 B.C.), which list 3240 chariots among his enemies, and in Thutmose III's claim to have captured 892 chariots at the battle of Megiddo. Other large numbers of chariots in biblical accounts can be found in 1 Samuel 13:5 (30,000/3,000 in Septuagint); 1 Kings 10:26 (1,400 chariots); and 1 Chronicles 19:7 (32,000 chariots). For more information on the use of iron fittings, see Judges 1:19.

4:5. holding court. Deborah is the only figure portrayed in the book of Judges as actually functioning in a judicial position. She hears and decides cases and provides answers to oracular inquiry under a palm tree which served as a landmark for that region. The description of her "court" is similar to that found in the Ugaritic epic of Aqhat (c. 1500 B.C.), which depicts King Danil sitting on a threshing floor before the city gates, judging the cases of the widows and orphans (Aqhat III.i.20-25).

4:5. between Ramah and Bethel. Ramah, in the tribe of Benjamin, is identified with er-Ram, three miles north of Jerusalem, and Bethel (Beitin) is another four miles north along the road into Ephraimite territory. This well-traveled route would be a likely place for a judge or prophet to sit and hold court.

4:6. Kedesh. See the comment on Joshua 12:22 for this site identified with Tell Qades, northwest of Lake Huleh in the upper region of the Galilee.

4:6. mustering at Mount Tabor. Its distinctive shape, a flat-topped promontory rising above the northeastern end of the Jezreel Valley (about two and a half miles from Nazareth), and its position at the juncture of the tribal territories of Zebulun, Issachar and Naphtali (Josh 19:22) made Mount Tabor a logical rallying point for troops from these tribes. From its summit it is possible to see south to Mount Gilboa and west to Mount Carmel. It would also be neutral ground where sacrifices and other cultic activities might be performed prior to a battle or at its conclusion (see Judg 8:18 and 1 Sam 10:3). Should an enemy detect their movements, the tribes would also hold high ground from which to fight and remain safe from Sisera's chariots. The actual battle, however, will take place to the south at the Wadi Kishon.

4:7. luring Sisera to Kishon. The Kishon River lies south of Mount Tabor near Taanach (see Josh 12:21). Although this is a flat plain that would ordinarily favor the use of chariots by Sisera's forces (see Judg 1:19), the river was apparently overflowing its banks due to heavy rainfall (Judg 5:20-21). This would have muddied the battlefield to the extent that the chariots would have been bogged down and become deathtraps. The genius of luring the enemy into an area where they would be overconfident and then surprised by the condition of the terrain provided the edge needed by the Israelites.

4:10. ten thousand men. It is difficult to determine whether this number should be read as ten thousand men or as ten divisions. The Hebrew terms are ambiguous. Often a clan would send a division of armed men, and these would likely have numbered far less than a thousand each. For more discussion see comment on Joshua 8:3.

4:11. Kenites. For discussion of these people, who ranged throughout the area from Galilee south to the Negev and the Sinai, see the comments on Numbers 24:21-22 and Judges 1:16.

4:11. tree of Zaanannim. Heber's campsite would be on the southern border of Naphtali (Josh 19:33), and its association with a landmark or sacred tree parallels it in the story to Deborah's palm (Judg 4:5). It was most likely near Mount Tabor and within the territory of Kedesh. This would place it north of the battle scene and within the capacity of a fleeing man like Sisera to reach.

4:12-13. Sisera's strategy. Having received reports of the deployment (possibly from Kenite allies—see Judg 4:17) of Barak's allied forces at Mount Tabor, Sisera marshaled his troops and chariots and sent them east through the Jezreel Valley into the Plain of Esdraelon.

They would have passed the sites of Megiddo (not yet reoccupied at this period) and Taanach as they drove toward the Kishon River. It is at this point that Sisera's strategy came apart due to the combination of rushing water in the wadi bed and the heavy rains that turned the plain into a quagmire.

4:14-16. Israel's strategy. Apparently, the strategy commanded by Deborah and carried out by Barak was to gather the combined tribal forces at Mount Tabor, a point on the fringe of their territories, from whose heights a clear view of the area could be seen. It provided protection should they be detected too soon and forested cover for their forces. Once they had been able to lure Sisera's army toward them through the Jezreel Valley and into the plain near the Kishon River, the Israelites could make a rushed attack on them as they floundered in the mud and water of the overflowing wadi. The strategy, as portrayed in Judges 4—5, is dependent upon divine intervention (a storm) and the giving of the exact moment in which to strike from Deborah, Yahweh's representative.

4:18-21. Jael's hospitality. In the "world-turned-upside-down" theme employed in Judges, many customs or everyday actions are reversed (see the correct sequence of events in a hospitality situation in Gen 18:2-8). Thus a woman instead of her husband offers Sisera hospitality. As a guest Sisera is not supposed to ask for anything, but he asks for both a drink as well as sentry duty on Jael's part. Finally, murdering a guest is never a part of the protocol of hospitality. However, Jael may have been justified in killing Sisera, since he was a potential threat to her as well as the honor of her household.

4:21. tent peg and hammer. The weapons Jael employed to kill the sleeping Sisera were ones with which she was quite familiar, since she undoubtedly used them to erect her tent each time they made camp. They would have easily come to mind, and the stroke, driving the peg through the skull into the ground, would have been a natural one for her.

5:1-31

Deborah's Song

5:1-3. singing victory songs. One way to celebrate victories and commemorate them for years to come is to compose and sing songs. They could be employed as immediate tributes to conquering heroes (see Judg 11:34 and 1 Sam 18:6-7) or serve as lasting parts of oral tradition (see the "Song of the Sea" in Ex 15:1-18). Victory songs are known in the an-

cient Near East such as that in the Epic of Tukulti-Ninurta (Assyria, thirteenth century B.C.) concerning his campaign against the Kassite king Kashtiliash. The song records how Tukulti-Ninurta requests divine aid on the basis of their previous relationship and how the gods come to his aid. It also includes a section of taunt against the enemy king who fled from the battle. Just as Deborah's song parallels the prose account in chapter 4, ancient Near Eastern literature offers several examples (in addition to the Tukulti-Ninurta Epic) of battle accounts being preserved in both prose and poetry (other examples come from Tiglath-Pileser I and Rameses II, both thirteenth century, and Thutmose III, fifteenth century).

5:6-7. troubled times. The lawless period associated with Shamgar and Jael, in which individual acts of heroism were the only moments of brightness, was characterized by roads so dangerous and subject to attack by bandits that merchants and farmers had to take hillside tracks and Israel's warriors were nowhere to be seen. Such troubled times are part of the "world-turned-upside-down" theme here and in the visions of Balaam found inscribed in plaster at Tell Deir 'Alla in the eastern Jordan Valley.

5:8. no shields or spears. The low level of technological development among the Israelites and their lack of the implements of war is also mentioned in 1 Samuel 13:19-22. They may have been forced to turn in all their weapons by their Philistine and Canaanite overlords, or they may simply have lacked the knowledge necessary to make them. In any case, Deborah's song implies their subjugation was also due to their worship of other gods and Yahweh's wrath.

5:10. riding white donkeys. Only the wealthy merchants could afford these prized animals. The call here is to have all classes, those who ride and those who must walk because of their poverty, to join in the song of praise for Yahweh who will deliver the people.

5:11. singers at watering places. The song to Yahweh is to be sung even louder than the cry of those who vied to water animals at wells and caravan stops. These men would cry out the news or a favorite story, perhaps accompanied by cymbals or other instruments. By entertaining travelers and carrying water, they could earn a small living and transmit stories.

5:14. roots in Amalek. In the list of tribes answering Deborah's call is a group from Ephraim associated with the hill country of the Amalek at Pirathon (see Judg 12:5). While it is possible that the wide-ranging Amalekites are referred to in this passage, it makes more sense to simply see this as an area within Ephraimite territory.

5:14. Makir. This passage and 1 Chronicles 7:14 both indicate that Makir (Machir) was a tribal group dwelling in the area between Ephraim and Zebulun, near the Kishon River.

5:19. Taanach. Five miles southeast of Megiddo and about the same distance west of Mount Gilboa, Taanach is one of the fortified cities that guarded the Valley of Jezreel (see comment on 6:33). It is mentioned in Pharaoh Thutmose III's reports of the Battle of Megiddo (fifteenth century B.C.) and possibly referred to in passing in the Amarna tablets. There was sparse occupation during the twelfth century, but there is a destruction layer dated about 1125.

5:20. the stars fought. In Near Eastern and Mediterranean traditions various gods (Egyptian Resheph; Mesopotamian Nergal; Greek Apollo) are associated with heavenly bodies (planets, stars, comets). They are occasionally viewed as leaving their courses to join in human battles, confound enemies and bring plagues to animals. As early as the end of the third millennium, Sargon's texts refer to the sun dimming and the stars going forth against the enemy. The Gebal Barkal stela of Thutmose III also mentions the aid of stars flashing from the sky to confuse and decimate his Hurrian enemies (see the use of stars and scepters in Num 24:7). It should be noted, however, that the stars in the Judges passage have no personalities connected to them and serve simply as Yahweh's messengers and tools, not as personified deities. See further the comments on Joshua 10:12-13.

5:21. the flooding of Kishon. The Kishon River is either the Wadi al-Muqatta, which serves as a drain for the Jezreel Valley flowing west to the Mediterranean, or the Wadi el-Bira, which flows east from Mount Tabor to the Jordan River. In Deborah's song, the river functions as an integral part of the battle strategy. With the aid of the stars in heavens, a source of rain in Ugaritic and Mesopotamian epic, the battle at the Kishon was decided by an unusual summer storm that sent torrents of water flooding in the Kishon River. As the banks overflowed, the saturated ground eliminated the effectiveness of Sisera's chariots. The story is very similar to that in Exodus 14:19-25, in which the pharaoh's chariots are disabled and destroyed by the returning waters of the Red Sea.

5:26. head crushing. In the Canaanite literature from Ugarit, the goddess Athtart (biblical Ashtaroth) is known as a warrior goddess who crushes the head of her opponents.

5:28. mother waiting at the window. There is a real poignancy about a woman, either mother or wife, standing and waiting for her husband or son to return from battle. While she must try to maintain her dignity and cast about for scenarios that will help rationalize the lateness of that return (vv. 29-30), she can only peer expectantly from the latticed window. Sometimes the window holds her captive in a cloistered universe, and sometimes it frames her as champion of a lost cause (see Michal in 2 Sam 6:16 and Jezebel in 2 Kings 9:30-32).

5:30. plunder. Warfare in the ancient world was justified by divine command or national honor. However, the impetus that drew kings and common soldiers to battle was the taking of plunder. The spoils of war meant riches, power and the subjugation of the enemy (see Deut 31:11-12; 20:14; Josh 11:14; 1 Sam 14:30-32).

6:1—8:35
Gideon

6:1. Midianites. The Midianites are a people living in the southern portions of the Transjordan region. They are described as the descendants of Abraham and Keturah (Gen 25:106), and in the Joseph narrative they operate as traders and caravaneers (37:25-36). Moses joins the Midianite clan of Jethro after fleeing Egypt (see comment on Ex 2:15), but the Midianites do not join the Israelites in the conquest of Canaan. In the Balaam narrative the Midianite elders are allied with the Moabites and participate in the hiring of the prophet to curse Israel (Num 22:4). Midianite territory originally centered in the region east of the Gulf of Aqaba in northwest Arabia, but Midianites ranged west into the Sinai Peninsula as well as north into Transjordan in various periods. Though their early history appears to be seminomadic or Bedouin in nature, archaeological study has revealed villages, walled cities and extensive irrigation in this region beginning as early as the Late Bronze period (the time of the exodus and the early judges). There is, so far, no reference to the Midianites in ancient texts, though they are sometimes identified with the *Shasu* mentioned frequently in Egyptian literature.

6:2. hiding in caves. With few fortified cities, the Israelites' only protection was to hide out in the hills, where they could preserve their supplies and their families. In this region they are most likely to have used the caves from the Carmel range into the Iron Hills flanking the Valley of Jezreel on the southwest.

6:3. invasion at harvest time. The timing of the invader was very important. If harvest time had passed, the villagers would have stored and hidden all of their grain and could withstand attack more easily. If the grain was still in the fields, the invader would have ample provisions and the villagers none. This would suggest April or May as the time of the invasions. The villages could easily be crippled if they were deprived of their year's supply of grain, so what the invaders did not use or steal, they destroyed. The trampling of the fields would also jeopardize future seasons.

6:3. Amalekites. See the comment on Numbers 24:20. The Amalekites wandered through vast stretches of land in the Negev, Transjordan and Sinai peninsula. The are unattested outside the Bible, and no archaeological remains can be positively linked to them. However, archaeological surveys of the region have turned up ample evidence of nomadic and seminomadic groups like the Amalekites during this period.

6:5. camels. It is important not to infer what the text does not state. It clearly indicates that the Midianites had innumerable camels, but it does not suggest that they used them as the equivalent of war horses in cavalry units. In fact evidence concerning the domestication of the camel does not suggest cavalry use for a couple of centuries yet. Nonetheless the saddle types used in this period do indicate that camels were being used effectively for transportation and as beasts of burden.

6:8. prophet. This is the first unnamed prophet in the biblical text. For discussion of various aspects of prophecy and prophets see the comments on Deuteronomy 18:14-22. Here he is seen as a defender of the covenant, and his message focuses on worshiping Yahweh exclusively. Ancient Near Eastern prophets often had messages that included admonitions regarding who should receive worship and how.

6:11. the Angel of the Lord. In the ancient world direct communication between heads of state was a rarity. Diplomatic and political exchange normally required the use of an intermediary. The messenger that served as the intermediary was a fully vested representative of the party he represented. He spoke for that party and with the authority of that party. He was accorded the same treatment as that party would enjoy were he there in person. While this was standard protocol, there was no confusion about the person's identity. All of this treatment simply served as appropriate recognition of the individual that he represented. Gifts given were understood to belong to the represented party, not the representative. Words spoken to the representative were expected to be reported back in accurate detail and were understood as having been spoken directly to the represented individual. When official words were spoken by the representative, everyone understood that he was not speaking for himself but was merely conveying the words, opinions, policies and decisions of his liege. In the same way the Angel of the Lord serves as the messenger or royal envoy endowed with the authority of the sender of the message.

6:11. Ophrah. The site of Ophrah has not been located with any certainty. The leading contender is the modern Affuleh between Megiddo and the Hill of Moreh in the Valley of Jezreel. Trees were often associated with oracles and theophanies, and sometimes marked places of worship (see Gen 12:6; 21:33; 35:4; Judg 4:5; 9:37; Is 1:29; Hos 4:13).

6:11. threshing wheat in a winepress. Threshing floors were large areas of dirt or stone that were usually out in the open so that the breezes could be used to blow away the chaff. They would generally be used by the whole community. Threshing was done mostly in June and July, using a stick or by walking cattle over the sheaves. A winepress was a square or circular pit hollowed out of rock big enough for a few people to walk around in. Threshing activity in a winepress would be much less conspicuous than on a threshing floor.

6:12. mighty warrior. The epithet used by the angel has often been translated "mighty warrior" (NIV), and that is acceptable when it is in a military context. There are, however, a number of people that are so described in community contexts (see Ruth 2:1; 1 Sam 9:1, both of which the NIV translates as "man of standing"). In these cases it designates the person as a responsible, upstanding individual in the community.

6:15. weakest clan, least in family. Gideon's comments about the impotence of his clan and his own lack of standing in the family have to do with authority. He has no authority to call out soldiers from his own clan or family, let alone from other tribes. The prerogatives of command came only with status, of which he is claiming to have none.

6:16. together/as one man. The NIV translates this phrase as if it applies to the Midianites' weakness before Gideon. An alter-native would be that despite Gideon's lack of official authority the Israelites would fight in concert, unified behind his leadership.

6:19. Gideon's offering. When Gideon describes what he wants to bring, he uses a general word for "gift" that is not necessarily indicative of a sacrifice, although when it is connected to a meal it usually has sacrificial overtones. It is the same word used for the offerings of Cain and Abel (see comment on Gen 4:1-7) and describes one of the categories in the sacrificial system (grain offerings, see Lev 2). The fact that the kid is prepared as meat and brought to the place rather than brought live and slaughtered there suggests more a meal than a sacrifice. The contents of this meal included goat meat and broth and unleavened bread (having been made quickly). An ephah is about half a bushel, which would make ten flat cakes of eight or ten inches in diameter, a very generous provision for the hard times they were experiencing.

6:20. put on rock. It is the angel that instructs Gideon to place the meal on a rock, where it is consumed, thus changing it from a meal to a sacrifice. Rocks were at times used as altars (1 Sam 14:32-34), but usually with the intention of allowing the blood to drain from the slaughtered animal, which would not be an issue here.

6:25. second bull, seven years old. The text may speak of two bulls (not in NIV, but see NASB). The second is offered as a sacrifice, and some infer the first must have been used to help tear down the altar. Only a few male bulls were needed to sustain a herd, so many males were slaughtered at a young age. Only the best stock would be kept for breeding. A seven-year-old bull must therefore have been a prime breeding bull. The sacrifice of this bull would have been extremely significant. Some bulls were kept for work animals, but these were usually castrated to make them more manageable and docile. If there are two animals here, the first was probably a gelded draft animal.

6:25. altar to Baal. Though the altar is said to belong to Gideon's father, the response of the town suggests it was a community shrine. There are a number of Canaanite temples that have been found in Israel (Hazor, Lachish) and a few open air sites from this period such as the "Bull Site" a few miles east of Dothan. Objects found at the sites, however, tend to be *masseboth* (standing stones, see comment on Gen 28:18-19) and incense stands rather than altars. One of the earliest Israelite altars is the tenth-century fieldstone altar at Arad that is about eight feet square and almost five feet high.

6:25. Asherah pole. Asherah can be either the name of a fertility goddess or the name of a cult object (as here). The goddess was popular in the polytheistic deviations in Israel and was sometimes considered a mediator of Yahweh's blessings. An indication of this belief is found in the inscriptions from Kuntillet Ajrud and Khirbet el-Qom. In Canaanite mythology she was the consort of the chief god, El. She appears in Mesopotamian literature as early as the eighteenth century, where she is consort of the Amorite god Amurru. The cult symbol may or may not have born a representation of the deity on it. The pole may represent an artificial tree, since Asherah is often associated with sacred groves and is portrayed as a stylized tree. Sometimes the cult object can be made or built, while on other occasions it is planted. We have little information of the function of these poles in ritual practice.

6:31. Joash's defense. Gideon's father, Joash, confronted with villagers seeking vengeance on behalf of the affronted Baal, suggests that this is not a matter for the community to punish but for Baal himself to avenge. When a desecration has taken place, it is deity's role to judge (see Lev 10:1-3; 1 Sam 6:19; 2 Sam 6:7). He declares that anyone who takes the matter of revenge into his own hands will be judged by his clan as guilty of bloodshed and subject to clan retribution. In the ancient Near East it is more common to see the god coming to the defense of his temple or image. So, for instance, the Weidner Chronicle reports how Marduk carried out his retribution on those whose performance of the rituals was unacceptable. In similar fashion Marduk seeks to restore to Babylon the image of himself that was carried off by the Elamites. These retributions, however, were all carried out by human beings claiming to be instruments of the gods' vengeance. It is this pretence that Joash wished to avoid.

6:33. Valley of Jezreel. The Valley of Jezreel gets its name from the town of Jezreel at the east end of the valley. This fertile plain divides the Carmel range from lower Galilee, extending southeast with the Kishon River from the Acco plain above Carmel to pass between the Hill of Moreh and Mount Gilboa and into the Jordan valley by Beth Shan. It ranges from five to ten miles wide across its fifteen-mile length (Jokneam to Jezreel). Major trade routes came into the valley by way of Nahal Iron at Megiddo, so the valley was sometimes referred to as the plain of Megiddo, or, later, Armegeddon. It was a natural staging ground for battles, and many took place there during biblical times, including Deborah and Barak's battle with the Canaanites (Judg 4), the battle of Mount Gilboa between Saul and the Philistines (1 Sam 31), and the battle between Josiah and Pharaoh Necho (2 Kings 23:29). It was also the location of Thutmose III's famous battle of Megiddo in the fifteenth century to subdue the land of Canaan.

6:34-35. the Spirit of the Lord in Judges. When the Spirit of the Lord is attached to any activity in Judges, it is usually to the calling up of an army. In a tribal society with no centralized government, it was difficult to get other tribes to stand with one or two that might be facing problems. The measure of a leader in such situations was his ability to compel others to follow even though he had no office of command over them. In Israel this was a mark of the power of Yahweh, for it was he alone who had the authority to call out the armies of the tribes. Yahweh was the only central authority. It was therefore a clear indication of the Lord's authority at work in someone when they exercised authority that was only Yahweh's by calling out the armies (see Judg 11:29; 1 Sam 11:6-8). This was one of the distinguishing features of the Judges of Israel.

6:36-40. fleece oracles. In an oracle a yes-no question is posed to deity and a mechanism of some binary nature is used so that deity can provide the answer. In Israel the priest carried the Urim and Thummim to use in oracular situations (see comment on Ex 28:30). That is apparently not available, so Gideon must be more creative and use a natural mechanism for the oracle (see Gen 24:14 and 1 Sam 6:7-9 for other occurrences). His yes-no question is whether or not the Lord is going to use him to deliver Israel. His oracular mechanism is based on what would normally happen to a fleece on a threshing floor overnight. Since the fleece is soft and absorbent and the threshing floor is rock or hard dirt, one would expect the fleece to be damp and the ground of the threshing floor dry. That would be the normal behavior of nature. In this case such a response would indicate a "yes" answer to his oracular question. Gideon has already been informed of the Lord's intentions by the angel and is just offering an opportunity for the Lord to inform him if the plan has changed. When the events of the first night turn out exactly how one would expect them to under normal circumstances, Gideon wonders if maybe this "silence" might just mean the Lord wasn't paying attention. He therefore switches the indicators so that the unusual occurrence would represent the "yes" answer—the fleece dry and the threshing floor wet. The thought behind this is that if deity is providing the answer, he can alter normal behavior and override natural laws in order to communicate his answer. In the ancient Near East,

when they wanted a natural mechanism for oracles, they tended to use the liver or kidney of sacrificed animals (a divinatory practice called extispicy; see comment on omens at Deut 18:10).

7:1. spring of Harod. The spring of Harod is at the base of the northern slope of Mount Gilboa, about a mile and a half east of the town of Jezreel. This is at the narrow pass at the east end of the Valley of Jezreel.

7:1. hill of Moreh. The hill of Moreh is directly north of Mount Gilboa and south of Mount Tabor. It blocks off the northeastern corner of the Valley of Jezreel. Traffic to Beth Shan and the fords of the Jordan there would swing south of the hill of Moreh to go through the pass where Gideon and his men are gathered. The Midianites were camped in the valley just west of Moreh about four or five miles from the spring of Harod and very close to Ophrah, Gideon's hometown (see comment on 6:11).

7:3. Mount Gilead. This is a very obscure reference that many believe represents a problem in the scribal transmission of the text. Mount Gilead usually refers to an area east of the Jordan which is difficult to fit in here.

7:5-6. styles of drinking water. Those who drink water in a kneeling position with their heads in the water to lap it up are (1) an easy target, (2) unaware of any enemy movement while they drink, and (3) susceptible to leeches. The alternative is to lie down flat (where one presents less of a target) and to keep alert, bringing water to the mouth while continuing to look around.

7:13. dream. Dreams were commonly believed to have significance in the ancient world. Not only did the Midianite soldiers take it as an omen, but so did the eavesdropping Gideon. Although the interpretation of dreams was often something best left to an expert because of the obscurity of the symbolism, some dreams were fairly transparent. It would not take an expert to discern that the barley loaf represented the farmer and the tent represented the nomad. For more on dreams see comments on Genesis 40:5-18; 41:8-16; and Deuteronomy 13:1-5. The concept of an overheard word as providing (inadvertently) an omen of encouragement is also found in the *Odyssey* as a slave girl expresses the wish that this would be the suitors' last meal.

7:16-21. Gideon's strategy. Gideon's three companies would have been positioned on the three sides of the camp, north, west and south (the hill of Moreh was on the east). The torches that they each have are made of material such as reeds that would smolder until exposed to the air and waved. The pitchers cover the glow of the smoldering torch until the proper moment. When all three divisions were deployed in their proper positions, the ram's horns were sounded. Usually only a few of the soldiers carried trumpets for signaling because hands were needed for weapons and shields. Likewise, for night battle, a certain number would be assigned to hold the torches that would illuminate the battle area and block retreat at the perimeter. It would be expected, then, that the trumpet blowers and torch holders would represent only a small percentage of the army, with the rest charging in to fight. Therefore, when the Midianites heard the blast of three hundred trumpets and saw the myriad of torches around the perimeter, they naturally assumed there was a massive army that would be charging into the camp, whereas Gideon had instructed his men to hold their positions around the perimeter.

7:22. fighting one another. It is a common motif that one of the ways a deity achieves victory is by throwing the enemy into confusion. An example in Egyptian literature occurs in the myth of Horus, where at Edfu Horus confuses the enemy so that they begin to fight one another until none remain.

7:22. Beth Shittah. The most common choice for the location of this town is the village of Shatta about six miles east of Jezreel heading toward Beth Shan. Therefore the Midianites have fled around the south end of the hill of Moreh to try to get across the fords of the Jordan along the Beth Shan Valley.

7:22. Zererah. Zererah is elsewhere known as Zarethan (Josh 3:16) and Zeredah. Most now identify it with Tell es-Sadiyeh eight miles further south from Abel Meholah, on the east side of the Jordan along the south side of the Wadi Kufrinje.

7:22. Abel Meholah, Tabbath. Abel Meholah is located on the west bank of the Jordan somewhere south of Beth Shan. The most likely candidate is Tell Abu Sus eleven miles south of Beth Shan at the southern end of the Beth Shan Valley where the Yabis river enters the Jordan from the east. Pottery shards from this period have been found in surveys at the site. Tabbath is less certain. It is often identified as Ras abu Tabat, though that seems too far south, very close to Tell es-Sadiyeh rather than Tell Abu Sus.

7:24. Beth Barah. The identification of this site is unknown, but it is obviously along the Jordan valley, apparently at a fording place near Abel Meholah.

8:1. Ephraim's complaint. Even though land had been assigned to each of the tribes, there were still frequent land disputes between them. Military activity of the sort conducted by Gideon could be expected to yield available territory that would previously have been controlled by the Midianites. The Ephraimites do not want to be left out should there be apportionment of additional territory. There is also the issue of plunder, which everyone could be expected to want a share of.

8:5. Succoth. Succoth is located at Tell Deir Allah about a mile north of the Jabbok River, about three miles east of the Jordan River. Remains from this period (Iron Age I) have been found on the site. The area on the top of the tell is comparable to one and a half football fields, about one and a quarter acres. It was a small settlement that was involved in a bronze-smelting industry.

8:6. hands in our possession. It was a common practice for a hand to be cut off each dead enemy so that a count of the casualties inflicted could be made. Egyptian monuments from this period depict piles of hands gathered after battle. Since the Midianite kings are not yet dead, the men of Succoth are unwilling to side with the resistance.

8:8. Peniel (Penuel). Penuel is located about five miles east of Succoth along the Jabbok River at modern Tell ed-Dhahab esh-Sherqiyeh. Surveys have provided evidence of settlement during this period, but the site has not been excavated.

8:9. tower in the town. Since the site of Penuel has not been excavated, remains of this tower have not been found. Iron Age sites, however, did often feature such towers as part of their fortifications. For example, excavations have shown that the town of Succoth had such a tower at the end of the judges period that was almost twenty-five feet in diameter. Such towers could be part of the gate structure, lookout posts along the walls, or, more frequently in this period, inner citadels in the area of the local shrine.

8:10. Karkor. The site of Karkor likely should not even be translated as a place name. In the text it has the definite article (which is unusual for place names), and the word means "level ground." It should almost certainly be identified as the Beqa'a basin. This is a broad, flat depression about five miles long, two miles wide, oriented on a southwest to northeast axis about seven miles northwest of modern Amman (biblical Rabbah).

8:11. route of the nomads. A local route climbed out of the Jabbok valley heading south from Penuel and moved southeast to intersect with the southwest corner of the Beqa'a basin. But the "route of the nomads" would be more off the beaten track. This verse says they went *east* of Nobah and Jogbehah. The location of Nobah is unknown, but Jogbehah is usually identified with Jubeihat about six miles northwest of Amman. It is located on an elevated ridge at about the middle of the southern side of the broad Beqa'a basin. If Gideon went to the east of Jogbehah, he must have been skirting the northeast end of the Beqa'a. This suggests that the "route of the nomads" followed the Jabbok east for several miles before heading south and swinging around to the south side of the Beqa'a from where the attack was made. This route would be about twenty miles from Penuel and about seventy from the initial encounter at Moreh.

8:13. Pass of Heres. Like Karkor above, the word "Heres" has a definite article and therefore is probably not a proper name. *Heres* means "sun," but that does not help identify the location. If the reconstruction of the comment on 8:11 is correct, the pass may be located heading out of the basin on the southwest. It may refer either to the ascent out of the basin itself or to the ascent along the road from the Beqa'a basin to the watershed a couple of miles northwest of Beqa'a toward Succoth.

8:14. writing among the general population. The languages such as Sumerian, Egyptian, Akkadian and Hittite that used cuneiform and hieroglyphics were syllabic and used hundreds of different signs. This made reading and writing something that only professional scribes could take the time to learn. Alphabetic script was invented in the middle of the second millennium and made popular literacy achievable, since it used less than thirty signs. Slaves in the mines of the Sinai region (the turquoise mines of Serabit el-Khadem) left alphabetic inscriptions (proto-Sinaitic) as early as the seventeenth century B.C. It is therefore not unlikely that Gideon could easily find someone who could write down the names of the leaders.

8:14. elders. The elders represent the ruling council of the town. In small towns this group may be comprised of the two eldest males from each household. That may be the case here, since 77 are identified and given the size of the site (see the comment above at 8:5) a population of 200-250 would be expected, 30 to 35 dwellings. Ugaritic uses 77 figuratively parallel to 66 to represent a large number. For another potentially representative use of 77, see comment on 8:30.

8:16. punishing with thorns. The verb used here and in verse 7 always means "to thresh" in the Old Testament. It is used figuratively of the destruction of enemies in a number of passages (see Mic 4:13). Gideon threatens to thresh/destroy the leaders *along with* briars and thorns. This may refer to a method of execution or, alternatively, to a dishonorable treatment of the corpses. Note that the men of Peniel are executed as well.

8:18. men killed at Tabor. There has been no mention of any fighting at Tabor. When the ambush occurred and the Midianites were backed up against the hill of Moreh, the main route of the flight took them to the south of the hill (see comment on 7:22). If there was fighting at Tabor, it means that some may have tried to escape around the north side of the hill to get to the Jordan via the Wadi Tabor. It can be inferred from verse 19 that Gideon had deployed some of his family to hold that pass and block their retreat.

8:20-21. execution by a minor. Execution with a sword can be very drawn-out and painful if the executioner does not know where to strike or lacks the strength or confidence to drive the sword home. Although it was an honor that Gideon offered to his son, it is easy to understand why the kings would prefer a skilled and practiced hand to do the job.

8:21. camel crescent ornaments. It is believed that these represented the moon. Some have been found in excavations at sites such as Tell al-Ajjul. Earrings also were often crescent-shaped, like the many examples found at Tell el Fara and Tell Jemmeh.

8:26. seventeen hundred shekels. In Genesis 24:22 a gold nose ring is said to weigh half a shekel. If earrings were about the same size, seventeen hundred shekels would represent thirty-four hundred earrings. This would be the equivalent of over forty-two pounds of gold.

8:27. golden ephod. An ephod was part of the priestly wardrobe (see comment on Ex 28:6-14) and in both Egypt and Mesopotamia was reserved for clothing images of deity and for high-ranking priests. Exodus 39:3 explains the process by which gold was worked into each thread used to weave the garment. It is likely that this ephod was also made of golden threads rather than of solid gold. Since Gideon had had success with oracles (6:30-36) and since the ephod is elsewhere closely associated with oracles (it contains the Urim and Thummim, see comment on Ex 28:30, and was used for oracular consultation in 1 Sam 30:7-8), it can be inferred that this ephod was intended to function as an oracular device. People who wanted to ask information of deity would come (pay their fee) and receive an answer (through the mediation of the specialists, Gideon and his family).

8:30. seventy sons, many wives. The wives of

an ancient ruler usually represented political alliances. Towns, city-states, tribes or nations who wished to ally themselves with a ruler or come under his protection sealed the treaty with a marriage of a daughter of their chief family to the suzerain. This was an act of loyalty on the part of the vassal, who would then have a personal stake in preserving the dynasty. The large number of sons indicated the strength of the family line, for with that many it would be assured of not dying out. This would be important for a ruler because the family usually occupied key positions in the administration. A large family would theoretically be able to secure the future of the dynasty. Some have considered seventy as simply a conventional indication of a large indeterminate number. Besides the several biblical examples, the Ugaritic myth concerning Baal's house speaks of the goddess Athirat (=Asherah) having seventy sons, and in the Hittite myth of Elkunirsa and Ashertu Baal claims to have killed Ashertu's (=Asherah) 77 (88) children.

8:32. family tomb. Burial practices of this period featured multiple burials in cave tombs. The body was laid out on its back with personal objects arranged around it.

8:33. Baal-Berith. Baal-Berith means "lord of the covenant" and is the designation of the deity worshiped in Shechem (about thirty miles south of Ophrah, where one of Gideon's concubines was from). There is no extrabiblical attestation of this epithet, but see comment on 9:46 on El-Berith.

9:1-57

Abimelech

9:1. Shechem. The site of Shechem has been identified with Tell Balatah, east of modern Nablus and thirty-five miles north of Jerusalem. Perhaps because of its proximity to two nearby peaks, Mount Gerizim and Mount Ebal, it has had a long history as a sacred site. The strategic position of Shechem, at the east entrance to the pass between these mountains, also made it an important trading center. As early as the Middle Bronze I Period Shechem is mentioned in the Egyptian texts of Pharaoh Sesostris III (1880-1840 B.C.). In the Amarna period (fourteenth century) Shechem was one of the major cities of Canaan and the city flourished. Jerusalem's governor complains to Pharaoh that Shechem's governor, Labayu, has given the area over to the Habiru (for more information see comments on Josh 5:1 and 9:1). The settlement was about six acres surrounded by a circular wall with a gate at

the east and a temple on the acropolis. The Iron Age of the judges period found little change in the city. It is not conquered by Joshua, and accordingly there is no evidence of destruction. It is likely that the temple on the acropolis is the temple of El-Berith mentioned in verse 46. The evidence of the destruction recounted in verse 49 can be seen in the form of debris and ash marking the end of stratum XI, dated to about 1125.

9:2. primogeniture in Israel. In the ancient Near East primogeniture is not always the rule. In many texts it is clear that the children divide the inheritance evenly. With regard to succession to rule, in some cultures brothers had priority over sons. In others it was up to the king to designate who his successor would be, and in some cases the subjects had to consent. In Israelite culture the firstborn was generally assumed to have certain advantages, but neither inheritance nor succession inevitably fell to the firstborn.

9:4. seventy silver shekels. The temple treasury pays out seventy shekels for the seventy lives of Gideon's sons. This is an indication of how cheaply they were valued (compare a fifty-shekel-per-male ransom price in Lev 27:3 and the typical twenty shekels for which a slave might be bought).

9:4. temple of Baal-Berith. For Baal-Berith see comment above at 8:33. For this period there is only one confirmed temple found by archaeologists inside the city of Shechem (though other buildings have been interpreted by some as possibly being temples). Whether this one is the temple of Baal-Berith or the temple of El-Berith (see v. 46), or whether these are two designations for the same temple, is a matter of some dispute that cannot be resolved based on the information available at this time.

9:4. use of mercenaries. A town of Shechem's size would have had a population of perhaps a thousand people and therefore a potential army of maybe two to three hundred. Nevertheless, most of these would have been uncomfortable with the task of execution for which these mercenaries were hired. Mercenaries are often motivated by the potential for plunder. In a situation such as this that would not be the case. In the Mari military organization in the eighteenth century B.C. it is thought that the temples provided the financial backing for military activity that was supported by the deity.

9:5. ritual execution. The comment that the sons of Gideon were executed "on one stone" suggests ritual execution. Sacrifices usually took place on an altar and a large rock was at times used for a makeshift altar (see comment on 6:20). This might further have connection to the huge standing stone that was the focus of the courtyard of the acropolis temple at Shechem in this period. The execution of competitors for the throne is well known through the ancient Near East and, indeed, throughout history. But there are no known examples of ritual execution of claimants to a throne as human sacrifice in the ancient Near East.

9:6. pillar in Shechem. The translation "pillar" represents an emendation of a difficult Hebrew word. An alternative that has been suggested on the basis of archaeology is that the word should not be emended but translated as a technical architectural term referring to a palisade.

9:6. Beth Millo. The Beth Millo makes most sense as the fortified temple precinct on the town's acropolis (see comment on 9:46). A millo is generally considered an area where fill dirt has been used to create an artificial elevated platform.

9:7. Mount Gerizim. There is no doubt that someone positioned on the flanks of Mount Gerizim could make themselves heard in Shechem. Gerizim is just south of the city and the natural acoustics would accommodate such a confrontation. There is a natural outcropping of rock on the lower section of the flank not far from Shechem that is often identified as a potential point. The ruins of a temple from centuries before would have been there at this time.

9:8. tree parables. There is an Old Babylonian fable from early in the second millennium called The Tamarisk and the Palm. The two trees are arguing which is superior by exploring what each has to contribute to the king's palace. Also of interest is the section of the Love Lyrics of Nabu and Tashmetu in which the shade of various trees (cedar, cypress, etc.) stands as a metaphor of protection for the king. In the Sumerian myth Lugal-e, Ninurta is opposed by an enemy that the plants have named king over themselves.

9:9-13. olive tree, fig tree and vine. These are three of the most productive members of the economy of Palestine. Olive oil, figs and wine are among the staple products of the region and constituted the primary exports. They therefore represented domestic prosperity and successful foreign relationships—both the result of a competent king's rule.

9:14. thornbush. Many consider this to be prickly boxwood, which, with its very tiny leaves, has no shade to offer unless one would sit in the middle of a thicket of it—a very unpleasant experience. In the dry climate of Palestine fires can be frequent in the brush. Such brush fires would in turn generate enough heat to kindle a fire among the larger trees. The Aramaic Wisdom of Ahiqar contains a conversation between the bramble and the pomegranate tree.

9:21. Beer. Be'er in Hebrew means "well," and there are many towns with names that include the word (such as Beersheba). It is therefore difficult to identify this town with any confidence. The most common suggestion is the town of el-Bireh north of Shechem in the Jezreel Valley near Gideon's hometown of Ophrah.

9:25. robbers in the hills. One of the advantages of a city strategically located on a trade route is the merchant traffic that flows through the town, selling goods, buying local goods to merchandise elsewhere and bringing business and tariffs to the town. Setting robbers in the hills would serve to make Shechem an unattractive station for traveling merchants and would deprive Abimelech of the tariff income that he would collect. This strategy then is designed to bring ruin to Abimelech by crippling trade.

9:26. Gaal and his brothers. The band of Gaal and his brothers has every appearance of one of the small dispossessed clans that were common during this period. Having been driven from their own cities or homeland, they take to the road as a traveling guild or as mercenaries for hire, looking for a new location in which to settle. In the Amarna letters this type of group is labeled "Habiru."

9:28. mixed population disputes. Hamor, Shechem's father, is taken as a reference to the native population that lived in Shechem since the days of the patriarchs (see Gen 34). It appears, then, that Gaal is stirring up dissension between the Israelite population and the Hivite (Hurrian?) population. Abimelech had made his case for being appointed as ruler on his own mixed heritage (see 8:31 and 9:2). Just as his membership in both groups had allowed for his acceptance by both, it now provides a basis for his rejection by both.

9:36-37. shadows from the mountains. Zebul and Gaal are standing at the east gate of the town looking east. From that vantage point there is the Askar plain directly in front of them and hills to the southeast (Mount el-Urmeh) and northeast (Mount el-Kabir). The rising sun would leave both the western flank of the northern hill and the northern flank of the southern hill (both forested) in shadow. The remains of a fortress settlement from this period have been found at the top of Mount el-Urmeh, which could have been the location of

Abimelech's headquarters (Arumah, v. 41).

9:42. attacking those who went out to the fields. The phrase used here to describe the activity of the people can refer to going out in the fields for agricultural activities (as in 9:27) but can also refer to "taking the field" in military campaign (see 2 Sam 11:23; 18:6). Though Gaal has been driven from the city, there is apparently a contingent that wants nothing more to do with Abimelech and is embarking on a military operation.

9:43-44. ambush. It is likely that the ambush group coming down to the gate of the city came off the flanks of Mount Gerizim, which is south of the city, to get behind those going out, who were met by frontal assault from the other two divisions.

9:45. scattering salt. Though this practice is not attested elsewhere in the Bible, early Hittite documents refer to scattering cress over a devastated city, and in thirteenth-century Assyrian texts Shalmaneser I scatters salt on a destroyed city. Both substances are referred to in one of the curses found in the Aramaic Sefire treaty. None of these texts offer explanation for the purpose of this action. Some have thought that its intention was to render the fields infertile. But not all salts accomplish that, and the part on which salt was scattered was not the fields but the city. Furthermore, this would not explain the alternate use of cress. In the Old Testament as well as the rest of the ancient Near East, salt is used for consecration (see comment on Lev 2:11-13). This would suggest that the practice was a ritual for purification or consecration of the city to deity. Additionally, salt impedes the action of yeast (leaven), and since leaven was a symbol of rebellion, salt could easily represent that which inhibited rebellion. Finally, salt is symbolic for that which is infertile. In a Hittite treaty, the testator pronounces one curse that says if the treaty is broken may he and his family and his lands, like salt that has no seed, likewise have no progeny.

9:46. temple of El-Berith. The comparable title *il brt* is attested in one of the Hurrian hymns among the tablets from Ugarit. El was the chief god of the Canaanite pantheon and "berith" means covenant. It has been suggested that there may have been a syncretism of religious beliefs among the mixed Israelite/Canaanite population of Shechem, combining elements of Yahweh, the covenant God of Israel, with El, the Canaanite deity. The remains of a temple of this period have been found on the acropolis at Shechem (see comments on 9:1 and 9:4). This temple was 108 feet by 92 feet and was fortified with walls 18 feet thick.

A standing stone *(massebah)* stood in the courtyard. Others have suggested that the sacred site on nearby Mount Ebal (see comment on Josh 8:30-31) should be identified with the El-Berith shrine (since the retreat there appears to take place after the city has been destroyed, v. 45), but there is no evidence of any fortress there.

9:47. Mount Zalmon. Mount Zalmon is otherwise unknown in the Old Testament. Some have suggested that it refers to Ebal or Gerizim, but it is difficult to understand why a different name would be used here. Another possibility is that it refers to the next ridge across the valley south of Gerizim.

9:50. Thebez. Thebez has been identified with modern Tubas, about nine miles northeast of Shechem, based on early Christian writings (Eusebius). No archaeological work has been done at the site.

9:51. central tower. A common feature of towns of this period was a second fortified area inside the town—a citadel of sorts. These often took the form of a tower at the highest point of the town, perhaps also including the temple area and the storehouses and treasuries.

9:53. upper millstone. The millstone was made up of two stones, usually basalt. The lower millstone was heavy (sometimes nearly one hundred pounds), a flat or slightly curved stone upon which the grain was laid and then ground into flour with the second, lighter, stone, which weighed four or five pounds and was shaped to the hand of the worker.

10:1-5
Minor Judges: Tola and Jair

10:1. "minor" judges. The text never refers to these as "minor" judges—that is a much more modern designation, used to refer to those judges who are not recorded as being involved in military activity. The nature of their "judging" must then be identified in other ways. It was the king's duty to establish justice, and that is also the nature of the role of these "judges." This is not so much done through a judiciary system, though that is included, but through all the many aspects of ruling. These then are local rulers. See comment on 2:16.

10:1. Shamir. Shamir has been identified by some as Samaria, the later capital of the northern kingdom. If it is not Samaria, the location is unknown.

10:3. thirty sons, thirty donkeys, thirty towns. Besides referring to physical sons, this terminology could refer to vassals (see 2 Kings

16:7) or those at one's service (see 1 Sam 25:8; 2 Kings 8:9). In this case Jair would be identified as having a territory of thirty towns under his control, each with its own ruler (they generally rode donkeys) who was his vassal. There is a Hittite myth that tells of the queen of Kanesh bearing thirty sons in a single year.

10:4. Havvoth Jair. Havvoth Jair means "settlements of Jair" and refers here to the settlements in the region east of the Sea of Galilee in Gilead between the Yarmuk and Jabbok rivers.

10:5. Kamon. Though there have been many different suggestions for the location of Kamon, there is little to go on for evidence for any of them.

10:6—12:7
Jephthah

10:6. list of gods. Baals and Ashtoreths (=Astarte) refer to the Canaanite deities, while all the other deities are referred to by nation rather than by name, though it is not necessary to think in terms of national gods with political associations. These were more likely fertility gods and other nature gods. This shows the syncretism within Israel and her continued polytheistic mindset. The polytheism of the ancient world was an open system. It was considered foolish to ignore or neglect any god who could potentially bring either harm or blessing.

10:8. Gilead. Gilead is the region in Transjordan bordered by the Jabbok River on the south (though at times extending as far south as the Arnon) and the Yarmuk River on the north.

10:9. Ammonites. The Ammonites lived north of the Moabites in the region around the Jabbok River. They are known from Assyrian records as Bit-Ammon and as the land of Benammanu. They were settling this territory just around the time of the Israelite wanderings.

10:17. Mizpah. There are several different sites that go by the name of Mizpah. The most familiar is located in the tribal territory of Benjamin and is identified as modern Tell

en-Nasbeh about six miles north of Jerusalem, but this is too far away to muster troops for a battle in Gilead. Mizpah in Gilead is most likely the place where Jacob and Laban had made their agreement (Gen 31), but this site is likewise unknown. The Gilead where the Ammonites camped may be the town of Gilead, modern Khirbet Jel'ad about six miles south of the Jabbok.

10:18. military governors. In times of military threat, territories governed by elders or tribal leaders were willing to submit themselves to a military governor who would provide protection and perhaps rid them of their enemies. A parallel to this political necessity can even be seen in the stories about the gods. In the Babylonian Creation Hymn to Marduk, Marduk becomes the chief of the pantheon when he agrees to take responsibility for meeting the military threat presented by the younger gods. It is this sort of arrangement that is believed to have been the sociological stepping-stone to the development of kingship in the ancient Near East.

11:1. mighty warrior. The text refers to Jephthah as a "mighty warrior" (NIV). The terminology used here is not just military in nature but can refer to a person of repute or one who has standing in the community—a responsible person. In this context, however, it is likely that his reputation is built on his military success. This is the same phrase used to describe Gideon in 6:12.

11:2. illegitimate sons driven from household. It should be noted that it was not any family shame or humiliation that resulted in Jephthah's being driven out. With the existence of temple prostitutes and polygamy it would be fairly common for children of different mothers to be in the same household. Here the text makes it clear that it was the inheritance that motivated the expulsion. Whether Jephthah, as the firstborn, had rights to a double portion, or whether they were dividing equally (see comment on primogeniture at 9:2), elimination of one party would increase the shares of the others.

11:3. land of Tob. Tob has been identified with et-Tayibeh in the region between Edrei (Der'a)

THE POLITICAL CLIMATE IN THE EARLY IRON AGE
In the Late Bronze Age (1550-1200 B.C.) there was an ongoing struggle between major political powers seeking control of Palestine (see comment on Josh 9:1). With the arrival of the Sea Peoples around 1200 (see comment on Judg 13:1), all of the major powers were either wiped out (e.g., the Hittites) or neutralized (Egypt). Moving into the Iron Age (just about this point in the book of Judges), the power stalemate has been replaced by a power vacuum. The absence of major powers vying for control of the region allowed the smaller states to test their strength, develop and build regional "empires." The Philistines were able to take advantage of this early in the period. Then David and Solomon were able to build a substantial empire in Syro-Palestine without needing to be concerned about political powers in Mesopotamia, Anatolia or Egypt.

and Bozrah (Busra ash-Sham) in western Gilead, about twenty miles west of Mount Hauron. Though no excavations have been conducted on the site, it is possibly named in Thutmose III's city list of this period.

11:8-10. position offered to Jephthah. The initial offer by the elders would have set Jephthah up as the military governor of Gilead, though apparently still operating under the authority of the elders. In verse 9 Jephthah negotiates to be in authority also over the elders, a step closer to the idea of kingship (compare how Abimelech was made king in the region of Shechem in chap. 9 and David's kingship over just Judah in 2 Sam 2:1-4).

11:12-13. negotiating territorial dispute. Basic to the understanding of the negotiation is the recognition that the Ammonites and Jephthah share a concept of divinely granted eminent domain. The gods are the ones who give rights and possession to the land, and appeal is made to the gods to judge the case and, eventually (in war), to defend the territorial distribution. The question of rights to the land did not turn on who was there first, but on the evidence that deity had given the land and on his ability to preserve the possession of the land for his people.

11:15-23. Jephthah's claims. The Israelites had taken the land from the Amorites, not the Ammonites. Though the Ammonites might be able to claim that the Amorites had taken the land from them, Jephthah's point would be that Yahweh had taken the land away from the Amorites and given it to Israel. Any prior claims the Ammonites may have had were nullified by the amount of time that Israel has been in possession of the land with no claim having been made. For details of the geographical issues presented by Jephthah, see the corresponding comments in Numbers 21.

11:24. Chemosh. Chemosh is best known as the national god of the Moabites, and in the ninth-century Moabite stone (Mesha Inscription) he is said to bring victory in battle, as Yahweh is depicted as doing for Israel. The Ammonite national deity is generally Milcom (1 Kings 11:5, 33; NIV, Molech). Although Chemosh was adopted as the national deity of the Moabites, the occurrence of the variant form, Kamish, in a deity list from Ebla, where he had a temple, suggests he was on the register of Semitic gods in third-millennium Syria, long before the Moabites. One Assyrian deity list associates Chemosh (Kammush) with Nergal, the god of the netherworld. There is not yet any firm identification of what natural phenomenon Chemosh was related to, nor is there any uncontested depiction of him on ar-

chaeological finds.

11:26. chronological note. Jephthah identifies the Israelite possession of the land as having already a three-hundred-year history to it. Although this is undoubtedly a round number, it supports a date for the conquest in the fifteenth rather than the thirteenth century (see sidebar concerning the date of the exodus at Ex 12). Jephthah is generally dated to around 1100 B.C. and cannot be placed much later if space is to be left for Samuel, Saul and David. Though the Bible's integrity would not be jeopardized if Jephthah were misinformed or exaggerating, it is difficult to believe his argument would carry any force if Israel had really been in the land only half that time.

11:29. Spirit of the Lord. The Spirit of the Lord is again associated with the raising of an army (see comment on 6:34-35). Though Jephthah has been given authority to command in Gilead, he has no such formal role in other areas of Manasseh, including the area of Bashan (north of Gilead) as well as considerable territory west of the Jordan.

11:29. troop movement. Since the site of Mizpah is uncertain, there is nothing here specific enough to reconstruct Jephthah's muster of the troops.

11:30. vows. A vow is a conditional promise, usually of a gift to be made to deity (for more information see comments on Gen 28:20-22; Lev 27:2-13; and Num 30:2-15). Parallels to Jephthah's vow can be found in classical literature in the vow of Idomenus, king of Crete (roughly contemporary with Jephthah). The storm that threatens him as he returns from the sack of Troy leads him to make a vow much like Jephthah's and results in his sacrifice of his son. Often appropriate sacrifices to request divine aid would be offered prior to battle (see 1 Sam 13:8-12). If there was no possibility or opportunity for this prior to battle, one might envision the type of vow made by Jephthah. An alternative for Jephthah could have been to devote the plunder to the Lord (compare Num 21:2), but perhaps that would be inappropriate for towns outside of Israelite territory.

11:31. what Jephthah expected to meet him. While it is true that the Israelite house accommodated animals, animals do not go out to meet someone. Dogs were not kept in houses, were not kept as pets and were unsuitable for sacrifice. Furthermore, a simple animal sacrifice would not be suitable for the extent and significance of the victory Jephthah has achieved. It can therefore be concluded that Jephthah is anticipating a human sacrifice (on human sacrifice in the ancient Near East see comments on Gen 22:1-2; Deut 18:10).

11:31. burnt offering. In all of the over 250 occurrences of the term used here, it refers to an actual sacrifice literally burnt on an altar. It is never used figuratively or symbolically. For a discussion of the burnt offering see comment on Leviticus 1:3-4. It is the word used in Genesis 22:2 and in 2 Kings 3:27, where human sacrifice is in view.

11:33. area of conquest. The area of Jephthah's conquest is said to include twenty towns, with three named specifically. Archaeologists have found many small fortified settlements in this region from this time that featured round watchtowers. It is likely that many of these twenty settlements were of this type. There is a well-known Aroer just north of the Arnon gorge where it turns south, on the southern border of Ammonite territory, but it is likely that this is a different town by that name closer to Rabbah (as in Josh 13:25). Abel Keramim probably is the town called *krmm* in Thutmose III's list of cities, but the identity of the site is unknown. Minnith, on the basis of later Greek sources, is placed between Heshbon and Rabbah. A tentative identification suggests Umm el-Basatin. Though there is some uncertainty about the sites, what is clear is that Jephthah did not simply expel Ammon from Israelite Gilead but invaded Ammon and conquered many of its fortified garrisons, mostly between Rabbah and Heshbon.

11:34. victory celebration. The practice of maidens going out to greet returning victors with song and dance is attested in the celebration for Saul and David (1 Sam 18:6-7) and partly by Miriam's song in Exodus 15:20-21. The "tambourine" his daughter played has been identified in archaeological reliefs as the tambour, a small drum (leather stretched over a hoop) that would not have the tinny rattle sound of modern tambourines.

11:34. only child. In the popular religious belief in the ancient Near East the veneration of ancestors by succeeding generations was important to the comfort one would enjoy in the afterlife. Such concepts were sometimes held by Israelites as well, though not endorsed. Within the context of the covenant, the end of a family line meant the forfeiture of the land that had been granted as a share of the covenant. In either worldview, the death of the only child was devastating on the philosophical as well as the personal emotional level.

11:35. tearing clothes in grief. Along with placing ashes in the hair, the tearing of clothing was a common form of mourning in the ancient Near East. One example outside the Bible is found in the Ugaritic epic of Aqhat (c.

1600 B.C.), in which the sister of the hero tears her father's garment as she foretells a coming drought. Such an act often implied grief over the death of a relative, friend or prominent individual (2 Sam 3:31). However, it also was a sign of impending ruin, as in the Ugaritic example, Numbers 14:6 and here.

11:35-36. breaking vows. Since a vow is a religious act, drawing the deity into compact with the worshiper, it may not be broken under penalty of God's displeasure (see Ex 20:7 and the injunction not to "misuse" God's name). Though a vow could not be broken, the law allowed for the mitigation of vows, especially those involving persons (see comment on Lev 27:2-8). This loophole was apparently unknown to Jephthah.

11:37. roaming the hills for two months. In Canaanite mythology from Ugarit *(Baal and Mot)* the virgin goddess Anat roams the hills mourning for lost fertility, since Baal is dead. The motif of roaming the hills for lost fertility is therefore a possible connection with Jephthah's daughter's request. In early Mesopotamian practice it was the god Dumuzi (Tammuz), the "quickener of the child in the womb," who had died and was lamented. The time period of two months likely correlates with one of Israel's "seasons." The Gezer calendar (tenth century) divides the year into eight periods: four of two months' length and four of one month's length. The second two-month period (for sowing) consisted of winter months when concerns about fertility would be most prominent.

11:39. fulfillment of the vow: women serving at tabernacle? It has been suggested by some interpreters that instead of being slaughtered as a sacrifice Jephthah's daughter was consecrated to serve in the tabernacle in a state of celibacy. There are examples of lifelong dedication to sanctuary service (Samuel in 1 Sam 1:28) and of women serving at the sanctuary (Ex 38:8; 1 Sam 2:22). But there are no examples of women serving the sanctuary in a vow of celibacy or in lifelong consecration. In the ancient Near East as a whole, dedication to the sanctuary generally involved prostitution rather than celibacy (see comment on Deut 23:17-18). This sort of dedication has been viewed as comparable to sacrificing a son. Perhaps most significant is the class of women referred to as *naditu* in the Old Babylonian period (1800-1600). They were connected with the temple as "bride of the god" and were therefore prohibited from marriage, though they were not necessarily celibate. Hammurabi's laws mention situations where a man marries a *naditu*, but in such situations she did not bear children.

11:40. commemoration. The verb that the NIV translates "commemorate" is uncertain (the only other occurrence is in Judg 5:11, NIV: "recite"), yet it offers the only description of this annual observance. As a result commentators can only speculate as to its nature. Without any clear indication of its nature, it is difficult to suggest parallels in the ancient world. In the Old Babylonian period the *naditus* (see above comment) yearly performed rites on behalf of those who had died childless. The context of this passage suggests the four-day observance was in some way a period of mourning for lost fertility (see comments on 11:37 above).

12:1. Zaphon. The general location of Zaphon is clear enough, but there is still no consensus about its precise location. Joshua 13:27 lists it next to Succoth in Gad's territory. It is commonly identified with Tell el-Qos a couple of miles north of Succoth (Tell Deir 'Allah).

12:1. Ephraimites' complaint. The Ephraimites are inclined to be contentious (see with Gideon, 8:1 and comment there), but while Gideon is able to assuage them, here the complaint escalates into civil war. None of the territory taken from the Ammonites had been allotted to Ephraim, but their allotted territory was across the Jordan from the Ammonite lands. It should also be remembered that the tribes of Israel were set up as individual entities joined together by their common faith and heritage. The only formal leadership they recognized was the leadership of their national God, Yahweh, and the tribal leadership of elders and clan heads. Jephthah represented a departure from that because he was given a formal position of rule (see comment on 11:8-10). This may have been viewed as a threat to other tribes.

12:4. Gileadites as renegades. The Ephraimites attempted to nullify any territorial claims by the Gileadites by negating their tribal status. Historically Gilead was one of the clans from the tribe of Manasseh. By identifying them as mixed stock (Ephraim and Manasseh), they were classifying them as squatters on the land with no rights to territory as full-fledged clans and tribes would have. This was a land grab by the Ephraimites.

12:5. fords of the Jordan. The fords referred to here would be those by the town of Adam just south of the confluence with the Jabbok River (see comment on Josh 2:7).

12:6. variations in ancient Hebrew pronunciation. Pronunciation of some consonants varies between the related Semitic languages of the ancient Near East. In one of these variations the Hebrew consonant *shin* (sh) combines two consonants from Ugaritic (similar to Canaanite), *sh* and *th*. So the Hebrew word for three, *shalosh*, in Ugaritic is *thalath* and in Aramaic is *talat*. Most significant is the fact that Ammonite also featured the *th* consonant variant. It is this type of variation in pronunciation that distinguished the Ephraimite and Gileadite speech. This is not so much dialectical as it is regional variation. As is always the case, consonant sounds that are not native to one's own speech dialect are difficult to reproduce without practice. G. Rendsburg has worked out the most likely scenario to fit the details of both linguistics and context. The Ephraimites would generally have pronounced the word "shibboleth," while the Gileadites, sharing Ammonite practice, would have pronounced it "thibboleth." When the Gileadites confronted the suspected Ephraimites, they challenged them to pronounce "thibboleth," for which the Ephraimites could only manage "sibboleth." The word *shibboleth* can mean either ears of corn or the torrent of a river. The latter makes more sense in the context.

12:8-15 Minor Judges: Ibzan, Elon, Abdon

12:8. "minor" judges. We know nothing of these three individuals from any other sources in or out of the Bible. For discussion of office see comments on 10:1 and 2:16.

12:8. Bethlehem. Bethlehem here is generally considered to be not the one in Judah a few miles south of Jerusalem but the one in the territory of Zebulun in the hills of Galilee just north of the Valley of Jezreel. The only indicator leading to this decision is that Elon and Abdon are also from this general area.

12:8. political marriages. The wives of an ancient ruler or his children usually represented political alliances. Towns, city-states, tribes or nations who wished to ally themselves with a ruler or come under his protection sealed the treaty with the marriage of a daughter of their chief family to the suzerain or his son. This was an act of loyalty on the part of the vassal, who would then have a personal stake in preserving the dynasty. The large number of sons indicated the strength of the family line, for with that many it would be assured of not dying out. This would be important for a ruler, because the family usually occupied key positions in the administration. A large family would theoretically be able to secure the future of the dynasty. Verse 9 indicates a vast web of political associations.

12:11. Aijalon in Zebulun. The well-known town and Valley of Aijalon is in the territory allotted to Dan and is therefore different from that referred to here. This site is unidentified.

12:13. Pirathon. Pirathon has been identified with the village of Farata six or seven miles south-southeast of Samaria.

12:14. forty sons and thirty grandsons on seventy donkeys. It is difficult to tell whether these sons and grandsons represent political alliances (see comment on 10:3) or the size of the clan that he ruled (see comment on 12:8 above). The reference to the donkeys favors the former and the reference to grandsons favors the latter.

13:1-25

The Birth of Samson

13:1. Philistines. The group of Philistines that are well-known through the narratives of Judges and 1 and 2 Samuel came into the Palestine area with the migration from the Aegean region of the group known as the Sea Peoples about 1200 B.C. It is the Sea Peoples that are generally thought to have been responsible for the fall of the Hittite Empire and the destruction of many cities along the coast of Syria and Palestine, such as Ugarit, Tyre, Sidon, Megiddo and Ashkelon, though the evidence for their involvement in those areas is circumstantial. Their battles with the Egyptian Pharaoh Rameses III are depicted on the famous wall paintings at Medinet Habu. It is this vast people movement that is also reflected in the Homeric Epic of the siege of Troy. Coming from Crete, Greece and Anatolia, they probably used Cyprus as a base from which to launch their attacks. Following the repulsion of the Sea Peoples from Egypt, the tribe that came to be known as the Philistines settled on the southern coast of Palestine, where they established their five capital cities of Ashkelon, Ashdod, Ekron (Tell Miqne), Gath (Tell es-Safi) and Gaza.

13:2. Zorah. Zorah is identified with the modern Sar'a about sixteen miles west of Jerusalem in the Sorek Valley, which was the major pass from the coastal plains through the Shephelah to the hills around Jerusalem.

13:2. barrenness. The inability of a wife to bear children often made her vulnerable to her husband's whims, for most marriage contracts allowed for her to be divorced on such grounds. Alternatively it often led to the taking of other wives, who, upon producing children, would assume a more favored status within the family. This text is not, however, concerned with family politics or psychologi-

cal tensions. The previous barrenness of Manoah's wife is one element that helps to demonstrate the supernatural aspect to Samson's life and career.

13:4-5. Nazirite vow. As with most vows in the ancient Near East, the Nazirite vow typically represented a conditional agreement with deity that was concluded with offertory gifts in response to a favorable answer to a petition. What distinguished the Nazirite vow was the period of abstinence preceding the offerings. Samson's situation is even more notable in that the period of abstinence is not the usual days or weeks, but his entire lifetime. For more information on the details of the Nazirite vow, see the comments on Numbers 6:1-21.

13:5. ritual importance of hair. There is a Phoenician inscription from the ninth century reporting the dedication of shaven hair by an individual in fulfillment of a vow made to the goddess Astarte. It is of importance that in the biblical text there is no discussion of what should be done with the hair that is cut. It is neither dedicated as in the above inscription, nor is it deposited in the temple as in some cultures. The dedicated hair is uncut, not cut. Hair (along with blood) was one of the main representatives in ancient thinking of a person's life essence. As such it was often an ingredient in sympathetic magic. This is evident, for instance, in the practice of sending along a lock of the presumed prophet's hair when the prophecies were sent to the king of Mari. The hair would be used in divination to determine whether the prophet's message would be accepted as valid.

13:15-16. hospitality meal. Hospitality custom required that all strangers who approached a dwelling were to be offered the opportunity to rest, refresh themselves and eat a meal. This was done to assure the friendship of the stranger. This would be particularly true of someone who was offering such prophetic portents as here described. What is particularly generous here is the fresh meat, an item not usually found in the daily diet.

13:17. importance of the name. Someone's name was believed to be intimately connected to their being and essence. A name was believed to be important for magical purposes or hexing. The giving of one's name was an act of favor, trust and, in human terms, vulnerability. The Ten Commandments had prohibited Israel from attempting to use Yahweh's name in magical ways to manipulate him. But here it is neither evil intent nor invocation that are intended by Manoah. The text indicates that Manoah did not realize that the visitor was supernatural. If a prophet, the individual's reputation could be enhanced and his sponsorship provided for by someone pleased with the accuracy and benevolence of his pronouncements. Such rewards could only be given if the individual's identity were known.

13:19. grain offering. The word used to describe the grain offering means "gift" or "tribute." The offering is used in situations where respect or honor are intended. The same term is used the same way in Ugaritic and Akkadian (Canaan and Mesopotamia). It is typically found on occasions of celebration rather than the context of sadness or mourning. In formal settings a small portion was burnt on the altar as a token of the gift to the Lord, while the remainder was given to the officiating priest. The ingredients of this offering were grain, oil and incense. The grain was the grits or semolina left in the sieve after wheat was ground into flour. The oil was olive oil, used as shortening in cooking and easily combustible. The incense was frankincense, which was made from the gum resin of a type of tree found only in southern Arabia and Somaliland. The grain offerings used a small amount that was entirely burnt in a slow smolder (For more information see comments on Lev 2).

13:19. sacrifice on rock. By placing the food on a rock, it is changed from a meal to a sacrifice and is consumed. Rocks were at times used as altars (1 Sam 14:32-34), usually with the intention of allowing the blood to drain from the slaughtered animal.

13:22. taboo of seeing God. The concept of deity having an awesome, unapproachable appearance was not limited to Israelite theology, for in Mesopotamia the gods displayed their power through their *melammu*, their divine brilliance. This display, however, though it struck terror in the heart, was not seen as being fatal. It is also clear in the biblical text that there is nothing like the *melammu* attached to the messenger, because his supernatural identity is not recognized by Manoah. Parallels to this taboo are unattested in ancient Near Eastern literature.

13:24. Samson's name. Samson's name is a form of the noun that in Hebrew means "sun." Just a couple of miles south of his home is the town of Beth Shemesh, house/temple of the sun. The solar cult is known to have existed among the religious aberrations in Israel (2 Kings 23:11), and some have suggested that Yahweh was at times depicted as the sun in relief (the incense stand from Taanach) and in literature (e.g., Ps 80:2-3; Deut 33:2).

13:25. Mahaneh Dan. Mahaneh Dan means "camp of Dan" and therefore most likely does not represent an established settlement. Zorah and Eshtaol (Khirbet Deir Shubeib) are only about a mile apart, but there is a spring by the Wadi Kesalon running between the two towns that may be the area referred to here.

14:1—16:31
Samson's Exploits

14:1. Timnah. Timnah is located about five and a half miles west along the Sorek Valley from Samson's home in Zorah. It is modern Tell el-Batashi, situated about halfway between Zorah and the Philistine city of Ekron. Excavations at the site show occupation during this period but offer little insight into the biblical narrative.

14:2. parent arranged marriages. Throughout the ancient Near East marriage was viewed more as a clan partnership (often with economical motivations) concerned with family status than as a romantic matching of couples who had feelings for one another. As a result the arrangements for these partnerships were in the hands of the head of the family. The parents decided when marriage should take place and who the mate should be. Often arrangements were made when the spouses-to-be were still children. Endogamy, marriage to someone from the same tribe or village, was the common practice, especially in Israel where land holdings were tied to tribal affiliation. Even when an individual would have the freedom to make a choice on his own, the parents would then have to carry out the negotiations for the financial arrangements concerning bride price (see comment on Gen 29:18-20) and dowry (usually property), both constituting assets that become attached to the wife. Bride price is discussed much more than dowry in the ancient Near East and in the Bible.

14:3. uncircumcised. Circumcision was practiced by many different peoples in the ancient Near East (see comment on Gen 17:9-14) but not by the Philistines. The comment here has little to do with physical attributes or sociological practices, but is an ethnic designation that for the Israelites is a sign of the covenant.

14:5-6. lion. Kings and heroes of the ancient world often boast of their lion-hunting skills. A familiar scene in Egyptian paintings is Pharaoh astride his chariot facing lions with bow or spear in hand. Assyrian kings likewise claim hundreds of lions as hunting trophies. A relief from Tel Halaf (about 900 B.C.) pictures a warrior using a sword to fight a lion. Killing a lion with bare hands is a feat attached to other ancient heroes as, for instance, the Sumerian king Gilgamesh and Heracles of Greek legend. Lions were common in the forested regions of Palestine, and in this time period the whole region surrounding the Sorek Valley between Zorah and Timnah was forested.

14:6. Spirit of the Lord. In previous appearances in the book the Spirit of the Lord has been involved at the point where the authority to raise an army was a strategic issue (see comments on 6:34-35 and 11:29). In those cases the Spirit endowed the judge with an authority that could only be given by God. In Samson's situation not authority but physical ability is involved. The Spirit of the Lord comes upon Samson on a number of occasions (see 14:19 and 15:14), but not every time he performs an unusual feat. The common denominator is that the Spirit is involved in each situation when he attacks or is attacked.

14:10. feast for bridegrooms. This was the second stage in the marriage process, which took place some time after the proclamation of espousal had been formally made. The traditionally seven-day feast was climaxed by the consummation of the marriage, which may have taken place after the first night of the feast. A ceremony under a canopy is indicated in biblical materials (Ps 19:4-5; Joel 2:16). The Ugaritic tale of King Keret features a wedding feast when he marries Huray, but little detail is given.

14:11. thirty companions. The bridegroom's companions would be those from the clan or village of the bride who came forth to support the union. Their obligations are unclear but may involve providing security for the bride by committing to see that she was treated fairly in her new family and perhaps by accepting liability for the woman's support should her husband abandon her. At the beginning of verse 11 there is a variant reading of "Because they feared him" instead of NIV "When he appeared." If this variant is correct, there may be an implication that there was some intimidation that brought out so many, thus also supporting the claim of verse 15 that the companions were coerced to come in order to be robbed.

14:12. riddles. Riddles are characteristically based on two levels of meaning inherent in the words used. One level would involve the common word usage, while the solution to the riddle would require unraveling a more obscure meaning of the words. It has been suggested that the common level of meaning in Samson's riddle would have been either something crude (related to the results of overindulgence at a banquet) or something erotic (related to the imminent consummation

of the marriage), though either of these would appear too metaphorical to be able to constitute a common level of meaning. In Greek legend of this period Mopsus engaged Calchus, a leader of the Achaeans leaving the sack of Troy, in a riddle contest. The intriguing connection here is that Mopsus is later credited with the founding of Ashkelon.

14:13. thirty sets of clothing. The thirty outfits spoken of here would be fine apparel used for special occasions. The equivalent today would be thirty three-piece suits. In the same way that a shirt would be worn under a suit, the linen garments referred to here would be worn under the embroidered outer cloak.

14:14. honey in the carcass. The motif of bees building their hive in the carcass of a large animal is known from literature in the Aegean region (where the Philistines originated), so this riddle should have been one the Philistines could solve.

14:18. riddles answering riddles. Samson's friends answer his riddle, while at the same time posing their own riddle that gives a clue as to how they procured the answer. Honey and the lion answers Samson's riddle. But what is it that is sweeter than honey and stronger than a lion? A woman's enticement, of course. Samson demonstrates his skill at riddles by immediately solving theirs and responding with his own wordplay. "Plowing with someone's heifer" could be analogous to our expression "walk a mile in his shoes" but it also has the more insidious meaning of meddling with his wife.

14:19. Ashkelon. Ashkelon is located nearly forty miles down the coast south of Tel Aviv. It is a one-hundred-and-fifty-acre site that was heavily fortified as one of the five major cities of the Philistines. The Canaanite ruler during the Amarna period (fourteenth century) was Yidya, who was responsible for seven of the letters of the Amarna archive. The Philistines settled on the site around 1175 B.C. During the period of Samson's exploits (Iron Age I) Ashkelon had fortifications at least on the northern slope as well as a glacis (sloped area outside the wall to prevent easy access to the wall) and a mudbrick tower. From Timnah to Ashkelon would have been a journey of twenty-five miles. It is unclear why he would have gone there rather than to Ekron, Gath or even Ashdod, all much closer.

14:20. outcome of wedding: wife given to another. The giving of the wife to the companion does not suggest a secret side romance but would have been the normal course of action. The role of the companions at the wedding was to guarantee continued support should the wife be deserted, as the family assumed had happened. A Babylonian prayer to Ishtar requests that an angry young man come back to his wife at his in-laws' house and the connected ritual is intended to result in conception.

15:1. wheat harvest time. The wheat harvest time was at the end of May in this section of the country.

15:1. taking young goat. Though the marriage was usually consummated the first night of the feast, the bride often did not go to live with the bridegroom at the end of the seven-day feast. For several months the husband would regularly bring a gift and visit the bride in her father's house (and stay the night) until all was ready for the move. In Babylon this was typically a four-month period, perhaps intended to be a probation period to see whether the bride could become pregnant.

15:4. three hundred foxes. The word translated by the NIV as "fox" is believed to be a more generic term that could also refer to jackals. From the practical standpoint it is likely that jackals are used here. Foxes hunt alone while jackals hunt in packs. Trapping this large a number of foxes would require not only great amounts of time but also cover a large range of territory. Acquisition of jackals would be a more manageable task in that whole packs could be captured at once. Both species were native to Palestine during this period.

15:5. shocks and standing grain. The stalks that have already been cut and are lying in piles awaiting the threshing process are the shocks. The standing grain is that which has not yet been cut. It was still some months until the grapes and olives would be harvested, but the fire did irreparable damage to those industries as well.

15:8. rock of Etam. There is a town near Bethlehem named Etam (2 Chron 11:6), but it is too far east to be involved here, and Samson is not in a town. The most common identification is with 'Araq Isma'in in the vicinity of Samson's hometown, Zorah, on the slopes of the Sorek Valley.

15:9. Lehi. It is uncertain whether Lehi (jaw) is a place name or a description. Akkadian uses the word for jaw to describe the boundary of a territory, and some have felt that the same occurs here in Judges, though it is unattested elsewhere in the Old Testament. Those who consider it a place name generally identify it with Khirbet es-Siyyagh in the hill country of Judah heading toward Jerusalem in the vicinity of Beth Shemesh. It is about two miles from Zorah and the rock of Etam.

15:13. new ropes. Ropes have been found pre-

served in Egyptian tombs made of green papyrus or of date-palm fiber. In Israel the stem of the sparrow-wort, a desert shrub, was one of the most suitable and convenient materials. New ropes would have been less brittle and therefore more resilient.

15:15. donkey's jawbone. The jawbone of a donkey would be about nine inches long and weigh a little less than a pound. It would be slightly curved and may well have had many of the teeth still in place to improve its effectiveness as a weapon.

15:19. provision of water. Sedimentary rock is known to feature pockets where water can collect just below the surface. By breaking through the surface the collected water can be released. The text does not explain in what way God opened up the rock.

15:19. En Hakkore. No spring has been located in this region that would suit the details of the passage.

16:1. Gaza. Gaza was one of the five major cities of the Philistines. It is located about twelve miles southeast of Ashkelon about three miles from the Mediterranean. In the Amarna period it was the most important center of Egyptian administration of the region. The 135-acre site is located at the southern entrance to the coastal plain, where it occupies the highest point in the region along the main trade route coming up from Egypt. Egyptian reliefs portray the city as well fortified in the thirteenth century, though the limited excavations have turned up little from the Old Testament period.

16:3. structure of city gates. The text mentions three parts of the gate: the gate itself, the posts and the bar. Two gate doors were generally set into stone sockets buried just under the ground. The posts flanked the gate on either side. They were made of wood and joined to the wall. During Iron Age I many cities did not have walls, but instead there were houses built close around the perimeter to serve that purpose. The bars slid across the gates and the end fit into an opening in the post. These bars could be locked in place by a series of small wooden dowels that slipped into holes on a block mounted on the gate. One could therefore not exit the city without a key once the gate was locked. Since the fortifications of ancient Gaza have not been found by archaeologists, it is difficult to be more precise about the details of this particular gate. Gate openings of this period were often as much as twelve feet wide, though some are as small as six feet.

16:3. hill facing Hebron. Hebron is nearly forty miles east of Gaza in a continual uphill climb. The text does not suggest that Samson carried the gates to the vicinity of Hebron. The phrase used can often mean "on the way to" (see for instance Josh 13:3). He headed off on the road to Hebron and dumped the gates on a hill on the way.

16:4. Valley of Sorek. The Valley of Sorek is the area of most of Samson's activity. The main valley is about thirteen miles west of Jerusalem and is part of the wadi extending about thirty miles in a northwesterly direction from the hills around Jerusalem to the Mediterranean. It serves as the main pass between the coastal plain and the hills of Judah near Jerusalem.

16:5. rulers of the Philistines. The five rulers of the Philistines appear to be equal in authority. The term used to describe them is likely the Philistine term, and most scholars believe it has its roots in the language of the Sea Peoples (Greek or another Indo-European language). Until more information is found it is impossible to offer a clearer political analysis.

16:5. eleven hundred shekels of silver. Eleven hundred shekels of silver is an exorbitant sum—a king's ransom (see 2 Sam 18:12). Compare the ten shekels that was the standard annual wage of a laborer and the four to six hundred shekels that was paid for tracts of land. The 5500 shekels would equal 550 times the average annual wage. If we took $25,000 as an average annual wage today, that kind of offer would be in the $15 million category.

16:5. Philistine beliefs about Samson's strength. The Philistines believed there was a secret to Samson's great strength that needed to be discovered and that could be exploited to weaken him. This demonstrates that they considered supernatural or magical elements to be the source of his abilities. Samson understands this in that he offers magical solutions for binding him. Just as modern superstitions maintain that only silver bullets can be used to slay a werewolf, so in the ancient traditions certain materials had magical properties that could be used to counteract supernatural phenomena. This falls into the category of magic designated "rite of contact and transference" known from Hittite texts. In these rites, wool or cords of various colors or materials were used to neutralize magical properties.

16:7. fresh thongs. The fresh thongs or bow strings were sometimes made of the intestines of cattle. Sumerian literature refers to deriving bow strings from a sheep's leg (presumably the tendons) or from ram's gut, while Ugaritic literature refers to tendons from a bull's leg. They were usually laid out to dry before being put to use. Others have preferred to think of vines being used. The fact that seven are used

also suggests a magical element to the procedure.

16:11. new ropes. See comment on 15:13.

16:13-14. loom weaving. There were two types of looms used in this period: the horizontal loom and the vertical loom. From the description given of Delilah's loom it appears to be the former type. Four stakes were driven into the ground in a rectangular pattern. The threads that would make up the warp of the fabric were tied at regular intervals to sticks on both ends, and the sticks were then used to stretch out the threads between the stakes. When the ends of each stick were braced behind the stakes, the threads would be stretched horizontal to the ground, taut for weaving. A shuttle would then be tied to the thread that was to be woven in as the woof of the fabric, with a bar being used to separate alternating threads of the warp to allow the shuttle with the woof thread to pass through. Once the woof thread was in place the pin would be used to tighten that row against the previous rows. Samson has now become quite creative for he is suggesting that his hair be substituted for the woof thread. This would, however, be a logical magical procedure in that the hair was considered to contain one's life essence and the weaving would be a binding action. When Samson jumps up, he pulls the whole loom with him, snapping the end sticks off the four stakes between which the fabric was stretched.

16:13. seven braids. It was a common style for men to have the hair bound or even curled in segments. Samson's hair was styled in seven such segments (one in the back and three on each side).

16:17. Nazirite. See comments in Numbers 6 for more information about the Nazirite vow and the significance of hair. Though Samson may have violated the vow on numerous occasions, such circumstances merely required the vow to be renewed. This was different in that the shaving of the hair was the way to bring the vow to an end.

16:17-19. cutting hair to deprive of invincibility. There are a few examples of this same concept known from early literature of the Aegean region reported by Apollodorus (second century B.C.). One account is of Nisus, king of Megara, whose long hair made him invincible. His daughter, Scylla, had fallen in love with his enemy, Minos, king of Crete (seventeenth century B.C.), so she cut off part of her father's hair so that Minos could achieve victory. A similar fate likewise befell Pterelaos, king of Teleboea (also reported by Apollodorus), whose hair, which made him immortal, was shaved off by a daughter in love with the enemy. These stories may well have been known by the Philistines who were from the Aegean region, in which case the suggested course of action would have made perfect sense to them.

16:21. blinding prisoners. Most evidence comes from Mesopotamia, where it was common practice for prisoners of war to have either their eyes gouged out or their tongues removed.

16:21. bronze shackles. Both manacles and fetters were used in the ancient Near East, and bronze would have been the logical material to make them out of at this period. Even later in the Iron Age bronze continued to be used for this purpose (see Jer 39:7). It is likely that Samson had both his hands and his feet shackled in this way.

16:21. grinding mill. Grinding grain into flour was usually done with millstones and was the job of the lowest members of society. One of the basic "appliances" of any ancient household would have been the handmill (called a saddle quern) with two stones for grinding (see comment on Judg 9:53). Larger milling houses often served as prison workhouses in Mesopotamia, but each prisoner still used a handmill for grinding. The large rotary mill that could be powered by donkey or slave labor was not invented until after the Old Testament period. The palace at Ebla had a room containing sixteen handmills, inferred to be a place where prisoners ground grain. Grinding houses would include prisoners of war, criminals and those who had defaulted on their debts.

16:23. Dagon. There is evidence of Dagon as a important god within the Semitic pantheon of deities as early as the third millennium B.C. in Mari. Assyrians worshiped him in the first half of the second millennium, and in Ugaritic literature he is positioned as the father of Baal Haddu. His temple in the town of Ugarit was bigger that the temple of Baal. It is generally assumed, then, that the Philistines did not bring this god with them from their Aegean homeland but adopted him upon their arrival in their new territory. Dagon is often identified as a god of grain or of storm, but both of these remain somewhat speculative.

16:25. brought to entertain. The "entertainment" provided by Samson was probably not connected to his wit or his strength, but to his blindness. Putting obstacles in the way and striking or tripping him would be only a few of the cruel possibilities for tormenting a blind person in an unfamiliar place.

16:29. temple architecture. The temples at Tell

Qasile (ancient name unknown, but occupied by Philistines; located within modern Tel Aviv) and at Beth Shan are the only Philistine temples from this time period that have been uncovered by archaeologists, though the temple at Lachish is also instructive. They commonly feature pillars that support the roof in a central hallway (perhaps partially open-air). The pillars in the temples of this period were often made of wood and stood on stone pedestals. They were held in place by the weight of the roof. The largest phase of Iron I temples at Tell Qasile was twenty-five by forty-five feet. The temple at Beth Shan features a central area with two pillars and measures nearly forty-five feet square. The Late Bronze acropolis temple at Lachish (Canaanite and slightly earlier) was of similar design, with two pillars in the central area, but was bigger, measuring about sixty by one hundred feet.

16:29-30. bringing down the house. The verb used in verse 30 suggests a twisting motion, from which we can infer that Samson turned the pillars off their stone bases, thus removing the support of the roof and causing its collapse.

16:31. Zorah and Eshtaol. Zorah is identified with the modern Sar'a about sixteen miles west of Jerusalem in the Sorek Valley, which was the major pass from the coastal plains through the Shephelah to the hills around Jerusalem. Zorah and Eshtaol (Khirbet Deir Shubeib) are only about a mile apart, but there is a spring by the Wadi Kesalon running between the two towns that may be the area referred to here.

17:1—18:31
Micah and the Danites

17:2. eleven hundred shekels. Although a very large amount (eight grams/shekel), it is not beyond the realm of possibility that this much silver could be involved here (compare the four hundred paid by Abraham for Machpelah and Gideon's spoils taken in Judg 8:26). It most likely represented the woman's dowry, received at marriage, that was to provide support should she be widowed or abandoned. It is also the amount paid to Delilah in 16:5 by the Philistine kings.

17:2. curse. The text is ambiguous enough to allow for either "oath" or "curse" with regard to the eleven hundred shekels of silver. It is possible that Micah's mother had pledged that amount to Yahweh, or it may be that she had placed a curse on whomever had taken it. In both cases God would have been called upon as witness (see Num 5:21 and Neh

10:29). The mother might well have been desperate to find her pledged funds and called upon God to help with the search. Micah's reassurance that he has the silver sounds less like a response of a dutiful son than it does of someone frightened of taboo (i.e. consecrated) items (see Josh 7:20-21).

17:2. changing curse to blessing. Like Balaam (Num 23:11), Micah's mother changes her curse into a blessing. She may have been disappointed to find that her son had taken the silver, but she quickly transposes one form of divine invocation into another. In this way, the potential harm is abetted (see 2 Sam 21:3).

17:3. consecrated to the Lord to make image. The making of sacred images was forbidden in Exodus 20:4. However, the lawlessness portrayed in the Judges period and common practice among the Canaanites makes it almost a certainty among the Israelites (see Gideon's ephod in Judg 8:27). Idols were carved out of wood or stone as well as cast from precious metals (see the golden calves in Ex 32:1-4 and 1 Kings 12:28). Molds for the casting of gods have been found at several Canaanite sites. It may be presumed that the material employed was consecrated at the beginning of the process, and certain rituals (the "mouth-opening" in Egyptian and Mesopotamian texts) and ceremonies were performed to bring the object to life. Then the final product was consecrated in the service of the god represented (see Ex 40:9-11 and Lev 8:10-11 for the consecration of the tabernacle).

17:5. shrine. Archaeological excavations at sites throughout Syro-Palestine have uncovered house-shrines. These private sanctuaries would have served the needs of households and perhaps extended families within a village culture (the plaster fragments from Tell Deir 'Alla may be associated with such a shrine as may the Kuntillet 'Ajrud inscriptions). In larger population centers, more formal temples and shrines also existed to serve as worship and sacrificial centers for all devotees and as a base of operations for the priestly community of the god. However, the biblical text makes a point that Micah's shrine was not a proper center for Yahweh worship, and the inclusion of an idol graphically demonstrates the danger of unsupervised local worship (see the law in Deut 12:2-7).

17:5. ephod. The ephod was part of the priestly garments to be worn exclusively by Aaron and other high priests (see the comment on Ex 28:6-14). It was probably an apronlike affair, made of special fabric and woven with a mixture of woolen and linen thread as well as gold. The breastplate containing the twelve

stones representing the Israelite tribes was attached to the ephod (Ex 28:25). The association of the breastplate with the Urim and Thummim, the lots used in divining God's will, makes the ephod a part of this oracular procedure. As such it could have eventually been so closely associated with the divine that it too was worshiped (see Gideon's golden ephod in Judg 8:27). Micah's ephod is designed to add legitimacy to his personal shrine, and the fact that it is listed in association with his idols suggests it was also an object of worship (see Judg 18:14-31).

17:5. idols. Graven images of any sort are strictly forbidden by Exodus 20:4-6; 34:17. Yet the existence of idols made of metal, wood and stone was a continual reality in ancient Israel (see Is 40:19-20; Hos 8:4-6). It is therefore not surprising that Micah has created idols. However, the official sanction given to them by the Levite raises the scandal of the lawless Judges period.

17:6. no king. Given limited central authority, the judges were not able to undertake significant spiritual or social reform among the people, nor were they in a position to adjudicate intertribal squabbles. The priesthood, the tribal leadership and the judges are seen in the narrative to be part of the problem rather than part of the solution. Inauguration of a central, civil authority had the potential to resolve some of these problems, but only the appropriate view of kingship would result in progress. As 1 Samuel 8—12 will point out, there are drawbacks to kingship as well, and it is a dangerous mistake to treat a spiritual problem with a political solution.

17:7-10. family priests. Micah's original choice was to appoint one of his sons as the priestly administrator of his shrine. However, when the opportunity arose to install a Levite, he jumped at this opportunity to legitimize his sanctuary (note how it has gained a reputation in Judg 18:14-15). The use of the term "father" here implies ability to make true oracular answers to the yes and no questions posed to God through him (see the use of this term in 2 Kings 6:21; 8:9; 13:14). It might also be compared to the title "mother in Israel" given to Deborah in Judges 5:7. However, the practice of using local or family priests is eventually forbidden as the monarchy attempted to centralize all worship in Jerusalem (see 2 Kings 18:4; 23:5-9).

17:7-9. itinerant Levite. The Levites did not receive a specific territorial allotment because they were to serve all of the tribes as priests (Josh 18:7). Thus it is not out of character in this period for a young Levite to go on a journey and seek employment in his profession. There are some problems here with his association with Judah, but the historical context is uncertain.

17:10. priest's salary. There is no provision in the law for a priest to receive a salary. Exodus 28:1 and 29:26-28 describe the portion of the sacrificial offering that is to be set aside for the priests, and Joshua 21:3-40 lists towns and pasturelands allotted to the Levites for this sustenance. However, the offering of a specific amount of precious metal as wages functions more as a bribe or retainer for a prized employee.

18:1-2. Danite migration. The allotment assigned to the tribe of Dan was between that of Ephraim and Benjamin along the coastal plain (Josh 19:40-48). They would have been closest to and most immediately affected by the Philistines (see Samson's exploits in Judges 13—16) and may have eventually felt that they would never be able to effectively compete with this much stronger people.

18:5-6. oracle. One of the most common forms of divination employed in the ancient Near East involved asking a god a yes or no question. This might require the casting of lots or, as in this instance, inquiring of a prophet or priest at a shrine. While this might seem to eliminate ambiguity, the Levite's answer suggests that a question could be answered with a noninformative statement. In Mesopotamia, the *baru* priest sometimes used a "divining cup" (see Joseph in Gen 44:5) or might consult a body of omen texts to provide answers.

18:7. Laish. Located at the foot of Mount Hermon in the extreme northern portion of Israelite territory (also known as Leshem in Josh 19:47), the city was about one hundred miles from Dan's assigned territory. Laish was conquered by the Danites and renamed Dan. The site, which contains one of the sources of the Jordan River, has a long history, attested by Egyptian execration texts and in the Mari letters. It would not be surprising to see Phoenician (Sidonian) influence in this northern city. For more information see the comment on Dan in 18:29.

18:12. Kiriath Jearim. Listed as a city within Judah (Josh 15:60), the site is commonly identified with Tell el-Azhar, nine miles west northwest of Jerusalem, but this is unsubstantiated by archaeological finds or extrabiblical references. Its association with Mahaneh Dan in this verse puts it in this general area (see the comment on 13:25). This location places it only six miles from Gibeon, with which it is also associated (see comment on Josh 9:17).

18:14-27. pillaging the shrine. The practice of attacking and looting shrines and temples was simply part of warfare in the ancient world. Since these places were often storehouses of grain and other commodities and contained valuable objects made of precious metals, they were a natural target. The collecting of sacred images as "hostages" was also common (see 1 Sam 5:1-2) and is documented in the Mari letters (eighteenth century B.C.) as well as in the Cyrus Cylinder from the Persian period (c. 540 B.C.).

18:28. Sidon, Beth Rehob. At the time of the Danite conquest of Laish, it was a village controlled by the Sidonians (on the Lebanese coast). The exact location of Beth Rehob is unknown, although it most likely is to be found "near the entrance to Hamath" (Num 13:21), in the Huleh valley where it links with the Bekah valley of southern Lebanon.

18:29. Dan. Tel Dan (Tell el Qadi) is located at the foot of Mount Hermon and is watered by a number of springs which serve as one of the sources of the Jordan River. Its identification has been proven by the discovery of an inscription which invokes "the god of Dan." However, its original name was Laish (see Josh 19:47; Judg 18:7), and by that name it was mentioned in the Egyptian execration texts and perhaps in the Mari letters. The Middle Bronze period at the site saw the construction cover over thirty acres. An arched mudbrick gateway from this era testifies to the remarkable culture of the city. The conquest of the city in the early Iron Age is not evidenced by a destruction level, but there is material evidence (pottery, storage pits) of the introduction of a new population group in the Iron Age. No temple or shrine has been found from this period, but Jeroboam may have been following earlier tradition when he constructed a temple when the nation was divided in the tenth century (1 Kings 12:29-30).

18:30. tribal priesthood. The Levites were to serve as priests for all of the tribes. Thus it is not out of character to speak of Jonathan, the son of Gershom, as priest of the tribe of Dan. Jonathan came to his position by first serving as a household priest in Ephraim and officiating before idols, and then by consenting to the confiscation of these sacred images from Micah's house. In that sense he perpetuated a form of false worship along the lines of those priests condemned by Hosea for failing to convey the true knowledge of God to the people (Hos 4:6).

18:31. house of God in Shiloh. The shrine at Shiloh operated as a cultic center during the Judges period (Judg 21:19) and in the time of Samuel (1 Sam 1:3), but it was apparently destroyed by the Philistines after the battle of Ebenezer (1 Sam 4:1-11). Mention in Psalm 78:60 and Jeremiah 7:12; 26:6-9 suggests the shrine there may have been rebuilt and used until Solomon built the Jerusalem temple. The site has been identified as Khirbet Seilun, about halfway between Bethel and Shechem. This seven-and-a-half-acre site is situated in a strategic location where it enjoys fertile land, a reliable water source and access to the main north-south route through the heartland of Israel. Substantial Iron Age I ruins have been found at the site, along with evidence of destruction by means of fire. Though remains of public buildings from this period have been found, no trace of the sanctuary has been identified. The probable location at the highest point of the tell has suffered from erosion and later settlement.

19:1—21:25
The Civil War Against Benjamin

19:1. Levites. For discussion of the role, function and provisions made for the Levites, see the comments on Numbers 16:10; Deuteronomy 14:27-29; 18:1-5; 18:6-8.

19:1. concubines. A concubine is a secondary wife who has probably come into the marriage without a dowry. Her children may only receive a portion of their father's estate if he chooses to publicly acknowledge them as his heirs (note how Abraham treated his sons by Keturah and his concubines in Gen 25:1-4). It is possible that this sort of arrangement became necessary when the first or principal wife was infertile (see the use of Hagar in Gen 16:1-4 and the maids of Leah and Rachel in Gen 35:21-22). However, in most cases in which a marriage contract is made with the father of a woman who will be considered a concubine, there is an assumption of a lesser status than a regular wife. Thus the Levite may have simply contracted for a sexual partner, since his social status would ordinarily have required a wife of certain attributes (see Lev 21:7). This may explain why he was in no hurry to bring his concubine home (Judg 19:2).

19:1. hill country/Bethlehem. The geographical distances involved are not great (perhaps thirty miles), but they do represent two tribal areas and in later terms the two kingdoms of Israel and Judah. In any case it would have required at least a full day's travel to cover and thus explains why they must stop for the night after a later afternoon departure only got them as far as Jebus/Jerusalem (Judg 19:8-11). The text actually refers to "Mt.

Ephraim" (NIV: the hill country of Ephraim) which may be identifiable as Jebel Asur, the most noticeable elevation in the region.

19:10. Jebus/Jerusalem. For discussion of the pairing of these city names see the comments on 1:7-8 and 1:21. The city would have been only about four miles north of Bethlehem.

19:12-14. Gibeah. Scholarly consensus now places the site of Gibeah at Jaba', about four miles northeast of Jerusalem. Jaba' sits on a hill above a canyon pitted with caves (see the Rock of Rimmon in Judg 20:47). Although it is described as a village in the tribal territory of Benjamin, Gibeah will later serve as Saul's fortress city when he becomes Israel's first king (see 1 Sam 10:26; Is 10:29). The travelers would likely have passed west of Jerusalem and then taken the road northeast through Anathoth to Geba.

19:15-17. city square hospitality. What is implied here is that no one met the Levite's party as they entered the village, unlike in Genesis 19:1, and they were forced to seek shelter in the *rehob* ("city square"). This place is a poor refuge for travelers. Having to spend the night there would be their last choice, and it would reflect on the poor hospitality of the town that strangers would have to shelter there. In Genesis 19 the angels' intention to go to the *rehob* suggests a testing of the community. The fact that the Levite in Judges 19 is forced to go to the *rehob* demonstrates a basic failure on the part of the citizens of Gibeah to offer him hospitality.

19:18. house of the Lord. It is possible that the Levite is either speaking of his own home in Ephraimite territory, where he may or may not perform any cultic functions, or to the shrine at Shiloh where the ark of the covenant is housed and a group of Levites provide official sacrificial duties (1 Sam 1:3).

19:21. foot washing. It is typical for the host to make a modest offer to the guest (usually water, food, shelter and a foot washing). This does not preclude more being given to the guest, but it does protect the host who may find himself in the dishonored position of offering more than he can deliver. In any case the host will make every effort to insure his guest's comfort, and this would include cooling and cleansing hot, dusty feet (see Gen 18:4; 19:2; 24:32).

19:24. daughter and concubine made available. The situation here may be intended to portray a skewed world in which no man or woman is safe from harm. The Ephraimite's invitation that the men do "what seems good to you" is suggestive of the final phrase in this narrative: Judges 21:25b—"everyone did as he saw fit." It should be noted that women are legal extensions of their husbands in ancient Israel and thus would come under the same legal protections guaranteed to their husbands—as long as their husbands identified them as such. In this instance the Ephraimite apparently shifts his role from hospitable to inhospitable host by "callously" offering the Levite's concubine to the crowd in order to save his honor and perhaps his own life. Technically the concubine could not be legally separated from the Levite and should have been protected by the customs of hospitality to the same degree.

19:25. Levite gives concubine to crowd. This interchange is less dramatic than that in Genesis 19:9. The citizens of Gibeah simply ignore the Ephraimite's offer without accusing him of "playing the judge." There is a sense of urgency in the text, brought on by a lack of reasoning in the actions of the mob, which may explain the Levite's action of thrusting his concubine out the door and into the hands of the crowd. In both cases the life of the host is saved by his guest(s), but clearly the solution provided by Lot's guests is preferable to the Levite's. What is clear in both narratives is that the guest is forced to save his own life and that of his host. The irony of this reversal climaxes the narrative, although a sense of disgust lingers over the violence done to the Levite's concubine. She is a victim whose only attempt to assert her independence (her flight from her husband in Judg 19:2) was thwarted by her father, her husband and the failure of the citizens of Gibeah to carry out their proper role as host. The Levite chooses to sacrifice her to save himself.

19:29. cut up pieces sent. The Levite will perpetrate one last indignity on his concubine's body by carving her up into twelve pieces and then using them as grisly invitations to a general assembly of the tribes. There are clear parallels between this action and Saul's call to arms in 1 Samuel 11:7, in which he carved his oxen into twelve pieces.

20:1. Dan to Beersheba. This is the traditional geographic range given in the text for the north-south political limits of Israel. It represents a distance of approximately 160 miles.

20:1-3. assembly in Mizpah. This site in the tribal territory of Benjamin was a common assembly point in premonarchic Israel (Josh 18:26; 1 Sam 7:16). The name means "to watch," and the site may have been a military outpost or border fortress, and thus a likely spot for the type of encampment described in Judges. It may be identified with Tell en-Nasbeh, about six miles north of Jerusalem.

20:2. four hundred thousand soldiers with swords. As in many of the other passages that mention the size of an army, it is difficult to ascertain whether the Hebrew word ought to be read as "thousands" or "divisions" (for more discussion, see comment on Josh 8:3). Whatever the case may be, this is a large turnout in response to the summons. Population estimates for this period generally run in the 200,000 to 250,000 range, based on the number of settlements, the size of the settlements and the average number of inhabitants per acre of city space. The swords that are mentioned are probably bronze swords, since we know that Israel did not develop iron technology until the monarchy period.

20:3-8. the hearing and verdict. Some aspects of Israelite judicial procedure are followed in this episode. The chiefs or elders of the tribes are assembled to hear testimony. Once this has been given, a verdict is rendered (compare the case of the prodigal son in Deut 21:18-21). One major variation on this process is the fact that only the word of the Levite is given. Ordinarily, two witnesses are required for a verdict to be given (see Num 35:30; Deut 19:15). The judgment of the tribes in this case includes taking an oath to stay in the field until punishment has been administered. Such a united front is unprecedented in the Judges period, when the tribes often fight among themselves (Judg 12:1-6) or refuse to join a combined military effort (see Judg 5:15-17). The idea that honor has been violated or a great affront done that requires military action may be compared to David's vow after being rebuffed by Nabal in 1 Samuel 25:21-22.

20:9,18. direction of the lot. The casting of lots prior to battle forms an inclusio in the book of Judges. At the beginning of the book, God responds to the Israelites' question of "who will be the first to go up and fight?" with the name Judah (1:1-2). And, again, in this final episode Judah is directed to "go first" in the battle against Gibeah and the Benjaminites (20:18). The use of lots is common in Israelite tradition in situations of land distribution (see Josh 14:2; 19:1-51) and judicial procedure (see Josh 7:14-21; 1 Sam 14:41-42). It is a form of divination in which the decision, based on the cases of lots (dice, knuckle bones, incised ivory palettes, etc.) is provided by God's answer to a question (see the comments on Judg 1:1-2 and 18:5-6).

20:15. twenty-six thousand swordsmen. For discussion of the large numbers see the comment at 20:2.

20:16. seven hundred left-handed slingers. The number may reflect a special or elite contingent of ambidextrous warriors (see the comment on Judg 3:15), who were such marksmen with their slings that they could turn the odds for an outnumbered army (see 1 Chron 12:2 for another group of Benjaminite heroes or elite troops who were experts with the sling).

20:26. fasting. Fasting is little attested in the ancient Near East outside of the Bible. It generally occurs in the context of mourning. In the Old Testament the religious use of fasting is often in connection with making a request before God. The principle is that the importance of the request causes an individual to be so concerned about their spiritual condition that physical necessities fade into the background. In this sense the act of fasting is designed as a process leading to purification and humbling oneself before God (Ps 69:10). After their second defeat by the Benjaminites, the other tribes gathered to seek God's advice, and in preparation for this query they fasted and made sacrifices in order to remove any sin or other obstacle that may have been the cause for this defeat. For similar efforts related to military action, see 1 Samuel 7:6 and 2 Chronicles 20:1-4.

20:26-28. ark at Bethel. This is the only reference to the ark in the book of Judges, and therefore for most of the book it is unknown where the ark is being kept or how it is being used. It is generally assumed that its location changed on a number of occasions during the period. In the beginning of 1 Samuel it is at Shiloh.

20:28. time period. Since the episodes in the book of Judges are not always in chronological order, it could be that these events occurred closer to the beginning of the settlement period. This would allow for a son of Aaron to still be alive and able to serve as priest before the ark at Bethel. If it relates to a later period, then this was probably Phinehas II, the predecessor to Eli at Shiloh.

20:29-36. ambush strategy. The use of decoying ambushes, such as that described in this episode, seems to have been a familiar part of Israelite military strategy. Joshua employs it in his second attack on the city of Ai (Josh 8:2-21), and Abimelech uses similar tactics in his capture of the city of Shechem (Judg 9:30-45). This strategy falls into the category of indirect warfare, characterized by ambush, pretend retreats, decoys, infiltration and the like, rather than lengthy siege or pitched battle. It would have been difficult for armies to besiege walled cities without siege engines or a large enough force to completely surround the city and prevent counterattacks or the escape of the citizens. Thus trickery was used to fool the city into opening its gates or into sending contingents of troops outside the walls that could be cut off by ambushes (see Jeroboam's unsuccessful strategy in 2 Chron 13:13-18). Such tactics are known from the ancient Near East in the Mari texts (eighteenth century B.C.), the Egyptian Papyrus Anastasi (thirteenth century B.C.) and a Middle Assyrian text (tenth century B.C.).

20:33. Baal Tamar. A site between Gibeah and Bethel which has not been conclusively identified. Among the possibilities are Khirbet Atarah, Ras et-Tavil and Sahre al Gibiyeh, all of which are within this general area. The city serves as the site of a diversionary battle which allowed another army of Israelites to attack Gibeah and destroy it.

20:35. 25,100 killed. The original Benjaminite muster was 26 divisions plus 700 trained warriors (v. 15). The number here in verse 35 is the total casualty count, which is broken down in the following verses. Of the divisions, 25 were wiped out, including 18 on the battlefield (v. 44), 5 during flight (v. 45) and 2 more in the "mop up" operation (v. 45). Of the 700 trained warriors, 100 were killed while 600 escaped and hid (v. 47).

20:45. rock of Rimmon. The limestone cliffs around the site of Gibeah/Geba are pitted with small caves from which ambushing soldiers could spring or in which these six hundred survivors could hide (see comment on Judg 19:12-14). This is the origin of the name "Pomegranate Rock," which is most likely identified with the el-Jaia cave in the Wadi es-Swenit, approximately one mile east of Gibeah/Geba.

20:48. decimating cities (incl. animals). Although the term is not used here, the action taken against the Benjaminite towns is precisely the same as a *herem*, a holy war in which all persons, animals and property are destroyed as a sacrifice to God (see Josh 6:17-21 at Jericho and 1 Sam 15:2-3 and the *herem* against the Amalekites). This would then account for the fact that only six hundred Benjaminites (hiding at the Rock of Rimmon) would have survived this devastation. It is an extreme form of warfare, and one that occurs only infrequently since it does not provide the conquering force any loot or slaves.

21:1. oath. Once again an unwise oath appears in the narrative (see previously Jephthah's oath in Judg 11:30-31). In their zeal to punish the Benjaminites, they had carried out a war of total devastation and had sealed the fate of their future existence by swearing not to intermarry with any survivors (see the importance of keeping a vow in Num 30:2-15). This may have also been a security measure should there be future conflicts with the Benjaminites. However, the destruction had been so complete that the six hundred survivors were left without wives or other women to marry. Since the Israelites could not violate their oath without bringing God's wrath upon them, an alternative source of brides for the Benjaminites had to be sought.

21:4. built altar. If Bethel was only an assembly point for this episode and not the permanent cultic site for the ark, it is to be expected that a new Yahweh altar would have to be constructed for the use of the Israelites (see the legislation on construction of altars in Ex 20:24-26). It is also possible that a new altar would have been built in an open area or on a high place to accommodate the large numbers of Israelites assembled (see Gideon's new altar in Judg 6:26).

21:4. offerings. In order to purify themselves and make themselves worthy of God's attention, a new altar is constructed and burnt, and peace offerings are made (see Ex 20:24). This is done because they have placed themselves in a difficult situation after making an unwise vow. They are responsible for the near-extermination of the tribe of Benjamin. Now they regret that act and want to seek Yahweh's guidance on how to save Benjamin from extinction. Their act of building an altar and making sacrifices is proper (as it was in Judg 20:26) and elicits a response from God.

21:8-12. Jabesh Gilead. Most likely located at Tell Maklub, on the Yabis River in the northern Gileadite hill country, just east of the Jordan River. It was a strategic site, commanding the well-traveled wadi immediately below the city. As such it controlled much of the merchant traffic in that area (see 1 Sam 11).

21:5, 10. death for not attending. The Israelite tribes had taken an oath of solidarity. The assumption was that anyone who failed to assemble was taking the side of their enemy and thus deserved the same fate. Thus Jabesh Gilead was targeted for punishment as a fulfillment of the oath and, conveniently, as a source of brides for the six hundred remaining

Benjaminites. Taking an oath such as this might be compared to Saul's statement in 1 Samuel 11:7 when he called for a mustering of Israelite tribes to save Jabesh Gilead from the Ammonites. He threatened to destroy the cattle of any man who failed to assemble for this campaign. The threat probably implied violence against the person as well. One Mari text provides a graphic example of this type of threat. The head of a criminal was carried on a pole as an indication of the fate of draft dodgers.

21:6. elders. In the absence of a king or other dominant leader, the tribes had to rely on the collective assembly of the tribal elders. They administered justice in the village culture (Deut 19:12; 21:2-6; 22:15) and served as representatives for the people at major gatherings (Josh 8:10; 1 Sam 4:3).

21:19. geography. The festival of Shiloh (Khirbet Seilun) must have been on the pilgrimage route between Bethel in the south and Shechem (Tell Balatah, about thirty miles north of Jerusalem) to the north. Lebonah was located north of Shiloh (possibly either El-Lubban or Lubban Sherqujeh). All of these directions by the elders suggest that none of them had been to this Canaanite festival.

21:21-23. girls of Shiloh. The idea of stealing brides also occurs in early Greek and Roman traditions and probably reflects a practice that was not uncommon in the ancient world. The festival in question was apparently a Canaanite fertility ritual associated with the harvest.

21:25. no king. This chapter concludes with the same statement which appears earlier, explaining the anarchic conditions in the Judges period by noting that no king ruled at that time (see the comment on Judg 17:6). This provides an exclamation to the entire book. The stories filled with violence and death were an obvious case for the necessity of the monarchy. The covenant was ignored, the people rebelled, and no law was above breaking in a time when everyone did what was right in their own eyes. Thus the only hope for peace and the rule of order was a reestablishment of the covenant and the imposition of strong leadership.

RUTH

1:1-22
To Moab and Back

1:1. chronological note. The story of Ruth is placed by the narrator in the time of the judges, but no indication is given as to when in this several-century period it took place. If the genealogy at the end of the book has no gaps (see comment on Gen 5:1-32), the events would best be placed in the second half of the twelfth century, roughly contemporary to Jephthah and Samson.

1:1. Bethlehem. Bethlehem is located about five miles south of Jerusalem. Bronze and Iron Age pottery has been found at the site, but little excavation can be carried out due to continuing occupation. The town was particularly susceptible to the climate because there was no spring and it relied on cisterns to gather water. The main produce of the area includes grain crops (wheat and barley) as well as olives and grapes.

1:1 going to Moab in time of famine. There are a number of wadis that cross the region of Moab, and the combination of adequate rainfall and porous soil makes it good for agriculture. The family of Elimelech would have traveled north to the area of Jerusalem and then taken the Jerusalem to Jericho road to cross the Jordan at the fords by Jericho. From there the road east up to Heshbon would connect them to the north-south King's Highway leading through the region of Moab. Depending on where they settled, the trip would have been seventy to one hundred miles and would have taken about a week.

1:1. Moab. The region of Moab, east of the Dead Sea, extended from the plains north of the Arnon River south to the Zered River. The region measures about sixty miles north to south and about thirty miles from the Dead Sea to the eastern desert. The "plains of Moab" north of the Arnon was a region that had belonged to Sihon (see Num 21) and had been distributed to the tribe of Reuben. Little is known of Moab during this period, though archaeological surveys have identified several dozen settlements during this time.

1:2. Ephrathites. "Ephrathite" could refer to either a geographical district or a clan ancestor. The fact that the designation could refer to individuals from differing tribes and clans would make it a potentially confusing designation, but geographical possibilities are equally uncertain.

1:3-5. plight of the widow. Widows in the ancient Near East had lost all social status and generally were also without political or economic status. They would equate to the homeless in our American society. Typically they had no male protector and were therefore economically dependent on society at large.

1:1-6. divine intervention. As would be the case for any natural occurrence, the Lord is seen as intervening to bring an end to the famine. In the ancient Near East, deity played the most important role in cause and effect, both in history and in nature. In our worldview we would be inclined to identify human or natural cause and effect first and then mention that "of course, God was behind it all." In the ancient Near East it would be the other way around. God would be identified as the cause behind famine or war, with natural or human causes given secondary notice, if mentioned at all. They would not rule out natural causes any more than we would rule out supernatural ones.

1:8. advantage of mothers' homes. Usually the place of protection is in the *father's* house rather than the mother's. Ruth 2:11 implies that Ruth's father is still alive. In its other appearances in the Old Testament (Gen 24:28; Song 3:4; 8:2) the mother's house has to do with preparations for marriage. This corresponds to the situation in both Mesopotamia and Egypt, where the mother was protector of the daughter and the one who advised and supervised in matters of love, marriage and sex. Therefore, Naomi's encouragement of the girls to return to their mother's home does not suggest seeking a place of legal protection, but rather a place that may provide a new family situation.

1:13. why would they wait for Naomi's sons? In Israel the law had established the institution of levirate marriage (see comments on Gen 38:6-26; Deut 25:5-10) wherein if a man died leaving his wife childless, his brother was responsible to impregnate the widow so that the family line of the deceased would not die out. Commentators have noticed, however, that in the scenario Naomi is presenting, the potential sons that could provide an heir for Ruth or Orpah would have a different father than their deceased husbands, so this would not qualify as levirate marriage. It is difficult to see, therefore, how this would preserve the line of Mahlon or Kilion. Nonetheless, such sons could at least provide legal protection and care for the women in old age.

1:16-17. the nature of Ruth's commitment.
Rather than having any evangelistic intentions, Naomi makes every attempt to chase Ruth back to her own gods. It was not unusual for women who married into foreign families to seek the continued protection of their native deities (see Gen 31:19; 1 Kings 11:8; 16:31). From the information the text gives, one could conclude that Ruth's acknowledgment of Yahweh just comes along with the adoption of a new people in a foreign land. Just as Ruth has stated that wherever Naomi travels or settles she will travel or settle, she has also affirmed that whoever Naomi's people or gods are will be her people and gods. This appears to be a commitment made to Naomi on the basis of a relationship with Naomi rather than a commitment made to Yahweh because she has been convinced of the theological superiority of monotheism and that Yahweh is the sole God of heaven and earth.

1:17. even death will not separate us. Contrary to many translations, Ruth here affirms that even in death she will not leave Naomi. What she means is that she intends to care for Naomi's burial and the rituals connected with death, and to be buried in the same place as Naomi. Being cared for in death would have been a typical concern to a childless widow, so this would be a significant commitment to Naomi. Ruth's decision to be buried in Naomi's land would show that she was totally setting aside her former allegiances and dependencies to cast her lot in with Naomi. Being buried in the same family tomb as Naomi would be further assurance that appropriate provisions would continue to be made for Naomi after death. Care for the dead was popularly believed to influence their existence in the afterlife.

1:19. the whole town. Bethlehem has never been a big town despite the important role it has in Israel's history. The population of the town would not have exceeded a couple of hundred in most periods and was likely considerably less at this time.

1:20. significance of names. In the ancient Near East a name was often given with a meaning in mind and with the hope that the name would characterize or imprint itself on the person's destiny. Unfortunately the name Naomi, "pleasantness," brings only irony as it appears to mock her ill-fortune. She suggests it would be a false claim to admit being Naomi after all the bitterness (Mara) she had experienced.

1:21. deity as cause of suffering. In the ancient world the gods were seen as behind all mundane daily occurrences and, therefore, certainly as determining the course of one's life. The cycle of nature (that had brought the famine) as well as disease and death were all in the hands of deity. It is natural, then, that Naomi identifies Yahweh as the source of her misery. It is important to note that this does not explicitly translate into blame. She does not proclaim her innocence or seek vindication, and she does not openly call into question God's justice. It is safe to assume, however, that she is not aware of any claim deity would have against her integrity and would be distressed that the reasons for Yahweh's actions against her were not evident. On the other hand, the general opinion in the ancient world was that the mortals rarely could discern what led the gods to do what they did. This puzzlement is a common theme of Mesopotamian wisdom literature.

1:22. beginning of the barley harvest. The barley harvest in this region would begin in mid- to late-April as the rainy season came to a close. It was the earliest of the major harvest seasons.

2:1-23
Ruth Meets Boaz

2:1. status of Boaz. Traditionally translations have identified Boaz as a "valiant warrior," but the NIV "man of standing" is probably a better choice. One's prominence could be achieved through military prowess (see Jephthah, Judg 11:1), but many of the people described by this phrase have no known military reputation. It is likely that the phrase has broader application (see comment on Judg 6:12).

2:2. poor gathering grain. Israel's law mandated provision for the poor and destitute by allowing them to follow the reapers in the fields to gather what was dropped or left behind (see comments on Lev 19:9-10 and Deut 24:19-22). This solution to a social problem required that the recipients work hard for their provision, and it therefore preserved the dignity that is sometimes forfeited by those who are entirely dependent on the generosity of others.

2:8. the field of Boaz. Since land was apportioned by tribe and clan and family, what would have looked like a single field may have had delineated tracts that belonged to various clan or family members. Stone markers would have identified the boundaries, and it would be very easy to pass from one family holding to another in what looked like one field. Indeed, it would have been easiest for the poor to roam over the whole field to improve their chances of adequate returns. In contrast, Boaz has intentions that Ruth be more than adequately provided for.

2:12. refuge under the wings. The metaphor of taking refuge under the wings of deity is found also in Psalms (36:8; 57:2; 61:5; 91:4) and is consistently related to issues of care and protection connected to the covenant. The metaphor is also known from other ancient Near Eastern cultures, particularly Egyptian, where even the disembodied wings represent protection. Deities with wings are often portrayed overshadowing the king. Likewise an ivory from Arslan Tash dated to the eighth century shows characters in human form with wings protecting a figure in the center.

2:14. dipping bread in wine vinegar. The morsel that Ruth dips would most likely have been a grain cake of some sort, usually cooked in oil. The substance she dips it in had as a base the byproduct of the wine fermentation process. It was bitter tasting if used for a drink but here is used as a dressing or condiment of sorts and would have been enjoyable.

2:15-16. additional gathering privileges. Verse 16 uses some very obscure terminology in relaying Boaz's instructions to his workers, but it is clear that he has purposed to make Ruth's labor productive. Best estimates conclude that the workers are instructed to take some stalks out of their own harvested handfuls and leave them for Ruth to retrieve.

2:17. threshing the grain. The hard surface of the threshing floor often served the needs of an entire community. A stick or a rock would be used to beat the stalks to separate the grain from the chaff.

2:17. ephah. An ephah would amount to about two thirds of a bushel of grain. This has been calculated to be between thirty and fifty pounds of grain, which would have represented about a month's worth of the grain ration usually allotted to male workers.

2:20. kinsman-redeemer. The kinsman-redeemer's role was to help recover the tribe's losses, whether those losses were human (in which case he hunted down the killer), judicial (in which case he assisted in lawsuits) or economic (in which case he recovered the property of a family member). Since Yahweh had granted the land to the Israelites as tenants, they could not sell it, and if they mortgaged a portion of it to pay debts, it was considered very important to regain ownership as soon as possible. In this way the land remained within the extended family as a sign of its membership in the covenantal commu-

nity. The importance of this inalienable right to land can be seen in Naboth's refusal to relinquish the "inheritance of my fathers" when King Ahab offered to buy his vineyard (1 Kings 21:2-3). In Mesopotamia (especially in the earlier periods) land was often owned by families rather than by individuals, so any individual would be limited in his ability to sell the property.

2:23. barley harvest and wheat harvest. The barley harvest ended in May and blended into the wheat harvest, which continued into June.

3:1-18
Ruth's Proposal

3:2. winnowing barley at the threshing floor. Winnowing was often done in the late afternoon, when the breeze had picked up after the day's heat. The process used a pronged fork on a long handle by which the threshed grain was tossed into the air. The breeze blew the lighter chaff a short distance away (it was later retrieved to be used as fodder), while the grain fell back to the threshing floor. The threshing floor was usually out in an open area to make maximum use of the breeze.

3:3. Ruth's ablutions. The perfume mentioned here consisted of scented oils that would have been commonly used at celebrations and other festive occasions. The scents were usually derived from imported plants.

3:3. why shouldn't Boaz know she is there? Some commentators have suggested that Ruth is fashioning herself as a bride, and thus to be seen would be to tip her hand. Most consider her remaining hidden to be an issue not of propriety but of appropriate timing.

3:7. lying at the end of the grain pile. The threshing floor would have been used by many members of the community, so there would have been others there winnowing besides Boaz. Each would have had his assigned traditional area, and each would sleep by his pile after the festivities so as to guard it until it could be carted away in the morning.

3:7-9. uncovering feet and the spreading of the garment. There are occasions in the Old Testament where the term "feet" is used euphemistically for the sexual organs. The expression "spread the edge of the garment" is likewise used with sexual overtones in a betrothal context in Ezekiel 16:8. The text of Ruth does not suggest a blatant sexual act but is provocative in its ambiguity.

3:9. what is Ruth asking? Ruth uses a phrase that elsewhere is used to refer to betrothal and marriage. It is also clear from Boaz's response in the next verse that she has requested marriage. Naomi had not advised her to be this bold, but the outcome of marriage was certainly what Naomi had in mind.

3:12. why does it matter that there is a closer relative? The benefits that derived from functioning as a kinsman-redeemer required that a sequence of priorities be established. Closer relatives were therefore given the opportunity to exercise that function first.

3:14. why should it not be known a woman was there? Aside from the natural desire to preserve the reputation of both Ruth and Boaz (the word used in v. 13 for staying the night does *not* have sexual connotations), Boaz was anxious not to jeopardize the legal matters of the following day by any shadow of immorality.

3:17. six measures. The unit of the six measures is unspecified and therefore uncertain. It is unlikely that it would be six ephahs—that would be far too much for her to carry. Boaz may just have used shovelfuls or double handfuls.

4:1-16

A Husband and a Son

4:1. seat at the town gate. The gate area in Israelite cities was an open space that was the hub of activity. Merchants, visitors, messengers and judges all frequented that area and conducted their business there. It was a logical place to find someone you might be looking for. Since people heading out to their fields would pass through the gate area, Boaz hoped to encounter the individual he sought. Numerous excavations have produced gate plans showing that often there were benches lining the whole area where people could meet for their various purposes. Since only limited excavation has been done at Bethlehem, no gate from this period has yet been uncovered.

4:2. ten elders as witnesses. The elders, usually clan leaders or heads of household, served as the governing body of the city. Judicial and legal matters were in their hands. Here there is no legal judgment to pass, but they would oversee the legal transaction to assure that all was done according to law and custom, as well as serve as witnesses to the transaction.

4:4. why would he want to redeem the land? By redeeming Naomi's land the kinsman would have prospects for very soon enlarging his own permanent landholdings. Since Naomi had no heir, when she died, the land would revert to his family and be passed on to his heirs. The money put forth for the land would be an investment on future returns. If this was just a case of land redemption, it would have been a very attractive business proposal.

4:5-6. Why does Ruth's involvement change the situation? Once Boaz interprets the kinsman responsibilities as including marrying Ruth, the economic picture changes considerably. One could forgive the other kinsman for not realizing that Ruth came with the package deal. Only by a significant stretch in custom would he be considered to have any levirate obligations to Ruth (for review of levirate laws see comment on Deut 25:5-10), yet it is clear that that is involved by the reference in verse 5 to maintaining the name of the dead. If the kinsman must marry Ruth, the son that may be born to her would then be the heir to the property of Elimelech's family. In this case the money that is used to redeem the land is not an investment but simply reduces his family assets. Instead of serving to eventually enlarge his holdings of land, his money would be going to a charitable cause. He would also incur additional cost in providing for Naomi, Ruth and who knows how many additional children. It is even possible that Ruth's children would have a claim to a portion of his inheritance along with any children he already had. It is likely he is married; the economic impact on his family of redeeming Ruth is thus a chief criterion in his decision.

4:7-8. removal of sandal. Sandals were the ordinary footwear in the ancient Near East, but they were also a symbolic item of clothing, especially in the relationship between the widow and her legal guardian. This may have been due to the fact that land was purchased based on whatever size triangle of land the buyer could walk off in an hour, a day, a week or a month (1 Kings 21:16-17). Land was surveyed in triangles, and a benchmark was constructed of fieldstones to serve as a boundary marker (Deut 19:14). Since they walked off the land in sandals, the sandals became the moveable title to that land. By removing the sandals of her guardian, a widow removed his authorization to administer the land of her household. Land transfers in the Nuzi texts also involved replacing the old owner's foot on the land with that of the new owner.

4:9-10. nature of the transaction. By purchasing all of Naomi's property and goods, Boaz has undertaken the total care of Naomi and the obligation to support her in life and provide for her in death. By acquiring Ruth, he has obligated himself to give her the opportunity to bear children, the first of whom would then become the heir of Elimelech and his sons.

4:11-12. blessing. Blessings connected to marriage rarely address the relationship between husband and wife; instead they focus on children. The blessing of creation as well as the covenant blessing anticipated reproduction as the blessing of God. In the ancient world as a whole this is also true as can be seen in the blessing on King Keret in the Ugaritic texts—that his new wife would bear him seven or eight sons. Examples in the blessing on Boaz are drawn from Israel's national history (Rachel and Leah, see Gen 30) as well as from the tribal history of Judah (Tamar, see Gen 38).

4:15. responsibility of children. It is here suggested that the son will lift Naomi's spirits and console her after the loss of her husband and sons. Her grief over her previous loss would have been not only in terms of personal relationships, but also in terms of economic hardship and possibly even of afterlife issues that were popularly associated with ongoing rituals by descendants (see comment on Num 3:1). This grief would then be addressed, since it was expected that children would care for their parents in old age (providing food and shelter, legal protection and proper burial).

4:17. Naomi's son. Some have concluded that there was an official adoption of the child by Naomi. While adoption for legal purposes was a very common practice in the ancient world, the legal situation here would not have required an adoption. Another suggestion has been that the son is actually being turned over to Naomi's custody for her to raise, since he is a substitute son for her. While this is possible, it is most likely that there is simply a recognition that Naomi is the legal mother of the child and that she will play a significant role in his upbringing, while he will continue to provide for her in the next generation.

4:17-21
Genealogy

4:18. importance of family line. Here we discover that this incident that nearly resulted in a family of Israel dying out concerned none other than the family of David. The great King David came that close to never having been born. The genealogy is demonstration that God resolved the family crisis. Not only did the family of Naomi survive, but it prospered to become one of the great families in Israel. Survival of the traumatic Judges period (setting from 1:1) was through faithfulness and loyalty; faithfulness and loyalty in turn resulted in individuals such as David (result of 4:21).

1 SAMUEL

1:1-28
Samuel's Birth

1:1. Ramathaim in the hill country of Ephraim. There is a town called Ramah (modern er-Ram) in the territory of Benjamin about five miles north of Jerusalem and four miles south of Bethel. Since Ramah is given as the place of Samuel's home in 1:19, some consider this to be the site. The text, however, clearly locates Ramathaim in the hill country of Ephraim. This has long been associated with New Testament Arimathea about fifteen miles west of Shiloh.

1:2. polygamy in Israel. In Israel, as in most of the ancient world, monogamy was generally practiced. Polygamy was not contrary to law or morals, but was usually not economically feasible. The main occurrence of polygamy would be when the first wife was barren, but there are several other factors that encouraged the practice, including (1) an imbalance in the number of males and females, (2) the need to produce large numbers of children to work herds and/or fields, (3) the desire to increase the prestige and wealth of a household through multiple marriage contracts, and (4) the high rate of death for females in childbirth. Polygamy is most common among pastoral nomadic groups and in rural farming communities where it is important that every female be attached to a household and be productive. In the Bible most cases of polygamy among commoners occur prior to the period of the monarchy.

1:2. shame of childlessness. Since bearing children was a sign of God's greatest blessing (Ps 127:3), the inability to bear children was often viewed as a sign of God's punishment. Additionally, a woman's status in the family would be very tenuous if she had not borne children. A barren woman could be and often was discarded, ostracized or given a lower status. Mesopotamian prayers and legal texts show that these same issues existed throughout the ancient Near East.

1:3. Shiloh. Whether Elkanah's home is Ramah in Benjamin or Ramathaim in Ephraim, the journey to Shiloh was about fifteen miles. For a family this would have been a two-day journey. The site of Shiloh has been identified as Khirbet Seilun, about halfway between Bethel and Shechem. This seven-and-a-half-acre site is situated in a strategic location enjoying fertile land, a reliable water source and access to the main north-south route through the heartland of Israel. Substantial Iron Age I ruins have been found at the site, along with evidence of destruction by means of fire. Though remains of public buildings from this period have been found, no trace of the sanctuary has been identified. The probable location for the sanctuary at the highest point of the tell has suffered from erosion.

1:3. annual sacrifice. The law called for three annual pilgrimages: at the Feast of Unleavened Bread, the Feast of Weeks and the Feast of Tabernacles. Many interpreters consider the last to be the occasion for Elkanah's visits. Since the text does not specify the occasion of a pilgrimage feast, however, some believe that this was a traditional family ritual reflecting the piety of Elkanah.

1:3. priestly line of Eli. Eli was from the line of Aaron through his fourth son, Ithamar. At the beginning of the Judges period, the high priest was Phinehas, son of Eleazar, the eldest son of Aaron. The two middle sons of Aaron, Nadab and Abihu, had been slain because of ritual violation (Lev 10). How the care of the tent of meeting and ark had switched from the Eleazar branch to the Ithamar branch is unknown.

1:4. giving portions of sacrifice. A number of the sacrifices provided an opportunity for a shared meal, especially the fellowship offering (see the comment on Lev 3:1-5). When a sacrificial meal was included, the officiating priest as well as the family of the celebrants would receive portions of the meat, a rare item in ancient meals. This would have the sociological status of a turkey dinner in America.

1:5. double portion for Hannah. The description of Hannah's portion is obscure in the Hebrew. Most translations identify it as a double portion (NIV, NASB, NKJV, NRSV), while other suggestions have been "only one portion" (RSV) and "special portion" (NLT). Many of the commentators favor "only one portion" because that sets up the contrast that makes most sense of the context.

1:7. sanctuary at Shiloh. Here the sanctuary is

referred to as the "house of the Lord," which is ambiguous regarding the nature of the structure. In verse 9 it is referred to as a "temple," which implies a building. In 2:22 reference is made to the tent of meeting, that is, the tabernacle. This variation in terms suggests that the tent has either had a more durable structure built around it or has been erected inside a sacred enclosure that perhaps was previously Canaanite.

1:8. husband better than ten sons. Elkanah's attempt to console Hannah is weak. While their relationship on a human level could be argued to meet Hannah's emotional needs, there is much more involved here. First, there is the social stigma of barrenness. Second, there is the extension of the family into the future. Children were relied upon to care for parents in their old age, to provide proper burial and to carry on their memory. In some cases it was believed that one's comfort in the afterlife was dependent on provisions carried out by succeeding generations. Hannah's status in society and hope for the future are dismal. These concerns give Elkanah's well-meaning question an empty ring.

1:9. priest's seat by the entrance. Eli was perhaps too advanced in years to continue officiating, but he could still serve a public relations function, greeting worshipers at the entrance and offering advice or instruction. The piece of furniture described here could be translated "chair" but in most places refers to a throne or a seat of honor. In public settings benches would often be provided, while in residences a couch or stools would be more common. Excavations at Mari have provided many examples of stools in residences.

1:11. vows. Vows are voluntary, conditional agreements that are common in most of the cultures of the ancient Near East, including Hittite, Ugaritic, Mesopotamian and, less often, Egyptian. In the ancient world the most common context for a vow was when a request was being made to deity. The condition would typically involve God's provision or protection, while that which was vowed was usually a gift to deity. The gift would most frequently take the form of a sacrifice, but other types of gifts to the sanctuary or priests would be options. Fulfillment of a vow could usually be accomplished at the sanctuary and was a public act. In Ugaritic literature King Keret makes a vow in requesting a wife who could produce offspring. In return he offered gold and silver corresponding to his bride's weight.

1:11. hair cutting. Refraining from cutting hair is the most important element in the Nazirite vow (see comments on Num 6). The Nazirite vow is usually restricted to a limited time period, but here, as with Samson, it is specified as being lifelong. The significance of hair to the vow is unknown, though hair (along with blood), was one of the main representatives in ancient thinking of a person's life essence. As such it was often an ingredient in sympathetic magic. This is evident, for instance, in the practice of sending along a lock of the presumed prophet's hair when the prophecies were sent to the king of Mari. The hair would be used in divination to determine whether the prophet's message would be accepted as valid.

1:13. silent personal prayer. Often prayers were accompanied by sacrifices. In this official act a priest would be paid a fee to offer the sacrifice and recite an appropriate prayer. Hannah, lacking funds for such an official undertaking, is praying on her own but is delighted to receive a favorable blessing from the priest, which she took as having the force of an oracle. In Mesopotamia the seer-priests would use divination to read omens on behalf of women praying for conception. There are numerous examples of spontaneous prayer in the Old Testament, though this is the only occasion where the prayer is specified as being silent. In the ancient Near East prayers tended to be formulaic and often had a basis in magical incantations. As a result we know little about silent spontaneous prayer.

1:19. nature of worship. The worship referred to here probably indicates participation in the daily morning sacrifice (see comment on Lev 6:8-13).

1:22-24. weaning age. Weaning generally took place between the ages of two and three and was accompanied by a celebration since it was a rite of passage. According to the Egyptian *Instruction of Any* a child was nursed for about three years.

1:24-25. nature of the sacrifice. The sacrifice offered by Elkanah and Hannah included a bull, flour and wine. According to Numbers 15:8-12 the flour and the wine were to accompany a bull offering. The text is more easily understood as referring to three bulls rather than to a three-year-old bull. This would be supported by the fact that they also bring three times the required amount of flour and wine. If there are three bull offerings to be made, this may indicate the generosity of Elkanah and Hannah.

1:28. lifelong dedication. As pointed out in the comment on 1:11, this length of dedication was abnormal for the Nazirite vow. Even so the length had been specified in the vow and

was being fulfilled accordingly. Hannah is not only fulfilling her vow but is carrying out an ancient tradition. The first male offspring born to any mother was considered as belonging to deity. In the ancient Near East this concept sometimes led to child sacrifice to ensure fertility. Alternatively, in ancestor worship the firstborn would have inherited the priestly function for the family. In Israel it led to consecration—transferring the firstborn to the domain of deity for cultic service or to the temple for holy use. From that status the son may be redeemed, and Israelite law saw his place being taken by the Levites (Num 3:11-13). Because of her vow, Hannah did not follow through on the redemption proceedings. In Mesopotamia slaves were sometimes given as gifts to the temple for the rest of their lives, and Akkadian literature attests to a particular class of women who were dedicated for life to serve the temple as prostitutes. Gifts of children to the temple are evidenced in Sumerian texts from the beginning of the second millennium.

2:1-10
Hannah's Prayer

2:1. horn. The imagery of the horn is at times used in relation to posterity (see especially 1 Chron 25:5, but also Ps 132:17). It is also used to represent visible strength as a weapon capable of goring the enemy. Ceremonial crowns of gods and kings in Mesopotamia often featured horns.

2:6. grave. The word translated "grave" is the Hebrew *Sheol*. It was common belief in the ancient Near East that there was continued existence beyond the grave in a netherworld of some sort. It was considered an act of God's judgment to be sent there, but it was not seen as a place of ongoing reward or judgment. Since the grave was the means of entry into the netherworld, Sheol is often simply another way of speaking of the grave.

2:8. world upside down. The actions of God were often seen as bringing reversal to the world. This reversal could be in terms of the created world (mountains reduced to dust, valleys lifted up, sun going dark); the social world (the poor receiving honor, as here, the mighty being deposed); or the political world (empires tumbling). This world-upside-down motif was a way of expressing God's sovereign control. It could be used to convey judgment or reward and came to be connected with the future kingdom of God, where wrongs would be set right and a new order would take shape.

2:8. foundations of the earth. The foundations of the earth are sometimes viewed as pillars (Ps 75:4) and other times as water (Ps 24:2). Both possibilities have been suggested by interpreters of this passage, which contains the only occurrence of the word here translated "foundations." Both water and pillars are part of the ancient view of the structure of the world.

2:9. thundering from heaven. Thunder and lightning were considered to regularly accompany the presence of a deity in the ancient Near East, often in a battle setting. From the Sumerian Exaltation of Inanna, to the Hittite myths about the storm god, to the Akkadian and Ugaritic mythologies, the gods are viewed as thundering in judgment against their enemies. Baal is depicted as grasping a handful of thunderbolts. Thundering terminology is picked up in royal rhetoric as Hittite or Assyrian kings portray themselves as the instruments of the gods, thundering against those who have violated treaties or stood in the way of empire expansion.

2:10. kingship in this period. The reference to kingship here is surprising since Israel has not yet instituted a monarchy. Nevertheless, kingship was well known in the ancient world of this time, and segments of Israel had already dabbled with the idea (Judg 9). Furthermore, that kingship was a future expectation is reflected in passages such as Genesis 17:6; Numbers 24:17; and Deuteronomy 17:14-20.

2:11-36
The Decline of the House of Eli

2:13. three-pronged fork. Examples of the three-pronged fork have been excavated by archaeologists at Gezer. These bronze implements are short-handled with long, straight tines (like a pitchfork with a short handle) and date to the Late Bronze period. The term used here describes a similar utensil in Old Assyrian texts.

2:13-16. priestly practices. The text contrasts the normal procedure at Shiloh to the procedures used by Eli's sons. Both differ from the prescribed procedure in the Pentateuch (see Lev 7:30-34). The Pentateuch details which parts comprise the priest's share. The normal practice at Shiloh was for the priest to receive whichever part came up from the boiling pot on the end of the fork. Eli's sons insisted on taking what they wanted, when they wanted it. Their ritual offenses came in three areas: (1) their selection of the best parts for themselves; (2) their preference for the meat being roasted rather than boiled; and (3) their refusal to yield

the fat for burning on the altar (Lev 3:16; 7:25).

2:18. linen ephod. The linen ephod is a garment reserved for the priesthood (see 2:28), so this is an indication that Samuel has become involved in an apprenticeship. The ephod was most likely a type of apron. Linen was the basic material, though higher ranking priests would have had gold thread woven into the fabric.

2:19. garment made by Samuel's mother. The robe described in this verse is likewise a priestly garment (see Ex 28:31-34) but is also worn by other people of standing and authority (kings, prophets, Job and his friends, God). It is identified as a garment characterizing priests in 1 Chronicles 15:27. It was typically fringed with a distinctive hem that indicated a person's standing.

2:22. women at the entrance of the tabernacle. In the ancient Near East there are many examples of women serving the temple in various capacities. From menial tasks to priestly duties, from celibacy to prostitution, from short-term periods as a result of vows to lifelong dedication—examples of all sorts are available. It is therefore difficult to identify the nature of the service that the women mentioned here are performing. The indictment of the sexual misconduct of Eli's sons suggests that the women were either involved in some duty of piety or were supposed to be virgins. It must be noted, however, that there is no evidence of religiously motivated celibacy in Israel, and the text does not describe the women as virgins. For further discussion see comment on Judges 11:39.

2:27. prophet. The role of prophet was well understood in the ancient Near East, as evidenced by over fifty texts found in the town of Mari that report various messages given by various prophets. Generally the prophet offered a message from deity. For more information see the comments on Deuteronomy 18.

3:1-21
Samuel Becomes a Prophet

3:3. the temple. The term used here suggests a building. For more information see comment on 1:7.

3:3. lamp of God. The menorah in the tabernacle was to remain lit all night (Ex 27:21; Lev 24:1-4), but it was never supposed to be extinguished, so the comment that it had not yet gone out would be pointless. On the other hand, we have seen that the practices at Shiloh did not necessarily follow what was stipulated in the Law. The phrase "lamp of God" is also used to refer to hope (2 Sam 21:17; 1 Kings 11:36; 2 Kings 8:19), and that would also make sense in this context.

3:3. incubation dreams in the ancient Near East. In the ancient world it was believed that a person sleeping in the temple or its precincts may become privy to divine plans. Some would perform sacrificial rituals and spend the night in the temple in order to receive such revelation. This process is referred to as incubation. In early literature kings such as Naram-Sin and Gudea sought information through incubation. In the Judges period this practice is observable in the Ugaritic epics of Aqhat (where Daniel is requesting a son) and Keret (where Keret is requesting a son). Though Samuel is simply performing his regular duties and clearly has no expectation of revelation, his experience would be understood in light of the common association between temple and revelation. There are no known examples in the ancient Near Eastern literature of such unintentional incubation dreams.

3:4-10. Samuel's dream? Since Samuel gets up to go to Eli and speaks when the Lord arrives (v. 10), modern readers would not usually characterize his experience as a dream. Yet these elements are not contradictory to dreaming by ancient definitions. In ancient Near Eastern literature (examples from Mesopotamian, Egyptian, Hittite and even Greek) there is a category called auditory message dreams. Well-known dreams in this category would include those of the Egyptian king Thutmose IV (fifteenth century), Hittite king Hattushilis (thirteenth century) and Babylonian king Nabonidus (sixth century). In these examples the dreams were meant to validate either their kingship or tasks they are undertaking. In auditory message dreams the god appears (see v. 10) and sometimes startles the person awake. The content of the dream is a spoken message by the deity rather than events or symbolic images. There are a number of examples of the person responding verbally to the deity (e.g., Nabonidus). By ancient Near Eastern standards, then, Samuel's experience could be classified as a dream.

3:11-14. importance of repeated messages. The message given to Samuel is virtually the same as that pronounced by the man of God in chapter 2. The repetition of the message indicates its importance and verifies its truth. It also serves to provide affirmation of Samuel's prophetic calling.

4:1—7:1

The Capture and Return of the Ark

4:1. political climate in the early Iron Age. In the Late Bronze Age (1550-1200) there had been an ongoing struggle between major political powers seeking control of Palestine (see comment on Josh 9:1). With the arrival of the Sea Peoples around 1200 (see next comment), all of the major powers were either wiped out (e.g., the Hittites) or neutralized (Egypt). Moving into the Iron Age, the power stalemate was replaced by a power vacuum. The absence of major powers vying for control of the region allowed for the smaller states to test their strength, develop and build regional "empires." The Philistines were able to take advantage of this early in the period. Then David and Solomon were able to build a substantial empire in Syro-Palestine without needing to be concerned about political powers in Mesopotamia, Anatolia or Egypt.

4:1. Philistines. The group of Philistines that are well known through the narratives of Judges and 1 and 2 Samuel came into the Palestine area with the migration from the Aegean region of the Sea Peoples about 1200 B.C. It is the Sea Peoples that are generally thought to have been responsible for the fall of the Hittite empire and the destruction of many cities along the coast of Syria and Palestine, such as Ugarit, Tyre, Sidon, Megiddo and Ashkelon, though the evidence for their involvement in those areas is circumstantial. Their battles with the Egyptian pharaoh Rameses III are depicted on the famous wall paintings at Medinet Habu. This international upheaval is also reflected in the Homeric epic of the siege of Troy. Coming from Crete, Greece and Anatolia, the Sea Peoples may have used Cyprus as a base from which to launch their attacks. Following the repulsion of the Sea Peoples from Egypt, the tribe that came to be known as the Philistines settled on the southern coast of Palestine. There they established their five capital cities of Ashkelon, Ashdod, Ekron (Tell Miqne), Gath (Tell es-Safi) and Gaza.

4:1. Ebenezer and Aphek. Both of these sites are in the area of an important pass between the hill country and the plain. The area is about twenty miles west of Shiloh and north of Philistine territory (about twenty miles north of Ekron, the furthest north of the five major Philistine cities). Aphek is identified with modern Ras el-Ain, also called Tell Aphek, by the Yarkon River. It is named in Egyptian texts as early as the nineteenth-century Execration texts and appears in the itineraries of Thutmose III (fifteenth century). Excavations have uncovered evidence of Philistine settlement on the site in this period. The identification of Ebenezer is less certain. Many now believe that it is the site called Izbet Sartah located on the edge of the hill country across the pass from Aphek and about two miles further east. The small settlement (half an acre) was established late in the Judges period and was abandoned early in the eleventh century. One of the oldest and longest proto-Canaanite inscriptions was found at this site. The ostracon has eighty-three letters but no coherent words, and has been identified as an abecedary (alphabet list). Some interpreters think it should be classified as early Israelite.

4:3-4. ark and cherubim. The ark was a wooden box, open at the top, approximately three to four feet in length and two and a quarter feet in both width and height, based on eighteen inches a cubit. It was overlaid inside and out with sheets of the finest gold. Four rings (also gold covered) were attached to the sides for the insertion of two gold-encrusted poles, which were used to carry the ark and protect it from the touch of all but the high priest. A golden cover, decorated with two winged cherubim, sealed the ark. The primary function of the ark was to store the tablets and to serve as a "footstool" for God's throne, thereby providing an earthly link between God and the Israelites. In Egyptian festivals the images of the gods were often carried in procession on portable barques. Paintings portray these as boxes about the size of the ark carried on poles and decorated with or flanked by guardian creatures. Biblical descriptions as well as archaeological discoveries (including some fine ivory pieces from Nimrud in Mesopotamia, Arslan Tash in Syria and Samaria in Israel) suggest the cherubim are composite creatures (having features of a number of different creatures, like the Egyptian sphinx), often four-legged animal bodies with wings. The cherubim appear in ancient art with some regularity, flanking the thrones of kings and deities. The combination of cherubim as throne guardians, chests as footstools and statements in the Old Testament concerning Yahweh being enthroned on the cherubim supports the concept of the ark as representing the invisible throne of Yahweh. The use of empty thrones was widespread in the ancient world. They were provided for use by deities or royal personages when they were present.

4:3-7. use of the ark in battle. In the divine warrior motif the deity is fighting the battles and defeating the deities of the enemy. In Assyria Nergal is the king of battle, and Ishtar is viewed as a war goddess. The Canaanite Baal and the Babylonian Marduk are divine warriors. This is not to be viewed as "holy war" because in the ancient Near East there was no other kind of war. In most situations prayers would be made and omens asked to assure the god's presence. Standards or statues of the deity were usually carried to symbolize their presence. Assyrian kings of the ninth and eighth centuries regularly refer to the divine standard that goes before them. The ark, as Yahweh's standard, represents the Lord as clearing the way before the Israelites and leading the armies into Canaan. This concept is not very different from the Assyrian belief that the gods empowered the weapons of the king and fought before him or at his side. Nearly every army in the ancient Near East included priests and diviners (as seen in the Mari texts), prophets (2 Kings 3) and portable sacred objects (Assyrian Annals of Shalmaneser III [858-824 B.C.]). In this way, the god(s) could be consulted on the battlefield or invoked to lead the soldiers to victory.

4:9-10. Philistine control of Israel. It is difficult to be certain how much of Israelite territory came under Philistine control at this time. Most estimate that it would have included from the Jezreel Valley south through the central hill country, skirting the Jerusalem hills but extending to much of the Negev.

4:10. thirty thousand Israelites slain. This is clearly a significant loss of life, but it is difficult to be certain of how to read the numbers. For further information see the comment on Judges 20:2.

4:12. Shiloh. The site of Shiloh has been identified as Khirbet Seilun, about halfway between Bethel and Shechem. This seven-and-a-half-acre site is situated in a strategic location where it enjoys fertile land, a reliable water source and access to the main north-south route through the heartland of Israel. Though this chapter does not say anything about the destruction of Shiloh by the Philistines, Jeremiah 7:12-15 suggests that it was destroyed at this time. Substantial Iron Age I ruins have been found at the site, along with evidence of destruction by means of fire.

4:12. dust on the head. Putting dirt, dust or ashes on one's head was a typical sign of mourning throughout the Old Testament and into the New Testament period. It is a practice also known from Mesopotamia and Canaan. Many mourning rites function as a means for the living to identify with the dead. It is easy to see how dust on the head would be a symbolic representation of burial.

4:21. names with significance. The giving of names in the ancient world was a significant act. A name was believed to affect a person's destiny; so the person giving the name was exercising some degree of control over the person's future. Often the name expressed hopes or blessings. At other times they preserve some detail of the occasion of the birth, especially if the occasion appeared significant. This name is built from the same noun/adjective that is attached to the ark as well as used to describe Eli (v. 18). Though the bearing of a son would have normally been viewed as significant, everything of national significance is gone—Eli, his sons and, especially, the ark. The future looks grim.

5:1. Ashdod. Ashdod is about three miles from the coast directly west of Jerusalem. The tell of the ancient site is about three and a half miles south of the modern city. It features a twenty-acre acropolis and a lower city of over one hundred acres. It is mentioned in the Ugaritic texts, where it is an important center of trade, and excavations have demonstrated a large Late Bronze Canaanite settlement on the acropolis. The Canaanite city was destroyed by the Sea Peoples. The site was then settled by the Philistines and became one of their five principal cities. The Iron Age settlement of Samuel's time period is represented in stratum X, which is Philistine in culture. At this time the city was well fortified and was beginning to expand from the acropolis to the lower city. No temple has yet been uncarthed in that stratum.

5:2. Philistine temples. The Philistine temples of this period feature a holy place where the statue of the god was prominently displayed on a raised platform. For further information about Philistine temple architecture see the comment on Judges 16:29.

5:2. Dagon. There is evidence of Dagon as a important god within the Semitic pantheon of deities as early as the third millennium in Mari. Assyrians worshiped him in the first half of the second millennium, and in Ugaritic literature he is positioned as the father of Baal Haddu. His temple in the town of Ugarit was bigger that the temple of Baal. It is generally assumed, then, that the Philistines did not bring this god with them from their Aegean homeland but adopted him upon their arrival in their new territory. Dagon is often identified as a god of grain or of storm, but both of these remain somewhat speculative.

5:2. ark as trophy of war kept in temple. The ark would have been placed in the temple to indicate that Yahweh, Israel's God, was a defeated prisoner of Dagon. His inferiority had been demonstrated on the battlefield, and his subordination was represented in his humble servitude before his master Dagon. It is possible that it was believed that continuing opportunities for humiliation would result. This is very similar to how conquering kings treated

captive kings (see comment on Judg 1:6-7). There are several examples in the ancient world of statues of a god being carried off as trophies of war. The Marduk statue is taken from Babylon by the Hanaeans (seventeenth century), by the Elamites (thirteenth century) and by the Assyrians (seventh century), and in each case is eventually recovered and restored to his temple. Additionally the statue of Shamash was taken from Sippar by the Suteans (eleventh century). In the eighth and seventh centuries this was a common practice of the Assyrians, and Isaiah prophesies that captivity will be the fate of the gods of Babylon (Is 46:1-2). Assyrian king Esarhaddon speaks of taking the gods of his enemies as booty.

5:3-4. importance of fall, hands and head. The repeated fall of Dagon was a clear indication that Yahweh was not defeated, inferior, subordinate or about to suffer humiliation. While the ark's presence in the temple of Dagon had been intended to humiliate, the cutting off of the hands and head of Dagon indicated destruction. The head of a conquered foe was typically displayed as evidence of his death (see 17:51-54) and cutting off hands was a way of counting casualties (see comment on Judg 8:6) as well as mutilation that demonstrated the powerlessness of the enemy. In a Ugaritic text, Anat, the goddess of battle, carries the heads and hands of her slain opponents away from the battlefield. In addition, this makes sense given how images were manufactured. In a Hittite prayer of this period, a promise is made to supply a life-sized statue of the king with head, hands and feet of gold, and the rest of silver. Since the images of the gods were generally clothed, more care and expense was afforded to the portions that would show. Images were often not cast in one piece but made in parts and joined together with tenons.

5:5. holiness of threshold. The threshold was typically made of a single stone that spanned the doorway, raised slightly from the level of the floor. Sockets were cut into the outer edges of the threshold on which the gates or door swung. The height of the threshold would prevent the doors from swinging out. Entryways were often considered both sacred and vulnerable. Superstitious belief held that stepping on the threshold would allow demons that haunted the entryway to gain admission. Perhaps that was the preferred explanation among the Philistines for Dagon's troubles. Similar superstitions have continued in the Near East and the Far East from Syria to Iraq to China, but ancient information concerning this superstition is lacking.

5:6. plague of the Philistines. The connection with rodents in the passage (5:6, in a sentence preserved only in the Septuagint; 6:4) suggests that the affliction is infectious and is possibly bubonic plague. The Hebrew term translated "tumors" could easily be used to represent the boils (buboes) that are symptomatic of the plague. There is some question, however, whether bubonic plague is attested in the ancient Near East at this early a date. As a result, others have proposed that the plague be understood as bacillary dysentery, which can be transmitted through food infected by mice. If this is correct, however, the connection of the swellings is unclear.

5:8. rulers of the five cities. The five rulers of the Philistines appear to be equal in authority. The term used to describe them is likely the Philistine term, and most scholars believe it has its roots in the language of the Sea Peoples (Greek or another Indo-European language). Until more information is found, it is impossible to offer a clearer political analysis.

5:8. Gath. Gath has been tentatively identified as Tell es-Safi, five miles south of Tell Miqne/Ekron. Of the five major cities of the Philistines it was the closest to Judah. There has been little excavation at the site, though it has been confirmed that there are Iron Age remains. The city was located by the Elah Valley, one of the principal passes from the coastal plain into the hill country surrounding Jerusalem.

5:10. Ekron. Ekron has been identified as Tell Miqne in the Sorek Valley, about twenty miles southwest of Jerusalem and fifteen miles from the Mediterranean. It features a forty-acre lower city, a ten-acre upper tell and a two-and-a-half-acre acropolis. Excavations since the early 1980s have given a good picture of this town, which, by the divided monarchy period, was known for its production of olive oil (with over one hundred processing plants). An inscription found on the site in 1996 (dated to the seventh century B.C.) provided the first example of the Philistine dialect of West Semitic using the Phoenician script. In this period it was fortified with a mud-brick wall over ten feet thick. A large public building (over twenty-five hundred square feet) from this period has been excavated that archaeologists believe to be a palace-temple complex. If they are correct, this is likely the building where the ark would have been housed and where the leaders would have met.

6:2. priests and diviners. Since it was now suspected that the supernatural power connected to Yahweh and the ark was more than the Philistines or their gods could handle, the specialists were consulted for their advice on what was to be done. Priests would have expertise in the treatment of holy objects and issues of purity, whereas diviners would be skilled in incantations, omens and magical procedures.

6:2. importance of proper procedures. The plagues that had followed the ark around Philistia made it clear that they were dealing with an angry god. Appeasement of the deity would require certain gifts and rituals. Popular belief would have expected that such appeasement would only work if acceptable gifts were offered, correct words were spoken, and appropriate actions performed. Incorrect procedures might prove entirely fruitless or might make the deity angrier still. This all took place in the realm of magic, a science that required precision.

6:3. guilt offering. For discussion of this offering see comment on 5:14-16 ("reparation offering"). One of the offenses this offering is designed to address is sacrilege, the desecration of sacred areas or objects. The crime addressed by the reparation offering was appropriating that which was holy into the realm of that which was profane. The Philistines were therefore admitting to desecrating the ark.

6:4-5. efficacious symbols of the plague. Making symbols of the mice and tumors was an act of sympathetic magic in which the representation of something stands for the reality. By sending the tokens back with the ark they were hoping to rid themselves of these divine punishments. Images of mice and other animals, believed to have been used in magical rituals, have been found in excavations throughout the ancient Near East.

6:4-5. role of rats. In the comment on 5:6 it was noted that some readings connect the plague to rodents. The Hebrew word used is often translated "mice" but is more generic and could refer to rats as well. Bubonic plague is spread through fleas that infest rats.

6:7-9. oracular mechanism. The success of this strategy would determine both whether they had assessed the problem correctly and whether their gift was acceptable to the deity they were seeking to appease. Besides offering a gift of appeasement and attempting to rid themselves of the plague through sympathetic magic, the Philistines are also asking for an oracle from Yahweh. They are doing this because sending the ark back is an admission that Israel's God is more powerful than theirs. Such an admission is humiliating, and they would not do it unless they were absolutely convinced that Yahweh was the cause of their problems. That is what the oracle is intended to determine. In an oracle a yes/no question is posed to deity, and a mechanism of some binary nature is used so that deity can provide the answer. In Israel the priest carried the Urim and Thummim to use in oracular situations (see comment on Ex 28:30). In the ancient Near East, when they wanted a natural mechanism for oracles, they tended to use the liver or kidney of sacrificed animals (a divinatory practice called extispicy; see comment on omens at Deut 18:10). Here the Philistines use a natural mechanism for the oracle (see Gen 24:14 and Judg 6:36-40 for other occurrences). Their yes/no question is whether or not Yahweh, Israel's God, is the one responsible for the plagues. Their oracular mechanism is based on the normal behavior of cows. If the answer to the question is "no," the cows will act like normal cows: they will go to the barn to nurse their calves, or they will wander into the field. If the answer to the question is "yes," the Lord will override the natural behavior of cows: they will ignore their bulging udders and their hungry, bleating calves, and will trot merrily along the road straight to Israelite Beth Shemesh (uphill). The thought behind this process is that if deity is providing the answer, he can alter normal behavior and override natural laws in order to communicate his answer, just as he had done in sending the plague.

6:9. Beth Shemesh. Beth Shemesh was located in the border region between Israel and Philistia. It occupied about seven acres on a ridge overlooking the Sorek Valley that ran along the north side of the city. The journey from Ekron to Beth Shemesh followed the Sorek Valley and was about nine miles. The archaeological site is Tell er-Rumeilah west of modern Ain Shems. There is an Iron Age occupation level at the site dated to the mid-eleventh century, the time of Samuel. In this level a residence has been found with a spacious courtyard paved with flagstone surrounded by several chambers.

6:13. wheat harvest. The wheat harvest occupies the months of May and June in this region.

6:15. rock as altar. Other passages where a rock serves as an altar include Judges 6:20-21; 13:19; and 1 Samuel 14:33-34. By elevating the sacrifice off the ground in this way, the blood could drain. More often Israelite makeshift altars consisted of a number of large stones piled up.

6:19. putting seventy to death. There is considerable controversy concerning the number who died at Beth Shemesh. The NIV translates

seventy, following a few Hebrew manuscripts. A more convincing array of manuscripts sets the number at 50,070. This is odd because the Old Testament generally rounds to even ten thousands. It is also unlikely because Beth Shemesh was a small country town that would have had a population of less than one thousand. Even the number seventy has been taken as a conventional indication of a large number (see comment on Judg 8:30).

6:19. punishment for looking into the ark. Despite popular modern speculation the text gives no indication of the mode of death for the offenders. Numbers 14:20 forbids even the priests to look *at* the ark. It would have been difficult for the people of Beth Shemesh to avoid that, but their curiosity led them to violate the sanctity of the ark by going well beyond an incidental glance. Restricted access to sacred space and holy objects was common in the ancient world (see comment on Lev 16:2), so treating the ark as a common object of curiosity would have been recognized as an act of desecration.

6:21. Kiriath Jearim. Listed as a city within Judah (Josh 15:60), the site is commonly identified with Tell el-Azhar, nine miles west-northwest of Jerusalem, but this is unsubstantiated by archaeological finds or extrabiblical references. Its association with Mahaneh Dan in Judges 18:12 puts it in that general area (see the comment on Judg 13:25). This location places it only six miles from Gibeon, with which it is also associated (see comment on Josh 9:17). It is about seven miles northeast of Beth Shemesh.

7:2-17

Defeat of the Philistines

7:3. foreign gods and Ashtoreths. Here the Ashtoreths are distinguished from the foreign gods. Ashtoreth is the name of the goddess known in Canaan as Ashtar or Astarte, the consort of Baal (see comment on Judg 2:13). The use of the plural here may suggest that all deities and their consorts should be disposed of.

7:5. Mizpah. Though several cities shared this name (it means something like "outpost" or "garrison"), this one in Benjaminite territory is the most well-known. It is often associated with the eight-acre site called Tell en-Nasbeh about eight miles north of Jerusalem. Mizpah at this time was an oval enclosure surrounded by a wall about three feet thick. It guarded the main north-south road between the hills of Judah and the hills of Ephraim.

7:6. pouring out water from a well. Though

wine libations are known from sacrificial texts, there are no other examples of ritualized water libations mentioned in the Old Testament. Rabbinic sources speak of water libation as one of the rituals practiced during the Feast of Tabernacles. In that context it is thought to accompany prayers for rain. In Mesopotamia water libations were among the offerings given to the dead, and they also poured out water from a well to ward off evil spirits when the well was dug. None of these possibilities makes sense in this context, where it is connected to repentance and purification.

7:6. fasting in religious practice. Fasting is little attested in the ancient Near East outside of the Bible. It generally occurs in the context of mourning. In the Old Testament the religious use of fasting is often in connection with making a request before God. The principle is that the importance of the request causes an individual to be so concerned about his or her spiritual condition that physical necessities fade into the background. In this sense the act of fasting is designed as a process leading to purification and humbling oneself before God (Ps 69:10). In connection with their repentance the Israelites fasted in order to remove any sin or other obstacle that may have led to their subjection to the Philistines. For similar efforts related to military action, see Judges 20:26 and 2 Chronicles 20:1-4.

7:6. Samuel's leadership. Samuel's leadership is described by the same term that serves as a title for the judges (see comment on Judg 2:16-19). This rounds out his credentials as prophet, priest and judge. The three roles are combined in this passage as he leads them in repentance in order to bring about their deliverance.

7:7. Philistine response. Why do the Philistines attack when the Israelites gather for a religious observance? In the ancient Near East rituals were generally performed prior to military initiatives. One of the ways that spies or informants could tell military action was afoot was when suspicious gatherings took place for rituals not connected with known festivals. Assyrian kings regularly received reports from their informants regarding a vassal king's involve-ment in rituals that could be suspected of being connected with battle preparations.

7:9. lamb for a burnt offering. Lambs were offered daily in the sacrificial system (see comment on Ex 29:38) and were also used for purification offerings (see Lev 12:6 and 14:10). Those offerings required one-year-old lambs. This lamb is a suckling, in Akkadian referred to as a spring lamb, and therefore offered the

most tender meat. In one Assyrian text from the time of Ashur-Nirari V (eighth century) a spring lamb is used in an oath-taking ceremony connected to the making of a treaty.

7:10. thundering from heaven. Thunder and lightning were considered to regularly accompany the presence of a deity in the ancient Near East, often in a battle setting. From the Sumerian Exaltation of Inanna, to the Hittite myths about the storm god, to the Akkadian and Ugaritic mythologies, the gods are viewed as thundering in judgment against their enemies. Baal is depicted as grasping a handful of thunderbolts. Thundering terminology is picked up in royal rhetoric as Hittite or Assyrian kings portray themselves as the instruments of the gods, thundering against those who have violated treaties or stood in the way of empire expansion. For further information concerning the divine warrior see comments on Exodus 15:3; Joshua 3:17; 6:21-24; 10:11.

7:11. Beth Car. This site is mentioned only here and remains unidentified.

7:12. memorial stone. In the ancient Near East it was common practice to use stones, often inscribed, to mark boundaries. Babylonian *kudurru* stones were boundary markers that were sometimes inscribed with the details of the royal grant assigning rights to the land. They were public and legal indicators of ownership and were believed to enjoy divine protection. Like this stone, the *kudurru* stones were sometimes given names (for example, "Establisher-of-Permanent-Boundaries"). The Egyptians also erected memorial stelae to indicate the borders of their territory, especially that which had come to them by conquest. Examples are known throughout the second millennium. Both Babylonian and Egyptian examples usually had lengthier inscriptions on the stone describing summary accounts of the victory or stipulations or curses regarding the continuing possession of the land.

7:12. Shen. Many versions and translations read "Jeshanah," and most commentators consider this more likely. Shen is otherwise unknown, while Jeshanah is usually associated with Burj el-Isaneh. It seems less likely, however, that the Philistines would flee straight north (though they did have garrisons in that direction). It is possible that Shen ("tooth") is just a reference to a natural formation.

7:12. Ebenezer. The Ebenezer mentioned in 4:1 (Izbet Sartah) was about twenty miles northwest of Mizpah. The location named Ebenezer in this chapter is likely at a different place. Samuel is giving the name here and using the meaning of the name ("tone of help") to show that this Ebenezer represents victory rather than the humiliating defeat that had become associated with the other Ebenezer.

7:14. Ekron to Gath. The line from Ekron (Sorek Valley) to Gath (Elah Valley) is about five miles north-south. The coastal plain of the Philistines lies to the west of the line and the Shephelah leading into the hill country of Judah to the east. This verse probably indicates that those towns in the Shephelah that the Philistines had taken over were recovered.

7:14. Amorites. The Amorites along with the Canaanites were the primary inhabitants of the land prior to the coming of the Israelites and the Philistines. For some information about their background see the comment on Numbers 13:29.

7:16. Samuel's territory. The Bethel-Gilgal-Mizpah circuit appears to be all in the territory of Benjamin. There are several towns named Gilgal, including one listed on the northern boundary of Judah. If this is the correct Gilgal, Samuel's circuit would have started by traveling from his home in Ramathaim about fifteen miles southeast to Bethel. Two miles further south would get him to Mizpah, and from there Gilgal was nearly ten more miles. The return trip home would have been about twenty-five or thirty miles. There are sites named Gilgal closer to Bethel and Mizpah that may be intended here. In the Mari documents there is a diviner named Asqudum who regularly makes a circuit of four towns providing his services to the citizens.

7:17. altar at Ramah. The text does not specify whether this is an altar for sacrifice or a memorial altar (see comment on Josh 22:9-34). If it is an altar for sacrifice, it may be replacing the one that was in Shiloh and had been destroyed by the Philistines.

8:1-22

The Request for a King

8:2. role of Samuel's sons. Samuel was "judging" on the circuit mentioned in 7:16. This was not the sort of judging he had been involved in earlier in the chapter (7:6) but would have involved giving decisions concerning disputes among the people (see comments on Ex 18:13-27 and Deut 16:18-20). Samuel's sons were serving this type of function, not the delivering type of judges found in the book of Judges. Their territory was very remote (see next comment), rather than central as Samuel's had been.

8:2. Beersheba. Beersheba is located at the southern extremity of the land in the northern

Negev at Tell es-Seba' (three miles east of the modern city). Archaeological finds from this period suggest that the site was in transition from being a temporary to a permanent settlement. Some of the first houses were just being built. The population would have been less than two hundred. Therefore this was a very minor appointment.

8:6. kingship in the ancient Near East. The kings of the ancient world enjoyed nearly limitless power and authority, and regularly claimed divine support for their rule. Kingship was believed to have been lowered from heaven and to have its roots in the original creation and organization of the world. The king functioned as vice-regent for the divine ruler, and it was his duty to preserve order and justice in society. He was entrusted with a divine stewardship over the people and the land. Kings were often considered to possess a divine office while they lived (understood differently in the various times and cultures) and to become gods when they died. Justice and law came from them. They often had priestly duties and were depicted as shepherds. The maintenance of the temples and provisions for them was an important obligation of the king. Throughout the ancient Near East kings were military leaders. They brought protection or deliverance for their people as well as acquiring other lands. These conquests brought access to additional natural resources and trade routes, as well as bringing plunder into the royal coffers and slave labor into the kingdom. Both of these would reduce the burden on the population of the country.

8:6. what the leaders want. The leaders of Israel have decided that they want a permanent head of government empowered with centralized authority over the tribes and commanding a standing army. They have concluded that their organization as a federation of tribes has put them at a military disadvantage. They believe that a king with a trained standing army at his command will level the playing field and enable them to successfully defend their land. They have been mistaken in assessing their problem as a political problem and consequently opting for a political solution. What Samuel seeks to clarify for them is that their problem is not political but spiritual. Their political solution will solve nothing unless it is accompanied by a spiritual solution.

8:7. divine king versus human king. In Israel's tribal structure there had been no provision made for a human centralized authority. Moses had provided prophetic authority and Joshua had been granted military authority, but no one had succeeded Joshua in such a position.

Moses had been understood to be the intermediary, giving God's instructions as God led the people. Likewise, as the book of Joshua repeatedly indicates, Joshua was subordinate to God's commander (Josh 5:13-15), and the victories were the Lord's victories. Each tribe had its leadership, but central authority belonged to the Lord and was his to give. The judges were those whom the Lord raised up and endowed with a recognized central authority (see comment on Judg 2:16-19). The fact that God was seen as raising up military leaders and that God was the one who brought the victories demonstrates that God was the one who was the king leading out the armies in battle. Victory in battle was assured if the Lord was pleased with Israel. By making their request, the leaders are implying that God has been less than successful in bringing victory and that somehow a king will do a better job.

8:11. prerogatives of kingship. Kingship requires a supporting administration. The administration must be housed and fed. Buildings need to be erected to house the administration, and land must be owned by the crown. A standing army must be raised, and it likewise must be housed and fed. The king must then have access to laborers and goods of every sort. Taxation and forced labor were the major means of providing for the monarchy and stood as royal prerogatives. This would bring about dramatic political and economic changes. This portrayal of kingship is similar to that known in the ancient Near East of this period, particularly observable in Ugaritic texts as the model of Canaanite kingship.

8:11. chariots and horses. Israel had not previously had cavalry or chariotry. This development within a standing army required the centralized authority of kingship. Training was required that only a permanent army could provide. Construction and care of the chariots and stabling and caring for the horses all required significant administrative oversight.

8:11. running before chariots. Those who run before chariots proclaim the presence of the king and protect the person of the king. In Hittite texts the gods are said to run before the king's chariot, leading to victory. The men who run before the king's chariot function as heralds (see 2 Sam 15:1; 1 Kings 1:5; 18:46).

8:12. infantry commanders. In the spontaneous calling out of an army in times of emergency (as previously practiced in Israel), trained commanders were not part of the picture. Part of a standing army, however, involves the permanent appointment of such

officers. Such military divisions are also known from Assyrian and Babylonian military terms, where, for instance, one of the lower officers is the commander of fifty.

8:12. working the king's fields. Once an administration is set up, certain lands become royal lands (2 Chron 26:10). Land can become forfeit to the throne as a result of criminal activity, or land can come to the throne through lack of heirs to inherit ancestral property. This land would be farmed to provide food for the administration as well as to supply stockpiles against emergency. Those who work the land may be forced laborers (in a form of taxation), slaves from foreign peoples or debt slaves who have no other way to recover from losses.

8:12. making the king's weapons. The king's weapons would have included bow and arrow, sword, dagger, shield and javelin. At this period the Israelites had either not yet acquired iron-working technology or had been effectively prohibited from producing iron weapons, so their weapons would have been bronze. It was common even into the Middle Ages to have a royal smith who would even travel with the army to service the weapons of the king. The Nuzi texts list carpenters and bronze-workers among the palace staff.

8:13. cooks, bakers, perfumers. Cooks and bakers staffed the royal scullery. The extended family of the king and his administration (often from the extended family) would have to be regularly fed in royal style. Additionally there may have been prisoners of the king and household servants who would need at least meager provisions. Perfumers performed a number of different duties at the court. The king's garments were regularly perfumed, and spices were burnt in order to maintain a pleasing aroma around the palace. Additionally some spices were recognized as having medicinal value, in which case the perfumer might be performing the task of pharmacist. Assyrian texts and Egyptian tomb paintings both portray elaborate procedures for preparing these spices and ointments.

8:14-15. land confiscation. Attractive properties were frequent targets of royal confiscation. The king's administrators and favorites were rewarded and kept loyal in this way (see comment on 22:7). This practice is well-known from Hittite and Ugaritic materials as well as from Kassite period Babylon, where land grants to courtiers were very common.

8:16. commandeering of donkeys and slaves. It was not unusual for a king to commandeer a slave who caught his attention or stock animals that were noteworthy. The commoner would have little choice but to offer as a gift that which had attracted the king.

8:17. tithe of grain and flocks as taxes. In Ugaritic literature the tithe is a fixed payment to the king made by each town and village. In earlier biblical passages the tithe was treated as something due the priesthood and the sanctuary. Here the tithe describes royal taxation.

9:1-27
Saul and Samuel Meet

9:1. status of Kish. Traditionally translations have identified Kish as a "valiant warrior," but the NIV "man of standing" is probably a better choice. Such prominence could be achieved through military prowess (see Jephthah, Judg 11:1), but many of the people described by this phrase have no known military reputation. It is likely that the phrase has broader application (see comment on Judg 6:12).

9:1. Benjamin. The tribe of Benjamin was descended from the youngest son of Jacob. Its more recent history was disreputable in that it had been nearly exterminated in a civil war during the Judges period (Judges 20—21). Its tribal allotment was small but strategically placed between the powerful tribes of Judah and Ephraim. Jerusalem, not yet in Israelite control but destined for greatness, was in Benjaminite territory.

9:2. Saul's appearance and stature. People in the ancient Near East placed high value on the stature and appearance of the king. The earliest kings were temporarily empowered warlords—mighty champions and fierce fighters. Even after kingship evolved into a permanent institution, the king who carried the aura of a great champion was the pride of his people. A few examples include Sargon of Akkad, described as mighty in battle; Tukulti-Ninurta of Assyria, who had no rival on the battlefield; Nebuchadnezzar, a valiant man strong in warfare; and Gilgamesh, a heroic warrior of great stature as well as beautiful in manhood.

9:2. Saul outside the Bible. As yet no mention has been found of Saul in any ancient Near Eastern inscriptions. He had little contact with other peoples except the Philistines, and there have been no significant finds of Philistine historical archives.

9:4-5. scope and distance of Saul's search. Saul lived in Gibeah, about six miles north of Jerusalem. The hill country of Ephraim was about fifteen miles northwest of his home. Though Shalisha and Shaalim are obscure, most interpreters identify them with Baal-Shalisha and Shaalbim respectively,

which stand at the northwest and southwest extremities of the Ephraimite hill country. Just the circumference of this area would entail a sixty-mile trek, a large area to cover in this three-day search (v. 20). The region of Zuph is generally inferred (from 1 Sam 1:1) to be the region of Samuel's hometown in the hill country of Ephraim.

9:6. Samuel's reputation. It is intriguing that Saul, who lives only a stone's throw away from Samuel's hometown and within the circuit of Samuel's territory, appears ignorant of this nationally renowned figure. Rather than suggesting that Samuel's renown was less than reputed, it likely indicates the spiritual and political naivete of Saul.

9:6-9. role of the local "man of God." Though Samuel had a national reputation, to the local people among whom he had lived all his life he was like a village holy man. These holy men were supported by the gifts of the villages they served and would have been consulted on any number of minor personal matters. Areas of expertise would include issues of health and illness, rituals and prayers, legal and political affairs and a variety of other personal and community matters.

9:8. gift of silver. A quarter of a shekel of silver would have been the equivalent of a week or so of wages for the ordinary working man. This would be appropriate considering the value of the donkeys that had been lost.

9:9. terminology for prophets. Three terms are used in this passage: man of God, seer and prophet. The first is a general term that could apply to either of the others. The seer and the prophet were engaged in basically the same activity, but the structuring of the role in society was different (much like the difference between the offices of judge and king). Nevertheless, it is a terminological change that is noted here, not a sociological one.

9:11. coming out to draw water. Towns were usually situated on high ground in the vicinity of a water source (spring or well). In later periods tunnels were built to give secure access to the water sources, but at this period one would have to go outside the city walls to get the daily supply of water. Typically this would be done in the early evening rather than in the heat of the day.

9:12. high place. The high place (Hebrew: *bamah*) is a place of worship where an altar is functioning. It is typically not an open-air shrine but an indoor facility, housing sacred furniture and precincts large enough to accommodate a priesthood (we cannot assume that all of them were on high ground). The Mesha Inscription shows that such shrines were also part of Moabite worship. Possible examples have been found at sites such as Megiddo and Nahariya.

9:12-13. sacrifice at the high place. Though the name of this town is not given, most assume that it is Samuel's hometown of Ramah (Ramathaim, see 1:1). After the fall of Shiloh he built an altar in Ramah (7:17), and with the ark in exile this was probably functioning as a central sanctuary. Sacrifices were typically occasions for meals, and that proves to be the case here as well. This may be a new moon sacrifice, which was a festive occasion (see comment on 20:5). Alternatively it could be an enthronement ceremony, specially called since Samuel had been forewarned of Saul's arrival.

9:13. blessing the sacrifice. No other passage in the Old Testament speaks of blessing the sacrifice. Blessing is usually the offering of kind words that it is hoped the deity will bring about. Since sacrifices were often associated with petitions, Samuel's blessing may have reflected the hope that the petition be granted.

9:21. Saul's objection. In the ancient Near East kings usually tried to attach some significance to their ancestry when none was evident, lest this weakness be used as a reason for revolt by some ambitious competitor. The lack of ancestry could label one as an imposter or pretender. The objection of genealogical unworthiness is not uncommon in the Bible, and, in fact, is sometimes worn as a badge (Amos 7:14). For information concerning the tribe of Benjamin, see the comment on 9:1. Nothing further is known of the status of Saul's clan.

9:22. hall where they ate. The portions of meat that were to be eaten by the priests and the worshipers were at times required to be eaten on the premises (for example, Lev 7:6). Since feasting was an important part of sacrifice and worship, sanctuaries provided rooms for that activity. The word used in this verse to describe this room is used elsewhere for the various rooms attached to the sanctuary in the temple complex. Archaeologists often find auxiliary rooms attached to the main sanctuary, but it is frequently not possible to determine what each room was used for.

9:23. choice cut of meat. The thigh (NIV "leg," v. 24) was considered one of the prime pieces of meat and was usually reserved for the officiating priest (Lev 7:32-34). Here Samuel yields it to his guest of honor.

9:25-26. sleeping quarters on roof. Though the presence of stairways and supporting pillars (among other evidences) show that many houses had second (or even third) stories, archaeologists are usually not able to recover

more than the floor plan of houses in the remaining rubble of occupation levels. Second stories (rooms on the roof) were desirable for family activities and sleeping because they offered better ventilation.

10:1-27
The Anointing and Selection of Saul as King

10:1. anointing with olive oil. Anointing a king was common practice in some parts of the ancient Near East. Much of the evidence comes from Hittite sources describing enthronement ceremonies. There is no evidence of kings being anointed in Mesopotamia. In Egypt the pharaoh was not anointed, but he anointed his officials and his vassals. His anointing of them established their subordinate relationship to him and indicated his protection of them. This model would fit the idea of Saul being anointed as a vassal to God. But in 2 Samuel 2:4 it is the people who anoint David. This anointing suggests some sort of contractual agreement between David and the people he will govern. In Nuzi, individuals entering a business agreement anointed one another with oil, and in Egypt oil anointment was used in wedding ceremonies. For information on royal coronations see comment on 11:15.

10:2. Rachel's tomb at Zelzah. Locating this site is extremely complicated. Detailed study including attempts to reconcile many variants and difficulties offer two main possibilities. One is that the tomb should be located in the vicinity of Kiriath Jearim (see comment on 6:21). Kiriath Jearim is about fifteen miles south-southwest of Samuel's home. The second follows the supposed course of Saul's journey in this passage as he appears to be traveling east from Ramah to Geba. This would place Rachel's tomb along that road.

10:3. great tree of Tabor. Judges 4:5 refers to the "Palm of Deborah" where she held court, and Abraham pauses at the great tree of Moreh (see comment on Gen 12:6). Trees served as landmarks, meeting places and even sacred sites. Where the sun is hot and shade is desirable, trees can take on special significance.

10:3. worship at Bethel. Throughout much of Israel's history, Bethel was considered an important sacred site. The ark was housed there for at least part of the Judges period, and it was a place of altar and sacrifice (see comments on Judg 1:22-23; 20:26-28; 21:4).

10:3. products for sacrifice. Goats, bread and wine were the basic makings of a sacrificial meal. By receiving consecrated bread, Saul is again being treated as a priest (see comment on 9:23) and being recognized as an honored personage.

10:5. Gibeah of God. The designation "of God" suggests there was some sort of shrine or sanctuary on this hill (Gibeah = hill), but it was currently also occupied by a Philistine garrison. Since 13:3 speaks of a Philistine garrison at Geba, many have identified the two as the same location, the modern village of Jaba about six miles north of Jerusalem. No excavations have been conducted there, but surface surveys have found Iron Age remains on the site. It overlooks the strategic pass across the deep canyon of the Wadi Swenit from Micmash that leads from the north into the region of Jerusalem. For discussion of Gibeah see comment on 10:26.

10:5. high place. There is a difference between outdoor cultic places and the "high place" (*bamah*) mentioned in many places as religious centers in the local towns and cities (1 Kings 11:7; Jer 7:31; Ezek 16:16; 2 Chron 21:11; Mesha's Moabite Stele). The high place could be outdoors but often was an indoor facility, built to house sacred furniture, an altar and precincts large enough to accommodate a priesthood.

10:5. musical instruments. These are all typical musical instruments of the time and are attested in ancient Near Eastern texts, reliefs and paintings as early as the third millennium. There is still some disagreement among authorities as to which of the Hebrew words in this passage ought to be translated "harp" and which as "lyre." The one the NIV translates "lyre" is a ten-stringed instrument, while the one translated "harp" is thought to have had fewer strings. Both are hand-held with frames made of wood. The tambourine has been identified in archaeological reliefs as the tambour, a small drum (leather stretched over a hoop) that would not have the tinny rattle sound of modern tambourines. The instrument translated as flute is likely a double pipe made of either bronze or reed.

10:6. connection between music and prophecy. One could be trained for the profession of prophet (or seer), and there was a prophetic guild in this early period of Israel's history usually identified as the "sons of the prophets." Typically these prophets would use various procedures in order to prepare themselves for receiving prophetic oracles. Music played an important role in inducing a trancelike state (ecstasy) that was seen as making one receptive to a divine message. In the Mari texts there is an entire class of temple personnel who were ecstatics and who often provided prophetic messages.

10:6. role of the Spirit of the Lord. When the Spirit of the Lord was attached to any activity in the Judges period, it was usually to the calling up of an army. In a tribal society with no centralized government it was difficult to get other tribes to stand with one or two that might be facing problems. The measure of a leader in such situations was his ability to compel others to follow though he had no office of command over them. In Israel this was a mark of the power of Yahweh, for it was he alone who had the authority to call out the armies of the tribes. Yahweh was the only central authority. It was therefore a clear indication of the Lord's authority at work in someone when they exercised authority that was only Yahweh's by calling out the armies (see Judg 11:29; 1 Sam 11:6-8). This was one of the distinguishing features of the judges of Israel. Saul's central authority is going to be permanent and more extensive than that possessed by the judges, but it still receives its endorsement by the empowerment of the Spirit of the Lord. In 11:6 the empowerment of the Spirit is going to result in Saul's raising an army, as the judges had done. Here it is associated with prophetic activity, specifically to his receptivity to divine guidance.

10:8. Gilgal. As noted in the comment on 7:16, there are several sites with the name of Gilgal. It is impossible to be certain which one is intended here.

10:8. purpose of sacrifices. Burnt offerings and fellowship offerings are two of the most general types of sacrifices. The former often accompanied petition, while the latter served as an opportunity for festive celebration and a communal meal before the Lord. It is likely, then, that these sacrifices would have been directed to either the initiation of kingship or perhaps toward military activity against the Philistines. Between the sacrifice offered in Samuel's town, the sacrifice of those going to Bethel, and these in Gilgal, it becomes evident that sacrifice in this period was not restricted to a central location.

10:10. Saul as a prophet. Kings in the ancient Near East were often considered to have prophetic gifts. This was especially true in Egypt, where the pharaoh was the representative of the gods and spoke for them. Civil leadership in Israel up to this time has also often combined authority for ruling with prophetic activity (Moses, Deborah, Samuel). Samuel accumulated priestly, prophetic and governing roles, but the governing role was the result of the other two. With Saul the issues concern to what extent someone chosen as king will also accumulate priestly or prophetic roles. Kingship in the ancient Near East was at times configured with those roles included. It is then very logical to ask, "Is Saul also among the prophets?"

10:17. Mizpah. Though several cities shared this name (it means something like "outpost" or "garrison"), this one in Benjaminite territory is the most well-known. It is often associated with the eight-acre site called Tell en-Nasbeh about eight miles north of Jerusalem. Mizpah at this time was an oval enclosure surrounded by a wall about three feet thick. It guarded the main north-south road between the hills of Judah and the hills of Ephraim.

10:20-21. process of choosing a king. Evidence from Mesopotamia suggests that divination was used to confirm a designated king but not to propose one. Divination was not considered acceptable in Israel. The process used here is more like an oracular process and is very similar to that used in Joshua 7 (see comment on Josh 7:14-18).

10:25. regulations of the kingship. This appears to be a document that frames a constitution or charter of some sort. One possibility is that it details the people's subordination to the king and the king's subordination to the Lord. In Egypt the coronation ceremony involved a proclamation by the god Thoth that gave the official approval of the gods for the king's accession. There is nothing in this chapter that actually depicts Saul as being crowned; he is merely acclaimed as the one that has been selected (see comment on 11:15).

10:26. Gibeah. Saul's hometown of Gibeah was long been identified with Tell el-Ful about three miles north of Jerusalem, though many have not been convinced despite a small fortress uncovered at the site that archaeologists dubbed "Saul's fortress." The archaeological, textual and topographical evidence are now all thought to favor the theory that Gibeah and Geba are one and the same and are to be identified with Jaba on the southern rim of the Wadi Swenit about six miles north of Jerusalem.

11:1-11

Saul Defeats the Ammonites

11:1. Jabesh Gilead. Jabesh Gilead was a city in the Transjordan, probably along the Wadi el-Yabis, a tributary of the Jordan River that cut through the north Gileadite hill country. A number of sites in the area have been proposed as the ruins of Jabesh Gilead, none of

which have proved convincing. The most likely candidate is Tell Maqlub, lying on the northern edge of a bend on the Yabis River. There is detailed evidence for Iron I Age (c. 1200-1000 B.C.) material remains in this area. The city is described as having a treaty relationship with Israel from the period of the judges (chap. 21; cf. 2 Sam 2:4-7). Jabesh Gilead was not incorporated into Israel until after the death of Saul. Cf. 1 Samuel 11:9-10.

11:1-2. Nahash. Ammon and Israel had continually fought over the area east of the Jordan River (see Judg 11:33). Based upon fragments from the Dead Sea Scrolls, a restoration of 1 Samuel 10:27b gives evidence that Nahash had also threatened the Israelite tribes of Gad and Reuben, a fact confirmed by the Jewish historian Josephus (A.D. 37-100). Nothing is known of Nahash from extrabiblical literature, no Ammonite historical documents from this period having survived.

11:1-2. Ammonites. Apart from the Bible, the Ammonites are only known from written sources from the Late Assyrian annals (c. 733-665 B.C.) and from local fragmentary epigraphic sources (to c. 590 B.C.). The Bible describes them as a Transjordanian people related to the Israelites through Abraham's nephew, Lot. From the period of the exodus and following, the Ammonites were perennial enemies of Israel until their conquest by Saul's successor, David (2 Sam 10—12).

11:2. gouging out the right eye. The practice of blinding one's enemies is found with the Philistines (against Samson; Judg 16:21) and Nebuchadnezzar of Babylon (against Zedekiah of Judah; 2 Kings 25:7). It was also a common Assyrian practice performed upon vassal kings who had broken treaties. The Jewish historian Josephus (A.D. 37-100) states that the right eye was gouged out in this case, which made the soldier unable to fight, since the shield was held over the left eye. However, in the context of 1 Samuel 11 the purpose of the gouging out of the eyes appears to have been reproach. Incapacitating mutilation of subjected individuals is also seen in the treatment of kings whose thumbs and big toes were cut off (see comment on Judg 1:6).

11:4. Gibeah. See comment on 10:26.

11:6. role of the Spirit of God. The Spirit of God rested upon Saul as it previously did upon the judges Othniel, Gideon, Jephthah and especially Samson (Judg 14:6, 19; 15:14). When the Spirit of the Lord was attached to any activity in Judges, it was usually to the calling up of an army. In a tribal society with no centralized government it was difficult to get other tribes to support one of their number that might be facing problems. The measure of a leader in such situations was his ability to compel others to follow though he had no office of command over them. In Israel this was a mark of the power of Yahweh, for it was he alone who had the authority to call out the armies of the tribes. Yahweh was the only central authority. It was therefore a clear indication of the Lord's authority at work in someone when they exercised authority that was only Yahweh's by calling out the armies. This had been one of the distinguishing features of the judges of Israel. In 1 Samuel 10, the Spirit had caused Saul to behave like one of the prophets, while here in 1 Samuel 11, Saul exercised the authority of calling out the armies of Israel. His Spirit possession was reflected immediately in his righteous indignation, similar to the situation where Samson in his fury killed thirty at Ashkelon (Judges 14:19), and it was confirmed by the response of the troops.

11:7. oxen pieces as messages. A biblical parallel to dismemberment as a message comes from Judges 19:29-30, where the unnamed Levite cut his concubine into twelve pieces, evidently an invitation to participate in the intertribal war against the tribe of Benjamin. The idea was that whoever did not come for the battle would be punished in like manner. A letter from the city of Mari has a certain Bahdilim asking the king of Mari if he can cut off the head of a prisoner and send it around as a warning to troops who are not being cooperative in assembling for battle.

11:8. Bezek. Bezek has been located at Khirbit Ibzik, a site west of the Jordan River, twelve miles northeast of Shechem and about fourteen miles west of Jabesh Gilead. It is placed on the southwestern slope of the Ras es-Salmeh, a steep mountain range overlooking the Manasseh hill country. It was thus a convenient place from which to cross the Jordan River to arrive at Jabesh Gilead.

11:8. size of army. The number of soldiers mentioned varies greatly in ancient versions of the Old Testament. The later texts, however, give expanded numbers for both Israel and Judah. Many archaeologists would estimate the entire population of Canaan at this time as being barely this many. The Hebrew term for thousand has often been viewed as a term denoting a unit of soldiers and not to be taken as referring to an actual number (see comments on Josh 8:3; Judg 20:2).

11:9. distance from Bezek to Jabesh Gilead. If both Bezek and Jabesh Gilead have been identified correctly by modern archaeologists, then the two cities were about thirteen or fourteen

miles apart. This could easily be covered in a march that began in the evening and concluded in the Ammonite camp in the early hours of the morning.

11:12-15
Saul Affirmed as King

11:14-15. reaffirmation of kingship at Gilgal. Gilgal, a cultic center on Samuel's circuit, remains unlocated, but most think it was near Jericho (see comment on 1 Sam 7:16). As the sacred site closest to the battle scene, it is chosen for the coronation. Even though Saul has been designated by two different processes as the one who will be king, it is only now, after he has proven himself in military affairs (remember, the people wanted a king who would lead their armies into battle), that he will actually be crowned. The text says nothing of reaffirmation but states that they made him king. In Mesopotamia there were ceremonies to celebrate enthronement each year connected to New Year's celebrations. Coronation in the ancient Near East would generally involve investing the king with the royal insignia and regalia and anointing him. There was commonly an aspect of the ceremony in which the king's legitimacy was affirmed by the chief deity. The anointing and the affirmation of legitimacy had already taken place in this case.

11:15. fellowship offerings. One portion of the fellowship offering was offered to God, and another portion was consumed by the worshipers. Typical use of this offering was for ratification of treaties or covenant agreements. For more information see comments on 10:8; Exodus 24:5; and Leviticus 3:1-5.

12:1-25
Samuel's Speech

12:15. Samuel clearing himself of claims. Politics has not changed much in three millennia. It is common for a ruler to blame the country's problems on a previous administration. It was also not uncommon in the ancient world for charges to be trumped up against anyone who might be seen as a threat to the power of the ruler currently in power. It was therefore understandable that Samuel would want to take steps to procure an affirmation of his innocence in matters of government. It was the ruling party's duty to maintain justice, and Samuel wanted verification that he had not been accused of any injustice. The legal process described here consisted of three parts: (1) the witnesses are listed (Yahweh, his anointed [i.e., the king] and the people, v. 3), (2) Samuel appealed to these witnesses, and (3) the witnesses responded. This pattern is also attested in Ruth (4:4, 11) and Joshua (24:22).

12:6-12. time span of recounted history. Exodus 12:40 says that the Israelites were in Egypt for 430 years. First Kings 6:1 says that it was 480 years from the exodus to the dedication of the temple. The coronation of Saul may be as much as eighty years prior to the dedication of the temple, meaning that Samuel is covering somewhere between 800 and 850 years of history in five short verses. That would be like a contemporary speaker addressing the failures of Christianity from the Crusades to the present in one hundred words or less.

12:12. divine kingship. Ever since the book of Exodus the text has been developing the idea of Yahweh fighting for the Israelites, resulting in the Lord being praised as warrior and king. The book of Joshua indicates repeatedly that the Israelites' victories are the Lord's victories. Yahweh was established as their king and champion and led them forth victoriously in battle. References to Yahweh as king of Israel abound in Scripture (e.g., Ex 15:18; Num 23:21; Judg 8:7; and 1 Sam 8:7; 10:19). The concept of deity as king was not unique to Israel, however. Both Marduk (Babylonian) and Baal (Canaanite) demonstrate their kingship by subduing the sea, which is personified in their divine foe (Tiamat and Yam respectively). The issues of bringing secure order out of conflict, being proclaimed king and establishing a dwelling are intertwining themes in the ancient Near Eastern literatures concerning cosmic battle. More specifically, the Assyrians, for example, claimed that the god Assur was the monarch and that the reigning king was in essence his earthly representative. The difference in Israel, until now, was that Yahweh did not have an earthly counterpart, as did the other nations. The fact that God was seen as raising up military leaders and that God was the one who brought the victories demonstrates that God was the one who was the king leading out the armies in battle (see comment on 8:7). Now Saul's kingship was to be an earthly reflection of Yahweh's rule in heaven.

12:17-18. rain during the wheat harvest. Rain during May and June in Palestine, the months of the wheat harvest, was almost unknown and thus was interpreted as a supernatural occurrence. Furthermore, it could endanger the crop (see Prov 26:1). Thus God was standing as divine witness against them.

12:19. Samuel's revised role. Like Moses and Deborah before him, Samuel, until this point, had exercised political leadership by virtue of his prophetic office. With the initiation of kingship, the role of the prophet would now become an advisory one. Rather than leading the people as the recipient of divine messages, the prophet would offer guidance to the king, who would retain the freedom to accept or reject it. This passage also emphasizes the intercessory role of the prophet (for more information see comments on Deut 18:14-22).

12:25. king and people identified. In the ancient Near East the king was often considered the personification of the state. As a result the king could be held accountable for the peoples' behavior, and the people could be punished or blessed based on the conduct of the king.

13:1-22
Saul Offers the Sacrifice

13:1. chronological note. The age of Saul at his accession is not precisely known since this verse has not survived intact in most ancient manuscripts. The Greek version of the Old Testament (called the Septuagint) added the number thirty here, but that is probably a secondary calculation, possibly based on David's age at his accession (2 Sam 5:4). Saul had an adult son, Jonathan, and at least one grandson before his death (2 Sam 4:4). Saul's length of reign is listed as two years, though most interpreters believe that part of the number has dropped out of the text (i.e., x-two years). However, the Jewish historian Josephus (A.D. 37-100) and Luke (Acts 13:21) both know a tradition that Saul reigned for forty years. Because of the unique spelling of the number in the earliest manuscripts, it is now believed by many that the original number for the length of his reign has been lost.

13:2. size and nature of standing army. Saul's selection of three thousand men probably represented a choice of men to serve as retainers or an imperial guard, rather than the total of the volunteers for the war, which would have been more. Standing armies in the ancient Near East were made up of professionally trained soldiers and mercenaries. They served garrisons and border posts as well as providing for a palace guard. The number of three thousand might simply represent three companies (one stationed with Jonathan and two with Saul). Geba is not a large site, and it is unlikely that it would have housed more than a few hundred men under normal circumstances, but the Israelites would soon have to face the combined military forces of the Philistines (see comment on verse 5).

13:2. Micmash. Rising about two thousand feet above sea level, the site of Micmash (modern Mukhmas) is about four and a half miles southwest of Bethel. Sparse Iron Age finds at the site have led some experts to prefer identification with Khirbet el-Hara el-Fawqa just over half a mile to the north, where more evidence of occupation at this time was found. The mountainous terrain in the area is an obstacle to chariot warfare.

13:3. Philistine garrison at Geba. Geba has been identified as the modern village of Jaba about six miles north of Jerusalem. No excavations have been conducted there, but surface surveys have found Iron Age remains on the site. It overlooks the strategic pass across the deep canyon of the Wadi Swenit from Micmash that leads from the north into the region of Jerusalem.

13:4. distance from Gilgal to Micmash. Again there are numerous sites named Gilgal, and their precise locations are unknown (see comment on 7:16). The Gilgal in 10:8 appears to be near Geba. If Saul's encampment is the Gilgal from Joshua's time, it was much further east, near the Jordan River, about twenty miles from Micmash. In this case he would have been far removed from the theater of operations.

13:5. Philistine army. The Philistines had overwhelming military superiority in this situation, with thirty thousand (often amended to three thousand) chariots and six thousand horsemen (charioteers). If the amended number is correct, there were two soldiers per chariot, known from contemporary Egypt, Anatolia and Assyria. For comparison, Shalmaneser III of Assyria (ninth century B.C.) claims to have crossed the Euphrates River with an army of 120,000. Provincial Assyrian governors were required to raise troops for the Assyrian army, often amounting to as much as 1,500 cavalry and 20,000 troops. Since there were over twenty provinces, the entire amount of Assyrian troops was very large.

13:6. hiding places. Pits and cisterns were dug for the collection of water and would have served as convenient hiding places if they were dry. These would typically have been in the area of towns. There were forested areas on either side of the Wadi Swenit in ancient times so thickets would have been available. Wadi Swenit and Wadi Kelt also feature many caves in the walls of the cliffs. Caves in Palestine often offered protection for people in danger. Sometimes caves were used for family tombs. These would have been well-known by the inhabitants of the area and protected from easy access. There is extrabiblical in-

scriptional evidence for cave-dwelling refugees in a cave near the Judean fortress city of Lachish. On the walls is written, "Spare me, O merciful God, spare me, O Yahweh," and, "Save, O Yahweh."

13:7. Gad and Gilead. Both the terms Gad and Gilead were employed as general designations for Israelite lands east of the Jordan River. Gilead was inhabited by the tribes of Reuben and Gad. The Israelites fled to these areas since they were somewhat removed from the base of Philistine operations.

13:8. Saul's conundrum. Offering a sacrifice to enlist a deity's favor before an impending battle was common in the ancient Near East. This favor would hopefully ensure the god's willingness to participate in the conflict. The *Iliad* provides many examples of this in contemporary Greek literature, and Hittite and Assyrian accounts (e.g., Esarhaddon of Assyria, seventh century B.C.) amply attest the use of sacrifices and omens to determine the will of the gods before going to battle as an essential part of military strategy. In Saul's case the need for the ritual was interfering with the strategic element of timing. His choice attempted to acquire the ritual benefit (by offering the sacrifice himself) and still try to take advantage of striking before the strategic military moment passed.

13:8-13. Saul's offense. In general it was not unusual for a king to serve some priestly functions (see comment on 2 Sam 8:18). In consideration of the dominant role Samuel has had, however, it is to be expected that the charter of Saul's kingship (10:25) drew distinct lines of delineation between their respective roles. It should be noted that Saul is not accused in verse 13 of violating priestly protocol or committing desecration, but of breaking the command of God.

13:9-10. function of the sacrifices. Burnt offerings and fellowship offerings are two of the most general types of sacrifices. The former often accompanied petition, while the latter served as an opportunity for festive celebration and a communal meal before the Lord. Additionally the peace offerings are sometimes thought to represent an acknowledgment of the deity's kingship—an important element prior to battle. For general information on the sacrifices, see the comments on Leviticus 1:3-4; 3:1-5.

13:14. man after his own heart. This statement means that God was now going to select someone of his own choosing (according to his own will or purpose rather than according to the will and purpose of the Israelites). This wording does not concern the piety of David but demonstrates God's exercise of will in rejecting Saul (a man fulfilling Israel's desire, 9:20) and replacing him with someone who was measured by a different criterion. Akkadian uses the same terminology when it speaks of the deity Enlil installing a king of his own choice. Even Nebuchadnezzar puts a king of his own choice in Jerusalem.

13:15. Gilgal to Gibeah. The distance for the army to travel from Joshua's Gilgal to Gibeah was about fifteen miles or a day's journey (for difficulties in identification see comment on 13:4).

13:16. Geba and Micmash. These two sites face one another across the deep canyon of the Wadi Swenit, along the strategic pass that crosses the wadi from the north into the region of Jerusalem. Micmash is a little over a mile northeast of Geba.

13:17-18. routes of raiding parties. The Philistine raiding parties turned in three different directions. The Ophrah road was due north and led to the town of Ophrah five miles north of Micmash. The Beth Horon road led west to the town of the same name, about twelve miles from Micmash. It went through Gibeon and would have been one of the major supply lines from the Philistine plains into the Jerusalem hills. Last, the border road overlooking the Valley of Hyenas (Zeboim) was southeast of Micmash, probably where the Wadi Swenit met the Wadi Kelt about halfway between Micmash and Jericho. This is the major pass into the Jordan Valley.

13:19-20. iron monopoly. For the ancients there were many technical difficulties in smelting iron, including maintaining a consistently high temperature, adequate draft, combining a proper amount of carbon and iron (called "carburization," which transforms the wrought iron into steel), and heavy tools to remove slag from the iron itself. Weapons made of uncarburized iron are inferior to bronze weapons. Consistent carburization is not evident in Palestine until the tenth century. It is not certain where iron smelting began, but it was widespread throughout the Near East (especially Anatolia and northern Iraq) by the end of the second millennium B.C. The widespread use of iron in place of bronze is now thought to be the result not only of the availability of the technology for smelting iron but also of the increasing difficulty of procuring the tin needed to make bronze. What must be noted, however, is that the text does not indicate an inferiority in iron technology but the absence of blacksmiths. Bronze weapons would have still been very useful to the Israelites. It is likely that these verses indicate that

blacksmithing had been outlawed so as to prevent the manufacture of metal weapons of any sort.

13:21. charges for smithing. The smithing charges here can be seen to be exorbitant when measured against the fact that the average monthly income was approximately one shekel. The implements that were sharpened (plows, mattocks, pickaxes, goads) were for agricultural enterprises. They may have been made of iron or bronze, but the Israelites were prohibited from operating the smithies needed for sharpening them. Iron plows have been uncovered throughout Palestine for this period. Iron mattocks (apparently a type of hoe) have been found at Tell Jemmeh in southwest Palestine. Goads were pointed implements used to encourage the oxen to continue plowing.

13:22. weapon shortage. This verse confirms that neither iron nor bronze manufacture was permitted to the Israelites. We must assume that the Philistine rule in the area had resulted in the confiscation of weapons and that the law against blacksmithing of any sort had made only the most primitive weaponry available to them.

13:23—14:48
Victory at Micmash Pass

13:23. Micmash pass. The Micmash pass is the strategic pass that leads from the north into the region of Jerusalem across the deep canyon of the Wadi Swenit. For more information on Micmash see comment on verse 2. A contingent had advanced from the Philistine camp to the slope of the ravine (or pass) which separated Micmash from Gibeah/Geba and the Israelite camp. The site was surrounded by the hills which formed the north side of the wadi. Micmash was inaccessible except for the pass which linked it to Gibeah/Geba.

14:1, 6, 17. armor-bearer. Jonathan's armor-bearer was more than a porter of military equipment. He fought together with him and probably served the function of a squire or apprentice. The closest parallel from ancient Near Eastern literature is the member of the chariot crew that holds the shield.

14:2. "pomegranate tree" at Migron. Though some commentators have identified Migron as a threshing floor, others have suggested that it is the ancient name for the Wadi es-Swenit. There is a rock of Rimmon (Hebrew for pomegranate) located one mile east of Gibeah/Geba (see comment on Judg 20:45) with a large cave that may have been serving as Saul's headquarters. On the other hand, if "threshing floor" is correct, there is an ancient threshing floor between Geba and Wadi Swenit, and Ugaritic texts attest to the threshing floor as a place where a king (Danil) met with the people. The open area of a threshing floor, however, would seem less likely in this context.

14:3. linen ephod. An ephod was part of the priestly wardrobe (see comment on Ex 28:6-14) and in both Egypt and Mesopotamia was reserved for clothing images of deity and for high-ranking priests. The ephod is elsewhere closely associated with oracles (it contains the Urim and Thummim, see comment on Ex 28:30, and was used for oracular consultation in Judg 8:27).

14:4-5. terrain: Bozez and Seneh. Khirbet el-Miqtara is a small settlement not far from the pass on the south side of the Wadi Swenit where the cliffs begin to get steeper. This area features some large outcroppings where someone could scale the cliffs without being seen.

14:6. divine warrior ideology. In the divine warrior motif the deity is fighting the battles and defeating the deities of the enemy. In Assyria Nergal is the king of battle, and Ishtar is viewed as a war goddess. The Canaanite Baal and the Babylonian Marduk are divine warriors. In this worldview human warfare is viewed simply as a representation of warfare among the gods. The stronger god would be victorious regardless of the strengths or weaknesses of the human combatants. Therefore, if Yahweh fights on their behalf, Jonathan is convinced that they will be victorious.

14:10. explanation of oracular mechanism. Oracular mechanisms of this period generally operated on a binary mechanism whereby designated occurrences could offer either a yes or a no answer from deity. The designated occurrences were typically options between an ordinary versus an extraordinary occurrence (see comments on Judg 6:36-40 and 1 Sam 6:7-9). In this case, however, either of the Philistine challenges could be seen as typical and appropriate. It would seem, instead, that Jonathan is looking for Yahweh's direction through an (inadvertent) invitation from the Philistines to come into the camp.

14:14. area of battle. The Hebrew text is very difficult, and translations vary greatly (NIV: "in an area of about half an acre"). The reference to half a furrow in the Hebrew text suggests that Jonathan cut a swath half a furrow wide (estimated at ten to fifteen yards) through a field of about one acre.

14:15. earthquake. In the ancient Near East the thundering in the sky and the trembling of the earth are commonly paired together as an indication of the divine involvement in battle (see comment on 2:9). Additionally, the dread of a deity as a divine warrior was often believed to precede a powerful, successful army into battle. Egyptian texts attribute this terror to Amun-Re in the inscriptions of Thutmose III, and Hittite, Assyrian and Babylonian texts all have their divine warriors who strike terror into the hearts of the enemy. It is a common motif that one of the ways a deity achieves victory is by throwing the enemy into confusion. An example in Egyptian literature occurs in the myth of Horus at Edfu: Horus confuses the enemy so that they begin to fight one another until none remain.

14:19-20. oracular use of the ephod. The Urim and Thummim were kept in a pouch in the priest's ephod (see above, verse 3). Information from the Urim and Thummim presumably would be gained by posing a yes-no question and then shaking out one of the stones. It is thought that the same stone would have to be shaken out three times in succession to confirm the answer. When Saul instructs Ahijah to withdraw his hand, he has made the decision to discontinue the oracular process and proceed without divine guidance.

14:23. aspects of divine intervention. Evidence for crediting the Lord with the victory would be seen in four elements that typically indicated divine intervention: direction through an oracle (v. 10); success by the outnumbered army (v. 14), earthquake (v. 15), and confusion and panic among the Philistines (v. 20). These are all connected to the work of Jonathan, while Saul was experiencing no such divine help or guidance even though he anxiously sought it.

14:23. Beth Aven. The town of Beth Aven has not been identified with any certainty. The way it is introduced in the texts suggests it was more prominent than Ai. Tell Maryam is often considered the prime candidate. It has not been excavated, but surveys have turned up Iron Age remains. Hosea is thought to use Beth Aven as a pejorative name (lit. "house of wickedness"; cf. Hos 4:15; 5:8; 10:5) for Bethel (house of God), north of Micmash. As still another alternative, some manuscripts of the Old Testament read Beth Horon, which was due east of Micmash. Any of these towns would have been on a route of pursuit to Aijalon.

14:24. fasting for battle. Fasting is little attested in the ancient Near East outside of the Bible. It generally occurs in the context of mourning. In the Old Testament the religious use of fasting is often in connection with making a request before God. The principle is that the importance of the request causes an individual to be so concerned about his or her spiritual condition that physical necessities fade into the background. In this sense the act of fasting is designed as a process leading to purification and humbling oneself before God (Ps 69:10). This would be a normal procedure to use in rituals preparing for battle but is incomprehensible as a requirement during the battle. The emphasis Saul places on the fast is for the sake of his own vengeance rather than for the sake of consecration to the Lord.

14:31. Micmash to Aijalon. Aijalon (modern Yalo) was a few miles southwest of Beth Horon and about twenty miles west of Micmash. The town was on the edge of the hill country.

14:32-35. eating without draining blood. Sacred literature from Ugarit and Mesopotamia, as well as Israel, identified blood as the life force of any animal. As such in Israelite tradition it belonged to the life-giver, the creator God Yahweh. Therefore the Israelites were prohibited from consuming meat which still contained blood. This sacred fluid had to be drained from the meat and "poured on the ground like water" so that it returned to the earth. In sacrificial contexts the blood was to be poured on the altar (see Lev 17:11-12). The prohibition against eating meat with the "blood still in it" in Leviticus 19:26 is tied to the injunction against participating in any form of divination or sorcery. Thus, rather than a dietary law, this decree involves the practice of draining blood from a sacrificial animal into the ground or a sacred pit, which was designed to attract the spirits of the dead (see 1 Sam 28:7-19) or chthonic deities, and to consult them about the future. Such practices are found in several Hittite ritual texts and in Odysseus's visit to the underworld (*Odyssey* XI, 23-29, 34-43). These practices were condemned (Deut 18:10-11) because they infringed on the idea of Yahweh as an all-powerful God, who was not controlled by fate.

14:33-35. rock as an altar. Having a stone function as an altar was not unprecedented. A stone served as an altar for the sacrifice at Beth Shemesh (6:14). Secular slaughter of animals was permitted as long as the animal's blood was poured out on the ground (Deut 12:15-24).

14:37. no reply by the oracle. It is generally assumed that the Urim and Thummim were being used for oracular inquiries (see next entry) and that for an answer to be affirmed it would have to be repeated a specified number of times.

14:40-43. binary process for determining guilt. Saul arranged a lot-casting ceremony similar to that used to elect him king (10:19-21) and to condemn Achan (Josh 7:16-18). According to a section of text provided by some reliable manuscripts, the decision was made through the use of the Urim and Thummim (see Ex 28:30; Lev 8:8; Deut 33:8), items kept in the priest's ephod. No description of these objects is found in Scripture, although traditions from the Hellenistic and later periods suggest they were markers, whose appearance and presentation when cast like lots would determine God's will (see Num 27:21; 1 Sam 14:37-41; 28:6). The practice of posing yes-no questions to the gods (asking oracles) is known throughout the ancient Near East. Particularly of interest are the Babylonian *tamitu* texts, which preserve the answers to many oracular questions. Positive and negative stones (thought to be bright stones and dark stones) were also used widely in Mesopotamia in a procedure called psephomancy. In one Assyrian text alabaster and hematite are specifically mentioned. The yes-no question would be posed and then a stone shaken out. The same color stone would have to be shaken out three times consecutively for the answer to be confirmed. *Urim* is the Hebrew word for "lights" and therefore would logically be associated with bright or white stones. One recent study has pointed out that hematite, because of its use for weights and seals, was termed the "truth stone" in Sumerian. The Hebrew word *thummim* could have a similar meaning. Hittite KIN-oracles feature a detailed description of the question, concluding with the request that the answer be favorable. Then there is a series of three castings of the lot to determine the answer. In this context a series of yes or no questions were posed, and after this binary inquisition the lot indicated Jonathan as the offender.

14:47-48. Saul's conquests. The narrator's selection has focused on the spiritual failures of Saul, but here he makes it clear that there were many victories. There is no suggestion in the text or evidence from extrabiblical materials to suggest that these victories represented an expansion of Israelite control or territory. Moab, Ammon and Edom are the neighbors to the east and south. Philistines and Amalekites border on the southwest and are the Israelites' archenemies during this period. Zobah is an Aramean state located in the Beqa Valley region of modern Lebanon. It is possible that these battles of Saul's were defensive rather than offensive.

15:1-35

Saul's Amalekite Failure

15:2-8. Amalekites. The Amalekites were a nomadic tribe inhabiting the desert south of Judah in the Negev and Sinai. The biblical writers saw them, like the Edomites, as descended from Esau. They were the traditional enemies of the Israelites, beginning in Exodus 17:8-13, where they attempted to block the Israelites from crossing into West Asia from Egypt. The passage here is the first recorded instance of the Israelites invading Amalekite territory. The Amalekites are not mentioned in any extrabiblical source.

15:3. the ban. The "ban" is sometimes chosen as the English word to represent the concept of total destruction that is commanded here. Just as there were some types of sacrifices that belonged entirely to the Lord while others were shared by priest and offerer, so some plunder was set aside as belonging solely to the Lord. Just as the whole burnt offering was entirely consumed on the altar, so the ban mandated total destruction. Since the warfare was commanded by Yahweh and represented his judgment on Israel's enemies, the Israelites were on a divine mission with Yahweh as their commander. Since it was his war, not theirs, and he was the victor, the spoil belonged to him. Although the divine warrior motif occurs throughout the ancient Near East, the *herem* concept is more limited—the only other occurrence of the term is in the Moabite Mesha inscription, but the idea of total destruction is also in the Hittite material. The best analogy for us to understand *herem* is to think in terms of radiation. A nuclear explosion would destroy many things and irradiate much more. The abhorrence and caution with which we would respond to that which has been irradiated is similar to what is expected of the Israelites regarding things under the ban. If radiation were personified, one could understand that once something was given over to it, it was irredeemable. It was this condition that Saul exposed himself to by not following the instructions for the ban. Although peoples outside the land were exempt from this, God had singled out the Amalekites for destruction because of their acts against God's people (15:2).

15:4. Telaim. Telaim (Telem in Josh 15:24) was a city of uncertain location in the Negev, but not far from Ziph (modern Khirbit ez-Zeifeh), about thirty miles south of Hebron. The city belonged to the tribe of Judah.

15:4. size of army. Saul had only used three thousand men in 1 Samuel 13, and David fought against the Amalekites with only four hundred men. The word translated "thousand" in these passages should be rendered by its alternate meaning, "companies" or "divisions." Rather than a specified number, it has been suggested that each clan supplied a division, with the number varying dependent on the size of the clan. Later in history these companies were standardized as having a thousand, but here there may be as few as ten in a division. Thus two hundred military divisions came from Israel and ten from Judah. The precise numbers of soldiers would not be known.

15:6. Kenites. The Kenites are mentioned in Scripture as having a nonaggressive relationship with Israel. It has been argued that the term *Kenite* is a reference to metalworking and that the Kenites were itinerant smiths. They were usually found on the southeast border of Judah near Edom. Many of the Kenites were linked to Moses (Judg 1:16, 4:11). Some have suggested that they enjoyed a status as ritual specialists.

15:7. Havilah to Shur. The location of Havilah is uncertain but was probably on the western edge of the Arabian Peninsula near modern Medina (see comment on Gen 25:18). Though it is not impossible that Saul chased them all the way to Egypt, other possibilities are allowed in the wording of the text. One is that Saul chased them along that road. A second is that the text is identifying a certain group of Amalekites, those working the trade route from Havilah to Shur.

15:12. king's monument. Ancient Near Eastern kings often commemorated a victory with a commemorative stele. These would typically offer the details of the successful military campaigns and proclaim the suzerainty of the king over the area. One of the most famous is a stele of the Egyptian king Merenptah (c. 1224-1214) commemorating a victory over the Libyans. They tended to glorify (and enhance) the king but additionally were usually intended to elaborate on how the deity had brought victory to his favored one. Saul's monument was at the Judean town of Carmel. Absalom set up a similar monument in the King's Valley (2 Sam 18:18).

15:22. obedience better than sacrifice. In the ancient Near East oracular instructions from the deity typically concerned ritual procedures for the king to perform. If there were instructions to carry out some military activity, it could easily be assumed that the deity would give such a command in order that his or her temple could benefit from the booty that would be taken. As a result, it would be difficult to separate the ideas of obedience and sacrifice. Obedience to most oracular instructions would inevitably result in sacrifices being offered to the deity. It is easy to understand how Saul would see obedience in terms of sacrifice rather than as an alternative possibility.

15:23. comparison of offenses in ancient Near East context. The Hebrew word that the NIV translates "rebellion" has to do with pressing one's case. It is used to describe the Israelites' contentiousness in the wilderness. Here it represents Saul's attempts to justify and excuse his actions. Samuel compares this to divination. Divination assumed that there was knowledge to be gained about the activities and motives of the gods through the use of various indicators (such as the entrails of sacrificed animals). It professed to be able to identify what would please the deity without specific input from the deity. In the same way Saul was contending that he knew what would be pleasing to deity (despite Yahweh's specific commands). His contentions claimed the same kind of information divination would offer—that he had an inside track on what would please God. The Hebrew word NIV translates "arrogance" is used when someone is trying to force a particular course of action. Samuel appropriately compares this to idolatry (specifically he refers to teraphim; see comment on Gen 31:19) in that the idols were typically used to manipulate and coerce the gods into particular courses of action (see comment on Deut 4:15-18). Food and gifts were presented to the gods so that the gods would be obliged to grant requests or bestow blessings. Samuel is suggesting that that is exactly the activity Saul intends to engage in as he plans to present all of these cattle to the Lord. Saul was attempting to manipulate with gifts in the same way that idol worshipers did.

15:27. Samuel's hem. As the high priest's garments had an elaborately decorated hem (Ex 28:33-34), Samuel's robe would also have had a distinctive fringe or design marking him as a prophet. It may have been specially dyed or contained a special stitching, and it symbolized his power and authority. Its importance for identification is indicated by the fact that a hem impressed on a clay tablet is used to identify a prophet in the Mari texts. A husband divorced his wife by symbolically cutting off the hem of her robe. Grasping the hem of the garment was a common phrase found in Ugaritic, Aramaic and Akkadian (languages related to biblical Hebrew). In Akkadian the phrase was "to seize the hem." Grasping

the hem of someone's garment was a gesture of supplication and submission, both in Israel and Mesopotamia. Saul's grasping of Samuel's skirt was a final plea for mercy. This is also the case in the Ugaritic Baal Cycle, where Anat seizes the hem of Mot's garment to plead for her brother Baal. Old Babylonian texts evidence the seizing of the hem as a means of forcing a person into a legal confrontation. When the hem ripped, the prophet recognized this as a symbolic act. The tearing of the garment represented the tearing of the kingdom from Saul's hands.

15:33. put Agag to death. The word used here is unique in the Old Testament and is sometimes translated "hacked to pieces." Dismemberment was a common procedure for the execution of high-ranking enemies and is depicted on a relief of the Assyrian king, Shalmaneser III.

16:1-12
David's Anointing

16:1-13. succession narrative and Hittite apology. The description of David's rise to the throne of Israel has some similarities with annalistic documents from Hittite Anatolia of the fourteenth and thirteenth centuries B.C. The Proclamation of Telepinu is a decree or an edict with a long prologue justifying the king's cause. Telepinu, a usurper, attempted to justify his accession to the throne by recalling events that actually happened generations before the reign of the king he overthrew. Although, like David, he did not claim any hereditary legitimacy, he showed that he belonged to a line of legitimate and successful predecessors whose principles were betrayed by the king whom he removed. A second example, the Apology of Hattusilis, was a document whose purpose was to justify the revolt that brought Hattusilis to the throne. Like Telepinu, he claimed to have taken the throne because of an unworthy predecessor. David's replacement of the unworthy Saul has superficial similarities with these two Hittite kings. The biblical text, however, is anxious to demonstrate that David did not usurp the throne and in fact did nothing to undermine the reign of Saul. He was not involved in any plot but was simply a pawn in the divine plan.

16:1. anointing with olive oil. Anointing a king was common practice in some parts of the ancient Near East. Among the Egyptians and Hittites, anointing was believed to protect a person from the power of netherworld deities. Much of the evidence comes from Hittite sources describing enthronement ceremonies.

There is no evidence of kings being anointed in Mesopotamia. In Egypt the pharaoh was not anointed, but he anointed his officials and his vassals. This anointing established their subordinate relationship to him and indicated his protection of them. In the Amarna texts there is reference to a king of Nuhasse (in modern Syria) being anointed by the pharaoh. This model would fit the idea of David being anointed as a vassal to God. In 2 Samuel 2:4 it is the people who anoint David. This anointing suggests some sort of contractual agreement between David and the people he will govern. In Nuzi, individuals entering a business agreement anoint one another with oil, and in Egypt, oil anointment is used in wedding ceremonies. For information on royal coronations see comment on 11:15. The spices used for anointing purposes were myrrh, cinnamon, cane and cassia (see recipe in Ex 30:23-25). Oil symbolized the gifts of God to the people and the responsibilities now laid on their leaders through this ceremony. In Israelite practice, anointing was a sign of election and often closely related to endowment by the Spirit. Additionally, throughout the ancient world anointing symbolized an advance of a person's legal status. Both concepts of protection and change of status may correlate to the king's anointing, for it would offer him protection on the throne and identify him with the divine realm.

16:4. Bethlehem. The village of Bethlehem was about six miles south of Jerusalem, lying on the border of the fertile region of Beit-Jalah and the dry region of Boaz near the Judean Desert. Bethlehem may be mentioned in a fourteenth-century letter of Abdi-Hepa, king of Jerusalem. He refers to a town called Bet-Ninurta, which some have suggested could be read as Bit-Lahama. There are meager Iron Age (c. 1200-586 B.C.) remains found at Bethlehem, primarily on the lower city.

16:5. sacrifices at local shrines. Before the construction of the temple in Jerusalem, it was acceptable for the Israelites to perform sacrifices at local sanctuaries, which were quite numerous. Though the term is not used here, this may be one of the high places (Hebrew *bamoth*), man-made installations in which cultic acts were performed. Such installations often included cultic furniture, such as a platform or an altar. In later periods the high places were condemned by the prophets.

16:7. deity searching the heart. It was a common understanding that the gods were not limited to what could be observed on the outside but were capable of deeper insight. In an intriguing Sumerian lament the moon god is portrayed as one who searches the bowels and the hearts of an anointed one who stands before him in supplication. In a Neo-Babylonian text, Shamash (the god of justice) is said to see into the heart of man.

16:10-11. eighth son. The motif of the youngest, eighth son as a hero is seen as early as the Sumerian epic called Lugalbanda in Khurrumkhurra (mid-third millennium), where Lugalbanda is the eighth son who joins his seven older brothers on an escapade to conquer the city of Aratta. Through a series of adventures he emerges the hero.

16:13-23
David at the Palace

16:13-14. role of the Spirit of the Lord. In the Judges period the Spirit of the Lord endowed an individual with central authority that only the Lord possessed (see comment on Judg 6:34-35). The Spirit of the Lord came on Saul in very similar circumstances (see comment on 11:6) and also associated him with prophetic activity (see 10:6). The role of the king represented a more permanent central authority and likewise relied on empowerment by the Lord. The king was an agent of deity and a heavenly functionary just as judges and prophets were. The Spirit did not empower two individuals for the same task at the same time. When David received the authorization for the role as representative, it was taken away from Saul. Just as the Spirit was able to give the positive attributes of courage, charisma, insight, wisdom and confidence, negative results could also be produced by spiritual influence. These would include fear, paranoia, indecisiveness, suspicion and shortsightedness. The term used to describe this spiritual influence in verse 14 does not necessarily suggest something morally evil but has a wide range of negative manifestations (see for instance Judg 9:23; Is 4:4; 37:7; 61:3). Just as God can punish with physical illness, he can discipline by means of psychological affliction. In Mesopotamia the king was seen as being endowed with the *melammu* of the gods (the visible representation of the glory of deity). It designated him as the divine representative and indicated that his legitimacy was approved by the gods. In Assyrian inscriptions it is pictured hovering over the king. The *melammu* could be revoked if the king proved unworthy or incompetent. So in the epilogue to Hammurabi's Laws the king utters a curse on anyone who does not heed the words of the law. If it is a future king, Hammurabi says, "May Anu revoke his *melammu*, break his scepter and curse his destiny."

16:16-18. court musicians. Court musicians, both male and female, are attested at many royal courts throughout the ancient Near East. They are attested in texts (including, for instance, Uruk and Mari) in the Tigris-Euphrates Valley, Hittite Anatolia and Egypt. Additionally, musicians are frequently portrayed in Egyptian tomb paintings. Musicians were usually retained for the ruler's entertainment or for cultic ceremonies. They were included among permanent palace personnel, as ration lists demonstrate.

16:16. harp. The musical instrument here is more precisely a lyre, a stringed instrument. It usually had two arms rising up from the sound box. The strings were attached to the crossbar at the top of the instrument. Examples of lyres have been found at Canaanite Megiddo.

16:20. gifts sent with David. One can assume that David's father Jesse was honored by the drafting of his son into royal service and thus sent gifts. Bread and wine are occasionally mentioned as gifts in the Old Testament. The precise purpose for gifts in this passage is unknown. However, without any formal taxation, David's family may have made a donation to the royal kitchen, since David himself was part of the king's house. There are many examples of subordinates in the Neo-Assyrian period bringing gifts of food to the Assyrian monarch.

17:1-58
David and Goliath

17:1. Philistines. The group of Philistines that are known through the narratives of 1 and 2 Samuel came into the Palestine area with the migration from the Aegean region of the Sea Peoples about 1200 B.C. It is the Sea Peoples that are generally thought to have been responsible for the fall of the Hittite Empire and the destruction of many cities along the coast of Syria and Palestine, such as Ugarit, Tyre, Sidon, Megiddo and Ashkelon, though the evidence for their involvement in those areas is circumstantial. Their battles with the Egyptian pharaoh Rameses III are depicted on the famous wall paintings at Medinet Habu. This international upheaval is also reflected in the Homeric epic of the siege of Troy. Coming from Crete, Greece and Anatolia, the Sea Peoples may have used Cyprus as a base from which to launch their attacks. Following the repulsion of the Sea Peoples from Egypt, the tribe that came to be known as the Philistines settled on the southern coast of Palestine,

where they established their five capital cities of Ashkelon, Ashdod, Ekron (Tell Miqne), Gath (Tell es-Safi) and Gaza. They had overrun Israelite territory in the battle in which the ark was taken (1 Sam 4) and again will do so in the battle in which Saul and his sons are killed (chap. 31). During the reign of Saul there is continual conflict as Saul tries to rid the land of their presence and prevent further incursions.

17:1. location of Philistine camp. Socoh (modern Khirbet Abbad) was a town in the Shephelah Valley about fourteen miles west of Bethlehem near Philistine territory. The site has been surveyed and has produced ceramic remains dated to this time period. Azekah (modern Tell ez-Zakariyeh) was a fortress three miles northwest of Socoh, which controlled the main road across the Elah Valley. The site was excavated earlier this century, uncovering a rectangular fortress with four towers that was dated to this period. This area was of strategic importance to both sides as the main pass between the Philistine plain and the Judean hills. The main road through the Shephelah region heads north from Lachish to Azekah, but about a mile south of Azekah a road goes east following the Wadi es-Sant that opens into the Elah Valley. Ephes-Dammim has not been positively identified but would logically be looked for in this area.

17:2. Israelite camp. The Valley of Elah ("Terebinth") was the broad north-south plain that had an opening where the Wadi es-Sant started its rise into the hill country of Judah, about two miles east of Socoh.

17:4. Gath. Gath has been tentatively identified as Tell es-Safi, five miles south of Tell Miqne/Ekron. Of the five major cities of the Philistines it was the closest to Judah. There has been little excavation at the site, though it has been confirmed that there are Iron Age remains. The city was located about five miles west of Azekah by the Wadi es-Sant that opens up into the Elah Valley.

17:4. Goliath's size. Goliath's height is given in the text as about nine and a half feet. It is suspected that he is of the same stock as the Anakim, the giant inhabitants of the land that the Israelite armies were able to defeat in the conquest. The descendants of Anak are generally considered "giants," though the description "gigantic" may be a more appropriate line of thinking. Champions of this size are not simply a figment of Israelite imagination or the result of embellished legends. The Egyptian letter on Papyrus Anastasi I (thirteenth century B.C.) describes fierce warriors in Canaan who are seven to nine feet tall. Additionally, two female skeletons about seven feet tall from the twelfth century have been found at Tell es-Sa'ideyeh in Transjordan.

17:5-7. Goliath's armor. Goliath's helmet was likely the typical Philistine feathered head-dress known from Palestinian and Egyptian art. His body armor ("plaited cuirass") was probably of a well-known Egyptian style of bronze scale armor that covered the entire body, weighing over 125 pounds. One of the best descriptions of scale armor comes from the Nuzi texts, where a mail coat was comprised of anywhere from seven hundred to over one thousand scales of varying sizes. These scales were sewn onto a jerkin of leather or cloth. The front and back were sewn together at the shoulders (with a space for the head) and probably reached to the knees. His greaves were probably made of molded bronze around the entire calf, padded inside with leather, a type known from Mycenaean Greece. His scimitar (NIV: bronze javelin) was probably a heavy, curved, flat sword with a cutting edge on the outer side of the blade (see comment on Josh 8:18). His spear was something like a javelin, with an iron spear point that weighed over fifteen pounds. It may have been equipped with a ring for slinging, a type known both in contemporary Greece and Egypt. Although most of the weapons were made of bronze, the spear point was made of iron. Goliath's shield was most likely a standing shield, which would have been larger that a round shield.

17:8-10. champion warfare. At times individual combat was used, with the individuals viewed as representatives of their respective armies, so that the divine will could be expressed. Examples of individual combat are known in Egypt on the Beni Hasan wall painting (early second millennium) and in the Egyptian Tale of Sinuhe. It is likewise depicted on a Canaanite vase from the first half of the second millennium. Nearer in time, parallels can be found in the *Iliad* (Hector against Ajax, Paris against Menelaus) and the Hittite Apology of Hattusilis III. A relief from the tenth century found at Tell Halaf depicts two combatants grabbing at one another's heads and thrusting with short swords.

17:11. role of king. The text undoubtedly wants to display Saul's incompetence. The people had sought a king to lead their armies into battle. It was not odd, however, for a king to send out a champion rather than going himself. Even in the event that the king was a great warrior, others would be given the opportunity to prove their skills first. In some senses it would resemble all of the prelimi-

nary bouts that precede the "main event" in boxing. As early as the Sumerian epic Gilgamesh and Aka, the practice is seen of the real champion holding back while he sends a capable fighter under his command to engage the enemy. This is also evident in the *Iliad*, where Patroclus dons the armor of Achilles in order to go out and challenge Hector. Nevertheless, given the amount of time that had gone by, Saul should by now have been willing to take up the challenge himself.

17:12. Ephrathite. The Ephrathites were probably a tribal subdivision of the Calebites from the Bethlehem region. Bethlehem was a village within the larger Ephrathah clan, and later the clan became synonymous with the village itself.

17:12. Bethlehem. See comment on 16:4.

17:17-18. food supplies. David came to the camp with about half a bushel of roasted grain (either wheat or barley), loaves of bread and cuts of cheese, all of which were favorites for common people. The grain would typically be fashioned into loaves for consumption, and some would likely be made into beer. In Egyptian texts ten loaves of bread, a half a pound of barley and a jug of beer represented a standard daily wage. The Assyrian annals describe soldiers traveling with grain and straw for their horses. Local governors in Assyria were required to open granaries for armies that were traveling through the region. Since the army is in the vicinity of the Judean hills, it is likely that the people from the area were expected to provide supplies.

17:18. what David is getting from them. David was told to ask how his brothers were doing and to "pick up their assurance." This was likely some sort of token returned with David to confirm that the goods had been provided. This would be proof that Jesse had met his obligations to supply the army and would be the brothers' way of collecting their rations. An Akkadian (a language from Mesopotamia related to Hebrew) pledge was often a cased clay tablet sent with a messenger.

17:19. distance between Bethlehem and Elah. Bethlehem was about fifteen miles from the Valley of Elah, which took most of the day for David to walk.

17:25. reward for killing Goliath. Ancient kings were often interested in procuring the allegiance of those who had demonstrated military prowess. Marriage agreements in the ancient Near East would often function as political or social alliances between families and thus benefit both parties. Thus the champion's family would receive important recognition from being connected to the crown, while the king would be allied to the renowned hero who had killed Goliath. The Hebrew says nothing about taxes, only that his father's house will be free in Israel. Some have compared the Hebrew word to its Akkadian cognate, which sometimes designates a social class. This then would probably describe a family that had become clients of the crown, supported by allocations of plots of land and supplies, which is implied in 1 Samuel 22:7. This type of client class is well known from Mari texts, the Code of Hammurabi and the Laws of Eshnunna. In these texts, individuals received land grants from the crown, likely based upon service rendered to the king. Perhaps more likely is the comparison to another term in Ugaritic texts that refers to a reward for an act of bravery. It exempts the recipient from mandatory service to palace.

17:36. lions and bears around Bethlehem. Recent excavations in Palestine have uncovered both the lion and the bear in Iron Age levels (early first millennium B.C.). Bears were typically found in the hilly wooded areas of the central hill country, where caves and forests provided their habitat. Similarly the lion would have made its home in the central hills, which were more heavily forested during this period. Although evidence for the lion is lacking in the modern era, the bear survived in the region until early this century. In this region in antiquity the lion was found in Greece, Turkey (Anatolia), the Near East, Iran and India, while there was a Syrian form of the widespread brown bear.

17:37. expectation of divine intervention. The idea that God fought as a partner in battle was a common theme in the ancient Near East. Victories were attributed to deities in both Egypt and Mesopotamia. In fact the encounter was initiated by the deity itself, who then fought alongside the monarch (see comment on 4:3-7). In Egypt regiments were named after the god under whose standard they fought. In Canaan the divine warrior was identified as one who devastated nature. However, it was recognized by these societies that the gods also participated through the use of individual agents who had been commissioned to do the god's bidding in battle. This aspect is seen clearly in contemporary Greek literature as the various gods aid and protect their favorites in the *Iliad*.

17:38-39. Saul's armor. The use of protective armor (shields, helmets, coats and greaves) is attested in Egypt and Mesopotamia by the early third millennium B.C. Though rarely found in archaeological contexts, even early portrayal of soldiers depict them wearing heavy armor (for example on reliefs from the Sumerian city of Lagash and from murals from Hierakonpolis in Pre-Dynastic Egypt). The palace of the Assyrian king Sennacherib (seventh century B.C.) exhibits numerous wall reliefs portraying Assyrian military dress and tactics. The king's tunic and armor would have been very distinctive. If David went out dressed in them, many would have thought that the king himself was going out. Perhaps such a misidentification would have seemed attractive to Saul, who had been sought out by the Israelites to lead them forth in battle. In the *Iliad* a similar switch occurred when Patroclus went out in the armor of Achilles, hoping to intimidate the Trojans. David's refusal would have reflected his recognition that without being trained on how to use the armor and weapons to his advantage, they would become a detriment.

17:40. sling. Although described simply as a shepherd's weapon here, the sling was also used in organized warfare, and Goliath would have been well aware of its deadly potential. Assyrian slingers are depicted on the walls of Sennacherib's palace at Nineveh. In the Babylonian Wisdom composition entitled *Ludlul Bel Nemeqi* the sufferer reports his deliverance by a variety of metaphors, one of which claims that Marduk took away his enemy's sling and turned aside his sling stone. Assyrian sling balls were found at Lachish, an Iron Age Judean fortress town. These were the size of a human fist (two to three inches in diameter) and had been used for the successful Assyrian siege of Lachish in 701 B.C. (possibly also by the Babylonians in their siege of Lachish in 587 B.C.). The Benjaminites were known to be deadly accurate with their slings (Judg 20:16), and it is estimated that a skilled slinger could hurl the rocks at more than one hundred miles per hour. The effective range would probably not exceed one hundred yards. The stone was held in a leather pouch with cords attached at opposite ends. The sling was whirled over the head until the person let go of one of the ends.

17:43-47. prebattle insults. Goliath's insults and curses against David and his God reflect a common rhetoric in these types of confrontations that is found throughout the Near East and eastern Mediterranean. Insulting bravado was intended to demoralize and intimidate the opponent. The curses that were included were not merely empty words but were presumably backed by the person's deity. Sennacherib's representatives at the gates of Jerusalem in 701 B.C. extolled the greatness of the gods of Assyria and ridiculed the God of

Judah as incapable of defending his city (2 Kings 18:17-36). In the Gilgamesh Epic the guardian of the cedar forest, Huwawa, tells Gilgamesh that he should have given his flesh to be eaten by birds of prey and scavengers.

17:43. names of Goliath's gods. Although Goliath's gods are not named, one of the primary deities of the Philistines mentioned in the Bible is Dagon, the patron deity of many West Semitic peoples from the Middle Euphrates region to the Mediterranean coast. Temples to Dagon have been found at the Philistine sites of Gaza and Ashdod. They also worshiped Baal-Zebub, whose temple has been found at Ekron, and the goddess Ashtoreth, who had a temple at Beth Shan (1 Sam 31:8-13). Archaeology, however, has also shown that the Philistines had cultic and architectural connections with the Aegean. Schematic representations of female deities similar to those found in the Aegean have been found at Ashdod, Ekron and Tell Qasile. Cultic vessels showing Aegean influence have also been found.

17:45-47. foundation of David's boast. David's claim would have been acknowledged within the broad theological framework of the ancient world. There are two concepts in tension here. The first is that the stronger, better-equipped warrior is a more effective agent for the gods who are battling. This would be the basis for Goliath's presumed superiority. David is simply following the logic to its inevitable end to arrive at the second concept. If the gods are, in actuality, doing battle with one another through the human agents, then the strength and weapons of the human combatants are irrelevant. Thus Yahweh is described as Yahweh of Hosts, paraphrased with a military description, "the God of the battle ranks of Israel" (author's translation), and David's boast is based on Yahweh's abilities, not his own. This claim would perhaps be psychologically sufficient to undermine Goliath's confidence. Similarly in the *Iliad* Hector acknowledges the superiority of Achilles but suggests that the gods may be on his side and allow him to kill Achilles. In another example, when Hector and Telamonian Aias have fought to a draw, Hector suggests they desist until another day, when the gods will have decided which should win.

17:49. David's shot. The text offers no information concerning the range between David and Goliath when David took his shot. A stone from a slingshot is capable of delivering a killing blow but only when striking a few strategic areas of the head (which was protected). David's shot targeted one of the few vulnerable areas that could render his opponent unconscious. This allowed him to approach and secure Goliath's sword, which he then used to kill his unconscious victim (despite the NIV's implication that the shot killed Goliath).

17:51. cutting off the enemy's head. Killing the enemy with his own weapon was not an unprecedented feat. Similarly, Benaiah took the Egyptian's spear out of his hand and killed him (2 Sam 23:30). In Egyptian literature, Sinuhe killed a soldier from Retenu with his own battle-axe. It can be assumed that Goliath's head was a trophy that was to be put on display. Assyrian king Ashurbanipal was reported to have dined with his queen in the garden with the head of the king of Elam on display in a nearby tree.

17:52. Gath, Ekron and Shaarim. Ekron, like Gath, was one of the five major Philistine cities. It was about five miles north of Gath. Shaarim was a city (and also the name of a highway) near Socoh and Azekah (see Josh 15:36). It is probably the modern site of Khirbit esh-Sharia, which is about one mile northeast of Azekah. Thus Shaarim was about six miles east of Gath and seven miles southeast of Ekron. The road from Shaarim went west and could be taken to either Gath or Ekron.

17:58. extrabiblical information on David. David as an individual is not mentioned by any ancient Israelite inscription, by any source outside of Israel or by evidence of any contemporary material remains at Jerusalem. However, a recent fragment of a ninth-century B.C. Aramaic inscription from Tel Dan has the phrase "House of David," denoting the royal house of the kingdom of Judah, the successor state to the united kingdom of Israel. Thus there is extrabiblical evidence from an enemy state that the Judahites understood their dynastic house to have been derived from a certain David, who most certainly was the famous David of the Bible.

18:1-30
David in Saul's Family and Court

18:4. Jonathan's gift to David. The word for the robe that Jonathan gave to David often denotes a royal robe. Ugaritic texts refer to a special robe worn by the crown prince. If Israel had the same custom, Jonathan would be renouncing his claim to the throne by giving David that robe. He also gave to him his daily warrior's garment and bow. The Israelite sword was carried in a sheath that hung from a belt. The bow was probably made of animal horn and sinews bonded with strips of wood. Jonathan's gifts to David may very well represent his willingness to give up and transfer his particular position as heir apparent to the throne of Israel. He thus was expressing loyalty and possibly submission to David.

18:5. David's office. The group of armed men over which David is given control here is the standing army made up of the professional military men. It is possible that this is not a field post but more of an administrative position ("secretary of the army"). The position is to be contrasted with the post given to David in 1 Samuel 18:13, which suggests a field command with active duty.

18:6-7. comparison between Saul and David. The comparison of Saul slaying "his thousands" and David "his tens of thousands" is a standard way of expressing a very large number in parallel lines of poetry. The same parallelism can be found in Psalm 91:7, where God protects an individual from a plague, and even in poetry from Ugarit, where the craftsman god, Kothar-wa-Hasis, is described as crafting silver by the thousands and gold by the ten thousands. The intention of these words is to convey large numbers, not to offer a comparison of one being greater than the other. In some cases the greater honor was placed in the last position, but Saul could have been angered simply because David was mentioned in the same breath as himself, thus placing him in the same rank as the king.

18:10. harp. See comments on 10:5 and 16:16.

18:10. spear. Saul's spear appears to have been a sign of his kingship, somewhat like a scepter (also see 22:6; 26:7). Saul stood with spear in hand with his troops in 22:6, in much the same way as the Egyptian monarch is artistically depicted with a scepter. The Assyrian kings were often depicted with weapons in their hands, which were occasionally spears. The spear was not designed to be thrown like the shorter javelins but was usually a thrusting weapon used by the infantry. Nonetheless the *Iliad* portrays mighty warriors hurling heavy spears effectively at their opponents.

18:13. David's office. David is said to be given rule over "one thousand," but the term probably refers to the military division supplied by a clan, with the number varying dependent on the size of the clan. Later in history these companies were standardized as having a thousand, but early on there may have been as few as ten in a division. Apparently Israel's army was divided into these "clans" (Num 31:5; Josh 22:21, 30; Judg 5:8). The army was further divided into "hundreds" (1 Sam 22:7) and even fifties (see comment on 1 Sam 8:12). David is now being put on active duty with a field command.

18:17. marrying the daughter of a king. Marrying the eldest daughter of the king would give David the title of "king's son-in-law," raising his status immensely. In some societies this would have been a potential stepping-stone to the throne, but no such practice is evidenced in Israel. David recognized that his family did not have the same social status as Saul. Saul would have been anxious to procure the loyalty and support of such a noteworthy warrior (see comment on 17:25). Thus David's lower social status was not considered a barrier to his marrying into Saul's family.

18:25. bride price. The bride price was a sum of money paid by the fiancé to the girl's parents (see comments on Gen 29:21-24; Ex 22:16-17; Deut 22:23, 25; 22:29) and typically provided for the wife ahead of time in case the husband deserted her or died. Such provision would not have been necessary for someone in the royal household, but the amount of the bride price would have reflected the status of the bride. David would not have had the means to enter into a royal marriage. However, the price appears to have been set by the father (see Gen 34:12), and thus Saul attached the bride price to the military prowess of the husband-to-be rather than to financial resources. It was not unusual in the ancient Near East for casualty counts to be kept by cutting off some body part: usually hands (see comment on Judg 8:6) or heads (2 Kings 10:6-8 and the practice of making piles of heads by Assyrian king Sargon II). The request for foreskins would have proven that the victims were Philistines, because many of the other neighbors of Israel would have practiced circumcision.

19:1-24
Saul's Pursuit of David

19:13. teraphim. The term *teraphim* refers to a household idol or idols that appear to have had a role in divination (Ezek 21:21; Zech 10:2) and were associated with luck and prosperity of the family. They were explicitly condemned by the biblical authors (Ex 15:23; 2 Kings 23:24). The narrator in Genesis 31 referred to Laban's gods as teraphim. The fact that Rachel was able to hide them under a saddle (Gen 31:19) suggests that some were quite small, though from this passage, it appears that David and Michal's teraphim were of human size and shape. Many of these small figurines have been found in Mesopotamia and Syro-Palestine. They were a part of the "popular" or local religion, not associated with temples or national cults for the major deities. One recent study has suggested they were figurines of the ancestors, but others see them more generally related to the family's patron deity.

19:18. Ramah. In his desire for safety, David moved only two miles east of Gibeah/Geba to Ramah, which was Samuel's hometown.

19:18-24. Naioth. The term Naioth is associated with Ramah and is used only here in this context. It is probably not a proper noun but a generic word for camps. In the Mari texts the Akkadian word related to this Hebrew term is used to describe the encampments of mobile shepherding communities on the outskirts of town. It is possible that Israelite prophetic groups may have occupied shepherd's residences or simply formed a similar type of camp outside Ramah.

19:20. entranced prophesying. One could be trained for the profession of prophet (or seer), and there was a prophetic guild in this early period of Israel's history, usually identified as the "sons of the prophets." Typically these prophets would use various procedures in order to prepare themselves for receiving prophetic oracles. Music played an important role in inducing a trancelike state (ecstasy) that was seen as making one receptive to a divine message. In the Mari texts there is an entire class of temple personnel who were ecstatics and who often provided prophetic messages. This ecstatic prophecy, or prophecy that appears to proceed from someone in a "possessed" or trancelike state, was conducted in Mesopotamia through a functionary labeled a *muhhu.* In Israel the phenomenon often resulted in the prophets being thought of as madmen (see for example 19:19-24; Jer 29:26). Here it is not resulting in prophetic messages from the Lord but serves as a sign of the power of God on the messengers. In that sense it could be compared to the tongues of fire in the upper room in Acts 2.

19:22. well at Secu. Secu denotes a bare height and is not to be taken as a proper noun, because it has a definite article (not usual for proper nouns). There are more than half a dozen wells or springs along the two-mile road from Gibeah to Ramah.

19:24. Saul's "nakedness." Even Saul was "infected" by God's Spirit and became possessed (had an ecstatic experience) resulting in stripping off his garments. This is yet another case of Saul being overcome by the Spirit in various ways (cf. 10:10; 11:6; 16:14). The term "nakedness" can denote the removal of the outer garment, not entire nakedness, and that is probably what is involved here. He not only shamed himself in front of Samuel but also laid aside his kingly regalia, confirming his rejection as king.

20:1-42
Jonathan Helps David

20:5. New Moon festival. Keyed to its use of a lunar calendar, ancient Israel marked the first day of the month, with its "new moon" phase, as a festival day (every twenty-nine or thirty days). As on the Sabbath all work was to cease (see Amos 8:5), and there were sacrifices to be made (Num 28:11-15). In the monarchy period the king became a prominent figure in these celebrations (see Ezek 45:17), and this may explain the political importance of Saul's feast. The festival continued to be observed in the postexilic period as well (Ezra 3:5; Neh 10:33). New Moon festivals were also prominent in Mesopotamia from late in the third millennium down to the Neo-Babylonian period in the middle of the first millennium B.C.

20:6. annual family sacrifice. The tradition of an annual family sacrifice had also been reflected in the family of Hannah and Elkanah (see comment on 1:3). This was separate from the agricultural festivals and pilgrimages (2 Chron 8:13). In David's time this meant an ingathering of the family at the clan site, Bethlehem. Since it represented a higher level of obligation and familial loyalty, the annual sacrifice could easily serve as a valid excuse for David to absent himself from Saul's monthly celebration of the new moon.

20:26. ceremonial uncleanness. Saul considers David's absence to be likely due to ritual impurity. No one could participate in cultic activity, like the New Moon festival, when in a state of uncleanness. This could occur in a variety of ways: contact with bodily discharges such as semen or blood; contact with the dead or the diseased; and contact with an object that has come in contact with something that is unclean (see the laws of impurity and the methods for ritual cleansing in Lev 11—15). Bathing, a waiting period, sacrifices and examination by a priest were the principal means of purification.

21:1-9
David's Flight Through Nob

21:1. Nob. Although its exact location is unknown, Nob is generally believed to lie just north of the city of Jerusalem. Possible locations include Ras el-Mesharif on the slope of Mount Scopus and Qu'meh (see Is 10:32). In David's time it served as the sanctuary site and was served by Aaron's descendants. Presumably it had been moved from Shiloh after the death of Eli and his sons (see 1 Sam 4:10-22).

21:4-6. bread from the table. Twelve loaves of freshly baked bread were placed on the table of the Presence to symbolize the twelve tribes of Israel (see Ex 25:23-30). They were replaced by new loaves each Sabbath, and the old loaves were to be consumed by the priests (see Lev 24:5-9). In this case, due to the need for supplies and David's assurance that his men were ritually clean, Ahimelech had the jurisdiction to allow for a variance.

21:5. purity of men. Since the "consecrated bread" was reserved for priestly consumption, David had to swear that his men were ritually pure before the priests would give him the loaves. Sexual intercourse or contact with women who were menstruating were among the ways that a man could become "unclean" (Lev 15:32-33).

21:7. chief shepherd. Doeg the Edomite is probably a mercenary in the employ of Saul. Many translations allow a slight emendation, rendering "runner" for this word. This would fit well with his function as a royal messenger or spy, whose job was to carry instructions throughout the kingdom and report unusual happenings like David's visit to Nob. A similar use for royal messengers is found in the Mari texts. Nevertheless, chief of shepherds is a common administrative designation, used, for instance, in the titles of the scribe who copied the Ugaritic Myth of Baal and Mot.

21:7. reason for Doeg's presence. Doeg is said to be detained "before the LORD" at Nob. It is possible that he is awaiting a reply to a question sent by the king or a personal oracle. If he is a messenger, the former seems most likely. If he is a herdsman, then he may have delivered a consignment of animals for sacrifice or be giving an account to the officials at Nob of his activities.

21:9. behind the ephod. The ephod, as described in Exodus 28:6-14, was a garment worn by the high priest. In the ancient Near East the ephod was one of the garments used to clothe the image of the deity. Since no image is mentioned here, another alternative is that it hung on a stand of some sort (also a possible explanation of Gideon's ephod in Judg 8:24-27). With the ark still out of the picture, the ephod may have become the holiest relic of the sanctuary. Captured articles of power such as Goliath's sword would therefore be kept there (just as the ark had been put in the temple of Dagon, see comment on 5:2).

21:10-15

David and Achish

21:10. Achish. This King Achish is not referred to in any extrabiblical sources, but the name Achish is attested as a Philistine royal name at a later date. Assyrian records of the seventh century list Ikausu, son of Padi, as the king of Ekron. Ikausu is the same as Achish, son of Padi, named on an inscription from the same period found at Ekron (Tell Miqne).

21:10. why would David go to Gath? Though over twenty miles from Nob, Gath was the closest of the major Philistine cities to Judah. It was most likely David's intention to offer his services as a mercenary to the Philistines. It could be anticipated that they would welcome a proven military man of David's reputation and the opportunity to have this renowned warrior fighting with them instead of against them. Additionally, David's allegiance might eventually give them the chance to launch a strike against Saul and depose him, putting David on the throne of Israel as their puppet. All of this would have argued for the Philistines welcoming David with open arms, but factors were at work for which he had not calculated.

21:11. song. David's notoriety as a mighty warrior and enemy of the Philistines is recalled by Achish's advisers. They quote the chant first mentioned in 1 Samuel 18:7 to warn their lord not to trust him. Its lauding of David has taken on the status of national anthem and neutralizes any positive potential David might have hoped for the Philistines to imagine.

21:13-15. feigned insanity. David was sharp enough to recognize that his negative status as an enemy warrior was obscuring his potential status as a mercenary, ally and potential puppet ruler. Thus he shrewdly reclassified himself by changing his behavior and acting insane. Though David's reputation was well-known, very few Philistines would have ever got a close enough look at David to identify him by appearance. The only evidence they have that he is the famous David is his own self-identification. By acting insane, he discredits that identification. Now he is just a madman claiming to be a famous person. In the ancient Near East, insanity was often identified with possession by a god. A sign of this is that the Hebrew word used here for David's actions, *shaga'*, appears in 2 Kings 9:11, Hosea 9:7 and Jeremiah 29:26 for ecstatic (i.e., "mad") behavior by prophets. These people, while accepted as signs of the presence and sometimes as the messengers of the gods, were not sought after. They must be allowed to live, which is what David was counting on here, but they were also excluded, when possible, from polite society.

22:1-5

David Gathers a Band

22:1. cave of Adullam. This site in the Shephelah (possibly Tell esh-Sheikh Madhkur, five miles south of Beth Shemesh and ten miles southeast of Gath) served as a rallying point and stronghold for David and his men during his period as an outlaw (see 2 Sam 23:13 for its association with David's exploits involving his thirty "mighty men"). It seems to lie in a sort of "no man's land" between Philistine and Israelite territory.

22:1-2. David's band. Like other political and social dissidents before him (see Jephthah's band of adventurers in Judg 11:3), David assembled a group of four hundred men during his outlaw period. This included some family members (since otherwise Saul would probably have imprisoned or killed them because of their association with David), but the majority of his band was probably made up of social outcasts (known in ancient Near Eastern literature as *habiru*), mercenaries and men who saw an opportunity to overthrow Saul. Their bitterness and discontent made them rally to David as their champion.

22:3. Mizpah in Moab. The exact location of this Mizpah ("watchtower") is unknown. Presumably it was a royal Moabite city or at least a fortress. Among the suggested sites are Kerak and Rujm el-Meshrefeh in Jordan.

22:3-4. why protection in Moab. Perhaps because of his Moabite ancestry through Ruth, David felt he could claim kin ties and safely place his parents in the protective custody of the king of Moab (see Ruth 4:17-22). It is also possible that David was counting on Moab's enmity toward Saul (see 1 Sam 14:47). An example of revolutionary fugitives seeking refuge in a mother's country can be seen in Idrimi, king of Alalakh (during the Judges period), who fled to his mother's family at Emar. Idrimi in exile became the leader of a Habiru band that eventually helped him regain his throne.

22:4. the stronghold. This most likely refers to David's base of operations near the cave of Adullam (see 1 Sam 22:1). Some have suggested that it is a reference to Masada.

22:5. Gad. This is the first appearance of this Israelite prophet or seer. His advice to David to return to Judah and thus face up to Saul provided the type of divine backing David needed to begin his pursuit of the throne. See his involvement with David's census in 2 Samuel 24:11-25.

22:5. forest of Hereth. The exact location of this forested area is unknown, although it

must have been in Judah. Suggestions include the site of Khirbet Khoreisa (approximately six miles southeast of Hebron) and Kharas, near Keilah (Khirbet Qila, about six miles northwest of Hebron).

22:6-23

Execution of the Priests

22:6. tamarisk tree at Gibeah. Once again a ruler is depicted as holding court under a tree (see Saul previously in 14:2 and the Ugaritic king Danil in the Aqhat epic). A tamarisk is a tree adapted to desert environments, with many slender branches and scaly leaves. It would be a rare site in the hill country near Gibeah. In this case it may also have marked a cultic site (see the sacred palm under which Deborah served as judge in Judg 4:5).

22:7. prerogatives of officers. One of the ways in which a king, chief or warlord maintained the loyalty and support of his military commanders was through the granting of land (a fief) and the right to its harvests and other resources (see 8:12-15). For instance, Hammurabi's laws and the Mari texts both describe the rights of fief holders and the obligations to the state. Thus Saul is reminding his officers here that their claims to these lands are based on his favor toward them. If they hoped to keep them, they should not consider giving their allegiance to David. Nor should they trust in David's ability to keep any promises of land grants and military commissions to his followers.

22:10. inquiring of God. Among the tasks assigned to the high priests in the ancient Near East was to seek an oracle from deity when requested. Babylonian and Assyrian religious texts mention the examination of animal entrails, the consulting of omen texts or the use of an object associated with the god to divine the future. This might have been done at Nob using the Urim and Thummim (see Ex 28:30) or the ephod (see Abiathar's use of the ephod in 1 Sam 23:5, 9). The giving of an oracle is not mentioned in 21:1-9, but Ahimelech admits that he "inquired of God" for David in 22:15.

22:14. David's office. Since kings seldom paid state visits to each other's capitals, messengers, functioning as royal envoys, served as royal surrogates. This role required them to function as diplomatic couriers, negotiators and occasionally as emissaries to the gods. Embodying as they did the authority and power of their state, kings' messengers were generally treated well by local officials. Their persons were protected, as well as their personal property. Ahimelech recites David's marks of distinction as his defense for aiding him, including his status as a member of the royal family and commander of the king's bodyguard. Only the most trustworthy and loyal men could be expected to rise to these offices (see 18:27; 2 Sam 23:22-23). Thus as a sign of courtesy, extended to couriers, David was provided with food. Texts from Mari and other Mesopotamian cities list food, garments and other necessities given to royal emissaries to meet their needs on the road and to please their master.

22:16-19. destruction of priesthood by angry king. Saul's order to kill Ahimelech and the entire priestly community at Nob was so outrageous a sacrilege that his own officers refused. Only the Edomite mercenary Doeg was willing to carry out the order and in so doing also massacred the entire population of Nob. Saul's order gave a further sign of his instability and, as he was to discover (28:6), effectively cut him off from any contact with Yahweh. Charges of offenses against deity were often made against kings by their political enemies. Thus the Assyrian king Tukulti-Ninurta charged Kashtiliash with "crimes against Shamash," and the Persian king Cyrus claimed to have been chosen by Marduk to punish Nabonidus for failing to honor the god or his priesthood. Akhenaten, the rogue Egyptian pharaoh of the fourteenth century, had disenfranchised the powerful priests of the god Amun-Re and had scratched out the name Amun in all inscriptions. Thus Saul's action would be seen as just as significant an act of desecration.

22:20-23. Abiathar. Only a single priest escaped the massacre at Nob. Abiathar, the son of Ahimelech, fled to David's camp, bringing with him the sacred ephod (23:6). Once Abiathar had told him what Saul had done, David accepted responsibility and added the priest to his company. This event is the crux of the episode, since it placed in David's camp a divine representative, while Saul was left with no further contact point with God. Subsequently Abiathar was to consult the ephod for David (1 Sam 23:9-12) and serve as the visible symbol of God's presence with the outlaw band. Additionally this episode shows the fulfillment of the prophecy concerning Eli's family (1 Sam 2—3) in that this priestly clan was the family of Eli.

23:1-29
David Pursued and Rescued

23:1. Keilah. Located in the eastern portion of the Shephelah, near the border of Philistine territory, Keilah (Khirbet Qila, six miles northwest of Hebron) must have been a frequent target of raiders. It was also mentioned in the El Amarna tablets as a city contested between the rulers of Jerusalem and Hebron.

23:1-5. Philistines. For the Philistines as a part of the population of Canaan and as enemies of Israel, see comment on 4:1.

23:9-12. oracular use of ephod. For a discussion of the use of the ephod for purposes of divination, see comment on Judges 8:24-27. Abiathar's ability to make oracular inquiries for David stands in stark contrast to Saul's lack of divine guidance.

23:7. walled city. Keilah is identified as a walled city with gates that could be barred. As an important link on the roads north-south through the Shephelah and east into Judah, the city would have to be fortified against attack. Note that it was the unprotected threshing floors, which would have been outside the city walls, that the Philistines attacked in 23:1. Saul saw David as trapped within these walls, assuming he would be easier to capture here than in the open countryside. The site has not been excavated, so archaeology has little light to shed on the text.

23:14. strongholds in the wilderness of Ziph. The site of Tell Ziph is located thirteen miles southeast of Keilah and five miles southeast of Hebron. Although in the tribal territory of Judah, it is within a steppe area that would have been sparsely inhabited and a place in which fugitives could easily hide. The strongholds were small outposts that served as signaling stations and contact points for herdsmen and villagers in the area.

23:15-18. Horesh. The term literally means "wood" or "wooded height," and it simply adds a further qualifier to help locate the region where David and his men were hiding in the Judean wilderness and a setting for his meeting with Jonathan. It is generally identified with Khirbet Khoreisa, about two miles south of Tell Ziph.

23:19. Hakilah/Jeshimon. The barren strip of land running parallel to the Dead Sea on the eastern edge of the Judean Wilderness was known as Jeshimon. Despite its arid nature, the ruggedness of the area provided many hiding places, such as the hill of Hakilah, for fugitives like David (see similar description in 26:1, 3).

23:24. wilderness of Maon in Arabah. David moves further south into the Judean Wilderness along the Dead Sea. The Arabah is simply a term for the entire Jordan Rift Valley and here is probably synonymous with the Judean Wilderness. Maon is probably to be identified with Khirbet Ma'in, eight miles south of Hebron and four and a half miles south of Tell Ziph.

23:29. En Gedi. The oasis of En Gedi lies midway down the Dead Sea and approximately thirty-five miles southeast of Jerusalem. Fed by a continuous spring, it is a splash of life and color in the midst of an otherwise barren landscape. It has served as a cultic site, military outpost and commercial center during its long history. David's choice of this area was probably based on the large number of nearby caves and the water supply. There are a number of fortresses from the period of the divided monarchy (eighth and seventh centuries) that have been discovered in this area. One is at the spring, while another is at the top of the cliff that offers a view of travelers for miles around.

24:1-22
Saul Spared by David

24:2. Crags of the Wild Goats. The name En Gedi means "spring of the young goat," and thus these crags probably take their name from the spring. Ibexes also live in these hills, adding one more possibility for the place name. However, it is a precarious region to take three thousand men on a search mission.

24:3. Saul's business in the cave. While the sheepfolds outside the cave suggested the presence of possible informants to question about the location of David, Saul's entering alone implies he simply planned to use its privacy to relieve his bowels.

24:4-5. significance of Saul's hem. Like the elaborately decorated hem on the high priest's garments (Ex 28:33-34), Saul's robe would also have had a distinctive fringe or design marking him as the king. It may have been specially dyed or contained a special stitching reserved only for the king's use, and it symbolized his power and authority. A hem impressed on a clay tablet is used to identify a prophet in the Mari texts. In Akkadian literature it was a sign of divorce for a husband to cut off the hem of his wife's robe. In diplomatic contexts it symbolized the breaking of an alliance.

24:6. the Lord's anointed. David's refusal to kill Saul when he had the opportunity (see also 26:8-11) is based on the king's status as the "Lord's anointed." He had been given his position by God and only God could take it from him. Political assassination is a very bad precedent for a claimant to a throne to employ (see the way in which it escalates in 1 Kings 15:25—16:27). Divine right to the throne could

serve as an extraordinary insurance policy for the king as long as the mystique of being the "Lord's anointed" was maintained. Thus David's refusal to act demonstrates his loyalty to God's original designation of Saul as king and also provides an argument against future attempts on his own life when he became king. The person of the king was typically seen as being under the protection of deity in the ancient Near East. This is reflected, for instance, in a Hittite blessing on the king that affirms that the storm god will destroy anyone threatening the person of the king.

24:14. dead dog. In Akkadian literature humility was often expressed by using terms of self-deprecation. Comparing oneself to a dead dog or a stray dog was one of the common options. Similar dog metaphors are used in the Amarna letters and the Lachish letters.

24:21. oath not to decimate descendants. It was the common practice in the ancient Near East that a king who did not come to the throne by inheritance would summarily execute the prior king's descendants in order to eliminate any potential competition or sedition. This political expediency, however, by wiping out the family line, was popularly thought to jeopardize the afterlife of those family members who had already died (for further information see comments on Num 3:12-13 and Josh 8:29).

24:22. stronghold. See comment on 22:4.

25:1-44
David Encounters Nabal and Abigail

25:1. wilderness of Maon. See the comment on 23:24.

25:2. Carmel. This town lies within the Judean Wilderness, about eight miles southeast of Hebron and a mile north of Maon. It was taken from the Amalekites by Saul in 15:12, and it is therefore not surprising that the people are inclined to be loyal to Saul (as suggested by Nabal's response to David in vv. 10-11).

25:3. Nabal. This personal name means "the fool." That is an unlikely name for a mother to give her son at birth and is more likely to be a name applied to the man by the biblical writers to indicate his role in the story. His foolishness is in stark contrast to the wisdom displayed by his wife Abigail.

25:7. protection of sheep. David implies in his message to Nabal that his group had voluntarily protected the owner's sheep from attacks by wild animals or raiders (see vv. 15-16). Now, at sheep shearing, a festival time when a count would be taken of the sheep and rewards would be given to the shepherds, David also asks for support for his men. Contracts between herdsmen and sheep owners during the early part of the second millennium have been found in Mesopotamia at the town of Larsa. Herdsmen would typically receive a fee or commission on the sheep and goats that were delivered safely at the shearing. David's men are claiming a portion of that compensation. It would usually include wool, dairy products or grain. Nabal spurned this request and insulted David instead.

25:18. provisions in Abigail's gift. Nabal had listed bread, water and meat as rewards for his servants (25:11), and now Abigail includes two hundred loaves, two skins of wine and five butchered sheep as part of her gift. This acknowledges the service David and his men had done in protecting Nabal's herds. In addition, as a sign of hospitality during a festival period, she also brings a bushel (five seahs) of roasted grain, one omer (two quarts) of raisins (following the preferred Septuagint reading), and two hundred pressed fig cakes. These latter items were stored food items and would serve David's company well.

25:23-31. persuasive oration in the ancient Near East. As is the case with Abigail's speech, persuasive oration generally appears in wisdom contexts. She suggests David disregard the words of fools (see Prov 26:2) in much the same way that Ptah-Hotep (2450 B.C.) and Amenemope (seventh century B.C.) do in Egyptian "instructions," and the seventh-century B.C. Assyrian sage Ahiqar does. They, like Abigail, also extol the virtues of loyalty and the obligations of rulers to their subjects. This latter trait is an integral part of one of the most famous pieces of persuasive oration in the ancient Near East, the Protests of the Eloquent Peasant from Middle Kingdom Egypt.

25:39-44. king's marriages as alliances. Diplomatic texts from throughout the ancient Near East contain marriage contracts that function as political alliances between countries. Zimri-Lim, the king of Mari during the eighteenth century B.C., successfully placed his daughters in the harems of nearby kingdoms and married several foreign wives himself to increase his power and the stability of his realm. In David's case, prior to becoming king of Israel, he made a series of marriages that strengthened his political and economic position. Thus the marriage to Saul's daughter Michal gave him connection to the royal family. His marriage to Abigail provided him with ties to the area around Hebron, and his marriage to Ahinoam of Jezreel established connections with

households in the vicinity of Megiddo and Beth Shan. This kinship network insured that David would have friendly voices in the council of elders from all over the country.

26:1-25
David's Second Chance to Kill Saul

26:1. locations. See the comments on 23:14 and 23:19.

26:8-11. the Lord's anointed. See the comment on 24:6.

26:11. spear and water jug. The spear was generally used by the infantrymen in the front ranks. This is hardly where one would expected to find a king. The fact that Saul always seems to have the spear near to hand (see for instance 18:10; 19:9; 2 Sam 1:6) suggests it may have been an insignia of his office. As a result, this may have been a ceremonial spear. It may also be significant that this is the same weapon he tried to kill David with in their early encounters. The jug or cruse may well have been one of the small disk-shaped vessels known from this period that featured two handles flanking the mouth so that they could be attached to a strap. Depriving a man of his water and weapon in this region would have constituted a threat to his life. David therefore demonstrated how Saul's life was in his hands.

26:19. forced to worship foreign gods. When exiled from their own country, fugitives were denied the opportunity to worship their god at familiar sacred sites. The only option for worship open to them was to serve the gods of other lands, adopting the ways of the people with which they were forced to dwell. Similar sentiments are expressed in the story of the Middle Kingdom Egyptian exile Sinuhe.

26:20. partridge of the mountains. Hunting partridges involved beating the bushes and chasing the birds until they were exhausted. This is an apt description of the manner in which Saul has been pursuing David. There is also a pun here based on the literal meaning of the Hebrew word for partridge, which is the "one who calls upon the mountain" (see Jer 17:11). David is doing this as he reproaches King Saul.

27:1-12
David as a Philistine Vassal

27:2-12. role as a Philistine mercenary. The use of mercenary troops was quite common in the ancient world (see Jer 46:20-21). Very often these men were political fugitives, like David, and their loyalty to their employer was based on their hatred of the ruler who had exiled them (many of the fifth-century B.C. Greek tyrants joined the Persian army after being expelled from their positions and fought against the Greeks at the Battle of Marathon). Thus Achish of Gath's misplaced trust of David is based on the known enmity between David and Saul, but it is reinforced by the amount of booty which David brings him from his raiding expeditions. David is using this opportunity to (1) escape Saul, (2) obtain wealth through raiding which he can use to ingratiate himself with the elders of Judah (30:26), (3) learn the military tactics and the iron technology of the Philistines and (4) eliminate some of Israel's enemies in his raids. By leaving no survivors, David eliminates any witnesses and thus maintains Achish's trust until the time when he will return to rule in Judah.

27:2-3. Gath. Although its exact location has not been firmly established, the current view places Gath at Tell es-Safi, five miles south of Tel Miqne-Ekron in the northern Shephelah. Its pre-Philistine existence is attested in the El Amarna letters and was traditionally tied to the Canaanite Anakim (see Josh 11:21). As one of the five principal Philistine city-states, Gath was the home of the giant warrior Goliath and one of the leaders in the campaign against Israel (see Judg 3:3).

27:2. Achish. This King Achish is not referred to in any extrabiblical sources, but the name Achish is attested as a Philistine royal name at a later date. Assyrian records of the seventh century list Ikausu, son of Padi, as the king of Ekron. Ikausu is the same as Achish, son of Padi, named on an inscription from the same time period found at Ekron (Tell Miqne).

27:6. Ziklag. The exact location of Ziklag is still in dispute. A number of sites have been suggested, but the two most likely are Tell esh-Shari'a (in the northwestern section of the Negev, about fifteen miles southeast of Gaza) and Tell es-Seba' (most often identified as the site of ancient Beersheba and four miles from the modern city; see comment on Gen 22:19). The dispute arises over possible breaks in occupation during the Iron Age (early monarchy) period at Tell esh-Shari'a and the likelihood that the original site of Beersheba was further west of Tell es-Seba'. While the occupation history of Tell es-Seba' generally matches the information we have on Ziklag, this identification would put Ziklag over thirty miles south of Gath. Both sites place David's stronghold in the Negev, where he could easily stage raids south in the Sinai or east into Edom and Midian. They would also be far enough from Philistine territory to allow him to operate without close scrutiny.

27:7. chronological note. This is the final period before David comes to the throne. His accession is usually dated about 1010 B.C.

27:8. Geshurites. These people lived in a region to the southeast of Philistia in the northern Sinai (see Josh 13:2). They are not to be confused with the inhabitants of Geshur in the southern Golan area of Bashan (Josh 13:11). That area would have been inaccessible to David's raiders. Presumably these southern Geshurites were allied with the Philistines and thus would have made appropriate targets for David's expeditions in the Negev.

27:8. Girzites. The Girzites only appear in this passage and are not mentioned in any other ancient source outside the Bible. Some variant readings identify the people referred to here as the Gezerites. The town of Gezer is ten to twelve miles northeast of Gath. This would seem to be an unlikely raiding area for David if Ziklag is twenty-five to thirty miles south of Gath.

27:8. Amalekites. See the comments on Deuteronomy 25:17-19.

27:8. Shur. The wilderness of Shur lay in the northern Sinai between Canaan and the northeastern border of Egypt (see comment on Ex 15:22). Pastoral nomadic tribes, such as the Geshurites and Amalekites, traditionally inhabited this region and used its arid environment as a defense.

27:10. Jerahmeelites. David's ambiguous response to Achish regarding his raids suggested he was looting villages in Judah. The Jerahmeelites were a Judahite clan associated with the area just to the south of Beersheba (see 30:29).

27:10. Kenites. See the comments on Numbers 24:21-22.

28:1-25

Saul and the Medium from Endor

28:2. David as personal bodyguard. As he was in Saul's service (22:14), David now is appointed as the head of the personal bodyguard of King Achish. This puts him in a difficult situation, since it almost assures that he will have to participate in the battle against Saul.

28:3. mediums and spiritists. For more information on divination as a whole, see the comments on Deuteronomy 18. The practitioners of spiritism and sorcery are condemned because of their association with Canaanite religion and because their "art" attempted to circumvent Yahweh by seeking knowledge and power from spirits. They represented a form of "popular religion." In this case the banned individuals participated in a form of divination employing ritual pits from which ancestral spirits could be raised to speak to the living about the future.

28:3. banning them. Saul's decision to ban mediums and spiritists from his realm would ordinarily be praised because of their close association with Canaanite worship practices. They functioned as conjurers of ancestral spirits who could speak of the future. Superstitions and the aura of the occult power made these individuals feared and often undesirable. Almost a millennium earlier King Gudea of Lagash had also banned mediums from his realm, so it is not an act connected solely to monotheism. In this instance Saul's ban is paralleled with the death of Samuel to demonstrate that he had no means at his disposal, whether legitimate or illegitimate, to divine God's will.

28:4. location of Philistine and Israelite camps. The eastern end of the Valley of Jezreel is about ten miles wide from north to south. The north end is blocked off by Mount Tabor, while the south end is blocked off by Mount Gilboa. The ten-mile stretch between the two is broken into two passes by the smaller Hill of Moreh. The town of Shunem where the Philistines make camp is on the southwest side of the Hill of Moreh just across the Harod Valley (the southern pass from the Valley of Jezreel to the city of Beth Shan) from Saul's camp at Mount Gilboa. The two camps are about five miles apart. Endor is located in the middle of the northern pass (between the Hill of Moreh and Mount Tabor), about six or seven miles north of the Israelite camp (about a two-hour trek). Saul would have proceeded around the eastern side of the Hill of Moreh and thus have avoided the Philistine camp. Note that Endor (Khirbet Safsafeh) is technically in the tribal territory of Manasseh, outside of the territory controlled by Saul (Josh 17:11). The fact that the battle takes place so far north of Philistia suggests that they were trying to cut the Galilee region off from Saul's kingdom. Saul's position takes advantage of the mountainous terrain and would favor his lightly armed forces.

28:6. means Saul used to seek information. Saul is rightly concerned about the upcoming battle with the massed forces of the five Philistine city-states. He first employs the usual divination methods to consult God and see if the Divine Warrior would give him a victory. These methods included incubation rituals in which the inquirer sleeps within a sanctuary or near a sacred object in order to receive a dream from a god (see comment on 3:3), the use of Urim to cast lots (see comment on Ex 28:30) and the visions of prophets (see Saul's previous association with prophets in 1 Sam 10:10-11). None of these inquiries was answered, and it is made clear that Saul is abandoned by God.

28:7. specialist Saul wanted to use. Since he had no other recourse to seek God's will about the coming battle, Saul broke his own law banning mediums and made a secret visit to the medium of Endor. She has established a reputation as one who could successfully consult ghosts and ancestral spirits. This specialist from Endor used a ritual pit to conjure up the spirits of the dead. Although the process is listed in Deuteronomy 18:10-11 as one of the "detestable acts" associated with Canaanite religion, the actual use of a pit is not mentioned in the Old Testament outside of the Endor episode. As in Hittite magic, the practitioner here is an "old woman." The pits were believed to be magical portals through which spirits could pass between the realms of the living and the dead. The practitioner was one who had special knowledge of the location of such a pit and who was familiar with the procedures necessary to summon the dead. There is no indication in these rituals that the practitioner was possessed by the spirit or that the spirit spoke through her, and so she was not a medium in the modern sense.

28:8-11. procedures for calling up spirits. Examples from Greek (Homer's *Odyssey*), Mesopotamian and, especially, Hittite literature provide the details: (1) done at night, (2) after the spot is divined a pit is dug with a special tool, (3) a food offering (bread, oil, honey) or the blood of a sacrificial animal is placed in the pit to attract spirits, (4) an invocation ritual, including the spirit's name, is chanted, and (5) the pit is covered to prevent spirits from escaping after the ritual is concluded. Both practitioner and client had roles to play in the procedure. The spirits who emerged were in human form and generally were able to communicate directly with the client. In Mesopotamian necromancy incantations, only the practitioner could see the spirit. This was accomplished through ritual ointments smeared on the face.

28:14. prophetic mantle. Since clothing is often a status marker in the ancient world (see Joseph's various changes of clothing in Genesis 37, 39—41), it may be expected that prophets were distinguished by a particular garment. The spirit of Samuel is recognized by his robe (see Elijah's mantle in 1 Kings

19:19 and 2 Kings 2:8, 13-14).

28:8-20. beliefs about afterlife. The spirits of the dead were believed to descend to the underworld known as Sheol. This was a nebulous region of continued existence, but it is not distinguished as a place of reward or punishment.

28:8-11. consulting dead in ancient Near East. Because of a well-developed ancestor cult that pervaded much of the ancient Near East (perhaps reflected in the emphasis on the role of the male heir to care for the father's shrine in Ugaritic documents), the dead were considered to have some power to affect the living. It was believed that if libations were poured out on behalf of dead ancestors, their spirits would offer protection and help to those still living. In Babylon the disembodied spirit (*utukki*) or the ghost (*etemmu*) could become very dangerous if not cared for and often were the objects of incantations. Proper care for the dead would begin with proper burial and would continue with ongoing gifts and honor of the memory and name of the deceased. The firstborn was responsible for maintaining this ancestor worship and therefore inherited the family gods (often images of deceased ancestors). Such care would have been based on a belief, as seen in Saul's consultation of the medium of Endor, that the spirits of the dead could communicate and had information on the future that could be of use to the living. These spirits were consulted through the efforts of priests, mediums and necromancers. This could be a dangerous practice since some spirits were considered demons and could cause great harm. While it is difficult to totally reconstruct Israelite beliefs about deceased ancestors and the afterlife, it seems possible that prior to the exile there existed a cult of the dead or ancestral worship. This is suggested by archaeological remains: (1) utensils, bowls and implements for eating and drinking found in Iron Age tombs in Israel, (2) references to deposits of food and drink offerings for the dead (see Deut 26:14; Ps 106:28) and (3) the importance placed on family tombs (see the ancestral tomb for Abraham and his descendants at Hebron) and mourning rituals performed at these tombs (see Is 57:7-8; Jer 16:5-7). The local and family ancestral cults were condemned by the prophets and the law.

28:24. meal prepared for Saul. There are elements of hospitality customs in the offering of a meal to Saul by the woman of Endor. Like Abraham, she provides a costly meal by slaughtering a calf and making bread (see Gen 18:6-7). It is unlikely that the woman owned more than this one animal, and so she is truly doing Saul great honor. Saul's reluctance to accept her invitation may be tied to her profession or her association with other gods. It may also be a sign of his depression over Samuel's words of doom. His eventual acceptance follows the pattern of indecisiveness and contradictory behavior so often found in his career. There is also a sense of resignation in eating a "last meal."

29:1-11
David's Help Rejected by Philistines

29:1. Aphek/spring in Jezreel. There are a number of different sites named Aphek in various parts of Canaan. This one is qualified by its identification with a spring in the Jezreel Valley. Most likely this Aphek is in the southern Sharon plain and specifically the site of Ras el-'Ain at the source of the Yarkon River. This then suggests that the Philistines first mustered their troops at Aphek (as they did prior to the Battle of Ebenezer in 4:1) and then moved up thirty-five or forty miles into the Jezreel to confront Saul. References in Josephus connect this Aphek with Antipatris (see Acts 23:31), twenty-six miles south of Caesarea Maritima.

29:3. Hebrews. The Israelites are referred to repeatedly by the Philistines as Hebrews (see comment on Gen 14:13). This may have been a generic term, as is the case with Habiru and Apiru in Akkadian and Egyptian texts, or a pejorative label applied to a people without leadership or a defined political state. David's role as a mercenary fits well with the term Habiru in the El Amarna texts.

29:5. David his tens of thousands. This is the third time this chant has been quoted in the text (see 1 Sam 18:7; 21:12). Originally it served as a mark of distinction for David and a source of Saul's jealousy and hatred toward him. In the episodes involving the Philistines, the chant is used as a reminder and a warning that David cannot be trusted to serve Achish loyally. In this instance it provides David with a plausible excuse not to participate in the final battle against the "Lord's anointed."

30:1-31
Disaster at Ziklag and Revenge on the Amalekites

30:1. distance from Aphek to Ziklag. The distance from the Sharon Plain to the southern Shephelah where Ziklag was located is approximately fifty miles. It would not be unusual for an armed group and their auxiliaries to take three days to travel this distance.

30:1. Amalekites. One of the curiosities of the Amalekites is that they always seem to be present to cause trouble no matter how many times the Israelites defeat them (see Ex 17:8-16; 1 Sam 15:1-9). In this case the Amalekites respond to David's raiding of their villages (1 Sam 27:8), taking advantage of David's presence at Aphek. The raid is immediately followed up by David's devastating defeat of the Amalekites and the rescue of his family and property. In this way the narrative demonstrates that David was nowhere nearby when Saul was killed. He is acting the role of hero, defeating Israel's enemies and saving his people from harm, while Saul is being defeated by the Philistines at Gilboa.

30:7-8. oracular use of Ephod. David's question is typical of oracular events in which a yes or no response is requested. For other examples of using the ephod for this purpose, see the comments on Judges 8:24-27 and 1 Samuel 23:9-12.

30:9. Besor Ravine. This was a deep wadi bed (three to four hundred feet wide) whose steep sides would have required a great deal of agility and energy to traverse. It is located in the western Negev and served, along with the Wadi Gerar, as the southern border of Canaan.

30:11-13. Egyptian slave. In their effort to escape, the Amalekite raiders had abandoned a sick Egyptian slave. David's hospitality to this man, giving him food, water and raisin cakes, is reminiscent of Abigail's offering to David in 1 Samuel 25:18. It once again displays David's adherence to traditional values and also provides him with the military intelligence his small force of four hundred men will need to defeat the much larger force of Amalekites.

30:14. Kerethites. These people were associated with the Philistines and the Pelethites, and their name suggests a Cretan origin. Their territory in the Negev probably adjoined that of Ziklag and Judah.

30:14. land of Caleb. The allotment given to Caleb and his family was in the area around Hebron and Debir (see Josh 14:6-15; 15:13-19) in southern Canaan. In later periods this was in fact within the territory of Judah (Josh 15:1-12).

30:17. fleeing on camels. For the Amalekites living in the steppe areas of the Negev and northern Sinai, the camel would have been a perfect beast of burden and swift form of transportation for raiding. In this case, they also served to provide a quick getaway for the remnant of the Amalekite band. For more information see the comment on Judges 6:5.

30:18-25. division of spoil. See the comment on Deuteronomy 20:10-15 for a discussion of the protocol associated with the division of spoils following a battle. David adhered to the sacred code that auxiliary troops, left to guard a fortress or the baggage train, should also share equally in the spoil. The two hundred men who were too exhausted after traveling from Aphek to continue in pursuit of the Amalekites still served as a rear guard in case David was forced to flee and thus deserved their share.

30:26. elders of Judah. David's generosity in sending a portion of the loot he had taken from the Amalekites has real political implications. Being able to distribute wealth is a sign of power in the Near East. It marks these local elders as David's clients, and it will be expected that they will support him in his bid for the kingship (see 2 Sam 2:4).

30:27-31. towns. The towns in addition to Hebron where David sent portions of his spoils include Bethel (Khirbet el-Qaryatein), just north of Arad (Josh 19:4); Beth Zur (Khirbet et-Tubeiqah), four miles north of Hebron and associated with Caleb (Josh 15:58); Ramoth Negev (possibly Bir Rakhmeh; named Baalath Beer in Josh 19:8), nineteen miles southeast of Beersheba; Jattir (Khirbet 'Attir), a Levitical city twelve miles southwest of Hebron (Josh 21:14); Aroer (modern 'Ar'arah), twelve miles southeast of Beersheba (Josh 15:22); Siphmoth, an unknown site; Eshtemoa (es-Semu), ten miles southwest of Hebron (Josh 15:50); Carmel (Tell el-Kirmil), seven miles south of Hebron (1 Sam 15:12); Hormah, possibly Khirbet el-Meshash, seven miles east of Beersheba (Josh 15:30); Bor Ashan (Khirbet 'Asan), just northwest of Beersheba and a Levitical city of Judah (Josh 19:7); and Ether (NIV: Athach; Khirbet el-'Ater) in the Shephelah, about fifteen miles northwest of Hebron. Most of these sites are in the area known as the hill country of Judah, though a few are further south in the Negev.

31:1-13
The Death of Saul

31:1. Mount Gilboa. See comment on 1 Samuel 28:4 for the position of the Philistine and Israelite forces within the Valley of Jezreel (see also 1 Chron 10:1-12). The fact that so many of Saul's men and three of his sons are slain on the slopes of Mount Gilboa demonstrates that his army was quickly forced to flee before superior Philistine tactics. They may have been seeking to restore order by regaining the high ground in the battle, but without the leadership of Saul's sons they were quickly cut down and Saul was faced with capture.

31:3-5. Saul's prospects if captured alive. In this period it was common for captured kings to be mutilated and subjected to a life of humiliation. Putting out the eyes or cutting off the thumbs and big toes were just a few of the procedures used. As a sign of their ignominy, they were doomed to spend miserable years begging and fighting for scraps under the triumphant king's table (see comments on Judg 1:6-7), or displayed in public places for whatever abuse passersby might invent. Torturous practices were continued by the Babylonians, Assyrians and Persians, and the literature is full of the gruesome acts performed on captured enemies. Other examples of a king requesting his armor-bearer to kill him exist in Assyrian records. The Elamite king and his armor-bearer stab each other simultaneously.

31:9. cutting off the head. A king's head was a treasured prize used as a means of boasting of one's conquests. Assyrian king Ashurbanipal was reported to have dined with his queen in the garden with the head of the king of Elam on display in a nearby tree. He describes the cutting off of the head as "making him more dead than before."

31:10. armor placed in temple. In addition to stripping the bodies of the slain for loot, Saul's armor (symbol of his position as king and well known to the enemy—see 1 Sam 17:38) was taken as a trophy in much the same way that Goliath's sword (1 Sam 17:54) and the ark of the covenant (1 Sam 5:2) were taken and displayed in a temple. In this way the gods of the Philistines were honored, and Saul and his God were graphically demonstrated to be defeated. See the comment on Judges 2:13 for the name Ashtoreths.

31:10. exposing the corpse. To dismember the body of Saul and leave it unburied was the height of disgrace and shame for the victim and the family/nation. Improper burial was popularly thought to jeopardize an individual's afterlife (for further information see comment on 1 Kings 16:4). The practice of impaling the bodies of their defeated enemies was commonly used by armies in the ancient Near East. For instance, the Assyrians considered it a psychological ploy and a terror tactic (as depicted on the walls of their royal palaces).

31:10-12. Beth Shan. In this period Beth Shan (Tell el-Husn) was either controlled by the Philistines or allied with them. Since it lies in a commanding position in the Jezreel Valley and is a very tall mound, it would be a perfect place to display Saul's dismembered body.

The ten-acre mound stands at the eastern end of the Jezreel Valley and guards that important trade route's entrance into the Jordan Valley. It continues as an independent Canaanite enclave into the monarchy period (1 Sam 31:10-12) but was incorporated into Solomon's administrative districts (1 Kings 4:12). This is a double site, with a Roman-Byzantine city (Scythopolis) built at the base of the tell. Archaeological investigations have shown almost continuous occupation of the site since Chalcolithic times (4500-3300 B.C.). The water supply (Wadi Jalud), arable land and strategic location have insured that its population prospered, generally under Egyptian rule (starting with Thutmose III in the sixteenth century) and later under the Sea Peoples and Israelites. From this period archaeologists found remains of twin temples that some identify as the temples of Astarte mentioned here and the temple of Dagon (see 1 Chron 10:10).

31:11-12. Jabesh Gilead. See the comment on 11:1 for the discussion of Saul's original connection with this Transjordanian city. Their rescue of Saul's body from Beth Shan reflects the obligation they felt because of his efforts to save their city from the besieging Ammonites (1 Samuel 11).

31:12. journey from Jabesh Gilead to Beth Shan. Although the exact location of Jabesh Gilead is unknown, it must have been along the Wadi el-Yabis in the northern Gileadite hill country. Tell Maqlub, thirteen miles from Beth Shan, is a likely candidate.

31:12. cremation. Cremation is not sanctioned as a burial rite elsewhere in the Bible (see Lev 20:14; Josh 7:25 for the use of burning as capital punishment). It is possible that the advanced state of deterioration and decay required extreme measure to purify the body. No embalming techniques would have been effective. The burning of the bodies of heroes in the *Iliad* might suggest a similar ritual honoring Saul. The only other peoples in the ancient Near East known to practice cremation were the Hurrians of Mitanni and the Hittites (both mid-second millennium).

31:13. tamarisk tree at Jabesh. A final ironic note in the Saul narrative has him buried beneath a tamarisk tree. He is portrayed as assembling his troops and exercising his power as king under or near a tamarisk tree in 1 Samuel 22:6. His grave is marked by this simple desert growth rather than a palace, capital city or kingdom. The tamarisk grows in sandy soil. It is deciduous and may reach over twenty feet in height, with small leaves that excrete salt. Its bark is used for tanning and its wood for building and making charcoal. Bedouin commonly plant this hearty tree for its shade and the branches which provide grazing for animals. In Mesopotamian incantations, the tamarisk was a holy tree with purifying qualities. Images were made from its wood and it was at times connected with cosmic stability.

---

2 SAMUEL

1:1-16
News of Saul's Death

1:1. chronology. The year is approximately 1010 B.C. This date can be arrived at by calculating back from more certain points in time later in the monarchy period.

1:1. Ziklag. Ziklag has not been identified with any certainty. For discussion of the possibilities see comment on 1 Samuel 27:6.

1:2. dust on head. The practice of putting dirt, dust or ashes on one's head was a typical sign of mourning throughout the Old Testament and into the New Testament period. It is a practice also known from Mesopotamia and Canaan. Many mourning rites function as a means for the living to identify with the dead. It is easy to see how dust on the head would be a symbolic representation of burial.

1:2. reverential prostration. The standard method of demonstrating obeisance in the ancient Near East was to bow to the ground. Egyptian tomb art is filled with examples of servants and royal officials prostrating themselves before the pharaoh. In the El Amarna tablets (fourteenth century B.C.) the format of each letter contains a greeting, followed by a set formula of honoring the pharaoh by bowing seven times forward and backwards.

1:2. news dissemination. The normal official means of spreading news was through the use of couriers. Nevertheless couriers would have only been dispatched to certain key locations. Since the administration had been nearly wiped out and the rest were in flight or in hiding, there were likely few if any official couriers to bring word of the results of the battle at Gilboa, especially as far away as Ziklag, some seventy-five or eighty miles south of the scene of battle. Other news carriers would be soldiers returning from battle or merchants traveling from city to city. In this case, however, it is evident that the Amalekite sought David out, expecting to gain favor.

1:6. leaning on his spear. The spear has been an important symbol of Saul, from use as a weapon against David (1 Sam 18:10-11) to an identifying emblem (1 Sam 26:11) to a crutch as he faces death.

1:8. Amalekite. See comment on Deuteronomy 25:17-19. Since it was the Amalekites who had just recently been responsible for the raid on David's town, Ziklag (see comment on 1 Sam 30:1), this man is already in jeopardy, and his message is not likely to be given any credibility.

1:9. Saul's request. Death is imminent and preferable to the alternative (see comment on 1 Sam 31:3-5). Saul's request reflects a desire to end his life with as little pain as possible.

1:10. crown and armband. The headwear mentioned here would more accurately be rendered "diadem," referring to an object hung at the forehead or on the front of a headpiece. It often is a symbol of authority. As early as the Sumerian period the diadem is one of the insignias of royal power bestowed on the king by the god Anu. Perhaps the best-known example of this in the ancient world is the serpent (uraeus) on the front of a pharaoh's crown, which was believed to be a protective device. In the descriptions of Israel's high priest's garments the diadem is generally associated with a "golden plate" (NIV; see comment on Lev 8:9). The armband is not referred to in any other Old Testament passages. Armbands were a frequent adornment in the first millennium. The earliest examples found by archaeologists in Israel date to the eleventh century. Armbands and a diadem are mentioned in a list of jewelry that the Assyrian king Sennacherib gave to his son (and successor) Esarhaddon.

1:11. tearing clothes as sign of mourning. Along with placing ashes in the hair, the tearing of clothing was a common form of mourning in the ancient Near East. One example outside the Bible is found in the Ugaritic Epic of Aqhat (c. 1600 B.C.), in which the sister of the hero tears her father's garment as she foretells a coming drought. Such an act often implied grief over the death of a relative, friend or prominent individual.

1:12. mourning rituals. Many mourning rituals find their origin in (1) identifying with the dead, (2) providing something for the dead or

(3) protecting the living from the dead. Yet it is not always possible to trace back and discover how these values may have been reflected in any particular ritual. Weeping, wailing and lamenting were important in the funeral rites of most peoples of the ancient Near East. Fasting, tearing clothes and setting aside regular clothes were all ways of expressing grief.

1:15. David's order. The execution of the Amalekite has many complex elements linked to it. As already mentioned, the fact that he was an Amalekite put him in grave jeopardy. Second, David had on two other occasions refused to take Saul's life because of his respect for Saul's status as being the anointed by God, and he would expect no less from others. Third, if he received the actions of the Amalekite as having been done in his service, he would be subject to the accusation that he had commissioned an agent to execute Saul. It was important for him to distance himself from the actual killing of Saul, even if it could be justified as a mercy killing.

1:17-27
David's Elegy for Saul and Jonathan

1:17. elegies. Examples of funeral laments have been found in the ancient Near Eastern literatures. Perhaps best known is Gilgamesh's lament for his deceased friend Enkidu in tablet eight of the Gilgamesh Epic. This calls on others to share in the mourning and eulogizes the good qualities and heroic deeds of the deceased.

1:18. Book of Jashar. It is inferred that the Book of Jashar contained ancient poetic accounts of heroic deeds (the only other reference to it is in Josh 10:13). It has not been preserved. The title *Jashar* could be the adjective "upright" or a form of the Hebrew verb "sing."

1:20. Gath, Ashkelon. Gath and Ashkelon were two of the five principal cities of the Philistines. For more information about them see comments on 1 Samuel 5:8 and Judges 14:19 respectively.

1:20. uncircumcised. Circumcision was practiced by many different peoples in the ancient Near East (see comment on Gen 17:9-14) but not by the Philistines. The comment here has little to do with physical attributes or sociological practices, but is an ethnic designation that for the Israelites is a sign of the covenant.

1:21. curse on Gilboa. The curse focuses on the fertility of the area. It is similar to curses such as that found in the Atrahasis Epic that are intended to result in famine. By becoming a place of death (dry, unproductive fields), it would serve as a memorial to the deaths that had occurred there.

1:21. shield rubbed with oil. Israelite shields of this period were made of wood with leather stretched over the surface. They were either round or rectangular with rounded top. Oil was used to wipe the blood off after a battle and to treat the leather so it remained pliable.

1:24. fine clothing. The clothing provided for the women of Israel simply reflects an improvement in the standard of living during the reign of Saul. Successful policing of the trade routes could increase merchant activity, which in turn made imports more accessible and provided outlets for exporting local goods.

2:1-7
David Made King

2:1. oracular inquiry. From chapter 23 through the end of 1 Samuel, David is making oracular inquiries of the Lord by means of the ephod under the guidance of Abiathar the priest. It is likely that is also what is happening here. In an oracular inquiry a yes-no question was posed to the deity, and a binary mechanism was used to determine what the answer was. The normative means laid out for this process in Exodus was the Urim and Thummim (which were kept in a pouch in the ephod).

2:1. Hebron. Hebron was centrally located in the hill country of Judah and was one of the most important towns in the region. It is located about twenty miles south of Jerusalem. This twelve-acre site, occupied about 1200 B.C., was very attractive because there are more than two dozen springs in the area. About the time of David the fortifications of the city were improved and expanded. It served as David's capital for seven years and enjoyed its greatest prominence during this period.

2:4. tribal king. In a previous attempt at kingship the process was initiated on the tribal level (see Judg 9). Since the Philistines had most likely overrun the central part of the land as a result of the battle at Gilboa (1 Sam 31), only a few of the tribes may have had the freedom to participate in designating a new king. It must also be remembered that tribal autonomy had a long history among the Israelites, and a city-state form of government had characterized the previous Canaanite residents of the region. Finally, with three of Saul's sons having been killed along with him, there was no clear information concerning succession to the throne, even if the tribal leaders were content with Saul's line and the Philistines would have allowed it. All of this makes the procedure of a tribe designating a king very logical. **2:5-7. procuring support.** The town of Jabesh Gilead in Transjordan would have still been free of Philistine control. It represented one of the strategic constituencies of Saul because of the deliverance that he had provided them (1 Sam 11). If the leaders of this pro-Saul enclave could be persuaded to acknowledge David, they would serve as bellwether for many of the other Transjordan cities and perhaps others from the northern regions. David suggests to them that they have repaid Saul in providing him proper burial—he is gone and there is no loyalty still due him or his family. David is just as willing to provide for their defense as Saul had been.

2:8—3:5
Conflict Between the Houses of David and Saul

2:8. Mahanaim. Besides serving as an administrative center for the government of Saul's son, this is where David sets up headquarters when he has to flee from Absalom (17:27). The town is also mentioned as one destroyed by Pharaoh Shishak's invasion during the time of Solomon's son. While it is clear that Mahanaim is in the Transjordan region, the precise location is unknown. The most common identification today is with Tell edh-Dhahab el-Gharbi on the northern bank of the Jabbok. There have been no excavations at the site, but surface surveys confirm that it was occupied during this period.

2:9. political control of Saul's house. Abner had been Saul's commander in chief and was his cousin. Rather than take the throne for himself, he procured it for one of Saul's surviving sons, Ish-Bosheth. He appears to have retained the support of a number of the northern tribes. Though Ish-Bosheth was king, the text gives the impression that Abner was in control. It was not that unusual for a military strongman to sponsor a weak heir to the throne. In earlier Egyptian history at the end of the Eighteenth Dynasty, Ay, a military commander (and perhaps father-in-law) of Akhenaten is the principal sponsor and advisor of young Tutankhamun son-in-law of Akhenaten.

2:12. Gibeon. The city of Gibeon is usually identified with the modern el-Jib, located six miles northwest of Jerusalem and seven miles southwest of Ai. The excavations there have discovered a double water system constructed

as early as the Judges period. The earlier of the two systems involved cutting straight down through the limestone some thirty-five feet (descended by a stairway spiraling down the wall) to a tunnel, allowing the inhabitants of the city to have access to spring waters at the base if the mound was besieged. A second, later system provided a stepped tunnel leading to another (more reliable) spring. This water system is strong evidence that the site is Gibeon because of the well-known "pool of Gibeon" mentioned here. The identification is further confirmed by jar handles found at the site with the city's name inscribed on them (although it should be noted that jar handles with other cities' names stamped on them were found as well, explained by the city's major industry: wine export).

2:12-13. reason for the battle. Gibeon was a principal city in the region that had been overrun by the Philistines and presumably was still under Philistine control. It is therefore difficult to imagine that either army would be free to initiate military action against the other in Philistine territory. More likely is the possibility that Abner is on his way down to make preliminary arrangements to transfer his support to David. Natural caution would lead David to dispatch a military escort since Abner was not foolish enough to come without his own military entourage. Joab intercepts Abner at Gibeon, and they decide to be entertained by a gladiatorial contest between some of the trainees or mercenaries. Though bloodshed was probably expected in these "games," tempers flare and a full-blown skirmish explodes.

2:13. pool of Gibeon. The pool of Gibeon was a well-known water system—a model of modern engineering. The builders tunneled down through the limestone about thirty-five feet, making the hole almost forty feet wide. Steps were carved into the side spiraling down to the bottom of this pool where a straight set of stone steps descended another forty-five feet through a tunnel to reach the water table (seventy-nine steps in all). This had been built to provide the inhabitants of the city with a secure water supply inside the walls during time of siege. It has been estimated that about three thousand tons of rock would have been removed to accomplish this engineering feat. Only later was a tunnel cut to the spring outside the city.

2:14-16. individual bouts. At times individual combat was used, viewing the individuals as representatives of their respective armies so that the divine will could be expressed (as in the fight between David and Goliath). It is unlikely that this is the case here because there are twelve pairs (not just one) and because the intent is cited as entertainment. It must be noted, however, that battle is at times portrayed as a festival (as early as Sargon and, closer to this time, in the Tukulti-Ninurta Epic). The NIV translation "fight hand to hand" obscures the fact that this is merely an exhibition. Examples of individual combat are known in Egypt on the Beni Hasan wall painting (early second millennium) and in the Story of Sinuhe. It is likewise depicted on a Canaanite vase from the first half of the second millennium. Nearer in time, examples are known from Mycenaean Greece and from Hittite literature. A relief from the tenth century found at Tell Halaf depicts two combatants grabbing at one another's heads and thrusting with short swords.

2:16. daggers. The weapons used by the combatants are described by the Hebrew word that is typically translated "sword." It can be used for shorter two-edged swords (usually less than sixteen inches) or longer one-edged swords. The context here would demand the former since the combatants are in close quarters and are stabbing one another.

2:21. stripping of weapons. The plunder from personal combat was the possessions of the slain. The rank or status of a warrior would be reflected in clothing, armor or the quality of the weapons. These would become trophies and status symbols for the victor. Asahel is unwilling to settle for any soldier's gear—he wants the commander's.

2:23. butt of the spear. Spears often were made with a metal casing on the butt end that was not honed to a point but was tapered down to a sharp edge. This could be used as a goad or to stick the spear in the ground. Many of these metal ends have been found in excavations and are portrayed on wall paintings.

2:24. geography. The place names mentioned in verse 24 cannot be identified with any confidence. It is likely that the "way to the wasteland of Gibeon" runs northeast toward the Jordan valley. Ammah and Giah are unknown. There is a hill rising out of the fertile valley around Gibeon on the way toward Geba that may be identified as Ammah.

2:29. Abner's itinerary. The Arabah refers to the Jordan rift valley. Abner would have descended into it through the Micmash pass (see comment on 1 Sam 10:5) toward the ford at Adam (see comment on Josh 2:7). Bithron may not even be a place name, and if it is, it remains unidentified.

2:31. buried in father's tomb. Iron Age burial practices featured multiple burials in cave tombs. The body was laid out on its back with personal objects arranged around it.

3:6-39
Abner's Defection and Execution

3:7. sleeping with concubine. Concubines are women without dowry who include among their duties providing children to the family. In the royal household they may represent minor political alliances. Since a concubine has been a sexual partner, a son who used his father's concubine was not only viewed as incestuous but was seen as attempting to usurp the authority of the family patriarch. In a similar way a successor to the throne at times sought to expropriate the authority of his predecessor by taking over his concubines. Israel was a tribal society in transition to a monarchy. The network of support for a king would have been found in the powerful clans and families. Acquiring concubines and wives would therefore be the mechanism for building up the backing of each local area. Support might also be found in wealthy merchants, military leaders or even in priestly families.

3:8. dog's head. This expression is not used anywhere else in the Old Testament. See comment on 1 Samuel 24:14 for information concerning self-deprecation using dog metaphors.

3:9. curse formula. This formula is common in curses in Samuel and Kings and is usually found in the mouth of royal figures. An exception is Ruth's use of this same formula in Ruth 1:17. The formula is also known from Alalakh and Mari. Abner has not specified what it is that God will do. Since this oath is sometimes associated with rituals in which animals are mutilated, it is assumed that the speaker calls down similar mutilation on himself.

3:10. transfer of kingdom by Abner. As mentioned in the comment on 2:9, Abner most likely held the reins of power in the provisional government for which Ish-Bosheth was the figurehead. If the military was loyal to Abner, his defection would leave Ish-Bosheth virtually unprotected. Abner would probably likewise succeed in bringing with him the allegiance of most of the northern tribes that had remained faithful to Saul's family.

3:13-14. Michal's status. As indicated in the comment on 3:7 above, royal harems were the accepted means of establishing a support base both nationally and internationally. Michal, the daughter of Saul, would have represented a certain amount of legitimation for David as he was attempting to lay hold of Saul's kingdom. Ancient law (evidenced in Hammurabi,

Eshnunna and the Middle Assyrian Laws) provides that a man who has been driven from his home by force may lay claim to his wife when he returns. He would retain this right even if she has remarried (often necessary for support) and had children.

3:14. one hundred foreskins. This was the bride price paid by David for Michal (see comment on 1 Sam 18:25). The accomplishment of killing one hundred Philistines would have identified David as a significant military ally meriting marriage into the royal family.

3:17-19. Abner's diplomacy. Abner is now functioning as an agent for David's kingdom. He is not only planning his own defection but intends to bring the northern tribes with him. Tribal decisions were made by the elders who are called together. It is strategic for him to speak to the Benjaminites personally and individually, both because he is a prominent leader in the tribe of Benjamin, and, even more importantly, because Saul was from the tribe of Benjamin, so they would be the most loyal to Saul's descendants.

3:20-21. agreement between Abner and David. It was typical of important transactions that they be sealed with a feast shared between the parties to celebrate the legal arrangements that have been concluded. The twenty men with Abner may be important representatives of the powerful factions in Israel as well as a small military entourage of high ranking officers.

3:22. raid with plunder. Most armies, whether made up of mercenaries, conscripts or professional members of a standing army, considered plunder to be part of the pay of being a soldier (much like a waitress would consider tips). Some raids were carried out with military objectives in mind (expansion, control of trade routes, etc.), but others would be intended to pester an enemy and, at the same time, provide extra pay for the soldiers. Since David had little means to finance an administration or military, plunder was probably the sole source of compensation for the army.

3:26. well of Sirah. This oasis is generally and traditionally located about two miles north of Hebron.

3:29. curse on Joab's house. The curse pronounced by David is wide-ranging. The first category refers to the most serious and humiliating forms of physical disease (for more details on these see comments on Lev 13). The second is the most obscure. The word the NIV translates "crutch" has been now identified from Ugaritic and Akkadian as the word for "spindle" or "distaff." The phrase used here was the common description of a woman in-

volved in menial tasks. A Hittite oath of a soldier, if broken, would result in the loss of manhood. The oath describes this penalty in terms of the violator holding the spindle and mirror. This second curse then threatens Joab's house with decreased virility. The third curse speaks of violent death and the fourth of suffering want or famine.

3:31. mourning rites. See comment on 1:12.

4:1-12
Assassination of Ish-Bosheth

4:3. Beeroth and Gittaim. Beeroth is generally looked for north of Kephireh toward the Bethel/Ai area, perhaps at el-Bireh or Nebi Samwil. It was one of the Hivite cities of Gibeon that deceived Joshua (see Josh 9). This verse tells us that the Hivite population fled to Gittaim (specific location unknown), apparently leaving Benjaminites as the sole population in Beeroth.

4:4. Mephibosheth's injury. Although the biblical text does not clarify the details, it is generally believed that the battle at Mount Gilboa in which Saul was killed led to Philistine control of the entire central region. If that is true, it is likely that the Philistines would have sacked Saul's capital at Gibeah. Such circumstances would explain the frantic flight of Saul's household and the subsequent injury of Mephibosheth. A neck or spine injury could have made Mephibosheth a paraplegic, but it need not have been so extensive as that. Broken legs or ankles improperly set or poorly treated could likewise lame him. Splinting to set bones was a practice known in the ancient world, but compound fractures were often considered hopeless.

4:5. noonday rest. In the semiarid climate of the Near East it is common for the hottest hours of the day (after lunch) to be set aside for rest or napping.

4:6. wheat in the king's house. Though it would not be difficult to document the presence of storehouses in proximity to royal quarters, there is a persuasive textual variant at this point in the text that makes reference to a guard (female) who has fallen asleep because she had tired herself out gathering wheat.

4:12. mutilation and exposure. To dismember the bodies of the assassins and leave them unburied is the height of disgrace and shame for the victim and the family. Improper burial was popularly thought to jeopardize an individual's afterlife (for further information see comments on Num 3:12-13 and Josh 8:29). Public display of enemies' corpses can be seen in the practice of impaling the bodies on a pike, which the Assyrians used as a psychological ploy and a terror tactic (as depicted on the walls of their royal palaces). The cutting off of the hands and feet was probably understood to extend their pain and suffering into the afterlife, but there is not enough attestation of the practice or the thought behind it to recover the reason with confidence.

5:1-25
David's Victories

5:1. flesh and blood. The actual Hebrew idiom is "bone and flesh," but it expressed the same concept as our "flesh and blood" does. Affirmation of their kinship is offered as a basis for political alliance. Compare the similar context in Judges 9:2.

5:3. role of the elders. The elders here are the clan leaders of Israel. In the absence of a king or other dominant leader, the tribes relied on the collective assembly of the tribal elders. They administered justice in the village culture and served as representatives for the people at major gatherings. The people would look for the endorsement of David by the elders before they would accept his leadership.

5:3. compact with elders. As in 2:4 where an agreement was reached with the leaders of Judah, here all the tribes subscribe to a formal declaration of David's kingship. This would likely have included a written ratification document such as that drawn up with Saul in 1 Samuel 10:25.

5:3. anointed. David had been anointed by the leaders of Judah in 2:4. Anointing designated a change in status and was symbolic of their affirmation of his kingship. For more information on the practice of anointing see comment on 1 Samuel 16:1.

5:4-5. chronology. David's reign is generally believed to take up the first third of the tenth century B.C. (about 1010-970). Forty can often be a round number, but the breakdown in verse five suggests that it should be taken as a precise reckoning.

5:6. Jerusalem. The city is strategically located along an east-west road that runs from the fords of the Jordan near Jericho to the coastal highway. It is also by the most significant north-south road that runs through the hill country from Beersheba to Beth Shan. Its location is also strategic because of its position by the border between Judah and Benjamin. The deep valleys on the east and west of the ridge and the reliable water supply found at the Gihon spring combined to make the location defensible and desirable. The earliest reference

to Jerusalem is in the Egyptian execration texts from early in the second millennium B.C., where its kings are named Yaqirammu and Shayzanu. The next reference is found in six letters in the Amarna texts from Abdi-Heba, king of Jerusalem, to the pharaoh requesting military support. Jerusalem was one of the key cities in the region and in the Amarna period was competing with Shechem for control of the hill country. Jerusalem was defeated by the Israelite armies at the time of the conquest, but the inhabitants had not been driven out and it had not been occupied by the Israelites (Judg 1:21). The city of Jerusalem in this period occupied only the north-south ridge covering about ten acres that runs south of the modern city walls. The top of the ridge is only about four hundred feet wide and about fifteen hundred feet long. The population would not have exceeded one thousand. The Canaanite city was built on an artificial platform that was supported by a series of terraces. Archaeologists have uncovered a stepped stone structure over fifty feet tall at the northeast corner of this ridge. This was most likely the platform for the Jebusite citadel referred to in verse 7, and was enhanced by David for use as the foundation of his palace built in verse 11. The city was surrounded by a ten-foot-thick wall that had first been built over eight hundred years earlier. There is little else that archaeologists have found in the city that is attributable to the time of David.

5:6. Jebusites. First mentioned as descendants of Canaan (Gen 10:16), the Jebusites were probably non-Semitic peoples, related to the Hittites or Hurrians, who moved into this region during the early second millennium. They inhabited the hill country along the southern border with Benjamin (Josh 15:8) and the city of Jebus (Josh 15:63; 2 Sam 5:6). After David captured Jerusalem, the Jebusites apparently were either assimilated or were enslaved and eventually lost their ethnic identity (2 Sam 5:6-9).

5:6. lame and blind. There has been some suggestion that this was a magical tactic involving a hex. By positioning lame and blind people on the walls the threat was posed that any who entered the city would become lame and blind. Most, however, have preferred the understanding that this is simply a taunting hyperbole: "Even the lame and blind could hold off your armies!"

5:7. Zion. The etymology of Zion cannot at present be traced, but here (its first occurrence) it appears to refer to the acropolis of the Jebusite city. It later came to represent David's city and was used to refer to the entire city of

Jerusalem through much of the poetic and prophetic literature of the Old Testament.

5:8. water shaft. For over a century many interpreters have identified David's means of entry into the city with Warren's Shaft, a rock-cut tunnel that gave the residents access to the water of the Gihon Spring. More recent archaeological work in the tunnel system by Reich and Shukron, however, has determined that the Warren Shaft was never used as a water tunnel and was not connected to the underground system in the time of David. The following comments explore the various elements involved in this interpretation.

The Gihon spring lies in the Kidron valley on the southeast side of the city. Three or four times a day it gushes water for about forty minutes. It can provide up to forty-five thousand cubic feet per day (enough to fill a pool that is seventy-five feet square and eight feet deep).

The strategic importance of water systems. In time of siege it was imperative for the inhabitants of the city to have access to a secure water supply, but the city walls were on the crest of the hill, while the spring was in the valley. For this reason much engineering creativity was directed toward the use of tunnels and shafts cut through the bedrock that could provide water for the city. Other water tunnels are known from Hazor, Megiddo, Gezer and Gibeon (see comment on 2:13). The earliest rock-cut water systems known from the ancient Near East are from thirteenth-century Mycenaea.

Jerusalem's water system. From inside the city one would enter a passageway that descended gradually by slopes and steps. A sharp right turn would enter a horizontal tunnel that ended in a steep stairway into a natural cave. The distance from the entrance to the cave is about 130 feet. A sharp turn from the cave led one into a fortified tower, where the water from the Gihon Spring collected in a large pool.

David's penetration of the city. The only entryway into the water system from the outside would have been through a channel that forked off from the tunnel that took water from the spring to the pool in the tower. This channel ran the length of the city. It was not a tunnel, but it was covered over by huge rocks. At this stage it is not possible to offer any clear idea of how Joab made his way into the city.

5:9. king's personal ownership of the capital. The title "City of David" may reflect the ancient practice that the capital city became not only the royal residence but the personal estate of the reigning king and his successors. From Tukulti-Ninurta of the thirteenth century to Sargon II of the eighth century, Assyrian kings were known to name capital cities after themselves. Sargon purchased the site of Dur-Sharrukin and built his capital there (Khorsabad) in much the same way that Omri bought the site for his new capital, Samaria (1 Kings 16:24). Such royal estate cities typically housed the administration (composed largely of relatives of the king) and enjoyed certain privileges, including exemption from taxation, corvee labor, military duty and imprisonment, as well as being beneficiaries of the most beautiful and elaborate building projects. Such privileges (*kidinnutu*) were enjoyed, for instance, by Babylonian cities such as Nippur, Sippar and Borsippa, based on their status as religious centers rather than as political capitals. Political capitals such as Nineveh and Babylon also were endowed with similar status.

5:9. supporting terraces (millo). It is now accepted by most that this important defensive structure should be identified with what archaeologists have called the "stepped stone structure" (see comment on 5:6). This structure is made of rock and earth, and allowed for the building area to be expanded by about two thousand square feet.

5:11. Tyre. Tyre was one of the major Phoenician seaports of the ancient world. It was located on a small island (about 150 acres) in the Mediterranean just off the coast about one hundred miles directly north of Jerusalem. The city and its mainland fortress are well represented in ancient sources from as early as Ebla and including Egyptian execration texts, Amarna letters, the Epic of Keret (Ugaritic), the Tale of Wenamon (Egypt) and down into Greek and Roman sources. Besides its significant role in the sea trade of the day, the textile and dye industry (see comment on Num 4:6) and the export of cedar were among the pillars of its economy.

5:11. Hiram. The dates of Hiram I of Tyre (Phoenician Ahiram; Assyrian Hirummu) are commonly cited as 969-936 B.C., based on the chronological reckoning of the Jewish historian, Josephus (first century A.D.). He claims to have extensive records of the history of Tyre and offers much information about Hiram's reign. This dating gives little if any overlap between David and Hiram and is suspect due to the methods of calculation available to Josephus. Contemporary Near Eastern sources offer no information about this Hiram but mention prominently his later namesake, Hiram II. The name is also well known from the sarcophagus of Ahiram, king of nearby

Byblos, around this same time period.

5:11. cedar wood. Cedar trees are slow growing and can live up to three thousand years and attain heights of 120 feet. Beautiful grain, sweet-smelling aroma and durability combined to make cedar the wood of choice for most temples and palaces of the ancient world. High resin content inhibited the growth of fungus. The forests of Lebanon on the west slope of the Lebanon range (at elevation levels of about five thousand feet) were one of the few places where it grew. Both Mesopotamia and Egypt were importing it beginning as early as the fourth millennium B.C. By the year 1000, there was little that remained of the legendary forests, making the rare wood all the more valuable.

5:11. David's palace. Though no remains of David's palace have been discovered by archaeologists, the assistance of Hiram of Tyre suggests that it would have been of Phoenician architectural design. Contemporary Phoenician examples excavated in Syria are identified by the Akkadian description *bit-hilani*, which refers to the characteristic porch with columns that are prominently featured. A palace of *bit-hilani* style has been excavated in Israel at Megiddo and has been identified as Solomon's palace. This most likely offers the closest example of what David's palace in Jerusalem would have looked like. The palace at Megiddo is about seventy feet square. Inside, a number of large halls, an audience chamber, an interior courtyard and about a dozen smaller rooms for residential or administrative use filled out the first floor. It was at least two stories tall and featured a guard tower.

5:13. royal marriages as political strategy. Marriage was a tool of diplomacy throughout the ancient Near East. Towns, city-states, tribes or nations who wished to ally themselves with a ruler or come under his protection sealed the treaty with a marriage of a daughter of their chief family to the suzerain or his son. This was an act of loyalty on the part of the vassal, who would then have a personal stake in preserving the dynasty. For instance, Zimri-Lim, the king of Mari during the eighteenth century B.C., successfully placed his daughters in the harems of nearby kingdoms and married several foreign wives himself to increase his power and the stability of his realm. Similarly Pharaoh Thutmose IV (1425-1412 B.C.) arranged a marriage with a daughter of the Mitannian king to demonstrate good relations and end a series of wars with that middle Euphrates kingdom. In David's case, prior to becoming king of Israel he made a series of marriages that strengthened

his political and economic position (see comment on 1 Sam 25:39-44). The marriages in this verse likely assured the support of some of the leading families of Jerusalem.

5:17. stronghold. The stronghold referred to here is not the same as that referred to in 1 Samuel 22:4 and 24:22, but is likely the Jebusite citadel in Jerusalem. The platform for this citadel and a few remnants of the wall have been found by archaeologists at the northern end of the Jebusite city in the area south of the modern walls of the Old City.

5:18. Valley of Rephaim. As the Sorek Valley moves eastward out of the Shephelah near Beth Shemesh, it breaks into several passes into the hills around Jerusalem. The Sorek Valley at one point turns northeast toward Gibeon, while the Valley of Rephaim turns east-southeast toward the area between Bethlehem and Jerusalem. It joins the north-south road from Jerusalem to Bethlehem and then heads northeast into Jerusalem. This would be a strategic location for the Philistines to cut David off from potential reinforcements from Judah.

5:19. oracular inquiry. From chapter 23 through the end of 1 Samuel, David is making oracular inquiries of the Lord by means of the ephod under the guidance of Abiathar the priest. It is likely that is also what is happening here. In an oracular inquiry a yes-no question was posed to the deity, and a binary mechanism was used to determine what the answer was. The normative means laid out for this process in Exodus was the Urim and Thummim (which were kept in a pouch in the ephod).

5:20. Baal Perazim. The "baal" element in this name (as a title for deity) is thought to identify the site as a sacred site and may have derived its name from Perez the son of Judah and progenitor of the line of David. Some identify the site as the ridge between Giloh and Beit Jala about two miles northwest of Bethlehem.

5:21. abandoned idols. Nearly every army in the ancient Near East included priests and diviners (as seen in the Mari texts), prophets (2 Kings 3) and portable sacred objects (Assyrian Annals of Shalmaneser III [858-824 B.C.]). In this way, the god(s) could be consulted on the battlefield or invoked to lead the soldiers to victory. In the divine warrior motif, the deity is fighting the battles and defeating the deities of the enemy. In most situations prayers would be made and omens asked to assure the god's presence. The idols would only be abandoned under the most critical circumstances. There are several cases in the ancient world of statues of a god being carried off as trophies of war. For examples see comment on 1 Samuel 5:2.

5:24. marching in the balsam trees. If balsam trees are mentioned here, they would be identified as bushlike shrubs called mastic terebinths, common in the hill country. While there are many reasons to be suspicious of that translation, no other suggestion has been persuasive either. There is agreement, however, that some sort of tree is referred to. It has been suggested that David is using a tree oracle in which observations of the trees are taken as divine guidance, but it is difficult to confirm this as a regular oracular procedure.

5:24. divine vanguard. In the divine warrior motif the deity goes out as the vanguard to vanquish the enemy. This is common throughout the ancient Near East. In Hittite accounts, Hattusilis III claims that Ishtar went out before him. In Egypt, Amun-Re is said to have gone out before the armies of Thutmose III. The deity terrifies and confuses the enemy, and at times sends thunder (see comment on 1 Sam 7:10) or earthquakes (see comment on 1 Sam 14:15).

5:25. Gibeon to Gezer. The Valley of Rephaim (where the Philistines were camped in verse 22) is southwest of Jerusalem. The Gibeon-Gezer corridor follows the Aijalon Valley, which is northwest of Jerusalem. Verse 23 suggests that David positioned his army to the west of the Philistines to block their retreat. This would have driven the Philistines toward Jerusalem (about two miles), which they would have passed to the west. Just north of the city they would have veered northwest to make for Gibeon (six miles). There may have been additional Philistine garrisons in this area, or they may simply be heading for the next corridor to the plain. Since the text mentions Gezer, they must have headed northwest out of Gibeon to the Beth Horon pass (about three miles; see comment on Josh 10:10) and down into the Valley of Aijalon (five miles). It is about seven more miles to Gezer, which means that David drove the Philistines completely out of the hill country.

6:1-23

The Installation of the Ark in Jerusalem

6:1. thirty thousand chosen men. David's standing army is now thirty divisions (see comment on Josh 8:3). The importance of the ark as well as its military significance is indicated by the size of the escort. Processions to showcase military might were common in the ancient world and continue in popularity to-

day. The Assyrian army likewise accompanied the statue of Marduk as it was restored to Babylon from Asshur in the seventh century.

6:2. Baalah. In 1 Chronicles 13:6 Baalah is identified as another name for Kiriath Jearim. The ark has been housed in Kiriath Jearim ever since its return from Philistia. The site is commonly (but tentatively) identified with Tell el-Azhar, nine miles west northwest of Jerusalem.

6:2. enthroned between the cherubim. The ark was a wooden box, open at the top, approximately three to four feet in length and two and a quarter feet in both width and height, based on eighteen inches a cubit. It was overlaid inside and out with sheets of the finest gold and had four rings (also gold covered) attached to the sides for the insertion of two gold-encrusted poles, which were used to carry the ark and to protect it from the touch of all but the high priest. A golden cover, decorated with two winged cherubim, sealed the ark. Its primary function was to store the tablets and to serve as a "footstool" for God's throne, thereby providing an earthly link between God and the Israelites. In Egyptian festivals the images of the gods were often carried in procession on portable barques. Paintings portray these as boxes about the size of the ark carried on poles and decorated with or flanked by guardian creatures. Biblical descriptions as well as archaeological discoveries (including some fine ivory pieces from Nimrud in Mesopotamia, Arslan Tash in Syria and Samaria in Israel) suggest the cherubim are composite creatures (having features of a number of different creatures, like the Egyptian sphinx), often four-legged animal bodies with wings. The cherubim appear in ancient art with some regularity, flanking the thrones of kings and deities. The combination of cherubim as throne guardians, chests as footstools and statements in the Old Testament concerning Yahweh being enthroned on the cherubim supports the concept of the ark as representing the invisible throne of Yahweh. The use of empty thrones was widespread in the ancient world. They were provided for use by deities or royal personages when they were present.

6:3. new cart. The use of a new cart would assure that there was no ritual impurity connected to the cart from previous usage (for instance, if it had been used to transport dung or dead animals). However, instructions for the transport of the ark always involved priests using poles to carry it rather than using a cart. The cart precedent was set by the Philistines (1 Sam 6:7).

6:5. worship music. These are all typical musical instruments of the time and are attested in ancient Near Eastern texts, reliefs and paintings as early as the third millennium B.C. There is still some disagreement among authorities as to which of the Hebrew words in this passage ought to be translated "harp" and which one as "lyre." The one the NIV translates "lyre" is a ten-stringed instrument, while the one translated "harp" is thought to have had fewer strings. Both are hand-held with frames made of wood. The tambourine has been identified in archaeological reliefs as the tambour, a small drum (leather stretched over a hoop) that would not have the tinny rattle sound of modern tambourines. The fourth instrument (NIV "sistrum") is the most difficult because it only occurs here. It is most commonly considered a shaker or rattle of some sort. The last, cymbals, are made of bronze and are in the percussion group, so the only remaining question concerns their size.

6:6. threshing floor of Nacon. The location of this threshing floor is unknown. The text puts it in the vicinity of Obed-Edom's house, which in turn is not far from Jerusalem, but it is impossible to be more precise.

6:7. Uzzah's irreverence. The ark is viewed as an object requiring respect and caution. Its very nature made it dangerous (compare electricity). The word translated "irreverence" occurs only here in the Old Testament, but the same root in related languages means "disdain" (Akkadian) or "negligence" (Aramaic).

6:10. house of Obed-Edom. The name Obed-Edom means "servant of Edom" (perhaps a deity's name; compare Obadiah = Obed-Yah[weh]). Additionally he is identified as a Gittite, that is, from Gath. A company of soldiers (mercenaries?) from Gath made up David's personal bodyguard (see 15:18), and it is possible that this individual is one of them. The house is generally considered to be in close proximity to Jerusalem, but evidence is lacking.

6:13. sacrifice every six steps. When the Assyrian king Ashurbanipal was restoring the image of Marduk to Babylon (seventh century), fatted bulls were offered every two miles along the way (Assur to Babylon is about 250 miles). David would have made about the same number of sacrifices as Ashurbanipal in about a half mile. The text does not specify what was used for an altar or how long the procession took. The word translated "bull" is a general term for cattle that can be male or female. The category of fatted calf is not used in the ritual instructions in the Pentateuch. It is presumed to be an animal that has been specially fed and pampered so the meat will be

tender. The text does not specify what type of sacrifice this is intended to be.

6:14. linen ephod. Though the ephod is a priestly garment, David is not necessarily portrayed as actually officiating in the role of the priest. Alternatively he may be taking the role of supplicant before the Lord and thus "offers" the sacrifices, not as priest but as any worshiper would (see comment below on verse 17).

6:14. dancing in the ancient world. Much of the dancing that is attested in the ancient world takes place in cultic contexts, though both Mesopotamian and Egyptian sources frequently depict dancers involved in entertainment. The dancing connected to festivals would probably resemble folk dancing of today, featuring the coordinated movements of a group of dancers. At other times the dances could more resemble ballet, where a scene or a drama is acted out. Single dancers usually performed either whirling, squatting, leaping, hopping-type dances or acrobatics approximating a modern gymnast's routine. Dancers sometimes performed either scantily clad or in the nude. In cultic contexts the participating officials (i.e., priests and administration) at times danced, not just the professionals. In one Hittite ritual this specifically included the queen. There are no known examples of dancing kings.

6:14-21. David's activity. The verb translated "danced" in verses 14 and 16 is used only in this passage. The use of the word in the related language of Ugaritic shows it to be something one does with fingers, thus suggesting snapping or waving fingers. The verb translated "leaping" in verse 16 is used only here and in a slightly different form in Genesis 19:24, where it is a description of the agility of the arms. In the parallel passage, 1 Chronicles 15:29, the verb translated "dancing" is only used of human activity twice (once parallel to singing and rejoicing, Job 21:11; and once opposite to mourning, Ecc 3:4). It generally conveys swaying, trembling or vibrating movements. It is possible, then, that David is not involved in dance at all but is swaying his arms and snapping or waving his fingers.

6:15. trumpets. The trumpet referred to here is the ram's horn (shofar). The shofar is capable of a variety of tones but cannot play a tune so is used primarily for signals either in worship or in warfare. The ram's horn was softened in hot water, then bent and flattened to produce its distinctive shape.

6:17. tent pitched for the ark. The text does not refer to this tent as the tent of meeting or the tabernacle, the two technical descriptions that typically identify the sanctuary that had been ordained at Sinai. Canaanite religious texts also speak of pavilions used for the dwelling of the gods. Archaeologists have found the remains of a Midianite tent shrine at Timnah that dates to the twelfth century B.C. It too was made of curtains draped over poles. Portable structures of similar design (curtains hung over gold-gilded beams or poles) are found in Egypt as early as the mid-third millennium both in sacred and secular use.

6:17. burnt offerings and fellowship offerings. Burnt offerings were totally consumed on the altar and usually were connected to petitions (see comment on Lev 1:3-4). Fellowship offerings provided a basis for a communal meal, and typical use of this offering was for ratification of treaties or covenant agreements. For more information see comments on 1 Samuel 10:8; Exodus 24:5; and Leviticus 3:1-5. The fellowship offerings are seen in contexts of coronation (1 Sam 11) and temple dedication (1 Kings 8). It is possible that the installation of the ark was combined with an enthronement celebration; see next comment.

6:17. enthronement celebration. Assyrian enthronement festivals from the time of Tukulti-Ninurta I (twelfth century) describe the king taking off his royal robes and praying humbly before the deity. Then the king is re-crowned and blessed. There follows a procession to the throne, concluding in gifts of allegiance being offered by high officials. The similarities in David's festivities can easily be seen. Here it is Yahweh whose enthronement is being celebrated. David sets aside his royal garments and leads the procession as a simple supplicant to the throne room (the tent). Then the sacrifices of petition and allegiance are offered. From verse 21 it might be inferred that on this occasion there was also a reaffirmation of David's election and kingship. Assyrian records also preserve several accounts of the founding of a new royal city (Ashurnasirpal, Sargon, Sennacherib, Esarhaddon). These feature the god being brought into the city accompanied by sacrifices and a banquet (including music), with food and drink being distributed liberally to the people.

6:18. blessings for the people. In the ancient world, blessings (as well as curses) were believed to have a power all their own that would result in their fulfillment. They were often given by the priests to someone leaving the sanctuary after participating in some ritual. In ancient Near Eastern practice a phrase invoking the gods to grant watch care and well-being is used regularly in Ugaritic and Akkadian salutations. Finally, the phrase "the

Lord bless you and keep you" is also found in the words (Hebrew) painted on a large storage jar from the ninth century B.C. found at Kuntillet Ajrud in the northern Sinai.

6:19. gifts for the people. The loaf of bread here is a braided ring bread that is perforated in the baking process. "Date cake" is a traditional translation—the word occurs only in this account, and the meaning is uncertain. The treat rendered "raisin cake" could be made out of any dried fruit. Hosea 3:1 specifies that raisins are used to make this morsel, but the context here does not give that information. This would be a block or ball of compressed dried fruit.

6:20. Michal's complaint. In verse 16 the text says that when Michal saw David performing whatever he was doing (see comment on 6:14-21) that she despised him. It is not until this verse that detail is given concerning what offended her. Michal's complaint did not focus on undignified behavior but on David's attire. There are two reasons already mentioned why David may have set aside his royal robes in favor of a simple linen ephod. If he is dancing as part of the procession (see 6:14 above), he may have adopted the attire of those who dance, which was often very little. If this resembles an enthronement festival (see 6:17 above), it was customary for the king to adopt the role of supplicant. Since Michal compares him to a "vulgar fellow," it is likely that the former represents her understanding.

7:1-29
A Covenant and a Dynasty for David

7:1, 11. rest. Here it is indicated that God has given David rest from his enemies, and throughout the Old Testament the Lord speaks of giving rest to his people. This is especially significant in this context where David wants to build a temple, because in the ancient Near East the temple of the deity was supposed to offer rest to the deity. Some of the temple names even suggest that as a primary function of the temple. This divine rest then often results in rest for the people in their land. In contrast the Bible says little about divine rest, and it is never the prerequisite for human rest except for the sabbath.

7:2-3. prophet as advisor. Prior to the time of Samuel, prophets had exercised political leadership by virtue of their prophetic office. With the initiation of kingship the role of the prophet had become an advisory role. Rather than leading the people as the recipient of divine messages, the prophet offered guidance to the king, who would retain the freedom to accept or reject it. For more information see comments on Deuteronomy 18:14-22.

7:2. cedar dwelling versus tent dwelling. It was a common occurrence in the ancient Near East for a victorious king to show his gratitude to the patron deity by building a temple. Examples go back into the mid-third millennium among the Sumerians and continue down into Assyrian, Babylonian and even Persian times. The temple (home of the god) was expected to bring the protection of the deity to the king and his land. A permanent and luxurious dwelling (cedar) would be intended to insure the Lord's presence and favor. In Ugaritic literature the father god, El, was believed to inhabit a tent shrine (as were many of the Canaanite deities). Baal, in contrast, built for himself a beautiful palace.

7:5. divine permission to build. In the ancient world it was important to procure divine permission to build a temple. If the king proceeded on his own without direction as to the location, orientation, size and materials, he could expect only failure. In the Neo-Babylonian period Nabonidus tells of a king who undertook such a project without the consent of the gods, with the result that the temple collapsed. In the Sumerian *Curse of Akkad*, Naram-Sin seeks an omen that will permit him to build a temple. Though he does not receive one, he proceeds anyway. His action is consequently blamed for the fall of the dynasty of Akkad.

7:8-11. deity as king's sponsor. It is common rhetoric in the ancient Near East for a king to claim the sponsorship of the national deity. Hittite and Mesopotamian documents are especially clear. The deity is acknowledged as having brought the king to the throne, given him the land and established his kingship. The god is relied upon to protect the king, give him victory over his enemies and establish his dynastic line, thereby determining the destiny of the king.

7:13. son to build temple. An inscription survives in which Adad-Guppi, the famous queen mother of the Neo-Babylonian empire (sixth century), reports a dream given by the god Sin. The god told her that it was her son who would construct the temple for him in the city of Harran. This was different to David's situation in that that was a work of restoring a sanctuary that had fallen into ruins.

7:14. father/son relationship between God and king. Egyptian kingship is particularly strong on this point, since the kingship of the pharaoh was seen as derived from the divine realm. More particularly he was conceived as the son of Re, the sun god. In Ugaritic litera-

ture, Keret, king of Khubur, is identified as the son of El, the chief god of the Canaanites. Among the Aramean kings the designation was even included in their throne names (Ben-Hadad means son of Hadad). In Mesopotamia, from Gilgamesh in the mid-third millennium through kings such as Gudea, Hammurabi, Tukulti-Ninurta and Ashurbanipal, just to name a few, it was part of the royal prerogative to claim divine heritage.

7:14-15. security despite discipline. In one Hittite treaty of the second millennium the Hittite king, Hattusilis III, guarantees his vassal, Ulmi-Teshup of Tarhuntassa, that his son and grandson will inherit the land after him. The text goes on to say that if Ulmi-Teshup's descendants commit offenses, they will be punished (even with death), but that the land will not be taken away from Ulmi-Teshup's family as long as there is a male heir.

7:15. covenant love. Hittite, Akkadian, Ugaritic and Aramaic examples all show that the positive action of the suzerain toward the vassal is expressed as love, kindness and graciousness, and in return the vassal is expected to respond with obedience and loyalty. In the Amarna letters (from vassal kings of Canaan to their Egyptian overlord) "love" is used as a characterization of friendly and loyal international relationships. It expresses the vassal's intentions to be loyal and to honor the terms of the treaty agreement between the parties. The biblical text shows a clear example of this usage in 1 Kings 5:15. There are rare instances in Mesopotamian literature where an individual is admonished to love a deity, but in general the gods of the ancient Near East did not seek love from their worshipers, nor did gods enter into covenant relationships with them.

7:18-29. observations about David's prayer. In a prayer of Ashurnasirpal I (an Assyrian king a generation earlier than David) to Ishtar he thanks Ishtar for her sponsorship. The benevolent acts he recognizes include raising him up from obscurity, appointing him as a shepherd to the people, making him a name and allowing him to establish justice for his people. These are also some of the same divine services that Nathan has identified to David (verses 8-11).

7:22. monotheism. The statement here that there is no God except Yahweh goes beyond previous statements. Though there were several attempts in the ancient world to magnify one god to the near exclusion of others, these do not come close to the ideal of monotheism represented in ancient Israel (see comments on Ex 20:3 and Deut 6:4).

8:1-18

David's Kingdom

8:1. Metheg Ammah. Many doubt that this is a place name, and a number of creative alternatives have been proposed. If it *is* a place name, the location has not been identified.

8:2-3. selective, proportional execution. The described means of choosing those who would be executed is unparalleled in both the Bible and the ancient Near Eastern records available to us.

8:2. tribute. When one state or other political entity conquered another or extended hegemony over its affairs, the result was the exaction of tribute payments from the subject people. This could take the form of precious metals (by weight or as jewelry or implements), farm produce (a significant portion of the harvest) or labor service. Not surprisingly, this draining of the economy was unpopular and was generally the reason for revolt or warfare. Extrabiblical documentation for this practice is widespread. For instance, the annals of the Assyrian kings often include lists of items received as tribute: the Black Obelisk inscription of Shalmaneser III (859-824 B.C.) contains Jehu's tribute to Assyria of silver, gold, lead and hard woods; Tiglath-Pileser III (744-727 B.C.) received elephant hide, ivory, linen garments and other luxury items from his vassals in Damascus, Samaria, Tyre and elsewhere.

8:3. Hadadezer. Hadadezer is identified as the son of Rehob, which may indicate his association with the important town of Beth Rehob (see 10:6). The Assyrian king who was contemporary to David, Ashurrabi II, reports significant trouble from an Aramean king who is seeking to expand into Assyrian territory. There is no mention of this king's name, but Hadadezer is the most likely candidate. The name itself is familiar since it is also the name of the Aramean king who opposed the Assyrians in the ninth century (Adad-Idri is the Assyrian form).

8:3. Zobah. This important Aramean kingdom was situated in the vicinity of the Anti-Lebanon range and the northern section of the Beqa Valley (southern section of the Orontes) and extended east to the plain of Homs. It is mentioned in Neo-Assyrian records of the eighth and seventh centuries.

8:3. Euphrates River. The bend of the Euphrates at Emar is most likely the area intended here. According to 1 Chronicles 18 this battle took place at Hamath on the Orontes river. NIV's "control" is the Hebrew word for "hand," which elsewhere refers to a stele or monument with a royal inscription (1 Sam 15:12; 2 Sam 18:18) being set up here by David. Verse 13 speaks of a "name" David makes (NIV "became famous"), which is another way that Hebrew speaks of a monument. Egyptian Pharaoh Thutmose III (fifteenth century) boasted of the steles they erected on the banks of the Euphrates.

8:4. chariots. The chariots of Syria during this period are similar to the Assyrian models depicted in reliefs of the ninth century. They featured two yoked horses with one or two others harnessed beside. Two spoked wooden wheels on a rear axle supported a small platform occupied by a driver and rider equipped with bow and spear. The sides only went up to mid-thigh on the standing occupants.

8:4. hamstringing. Horses could not be mercifully shot as they are today, and the Israelites had no use for them and no means to care for them; they certainly did not want their enemies to have continued use of them. Hamstringing involves cutting through the rear tarsal tendon in the hock joint (equivalent of human Achilles tendon), leaving the horses unable to walk.

8:5. Arameans of Damascus. The movement of Arameans into the Levant took place in the eleventh century. Based on other examples from cuneiform literature, the name Aram may in fact have originally been that of a region (cf., Sippar-Amnantum of the Old Babylonian period) that was later applied to people living there. Current evidence suggests that the Arameans inhabited the upper Euphrates throughout the second millennium, first as villagers and pastoralists, then as a political, national coalition. In this text there is no mention of a king of Damascus, suggesting that Damascus has not yet emerged as a major power in the region.

8:5. Damascus. Damascus is located in an oasis watered by the Barada River in the shadow of the Anti-Lebanon range to the west and with the Syrian desert stretching out to its east. It is first mentioned in the lists of Thutmose III in the fifteenth century and is named, though not in a major role, in the Amarna texts. Its major prominence comes in the conflicts with Assyria in the ninth and eighth centuries. The continuing occupation of the site has offered few opportunities for excavation, resulting in no information to illuminate the biblical period.

8:7. gold "shields." The Hebrew term here was long obscure but is now recognized as a technical term borrowed from Aramaic referring to a bow case. Ceremonial bow cases are pictured in later Persian reliefs.

8:8. Tebah and Berothai. Tubikhu is men-

tioned in the Amarna texts as a city south of
Homs and may be the Tebah mentioned here.
It is also known from Egyptian itineraries.
Berothai is Bereitan in the Beqa Valley south of
Baalbek. 1 Chronicles 18:8 adds Cun (Kunu) to
the list, which was the ancient name of Baalbek (almost fifty miles north of Damascus).
8:9. Tou of Hamath. Tou of Hamath controlled
the region north of Zobah and was apparently
pleased to see the influence of the kingdom of
Zobah checked by the Israelites. While
Hamath (modern Hama, about 130 miles
north of Damascus) is the name of a city on
the Orontes, it also identifies a nation in
Neo-Assyrian records. Tou is unknown outside the Bible, but the name is common in the
Hurrian language. This suggests that Hamath
was not at this time an Aramean state.
**8:10-11. dedicating precious metals to the
Lord.** Dedication of the precious metals to the
Lord means that they were donated to the
sanctuary's treasury and became part of the
assets administered by the priests rather than
going into the royal treasuries. Specially selected objects such as ceremonial weapons or
important cultic objects would have been
kept, while many of the smaller items would
be melted down.
8:12. extent of David's control. David's kingdom included Transjordan at least as far south
as the Arnon. Territory of Edom focused on
the region southwest of the Dead Sea. David's
conquests targeted the two major trade routes
through the region.
8:13. Valley of Salt. Wadi el-Milh is one possibility, halfway between Beersheba and the
Dead Sea, though only the name supports the
identification.
8:14. building garrisons. Placing garrisons in
annexed territories or in vassal countries allowed a country to extend its supply line and
to monitor activities and maintain control.
Food supplies and arms could be stored there,
and the military personnel could be ready to
deal with any deviation from treaty stipulations or to put down any uprisings. Likewise
tribute could be collected and merchant activity controlled.
**8:16-18. administrative officers and organiza-
tion.** Joab is listed first, reflecting the reality
that the military commander was second in
command in the administration. This was normal in the Levant. The recorder would have
charge of the records and documents of state
and could be viewed as a herald or even as the
equivalent to the modern press secretary. He
also had control of who was admitted to see
the king and would have been the protocol officer. The secretary would have been in charge

of diplomatic correspondence and would
have been comparable in some ways to the
Secretary of State. There has been some suggestion that these offices are tailored to Egyptian models of administration, but Canaanite
models are equally defensible.
8:17. two high priests. Abiathar descends
from the line of Eli (see comment on 1 Sam
1:3), which held the high priestly office at the
beginning of this period. Zadok is later identified as representing the line of Aaron through
his firstborn, Eleazar (1 Chron 6:8). There is no
information concerning how the transfer of
power had occurred during the Judges period.
It is not impossible that the Zadok line had retained priestly prerogatives in Judah, but one
can only speculate. Competing priesthoods
are not unusual in the ancient Near East, but
typically would represent priesthoods for different gods.
8:18. Kerethites and Pelethites. These were
groups of mercenaries who served David as
vassals rather than as members of the standing
army. The Kerethites are identified as immigrants from Crete and are closely associated
with the Philistines, who were believed to
come from the same area of the Aegean. The
Pelethites are known only from passages such
as this, where they are associated with the
Kerethites.
8:18. sons as "advisers." The Hebrew text
uses the word "priests," but this is not the
problem it has been portrayed as. Although
the tribe of Levi had been exclusively assigned all of the duties related to the sanctuary (see comments on Lev 10:10 and Num
18:1-7), there is no text that prohibits non-
Levites from performing other priestly tasks
(see comments on Ex 28:1). It is just that as
time went on, priestly tasks not related to the
sanctuary were gradually eliminated (see
2 Kings 23:8). The existence of priestly duties
carried out within the family context are indicated in post-Sinai contexts (Judg 6:24-26;
13:19; 1 Sam 20:29), and in the general culture
of the ancient Near East the oldest son frequently had priestly duties in the veneration
of ancestors (see comment on Num 3:1). Saul
had been reprimanded for his involvement in
a priestly function, but that may have been because it violated the charter (1 Sam 10:25) that
delineated his role with respect to Samuel's
(see comment on 1 Sam 13:8-13). David's
priestly prerogatives may have been attached
to the traditional roles in Jerusalem. The existence of such a royal priestly tradition is recognized in places like Psalm 110:4 and perhaps
in David's participation in the ceremony of installing the ark (above, 6:14).

9:1-13

David's Care for Mephibosheth

9:3. lame in both feet. See the comment on Mephibosheth and his disability in 2 Samuel 4:4.

9:4. Lo Debar. This was an area north of the Yarmuk River in Transjordan that was allied with Saul and later transformed into a vassal state by David. The site of Tell Dober, which has evidence of occupation in the Iron I and II periods, may well be the city that controlled this region. It lies at the southwestern tip of the Golan and is north of the Yarmuk.

9:7. David's action contrasted to normal. Mephibosheth had good cause to be afraid of David. There is wide precedent in Mesopotamian texts for the elimination of all rival claimants to the throne when a king comes to power (compare Baasha's murder of Jeroboam's family in 1 Kings 15:29). Such purges also occurred years later as a form of revenge for political opposition or rebellion attempted against previous rulers. For example, Ashurbanipal mutilated, executed and fed the bodies of his grandfather's rivals to dogs as part of his first official acts as king of Assyria. David, however, treats Mephibosheth, the only surviving male member of the royal family, as the rightful heir to Saul's estates. His generosity is coupled with the command to eat at David's table. In this way Mephibosheth is treated with honor, though some have noted it also keeps him under observation should he be inclined to subversion.

9:7. eating at the king's table. Political prisoners were seldom kept in prison cells. It was more advantageous for the king to hold them in confinement within his palace or royal city, treating them to the pleasures of the "king's table" but always keeping a close eye on their activities. Reports in ration lists from the Babylonian and Assyrian periods provide evidence of food, clothing and oil provided to "guests" of the king. Persian courts contained political detainees as well as "allies" who were kept in the king's presence to insure a continual flow of taxes and soldiers for the army. Thus Mephibosheth, like Jehoiachin many years later (2 Kings 25:27-30), enjoyed the largesse of the king's court but was not truly free.

10:1-19

War with the Ammonites

10:2. David's intended treatment of Hanun. During David's outlaw period he not only spent time as a Philistine mercenary but also sought out help from Saul's enemy Nahash of Ammon. This would have involved a pact of mutual nonaggression and support, and would have been of benefit to both David and Nahash. Most treaties found in ancient Near Eastern documents are suzerain treaties in which a stronger state imposes tribute and other obligations on vassal states (see the vassal treaties of Esarhaddon). Some, like the treaty ending the war between Egypt and Hittites in the thirteenth century B.C., recognize "brotherhood" or parity between the two sovereigns (Rameses II and Hattusilis III). Since treaties were considered to be "eternal," it is not unusual that David would have sent a delegation to Hanun to renew the elements of this agreement. The hostile reaction the diplomats received suggests Ammon's fear that David wished to transform the treaty from a parity agreement to a suzerain treaty.

10:3. Hanun's treatment of David's men. David's messengers have half their beards shaved (symbolically emasculating them and by extension David) and "their garments [were cut] in the middle at their hips," leaving them naked like slaves or captives (see Is 20:4). These men were ambassadors and as such were entitled to both respect and diplomatic immunity. What may seem like a "prank" was in fact a direct challenge to David's power and authority, and precipitated a war between the two nations. David could not allow such an obvious "rape" or symbolic castration of his representatives to go unavenged. A review of Assyrian royal annals (Sargon II, Sennacherib and Ashurbanipal) contains justifications for a declaration of war based on a violation of a sworn agreement or the physical challenging of Assyrian authority. Although the annals are not as graphic as this example, they also serve as a "dropping of the gauntlet" in political terms.

10:5. till beards grow back. Beards were a symbol of virility (compare the Assyrian king Shamshi Adad's taunting of his son Yasmah-Addu, saying "Are you not a man—have you no beard?" in the Mari letters). The physical message conveyed by Hanun's act is that Israel would be deprived of its strength and thrown into mourning, with garments torn and heads and beards shaved (see Is 15:2). As representatives of the king, these ambassadors were personally embarrassed by their treatment. However, by extension, David was also shamed, and thus he kept them from public view until the "damage" was no longer visible.

10:6. coalition. Very often small states or kingdoms would ally together against a common enemy. In this case, Ammon, feeling the need to strengthen its position against David, enlisted the help of the Arameans. Twenty divisions of troops came from Beth Rehob on the border between Syria and Israel (in the vicinity of the Huleh Valley near Tel Dan—see Judg 18:28), and from Zobah in the northern Beqa Valley. The former city is also mentioned in Egyptian records from the time of Thutmose III. See the comment on 2 Samuel 8:3 for other conflicts between Israel and the Aramean king Hadadezer. Maacah also lies southeast of Beth Rehob, south of Mount Hermon and east of the Jordan. The last group of soldiers (twelve divisions) come from Tob (et-Tayibeh, twelve miles southeast of the Sea of Galilee in Gilead). The list of allies thus names the regions from north to south, covering the territory from the Orontes to the territory of Ammon.

10:7-12. battle situation. The presence of two separate forces (Ammonites defending the gates of their city [probably Rabbah] and Arameans deployed in the adjoining area) required Joab to divide his own army and make contingency plans with his co-commander, Abishai, in case of a collapse by either Israelite group (compare the account in 1 Chron 19:9-13). This strategy suggests he was surprised by the enemy position and did not have sufficient forces to effectively fight a sustained two-front battle. Although he was in a dangerously untenable position, with enemy troops on two sides, his strategy appears to have worked, at least to the extent of a draw. This may explain why he was not able to follow up his efforts but withdrew to Jerusalem.

10:16. Helam. Although its exact location is uncertain, the city or district of Helam was probably in northern Transjordan, perhaps between Damascus and Hamath (supported by a variant reading in Ezek 47:16)—a site that could serve as a staging area for Hadadezer's Aramean troops from across the Euphrates and an area close enough to be a threat to David's control of the region. The site is mentioned almost a millennium earlier in an Egyptian execration text, but that does not help locate it.

10:17. battle lines. Military formations were designed to take advantage of terrain and the weaponry employed by the army. The text indicates that Shobach, the Aramean commander, had both chariots and infantry. The ranks of infantry, deployed in mass formations led by "commanders of fifty," included spearmen with shields in the front rank and bowmen and slingers placed immediately behind them. When the armies came together, hand-to-hand combat would have employed flat-bladed axes and daggers. The chariots

were often placed on the flanks for easier maneuverability.

10:19. subjects of Israel. It was not uncommon in the ancient Near East for the fortunes of war to lead to political shifts of allegiance. With the defeat of the Aramean army, many of the villages and towns that had formerly sworn allegiance to Hadadezer now offered their support and tribute to David. Parallels to this practice can be found in the Vassal Treaties of Esarhaddon as well as in the campaign lists of most of the Assyrian monarchs. It should not be assumed, however, that David was able to take total, structural command of this region of northern Transjordan. Coerced support, won one day in battle, may disappear at the first sign of weakness.

11:1-27
David and Bathsheba

11:1. the time when kings go off to war. Military campaigns, while seldom officially declared, came predictably in the ancient Near East with the end of the winter rains. A period of several months was then available during the spring season, prior to the harvest, when every able-bodied man was needed to work in the fields. Many of the Assyrian and Babylonian royal annals include the notation that a military campaign began in either the first month (Nisannu) or the second month (Aiaru) of the year (the period from March-May).

11:1. king remained behind. Kings, because of the duties of state or physical reasons, could not always accompany the army in every campaign. For instance, the Assyrian king Sennacherib employs an official known as the Rabshekah to besiege Jerusalem in 2 Kings 18:17-35. David's decision to remain behind may reflect his confidence in Joab's military skill, a pressing diplomatic matter or his concern with domestic affairs.

11:1. Rabbah. Rabbah was the capital city of the ancient Ammonites. It was located at the same site as modern Amman in Jordan on the north bank of the Zerqa at the sources of the Jabbok River, about forty miles east of Jerusalem. Because of continued occupation of the area, archaeological excavations have been limited. The ancient acropolis, however, has been investigated but has yielded little about the city at the time of David (perhaps a wall constructed by him).

11:2. roof of the palace. Because of the cool breeze that refreshes Jerusalem in the early evening, many people come out to socialize or to enjoy the air from the privacy of their roof tops. The palace's architecture was most likely similar to that of more common dwellings, with a large living or sleeping area on the roof (1 Sam 9:25).

11:2. bathing. Bathsheba's bathing is probably an act of purification following her menstrual cycle (see 2 Sam 11:4). This would be based on the laws of ritual purity as described in Leviticus 15:19-24. It is uncertain whether her intent in bathing on the roof was simply to use the air to help dry herself or whether she used the opportunity to bring herself to the attention of the king.

11:3. family of Bathsheba. The father of Bathsheba is Eliam, a member of David's special cadre of "mighty men" (2 Sam 23:34) and therefore the head of an influential household. This Eliam is the son of Ahithophel, one of David's most respected advisors (2 Sam 15:12; 16:23). This information, along with the fact that her husband, Uriah the Hittite, is also one of the "mighty men" (2 Sam 23:39), suggests that David knew exactly whose house he was looking at and was well acquainted with Bathsheba (an alternative translation suggests that it was David who said "Is this not Bathsheba?").

11:4. purification from uncleanness. The reference to Bathsheba's bathing refers to a ritual of cleansing after the completion of the seven days of impurity following her menstrual cycle (see Lev 15:19-24). It also establishes that she was within the most likely time for conception when she had sexual intercourse with David (10-14 days after commencement of menstruation). This also meant that it was impossible for Uriah to be the father of her child.

11:6-7. Hittite in army. As one of the seven major peoples of Canaan (Deut 7:1), the Hittites could easily have been hired as mercenaries, served on labor gangs or intermarried with Israelites during the period of the judges and the monarchy. They may represent descendants of immigrants from the Anatolian empire or the more recent, northern Syrian Neo-Hittite states.

11:9-11. Uriah's behavior. The presence of the ark of the covenant (v. 11) with the army suggests that they were engaged in a form of "holy war" and therefore special restrictions may have been imposed on the military (see the mass circumcision of the men prior to the beginning of the conquest in Josh 5:4-8 and the purity rites required of encamped soldiers in Deut 23:9-11 and 1 Sam 21:5). If Uriah had taken advantage of the opportunity David gave him to have intercourse with Bathsheba, it would have been possible to claim he was responsible for her pregnancy. However, Uriah's insistence on maintaining his ritual purity by sleeping in the guard barracks

forced David to take more drastic measures.

11:14-15. letter of doom. Since Uriah was originally sent to David to bring a first-hand report of the military situation, it is not unusual that David would have sent him back to Joab with official dispatches and orders. As a story element, having a victim deliver his own death warrant is found in folklore from many cultures (see the *Iliad*, where the story is reported of Bellerophon, who, falsely accused, carried his own death warrant to the king of Lycia), but this is the only occurrence in the Bible.

11:15-16. deployment of Uriah. As one of David's "mighty men," Uriah would have regularly been placed at the head of a contingent of soldiers and may have been expected to hold a strategic position in the battle plan (see the description of these "mighty men" in 2 Sam 23:8-39). In this case, however, he was intentionally placed opposite an elite force of Ammonite troops and badly outmatched. Uriah's portrayal as the immaculate soldier suggests that he would accept this assignment without question, but he must have wondered at the tactics.

11:16-24. battle tactics. The tactics on each side seem to involve feints and traps. With the city under siege, it would have been unnecessary to launch offensives. It may be that Uriah's troops were sent on a mission to attempt a breach of the walls. Israelite casualties occurred when Uriah's division was met by a foray coming out to engage the would-be breachers and because they were drawn too close to the walls, where they were within range of missiles thrown or fired from above. Joab's anticipation of David's recitation of the well-known incident of Abimelech's death (Judg 9:50-53) shows that this may have either been a calculated risk or a tactical mistake, if the Israelites were simply fooled into a murderous crossfire. However, it also provided a plausible explanation for Uriah's death and probably did not cost the lives of too many other Israelite soldiers.

11:26-27. time of mourning. The standard period of mourning was seven days (Gen 50:10). Only exceptional persons merited a longer time (thirty days for Moses and Aaron in Deut 34:8 and Num 20:29). In the case of a grieving widow, this would allow her the usual amount of time associated with other forms of impurity before she could consider remarriage (see Lev 12:2; 15:19).

12:1-13
Nathan's Rebuke

12:2-4. purpose of the parable. Nathan's parable of the ewe lamb provides a juridical setting for the indictment of David for his adultery with Bathsheba. As chief advocate for the rights of his people (see 2 Sam 15:4; 1 Kings 3:4-28), the king was expected to render judgment and to demonstrate his wisdom. While David does judge the actions of the "rich man," he is not wise enough to discern that he is judging himself.

12:2-12. nature of the indictment. The case presented by Nathan for David's decision may appear to the reader to have nothing to do with David's crimes, since it deals with neither adultery nor murder. What this case demonstrates is that adultery and murder were only the end results of a more serious crime: abuse of power. David is formally indicted by the divine tribunal (God speaking through the prophet) not only for taking another man's wife but for believing that he could take whatever he wanted and being dissatisfied with what God had given him. It is thus made clear that the king is not above the law and will be called to judgment by God, if not by the civil authorities.

12:5-6. deserves death/quadruple compensation. In his outrage, David would like to be able to sentence the offender to death because of his pitiless attitude, but the law was clear enough. The fourfold compensation is consistent with the law in Exodus 22:1 for the theft of a sheep (Hammurabi's Code requires a fine ten times the value of the stolen livestock).

12:8. master's house and wives. Since royal marriages were a reflection of the power of a monarch and represented political and economic alliances made in the name of the state, it would have been necessary, at the succession, for the harem of the former king to become the responsibility of the new monarch. In this way there was continuity of treaty obligations. After the death of Ishbosheth (2 Sam 4:5-7) and David's rise to kingship, it would have been expected that he would extend his protection to Saul's family, including his harem. Thus it is possible that the brief reference to David's marriage to Ahinoam in 1 Samuel 25:43 is a reference to his taking Saul's wife Ahinoam (1 Sam 14:50).

12:11. curse. This punishment follows the crime by suggesting that David's power will be usurped and his wives will be taken from him (see Absalom's taking of David's wives in 2 Sam 16:21-22). This even hints at the possibility that the throne would be taken from him. His violence and sexual misconduct will be matched by the violence and sexual misconduct of his household.

12:15-25
The Death of David and Bathsheba's Child

12:16. David's plea. In the Old Testament the religious use of fasting is often in connection with making a request before God. The principle is that the importance of the request causes an individual to be so concerned about his or her spiritual condition that physical necessities fade into the background. In this sense the act of fasting is designed as a process leading to purification and humbling oneself before God (Ps 69:10). Babylonian prayers include similar expressions of supplication and a sense of dependence on the power of the gods to remove evil and restore health.

12:20-23. David's conduct. David's servants did not know the judgment that had been uttered against the child by God. As a result, David's actions were misinterpreted by them. Fasting can be a response to mourning (as David's servants assumed in this case). But David strove to change God's mind, and his fasting was part of the procedure to enhance David's petition. Once he sees that the petition has been denied, he ceases his fast.

12:23. I will go to him, he will not return to me. This is simply David's acknowledgment that his efforts to save his son have failed. He does not expect any petition to bring his son back to life but recognizes that they will only be together in death. It is therefore a poignant expression of the ultimate fate of all humanity, similar to Jacob's mournful reply in Genesis 37:35. Gilgamesh's mourning for his dead companion Enkidu includes the statement that he "has now gone to the fate of mankind," and the hero is reminded by Siduri in the same epic that "when the gods created mankind, they ordained death for him." For more information on afterlife, see the comment on Job 3:13-19.

12:26-31
The Fall of Rabbah

12:26. royal citadel. This verse refers to a citadel, while the next refers to the water supply. It is generally assumed that the water supply for ancient Rabbah was the powerful spring by the city. Whether there were separate fortifications to guard the acropolis and the water supply or whether they were both guarded by a single fortification is unknown. One way to capture a walled city is to cut off its access to water. It may be that the citadel was captured because the Israelite army gained control of the water supply. This was the tactic used by

Antiochus III in Hellenistic times when he captured the same city.

12:27. water supply. Due to the often meager rainfall and the fact that it only comes during the winter months, cities and towns were dependent on wells, springs and cisterns during much of the year. The kings of Mesopotamia often boasted in their annals about their efforts to build canals, aqueducts and water-lifting devices (see also 2 Kings 20:20). Thus the capture of a city's water supply generally meant a quick end to a siege. Nothing is known of the means by which the water supply of Rabbah was protected.

12:28. king accomplishing last phase. The royal annals of ancient kings and pharaohs seldom mention their generals by name and always ascribe victories that the gods have granted to the crown. Kings did not always go on campaigns with the army. Assyrian records speak of the king remaining at home while a high-ranking general or the crown prince was entrusted with accompanying the army. This often happened when there were matters at home that were too pressing for the king to be absent. David's absence from the battlefield might therefore lead his subjects (or detractors) to infer that he is incapacitated, threatened or in some way unable to conduct the duties of king. Even when the king led the campaign, he would often not be the one leading the charge in battle but would be back at camp headquarters planning strategy. It would still be normal procedure, however, when possible, for the king to lead the march into the conquered city. David had himself seen the divided loyalties that resulted when his own victories won him a popular following among the people. These eventually contributed to bringing him to the throne. Joab's pointed statement regarding whose name would be invoked as Rabbah's conqueror might therefore be expected to get David's attention and send him quickly into the field.

12:30. king's crown. The word used here usually refers to a ceremonial headdress. Conical caps or turbans were common among the kings and deities of the ancient world. Those worn by kings were often made of embroidered cloth brocaded with gold and gems. At times an additional gold diadem was worn encircling the turban. The weight of this particular crown suggests that it was made entirely of gold and not worn by the Ammonite king but perhaps sat upon the brow of a statue of the god Milcom (an attractive variant reading in the text). Many of the statues of Canaanite gods feature a coni-

cal headdress, so it would not be unlikely for the Ammonite god to be so adorned. It is grammatically possible that it was the jewel in the crown that was taken as plunder and worn by David, rather than the seventy-five-pound crown, which would have been difficult to wear for even a short ceremony.

12:31. labor of captives. One of the sources of heavy labor in Mesopotamia and Syro-Palestine was war captives. While royal annals and inscriptions (such as the Mesha stele from Moab) describe large numbers of captives, these may be exaggerations. More reliable, however, are administrative documents listing rations, clothing and the deaths of slaves. It is likely that these persons were put to immediate use restoring the damage caused by wars but eventually settled and became citizens, tilling farms or serving in the military.

13:1-22
Amnon and Tamar

13:8-9. bread making. The use of a special pan (mentioned in later Jewish literature) in which the kneaded dough is boiled to make a sort of dumpling suggests more than just bread making. Amnon's feigned illness, coupled with the suggestion that he needs someone to prepare nourishing food, calls for an easily digestible item and evident precautions against suspected poisoning.

13:12-13. Tamar's plea. There are four elements to Tamar's plea. The first is that such behavior is not the custom among the Israelites. Obviously taking brides by force is not unknown (see Shechem's rape of Dinah in Gen 34:2 and the abduction of the female dancers of Shiloh in Judg 21:19-23), but apparently it was considered an unacceptable "non-Israelite" custom. When Tamar describes this act of rape, she uses a "shock" word that is designed to bring someone to their senses. The second and third elements of her plea concern personal honor, hers and Amnon's respectively. She realizes that without witnesses there can be no case made against him, and therefore her only hope is to play upon his better judgment and his character as a prince of Israel. She tells him that he will be counted among the fools, a term that applies to men without principle or personal honor who come to a bad end. In Tamar's final attempt (v. 13) she suggests her willingness to join Amnon's household as his wife.

13:18-19. Tamar's garment. The costly, embroidered robe (the term only appears elsewhere in the Joseph narrative [Gen 37:3]) worn by

Tamar marked her as one of the virgins of the household of David. It implied that she was pure and not yet spoken for, and therefore still under the care and protection of the royal house. Now, by tearing her robe, Tamar demonstrates her grief and the fact that her honor has been compromised. Her right to wear this special garment has ended, and her future prospects have been dramatically changed.

13:19. ashes on head. Like tearing one's garment and wearing sackcloth, placing ashes on the head is a sign of mourning (Esther 4:3; Jer 6:26). The gesture of placing her hand on her head has perhaps been illustrated by the mourning female figures on the Phoenician sarcophagus of Ahiram, thirteenth-century king of Byblos, but there the mourning women are putting both hands on their head. The Egyptian *Tale of Two Brothers* also describes this gesture as an indication of mourning.

13:20. Tamar's fate. Because she was no longer a virgin, her worth to her household was diminished, and it is quite possible that no marriage was contracted for her. This is suggested by the comment that she came under the care of Absalom's household rather than David's. She would have lived an unfulfilled existence. The El Amarna texts equate a woman without a husband with an unplowed field.

13:23-39
Absalom's Execution of Amnon and His Exile

13:23. Baal Hazor. This site is usually identified with Jebel el-'Asur, five miles northeast of Bethel, in a rugged part of the Central Hill Country.

13:23. sheepshearing. The wool industry was extremely important in the ancient Near East. For instance, a large percentage of the administrative tablets from the Sumerian city of Nippur deal with the wool industry and the wool trade. Sheep were sheared in the early summer, generally near sites associated with dyeing and weaving (for instance, a large quantity of loom weights was discovered at Timnah). Since this labor required large numbers of laborers, like the grain harvest, the burden was lightened by associating it with a holiday time as well (see 1 Sam 25:7-8).

13:34. geography. The flight of David's sons from Baal Hazor cannot be reconstructed with any confidence. Undoubtedly it was circuitous, but the text of this verse is too uncertain to provide details. It is possible that the location Horonaim included from the Septuagint in NIV may represent Upper and Lower Beth Horon, where there was a major pass from the

Northwest. These sites are identified with Beit 'Ur el-Foqa' and Beit 'Ur et-Tahta, both about ten miles northwest of Jerusalem. Neither city can be seen from Jerusalem, but it can be expected that sentries would have been stationed westward to guard this important approach. The text merely indicates this approach as the road that the travelers were using.

13:37-38. Absalom's flight. After Amnon's murder, Absalom fled back to his grandfather's kingdom in Geshur, in the southern portion of the Golan Heights in Bashan. This independent kingdom and its cities just east of the Sea of Galilee are known from the El Amarna and Egyptian execration texts. David's marriage to Talmai's daughter is just one of several diplomatic alliances created by such unions (2 Sam 3:3).

14:1-20
The Wise Woman of Tekoa

14:2. wise woman. The context of the story and of the political situation requires a person skilled in speaking (see also the wise woman of Abel in 2 Sam 20:16-19). However, for a woman to have an authoritative voice, as each of these women do, a special status is also required. Educated women as well as women in positions of authority (priest, scribe and prophet) occasionally occur in the ancient Near Eastern material, but the category of "wise woman" has not yet been isolated.

14:2. Tekoa. Located about ten miles south of Jerusalem, Khirbet Tequ'a lies in the hill country of Judah and borders on the wilderness. The small size and relative remoteness of this village allowed the wise woman to present a case which might not be known to persons in Jerusalem.

14:2. strategy of the wise woman. The strategy used by the wise woman follows a well-known motif of disguise and legal fiction. For instance, in an Egyptian myth (twelfth-century text) the gods Horus and Seth are each trying to seize the throne left empty by Osiris. Horus's mother, Isis, disguises herself as a herdsman's widow and brings a fabricated case before Seth in which strangers are trying to confiscate her son's property and evict him. Seth becomes indignant on her behalf and by his verdict condemns himself.

14:4-11. king as court of last resort. One of the prime responsibilities of the kings of the ancient Near East was to establish justice and righteousness for the people (prologue to Hammurabi's Code; 2 Sam 8:15; 1 Kings 10:9). To deal with the load of cases that arose, kings delegated authority to elders and judges who heard most disputes (2 Sam 15:4). Still there are a number of texts (Mari letters and the Code of Ur-Nammu), many of them dealing with the plight of widows and orphans, which identify the king as the court of last resort.

14:7. clan responsible for capital punishment. According to Exodus 21:12 murder is a capital crime (also evidenced in the Ur-Nammu code). It would ordinarily be within the rights and jurisdiction of the clan to carry out this sentence (as in the Middle Assyrian Laws). However, it is possible that the "avenger of blood" (2 Sam 14:11) is not a member of the clan and has been hired to carry out the sentence. This case is further complicated by the lack of witnesses (Num 35:30). Even more serious is the elimination of the heir. This would leave the widow without a caregiver, and the family's land would revert to the clan and nearest male kin.

14:7. advantage to clan of extinguishing line. If a man's last descendant was executed or died, his property would remain within the clan and would be redeemed by the nearest male kin (see Jer 32:6-16). There are economic advantages to be gained from this, since it would strengthen the holdings of a prominent member of the clan (compare Ahab's acquisition of Naboth's vineyard in 1 Kings 21 and 2 Kings 25—26) and would ensure the land would remain under cultivation.

14:11. avenger of blood. The legal role of the avenger of blood is described in Numbers 35:16-28 and Deuteronomy 19:6-12. There is some disagreement about whether this person is hired by the clan to carry out sentence or is a member of the clan involved. Blood feuds, even internal ones, were so disruptive that the cities of refuge were established to provide a "cooling down" period and a reexamination of the circumstances of the case (see comments on Num 35).

14:13-17. analogy to Absalom's case. The wise woman skillfully ties her hypothetical case to Absalom's situation. In the analogy the woman stands for the nation (or the people), and David himself has become the avenger of blood who is portrayed as threatening the future of the kingdom and of the inheritance of the covenant by his actions against Absalom. There is also a veiled reference to plotters who stand to gain from Absalom's exile or death as eventual inheritors of David's authority and power. Now, using a wisdom plea, the woman calls on David to be a "just king" who provides a righteous solution to her "case."

14:20. king knows everything. Egyptians also considered their kings to be endowed with all knowledge and capable of discerning what anyone's thoughts were. This was believed to be the basis on which the king was able to rule justly and pronounce righteous judgments.

14:19-20. Joab as Absalom's sponsor. Throughout David's career Joab served as commander of the army and chief political advisor to the king. At times, when it was apparent that David was incapable of making a decision (as with Absalom) or was in danger of harming the authority of the monarchy (see 2 Sam 19:1-8), he used independent judgment. Such autonomy both benefited David and made him wary of Joab's power. In this instance, Joab may have perceived the growing popular support Absalom had with the people and felt it would be better to have him where he could be watched, at court, than working to undermine David's authority in exile. As a "company man," Joab is also interested in securing a smooth and legitimate succession to the throne when the time comes. Thus it is not wise to leave this loose end unattended.

14:21-33
Absalom Restored to Favor

14:24. Absalom's partial restoration. It was not uncommon for persons to be exiled for political reasons. For instance, the Middle Kingdom Egyptian courtier Sinuhe spent over twenty years in forced exile, and Ahiqar, the advisor to the Assyrian king Sennacherib, lived for a time in exile in Egypt. On their return, however, they expected honorable treatment and a restoration of former status. But even though David agreed to Joab's request to return Absalom to the royal court, he was not yet prepared to restore his status (as crown prince?). This suggests that though the death sentence had been lifted, David had no intention of offering a full pardon and was simply keeping Absalom where he could be carefully monitored.

14:26. Absalom's hair. Absalom's virile handsomeness is epitomized by his long hair. Its thickness and weight (between two and four pounds) were considered remarkable. There is a Phoenician inscription from the ninth century reporting the dedication of shaven hair in fulfillment of a vow made to the goddess Astarte. In ancient thinking, hair (along with blood) was one of the main representatives of a person's life essence. As such it was often an ingredient in sympathetic magic. This is evident, for instance, in the practice of sending along a lock of the presumed prophet's hair when prophecies were sent to the king of

Mari. The hair would be used in divination to determine whether the prophet's message would be accepted as valid. Absalom's hair is not connected to any such functions in this text. Instead the reference to the hair simply serves as a foreshadowing of his unusual death (2 Sam 18:9-15), a concept that may be strengthened by an omen text that says that if a man has beautiful hair, the end of his days is near.

14:26. shekels by the royal standard. The standardization of measures in Judah is most likely based on shekel weights first established in Ugarit, Babylonia or Egypt (approximately 3.5 ounces to 1 shekel). There is some variation in these standards, with as much as 4.5 ounces to a shekel occurring.

14:33. Absalom's full restoration. Full parental acceptance is seen in Absalom's long-delayed audience with the king and David's kiss (see Gen 33:4 and Ex 18:7 for the kiss as an affectionate greeting and sign of kinship). A public display such as this demonstrated full reconciliation, but it did not promise Absalom the position of heir to the throne.

15:1—19:43
Absalom's Revolt

15:1. chariot and horses. It is possible that having a chariot and horses and an entourage of fifty runners could be construed as official language for status as either a king or the heir to the throne. The chariots featured two yoked horses with one or two others harnessed beside. Two spoked, wooden wheels on a rear axle supported a small platform occupied by a driver and rider equipped with bow and spear. The sides only went up to midthigh on the standing occupants. The word used here suggests an ornamental chariot of the sort used both in Egypt and Mesopotamia. The luxury transportation of the day, these were typically gilded with all variety of gold, lapis lazuli and precious stones.

15:1. fifty runners. Those who run before chariots proclaim the presence of the king or prince and protect his person. In Hittite texts the gods are said to run before the king's chariot leading to victory. The men who run before the king's chariot function as heralds. Fifty was a regular unit within the military. Having such an entourage gave Absalom a bodyguard as well as the rank of captain. Wherever he went, his fifty runners would have raised attention and given credence to his claim to his status as heir apparent.

15:2-6. Absalom's currying favor with the people. When a prince wishes to displace his father the king, it is inevitable that he will attempt to undermine the king's authority with public statements about corruption or governmental malpractice. For example, the Ugaritic king Keret is denounced by his son for not hearing the cases of widows, the poor or the oppressed. Absalom employs this same strategy, taking advantage of a lack of leadership on David's part (failure to appoint judges) and of growing discontent among the northern tribes. In addition to offering them a model of efficient administration of justice, Absalom also plays the "common man," not allowing supplicants to bow to him but kissing them as an equal or friend.

15:7-10. Hebron. It is shrewd political maneuver on Absalom's part to be crowned in Hebron (nineteen miles southeast of Jerusalem). In addition to being the site of the ancestral burial cave at Machpelah, it was also David's capital city when he was king of Judah. Absalom thereby associates himself with the covenant and the roots of David's original power center. He also puts enough space between himself and Jerusalem to prevent interference and set the stage for his march on the capital.

15:8-9. fulfilling vow. Information concerning vows can be found in most of the cultures of the ancient Near East, including the Hittite, Ugaritic, Mesopotamian and, less often, Egyptian. Vows are voluntary agreements made with deity. Vows would typically be conditional and accompany a petition made to deity. Since this is a religious act, drawing the deity into compact with the worshiper, it may not be broken under penalty of God's displeasure. This may explain why David would accept Absalom's request, even though six years had passed since the vow was spoken.

15:10. sound of the trumpets. The blowing of trumpets or the ram's horn (shofar) was used as a signaling device in battle, for celebration and as preparatory to a major announcement, as in the coronation of a king. The shofar is capable of a variety of tones but cannot play a tune so is used primarily for signals. The ram's horn was softened in hot water and then bent and flattened to produce its distinctive shape. Trumpet signals are attested in Egypt in the Late Bronze Age (this time period) in both military and religious contexts. A preset code would include some combination of long and short blasts.

15:10. king in Hebron. David had been king in Hebron for seven years before moving his capital to Jerusalem. Drawing on this dynastic tradition, Absalom has himself declared king in Hebron. This gives his rebellion greater legitimacy and provides ample indication that he was drawing support from Judah as well as the northern tribes. Hebron was centrally located in the hill country of Judah and was one of the most important towns in the region. It is located about twenty miles south of Jerusalem. For more information see comment on 2:1.

15:12. offering sacrifices. As in 1 Samuel 10:8 it is likely that the sacrifices were burnt offerings and fellowship offerings, two of the most general types of sacrifices. The former often accompanied a petition, while the latter served as an opportunity for festive celebration and a communal meal before the Lord. These sacrifices would have been directed to the initiation of kingship and perhaps toward military activity against David. The sacrifices were being offered to make petition for God's blessing and in preparation for a feast that would create an alliance between Absalom and those in attendance.

15:12. Ahithophel. This is the first introduction to Ahithophel, one of David's chief advisors. As suggested in the comment on 11:3, he is likely the grandfather of Bathsheba. In nations where kingship is either inherited or won on the battlefield, advisors were essential for providing educated, wise and diplomatic strategies and counsel. Often adorned with titles such as vizier, prime minister or royal steward, these individuals were entrusted with many of the responsibilities for operating the kingdom. During this period the Israelite kings did not designate such an office, and Ahithophel is never listed among the officials of the administration, but his status as royal counselor suggests that he may have enjoyed some of that function.

15:12. Giloh. Although sometimes identified with Khirbet Jala, five miles northwest of Hebron, this hometown of Ahithophel is more likely to be found further south and west, near Debir. It was assigned to the tribal territory of Judah (Josh 15:51).

15:16. concubines caring for palace. Since royal marriages were a reflection of the power of a monarch and represented political and economic alliances made in the name of the state, it would have been necessary, at the succession, for the harem of the former king to become the responsibility of the new monarch. In this way, there was continuity of treaty obligations. It is possible that the concubines left behind were those that David had taken into his harem from the leading Jebusite families of Jerusalem (see 5:13) or from some of the families that were supporting Absalom in Hebron.

15:18. Kerethites, Pelethites, Gittites. These were groups of mercenaries who served David as vassals rather than as members of the standing army. The Kerethites are identified as immigrants from Crete and are closely associated with the Philistines who were believed to come from the same area of the Aegean. The Pelethites are known only from passages such as this where they are associated with the Kerethites. The Gittites may be a brigade of troops formed during David's service with Achish of Gath (1 Sam 27:1-12) or simply a group formed as his personal bodyguard after becoming king. All of these troops seem to be of Philistine or Cretan origin. It is unclear from the text whether these special units of mercenary troops (see 2 Sam 8:18) represented the sum total of the army which David was able to command in his retreat from Jerusalem or simply additional contingents.

15:19-22. mercenaries' loyalty. It became common practice in the ancient Near East to employ mercenary troops to augment native forces (for instance, Egyptian use of Nubians starting with the New Kingdom). However, as David suggests, the loyalty of mercenary troops is generally based on regular payment and, when possible, choosing to fight on the winning side. The remarkable statement by Ittai the Gittite expressing personal loyalty to David implies a long-standing relationship and a fealty that transcends monetary gain.

15:23. geography. David leaves Jerusalem traveling east across the Kidron Valley toward the Mount of Olives, the hill across the valley from Jerusalem. He then continues northeast to Bahurim following the Jerusalem to Jericho road to the Jordan Valley across the region the text refers to as the wilderness. He eventually would have crossed the Jordan at the fords of Jericho and then proceeded north to Mahanaim.

15:24-25. role of the ark. It would be logical to bring the ark along because the ark represents the presence of Yahweh and as such is a powerful talisman (for the significance of the ark in battle see comment on 1 Sam 4:3-7). However, David is discerning enough to recognize that if he is out of favor with God, the ark will do him no good and may even pose a threat. There is also a potential advantage to be gained by leaving the ark in Jerusalem, as he shrewdly uses its continued presence as a cover for the spying efforts of Zadok, Abiathar and the priesthood (2 Sam 15:35-36; 17:15-16).

15:25-26. testing the Lord's favor. Israelites believed that God's favor or disfavor was evidenced in the good or evil that came into a person's life. David's expulsion from Jerusa-

lem is therefore described almost as a trial by
ordeal. The king's speech suggests that he is
resigned to leave the course of events in God's
hands. Remembering the pronouncement of
judgment by Nathan, recorded in 12:10-12,
David cannot be certain that these tragic
events are not punishment for his crimes.
David is relying on Zadok's ability as a seer to
obtain a word from Yahweh on the king's ultimate fate (compare Saul's use of the witch of
Endor in 1 Sam 28:3-8). One Mari prophetic
text provides a warning of a revolt and the
need to surround the king with trustworthy
officials; this might be the type of message
David was hoping to receive.

15:28. fords in the desert. The "fords in the
desert" is a reference to the fords near Jericho,
about a day's journey from Jerusalem. Rather
than taking the symbolic step of leaving his
kingdom entirely, David plans to encamp on
the west bank of the Jordan River, about four
miles from the mouth of the river as it empties
into the Dead Sea. He would rest here and
await news of the developments in Jerusalem
(see 2 Sam 17:16).

15:30. Mount of Olives. When dealing with
ancient geographic names, it is always possible that the reference is to a landmark or trail
that is no longer in existence. In this case, the
place name may refer to the Mount of Olives
(see Zech 14:4) or perhaps to a specific path up
the middle slope of one of the three ridges of
the Mount of Olives leading to the northeast.
This is less than a mile from the city walls.

15:32. summit where people used to worship.
This place of worship is not previously mentioned in the text but probably represents a
traditional open-air altar or an abandoned
shrine. Some suggest this is to be identified
with Nob (1 Sam 21:1, 19), but that is uncertain, and Nob is generally thought to be further north.

16:1-2. food supplies. Any army in the field
needed provisions and a supply line. Local
governors in Assyria were required to open
granaries for armies that were traveling
through the region. It is common that the people from the area were expected to provide
supplies. In this case, the food also functions
as tribute to a sovereign and recognition of
David's right to rule. Ziba's gift is less generous than Abigail's in 1 Samuel 25 but is not of
inappropriate size.

16:3-4. Mephibosheth's absence. While David's immediate concern is the rebellion within
his own household, this chapter reminds us
that there is a deposed dynastic house (Saul's)
lurking in the background and willing to capitalize on David's weakness to its own advan-

tage. Ziba categorizes Mephibosheth with the
disgruntled in a ostensibly successful attempt
to curry favor with David. Ziba's accusation is
sufficiently believable that David confiscated
Mephibosheth's lands. The Sumerian code
calls for an adopted son to forfeit land in cases
where he has repudiated his legal obligations
to the family that adopted him. David had always had the option to confiscate the lands
belonging to his predecessor. Here he exercis-
es that option but does not take them for the
crown, instead giving them as a grant to a loyal servant.

16:5. Bahurim. Located north of the Mount of
Olives, Bahurim was a Benjaminite village
(probably Ras et-Tmim or Khirbet Ibqe'dan).
Saul had been from the tribe of Benjamin, so it
would be expected that here among his kin
one would find an enclave of loyalists. This is
still practically on the doorstep of Jerusalem,
which itself is in the territory of Benjamin.

16:11. the Lord has told him. David is not
claiming to have been privy to a discussion
between the Lord and Shimei, nor is he suggesting that Shimei has been the recipient of a
prophetic oracle of some sort. The way that
the Lord had "told" Shimei to curse David
was through the events that had transpired.
With David's own son driving him from the
throne, it would be very easy to infer that
David was suffering judgment at God's
hands. All that is left to deduce is what the offense might have been that led to the punishment. David is simply acknowledging that
Shimei is absolutely justified in thinking that
God had cursed him and therefore cannot be
blamed for wanting to jump on the bandwag-
on. Only a future vindication would free David to consider Shimei's acts to be in the
category of treason rather than simply a voice
recognizing the circumstances through which
God is carrying out retribution.

16:21. Absalom and David's concubines. It
can be shown in a number of instances that
the royal harem is considered the exclusive
property of the reigning king. Any attempts to
obtain women from the harem are seen as a
sign of rebellion or usurpation of power (see
Ishbaal's reaction to Abner in 2 Sam 3:6-11 and
Adonijah's request for Abishag in 1 Kings
2:20-21). The loss of the harem to another
monarch, as described in the Assyrian annals
of Sennacherib, was a sign of submission or
being deposed. For more information see the
comment on 3:7.

17:1. twelve thousand men. This number may
actually refer to a levy from all twelve tribes
rather than an exact figure. Some scholars
suggest that the word translated as "thou-

sand" was simply a military unit. For more information see comment on Joshua 8:3.

17:1-3. Ahithophel's strategy. By eliminating David, Ahithophel believed that any opposition to Absalom's rule would collapse. A quick attack on the disorganized, exhausted "army" of David might well be successful in killing the king and routing his already demoralized forces in a place of their choosing. This was not to be a pitched battle but a surgical strike with a fixed purpose.

17:5-13. Hushai's strategy. Carrying out the role of double agent assigned him by David (2 Sam 15:32-36), Hushai argues against Ahithophel's immediate strike against David. He suggests a militarily sound strategy of consolidating Absalom's control over the capital and the nation before moving in great force against the deposed king. He also raises the specter of a possible defeat early in Absalom's rule that could raise questions about his fitness and restore David's chances of return. He skillfully manipulates Absalom's pride as he paints the grand picture of the new king riding at the head of an endless sea of soldiers ready to overwhelm any meager opposition. Procrastination and additional time for strategic planning are accepted as wisdom here despite the advantages inherent to Ahithophel's strategy (see Amasa's fate when he failed to respond to Sheba's revolt with dispatch in 2 Sam 20:4-13).

17:13. drag the city down with ropes. One of the strategies employed in siege warfare was the use of scaling ladders. It is possible that grappling hooks, attached to ropes, may also have been used for this purpose. These could be climbed as attackers swarmed over the walls or used to dislodge stones from the walls and make them more vulnerable to battering rams. Depictions of sieges in Assyrian palaces include the demolition of walls using picks, but hooks and ropes may also have been used by attackers.

17:17. En Rogel. A spring half a mile south of the Gihon Spring, near the junction of the Hinnom and Kidron Valleys, En Rogel most likely shared the same water source as Gihon (associated with Bir Ayyub, "Job's Well"). It served the needs of the people immediately outside the walls of Jerusalem. Since it was frequented by many people, it would be a place to hear the gossip and it would not be suspicious for Jonathan and Ahimaaz to be stationed here, waiting for word from the city.

17:18. Bahurim. Located north of the Mount of Olives, Bahurim was a Benjaminite village (probably Ras et-Tmim or Khirbet Ibqe'dan). It is a bit ironic that David's spies would be

aided and hidden in a well by an inhabitant of Bahurim, since it was also the home of Shimei ben Gera, who had cursed the king (2 Sam 16:5).

17:23. Ahithophel's actions. Suicide is not condemned in the Hebrew Bible. The six examples (Abimelech, Samson, Saul, his armor-bearer, Ahithophel and Zimri) that appear in the text even suggest a measure of honor and courage is attached to the act, in much the same way as it is described in Seneca (*70th Epistle*). The Roman philosopher says, "The wise man will live as long as he ought, not as long as he can." Thus Ahithophel's departure is a reasoned journey. He clears up his affairs at home, presumably writing a will and insuring orderly transference of property to his heirs, and then hangs himself. He also cheats the executioner, since his support of Absalom would be interpreted as treason against the Lord's anointed.

17:24. geography. It may be presumed that Absalom did not cross the Jordan until some time after David had left the fords and traveled to Mahanaim, about thirty-five miles from the fords at Jericho. Mahanaim is identified with Telul ed-Dhabab el-Garbi on the north bank of the Jabbok. Its importance as an administrative center is attested by its use by Ishbaal (2 Sam 2:9) as his capital and its mention in the records of Pharaoh Shishak. There have been no excavations at the site, but surface surveys confirm that it was occupied during this period.

17:28-29. provisions. Once again David receives provisions for himself and his men (see Abigail's supplies in 1 Sam 25:18 and Ziba's proffered provisions in 2 Sam 16:2). In each of these cases, these foodstuffs could be construed as tribute or as the duty expected of a vassal. The Ammonites had been subdued by Saul (1 Sam 11) and later by David (2 Sam 10). Thus the king is acknowledged by his allies with hospitality and respect despite his forced departure from Jerusalem.

18:1-2. military organization. This division of the military into three fighting units made up of sections of one hundred and one thousand is typical of Israelite military structure (see Num 31:48; Judg 9:43; 1 Sam 11:11). Mesopotamian sources, such as the Mari texts, speak of a variety of military groups commanded by officers of differing rank and status. In addition to these regular contingents of troops, special lightly armed forces used in ambushes and reconnoitering, and troops assigned to protect commanders or the king are also mentioned.

18:6. forest of Ephraim. The most likely area

for this battle site is in Transjordan near Mahanaim (see 2 Sam 17:27). This would fit the
scene of Absalom bringing the conflict to David rather than David invading Israel by crossing the Jordan. The density of this "forest" is
somewhat in dispute, since deforestation and
erosion have drastically changed the area
south of the Jabbok. The word used here
could refer to rugged country with isolated
groves as well as a true forest. It is unusual to
see the forest attributed to Ephraim, since
Ephraim's assigned territory was all west of
the Jordan. But the tribe may have made some
claims to that territory or had settlers there
(see Judg 12).

**18:8. forest claimed more lives than the
sword.** When the Old Testament speaks of
land devouring people (as the forest does
here), it is indicating a hostile, inhospitable
environment that threatens survival. Since
this was a battlefield chosen by David and not
Absalom, it may be expected that the king's
forces utilized the rough terrain and forested
areas to their advantage. Ambushes, feints
drawing troops into ravines or wadis, and
other guerilla tactics may have been employed. Divisions can get disoriented, lost or
isolated and become easy targets.

18:9. Absalom's predicament. The text says
that it was Absalom's head that got caught,
not his hair as commonly assumed. The situation is pregnant with symbolism as the royal
mule (the designated mount of kings) deserts
the would-be king and leaves him hanging in
a tree, a condition for one cursed of God (Deut
21:23).

18:11. ten shekels and a warrior's belt. A bo-
nus of one year's worth of pay and a distinctive article of clothing constituted a significant
reward and indicates how strategic Absalom's
death was to Joab. Gilgamesh's military attire
included both a belt for his dirk and a sash or
girdle of some sort, but the word used here
(feminine form) is never used elsewhere as a
piece of military gear (despite the NIV's addition of "warrior"), usually conveyed by the
masculine form. It is used for a woman's sash
in Isaiah 3:24 and may refer to a fancy sash or
belt worn on special occasions (see comment
on 1 Kings 2:5).

18:14. javelins. The "javelin" used by Joab everywhere else refers to a blunt rod used to
beat someone. The verb is one that usually
means to strike (exception, Judg 3:21). The
heart is not always internal, but can refer to
the chest or the midsection. If Joab's intention
was to stab Absalom, a sword or spear would
have been the more likely choice. It seems instead that Joab intends to dislodge Absalom

from the tree by whacking him in the midsection. A single rod might have broken under
such rigorous use (see Is 14:29), so he uses
three. Once the (probably unconscious) victim
was brought to the ground, Joab's ten assistants collectively finished the job.

18:14. armor-bearers. Commanders and officers within the army were accompanied by armor-bearers (see examples in the *Iliad*). These
trusted individuals formed a bodyguard during battle (see 1 Sam 31:4-6), provided substitute weapons should the commander break or
lose one, and apparently even functioned as
"friends" and advisers (see David as Saul's armor-bearer in 1 Sam 16:21 and Jonathan's armor-bearer in 1 Sam 14:12-17).

18:16. sounded the trumpet. As part of the
preparations for battle, ancient armies
throughout the Near East broadcast to their
troops a set of designated signals that would
call for advance or retreat. The use of trumpets (shofar) and runners might be the only
means to control troop movements. They
were also used as a rallying sound to assemble
troops for battle or, like the fire signals of the
Mari texts, as a signal of approaching danger.

18:17. burial practice. Assyrian texts indicate
that punishment of rebels regularly included
impalement, leaving the bodies unburied. Israelite leaders also engaged in these forms of
"display" (see the execution of the five enemy
kings in Josh 10:27), but the bodies were not to
be left hanging indefinitely (Deut 21:23). Thus
even accursed individuals would be buried
under a pile of stone (see comment on Josh
8:29)—not to be confused with the honorable
funerary mounds of Mesopotamian kings.

18:18. pillar as monument. The Ugaritic Epic
of Aqhat (c. 1600 B.C.) mentions that one of the
duties that a son owes to his father is to erect a
stele or pillar in honor of the ancestor gods.
Since Absalom has no [living?] son to do this
for him, he does the job himself. This is rather
ironic considering that he was not buried in
the family tomb. His personal monument becomes a sad marker of a failed life. The tomb
in the village of Silwan (across the Kidron valley from Jerusalem) today called Absalom's
tomb is from a much later period (Herodian).

18:18. King's Valley. The exact location of this
site is unknown. It is often identified with the
Kidron Valley, east of Jerusalem, or the conflu-
ence of the Hinnom, Tyropoeon and Kidron
Valleys. It is also referred to as the Valley of
Shaveh in Genesis 14:17.

18:19-23. messengers bringing news. Runners
were used by armies and government officials
in the ancient Near East. The Mari texts describe battlefield movements being partially

directed by messengers as well as diplomatic dispatches and news of the approach of delegations and caravans. It seems apparent from these texts as well as the biblical narrative that messengers had different ranks. Some, like the *suharum* of Mari, were young men employed for their stamina and speed. However, there were also messengers in the lower levels of the diplomatic corps (perhaps comparable to the priestly status of Ahimaaz) who were trusted with more important missions.

18:24. between inner and outer gate. Starting with the Middle Bronze period, city fortifications included both massive wall systems and elaborate, multichambered city gates. The patterns in the Iron Age varied from site to site (both casemate and solid wall construction), but generally a stepped approach and narrow entrance restricted the types of vehicles and the amount of traffic through the gateway. Additionally there was often a right-angle turn inside the outer gate before entrance was gained to an inner gate. Within this area between the gates were guardhouses and meeting places used by legal and business officials. Excavations at the city of Dan have revealed an elevated platform between the two gates where it is thought that the ruler of the city sat when public court was in session.

18:24. roof of the gateway. Whether rectangular or circular in construction, gates were guarded by multistoried towers that could be used as lookout posts. Evidence from Megiddo, Timnah, Hazor and Lachish demonstrates the use of tower fortifications for defense and as platforms for sentries.

18:33. room over the gateway. Since the gates and their attendant towers were multistoried, there would be ample room within their walls for guardhouses and chambers used for quartering troops and as meeting places. David's retreat after the news of Absalom's death into one of these rooms places him in a position to see the disposition of his army while still having privacy. The fact that he did not go back into the city suggests his awareness of the delicate political situation, while at the same time indicates he is not ready to resume his regular schedule.

19:8. king's seat in the gateway. Recent excavations at Tel Dan have revealed what appears to be a stone platform set inside the gate area, which once was canopied and may have held a throne. It could have been used for ceremonial or diplomatic occasions or legal proceedings (see 1 Kings 22:10). The Ugaritic Epic of Aqhat describes King Danil sitting in the gate area judging the cases of widows and orphans. Thus a king enthroned is a king carry-ing out the duties of the position—an image David now wanted to portray.

19:11-15. process for reinstallation of David. Because Absalom had been anointed king, and because the tribal elders of both Judah and Israel were divided on whether to take David back as king, certain compromises and assurances had to be made. For instance, Absalom's chief general, Amasa, is now given charge of David's army (although not the elite and mercenary troops, which remained under Joab's command). David also has to cajole his own tribe, reminding them of blood ties and previous oaths of loyalty. David's exile and eventual return to kingship could be compared to the similar experiences of Idrimi, the fifteenth-century B.C. king of Alalakh, who was forced from his throne for seven years before regaining the loyalty of his vassals.

19:15. Gilgal. During much of the early monarchy, Gilgal apparently served as a cultic center. Perhaps because of its previous association with the installation of Saul as king and its proximity to the Jordan River (possibly identified with sites near Khirbet Mefjir, about a mile northeast of Jericho), this was an appropriate place for the tribal elders to welcome David back as king. See comments on 1 Samuel 7:16; 11:14-15.

19:24. caring for feet and mustache. The NIV translation suggests a neglect of personal appearance that frequently accompanied mourning. This would also serve as evidence that Mephibosheth had entertained no thought of promoting himself for the throne, for otherwise he would have taken special care to appear kingly. Alternatively, Ezekiel 24:17 identifies bared feet and covered mustache as signs of mourning. The actions attributed to Mephibosheth allow this possibility, because the text simply says he had not "done" his feet or mustache.

19:22, 29. pardon granted on special occasions. The king serves as "head of household" to his nobles and royal court. As such he may operate as a *paterfamilias*, granting life or sentencing them to death for political crimes or disloyalty (see 1 Kings 2:19-46). Shimei and Mephibosheth have both committed crimes against David that could justify the death penalty. However, David chooses on the day of his accession to pardon them as a sign of his magnanimity and willingness to forgive his political enemies (see Saul's similar statements in 1 Sam 11:12-13). It was typical in Mesopotamia for the king to declare *anduraru*—a release of prisoners and debt slaves—connected to his accession to the throne. Similar release could also extend to those guilty of political crimes as seen in the reform document of the Sumerian king Uruinimgina (twenty-fourth century B.C.), in which even thieves and murderers are freed. In Egypt the coronation of a new pharaoh was often accompanied by proclamations of amnesty.

19:42. eating the king's provisions. Those who eat from the king's table or storehouse are his dependents and must therefore demonstrate their loyalty based on this payment (evidenced in the listing of provisions provided to nobles and members of the bureaucracy in Mari and Babylonian administrative texts). This is the basis of Mephibosheth's crime, since he is one who had accepted David's provisioning (2 Sam 9:6-7). The leaders of Judah disclaim any such ties, insisting that their welcome of David is based on his ability to rule, not bribes or favors granted to them.

19:41-43. basis of intertribal argument. The presence of favoritism and discrimination is bound to end up being reflected in policies and privileges. At the heart of this dispute is whether the monarchy is built around the person and family of David (a position the elders of Judah take, referring to their kin ties) or whether the kingship is an institution deserving loyalty no matter who reigns (Israel's position). This argument foreshadows Sheba's revolt and the eventual secession of the northern tribes under Jeroboam's leadership. The dispute also is reminiscent of the arguments between tribes so common in the Judges period. Both examples indicate that the idea of centralized government under a monarchy has not yet taken firm root among the Israelites. It is easy to think of Israel as having a natural unity reflected in the united monarchy, while the divided monarchy is considered an aberration. In fact, however, until the postexilic period it was tribal loyalties more than unified national loyalties that tended to govern political decisions.

20:1-25
Sheba's Revolt

20:1. Sheba's declaration. The troops of all the tribes but Israel, feeling like outcasts in the reinstallation process, do not initiate military action against Judah or David but simply abandon David under the leadership of Sheba (he sends them "to their tents" rather than mustering them for battle). Sheba's declaration effectively announces withdrawal of support of David's kingship, but it does not indicate support for another king. Since Sheba is a Benjaminite, it is possible that there is still some linkage to the house of Saul and that a

Saulide would be sought, but the text does not reveal that element.

20:3. treatment of the ten concubines. Because Absalom had taken sexual possession of these women, they could no longer serve as sexual partners of the king. If they had been in the harem to represent political allies who had supported Absalom, their status as persona non grata would be doubly justified. David maintained his obligation to them, but they would never have children by him. Hammurabi's code requires that widows receive "food, oil and clothing" as their due, and Exodus 21:10 addresses similar rights of concubines.

20:4-5. mustering the army. The short period of time allotted for Amasa to assemble an army from the clans of Judah may be a test of his and their loyalty. Amasa had served Absalom, and the elders of Judah had only recently renewed their oath of loyalty to David. Runners may have been used to gather the troops (see the seven-day mustering of 1 Sam 11:3-5), but the Mari texts indicate the use of inscribed lists that were to be taken to villages and encampments to enlist soldiers. This procedure would have required much more than three days to gather a large force.

20:6. master's men. Joab is the one identified here as Abishai's master. Since Joab is out of favor and perhaps demoted, Abishai is given command of the standing army. The army was divided into three groups. First were the mercenaries, who served as the king's personal army and bodyguard; these were the Cherethites and Pelethites, of which there were probably several hundred. Second was the standing army, which probably included both Israelites and mercenaries; these were the trained professional soldiers who had been under Joab's command and were now being led by Abishai. At this point perhaps only those of Judah had remained loyal, so this may also be only a few hundred, though the standing army would generally have consisted of a few thousand. The third group was all those who were eligible for being enlisted in times of crisis. This was the group that Amasa was trying to organize.

20:8. great rock in Gibeon. Many times the biblical text makes reference to landmarks known in that time but no longer familiar to us (see Deborah's palm in Judg 4:5). Thus the writer here may be referring to an altar or high place such as Nebi Samwil (about a mile south of el-Jib; see 1 Sam 14:33; 1 Kings 3:4) or simply a particularly unusual rock formation near Gibeon (el-Jib, four miles northwest of Jerusalem).

20:8. Joab's gear. It is difficult to reconstruct Joab's ruse. He is wearing his soldier's tunic with the normal warriors' belt and sheath for his sword. The most common understanding is that Joab contrived somehow to tip his sword out of its sheath in a way that appeared accidental. He retrieved it with his left hand and was holding it nonthreateningly when he came up to Amasa.

20:9. taking by the beard. Greeting a nonrelative with a kiss is not often attested except in situations of obeisance (i.e., kissing the feet; found in many ancient texts, including the Epic of Gilgamesh). There are instances in which the kiss is a form of reconciliation (see Joseph and his brothers in Gen 45:15), and this may be the case with Joab and Amasa. It also could be an expression of concern or commiseration with a common problem, as in 2 Samuel 15:5. When men kissed, it would not have been unusual for one to grasp his fellow's beard. This act makes each man vulnerable and is more often associated with aggressive action in battle. Here it is a sign of trust to allow the kiss. In this case, Amasa's trust was misplaced, and Joab used the opportunity to eliminate his rival.

20:14. Abel Beth Maacah. Typically identified with Tell Abel el-Qamh, three miles northwest of Dan in the northernmost part of Israel, Abel Beth Maacah also appears in the list of Thutmose III's conquests. Its strategic importance is attested to by the recording of its capture by Tiglath-Pileser III in 1 Kings 15:29 and the Assyrian annals.

20:15. siege ramp. One of the common methods in siege warfare was the construction of a ramp that could be used as an assault platform for siege towers as well as a means of gaining approach for battering rams (2 Kings 19:32; Jer 6:6; Ezek 4:1-8). The ramps were made necessary because of the common construction of a slopping glacis and high walls that made it difficult to attempt a frontal assault. Archaeological investigations have found evidence of the construction of these ramps (such as at Masada), and depictions of the use of the siege ramp are found in Assyrian bas-reliefs and are described in the annals of Sennacherib and other Assyrian kings. The earliest archaeological remains of a siege ramp were found in connection with the Assyrian siege of Lachish in 701. Though evidence of ramps has not been found for this period, the battering ram had already been in use for nearly a thousand years, so ramps must also have been in use.

20:16. wise woman. See the comment on 2 Samuel 14:2.

20:19. city that is a mother in Israel. Phoenician, Ugaritic and Old Babylonian word parallels to *'em*, "mother," are kin terms related to clan groups. It is therefore likely that the wise woman's argument is related to the extermination of one of Israel's clans, not a "founding city." This is coupled with a long tradition of common sense by the inhabitants of Abel. Joab is therefore encouraged to be "wise" like them and spare his fellow covenantal partners.

20:23-25. administrative offices. This list of officials within David's inner circle is an indication of the growing complexity of David's growing bureaucracy (compare Solomon's administrative lists in 1 Kings 4:1-19). It and the list in 2 Samuel 8:15-18 are typical of similar rosters found in Neo-Babylonian administrative documents. While these offices are unrelated to the story of Sheba's revolt, it would be appropriate for the editor to insert the list here as an indication of the restoration of political order. The inclusion of a new office, that of chief of forced labor, also suggests new policy objectives to strengthen fortresses and improve communication and travel within the kingdom.

21:1-14
Revenge of the Gibeonites

21:1. previous administration offenses as cause for present distress. In the ancient Near East it is common for the king to be understood as the embodiment of the state and the representative of the people. During the reign of the Hittite king Mursilis, a twenty-year plague was determined to have been the result of offenses committed by his predecessor, and attempts were made to appease and make restitution. Likewise the Babylonian king Nabonidus discerned by oracle that some of his difficulties were the result of the neglect of the moon god, Sin, and he sought to rectify that situation. Perhaps most notable among ancient documents for the condemnation of previous kings' conduct is the Weidner chronicle. In this document thirteen kings are criticized for their failure to give due honor to the Esagil sanctuary of Babylon. This becomes the basis for the advice to the current administration to be more faithful.

21:1. famine leading to oracular inquiry. Famine or plague was often looked upon as a sign of divine disapproval or wrath. The Hittite king Mursilis composed a body of Plague Prayers in order to avoid the wrath of the gods. Seeking the "face of the Lord" is a common expression also found in Babylonian and

Hittite sources. Seeking the face of a superior normally meant to have an audience with that personage for the express purpose of seeking his counsel or direction. It is not certain in this instance whether David sought God's presence by means of an oracle, or whether he entered a holy place to speak to God.

21:2-4. Gibeonites. The city of Gibeon (modern el-Jib) is six miles northwest of Jerusalem in the tribal territory of Benjamin. For more information see comment on Joshua 9:3. The Gibeonites were protected by treaty as a result of the incident recorded in Joshua 9. It can be understood that they could easily become the target of nationalistic zeal, but there is no information from the biblical records of Saul's reign detailing his actions against them.

21:5-9. seven of Saul's line executed and exposed. The execution and exposure of criminals and covenant breakers was common in the ancient Near East. Some exposed corpses have been found at Terqa (Tell Ashara) in Syria from about this time period, when seminomadic Arameans traveled to the site to give tribute to the Assyrians. Moreover, many Kassite period boundary stones from Babylonia (late second millennium B.C.) contain curses which include exposure of the corpse in the event of someone transgressing the stipulations of the boundary agreement in question.

21:6, 9. on a hill before the Lord. The hill before the Lord was presumably the Gibeonite high place mentioned in 1 Kings 3. It is normally identified with Nebi Samwil, which is about one mile south of Gibeon. The fact that it was performed before the Lord may indicate a sort of ritual act. The aforementioned Kassite treaty curses were also performed in the audience of a deity.

21:9. harvest time. The beginning of the barley harvest is in April, corresponding to the Hebrew month Ziv. The month name was borrowed from the Canaanites and corresponds to the Babylonian month Iyyar, the second month of the agricultural year. An ancient description of harvest time in Palestine can be found in the Gezer calendar (tenth century B.C.). The calendar mentions a month of harvesting barley followed by a month of harvesting wheat. The crops were either pulled out by hand or cut with a sickle.

21:12-14. treatment of bones and bodies. It can be assumed that only the ashes of Saul and Jonathan were buried here, since their bodies had been burned (1 Sam 31:11-13), which was an unusual custom in ancient Israel. Israelites considered that a person's body ("flesh") and spirit were in principle inseparable. Thus, the individual was both spirit and

flesh. Because of this the dead corpse was very carefully treated, as it was still considered part of the person's existence. If the dead person's body was somehow destroyed (e.g., by exposure), that person's existence was severely threatened (for more information see comment on 1 Kings 16:4). This idea is implied in literature and in the material remains from the Mesopotamian city of Ur in the early second millennium B.C. The bodies of dead relatives were buried underneath the shrine room of private residences. They were still considered in some sense part of the family and required eating utensils and other daily life implements. Thus it was important to treat the bones of the corpse with great care. In a similar fashion, David was concerned to take care of the remains of Saul and Jonathan.

21:15-22
Exploits Against the Philistines

21:16. weapons. Either the Philistine's spear or spearhead (the shaft of the spear was not normally made of bronze) weighed three hundred shekels, roughly equivalent to seven and one half pounds, half the weight of Goliath's (1 Sam 17:7). He was girded with a "new sword," an ambiguous term which may have been a special distinction.

21:17. lamp of Israel. The temple was to have a perpetually burning lamp (Ex 27:20). The lit lamps symbolized the presence of God in their midst and the resulting life and hope that they enjoyed because of it. The phrase "lamp of God" is also used to refer to hope (1 Kings 11:36; 2 Kings 8:19), and that would also make sense in this context as the Davidic dynasty represented God's provision of kingship. Similar uses of the word in Ugaritic and Akkadian are tied to perpetuation of rule or divine presence. Assyrian king Tiglath-Pileser III is referred to as the light of all mankind. An Old Babylonian idiom expresses a family having no descendants by the image of its brazier going out.

21:19. spear shaft like a weaver's rod. The spear in question must have been equipped with a thong and a ring for slinging which resembled the wooden rod and rings, tools used to lift the heddle in weaving. This type of spear was a weapon used in the Aegean and in Egypt in the early Iron Age (c. 1200-900 B.C.). There are artistic depictions in both Egypt and Greece of women weaving with the aforementioned tools.

21:20-22. twelve fingers and twelve toes. Deformities were the object of intense curiosity and speculation in the ancient world. There is an entire series of Mesopotamian omen texts that describe birth anomalies, including those with extra digits on hands and feet.

22:1-51
David's Hymn of Victory

22:1-51. singing a victory song. One way to celebrate victories and commemorate them for years to come is to compose and sing songs. Songs of all sorts are known throughout the ancient Near East from the first half of the third millennium. One Assyrian list of songs about a century before David includes titles of about 360 songs in dozens of different categories. The singing of a song in response to divine help resulting in victory is a common theme in the Bible. Though they may not be the same genre as the Hebrew Psalms, kings from both Mesopotamia and Egypt composed dedicatory hymns to gods, thanking them for victory over their enemies. For example, Tukulti-Ninurta I of Assyria (c. 1244-1208 B.C.) composed a long epic hymn to Ashur thanking him for victory over Babylon, while justifying his conquest of Babylon because of the unworthiness of their ruler.

22:2-3. rock metaphor. The rock in the Old Testament often symbolized security and the defense of an impregnable refuge. God was the rock (or mountain) who gave security and safety to his people. Some of the most important Anatolian and Palestinian deities of the late second millennium B.C. (such as El, the divine creator) were described as deified mountains.

22:5. waves of death metaphor. Here, as in the book of Jonah (2:6-7), the writer equates his circumstances with a watery covering at the entrance to death, which is a synonym to Sheol, the abode of the dead. Swirling waters represented the chaotic, destructive waters that jeopardize not only life, but creation.

22:6. cords of the grave. Noose snares were commonly used by hunters in the ancient Near East. In this metaphor, death or Sheol is the hunter. For many cultures in the ancient Near East, Sheol, the abode of the grave (i.e. underworld) was a very real place where individuals led an amorphous existence, eating clay and dust, hoping that their descendants would take care of their needs. There were gates and gatekeepers to keep the dead inside; thus it was called "the land of no return." This description can be found in the second-millennium Akkadian epic The Descent of Ishtar. Apparently the Hebrew view of the grave was not unlike this, although there is no elaborate description of it in the Old Testament.

22:14-16. Yahweh as a warrior. In the divine warrior motif the deity is fighting the battles and defeating the deities of the enemy. In Assyria, Nergal is the king of battle, and Ishtar is also viewed as a war goddess. The Canaanite Baal and the Babylonian Marduk are divine warriors. Thunder and lightning were considered to regularly accompany the presence of a deity in the ancient Near East, often in a battle setting. From the Sumerian Exaltation of Inanna, to the Hittite myths about the Storm God, to the Akkadian and Ugaritic mythologies, the gods are viewed as thundering in judgment against their enemies. Baal is depicted as grasping a handful of thunderbolts. Thundering terminology is picked up in royal rhetoric as Hittite or Assyrian kings portray themselves as the instruments of the gods, thundering against those who have violated treaties or stood in the way of empire expansion.

22:34. feet of a deer. There were fairly large populations of Iranian deer in Palestine during the period of the Israelite monarchy (although they became extinct sometime last century). They were never domesticated and represented only a small percentage of the meat supply at the Bronze and Iron Age sites in the region. Some deer were kept in captivity, as described by a fifteenth-century ration list from coastal Alalakh (see comment on Ps 18:33).

23:1-7
Last Words of David

23:1. oracle of David. The introductory term translated "oracle" is most commonly used to introduce speeches of the Lord, but it is also sometimes used to introduce wise sayings (Agur's oracle, Prov 30:1) or prophetic speeches (Balaam's oracle, Num 24:3, 15), as verses two and three suggest this is. This is the only insinuation in the Old Testament that David could be classified among the prophets.

23:1. singer of songs. It is unclear whether this phrase represents a description of David or a description of the "God of Jacob." Both can be justified from usage of this terminology in the Ugaritic texts. The former would describe David's singing talents, and the latter would describe God as the treasured object of the songs or perhaps the cherished defender of Israel.

23:5-7. metaphors of kingship. The metaphor begun at verse five has a solar flavor. The rule of a just king is like the warmth of the sun for crops but is devastating to the unjust. Representing the king's justice as the sun (Yahweh is the king in this case) is found among the Hittites and especially for the kings of Egypt. A Middle Kingdom hymn to the god Amun-Re describes the king as the lord of rays, who gives life-giving rays to those whom he loves but is a consuming fire to his enemies. In Mesopotamia it is Shamash, the sun god, who is the god of justice. Thorns symbolize rebels, who are simply poked into the fire (the result of the sun's heat).

23:8-39

Accounts and List of David's Mighty Men

23:8. David's mighty men. It is generally thought that the thirty were a special group of retainers—champions who had attached themselves to David (see comment on 1 Sam 17:25) and served as his "special forces" group—an elite group of operatives that did not necessarily function within an organized military structure.

23:11-12. Pas Dammim. Pas Dammin, or Ephes Dammin (1 Sam 17:1), was described in Scripture as being between Socoh and Azekah near the Valley of Elah. Thus it was west of Bethlehem towards the Philistine coast. Damun, four miles northeast of Socoh, is one candidate for the modern site of Pas Dammin, but it is difficult to see how that could be described as between Socoh and Azekah.

23:13. geography. Adullam was about sixteen miles southwest of Jerusalem. It is identified with modern Tell esh-Sheikh Madhkur. It is not certain whether the "cave" of Adullam is to be identified with the city itself or with a nearby site. The location of the Valley of Rephaim is uncertain but may be the modern el-Baq'a, an area southwest of Jerusalem (see comment on 5:18). Thus the cave of Adullam was somewhere north and east of the Valley of Rephaim.

23:14. stronghold. The stronghold mentioned here is likely near the site of Adullam (see 1 Sam 22:4). Some have suggested that it is a reference to Masada. The context for this section seems to be when David was in flight and thus was not yet king. During David's rule the "stronghold" was Zion (2 Sam 5:17).

23:15-17. gate of Bethlehem. Neither a well nor a gate has been located in the sparse Iron Age remains at Bethlehem. The remaining Iron Age remains have been located on the slope of modern Bethlehem near the Church of the Nativity. The upper part of the mound does not seem to have been occupied during the Iron Age. Thus David's gate and well were probably on the lower part of the town.

23:20. lion pit on snowy day. Lions, though probably not plentiful, were still roaming the countryside in the Iron Age and became extinct only in modern times. Hunting lions was a favorite sport of kings and heroes. Both Egyptian and Assyrian kings chose lion-hunting scenes to depict their manliness. One of the techniques used to hunt lions was the use of a pit. The lion would be pursued into the pit, where often a net would be used to entangle it. The hunter would then go into the pit with a spear and finish the kill. The likely reason for mentioning the snow would be that it made the footing more difficult. Snow was not an altogether extraordinary occurrence in the highlands of southern Palestine.

23:23. king's bodyguard. The position that Benaiah held here, captain of the king's bodyguard, was the same that David held in Saul's administration (see 1 Sam 22:14). This was probably the mercenary force described as "the Cherethites and the Pelethites" (see comment on 15:18). Captains of the king's bodyguard are well-known from Assyrian records and from Greek sources (e.g., Herodotus) describing the Persian army of Darius I and Xerxes I (521-465 B.C.).

24:1-17

David's Census

24:2. census. Taking a census was a practical measure utilized by governments in the ancient Near East, perhaps as early as the Ebla tablets, c. 2500 B.C. (though the evidence here is scant), and clearly by the middle of the second millennium. However, the benefits derived from this practice were not necessarily appreciated by the people since they led to increased tax levies as well as military or forced labor service. Viewed in this light, it is not surprising that popular notions existed that the census was a source of bad luck or the basis of divine displeasure. Mari texts (eighteenth century B.C.) from Mesopotamia describe men fleeing to the mountains to avoid being counted.

24:5-8. itinerary. The census takers begin by heading east into the Transjordan region to the southeast extremity of the land at Aroer along the Arnon and then proceed north to the northeast extremity at Dan. Tahtim Hodshi is obscure, but the logic of the itinerary would suggest something in the region of Mount Hermon, often considered a northeast boundary. From there they head northwest to the Phoenician coast at Sidon and then begin to move south through the main sections of the country.

It is interesting to note that after the mention of Tyre (outside of Israel proper), the Hivites and Canaanites are mentioned, and then the list skips to Beersheba at the southern extremity of the land. In so doing it fails to mention by name any districts, towns or territories on the west side of the Jordan.

24:9. census results. The total of 1.3 million fighting men has seemed high to the archaeologists who study population density. Estimates of the population of the land at the time of David run between three and nine hundred thousand. While granting that the methods by which such estimates are arrived at can be contested, it must also be remembered that the word translated "thousands" in the text may also mean divisions made up of much fewer than a thousand.

24:10. conscience-stricken about census taking. It was because of God's anger (for undisclosed offenses, v. 1) that David decided to take a census. If he is now conscience-stricken concerning that decision, it suggests that his motive for taking the census may have been to appease God's anger. One way to appease the anger of deity in the traditional Near Eastern way of thinking was to pay him off, that is, offer generous gifts to the sanctuary. Since a census generally levied a head tax to be paid to the temple (see comment on the census temple tax in Ex 30:11-16), it is possible that the census was an attempt to appease God by pouring money into the temple coffers. This was not how Yahweh desired to be treated, and rather than appeasing his anger, it increased it. The punishment was the result of both his original anger and David's attempted appeasement.

24:11. seer. The seer and the prophet were engaged in basically the same activity, but the structuring of the role in society was different (much like the difference between the offices of judge and king). The seers appear to be able to pass on their office either to students or to sons, whereas the prophet is spontaneously called by God.

24:12-15. king and people identified together. In the ancient Near East it was common for the king to be the embodiment of the state and the representative of the people. In Hittite literature, for instance, an offense committed by the king could bring punishment on all the people. Royal prayers were often directed toward the deities to seek forgiveness for past or present royal offenses that were viewed as being the cause of present distress.

24:16. angel afflicting the people. This is the same terminology used for the destroying angel in the Passover account in Exodus 12. In the Mesopotamian epic called Erra and Ishum the plague god (Erra or Nergal) embarks on a massive campaign of destruction and is finally calmed by a subordinate, Ishum, preventing total decimation of the land. An obvious difference (among many) is that here in Samuel the destroying angel is under the absolute control of the Lord, while in the Erra epic, Marduk, the chief god of Babylon, is distant and ambivalent.

24:18-25
Altar and Threshing Floor

24:18. Arauna the Jebusite. When David conquered Jerusalem he did not drive out the Jebusite inhabitants. Arauna, having retained a significant tract of land north of the city, is sometimes identified as the Jebusite governor. In fact the Hurrian word (the Jebusites are usually considered of Hurrian extraction) for a feudal overlord is *ewrine*, leading some to believe that Arauna (variant: Awarna) is a title rather than a name.

24:18. threshing floor. Since the threshing floor was a large, flat, open area, it was a natural gathering spot for the townspeople. Since it was so intimately connected with the harvest, it was a natural site for religious ceremonies and festivals. These combine to make it likely that Arauna's threshing floor already had some sacred traditions attached to it from earlier periods.

24:22. threshing sledges and ox yokes. The threshing sledge was a platform made of boards with pieces of iron stuck through holes. This would be hitched behind the threshing animals and loaded up with rocks. When dragged over the wheat it would aid in the threshing process. For this text they, along with the yokes, become a convenient source of wood for the sacrifice.

24:24. fifty shekels of silver. This is not a great amount of money compared to the four hundred shekels that Abraham paid for the cave of Machpelah (Gen 23). Additionally, 1 Chronicles 21:25 reports that six hundred gold shekels were paid for the entire site.

1 KINGS

1:1-53

Solomon Gains Throne over Adonijah

1:3-4. Abishag's status. The fact that David is said to have had no relations with Abishag indicates that she was never officially taken into the royal harem. Though neither wife nor concubine, her role as final companion to the king provided enough ambiguity to later place her in the middle of a power struggle (see comment on 2:13-21).

1:3. Shunammite. Located in the territory of Issachar (Josh 19:18), Shunem (modern Solem) was seven miles southeast of Nazareth. It is mentioned in Thutmose III's conquest list of the fifteenth century B.C. and in the four teenth-century B.C. El Amarna letters.

1:5-6. primogeniture in Israel. In the ancient Near East primogeniture is not always the rule. In many texts it is clear that the children divide the inheritance evenly. With regard to succession to rule, in some cultures brothers had priority over sons. In others it was up to the king to designate his successor, and in some cases the subjects had to consent. In Israelite culture the firstborn was generally assumed to have certain advantages, but neither inheritance nor succession inevitably fell to him. See the comment on Deuteronomy 21:15-17 for the ancient Near Eastern context of inheritance rights of the firstborn.

1:5. fifty runners. It was common practice for persons of high political status to display their authority by riding in a chariot, accompanied by an entourage of runners (see comment on 2 Sam 15:1). In battle formation this provided a set fighting unit, as noted in the annals of Sargon II and other Assyrian kings.

1:7-8. support of army and priesthood. In the Ugaritic Epic of Keret, Prince Yassib, Keret's son, makes the argument that the invalid king is no longer capable of carrying out his duties and that he should therefore yield the throne to his successor. Similarly, David's sons positioned themselves to take the throne from their declining father. They went about this by soliciting the support of power groups within the state—specifically, the leaders of the military and the priestly community. Opposition from either of these groups could make for a short reign (see respectively 1 Kings 16:15-18 and 2 Kings 11). Since the dynastic line was staying in power, there was no need to reenlist support among the tribes and clans. With their

pressing for the establishment of a coregency (a common practice in Egyptian and Mesopotamian monarchies), rather than seeking to forcibly depose David, Nathan and Bathsheba win the throne for Solomon.

1:9, 19. sacrifices. It is likely that the sacrifices were burnt offerings and fellowship offerings, two of the most general types of sacrifices. The former often accompanied a petition, while the latter served as an opportunity for festive celebration and a communal meal before the Lord. These sacrifices would have been directed to the initiation of kingship (coronation). The sacrifices were being offered to make petition for God's blessing and in preparation for a feast that would create an alliance between Adonijah and those in attendance, following the pattern used by Absalom. Such covenantal meals are a part of treaty and alliance agreements, as exemplified in texts from Mari and the Amarna letters.

1:9. En Rogel. This spring is only about 650 yards south of the Gihon Spring in the Kidron Valley (see comment on 1:33) and only about a half mile from David's palace. The choice of this location for the ceremony is probably due to the fact that the spring lies at the junction of the territory of Benjamin and Judah (presumably suggesting both would have access to its water supply). Adonijah's support base can therefore be inferred as comprising the tribal alliances that brought David to power. His support by Joab and Abiathar would also represent this traditional element. The stone of Zoheleth is sometimes translated Serpent Rock and likely refers to a distinctive rock that had some ritual traditions associated with it.

1:21. treatment of claimants to the throne. There is wide precedent in Mesopotamian texts for the elimination of all rival claimants to the throne when a king comes to power. Such purges also occurred years later as a form of revenge for political opposition or rebellion attempted against previous rulers. One way to better understand Bathsheba's fears for herself and her son Solomon is to look at the murder of the Assyrian king Sennacherib in 681 B.C. by his sons. Although the king had designated his son Esarhaddon as his successor, civil war broke out with portions of the military taking sides. Esarhaddon finally secured the throne and had those guilty of the murder of their father executed. Such intrigue surrounding the succession to the throne was not unusual in the ancient

Near East. There had been bloody strife between David's sons in the past (see 2 Sam 13—
15), and a general purge of other claimants
might well occur after David's death. Esarhaddon solved the problem for his successor
by having his treaty partners sign an agreement to support the disposition of his two
sons as king of Assyria and of Babylonia respectively.

1:33. the king's mule. During the early monarchy the proper animal for the king to ride
was the mule (see 2 Sam 18:9). Precedent for
this practice is found in a Mari letter containing a suggestion to King Zimri-Lim that it
would be more in keeping with the dignity of
the monarch if he rode in a cart pulled by
mules rather than by horses. It is also possible
that horses were not in general use by the Israelites until later periods. During this period
mules were two or three times more expensive than horses. They were imported and, of
course, could not reproduce.

1:33. Gihon. This is a spring now known as
'En Sitti Maryam in the Kidron Valley just below the east slope of David's Jerusalem (see
comment on 2 Sam 5:8). In contrast to Adonijah's support base in the traditional tribal
groups, Solomon's base appears to be in the
royal city, Jerusalem, itself. The Gihon spring,
as Jerusalem's water supply, is therefore a fit
setting for this ceremony.

1:34. anointing by priest and prophet. The pattern to this point had been for a prophet to
anoint the prospective king (see the comment
on 1 Sam 16:1). This provided divine sanction
for him to rule. In the ancient Near East, priests
often played significant political roles, but no
prophets from the ancient Near East are known
to have played the role of kingmaker. Now,
with the first example of hereditary succession,
it was appropriate that both the high priest and
a prophet participate in this ceremony. In this
way, both God (through the prophet) and the
religious community that served the people
and Yahweh (especially the Jerusalem sanctuary) recognized the king's right to rule.

1:38. Kerethites and Pelethites. See the comment on 2 Samuel 15:18 for discussion of these
mercenary troops (probably Cretans and other
Sea People descendants). They served as a
praetorian guard, whose duties and loyalties
were strictly to the king. Use of highly trained,
mercenary soldiers is also found in Egyptian,
Mesopotamian and Roman sources.

1:41. noise in the city. Though En Rogel is
only 250 yards from the southern wall of the
city, it is much lower in elevation (near the
southwestern end of the foot of the modern
village of Silwan). Neither the activity in the
city nor that at Gihon can be observed from
that vantage point. Nonetheless, the commo-
tion would easily carry across the valley.

1:49. Adonijah's guests disperse. Adonijah's
supporters apparently were willing to try to
force the succession issue but had no stomach
for civil war. Nor did they desire to be personally aligned with one who would undoubtedly now be labeled a rebel. It was clear that
Solomon had gained the support of both the
king and the political establishment of Jerusalem, and Adonijah's cause was a lost one.

1:50. taking the horns of the altar. Adonijah
claims the right of sanctuary when he grabs
the horns of the altar (see Ex 21:13-14). Archaeological evidence of horned altars has
been found at sites such as Beersheba (see
comment on 2:28). Asylum, however, was
supposed to be granted for unintentional homicide, and Adonijah's "crime" was presuming
his right to rule as king. It seems likely that
the altar, because of its tie to sacred space and
association with the deity (see the comment
on Ex 27:1-8), could be used to take oaths of
innocence in the face of possible punishment
(as seen in Hammurabi's code).

2:1-11
David's Instructions to Solomon

2:1-11. dying king's instructions. A number of
pieces of Egyptian wisdom literature, notably
the Instruction of Merikare (from about 2100
B.C.), take the form of instructions to a newly
crowned king from his predecessor. As here,
the instructions given to Merikare by his father offer advice concerning how certain situations should be dealt with in order to secure
a just and unthreatened rule. The new king's
responsibility is to deal wisely with those who
have shown rebellious tendencies. Even the
categories of rebels mentioned show some
similarity to the individuals David advises Solomon to act against.

2:5. Joab's crimes. Abner (see the comment on
2 Sam 3:29) and Amasa (see comment on
2 Sam 20:9) had both been military and political rivals eliminated by Joab in defiance of
David's intentions. In both instances, David
was politically embarrassed and had to publicly denounce Joab's actions. Given Joab's
past treatment of opponents, the stability of
the kingdom required that he be punished as
a criminal.

2:5. blood-stained belt and sandals. The
words used for belt and sandals in this verse
are never clearly used for military dress (see
comment on 2 Sam 18:11). The idea here may
be that the clothing stained with blood indi-

cated that the killings were not in battle contexts.

2:7. eating at the king's table. Those who eat from the king's table or storehouse are his dependents and those he chooses to sponsor. It is expected that they will demonstrate their loyalty based on this payment (evidenced in the listing of provisions provided to nobles and members of the bureaucracy in Mari and Babylonian administrative texts). Those sponsored in this way would generally be members of the administration and champions of military repute. Many of these would either be already part of the king's family or would marry into the family (see comment on 1 Sam 17:25).

2:8. Mahanaim. Besides serving as an administrative center for the government of Saul's son (2 Sam 2), this is where David set up headquarters when he had to flee from Absalom (see the comment on 2 Sam 17:24). The town is also mentioned as one destroyed by Pharaoh Shishak's invasion during the time of Solomon's son. While it is clear that Mahanaim is in the Transjordan region, the precise location is unknown. The most common identification today is with Tell edh-Dhahab el-Gharbi on the northern bank of the Jabbok. There have been no excavations at the site, but surface surveys confirm that it was occupied during this period.

2:8. Shimei's crime. See the comment on 2 Samuel 16:11.

2:10. royal tombs. By right of capture, the citadel area of Jerusalem was David's private domain and thus a proper burial site for himself and his successors. Ugaritic shaft tombs within their palace precinct indicate this was a familiar royal practice. Early Iron Age (1200-1000 B.C.) and Iron Age II (1000-600 B.C.) tombs, based on archaeological investigation along the coastal plain in the area of Judah, seem to have been primarily either cave tombs or rectangular chamber tombs, some with forecourts and raised benches for the internment of the corpse. The quality and quantity of grave goods can only be speculated on since there is no trace of the royal tombs from the monarchy period. However, it may be presumed, based on the royal tombs of Mycenae, Egypt and Ugarit, that they would have contained treasures representative of the status of the dead. The place often identified to tourists as David's tomb on present day Mount Zion is a late tradition. The only monumental tombs from the First Temple period are in the modern village of Silwan across the Kidron Valley from David's Jerusalem. These do not date back as early as David (who was buried *in* the City of David) and are not royal tombs.

2:11. chronology. Typical of ancient Near East-

ern annals, the narrative describing each of Israel and Judah's kings ends with a summary statement that takes note of the number of years the king reigned and sometimes a mention of contemporary monarchs. Though the number forty is often a round number, here it is broken into very precise divisions, suggesting an actual forty-year reign. David's reign would have extended from about 1010 to 970.

2:12-46
Solomon's Accession to the Throne

2:19. queen mother's throne. There were three different types of queens in the ancient world. The most familiar to our way of thinking is one who is the primary wife of the king (e.g., Queen Esther). While sometimes these royal consorts were little more than ornamentation, in other contexts (such as among the Hittites of the second millennium) they served as royal deputies with extensive power (compare the role of Jezebel in Ahab's court). A second type is the wife (or mother) of the king who accedes to the throne after his death and rules in his place (e.g., Athaliah of Judah, Hatshepsut of Egypt). The third is the queen mother whose royal husband has died but who continues to exert significant political influence over the new king, her son (e.g., Sammuramat of Assyria, Maacah of Judah, see 1 Kings 15:13). That is the role depicted for Bathsheba here. The extent to which the queen mother exercised a significant or powerful role in judicial, economic or social matters would have depended on the personality of the individual. The fact that the mother is named for nearly every king of Judah (though not for kings of Israel) suggests that the role of queen mother was an important one throughout the Davidic monarchy.

2:13-21. Adonijah's request. The network of support for a king would have been found in the powerful clans and families. Acquiring concubines and wives would therefore be the mechanism for building up the backing of each local area. Support might also be found in wealthy merchants, military leaders or even in priestly families. Royal marriages were a reflection of the power of a monarch and represented political and economic alliances made in the name of the state. It would therefore have been necessary, at the succession, for the harem of the former king to become the responsibility of the new monarch. In this way there was continuity of treaty obligations. Consequently a potential successor to the throne at times sought to expropriate the authority of his predecessor by taking over his harem. As a result any attempts to obtain women from the harem are seen as a sign of rebellion or usurpation of power. The loss of the harem to another monarch, as described in the Assyrian annals of Sennacherib, was a sign of submission or being deposed. Abishag's status would have been ambiguous if she had never officially become part of the harem, in which case Adonijah's request would not have constituted an overt attempt to procure the throne. It is possible, however, that Adonijah wished to position himself for an attempt to take over the kingship by acquiring David's last companion. Certainly Solomon chose to interpret the request as having that intent.

2:26. Abiathar's banishment to Anathoth. The Iron I village of Anathoth was located at Ras-Kharrubeh, about three miles northeast of Jerusalem. In the Persian period the site was moved slightly north to the village of Anata. Apparently Abiathar and his family continued to hold estates in this area (note Jeremiah's ties to Anathoth and the field of Hanamel in Jer 1:1 and 32:7-9). As part of Solomon's purge of Adonijah's supporters, Abiathar was banished to the "country life" and forced to resign his duties as high priest. Solomon's reluctance to execute Abiathar or his priestly family is understandable in light of Abiathar's faithful service as priest and diviner for David (see 1 Sam 23:9-12).

2:28. horns of the altar. See the comment on 1 Kings 1:50. Horned altars have also been found in excavations of Canaanite sites and in Cyprus. The horns may have been used to tie down a sacrifice or support a bowl of incense. Joab's attempt to claim asylum by grasping the horns was rejected, because of his treason against Solomon and his unauthorized murders of Abner and Amasa. The charge and curse for "shedding of innocent blood" in verses 31-33 is an oath of clearance for David's family and a condemnation of Joab's. Egyptian legal documents from the time of Rameses IV, twelfth century B.C., charge officials to be careful not to inflict punishment on a person without proper authorization. The text states that "all that they have done [should] come down upon their own heads."

2:34. buried on his land in the desert. It is likely that Joab was buried in a family tomb near Bethlehem (his brother Asahel was buried there in 2 Sam 2:32). The description is of open pasture land rather than desert, and that would fit the area of the Judean hill country.

2:36-37. Shimei's house arrest. Based on Shimei's earlier cursing of David (2 Sam 16:11) and David's final instructions (1 Kings 2:8-9), Solomon places him under close house arrest—a condition in which the prisoner is responsible for maintaining his own defined boundaries. Apparently there was some concern that Shimei might rally support against Solomon among the Benjaminite tribesmen if he was allowed to travel north of Jerusalem. This compares to the restrictions placed on the movement of slaves in the Ur-Nammu and Hammurabi codes and suggests that Shimei had lost rights as a full citizen. In the Instruction of Merikare (see comment on 2:1-11) those vassals who had a history of rebelling but were not currently involved in rebellion were to be exiled.

2:37. Kidron Valley. Mention of the Kidron as Shimei's northern boundary is a clear indication that he is not to have contact with other members of the Benjaminite tribe—a group that had been a part of Sheba's revolt in 2 Samuel 20. The Kidron wadi is located just east of the Ophel, separating Jerusalem from the Mount of Olives.

2:39. geography. Although a conclusive identification of the Philistine city of Gath has not yet been established, the general consensus is that it is at Tell es-Safi, ten miles southeast of Tel Miqne-Ekron. David's association with Achish and his inclusion of mercenaries from Gath (2 Sam 15:18-23) suggest it was part of Israel's political sphere—at least by treaty agreement. Shimei's journey there to recover his two slaves would have taken him west of Jerusalem as far as the Shephelah and easily outside the confines of his house arrest.

3:1-3
Summary of Solomon

3:1. identity of Pharaoh. The biblical narrator chose not to mention the pharaoh by name, but most likely this would have been Siamun, the next to last ruler of the relatively weak Twenty-First Dynasty. Since this pharaoh was faced with difficulties with the Theban priesthood at home, he was unable to conquer either Philistia or Israel. He therefore chose to ally himself by marriage with Solomon, perhaps as a way of weakening the Philistines along the southern coast of Palestine (c. 960 B.C.).

3:1. marriage alliances. The policy of using royal marriages as a diplomatic tool, tying local leaders as well as foreign monarchs together in treaty and familial alliance, has a long history in the ancient Near East (see the comments on 11:1). The fact that Solomon received a daughter of the pharaoh demonstrates he is in a stronger position than the monarch of Egypt at that time. Her dowry included yielding Gezer to Solomon, thereby giving the king of Israel a strategic site overlooking the northern Shephelah and guarding one of the principal roads between the coast and the hill country around Jerusalem.

3:2-3. sacrificing at high places. The picture portrayed in the biblical narrative is that prior to the construction of the temple in Jerusalem, sacrifice and religious ritual commonly took place at local shrines or *bamoth*. They were constructed for this purpose and in most cases appear to be an installation that could be entered and within which cultic activity took place (see the comment on 1 Sam 9:12-13). Many of them may have had an urban setting, although this does not preclude their existence outside city walls on nearby hills (2 Kings 17:9-11). Their actual appearance and the furnishings associated with the high places are unknown, but the large number of references to them as sacrificial sites suggest some may have been quite elaborate. Eventually the monarchy and the Jerusalem priesthood attempted to suppress the use of the high places because of their desire to emphasize Solomon's temple as "the place which Yahweh will choose."

3:4-15
Solomon's Dream

For information on this section see the comments on 2 Chronicles 1.

3:16-28
Example of Solomon's Wisdom

3:16. prostitution. Despite being prohibited by law (Lev 19:29; Deut 23:18), prostitution was apparently tolerated among the Israelites. In fact, several narratives exist in which a prostitute is a heroine (Rahab in Josh 2 and Tamar in Gen 38). Certainly their social status would have been extremely low, but that may well be an integral part of the Rahab episode, where several unexpected events occur. Solomon's willingness to hear the case of the two prostitutes in here fits in well with his image as a "just king" (making up for the judicial failures of David—2 Sam 15:2-4). It is also in keeping with the legal protections afforded prostitutes in the Mesopotamian law codes (Lipit-Ishtar and Middle Assyrian Code).

3:16-28. royal wisdom in judging. Solomon's wisdom is demonstrated in his ability to discern true justice, a quality which marks him as a "just king." This attribute is claimed by nearly every ancient Near Eastern king as he ascends the throne and establishes his rule as one concerned for the welfare of the state and even the weakest of its citizens (see the prologue to Hammurabi's Code in which he is charged by the gods "to cause justice to prevail in the land"). Other examples of the expectation of royal wisdom are found in the Egyptian Protests of the Eloquent Peasant (twentieth to eighteenth centuries B.C.) and in the appeal of the eleventh-century B.C. Egyptian priest Wenamon, who asked the prince of Byblos for a resolution of his case.

4:1-28
Solomon's Administration

4:7. district system. In an attempt to centralize his authority as king and begin the process of weakening local, tribal loyalties, Solomon reorganized his kingdom. The tribal districts that had been created after the conquest and during the settlement period could be dangerous to the Davidic dynasty. The northern tribes under Sheba had already attempted to secede from the united kingdom (2 Sam 20:1-2). If new political boundaries could be redrawn so that tribal populations and the new Canaanite cities added to the nation were mixed together, then the king might forestall future political problems. This restructuring also aided in financing national works projects (see 1 Kings 9:15-19), the national defense and the initiation of international commercial ventures (1 Kings 9:26-28). Since each district was responsible for maintaining the king's household one month each year, a regular system of taxation (other than the religious tithe) could be initiated, further weakening local autonomy in favor of a centralized national perspective on administration.

4:7. provisions for royal household. The king's household consisted of his immediate family as well as his major government officials and their extended bureaucracy (see the list in 1 Kings 4:1-6). In this way each of the twelve officials given charge of Israel's administrative districts (see the list in 1 Kings 4:8-19) helped finance Solomon's government. Their responsibilities would have included marshaling the natural and human resources of their districts to insure a more efficient and profitable use of their local resources in the national interest. Such provisioning also served as a form of taxation, directing the local districts to give service to the national government. Administrative documents from Ugarit, Mari and Babylon give some indication of royal expectations from local governors. A quota of raw and manufactured goods and materials are listed, sometimes side by side with previous years' offerings.

4:8-19. geography. Ugarit and Alalakh both yielded administrative texts with a literary form similar to that found here. The geographical designations for the various provinces of Solomon's kingdom are not sufficiently delineated so that exact boundaries can be established for each of them. Each governor apparently had a seat or seats of administration: for example, Ben-Abinadab at Dor and Baana at Taanach and Megiddo. Some of the districts apparently encompassed previous tribal area: Dan's original area in the central highlands, Naphtali in eastern Galilee and Asher on the western slopes of the Galilee. However, what is distinctive is the inclusion of Canaanite and Philistine territory: Dor, a port city of the Sea Peoples mentioned in the Egyptian tale of Wenamon (eleventh century B.C.) and Canaanite Hepher (Tell Ibsar) in the Sharon Plain (Josh 12:17). The placement of Judah at the end of the list (v. 20) suggests that its administration and fiscal responsibilities may have differed from the rest of the districts because of its association with the Davidic house.

4:21. boundaries of Solomon's kingdom. The description of Solomon's kingdom stretching from the Euphrates River in the east (refers to the area where the river turns north in the region of Emar) to the Wadi al-Arish on the border of Egypt is intended to demonstrate the magnitude of Solomon's rule and correlate it to the boundaries of the covenantal promised land of Deuteronomy 1 and Joshua 1. Mesopotamian annals from the time of Sargon of Akkad (third millennium) to the later Assyrian rulers included statements of the extent of their kingdoms. In general they reflect either military campaigns that have taken the king into areas beyond his actual boundaries or an extension of economic hegemony in which the ruler is able to extract tribute or tolls from neighboring kingdoms or foreign merchants. The reality is that there are various levels of what constituted "control" or "boundaries." The text here does not offer the details of the level of control Solomon exercised over each area, but nevertheless several different relationships may be identified. In addition to the traditional territory from Dan to Beersheba, Solomon had provinces (conquered states such as Moab, Edom and Ammon), vassals (tribute-paying, but having native rulers such as Hamath, Zobah and Philistia), and allies (treaty partners such as Egypt and Tyre).

4:22. daily provisions. Such a notation of the quantities of grain and animals made available daily to feed Solomon and his court fits in well with the picture of a monarch on a par with the Egyptian pharaoh. The use of some Egyptian loan words (cor = homer = 6.3 bushels) suggests that the form of this statement may have been modeled after the official records of Egypt or the Canaanite or Philistine kingdoms. Note that all of the items listed could be stored or kept in pasture or corral until they were needed. Perishable foods were also a part of their diet, but these (other than oil) seldom appear as weighed or measured items on administrative lists such as the ration lists found in the Mari texts that keep track of the exact amounts given to slaves, officials and traveling dignitaries.

4:25. own vine and fig. This is a stock phrase that appears in the historical annals and many of the prophets as a sign of peace and prosperity for Israel. When God is angry, then the reverse occurs, and the vine and fig tree are destroyed along with the peace. The idiom refers to the security and moderate prosperity that allow one to enjoy life's little pleasures. The vine and fig provided some shade as well as fruit and enjoying them indicated some long-term prospects—each took several years to become productive.

4:26. horses and chariots. Typically a chariot team included three horses with only two being used at any one time and the third kept as a reserve. The three would be stabled together, so twelve thousand horses for four thousand pens is the correct proportion indicating the potential for four thousand chariot teams (though some may have been used for cavalry). Nevertheless, 1 Kings 10:26 reports that Solomon had fourteen hundred chariots. This is a large contingent of chariots but is not as large as the two thousand that Ahab contributed to the western alliance that met the Assyrians at the Battle of Qarqar in 853 (see comment on 22:1). In the thirteenth century the Hittites and their allies had amassed twenty-five hundred chariots to confront Rameses II at the Battle of Qadesh.

4:30. wisdom of the men of the east. There was a longstanding tradition of wisdom in the ancient Near East. Proverbial statements, such as those by the Egyptian sages Ptah-Hotep (2450 B.C.) and Amenemope (c. 1100) and the Assyrian courtier Ahiqar (c. 700), closely parallel portions of the book of Proverbs. In addition, the longer wisdom pieces, such as Job and Ecclesiastes, are very similar in form and content to the Egyptian Dispute over Suicide (c. 2100) and the Babylonian Dialogue about Human Misery (c. 1000). Even more classical epic poetry, such as the Gilgamesh cycle and the tale of Ishtar's descent to the underworld, contains elements of wisdom literature that explore issues like human mortality and concern for personal achievement. With such a rich body of literature and tradition, it is a remarkable statement to say that Solomon surpassed all of these ancient sages.

4:31. Ethan, Heman, Calcol, Darda. These renowned wisdom figures are also tied to the genealogy of Judah and Tamar through their son Zerah (Gen 38:30). Mahol (Hebrew *mahol* = dancers) may actually refer to their role as musicians, a profession which is associated both with worship as well as wisdom performance. Ethan and Heman appear in Psalm titles (Ps 88 and 89) and thus have been incorporated into the formal aspects of temple worship, even though they are not listed here among the Levites.

4:32. three thousand proverbs. The *mashal* or proverb fits into a genre of writing in the ancient Near East which is marked by short, pithy statements expressing common sense or well-known values. Three thousand is a round number and is described as the number that he spoke, not the number he composed. As today, wisdom can often be the result of research and gathering of information rather than reflective of some creative enterprise.

4:32. 1005 songs. It was not uncommon in the ancient world to express "more than" with an x plus one progression or the use of a round number plus one or plus a digit (see Prov 6:16; Amos 1:3). But if the five in this number is functioning the same way, it is unusual. This oriental mode of expression is also observable in something as familiar as 1,001 Arabian Nights. Around 2000 B.C. Shulgi, king of Ur, also had a literary reputation. In hymns to himself he boasts of his education and literary skills, and bears the title of first royal musician.

4:33. plant life. Botanical wisdom in the ancient world did not concern the issues that modern day biologists would study. One area of interest was herb lore, which included medicinal functions as well as use in industry (dyes) and food production. In other cultures it would also include magical properties of various herbs. Another area of botanical wisdom would be agricultural in nature—the wisdom of a farmer concerning seeds and the whole planting, nurturing, fertilizing and harvesting process. Since the statement concerning Solomon's wisdom targets trees, however, and occurs in the context of proverbs and songs, it is more likely that Solomon's wisdom was expressed by using trees in parables or fables with wisdom teachings. Such parables

are known in the Old Testament (Judg 9:8-15) as well as in the ancient Near East (e.g., the Sumerian Fable of the Tamarisk and the Palm) and required insight into the nature of the trees and bushes.

4:33. animal life. Though the NIV uses verbs like "described" and "taught," the Hebrew simply says Solomon "spoke about" plant and animal life. As in the previous entry, this suggests that he used his insight to tell stories—parables and fables about animals for the purpose of teaching wisdom. Aesop was not the first to use this medium, and more than a millennium before Solomon the Sumerians were producing animal debates and fables. The most prominent Akkadian fable known to us is The Snake and the Eagle. Additionally, wisdom speech in ancient Egypt (e.g., the Instruction of Amenemope) and Mesopotamia (as in the first-millennium Aramaic Words of Ahiqar) was filled with analogies and parables involving animals and plants.

5:1—6:38
Building the Temple

For more information on chapter 5 see comments on 2 Chronicles 2:1-18.

5:1. relationship between Israel and Tyre. The Phoenicians of Tyre, located twenty miles south of Sidon on an island half a mile off the Phoenician coast, prospered from their control of the naval mercantile trade throughout the Mediterranean. Their independence is attested in the Egyptian Wenamon's report (c. 1080 B.C.), and their influence is found in archaeological levels on Cyprus and later at Carthage on the North African coast. However, their preoccupation with trade and their lack of sufficient farmlands made it necessary for them to establish relations with neighboring nations who were interested in the goods brought by Phoenician ships and could pay for them with grain and other natural resources. Solomon's consolidation of the region of Palestine made him a good trading partner for Hiram and a constant source of income for Phoenician builders and contractors.

5:1. Hiram. The dates of Hiram I of Tyre (Phoenician Ahiram; Assyrian Hirummu) are commonly cited as 969-936 B.C., based on the chronological reckoning of the Jewish historian Josephus (first century A.D.). He claims to have extensive records of the history of Tyre and offers much information about Hiram's reign. This dating gives little if any overlap between David and Hiram and is suspect due to the methods of calculation available to Josephus. Contemporary Near Eastern sources offer no information about this Hiram but mention prominently his later namesake, Hiram II. The name is also well known from the sarcophagus of Ahiram, king of nearby Byblos, around this same time period.

5:3. under his feet. The Assyrian king Tukulti-Ninurta I (thirteenth century) "puts his foot on the neck of" individual conquered kings as well as (symbolically) on that of conquered lands, clarifying that they have thus become his footstool. This is graphically depicted in a tomb painting from the fifteenth century B.C. showing Thutmose IV seated on the lap of his mother (?) with his feet resting on a box that is filled with enemies laid out in a pile. For further information see comment on Psalm 108:13.

5:17. quarrying stone. Limestone from the hill country was quarried for the temple in Jerusalem. This involved simply extracting the stone from the cliffs, not the finishing process of dressing and shaping the stones that would have been done by master craftsmen from Phoenicia (see 1 Kings 7:10).

6:1. chronology. This chronological note attached to Solomon's construction of the Jerusalem temple is at the heart of the discussion of the date of the exodus and conquest periods (see sidebar on the date of the exodus). Most historians would place the dedication of Solomon's temple in 966 B.C. By adding 480 years to this, you get 1446 B.C. as the date for the departure from Egypt. Archaeological difficulties and the strength of the Egyptian hold on Syro-Palestine during the fifteenth century B.C. have brought this date into question. As a result many now see 480 as a stylized number, symbolic of forty years (a typical round number) for each of twelve judges or indicating twelve generations (40 x 12 = 480). Based on the dates for Hiram I and the founding date for the Phoenician colony at Carthage, the temple's construction most likely took place between 967-957 B.C. The note uses typical Phoenician phrasing.

6:1. Ziv. This is the second month of the Canaanite and Israelite calendar. It corresponds to portions of April and May in our own calendar. The fact that the passage identifies this as the second month may indicate that Ziv was not the usual Israelite month name used but represented an official designation known to a larger, non-Israelite audience.

6:4. clerestory window. Because the architectural terms found in the Hebrew are technical terms, their exact meaning is uncertain. Some suggest that the windows were constructed with a narrow opening on the outside and a wider opening on the inside (see Ezek 40:16).

It is also possible that latticed windows are meant here. The lack of windows in Mesopotamian temples, however, argues against natural light entering Solomon's temple (see 1 Kings 8:12). The 'Ain Dara temple had false windows carved into the stone with a lattice-work design.

6:5. six side-rooms. This portion of the temple's structure is clouded by the uncertainty over the Hebrew terminology generally rendered "side buildings" or "wings." These may be part of the earliest construction of the building, serving first as storage areas and later expanded upward as the temple grew. Whether they were intended as permanent structures or even buttresses is unclear, as is the materials from which they were built. The architecture of the contemporary temple at 'Ain Dara features tall corridors flanking the hall. It is possible that this verse describes such corridors.

6:6. offset ledges. The side chambers along the outer walls of the temple were offset or recessed as they followed the wall upward. V. Hurowitz provides two interpretations of this architectural feature: (1) a means of enclosing the temple within a "cedarwood crate" (with cedar boards laid horizontally on the recesses) or (2) a sort of "reverse pagoda" shape, creating the visual effect that the outer wall of the temple widened from bottom to top.

6:7. tools used. Earlier taboos against using iron tools in the construction of sacred altars or buildings (see Deut 27:5; Josh 8:31) are somewhat tempered by their apparent use at the quarry but not near the temple site. An early Sumerian account of Gudea's building a temple for his god insisted that there be no noise around the area of the temple during the building project. Masons used large picks (weighing thirty or thirty-five pounds) for quarrying and smaller picks (weighing twelve or fifteen pounds) for the shaping of the stone. Those found in excavations have iron heads of various shapes with wooden handles. Iron-headed sledge hammers and long double-handled saws were also portrayed on Assyrian reliefs.

6:14-35. See comments on 2 Chronicles 3.

6:36. three courses of dressed stone. Perhaps as an architectural buffer against earthquake damage, the walls of the inner court were constructed with a row of cedar planks (in known examples these are about four inches thick) interspersed after every three horizontal courses of stone. This would help compensate for slight irregularities in the stone size and smoothness. This style is also attested at Ugarit, throughout Anatolia, in the palace at

Knossos on Crete and at other Mycenaean sites. See its mention in Ezra 6:4 with regard to the postexilic Second Temple.

6:38. month of Bul. The Canaanite calendar names are used here as well as the older name for month (*yeraḥ,* meaning "moon"). Bul is also found as a month name in Phoenician inscriptions. It means "moisture" and is tied to the rainy season of autumn in the Mediterranean climate. As the eighth month it corresponds to October-November.

7:1-12
Building the Palace

7:1-12. dimensions and architecture of palace. Like other palace complexes in the ancient Near East (such as those at Mari, Nineveh, Babylon and Susa), Solomon's royal precinct would have covered several acres, and the palace itself was larger than the temple. It served as an administrative complex as well as a hall of justice and an armory. Of the structures mentioned here, the "Palace of the Forest of Lebanon" is most fully described (150 feet long, 75 feet wide, 45 feet high), with its three rows of forty-five cedar pillars making it very much like a "forest." The overall style of construction is much like that of the *Bit-Hilani* of Syria and Mesopotamia (see comment on 2 Sam 5:11), with chambers on three sides surrounding a central meeting hall (75 feet long and 45 feet wide). The side rooms would have contained three stories, while the hall would have been open to the flat ceiling. Doors are found at the sides and at either end, and windows in the upper stories allowed light to cascade down into the audience chamber and assembly hall. The other two palaces (v. 8) are not described in any detail, but since they served as living quarters, their monumental character would not have been as important to the prestige of the monarchy as public buildings.

7:9. dressing of stone. The stone for the palaces was to be cut to specific size and shape so that they could be fitted into a "headers and stretchers" pattern, with cedar logs providing additional stability. It was necessary to first saw the soft limestone from the Judean cliffs (it would harden after exposure to air). This would provide a dressed block (ashlar masonry), finer than could be created with hammer and chisel, that would fit together as closely as possible.

7:10. size of stones. The massive foundation blocks were between twelve feet and fifteen feet in length, weighing many tons. The even larger blocks found in the foundation of

Herod's temple platform in Jerusalem (one block was over forty feet long and weighed about one hundred tons) suggest this was not an unusual size for monumental construction.

7:15-22. free-standing pillars. These two hollow, bronze pillars are thirty-four feet high (counting the capitals) and nearly five feet in diameter. The description of the free-standing pillars of a temple in the Assyrian city of Kar-Tukulti-Ninurta also contains the details of length, circumference and the design of the capitals with which they were crowned. Of particular interest is the additional fact that they were engraved with inscriptions. This feature would be typical for entryways, and it is likely that these pillars were considered gateposts. One possibility is that Jachin and Boaz may have been the first word of the respective inscriptions and therefore came to be considered their names. Pomegranates and lotus flowers (NIV: "lilies") are often used in architectural decorations.

7:23-51. See comments on 2 Chronicles 4.

8:1-66
Dedication of the Temple

8:2. month of Ethanim. This autumn month (corresponding to September-October) was a part of the rainy season and is tied into the Feast of Tabernacles (see the comments on Ex 23:16b and Deut 16:13-17). The dedication of the temple during the seventh month (its completion is noted in 1 Kings 6:38 in the eighth month) may reflect a year-long celebration after the completion of work or a delay of nearly a year in order to officially tie it into the harvest festival.

8:14-66. See comments on 2 Chronicles 6.

9:1-9
Response of Yahweh

For information on this section see comments on 2 Chronicles 7.

9:10-28
Deeds of Solomon

9:11. twenty towns in Galilee. Since the Galilee is defined various ways (see Josh 20:7; Is 9:1), it is possible that the territory given to Hiram included portions of the western foothills as far as Megiddo. Most likely it would have involved the buffer area between Phoenicia and Israel. Note the return of these lands and cities to Solomon in the Chronicler's account (2 Chron 8:2). Precedent for exchange of territory and cities is to be found in Mesopotamian and Egyptian royal records, treaties and annals. For instance, in the Assyrian annals of Sennacherib, the king describes capturing towns in Hezekiah's territory and transferring them to Philistine kings in Ashdod, Ekron and Gaza.

9:14. 120 talents of gold. In the system of weights and measures used in the ancient Near East the talent was the highest unit of weight (equivalent to sixty minas or three thousand shekels). One hundred twenty talents is therefore about four tons of gold. For statistics concerning gold see comments on 1 Chronicles 22:14.

9:15-19. building projects. Both as a part of his consolidation of control over all of Israel and as a check against any armed incursion by the Egyptian pharaoh Shishak, Solomon initiated a program of public works using a corvee or forced labor system. The list found here, which stretches geographically north-south, is similar in style to that found in the Mesha inscription from Moab and in Assyrian royal annals. This program transformed Jerusalem, expanding its living area and defense. It also strengthened the defensive posture of the nation in strategic commercial and military centers such as Hazor, Megiddo and Gezer as well as in the southern border towns of Baalath and Tamar ('Ain Husb). The consistency of building style (casemate walls and six-chambered city gates) at many of these sites helps archaeologists establish architectural links to this period despite the lack of documentary evidence outside the Bible. The infusion of capital necessary to make such vast improvements in the infrastructure would have been a boost for the local economy and kept potentially hostile, Canaanite populations employed more constructively.

9:15. supporting terraces (Millo). The city of Jerusalem in the period of David had occupied only the north-south ridge covering about ten acres that runs south of the modern city walls. The top of the ridge is only about four hundred feet wide and about fifteen hundred feet long. The previous Canaanite city had been built on an artificial platform that was supported by a series of terraces. Archaeologists have uncovered a stepped stone structure over fifty feet tall at the northeast corner of this ridge. This was most likely the platform for the Jebusite citadel referred to here in 2 Samuel 5:7 and was extended by David for use as the foundation of his palace and again by Solomon as the city expanded north to include his palace and the temple complex. It is now accepted by most that the "Millo" (NIV footnote) should be identified

with the retaining walls (including the "stepped stone structure") that provided the foundation for these monumental buildings. There is little else that archaeologists have found in the city that is attributable to the time of David and Solomon.

9:20-28. See comments on 2 Chronicles 8.

10:1-13
The Visit of the Queen of Sheba

For information on this section see comments on 2 Chronicles 9:1-12.

10:14-29
The Wealth and Splendor of Solomon

For information on this section see comments on 2 Chronicles 9:13-28.

11:1-13
Solomon Led Astray by Wives

11:1-3. marriage alliances. Marriage was a tool of diplomacy throughout the ancient Near East. For instance, Zimri-Lim, the king of Mari (eighteenth century B.C.), used his daughters to cement alliances and establish treaties with his neighboring kingdoms. Similarly, Pharaoh Thutmose IV (1425-1412 B.C.) arranged a marriage with a daughter of the Mitannian king to demonstrate good relations and end a series of wars with that middle Euphrates kingdom. The wives of an ancient ruler therefore usually represented political alliances. Towns, city-states, tribes or nations who wished to ally themselves with a ruler or come under his protection sealed the treaty with a marriage of a daughter of their chief family to the suzerain or his son. This was an act of loyalty on the part of the vassal, who would then have a personal stake in preserving the dynasty. In David's case, prior to becoming king of Israel, he made a series of marriages that strengthened his political and economic position. Thus the marriage to Saul's daughter Michal gave him a connection to the royal family, his marriage to Abigail provided him with ties to the area around Hebron, and his marriage to Ahinoam of Jezreel established connections with households in the vicinity of Megiddo and Beth Shan. This kinship network insured that David would have friendly voices in the council of elders from all over the country. The huge number of wives and concubines are designed as a reflection of the wealth and power of Solomon in relation to his nobility and neighbors. The author does not condemn Solomon for polygamy—it was a necessary part of his political activities. Condemnation is for the way Solomon allowed his wives to turn him away from the Lord.

11:2. prohibition against intermarriage. A chief concern of the biblical writers was syncretism. If Israel was to remain true to Yahweh, then it must be free of foreign influence. According to this viewpoint, intermarriage and the training of children by mothers who were not Israelites could only weaken the covenantal bond (see the comment on Deut 7:3).

11:3. wives of royal birth. Distinction is drawn between those wives who were of higher status or rank than concubines. The Ugaritic texts provide a similar example of division within the harem. In Arhalba's court, wives whose children were in the line of succession (such as Kubaba), were considered truly royal women and distinguished from those who had lesser status.

11:3. three hundred concubines. The harem served both political as well as sexual functions. Wives were part of the alliance system between nations, and they were the means of obtaining an heir to the throne. Many wives were a reflection of power and a hedge against female infertility. Not all wives in a harem, however, were of similar social rank, and those from lesser families would have been designated as concubines, whose children would not have been in the royal succession.

11:5. Ashtoreth. See the comment on Judges 2:13 for this Canaanite fertility goddess, the consort of the storm god Baal. In Ugaritic texts (the Keret epic and the Baal and Anath cycle) she is known as Athtar or Astarte, and in Mesopotamia religious documents she is called Ishtar. Ashtoreth/Astarte was worshiped as the chief goddess of both Tyre and Sidon in Phoenicia, and they took her worship throughout the Mediterranean, where she was identified with the Greek goddess Aphrodite.

11:5, 7. Molech. The Ammonite god Milcom (= Canaanite Baal) is actually named in verse 5 (as well as in v. 33) though referred to as Molech in verse 7. (See the comment on Lev 18:21 for the association of Molech, a Canaanite and Phoenician deity, with child sacrifice.) The name Milcom has been attested in Ammonite inscriptions and personal names, and makes more sense than Molech in this context, since this is a listing of national gods. It is difficult to tell whether Molech in verse 7 is a misspelling or a variant form of the name.

11:7. Chemosh. Described in terms very much like Yahweh in the Moabite inscription of King Mesha (c. 830 B.C.), Chemosh is a national deity who punished his people by allowing them to be controlled by Israel during Omri's reign (see 2 Kings 3), called for a holy war of liberation (much like the use of *herem* in Josh 6:17-21), and fought, like Yahweh, as a divine warrior for the Moabites (Josh 10:42). Outside of Moab, Chemosh may have been worshiped as Kamish at Ebla and, based on an Assyrian text equating him with the underworld god Nergal, appears to have been part of the pantheon of gods in Mesopotamia.

11:14-43
Solomon's Political Adversaries

11:14. Hadad the Edomite. Edom had been conquered by David during his wars to subdue his neighbors (see 2 Sam 8:13-14). David's garrisons had probably been meant to secure control of the trade routes and access to the port on the Gulf of Aqaba. Now, perhaps with half-hearted support from the Egyptians (see comment on v. 22), a new Edomite leader was jeopardizing Israelite control. There is little information to suggest that Edom was a national entity at this time. Hadad more likely represented one of the more powerful tribes in the region. His opposition may have taken the shape of raids on caravans rather than wars of independence. There are no references to him in contemporary extrabiblical sources.

11:15-16. Joab's action against Edom. Such wholesale extermination is known from Assyrian records and the evidence of the mass grave uncovered at Lachish that dates to Sennacherib's 701 B.C. campaign against Judah. Many of the fifteen hundred bodies in that grave were civilians, indicating both the loss of life during the siege and the manner in which much of the garrison was exterminated.

11:17-18. Hadad's journey. Like Jeroboam in verse 40, Hadad sought asylum in Egypt. His flight took him south and east of Edom to Midian in the northern Arabian peninsula and then on to Paran in the northwestern Sinai (possibly the oasis Feran; see Num 13:3). The rough terrain and circuitous route would have protected the refugees from pursuit.

11:18. identity of pharaoh. Unlike verse 40, where Shishak is named as pharaoh of Egypt, the monarch is anonymous here. He is most likely a member of the Twenty-First Dynasty, but there is no indication of his identity. Since Hadad was in Egypt from his childhood to his manhood, he would have had association with several pharaohs, including at least Osorkon (984-978) and Siamun (978-959). All of the pharaohs of this period would have welcomed political refugees from Palestine and Transjordan in their attempt to balance and counterbalance the growing power of Solomon and Hiram in the region.

11:18. Hadad's exile. It is an interesting fact of political life in the ancient Near East that political dissidents and royal refugees were often taken in by kings (Egypt, Babylon, Persia and even petty chiefs of Palestine, according to the Tale of Sinuhe). These persons were part of a larger game played by rival monarchs, and what was at stake was the economic and political control of the entire region. The refugees were housed, tied to their patron by marriage and then let loose with some financial or military support to cause as much trouble as they could on a rival king's borders. In this way one power could drain the resources of its rival and eventually set it up for conquest.

11:19. Tahpenes. This word is based on the Egyptian term *t.hmt.nsw,* and it is likely not a personal name but a title. It would be comparable to the Hebrew *gebira* ("queen mother"), which follows it as an explanation in the Hebrew text. Her status is therefore indicated as the "wife of the king" and mother of the heir to the throne.

11:22. Pharaoh's attempt to retain Hadad. If this pharaoh is Siamun, as seems likely, he is the same one who had made a treaty with Israel (see 3:1) sealed by the marriage of his daughter to Solomon. This represented a change in policy from the days of David, when he had been undermining Israelite expansion by harboring enemies such as Hadad. Hadad's resolve to go back and organize opposition against Solomon puts Siamun in a very awkward position.

11:23. Rezon. This name, which is etymologically similar to *rozen* ("ruler"), may be a royal title. Though some have suggested that his actual personal name is Hezion (see 15:18), there is little to support that, and he is more likely a father or even grandfather of Hezion. Apparently this former vassal of the Aramean ruler Hadadezer escaped David's slaughter (2 Sam 8:3-8) and spent some time as a brigand chief. Then during Solomon's early reign he was able to establish himself as ruler of Damascus and create a kingdom (Aram) that would rival Israel throughout the tenth and ninth centuries.

11:24. Hadadezer of Zobah. See the comments on 2 Samuel 8:3-8 and 10:6 for the rivalry between David and the Aramean states in northern Transjordan and western Galilee. Zobah was located north of Damascus (see comment on 2 Sam 8:3). It was one of several Aramean kingdoms that controlled portions of Syria and northern Mesopotamia until the expansion of Israel's control under David and Solomon.

11:24-25. Aram of Damascus. This is the name of the small state centered around the Syrian city of Damascus (see 2 Sam 8:5-6). The growth of its power in the period after the division of Israel into two states made it the most influential state in the area of Syro-Palestine. Assyrian sources from the reign of Shalmaneser III mention it as a significant rival and the head of a coalition of states (Battle of Qarqar in 853, see comment on 22:1).

11:26. Zeredah. The birthplace of Jeroboam may be identified with 'Ain Seridah, about fifteen miles southwest of Shechem in the tribal territory of Ephraim.

11:27. supporting terraces (Millo). See the comment on 9:15 for the structural purpose of the Millo.

11:28. Jeroboam's office. As a member of Solomon's bureaucracy, Jeroboam was a local leader of the regional corvee, a corps of men drafted into temporary service (porterage, construction), within the district of "the House of Joseph" (Ephraim/Manasseh). Since the term for "forced labor" is not used, it may be presumed that Jeroboam's work was with Israelites, not slaves. His position might be compared to the *rabi Amurrim* (head of the Amorites) in the Mari texts, whose tasks included both military commands as well as being a local labor organizer, supervising construction projects on dams and the renovation of temples.

11:29. Ahijah. Though Shiloh (see comment on 1 Sam 1:3) had been destroyed at the time of Eli and much of its cultic standing had been lost, it retained its religious heritage because of its ancient tradition. There may be no significance to the fact that Ahijah hails from the northern territory, but he is playing the role of kingmaker that was familiar in this early period of the prophetic office. Both Saul and David had been anointed by the prophet Samuel, who also was trained in Shiloh. This precedent continued throughout the next century as each of the major dynasties of the northern kingdom (Jeroboam, Baasha, Omri, Jehu) rose and fell in accordance with prophetic pronouncement. Sometimes the designated king was content to wait for the proper time (as Jeroboam does), while for other individuals (such as Jehu), the prophetic proclamation initiated a coup. In the ancient Near East priests often play significant political roles, but no prophets from the ancient Near East are known to have played the same role as these Israelite kingmakers. Nonetheless, throughout the ancient world it was believed that prophets not only proclaimed the message of deity but in the process unleashed the divine action. In Assyrian king Esarhaddon's instructions to his vassals, he requires that they report any improper or negative statements that may be made by anyone, but he specifically names prophets, ecstatics and dream interpreters. It is no wonder, then, that this action by Ahijah immediately put Jeroboam in jeopardy (v. 40).

11:30. division of the prophet's cloak. The cloak Ahijah tears is a normal garment (see Deut 22:26) rather than a garment of office. This is a startling action considering the cost of clothing and the likelihood that most people had only one additional set of clothing. Symbolic gestures become one of the common methods used by the prophets to convey a message. Some gestures are common, normal activities, though usually they take a more eccentric turn (see comments on Ezek 4:1). By accompanying the prophetic pronouncement with a gesture, there was a stronger suggestion that the prophecy was being effectuated and brought into reality. There is some similarity to the way the rest of the ancient world viewed the magical realm. In magical practice ritual actions often needed to accompany the incantations that were intended to bring about the desired result. For more information concerning the relationship between the prophets and magical procedures, see comments on 2 Kings 4:34; 5:11.

11:33. Ashtoreth, Molech, Chemosh. See the comments on 1 Kings 11:5 and 7 for these Canaanite gods.

11:36. lamp in Jerusalem. As an eternal flame is a symbol of endurance and remembrance, the reign of a descendant of David in Jerusalem provides a link to God's promise to David's dynasty (2 Sam 7:8-16). Similar uses of the word in Ugaritic and Akkadian are tied to perpetuation of rule or divine presence. Assyrian king Tiglath-Pileser III is referred to as the light of all mankind. An Old Babylonian idiom expresses the concept of a family having no descendants by the image of its brazier going out.

11:40. Shishak. Shishak (Sheshonq I) was the chief of a prominent Libyan family that had been settled in the Egyptian delta region (Bubastis) as a result of conquests several centuries earlier (twelfth century). He married into the family of the Twenty-First Dynasty pharaohs, and when their line died out, he was positioned to accede to the throne as the founder of the Twenty-Second Dynasty (c. 945). He established himself on the throne through the placement of family members in

key posts and through further marriage alliances. Once enthroned, he made a determined effort to restore Egyptian power by inaugurating a monumental building program in several areas: the Delta region (including both the area of Tanis and Memphis) and Herakleoplis. The biblical account as well as his statue at Byblos indicate a strong interest in extending Egyptian hegemony into Syro-Palestine. His inscription at Karnak describes his invasion of Palestine in 925 (including a list 154 towns destroyed) and is also commemorated on a stele erected at Megiddo. Jerusalem is spared because of Rehoboam's payment of a huge ransom for the city (1 Kings 14:26).

11:40. Egypt as protector. Just as Hadad sought political refuge in Egypt (see comment on 11:18), Jeroboam turns to Shishak for support and protection. It would have fit quite well into the pharaoh's plans for his own incursion into Palestine to aid Solomon's rival. It is even possible that the price extracted from Jeroboam for this assistance was to step aside when Shishak campaigned along the coast as far north as Taanach and Megiddo and inland to Beth Shan.

11:41. annals of Solomon. It is common practice to end an account of a king with a reference to additional works from which the narrative had been drawn—generally the "Book of the Annals of the Kings of Israel" (see 1 Kings 14:19; 16:14). The source listed here, however, seems to be a separate compendium dealing specifically with events in Solomon's life and additional accounts of his wisdom. From a historical standpoint it is unfortunate that we no longer have access to these materials. In the ancient world royal annals were often kept not just as an unbiased repetition of events but as a means by which a king established his reputation before the gods and for the benefit of later kings. Whether theological or propagandistic or both, they were usually composed with legacy in mind.

12:1-24
Rebellion Against Rehoboam

For information on this section see comments on 2 Chronicles 10—11.

12:25-33
Jeroboam Establishes His Kingdom

12:25. fortification of Shechem. Jeroboam's choice of Shechem (Tell Balatah) as his first capital city was based on its strategic location (thirty miles north of Jerusalem in a narrow pass between Mounts Ebal and Gerizim), its available water supply and its rich agricultural resources. Its location also allowed it to dominate all commercial and military travel through the Ephraimite region. Archaeological evidence for Jeroboam's refortification of the site is scarce, although there are indications of a casemate wall and towers built in Strata IX following the old Late Bronze fortification line. Destruction layers ending both Strata IX and X may be indications of the incursions of the Egyptian pharaoh Shishak. For the earlier history of Shechem see comment on Judges 9:1.

12:25. Peniel. Peniel/Penuel has been identified with Tell edh-Dhahab, "Mounds of Gold," on the Jabbok, five miles east of the Jordan River. Jeroboam may have relocated here during Shishak's invasion of Palestine, but the appearance of Peniel on Shishak's list of conquests at Karnak suggests it was not a distant enough refuge. Jeroboam may have also used the fortress here to help him control that portion of Transjordan (Gilead) which had previously been ruled by David.

12:26-27. Jerusalem and house of David connection. Since Jerusalem had been conquered by David and the sanctuary there established by David and Solomon, there were strong ideological ties between the house of God and the house of David, both inseparably tied to Jerusalem (for information concerning Jerusalem as personal property of the Davidic dynasty see comment on 2 Sam 5:9). It was the Yahweh who had established the Davidic dynasty who was enshrined at the temple in Jerusalem. Jeroboam therefore had to seek a way to break the political ties with the Jerusalem worship of Yahweh without breaking the traditional ties with Yahweh of the covenant who had brought them out of Egypt and given them the land.

12:28. golden calves. Like the ark of the covenant the golden calves are not idols. Rather both the ark and the calves function as thrones or pedestals upholding the glory of God. Calves were a reflection of syncretism, the religious and cultural borrowing from the Canaanites, so prevalent among the Israelites. Bulls or calves were associated with the god Baal and the fertility cult in Ugaritic texts. El is often referred to as "Bull El," and there is a tale of the mating of Baal and Anat which produced a steer. Quite likely, Jeroboam saw this as an excellent political maneuver, pleasing Israelites who were more comfortable with a mixture of Yahwist and Baalist imagery. Bronze or composite bull or calf figurines have been found in several archaeological excavations (Mount Gilboa, Hazor, the Bull Site and Ashkelon; as well as a ceramic one at Shiloh) but only three to seven inches long.

12:28. calves as thrones. Since Jeroboam's intent was to provide alternative worship centers to Jerusalem, it would have been necessary to furnish those shrines with a religious symbol just as powerful as the ark. The calf symbol was well-known in the Canaanite context of the second millennium and represented fertility and strength. However, so that the calves would not be considered idols, the argument was made that they were instead merely the throne of Yahweh. This is based on the portrayal of Canaanite and Ugaritic gods in sculpture and reliefs standing on the body of a bull. In addition, Mesopotamian moon gods Sin and Nannar are both represented on cylinder seals and in religious texts either with a bull or portrayed as a rampant "ferocious bull." Thus one possibility exists that the golden calves placed in the shrines at Dan and Bethel by Jeroboam were intended to function as thrones or divine pedestals for the invisible Yahweh. Some have noticed that in third-millennium depictions (mostly on cylinder seals) the deity would be depicted standing on the back of a winged composite creature (such as the cherubim were). It was in second-millennium Syria that the bull became the more common "pedestal animal."

12:28. calves' relation to Yahweh. It has been commonly accepted by many scholars that Jeroboam's golden calves were connected to a (syncretistic) worship of Yahweh. This argument is based on the lack of another divine name associated with the calves and the reference to the "gods who brought you out of Egypt." This latter phrase seems to negate the possibility of association with the Egyptian bull-god Apis (despite Jeroboam's Egyptian ties; see 1 Kings 11:40). Ugaritic parallels suggest ties between the calves and either Baal or El. Attempts to tie the calves to Sin, the moon god of Haran and Ur, and to vestiges of the ancestral religion within the Joseph tribes is bolstered by a great deal of textual and archaeological evidence, but they are still open to speculation. Whatever its original intent or background, the calves ultimately became associated with false worship by the Israelite community, whether as a violation of commandment one or two. The latter seems more likely in that even a century later, when Jehu eliminates Baal worship from Israel, he takes no action against the calves (see 2 Kings 10:28-29).

12:29. Dan and Bethel. Jeroboam's choice of

these two sites for his national religious centers was based on their previous association with cultic activity. Bethel was the site of Jacob's theophany (Gen 28:10-22) and an altar (Gen 35:1), while Dan became the shrine for the tribe of Dan in Judges 18:27-31. Geographically, the cities were located at either end of the nation and thus facilitated the peoples' religious pilgrimages and sacrifice.

12:30. Bethel. See the comments on Joshua 8:9 and Judges 1:22-23. Lying only eleven miles north of Jerusalem on the dividing line between the two kingdoms, Bethel (Beitin?) was a natural choice for Jeroboam's shrine. Its sanctuary could attract pilgrims who might otherwise travel south to worship in Solomon's temple. Ultimately, Bethel will eclipse Dan in importance as the "king's sanctuary."

12:30. Dan. See the comment on Judges 18:29. Jeroboam built upon Dan's (Laish) traditions as a cultic site, both from the time when it was a Phoenician colony and later when the tribe of Dan migrated to the area (Judg 18:27-31). Situated in the extreme north and on the border with Phoenicia and Syria, Dan probably served as a site for treaty negotiations as well as a border outpost. Its somewhat isolated position in the foothills of Mount Hermon and the distance to Israel's power center at Samaria, however, may have contributed to a loss of status after Jeroboam's time. Excavations at Dan have uncovered the high place constructed by Jeroboam for the calf. The sanctuary complex was about 195 by 145 feet and featured a large altar in an open-air courtyard. One large horn from the main altar was found as well as a smaller horned altar.

12:31. shrines on high places. Since Jeroboam's strategy has an underlying political agenda, it seems natural that he would have certified the continued use of traditional, local shrines or "high places." This was an acknowledgment of the desire for a greater measure of local autonomy (see the plea made by the tribal leaders in 1 Kings 12:4) and a popular ploy, allowing "popular" forms of religious expression to flourish without undue restriction in places like Mount Carmel, Gilgal, Mizpah and Mount Tabor. While some of these may have been open-air altars, the mention of "houses" suggests a more elaborate cultic installation associated with urban centers (2 Kings 17:9-11; 2 Chron 1:3). The lack of central control over religious practice could of course only facilitate syncretism.

12:31. new priesthood. There is precedent elsewhere in the ancient Near East for deemphasizing one community of priests in favor of another one. For instance, the Egyptian pharaoh Akhenaten attempted to break the power of the Amon priesthood in order to magnify Aten worship. Similarly, the Neo-Babylonian king Nabonidus replaced Marduk as the principal deity of worship in his empire with the moon god Sin. In both cases the revenge taken by the slighted priesthood cost the ruling dynasty its position. Jeroboam's treatment of the Levites in his new kingdom is an indication that he does not trust their loyalties to him. He felt that by appointing a non-Levitical priesthood he could insure that his policies (shrines at Bethel and Dan, golden calves, use of high places, new religious calendar) would be carried out without question. Priests and Levites in Israel exercised significant political influence, so Jeroboam felt it mandatory to appoint loyalists who were dependent on him for their position.

12:32-33. new festival. The eighth month (Marchesvan) spans our October-November, a month later than the principle festivals in Jerusalem, when the New Year and the Feast of Tabernacles were celebrated. The Feast of Tabernacles was a harvest festival (see comment on Deut 16:13-17), so some suggest that Jeroboam's adjustment to the calendar reflected a later fruit harvest in Ephraim than in Judah. Alternatively, the festival period in the seventh month may have taken on certain political elements. 1 Kings 8:2, 65 make it clear that the dedication of the temple in Jerusalem took place in connection with this period. In Babylon the New Year was an occasion for celebrating the enthronement of the national god and the king. Since temple dedication involved the enthronement of Yahweh in his temple, there is at least some level of continuity here. If this festival included celebration of kingship, the Jerusalem practice would, of course, have focused on the elect status of the Davidic dynasty.

13:1-34

The Shrine and the Prophet

13:1. man of God. For discussion of various aspects of prophecy and prophets see the comments on Deuteronomy 18:14-22. As in Judges 6:8 this nameless prophet is a defender of the covenant. His message denouncing Jeroboam and his altar at Bethel clearly infers that this shrine is illegitimate. Ancient Near Eastern prophets often had messages that included admonitions regarding who should receive worship and how, and what were and were not legitimate shrines.

13:2. human sacrifice. See the comments on Genesis 22:1-2 and 22:13-19 for the case against human sacrifice among the Israelites (contrast Judg 11:30-40). While human sacrifice, especially of infants, was practiced by some of the peoples of the ancient Near East (archaeological evidence from Carthage, Nuzi and Tepe Gawra; see Lev 18:21; 2 Kings 3:27), the curse of the man of God in this narrative relates to the defiling of the Bethel altar. The term "sacrifice" is clarified by the next phrase that explains that it is dead men's bones, not executed victims, that will be burned. Any sacred installation would have to maintain its ritual purity. Burning the bones taken from crypts would so utterly corrupt it that it would be difficult to ever use it again.

13:3. the sign. The credentialing of a "true" prophet could come if his/her pronouncements came true or, in a more spectacular mode, when Yahweh sent a "sign" as a verification that the prophet was sent from God. In this case, what was needed was an unmistakable sign of divine wrath against the altar at Bethel. It would not be enough simply to call for its eventual disuse. Instead the immediate destruction of the altar was declared, along with the desecration of the sacred ash from the sacrifice. These ashes contained the fatty residue reserved for God (see Lev 1:16; 6:10 for proper disposal of these ashes). In this way both the vehicle of sacrifice (the altar) and the sacrifice of dedication itself are to be invalidated by divine command. Many of the altars found by archaeologists have been made of limestone, a soft stone that is easy to quarry and readily available. Impurities or inadequate time to cure could be among the causes for the stone to crack when exposed to heat.

13:4. shriveled hand. Most interpreters have identified this physical condition as resulting from some sort of hemorrhage or clot, but these conditions do not explain why the arm remained extended. The latter has been described as a condition today termed "cataplexy" (a shock to the nervous system that causes muscle rigidity).

13:7-9. shared meal and gift. Meals and gifts were often used in the treaty or covenant making process (see Gen 24:52-54; 31:43-46; Ex 24:9-10). Meals were also an integral part of the protocol of hospitality, which, for a time, set aside any enmity between the parties involved (see Judg 19:1-9). The man of God's refusal to make peace with Jeroboam is a further sign of Yahweh's denunciation of the king and his policies. Some similarity can be identified in the scene between Samuel and Saul in

1 Samuel 15:24-31, where worshiping the Lord would have likely involved a festive meal settling their differences and renewing their alliance. In this case, however, the Lord's instructions had clearly prohibited any such rapprochement.

13:11-18. behavior of the old prophet. Though the man of God had successfully repudiated Jeroboam's attempt to enlist his allegiance, he was not as successful in avoiding the overtures of the prophetic community at Bethel. The shared meal would have carried the suggestion of alliance between the man of God from Judah and the prophet(s) of Bethel.

13:21-22. oracle of judgment. Prophets were known to receive messages that were uncomfortable for them and that they preferred not to deliver. This particular oracle showed the old prophet from Bethel to have been deceptive, but that does not prevent God from using him to pronounce judgment on the man of God who had disregarded his original instructions from the Lord.

13:26-32. burial of prophet. The unusual manner of death for the man of God (vv. 24-25) and the witnesses who saw a lion simply standing beside the body and not even attacking his donkey, testify to a judgment of God. This "sign," more than the one that destroyed the altar at Bethel, convinces the "old prophet" that he had been responsible for his colleague's death. In fact his statement in verse 32, certifying the validity of the man of God's curse against the altar and the high places in Samaria, serves as a reinforcement by a "northern" prophet of its inevitable enactment. To honor the man he had betrayed, the prophet provides him with a tomb (in essence adopting him into his family), which he in turn will share—forever intertwining their dual curse. While one interpretation of the unusual death of the man of God might have been that his curse of the altar was ill-founded, the story preserved here simultaneously validates the curse and explains the death.

14:1-20

Jeroboam I of Israel

14:3. gift for the prophet. See 1 Samuel 9:6-8; 2 Kings 5:5; and comment on 2 Kings 8:9 for other examples of bringing a token gift to a prophet. It may be that prophets, like Levites, were landless and depended for their food and livelihood on the gifts of those who consulted them. This gift may have been relatively insignificant since the king's wife was in disguise. Whatever the amount, the gift showed a sense of respect for the God the prophet represented (see Gideon's "present" for the angel in Judg 6:18-21). The large number of votive images found by archaeologists in Canaanite and Israelite contexts suggest both food offerings and fertility symbols were commonly offered when an oracle or god was consulted.

14:2, 4. Shiloh. For information concerning Ahijah and Shiloh see comment on 11:29. Whether Shiloh (Khirbet Seilun, between Bethel and Shechem) contained an open-air shrine or was the site of a more elaborate temple complex in the period of the early monarchy and divided kingdom is uncertain. In any case the presence of a priestly community affiliated with the family of Eli stems from the time of the judges (1 Sam 1:7-9) and continues into the monarchy (see Jer 7:12-15 for mention of its destruction). Such a center would have also attracted prophets, like Ahijah, associating themselves with the presence of God.

14:9. indictment of the king. There is a long tradition in Mesopotamia recognizing the stereotype of the king who makes disastrous choices and brings on himself the wrath of the gods and the doom of his kingdom. The classic example in Mesopotamia is Naram-Sin of the dynasty of Akkad at the end of the third millennium. In a work known as the Curse of Agade, his desecration of the famous Ekur temple of Enlil in the holy city of Nippur is blamed for the fall of the kingdom (which doesn't happen for several more decades).

14:10-11. curse on the house of Jeroboam. For a ruling dynasty the worst possible curse is one that predicts the extinction of the family and the passing of the kingship to another group. This may explain why the Assyrian kings were always careful to list the kings they had violently deposed as a visible threat to any others that might think to revolt or even "did not bow at the king's feet quickly enough" (Sidqia of Joppa in the annals of Sennacherib). The colorful language describing the complete annihilation of Jeroboam, his sons and all of his clients/bondsmen provides images of them all going up in smoke and leaving no more trace than a dung fire. The further humiliation of their bodies being left unburied and devoured as garbage by scavenging dogs dishonored Jeroboam's house, cutting its members off from their ancestors (see Deut 28:26). For similar curses against a royal house in Israel, see comment on 1 Kings 16:4.

14:15. Asherah poles. See the comments on Asherah and the poles which symbolized her presence in Canaanite cultic sites in Deuteronomy 7:5 and Judges 2:13.

14:17. Tirzah. See the comment on Joshua 12:24 for the premonarchic background of this city. It seems likely that Jeroboam ruled from Tirzah, as did his immediate successors—Baasha, Elah, Zimri and Omri. Tirzah has been identified as Tell el-Farah, seven miles northeast of Shechem on the road to Beth Shan. It is favored by good elevation, a consistent water supply (two springs that feed the Wadi Farah) and a strategic location on the trade route. It also has ready access to the fords of the Jordan at Adam. The gate and fortifications were rebuilt from the Middle Bronze remains, and there is evidence of central planning in the building of new residences throughout the city. Its political importance may also be inferred from its mention in Shishak's list of conquests during his invasion of Palestine.

14:19. annals. The standard method of recording the major events and accomplishments, year by year, of the ancient Near Eastern kings was the production of royal annals. Some of the known chronicles of the ancient world (such as those of the Assyrian kings), while useful in reconstructing chronology and geographic locations, very often are a blatant example of official propaganda. Others (such as those from the Neo-Babylonian period) simply offered unembellished information. The reference to the annals of the kings of Israel again demonstrates that the biblical writers drew their account from larger, more detailed sources.

14:21-29
Rehoboam of Judah

For more information on this section see comments on 2 Chronicles 12.

14:23. high places. Apparently the use of outdoor shrines was common among the Canaanites. This was considered abhorrent to the Deuteronomic writer(s) because these local cult sites promoted a "popular" brand of religion that contained elements of Canaanite worship deviating from the established Yahweh-only doctrine. Thus local altars, sacred poles dedicated to Asherah, sacred groves and any place associated with a Canaanite god (Baal, El, etc.) or the worship of god outside of Jerusalem, "the place the Lord your God will choose" (Deut 12:5), were forbidden. There is a difference between these outdoor cultic places and the "high place" (*bamah*) mentioned in many places as religious centers in the local towns and cities (1 Kings 11:7; Jer 7:31; Ezek 16:16; 2 Chron 21:11; Mesha's Moabite Stele). The "high place" was apparently an indoor facility, built to house sacred furniture, an altar and precincts large enough to accommodate a priesthood. A clear differentiation is drawn between these two types of religious sites in 2 Kings 17:9-11.

14:23. sacred stones. Standing stones or *maṣṣebot* were apparently a common feature of Canaanite religion and also appear as memorials in a number of Israelite covenantal contexts (see Ex 24:3-8; Josh 24:25-27). Their association with Asherah, Baal and other Canaanite deities is the basis for their being condemned as a rival and threat to Yahweh worship. Archaeologists have discovered sacred stones at Gezer, Hazor and Arad. In the latter two cases, they are clearly within a sacred precinct and part of the cultic practices at these sites. The Hazor stones include incised representations of upraised arms and a sun disk. From basins sometimes found near the foot of such pillars it is inferred that libations (liquid offerings) were poured over them.

14:23. Asherah poles. One common feature of Canaanite worship and syncretized Israelite worship on "high places" and in city shrines is the erection of Asherah poles (Judg 3:7; 1 Kings 14:15; 15:13; 2 Kings 13:6). There is some uncertainty about whether these were simply wooden poles, erected to symbolize trees, or whether they contained a carved image of the fertility goddess or were a part of a sacred grove. The reference in 2 Kings 17:10, which refers to Asherah poles beside "every spreading tree," seems to indicate that these were poles erected for cultic purposes rather than planted trees. As the consort of El, Asherah was clearly a popular goddess (see 2 Kings 18:19), whose worship is mentioned in Ugaritic texts (1600-1200). Her prominent appearance in the biblical narrative indicates that her cult was a major rival to Yahweh worship (see the prohibition in Ex 34:13; Deut 16:21). This explains both the number of examples in which Asherah poles are erected and venerated as well as the strong condemnations of this practice and the depictions of these poles being cut down and burned (Judg 6:25-30; 2 Kings 23:4-7). For more information see the comment on Deuteronomy 7:5.

14:24. male prostitutes. For more information concerning cultic prostitution see the comment on Deuteronomy 23:17-18. The term used here occurs in both feminine and masculine forms and refers, perhaps euphemistically, to ones who have been set apart for particular functions. This same term is used in Akkadian literature to refer to those who have been consecrated as functionaries serving at the shrines or temples. The prostitute was among those functionaries, as was the wet nurse and the midwife. It is unclear what functions the males might have served.

15:1-8
Abijah of Judah

For information on this section see comments on 2 Chronicles 13:1-22.

15:9-24
Asa of Judah

For information on this section see comments on 2 Chronicles 14—16.

15:18. Tabrimmon, Hezion. These two names are known only from this context. Aramaic sources from this period are nonexistent, and Assyrian records do not involve Aramean kings at this time. The names represent logical and legitimate Aramean forms, but no other historical information is available.

15:25-32
Nadab of Israel

15:25. chronology. The attempt on the part of the biblical writer to correlate the reigns of the kings of Israel and Judah is not always easy to synchronize. Most likely, Asa's first year was 914 B.C., but Nadab's first year very likely did not begin until 911 B.C. In addition, Nadab's reign, while it comprised portions of two years, actually only lasted a few months before he was assassinated in the autumn of 910 B.C.

15:27. Gibbethon. Lying about two miles west of Gezer in Philistine territory, Tell el-Melat was likely only a military outpost on the border with Israel (note it is listed in Danite territory in Josh 21:23). Its strategic location is attested by its mention in the campaign list of Pharaoh Thutmose III (1468 B.C.) and of the Assyrian king Sargon II, as part of his suppression of the Ashdod revolt (713 B.C.; Is 20:1).

15:29. wiping out predecessor's family. See the comment on 1 Kings 1:21 for a discussion of political purges at the time of change of administration. By eliminating all future claimants to the throne, Baasha made it more likely that his family would succeed him. The fulfillment of the curse (1 Kings 14:7-16) against Jeroboam's house is similar in form to the Ur III "Curse of Agade" about the Akkadian king Naram-Sin, whose desecration of a shrine in Nippur brought the wrath of the gods down on him and his kingdom.

15:33—16:7

Baasha of Israel

15:33. Tirzah. See the comment on 1 Kings 14:17. Tirzah officially becomes the capital of the northern kingdom of Israel during Baasha's reign. It will remain there until Omri moves it to Samaria (1 Kings 16:24).

15:33. chronology. The reign of Baasha presents one of the most difficult chronological problems in the Bible. If, as this verse states, Baasha came to the throne in Asa's third year and reigned twenty-four years, he would have died in Asa's twenty-sixth year (see 16:8). The problem comes when 2 Chronicles 16:1 has Asa and Baasha at war in Asa's thirty-sixth year. Suggested solutions have been numerous, but none very convincing. Thiele's dates for Baasha are 909-886. He is contemporary with Asa of Judah and Ben-Hadad I of Damascus. This is the beginning of a century-long period when the Arameans of Damascus begin taking a leading role in the region.

16:4. dogs, birds and no burial. The fate assigned to Baasha's family (notice, not to Baasha himself) was the worst that could befall someone in the ancient world. Exposing the corpse represented a final humiliation and a desecration, for most ancient peoples believed that proper, timely burial affected the quality of the afterlife. In the Gilgamesh Epic, Enkidu, returned from the netherworld, reports to Gilgamesh that the one who died unburied has no rest and that the one who had no living relatives to take care of him could only eat what was thrown into the street. A Babylonian curse relates burial to the uniting of the spirit of the dead with loved ones. We know that even Israelites believed that proper burial affected one's afterlife, because they, like their neighbors, buried their loved ones with the provisions that would serve them in the afterlife; most often pottery vessels (filled with food) and jewelry (to ward off evil), with tools and personal items sometimes added. Israelite law required even the body of an impaled criminal to be removed and buried at sunset rather than left to be devoured by birds and other animals. First-millennium Assyrian records demonstrate these concerns as Ashurbanipal punishes his opponents by having their bodies thrown in the streets and dragged around. Being devoured by scavengers made burial impossible and was the most dishonorable punishment possible. From the same period an Assyrian curse declares, "Let dogs tear his unburied body to pieces." On one occasion the corpses were chopped up and fed to dogs. The intention of this atrocity was typically to eliminate any possibility of proper burial and thus to doom the individual's spirit to wander restlessly rather than enjoy a peaceful afterlife. Exposing the corpse was also occasionally practiced by the Egyptians.

16:6. Tirzah. Tirzah was a royal residence of Jeroboam and then the capital city of the northern kingdom, probably beginning in the time of Baasha. It has been identified as Tell el-Farah seven miles northeast of Shechem on the road to Beth Shan. It is favored by good elevation, a consistent water supply (two springs that feed the Wadi Farah) and a strategic location on the trade route. It also has ready access to the fords of the Jordan at Adam. The gate and fortifications were rebuilt from the Middle Bronze remains, and there is evidence of central planning in the building of new residences throughout the city. Its political importance may also be inferred from its mention in Shishak's list of conquests during his invasion of Palestine.

16:8-14

Elah of Israel

16:8. chronology. Elah's reign was brief and apparently uneventful. As with his predecessors, there is as yet no mention of him in extrabiblical records. Thiele places him in 886-885.

16:11. killing predecessor's family. Leaving any living relatives of a king who had been forcibly deposed from the throne by assassination was an invitation to civil war. The relatives would be honor-bound to avenge the death of the previous king, and they would be certain to find those who would support their bid to regain the throne. Such annihilation of ruling families was common practice both in Israel and in the ancient Near East at large.

16:13. worthless idols. The text here speaks only of "worthless things," but that is a common designation of idols in the ninth through the sixth century. It expresses the biblical perspective that the idols are powerless nothings and that the belief in them is conceptually flawed.

16:14. annals. Royal annals were kept throughout the ancient Near East, with most examples coming from mid-second millennium Hittite kings and from ninth- to sixth-century Assyria and Babylon. The annals could be represented by annalistic royal inscriptions that give detailed accounts of military campaigns. In addition there are court chronicles that give information of important events in each year. There are currently no annals from Israel or Judah that have been discovered by archaeologists.

16:15-20
Zimri of Israel

16:15. chronology. Zimri's seven days are dated by Thiele to 885.

16:15. Gibbethon. Gibbethon was one of the cities listed among those taken by Thutmose III on his campaign into Palestine in the first half of the fifteenth century B.C. Over seven hundred years later it was an important conquest of the Assyrian king Sargon II in his campaign against Ashdod (713-712). If the city is to be identified with Tell Malat, it is strategically located near the intersection of the Philistine plain with the foothills of Judah nearly twenty miles west of Jerusalem and about four miles west of Gezer. Extensive excavations have not been conducted, but there are finds dating to this period on the site, and it is clear that it was a fortified city.

16:16. army naming king. While it was not typically the army's task to designate the king, the support of the military was an important link to securing a contested throne. Military coups were probably more frequent in the Near East than our sources indicate, because most kings desired to present themselves as having come to the throne through legitimate means. Using the might of the military to seize power and enforce one's rule is not a precedent that many would seek to establish. Nevertheless prominent examples of militia-backed takeovers from one's own countrymen can be found in the Assyrian kings Tiglath-Pileser III (745) and Sargon II (722), and the Persian king Darius the Great (522), though each puts a different twist on the story of his succession that suggests a legitimate claim to the throne.

16:18. citadel of the royal palace. Tell el-Farah, ancient Tirzah, shows evidence of destruction and abandonment at this time. There is a fortified citadel that has been found at the northwest corner of the site that is possibly the one that Zimri set aflame. The practice of a king burning down the palace around himself is also seen in 648, when Babylon succumbs to the siege of Ashurbanipal and Shamash-shuma-ukin throws himself into the flames of the burning palace.

16:21-28
Omri of Israel

16:21-22. contesting succession to the throne.

When succession to the throne was not a case of a son taking the place of his father, it could be expected that there would be several claimants, each with supporting factions. Nothing is known of the nature of Tibni's claims or who made up his constituency. Likewise the details of the civil war are not given.

16:23. chronology. Thiele's dates for Omri are 885-874. This is a critical juncture in the history of the region because the Assyrians are ready to begin their attempts at western expansion. Ashurnasirpal II came to the throne in 883 and extended his control over the entire course of the Euphrates, thus putting him on the doorstep of the western nations. The Aramean state of Bit-Adini by the western reaches of the Euphrates came under his control, and in 877 he marched to the Mediterranean and then south between the Orontes/Litani rivers and the Mediterranean, collecting tribute from cities as far south as Tyre. Additionally the Arameans of Damascus under Ben-Hadad have become a force to reckon with, and all of this will force Israel to find its niche through international alignment.

16:24. Samaria. It was Omri who built Samaria and established it as the capital of the northern kingdom, Israel. About twelve miles west of the previous capital, Tirzah, the city is located at an important crossroads with easy access to the Jezreel Valley to the north, Shechem to the southeast and the coast to the west. It is near both major north-south routes that run west of the Jordan. The excavations at the site have uncovered what is believed to be Omri's palace on the acropolis as well as parts of the wall separating the acropolis from the lower city. The wall was about five feet thick and built using the finest masonry of the day (ashlar stones set in a trench using headers and stretchers). Ahab improved the fortifications by adding a casemate wall over thirty feet thick.

16:24. two talents of silver. Two talents of silver equals six thousand shekels. This is considerably more than David paid for the eventual temple site in Jerusalem, but it is a substantially larger portion of real estate as well. It is about 150 pounds of silver. Its economic equivalent in buying power today would be between fifteen and twenty million dollars. Even if the entire upper and lower city (which comprised 160 acres in Roman times) was included, this was still expensive real estate.

16:27. Omri in the ancient Near East. Though there are no contemporary sources that record interaction with Omri, sources from the middle of the ninth century refer to Omri in a number of different ways. The Moabite inscription of King Mesha recounts Omri's past oppression of Moab as the historical background of Mesha's claims of his more recent domination of Omri's successors. Assyrian inscriptions of Shalmaneser III identify Israel as the land of Omri. Since Omri was on favorable terms with pro-Assyrian Tyre and Sidon, it is likely that he also adopted a pro-Assyrian stance. His alliance with the Phoenicians was sealed by the marriage of the crown prince, Ahab, to the Sidonian princess, Jezebel. This strategy aligned him against the Arameans, who stood against the Assyrians and were the most active threat against Israel. Nevertheless it appears that Omri did negotiate a working relationship and maintained an uneasy peace with the Arameans, who were feeling the pressure of the Assyrians and needed friends in the region.

16:29-34

Succession of Ahab of Israel

16:29. chronology. Thiele's dates for Ahab are 874-853. It is certain that he was still on the throne in 853 because he is listed in Shalmaneser III's records as one of the principle members of the western coalition that opposed the Assyrians at the battle of Qarqar in that year.

16:31. Jezebel. The only possible reference to Jezebel in contemporary records is a seal from this time period inscribed with the name "yzbl." It is a large seal featuring Egyptian motifs accompanied by the Phoenician inscription of the name. As the king's daughter, it has been suggested that she could have enjoyed a status as the high priestess of the national deity, Baal Melqart.

16:31. Ethbaal of Sidon. Ethbaal was the king of the Sidonians from 887 to 856. He ruled over the entire region of Phoenicia and actually used Tyre as his capital city. Josephus, writing many centuries later, describes him as a priest of the goddess Astarte who had usurped the throne. Josephus is not always reliable on such matters, but he appears to be using some Greek sources that may be translations of Phoenician records. Ethbaal is given much credit in the development of Tyre as an island port and probably built the southern harbor with its accompanying breakwater. No mention of him has yet been found in contemporary records.

16:31. Baal Melqart. Melqart was the chief god of Tyre as early as the ninth century B.C. He is equated with the Mesopotamian god Nergal, lord of the netherworld, and later with the Greek god Heracles. He is at times referred to as the Baal of Tyre and thus his identification with the Baal who enjoys Jezebel and Ahab's loyalty. It should be understood that this is therefore a different god from the Canaanite Hadad, who is usually referred to as Baal in the biblical text. In the ninth-century Aramean inscription of Bir-Hadad, Melqart is a warrior god, but no myths concerning his activities have survived from the Old Testament period. In later texts, Melqart is seen as a dying-rising god (correlating to the cycles of nature), who appears to be brought back to life by fire.

Since the biblical text never uses the title Melqart, there are alternative possibilities. The most common is that Baal is Baal Shamem (lord of the heavens), who is known throughout the first millennium as one of the chief gods of Phoenicia. Most information on him, however, comes after 800, and therefore little can be determined about him from the period of this narrative.

16:32. temple of Baal in Samaria. Excavations in Samaria have not yet located any remains from Ahab's temple of Baal. It has been suggested that the temple contributed to the concept being promoted by Ahab and Jezebel that the city was the sacred precinct of Baal (for the privileges of such status, see comment on 2 Sam 5:9). This would mean it functioned as an independent political unit, just as Zion often did in the south. For the implications of this see the comments in 2 Kings 10:21.

16:33. Asherah pole. Asherah can be either the name of a fertility goddess or the name of a cult object (as here). The goddess was popular in the religious deviations in Israel and was sometimes considered a consort of Yahweh. An indication of this belief is found in the inscriptions from Kuntillet Ajrud and Khirbet el-Qom. In Canaanite mythology she was the consort of the chief god, El. She appears in Mesopotamian literature as early as the eighteenth century, where she is consort of the Amorite god Amurru. The cult symbol may or may not have born a representation of the deity on it. The pole may represent an artificial tree since Asherah is often associated with sacred groves. Sometimes the cult object can be made or built, while on other occasions it is planted. We have little information of the function of these poles in ritual practice.

16:34. rebuilding Jericho. Joshua had pronounced a curse on anyone who would rebuild the city of Jericho. Many interpreters have thought that a practice of the day was that the dedication of a house would feature the sacrifice of a child from the family. This was used to explain the skeletal remains of children found buried under the thresholds of houses (foundation sacrifices). In similar manner the builder of a city would sacrifice a child who would be buried in a significant location in the city. This interpretation has been largely abandoned, and some researchers now see a connection between the curse and the disease schistosomiasis (bilharziasis). This disease is caused by a blood fluke carried by snails of the type found in abundance at Jericho. It infects the urinary tract and affects fertility and child mortality.

17:1—18:15
Elijah and the Drought

17:1. Tishbe in Gilead. Tishbe is mentioned nowhere else in the Old Testament, and its location is unknown. The traditional identification with Istib, eight miles north of the Jabbok River, has little to commend it.

17:1. withholding of rain and Baal. The policies and actions of Ahab and Jezebel are intended to promote Baal as the national deity of Israel in place of Yahweh. The dispute championed by Elijah concerns which deity is king—which is more powerful. In the Canaanite material available from ancient literature (particularly the information provided by the Ugaritic tablets), Baal is a god of lightning and storm, and responsible for the fertility of the land. By withholding rain, Yahweh is demonstrating the power of his kingship in the very area of nature over which Baal is thought to have jurisdiction. Announcing this beforehand to Ahab is the means by which Yahweh's kingship and power are being portrayed. If Baal is the provider of rain and Yahweh announces that he will withhold it, the contest is on.

17:3. ravine of Kerith. This incident demonstrates Yahweh's control in that he shows he can provide for whomever he wishes. The Wadi Kerith has not been identified with confidence. NIV translates the description as "east of the Jordan," but the Hebrew phrase often means "on the way to," suggesting that the wadi is one that drains into the Jordan from the west. Matching this description and known for its desolate terrain is the Wadi Kelt. Wadi Swenit runs past Micmash and halfway to Jericho meets the Wadi Kelt, which is the major pass into the region of the Jordan. This would be about thirty miles southeast of Samaria. An alternative in the region of Samaria would be the Wadi Faria, which meets the Jordan at the fords at Adam.

17:4. fed by ravens. Ravens are known to roost in desolate rocky areas like the wadi.

Their habit of storing excess foods in rocky crags worked to Elijah's benefit. He could observe where they put the food and retrieve it. While much of the diet of ravens consists of carrion, they also eat fruit such as dates.

17:9. Zarephath. Zarephath (modern Sarafand) is a town near the coast of the Mediterranean between Tyre and Sidon. It is listed as a harbor city in thirteenth-century B.C. Egyptian texts. It was a flourishing manufacturing and industrial center throughout the first millennium B.C. and down into Roman times. Its importance here is that it shows that Yahweh had also produced a drought in Baal's own home territory.

17:10. gathering sticks at the town gate. The woman is gathering twigs to start a small fire. The verb suggests foraging for discarded stubble. The traffic through the town gate and jostling of loads there would make it a likely place for one to find small pieces that had been dropped by others.

17:10. widow. In a society that is subject to disease and warfare, it is not uncommon to find widows. Since a widow had no inheritance rights, special provisions were typically made for them under the law, allowing them to glean in harvested fields and protecting them from being oppressed. They needed protection under the law because they were powerless to protect themselves and were often dependent on charity for survival. Based on the statements in the prologues of the Ur-Nammu Code and the Code of Hammurabi, it is clear that kings considered it part of their role as "wise rulers" to protect the rights of the poor, the widow and the orphan. Similarly, in the Egyptian Tale of the Eloquent Peasant, the plaintiff begins by identifying his judge as "the father of the orphan, the husband of the widow." If a god is going to demonstrate his role as a king, one clear way of doing so is to show his concern for the vulnerable by caring for the needs of a widow in desperate need.

17:10-11. Elijah's request. Elijah's request would have been very modest within the range of normal hospitality (which was often offered at the gate of the city). In this time of drought and famine, however, it served only to expose the corporate and personal crises that existed.

17:12. LORD your God. Here the woman clearly refers to the Israelite God, Yahweh. There must have been something recognizably Israelite in Elijah's appearance, and the woman follows standard protocol by pronouncing her oath in the name of the deity of the person to whom she is speaking. Though she uses a common oath formula, she also unwittingly offers affirmation of Yahweh's vitality. Her phrase betrays nothing of any personal belief in Yahweh.

17:12. flour and oil. One of the typical baked products that formed a basic part of the meal was a small flat cake made of wheat flour and cooked in oil.

17:14. provision of flour and oil: fertility. Grain and oil were two of the major exports of the city of Zarephath. The fact that they were in short supply is an indication of how severe the drought was. They are also two of the most basic commodities for survival. As staple products they represent the major arena where fertility can be observed. The contest between Yahweh and Baal continues as Yahweh demonstrates that he is able to provide for "Baal's people" in "Baal's territory" just as easily as he is able to provide for his own people and just as easily as he is able to withhold from whomever he chooses.

17:18. death of son connected to prophet. Prophets were often considered dangerous and having one around posed considerable risk. The gods could be harsh taskmasters as often as they could be generous benefactors, and the prophets represented them. Additionally, if the prophet were to become angered or offended at any little thing, he might, in an uncontrolled moment, pronounce some sort of curse that would inevitably come true. The woman assumes that her child's death is punishment from some presumed (though unknown) offense that has come to the attention of the deity because of the prophet's presence. She had thus far benefited from Elijah's presence, but now she judges that the cost was too high.

17:21. stretched himself on boy three times. Some have taken this as an example of mouth-to-mouth resuscitation, since in ancient times death was determined as having taken place when the person stopped breathing. But the full weight of a man on a child would be counterproductive to that procedure. The more complete description of the procedure in 2 Kings 4:34-35 suggests a different explanation. In Mesopotamian incantation literature the touching of part to part is a means by which demons exercise power over their intended victims—it is the idiom of possession. In this belief, vitality or life force can be transferred from one body to the other by contact of each part. By imitating the procedure believed to be used by demons, the prophet is able, through the power of Yahweh (notice the prayer), to drive the demons out and restore the boy's life. This is often consid-

ered to be one of the clearest cases of sympathetic magic in the Bible.

17:22. return of life versus Baal. Part of the profile of fertility gods was the dying and rising cycle that was related to vegetation and to the seasons. The deity would "die" during the winter months and descend to the netherworld. He would be brought back out of the netherworld and restored to life in the spring to bring fertility back to the land. His power to enable fertility extended beyond crops to animals and people as well. As a god who regularly returned from death, it was believed that these fertility gods also had the power to occasionally restore life to someone who had died. Therefore, by restoring the boy's life, Yahweh is again showing his power in the realm considered to be Baal's central arena (see comment on 2 Kings 4:16-35).

18:1-46
The Contest on Mount Carmel

18:3. Obadiah in charge of the palace. Obadiah holds one of the highest offices in the administration (see comment on 4:6). Though this post later becomes the equivalent of prime minister, at this stage it most likely designates stewardship of royal lands and possessions. It is claimed as a title of an official named Gedaliah on a seal from sixth-century Lachish.

18:4. killing Yahweh's prophets. The standard religious systems of the ancient Near East were openly tolerant of worship of any deities. To ignore a potentially powerful deity or to persecute his worshipers would make one vulnerable to divine anger and punishment. Religious intolerance or persecution do not arise until much later in history. Policies that may look like religious persecution in the ancient world are usually political in nature. When the Egyptian pharaoh Akhenaten took action against the priests of Amun-Re, it was because of their substantial political and economic influence. He was seeking to defuse their power. The agenda of Jezebel was to enthrone Baal as the king and national god of Israel instead of Yahweh. This would have been her act of loyalty to Baal. The prophets of Yahweh would have, of course, contested this move on religious, political, personal and traditional grounds. They would be most capable of mobilizing formal and large-scale opposition among the general population. On political grounds, then, they had to be eliminated.

18:19. Mount Carmel. It is likely that Mount Carmel, south of the modern port of Haifa, had long served as a boundary between Israel and Phoenicia and was, like many mountains, considered a sacred site. As early as the lists of Pharaoh Thutmose III (fifteenth century), Carmel is probably the one identified as a holy mountain in the vicinity of Acco. It is also the location where Assyrian king Shalmaneser III collected tribute from both Tyre and Jehu of Israel in 841. Carmel actually refers to a mountain range that stretches about thirty miles from the outcropping into the Mediterranean southeast toward Megiddo and stands at the northwestern end of the Valley of Jezreel. It is uncertain which summit in the range is the location of the contest. It is possible that the contest took place at the foot of the mountain rather than on its summit. Sacred mountains usually featured the places of worship at their base rather than at the summit, which would have been considered holy ground inaccessible to the populace. Elijah eventually ascends to the summit to offer his prayer for rain (v. 42).

18:19. eating at Jezebel's table. It is interesting that it is Jezebel's table, not Ahab's, that hosts the prophets of Baal and Asherah. This suggests that she has her own dining accommodations and resources and that she is the sponsor and benefactor of these prophets.

18:23-24. nature of the contest. There are three significant concepts involved in centering the contest around the ability of the deity to send fire. (1) *Fire is an indication of the presence of God*. In biblical texts, from the burning bush and the pillar of fire to the throne vision of Ezekiel (1:4), fire is seen as accompanying theophanies (appearances of God). In this way the contest asked the respective deities to show themselves. (2) *Fire is connected to the lightning of the storm god*. As the storm god, Baal is depicted with lightning bolts in his hand and is spoken of in the texts as flashing forth with fire or lightning. In one text fire is even used by Baal as a means of constructing his house. Baal was therefore considered by his worshipers as the lord of fire. In the continuing agenda of the narrative that Yahweh show his superiority in every area of Baal's domain, the ability to bring fire is strategic. (3) *Fire represents the acceptance of the sacrifice.* Burnt offerings of this sort typically accompanied petition. In this case the petition on everyone's mind was for the drought to end. If both parties had been praying for the drought to end, the resulting rain could be attributed by either group to its own god. As a result the contest is set up to demonstrate which deity is responding to the petition of his followers. If fire is sent, the petition has been granted, and

the rain that follows can be attributed to the correct deity. It is therefore important to recognize the close connection between the sending of the fire and the sending of the rain.

18:26-29. prophets' appeal to Baal. The NIV speaks of the prophets "dancing around the altar" (v. 26) and "slashing themselves with swords and spears" (v. 28). In the first description the verb is controversial. It is the same verb as that translated "passover" in Exodus 12 (see the comment on Ex 12:11) and may be better understood as protectively standing vigil. Certainly there is plenty of evidence of ritual dances in the ancient world; however, none of them come from the literature connected with the Canaanites. The self-laceration of this verse is part of a mourning ritual. In Ugaritic literature the gods are portrayed as practicing this when they hear of the death of Baal. Additionally an Akkadian wisdom text from Ugarit compares the bloodletting of mourning rites to that practiced by ecstatic prophets.

18:27. Elijah's taunts. The biblical text offers four activities that Elijah suggests for Baal: thinking, busy, traveling and sleeping. These can be compared to some of the activities in which Baal is engaged in the Ugaritic texts. When the goddess Anat comes to look for Baal, she is told he has gone hunting. Ugaritic literature that portrays the death of Baal features the repeated strain that he needs to be awakened. The classical source used by Josephus, Menander of Ephesus, reports that the Tyrian king, Hiram, contemporary of David, instituted the ritual for the awakening of Herakles (=Melqart, see comment on 16:31). The mythology of the ancient world understood the gods to be involved in a variety of activities similar to those that engage human beings. Though Elijah's words are meant to be taunts, they are not unrealistic depictions of Canaanite beliefs. The prophets of Baal would not have viewed his suggestions as ridiculous or unworthy of deity.

18:30. Elijah's repair of the altar. The terms used suggest a previous altar for the worship of Yahweh that was in disrepair due to an act of destruction. It can probably be inferred that the altar had been torn down as a result of Jezebel's promotion of Baal worship. Destruction of competing or unacceptable high places was often a part of religious reform. It was often believed that the precise location and orientation of a sanctuary or altar had been determined by deity and was significant. Therefore, even though Elijah "builds" the altar in verse 32 with twelve stones that probably make up the entire altar, it can be viewed as "repair" in the sense that it enjoys continuity with the altar previously operating on the site.

18:32. size and purpose of the trench. The trench size is described in terms of something that holds about half a bushel of grain. A trench that held half a bushel would not be very large. Perhaps the text is making reference to a standard container that holds (Hebrew text: "houses") this amount of grain (the way we would speak of a two-liter bottle) and is suggesting that is how deep the trench was dug all around the altar. The purpose of the trench is to collect the runoff, which otherwise would have simply been absorbed into the dry earth.

18:33-34. soaking of the sacrifice. Some have thought that the pouring of water on the altar would have seemed a great waste to those who were languishing through a third year of drought. It must be remembered, however, that there is no suggestion that this was fresh water. The nearby Mediterranean was full of water—it was just undrinkable.

18:38. fire of the Lord. The storm gods of the ancient Near East are typically equipped with lightning bolts that are their means of sending fire. Assyrian kings throughout this period speak of the gods as a burning flame and of sending fire before them. Esarhaddon (seventh-century Assyria) speaks of his march and attack in terms of an unquenchable fire. All of this is the way that the deity was believed to enter into battle. Fire brought about by his thunderbolts was one of his principal weapons. While the events on Carmel do not show Yahweh using fire to destroy his enemies, he is using it as a means to defeat his opponent, Baal. Another occurrence of fire from the Lord consuming a sacrifice is in the ordination of Aaron and his sons (Lev 9:24).

18:40. Kishon Valley. The Kishon River flows northwest from the northern end of the Jezreel Valley to the Mediterranean just east of Haifa. It is fed from the mountains in the Carmel range and from the hills of Galilee around Nazareth.

18:44. cloud. The text has given no indication of the time of year this event takes place. Summers are usually devoid of rain in Palestine, though there can occasionally be clouds in the sky. The winter is the rainy season. Rain usually comes from the west (the sea), as indicated here. When the rainy season begins in the autumn, showers often come on quite quickly from the west. Comparing the size to a man's hand is indicative of how far away the cloud is—when he holds up his outstretched hand, he can obscure it from his sight.

18:45. Jezreel. Jezreel was between fifteen and twenty miles from the Carmel area. This fifteen-acre site was situated at the southeastern entrance to the Jezreel Valley between the Hill of Moreh and Mount Gilboa. It was here that Ahab had built a winter capital. Excavations have unearthed a large royal enclosure from this time period occupying a large portion of the mound (see comment on 21:1).

18:46. tucking cloak into belt. The "girding of one's loins" typically involves belting tight a loose garment or folding up a long one in preparation for some strenuous activity. This particular passage is difficult because the verb that is used is unique to this verse and its meaning is uncertain. So, for instance, if Elijah had "girded his loins" for the slaughter of the prophets, he could just as well be ungirding them here. Despite the NIV translation, no garment is mentioned here.

18:46. Elijah running ahead of Ahab. This verse does not speak of outrunning but of running before the chariot of Ahab until he came to Jezreel. Those running before the chariot of a king or prince constitute his entourage (see comment on the same phrase in 2 Sam 15:1). Elijah, under the power of Yahweh, was playing the role of prophetic herald, apparently proclaiming the changed attitude of Ahab and his loyalty to Yahweh. The power of Yahweh brings blessing, success and victory. In Hittite texts it is the gods who run before the chariot of the king—here Elijah does so as the representative of God. The eighth-century Aramean king, Bir-Rakib, portrays himself as a loyal vassal to the Assyrian king Tiglath-Pileser III by "running at his wheel."

19:1-18
Elijah's Flight

19:3. Beersheba. Beersheba is the southernmost extremity of the land. It is located in the northern Negev at Tell es-Seba' (three miles east of the modern city). Its name derives from its association with the wells dug to provide water for the people and flocks in this area (see Gen 26:23-33). Archaeological evidence has been found of occupation during the monarchy through the Persian periods.

19:4. day's journey into the desert. Elijah is apparently heading southwest toward the Sinai Peninsula. One day's journey would have taken him about a third of the way to Kadesh-barnea.

19:4. broom tree. The white broom tree (*retama raetam*) is common in this region and grows anywhere from five to ten feet in height. It is the only shrub to offer shade in this dry, desolate region.

19:5-7. angel's provisions. There is nothing striking about the description of the food provided by the angel. It is the same as what Elijah had asked the widow to make for him (see 17:13). Perhaps most significant is that the Israelites in the wilderness were reported to have made such cakes out of manna (Num 11:8).

19:8. trip to Horeb. Horeb is another name for Mount Sinai. If Sinai is to be found down in the southern region of the peninsula, as the text seems to necessitate (see comment on Ex 19:1-2), he must travel another two hundred miles and could therefore easily take forty days. It is true that a caravan could often make seventeen to twenty miles a day, but Elijah is not accustomed to this type of travel and is traveling on his own. Five miles per day under such conditions in this climate would not be unusual.

19:11-13. fire, wind and earthquake with theophany. A theophany is an appearance of the divine presence. In the ancient Near East theophany was often connected with battle, and the warrior god was believed to fight on behalf of his people using thunder bolts (lightning, fire), the stormwind and the trembling earth to terrify the enemy. From the Sumerian *Exaltation of Inanna*, to the Hittite myths about the storm god, to the Akkadian and Ugaritic mythologies, the gods are viewed as thundering in judgment against their enemies. Baal is depicted as grasping a handful of thunderbolts. Thundering terminology is picked up in royal rhetoric as Hittite or Assyrian kings portray themselves as the instruments of the gods, thundering against those who have violated treaties or stood in the way of empire expansion. Israel's Yahweh is also viewed as a warrior God, but here Elijah is shown that there is much more (see next comment).

19:12-17. Yahweh's plan. In the ancient Near East the gods were believed to be active in the events of history. Kings claimed that they were put on the throne by their patron deity and that that deity supported them, gave them guidance and brought them victory and success. It is interesting to note, however, that this involvement of the gods always seems to have the tone of political propaganda. The gods of the ancient Near East do not have a plan that they reveal. While they are believed to be active throughout the scope of history, there is no indication that they had a plan for the direction of history. Here it is made plain to Elijah that Yahweh is not simply a hot-blooded warrior defending or dethroning kings on an arbitrary whim like the gods of the ancient Near East. He has an agenda for

history. His warfare is not just wrathful blood-letting—there is a long-term plan that is being carefully worked out. Once all the fire and storm and earthquake are past, the plan can be articulated. The "gentle whisper" in verse 12 is not describing how the Lord speaks. It is descriptive of the resonating silence after all the clamor of destruction. It is with silence hanging in the air that Yahweh's voice of direction may be heard.

19:15-16. anointing three replacements. Elijah made the mistake of thinking that he was indispensable, God's last and only hope. By announcing three successors, the Lord is making it clear that he is never without recourse. The Aramean king, Hazael, will be God's instrument of judgment on Israel (for more information see comment on 2 Kings 10:32). Jehu will become king of Israel and in the process bring God's punishment on the house of Ahab (for more information see comments on 2 Kings 10). Elisha will continue the prophetic work of Elijah.

19:15. Desert of Damascus. The Desert of Damascus refers to the great Syrian desert that stretches from Damascus to the Euphrates river basin. It was this desert that the "fertile crescent" went around.

19:16. Abel Meholah. Abel Meholah is located on the west bank of the Jordan somewhere south of Beth Shan. The most likely candidate is Tell Abu Sus, eleven miles south of Beth Shan at the southern end of the Beth Shan Valley, where the Yabis River enters the Jordan from the east.

19:18. mouths not kissing Baal. On the black stele of Shalmaneser III, the Israelite king Jehu is portrayed kissing the ground before the Assyrian king. In *Enuma Elish* the tribunal of gods kisses the feet of Marduk after he has put down the rebellion and established himself as head of the pantheon. This was the common act of submission offered to kings and gods. Likewise the kissing of the idol involved kissing its feet in an act of homage, submission and allegiance. In the Mari letters the governor of Terqa, Kibri-Dagan, advises Zimri-Lim, king of Mari, to come to Terqa to kiss the feet of the statue of the god Dagan.

19:19-21
Elisha Chosen as Apprentice

19:19. plowing with twelve yoke of oxen. Large landowners could accomplish the task of plowing much more quickly using multiple plows, each pulled by a team of oxen driven by a worker. Here Elisha is in charge of twelve such teams.

19:19. prophet's cloak. The cloak referred to here is an outer garment, not the same as the robe discussed in 1 Samuel 15:27. The distinctive prophet's cloak is most likely made of animal skin and is hairy in appearance (see Zech 13:4), though not all cloaks were so made. Very little is said about prophetic garb in the ancient Near East, so comparison is difficult. It may be of interest that Assyrian inscriptions beginning at this period portray a few individuals wearing lion-headed cloaks. Some of these individuals are involved in ritual activities (dance) and accompany deity. It is guessed that they may be exorcists.

19:21. Elisha's response. Kissing is more often used in greeting than in saying goodbye (a word supplied here by the NIV translators, not in the Hebrew text). Kissing between a father (or grandfather) and a son or daughter is found in several contexts as a prelude to receiving a blessing (Gen 27:26; 31:28, 55; 48:10) and may be implied here. The butchering of the oxen supplies the meal for the celebration that also accompanied the blessing. It would appear, then, that Elisha has requested the opportunity to receive his parents' blessing.

20:1-43
Ahab and Ben-Hadad

20:1. Ben-Hadad of Aram. Aramean history at this time is still in need of much clarification, with at least part of the problem caused by several rulers with the name of Ben-Hadad ("son of [the god] Hadad"). The issue is further complicated by the fact that Shalmaneser III's inscriptions name the ruler of this time Hadadezer (see comment on 2 Sam 8:3). The first Ben-Hadad has been referred to earlier in chapter 15 and ruled during the first part of the ninth century, though no precise dating is possible. In 2 Kings 8 the king murdered by Hazael (about 842) is named Ben-Hadad, and Hazael is later succeeded by a king named Ben-Hadad. The name Bir-Hadad occurs in an inscription dedicated to the god Melqart, but again it is unclear which Ben-Hadad this refers to. It has been suggested that the sequence may be Ben-Hadad I (1 Kings 15), Ben-Hadad II (1 Kings 20), Hadadezer (Shalmaneser Inscription, considered by some a variant name of Ben-Hadad), Ben-Hadad III (Melqart inscription), Hazael, Ben-Hadad IV. There is no other material from the ancient Near East to help unravel this at this time.

20:1. thirty-two kings. Coalitions of many small kingdoms were frequent in these times. When Shalmaneser III invaded the west in 853 at the Battle of Qarqar, he was greeted by a coalition of twelve major kings. Shalmaneser's inscription lists the number of cavalry, infantry and chariots provided by the various members of the coalition. There were still many city-states and tribal groups around at this time, who each would have had a "king," so it is not difficult to imagine thirty-two of them banding together.

20:5-6. terms of tribute. Ahab is initially prepared to meet the demands for tribute and peaceful surrender imposed by Ben-Hadad. The resulting vassal relationship would involve members of Ahab's family being taken as hostages to insure that the terms were met. Assyrian practice of this time was to take princes hostage to provide incentive that good behavior would result, and here the Arameans are doing the same. When Ben-Hadad finds Ahab so agreeable, he insists further that the right of seizure be extended to anything of value that is found in the palace.

20:13-14. role of the prophet. In this period of preclassical prophecy the prophets of Israel served in very much the same role as their ancient Near Eastern counterparts (see comment on Deut 18:14-22). One of the most frequent areas addressed concerned, as here, the advisability of military activity. Since it was believed that God's involvement was essential for the success of the military, the entire sequence begins with the divine command to go into battle. This divine command can be seen as typical in the royal inscriptions of the Assyrians. It was also important to consult the deity about timing and strategies. During the time of Saul and David this type of information was usually gained through the priest's manipulation of oracular devices (see comments on 1 Sam 14:10; 22:10; and 23:9-12). Now, instead of asking questions of a priest to receive oracular responses, the questions are being posed to the prophet, who, as a representative of God, offers the prophetic oracles as responses from God.

20:23, 28. god of the hills, god of the valleys. In the polytheistic setting of the ancient Near East, gods were generally considered as having defined territorial jurisdiction, just as political leaders would have. This jurisdiction could be divided up along national lines (each nation having its patron deities) or by topographical areas or boundaries (rivers, mountains, lakes, plains, as here construed). The fact that Israel was a mountainous country and that the capital cities, Samaria and Jerusalem, were both in mountain regions, would fuel the speculation that Yahweh's jurisdiction was in the mountains.

20:24-25. planned strategy. The tactics that will be used for the second campaign are significantly different. In the first round the Aramean coalition attacked Samaria directly. This was intended as siege warfare. In the second phase the emphasis was not on starving the people out or on breaching the walls of a city, but on pitched battle in open terrain where the Arameans intended to take full advantage of their chariotry and cavalry. Whether because of the different battle tactics or because of the failure of the first campaign, the Arameans assigned a new group of field commanders and filled the ranks with new recruits.

20:26. Aphek. Identification of the site of this battle is complicated by the fact that there are several different towns named Aphek in ancient Israel (perhaps as many as five). The one that has most commonly been proposed as the site for this battle is located just east of the Sea of Galilee on the route from Damascus to Israel. The problem with this is that it is hard to imagine the Arameans choosing a site that far from Samaria or the Israelites going that far afield to engage them. Somewhere in the vicinity of the plain of Jezreel is most logical, and the use of Aphek as a muster point for the Philistines at the battle of Gilboa would likewise raise this possibility (compare the comments on 1 Sam 28:4 and 29:1).

20:30. escape to Aphek. Since the site of Aphek has not been identified, it is impossible to comment on the archaeological record of the fortifications. The collapse of walls is not specifically attributed to siege and breach, or to divine intervention. One of the principal tactics for bringing about the collapse of walls was tunneling beneath them. In fact it has been suggested that the very purpose of dry moats (dug to bedrock) and earthen ramparts was to prevent tunneling to undermine the walls. If the foundation of the wall could be weakened, the superstructure would collapse.

20:31. sackcloth and ropes. Sackcloth is a familiar sign of mourning. The sarcophagus of Ahiram depicts mourning women with what is likely sackcloth wrapped around their hips over their skirts. The ropes are probably a symbol that they consider themselves captives. Both Assyrian and Egyptian reliefs depict captives from Syria with a tether bound around the neck.

20:33. taken up into chariot. A vassal would have run by the wheel of the chariot (as in the Aramean Bir-Rakib inscription), whereas an equal is taken up into the chariot. By referring to Ben-Hadad as his brother and taking him up into his chariot, Ahab is expressing his

willingness to renegotiate their former relationship. It is likely that previously Ahab was considered a vassal to Ben-Hadad, in which case there would have been a suzerainty treaty between them. This would have required Ahab to pay tribute and be under the general authority of Aram. In this new "brother" relationship there would be a parity treaty between them that would not require tribute. It would put them on equal terms, providing mutual support militarily and opening up trade routes and merchant opportunities on an equal footing. Ahab's leniency is seen in his settling for equal status rather than pushing his advantage to make Ben-Hadad his vassal.

20:34. terms of treaty. The return of conquered territory would have restored the traditional boundaries between the two nations. The other concession by Ben-Hadad concerned trade opportunities. One of the actions taken when a major city came under the control of a new king was to construct a marketplace for his merchants in a square set up in his honor. A colony of merchants would then take up residence in the city to carry on their trade. This practice is illustrated by the courtyard outside the city gate of Dan. There the archaeologists excavated a series of buildings that has been identified as a bazaar area set up to honor the Aramean conqueror, whose stele (now referred to as the "House of David Inscription") was prominently featured there.

20:35-40. actions of the prophet. The initial encounter with the man who refused to wound him made it clear that even an act of mercy that disobeyed God's command brought forfeiture of life. The wound the prophet requests is apparently one to the head, which would then make very realistic the bandage that he wore. While the bandage serves as his disguise, the wound may have gained him access to the king. It is interesting that while the king has a reputation for mercy (v. 31) and shows mercy to Ben-Hadad, his judgment in this wounded man's case is anything but merciful. A talent of silver is exorbitant and would suggest that the prisoner is a very important person. For "sons of the prophets" see comment on 1 Samuel 19:20.

21:1-29

Naboth's Vineyard

21:1. Jezreel palace. For general comments about Jezreel see 18:45. The palace at Jezreel was excavated in the early 1990s. The rectangular enclosure covers about eleven acres and is surrounded by a casemate wall with towers at the corners. It featured a six-chambered gate, a moat and earthen ramparts. The moat was cut from rock and averaged thirty feet wide and at points was nearly twenty feet deep. The moat used in Palestine was a dry moat (called a fosse) probably intended to prevent tunneling under the walls of the city. Jezreel was about twenty-three miles from Samaria.

21:3. vineyard as part of inheritance. Ahab's offer is more than fair and even generous. Naboth's refusal is not just based on traditional "family homestead" type of feelings but on theological issues. Possession of the land had been a gift of the covenant. Distributed to tribes, clans and families, the patrimonial landholdings constituted each family's part of the covenant promises and benefits (for more information see comment on Lev 25:23). Documents from both Mari and Ugarit attest to a practice of perpetual ownership of land and strict rules about the transfer of property—but these are not given a religious explanation. It is also possible that, as a royal residence, Jezreel enjoyed a privileged status in which all residents enjoyed certain benefits (see comment on 2 Sam 5:9). Among these was protection from royal expropriation of land even in exchange for other property.

21:7. rights of the king. This passage is believed to represent a true distinction between the rights extended to the king in Israel and those current in Phoenicia. Differences involve issues concerning (1) the ultimate ownership of land and (2) the absolute power of the king. In the first category, Israelites believed that all the land was Yahweh's land, while the Phoenicians would have seen land as royal fiefdoms—all land was on grant from the king. In the second category, Israelite kingship was designed to be less despotic than most monarchies—the king was not above the law. Jezebel would not have been accustomed to such niceties.

21:9. declaring a fast. Fasts could be declared by the king and generally were proclaimed in the context of some sort of critical petition (see 1 Sam 7:6). For instance, in the drought that was experienced in these times a day of fasting would have served the purpose of praying for rain and perhaps seeking out the offenses that could potentially have brought the drought. Just as David arranges for the deaths of Saul's family members to rectify the offense in 2 Samuel 21, so here Naboth's death would be an attempt to bring an end to whatever situation was the basis for the fast.

21:9. seating arrangement. The prominent seating of Naboth would reflect his status in the community and sets him up for the contention that his actions were capable of affecting the entire community. The two false witnesses are seated near him so that they can claim to have heard his words.

21:11-13. Naboth's crime. Cursing the king usually entails a forthright renunciation of loyalty to the king (as in Judg 9:27-28 and 2 Sam 16:7-8) by fixing blame for the situation squarely on his shoulders. Cursing God is likewise associated with disloyalty to him and involves maligning or discrediting him, at times by fixing blame. Isaiah 8:21 features the combination of cursing both God and king in the context of fixing blame for hardship or crisis. As the community is being led in this fast to seek the cause of their crisis, these two planted witnesses claim that they heard Naboth fixing blame for the crisis on God and the king. This is judged as treasonous, and he is sentenced to death by the officials, who have been prompted to respond to the case in that way. An Alalakh text indicates that if a man is put to death for treason, ownership of his property reverts to the palace.

21:19. dogs licking blood. Dogs were scavengers who roamed the streets and alleys feeding on garbage. That anyone's (let alone a king's) body should be so exposed meant that there would be no honor in death or even a proper burial. Improper burial was popularly thought to jeopardize an individual's afterlife (for further information see comment on 1 Kings 16:4). Israelites considered that a person's body ("flesh") and spirit were in principle inseparable. Thus the individual was both spirit and flesh. Because of this the dead corpse was very carefully treated, as it was still considered part of the person's existence. First-millennium Assyrian records also demonstrate these concerns, as Ashurbanipal punishes his opponents by having their bodies thrown in the streets and dragged around. From the same period an Assyrian curse declares "let dogs tear his unburied body to pieces."

21:27. Ahab's response. Sackcloth and fasting were considered some of the basic elements of repentance as well as mourning in ancient Israel. Fasting is little attested in the ancient Near East outside the Bible. It generally occurs in the context of mourning. In the Old Testament the religious use of fasting is often in connection with making a request before God. The principle is that the importance of the request causes an individual to be so concerned about his or her spiritual condition that physical necessities fade into the background. In this sense the act of fasting is designed as a process leading to purification and humbling oneself before God (Ps 69:10). Sackcloth was made of goat or camel hair and was coarse and uncomfortable. In many cases the sackcloth was only a loin covering. The sarcophagus of Ahiram depicts mourning women with what is likely sackcloth wrapped around their hips over their skirts.

22:1-40
Battle at Ramoth Gilead

22:1. chronology: Battle of Qarqar. Since the alliance of Ahab and Ben-Hadad at the end of chapter 20, three years have gone by. It is generally assumed that the reason their alliance remained strong was because of the threat of the Assyrian king Shalmaneser III who was making his way westward. He finally posed a threat to southern Aram in 853, where he was met by a coalition of twelve western nations at the Battle of Qarqar. Shalmaneser lists Ahab of Israel and Hadadezer of Damascus as two of the most significant parties in the alliance which was led by Iarhuleni of Hamath. Qarqar is on the Orontes River about 150 miles north of Damascus, but only 25 miles north of Hamath. Though Shalmaneser claims victory, study of subsequent history suggests that the western coalition succeeded in their major objective. It was not until ten or twelve years later, after the confederacy had eroded, that Shalmaneser finally shows any indication of control in the region. It is most likely the general success against Shalmaneser that gave Ahab the confidence to take military action against the Arameans and try to regain Ramoth Gilead.

22:12-38. Micaiah and Ahab. See comments on 2 Chronicles 18.

22:38. pool in Samaria. In the excavations of Samaria a large pool (sixteen by thirty-three feet) was discovered inside the northwest corner of the wall by the palace, but it is impossible to say whether this is the pool referred to here. It is uncertain whether the prostitutes are bathing in the pool or the blood or both.

22:39. palace of inlaid ivory. Ivory decor was very popular at this time for inlays in furniture and for wall panels. One of the principal sources of ivory was elephant tusks, which were imported from Aram (where Syrian elephants were not yet extinct). Elephant hides and tusks, as well as live elephants, were at times included in tribute payments. Excavations at Ashurnasirpal's palace at Kalah produced some very fine ivory carvings decorating the walls. Over five hundred ivory fragments have also been found in the excava-

tions at Samaria dating to the ninth and eighth centuries B.C. Many feature Egyptian and Phoenician artistic motifs.

22:41-50
Jehoshaphat of Judah

22:42. chronology. Thiele's dates for Jehoshaphat are 872-848, with other systems generally coming within two years of that. No reference to Jehoshaphat has yet been found in extrabiblical inscriptional material from the ancient Near East.

22:46. male shrine prostitutes. For more information concerning cultic prostitution, see the comment on Deuteronomy 23:17-18. The term used here occurs in both feminine and masculine forms and refers, perhaps euphemistically, to ones who have been set apart for particular functions. This same term is used in Akkadian literature to refer to those who have been consecrated as functionaries serving at the shrines or temples. The prostitute was among those functionaries, as was the wet nurse and the midwife. It is unclear what functions the males might have served.

22:48. fleet of ships. Trade by means of seagoing vessels was already taking place in the first half of the third millennium B.C. By mid-second millennium a fleet of ships from Ugarit numbered 150. Excavations of a sunken merchant ship (off the coast of Uluburun, Turkey) from the period give a good idea of the variety of items being shipped. Trading ships of the first millennium were single-masted with a crow's nest and could feature either one or two banks of oars. Typical length would be about fifty feet, though larger ones are known.

22:48. Ophir. Gold from Ophir is mentioned in an eighth-century inscription from Tell Qasile. The precise location of the site is unknown. The fact that it was shipped in at Ezion Geber suggests an Arabian location, though sites in India and East Africa have been considered.

22:48. Ezion Geber. Ezion Geber was a port city located at the head of the Gulf of Aqaba and may be either Tell el-Kheleifeh (which some identify as Elath) or on the island of Jezirat Far'on (Coral Island), the only site in the region with evidence of an ancient harbor area. The latter has been substantiated by underwater archaeological work that shows massive walls and jetties (though not Iron Age) and a small amount of Iron Age pottery. The technology used for the artificial harbor is similar to that found at Phoenician Tyre.

22:51-53

Ahaziah of Israel

22:51. chronology. Thiele's chronology for

Ahaziah places him in 853-852. He is not mentioned in any extrabiblical records.

2 KINGS

1:1-18

Ahaziah, King of Israel

1:2. lattice of the upper room. The excavations in Samaria have demonstrated that the royal palace at this time did have a second story. The style of architecture featured open areas, and the lattice described here would have been a wooden grid offering both shade and air circulation.

1:2. Samaria. Samaria was the capital city of the northern kingdom of Israel. For more information see the comment on 1 Kings 16.24.

1:2. Baal-Zebub. For many years it has been suggested that this name is an intentional corruption of Baal Zebul (Chief Baal), often identified in Ugaritic literature as lord of the underworld. This would explain the Greek form used in Matthew 10:25; 12:24; and elsewhere, "Beelzebul," and the attachment of the title to Satan in the New Testament. "Zebub" means "flies," and if it is a complimentary title, it may refer to the ability to drive away flies who carry disease and infection. A deity named El-Dhubub is known at Ugarit and may mean something similar. Incantations known from Ugaritic invoke Baal Zebul to exorcise demons of disease. Ahaziah, however, is not requesting an incantation effecting healing but only an oracle providing information concerning whether or not he will recover. This is also what is offered by Elijah in verse 6.

1:2. Ekron. The Philistine town of Ekron (Tel Miqne) is about a sixty-mile trip from Samaria. For more information on the site see comments on Judges 1:18 and 1 Samuel 5:10.

1:8. Elijah's clothing. See comment on 1 Kings 19:19 for a discussion of Elijah's mantle. The text here, however, makes no specific mention of Elijah's mantle but describes him as distinguished by hairiness, which could refer either to his garment or his person. The latter is more likely here, because what the NIV translates "belt" is everywhere else a loincloth, which would not be visible if he wore another garment. Certainly another option would be that he is cloaked in the hairy mantle but can be seen to be wearing only the leather loincloth beneath the cloak.

1:10. fire from heaven. The storm gods of the ancient Near East are typically equipped with lightning bolts which are their means of sending fire. Assyrian kings throughout this period speak of the gods as a burning flame and of sending fire before them. Esarhaddon (seventh-century Assyria) speaks of his march and attack in terms of an unquenchable fire. All of this is the way that the deity was believed to enter into battle. Fire brought about by his thunderbolts was one of his principal weapons.

1:17. chronology. Ahaziah's brother, Joram, succeeded him and reigned, according to Thiele, from 852 to 841. As a result, Judah and Israel had kings with virtually identical names ruling over the same period of time.

2:1-18

Elijah Taken Up

2:1. Gilgal. There are several sites named Gilgal, and it is difficult to be certain which is intended here. The best known is in the region of Jericho (see comment on Joshua 4:19), but it would be unusual for their trip to lead them over to Bethel first and then back to Jericho. Additionally, verse 2 speaks of going *down* to Bethel, which would not make sense with this Gilgal. The other possible Gilgal is the one in the vicinity of Geba and Micmash (see comment on 1 Sam 13.4), which is just a few miles south of Bethel and would require a descent to go toward Bethel.

2:2. Bethel. Bethel was the location of one of the calf shrines and was an important religious center. Its history included the patriarchs (Gen 28), the conquest and settlement (Josh 8; Judg 1), and Samuel (1 Sam 7), and, for at least a short time, it housed the ark (Judg 20:26-28).

2:3. company of the prophets. One could be trained for the profession of prophet, and there was a prophetic guild in this early period of Israel's history, usually identified as the "sons/company of the prophets." Typically these prophets would use various procedures in order to prepare themselves for receiving prophetic oracles. Music played an important role in inducing a trancelike state (ecstasy) that was seen as making one receptive to a divine message. In the Mari texts there is an entire class of temple personnel who were ecstatics and who often provided prophetic messages. Akkadian texts also use the designation *mar bari* (son of a *baru*) to designate a member of the guild of diviners who sometimes offered prophetic oracles.

2:4. Jericho. The trip from Bethel to Jericho was about twelve miles (mostly downhill) and would have taken about half a day. A settlement had reoccupied the site during the time of Ahab (see comment on 1 Kings 16:34).

2:6. Jordan. The Jordan is about five miles beyond Jericho. This would be about the place where Joshua crossed the Jordan.

2:9. double portion. By asking for a double portion, Elisha is not asking for twice as much as Elijah had, but for twice as much as any other successor would receive. This is the normal inheritance right of the firstborn, who would "carry the torch" for the family. Elisha is requesting that he receive the status as the principal successor to Elijah.

2:11. location of Elijah's ascension. Throughout his career Elijah has been mirroring some of the events in Moses' life. As they have now crossed to the east side of the Jordan, they are going toward Mount Nebo (where Moses died), which is about ten miles from the Jordan. The text does not name Nebo, or even suggest they were on a mountain, but it does place them in roughly the same vicinity.

2:11. chariot and horses of fire; whirlwind. The word translated "whirlwind" is typically connected directly to God's activity (the storm of Jonah 1) and at times to his presence (Job 38:1). The chariot imagery is more difficult to assess, because no role is given to the chariot and horses in the passage. In ancient Near Eastern imagery, major deities are at times accompanied by charioteers. There is a deity known as Rakib-El, who is the charioteer of the Canaanite god El. He is textually associated with Hadad, the storm god, but too little is known to elaborate any further on that interesting connection (chariot with storm, as here). In Akkadian literature, Bunene, the advisor to the sun god Shamash, is designated the charioteer. Connection to a sun god offers possible explanation for a chariot of fire. The charioteer would be responsible for transporting the deity, especially into battle. In Israelite religious belief, Yahweh is sometimes portrayed or manifested in ways familiar to an-

cient Near Eastern thought. For instance, in Elijah's contest with the Baal prophets, Yahweh is shown to be a God who controls fertility and responds with fire, and figurative language often associates him with the sun (Ps 84:11). Here his portrayal may share elements with Hadad, the storm god who is accompanied by a charioteer. These similarities suggest the possibility that familiar imagery was being used to clarify the involvement of deity in this unprecedented event.

2:12. my father. The title "father" is used to designate the leader of a group in both Hebrew and Akkadian. Likewise a "son" is therefore a member of that group.

2:12. chariots and horsemen of Israel. It is uncertain whether Elisha is exclaiming at what he is seeing or is ascribing this title to Elijah. If it is the latter (as 13:14 suggests), the title may be indicating an identification of Elijah's status as the charioteer, a close associate of the deity (cf. Bunene in the comment on 2:11) and the one that brings him into battle.

2:12. tearing clothes. Along with placing ashes in the hair, the tearing of clothing was a common form of mourning in the ancient Near East. One example outside the Bible is found in the Ugaritic Epic of Aqhat (c. 1600 B.C.) in which the sister of the hero tears her father's garment as she foretells a coming drought. Such an act often implied grief over the death of a relative, friend or prominent individual.

2:13. prophet's mantle. Elijah had cast his cloak over Elisha to select him for the task in 19:19. The cloak referred to here is an outer garment, not the same as the robe discussed in 1 Samuel 15:27. The distinctive prophet's cloak is most likely made of animal skin and is hairy in appearance (see Zech 13:4), though not all cloaks were so made. Very little is said about prophetic garb in the ancient Near East, so comparison is difficult. It may be of interest that Assyrian inscriptions beginning at this period portray a few individuals wearing lion-headed cloaks. Some of these individuals are involved in ritual activities (dance) and accompany deity. It is guessed that they may be exorcists. Elijah's mantle is here indicative of his spirit and power that Elisha is inheriting.

22:19-22

Waters of Jericho

2:19. bad water. The history of the water problem at the Ain es-Sultan spring by Jericho can be reviewed in the comments on Joshua 6:26 and 1 Kings 16:34. An alternative to the parasite theory suggested in those comments is that the geological shifts that could possibly have been related to the fall of Jericho brought the spring water into contact with radioactivity in the rock layers that polluted the water and caused sterility.

2:20. new bowl and salt. The use of a new container suggests one untainted by impurities, thus indicating that this is a ritual undertaking. "Flask" is preferable to NIV's "bowl," though the word is used only here in the Bible and is of uncertain meaning. Salt is used to combat the curse because curse is connected to rebellion and salt is seen as symbolically counteracting rebellion (see comment on Judg 9:45).

2:23-25.
Boys and Bears

2:23. age of mockers. Two different descriptions are used for this group. The first (v. 23) uses a noun and adjective combination that elsewhere refers to children or prepubescent youths. The second (v. 24) typically refers to the younger generation, from babies (e.g., Ruth 4:16) to middle-aged men (e.g., 2 Kings 12:8; Rehoboam was over forty, and these are his peers). This is probably a group of young teens. It was Elisha's curse but God's judgment.

2:23. baldhead. If Elijah was a hairy man (see comment on 1:8), Elisha's baldness would be a stark contrast and perhaps suggest to some that he could never have the same powers as his master. This taunt would therefore be a disavowal of his prophetic office and calling and would be strikingly refuted by the immediate fulfillment of his curse. Therefore in verses 19-22 Elisha removed a curse, while in 23-24 he effectuated a curse.

2:24. bears. Syrian bears were not yet extinct in this period and inhabited the forested regions in Israel. Bears were typically found in the hilly wooded areas of the central hill country, where caves and forests provided their habitat. The forested areas would be closer to Bethel than to Jericho. Ravaging wild beasts were often seen as punishment sent from God (see comment on 17:25).

2:25. Elisha's journey. The trip from Jericho to Bethel is about twelve miles, while Bethel to Mount Carmel is nearly seventy-five miles. From Mount Carmel back to Samaria is nearly forty miles.

3:1-27
War with Moab

3:1. chronology. Joram's succession has been previously mentioned in 1:17, but there it was related to the second year of Jehoram, son of Jehoshaphat. Here it is correlated to the eighteenth year of Jehoshaphat. This led Thiele to identify a period of coregency between Jehoshaphat and his son. The year, according to Thiele, is 852.

3:2. sacred stone of Baal. Standing stones were often used in shrines and temples in the niche where the idol otherwise would stand. Sometimes these could have reliefs of the deity inscribed on them, but often they would be blank. Such stones have been found in many excavations in Israel, including those at Dan, Gezer and Arad.

3:4. Mesha of Moab. Mesha is known from the inscription (the Moabite Stone) that details the past control of Israel over Moab and celebrates Mesha's breaking free of that control. The four-foot-high inscription was found at the site of Dibon, just north of the Arnon river, in 1868. It commemorates the building of a sanctuary, and it mentions Omri by name and refers to his son (Ahab, or perhaps his grandson, Joram) without naming him. It makes reference to the Moabite national god Chemosh who had used Israel for punishment of his land but now had brought victory. The next verse makes reference to Mesha's successful revolt against Israelite control (during the reign of Ahaziah?), so the events of the Moabite stone precede the events of this chapter.

3:4. tribute. While one hundred thousand lambs is an immense amount of tribute, it pales in comparison to the over eight hundred thousand sheep that Assyrian king Sennacherib claims to have taken from Babylon.

3:6-8. battle strategy. The allies cannot easily come against Moab from the north because Mesha has fortified the Medeba plains north of the Arnon. As a result they march south through Jerusalem, Hebron and Arad, around the south end of the Dead Sea (through the desert of Edom) and come at Moab from an unexpected direction. The march from Samaria to Arad is about eighty-five miles. From there it may be as many as fifty more to Kir Haresheth if a fairly direct route is taken.

3:8. desert of Edom. The desert of Edom is difficult to identify, but the comment in verse 9 that they had a seven-day march suggests that it refers to the area east of Edom. Perhaps they skirted to the south of the Wadi Zered and moved around to attack Moab from the east.

3:9. lack of water. From the time they left Jerusalem, they would have been traveling through arid, inhospitable land with few water sources. Dehydration comes very quickly in this climate and can be deadly.

3:11. presence of a prophet. It was typical procedure in the ancient Near East for an army to be staffed with some religious personnel (priests or prophets) for the purpose of making oracular requests, reading omens, making appropriate sacrifices and representing God's presence with the army.

3:11. pouring water on the hands of Elijah. Elisha is here identified as the personal attendant of Elijah. Though he performed menial tasks, his mere association with the already legendary prophet offered some hope for divine aid.

3:13. prophets of father and mother. Joram's father and mother, Ahab and Jezebel, had favored the prophets of Baal and Asherah. It is interesting that Joram does not disavow those prophets or the gods they serve, but only replies that Yahweh was the one who had instigated the campaign, so he must be dealt with. This may suggest that oracles had been sought from Yahweh by this northern king and that the oracles had answered favorably concerning this military action, though, alternatively, the alliance may have taken shape only because Jehoshaphat consulted Yahweh concerning his involvement (see 2 Chron 18:4-7). This divine direction, however it came, is now interpreted by Joram as Yahweh's intention to bring about their destruction.

3:15. harpist. The translation of "minstrel" would be preferable here since the instrument is not mentioned. It is most likely a lyre of the same type that David played for Saul. Typically, especially in this early period, prophets would use various procedures in order to prepare themselves for receiving prophetic oracles. Music played an important role in inducing a trancelike state (ecstasy) that was seen as making one receptive to a divine message. In the Mari texts there is an entire class of temple personnel who were ecstatics and often provided prophetic messages. The lyre usually had two arms rising up from the sound box. The strings were attached to the crossbar at the top of the instrument. Examples of lyres have been found at Canaanite Megiddo.

3:17. provision of water. It is likely that the army was in the vicinity of the Wadi Zered. Like all wadis, Zered fills up seasonally with the runoff from the higher elevations. As a result, it can suddenly course with water even though no rain has been experienced at the lower elevations. The digging of pits in the wadi would be a means of capturing the runoff for their use lest it all surge right past them. Prophetic knowledge of rain in high elevations that would bring water into the area is

also demonstrated by Deborah (see comment on Judg 4:14-16).

3:22. water appearing as blood. It is not hard to imagine the water having the appearance of blood in a sandstone water course under a rising sun on a hot, hazy day—especially if the Moabites had no reason to think there would be any water scattered in the pits throughout the wadi. But if they actually thought it was blood, where were the corpses? If they come charging in expecting plunder, it is more likely that the Moabites see what appears to be a deserted camp. They therefore take the appearance of the water as an omen that internal rivalries have resulted in the desertion of the camp as the armies fought one another. In fact a Mesopotamian omen series of popular beliefs contains the indication that if a river carries blood, internal strife will lead an army to do battle with itself, brother against brother. The imagery of blood flowing like water is used in Assyrian descriptions of battles.

3:25. treatment of Moab. The ecological destruction was intended to cripple the economy for years. The springs and fields could eventually be cleared of stones, but needing to do so would make it a long, slow process to reestablish a productive agriculture. Sometimes springs would find other, less usable outlets and fields would be so damaged as to have greatly reduced fertility. The cutting down of trees would have even more devastating effects on the ecological balance. Not only would shade and wood supply be lost, but topsoil erosion would increase and the loss of forestation's contribution to the environment would accelerate the development of wasteland conditions. Some fruit trees (such as the date palm) take twenty years of growth before they become productive. Agricultural devastation and deforestation were typical tactics of invading armies seeking to punish those they conquered and as an attempt to hasten their surrender. The Assyrian records and reliefs especially detail punitive measures that include felling trees, devastating meadowlands and destroying canal systems used for irrigation.

3:25. Kir Haresheth. This is a designation for the capital city in the southern section of Moab, otherwise known as Kir-Moab, and identified with modern Kerak, seventeen miles south of the Arnon along the King's Highway. There has been no major excavation at the site, but surface surveys show some slight remains from the Iron Age.

3:27. child sacrifice. Evidence of child sacrifice has been recovered from Phoenician sites in North Africa (Carthage) and Sardinia, and it was also practiced in Syria and Mesopotamia during the Assyrian period (eighth to seventh centuries B.C.). Dedicating children to a god as a form of sacrifice is found in several biblical narratives. They can be explained as a means of promoting fertility (Mic 6:6-7) or as a way of obtaining a military victory (Judg 11:30-40), as here. In no case, however, does Yahweh consider this an acceptable sacrifice (Deut 18:10). An eighth-century B.C. Phoenician inscription speaks of sacrifices made to Molech before battle by the Cilicians and their enemies.

4:1-7
Provision of Oil for Destitute Woman

4:1. company of the prophets. See comment on 2:3.

4:1. debt slavery. Because of the fragile nature of the environment in much of the ancient Near East, farmers and small landowners often found themselves in debt. Their problems could magnify if a drought and resulting poor harvests continued over more than one year, and they could be forced to sell their land, goods and eventually even their family and themselves into debt slavery. Israelite law takes this situation into account by providing a fair period of labor service to the creditor as well as a time limit on servitude for the debt slave. No one could serve more than six years, and when slaves were freed they went out debt-free. This would have been a good solution for some, but without their land to return to, many may have chosen to remain in the service of their creditor or to move to the cities to find jobs or to join the military.

4:2. oil. The oil was olive oil, used as shortening in cooking. It was usually mixed with the grain before baking but was sometimes spread over the dough.

4:8-37
Elisha and the Shunammite Woman

4:8. Shunem. Shunem was located at the eastern end of the Valley of Jezreel on the southwest slope of the hill of Moreh. The town is listed in Egyptian itineraries and shows remains from the Iron Age.

4:10. room on the roof. The typical Israelite house of the Iron Age was what is referred to as the "four-room house." On the ground floor it featured a room that stretched the whole width of the house. The front section

was divided into three parallel rooms perpendicular to the back room. The center of these three was often an open courtyard area. Most of these houses are believed to have had second stories, though these are rarely preserved for archaeologists' view. The particular architectural terminology used in this verse remains obscure.

4:16-35. giving son, taking son, reviving son. In the Ugaritic Epic of Aqhat, the upright king, Danil, was given a son (Aqhat) by the gods. Falling into disfavor with the gods, his life is taken, but then apparently restored again, revived by the gods. Though none of the details of the Aqhat narrative show any similarity to the account here, the basic motif concerning the power of deity to give, take and give back is a familiar one.

4:18-20. cause of death. The death of the son is usually attributed to sunstroke, though other suggestions range from cerebral hemorrhage or cerebral malaria to meningitis. The few details given make it difficult to achieve any confidence in diagnosis.

4:23. New Moon or Sabbath. Keyed to their use of a lunar calendar, ancient Israelites marked the first day of the month, with its "new moon" phase, as a festival day (every 29-30 days). As on the Sabbath, all work was to cease (see Amos 8:5), and there were sacrifices to be made (Num 28:11-15). In the monarchy period, the king became a prominent figure in these celebrations (see Ezek 45:17). New Moon festivals were also prominent in Mesopotamia from late in the third millennium down to the Neo-Babylonian period in the middle of the first millennium B.C. This would have been a convenient opportunity for people to consult a seer to seek an oracle, which might explain the connection between Elisha and these holy days.

4:25. Mount Carmel. Since there is no information concerning where Elisha is staying in the Carmel range, it is difficult to be precise, but the distance from Shunem to the area of Carmel is about twenty miles.

4:27. taking hold of feet. Taking hold of the feet was a gesture of self abasement and entreaty. Though this gesture occurs nowhere else in the Old Testament, in Akkadian literature a wide range of fugitives or supplicants take hold of the king's feet to demonstrate their submission or surrender and make their petitions.

4:29. tucking cloak into belt. In order to make sure that a longer garment did not interfere with more strenuous activity, the lower edge of the cloak could be turned up and tucked into the belt.

4:29. laying staff on boy's face. There is no other reference to a prophet being equipped with a staff (the rod of Moses is a different Hebrew word), and the other passages where this word is used speak only of a nondescript stick used for support—often a crutch or cane. From verse 31 it would appear that Elisha and Gehazi considered it possible that the staff would revive the boy. In Akkadian incantation texts a staff is sometimes the instrument by which exorcisms against the *asakku* demons (bringing disease and fever) are effected. Since it was the boy's head that hurt, the staff is laid across his face.

4:34. Elisha's procedure. In Mesopotamian incantation literature the touching of part to part is a means by which demons exercise power over their intended victims—it is the idiom of possession. In this belief, vitality or life force can be transferred from one body to the other by contact of each part. By imitating the procedure believed to be used by demons, the prophet is able, through the power of Yahweh (notice the prayer), to drive the demons out and restore the boy's life. This is often considered to be one of the clearest cases of sympathetic magic in the Bible.

4:35. sneezing seven times. The word translated "sneezed" occurs only here and its meaning is uncertain. From the context, other possibilities would include "convulsed" or "moaned."

4:36-41
Poison Stew

4:36. Gilgal. Uncertain location; see comment on 2:1.

4:38. pot. This is a wide-mouthed cooking pot that could be made of either pottery or metal.

4:39. ingredients of stew. The poisonous ingredient is generally considered the yellow gourds known as colocynths, popularly referred to today as apples of Sodom. They can be fatal.

4:41. adding flour. Flour or meal was believed to possess magical power able to remove evil magic. It is often used in magical incantations and rituals in the ancient Near East, but not quite in this way. Sometimes a flour paste is used to make a figurine that is then used in a magical ritual. Other times the flour is sprinkled in a circle around something that the ritual is to be performed on. As is often the case, Elisha is using procedures that would have some familiarity with the world of magic, but never quite in the common way or with the ritualistic elements.

4:42-44
Feeding the People

4:42. Baal Shalishah. Baal Shalishah is traditionally located at Bethsarisa on the plain of Sharon about fifteen miles west-northwest of Joppa. Other interpreters, however, favor a site closer to Gilgal such as Ein Samiya in the eastern part of the hill country of Ephraim about six miles northwest of Bethel.

4:42. gift for Elisha. The gift is comprised of the firstfruits that would generally be given as an offering to the sanctuary for use by the priesthood. As a man of God, Elisha apparently qualified as a recipient of these gifts.

5:1-27
Elisha and Naaman

5:1. Aram/Syria. The land of Aram, north of the land of Israel, was known by the Greeks as Syria. Current evidence suggests that the Arameans inhabited the upper Euphrates throughout the second millennium, first as villagers and pastoralists, then as a political, national coalition. During this period they are alternately allies and the most troublesome foes of Israel.

5:1. leprosy. Those studying the language have concluded that the term often translated "leprosy" is more accurately rendered "lesion," or, less technically, "scaly skin." Such patches could be swelled or weeping, as well as flaking. Similar broad terminology also exists in Akkadian, where the Babylonians likewise considered it an unclean condition and the punishment of the gods. Clinical leprosy (Hansen's disease) has not been attested in the ancient Near East prior to the time of Alexander the Great. None of the most prominent characteristics of Hansen's disease are listed in the ancient texts, and the symptoms that are listed argue against a relationship to Hansen's disease. The condition discussed in the text is not presented as contagious. Descriptions would suggest that modern diagnoses would include psoriasis, eczema, favus and seborrheic dermatitis, as well as a number of fungal-type infections. The great cultural aversion to skin diseases may be that in appearance and sometimes odor they resemble the rotting skin of the corpse and are therefore associated with death. This natural revulsion adds considerably to the victim's outcast status when combined with the quarantine that is ritually rather than medically motivated.

5:5. Naaman's gift. The gift accompanying Naaman is exorbitant—a king's ransom. Ten talents equals thirty thousand shekels, about seven hundred fifty pounds of silver. The six thousand shekels of gold equals about one hundred fifty pounds (one gold shekel equaled fifteen silver shekels). Converted to today's buying power, it would be in the vicinity of three-quarters of a *billion* dollars. One can get an idea of the proportions by understanding that a typical wage would have been ten silver shekels per year, and one gold shekel would purchase one ton of grain.

5:6. request to foreign king for healing. A number of examples exist of kings sending to other kings for help in the area of healing sickness. Babylonian exorcists were prized by the Hittites, and Egyptian doctors were famed for their healing skills, especially in their treatment of eye diseases.

5:7. tore robes. The tearing of robes, especially royal robes, was a sign of mourning. This would have signaled a national crisis or tragedy. We are never told which king of Israel this is, though much of Elisha's interaction is with Jehoram.

5:10. trip to the Jordan. Since Elisha is probably in Samaria (see comment on verse 24), the trip to the Jordan would have been about forty miles. There is no easy, direct route from Samaria to the Jordan. He probably would have gone back the way he came: north to Dothan, through the Dothan Valley to the Valley of Jezreel, from Jezreel through the Gilboa pass to Beth Shan and then on to the Jordan.

5:10. washing in the Jordan. In the Mesopotamian *namburbi* rituals protective purification is accomplished by dipping seven times in the river facing upstream and seven times facing downstream. This ritual also includes releasing gifts for the god Ea into the river. The flowing water was believed to carry the impurities to the netherworld. Again, Elisha's chosen procedures are ones that would ring a note of familiarity to those who lived in this world of magical rituals. On the medical level there are a number of locations in Israel (e.g., near Tiberius) that boast of hot springs capable of restoring healthy skin from any number of conditions. Nevertheless, the text refers specifically to the Jordan River, which could not be confused with a mineral spring.

5:11. expected procedure. Naaman obviously had expected different methods to be used. The elevation of the hand here ("elevation" preferred rather than "waving") often accompanied invocations or incantations. Praying with raised hand is referred to in the Aramaic Zakkur inscription and is depicted in numerous reliefs (right hand, palm inward, elbow bent). There is a series of Akkadian incantations called *shuilla* (raising of the hand). The

extant copies date to about this period. These compositions include invocation and praise of deity leading up to a prayer seeking appeasement, protection and the removal of evil. It would have been unusual in the ancient worldview for rituals to be performed without the presence of the specialist reciting incantations, accompanied by appropriate gestures, and orchestrating the procedures. The absence of the specialist leads Naaman to think that any body of water could serve the purpose of cleansing. He expected Elisha, the practitioner, to make the difference, while Elisha is careful to remove himself from such a role.

5:12. Abana and Pharpar. The variant reading Amana is probably to be preferred in light of Mount Amana in the Anti-Lebanon range and the Amana River (today known as the Barada) that flows into the plain of Damascus from its flanks. The Pharpar is less certain, though it may be the river el-Awaj, which flows down from the flanks of Mount Hermon to the marshes southeast of Damascus.

5:17. carrying earth back. Naaman makes it clear that his reason for carrying the dirt has to do with sacrifices. This suggests that he intends to build an altar of the earth that he has brought back with him (the word for "earth" here is the same that is commanded for use in altar construction in Ex 20:24; see comment there for further information).

5:18. temple of Rimmon. Rimmon (=Ramman, "thunderer") is believed to be a title of the storm god, Hadad, the head of the Aramean pantheon. Though this association is confidently made, there has been no occurrence of this title outside the Bible (but see Hadad Rimmon in Zech 12:11). The limited excavations in Damascus have not unearthed the temple referred to here, but a basalt orthostat (an engraved standing stone) from this period found incorporated into the substructure of the Umayyad mosque suggests that the mosque was built over the site of this temple.

5:22. company of the prophets. See comment on 2:3.

5:22-23. Gehazi's request. Considering what Naaman had been prepared to offer, Gehazi's request is extremely modest, yet it is still a considerable sum. A talent of silver is three hundred years of wages (for someone making thirty to thirty-five thousand a year, that would be like getting about ten million dollars), and Naaman doubles it. Gehazi is trying to set himself up for life.

5:24. the hill. The word NIV translates "hill" is a technical term for the acropolis area usually connected to a royal city. This suggests that Elisha is currently living in Samaria.

5:26. rebuke to Gehazi. Whether the money was from Naaman's personal wealth or from the treasury of the Aramean king, Gehazi could have reasoned that he was simply taking back what had been plundered from Israel. But Gehazi does not have charity or replenishment of the national coffers in mind. Elisha's reference to olive groves, vineyards, livestock and servants all reflects what Gehazi could purchase for himself with the money. His newfound wealth would have bought him a life of luxury and leisure. Thus Gehazi was reducing the high prophetic calling to a mercenary vocation that exploited divine power for personal gain.

5:27. transfer of disease. In the ancient world, witches and sorcerers were believed to be able to impose disease through hexes and curses. Rituals to remove various ills (the *namburbu* rituals for instance) usually involved transferring the evil to an object of some sort and then disposing of the object. One would have thought that in the ritual washing, Naaman's disease would have been transferred to the water and carried away. Naaman, however, has also been in contact with the gifts he brought, and here they are treated as a means of transfer of the evil from Naaman to Gehazi. This resembles what we would call contagion (though no medical contagion connected to the infections of skin diseases could have been contracted through natural means so quickly).

5:27. Gehazi's doom. See the comment on leprosy at 5:1. This is not a death sentence, for this condition is not life threatening or even health threatening. It could be categorized as a social disease in that its main consequence is that the victim is excluded from society as an undesirable outcast. Comparison to "snow" most likely concerns the flakiness rather than the color ("white" is added in the NIV).

6:1-7
Recovery of the Axhead

6:1. company of the prophets. See comment on 2:3.

6:2. poles (beams) for houses. Their problem is that the place where they assemble to be instructed by Elisha is too small, so they determine to work together to build a more adequate facility. The Jordan valley, being heavily forested, would be the natural place to find the necessary wood (acacia, tamarisk and willow would be the most likely).

6:5. iron axhead. Though this period is already well into the Iron Age and iron is be-

coming more widely available as technology and smelting procedures are being improved, implements of iron remain expensive and valuable.

6:6. "floating" axhead. One category of magic involved rites of contact and transference. Through contact with magically endowed objects, properties or characteristics were believed to be transferred from one object to another. The biblical text does not mention what type of wood Elisha cut, but in Mesopotamian practice tamarisk wood was often used in such rituals. Though some may be reluctant to see God's prophet making such extensive use of what appear to be magical practices, the fact remains that these would have appeared as magical to the ancient observer; see comments on 4:34; 4:41; and 5:11.

6:8-23
Blinded Arameans Captured by Elisha

6:9-11. prophets giving military information. In the examples of prophetic activity in the ancient Near East, military advice is commonly given by prophets to kings. The information given by Elisha is far more specific than the examples known from other literature.

6:13. Dothan. Located at Tell Dothan, this is an imposing site covering about twenty-five acres. It is ten miles north of Samaria on the main route used by merchants and herdsmen going north to the Jezreel Valley. The area around the city (the Dothan Valley) provided choice pasture land, so it developed into a major city site as early as the Early Bronze Age (3200-2400 B.C.) and would have served as a natural landmark for travelers. Though it is not mentioned in extrabiblical material, archaeology of the site has confirmed a major settlement on the site for Iron Age II.

6:17. horses and chariots of fire. The text does not say the horses and chariots fill the mountains (plural), but the mount (singular) and that they surround Elisha. This suggests that the "mount" is the tell on which the city of Dothan is located (some two hundred feet above the surrounding plain). They represent a protective bodyguard for the prophet. Yahweh is often portrayed as the "Lord of Hosts"—the com-mander of the heavenly armies. One contingent of his chariotry is here to engage in battle. For more on the horses and chariot of fire see comment on 2:11-13. For information about Yahweh as a divine warrior see comment on 1 Samuel 4:3-7.

6:18. blindness. The word for blindness here is used elsewhere only for those gathered outside Lot's house in the town of Sodom (Gen 19). It is a term related to an Akkadian word for day-blindness and also serves in Hebrew (as in Aramaic) to refer to night-blindness (pertinent to Gen 19). Both of these conditions are seen in Akka-dian texts as requiring magical remedies. Day-blindness (hemeralopia) and night-blindness (nyctalopia) have vitamin A deficiency as their principal cause, and vitamin B deficiency may contribute to the sense of confusion evident in both passages. It is therefore of interest that liver (rich in vitamin A) figures prominently in the magical procedures used in Mesopotamia to correct the condition. In an interesting section of the Epic of Tukulti-Ninurta the Assyrian king reports how the gods took his side in the battle. Shamash (the sun god and the god of justice) is said to have blinded the eyes of the enemy.

6:19. trip from Dothan to Samaria. The ten-mile trip would have taken some time when trying to lead a debilitated army of confused men who cannot see very well.

6:21. "father" as title. The title "father" is used to designate the leader of a group in both Hebrew and Akkadian. Likewise a "son" is therefore a member of that group. The king's use of the title indicates his recognition of Elisha's status and reflects his respect for the man of God.

6:22-23. treatment of prisoners. "Captives of the bow" is an expression found in Akkadian texts to describe persons who have been taken as part of the plunder. They are then at the disposal of the victor, who can employ them in slave labor, sell them or set them free. It is Elisha's intention to make use of this opportunity to create friendly relations with the Arameans. The feast laid before them is a banquet or even a ceremonial meal usually accompanying a special occasion or establishing a treaty agreement.

6:24—7:20

Siege of Samaria

6:24. Ben-Hadad. Aramean history at this time is still in need of much clarification, with at least part of the problem caused by several rulers with the name of Ben-Hadad (meaning "son of [the god] Hadad"). The issue is further complicated by the fact that Shalmaneser III's inscriptions name the ruler of this time Hadadezer (see comment on 2 Sam 8:3). The first Ben-Hadad has been referred to in 1 Kings 15. He ruled during the first part of the ninth century, though no precise dating is possible. In 2 Kings 8 the king murdered by Hazael (about 842) is named Ben-Hadad, and Hazael

is later succeeded by his son, also named Ben-Hadad (2 Kings 13:24). The name Bir-Hadad occurs in an inscription dedicated to the god Melqart, but again it is unclear which Ben-Hadad this refers to. It has been suggested that the sequence may be Ben-Hadad I (1 Kings 15), Ben-Hadad II (1 Kings 20), Hadadezer (Shalmaneser Inscription, considered by some a variant name of Ben-Hadad), Ben-Hadad III (Melqart inscription, 2 Kings 8), Hazael, Ben-Hadad IV (2 Kings 13). There is no other material from the ancient Near East to help unravel this at this time. If this passage is in its proper chronological place, Ben-Hadad III would be the necessary identification. If the arrangement is viewed as more thematic than chronological, the besieging king may be the successor of Hazael.

6:25. siege leading to famine. The whole idea of siege is to drive the population to the extremities of hunger and thirst so that they capitulate without a fight. Famine in this case is not an environmental condition, but the results of the siege when food supplies have been exhausted.

6:25. prices of undesirable foods. The "donkey's head" would have been one of the least desirable things imaginable to eat for food, yet here it is selling for exorbitant prices. Recall that the standard wage was only about one shekel per month. The second item, literally "dove's dung" (NIV note), may really be pigeon manure, which has been known to be used for food in dire times, or it could refer to pods from a thorny variety of acacia, as it does occasionally in Akkadian. Whether it was being used for food or fuel, even a few ounces of it cost many months pay. In the Cuthean Legend of Naram-Sin (who ruled in Mesopotamia toward the end of the third millennium), six and a half quarts of barley (less than a week's worth of meals) was said to be worth fifty shekels of silver (five years pay) during time of siege.

6:29. cannibalism. Cannibalism is a standard element of curses in Assyrian treaties of the seventh century. It was the last resort in times of impending starvation. This level of desperation could occur in times of severe famine (as illustrated in the Atrahasis Epic) or could be the result of siege (as during Ashurbanipal's siege of Babylon, about 650 B.C.) when the food supply had become depleted, as mentioned in this text and anticipated in the treaty texts. Siege warfare was common in the ancient world, so this may not have been as rare an occasion as might be presumed.

6:32. elders. The elders represent the influential families of a town or tribe. They are sitting with Elisha as one likely to receive an oracle concerning a suggested course of action or a proclamation that deliverance is near. Meanwhile the unidentified king has lost patience with what has apparently been a long wait for the oracular information (v. 33) and has decided that the siege is punishment from Yahweh. In Israel the distinction was not always sharply drawn between the prophet as *proclaimer* and the prophet as *instigator*. This confusion occurs because the widespread belief in the ancient world still persisted in Israel that the utterance of words by skilled individuals had the power to coerce the gods to act accordingly. The Israelite king has decided that Elisha must have had some role in inducing Yahweh to take this action against Samaria.

7:1. change in prices. A seah is about seven and a half quarts and would be enough to make about a week's worth of meals for a single adult, so the cost is still inflated (but see comment on 6:25 to see how much better it is). Information on prices is provided in Babylonian literature. Whereas in normal circumstances a shekel would buy about a hundred quarts of barley, here it buys only fifteen. During Ashurbanipal's siege of Babylon, barley was going for ten quarts for a shekel. Basic subsistence level for a family of four would be about four quarts of barley per day.

7:2. officer. The term used here is thought to originally have described the third man in a chariot crew who was responsible for holding the shield to protect the driver and the archer. As time goes on it is used outside of chariotry contexts and probably refers to an armor-bearer or, in an administrative role, the king's adjutant.

7:2. floodgates of heaven. The text uses the poetic phrase "windows of heaven" to describe the openings through which the rain came down. This is not scientific language but reflects the perspective of the observer, much as we would speak of the sun setting. The only other occurrence of such a term in ancient Near Eastern literature is in the Canaanite myth of Baal building his house, where the "window" of his house is described as a rift in the clouds. But even there it is not associated with rain. The officer is speaking generally of God's provision, because the issue under discussion is food, not water.

7:3. leprosy. For information on the skin conditions translated here as "leprosy" see the comment on 5:1. These outcasts have even fewer resources at their disposal than the people of the city.

7:6. Hittite and Egyptian armies. The Hittites had left their Anatolian homeland several centuries earlier and had resettled in regions north of Aram, centered in the city-states of Carchemish and Karatepe. It is likely that even Hamath would still be considered a Hittite state at this time. There was already a history of warfare between these Hittite states and the Arameans. Egypt is more difficult here, for there is little evidence to suggest Egypt was active or interested in the Levant during this period. Additionally, the reference to kings (plural) of Egypt (obscured by the NIV) would be odd. Some have suggested that rather than Egypt (Hebrew: *mṣrym*) the text refers to Musri (*mṣry*), though there has been no consensus on where that might be located. The party referred to here should be understood as the same Musri appearing in the inscriptions of Shalmaneser III from this period. Musri is included among the allies from the "Land of Hatti" that fought against Shalmaneser III at Qarqar in 853 and is listed right after Jehu of Israel in the tribute list on the Black Stela of Shalmaneser III from 841. If this Musri is Egypt, as many suppose, then it demonstrates that Egypt was active in the region. If it is a location in north Syria, its identity remains unknown. Some favor this option because it is also named as a neighbor of Arpad (north of Aleppo in North Syria) in the Aramaic Sefire treaty of the eighth century, though others see this Musri as the king's name rather than a place name.

7:10. gatekeepers. The gates of an enclosed city were always locked at night, and, of course, they have been barred during the length of the siege.

7:15. Aramean retreat. The leaders of Samaria suspect a ruse well known in the ancient world—an ambush set by appearing to have given up and gone home. Perhaps the most well-known application of this ruse was its use by the Greeks against Troy in the war several centuries earlier recorded in the *Iliad*. The fleeing Arameans were trailed as far as the Jordan, some forty miles away.

8:1-6

The Shunammite Woman's Land

8:2. land of the Philistines. Though Samaria typically experiences slightly more rainfall per year than the southern coastal plain (land of the Philistines), the alluvial flood plain of the coast is less dependent on the rainfall and would be the logical area to try to weather a famine.

8:3-6. confiscation of land. Land that had been deserted typically reverted to crown

property until a claim was made. The fact that
the woman is making the claim suggests that
her husband had died, in which case she
would be able to claim the land on behalf of
her son, who would be the rightful heir to the
property.

8:6. income from land. Generally a person
would not expect to receive back income from
the land for the period of absence. That would
be considered the reimbursement to those
who had kept the land up and worked it.

8:7-15
Hazael Becomes King of Aram

8:7. Damascus. A trip from Samaria to Damascus was about 125 miles and would have
taken a little over a week on foot. Damascus is
the capital of Aram and the royal seat. For
more information on the site see comment on
2 Samuel 8:5.

8:7. Ben-Hadad. For the confusion concerning
the identification of any given Ben-Hadad see
the comment on 6:24. Since this is the time of
Hazael's accession to the throne, the year is
842 B.C. Shalmaneser indicates that Hazael
murdered Hadadezer.

8:8. Hazael. Hazael is referred to in the
records of his contemporary, Shalmaneser III
of Assyria, where he is identified as a usurper.
He reigned from 842 to about 800 B.C. He is
also named on a couple of fragmentary Aramaic and Assyrian inscriptions. When the
western coalition that had withstood Shalmaneser III at Qarqar fell apart during the
840s, Hazael remained anti-Assyrian and held
out for a number of years both in pitched battle and under an unsuccessful siege of Damascus (though he paid heavy tribute). From
836 on Shalmaneser was busy elsewhere
(mostly in Urartu) and then was succeeded by
weak rulers, leaving Hazael free to focus his
attention on Israel for most of his reign. For information concerning his military actions
against Israel see comment on 10:32.

8:8. consulting Yahweh. Even though the
Arameans did not worship Yahweh, they
would not have denied his existence or power.
The polytheism of the ancient world was an
open-ended system in which divine power
was respected no matter what the source.
Likewise prophets were held in high esteem
and a chance to consult one in time of sickness
was not to be missed. Though it is possible
that the religious personnel connected to the
worship of Baal might have been offended
(see comment on 1:2), people would often take
that risk to get oracular information from the
divine realm.

8:9. gift. As in the case of Naaman, the gift offered is exorbitant. In the ancient world gifts
to deity were often attempts to manipulate
and obligate, and this must be viewed in the
same way. Since prophets were believed to
have influence over the gods they represented, this was the king's way of procuring a favorable oracle. He was trying to buy not a
falsified report but the prophet's words of
power that would carry divine power in their
train.

8:12. treatment of conquered cities. The tactics listed here are all standard procedure for
eliminating the possibility of future rebellion.
The burning of fortified cities would destroy
any hope that one might be used for a defensible rallying point for later revolution. The execution of men, children and even unborn
babies decimates any present or future army.
Ninth-century Assyrian conquest accounts
speak of burning the young boys and girls.
The practice of ripping open pregnant women
is mentioned very rarely. It is a practice attributed to Assyrian king Tiglath-Pileser I (about
1100) in a hymn praising his conquests. It is
also referred to in passing in a Neo-Babylonian lament.

8:13. dog. Dogs were considered general
pests, making this comparison a common one
in statements of humility or self-depreciation.
Similar use is found in the Lachish letters and
the Amarna correspondence.

8:16-24
Jehoram of Judah

For information on this section see comments
on 2 Chronicles 21.

8:25-29
Ahaziah of Judah

For information on this section see comments
on 2 Chronicles 22.

9:1-29
Jehu's Coup

9:1. anointing of kings. Anointing a king was
common practice in some parts of the ancient
Near East. Among the Egyptians and Hittites,
anointing was believed to protect a person
from the power of netherworld deities. Much
of the evidence comes from Hittite sources describing enthronement ceremonies. There is
no evidence of kings being anointed in Mesopotamia. In Egypt the pharaoh was not
anointed, but he anointed his officials and his
vassals. His anointing of them established

their subordinate relationship to him and indicated his protection of them. In the Amarna texts there is reference to a king of Nuhasse (in modern Syria) being anointed by the pharaoh. This model would fit the idea of Jehu's anointing as an indication that he would have the support of the prophets and, presumably, Yahweh. In 2 Samuel 2:4, when the people anoint David, some sort of contractual agreement between David and the people he will govern is suggested. In Nuzi, individuals entering a business agreement anoint one another with oil, and in Egypt, oil anointment is used in wedding ceremonies. In Israelite practice, anointing was a sign of election and often closely related to endowment by the Spirit. Additionally, throughout the ancient world anointing symbolized an advance of a person's legal status. Both concepts of protection and change of status may correlate to the king's anointing, for it would offer him protection on the throne and identify him with the divine realm.

9:1. Ramoth Gilead. The site of Ramoth Gilead has not been identified with certainty, but most accept Tell Ramith for its size, location and Iron Age pottery found in surveys. It has yet to be excavated. If this is the correct identification, it is located on the King's Highway at the juncture where the road south from Damascus would turn west to cross the Jordan near Beth Shan and enter the Jezreel Valley to connect with the main route of the Trunk Road (see sidebar on Trade Routes in Genesis 38).

9:6-10. prophets and inspired coups. In the southern kingdom of Judah, succession to the throne was permanently established by the covenant with the Davidic line. The northern kingdom, Israel, had come into being by means of a prophetic pronouncement (1 Kings 11:29-39), but there was no guarantee of dynastic succession. Each of the major dynasties (Jeroboam, Baasha, Omri, Jehu) rose and fell in accordance with prophetic pronouncement. Sometimes the designated king was content to wait for the proper time (Jeroboam), while in other cases, such as this one, the prophetic proclamation initiated a coup. In the ancient Near East priests often play significant political roles, but no prophets from the ancient Near East are known to have played the same role as these Israelite kingmakers. Nonetheless, throughout the ancient world it was believed that prophets not only proclaimed the message of deity but in the process unleashed the divine action. In Assyrian king Esarhaddon's instructions to his vassals, he requires that they report any improper or negative

statements that may be made by anyone, and he specifically names prophets, ecstatics and dream interpreters. It is no wonder, then, that a prophet negatively disposed toward a king must somehow be controlled lest he bring about all sorts of havoc. One can perhaps understand why a king would be inclined to imprison such a prophet, whose very words might incite insurrection or impose doom.

9:14. battle at Ramoth Gilead. The sequence of events is very complex here, because this is 841, the same year that Shalmaneser III of Assyria invaded Aram and engaged in a series of military encounters with Hazael. According to Shalmaneser's records, Hazael met him in pitched battle at Mount Hermon and was defeated. Hazael then safely retreated to Damascus, which was unsuccessfully besieged. Upon failing to overthrow Damascus, Shalmaneser vented his fury on the area of Hauran, just east of Ramoth Gilead, from where he marched to Mount Carmel and received tribute from Jehu. The march from Hauran to Carmel must have gone through the Jezreel Valley. If these events are all to fit together, one would have to suppose that Aram had moved against Ramoth Gilead in the early spring and was met by the combined forces of Judah and Israel. Shalmaneser typically left for his campaigns about May first, and it is about 550 miles from Assyria to Damascus, so he would not be arriving until maybe mid-June. As soon as Hazael received word that Shalmaneser was coming, he rushed north and met the Assyrian army at Mount Hermon. Jehu, still at Ramoth Gilead, likewise got the news of the Assyrian advance and was faced with the question of what Israel's position would be. Gathering the support of the pro-Assyrian party and strengthened by the prophetic anointing, he proceeded with the coup. During the period that Shalmaneser was failing in his siege of Damascus and laying waste the area of Hauran, Jehu was exterminating the house of Ahab and the followers of Baal. Once he established his control, he willingly gave Shalmaneser access across Jezreel and paid tribute at Carmel.

9:14-16. Trip from Ramoth Gilead to Jezreel. It is about forty-five miles from Ramoth Gilead to Jezreel. Jezreel is a fifteen-acre site situated at the southeastern entrance to the Jezreel Valley between the Hill of Moreh and Mount Gilboa. It was here that Ahab had built a winter capital. Excavations have unearthed a large royal enclosure from this time period occupying a large portion of the mound (see comment on 9:30).

9:17-20. sending messengers to approaching

rider. The rapid approach of a small chariot contingent only allows for a few possibilities, and none of them are good. They are either in flight from the enemy or are coming with evil intent. The rider sent out could serve either as a messenger to bring word back to the king or as a negotiator. What is unusual is that in such an uncertain situation the kings would ride out (apparently with no bodyguard) to meet Jehu (v. 21) and thus expose themselves to danger.

9:21. Naboth. For the background of the events concerning Naboth see comments on 1 Kings 21.

9:22. idolatry and witchcraft. This accusation is given as a cause for deposing a queen mother as early as the mid-second millennium, when the Hittite king Murshili II opposed his late father's Babylonian wife on the claim that she practiced sorcery. It should be remembered that both of these kings are related to Jezebel in that she is the mother of Jehoram and the grandmother of Ahaziah.

9:27. Beth Haggan-Gur/Ibleam-Megiddo. Ahaziah takes the road south from Jezreel. This is the direction of home (Judah) but is also the direction toward the northern capital city, Samaria, where he could expect to find protection. The road south skirts the eastern edge of the Jezreel Valley along the foot of the Gilboa mountains. Beth Haggan is where the road climbs out of the valley to the plain of Dothan and then into the hills of Samaria. Ibleam is at the top of the rise at the northern end of the plain. It is nearly ten miles from Jezreel. In full flight in a chariot this distance could have been covered in less than half an hour. But he is still fifteen miles from Samaria. When the decision is made to head for Megiddo, he must turn to the northwest, but it is only twelve miles away and could likewise offer sanctuary to the wounded king. It is also an easier road on level ground as it travels along the southwestern edge of the Valley of Jezreel. Beth Haggan is modern Jenin and is referred to in the Egyptian execration texts and called Gina in the Amarna texts. There is a seven-acre tell there with Iron Age pottery. Ibleam is named in Thutmose III's annals and is identified with Khirbet Belameh. Neither of these sites has been excavated.

9:30—10:17
Extermination of Ahab's Family

9:30. Jezebel's actions. In the ancient world powdered kohl (either galena [lead sulfide] or stibnite [antimony trisulfide]) mixed with oil or water was used as makeup to outline the eye and accentuate its almond shape. Hair-dressing may have included scenting, coloring or plaiting. Jezebel's purpose was to be seen as attractive in every way: physically, socially and politically. There is a familiar motif of a woman looking out the window that is represented beautifully in ivory carvings found at Nimrud, Samaria and Arslan Tash (in which she is adorned with an Egyptian wig). In literature the woman is gazing into the distance awaiting news of a husband or son who has gone off to war (see comment on Judg 5:28). In contrast, the ivories are often thought to represent a prostitute, perhaps connected to the worship of Astarte. This could then be a subtle reminder of Astarte and the foreign worship sponsored by Jezebel (note the accusation Jehu made against her in v. 22).

9:30. Jezreel palace. The palace at Jezreel was excavated in the early 1990s. The rectangular enclosure covers about eleven acres and is surrounded by a casemate wall with towers at the corners. It featured a six-chambered gate, a moat and earthen ramparts. The moat was cut from rock and averaged thirty feet wide and at points was nearly twenty feet deep. The moat used in Palestine was a dry moat (called a fosse), probably intended to prevent tunneling under the walls of the city. Jezreel was about twenty-three miles from Samaria.

9:31. calling Jehu "Zimri." The dynasty of Omri, of which Ahab and Jezebel were a part, had seized power from the usurper Zimri (see 1 Kings 16). By alluding to this incident, she may be warning Jehu that his coup will not necessarily lead to a secure hold on the throne but that he in turn is likely to be overthrown. Her question, "Is it peace?" not only suggests negotiation but also queries whether he really believes his destruction of the house of Ahab will bring peace for the country or for him. The alternative would be to ally himself with her and thus take advantage of some continuity. If her makeup has been applied to make her alluring, she may be suggesting that he take over the harem of the former king and thereby establish his legitimacy (for this practice see comment on 2 Sam 3:7). The loss of the harem to a claimant to the throne is described in the annals of Sennacherib as a sign of being deposed.

9:32. eunuchs. Eunuchs were those officers entrusted with the care and supervision of the royal harem. Having been castrated, they posed no threat to the women of the harem and could not engender children by the harem women who might be mistaken for royal heirs. It should be noted that the Hebrew word used here may not be limited to eunuchs—some believe it extends more broadly to administrative officials. It is logical in this context, however, to think of the queen being accompanied by keepers of the harem.

9:36. devoured by dogs. Assyrian practices (especially Ashurbanipal) include leaving corpses in the street for dogs to devour (as well as pigs, jackals and birds). On one occasion the corpses were chopped up and fed to dogs. Treaty curses also included invoking this doom on rebels. The intention of this atrocity was typically to eliminate any possibility of proper burial and thus to doom the individual's spirit to wander restlessly rather than enjoy a peaceful afterlife. Perhaps most interesting is the Akkadian text in the Maqlu collection of incantations that places a curse on a sorceress (see v. 22) that dogs would tear her to pieces. For more information see comment on 1 Kings 16:4.

10:1. Jezreel. See comment on 9:14-16.

10:6. wiping out predecessor's line. Leaving any living relatives of a king who had been forcibly deposed from the throne by assassination was an invitation to civil war. The relatives would be honor-bound to avenge the death of the previous king, and they would be certain to find those who would support their bid to regain the throne. Such annihilation of ruling families was common practice both in Israel and in the ancient Near East at large.

10:8. heads in baskets. The Assyrians made a practice of piling up the heads of those that had been killed in battle or punished for their rebellion. It was common in this period for such piles to be placed just outside the city gates as a warning to the inhabitants that rebellion was treated harshly.

10:11. group executed. The term translated "close friend" here is a technical term used both in Akkadian and Ugaritic sources describing those who enjoy the sponsorship of the court. They are royal wards who enjoy court privileges and were probably non-Israelite. Additionally Ahab's family, administration and religious personnel were executed.

10:12. Beth Eked of the Shepherds. This location must be somewhere along the nearly thirty-mile route between Jezreel and Samaria, but it has not been identified with any confidence. If it refers to a place where shepherds congregated or gathered their sheep, somewhere around the plain of Dothan would be logical.

10:12-14. treatment of Ahaziah's relatives. Since Jehoram of Israel was the uncle of Ahaziah of Judah, all of these relatives of Ahaziah are at least indirectly associated with the bloodline of the house of Ahab. That is sufficient to bring a death sentence on their heads. The well here is a cistern that would have been very natural in an area where shepherds gathered. It was just such a cistern in which Joseph's brothers imprisoned him around this same area of Dothan.

10:15. alliance with Jehonadab. Jehonadab is the leader of the Rechabites, a rather obscure clan in Israel that apparently lived an ascetic lifestyle and was known for its commitment to a seminomadic existence (some think because of their vocation as itinerant craftsmen) and for its religious conservatism (see the reference to them in Jer 35 some two centuries later).

10:18-27
Extermination of the Cult of Baal

10:19. the great Baal (enthronement) sacrifice. Part of the rhetoric that accompanied the promises of new kings in the ancient world was that they would be more devoted to the national or local gods than their predecessors. This often included commitments to repair, restore, enlarge or embellish the sanctuary. This strategy would gain the support of the priesthood and the pious populace, and, hopefully, bring divine approval of the new reign as well. It was politically correct for the king to take his place as royal patron and foremost of the supporters of the local deity. It is possible that Jehu is calling for an enthronement celebration in which he will take the throne as the vassal of Baal, whose enthronement as king of the gods would likewise be recognized. To be absent from such an event could easily be considered treason.

10:21. temple of Baal in Samaria. Excavations in Samaria have not yet located any remains from Ahab's temple of Baal. It has been suggested that the temple contributed to the concept being promoted by Ahab and Jezebel that the city was the sacred precinct of Baal. This would mean it functioned as an independent political unit, just as Zion often did in the south. Therefore, even after Jehu had been made king of Israel and Ahab's line had been wiped out, control of Samaria, especially the temple precinct, had to be approached separately.

10:22. robes from the keeper of the wardrobe. These robes would have been cultic vestments for the worship of Baal (see Zeph 1:8). It is additionally likely that the occasion and the use of the sacred robes would have prohibited any weapons from being worn—a distinct advantage for Jehu's men.

10:26. sacred stone. Standing stones often occupied the place of the sacred niche in Canaanite sanctuaries in place of an image. These stones were often plain but occasionally had a figure of the deity carved in relief on the face of the stone.

10:27. use as latrine. It was the practice to rebuild temples on the sites where they had traditionally been because it was believed that the god had revealed the location and it was holy ground. By making it into a latrine area (or perhaps a garbage dump), Jehu was insuring that it would never be the site of a temple again. This greatly reduced any possible resurgence of the official Baal cult in Samaria.

10:28-36
Jehu of Israel

10:32. Hazael's actions against Israel. No military details are given here, but the text describes the loss of the entire Transjordan region to Hazael. After 838 the Assyrians were absent from the west for several decades, and this allowed the Arameans to begin to build their own little empire. This continued during the reign of Jehu's successor, Jehoahaz (see comments on 2 Kings 12—13).

10:34. Jehu in Assyrian records. The fact that Jehu quickly paid tribute to Shalmaneser III upon his accession to the throne of Israel suggests that he probably enjoyed the support not only of the religiously conservative Yahwist party but also of the pro-Assyrian faction of the government (see comment on 9:14). This party saw the breakdown of the western coalition as leading inevitably to defeat by the Assyrians and was tired of the perpetual warfare. Jehu is portrayed in the uncomplimentary posture of prostration on the Black Stela of Shalmaneser that reports the tribute he brought to the Assyrian king in 841. His tribute consisted of items of silver and gold and some javelins.

11:1-21
Athaliah

For information on this section see comments on 2 Chronicles 22—23.

12:1-21
Joash of Judah

For information on this section see comments on 2 Chronicles 24.

13:1-9
Jehoahaz of Israel

13:1. chronology. According to Thiele, Jehoahaz of Israel came to the throne in 814 B.C. in the twenty-third year of Joash of Judah. He reigned until 798 B.C. This was a period when the Assyrians had focused their attention elsewhere. As a result the Arameans under Hazael were trying to enlarge their control of the area.

13:3. Hazael's control of Israel. Hazael was king of Aram-Damascus around 842-800. He is also known from an ivory fragment from Arslan Tash in Syria and from a cylinder seal found at the Assyrian city of Assur. The Assyrians claimed to have taken booty from Hazael. The Aramean king fought with the Assyrian king Shalmaneser III in 841 and was defeated, although the Assyrians were unsuccessful in taking Hazael's leading city of Damascus. The Assyrian threat diminished after 836, and Hazael was able to concentrate on attacking Israel and Philistia.

13:5. deliverer from Aram. The "deliverer" (coming from the same Hebrew root as Messiah) in this case is not mentioned by name. The phrase is reminiscent of the deliverers in the period of the judges. It may have been a neighboring ruler, such as Zakur of Hamath or Adad-Nirari III of Assyria, both of whom were powerful at this time. Even Joash of Judah has been suggested as a possibility.

13:6. Asherah pole. One common feature of Canaanite worship and of syncretistic Israelite worship on "high places" and in city shrines is the erection of Asherah poles. There is some uncertainty about whether these were simply wooden poles, erected to symbolize trees and perhaps containing a carved image of the fertility goddess, or whether they were part of a sacred grove. The reference in 17:10, which refers to Asherah poles beside "every spreading tree," seems to indicate that these were poles erected for cultic purposes rather than planted trees. As the consort of El, Asherah was a popular goddess whose worship is mentioned in Ugaritic texts (1600-1200 B.C.). The Asherah cult continued to be prominent in Phoenicia in the first millennium B.C., when it presumably was introduced into Israel during the dynasty of Omri and Ahab. Her prominent appearance in the biblical narrative indicates that her cult was a major rival to Yahweh worship. For more information see the comments on Exodus 34:13 and Judges 6:25.

13:10-25
Jehoash of Israel

13:10. chronology. By Thiele's reckoning, Jehoash began his reign in 798 B.C. (the thirty-seventh year of Joash of Israel) and ruled for sixteen years (until 782). During this period the Assyrians became more active, and their influence in the west occupied the attention of the Arameans (see comment on 13:22-25). Joash is mentioned by name in the inscriptions of the Assyrian king Adad-Nirari III (810-783).

13:14. chariots and horsemen of Israel. This phrase, also found in 2 Kings 2:12, appears to have been a popular slogan during the period of the Aramean wars. Elisha was active in the military affairs of Israel and had gained a reputation for mediating Yahweh's participation in Israel's wars. In the mythology of the period there were deities who served as the charioteers to bring the divine warrior into battle (see comment on 2:11). This title may have recognized Elisha's role as a similar one—when he came, Yahweh came with him.

13:15-19. arrow symbolism. Although the acts here performed by Elisha resembled non-Israelite magical phenomena, and no explicit reference to the God of Israel is mentioned, there is an undercurrent of divine will. This particular ritual, apparently in imitation of belomantic (divination by means of arrows) practices, is not attested in Mesopotamian sources, although bows and arrows were often used in their magic rituals.

13:22-25. encounters with Aram. Here the biblical text concurs with Assyrian sources. During the reign of the Assyrian king Shamshi-Adad IV (824-811 B.C.) the Assyrians were concerned with campaigning in Babylonia to the exclusion of the west. Thus the Aramean states were able to thrive. By the reign of Adad-Nirari III (811-783) the Assyrians shifted their emphasis to the west once again. A number of commemorative inscriptions of Adad-Nirari describe the defeat of Damascus and Arpad (other powerful Aramean states) and the collecting of tribute. Jehoash is also recorded as having given tribute to the Assyrians in a stele from Tell al-Rimah. Thus Damascus was weakened by Assyria enough to allow for the deliverance of Israel, which in turn became a client state of Assyria.

14:1-22
Amaziah of Judah

For information on this section see comments on 2 Chronicles 25.

14:23-29
Jeroboam II of Israel

14:23. chronology. Jeroboam II became king in 782 by Thiele's chronology. He may have been coregent with his father Jehoash for eleven years previous to this (793), which was counted as part of his reign. During this time Israel was free of threat from both Aram and Assyria, allowing prosperity and expansion in a time of relative security.

14:25. restoration of borders. Jeroboam's expansion restored Israel to the size it had been during the reign of Solomon. Lebo-Hamath (modern Lebweh [Ematu in the Ebla texts; Lab'u of Assyrian sources]) on one of the sources of the Orontes is in the northern Baqa' of Lebanon, forty-five miles north of Damascus. This was the southern border of the land of Hamath and therefore the northern border of Canaan, and designates the northern corner of the empire. The name appears in city lists of the Egyptian king Thutmose III (fifteenth century B.C.) and the annals of Tiglath-Pileser III of Assyria (eighth century B.C.). The Sea of Arabah (or Wadi Arabah, Amos 6:14), now the Dead Sea, was the southern border of the kingdom.

14:25. Gath Hepher. Gath Hepher is only mentioned here as the home of Jonah. It has been identified with el-Meshed, a site a few miles northeast of Nazareth.

14:27. preclassical prophecy. In the early periods of the monarchy the prophets primarily addressed the king and his court, much as their ancient Near Eastern counterparts did. These prophets have been termed "preclassical." Beginning in the eighth century, however, the prophets increasingly turned their attention to the people and became the social-spiritual commentators that we most readily identify with the prophetic institution; these are the classical prophets and the writing prophets. Their role was not to predict as much as it was to advise of God's policies and plans. In this context, Jonah is in the role of the preclassical prophet, while in the book of Jonah, his role is more like the classical prophet developing at this time. For more information about prophecy in the ancient Near East see comment on Deuteronomy 18:14-22.

14:27. blotting out. The phrase "blotting out" stems from the image of washing a papyrus scroll clean in order to use it again, typical of Egyptian practice. Moreover, erasing the name of an ancestor from an inscription in Mesopotamia angered the gods. Thus Yahweh decided not to erase Israel's name (i.e., destroy it) but promised salvation.

14:28. Damascus, Hamath, Yaudi. Damascus and Hamath were well-known Aramean polities (for more information see comments on 2 Sam 8). Yaudi, however, is not so easily identified. Yaudi is likely the Iaudi of Assyrian sources, which is always identified with Judah. Assyria was in no position to oppose Israelite expansion from about 773 to 745 B.C., during the reign of Jeroboam.

15:1-7
Azariah (Uzziah) of Judah

For information on this section see comments on 2 Chronicles 26.

15:8-12
Zechariah of Israel

15:8. chronology. The brief reign of Zechariah was in 753 B.C. He was a contemporary with Azariah (Uzziah) of Judah (c. 792-740 B.C.).

15:13-16
Shallum of Israel

15:13. chronology. Shallum succeeded Zechariah in 752 B.C. and reigned for only one month. Azariah was still on the throne of Judah.

15:16. Tirzah. Tirzah was a royal residence of Jeroboam I. It probably became the capital city of the northern kingdom in the time of Baasha and remained the capital until Omri gave the position to Samaria. It has been identified as Tell el-Farah seven miles northeast of Shechem on the road to Beth Shan. It is favored by good elevation, a consistent water supply (two springs that feed the wadi Farah) and a strategic location on the trade route. It also has ready access to the fords of the Jordan at Adam. The gate and fortifications were rebuilt from the Middle Bronze remains, and there is evidence of central planning in the building of new residences throughout the city. Its political importance may also be inferred from its mention in Shishak's list of conquests during his invasion of Palestine.

15:16. Tiphsah. Tiphsah (or Tappuah) may have later been called Thapsacus in Syria, a city on the bend of the northern Euphrates River. The name Thapsacus is not attested until the Greek writer Xenophon in the fourth century B.C. The city of Tiphsah is also listed as one of Solomon's cities (1 Kings 5:4). Tiphsah's distance from Israel shows that Menahem had great influence during a period of Assyrian decline.

15:16. treatment of pregnant women. The practice of ripping open pregnant women is mentioned very rarely. It is a practice attributed to Assyrian king Tiglath-Pileser I (about 1100) in a hymn praising his conquests. It is

also referred to in passing in a Neo-Babylonian lament.

15:17-22
Menahem of Israel

15:17. chronology. Menahem's reign is attributed by Thiele to the years 752-742 B.C. Like the three previous Israelite kings, he was a contemporary of Azariah of Judah. His reign overlaps with the beginning of the Neo-Assyrian empire under Tiglath-Pileser III.

15:17-22. Menahem in Assyrian inscriptions. Menahem is mentioned along with other Levantine kings in the Assyrian annals as paying heavy tribute to Tiglath-Pileser III (also known as Pul or Pulu). He also appears on an Assyrian stele found recently in Iran. The tribute list includes silver, gold, tin, iron, elephant hides, ivory, blue-purple and red-purple garments, multicolored linen garments and camels. Menahem, presumably, did not send all of these items but only a portion of them.

15:23-26
Pekahiah of Israel

15:23. chronology. Pekahiah, son of Menahem of Israel, began his reign in 742 B.C. and reigned for two years. Azariah was still the monarch in Judah.

15:25. citadel of the royal palace. This term is also found in Isaiah 13:22, where it is parallel to "palaces of pleasure." There the context appears to refer to a specific structure within the palace complex. It is likely a type of fortification. The Assyrian kings constructed major palatial complexes that were often called "fortresses of the king." They would provide a defensible area inside the city in case the walls were breached or there was a revolt within the city.

15:27-31
Pekah of Israel

15:27. chronology. The text states that in Azariah's last year as king of Judah, Pekah became king of Israel. He is credited with twenty years of rule. Thiele dates his reign from 752 to 732 B.C., thus making him a contemporary of Menahem and briefly Pekahiah. If this is true, then there was more than one person who claimed to be monarch in Israel during this period, which would be consistent with the turmoil described by the writer(s) of 2 Kings. The writer(s) of 2 Kings may have dated Pekah's reign from the establishment of a separate kingdom on the east of the Jordan. This complexity has yet to be unraveled.

15:25-31. Pekah and Assyrian campaigns. Pekah is found in the Assyrian annals of Tiglath-Pileser III as Paqaha. The Assyrian king claims that when the Israelites overthrew Pekah, Tiglath-Pileser replaced him with Hoshea, the last king of Israel (732 B.C.). Subsequently, the Assyrians demanded heavy tribute from Israel. Pekah is also mentioned on a jug fragment from Hazor. The text simply reads, "wine belonging to Pekah."

16:1-20
Ahaz of Judah

For information on verses 1-9 see comments on 2 Chronicles 28.

16:10. Ahaz and Tiglath-Pileser at Damascus. This meeting took place after Damascus fell in 732. Ahaz, as a loyal vassal, was expected to be present to reaffirm his submission and join the celebration over the king's victory.

16:10. Damascus altar. The reproduction of this altar appears to result from Ahaz being impressed with it rather than from Assyrian compulsion. Judging from what is known of Assyrian practice of this time, it appears that they did not force their vassals to adopt the worship of their chief god, Assur. Thus it should be considered artistic innovation rather than ritual syncretism. Currently no archaeological or textual information exists to provide for an informed delineation of the features.

16:14. bronze altar. See comment on 2 Chronicles 4:1. This is the main altar of the courtyard, used for all of the animal sacrifices.

16:14. rearrangement of altars. The bronze altar had been positioned directly east of the temple, that is, in front of the entrance. Ahaz's new altar had originally been placed between the entrance to the courtyard and the bronze

altar, but now became the central focus as the bronze altar was moved out of the east-west axis to a side location north of the new altar. The new altar thus effectively replaced the bronze altar.

16:15. divided functions. The rituals performed on the new altar are characteristically Israelite. There is no cultic innovation here, nor are foreign rituals being incorporated into Israelite practice. The new altar picks up all of the prescribed functions of the sacrificial system. The one function that is left to the bronze altar is one that is not described in Israel's ritual literature. The verb that is used (NIV: "seeking guidance") means to examine or inspect, and may suggest sacrifices in which the entrails of sacrificed animals were examined for omens. It is unclear why Ahaz should reserve that function for the traditional altar.

16:17. tribute. The activity described here is part of the process of tribute gathering. Basins for transporting water from the main laver stood on carts featuring side panels and wheels. Similar objects have been found in Cyprus dating to about the time of Solomon. The bronze bulls that supported the laver (see 2 Chron 4:2-5 for description) would have gone far to make up the quota of bronze that was wanted for the tribute payment. In the ninth century Assyrian king Ashurnasirpal received bronze bulls as part of a tribute payment.

16:18. adjustments for the king of Assyria. It is difficult to be certain whether the described actions are undertaken in order to gather additional tribute for the Assyrians or whether they reflect changes that will underline and confirm Ahaz' submission to Assyrian suzerainty. The reference is to obscure architectural terms.

17:1-6
Hoshea of Israel

17:1. chronology. Hoshea became king in 732

THE WESTERN CAMPAIGNS OF TIGLATH-PILESER III, 734-732

From early in his reign (starting about 743) Tiglath-Pileser was active in Syria attempting to control the trade routes through this economically strategic region. By 738 he had collected tribute from most of the major parties in the area (including Damascus, the port cities and Samaria). During the next few years he was occupied in Urartu (in the Lake Van area to the north), and by 735 he had brought control to that region. In 734 he began what is known as the second western campaign. His initial objective was to march through the region as a show of power to reiterate his control (especially of the trade route) and collect tribute. His route took him down the Great Trunk Road to Gaza. No opposition is noted in any of the sources. In 733 the Assyrian armies returned, with Damascus as the main target. Though the Arameans suffered serious losses, Damascus successfully withstood a forty-five-day siege by the Assyrians. In this campaign Tiglath-Pileser ranged down into the region of Israel. Large sections of Israel were annexed and made into Assyrian provinces, and fortified cities such as Hazor and Megiddo were destroyed. Over thirteen thousand Israelites were deported, but no replacement inhabitants were shipped in, thus depleting the population of Lower Galilee for several generations. The final stage of the campaign came in 732, when Damascus fell and was annexed. In Israel Pekah was executed in favor of the pro-Assyrian Hoshea.

B.C. as a result of the Assyrian decimation of much of the northern kingdom. The synchronisms between the northern and southern kingdoms during this period are very complex, and there are no easy resolutions. It is generally supposed that there were several coregencies that are one cause of the apparent confusion. Assyrian king Tiglath-Pileser III claims in his annals to have put Hoshea on the throne of Judah.

17:4. relations between Hoshea and Assyria. Because of the reestablishment of Egyptian power in the Levant, Hoshea saw fit to negotiate with Egypt in order to be free of Assyrian power. The Egyptian king So has not been absolutely identified, but Osorkon IV who ruled in the eastern delta region of Egypt (Tanis, Bubastis) from 730 to 715 B.C. has been considered a likely match. Nonetheless, Hoshea's appeal to Egypt was unsuccessful. It is not certain exactly when Hoshea was arrested by the Assyrians (or deported). The records of the brief reign of Shalmaneser V (ruled 727-722) are comparatively poor. Sargon II (ruled 721-705) mentions the Samarians (i.e. Israelites) but not a king, suggesting that the king may have already been deported.

17:5-6. the fall of Samaria. The Assyrian sources describe the "ravaging" of Samaria (c. 724-721), which may have denoted the entire land. Some archaeological evidence for the destruction has been found at the Israelite city of Shechem. This accords with the typical Assyrian strategy of wasting the territory of a particular state and then surrounding the main city, which had now been cut off from its resources. Both Sennacherib and Nebuchadnezzar II used this policy against Jerusalem. The fact that the siege of Samaria lasted three years although the Assyrians were unmatched in siege warfare shows that it was heavily fortified. The city fell in 722/721. Although Shalmaneser III is given credit for the conquest of Samaria in the Bible, his successor Sargon II claimed the credit in the Assyrian annals. Sargon also claims to have rebuilt the city.

17:6. policy of deportation. The Assyrian deportation policies had been in effect for nearly four centuries by this time. Sargon claimed to have deported 27,290 people from Samaria. The record is not clear as to whether these were all men and whether they came from the land of Samaria or just the main city. The Assyrian king claimed that he took enough men to form a regiment of fifty chariots. The Assyrians also had a policy of relocating other conquered peoples into Samarian territory (though Tiglath-Pileser appears to have departed from that policy by not repopulating

Galilee in 733). Sargon claims to have repopulated the city of Samaria with other deportees. The deportation policy was intended to remove from conquered peoples anything that they might rally in defense of. If they have no land and no nation, and their ethnic identity has been compromised (through forced assimilation), there is no identity to fight for.

17:7-41
The Sins and Fate of Israel

17:9. high places. The picture portrayed in the biblical narrative is that prior to the construction of the temple in Jerusalem, sacrifice and religious ritual commonly took place at local shrines or *bamoth*. They were constructed for this purpose and in most cases appear to be an installation that could be entered and within which cultic activity took place (see the comment on 1 Sam 9:12-13). Many of them may have had an urban setting, although this does not preclude their existence outside city walls on near by hills. Their actual appearance and the furnishings associated with the high places are unknown, but the large number of references to them as sacrificial sites suggests that some may have been quite elaborate. Eventually the monarchy and the Jerusalem priesthood attempted to suppress the use of the high places because of their desire to emphasize Solomon's temple as "the place which Yahweh will choose" and to eliminate the syncretism that thrived at the high places. For more information on high places, see the comments on Deuteronomy 12:2-3.

17:10. sacred stones. Standing stones or *massebot* were apparently a common feature of Canaanite religion and also appear as memorials in a number of Israelite covenantal contexts (see Ex 24:3-8; Josh 24:25-27). Their association with Asherah, Baal and other Canaanite deities is the basis for their being condemned as a rival and threat to Yahweh worship. Archaeologists have discovered sacred stones at Gezer, Dan, Hazor and Arad. In the latter two cases, they are clearly within a sacred precinct and part of the cultic practices at these sites. The Hazor stones include incised representations of upraised arms and a sun disk. The stones at Dan are in the gateway, and the clear remains of the presentation of votive offerings were evident.

17:10. Asherah poles. One common feature of Canaanite worship and of syncretized Israelite worship on "high places" and in city shrines is the erection of Asherah poles. There is some uncertainty about whether these were simply wooden poles, erected to symbolize trees or perhaps containing a carved image of the fertility goddess, or whether they were a part of a sacred grove. The reference here to Asherah poles beside "every spreading tree," seems to indicate that these were poles erected for cultic purposes rather than planted trees. As the consort of El, Asherah was a popular goddess whose worship is mentioned in Ugaritic texts (1600-1200). Her prominent appearance in the biblical narrative indicates that her cult was a major rival to Yahweh worship. Pictures on seals excavated in Palestine show Asherah as a stylized tree in the Iron Age. For more information see the comments on Exodus 34:13 and Judges 6:25.

17:11. burning incense as pagan ritual. Incense was used for a variety of reasons in the extrabiblical world. The Phoenicians used it to prepare the body of the king for future life. One inscription from Byblos has a king describing himself as lying on incense. It was also used in the cult of the dead at Canaanite Ugarit. In Mesopotamia, incense was used for dedicatory and propitiatory offerings. They believed that the incense helped transport prayers to the deity, who would then inhale the incense. All of these practices were condemned by the writers of Scripture.

17:16-17. unacceptable worship practice. The molten images of calves or bulls were typical cult items in Canaan. Calf images have been found at a number of sites in this region (for more information see comments on 1 Kings 12:28). Worship of the starry hosts refers worship of the celestial gods (sun god, moon god and Venus particularly; in Babylonia, Shamash, Sin and Ishtar respectively), who were primary in most ancient religions. Controlling the calendar and time, seasons and weather, they were viewed as the most powerful of the gods. They provided signs by which omens were read and they looked down on all. The Zodiac is not yet known at this time. For information concerning Baal see comments on Judges 2:11-13. Evidence for "passing [or burning] children through the fire" outside of Scripture is scant but known in the Assyrian and Aramean world (see comment on Deut 18:10). Divination and enchantments were also well-known in Mesopotamia. Divination assumed that there was knowledge to be gained about the activities and motives of the gods through the use of various indicators (such as entrails of sacrificed animals). Thousands of omens and incantations have been uncovered in the past one hundred and fifty years of archaeological research.

17:24. resettlement of Samaria. Although the king of Assyria is not mentioned here, Assyri-

an sources claim that Sargon II reorganized the area in 720 B.C. These same texts do not cite the specific people groups that were deported to Samaria. However, some Arab tribes were transported to Samaria within five years of the reorganization. Babylon was under Assyrian control during this period. Cuthah is identified with Tell Ibrahim, twenty miles northeast of Babylon. Avva is now identified with the town of Awa (Ama, Akkadian, Amatu in eastern Babylonia). Hamath was the major Aramean city on the Orontes River in Syria. Sepharvayim has been tentatively identified as Sipirani, south of Nippur, though Shabarain in Syria is still a possibility. Whatever the case, Assyrian policy was to resettle an area with a diverse population.

17:25. god-sent lions. Ravaging wild beasts were considered one of the typical scourges that deity would send as punishment. As early as the Gilgamesh Epic in Mesopotamia the god Ea had reprimanded Enlil for not sending lions to ravage the people rather than using something as dramatic as a flood. The gods used wild beasts along with disease, drought and famine to reduce the human population. A common threat connected to negative omens in the Assyrian period was that lions and wolves would rage through the land. In like manner devastation by wild animals was one of the curses invoked for treaty violation (see also Deut 32:24).

17:25-29. syncretism in Samaria. Assyrian inscriptions from the age of Sargon II state that the new settlers were taxed as if they were Assyrians. Furthermore, they were instructed in the proper way to revere God and king. Most groups in antiquity believed that gods had jurisdiction over precise geographic areas. Thus Yahweh had ownership of Samaria and was worthy of worship. Nonetheless the settlers brought their own deities. In the open-ended thinking that accompanied ancient polytheism, there was always room for more gods. If a god had demonstrated power, it would be dangerous not to acknowledge him (see comment on Josh 2:11). Sargon had effected a religious syncretism in the area, with the express purpose of lessening the impact of nationalistic tendencies.

17:30-31. list of gods. The deity Succoth Benoth is not known from Mesopotamian sources. Benoth may be Banitu (fem. "the creator"), often used as a term for Ishtar. Nergal was the Mesopotamian god of plagues and of the underworld. His principal cult center was in fact at Cutha (twenty miles northeast of Babylon). Ashima is known from an inscription from Teima in Arabia as well as from some Aramaic personal names, but nothing is known about the deity. The Avvites are now identified with the town of Awa (Ama, Akkadian, Amatu in eastern Babylonia). Nibhaz and Tartak have been identified with the Elamite deities Ibnahaza and Dirtaq (Dakdadra). Adrammelech is thought to represent Addir-Melek. Addir is a title meaning "mighty one" and is applied to both Baal and Yahweh. Melek means king and would refer to the divine king. Lastly, Anammelech is believed to represent an assimilation of the Canaanite goddess, Anat (or her male counterpart, An) with Melek (a title often applied to the West Semitic deity Athtar). Little is known of these last two gods, but some associate them with the god Molech (see comments on Lev 18:21; Deut 18:10).

18:1—20:21
Hezekiah of Judah

18:1. chronology. See comments on 2 Chronicles 29.

18:4. bronze serpent, Nehushtan. Nehushtan is not attested outside Scripture. The term is apparently a conglomeration of the Hebrew terms for bronze *(nehoshet)* and serpent *(nahash)*. Figures of serpents crafted in copper or bronze have been found in numerous locations in the ancient Near East. They were apparently cultic images. Often the image of the serpent is held by a deity. It was especially prevalent in Syro-Palestine in the late second and first millennia B.C. Nehushtan appears to have been a deity of healing (especially snake bites), possibly considered an intermediary between Yahweh and the people of Israel (see comment on Num 21:8-9). A well-known bronze bowl from Nineveh with Hebrew names on it depicts a winged snake on a pole of some sort.

18:8. defeat of the Philistines. The Philistine seaports had been in Assyrian control since Tiglath-Pileser III (745-727 B.C.). Hezekiah likely invaded this area in 705 after the death of Sargon II of Assyria in battle. Counting on the vulnerability of Assyria, Hezekiah probably commandeered anti-Assyrian groups in the area to begin open rebellion against the powerful state. The purpose of the attack was to loosen Assyria's hold on the trade routes to Egypt. Sargon's successor, Sennacherib, however, was able to establish pro-Assyrian governors in Philistia.

18:11. places of northern deportation. The areas of deportation of the Samarians are not all precisely known. Halah was a city and province northeast of Nineveh. Sargon's capital was built there using enemy captives as laborers, probably including Israelites. Habor (Habur) was a large tributary of the Euphrates in eastern Syria. The area had a large Aramean population. Gozan (Tell Halaf) was a city by the headwaters of the Habur River and was the chief city of the Assyrian province of Bit Bahian. Israelite personal names have been found in the Assyrian documents from Gozan. These areas had suffered a decline of population because of the constant Assyrian incursions in the region in previous centuries. In this region the deportees were probably farming the king's lands. The "cities of the Medes" were probably regions of Media in northwest Iran that were controlled by Assyria. Sargon's campaigns to Media are well documented. Sargon's inscriptions record the resettlement of the fortress cities of Harhar and Kishessu by deportees. These Israelites would have been serving in a military capacity on the front line.

18:14-16. Hezekiah's tribute. The inscriptions of Sennacherib state that Hezekiah paid thirty talents of gold (about one ton) and eight hundred talents of silver (about twenty-five tons). The Assyrian texts are more detailed, as they claim that Hezekiah was required to send his daughters, concubines, male and female musicians, ivory, elephant hides and various other objects.

18:17. Sennacherib's officials. Tartan, Rabsaris and Rabshakeh appear in some translations, while the NIV refers to them as "supreme commander," "chief officer," and "field commander." The NIV is correct that these are titles rather than names. They are well-known from Assyrian texts. The first, Tartan (Akkadian, *turtan*), the "field marshal," was the chief military officer. He represented the king and was sometimes the crown prince. The second, Rabsaris (Akkadian, *rab sha reshi*), the "chief eunuch," was probably the representative of the separate military division, the king's bodyguard. The third, Rabshakeh (Akkadian, *rab shaqe*), the "chief cupbearer," is thought to be the provincial governor.

18:17-37.
Sennacherib Threatens Jerusalem

For information see comments on 2 Chronicles 32.

19:2. Shebna the secretary. Shebna was a high-level bureaucrat during the reign of Hezekiah. He was at one point a "royal steward," a position of uncertain function. The royal steward was probably the top civil servant in the administration. The office is documented numerous times in the text as well as in the corpus of official seals and their bullae (see sidebar in Jer 32). Shebna was later demoted to scribe or secretary (presumably because of some unknown scandal). A tomb has been found near Jerusalem with a fragment of a personal name (with Yahweh as an ending) and the title royal steward. Some believe this to be the tomb of Shebna referred to in Isaiah 22:15-16.

19:8. Sennacherib against Libnah. Libnah was in the Judean Shephelah eight miles northeast of the fortress city of Lachish. It is probably to be identified either with Khirbet Tell el-Beida or Tell Bornat (five miles further west), strategically located by the Wadi Zeita guarding the best route to Hebron from the coast. The Assyrian annals describe Sennacherib besieging Gath and Azekah, and wall reliefs at Nineveh show the siege of Lachish. Libnah was in this vicinity, showing that the Assyrian monarch was slowly moving towards the intended victim, Jerusalem.

19:9. Tirhakah. Tirhakah (Nubian: Taharqa) was a Kushite king of Egypt in the Twenty-Fifth Dynasty (reigned 690-664 B.C.). For geographical identification of Cush see comment on Numbers 12:1. Although no extrabiblical text confirms this, the biblical title "King of Kush" may have been given to him while he was crown prince. He was an energetic builder in Egypt, refurbishing temples and city walls at Memphis (his royal residence), Thebes and Napata. He left numerous inscriptions throughout Egypt. Tirhakah campaigned vigorously in the Levant preceding 674 B.C. In that year, Esarhaddon of Assyria attacked Egypt, only to be driven back by Tirhakah's forces. Three years later, however, Esarhaddon captured Memphis, causing the Egyptian monarch to flee to the south. Another Assyrian force came in 666 B.C., causing him to flee to Nubia. He was still recognized as king of Egypt until his death in 664.

19:12-13. list. Gozan was in Syria, where deportees from Israel had been sent (see comment on 18:11). Haran was west of Gozan along the Balikh River in present-day Turkey. Rezeph (Rasappa) mostly likely was the city that became an Assyrian provincial capital in Syria east of Emar and west of Mari along the upper Euphrates. The Aramean tribe of Bit-Adini (Eden) in northwest Syria had been conquered by Shalmaneser III (reigned 858-824 B.C.) and resettled in Telassar, which was most likely Til-Ashshuri ("mound of the Assyrians"), a site in the Zagros Mountain range near the Diyala River in Iraq. Hamath and Arpad were major Aramean city-states in

Syria conquered by Tiglath-Pileser III (reigned 745-727 B.C.). Sepharvayim has been tentatively identified as Sipirani, south of Nippur, though Shabarain in Syria is still a possibility. Hena and Ivvah are unknown.

19:15. enthroned between the cherubim. The cherubim were winged creatures associated with the Israelite ark of the covenant and Yahweh's presence. They also accompanied Yahweh in his travels through the heavens (see Ps 18:11). They appear in Assyrian mythological texts as Karibu, angelic intercessors. In Assyrian art they are shown as various composite creatures with one or more faces (human, bovine, aquiline, lionlike) and two or four legs. For more information see comment on Exodus 25:18-20.

19:23. cutting down the cedars of Lebanon. Isaiah is paraphrasing the boasting of the Assyrian king Sennacherib. The Assyrian royal annals of the ninth and eighth centuries B.C. employed the motifs of traveling through difficult passes, cutting mighty trees and supplying the army with water. Sennacherib claimed to have felled the Lebanon cedars and used them to build his royal palaces and public buildings in Nineveh.

19:28. hook in the nose. This image has parallels in Assyrian literature and iconography. Esarhaddon is depicted on a stele from Zinjirli in Syria as leading Baal of Tyre and Tirhakah of Egypt by a rope tied to a ring through their lips. Ashurbanipal claims to have pierced the cheeks of Uate' (king of Ishmael) with a sharp edged tool and put a ring in his jaw. Thus Isaiah is again mocking Assyrian practices.

19:29 renewed agriculture. The verse implies that the countryside had been ravaged by the Assyrian army. That the Assyrians intentionally devastated an enemy's countryside is well attested in their annals. Tiglath-Pileser III destroyed the surroundings of Damascus by cutting its orchards. His annals describe similar destruction during his campaigns in Babylonia. In spite of all this, Isaiah tells Hezekiah that the "aftergrowth" would be sufficient for two years, before normal fieldwork resumed.

19:32. no arrow or ramp. Sennacherib has a detailed description in his annals concerning the sieges of forty-six cities and towns of Judah. Furthermore, the Assyrian king claims to have "caged up" Hezekiah in Jerusalem and surrounded the city with "earthwork." However, nowhere in the annals does Sennacherib claim to have begun a siege at Jerusalem, as he did at the other towns. He continues to describe the tribute sent to him by Hezekiah but not the capture of the city itself. For more information see the sidebars in

2 Chronicles 32.

19:35. deity wiping out enemy. In one of Ashurbanipal's inscriptions he claims that Erra (the deity representing plague) struck down Uaite (Arab king of Shumuilu) and his army for failing to keep the terms of their treaty agreement.

19:37. Nisroch. No divinity by this name is known from Mesopotamia. It may be an intentional alteration of a deity's name, such as Marduk, Nusku or Ninurta. This event took place on the twentieth day of the tenth month in the year 681, twenty years after the siege of Jerusalem.

19:37. Ararat. Ararat (or Urartu) was a powerful kingdom in present-day Armenia around the vicinity of Lake Van, Lake Urmia and Lake Sevan. Esarhaddon mentions his brothers who fought against his succession but does not state where they sought refuge. However, Esarhaddon demanded from the king of Shurpia in southern Ararat that he extradite runaway Assyrians, some of whom may have been the brothers in question. The kingdoms of Ararat posed a constant threat to the Assyrian's northern border for about three centuries (c. 900-600 B.C.). Excavations there have exposed a thriving civilization with sophisticated iconography and literature.

20:3. Hezekiah's prayer. A prayer of the Assyrian king Ashurnasirpal I (mid-eleventh century B.C.) is preserved in which he asks for healing from an illness on the basis of his faithfulness to the goddess Ishtar. Besides identifying himself as humble, reverent and beloved by the deity, he speaks of the many rituals that he has faithfully carried out. He mentions his tears and anxiety, and begs for gracious healing. The text of Hezekiah's prayer is found in Isaiah 38:9-20; see comments there.

20:7. poultice of figs. Fig cakes may have been used as condiments and for medicinal purposes at Ugarit. Both later rabbinical Jewish and classical sources (e.g., Pliny the Elder) shared the belief that dried figs had medicinal value. Poultices were sometimes used for diagnosis rather than for medication. A day or two after the poultice was applied, it would be checked for either the skin's reaction to the poultice or the poultice's reaction to the skin. One medical text from Emar prescribes the use of figs and raisins for such a process. They helped determine how the patient should be treated and whether or not he would recover.

20:11. shadow of the stairway of Ahaz. The "shadow of the stairway of Ahaz" may have been a type of sundial. The Qumran Scroll of Isaiah 38:8 renders this phrase "on the dial of the Ahaz roof chamber." A similar idea may be a house model excavated in Egypt that contains two flights of stairs for telling time. On the other hand the structure may have been simply steps leading to a roof or higher structure where shadows were cast at a certain time of the day. The text here does not mention that the structure was used to tell time. Alternatively it may have been something that was used to worship astral deities. If it does represent a mechanism for telling time, it would be the only mention of such a device in the Old Testament. Sundials are known in the Old Testament world from Babylon and Egypt, with archaeological samples going back to the fifteenth century B.C.

20:12. Merodach-Baladan. Merodach-Baladan (or Berodach Baladan) is the Marduk-apla-idinna II of Assyrian and Babylonian sources. He was a Chaldean sheikh of the Bit-Yakin tribe who was allied with Tiglath-Pileser III of Assyria against another Babylonian ruler (c. 731 B.C.). Ten years later Merodach-Baladan took the throne of Babylon, and Sargon II was unable to remove him until 710 B.C. Once again he became a local Chaldean sheikh and was vassal to the Assyrian king. Upon Sargon's death in battle in 705 B.C. Merodach-Baladan helped to instigate a rebellion against Assyrian rule. It is here that the narrative of 2 Kings is likely to be placed. Based upon Hezekiah's actions against Assyrian rule, he apparently did act in concert with Merodach-Baladan's strategy. The Babylonian sheikh deposed the Assyrian appointee to the Babylonian throne and ruled from nearby Borsippa (703 B.C.) until he was deposed by Sennacherib, the new king of Assyria, in the same year. Merodach-Baladan fled to Elam, where he soon died.

21:1-26
Manasseh of Judah

For information on this section see comments on 2 Chronicles 33.

21:13. plumb line. The measuring line and plummet were ordinary tools used for the construction of mud-brick buildings throughout the Near East. A site was surveyed with a measuring line (usually a rope, cord or thread). The chief builder used a plumb line, weighted with tin or a stone, to test the integrity of the structure.

21:18. garden of Uzza. The garden of Uzza has not been located with any certainty. Some have speculated that it was at the cemetery located in the village of Siloam, east of the City of David. However, Uzza may be a short form of Uzziah, the leper king of Judah. Thus this may have been Uzziah's private garden that was used by later kings.

22:1—23:30
Josiah of Judah

For information on this section see comments on 2 Chronicles 34.

23:1. function of the elders. The elders (patriarchal family heads) played a major role in the early tribal organization of Israel and evidently still had a function during the monarchy. Elders had been given authority in their local communities and may still have played a limited role in the political leadership during the monarchy. City elders also played a limited role in preserving stability and enacting laws in their communities in Babylonia. However, they did not initiate policy, as the central monarchy controlled the power source of the state, the economy and the armed forces.

23:2. public reading of documents. Even after the invention of the alphabet, many of the people in the ancient Near East were illiterate, and thus the public reading of documents had an important function. Assyrian sources describe heralds standing at city gates reading royal pronouncements to groups of onlookers.

23:3. pillar. The king stood near a pillar or column (platform, according to the Jewish writer Josephus). It may have been a standing structure in the temple reserved for royalty. No clear parallels for this custom exist elsewhere in the Near East.

23:4. constellations and starry hosts. Worship of the starry hosts refers to the worship of the celestial gods (sun god, moon god and Venus particularly; in Babylonia, Shamash, Sin and Ishtar respectively), who were primary in most ancient religions. Controlling the calendar and time, seasons and weather, they were viewed as the most powerful of the gods. They provided signs by which omens were read, and they looked down on all. By the end of the second millennium a major compilation of celestial omens, the seventy tablets of the work known as *Enuma Anu Enlil*, had been compiled and was consulted for nearly a thousand years. Stamp seals from Israel in this period show that astral deities were very popular. There were many constellations recognized by the Mesopotamian astrologers (many, though not all, the same we recognize today, transmitted through the Greeks), but the Zodiac is not yet known at this time. For more information see comment on 2 Chronicles 33:5.

23:4. Kidron Valley to Bethel. Kidron Valley was east of the City of David. Bethel was about ten miles along a main transportation route due north of Jerusalem. Bethel had been the site of the shrine of the golden calf until a century earlier, when the northern kingdom had fallen to Assyria. Josiah also desecrates the altar there (see vv. 15-16), so that is an appropriate place to dump the desecrating ashes of these religious articles.

23:5. pagan priests. The term "pagan, idol priests" (Hebrew, *komer*) has many parallels in the ancient Near East, especially from Assyria. Kumru priests are known from Old Assyrian Period documents from Cappadocia (c. 2000-1800 B.C.) and from a single document from Mari during the reign of the Assyrian king, Shamshi-Adad I (reigned 1814-1781 B.C.). An Arabian queen was given the title of kumirtu priestess in an inscription of the Assyrian king Ashurbanipal (668-631 B.C.). *Kumra'* is also the word for priest in Aramaic in the first millennium B.C. It is plausible that these priests mentioned here served the shrines of West Semitic deities such as Baal and Asherah, though some consider them renegade priests of Yahweh.

23:6. scattering of the dust over graves. The sequence of burn-grind-scatter-eat is also found in a Ugaritic text to indicate total destruction of a deity—every destructive action is being carried out. The scattering of the dust on the graves is a final act of desecration on the image.

23:7. male shrine prostitutes. The Hebrew term, *qedeshim*, refers to "sacred males." Little is known about this practice, but it was thoroughly condemned and may well have had to do with cultic prostitution (see Deut 23:18-19). Cognate terms are found in Akkadian and Ugaritic, where they are also not clear in terms of function. The root means to be ritually clean. A *qadishtu* in Akkadian was a woman of special status. She had particular functions in the temple (midwife, wet-nurse and devotee of the god of the temple) none of which appear to be obviously of a sexual nature. A similar situation can be found at Ugarit. The condemnation of the males here in 2 Kings 23:7 may have had to do with the fact that they were devotees of foreign deities.

23:7. weaving for Asherah. Apparently the women were weaving types of coverings or vestments to adorn the Asherah statue (or pole). The fashioning of woven and embroidered garments used to place on the statues of gods in Mesopotamia is well known.

23:8. desecrating high places. Desecration of sacred places occurs when forbidden cultic practices are performed there. The laws for preserving the purity of Yahweh's sacred places are outlined in the book of Leviticus, but these desecrate the temple because they represent things not acceptable in Yahweh's presence. Other actions may cause desecration to the shrines of other gods. There were, however, certain common desecrating actions. Turning what had once been a sacred area into a graveyard (see v. 14) or a latrine (see 10:27) would bring permanent desecration.

23:8. Geba to Beersheba. Geba (modern Jaba) was a small village in the territory of Benjamin about six miles north of Jerusalem. No excavations have been conducted there, but surface surveys have found Iron Age remains on the site. It overlooks the strategic pass across the deep canyon of the Wadi Swenit from Micmash that leads from the north into the region of Jerusalem. It probably functioned as a border shrine city. It is paralleled with Beersheba, the southernmost town in Judah. Archaeologists found a dismantled horn altar there that may have been destroyed during the period of Josiah. At any rate the phrase here makes it clear that Josiah purged the entire land of Judah (from north to south) of foreign worship practices.

23:8. shrines at the gates. At Dan standing stones were found at a shrine just inside the city gate, and the clear remains of the presentation of votive offerings were evident. It is thought that the standing stones represented some of the deities of cities that had fallen to Israel. The votive offerings would be in fulfillment of vows made to those deities (perhaps for their aid in overthrowing the city the Israelites were fighting against). For more information on standing stones see comment on 17:10.

23:8. gate of Joshua. The gate of Joshua is not mentioned elsewhere in Scripture, and its precise location is not known. It may have been an alternative name for one of the Jerusalem gates. This was presumably the gate of the governor of the city, who was the highest official in the city administration. A seventh-century B.C. seal from Judah has been found with an inscription in a cartouche reading "governor of the city." There is an artistic scene on the seal that is reminiscent of Assyrian symbolism.

23:9. eating unleavened bread. The term here for unleavened bread is either a generic term for grain offerings or unleavened cakes to be eaten at the Passover celebration. Since leaven was associated with spoilage, and therefore impurity, unleavened bread was used in most sacred ceremonies.

23:10. Topheth, Ben Hinnom, Molech. Topheth was the cultic installation where children were offered to the god Molech. The word is thought to signify the hearth where the child was placed. The Hebrew term has parallel terms in both Ugaritic and Aramaic with the meaning "furnace, fireplace." Scholars have thought that Topheth was at the edge of the valley of Ben Hinnom before connecting with the Kidron Valley. The valley of Ben Hinnom has been identified with Wadi er-Rahabi southwest of the City of David. Many consider Molech to be a netherworld deity featuring rituals with Canaanite origins focusing on dead ancestors. An eighth-century B.C. Phoenician inscription speaks of sacrifices made to Molech before battle by the Cilicians and their enemies. The name Molech appears to be related to the Hebrew term *mlk* ("to rule"). Sacrifices to Molech were done at the installation of Baal, which may mean that the term was an epithet of Baal himself, as well as other deities (Jer 32:35).

23:11. horses and chariots dedicated to the sun. White horses were used in important ritual functions in Assyria and were usually associated with Ashur and Sin, major deities in the Assyrian pantheon. White horses were dedicated at the feet of a certain deity. Moreover a number of Assyrian deities rode a horse-drawn chariot on festival days. In Assyrian mythology the sun (god) was carried across the sky in a chariot driven by his charioteer Rakib-il. In the syncretism referred to here, Yahweh was probably being worshiped as a sun god, and the chariot and horses represented his vehicle. Archaeological evidence is provided by Iron Age horse figurines with solar disks and by the Taanach cult stand, which portrays a horse with a sun-disk on its back. This would have some similarity with the golden calf imagery where the calf served as a pedestal or the ark of the covenant that functioned as a footstool. None of these portray deity, but they represent his throne.

23:12. upper room of Ahaz. The upper room typically functioned as an audience chamber, so these were in a prominent location in the palace.

23:13. hill of corruption. The Hebrew phrase for "Hill of Corruption" is probably a wordplay on "Mount of Ointment, or Olives." It has been precisely identified as the hill rising above the modern Arab village of Silwan.

23:13. Solomon's idols. The amenities that Solomon had provided for his foreign wives included the construction of altars and shrines for their worship of their own gods (see the comments on 1 Kings 11:5-7).

23:14. covered with human bones. It is presumed that the human bones were thrown onto the refuse so no one would try to retrieve the items. This was because of the taboo of coming into contact with dead bodies (see comment on Num 19:11).

23:16. exhumation. Josiah is fulfilling the prophecy in 1 Kings 13:2. In both Mesopotamia and Israel the worst criminals were not accorded a proper burial, and their bones were either burned or discarded. This was the worst possible thing for an individual, since one's spiritual existence was intertwined with their physical existence (for more information see comments on Num 3:12-13 and Joshua 8:29). Thus if one's bones were destroyed, the individual's existence was also extinguished.

23:21-30. Passover celebration. For information see comments on 2 Chronicles 35.

23:31-35
Jehoahaz of Judah

23:31. chronology. Jehoahaz began and ended his short reign of three months in 609 B.C., not long after the final collapse of the Assyrian empire at Harran and on the verge of the monumental struggle between Egypt and Babylon for supremacy in the Near East.

23:33. relations with Egypt. The Levant was an unstable area after the collapse of Assyria in 612-610 B.C. Egypt and Babylon now fought a furious war for supremacy in the area. Egypt apparently tried unsuccessfully to lift the siege of the last Assyrian center at Haran in 610-609 B.C. Four years later Josiah of Judah tried to block Egypt's invasion of Syria but was wounded at the battle of Megiddo and subsequently died. Because of the power vacuum in the area, Judah became an Egyptian protectorate (609-608 B.C.). The Egyptians, although delayed, now traveled north and battled the Chaldeans at Carchemish, suffering a tremendous defeat (605 B.C.). The Chaldeans followed by invading Egypt in 601-600 but suffered heavy casualties. At any rate, Judah was only temporarily under the leadership of Egypt.

23:33. Riblah in Hamath. Riblah (modern Tel Zerr'a) was an important administrative and military town near Kadesh on the Orontes River in Syria about twenty miles south of the major Aramean center of Hamath. The Assyrians had set up a fortress here in the eighth century. Later Nebuchadrezzar II of Babylon used it as headquarters during his campaigning in the west.

23:33. tribute imposed on Judah. This is considerably less than the fine imposed upon Hezekiah (three talents of silver and thirty talents of gold; 2 Kings 18:14). The percentage of silver (seven thousand five hundred pounds) to gold (seventy-five pounds) is also different (100:1 instead of 10:1).

23:34. name changing. The name change was somewhat minimal, as the theophoric element (God's name contained in the name) was altered, from El- (generic for god) to Jeho- (for Yahweh). The name change probably had to do with a loyalty oath to a new overlord, which the Assyrian kings had also done. In the previous generation, Psammeticus I of Egypt (father of Necho) was renamed Nabushezibanni by the Assyrian king Ashurbanipal when he was installed as a district ruler. Notice also the name change for Daniel and his friends (Dan 1:6-7).

23:36—24:7
Jehoiakim of Judah

23:36. chronology. Jehoiakim's reign of eleven years was from 609 to 598 B.C. During this time, Nebuchadnezzar of Babylon fought a fierce battle at the Egyptian border in 601-600 with unclear results. Both armies were severely depleted, and the Chaldean king was unable to invade Egypt. This may have encouraged Jehoiakim to rebel against Babylon.

24:1. Nebuchadnezzar and Jehoiakim. Nebuchadnezzar II took the throne of Babylon in 605 B.C. after his victory against Egypt at the Battle of Carchemish in the same year. From that time on Jehoiakim was vassal to Babylon during most of his reign. The Babylonian Chronicle states that the Chaldeans were able to wrest control of the Levant from Egypt after this. Nebuchadnezzar attempted to follow up with an invasion of Egypt (601-600). This attack apparently crippled the Chaldeans for a brief period, possibly causing Jehoiakim to ally himself with Egypt. Nebuchadnezzar's response was to attack Judah with garrison troops from the west. Jehoiakim was captured and shackled (see 2 Chron 36:6), but appears to have avoided exile since he died in Judah.

24:2. invading raiders. The Chaldeans were the designation of the Semitic-speaking people of Nebuchadnezzar II of Babylon. They are mentioned in Assyrian records as inhabiting Babylonia by the beginning of the first millennium B.C. Though we are most familiar with the Arameans connected to the Aramean state north of Israel, there were also eastern Arameans, a Semitic-speaking people who inhabited much of the Tigris-Euphrates Valley, who often appear alongside the Chaldeans. It appears that the Chaldeans were more of a town-based group, while the Arameans were seminomadic. According to Babylonian sources, the Moabites and Ammonites were subjects of Babylon and were thus required to send troops against a recalcitrant neighbor.

24:7. Babylon versus Egypt. Nebuchadnezzar II attempted to follow up his victory over the Egyptians at Carchemish by invading Egypt in 601-600. They met at the Wadi of Egypt (probably the Wadi el-Arish on the eastern edge of the Nile Delta region). There was evidently a fierce battle, and the troops of Nebuchadnezzar were unable to conquer Egypt. However, the Babylonians were able to regroup for another campaign in the Levant soon thereafter, and the Egyptians were unable to muster a defense against them.

24:8-17
Jehoiachin of Judah

24:8. chronology. Jehoiachin's brief reign was in the last month of 598 and the first two months of 597. Since Jehoiachin appears to have come to the throne while Nebuchadnezzar's army was on the way to Jerusalem, his father, Jehoiakim, can be seen as instigating the trouble that brought the Babylonians west.

24:10-11. 597 siege of Jerusalem. In response to Judah's rebellion, the Chaldeans attacked Jerusalem in 597. The Babylonian Chronicle states that the siege lasted a mere three months, probably the entire reign of Jehoiachin. Although Nebuchadnezzar took credit for the victory in his annals, he did not preside over the campaign but left it to his generals. The relative ease with which the city was captured may be explained by the fact that it was during winter and food would have been scarce. The city's population would have been much larger than normal, since those in the outlying areas of Judah sought refuge in Jerusalem.

24:12. Jehoiachin's imprisonment. The quick surrender by Judah may be the reason why the Babylonians were somewhat lenient in their treatment of the Judahites. The deportation of a rebellious monarch was common treatment by both the Assyrians and Babylonians. They were looked upon as rulers that had broken a loyalty oath with the Babylonians (or Assyrians) and were duly punished. The conquerors normally installed a monarch who was sensitive to their cause, often from the same royal house in order to preserve some sense of continuity with the local population.

24:14. deportation. Though we have no records from Babylon concerning deportation practices, it can be assumed that they inherited Assyrian administrative practices to a certain extent. It was typical policy to deport influential people (rich and the military) as well as skilled workers, who could be employed cheaply in Babylon. The "poor of the land" were either not useful or were not considered a threat by remaining in the land of Judah.

24:17. name changing. As with Jehoiakim, Mattaniah was required by the Babylonians to change his name. The Babylonian Chronicle simply states that Nebuchadnezzar II appointed a king of his choice in Judah and that the new king "was after his heart," meaning that he had been "domesticated" by the Babylonians. As before, the Babylonians thought it in their own best interest to give the king another Hebrew name, so as not to incite rebellion.

24:18—25:26
Zedekiah of Judah and the Fall of Jerusalem

24:18. chronology. Zedekiah, the last king of Judah, reigned from 597 to 586. Necho II (r. 610-595), Psammeticus (r. 595-589) and Apries (r. 589-570) were rulers of Egypt, while Nebuchadnezzar II (r. 604-562) ruled the Chaldean empire.

25:1. siege of Jerusalem. The Babylonians evidently used a siege "wall" (as opposed to a ramp) to attack Jerusalem in 587-586. Assyrian sources describe Esarhaddon using the same type of contraption for his conquest of Shurbia, a Urartian kingdom south of Lake Van, in 672. Esarhaddon claims that his troops "climbed over the siege wall to do battle." This siege wall was probably made higher than the city wall, so as to allow the soldiers to climb atop the defender's wall. As with the Assyrians during Sennacherib's siege of 701, the Babylonians systematically destroyed the Judahite fortresses on the countryside, including Lachish (see Jer 34:7). Another purpose in removing the military threats surrounding Jerusalem was to discourage any Egyptian interference.

25:4. flight of army. It can be assumed by the context of this difficult verse that the king and his bodyguard attempted to escape by the east. The "men of war" may refer to the Babylonian soldiers who made a breach in the city wall, causing Zedekiah to flee.

25:5. plains of Jericho. The king took the Arabah Road (see v. 4), the road from Jerusalem to Jericho, which was in the steppe land of the Jordan Valley rift. The plains of Jericho are stretches of flat and dry ground east of Jericho. It was an open area, which made it easy for the Babylonian troops to retrieve the fugitives.

25:7. Zedekiah's treatment. Blinding was a common treatment of rebellious slaves (even subject kings) in the ancient Near East. The Assyrian vassal treaties mention blinding as a curse for a future violator of a loyalty oath. Other Assyrian sources mention the blinding of one eye of prisoners of war, in order that they could still be used as a work force but would have been rendered incapacitated in war. Zedekiah was put in a "house of punishment," corresponding to an Assyrian word for prison.

25:8-10. fall of Jerusalem. Nebuzaradan, the commander of the Babylonian armed forces, was the "chief cook" mentioned in a list of high officials of Nebuchadnezzar II. The title "chief cook," like that of "chief cupbearer," was an archaic term for those in high positions in Assyrian and Babylonian courts. They were often sent on military and diplomatic missions (e.g, the Rabshekah was the "chief cupbearer" to Sennacherib, 2 Kings 18:17). Nebuzaradan was responsible for the destruction of the city of Jerusalem, for sending Judahite high officials to be executed (vv. 8-12, 18-21) and for the deportation of a number of the Judahites a few years later (c. 582 B.C.; Jer 52:24-30). Typical of Assyrian and Babylonian practice, Nebuzaradan destroyed the major public centers in the city and the protective walls of the city to make it vulnerable to further attack.

25:13-17. plunder of Jerusalem. The writer of 2 Kings is probably reciting this list of items from nonextant official temple records of Judah. It can be compared to 2 Kings 17:15-50, where the original manufacture of the items was recorded. The large list of bronze objects may be a booty count. The items in 2 Kings 17 that were omitted here had been sent to Assyria in previous years (e.g., twelve bronze bulls were sent by Ahaz to Tiglath-Pileser III; 2 Kings 16:17). No Babylonian sources describe the inventory taken from Jerusalem.

25:22. governorship. It is possible that Gedaliah had previously been in the service of King Zedekiah, based upon a seal impression of the late seventh century B.C. from Lachish that reads, "belonging to Gedaliah, the Royal Steward." Alternatively, however, that bulla may refer to another Gedaliah of this period (see Jer 38:1). The name Gedaliah is also found on an ostraca from Arad. He was probably a ranking member of the "pro-Babylonian" party in Jerusalem. Similar to the Assyrians, the Babylonians desired to found an administrative core with a strong Babylonian presence in Judah. Contrary to Assyrian practice, however, the Babylonians did not repopulate Judah with people from other parts of the empire.

25:23-25. Mizpah. This was the capital of what was left of Judah. Mizpah is an eight-acre site located about eight miles north of Jerusalem. For information concerning its earlier history see comments on 1 Samuel 7:5 and 2 Chronicles 16:6. Recent reassessment of excavation reports have identified an occupation level from this period. One of the artifacts found at the site was a seal belonging to "Jaazaniah, the servant of the king"—likely the same individual mentioned in verse 23.

25:27-30
The Release of Jehoiachin

25:27-30. Jehoiachin in Babylon. The thirty-seventh year of Jehoiachin's exile was 560 B.C. Evil-Merodach (Babylonian, Amel-Marduk, "the man of Marduk") ruled Babylon from 562 to 560. He was the son and successor of Nebuchadnezzar II. He was assassinated by his successor Neriglissar. Very few sources remain from his brief reign. Jehoiachin was given the "seat of seats" by Evil-Merodach, implying that there were other royal prisoners in Babylon. The Unger Prism gives a list of kings who were prisoners in Babylon during the reign of Evil-Merodach. They include the kings of Tyre, Gaza, Sidon, Arvad and Arpad. Jehoiachin is mentioned on a rations list from Babylon, confirming the biblical information that he was fed at the king's table.

1 CHRONICLES

1:1-37
Genealogies: Adam to Abraham

1:1-54
Genealogies of Adam Through Jacob and Esau

1:1-4. Adam's sons. More detail of this section of the genealogy may be found in Genesis 5.

1:5-27. Noah's sons. More detail of this section of the genealogy may be found in Genesis 10 and 11.

1:13. peoples of Canaan. For more information on these people groups see comment on Exodus 3:8.

1:29-54. non-Israelite descendants of Abraham. Comments on these genealogies can be found as follows: Hagar (Ishmael) in Genesis 25:12-18; Keturah, Genesis 25:1-6; Esau, Genesis 36.

2:1—7:40
Genealogies of the Twelve Tribes

2:42-55. prominence of Caleb. Caleb and Joshua were the only representatives of the exodus generation to enter the land of Canaan. Caleb was given a special land grant within the tribe of Judah's holdings in the vicinity of Hebron (Josh 14:6-15). Since the genealogies are being used for land claims, it is important for Caleb's standing to be recognized.

3:1-16. royal line of David. The other prominent line in the tribe of Judah was, of course, the royal line. A number of these names are represented in variant forms from those that were used in Kings: Abijah/Abijam; Joram/Jehoram; Azariah/Uzziah; Shallum/Jehoa-

haz; Jehoiachin/Jeconiah. Most of these can be explained in one of three ways: (1) variations within spelling of the divine name in the name; (2) variant words with the same meaning; or (3) throne name versus personal name.

3:17-24. postexilic descendants of David. Most of these individuals are unknown outside of this list. Exceptions are Zerubbabel, of whom considerably more is known (see comment on Ezra 3:2), and Hattush (v. 22) who is known only as one who returned with Ezra (Ezra 8:2).

4:21. linen workers at Beth Ashbea. The reference to Mareshah earlier in the verse leads to the suspicion that Beth Ashbea too should be located in the Shephelah between the Jerusalem hills and the coastal plains, but it is impossible to be more specific at this time. Guilds of craftsmen were typically connected with particular towns that had chosen to specialize in that industry. Knowledge of the craft would be passed on from generation to generation. An Alalakh text lists over sixty such house industries as early as the fifteenth century B.C. Textile production was a common industry that was done on a small scale in most homes, but also could support large industrial centers. Linen technology required the processing of flax as well as spinning, dying and weaving facilities.

4:21. men of Cozeba. If it can be identified at all, Cozeba is likely a variant spelling of Achzib in the Shephelah. This has tentatively been associated with the modern site of Tel el-Beida, about five miles from Mareshah.

4:21. king's potters at Netaim and Gederah. It can be assumed that the palace or temple sought to attract to itself the best artisans of

---

SIGNIFICANCE OF GENEALOGIES TO POSTEXILIC AUDIENCE
Though most of the material of Chronicles covers the history of the preexilic period, it is written for those who returned from the Babylonian exile in the sixth and fifth centuries, and reestablished themselves in the land. Genealogies to them represented the charter of their identity. Their covenant with the Lord had established them as an elect people of God living in the land promised by him. Their family lineage was their certificate of membership. It was their heritage and their legacy. Often in the ancient world genealogies served sociological rather than historical functions. Instead of offering a strictly sequential report of the order of generations, they were designed to use continuity with the past as an explanation of the current structure and condition of society. Israel carried along with this an additional theological emphasis and significance that was inherent in their genealogical reports. Continuity with the past would give meaning to their current theological situation. Individuals in the ancient world found their identity not in their individualism but in their solidarity with the group. This included not only those that made up their contemporary kinship group but extended throughout the generations. The genealogies were their way of fitting themselves into this pangenerational solidarity. Every generation is not necessarily represented. One might compare the selective list of heroes of the faith in Hebrews 11. Americans today take pride in being able to trace their ancestry back to those who crossed on the Mayflower or those who signed the Declaration of Independence. The difference is that in Israel these connections gave rights and privileges rather than being simply status symbols.

the trades that they had need of. Sponsorship would have included providing supplies, workshops, equipment and perhaps some slave labor to help with menial tasks. Additionally they would receive rations, clothing and other needs. The towns mentioned here are again to be found in the Shephelah, but there is no consensus concerning their specific identification.

4:41. Meunites. A number of very different opinions exist concerning the identification of this group. The first is that it should be identified with the Minaeans of South Arabia. Their control of the incense trade had extended up into the region of Palestine by the fourth century. Others would identify the group with the Mu'unaya mentioned in the inscriptions of Tiglath-Pileser III. A third possibility links them to the town of Maon south of Hebron in the hill country of Judah.

4:42-43. new Simeonite territory. The new territory occupied by the Simeonites is due south of their assigned territory in the Negev but probably still west of the Arabah and east of Kadesh-barnea. Moving to this area entails a migration of perhaps forty or fifty miles.

5:1. Reuben's forfeiture. For information on this incident see Genesis 35:21-22.

5:8-9. area of settlement. The Reubenite settlement is in Transjordan alongside the north half of the Dead Sea from the Arnon River (Wadi Mujib) on the south to the Medeba plateau and Mount Nebo on the north. An area often held by the Moabites, it is about twenty miles square.

5:10. Hagrites. The inscriptions of Tiglath-Pileser III mention a tribe of Arameans called the Hagaranu that some have associated with the Hagrites. At this time, however, little is known of them.

5:16. territory of Gadite settlement. Gilead and Bashan are two areas that cover nearly one hundred miles (north-south) of Transjordan. Gilead is the hilly section of Transjordan between the Jabbok on the south almost to the Yarmuk on the north. Bashan is in the area (known today as the Golan Heights) bordered by Mount Hermon to the north, Jebel Druze (Mount Hauran) to the east, the Sea of Galilee to the west and the Yarmuk region to the south. Bashan proper, more limited to the region of the (upper?) Yarmuk, is a broad, fertile plateau region noted for its grazing. Salecah (v. 11) is about sixty miles east of the Sea of Galilee, south of Mount Hauran. The pasturelands of Sharon refer to a location in Transjordan that remains unidentified. The Moabite Inscription also refers to such an area, but does not locate it.

5:19. battle against the Hagrites and allies. The allies with the Hagrites are Arabian tribes. Jetur (by Roman times, Itureans, northeast of Galilee, see Luke 3:1) and Naphish are known from Ishmael's descendants (Gen 25:15). The region of Naphish is referred to in a seventh-century letter to the Assyrian king Ashurbanipal. Nodab (perhaps Adbeel in Gen 25:13) may also be listed in Assyrian records (Tiglath-Pileser III) as a tribal group in Transjordan. Aside from these passing references, nothing is known of these peoples or of this battle.

5:21. plunder. The numbers of livestock and human captives are incredibly large. In comparison, the totals from twenty years of campaigning by the extremely successful Shalmaneser III produced 110,610 prisoners, nearly 10,000 horses and mules, over 35,000 cattle, nearly 20,000 donkeys, and nearly 185,000 sheep. Sennacherib's campaign to Babylon netted 20,000 people, 11,000 donkeys, 5,000 camels, and 800,000 sheep.

5:26. Assyrian relocation of Transjordanian tribes. Tiglath-Pileser III (originally named Pulu) invaded Upper and Lower Galilee in 733 B.C. and reported that he deported 13,520 people (see comment on 2 Kings 15:29). In this campaign the northern kingdom of Israel was reduced to only Samaria and its surroundings, which survived independently for another twelve years. The relocation sites focus on the middle Euphrates, where Gozan (Guzanu=Tel Halaf, about one hundred miles east of Carchemish) is located on the Habur River. Halah is identified as Halahhu of the Assyrian inscriptions, which was located about eight miles northeast of Nineveh.

6:31-46. Levitical musicians. David's three chief musicians, Heman, Asaph and Ethan, all have long and distinguished pedigrees going back to their ancestor Levi through various lines. In the ancient world there were musicians' guilds that serviced shrines and sanctuaries. As early as the third millennium in Egypt there were priests that oversaw the musicians who performed in worship. Hittites and Babylonians both had musicians among temple personnel. Many religious situations from individual rituals, to ceremonies, to festivals were accompanied by musical performance (both vocal and instrumental). For more information see comment on Amos 5:23.

6:48-49. respective duties of Levites and Aaronide priests. The Aaronide priests were more directly involved in the performance of sacrifices and the duties connected to the holy place. The Levites were more directly connected with the other aspects of the sacred enclosure. These would include controlling access to the sacred area and providing for the supply and upkeep of the sanctuary (see details in 9:22-33).

6:55-56. distinction between villages and pasturelands. The land immediately surrounding Hebron was part of the grant to the Levites. This verse clarifies, however, that the settlements in the Hebron region, including the arable land around them, was still the portion of Caleb.

6:64. Levitical cities. For information on the Levitical cities see comments on Numbers 35:1-5 and Joshua 21:3-40.

7:28-29. territory of Ephraim and Manasseh. Ephraim's settlements ranged from Bethel in the south to Shechem in the north and did not include either the coastal plain (Gezer was the western limit) or the Jordan Valley. Manasseh was positioned north of Ephraim, and included the Samarian hills (up to Gilboa) and the Carmel range skirting the southern end of the Jezreel Valley (thus including Taanach and Megiddo). Manasseh territory included the Jordan Valley (Beth Shan) and the coastal plain (Dor) up to the Carmel promontory.

9:1. royal genealogical lists. There would be a number of reasons to keep genealogical lists in the official palace archives. First, whether land possession was on the basis of royal grant or divine grant, it was tied to families. Therefore property disputes often had to be settled by reference to genealogical records. Second, conscription for government service, whether in labor corvees or for military duty, was conducted on the basis of census figures, as was taxation. Census records typically would have been organized by genealogical categories.

9:3. significance of resettlement lists. This list is composed of those who settled in Jerusalem. It is distinct from the previous lists because they all addressed ancestral holdings being resettled. The reason Jerusalem had so few to live in it is that many of the families of Jerusalem had been decimated in the Babylonian destruction of that city. For people of other tribes to live in Jerusalem, they would have to neglect (if not give up) their ancestral lands in their tribal territories. Willingness to make that sacrifice in order to repopulate Jerusalem merited special notice.

9:22-27. gatekeepers. One of the most important tasks assigned to priestly personnel was controlling access to the temple precinct, the inner circle of the "sacred compass" (on this concept see comments on Lev 16:2 and Num 18:1-7). Defiling the sanctuary with impurity required a purification offering ("sin" offering, see comment on Lev 4:1-3) and could bring punishment on the individual as well as the people. The gatekeepers had to prevent unqualified intrusion. There were also many valuable items in the temple precinct. Gold and silver were plentiful and a temptation to the unscrupulous individual who may not have feared divine retribution for trespass or theft of temple property. These valuables also had to be guarded. Misappropriation of that which was sacred required a reparation offering ("guilt" offering, see comment on Lev 5:14-16). The gatekeepers were charged with guarding against these offenses.

9:28-33. other Levitical duties. All sorts of skills were useful within the priestly ranks. Accounting for the sacred vessels (remember, mostly made of gold) involved inventory procedures, a control and record of usage, and care for and storage of the vessels. The consumables also had to be inventoried and replenished, and there were special sacred recipes for some of the mixtures that were used (see comment on Ex 30:23-25).

10:1-14
The Death of Saul

For comments on the details of this section see 1 Samuel 31.

11:1-9
David Becomes Kings and Conquers Jerusalem

For comments on the details of this section see 2 Samuel 5.

11:10-47
David's Mighty Men and Their Exploits

For comments on the details of this section see 2 Samuel 23:8-39.

12:1-40
David's First Army

12:2. ambidextrous warriors. Left handedness was not acceptable in the ancient world because it was generally associated with evil or demons. As a result, anyone who was left-handed became ambidextrous because the use of the left hand in many situations was not approved. In battle, however, the ability to use either hand could become a distinct advantage. For instance, battle strategies were often designed to force the enemy to be moving to their left while fighting. For a right-handed soldier, this would put his shield (in his left hand) away from the enemy and expose him to attack. An ambidextrous soldier could easily switch the shield to his right hand without compromising his ability to fight as he moved. An ambidextrous bowman using a tree or rock for protection would have a wider range of target available because he could shoot from either side without exposing himself to the enemy.

12:15. crossing the Jordan at flood stage. The first month begins in March, when the spring temperatures were melting the snow in the mountains and causing the Jordan to reach flood stage. There is an interesting inscription of Sargon II of Assyria (eighth century) where he claims that he led his army across the Tigris and Euphrates at flood stage as on dry ground. On the one hand, this posed considerable risk to those crossing, but on the other hand (for that very reason), it often made surprise attacks possible because no one would be expecting the crossing to be made.

12:23-40. tribal alliance as foundation for kingship. Israel was still a tribal society despite the decision to have a king at their head. As a result, any potential king needed to procure the backing of the tribal leadership and the military contingents of the clans to support his bid for the throne.

13:1-14
Failed Attempt to Bring the Ark to Jerusalem

For comments on the details of this section see 2 Samuel 6:1-11.

14:1-17
Victory over the Philistines

For comments on the details of this section see 2 Samuel 5:17-25.

15:1—16:43
Bringing the Ark to Jerusalem

15:1. David's building projects in Jerusalem. The only project the biblical text names is the royal palace. Archaeology has, unfortunately, not been able as yet to identify any other buildings built in Jerusalem in the time of David. For the royal palace see comment on 2 Samuel 5:11.

15:20-21. music styles. The terms "alamoth" (used in the titles of Psalm 46 with a possible variation in Ps 48:14 and the title to 9) and "sheminith" (psalm titles to 6 and 12) are left untranslated in the NIV because there is still uncertainty concerning their technical mean-

ings. The former term in its nontechnical use means "maidens" and is therefore sometimes interpreted as being in the soprano range. The latter term means "eighth" and is thought to suggest a certain placement on the octave. Akkadian texts demonstrate the knowledge of the seven-note scale and various keys ("tunings"). Some of the Akkadian notations also concern the intervals used for filling out the chords (e.g., thirds).

For comments on the remaining details of this section see 2 Samuel 6:12-23.

16:26. gods are idols. See comments on Leviticus 26:1 and Deuteronomy 4:15-18.

16:39. tabernacle at high place in Gibeon. Outside of Chronicles there is no specific mention of the tabernacle being at Gibeon. Gibeon is located just six miles northwest of Jerusalem, and 1 Kings 3:4 identifies it as the most important high place and indicates a functioning altar there.

16:42. instruments in worship in the ancient Near East. See comments on 6:31-46.

17:1-27
Covenant Promises to David

For comments on the details of this section see 2 Samuel 7.

18:1-17
Establishment of David's Kingdom

For comments on the details of this section see 2 Samuel 8.

19:1-19
Ammonite War

For comments on the details of this section see 2 Samuel 10.

20:1-3
Defeat of Rabbah

For comments on the details of this section see 2 Samuel 11:1; 12:29-31.

20:4-8
Battles with the Philistines

For comments on the details of this section see 2 Samuel 21:15-22.

21:1-30
David's Census

For comments on the details of this section see 2 Samuel 24.

22:1-19
Preparations for the Building of the Temple

22:2. stonecutters. The dressed stone used in this period is known as ashlar masonry. An iron chisel was used to dress the margin around the edges, while the central part of the rock face was left unworked. In the area around Jerusalem limestone was particularly abundant and could be quarried nearby, but harder stone had to be brought from greater distances. Basalt was available in quantity in the Galilee and the Golan; granite was available in the southern Arabah near Eilat under a cover of sandstone. To quarry large blocks, wooden wedges were driven deeply into cracks and then soaked with water. As the wood expanded it would split the rock. Heavy blocks were moved into place by means of lead balls being spread on the block below. Subsequent blocks would flatten the lead balls.

22:3. iron nails and fittings. At this period iron was being widely used but was still considered decorative. The fittings were most likely decorated plates or bands attached to the door by the nails.

22:3. bronze work. Bronze was refined in a crucible, and then molds were used to give it its shape.

22:4 cedar wood. The principal use of cedar was for making the intricate paneling in the interior rooms. A second possible use was in the beams that would have been interspersed between the courses of stone work. Many of the carvings that were done for the temple used olive wood rather than cedar.

22:14. one hundred thousand talents of gold. This is an immense amount of gold. Its weight of 3750 tons would fetch about $45 billion at today's prices, but it represents far more in buying power equivalence. This is by far the largest amount of gold referred to in the Old Testament. Elsewhere in Chronicles there is mention of 3000 talents (112 tons) of gold (1 Chron 29:4). Outside of Chronicles the largest number is 666 talents (25 tons) of gold, which was the amount Solomon was said to receive yearly. In Egypt the largest known donation of gold and silver made by a pharaoh to the gods is the 200 tons by Shishak (who got lots of it from Jerusalem). In Assyrian inscriptions, kings such as Tiglath-Pileser III, Sargon II and Shalmaneser III rarely list the specific amount of gold taken in tribute or plunder, and when they do it is usually between ten and fifty talents. Centuries later Persepolis was believed to possess the richest hoard in the ancient world. At the time of Alexander's conquest its treasure of gold and silver was valued at 120,000 talents (=4,500 tons) of silver.

22:14. how much gold? In 1993 the statistics for the world mineral reserve base listed a total of 55,435 tons. The United States Central Bank gold reserve was about 9000 tons. A cube of pure, solid gold that is one foot per side weighs 1200 pounds (worth over $7 million in today's market). Solomon's contribution would have filled a standard two-car garage floor to ceiling with such blocks (6250 of them). If the builders would have stacked up blocks such as this they could have built the outer walls of the two main chambers of the temple one foot thick around three sides (with dimensions of 90 by 30 by 30.

22:14. one million talents of silver. As with the number in the last entry this is an enormous amount (almost 40,000 tons) and far exceeds anything else from biblical or extrabiblical sources.

23:1—26:32
Levites and Their Duties

23:28-31. duties of the Levites. See comments on 9:22-33.

24:6. scribe. Scribes in the ancient world were the accountants, the historians, the journalists, the personal secretaries, the tutors and the librarians of their day. Much of a scribe's training involved language and writing, and his apprenticeship would give him additional specialized skills. While many scribes were never more than clerks or middle-class functionaries, some scribes gained wide renown as sages, and others could rise to the rank of prime minister, as is evident in the texts form Ugarit.

25:1. connection between music and prophecy. Typically prophets would use various procedures in order to prepare themselves for receiving prophetic oracles. Music played an important role in inducing a trancelike state (ecstasy) that was seen as making one receptive to a divine message. In the Mari texts there is an entire class of temple personnel who were ecstatics and who often provided prophetic messages.

26:15. storehouse. This term occurs only here and in Nehemiah 12:25. In Akkadian the term refers to the outbuildings at the gates of temples, which fits well the more specific usage in Nehemiah.

26:16. Shalleketh gate. This is the only reference to this gate, and its positioning and function are obscure. From the context it appears to be on the west side (the rear) of the temple area but is not the west gate. Since there is a forum area to the west (see comment on 26:18), perhaps this gate led into the west end of the forum area while the west gate led from the forum into the temple area.

26:16-18. role of the gatekeepers. One of the most important tasks assigned to priestly personnel was controlling access to the temple precinct, the inner circle of the "sacred compass" (on this concept see comments on Lev 16:2 and Num 18:1-7). Defiling the sanctuary with impurity required a purification offering ("sin" offering, see comment on Lev 4:1-3) and could bring punishment on the individual as well as the people. The gatekeepers had to prevent unqualified intrusion. There were also many valuable items in the temple precinct. Gold and silver were plentiful and a temptation to the unscrupulous individual who may not have feared divine retribution for trespass or theft of temple property. These valuables also had to be guarded. Misappropriation of that which was sacred required a reparation offering ("guilt" offering, see comment on Lev 5:14-16). The gatekeepers were charged with guarding against these offenses.

26:18. court (parbar). This obscure architectural term is thought (on the basis of the Temple Scroll from the Dead Sea Scrolls) to refer to an open area (similar to a forum) just west of the sanctuary (that is, at the rear of it) featuring free-standing pillars.

26:20. temple treasuries. See comment on 26:16-18.

27:1-24
Army Divisions and Officers

27:1. significance of lists. Part of the duty of Israelites to their king and country involved service in the army when necessary and regular duty on the corvee labor crews. This latter used forced labor as a form of taxation. This list, however, concerned the organization of the former along militia lines that were not organized strictly by tribe. In the transition to a standing army, the militia system called upon each division to serve one month of "active" duty, thereby forming a rotating standing army in addition to the professional full-time troops and the mercenaries.

27:24. wrath on Israel. For information concerning this see comments on 2 Samuel 24.

27:25-34
Administration

27:25-31. king's property. These stewards had oversight of the estate and assets of the king. Royal holdings existed throughout the land be-

cause property that had no heirs reverted to the crown. Likewise, those who had become debtors to the king for one reason or another worked the land for the king. Besides real property and its produce the king also owned flocks and herds that were grazed throughout the land.

28:1-21
Charge to Solomon to Build the Temple

28:1 royal administration in the ancient Near East. The categories listed in this verse include representatives of each tribe (a vestige of the twelve-tribe system that preceded the monarchy), all officers of the military (both king's bodyguard and national army), royal stewards, administration of the palace (scribes, eunuchs, advisers, "cabinet" officials) and David's special forces (an elite group of operatives that did not necessarily function within an organized military structure). No reference is made to priests or Levites, but perhaps their presence is assumed (v. 21). Bureaucratic structures are evident in the ancient Near East as early as the fourth millennium B.C. Magistrates, bailiffs, judges, heralds and inspectors all were part of urban and village administration. But the list in this passage is the administration of the king and state—royal administration, not social administration. One could compare and contrast the Assyrian structure a few centuries later that featured three major officials under the king, roughly equivalent to American secretary of state, president's chief of staff and chairman of the joint chiefs of staff. A second layer would have included much of the palace administration.

28:2. footstool symbolism. The ark was a wooden box, open at the top, approximately three to four feet in length and over two feet in both width and height (based on eighteen inches per cubit). A golden cover, decorated with two winged cherubim, sealed the ark, securing the tablets of the law within it. Its primary function was to store the tablets and to serve as a "footstool" for God's throne. In Egypt it was common for important documents that were confirmed by oath (e.g., international treaties) to be deposited beneath the feet of the deity. The Book of the Dead even speaks of a formula written on a metal brick by the hand of the god being deposited beneath the feet of the god. Therefore the footstool/receptacle combination follows known Egyptian practice. In Egyptian festivals the images of the gods were often carried in procession on portable barques. Paintings portray these as boxes about the size of the ark carried on poles and decorated with or flanked by guardian creatures. A similar-sized chest with rings (for carrying with poles) was found in Tutankhamun's tomb.

28:11. temple architecture. Temples are typically classified by archaeologists on the basis of the arrangement of the chambers through which one gains access to the inner recesses and by the orientation of the main chamber where the presence of the god is represented. "Direct axis" architecture allowed one to walk in a straight line from the altar to the inner shrine (cella). "Bent axis" required a ninety-degree turn between the altar and the place where the image stood. The door through which one entered the rectangular cella in the direct access arrangement could either be on the short wall ("long room") or the long wall ("broad room"). Solomon's temple was of the "direct axis" style, but it was neither long room nor broad room because the holy of holies (cella) was square, not rectangular. Solomon's temple also featured an antechamber between the altar and the cella as well as a portico, courtyard and many siderooms. These were also common elements in ancient Near Eastern temple architecture. A ninth-century temple at Tell Tayanat in Syria features the exact structure of a portico with two free-standing pillars, a long antechamber and a small cella all on a direct axis, thirty-eight feet by eighty-three feet (Solomon's was thirty by ninety).

28:15-17. temple accessories. Archaeologists have unearthed many examples of temple accessories in excavations throughout the ancient Near East including a variety of braziers, shovels and containers. For more information on specific implements see comments on 2 Chronicles 4.

28:18. cherubim as chariot. This verse has the only explicit connection between the cherubim and a chariot motif. In Ezekiel 1 and 10, creatures that are identified with cherubim accompany Yahweh's mobile throne, but that is never called a chariot. Biblical descriptions as well as archaeological discoveries (including some fine ivory pieces from Nimrud in Mesopotamia, Arslan Tash in Syria and Samaria in Israel) suggest the cherubim are composite creatures (having features of a number of different creatures, like the Egyptian sphinx), often four-legged animal bodies with wings. The cherubim appear in ancient art with some regularity, flanking the thrones of kings and deities, for instance on the side of the throne picture on Ahiram's sarcophagus.

29:1-9

Donations Toward the Temple

29:2. onyx. Sometimes translated "carnelian" or even "lapis lazuli," the precise identification of this stone is unknown.

29:2. turquoise. Another possibility here is "antimony," and some believe it represents the mortar that was used to set mosaic patterns (see next entry).

29:2. stones of various colors. The reference to stones of various colors suggests the use of mosaics. In the classical world mosaics were very popular. The stone was not artificially colored, but rather stones of different shades were imported from wherever they could be found to give color to the mosaic. The earliest mosaic floors were made from colored pebbles laid out in geometric designs. Only later did they begin cutting the stone into cubes (tessellation) and forming them into pictures. No examples of mosaics in the Near East have been found earlier than the eighth century B.C. (Gordion in Asia Minor), though the art of inlay was known as early as the third millennium (as in the royal standard of Ur).

29:2. marble. Some translations call this alabaster. Marble had to be imported from Greece and is not evident in the ancient world until its introduction into Phoenicia in the Persian period. Marble capitals (the decorative tops of pillars) are not attested archaeologically in the Near East until the first or second centuries A.D., though pillars of the material referred to in this verse are mentioned in Esther 1:6, where the same material is used in an inlaid floor. Oriental alabaster was a calcium carbonate-like marble, unlike European alabaster, which is gypsum. It was used for fine vessels throughout the region during the biblical period, as well as for columns in architecture. In Sennacherib's "palace without rival" mostly white limestone was used, though he had some access to alabaster.

29:4. amount of precious metals. This comes out to over one hundred tons of gold and over 250 tons of silver. In Egypt the largest known donation of gold and silver made by a pharaoh to the gods is the two hundred tons by Shishak (who got lots of it from Jerusalem). In Assyrian inscriptions, kings such as Tiglath-Pileser III, Sargon II and Shalmaneser III rarely list the specific amount of gold taken in tribute or plunder, and when they do it is usually between ten and fifty talents. More comparable is the amount of 9,000 talents of gold and 40,000 talents of silver Alexander the Great is said to have taken from the Persian capital, Susa.

29:4. Ophir. Gold from Ophir is mentioned in an eighth-century inscription from Tell Qasile. The precise location of the site is unknown. The fact that it was shipped in at Ezion Geber suggests an Arabian location, though sites in India and East Africa have been considered.

29:7. amount of leaders' gifts. Five thousand talents of gold is nearly 200 tons and the amount of silver is twice that. Another amount of gold is measured in darics—the coined money of the Persian empire. Clearly the author of Chronicles has converted this amount to his own contemporary units. A daric is a gold coin that probably got its name from its originator, the Persian king, Darius the Great, toward the end of the sixth century B.C. This was the first coining of money in the Near East (though the Greek world had been coining money for over a century). The daric bore the image of an archer and weighed about .3 ounces. Ten thousand darics would therefore equal about one hundred eighty-five pounds (about two and a half talents). Perhaps the Chronicler did not just include this with the other gold talents because that part of the donation was given in ingots that had already been sized for merchant transactions. Even before money was being coined, there was limited use of standardized weight pieces either in ingot currency (no decoration or consistent shape), or ring money (in various ring shapes) as early as the second millennium.

29:10-30
Solomon's Coronation

29:21. coronation sacrifice. Burnt offerings and fellowship offerings are two of the most general types of sacrifices. The former often accompanied petition, while the latter served as an opportunity for festive celebration and a communal meal before the Lord. Typical use of this offering in a national context was for ratification of treaties or covenant agreements. Here, the sacrifices were being offered to make petition for God's blessing and in preparation for a feast that would create an alliance between Solomon and those in attendance.

29:29. sources in Chronicles. The Chronicler cites many different sources that he used in the compilation of his work. Most of these have not survived, though the canonical books of Samuel and Kings would have been among them. The sources mentioned here are records of three famous prophets of the period of David, though we do not know whether they are memoirs, anthologies of prophecies or some other type of document. There is no extant literature from the ancient world that is attributed to a court prophet, except those found in the Bible, so there is little precedent for identifying the nature of these works.

2 CHRONICLES

1:1-17
God's Blessings on Solomon

1:3. high place at Gibeon. Located about four miles northwest of Jerusalem, Gibeon (el-Jib) lies in the Benjaminite hill country with several nearby springs and an elaborate tunneled water system making it an important local settlement. The cultic site or high place where Solomon made his huge offering of one thousand sacrifices (1 Kings 3:4) may have actually been on a promontory called Nebi Samwil, about a mile south of Gibeon. The city's prominence is also found in its inclusion in Shishak's list of cities during his Palestine campaign. The use of a high place is not condemned by the biblical writer prior to the construction of the Jerusalem temple and the implementation of "Jeroboam's sin" (see comments on 1 Sam 10:8; 1 Kings 12:28-31).

1:3. Tent of Meeting. See the comments on Exodus 27:21 and 33:7-10 on the construction and use of this sacred installation during the wilderness period. The fact that it has been separated from the ark is only found in this narrative.

1:4. Kiriath Jearim. This village had served as the storage place for the ark of the covenant after its return from the Philistines (1 Sam 7:1-2). The town has been identified with Tell el-Achar, nine miles west-northwest of Jerusalem, but this is unsubstantiated by archaeological finds or extrabiblical references. Its association with Mahaneh Dan in Judges 18:12 puts it in that general area (see the comment on Judg 13:25). This location places it only six miles from Gibeon.

1:5. bronze altar. See Exodus 38:30 and 39:39

for the construction of this altar, which was supposed to stand in front of the tent of meeting (see also 2 Kings 16:14). The presence of the tent of meeting and the bronze altar at Gibeon while the ark was moved to Jerusalem suggests two different, major religious centers prior to the construction of the Jerusalem temple.

1:5. assembly inquiry. Inquiry usually refers to posing an oracular question to the deity, but no question is stated or implied here. A persuasive variant reading understands the search ("inquiry") to be for the altar rather than for an oracle from the Lord. This would make sense prior to the temple-building activities in the following chapters. With the anticipated construction of a new sanctuary, it is important to collect the relics that had been associated with the traditional shrine. Significant holiness would be attached to this altar that had been used by Aaron himself several centuries earlier. If there is an oracle being sought here, it likely concerns the desire to build a temple. Such work was not begun without specific divine approval (see comment on 2:1).

1:6. one thousand burnt offerings. In its magnitude, this can be compared to the mass sacrifices in Exodus 24:5-8 and 1 Kings 8:5. Such extravagance generally marks major covenantal events or the initiation of a new relationship with Yahweh. The huge piles of offerings on tables depicted in Egyptian tomb paintings may parallel, at least in terms of quantity, the devotion and power exemplified in Solomon's offerings at Gibeon.

1:7-12. incubation dreams. Though the passage in Chronicles does not mention a dream, 1 Kings 3 provides that detail. It was common practice for individuals or groups to travel to shrines, make offerings and then sleep before the altar in the hope of obtaining a dream message from the god of that place (see the comments on Gen 28:13-15 and 1 Sam 3:3). The setting therefore was extremely important to incubate a dream theophany (as in the dream of the Ugaritic hero-king Keret). In the vision the person is aroused by the god's appearance and a call to be alert to their pronouncement. Among the many examples from ancient Near Eastern literature, the Assyrian king Ashurbanipal describes a dream in which Ishtar appeared to him, and the Neo-Babylonian king Nabonidus records several dreams in which Marduk or Sin stood before him in all of their glory.

1:7. God's offer. In auditory message dreams such as this (see comment on 1 Sam 3:4-10), it is not unusual at all for conversation to take

place between the deity and the king. The dream functions to validate either the kingship or a proposed undertaking of the king.

1:8. Solomon's acknowledgment of God's patronage. Similar phrasing can be found throughout the ancient Near East as kings recognize the deity who has established them. The Hittite king, Muwattalli II, for instance, cites his own unworthiness in comparison to his father's status and accomplishments. He then recognizes the deity as having raised him up and established him on the throne.

1:12. granting of wisdom. Kings of the ancient Near East were supposed to be wise, and it was not unusual for them to credit deity for bestowing wisdom on them. The Assyrian king Sargon was proclaimed to be the wisest ruler in the world thanks to the gods Ea and Belet-ili. The god Asshur assures Sennacherib in a dream that his wisdom had surpassed the wisdom of the experts. Ashurbanipal boasts not only of his great learning and wisdom, but of his technical knowledge and his ability to debate the learned. He credits Shamash and Adad for granting him his wealth of wisdom.

1:14. Solomon's chariots and horses. The accumulation of such a large force of chariots indicates his intention to emulate the grand military displays of his neighbors and rivals. For conflicts in open country and on broad plains, the chariot, accompanied by detachments of infantry and cavalry, was both a shock weapon and a mobile platform for archers. The huge numbers of chariots recorded in the Assyrian annals at the Battle of Qarqar (853 B.C., see comment on 22:1) indicate just how important commanders considered them in their military planning. Solomon's contingent of chariots is not as large as the two thousand that Ahab contributed to the western alliance at that battle. In the thirteenth century the Hittites and their allies had amassed twenty-five hundred chariots to confront Rameses II at the Battle of Qadesh.

1:14. Solomon's stables. The wide distribution of stable facilities uncovered by archaeologists throughout Israel (Megiddo, Tell el-Hesi, Lachish, Beersheba, Hazor) suggests extensive use of chariot corps in the armies of Israel and Judah. The common architectural style found in most of these stables (long hall, divided lengthwise into three aisles by pillars, and a single door) indicates both attention to function and a common building program. They featured low stone pillars with holes for tethering, and large, shallow stone mangers (similar to those depicted on Assyrian monuments). Large installations would have been necessary to house and exercise these trained stallions. The Megiddo stables (those found generally dated to Ahab's time) could have housed up to 480 horses. When other stable facilities found by archaeologists are included, nearly 800 stalls can be identified.

1:15. Solomon's gold. For statistics concerning the gold of David and Solomon, see the comments on 1 Chronicles 22:14.

1:16-17. trade with Egypt. Solomon's role seems to have been as a "middleman" between Egypt and Anatolia in the horse and chariot trade. The Phoenicians had established most of the commercial links and provided the ships to carry goods throughout the Mediterranean. With them as his trading partners and Solomon's strategic location on the land link between Africa and Asia (see his horse farms in 2 Chron 8:3-4), it would be a natural expectation that Israel would tap the financial markets during a period of relative peace. As early as the Amarna period fine horses were being imported from Egypt, and the Hittites also imported from Egypt. Both Assyrian and Hittite sources differentiate between the large horses available in Egypt (Nubian horses) and their own smaller horses.

1:16. Kue. Located in the lowlands of southeastern Turkey in what is known in classical sources as Cilicia, Kue emerged from the destruction of the Hittite empire in 1200 B.C. to become a major trading center. In addition to its mention as one of Solomon's trading partners, Kue is found in the Assyrian annals as one of the participating states at the Battle of Qarqar (853 B.C.) and in the Karatepe inscription of Azitawada (late eighth century B.C.).

1:17. cost of chariots and horses. The cost of chariots found in inscriptional material ranges from sixty to one hundred shekels per chariot. The fact that Solomon is paying many times that price suggests that these are not ordinary chariots but ornamental chariots used in display and procession contexts. These are widely attested in both Egypt and Mesopotamia. The luxury transportation of the day, these were typically gilded with all variety of gold, lapis lazuli and precious stones. The Amarna letters refer to a chariot of the Mitannian king that was gilded with over three hundred shekels of gold. The price for the horses is also high but not outrageous for a good quality animal. In second-millennium Hittite sources a chariot horse could be bought for twenty shekels. But there are examples in Syria and Babylon from early in the second millennium to the middle of the first millennium where two to three hundred shekels were paid.

1:17. export trade with Hittites and Ara-

means. For them to receive horses and chariots by any overland route, the Hittites (see comment on 2 Kings 7:6) and Arameans would have had to deal with Solomon and his Phoenician trading partners. During the eleventh and tenth centuries B.C., the Aramean tribes had taken advantage of the weakness of Assyria and Babylonia to establish small states, such as that at Damascus (see the comments on 1 Kings 11:23-25). Realizing that the Assyrians were still capable of reemerging as a major force (as they were to do in the ninth century), it would have been good policy for both Cilicia and Aram to continue to train and equip strong armies, even in the face of inflated prices.

2:1—4:22
Solomon Builds the Temple

2:1. temple building in the ancient world. Early in the second millennium, Gudea, ruler of Lagash, receives instructions through incubation dreams that he is to build a temple for the goddess Ningirsu. The text reports his gathering of materials (wood, stone, gold and silver) and assembling a work force. At the completion of the work there is a dedication feast lasting seven days. As a result of his labor, Gudea is promised long life and a successful reign. Similar details are given over a millennium later when Esarhaddon is instructed to rebuild the famous Esagila temple in Babylon. Another interesting account of temple building is found in the Ugaritic epic in which the god Baal is building a house for himself. Again the elements of gathering appropriate materials, amassing a work force and celebration upon completion are all present.

2:2. conscript labor. The corvee for public works projects like the construction of the temple would be conscripted on the basis of a census. Considering the huge number of projects undertaken during Solomon's reign, it seems likely that native Israelites as well as resident aliens would have served in the corvee. Indications of this are found in Jeroboam's position as chief of the corvee in the Joseph tribes (1 Kings 11:28) and the stoning by the northern tribes of another corvee officer, Adoniram (1 Kings 12:3-4). The use of forced labor was already widespread in Syria in the second half of the second millennium. The excesses associated with "forced labor" are also used as one of the charges against the Neo-Babylonian king Nabonidus in the Cyrus Cylinder.

2:2. carriers. As with any labor group, there would have been a division of labor between the skilled and the unskilled. Presumably those delegated to the task of "carrying" would have been unskilled "strong backs," who would have hauled stone, timber and building materials and tools. Such heavy labor generally fell to prisoners of war or slaves in Mesopotamian documents. In this case, where resident aliens were involved, they may have served in this capacity, but that would depend on individual skills or background.

2:2. stonecutters. The parallel passage in 1 Kings 5:15-18 indicates the need for quarriers who wrenched the stone from the cliffs as well as more highly trained Phoenician Gebalites (from Byblos) who dressed the stone for use in the construction of the temple. The work at the quarry was accomplished by cutting trenches (about two feet wide all around) to isolate the stone that was to be used. Then wooden wedges were driven in at the bottom and drenched with water. The resulting expansion of the wood freed the bottom of the stone. Though this took no great skill on the part of the laborers, a supervisor with training would be needed to determine where the trenches should be cut so as to procure the best pieces of stone. The next stage was rough shaping. After this the true masons took over as they dressed the stone surfaces and gave it the proportions needed. The work was done with such precision that no mortar was needed. The Egyptian "satire on the trades" describes the cramped back and thighs of the stonecutter who destroys his arms fashioning "costly stones" for buildings. The work of stonecutters is depicted on some of the wall panels decorating Sennacherib's palace in Nineveh.

2:2. size of work force. The total work force is 153,600 (vv. 17-18), divided into three groups: carriers, stonecutters and officers. Numbers such as these may reflect approximate totals of all those who were recruited to work on the temple over the years it took to build, rather than the number working at any given time. Assyrian and Babylonian kings typically got their work force through their military campaigns. In fact, it was the need for a work force that sometimes instigated military activity. In one report, Ashurnasirpal gathered nearly fifty thousand to work on the city of Kalhu.

2:3-16. royal correspondence. There are many examples of royal correspondence from the ancient Near East, which contain requests for building supplies (such as the cedars of Lebanon), luxury items and diplomatic exchanges. The letter carried by the eleventh-century Egyptian priest Wenamon contained a request for cedar logs and made mention of the long-standing, multigenerational relationship between the pharaoh and the kings of the Phoenician coast. The kings of Mari regularly wrote to their vassals and allies, exchanging news and describing the arrival of manufactured goods, animals and raw materials that they had requested or purchased. In this context, Solomon's exchange of letters with Hiram, although not structured in the formal style typical of extrabiblical correspondence, provides a sense of business as usual.

2:4. burning incense. See the comment on Exodus 30:7-8 for the use of incense in the tent of meeting and evidence of its use elsewhere in the ancient Near East. The burning of incense was a regular part of worship of the gods throughout the ancient Near East, so this is a necessity that would be familiar to Hiram.

2:4. consecrated bread. See the comment on Leviticus 24:5-9 on the preparation and weekly presentation of the "show bread." This sacrifice symbolized both God's presence as well as the promise of fertility found in the covenant. It was common practice in the ancient Near East to set food before the gods, though Israelite practice in this regard was quite different from that of her neighbors (see comment on Lev 1:1-2).

2:4. Sabbaths, New Moons, feasts. See the comments on Numbers 28 and 29, which discuss Israel's religious calendar. Though the recognition of Sabbaths is so far unique to Israel, observances at the New Moons and annual festivals would have been familiar obligations to Hiram and the Phoenicians.

2:5. basis for the claim of Yahweh's superiority. Similar claims of superiority for their patron gods can be found in the Assyrian annals for Ashur and the *Enuma Elish* creation story for Babylon's god Marduk. Such would be the expected rhetoric for any nation in internal documents. When one nation claims superiority of its god(s) over the god(s) of another nation, it is usually based on military supremacy or acts of power. Such claims have greatest credibility when they are found in the mouths of those who have worshiped the other god(s) now being considered inferior. Such is the case in Rahab's statement (based on military supremacy and acts of power; Josh 2:11) and Naaman's exclamation (based on healing act; 2 Kings 5:15).

2:7. imported craftsmen. When Assyrians or Babylonians went on campaigns intended to round up a labor force, a prime objective was to procure skilled craftsmen (see the list of those exiled in 2 Kings 24:14, 16). On the one hand the sheer demand often required more craftsman than were available locally. Additionally, however, some peoples had further developed certain technologies because of the natural resources that were available to them. Craft guilds often were made up of families that had developed their own techniques and trade secrets that would be practiced and passed on from generation to generation. Such skills were desirable, and merchant trade could establish a reputation that would put such craftsmen in high demand.

2:7. blue and crimson yarn. These were the most exotic and desirable dyes that were available in the ancient world and were very expensive. They had been used in decorating the tabernacle and in embroidering the priestly vestments. The "blue cloth" has more recently been interpreted as a blue/purple or violet color. The dye for this color was one of the major imports of Phoenicia where it was extracted from the murex snail (*murex trunculus*) which inhabited shallow coastal waters of the Mediterranean. An ancient refinery has also been found at Dor along the northern coast of Israel. One chemist estimated that a quarter of a million snails would be needed to produce one ounce of pure dye. This dye was used in the manufacture of the most sacred objects.

2:8. types of lumber. Essentially cedar and cypress trees were to be used for the beams and other structural supports. This usage follows the pattern set by other ancient Near Eastern kings like Nebuchadnezzar of Babylon for their monumental buildings. Almug in 1 Kings 10:11-12 is red sandalwood imported from Ophir (native to India and Ceylon) and is a luxury hardwood used for furniture since it can be highly polished. The algum of Chronicles may be Grecian juniper, a tall coniferlike fir used for timber. Typically they used hardwoods that polished to a fine finish with nice grain or fragrant odor. A number of these woods are also impervious to bugs or mildew. Iron-headed axes and two-handed copper pullsaws were among the principal tools used to prepare the timber. Egyptian tombs and tomb paintings provide much information concerning these and other tools.

2:10. payment of woodsmen. While the wages to be paid to the Phoenician woodsmen are set in an agreement for the totality of the project, it may be assumed that each worker received a daily wage/ration for his labor. These men, while they might have belonged to a guild of woodsmen, may have also included ḫupshu laborers (mentioned in Amarna, Nuzi and Assyrian texts), who depended for their livelihood on what they could earn each day. The 125,000 bushels each of wheat and barley and the 120,000 gallons each of wine and oil would have served as rations for six to eight thousand workers for three years.

2:14. engraving. Engraving could be done on bone, ivory, shells, stone, gems, wood and metal of various sorts. The art of engraving included the shaping and inscribing of precious and semiprecious stones as seals and insignia. These cylinder seals and stamp seals were used throughout the ancient Near East as personal identification and the means of sealing official documents and contracts with the names of the participants. In the temple much of the furniture as well as the paneling required engraving work.

2:16. wood delivered by raft. The trade in cedar logs from Lebanon is well attested in Egyptian (Old Kingdom through the eighth century) and Assyrian sources. For a time Tiglath-Pileser III ordered the trade stopped between the Phoenicians and their Egyptian and Philistine trading partners, fearing the construction of a fleet or a growth in wealth sufficient to make them dangerous. Transport of the logs along the Palestinian coast south would have involved either tying them together into rafts, which required staying very close to shore for fear of storms breaking them up, or loading them on ships. Assyrian reliefs show Phoenician ships both loaded with logs and towing them. Reliefs at Sargon's palace show cedar-log rafts being floated down the river for use in his building projects, a process that was used as early as 2000 B.C. in Gudea's temple project. Joppa was the closest port to Jerusalem in antiquity and was the natural debarkation point for the logs. From Tyre to Joppa was nearly one hundred miles; the inland trek from Joppa to Jerusalem was about thirty-five miles.

2:17-18. aliens as conscript labor. See the comment on 2:2 and 2:7 on the use and acquisition of conscript labor.

3:1. Mount Moriah. This identification is intended to associate the site of the temple with the sacrifice of Isaac (see the comment on Gen 22:2) even if it is in name only.

3:1. threshing floor of Araunah. See the comments on 2 Samuel 24:18-25 for David's purchase of this facility. The threshing floor, like the city gate, served as a legally significant spot where grain was distributed, disputes settled (see 1 Kings 22:10), and where God's manifestation might occur (see Judg 6:36-40). A threshing floor would also be outside the walls of the city and elevated to take advantage of the winds to blow away the chaff. The choice of a temple site in the ancient world was an important matter that often absorbed a good deal of time and energy. It was believed that the deity was the one who would designate the spot. No such process is indicated here. Instead a site with already long-established sacred traditions serves the purpose. There are no oracles asked or any designation of location offered through divine messages.

3:2. chronology. The building begins early in Solomon's reign in the mid-960s. The second day of the second month is in the spring when the rainy season and the early festivals are past. The first day of the month would probably have been the New Moon festival, so the second day begins the work.

3:3-4. dimensions. The text in Chronicles describing the physical dimensions of the temple is incomplete, and the measurements given are different from those found in 1 Kings 6:2 (sixty cubits long by twenty cubits wide by thirty cubits high). Chronicles omits the height for the main structure but lists twenty cubits for the height of the portico in verse 4. This measurement may then be based on simply the foundations. There is also some variation in terminology, but that may be explained by the changes in language usage over time. The cubit "of the old standard" is slightly shorter than the common standard in Deuteronomy 3:11. Unlike Mesopotamian descriptions of temples that intend to glorify the king who built the temple, the biblical text gives information sufficient for the reader to visualize (if not precisely reconstruct) the building.

3:4. portico. The portico was the outermost section of the three parts of the Jerusalem temple. This would be consistent with the pattern found in the temple at Tainat and elsewhere in Syria and Phoenicia. It seems to be an "attachment" rather than an integral part of the temple complex and, unlike the two inner chambers, has no doorway. In construction it most resembles the great court of the palace (see 1 Kings 7:12). While the main inner chamber and the holy of holies effectively comprise the "house of Yahweh," the portico matches traditional Near Eastern architecture as the courtyard attached to major dwelling places.

3:5. palm tree and chain designs. The use of a palm tree motif in monumental construction in the ancient Near East also appears most graphically in the wall paintings of the palace of Mari during the reign of Zimri-Lim (eighteenth century). The palm symbolizes fecundity and is the source of the date, a major asset to the economy and food supply of the entire area. The chain design is expanded in the Chronicles version, while it only adorns the capitals of the bronze pillars in 1 Kings 7:17. In Egyptian temples, the palm and lotus pillars represent the conceptualization of the temple as a microcosm of the earth that is the domain of the deity.

3:6. gold of Parvaim. While Parvaim is most likely a place name, its location is unknown. Suggestions have identified it with Yemen and northeast Arabia, but there is no site associated with the term. Its relation to gold may be based on a standard of purity, either associated with etymological links to *parim*, "young bulls," or *para*, a fruit-bearing tree. In both cases the color of the blood or fruit may have given rise to styling this gold as particularly high grade.

3:7. carved cherubim. The description of the wall carvings parallels 1 Kings 6:29. These winged beings, symbolic of God's presence, were also embroidered into the curtains as well as the veil covering the Holy of Holies in the tabernacle (Ex 26:1). An inscription of Agum-kakrime in the second half of the second millennium refers to his contributions and building of a shrine for the gods Marduk and Sarpanitum. The doors to this shrine are decorated with pictures of a horned serpent, a bison, a dog, a scorpion man and several demons, including the protective laḥmu-demons. The contemporary temple at 'Ain Dara in Syria also featured many carvings of sphinxes and lions.

3:8. six hundred talents of gold. For the relatively small chamber of the Holy of Holies alone to be inlaid with six hundred talents (39,600 pounds) of gold would have been quite extravagant. It seems more likely that this amount would have been applied as thinly beaten sheets to the decoration of the entire inner walls of the temple. For comparisons concerning amounts of gold see comments on 1 Chronicles 22:14.

3:9. gold nails, fifty shekels. Contrary to the NIV rendering, this difficult text probably conveys that fifty shekels worth of gold was used to plate iron nails used to attach the gold inlay to the walls. Nails weighing fifty shekels (14.75 ounces) would be too heavy, while fifty shekels weight of gold nails would not be enough to do the job.

3:10-13. sculptured cherubim. These freestanding figures made of olive wood served as guardians or wardens of the Holy of Holies (compare 1 Kings 6:23-28), much as they do the Garden of Eden (Gen 3:24). The architecture of ancient Near Eastern temples evoked images of the Garden (as a residence or audience hall of deity) in several particulars. Composite winged creatures positioned by pillars stylized to look like trees (usually date palms) were common especially in Syria-Palestine and the upper Euphrates region. Like those whose wings cover the ark of the covenant within the Holy of Holies, these gold inlaid cherubim also function as the symbol of God's presence and a sort of throne. Ancient Near Eastern iconography frequently pictures the thrones of kings and deities flanked by composite winged creatures. The Canaanite equivalent for the storm god Baal was the figure of a bull upon which he is often depicted as standing (compare Ps 18:10 for Yahweh "riding" the cherubim). For more information see comment on Exodus 25:18-20.

3:14. curtain. According to the account in 1 Kings 6:31-32, the two sections of Solomon's temple were divided by a wooden door, which was inlaid with gold and decorated with carvings of cherubim, palm trees and flowers. The Chronicler describes also how the curtain served as a second barrier. In New Testament times the temple also had both doors and a curtain. Separating the holy precincts from the secular world and its impurity was required in the architectural design of ancient temples.

3:15-17. free-standing pillars. For more information see comments on 1 Kings 7:15-22. Their placement may be compared to the sacred architecture of the shrines at Shechem, Hazor and Tyre.

3:16. chains with pomegranates. Pomegranates are a symbol of fertility both in the ancient Near East and in the promises of the covenant (Deut 8:8). Ancient reliefs show a pomegranate-topped scepter used by kings and priests bringing sacrifices. A recently recovered ivory pomegranate (probably the top of just such a scepter) contains the Hebrew inscription "belonging to the temple of the Lord," suggesting its use by priests.

4:1. bronze altar. The use of bronze for sculptured items appears to have begun during the monarchy period. This sacrificial platform was a square, thirty feet to a side, with smaller levels forming steps to its altar. Like other altars, this one functioned symbolically as "God's table," upon which sacrifices were placed in acknowledgment of Yahweh's gifts of fertility (see 1 Kings 8:64 and 2 Kings 16:14). The huge size of this platform and altar most likely precludes it being cast as a single object. Instead it was probably constructed of wood and overlaid with bronze (compare the smaller altar described in 2 Chron 6:13).

4:6. basins. Archaeologists have found a bronze stand that would have held just such a basin dating from the twelfth century B.C. The

stand had wheels and was decorated with winged composite creatures (see 1 Kings 7:29). **4:2-5. the "Sea."** The "molten sea" (see 1 Kings 7:23-26) has parallels in Assyrian reliefs from the time of Sargon II (eighth century B.C.). There two massive cauldrons are portrayed, resting on the forelegs of bulls at the entrance to the Musasir temple. Its practical function was, like the laver in the tabernacle (Ex 30:18-21) and the ten basins (v. 6), for ablutions by the priests. Additionally, some have attributed to it a symbolic value. With its twelve bulls representing the twelve tribes and its monumental size (forty-five feet in circumference), it may have evoked images of Yahweh's role as Creator God and Lord over the chaotic waters of the earth. In this way, Yahweh eclipses the Canaanite deities Yamm and Baal and the Babylonian god Marduk, who represent sea and storm (see Ps 29:10; 104:1-9; Is 51:9-10).

4:7. lampstands. The ten golden lampstands (see 1 Kings 7:49) are a significant difference from the single lampstand in the tabernacle (Ex 25:31-38). They were probably cylindrical in shape, made of wood and covered with gold leaf. Placed on either side of the temple's interior, their light and golden reflection magnified the sense of splendor and glory inherent in Solomon's temple and God's presence (see Jer 52:19; 2 Chron 13:11; 29:7 for additional references to these "specified" objects). Along with the tables and incense altars or braziers, these furnishings provided the sense of this place being the "house of Yahweh."

4:8. tables. For information on the function of the tables and the use of the bread see comment on Leviticus 24:5-9.

4:8. sprinkling bowls. The golden bowls are also mentioned in 1 Kings 7:50, but the Chronicler supplies the figure of one hundred for them. Their exact function is unclear, but they may have been used to dip water from the basins (v. 6) or to collect blood from sacrifices (see Ex 24:6, 8; 27:3).

4:9-10. layout of the courts. This Phoenician-style, tripartite plan is also found in the temple at 'Ain Dara in northwest Syria. In this way the sacred precincts will be noted as restricted to priestly function and clearly divided from that portion of the temple complex that may have adjoined more secular buildings.

4:11. pots, shovels, sprinkling bowls. Completing the list of cultic objects fabricated by Hiram are those associated with sacrificial offering and incense. Incense shovels have been discovered in excavations at Tel Dan (see Lev

16:12-13). The pots were used to store ashes from the incense altar, and the bowls held blood from the sacrifices (Ex 38:3; Num 4:14). All of these dedicatory objects are designed to properly deal with the remains of sacrificial offerings. The disposal of ashes and the proper collection and use of blood were necessary to insure the purity of the altar and the temple.

4:16. meat forks. Archaeologists have discovered a number of large forks and these may be the items described by the Chronicler (see their inclusion in the lists in Ex 27:3 and Num 4:14). The priestly portion of the sacrifice was prescribed in Leviticus 7:28-36 to be the right thigh and the breast. However, in the story of the premonarchic shrine at Shiloh an instance is found of priests drawing sacrificial meat out of a common, boiling pot (see the comment on 1 Sam 2:13).

4:17. geography. Zarethan is located "in the plain of the Jordan," east of the river and halfway between the Dead Sea and the Sea of Galilee in Joshua 3:16 and 1 Kings 4:12. The exact site is not yet determined, although Tell es-Sa'idiyeh and Tell el-Meqberah are among the suggested locations. Succoth is located at Tell Deir Allah about a mile north of the Jabbok River and about three miles east of the Jordan River. Remains from this period have been found on the site. The area on the top of the tell is comparable to one football field, about one and a quarter acres. It was a small settlement that was involved in a bronze smelting industry.

4:21. floral work. A much more graphic description of the floral design on the lampstands (almond blossoms) can be found in Exodus 25:31-40 and 37:17-24. A similar example of a blossom motif has been found on a lampstand from Megiddo and on miniature pillars found at Arslan Tash. The lotus pattern is also common in Canaanite and Egyptian decor. The sense of constant fertility, here a reminder of the covenant, might be the purpose for this design.

4:21. lamps and tongs. The list provided by the Chronicler of golden sacred utensils includes the lamps attached to the multistemmed lampstands and the tongs used to carry coals to and from these lamps and the incense altars (see 1 Kings 7:49; Is 6:6). These tongs may have also been used to remove extinguished wicks, which would be relit and replaced within the lamp. The quality of the "fine" or "pure" gold used to plate even utilitarian objects like tongs or "snuffers" is a testament to their importance in cultic ritual.

4:22. wick trimmers. Wick trimmers would

have been employed to prevent the wicks, floating in the cups containing oil on the lampstands (Ex 27:20), from sputtering or refusing to ignite (see Is 42:3). It would have been a regular task of the priests to tend the lamps (Ex 30:7), and they may have employed a trimmer to insure that there was no interruption of ritual or an extinguishing of the light (Is 42:3; 43:17). Since this is an unusual Hebrew term, some scholars translate the word as "musical instruments," based on Mesopotamian texts and Assyrian reliefs depicting the use of music accompanying temple ritual and the "divine meal."

4:22. ladles and censers. The word used here and in 1 Kings 7:50 for censers is one of two types of fire pans—in this case one with a long handle (see Lev 10:1; Num 16:6). Incense and a hot coal would be placed on the implement and carried about to censer a room or altar. The Qumran texts mention such a firepan used to carry fire into the temple. New Kingdom Egyptian drawings depict the use of handled censers as part of a ritual to ward off evil or being carried in procession. Ladles were used to dispense oil into the lamps or carry incense to the altars or censers (1 Kings 7:50).

5:1—7:22
Solomon's Dedication of the Temple

5:3. festival of the seventh month. The Chronicler mentions only the number of the month, not its name, Ethanim. See the comment on this autumn month in 1 Kings 8:2. One of the common systems of calendars simply used numbers rather than names to designate the months. The festival referred to is the harvest festival of Booths (Succoth).

5:12. linen clothing. Although linen garments were generally reserved for the use of priests (Lev 6:10; 16:4), on this special occasion, the Levites and musicians are also clothed in linen. The linen for the clothing worn by the priests was imported from Egypt where it was also distinctively used for priests' garments. Angels, too, are said to be dressed in linen.

5:12. musical instruments. Cymbals, harps, lyres and trumpets are all typical musical instruments of the time and are attested in ancient Near Eastern texts, reliefs and paintings as early as the third millennium B.C. There is still some disagreement among authorities as to which of the Hebrew words in this passage ought to be translated "harp" and which one as "lyre." The one the NIV translates "lyre" is a ten-stringed instrument, while the one translated "harp" is thought to have had fewer strings. Both are hand-held with frames made of wood. Cymbals are made of bronze and are in the percussion group, so the only remaining question concerns their size. The trumpets are not the ram's-horn trumpets that are referred to in other contexts. Tubular flared trumpets were used in this period in military as well as ritual contexts. This is depicted on Egyptian reliefs as well as evidenced by actual instruments found, for example, in the tomb of King Tut (a silver trumpet nearly two feet long).

6:12-13. prayer posture. Solomon's posture in verse 12 and in 1 Kings 8:22 is initially standing with his arms upraised and palms opened upward as he addresses the assembly and prays a dedicatory prayer for the temple. It is implied from 1 Kings 8:54 that Solomon at some point had knelt down, and that detail is supplied in 2 Chronicles 6:13. The incantation prayers of Mesopotamian sources, such as that to Ishtar, imply prostration of the supplicant as well as a ritual of raising the hands. Hittite sources suggest similar postures and gestures. Royal prayers are not uncommon, though it is difficult to discern whether they are precomposed or spontaneous.

6:22. role of oaths in judicial process. See the comments on Deuteronomy 1:9-18 for background on the use of oaths. They are quite common in ancient Near Eastern law codes, where they appear in cases of theft and instances of damage to property. They also appear in treaty-making contexts, where the god(s) are called as witnesses to the agreement.

7:5-7. number and types of sacrifices. Burnt offerings, grain offerings and fellowship offerings are all mentioned here. See the comment on Leviticus 3:1-5 on the fellowship offerings and the burning of the fat prior to consumption of the sacrificial meat, and the comment on Leviticus 2:1-3 and 6:14-23 for the regulations regarding the grain offering. We are not told how many of the sacrifices were burnt offerings (which were totally consumed on the altar) and how many were fellowship offerings (which were used for festival meals). It appears that the king is providing much of the meat for a religious communal feast for those in attendance. These numbers are large but are not out of proportion with some of the other figures found in ancient Near Eastern literature. When in 879 B.C. King Ashurnasirpal II threw a dedication party for his palace in the Assyrian capital city of Calah, he provided five thousand sheep, one thousand

lambs and cattle, five hundred deer, five hundred gazelles, thirty-four thousand fowl and ten thousand fish.

7:8. Lebo Hamath to Wadi of Egypt. See the comment on 1 Kings 4:21 on the boundaries of Solomon's kingdom. The "entrance" to Hamath (Ematu in the Ebla texts), Lebo Hamath, is most likely modern Lebweh on one of the sources of the Orontes. This was the southern border of the land of Hamath and therefore the northern border of Canaan, and designates the northern corner of the empire, about forty-five miles north of Damascus. The Wadi of Egypt would be the Wadi al-Arish.

7:12-22. God's response. There are a number of interesting features to this divine speech. First, rather than the typical ancient Near Eastern practice of choosing the site prior to the construction (see comment on 3:1), God's choosing is indicated at the dedication. Second, even though the temple was seen as the place of God's presence, in verse 14 he still makes it clear that he will hear their prayers *from heaven*. Nonetheless, third, his name, eyes and heart will be in the temple. "Name" represents an extension of self. Eyes were understood as representing gathering of information and, therefore, "knowing." In English, "heart" is used metaphorically for the seat of emotions in contrast to logic and reason. Hebrew uses it as the center of both emotions and reason/intellect. This usage is also true of the related Semitic languages such as Ugaritic, Aramaic and Akkadian. For more information on temple ideology see next comment. The prayers that God will hear at the temple would not come from organized prayer meetings once a week but from the petitions (national, royal, priestly or individual) that would be associated with the burnt offerings. Finally, the threat against the temple and the people who would neglect it is paralleled in the ancient Near East in the gods who abandon their temples and their cities because of offenses, typically in the category of ritual neglect. Here Israel is warned against neglect of the law, which included rituals, but was much more extensive.

7:16. temple ideology in the ancient Near East. The temple here is seen as the receptacle of God's power on earth. It is from there that he will see what is happening and from where he will act (emotions and decisions). In the ancient Near East the temple was considered to be a microcosm of the land. It represented either the cosmic mountain (Mesopotamia) or the primeval hillock (Egypt) out of which all else emerged. It was a palace that paralleled the palace where the deity dwelt either in heavenly places or on the heavenly mountain. The deity was believed to be "in" the statue that was his representation in the temple; but the idol was not the deity (for more information on idols, see comments on Deut 4).

8:1-18
Solomon's Accomplishments

8:2. villages given by Hiram. See the comment on 1 Kings 9:11, which describes how Solomon transferred twenty cities in the Galilee region to Hiram of Tyre. If these are the same cities referred to there, it is possible that Hiram is returning them for any of several reasons. If this is referring to a different incident, the text offers no information concerning the location of the cities or the arrangements that led to their transfer.

8:3. Hamath Zobah. In earlier passages these are two separate areas (see comments on 2 Sam 8), but by the time of Solomon they appear to have been joined under one ruler. Zobah and Hamath were at the extreme northern border claimed for Solomon's kingdom. Any expedition there would be more likely in the form of a pacification campaign or show of force, such as the Mesopotamian kings' claims of expeditions "to the sea." Hamath was known for its pasturage and was later used by Assyrian kings as a way station for grazing horses. It is not unlikely that Solomon could also have made this use of it, as he imported horses from Kue (see comment on 1:16).

8:4-6. building projects. See the comment on 1 Kings 9:15-19 on Solomon's building projects. Tadmor is the oasis of Palmyra (about 125 miles northeast of Damascus) on the caravan route linking Palestine to northern Arabia. The twin cities of Upper Beth Horon, Beit Ur el-Foqa (about two miles northwest of Gibeon), and Lower Beth Horon, Beit Ur et-Tahta (about a mile and a half further to the northwest, and about one thousand feet lower in elevation), guard the Beth Horon pass. The pass leads into the Aijalon Valley (referred to in the Amarna texts as Ayyaluna), the major route from the hill country to the coastal plains. It has been suggested that Beth Horon is the city referred to as Bit Ninurta in the Amarna letters. Baalath is generally identified with Kiriath Jearim or a site in its vicinity east of Jerusalem (Josh 15:9; 18:14). Listed as a city within Judah (Josh 15:60), the site is commonly identified with Tell el-Azhar, nine miles west-northwest of Jerusalem, but this is unsubstantiated by archaeological finds or extrabiblical references. The effect of all this effort is to fortify strong points, establish

trading stations along major commercial routes and make it clear that Solomon's jurisdiction is recognized along his borders.

8:7-10. forced labor. See the comments on 2 Chronicles 2:2, 7 regarding the use of resident alien populations on forced labor projects.

8:13. Sabbaths, New Moons and three annual feasts. See 2 Chronicles 2:4 for a similar list of major religious obligations from weekly to yearly. For the three annual feasts see the comments on Deuteronomy 16:1-17.

8:17. Ezion Geber and Elath. Ezion Geber was a port city located at the head of the Gulf of Aqaba and may be either Tell el-Kheleifeh (which some identify as Elath) or on the island of Jezirat Far'on (Coral Island), the only site in the region with evidence of an ancient harbor area. The latter has been substantiated by underwater archaeological work that showed massive walls and jetties (though not Iron Age) and a small amount of Iron Age pottery. Study has shown its use by Egyptian mariners and the technology used for the artificial harbor is similar to that found at Phoenician Tyre. Elath is a settlement on the north coast of the Gulf of Aqaba that served as a trading port for the Red Sea and Arabian shipping.

8:18. Ophir. This nation supplied large quantities of exotic wood and precious stones (1 Kings 10:11), as well as serving as either a source or market for gold (1 Kings 9:28). Outside the Bible the only mention of Ophir is in an inscription from Tell Qasile (eighth century B.C.), and it does not aid in establishing its location. Suggestions for Ophir's location include Arabia, India and the Somali region of Africa.

9:1-12
The Queen of Sheba

9:1. Sheba. Suggestions on locating Sheba most often place it in the southwestern corner of the Arabian peninsula (possibly Yemen). This would place it in close proximity to the trade routes from Mesopotamia, as well as the links, through shipping on the Red Sea, with Africa and India. Sheba had contact with Syria-Palestine as early as the mid-second millennium. Solomon's new trading center and harbor at Ezion Geber in the Gulf of Aqaba may have threatened Sheba's camel caravans with competition. It would be only natural that the ruler of this area would want to establish friendly relations with a growing commercial power. The queen here is not mentioned by name, though Assyrian contacts with Arabia in the first half of the first millennium often dealt with powerful queens. She may have been either the ruler or the consort of the ruler, dispatched by her husband on this important diplomatic mission. The journey was about fourteen hundred miles long and would have taken many weeks.

9:1-4. test of wisdom. The wisdom contest is a familiar theme in ancient Near Eastern literature. Babylonian literature represents it in the context of fables that use animals or plants as the combatants. Even from Sumerian times the literature reflects the staging of debates that will determine which party is the wisest. Kings were supposed to be characterized by wisdom—it came with the territory, though typically the gods were credited with having bestowed it. Ashurbanipal boasts not only of his great learning and wisdom, but of his technical knowledge and his ability to debate the learned. He credits Shamash and Adad for granting him his wealth of wisdom. Proofs of wisdom included rebuilding cities and temples, developing previously unused land, constructing irrigation works and conducting ritual observances. Most of these were construed as acts of piety.

9:4. food on his table. One expression of extreme wealth would be the display of quantities and varieties of food on the royal table. It was a singular honor to eat at the king's table and the number of persons who could be accommodated there was a sign of the power of the ruler. It also functioned as a human parallel to the divine banquet table so often portrayed in Mesopotamian epic texts (such as in the Tale of Adapa). Royal banquets in the ancient Near East featured an extensive and sophisticated *haute cuisine*, as has been demonstrated by the tablets preserving many ancient recipes.

9:4. seating of his officials. The size of Solomon's bureaucracy and power as a monarch might be estimated by the number who would regularly be seated at his table. It was also a further expression of the wealth of his kingdom that he could continuously provide for these men (note Jezebel's accommodation of 450 prophets of Baal and 400 prophets of Asherah in 1 Kings 18:19).

9:4. attendants and cupbearers. The multitude of Solomon's retainers and the sumptuousness of their official liveries provided the queen of Sheba and others with graphic proof of his wealth and power. It also established Solomon's court as being on a par with those of Egypt, Mesopotamia and Persia, who also judged power by the number of servants in evidence.

9:9. 120 talents of gold. Among the gifts brought by the queen of Sheba is a quantity of gold amounting to nearly eight thousand pounds (four tons). Such an amount would perhaps better be termed a tribute payment or a share contributed in the establishment of a business partnership. In 1 Kings 9:14 this is the same amount received from Hiram of Tyre. For information concerning amounts of gold see comment on 1 Chronicles 22:14.

9:9. spices. Sheba would have been set right on the principal trade routes for frankincense and myrrh, both of which were on a par with gold in terms of value. Evidence of the incense trade can be found in the reliefs at Deir el-Bahari depicting the pharaoh-queen Hatshepsut's expedition to Punt in southern Egypt. Similarly, the aromatic oils, perfumes, medicinal and embalming substances followed these same trade routes. They would be a fitting gift to add to the king's treasury. For more information on frankincense see comment on Leviticus 2:1. For more information concerning the use of spices see comment on Exodus 30:23-24.

9:9. precious stones. Hoards of precious stones have been found in excavations at Megiddo, Gezer and Ezion Geber, including carnelian, agate and alabaster. Engraved gems, used as signets or jewelry, have appeared at Phoenician sites as well as at Ugarit and Byblos, and Egyptian scarabs made of steatite or faience are found at many sites. In the ancient Near East stones (including gemstones of various sorts) were believed to have apotropaic value (offering protection from spirit forces). A seventh-century B.C. Assyrian handbook preserves a list of various stones and what they "do"—possibilities range from appeasing divine anger to preventing migraine headaches. One ritual text lists twelve precious and semiprecious stones that are to be used to make a phylactery to be worn as a necklace. Additionally, unusual nonprecious stone was treasured for use in mosaics (see comment on 1 Chron 29:2).

9:10-11. algumwood. See the comment on 2 Chronicles 2:8 on this species of juniper and its relation to almug wood, sandalwood, in 1 Kings 10:11-12.

9:11. harps and lyres. Musical instruments can be constructed of a variety of different woods, and this could effect their sound quality (see sandalwood and juniper in the comment on 2 Chron 2:8). Images of the lyre have been found on a Megiddo ivory plaque (twelfth century B.C.) and coins. Harps appear in many contexts, including the Egyptian relief from the time of Rameses II (thirteenth century B.C.)

of a blind harpist. For more information on harps and lyres see comment on 5:12.

9:13-31
Solomon's Wealth

9:13. 666 talents of gold. This is an incredible amount equal to about twenty-five tons of gold. Perhaps one way to make comparison would be the tribute lists of the Assyrian annals (Sennacherib is said to have demanded thirty talents [nearly a ton] of gold from Hezekiah). This amount represents a vast trading network generating revenues far beyond those of most other nations (note the amounts recorded in 1 Kings 9:14, 28 and 10:10). For information concerning amounts of gold see comment on 1 Chronicles 22:14.

9:15-16. gold shields. The five hundred shields of "hammered gold" (a term peculiar to this context) were designed for ceremonial purposes and as a demonstration of Solomon's wealth. The larger shields weighed 7 1/2 pounds, while the smaller shields contained 3 3/4 pounds of gold. They are mentioned in the story of Shishak's looting of Jerusalem in 1 Kings 14:25-28 along with their replacement by bronze shields (clearly a sign of changed economic posture and a step away from Israel's "golden age"). Ceremonial showpieces (such as the gold swords and axes at Ur) have been found at excavations. Ceremonial bronze shields have been found by archaeologists in the ancient Near East, but no gold ones as yet. Nevertheless, Sargon II lists six gold shields in his booty list from Urartu, each said to weigh over fifty pounds.

9:17-19. throne. The magnificent throne of Solomon's palace can be compared, at least in materials and construction, with Phoenician furniture, such as the eighth-century ivory throne recovered from tomb 79 in Salamis, Cyprus. On the sarcophagus of the Phoenician king, Ahiram, he is portrayed on a throne flanked by winged lions. Sennacherib's reliefs depicting the plunder taken from Lachish (701 B.C.) include images of decorated thrones. Like the throne of the Ugaritic Epic of Baal, Solomon's was elevated above all others, demonstrating his position of power. The golden footstool also has a Ugaritic counterpart, indicating that only the king could sit in a relaxed position, totally secure in his authority and possession of the land (for the ark as Yahweh's footstool see comment on 1 Chron 28:2).

9:20. Palace of the Forest of Lebanon. See the comment on 1 Kings 7:1-12 for the description of this palace. The likelihood that it func-

tioned as both a royal residence as well as an arsenal is indicated by the golden shields displayed there (vv. 15-16) and the storage of more practical weapons in Isaiah 22:8.

9:21. trading ships. The mention of large cargo vessels known as Tarshish ships seems to indicate a type of ship employed in the Red Sea and Arabian coastal trade (see Is 2:16). Here the Chronicler refers to ships dispatched to Tarshish (a source of precious metals in Jer 10:9 and precious stones in Ezek 28:13, probably located in the western Mediterranean—possibly Carthage or southwestern Spain). This would greatly expand Solomon's trading links and suggests an even broader commercial partnership with the Phoenicians. For more information about ships see comment on 1 Kings 22:48.

9:21. ivory, apes and baboons. In addition to the large quantities of gold generated by Solomon's commercial enterprises, luxury items were also transported from exotic places to Israel. The Hebrew terms of the "ivory, apes and baboons" only appear in this passage and are probably loan words or Hebrew approximations of the native words. For example, there is some uncertainty whether to translate the third term as "baboons" or "peacocks." Eleventh- and tenth-century Assyrian kings also boasted of collections of exotic animals, specifically including the mention of apes.

9:25. chariot cities. Typically a chariot team included three horses with only two being used at any one time and the third kept as a reserve. The three would be stabled together, so twelve thousand horses for four thousand pens is the correct proportion, indicating four thousand chariot teams. Nevertheless, 1 Kings 10:26 reports that Solomon had fourteen hundred chariots. This is a large contingent of chariots but not as large as the two thousand contributed by Ahab to the western alliance that met the Assyrians at the Battle of Qarqar in 853 (see comment on 1 Kings 22:1). In the thirteenth century the Hittites and their allies had amassed twenty-five hundred chariots to confront Rameses II at the Battle of Qadesh. The implication is clear that Solomon had stationed sufficient forces on his borders to insure adequate protection and a strike force capable of quick retaliation or punitive campaigns.

9:29. sources. The parallel text to this summary statement on Solomon's reign is found in 1 Kings 11:41-43 (see comment for information about royal annals). However, the Chronicler's list of additional sources of information includes the writings of two of Solomon's contemporaries, the prophets Nathan and Ahijah. The third source, the visions of Iddo the seer, may refer to the figure in 2 Chronicles 12:15. Their citation is both an indication that the Chronicler drew his account from a variety of written and oral sources and may also suggest a direction or perspective he would encourage the reader to pursue further.

10:1—12:16
The Reign of Rehoboam

10:1-2. chronology. The year of these events is pretty firmly established at 931 B.C. (see comment on 12:2).

10:1. Shechem. The choice of Shechem for this political summit meeting suggests two things: (1) Rehoboam is in a weak political situation in comparison to David, since in 2 Samuel 5:1 the tribal leaders came to David's capital at Hebron to acknowledge him as king, and (2) having the meeting in the heart of territory associated with the premonarchic leadership of Joshua (Josh 24) and cultically a rival to Jerusalem (see the comment on 1 Kings 12:25) put Rehoboam at a further disadvantage. In fact Rehoboam was taking a chance in coming here away from his own power center. His lack of insight and administrative finesse in the negotiations are thus presaged by the meeting site.

10:4. Solomon's harsh labor. Just as the Persian king Cyrus charges his Babylonian rival Nabonidus with inflicting "forced labor service" on his people, the elders of Israel ask for a reduction in this practice by Rehoboam's administration. There is precedent in Mesopotamian documents for a new king to issue a *mesharum* decree manumitting a class of slaves or reducing the tax burden for a city or a district. Clearly there were grounds for discontent among the tribes, and a compromise was needed to hold the kingdom together.

10:6-8. elders. There seems to have been a division within the royal household/bureaucracy between "new" and "old" men (i.e., those who had been elevated to the status of adviser to the king recently and those with long service). The "elders" would represent those who had been in office during the time of Solomon. They may have come either from the royal family (half brothers, cousins like Jonadab in 2 Sam 13:3) or the civil service. The newcomers would most likely be made up of Rehoboam's own cousins and half brothers that were his contemporaries. The Sumerian Epic of Gilgamesh and Aka also features a situation in which Gilgamesh seeks advice first from the elders (who advise against rebellion), and then the young men of the city (who make up

the armed forces, and advise rebellion). There also the advice of the young men is followed.

10:11. whips/scorpions. The practice of using whips to drive slaves or animals, or as an instrument of torture has a long history. Some have identified the scorpions here as the type of whip that has fragments of metal or glass attached to the tip (which the Romans called "scorpions"). So far this type of whip is not attested either in excavated finds, reliefs or literature prior to Roman times. In one Akkadian word list, however, a copper scorpion is listed along with copper fetters for slaves. Akkadian scholars have tentatively identified this as a barbed metal tip of a scourge.

10:16. tenuous union of Israel and Judah. The rallying cry of the northern tribes had been raised once before during Sheba's revolt (see the comment on 2 Sam 20:1). It is easy to think that the unity of the twelve tribes of Israel as a single people was natural and intrinsic. But that is not the case. In fact they were twelve independent tribal units with much to drive them apart. The unity that had been achieved during the time of David and Solomon was achieved only with great skill and effort, and in a time of prosperity. However, the elements that hold such political entities together were only a generation old and, like chiefdoms (such as that organized by Saul among the Israelite tribes), it is still too dependent on the personality of the ruler. The tendency of chiefdoms and empires is to fragment at the least provocation. Now the cost of unity and the differing perspectives of north and south easily drove a wedge between them when it became clear to the northern tribes that Judah and the Davidic house had no intention of compromising with their requests for more local autonomy and lower taxes.

10:18. death by stoning. See the comment on Deuteronomy 13:10 for stoning as a method of capital punishment. Adoniram's death is like the first shot of a rebellion or a riot. It is almost poetic justice that the man in charge of public works (including the movement of rocks) should die in a hail of stones.

11:1. 180,000 fighting men. This is an extremely large number for just the tribes of Judah and Benjamin. It is about the same number of soldiers that served in the combined armed forces of America during the entire course of the Revolutionary War. Modern estimates of the actual total population size during this period suggest that there were no more than three hundred thousand inhabitants in the southern kingdom. In Neo-Assyrian records from the ninth and eighth century the size of the Assyrian army increases from about forty-five thousand (Shalmaneser III) to over two hundred thousand (Sennacherib). The twelve-nation western coalition confronted Shalmaneser at the Battle of Qarqar with as many as sixty thousand. The largest Hittite force reported was nearly fifty thousand (for the Battle of Qadesh, thirteenth century). All of this suggests that the word translated "thousand" in these passages should be rendered by its alternate meaning, "companies" or "divisions." Rather than a specified number, it has been suggested that each clan supplied a division with the number varying dependent on the size of the clan. Later in history these companies were standardized as having a thousand, but here there may be far fewer in a division.

11:2-4. prophetic oracle related to battle. In this period of preclassical prophecy the prophets of Israel served in very much the same role as did their ancient Near Eastern counterparts (see comments on Deut 18:14-22). One of the most frequent areas addressed concerned, as here, the advisability of military activity. Since it was believed that God's involvement was essential for the success of the military, the entire sequence begins with the divine command to go into battle. This divine command can be seen as typical in the royal inscriptions of the Assyrians. It was also important to consult the deity about timing and strategies. Sometimes, however, oracles were received unsolicited or unexpectedly. One example of this is found in a Mari text that describes a dream warning King Zimri-Lim not to go on campaign.

11:5-12. fortified cities of Judah. All of the cities listed, except Adoraim (modern Dura, three miles west of Hebron), are known from other sources (for instance, in the invasion of Shishak, see 12:2) and are located in Judah. They form an inner line of defense of the Jerusalem hills. There are four groups, ranging north to south, at strategic points guarding major approaches and highways: (1) Bethlehem, Etam, Tekoa and Beth Zur guard the eastern boundary; (2) Soco, Adullam, Gath and Maresha guard the west; (3) a southern line of defense includes Lachish, Ziph and Adoraim; (4) Zorah and Aijalon seem to function as northwestern fortresses, while Hebron (David's old capital in 2 Sam 2:1) may function as a staging point or regional center for both the south and the west. Archaeological research has not provided much help in identifying the building that Rehoboam did, though a few of the sites (particularly Lachish) show some evidence of this fortification work.

11:11-12. provisions for fortified cities. The garrisons within Rehoboam's fortress cities had to maintain a good stock of provisions and weapons in order to be effective guardians of the border. Like the Mari administrative lists detailing the amount of food, oil and beer necessary to sustain troops for various periods of time (ten or fifteen days or a month), the Chronicler has provided an abbreviated summary (lacking quantities and the times for regular delivery) of rations.

11:15. goat and calf idols. For information concerning the calves see comment on 1 Kings 12:28. Goat idols most likely refers to satyrlike demons who were believed to haunt the open fields and uninhabitable places. They are referred to only a few times in the Old Testament and have no known parallels in the ancient Near East.

11:22-23. princes as administrators. One of the principal methods of training the crown prince as well as other members of the royal family was to appoint them to administrative positions. Abijah's position might even be considered a coregency with his father Rehoboam (see 21:2-4). The Egyptian records and Mesopotamian annals regularly describe the appointment of royal sons as governors or district administrators (for example, see the Assyrian king Shamshi-Adad's appointment of his sons Yasmah-Addu and Ishme-Dagan to rule portions of his kingdom).

12:2-4. Shishak's invasion. Shishak's own account, recorded on the walls of the temple complex dedicated to Amon at Karnak (Thebes), contains a list of over 150 cities that he claims to have conquered, along with vague references to tribute garnered from the land of Syria. Jerusalem is not mentioned in the list, and the sites that are chronicled are in both southern and northern Israel. Using Gaza as a base, several divisions proceeded through the Negev, while the main force went through the Shephelah toward Jerusalem. It then turned north through the central hill country, went westward through the Jezreel Valley to Megiddo, and then followed the Trunk Road south along the coast. His itinerary also included a foray into Transjordan, crossing east at Adam and then back west heading to Beth Shan. Archaeologists have identified destruction levels at many of the named towns coinciding with this time period.

12:2. chronology. Egyptian sources place Shishak's reign and the founding of the Twenty-Second Dynasty between 945 and 924 B.C. Rehoboam's accession to the throne came in 931, so his fifth year would be 927, a plausible time after the death of Solomon and the division of the kingdoms.

12:3. Libyans, Sukkites, Cushites. Among the Egyptian troops are levies from southern and western areas bordering on Egypt (Libya, Nubia). Since Shishak is a Libyan, it seems reasonable to expect he would include regiments of his own tribal peoples in his campaign. It is also known that he conducted campaigns in Nubia and probably had coerced their cooperation in this joint venture. The Sukkites do not appear elsewhere in the Bible but are known from thirteen and twelfth-century Egyptian sources (there called *Tjukten*) as a people related to the Libyans. Their twelve hundred chariots are comparable to what Solomon's force had been (see comment on 1 Kings 4:26).

12:9. Shishak's booty. Many of the gold and silver objects that had been manufactured for the temple, including the famous golden shields (see comment on 9:15-16), were carried away as tribute paid to avoid the destruction of Jerusalem. This may have made up the lion's share of the two hundred tons of gold and silver that Shishak reports having contributed to the temples of his gods.

12:13. Rehoboam's mother. Since Solomon is known to have married women from many countries, including Ammon (see 1 Kings 11:1), it is not unusual that Rehoboam's mother, Naamah, should be an Ammonite. Her marriage would most likely represent a political alliance between the two countries. The practice of regularly naming the mother of the kings of Judah may indicate that the office of queen mother was significant (see comment on 1 Kings 2:19).

12:15. sources. The genealogical lists of Iddo the seer may be compared to other works associated with this prophetic figure (2 Chron 9:29 and 13:22), but he is not named in any of the narratives of this period. The "records of Shemaiah" are probably a separate, extrabiblical history that the Chronicler drew on in creating his summary of events. Shemaiah is the prophet who warns Rehoboam against civil war and who exhorts him to repentance in the context of Shishak's invasion (see 2 Chron 11:2; 12:5).

12:15. wars between north and south. There were no full-scale wars between the two states, but the continual border skirmishes, lasting until the reign of Jehoshaphat (1 Kings 22:44), would have been troublesome and bloody enough to cause a continual drain on their resources. They might be compared, on a smaller scale, to the conflict between David and Ishbaal in 2 Samuel 2:12-32.

13:1-22
The Reign of Abijah

13:1-2. chronology. This is the first appearance of the synchronistic recording of Israel's and Judah's kings (see 1 Kings 15:1). However, unlike the writer(s) of Kings, the Chronicler only uses this dating formula in this single instance. Based on Jeroboam's accession in 930 B.C., Abijah's rule began in 913.

13:2-20. battle between Abijah and Jeroboam. The location of the battle, Mount Zemaraim, has not yet been positively identified but is usually placed in the vicinity of Bethel. The most familiar identification is with Ras et-Tahuneh. The rhetoric in Abijah's speech suggests that his intention is to reunite the north and south, by conquest if necessary. This is open pitched battle rather than the siege of a city. As is common in Chronicles, the size of the armies (1.2 million) is much larger than expected but is not the largest in ancient reports. Herodotus has usually been considered guilty of gross exaggeration when he reports that the army Xerxes fielded against the Greeks was comprised of five million people. For comparison, consider the Battle of Gettysburg with combined forces of 165,000. Additionally, the half-million casualties for the northern kingdom in this one battle would rival the bloodiest battles in history. In ancient records the Assyrian king Arik-den-ili claims to have killed 254,000. His nearest rival is Sennacherib, who claimed he inflicted 150,000 casualties at the Battle of Halule. Allied casualties in the First Battle of the Somme (France, 1916) were about 623,000. This battle lasted six months and is listed in the Guinness Book of World Records as the bloodiest ever. At the Battle of Gettysburg combined losses were reported at 50,000, only one-tenth of what is reported here. One of the bloodiest battles of ancient history was between the Romans and the Huns at Châlons-sur-Marne (France, 451) where there were 200,000 casualties. For more information see comment on 11:1.

13:5. covenant of salt. In the hot climate of the ancient Near East, salt was necessary for the health of humans and animals, and was the principal food preservative (texts from ancient Mari describe its trade value). When treaties or alliances were made, salt was employed to symbolize that the terms would be preserved for a long time. Babylonian, Persian, Arabic and Greek contexts all testify to this symbolic usage. In the Bible, likewise, the covenant between the Lord and Israel is identified as a covenant of salt—a long-preserved covenant. Allies entering into such an agreement would generally share a communal meal in which salted meat was featured. Thus the use of salt in the sacrifices was an appropriate reminder of the covenant relationship. Additionally, salt impedes the action of yeast (leaven), and since leaven was a symbol of rebellion, salt could easily represent that which inhibited rebellion.

13:8. golden calves in battle. There is ample precedent for an army to bring their divine images with them into battle. In the divine warrior motif the deity is fighting the battles and defeating the deities of the enemy. Standards or statues of the deity were usually carried to symbolize their presence. Assyrian kings of the ninth and eighth centuries regularly refer to the divine standard that goes before them. The ark, as Yahweh's standard, represents the Lord as clearing the way before the Israelites and leading the armies into Canaan. This concept is not very different from the Assyrian belief that the gods empowered the weapons of the king and fought before him or at his side. Nearly every army in the ancient Near East included priests and diviners (as seen in the Mari texts), prophets (2 Kings 3) and portable sacred objects (Assyrian Annals of Shalmaneser III [858-824 B.C.]). In this way, the god(s) could be consulted on the battlefield or invoked to lead the soldiers to victory.

13:11. priestly rituals. For further information on these ritual activities see comments on Leviticus 6:8-13 and Exodus 25:23-30.

13:19. towns taken by Judah. Bethel, as the site of Jeroboam's southern cult center, was a significant conquest. Later biblical texts make it clear that it was firmly back in Israel's control by the time of Jeroboam II and Amos (Amos 7:10). Jeshanah, near Bethel and seventeen miles north of Jerusalem, has been identified with Burj el-Isaneh, and Ephron (Ophrah in Josh 18:23) is generally identified with et-Taiyibeh, four miles northeast of Bethel. Rehoboam's victory gains him control of the two major routes crossing from the territory of Judah into Israel. These routes run north on either side of Bethel and converge just south of Shiloh. The territory involved comprises about twenty square miles.

13:22. source. The "annotations of the prophet Iddo" is probably by the same prophet mentioned earlier in 2 Chronicles 9:29 and 12:15. Curiously, the only appearance of this prophet's name is in connection with these source materials. He does not appear in any of the narratives.

14:1—16:14

The Reign of Asa

14:3. foreign altars. The amenities that Solomon had provided for his foreign wives included the construction of altars and shrines for their worship of their own gods (see the comments on 1 Kings 11:5-7). These may have been some of the altars destroyed by Asa.

14:3. high places. For more information on high places, see the comments on 1 Kings 3:2-3 and Deuteronomy 12:2-3.

14:3. sacred stones. Standing stones or *masse-bot* were apparently a common feature of Canaanite religion and also appear as memorials in a number of Israelite covenantal contexts (see Ex 24:3-8; Josh 24:25-27). Their association with Asherah, Baal and other Canaanite deities are the basis for their being condemned as a rival and threat to Yahweh worship. Archaeologists have discovered sacred stones at Gezer, Dan, Hazor and Arad. In the latter two cases they are clearly within a sacred precinct and part of the cultic practices at these sites. The Hazor stones include incised representations of upraised arms and a sun disk. The stones at Dan are in the gateway, and the clear remains of the presentation of votive offerings are evident.

14:3. Asherah poles. One common feature of Canaanite worship and of syncretized Israelite worship on "high places" and in city shrines is the erection of Asherah poles. There is some uncertainty about whether these were simply wooden poles, erected to symbolize trees or perhaps containing a carved image of the fertility goddess, or whether they were a part of a sacred grove. The reference in 2 Kings 17:10, which refers to Asherah poles beside "every spreading tree," seems to indicate that these were poles erected for cultic purposes rather than planted trees. As the consort of El, Asherah was a popular goddess whose worship is mentioned in Ugaritic texts (1600-1200). Her prominent appearance in the biblical narrative indicates that her cult was a major rival to Yahweh worship. For more information see the comments on Exodus 34:13 and Judges 6:25.

14:7. fortification. Although the Chronicler does not list any of the cities fortified by Asa, it is clear that he had a solid reputation as a builder. Mesopotamian annals and regnal-year titles regularly comment on the king's building activities as evidence of his success. The Chronicler also wishes to include "building" as the hallmark of a "good king," the result being a time of peace and prosperity.

14:8. army equipment. The division of task

within the military is illustrated by Asa's infantry used as shock troops (carrying large shields and spears) and his Benjaminite archers (compare the equipment issued to Uzziah's troops in 2 Chron 26:14). The palace reliefs of the Assyrian king Sennacherib include depictions of soldiers armed with lances and a circular shield used for defense and as a weapon in close fighting. The reliefs of Shalmaneser III portray his archers in long coats of mail and accompanied by a shield-bearer to keep the bowman's hands free and to protect him from missiles. Perhaps the Benjaminite forces did not utilize these auxiliaries, or they attached their smaller shield to their arm so that they maintained some protection while they shot their volleys.

14:9. Zerah the Cushite. Since the Cushites are often identified with the Nubian Egyptian pharaohs (see comment on 2 Chron 12:3), some scholars have identified Zerah with Osorkon I, the Egyptian pharaoh at this time (about 897). Osorkon, the son of Shishak, however, is Libyan, not Nubian. Therefore, if Zerah came with Egyptian forces, he must be a Nubian general working in cooperation with the Twenty-Second Dynasty (who had exerted some control over Nubia during the days of Shishak). Others think it more likely that Zerah was a chief of a Bedouin tribe (see comment on Num 12:1 for this variation of "Cush"). For discussion of the size of the armies see comment on 13:3-20. Hebrew has no word for "million"—the text here refers to "a thousand thousands" (or, a thousand divisions) and would be expressive of an innumerable force. Compare to how we might use "a month of Sundays" to talk about a long, long time.

14:9. chariotry. Considering the number of troops marshaled by Zerah, there is a surprisingly small number of chariots. Even so, each army had its own strengths, and three hundred is still a strong force of chariots. As we know from Mesopotamian and Egyptian records and palace reliefs, two- or three-man chariot crews worked from these mobile platforms to fire volleys of arrows, to carry commanders or messengers about the battlefield and for frontal attacks. Armies often were organized around chariot groups, with contingents of infantry attached to each chariot commander. For comparative sizes of chariot forces see comment on 1:14.

14:10. geography. The battle between Asa and Zerah takes place near Mareshah, a city fortified by Rehoboam and identified with Tell Sandakhanna on the southwestern border of Judah. It is located about four miles northeast

of Lachish and nearly thirty miles southwest of Jerusalem. Zephathah (perhaps to be identified with the Zephath of Judg 1:17) only appears in this text. Since it is said to be a valley north of Mareshah, it is probably to be identified as Wadi Guvrin, just north of Mareshah and Beit Guvrin.

14:12-14. Gerar. See the comment on Genesis 20:1 for this site in the western Negev region, whose exact location is still undetermined (Tel Haror, about twenty-five miles southwest of Beersheba, is the most likely choice). Gerar may be the name of a region rather than a city-state, thus explaining the devastation of its cities by Asa.

15:8. detestable idols. Idols are not referred to specifically. The word refers to anything that is utterly revolting or disgusting from a ritual or religious standpoint, particularly prohibited food and objects used in unapproved foreign worship practices.

15:10. chronology. If Asa is attempting to tie his assembly and sacrifice to a major religious festival or event, then the third month contains the theophany at Mount Sinai (Ex 19:1) and the Feast of Weeks (Lev 23:15-16). Since a renewal of the covenant is also part of this event, Asa may be commemorating the covenant renewal at Mount Sinai (Ex 24). The year date places this celebration in 892.

15:16. Asherah pole. See the comment on 14:3 for discussion of the Asherah pole. The influence and political status of the queen mother (see comment on 1 Kings 2:19) could have undermined Asa's reform measures, and this may explain why he so utterly rejected her action and totally destroyed the object.

15:16. Kidron Valley. Located just east of the walls of the city of Jerusalem and containing one of the principal water sources for the city, the Gihon Spring, this would be an excellent staging area for King Asa's destruction of idols. Solomon had erected cult places for Ashtoreh, Chemosh and Molech here (1 Kings 11:7), but later reforming kings like Asa, Hezekiah (2 Chron 29:16) and Josiah (2 Kings 23:13) used the valley to make a show of ridding the nation of corruption.

15:19—16:1. chronology. There are some problems in reconciling the date provided here for the conflict between Asa and Baasha and the information in the parallel text in 1 Kings. For more information see comment on 1 Kings 15:33.

16:1. Ramah. Located just five miles north of Jerusalem, Baasha's incorporation of Ramah (er-Ram) into his territory would have been a cause of great concern for Judah. Just as Rehoboam had extended his control of the main north-south arteries between Israel and Judah five extra miles (see comment on 13:19), so now Baasha pushes his control of the same arteries five miles south of the traditional line between the nations. There have been no excavations on the site.

16:2-3. treaty with Ben-Hadad. Based on the manner in which this treaty is described here and in the parallel text in 1 Kings 15:18-19, it would appear that Aram had been maintaining a policy of nonintervention, perhaps awaiting the best offer from the warring parties. Ben-Hadad I ruled during the first part of the ninth century, though no precise dating is possible. For information concerning the difficulties of Aramean history of the ninth century see comment on 1 Kings 20:1.

16:4. conquests of Aram. Ben-Hadad's attack on northern Israel, at the instigation of Asa, cost Baasha an important trade corridor. The cities captured in this campaign (see 1 Kings 15:20) include Dan (the northern cult shrine), Ijon ('Ayyun) at the northern end of the Huleh Basin (about ten miles north of Dan), Abel Maim (Abel Beth-Maacah in 1 Kings), all of which are on the road between Syria and the Phoenician coastal cities of Tyre, Sidon and Acco. The fact that Ijon is mentioned first suggests an attack from the west and ranging south. It is unknown how long Aram was able to hold these towns, but they are clearly back in Jehu's hands a few decades later, according to 2 Kings 10:29. The inscription from Dan mentioning another Syrian campaign against northern Israel suggests that this was a continual threat that had to be faced by Israel's rulers.

16:6. Geba and Mizpah. These two cities, now refortified by Asa with materials taken from the defenses at Ramah, guard the northern border of Judah. Geba (modern Jaba', four miles northeast of Jerusalem) appears elsewhere as the northern limit of Judah (2 Kings 23:8) and functions as the guardian of the Micmash Pass. Mizpah (Tell en-Nasbeh, eight miles north of Jerusalem) stood as the fortress dominating the watershed highway on the frontier between Israel and Judah. By fortifying these cities Asa cut off further action against Ramah. Mizpah is about three miles north of Ramah guarding the road from Bethel to Ramah. The excavations at the site have uncovered a wall with eleven towers dating to this period. The wall was twelve to fifteen feet thick and thirty-five to forty feet high. Geba is about two miles east of Ramah blocking access from that direction.

16:7. seer. Although Hanani the seer only appears in this passage, he is mentioned as the father of Jehu the prophet in 1 Kings 16:1; 2 Chronicles 19:2; 20:34. The title seer, *ro'eh*, apparently was an alternative term for prophet (*nabi'*; see the comment on 1 Sam 9:9).

16:9. eyes of the Lord. This imagery provides a sense of the universality of Yahweh's vision (equivalent to omnipresence) and involvement (reflecting his sovereign control). A Babylonian boundary stone from the end of the second millennium speaks of the moon god Sin as "the eye of heaven and earth."

16:12. foot disease. Some attempts have been made to diagnose Asa's foot disease as gout (uncommon in biblical times) or gangrene brought on by the obstruction of blood flow. The fact that Asa chose to consult only physicians, who were at times associated with magical rituals or, at best, herbal remedies, further demonstrates his failure to seek God's aid and thereby contributed to his own death.

16:14. fire in his honor. Royal tombs were hewn into the sides of cliffs. The funeral rites for Asa are quite elaborate and include the burning of spices in his honor as well as a general lamentation and internment in his family tomb. The fire does not imply cremation of the body or an attempt to mask the odors associated with a diseased body, but was rather an expensive display of the king's wealth. The practice is well known among Assyrian kings, where it was used as an apotropaic ritual.

17:1—21:3
The Reign of Jehoshaphat

17:2. fortified towns in Ephraim. As noted in 2 Chronicles 15:8 Asa had extended his control northward into the Ephraimite hill country. It seems a natural continuation of this policy for Jehoshaphat to fortify these unspecified cities. There is also no specific mention of the number of troops stationed here. We know from the Lachish letters of a later period that regular correspondence was maintained with these types of outposts and that fire signals were used as an early warning system.

17:3. consulting Baal. "Consulting" refers to asking the deity for oracles. This would usually occur at a shrine dedicated to the deity, and the oracle would be mediated by the priests of that deity. In the ancient world oracular answers were often given by diviners, who would read favorable or unfavorable answers in the entrails of a sacrificed animal. Even while the Israelites fully acknowledged Yahweh as their national patron deity, some were inclined to continue to associate Baal with fertility and to consult him regarding agricultural issues. Also on daily issues such as sickness and health, they sometimes chose to look for information from Baal rather than from Yahweh (see 2 Kings 1:2).

17:6. removed high places and Asherah poles. See comment on 14:3.

17:11. Arabs. The Arabs referred to in the Old Testament inhabited the fringes of the Syrian desert, extending also into the Negev and the Arabian peninsula. Arabs begin to be mentioned in Assyrian royal inscriptions at about this time (for instance, they were one of the allies in the Battle of Qarqar).

17:12. building projects. Most of this building was military in nature providing garrisons, supply centers and border outposts to guard the entries into the land. Archaeological evidence of a line of fortresses in the Jordan Valley and adjacent to the Dead Sea may be associated with his reign. Supply centers were meant to stockpile food and other necessities in case of siege or famine.

17:14-19. Jehoshaphat's army. The conscript army of Jehoshaphat is exactly twice as large as that of his father Asa, well over one million men (see 2 Chron 14:7). For discussion of army sizes see comment on 13:2-20. Its divisions into clans follows the pattern found in other levies (1 Chron 27:1). Looking beyond the large numbers, the style of listing the contingents suggests a form of regimentation and a careful report reflecting proper protocol with regard to rank and organization.

18:1. marriage alliances. The wives of an ancient ruler or his children usually represented political alliances. Marriage was a tool of diplomacy throughout the ancient Near East. Towns, city-states, tribes or nations who wished to ally themselves with a ruler or come under his protection sealed the treaty with the marriage of a daughter of their chief family to the suzerain or his son. For instance, Zimri-Lim, the king of Mari (eighteenth century B.C.) used his daughters to cement alliances and establish treaties with his neighboring kingdoms. Similarly, Pharaoh Thutmose IV (1425-1412 B.C.) arranged a marriage with a daughter of the Mitannian king to demonstrate good relations and end a series of wars with that middle Euphrates kingdom. Solomon's seven hundred wives and three hundred concubines were a measure of his power and wealth, especially his marriage to the daughter of the pharaoh. The marriage alliance between Jehoshaphat and Ahab matched Ahab's daughter, Athaliah, with Jehoshaphat's son, Jehoram.

18:2. down to Samaria. Jerusalem is quite a bit higher in elevation than Samaria, but even if they had been equal, one would still have gone down to Samaria because of the descent out of the Jerusalem hills to go in most any direction. The distance between these two capital cities was about forty miles.

18:2. slaughtering sheep and cattle. Treaties were typically concluded amidst a great feast that would feature a ceremonial meal. These animals would have been sacrificed as an offering bringing divine sanction to the agreement.

18:2. Ramoth Gilead. The site of Ramoth Gilead has not been identified with certainty, but most accept Tell Ramith for its size, location and Iron Age pottery found in surveys. It has yet to be excavated. If this is the correct identification, it is in Transjordan about forty-five miles east of Jezreel. It is strategically located on the King's Highway at the juncture where the road south from Damascus would turn west to cross the Jordan near Beth Shan and enter the Jezreel Valley to connect with the main route of the Trunk Road (see sidebar on Trade Routes in Genesis 38). In 1 Kings 20:34 the Aramean king had promised to return the cities taken from Israel. It is possible that this has not been done, and Ramoth Gilead has remained under Aramean control. This battle brings the death of Ahab and therefore must be in 853 after the Battle of Qarqar against the Assyrians (see comment on 1 Kings 22:1) in which Israel and Aram were allies.

18:4. role of the prophet. In this period of preclassical prophecy the prophets of Israel served in very much the same role as their ancient Near Eastern counterparts (see comments on Deut 18:14-22). One of the most frequent areas addressed concerned, as here, the advisability of military activity. Since it was believed that God's involvement was essential for the success of the military, the entire sequence begins with the divine command to go into battle. This divine command can be seen as typical in the royal inscriptions of the Assyrians. It was also important to consult the deity about timing and strategies. During the time of Saul and David this type of information was usually gained through the priest's manipulation of oracular devices (see comments on 1 Sam 14:10; 22:10; and 23:9-12). Now, instead of asking questions of a priest to receive oracular responses, the questions are being posed to the prophet who, as representative of God, offers the prophetic oracles as messages from God in response.

18:7. prophesying ill. Throughout the ancient world it was believed that prophets not only proclaimed the message of deity but in the process unleashed the divine action. It is no wonder, then, that a prophet negatively disposed toward a king must somehow be controlled lest he bring about all sorts of havoc. In Assyrian king Esarhaddon's instructions to his vassals he requires that they report any improper or negative statements that may be made by anyone, but he specifically names prophets, ecstatics and dream interpreters. One can perhaps understand why a king would be inclined to imprison a prophet whose very words might incite insurrection or impose doom.

18:9. thrones at the threshing floor. Because of the importance of agriculture and fertility the threshing floor was often a place of ritual importance. Threshing floors were large, flat, open areas and certainly could have been useful for other purposes besides threshing. It is no surprise, therefore, that they should double as an open-air facility when space constraints or the desire for public visibility rendered the palace facilities inadequate. In the Ugaritic Epic of Aqhat, Danil, the king, publicly judges cases at the threshing floor outside the gate of his city.

18:16. scattered like sheep without a shepherd. An inscription of Sargon II of Assyria reports that the commander of the enemy troops fled like a shepherd whose flock had been stolen but later was captured and carried away in fetters.

18:18. vision of the throne room of Yahweh and his council. The familiar picture of a heavenly throne surrounded by the heavenly council is well known from the Ugaritic texts (most notably the Epic of Keret), though this Canaanite council is made up of the gods of the pantheon. Examples occur also in the tenth-century building inscription of Yehimilk from Byblos and the Karatepe stele of Azitawadda. In the Akkadian *Enuma Elish* it is the assembly of the gods that appoints Marduk as their head. Fifty gods made up this assembly, with seven in the inner council. In Israelite belief the gods were replaced by angels or spirits—the sons of God or the heavenly host. Usually one would expect this council to be plotting strategies to go to war on behalf of Israel, but instead the discussion is directed against Ahab.

18:19. council seeking volunteers. In the Ugaritic Epic of Keret the head of the assembly, El, asks for volunteers from the assembly to drive out the illness of Keret. In the end, however, El ends up taking the task on himself and creates a being to effect the healing.

18:19-22. luring spirit. This is a "mole" operation. When David wanted to undermine the success of his rebellious son, Absalom, he plants one of his advisors, Hushai, in Absalom's inner circle. His assignment is to suggest a strategy that will suit Absalom's natural inclinations but will actually work to David's advantage and accomplish David's plan (2 Sam 15:32 37; 16:15—17:14). Here the same process is at work. God has planned to act against Ahab who is seen as being led to his intended doom through the strategies suggested by trusted advisors (the prophets) that will coincide with his natural inclinations.

18:24. hiding in an inner room. The term used here refers to the place of utmost privacy. One usually retreats there to be alone or to find shelter.

18:26. Micaiah's imprisonment. Prisons were not used in the ancient world for reforming criminals. A hardened criminal might more likely find himself on permanent assignment on a labor crew. Prisons not connected with a labor crew were often located in the palace or temple, though they were sometimes simply pits. Some prisoners were in custody pending a trial, but most prisoners were either working off a debt or were political prisoners. This latter group was considered dangerous to the stability of the state rather to the health of the society. Punitive measures for this group often involved humiliating public display rather than isolated incarceration. Micaiah is being imprisoned to await the outcome of his prophecy and the battle—that will constitute his hearing and trial.

18:29. Ahab in disguise. In Assyria, when there was a bad omen (usually an eclipse) warning of evil tidings for the king, the ritual of the substitute king was sometimes performed. This is attested as early as 800 B.C., but is best known from the seventh century. In this ritual another individual was dressed in the robes of the king, and various rites and incantations were performed to identify this individual with the king. This person then took the brunt of the ill-fate that was to befall the king (usually death). It was believed that in this way the evil tidings could be redirected and the king could avoid his fate. While there is little here that would suggest a substitute king ritual, a similar mentality is minimally reflected in Ahab insofar as he expects to avoid the proclaimed doom on the king by not dressing as the king. It must be noted, however, that the avoidance of evil is more prominent here than the transfer of evil represented in the substitute king ritual (for more information on the ritual transfer of evil see comment on 2 Kings 5:27). Most significantly, there is no designated substitute unless Jehoshaphat, by retaining his royal regalia, is intended to function in that role. He became, at the very least, a lightning rod for the doom, just as it was planned for the substitute to be. While Ahab's disguise may in fact fool the enemy soldiers, the greater intention may be to deceive the supernatural forces that would fulfill the destiny which had been prescribed against him.

18:30. Aram's strategy. While the infantry was absorbed in hand-to-hand combat, the Aramean chariotry was specifically targeting the king of Israel. Chariotry typically had very particular objectives in the course of the battle, rather than becoming entangled in the general melee. They might make the initial charge into the infantry, but then would be used to contain the parameters or to pursue certain targets, as here. The strategy of targeting the king was to be able to inflict punishment on him that would prevent future incidents.

18:33. sections of the armor. Armor is described here as made up of two parts: a solid breastplate and a scale-armor kilt. The arrow struck either between the two or between the joints of the scale armor. One of the best descriptions of scale armor comes from the Nuzi texts, where a coat of mail was made up of anywhere from seven hundred to over a thousand bronze scales of varying sizes. These scales were sewn onto a jerkin of leather or cloth. The front and back were sewn together at the shoulders (with a space for the head) and probably reached to the knees. By the ninth century some iron scales were being used.

19:5. appointment of judges. In the Mari documents from the Old Babylonian Period in Syria (c. 2000-1600 B.C.), judges were appointed by the king to perform special tasks, such as assisting in the administration of a territory, acting as a territorial governor, conducting military campaigns and intervening in domestic legal affairs. One can assume that the judicial appointments of Jehoshaphat had more narrowly focused tasks, primarily in the arena of legal affairs. As evidenced by the preface to the Code of Hammurabi (c. 1750 B.C.) and the statements made by the "Eloquent Peasant" in Egyptian wisdom literature (c. 2100 B.C.), the standard for behavior for those in authority is to protect the rights of the poor and weak in society. "True justice" (see Lev 19:15) is expected of kings, officials and local magistrates. In fact, the "world turned upside down" theme found in the book of Judges and in prophetic literature (Is 1:23), de-

scribes a society in which "laws are enacted, but ignored" (for example, in the Egyptian Visions of Neferti [c. 1900]). An efficiently administered state in the ancient Near East depended on the reliability of the law and its enforcement. To this end every organized state created a bureaucracy of judges and local officials to deal with civil and criminal cases. It was their task to hear testimony, investigate charges made, evaluate evidence and then execute judgment (detailed in the Middle Assyrian Laws and the Code of Hammurabi). There were some cases, however, that required the attention of the king (see 2 Sam 15:2-4), and appeals were occasionally forwarded on to that highest magistrate (as in the Mari texts).

19:6-7. judicial system. The term for "judges" was used for both God and humans. Their authority came from God, and their main role was to keep harmonious relations between Israelites (or Judahites in this case). During the monarchy the judges were clearly subordinate to the monarch who appointed them. Thus they did not rule as they did in the period of the judges but governed under the auspices of the king. In the ancient Near East, leaders, whether tribal, military, city, provincial or national, had the obligation of judging the cases under their jurisdiction. There was no trial by jury, though at times a group of elders may have been involved in judging a case. When only one individual judge was involved, the danger of favoring the powerful or the wealthy was very real. Both in ancient Near Eastern documents and the Bible impartiality is valued, along with discernment. There were no lawyers, so most people represented themselves in court. Witnesses could be called, and oaths played a very significant role since most of our scientific means of gathering evidence were not available.

19:8-11. role of Levites and priests. After the division of the monarchy many Levites and priests in the north were cut off from Jerusalem and other southern sanctuaries. Jehoshaphat required the Levites and priests, along with the patriarchal family head, to take over the functions of the judges in Jerusalem (i.e., judging disputes). The Levites were in essence court functionaries who carried out the decisions of the court (see comment on Deut 18:6-8). The roles of priests and judges often overlapped, because oracles were frequently used to decide cases. In situations where physical evidence was not present or was insufficient, a verdict could be determined by the reading of omens. This meant that plaintiffs had to consult religious professionals (Levitical priests in Deut 17:9), whose service included seeking divine verdicts. Many who would come to the capital city of Jerusalem with a legal case would be seeking this type of assistance, so it is logical for this Levitical judiciary to be set up there.

19:11. administrative structure. The Jerusalem court was thus composed of Levites, priests, family heads and judges. There are some parallels with the Egyptian administrations in Dynasty 22 (eleventh to eighth centuries B.C.).

20:1. Moabites and Ammonites. Shalmaneser III of Assyria mentions in his annals an Ammonite king, Ba'sa son of Ruhubi, who contributed soldiers to the Aramean confederacy that fought against Assyria in 853 and 841 B.C. The Moabite king was probably Mesha, known from 2 Kings 3 and from a long inscription in Moabite in which he describes his rebellion against Israel (see comment on 2 Kings 3:4). This particular invasion cannot be found in any extrabiblical source. It may have been during a period in which the western coalition against Assyria had broken down and individual states were fighting against one another.

20:1. Meunites. A number of very different opinions exist concerning the identification of this group. The first is that it should be identified with the Minaeans of South Arabia. Their control of the incense trade had extended up into the region of Palestine by the fourth century. Others would identify the group with the Mu'unaya mentioned in the inscriptions of Tiglath-Pileser III. A third possibility links them to the town of Maon south of Hebron in the hill country of Judah. They appear with other groups that inhabited the southern border of Judah.

20:2. Edom. The heartland of Edom is east of the Arabah (the deep gorge extending south from the Dead Sea to the Gulf of Aqaba) from the Zered (Wadi el Hasa) to the Gulf of Aqaba. During most of the period from David until Jehoshaphat, Edom had been an annexed territory of Judah. Here it appears the Edomites have gained some degree of independence, and their territory served as the strategic base for this raid against Jerusalem.

20:2. Hazazon Tamar/En Gedi. The location of Hazazon Tamar is unknown, but some have placed it near the southern end of the Dead Sea, possibly at el-Hasasa, between En Gedi and Bethlehem. The oasis of En Gedi lies midway down the Dead Sea and approximately thirty-five miles southeast of Jerusalem. Fed by a continuous spring, it is a splash of life and color in the midst of an otherwise barren landscape. It has served as a cultic site, military outpost and commercial center

during its long history. There are a number of fortresses from the period of the monarchy that have been discovered in this area. One is at the spring, while another is at the top of the cliff that offers a view of travelers for miles around.

20:10. Mount Seir. Mount Seir was in Edom. Seir is generally considered the mountainous central region of Edom (elevations generally over five thousand feet) between Wadi al-Ghuwayr on the north and Ras en-Naqb on the south. In this case, the term probably referred to the entire land of Edom itself.

20:16. pass of Ziz. The pass of Ziz has often been associated with the Wadi Hasasa, which drains about nine miles southeast of Tekoa into the Dead Sea. The context of the passage suggests that the pass was an important link between Jerusalem and En Gedi.

20:16. desert of Jeruel. The wilderness of Jeruel was southeast of Tekoa on the descending plain to En Gedi.

20:19. Kohathites and Korahites. The Kohathites and the Korahites were two of the principle families that were involved in the leadership of the Jerusalem temple during the period of the monarchy. They were also two of the most important Levitical families (or clans). In the genealogy of 1 Chronicles 6:22-24 (also see Ex 6:18, 1 Chron 6:31), the Korahites were descended from the Kohathites.

20:20. Desert of Tekoah. The Desert of Tekoah extended east of Tekoa (Khirbet Tequ'a), a town in the highlands of Judah. The area was approximately twelve miles south of Jerusalem.

20:26. Valley of Berakah. The location of the Valley of Berakah ("blessing, praise") is not precisely known. Some scholars believe it may have been Wadi Berekut, between Tekoa and En Gedi.

20:28. harps, lutes and trumpets. The lyre had a widespread use in the ancient Near East. Egyptian tomb paintings show individuals from the Transjordan playing the lyre. The harp was evidently used in Nebuchadnezzar's orchestra (see Dan 3). In Israel it was a wooden instrument with eight strings (see 1 Chron 15:21). There were different types of trumpets used in ancient Israel. This particular type of trumpet was used on military and religious occasions to summon the people. Trumpets are occasionally depicted in the art of the ancient Near East, including the bronze figure of a trumpet player from Caria in southwest Turkey (c. 800 B.C.).

20:31. chronology. According to Thiele, Jehoshaphat ruled 872-848 B.C., and most other reckonings only differ a year or two from those dates. It has been suggested that he was coregent with his father Asa for the first three years of his reign. Contemporary kings in Israel were Ahab, Ahaziah and Joram. Ashurnasirpal II and Shalmaneser III ruled Assyria. No references to Jehoshaphat have yet been found in extrabiblical materials.

20:33. high places. For more information on high places, see the comments on 1 Kings 3:2-3 and Deuteronomy 12:2-3.

20:34. annals. The various annals mentioned in 1 and 2 Kings and 1 and 2 Chronicles that were recorded in the Book of the Kings of Israel are no longer extant. However, one can surmise that they were similar in structure and context to annals of kings from other areas in the ancient Near East. The Assyrians left detailed military annals of their later kings (from about 1100 B.C. onwards), describing military campaigns, strategy, relations with client kings and piety toward national gods. Hittite, Egyptian and Babylonian annals from the mid-second millennium B.C. are similar in nature. It can be assumed that other kingdoms in Syro-Palestine also composed annals.

21:1. chronology. By Thiele's reckoning, Jehoram ruled 853-841 B.C. It has been suggested that he was coregent with his father Jehoshaphat for the first five years of his reign. Contemporary kings in Israel were Ahaziah and Joram. This is a critical period featuring numerous western campaigns by the Assyrian king Shalmaneser III (see comment on 1 Kings 22:1).

21:3. gifts. Jehoshaphat followed a precedent of Rehoboam by placing his sons in fortified towns where they were well provided for (by means of the gifts, see 2 Chron 11:23). This was a well-known Assyrian practice. For example, Esarhaddon (reigned 681-668 B.C.) placed his elder son, Shamash-shum-ukin, on the throne of Babylon, while his younger son, Ashurbanipal, was given the throne of Assyria. Nonetheless, the elder son did not find this "gift" satisfactory and began a civil war soon thereafter.

21:4-20

The Reign of Jehoram

21:4. killing brothers. The practice of removing all other possible claimants to the throne was a well-known practice in the Old Testament (see Judg 9:5 and 2 Kings 11:1) and the ancient Near East. Because of monarchs having multiple marriages (or multiple concubines) and therefore many sons, there were often a large number of claimants to the throne. Rameses II of Egypt (reigned c.

1292-1225 B.C.) had over fifty sons, for example. Since most kingdoms did not always employ the practice of primogeniture, the succession to the throne was often in question.

21:6. relations to Ahab. Marriage alliances between kingdoms was not only a common custom but was considered indispensable for forging good relations with potentially hostile neighbors. One can reconstruct the present scenario here in 2 Chronicles. Jehoshaphat was a close ally of Ahab and thus cemented this alliance with the marriage of his son Jehoram to Ahab's daughter, Athaliah, daughter of Jezebel. Of course, this also brought in Baalistic worship to Judah from Phoenicia, the homeland of Jezebel. See comment on 18:1.

21:7. lamp for David. Lamps were often used metaphorically in Israel to symbolize life and prosperity. They were often placed in tombs for this reason. The expression "his lamp" is often used in Scripture to symbolize life. As an eternal flame is a symbol of endurance and remembrance, so the reign of a descendant of David in Jerusalem provides a link to God's promise to David's dynasty (2 Sam 7:8-16). Similar uses of the word in Ugaritic and Akkadian are tied to perpetuation of rule or divine presence. Assyrian king Tiglath-Pileser III is referred to as the light of all mankind. An Old Babylonian idiom expresses a family having no descendants by the image of its brazier going out.

21:8-10. Edom's revolt. Although this revolt is not described elsewhere in Scripture or in extrabiblical sources, there are destruction levels at Ramet Matred Negev dating from either the raid of Shishak (late tenth century B.C.) or the revolt mentioned in this passage.

21:10. Libnah. Libnah was a major fortress city in Judah that was one of the line of defenses of the capital city, Jerusalem. Thus, if the city revolted, the entire land of Judah was left vulnerable. The town of Libnah is usually identified with either Khirbet Tell el-Beida (nine miles northeast of Lachish) or Tell Bornat (about five miles further west), strategically located by the Wadi Zeita guarding the best route to Hebron from the coast.

21:15, 18. Jehoram's disease. One opinion is that Jehoram's "disease of the bowels" may have been chronic amoebic dysentery. Additionally, some suggest the more specific consequence of a massive rectal prolapse.

21:16-17. invasion of Philistines and Arabs. The invasion here was probably a series of raids from the west (Philistines) and south (Arabs), from well-known enemies of Judah. From the context of the passage it may be assumed that the raid was in response to the vulnerable situation that Judah was in because of the Edomite rebellion.

21:19. fire in his honor. The funeral rites denied Jehoram were often quite elaborate and include the burning of spices in honor of the dead as well as a general lamentation and internment in the family tomb. The fire does not imply cremation of the body or an attempt to mask the odors associated with a diseased body, but was rather an expensive display of the king's wealth. The practice is well known among Assyrian kings where it was used as an apotropaic ritual.

21:20. tombs of the kings. The Judahite kings were buried in the City of David, a small ridge bordered by Kidron, Hinnom and Tyropoeon Valleys. The kings from Rehoboam to Ahaz were buried here (except for some notable exceptions). Later kings were either buried in the "garden of Uzziah" (Manasseh and Amon) or in their own tomb (Josiah). The burial place of Hezekiah and the successors of Josiah is not mentioned. The site of the royal burials in the City of David has not been determined with certainty. Many of the Egyptian kings of the New Kingdom (c. 1550-1050 B.C.) were buried in the Valley of the Kings in separate tombs. There was apparently no such common royal burial place for the kings of Assyria.

22:1-9
The Reign of Ahaziah

22:1. raiders with Arabs. The raiders mentioned as having come with the Arabs are likely related to those mentioned in 2 Chronicles 21. Thus they may have been Philistines and other diverse groups who sought to capitalize on the weakness of the Judahite monarchy. They certainly concluded that Judah was weaker without the Davidic dynastic line in power.

22:2. chronology. Ahaziah ruled in 841 B.C. and was a contemporary of Shalmaneser III of Assyria (reigned 858-824 B.C.). By this time most of the coalition that had withstood Shalmaneser at the Battle of Qarqar had been dismantled, and anti-Assyrian sentiment was becoming less and less popular.

22:5. war against Hazael. The family ties between Judah and Israel explain the joint attack against Hazael of Aram of Damascus. The parties of the western coalition had broken down and were now fighting amongst themselves.

22:6. Jezreel. Jezreel has been identified with Zerin/Tel Yizra'al at the east end of the Jezreel Valley in the territory of Issachar. The city was about fifteen miles southeast of Megiddo. It was the winter capital of the Israelite kingdom by the reign of Ahab. With the destruction of the northern kingdom by the Assyrians (722/21 B.C.), Jezreel lost its importance, which it failed to regain. For more information see 1 Kings 21:1.

22:9. Samaria. Samaria was the capital of the northern kingdom of Israel for two centuries. Omri constructed the city in the early ninth century B.C., and it was destroyed by the Assyrians in 722/21. The city was built on a hill rising three hundred feet above the nearby valleys. It was located along the crossroads of major trade routes that lead to Shechem, the Jordan Valley, Megiddo, Jezreel and Jerusalem. The site has been extensively excavated in this century. For more information see comment on 1 Kings 16:24.

22:10—23:21
Athaliah the Usurper

22:10. Athaliah's executions. As queen mother (see comment on 1 Kings 2:19) during the reign of her son Ahaziah, Athaliah enjoyed an exalted position as "sovereign," which was evidently an official title. This afforded her a special influence on ceremonial and political matters. Following the custom of other dynasts, the usurper Athaliah attempted to destroy the members of the previous Davidic dynasty, in the same fashion that usurpers in the northern kingdom had killed off members of the previous dynasty. Such annihilations of ruling families was common practice both in Israel and in the ancient Near East at large. There is wide precedent in Mesopotamian texts for the elimination of all rival claimants to the throne when a king comes to power.

22:11-12. hiding in the temple. It is not certain where the last remaining Davidide was hidden. Medieval scholars theorized that there was a penthouse where the priests retired that was off-limits to Athaliah. However, no temple bedroom is ever mentioned in Scripture. At any rate the boy was concealed in the lodgings of the high priest in the temple precinct. Besides being a place to which very few would have access, temples in the ancient world were a place of sanctuary and protection.

23:1-3. priests' political power. In much of the ancient Near East the priesthood wielded considerable political power. They had land holdings, independent assets that came as gifts to the temple and an emotional hold on the people. In Israel the power of the prophetic institution is more evident than that of the priests, but it is likely that the priests also carried some political clout. The wife of the high priest Jehoiada, Jehosheba, was the daughter of Joram, the previous ruler, and thus Jehoiada was connected to the royal line by marriage.

23:5. Foundation Gate. The Foundation Gate is called the Sur Gate in 2 Kings 11:6. Its location cannot be determined with certainty.

23:9. weapons from the temple. It is not certain where these weapons were stored, as there is no mention of a temple armory in Scripture. Likely these are ceremonial pieces used by the king in processionals and kept on display. It is possible that they also included important weapons that had been captured in battle or taken as tribute. The Hebrew terms used for the weapons are rare. The Hebrew term that the NIV translates as "small shield" was long obscure but is now recognized as a technical term borrowed from Aramaic referring to a bow case. Ceremonial bow cases are pictured in later Persian reliefs.

23:10. temple geography. The palace guard apparently surrounded the palace on all sides and protected the route from the palace to the temple. From its description in 1 Kings, the temple of Solomon appears to have been enclosed in the larger palace complex. Very little is known of the layout of the temple precinct and palace complex of this time.

23:11. copy of the covenant. This appears to be a document that frames a constitution or charter of some sort. One possibility is that it details the people's subordination to the king and the king's subordination to the Lord. In Egypt the coronation ceremony involved a proclamation by the god Thoth that gave the official approval of the gods for the king's accession. The theme of a covenant between king, subject people and god can also be found in the Hittite annals of the late second millennium B.C. and Assyrian vassal loyalty oaths during the mid-first millennium B.C. In Assyrian records there is a ceremony where Esarhaddon of Assyria made a binding covenant with the people of Assyria to be loyal to his successor, Ashurbanipal. What is different in Scripture is the mention of a document that was physically handed over to the king, which is not mentioned in the extrabiblical sources.

23:11. anointing. The acts here are regular features of the accession ritual of the kings of Israel and Judah. First, the ram's horn was blown to signify the people's recognition and submission to the new king. The phrase "long live the king" is attested in a number of places in the historical books of Scripture and in the enthronement psalms (47, 93, 96, 97, 99). It was used after the accession of the king to the throne. The anointing of the king was also a symbolic gesture of the divine favor of the king before Yahweh. For more information on anointing see comment on 1 Samuel 16:1.

23:13. king's pillar. This may have been one of the two entry pillars at the entrance of the temple, Jachin and Boaz (see comment on 1 Kings 7:15-22). Ezekiel describes the "prince's station" at the "doorposts of the gate" of the temple (Ezek 46:2). The king may have stood on some kind of a platform reserved only for himself.

23:15. Horse Gate on the palace grounds. The Horse Gate was a gate of the temple enclosure and not the Horse Gate of the city. It may have been a passage through which mounted riders entered the city from the east (Jer 31:40).

23:17. destruction of temple (=house) of Baal. This is the only reference to the "House of Baal" in Jerusalem (parallel to 2 Kings 11:18). Thus its location can only be a source of speculation. It may have been a private shrine in the vicinity of the palace. There is, however, a large structure excavated at Ramat Rahel, two miles south of Jerusalem, that has similarities to the palace at Samaria. Its location compares to the location of the Baal Temple of Samaria, which was outside the acropolis of the city. The reaction of the populace to the destruction of the temple of Baal is similar in nature to the purge orchestrated by Jehu some years earlier. All evidences of the previous regime were eliminated. In New Kingdom Egypt, Thutmose III attempted to destroy all vestiges of the reign of Hatshepsut, while Horemheb (and others) did the same to the Aton kings.

23:19. doorkeepers. The doorkeepers were evidently royal guards who were responsible for the entrance to the temple precinct by which the king normally passed (see also 1 Kings 14:28; 2 Kings 11:19). The exact route from the temple to the palace is unclear. It may have been south between the temple mount and the City of David.

23:20. Jerusalem geography. The temple mount was at the highest point on the northern end of the City of David. The palace was situated just south of (and probably adjoining) the temple complex. Immediately southeast was the Kidron Valley, which separated the Temple Mount from the Mount of Olives. Southwest of the City of David was the Ben Hinnom Valley.

24:1-27

The Reign of Joash

24:1. chronology. Joash ruled from 835 to 796 B.C. and was a contemporary of Jehu, Jehoahaz and Jehoash of Israel. Shalmaneser III, Shamshi-Adad V and Adad-Nirari III ruled Assyria during this period.

24:4. ideology of temple restoration in the ancient Near East. The temple was the center of culture, economy and society in Syria, Mesopotamia and Israel. It served as the house of the city's patron deity, and thus the god's presence was considered to exist there. It was incumbent upon the ruler of the city to attend to the "care and feeding" of the deity. The statue of the god was bathed, clothed and fed daily. Just as important as the king's military success was his attention to the upkeep of the god's house. Countless building inscriptions from both Assyria and Babylonia attest to the king's piety because of his restoration of a certain god's house. Similarly, those who rebuilt or restored Yahweh's were accorded this same type of piety. Restoration entailed both physical and ritual aspects. A neglected temple would need structural repairs (see comment on v. 13) and perhaps the restoration of pilfered furniture and accessories. It is possible that gold objects or gold plating on walls would need to be replaced. Then the temple would need to have its sanctity reestablished through appropriate rituals. Finally, it would need to be provided with funding and personnel so that it could operate.

24:5. collection of funds. The collecting of funds for the restoration of a temple was a common occurrence by monarchs in the ancient Near East. Often, though, the monarch would restore the temple by means of corvee labor or by collecting building materials from his subjects. The initial collection procedure is described only in 2 Kings 12:5-7 and was unsuccessful. It entailed receiving funds from the "treasurers" (NIV). This word only occurs in this context and has now been identified in both Ugaritic and Akkadian texts dealing with temple treasuries. It could refer either to officers who distributed temple assets or to the assets themselves.

24:5. taxation in Israel. There are surprisingly few words in Scripture for "tax." The most common term was a generic word meaning to "evaluate for taxation." The term is used for the tribute that Israelite kings were obliged to pay ruling overlords. It was also used in connection with collecting funds for the temple, as here. The process of taxation is described in 1 Samuel 8:15-17. The king could also exempt a household from taxation (see 1 Sam 17:25). Solomon had a core of governors who periodically collected taxes (1 Kings 4:7-19). It appears that the rebellion against Rehoboam was motivated by tax abuse. Ostraca from Samaria record deliveries of wine for the use of the king, with the phrase, "for the king." These ostraca were from several sites that were probably depots where the local taxes were gathered. Another aspect of taxation was forced labor (see Ex 1:10; Josh 16:10; 2 Sam 20:24). Although taxation in Mesopotamia is much better documented, it appears to have similar attributes to taxation practices found in Israel.

24:6. Tent of the Testimony. The Tent of the Testimony was more commonly called the Tent of Meeting or tabernacle (see comment on Ex 33:7-10). It was the central place of worship for the Israelites before the construction of the temple of Solomon. It was the shrine that housed the ark of the covenant and various other cultic objects. The tabernacle continued to play an important link to Israel's history, even during the monarchy, and one gets the impression that somehow the tent was set up inside the temple precinct (see 1 Kings 8:4 = 2 Chron 5:5).

24:11. shared custody of funds between king and priests. The sharing of custody for funds used in temple restorations is attested in the records of Assyrian king Esarhaddon (seventh century). Here also there are accusations on both sides regarding who is responsible for the delay in the project.

24:12. repair crew. The regular maintenance of the temple complex was the responsibility of the "workmen in charge of the temple." Major repairs had to be contracted out to skilled workers. The listing of these skilled laborers is typical of contemporary Assyrian records.

24:13. nature of the work. It appears that the skilled workers restored the temple to its original foundations. The skilled workers were carpenters, builders, masons and stonecutters. The term for "builder" was used for both skilled and unskilled laborers who worked primarily with mudbrick. The carpenter was responsible for all of the wood items in construction, including the roof, door, window and stair fittings, and various cultic objects in the temple. The mason/stonecutter quarried the stones from natural caves or drove shafts in the hillside. Then the stones were cut and fitted into place. It will be remembered that Solomon contracted Phoenician craftsmen to build the temple. It is not expressly stated that foreign workers were used to refurbish the temple during the reign of Joash.

24:14. articles for the temple. The cultic vessels mentioned here were made by Solomon's craftsmen (1 Kings 7:50) and were distinct from those made by the Phoenicians (1 Kings 7:13-47). They became booty for Nebuchadnezzar II during his capture of Jerusalem more than two centuries after Joash. The terms are best described as "vessels for the service and for the burnt offering, bowls and gold and silver vessels."

24:15. Jehoiada 130 years old. Jehoiada lived longer than Moses (120 years) and Aaron (123 years), showing his great favor with God. The fact that the Chronicler called attention to Jehoiada's age shows his great importance, equal to any of the Judahite monarchs. Egyptian texts considered 110 to be the ideal old age, while Mesopotamian ideas targeted 120. In the sixth century, Adad-Guppi, the mother of the Babylonian king Nabonidus, is said to have lived to the age of 104.

24:18. Asherah poles. The Asherah poles were apparently man-made objects and often were situated near trees (see Jer 17:2), although they may have actually been living trees on occasion (see Deut 16:21). The Asherah cult object symbolized the goddess herself. The poles were often associated with the image of the goddess, which was a separate item altogether. For more information see comment on 2 Kings 13:6.

24:23. war in spring. In the ancient Near East spring was a popular time in which to commence military ventures. First of all, the weather in the winter was prohibitive for extensive military travel. Second, because of harvesting in the spring, invading armies were able to forage for food. The Assyrian annals make a point of describing any particular military campaign that happened during the winter or the dead of summer, when there was unbearable heat for the soldiers.

24:23-24. war with Aram. In the last decades of the ninth century the Aramean kingdom of Damascus was relieved of Assyrian pressures and was able to assert its influence south and west into Judah (see comment on 2 Kings 10:32). There was an attack on Gath (probably Gittaim in the northern Shephelah, not Philistine Gath), which posed a direct threat on Jerusalem (see 2 Kings 12:18). The Aramean king at this time was Hazael (see comment on 2 Kings 8:8), who ruled from 843 B.C. to near the end of the ninth century.

25:1-28
The Reign of Amaziah

25:1. chronology. Thiele assigns to Amaziah the years 796-767 B.C. He was contemporary with Jehoash and Jeroboam II of Israel. Adad-Nirari III, Shalmaneser IV and Ashur-Dan III ruled Assyria during his time.

25:5. size of military. The term in Hebrew for thousand, 'eleph, is also employed for "unit,"

which makes more sense in this passage. Thus Amaziah's census found three hundred units of available men to be soldiers, and there is no precise number of available soldiers given in the text. For more information on numbers see comments on 2 Chronicles 11:1; 13:2-20.

25:6. mercenaries. The use of mercenaries in ancient Near Eastern warfare was widespread. The Assyrians began to rely heavily on mercenaries by the reign of Tiglath-Pileser III (reigned 745-727 B.C.). Although mercenaries were experienced and well trained, their loyalty was often called into question when they did not get their pay in a timely fashion, or if they were fighting against a kindred foe. Ionian mercenaries left the Persian camp and fought for the Greeks at the Battle of Plataea during the Persian wars (480 B.C.).

25:6. hundred talents of silver. The talent was the largest weight measure used in the Near East. It was comparable to three thousand shekels at Alalakh and Ugarit in Syria and in the Old Testament (Ex 38:25-6). One hundred talents of silver weighed about three and one quarter tons. Obviously this was the total amount spent hiring the mercenaries and comes to one talent of silver for each division. This is not exorbitant pay and was just "earnest money"—the real payoff would come in the plunder.

25:11. Valley of Salt. The Valley of Salt has been identified with Wadi el-milh, east of Beersheba, about three miles due south of the Dead Sea. There are numerous areas in the region where the cliffs are high enough for people to be thrown to their death.

25:11. Seir. Seir was the biblical name for part of the country of Edom and was often used as a synonym for Edom. So "the sons of Seir" would be another name for the Edomites. Seir is listed as a geographic toponym in the Amarna letters from Egypt (fourteenth century B.C.).

25:12. styles of execution. Throwing enemy prisoners off a cliff is not known as a style of execution outside of this passage. It was likely the most convenient form of execution because of the geographical circumstances. In A.D. 67, during the Jewish revolt against Rome, thousands of Jews from Gamla hurled themselves off the cliff rather than be captured by the Romans.

25:13. Samaria to Beth Horon. Beth Horon is at the ascent between the Valley of Aijalon and the hill country, about twelve miles northwest of Jerusalem. From where the armies are, the main road home goes north from Arad to Hebron where it swings a bit to the west and then proceeds north through the Shephelah. From Arad to Beth Horon along this road is about fifty miles. The city of Samaria was over fifty miles further north of Beth Horon and was the capital of the northern kingdom, so cannot be the city intended here. Either there was another "Samaria" in Judah, not known elsewhere in Scripture, or the text originally read something like "Hebron." Since most of the mercenaries' pay came from plunder, this was their way of collecting.

25:14. gods of Seir. It is generally assumed that these would be the images of the Edomite gods. The national god of the Edomites was Qos. It is not unusual that worship should be offered to deities of defeated nations. At Dan standing stones were found at a shrine just inside the city gate, and the clear remains of the presentation of votive offerings were evident. It is thought that the standing stones represented some of the deities of cities that had fallen to Israel. The votive offerings would be in fulfillment of vows made to those deities (perhaps for their aid in overthrowing the city the Israelites were fighting against).

25:21. Beth Shemesh. Beth Shemesh was a town about fifteen miles west of Jerusalem in the Shephelah region between Jerusalem and the coastal territory of Philistia. It was an important fortress town that guarded the Sorek pass from raiders who desired to plunder Jerusalem. The site of Beth Shemesh (Tell er-Rumeliah) has remains showing an extensive Canaanite occupation of the city before the Israelite conquest.

25:23. topography of Jerusalem. Scholars have supposed that the Ephraim gate was located at the northwest corner of the city of Jerusalem, while the corner gate was at the northeast corner. The northern portion of Jerusalem was the only direction that allowed easy accessibility to the town. Other areas of the wall did not make for easy access because of the Valley of Ben Hinnom to the southwest and the Kidron Valley to the southeast.

25:24. plunder of Jehoash. Assyrian records often show that the family of the defeated king was sent under guard to Assyria to be hostages in order to guarantee the good behavior of the king. Ashurnasirpal II (reigned 883-859) is described as "taking hostages and establishing victory." Here the identity of the Judahite prisoners is not mentioned, but it can be assumed they were either part of the royal family or important members of the nobility.

25:27. Lachish. Lachish (Tell ed-Duweir) was a major fortress city in the Judahite Shephelah. It is not surprising that Amaziah went to this town, since it was in the line of defense surrounding Jerusalem. Both the Assyrians and the Babylonians captured Lachish in their invasions of Judah in the eighth and seventh centuries B.C. Located about thirty miles southwest of Jerusalem, the site covers some thirty acres.

26:1-23
The Reign of Uzziah

26:2. Elath. Elath (or Eloth) was the seaport constructed by Solomon at the head of the Gulf of Aqaba (see comment on 2 Chron 8:17). It was closely associated with the nearby port of Ezion Geber. It opened trade for Judah with Arabia, Africa and India. Uzziah apparently attempted to revive the Red Sea trade instituted by Solomon.

26:3. chronology. Uzziah's long reign is calculated by Thiele as lasting from 792 to 740 B.C. Scholars postulate that he had a long coregency with his father Amaziah on one end of his reign and with his son, Jotham, on the other. He was a contemporary with Jeroboam II (for forty of the fifty-two years), Zechariah, Shallum, Menahem, Pekah and Pekahiah of Israel. Adad-Nirari III, Shalmaneser IV, Ashur-Dan, Ashur-Nirari V and Tiglath-Pileser III ruled Assyria. Assyria was weak during most of this period, allowing for expansion and prosperity for both Israel and Judah. Uzziah's name has been found on a seal from Tell Beit Mirsim. Tiglath-Pileser's records mention a king named Azriau of Yaudi, but most do not equate this individual with Uzziah.

26:6-8. military successes. Although there are no other literary sources which describe Uzziah's victories over the Philistines, Arabs and Meunites, there is archaeological evidence of destruction at the Philistine city of Ashdod, which may have been done during the time of Uzziah. There is also evidence that Uzziah constructed fortresses in these newly conquered territories. Gath (Tell es-Safi; see comment on 1 Sam 5:8), Ashdod and Jabneh form a triangle about ten or fifteen miles on each side that dominates the northern section of the Philistine plain directly west of Jerusalem. Tell Mor near the Philistine city of Ashdod provides one example of such a fortress. Since Uzziah was not able to expand north because of the power of Israel under Jeroboam II, he turned his attention to the west and south, subduing people groups that had taken advantage of previously unstable conditions in Judah. For more information on the Meunites see comment on 20:1. The site of Gurbaal remains unidentified.

26:9. Jerusalem towers. Although the towers

built by Uzziah have not been identified, they were presumably similar to the towers built by the Assyrians at their major cities of Nineveh, Calah, Assur and Dur-Sharrukin. Dur-Sharrukin was a fortress built by Sargon II (reigned 721-705 B.C.), with towers strategically placed at the four corners of the city. See 2 Chronicles 25:23 for a description of the gates where the towers of Uzziah were built. Recent discovery of a massive tower in the vicinity of the Gihon Spring may yet prove to be part of these fortifications.

26:10. towers in the desert. There is archaeological evidence of Uzziah's building activity in Judah. The tower in the stratigraphic level IIIB at Gibeah was probably built in this period. The intensive building activity at Tell Abu Selimeh may also date from this period. There is evidence of early buildings and cisterns at Qumran and Ain Feshkha that date to Uzziah's reign. Fortifications, cisterns and farms have also been located in the Negeb area near Beersheba.

26:11-13. Uzziah's army. Evidence of Uzziah's power is shown by the fact that he had a standing army and did not have to rely upon conscripting soldiers during times of conflict. Assyrian sources indicate that Uzziah's army was significant enough to have taken part in a coalition against Tiglath-Pileser III during his invasion of the Levant in the mid-eighth century B.C.

26:14. arms. The wealth of Uzziah afforded him the opportunity to arm his soldiers with the traditional weaponry in the Near East in the Iron Age. The weapons mentioned here were also those listed as ones used by the Assyrian army. The Assyrians describe their weaponry in detail in their annals, and they are often depicted in wall reliefs at the king's palace. It can be presumed that Uzziah began to build up his army because of the threat of Assyria and of neighboring Israel.

26:15. machines. The "machines" made by Uzziah were probably protective shielding devices mounted on the walls providing protection for defenders to throw stones and shoot arrows at the enemy. The material remains from the Judahite fortress at Lachish attest to the nature of Uzziah's constructions. Additionally, they are represented in the Assyrian wall reliefs at Sennacherib's palace at Nineveh. In the past some interpreters had suggested that these were catapults, but there is no evidence of the use of catapults this early.

26:16-19. Uzziah's offense. Uzziah's offense was a direct violation of priestly prerogatives concerning the temple worship (Num 16:40). The altar of incense was located inside the outer chamber of the temple which denied access to all but officiating priests. The sacrilege he was charged with ("unfaithful," NIV v. 18) is the offense that was addressed by reparation offerings (see comment on Lev 5:14-16).

26:19. leprosy. Mari king Yahdun-Lim calls down a curse of leprosy on whoever desecrated the temple that he was dedicating, so it is clear that this is a common connection. Those studying the ancient Near Eastern languages have concluded that the term often translated "leprosy" is more accurately rendered "lesion," or, less technical, "scaly skin." Such patches could be swelled or weeping, as well as flaking. Similar broad terminology also exists in Akkadian, where the Babylonians likewise considered it an unclean condition and the punishment of the gods. Clinical leprosy (Hansen's Disease) has not been attested in the ancient Near East prior to the time of Alexander the Great. None of the most prominent characteristics of Hansen's disease are listed in the text, and the symptoms that are listed argue against a relationship to Hansen's disease. The condition discussed in the text is not presented as contagious. Descriptions would suggest that modern diagnoses would include psoriasis, eczema, favus and seborrheic dermatitis, as well as a number of fungal-type infections. Because of this, it is not clear exactly what type of skin disease Uzziah had. Comparison to "snow" most likely concerns the flakiness rather than the color ("white" is added in the translations that contain it). The great cultural aversion to skin diseases may be that in appearance and sometimes odor they resemble the rotting skin of the corpse and are therefore associated with death. This natural revulsion adds considerably to the victim's outcast status when combined with the quarantine that is ritually rather than medically motivated. It is not certain whether Uzziah was quarantined because of the disease or because of his cultic offenses. Naaman had a similar disease and was able to continue his duties as commander in chief. It is presumed that Jotham, son of Uzziah, took over official duties as coregent after Uzziah's cultic offense.

26:23. Uzziah's tomb. There is an epitaph now preserved in the Israel Museum marking the burial place of Uzziah, king of Judah. It represented a secondary burial of his bones.

27:1-9

The Reign of Jotham

27:1. chronology. Jotham ruled from 750 to 732 B.C. and was possibly coregent with his father Uzziah for ten years and with his son Ahaz for three years. Extrabiblical evidence of Jotham's reign includes a signet ring found at Tell el-Kheleifeh with his name and the picture of a horned ram. He is also named on a bulla found of Ahaz's royal seal.

27:3. Upper Gate of the Temple. Little is known of the architectural history of the temple after Solomon. The Upper Gate of the temple was located at the north entrance to the temple enclosure. Jeremiah was confined to the Upper Benjamin Gate, which was probably the same as the Upper Gate.

27:3. hill of Ophel. The hill of Ophel is identified as the section between the temple mount and the southern ridge known as the city of David. Apparently it featured fortifications that surrounded the temple-palace complex. Some believe that there was a citadel located here that was itself designated "the Ophel."

27:4. forts. Jotham continued his father's extensive building programs in Judah by constructing fortress cities in the highlands of Judah, most likely as a line of defense against invasion. Not only did he build forts in the wooded areas, he may have engaged in a program of forestation. No excavations have as yet identified fortifications that can be definitively connected to Jotham. It is in his reign, however, that the Neo-Assyrian Empire takes shape under Tiglath-Pileser III. Undoubtedly the renewed emphasis on defense projects reflects the rising threat.

27:5. Ammonites. The Ammonites lived north of the Moabites in the region around the Jabbok River. They are known from Assyrian records as Bit-Ammon and as the land of Ben-ammanu. At the end of Jotham's reign, the king of Ammon was Sharib. No Ammonite or Assyrian records illumine the history of the Ammonites prior to 733. They had paid tribute to Uzziah but apparently tried to break free of Judah's control and had to be suppressed with force.

27:5. amount of tribute. The amount of tribute given by the Ammonites is very large and compares with the terms that the Assyrians gave to Judah during the reign of Hezekiah (2 Kings 18:14-17). A hundred talents of silver was over three tons, while ten thousand cors each of wheat and barely were about sixty-five thousand bushels each (see comment on 2:10).

28:1-27

The Reign of Ahaz

28:1. chronology. Thiele places the rule of Ahaz from 735 to 715 B.C. This would make

him a contemporary of Hoshea, the last king of Israel, as well as of the Assyrian kings Tiglath-Pileser III, Shalmaneser V and Sargon II. The chronology of this period is very complicated, and the numbers from one system to another vary considerably. Most systems depend on a complex combination of coregencies. One possibility with Ahaz is to see him as being thrust onto the throne by a pro-Assyrian faction within the administration of Judah as early as 741 with the hope that cooperation with Assyria could maintain peace. Ahaz is named (referred to by the longer form of his name, Jehoahaz, in Assyrian, Iauhazi) in one of Tiglath-Pileser's building inscriptions as having paid tribute. A bulla (seal impression) of his royal seal has also been found.

28:2. cast idols. Ahaz cast idols of the Baals of Canaan, not to local representations. The plural (Baals) may be used as a parallel with the plural Elohim, the generic name for the Hebrew God. Casting idols for worship was specifically condemned in the Mosaic Law (see Ex 34:17). Metal casts of Canaanite deities (including Baals) have been found at numerous sites in Palestine.

28:3. Valley of Ben Hinnom. The Valley of Ben Hinnom was on the south side of Jerusalem and joined the Kidron Valley at the southeast corner of the city. Access from the city to Ben Hinnom came from the Potsherd Gate and the Valley Gate. The valley became infamous for Baal worship because of the acts of Ahaz and Manasseh. Josiah defiled the region in order to prevent future idolatrous acts (2 Kings 23:10).

28:3. sons passing through the fire. The biblical writers distinguished between the practice of the nations of burning their children in the service to their gods (Deut 12:31 and 2 Kings 17:31) and the idolatrous Israelites who "passed their sons and daughters through the fire." If "passing through the fire" was something different than child sacrifice, it is not certain what it was. In Deuteronomy 18:9 "passing through the fire" appears with other Canaanite divination practices. There are hints from contemporary Assyrian sources of burning children in this period. In some Assyrian economic documents the penalty clauses include "burning children to Sin."

28:4. high places, spreading trees. The worship at high places is not attributed to other Judahite kings but to the people of Judah (e.g., 1 Kings 22:44). A different verbal form is used in Hebrew to denote illegal sacrifices at shrines opposed to legal sacrifices at the Jerusalem temple. Ahaz, of course, was condemned for his illegal sacrifices. For more information on high places see comment on 2 Kings 17:9.

28:5. defeat by Arameans. This is a description of what is called the Syro-Ephraimitic War. One popular reconstruction maintains that states in the region of Syria and Palestine (including Israel and Aram) had forged a coalition to fight against the rising power of Assyria under Tiglath-Pileser III. Rezin of Aram-Damascus headed this coalition in 733 B.C. One year earlier, Aram and Israel attempted to force Ahaz of Judah to join the coalition against Assyria. The two states sought to dethrone Ahaz (see Is 7:6). Upon an appeal from Ahaz, Assyria marched west in 733-732 B.C. and devastated the area, ending the Damascene state and setting up a puppet king in Israel (Hoshea). Others believe that the aggression of the Syro-Ephraimite coalition reflected only their own ambitions for expansion and had nothing to do with a coalition against Assyria. The Assyrian annals of Tiglath-Pileser III are badly mutilated, but a general picture of the Assyrian conquest can be obtained.

28:14-15. treatment of prisoners. The Assyrian annals and wall reliefs depict the harsh conditions of those who were deported from their own territory. The males are normally naked, often with hooks in their nose or lips, and some are missing limbs. Others are carrying their worldly belongings with them. It appears that the Israelites had a similar policy, which was condemned by the prophet Oded. The extent of care and mercy described in these verses is, therefore, remarkable.

28:16. Ahaz asking help of Assyrians. In response to the invasion of Judah by the other Syro-Palestian states, Ahaz appealed to Assyria. Although the Assyrian annals do not explicitly state his appeal, he is listed as one of the kings who gave tribute to Tiglath-Pileser III.

28:17-18. military difficulties. Not only was Ahaz fearful of Aram-Israelite invasions, it appears his appeal to Assyria was for his war against Edom and Philistia. Recent excavations along the ancient border between Edom and Judah have confirmed the expansion of Edom into the Negev of Judah at towns such as En Hatzeva and Qitmit. Pottery ostraca from Arad that contain military correspondence from this period also show that Edomite invasions were considered imminent. The Philistines expanded their presence into the Shephelah region, regaining control of the area that had been under Judean control during the reign of Uzziah (see comment on 26:6-8). The description includes the three main passes into the Judean hills (the Aijalon,

Sorek and Elah Valleys). There are no archaeological finds that illumine this Philistine conquest in any of the sites mentioned here. Tiglath-Pileser's campaign of 734 included the Philistines among his targets. This led to setting up a stele in Gaza in 734 and the conquest of Ashkelon in 733. An Assyrian letter from Nimrud indicates the unstable conditions that existed in Palestine at this time. The territories lost by Ahaz were not returned to him but organized into Assyrian provinces.

28:23. gods of Damascus. Most of the people groups in the ancient Near East believed that the gods had limited geographic jurisdiction. The god's land was in effect under the stewardship of the monarch. Normally the gods did not have control of events occurring in other regions (where other gods had jurisdiction). Since most wars were conducted as holy wars, credit was given to the god(s) of the victorious army. As early as the mid-third millennium B.C. the Sumerian city of Lagash claimed that their gods gave them victory over neighboring Umma. Here Ahaz is making a frank admission that since the Arameans had been victorious over him, their gods were more powerful and in the right. The gods of Damascus were from the Aramean pantheon and included Hadad (the storm deity), which was most probably the proper name of Baal, known from Canaanite sources. Ahaz also made a large altar to the "gods of Damascus" (see 2 Kings 16:9-16). It is not clear whether the altar was Phoenician, Aramean or even Assyrian. It was to replace the bronze altar built by Solomon. The temple that Ahaz visited was probably that of Hadad-Rimmon (cf. 2 Kings 5:18). However the rites described here are typically Israelite.

28:24. furnishings of the temple. The furnishings of the temple probably included vessels, utensils, furniture and tools. According to 2 Kings 16:17-18 Ahaz was required to send very precise items, including the "Sabbath canopy," to the king of Assyria. The Assyrians did not normally interfere with local cultic practices. It appears that Ahaz sent them to satisfy a metal tribute obligation.

28:24. altars at every street corner. Babylonian texts speak of small open-air shrines or niches on street corners or courtyards. One text says that there were 180 of them in the city of Babylon to the goddess Ishtar. These shrines featured a raised structure with an altar on the top and seem to have been frequented primarily by women. In this sense the word "corner" may refer to what is basically a cultic niche.

28:25. each town with a high place. The

whole land of Judah was now made a center of foreign cultic practices. The Assyrians (and Arameans, for that matter) did not require any people group to switch allegiance to different gods, but a tributary group may have felt that their relationship with the conquerors would improve if they followed their deities. For information about high places see comment on 2 Kings 17:9.

29:1—32:33
The Reign of Hezekiah

29:1. chronology. Hezekiah's dates are the most controversial, and Thiele, in acknowledged contradiction to some of the biblical synchronisms, assigns him the date of 715-687 B.C., contemporary with Sargon II and Sennacherib of Assyria. Egyptian monarchs of this period were Shabako, Shebitku and Taharqa. Many consider it more likely that Hezekiah came to the throne in 727 and that his encounter with Sennacherib in his fourteenth year (2 Kings 18:13) took place when Sennacherib was still only the crown prince leading the armies for his father, Sargon II. Assyrian records confirm that there was a campaign to the west against Ashdod in 713. This represents the beginning of a lengthy series of conflicts between these protagonists that came to a climax in the siege of Jerusalem in 701 after Sennacherib had ascended to the throne. Archaeological evidence of Hezekiah's reign includes a seal found at Tell Beit Mirsim with Hezekiah's name that dates to his reign. The royal jar-handle stamps found in Syro-Palestine from the late eighth century onward probably also originated during Hezekiah's reign. Along with the expansion and building at Jerusalem (see the comment on 32:5), there is a great shaft at Lachish that was probably built in this period.

29:3. ideology of temple restoration in the ancient Near East. The temple was the center of culture, economy and society in Syria, Mesopotamia and Israel. It served as the house of the city's patron deity, and thus the god was believed to be present there. It was incumbent upon the ruler of the city to attend to the "care and feeding" of the deity. The statue of the god was bathed, clothed and fed daily. Just as important as the king's military success was his attention to the upkeep of the god's house. Countless building inscriptions from both Assyria and Babylonia attest to the king's piety because of his restoration of a certain god's house. Similarly, those who rebuilt or restored Yahweh's house were accorded this same type of piety. Restoration entailed both physical and ritual aspects. A neglected temple would need structural repairs and perhaps the restoration of pilfered furniture and accessories. It is possible that gold objects or gold plating on walls would need to be replaced. Then the temple would need to have its sanctity reestablished through appropriate rituals. Finally, it would need to be provided with funding and personnel so that it could operate.

29:4-15. the Levites. The Levitical families had not played a major role in the Jerusalem cult since the time of Jehoshaphat, over a century earlier. In accordance with typical restoration procedures, Hezekiah used the traditional priestly families to cleanse the temple and restore it to ritual purity. He then restored them to their original functions (see comment on 19:5).

29:15 consecration. Consecration is a process of ritual purification to prepare someone for association with that which is holy. Procedures varied from one culture to another, but most shared the idea that some ritual process was necessary so that impurity could be removed and the sanctity of the deity's house preserved. The priests were presumably consecrated based upon the detailed rules found in Exodus 29.

29:16. Kidron Valley. The Kidron Valley southeast of the temple was connected to Ben Hinnom, which had long been a dumping ground for the people of Jerusalem. Hezekiah, like Josiah, attempted to cleanse the Jerusalem temple complex by taking all of the illegal cultic items to this valley. The Kidron Valley was also used as a burial ground for the common people.

29:17. calendar. The first month was Nisan, which spanned our spring months of March and April. This was the beginning of the religious calendar of festivals. The purification procedure moved from the outer areas toward the inner ones, because each area had its own ritual requirements. When one level of purity was reached, an area could be entered. The next level of purity would allow access to the next, and so on. It took eight days to consecrate the areas contiguous to the temple, and eight more to carry out the procedure on the temple structure itself.

29:17. consecration of articles. The temple was rededicated in three steps; the temple was cleansed, it was then reconsecrated, and then there was the inaugural dedication ceremony. The articles that Ahaz removed had to be reconsecrated, because they had been removed from the sacred precincts and so were no longer pure.

29:21-24. sacrificial ritual. There were no sacrificial rituals used in the dedication of the tabernacle. When the temple of Solomon was dedicated, the animals sacrificed were too numerous to count. Nowhere does the text offer instructions for the numbers reflected here. For information about the sin offering see comments on Leviticus 4:1-3 and 4-12.

29:25. musical instruments. For harps and lyres see the note on 2 Chronicles 20:28. There were two kinds of cymbals used in the ancient Near East. One consisted of two shallow metal plates held with one in each hand and struck together. The others were shaped like a cup. One cymbal was held stationary while being struck with the other one. It is not certain which type of cymbal was employed here, but they were probably made of bronze.

29:27-30. singing. Reference to the words of David and Asaph suggests the Levites probably used a hymnal or psalter, possibly somewhat like the book of Psalms. Most ancient Near Eastern monarchs employed singers (both male and female) for use in the palace and temple. The Mari archives describe in detail the female singers and the daily food supplies that were needed for their sustenance. Over twenty-four classes of singers are known in Israel (1 Chron 25). The names of the three heads of families of singers are also known (Asaph, Heman and Ethan; 1 Chron 6:18-32). The singers were presumably free men, but slaves were also attached to the temple (Ezra 2:43-58; Neh 7:46-60). Women played a role in the music of the tabernacle (Ex 38:8), but there is no clear reference to there being female singers associated with the temple.

29:29-30. posture of worship. Some texts indicate that the Israelites prayed standing upright (1 Sam 1:26; 1 Kings 8:22; Jer 18:20). Other texts describe a kneeling posture (e.g., 2 Chron 6:13), the raising of the hands (Ps 28:2; Is 1:15; Lam 2:19) and even total prostration (Ps 5:8; 99:5, 9). Posture may have varied depending on the nature of the prayer. The Israelites were not unique with regard to their posture in prayer. There are many examples from Mesopotamia describing individuals in all of the postures mentioned above. For example, the incantation prayers of Mesopotamian sources, such as that to Ishtar, imply prostration of the supplicant as well as a ritual of raising the hands. Hittite sources suggest similar postures and gestures.

29:29-30. worship in the outdoors. The Israelites of Jerusalem normally prayed at the temple courts, facing the sanctuary itself (Ps 5:8; 28:2; 138:2). The Jew outside Jerusalem faced in the direction of the city of Jerusalem and temple (1 Kings 8:44-48). In most ancient Near

Eastern cultures the common person did not have access to the inside of a temple but did his worship in the temple courts. The temples of the ancient world were not built to be houses of worship but residences for the divine presence. Worship (prayers and sacrifices) was carried out at the temple, but there were no regular worship services at which all of the faithful gathered.

29:31. thank offerings. The thank offerings were types of fellowship offerings (see comment on Lev 3:1-5). Portions of this offering were consumed on the altar, while the worshiper ate the remainder.

29:32-33. animals for burnt offerings. The provisions for the burnt offerings are found in Leviticus 1:1-17. Verse 32 numbers the burnt offerings, which were fully consumed by fire, while verse 33 enumerates the thank offerings, which included a token burnt portion with the rest used as a basis for a communal meal. This combination of offerings was common in public ceremonies.

29:35-6. sacrifice and feasting. Biblical feasts were different in purpose, content and origin from those of other peoples in the ancient Near East. Ancient Near Eastern feast days coincided with the New Year or the change of seasons. The Israelite took part in the feast as one who was indebted to the grace of Yahweh. The feasts of their neighbors typically included periods of mourning, processions, the performance of sacred dramas (as well as other entertainment) and an opportunity to ask oracles of the deity.

30:1. Hezekiah's initiative toward northern kingdom. The northern kingdom of Israel had been conquered by the Assyrians (see comment on 2 Kings 17:5-6), who were now bearing down on the remainder of the western states. Hezekiah's father, Ahaz, had instituted a policy of cooperation with Assyria, which is documented by his incorporation into the Assyrian tribute lists. Hezekiah attempted to reclaim some of the territory of Israel which had been gained by Uzziah and lost by Ahaz (see 2 Kings 18:4-8). Hezekiah's political ambitions could only be accomplished with the establishment of a religious base in the north. Hezekiah probably began these initiatives as a result of the death in battle of Sargon II of Assyria (705 B.C.). With Assyria in turmoil, Hezekiah began to expand his territorial horizons. This eventually results in the invasion of Syro-Palestine by Sennacherib (701 B.C.).

30:1-3. reinstitution of Passover. The disaster of the fall of Samaria likely caused an internal reformation in Israel that was sympathetic to Hezekiah's policies and his attempt to reunify the nation in the worship at Jerusalem. Refugees from the north had no doubt fled to Judah after the Assyrian conquest, especially since Israel had now taken on aspects of syncretism (the mixing of worship with foreign religious elements). The national celebration of Passover fit well into Hezekiah's designs to reunify the nation. Both the Israelites and Judahites were able to hearken back to a past event which both groups shared, the exodus.

30:2-3. timing of Passover. The Passover was normally held on the fourteenth of the first month in the Hebrew calendar. However, there was a provision (Num 9:6-13) that allowed those who were either unclean or absent on a distant journey to observe the Passover in the second month. Hezekiah delayed the celebration to allow the northerners to attend.

30:13. pilgrimage feasts. There were three major feasts in the Hebrew calendar that called for pilgrimage to Jerusalem (for discussion see comments on Ex 23.15-17). During these feasts the number of pilgrims in Jerusalem made for very crowded conditions. Pilgrimage was more limited in the ancient Near Eastern religious practice, because most worship took place at local shrines of patron deities. Nevertheless people in outlying regions would make pilgrimage to shrines. Possible evidence of this occurs in the discovery of caravanseria, such as that at Kuntillet Ajrud, where graffiti was left by travelers who may have been pilgrims (though maybe merchants). In Babylonia some may have traveled to the capital to participate in New Year's Enthronement festivals, but it was not part of the religious expectation. In Egypt it was more likely for the gods to travel around to their various shrines in procession rather than for people to travel to any sort of centralized shrine.

30:15-17. Passover rituals. Hezekiah's Passover deviated from the general practice in two ways. First, the time of the celebration was different (see the note 2 Chron 30:2-3), and second, the Israelites were exempted from certain ritual prescriptions. Because many in the assembly had not sanctified themselves, the Levites presided over the slaying of the paschal lambs, a task normally done by the heads of families, most of whom were not sanctified in this instance (Num 9:6). However, those who were unclean were allowed in some instances to eat the paschal lamb.

30:21. Feast of Unleavened Bread. The Feast of Unleavened Bread was established to memorialize the deliverance of the Hebrews from Egypt (see comment on Ex 12:14-20). It was one of three annual festivals and was normally observed on the fourteenth day of the first month. For seven days unleavened bread was eaten and no manual labor was done. Sacrifices were offered on the first and last days of the month (Num 28:16-25; Deut 16:1-8).

30:23-24. Hezekiah's provision of animals. It appears that the king is providing much of the meat for a religious communal feast for those in attendance. These numbers are large but are not out of proportion with some of the other figures found in ancient Near Eastern literature. When King Ashurnasirpal II throws a dedication party for his palace in the Assyrian capital city of Calah, he provides 5,000 sheep, 1,000 lambs and cattle, 500 deer, 500 gazelles, 34,000 fowl, and 10,000 fish (879 B.C.).

31:1. sacred stones and Asherah poles. See the comment on 2 Kings 17:9.

31:1. high places and altars. See the comment on 2 Kings 17:9.

31:2. functions of the Levites. Hezekiah reaffirmed the functions of the Levitical order established by Solomon. Thus the priests were in charge of the offerings, and the Levites were in charge of the worship (also see the comment on 2 Chron 29:15).

31:3. king's contributions. In contrast to the contributions for the festival in 30:23-24, this verse speaks of regular and ongoing contributions funding the operation of the temple. Hezekiah followed the precedent of Solomon by providing burnt offerings on a regular basis for the temple services (2 Chron 2:4). The provisions for the offerings are described in Numbers 28—29. In the ancient Near East the king (representing the corporate nation) was the foremost worshiper of the national god. Therefore it would be expected that the palace would play a major role in supplying the regular sacrifices.

31:4. Levites' portions. The portion for the priests and Levites was delineated in Numbers 18 (see comments there), where the gifts were for the priests (v. 12) and the tithes were for the Levites (v. 21). Clearly Hezekiah was making a great attempt to have the religious officials devote themselves to the duties proscribed in the five books of Moses.

31:7. calendar. The third month corresponded to mid-May through mid-June on our calendar. Although this month was called Sivan in the postexilic period, the name is not known during Hezekiah's time. The seventh month, Ethanim (Tishri in the postexilic age), corresponded to mid-September through mid-October. The fact that the ingathering lasted from the third to the seventh month means that it included the harvest of every major crop

(May, lentils, barley; June, wheat; September, dates, grapes; October, olives).

31:11. storerooms in the temple. Most ancient Near Eastern temple complexes contained auxiliary rooms for storage, kitchens, priestly quarters and other various nonreligious functions. For example, the temple of Ninkarrak at Terqa in Syria (c. 1600 B.C.) had a large kitchen storage complex and priestly quarters (for dressing, not as a residence). Thus the new storerooms of Hezekiah were probably in addition to previously existing rooms.

31:14. keeper of the East Gate. One of the most important tasks assigned to priestly personnel was controlling access to the temple precinct, the inner circle of the "sacred compass" (on this concept see comments on Lev 16:2 and Num 18:1-7). Defiling the sanctuary with impurity required a purification offering ("sin" offering, see comment on Lev 4:1-3) and could bring punishment on the individual as well as the people. The gatekeepers had to prevent unqualified intrusion. There were also many valuable items in the temple precinct. Gold and silver were plentiful and a temptation to the unscrupulous individual who may not have feared divine retribution for trespass or theft of temple property. These valuables also had to be guarded. Misappropriation of that which was sacred required a reparation offering ("guilt" offering, see comment on Lev 5:14-16). The gatekeepers were charged with guarding against these offenses. An additional task clarified here is disbursing officer. The east gate is the most important since the temple faces east.

32:1. Sennacherib's campaigns. Sennacherib conducted military campaigns primarily in two regions during his reign (705-681 B.C.). He had at least one major campaign in Syro-Palestine which centered around Jerusalem and Hezekiah's rebellion (701). He also campaigned vigorously in Babylonia, another major problem area during his reign. He was confronted with constant opposition by Chaldean rebels under the direction of Merodach-Baladan (see comment on Is 39:1), culminating in Sennacherib's brutal sack of Babylon in 689 B.C.

32:3. water supply. The water supply included springs, wells and conduits. The springs and wells outside the city were stopped up in order to prevent the Assyrians from using them. The Assyrian threat caused Hezekiah to secure Jerusalem's water supply. This is what is referred to as Hezekiah's tunnel. It is cut through bedrock for 1750 feet from the Gihon spring on the east of the city by the Kidron Valley to the Pool of Siloam on the western flank of the southern tip of the city. In the late 1800s an inscription was found inside the tunnel that describes the diggers' meeting as they dug from both ends. For more information on water systems see the comment on 2 Samuel 5:8.

32:5. expansion of wall of Jerusalem. Recent archaeological study has shown evidence of the enlargement of the city of Jerusalem dur-

---

SENNACHERIB'S INSCRIPTIONS

Our material for Sennacherib's reign is derived from various sources. The "annals" are not precisely annals as such, as they were not contemporary with the campaigns they described but are referred to in this way because they were in a formal chronological succession. Many of the inscriptions were deposited in the compartments of building foundations; some were even found in their original locations. The annals generally passed through a number of editions. One intriguing nonannalistic text is a fragment of a literary type called a "letter to God."

The account of the campaign against Jerusalem was probably composed several months after the campaign itself (c. 700 B.C.). In addition to depositing the texts in building foundations, the Assyrians displayed their inscriptions as bas reliefs illustrated on the palace walls. There are a number of copies of this campaign inscribed upon large barrel-shaped cylinders. There are also stone carved reliefs at Nineveh relating to the Assyrian siege of Lachish (an important fortified city of Judah), which were found in room 36 of Sennacherib's palace. The annals describe the destruction of a wide area of Judah but do not mention the taking of Jerusalem, as drastic operations against the Judahite capital were never completed, although Sennacherib claims to have encircled Jerusalem with watchtowers. Forty-six cities of Judah were plundered, many of which were given over to their rival, Philistia. There is no statement about Sennacherib being magnanimous with Hezekiah as he was with the king of Tyre. Other rulers were replaced in this area (e.g., Sidra of Ashkelon). The testimony of the Assyrian sculptures is important; Lachish was exhibited, but not Jerusalem. The annals claimed that over two hundred thousand Judahites were taken captive (but not necessarily into captivity), and a number of Philistine cities that rebelled were also identified as having been taken. Sennacherib placed responsibility for Judah's fate in the hands of Hezekiah (the Assyrians typically blamed the enemy monarch for the invasion). We are told that the Assyrians demanded from Hezekiah his daughters, weapons, women, gold and numerous other artifacts. The lists of tribute are the longest and most detailed of any of Sennacherib's inscriptions, suggesting that the author sought to draw attention away from the fact that Jerusalem had not been taken. Hezekiah, however, was subdued. This battle had been won, but Hezekiah was still an Assyrian vassal, and he sent tribute to Sennacherib back at Nineveh.

ing Hezekiah's time, as well as an expansion of the city's population. He appears to have augmented fortifications and probably established administrative centers and command posts. Excavations in the Jewish Quarter of the Old City of Jerusalem have found segments of Hezekiah's wall that extended the enclosed portion of the city perhaps as much as seven hundred yards to the west of the north-south ridge that the city had occupied prior to this time.

32:9. siege warfare. The Assyrian reliefs at Nineveh depicting the siege of Lachish show battering rams, seven siege engines and Judahite deportees, as well as Sennacherib, seated on a lounge chair, watching the booty of Lachish pass by. The panels assert the expert military technology of the Assyrians. Their army was very orderly, with bowmen, spear throwers, slingers, ramps and siege engines. The siege engines were heavily armored four-wheeled vehicles (earlier models had six wheels) with a long, pointed, iron-headed shaft protruding from the front. They were ten to twenty feet long and four to six feet high. From the top they were open in the back and closed in the front. Sennacherib's innovations to this war machine included covering it with leather. Additional mobile towers were used to move archers close to the ram to protect it with cover fire. There are numerous other wall reliefs depicting Assyrian siege warfare throughout the ancient Near East. Nevertheless, the Assyrians preferred the technique of negotiation, as described in 2 Kings 18—19.

32:11. deity's role in battle. It was not unusual in the ancient Near East for military events to be directed by foreign gods. Yahweh was thus presented as being on the side of Assyria, and Judah was to be defeated (see Is 7:19; 10:5-6; 2 Chron 35:20-2)! This is paralleled in texts that show enemy gods calling upon the Assyrians. In one Assyrian text, Marduk calls upon Sargon II to come and invade Babylon. In a Babylonian text, Marduk calls upon Cyrus of Persia to come and take the city. In a similar manner, Yahweh is viewed as mustering the armies that will come and overthrow Babylon (Is 13:4). For more information on the divine role in battle see comments on Exodus 15:3; 1 Samuel 4:3; 8:7; 17:37.

32:12. god's high places removed. This action had been part of Hezekiah's reform designed to establish centralized worship only in Jerusalem. From the biblical author's standpoint, this would have been a positive accomplishment. From the Assyrian perspective, however, this action could be used against Hezekiah in a couple of ways. First of all, Assyrians would have considered it a negative thing to reduce the shrines at which a deity could be worshiped. From their perspective, the more worship the better. Second, it is possible that they would also have understood Hezekiah's action in light of a common practice in the ancient world: when invasion was imminent, the images of gods were often gathered from outlying shrines and collected in the capital city.

LACHISH

The city of Lachish (Tell ed-Duweir), was a powerful garrison city or royal citadel. Fortified by Rehoboam (c. 920), it was strategic because it strengthened a weak northern boundary. The city was a rectangular mound located in the Shephelah foothills between the Judahite hills and the coastal plain, resting on a natural promontory, surrounded by deep valleys on all sides. Lachish had an outer and inner gate complex, with an inner wall that was over twelve feet thick. The gate chambers had bronze pieces in debris dated to the Assyrian period. Eighteen ostraca (pottery shards with writing on them) from the Chaldean period relating to Nebuchadnezzar's invasion have been found. Lachish was subject to two sieges in the period of just over one century; many of those levels are mixed and hard to separate. As the city is enveloped by hills on all sides, the possible Assyrian siege site exists only at the southwest corner, although there is presently no archaeological evidence placing the position of the Assyrian camp. Over the whole area of the town is indication of destruction, including much charcoal debris. There is a siege ramp with heaped stones. It is the oldest attested in the Near East and the only one that is archaeologically attested in Israel. Similar-looking ramps have been depicted on Assyrian wall reliefs. The city was demolished within a few feet of its foundation. All buildings were consumed by fire and show an intense burning, along with reddened bricks. The floors were strewn with smashed vessels and utensils. The city was ransacked; only unimportant and heavy items remained. Hundreds of arrowheads were found, as well as twenty pieces of scale armor, and a bronze crest mount for a helmet. A mass of fifteen hundred human bones and decapitated human skulls (considered by the excavators to be civilians) which had rolled down the apex into a large pit were found. Thrown on top of the bones were many animal bones (including pig) and many pottery vessels. Over four hundred of the jars were also found here stamped *lmlk* ("for the king"); the only dated context for these jars is at Lachish. The Assyrians felt that this siege was of paramount importance. As stated, they created an entire room of reliefs at Nineveh commemorating the venture. The Lachish room (36) was situated in a strategic place in the palace, intending to show the conquest of Judah and Lachish. The panels show the Assyrian army advancing toward the city in three columns, with a landscape similar to that of Lachish behind the host; thus scholars were given an unprecedented opportunity to compare a Neo-Assyrian stone relief depicting an ancient city and the site itself.

This was one of the steps taken by Mero-dach-Baladan in the days of Sargon. The rhetoric of the invader would follow the line of thinking that these gods were upset and deprived because of having been removed from their shrines. The invader can then fashion himself as having been called in by these gods to restore them to their rightful place.

32:18. Hebrew versus Aramaic. The Judahite scribes told the Rabshakeh (see comment on 2 Kings 18:17) to stop speaking Hebrew, since they did not want the people on the wall to hear this message. He was asked to speak in Aramaic, which was the language of the Judahites after the exile, but not at this point. He surprised them with his knowledge of Judahite (biblical Hebrew). The crude response by the Rabshakeh showed that his role was to persuade and to agitate. The Rabshakeh (as provincial governor) may even have been an Israelite employed in the service of Sennacherib, like Nehemiah and Ahiqar (a "wise sage of Esarhaddon" identified as an Israelite in the book of Tobit). Aramaic is a language closely related to Hebrew. At this period it had already become the diplomatic language of the ancient Near East.

32:27-29. Hezekiah's prosperity. Hezekiah's prosperity is described in terms of the increase in royal assets. The gold, gems and spices suggest success in trade and perhaps in collection of tribute. The crops and herds suggest bountiful harvests and the administrative savvy to collect and stockpile effectively. Such success is surprising in light of his vassal status and would serve as evidence of God's blessing.

33:1-20
The Reign of Manasseh

33:1. chronology. Manasseh's long reign is placed by Thiele from 696 to 640 B.C. This may include a coregency with his father. Contemporary Assyrian kings were Sennacherib, Esarhaddon and Ashurbanipal. Significant Egyptian kings were Taharqa and Psammeticus I. Assyria continues to exercise strong influence in the west during most of this period.

33:4-5. altars in the temple. The location of the two temple courts has puzzled scholars. The floor plan of the temple in 1 Kings 6 describes only the inner court in any detail. Thus the exact placement of these altars in the very large enclosed area of the outer court is not known.

33:5. Manasseh's pagan practices. The heavenly host (sun, moon, stars and constellations) was worshiped at the altars in the temple courts and on the roof of the palace (see 2 Kings 23:12). There are ancient Near Eastern

texts from Syro-Palestine as early as the second millennium B.C. that describe astral worship. This practice was also common throughout Mesopotamia at this time, and stamp seals from Israel show that astral deities were very popular there as well. The stars were believed to be mediators between gods and men, and able to control events on earth. Assyrian kings are occasionally portrayed wearing emblems of the planets, which, of course, were closely associated with particular deities (for more information see comment on 2 Kings 23:4). Assyrian policy of this time did not override or restrict local religious practice, so there is no reason to think that Manasseh was being forced to set up these worship practices.

33:6. sons passing through the fire. Evidence for this practice outside of Scripture is rare indeed. Assyrian legal texts describe a penalty clause as "he will burn his son to Sin (a lunar deity), and his daughter to Belet-seri." Also see the comment on 2 Chronicles 28:3.

33:11. Manasseh's relations with Assyria. Manasseh inherited from his father Hezekiah a small vassal state subject to Assyria. The annals of Esarhaddon of Assyria (reigned 681-668) mention Manasseh along with a group of kings from the Syro-Palestine region who were required to transport material to Nineveh for a building project. Esarhaddon's successor, Ashurbanipal, also lists Manasseh in a group of rulers who sent gifts to him. In both of these texts, Manasseh is described as a loyal vassal.

33:11. Manasseh's imprisonment. When Esarhaddon died, the rule of Assyria was divided between his two sons. Ashurbanipal was given Assyria and soon dominated his brother, Shamash-shum-ukin, who had been given control over Babylonia. In actuality, Shamush-shum-ukin was little more than a governor, and, by 652, apparently tired of his subordinate role, he led a bloody civil war (supported by the Elamites) that lasted for five years. It ended when Shamash-shum-ukin was killed in the fire that swept through the city of Babylon after a two-year siege. It is documented that Shamash-shum-ukin had attempted to recruit support among the vassal states, and some have speculated that Manasseh had aligned himself with the Babylonian governor during the revolt. It is interesting that Manasseh was imprisoned by the Assyrians at Babylon (with other rebels to witness the result of a failed revolt?), rather than at Nineveh. Rebellious client kings were often deported by the Assyrians for undetermined periods. There is evidence that those who "repented" (i.e., were domesticated by the Assyrians) were often returned to their throne.

33:12. Manasseh's prayer. The text of Chronicles records nothing concerning the content of Manasseh's prayer, but later Apocryphal literature preserves an elegant prayer that is attributed to him.

33:14. expansion of Jerusalem. The expansion of the Jerusalem fortifications by Manasseh may not have been for the same reasons as his father Hezekiah (see comment on 32:5). The rising power of Egypt under Psammeticus I may have caused the Assyrians to help fortify Judah, which was fast becoming a buffer state. Remains of fortifications that may have been constructed during the reign of Manasseh have been found at Tell el-Hesi and Arad.

33:21-25
The Reign of Amon

33:21. chronology. Amon's brief reign was from 642 to 640, during the rule of Ashurbanipal of Assyria.

34:1—36:1
The Reign of Josiah

34:1. chronology. Josiah was king of Judah from 640 to 609. Ashurbanipal's reign was followed by a period of anarchy in Assyria, ending in that nation's collapse in 610. Psammeticus I and Necho II were kings in Egypt. Nabopolassar was the king of Babylon (626-605). This was a period in which Assyria was collapsing and Babylon was moving into Assyrian territory. Egypt was attempting to take advantage of the confusion to stake a claim to Palestine.

34:3-5. religious purge. The most famous purge of antiquity was when the Egyptians rejected the religious reforms of Akhenaten in the fourteenth century. It was during the brief reign of Tutankhamun that the attempt was made to return to the worship of the traditional gods through the traditional priests and to eradicate the heresy of Akhenaten. This included restoring the ancient shrines and temples, providing them the assets and personnel needed to operate and returning that which had been confiscated. The competing shrine and capital city that had been established by Akhenaten at Amarna was abandoned. Horemhab destroyed the temples at Amarna, dismantled the site and recycled the materials into other building projects. What was left was burned. Evidence of Josiah's purge is found in the record preserved in Israelite

stamp seals. The seals portraying familiar symbols of fertility gods, sun god and astral deities of earlier periods are replaced in this period with seals that contain only the inscription identifying the individual, with occasional decoration such as pomegranates.

34:6. purging of north. Though there had been purges of high places and pagan altars in the past (e.g. by Hezekiah), Josiah's purge was unprecedented for its thoroughness. Second Kings 23:15 adds that he burned the high places in the north, which had not been done before. He was able to do this because of the weakened Assyrian hold on the region.

34:8. ideology of temple restoration in the ancient Near East. The temple was the center of culture, economy and society in Syria, Mesopotamia and Israel. It served as the house of the city's patron deity, and so the god was believed to be present there. It was incumbent upon the ruler of the city to attend to the "care and feeding" of the deity. The statue of the god was bathed, clothed and fed daily. Just as important as the king's military success was his attention to the upkeep of the god's house. Countless building inscriptions from both Assyria and Babylonia attest to the king's piety because of his restoration of a certain god's house. Similarly, those who rebuilt or restored Yahweh's temple were accorded this same type of piety. Restoration entailed both physical and ritual aspects. A neglected temple would need structural repairs and perhaps the restoration of pilfered furniture and accessories. It is possible that gold objects or gold plating on walls would need to be replaced. Then the temple would need to have its sanctity reestablished through appropriate rituals. Finally, it would need to be provided with funding and personnel so that it could operate.

34:9. funding of restoration. Information given here suggests that some sort of temple tax was levied to provide for the necessary funds. The collecting of funds for the restoration of a temple was a common occurrence by monarchs in the ancient Near East. Often, though, the monarch would restore the temple by means of corvee labor or by collecting building materials from his subjects.

34:10-11. workers and materials. The regular maintenance of the temple complex was the responsibility of the "workmen in charge of the temple." Major repairs had to be contracted out to skilled workers. The listing of these skilled laborers is typical of contemporary Assyrian records. The skilled workers were carpenters, builders, masons and stonecutters. The term for "builder" was used for both skilled and unskilled laborers who worked primarily with mudbrick. The carpenter was responsible for all of the wood items in construction, including the roof, door, window and stair fittings, and various cultic objects in the temple. The mason/stonecutter quarried the stones from natural caves or drove shafts in the hillside. Then the stones were cut and fitted into place.

34:12-13. role of the Levites. These were all typical functions for temple personnel in the ancient Near East. For more on the role of the Levites see comment on 19:8-11.

34:14. finding of the Book of the Law. The discovery of old documents found during the repairs of temples is known from both Egypt and Mesopotamia. Scrolls were found located in the masonry of buildings in Egypt, while foundation deposits and stelae were often found in Mesopotamia. In earlier times foundation inscriptions (for instance, inscribed on bricks) had been used to dedicate the building project to the deity. These gradually became more elaborate, and by this period it was common to bury a foundation box when building a temple or palace. These would include royal inscriptions describing the king's military and building accomplishments. One purpose of these documents was to offer information to any king who might undertake the restoration of the building in future days. These recoveries were often duly recorded. Nabonidus, the last king of Babylon (reigned 556-539) is well known for his search for ancient documents buried in buildings. Shabaka, an Egyptian pharaoh from about 700, claims to have found a forgotten theological text concerning Ptah's creation of the world on a badly damaged ancient papyrus. He had the text (today called the Memphite Theology) inscribed on stone. The Book of the Law (or teaching) may have been a document that had been enshrined in a foundation box or concealed in the walls of the temple. Alternatively, it could have been found in the temple archives. It is not certain which books of the Old Testament it contained, but it at least included Deuteronomy.

34:22. prophetesses. Prophetesses, though somewhat rare, are known from Mesopotamia. The Mari texts from Syria in the early second millennium give evidence of both male and female prophets. Women are also known to have spoken out as prophetesses during the reign of Esarhaddon of Assyria. The females appeared to have served in the same function as the male prophets.

34:22. keeper of the wardrobe. One of the functionaries of the Baal temple in Samaria had a similar title (see 2 Kings 10:22). There is also a Babylonian text from this period with a similar title. These robes would have been cultic vestments for the worship of the deity (see Zeph 1:8). But in these situations there was an image of deity in the temple to clothe, and that was not the case in the Jerusalem temple. The only wardrobe here would have been that which housed the priestly garments. These would require special care so that they would not become defiled.

34:22. second district. The Second District is also mentioned in Zephaniah 1:10 in connection with the "hills of the city" and the Maktesh quarter. Some have identified this area as the suburbs of the City of David, which grew on the western hill of Jerusalem. Excavations in this area have exposed a large urban settlement dated to this period. For more information see comment on 32:5.

34:29-33. Josiah's reform. See comments on 2 Kings 23:1-20.

35:7. king's contribution. Josiah's contribution to the Passover is comparable to that of Hezekiah. See the comment on 2 Chronicles 30:23-24.

35:10-14. Passover procedures. For more information on the procedures for the Passover see comments on Exodus 12:1-11. For its observance in Hezekiah's day see the comment on 30:15-17.

35:18. unique celebration. This was the first centralized celebration of the Passover since that mentioned in Joshua 5:10-11. The Passover had basically remained a family rite from that date until Josiah's policy change (though see the observance in the time of Hezekiah in 30:15-17). An example of restoring ancient festivals that had been discontinued can be found in the Babylonian Akitu festival. For twenty years (689-669) this enthronement ceremony (the most important of the Babylonian festivals) was not celebrated. It was reestablished by Esarhaddon when Babylon regained its prominence.

35:20. Necho's march to Carchemish. The Babylonian Chronicle states that in 609 Necho was on a mission to aid Assyria, which was attempting to retake the provisional capital of Harran in Syria that had been captured by the Medes and Babylonians the year before. Necho's troops would reinforce the garrison base at Carchemish. The Egyptians had transferred their allegiance to Assyria when they saw that the balance of power had changed from Assyria to Babylon. It can thus be presumed that Necho saw greater opportunity for his own expansionist ambitions in Palestine and Syria if Assyria successfully fended off the Babylonians and Medes. It is easy to understand Josiah's anti-Assyrian stance, since Judah had been under Assyrian domination for over a century. However, even with Egyptian aid, the Assyrians were unsuccessful in dislodging the Medes and Chaldeans from Harran.

35:22. Battle of Megiddo. The Great Trunk Road (see sidebar on Major Trade Routes in Gen 38) that went across the fertile crescent from Egypt to Babylon proceeds along the coast of Palestine until it reaches the obstacle of the Carmel range. It then moves inland past the city of Megiddo (see comment on Josh 12:21) and into the Jezreel Valley (see comment on Judg 6:33). This is the logical place to intercept an army passing through the region, and many battles have taken place in this famous geographical arena. Nothing is known of this battle outside of Scripture. Although Josiah failed to block the Egyptian movement northward, he may have delayed them long enough so that they were of limited use to the Assyrians in the war against the Medes and Babylonians.

35:25. composition of laments. The lamentation composed by Jeremiah is no longer extant. Lamentation dirges were common for monarchs who had died (especially untimely deaths) and cities that had been taken and destroyed. Aside from the book of Lamentations in Scripture, there are Sumerian lamentations from the early second millennium concerning ruined cities, such as Ur, Eridu, Nippur and Uruk, as well as ruined temples. The literary pattern of the Sumerian lamentations is strikingly similar to the biblical models. The city in question has been allowed to be destroyed by its own god, resulting in a spiritual and physical crisis. Both the Sumerian and biblical lamentations expect a reversal of fortune of the city in question in the future.

36:1-23
The Reigns of Jehoahaz, Jehoiakim, Jehoiachin, Zedekiah and the Fall of Jerusalem

See comments on 2 Kings 23:31—25:30.

36:22-23. For information concerning Cyrus and his decree see comments on Ezra 1.

EZRA

1:1-11
The Decree and Provision of Cyrus

1:1. chronology. Based on the proclamation in the Cyrus Cylinder that calls for the rebuilding of the temples of the gods held captive in Babylon, the "first year of Cyrus" most likely refers to 539 B.C., the year he conquered Babylon and issued his decree. Cyrus had become king of Persia (Anshan) in 559 and had spent twenty years consolidating the kingdoms as far north as Lydia in Asia Minor (capturing Sardis in 546 B.C.) before turning against Babylon and its king, Nabonidus.

1:1. Cyrus. Careful use of Herodotus's *Persian Wars* (see sidebar in the book of Esther) and the Babylonian Chronicle reveal that Cyrus was the chief of a Persian tribe (Achaemenid) who won a struggle for power with Astyages, the last king of the Medes, in 550 B.C. By combining the force of these two areas east of the Tigris (modern Iran), he was able to eventually stage campaigns against Lydia (547 B.C.) and, after the capture of Sardis in western Asia Minor, Ionia. He consolidated his northern and eastern borders between 546 and 540 and then turned west to conquer Babylon, adding the Neo-Babylonian kingdom to his domain in 539 B.C. The city of Babylon opened its gates to Cyrus in October of that year, and in return he protected the sanctuary of Marduk from destruction or desecration. His administrative strategy permitted the worship of local gods and the recognition of native cultures. An excellent example of this policy is preserved on what is called the Cyrus Cylinder (see next comment). Cyrus was killed fighting the Scythian tribes on his northeastern border in 530 B.C. and was succeeded by his son Cambyses.

1:2-4. Cyrus Cylinder and Persian policies. It is evident that Persian administrative policy differed from that of Assyria or Neo-Babylonia with regard to the treatment of vassals and their cultures. The Cyrus Cylinder preserves a decree that reflects Cyrus's tolerance of a degree of autonomy for the peoples of his empire. Although it does not specifically mention Judah, it decrees that repairs be made to the shrines and temples that had been damaged, that all that had been destroyed be rebuilt, and that all sacred images that had been held hostage in Babylon be returned. Excavations of the temple at Uruk have yielded bricks used for restoration of the shrine stamped with the name of Cyrus. Captive peoples were allowed to return to their homelands and were encouraged to serve the Persian empire under royal governors, who in many cases were natives of those countries. All this suggests that rather than ruthlessly condemning and dismantling native cultures, the Persians chose a more benevolent approach. The expectation was that recognition of regional identities and a measure of local autonomy in the form of religious freedom would prevent the breakup of the empire and the almost continuous revolts that the Assyrians and Babylonians faced. It is possible that these policies were due in part to the inclusive nature of Zoroastrianism, the official religion of the Persian court. It should also be understood that the Persians did not turn a blind eye to local rulers who overstepped their bounds or made statements condemning or criticizing the Persian government (see Zerubbabel's reluctance to act despite the urging of the prophets Haggai and Zechariah).

1:2. "God of heaven" in Zoroastrianism. In the Cyrus Cylinder, King Cyrus gives credit for his victory over Babylon to the chief god of Babylon, Marduk. Isaiah 45:1-5 adopts this theme but gives Yahweh the credit even though Cyrus does not "know" him. Both statements fit well with the inclusive nature of Zoroastrianism in which the chief god, Ahura Mazda, is in continual struggle with the dark forces of the evil god Ahriman. Those gods who are perceived as aiding the Persian king, such as Marduk or Yahweh, would be recognized by the Persians as members of Ahura Mazda's heavenly army of the forces of light. The biblical writer in Ezra presses the same point as Isaiah, not mentioning Ahura Mazda but instead proclaiming Yahweh as the God of heaven. The phrase "God of heaven" also appears in the Elephantine papyri, Jewish documents from Egypt from the end of the fifth century. The fact that Yahweh is here called the God of heaven does not reflect Cyrus's personal beliefs. Similar deference was given to other gods when decrees were made concerning the restoration of their shrines.

1:3. God who is in Jerusalem. The reference to the God in Jerusalem reflects the language in the Cyrus Cylinder directing the hostage peoples and their gods to return to their homelands. There is a sense in this verse both of a

universal God, motivating the actions of the world's most powerful leader, and of a God whose seat is still, as always, in Jerusalem.

1:4-6. provision of goods and offerings. Since not all of the Israelites chose to return from exile, this statement may refer either to those who remained behind or to their non-Jewish neighbors. If it is the latter, then there is a strong tie to the "despoiling" of Egypt during the exodus, when the Israelites took gold and silver on their departure from Egypt (Ex 11:2; 12:35-36). The "freewill" offerings may be compared to those made to equip the Tent of Meeting in the wilderness (Ex 25:2-9). In this way, both the needs of the returnees (livestock and other provisions) as well as the means of rebuilding the temple in Jerusalem were provided for.

1:7-10. articles of the temple. As we know from references in the Mari texts as well as the Cyrus Cylinder, sacred objects, including idols and the many types of vessels used in worship, were taken hostage when a people was conquered. A way of demonstrating the power of your god over the god of conquered people was to desecrate their sacred objects or place them in a position of submission (see Dan 5:1-4 and 1 Sam 5:1-2). Now, as part of the restoration of the temple and proper Yahweh worship there, all of the sacred objects are inventoried, numbered to insure that none are missing and returned to Jerusalem (see comments on 2 Chron 4:8-11 for description of some of these bowls).

1:11. Sheshbazzar. Despite attempts to equate Sheshbazzar with Shenazzar (1 Chron 3:18), in order to give him a Davidic tie as a "prince of Judah" (Ezra 1:8), or with Zerubbabel, in order to reconcile events in Ezra with those in Haggai and Zechariah, it seems that this little known individual has his own separate identity. The title "prince of Judah" may indicate royal ancestry, in which case he should be viewed as a ranking member in the Davidic line. Alternatively the title could refer to a function, in which case he could be seen as the Persian who served in the official capacity of accompanying the exiles back to their land and supervising the transition to a local governorship (turned over to Zerubbabel). He is the first governor appointed by the Persians to administer Judah (Yehud) and is given charge of the sacred vessels as well as the task of laying the foundation for the restored temple in Jerusalem. Archaeologists have recovered jar handles and seals containing the names of three more governors of Judah about which we know nothing else and who were not even mentioned by Ezra and Nehemiah.

1:11. journey from Babylon to Jerusalem. The

most likely route would have taken the returning exiles north, up the Euphrates to either Mari or Carchemish and then south and west to Damascus and on down the caravan route to either the coastal road or perhaps back through the Jordan Valley to Jericho and then northwest to Jerusalem. The distance between Babylon and Jerusalem was roughly nine hundred miles, so the journey would have taken eight to ten weeks.

2:1-70
The Returning Exiles

2:1. province. The province of Judah (Yehud) was part of the satrapy of Babylon until the reign of Xerxes, when it became a portion of the satrapy "Beyond the River" (Trans-Euphrates). The text is thus talking about exiles originally of the province of Judah now returning to Jerusalem. Archaeological finds based on the distribution of coins suggests the province of Judah extended south as far as Beth Zur (six miles north of Hebron), west to Gezer, north to Mizpah and east to the Jordan.
2:2. what is known about leaders. Zerubbabel is known to have been governor under Darius, but Sheshbazzar preceded him. Bigvai (a Persian name) was a governor of Judah following the administration of Nehemiah. Of the others, Jeshua (Joshua in Haggai and Zechariah) served as high priest during the time of Zerubbabel (Zech 3:1-10). It is interesting to find the names Nehemiah and Azariah (an alternative form of the name Ezra) in the list, but possibly they were common ones. Mordecai should not be confused with the relative of Esther, and Mispar and Bilshan are unknown elsewhere. Rehum is mentioned in Ezra 4:7-24 as one of the officials ("commanding officer") who wrote a letter complaining to King Artaxerxes about the activities in Jerusalem.
2:3-67. classes of individuals. The principal groups of returnees consisted of members of clans or kinship groups (17 in vv. 2-19), some listed by geographical region, most of which are north of Jerusalem (22 names in vv. 20-35), as well as members of four priestly families (totaling 4,289, vv. 36-39), and a small number of Levites (just 74 listed in v. 40). The remainder of the inventory of names includes persons associated with the temple or service to the priesthood: musicians, gatekeepers, and 35 temple servants (vv. 43-54), who may have been non-Israelite in origin (there are possible comparisons to be made with Ugaritic and Neo-Babylonian guilds of designated temple servants). A group descended from "Solomon's servants" (vv. 55-58) was also of non-

Israelite origin (see forced labor groups in 1 Kings 9:20-21) and was probably attached to the temple community as the need for labor increased. The final group (vv. 59-63) could not maintain their family genealogies far enough back to be able to claim a position in the priesthood but had otherwise escaped assimilation into Babylonian culture.
2:69. amount of gifts. The drachma was equal to approximately half a shekel. The Babylonian shekel weighed about 8.4 grams and was represented in the Persian coin known as the *daric* once it began to be minted in the time of Darius (a few decades after the time of Cyrus). In this way about 565 pounds of gold and 3 tons of silver were provided for the rebuilding.

3:1-13
Rebuilding the Altar and Temple

3:1. seventh month. The seventh month in the calendar year is known as Tishri and is in the autumn (September-October). The tie to the Feast of Tabernacles is also found in Ezra's covenant renewal ceremony in Nehemiah 7:73—8:2.
3:2. Jeshua. Jeshua is the high priest in the early postexilic period. His grandfather, Seraiah, had been executed by Nebuchadnezzar when Jerusalem fell to the Babylonians (2 Kings 25:18-21; note that Ezra is also from the line of Seraiah, see 7:1). Judah's heir to the throne, Zerubbabel (see next entry), served as governor, but since Judah was still under Persian control, there were restrictions on the extent of his control (so as not to compete with the Persian king). Consequently, rule in the community was now divided between the governor and the high priest, giving the priest a more prominent role. Little is known about him except that he was one of the leaders who helped get the temple rebuilt. There are no contemporary extrabiblical references to him.
3:2. Zerubbabel. Zerubbabel was the heir to the Davidic throne (grandson of Jehoiachin, see comments on 2 Kings 24) and served as governor of Judah under the Persian king Darius I. There was a significant amount of expectation surrounding him that had a messianic flavor to it. Undoubtedly some expected him to set up the promised kingdom and bring freedom from their slavery (to the Persians). While his duties were primarily secular, he is described in Ezra, along with the priest Jeshua, as the force behind the rebuilding of the temple in Jerusalem. Governing under the auspices of the Persian king, he was responsible for maintaining law and order,

and for the collection of taxes. Though Zerubbabel is the last Davidic heir to serve in the role of governor, archaeologists have found a seal of Shelomith (listed as a daughter of Zerubbabel in 1 Chron 3:19), where she is designated as either a wife or an official of Elnathan, the governor who is thought to have succeeded Zerubbabel.

3:2. burnt offerings. The restoration of the temple and the proper worship of Yahweh began with the construction of an altar and the resumption of burnt offerings (see the precedent in Deut 27:6-7). Interestingly, the Elephantine papyri refer to the desire of that community to rebuild their destroyed temple, but they pledge not to stage burnt offerings on their altar so that the preeminence of Jerusalem could be maintained. For general information on the burnt offerings, see comments on Leviticus 1.

3:3. foundation. In order to maintain continuity with worship in the temple in Jerusalem prior to the exile, it was essential that the altar be constructed upon the foundations of the old one (see similar reconstruction in 2 Chron 24:12-13). In this way, the sacred space was revived as the one true spot for the sacrificial rituals of Yahweh worship. In the ancient world the choice of a site for a shrine or temple was never arbitrary. As early as 2000 B.C. the tablets of Gudea record an elaborate dream through which he was instructed concerning the intimate details of the location, dimensions and orientation of a temple. As a result, once an appropriate spot had been identified, rebuilding would always seek to recover the original plan and location. In one of his inscriptions, Nabonidus, the last king of Babylon, reports that he rebuilt the temple of Sippar on the foundations laid by Sargon nearly a century earlier without deviating even an inch. Some archaeological sites in Mesopotamia preserve over a dozen levels of building and rebuilding of temples on the same spot.

3:3. morning and evening sacrifices. Maintaining the continual observance of the daily morning and evening sacrifices was a signal of complete compliance to the temple regimen. According to Exodus 29:38-42 and Numbers 28:3-8 (see comments on both contexts for additional information) this involved the sacrifice of a year-old lamb along with flour, oil and wine each morning and evening. On two other occasions the practice had had to be revived (by Joash in 2 Chron 24:14 and Hezekiah in 2 Chron 29:7, 27-29) after a period of neglect or suppression due to pressures from Assyria.

3:4. Feast of Tabernacles. See the comments on Exodus 23:16b; Leviticus 23:33-43; and Deuteronomy 16:13-17 for information on this major religious festival. Its celebration is also tied to the dedication of the temple by Solomon (2 Chron 5:3) and to the covenant renewal ceremony of Ezra (Neh 8:13-18). In all three cases a new beginning for the people is signaled, and a celebration involving a feast has always been a means of solemnizing a covenant or treaty agreement (see the comment on Gen 31:54).

3:5. New Moon and other sacred feasts. See the comment on Numbers 28:1-30 for background on these religious festivals in the Israelite religious calendar (note also 1 Sam 20:5). What is evident here is the determination to once again regularize religious practice through the restoration of all of the previous sacrificial rituals.

3:7. food, drink and oil. Standard wages for laborers always included a daily ration of food, drink and olive oil (see the list in 2 Chron 2:10). Evidence of this is found in ration lists from Babylon, Mari and many other Mesopotamian cities (including amounts for both free laborers and slaves).

3:7. cedar logs by sea. Just as the eleventh-century Egyptian priest Wenamon contracted with the ruler of Syria for cedar logs that would be transported by sea, here a similar arrangement is made for the transport of logs to the port of Joppa to rebuild the temple (see the comment on 2 Chron 2:16 for additional examples of this practice).

3:8. chronology. Like the temple of Solomon, the construction of this second temple will begin in the spring during the second month, Ziv (1 Kings 6:1, 37). The work is said to begin in the second year of Zerubbabel's arrival at the temple. But the text is never very clear about when Zerubbabel came. He is never explicitly identified as a contemporary of either Shesh-bazzar or Cyrus (though 4:1-5 could suggest such an association), but is always tied to Darius. Ezra 2 is often thought to refer to a separate return, perhaps fifteen years later than the one described in chapter 1. As a result it is not easy to identify which year the second year is.

3:10. importance of foundation. See the comment on 3:3 for the significance of the foundation laid on sacred space. In addition it was the common practice in Mesopotamia to make a foundation sacrifice and bury tablets or cylinder cones describing the laying of the foundation by a king (much like our own practice of including a time capsule in the corner stone of a public building). For example, the foundation inscription of Yahdunlim, a nineteenth-century B.C. king of Mari, describes not only the building of the temple of Shamash but also a campaign to the Cedar Mountains and the Mediterranean Sea. The interest of the Persians in relaying foundations at traditional sanctuary sites is evidenced in Cambyses' personal role in the celebrations for the newly laid foundation of the Neith temple in Egypt around 525.

3:10. trumpets and cymbals. Musical instruments, such as trumpets, cymbals, lyres and harps, are often mentioned as the means of punctuating the start and the procession accompanying religious ritual (see 1 Chron 16:5-6; 2 Chron 25:11-13). The clashing of cymbals might be used to symbolize the clapping of thunder or as a means of marking time for the procession. Trumpets functioned as signaling devices on the battlefield and on occasions of great importance.

3:12. comparison of first and second temple. The splendor of ancient temples was based on several factors. While size could be of some significance, more important were the materials used in construction and the artistry of the craftsmanship. Solomon had far greater resources to commit to the materials than the postexilic community had—even with the sponsorship of the Persian government. The amount of gold, the quality and the size of the stones and the skill of the stonecutters and metal workers were all aspects in which the second temple could not hope to compare favorably with the first. The disappointment of the older generation does not necessarily reflect an obsession with external appearances. It was true then, as it had been at the time of the exodus, that the expense and grandeur of the edifice and its furnishings were a legitimate way to give honor to the God who inhabited the sanctuary. The people felt sadness at their own inability to provide surroundings with splendor commensurate to God's glory.

4:1-24

The History of Opposition to the Rebuilding Program

4:1. enemies of exiles. The land of Israel and Judah was not uninhabited at the time of the return from exile. The descendants of those people who had not been taken to Babylonia as well as those who had been brought into that area by the Assyrians (2 Kings 17:1-6) would have existed as distinct population groups. The fact that the writer of Ezra identifies them as "enemies" suggests that there had

already been clashes with these people (Ezra 3:3) and that their offer of help in rebuilding the temple was not an honest one. In any case it is likely their understanding of Yahweh worship differed from that of the returned exiles (see 2 Kings 17:33). That would help explain Zerubbabel's curt answer to them.

4:2. Esarhaddon's relocation. After the fall of Samaria in 722 B.C., the Assyrian king Sargon II had ordered the relocation of the bulk of the Israelite population to Halah and to Media (see the comment on 2 Kings 17:6). In their place, peoples from within the Assyrian empire were settled in Israel (see comment on 2 Kings 17:24). Additional deportations must have taken place under the reign of Esarhaddon (681-669 B.C., see comment on Isaiah 7:8). The descendants of these people, possibly taken from Sidon after the campaign of 676 B.C., are described as "enemies of Judah and Benjamin," but they are not in this early Persian period known as the Samaritans.

4:5. Cyrus to Darius. The Persian king Cyrus reigned until 530, when he was killed in battle against the Scythians on the northeastern border of his empire. He was succeeded by his son Cambyses, whose major accomplishment was the conquest of Egypt. However, he was murdered shortly thereafter, and a struggle ensued that eventually resulted in the accession of Darius, who had gained the support of the majority of the Persian nobility and married Cyrus's daughter. He began his reign in 522, and it will be during his administration (515 B.C.) that the Jerusalem temple will be finished.

4:6-23. chronological sequence. The author is writing from the time of Ezra-Nehemiah, about 440 B.C. These early chapters have looked back at the events that occurred nearly a century earlier between 538 and 518. At the mention of the opposition and delay in verse 5, the author digresses to recount the long history of opposition that continued from this initial incident down to his own time, before going back and resuming his story where he left off, about 520 B.C. The common theme throughout this digression is the continual opposition to the desires of the returned exiles in Jerusalem. His digression takes him from Darius through Xerxes and Artaxerxes (who was king in the author's time). Xerxes (Ahasuerus) began his reign in 486/485 B.C. and immediately became embroiled in suppressing revolts in Babylon—an event that may have also sparked uprisings in the western provinces, perhaps even in Yehud. In any case, a general sense of disturbance would have been sufficient reason to delay action on the Jerusalem construction projects, even into the reign of Artaxerxes (465-424 B.C.), and to cast suspicion on its leaders, given the continued stream of letters charging the Israelites with disloyalty.

4:6. Xerxes. Xerxes (Ahasuerus), the son of Darius, came to the Persian throne in 486/485 B.C. His early years were taken up with putting down revolts in Babylon and in Egypt. The result was the establishment of Babylon as a separate satrapy under the direct control of the Persian government. Subsequently Xerxes continued his father's ambition of conquering the Greeks. His massive army crossed the Hellespont into northern Greece and succeeded in burning Athens. However, the destruction of his fleet at the naval battle of Salamis left his army without an adequate supply line and the death of his general Mardonius in 479 at the Battle of Plataea ended any chance of a victory. Xerxes is known for a number of monumental building projects, but his reign ended in assassination in 465 B.C. For more information see comment on Esther 1:1.

4:7. Artaxerxes. Three Persian kings were named Artaxerxes. The one mentioned in Nehemiah is most likely the successor of Xerxes I, Artaxerxes I (465-424 B.C.). Outside of Scripture, little is known of this king. The Greek historian Herodotus described a taxation list and some poor economic policies that occurred during this king's reign. The Greek city-states, fresh from their victories against the Persians at Salamis and Plataea (480-479 B.C.), used every occasion to undermine Persian authority in the Near East. Thus, Artaxerxes endured two revolts during his reign (see the note on Nehemiah 1:1). He was, however, able to rule for forty years.

4:7. use of Aramaic. Aramaic, a close relative of Hebrew, was already an important language in the Assyrian period (see comment on 2 Chron 32:18), and both the Babylonians and the Persians employed it as the international diplomatic language. While they kept internal documents in Persian (often translated from the Aramaic), correspondence from officials like Tabeel would have been written in Aramaic. In this way, bureaucrats in every part of the empire had a common language for use in carrying out the king's business (compare the Roman use of Greek and modern diplomatic use of French).

4:9-10. titles used by speakers. The title for Rehum, translated as "commanding officer," applies to a civilian official with the power to issue orders or royal edicts. Shimshai's office of "secretary" (*sapar*) required him to make copies of official documents, translate them into Aramaic or some other language, and create tax roll records. These individuals were found throughout the empire, including Elephantine, since their services were always needed by higher ranking officials. The other titles ("judges and officials") are less well defined and probably refer to members of Rehum's entourage.

4:10. Ashurbanipal's relocation. The biblical text does not make any other specific mention of this deportation by the Assyrian king. However, there were many campaigns by each of the Assyrian kings to suppress revolts or to deal with coalitions of opponents (such as the Ashdod Revolt of 711 B.C. referred to in Is 20:1-4). It is easily possible that Ashurbanipal's expedition against the rebellious Babylon in 648 B.C. extended into the western provinces and resulted in a relocation of Israelites implicated in the uprising.

4:12-16. nature of the accusation. The reference made to the returned exiles may mean those who came to Jerusalem during the reigns of Cyrus and Darius or else those who arrived more recently during the time of Artaxerxes I. The officials' concern about the rebuilding of the city seems to imply, based on past experience, that Jerusalem had a history of being a rebellious and troublesome people who will spark further revolts throughout the region. It is also possible that the true threat was from the rebellious satrap, Megabyzus (c. 448 B.C.), who might easily have found Jerusalem a willing ally. The charge that they will withhold taxes is equivalent to treason (a similar charge was made against Hezekiah in the Assyrian annals of Sennacherib). Exaggeration of the situation may be a diplomatic ploy to gain the king's attention and force the people of Jerusalem to go through channels such as requesting permission of royal officials before starting construction.

4:15. nature of the royal archives. Archives would have included annals and chronicles. Royal annals were kept throughout the ancient Near East, with most examples coming from mid-second millennium Hittite kings and from ninth- to sixth-century Assyria and Babylon. The annals could be represented by annalistic royal inscriptions giving detailed accounts of military campaigns. In addition there are court chronicles that give information of important events in each year. No annals from Achaemenid Persia have as yet been discovered by archaeologists, though it is likely that the Persian bureaucracy would also have made an effort to amass as much as possible of the official records of the Assyrians and Babylonians. This would have given them historical perspective on the peoples they now ruled. It is thus possible that the request that the royal archives be searched would have included previous dealings with Israel and Judah (particularly the annals of Sargon II, Sennacherib and Nebuchadnezzar) as well as more recent events recorded by the Persian scribes.

4:16. Trans-Euphrates. The region west of the Euphrates river, excluding Babylon, which was a separate satrapy, comprised a very large Persian province ruled by a governor (satrap) as well as subordinates with the title *paḥat* (see Tattenai in Ezra 5:3) and royal investigators known as *patifrasa*. Within the satrapy were smaller administrator units, such as Yehud, which had their own royal appointee governing them.

4:18. translated to what. Although Aramaic was used for all diplomatic exchanges (correspondence, treaties), the official language of the Persian court was Persian. As a result, when the letter was read to King Artaxerxes, the scribe would have translated the Aramaic into Persian for the king's benefit and to maintain a sense of official decorum within the inner circle of the king's court.

4:24. second year of Darius. The narrative now resumes, following the interlude dealing with the construction of the wall system, with the reign of Darius and the issue of rebuilding the temple in Jerusalem. The second year of Darius would have been 520 or the beginning of 519 B.C. By that time the disputes over his succession to the throne after the death of Cambyses had subsided, and he would be ready to consider matters like the Jerusalem temple.

5:1-17
Tattenai's Letter to Darius

5:1. Haggai. Among the returned exiles were the prophets Haggai and Zechariah. Both expressed fervent messianic hopes with regard to Zerubbabel's leadership of the people and both actively promoted the rebuilding of the temple in Jerusalem. Haggai is particularly concerned that the returnees had spent their time and energy rebuilding their lives and homes while neglecting the temple (Hag 1:2-11). The name Haggai appears a number of times in the Elephantine papyri (over a century later), but that simply proves it was a fairly common personal name in this period.

5:1. Zechariah. With the meaning "Yahweh remembers," Zechariah was a common name in the exilic and postexilic period. This sixth-century prophet is identified as a member of a prominent priestly family descended from Iddo (see Zech 1:1). His message, like Haggai's, emphasized the rebuilding of the Jerusalem temple, but he also promoted the increased political role of the high priest alongside the Persian-appointed governor in the province of Yehud.

5:3. Tattenai, governor of Trans-Euphrates. Tattenai was a *paḥat* or *peḥu*, who served under the satrap Ushtannu. He is later appointed as a satrap in a Babylonian source dated to 502 B.C. As the local official on the scene, he took the responsibility for investigating the temple building process and asked for confirmation from Darius as to whether it was legitimate activity. Once he receives affirmation, he demonstrates that he is a good bureaucrat by diligently carrying out the king's orders (Ezra 6:13).

5:3. Shethar-Bozenai. If this is a personal name, it refers to an associate of Tattenai (possibly a scribe) who participated in the investigation of Jerusalem's temple building activities. It is also possible that the name is a title applied to Tattenai meaning "chief clerk of the chancery."

5:8. large stones and timbers in the walls. There is some difference of opinion on the meaning of the Aramaic word translated "large stones." Some commentators tie it to the root meaning "roll" and thus speculate that the large stones were cut in such a way that they could be rolled into place before they were shaped to fit together. Others point to an Akkadian phrase, *aban galala*, meaning ashlar stones. The timbers may have been designed for either earthquake protection or a mimicking of the style of building in Solomon's temple (see comment on 1 Kings 6:36).

5:12. God of heaven. See the comment on Ezra 1:2.

5:12. Nebuchadnezzar's destruction of Jerusalem. It is interesting to compare the arguments made by the elders of Jerusalem for the rebuilding of the temple with those found in the Elephantine letter requesting permission to rebuild the destroyed temple in that Egyptian military colony about 400 B.C. In both cases the "God of heaven" is invoked, as well as arguments of past history. The case in Ezra makes use of an explanation that blames the Babylonian destruction on the unfaithfulness of the people of Judah and the need for a period of cleansing (see Jer 25:8-14). The Persian king is now called upon to serve as the instrument of their religious restoration as his predecessor Cyrus had (see Is 45:1-3).

5:14. Sheshbazzar. See the comment on Ezra 1:11.

6:1-12

Darius Grants Permission

6:1. archives in the treasury of Babylon. See the comment on Ezra 4:15 on archive keeping in the Persian empire. During the reign of Darius, Babylon was still the capital of the satrapy of Trans-Euphrates and thus would be the repository of all records concerning its provinces. Many of these documents would have been on clay tablets or cylinders, although some might have been on papyrus or leather scrolls.

6:2. citadel of Ecbatana. Until 550 B.C. Ecbatana had been the capital of the Medes. It was located in the Zagros mountains in northwestern Iran, at the foot of Mount Orontes. After its capture by Cyrus it became the summer residence of the Persian kings, as they moved their court back and forth between Susa and Ecbatana to take advantage of more temperate climates. The extent of the search for the record of Cyrus's dealings with the Israelite exiles was broadened to this royal archive when nothing was found in the regional center at Babylon. Scrolls of leather were widely used in the Persian empire for this type of document.

6:3. dimensions. The numbers given for the dimensions are generally considered to have confused by a scribe, since the temple of Solomon had been only sixty cubits long, twenty cubits wide and thirty cubits high. Since this temple was to be built on the foundations of the former, it would be expected that it would have the same dimensions. Alternatively, the numbers in the text of the decree may represent ideal figures or maximum allowable dimensions. It is interesting that Cyrus and Darius took such an interest in sponsoring temple building, since temples are not attested (in either literature or archaeology) as playing any significant role in Zoroastrianism, the religion of Achaemenid Persia. Herodotus likewise notes the absence of temples in Persian religious practice.

6:7. rebuilt on its site. One of the tasks most often recorded in Mesopotamian royal annals was temple restoration (for example, those of Ur-Nammu from Ur III and the Kassite king Kurigalzu). Once sacred space has been identified and used for religious purposes, it becomes essential that it remain in use. Thus, kings like Cyrus would expect that the only appropriate site for the restoration of a temple would be on the foundations of the old one (see the comments on Ezra 3:3 and 3:10). This practice also explains why conquering nations or religions tend to build their places of worship on the sites of earlier temples and churches.

6:8. payment out of the royal treasury. The inclusion of dimensions for the restored temple (see v. 3) implies a concern for cost overruns on the part of the Persian government. It is possible that a special tax or levy on the satrap of Trans-Euphrates was exacted to help pay for the restoration project, but these funds would have first been sent to the general treasury and then disbursed as needed to the contractors in Jerusalem. There is also an official stamp given to the project since it has a line in the royal budget. The Cyrus Cylinder (see comment on 1:2-4) is unclear about the extent to which the royal treasury contributed to the rebuilding projects mentioned there, though excavations in a number of sites throughout Babylonia have recovered bricks used for sanctuary rebuilding that are stamped with Cyrus's name. This suggests that the royal treasury financed the project.

6:9-10. use of the goods provided in sacrifice. Darius's generosity as reflected here is also evidenced in inscriptions throughout the empire. In fact, the Egyptians who benefited from his magnanimity dubbed him "the friend of all the gods." The animals mentioned are specifically designated for burnt offerings (see comment on Lev 1:3-4). The ration of wheat, salt, wine and oil may have been divided between the priests and the construction workers, since this is a daily portion, but may have been used in offerings as well. Grain offerings (made with oil and semolina) often accompanied other offerings, and portions were given to the officiating priest (for the use of wheat, oil and salt in these offerings see the comments on Lev 2). For the use of wine for libations see the comment on Leviticus 23:12-13. Josephus reports the provision of funds for temple construction and of these same ingredients for sacrifices to the Jews several centuries later by Antiochus the Great.

6:10. praying for the well-being of the king. This request parallels similar remarks in the Cyrus Cylinder, asking the gods and presumably their worshipers to "recommend" Cyrus and his son to the god Marduk so that they would be granted "a long life." While this may represent a simple desire to receive the blessing of the god, it may alternatively be designed to prevent petitioning the gods to overthrow or curse the king. In fact, Herodotus reports that prayers for the king had to accompany every sacrifice. The Elephantine papyri also offers prayers to a Persian official if he would aid them in the reconstruction of their destroyed temple. The drafting of a decree so as to portray the king as knowledgeable and concerned about the religious practice of the subjects involved is demonstrated in the Xanthos Charter. This document from Lycia (in modern day Turkey) dated to 358 B.C. formalizes Persian support for the cult there with some of the same issues addressed as here.

6:11. punishment for disobedience. It is common for treaties and royal decrees to end with a curse or clause threatening punishment for disobedience to the stipulations of the document. It would be possible to compare Joshua's curse on the man who would rebuild Jericho in Joshua 6:26 and the curse on any prince who replaces the gate constructed by King Azitawada of Karatepe with this injunction. Such a statement is also found in the epilogue to the Code of Hammurabi, charging future rulers to provide justice or face a curse from the gods. The punishment of impalement is depicted in Assyrian Lachish reliefs and mentioned in a number of royal archives. The practice was to impale the corpse of the executed victim on a pointed stake in public view. Impalement is known in Persia, for instance in Amestris's execution of Inaros (leader of a Libyan revolt) during the reign of her son, Artaxerxes. The victim was thus denied proper burial, as the birds and insects devoured the remains. One curse used by Darius in his inscriptions is: "If you should blot out these words, may Ahura Mazda slay you and your house be destroyed," while another says "What you make, may Ahura Mazda pull down."

6:12. curse in the name of local god. Since many of the peoples of the ancient world believed that gods were localized, that is, tied to particular places and peoples, it would be appropriate that events within that divine "jurisdiction" should be handled by the local deity.

6:13-22

Completion, Dedication and Passover Celebration

6:15. date of completion. Such an important event as the completion of the second temple required careful recording. The date provided places it in the twelfth Babylonian calendar month, Adar, which would have been in February-March. The sixth year of Darius would have been 515 B.C., and the third day of the month of Adar would make the completion date March 12, 515. It should be noted that 1 Esdras 7:5 and Josephus both place the date

on the twenty-third of Adar, and this has been preferred by some since the third was a Sabbath.

6:17. dedication sacrifice compared to 1 Kings. See the comment on 2 Chronicles 7:5-7 for dedicatory activity for Solomon's temple. The actual number of sacrificial animals in the dedication ceremony for the second temple is much smaller than at the time of Solomon (1 Kings 8:63): 22,000 oxen versus 100 bulls; 120,000 sheep versus 200 rams and 400 male lambs. The sin offering of twelve male goats is according to priestly ritual (Lev 4:22-26; see the comment on Lev 4:13-32) and fits into Ezra's attempt to reestablish the idea of a twelve-tribe coalition, now reborn through the exile experience and prepared to resume its covenantal relationship with Yahweh in Judah and Jerusalem.

6:19. Passover. There has been no mention of a celebration of Passover since the time of Josiah (over one hundred years earlier; see comment on 2 Chron 35:18). Now, as a part of the rejuvenation of the restored Jewish community in Judah, this ritual (see the comment on Ex 12:1-28), which parallels the escape from bondage just experienced by the returned exiles, must be reinstituted. The date of the fourteenth of Nisan (the first month) is based on the religious calendar (Ex 12:2-6; Lev 23:5). Note the previous celebrations of Passover following the cleansing or renovation of the temple (see comments on 2 Chron 30).

6:21. separated from unclean Gentiles. There are several possibilities for this group of people. It is possible that they were remnants of the people of the northern kingdom or those from Judah who were not taken into exile (see 2 Chron 30:17-21). Their contact, during the period of the exile, with non-Israelites could have been perceived as a contamination from which they would have to consciously separate themselves. It is also possible that the Passover ceremony was, as in Exodus 12:48, extended to proselytes (*gerim*) who had converted to Yahweh-only worship.

6:22. Feast of Unleavened Bread. See the comments on Exodus 12:14-20 and Leviticus 23:6-8. Since the celebration of this festival is also attached to Hezekiah's (2 Chron 30:13) and Josiah's (2 Chron 35:16-17) celebration of the Passover, it is appropriate here as well. The joy expressed in this seven-day celebration is tied to the act of God in "changing the attitude of the king of Assyria" (a symbol for the Persian rulers of Mesopotamia), which has made the restoration possible.

7:1-28
Ezra's Arrival with Commission from Artaxerxes

7:1, 7-8. chronology. If these events occur during the reign of Artaxerxes I, then the seventh year of that king would be 458 B.C. This is nearly sixty years after the events described in the last chapter. The departure date given is the first day of Nisan (April 8) and the date of their arrival in Jerusalem is the first of Ab, the fifth month (August 4). This time of year, spring through midsummer, is dry and hot, and would have required a northern route, avoiding the desert and careful planning to insure adequate water resources were available for the returnees.

7:1-5. Ezra's ancestry. It was important that Ezra be recognized as having the proper credentials so that his mission would be sanctioned and his actions would have the force of law. Unlike Jeshua (see comment on 3:2) there is no suggestion that Ezra was a high priest, but the Aaronide genealogy provided for him (that only provides sixteen generations between Aaron and Ezra; for complete list see 1 Chron 6:5-53) shows that he is of prominent ancestry. The text likely suggests that he is a descendant of the Seraiah who was high priest at the time of the destruction of the temple in 586 B.C. Since Jeshua is not mentioned in his ancestry, it is likely that he was either from a different part of Seraiah's line or that this is a different Seraiah (a common name of the period).

7:6-12. Ezra's expertise. Ezra is given a variety of attributes, most of them centering around his ability as a scribe and teacher of the law of the God of heaven. As a scribe, Ezra was possibly a member of the Persian bureaucracy. It was a common practice for ancient Near Eastern governments to employ persons trained not only as secretaries or clerks, but as diplomats and lawyers. These individuals were used to interpret documents from subject and allied peoples. They were also sent on investigative missions to aid the king and his advisors in making decisions (for more information see comment on Neh 8:1). Examples include the seventh-century Assyrian scribe Ahiqar and the description of the scribal profession in the Middle Kingdom Egyptian "Satire on the Trades" where the profession of scribe is praised as a worthy vocation with benefits that far exceed other types of employment.

7:8. four-month journey. As is so often the case, the actual events of a long journey are not recounted here (see Gen 12:1-9). Since they departed in April and arrived in early August, this would have been a dry and hot trek. Most likely they would have taken the northern caravan route (approximately nine hundred miles) up the Euphrates, perhaps turning west at Mari across to Tadmor, then southwest through Damascus and on into Palestine. Considering the size of the company, including whole families, an average of ten miles a day could be expected.

7:14. seven advisors of the king. Based on the reports of Esther 1:14 and the ancient historians Xenophon and Herodotus, we know that the Persian kings relied on a group of seven princes or advisers as their privy council. It would be natural that an investigative commission, such as that given to Ezra, would come in the name of the king and his advisers.

7:14. nature of commission. The Persian kings showed a consistent interest in insuring that their subject peoples maintained the favor of their gods. Restoring temples had been one way to accomplish that, and here we find that obeying religious mandates was another. If the God of Israel was pleased by the people's obedience to his instructions, then by all means they should be enforced. Personnel should be put in place to instruct as well as monitor and assess compliance. It is, therefore, Ezra's commission to determine whether the Jews in the Persian province of Yehud are obeying the law found in the Torah. There had been enough complaints and queries sent from persons there to suggest such an investigative mission was necessary. As a scribe, Ezra has the expertise to handle this mission and to make judgments about compliance. In this way, the Persian king used a member of a subject people (just as Nehemiah was used) to try and insure continued divine approval for his empire and avoid the wrath of God (see v. 23).

7:15-17. Persians offering sacrifices to Yahweh. The Persian kings are known to have made public sacrifices to local deities as a way of showing respect, as well as for the political advantage it would give them in placating the newly conquered people (such as Cyrus's actions for Marduk in the Cyrus Cylinder). The actual list of sacrificial animals and the addition of cereal and drink offerings (see Num 15:2-10) suggests that Jewish experts had been consulted in order to draft the Persian decree. Such a practice is evidenced during the reign of Cambyses (530-522). An Egyptian priest of Sais, Uzahor, played a significant advisory role in attracting the king's interest in the restoration of the sanctuary of Neith and overseeing the process of restoration. This restoration included laying a foundation, reestablishing the rituals and festivals, and providing for government grants to fund the operation of the temple.

7:22. amounts provided. The ration list issued by Artaxerxes to his provincial officials has limits, but the numbers are still amazingly high: 3 3/4 tons of silver, 650 bushels of wheat, 600 gallons of wine, 600 gallons of oil, and unlimited quantities of salt. These amounts are not necessarily based on an assessment of what is required to operate the temple. Instead, as the next verse suggests, it was calculated as what was necessary to avert the wrath of Israel's god.

7:23. theological mentality. In the appeasement mentality of the ancient world, if God's wrath were not appeased, rebellious factions in Israel could claim that their actions against Persia were taken at the instigation of Yahweh. There was revolt in progress in the Persian empire at the time of Ezra. Inarus, a Libyan, had seized control of Egypt in 460 and had found ready support from the Athenian fleet in the Mediterranean. The revolt was crushed by Megabyzus between 456 and 454, so Ezra's journey (458) comes right at its height. By showing great respect for Yahweh, the temple and the priesthood, Artaxerxes followed previous Persian policy (Cyrus Cylinder), acknowledging the power of the God of heaven and adding a sense of urgency to the decree: "let it be done with diligence."

7:24. temple personnel tax exempt. There may have been a dual purpose behind this exemption from taxation. Ezra was coming into a situation where he was unknown and was associated with a foreign power. Tax exemption would have helped him gain some support from the Jerusalem temple community. Precedent for this practice by the Persians is found in the Gadatas Inscription from the reign of Darius, which granted tax exemption to the priests of the Greek god Apollo.

7:25. appointment of officials. It seems very appropriate that Ezra would have been given the right to appoint magistrates and judges within the area of his jurisdiction. In that way he would not have to contend with judicial opposition, and he could insure a common set of policies (see Jehoshaphat's judicial reform in 2 Chron 19:4-11). Persian administrative structure consisted of a dual set of officials—one for local and customary issues and the other charged with enforcing royal decrees and statutes. It is possible that Ezra would have jurisdiction to appoint both within the Trans-Euphrates satrapy, but more likely, given the reference to the "laws of your God," his prime concern was with local magistrates, who would be dealing with Jewish law throughout the province.

7:26. empowered to punish. Since Ezra is operating under the aegis and with the power of the Persian government, the list of penalties match those of the Persian penal code. Capital punishment and confiscation of goods do appear in Israelite law, but there is no mention of imprisonment, other than house arrest (Lev 24:12), except for prisoners of war and those in protective custody for political reasons (Jer 37:11-16). The word translated "banishment" might better be rendered "flogging" or "corporal punishment" based on its common usage in Persian law. The right to punish signifies the seriousness of Ezra's mission, whether or not he is ever forced to exercise this power.

8:1-36
Ezra Leads the Return to Jerusalem

8:2-14. size of returning group compared to first return. The total number of males listed in Ezra's returning group is 1,513. An estimate of 5,000 total returnees (based on a conservative number of wives and children) would make this group about one seventh the size of that listed in Ezra 2:64-65 (42,360).

8:15. canal of Ahava. This is most likely one of the many canals that radiated out from the Euphrates River near Babylon (at least within a radius of ninety miles). It may also be a settlement along one of these water channels, but variations in the sources (LXX; 1 Esdras 8.61 has Theras as the site) have confused the issue. As a result the exact site is still unknown.

8:17. Casiphia. If this is a place name, then it is in the vicinity of Ahava, but neither site has been identified beyond the general direction north of Babylon. It is also possible, based on the LXX reading, that this is a noun (a variant of Hebrew kesep, "silver") and thus reflects either that Iddo was the leader at a treasury site or of a guild of silver smiths.

8:20. temple servants. In addition to the 38 Levites who were induced to join Ezra's returning group, a body of 220 temple servants are also enrolled. The importance of these individuals as assistants to the Levites should not be overlooked. With such a small number of Levites available, their servants would have been essential to proper ritual activity, since there were many menial tasks to be done. Ezra certifies them by the mention of a list of names with their ancestry.

8:21. fasting. Fasting is little attested in the ancient Near East outside the Bible. It generally occurs in the context of mourning. In the Old Testament the religious use of fasting is often in connection with making a request before God. The principle is that the importance of the request causes an individual to be so concerned about his or her spiritual condition that physical necessities fade into the background. In this sense the act of fasting is designed as a process leading to purification and humbling oneself before God (Ps 69:10). As indicated in the text, the Jews are here concerned about their safety. Their request is to procure the protection of God so that their journey may be seen to have been undertaken at his bidding.

8:21-23. danger of being robbed. Since Ezra's group will be traveling without a military escort (compare Nehemiah's entourage in Neh 2:9), the dangers of the road were a serious matter. Political forces were at work upsetting the balance in the western portions of Persia's empire. Plus, an unarmed group, transporting large quantities of gold and silver, might have easily been picked apart by a determined band of outlaws.

8:26-27. amounts. In weighing out and recording the gifts given by the Persian king, Ezra fulfills that portion of his mission. The 650 talents of silver equal 24$\frac{1}{2}$ tons, while the 100 talent weights of silver objects and 100 talents of gold each weigh approximately 3$\frac{3}{4}$ tons each. The 20 golden bowls weighing 1,000 darics are equal to 19 pounds. While this is an extremely large amount, it does represent both royal gifts as well as those from exilic Jewish families.

8:31. length of journey. Since it was April at the time of departure, a journey directly across the desert (approximately five hundred miles) would not have been possible. Thus the travelers took a longer, northern route, up the Euphrates and then west to Damascus and on to Palestine (approximately nine hundred miles). See the comments on 1:11 and 7:8.

8:35. sacrifices. See the comment on Ezra 6:17 on the dedicatory sacrifices for the second temple. The Persian king had ordered that these sacrifices be made when the exiles returned to Jerusalem (Ezra 7:17). Ezra is now recorded carrying out these orders. The mention of "sin offering," as in Ezra 6:17, is a further indication of the need to purify each returning group.

8:36. satraps and governors. The Persian empire was divided into twenty-one satrapies (twenty-two after Babylon became a separate province). Each was administered by a governor or satrap. However, considering the huge size of some of these provinces, it was neces-

sary to have a secondary layers of officials, each known as a *peḥa*, to aid in carrying out tax collection and enforcement of royal decrees (see the comment on Ezra 5:14).

9:1-15
The Problem of Intermarriage

9:1-2. nature of accusation. Ezra is soon informed of a major violation of the Law that he had come to establish: intermarriage with a standard list of non-Jewish people, a practice that endangered the cultural and religious existence of Israel. Endogamy, or marriage only within a select group (which did include converts), had become a tenet for the exilic community (see comment on 9:10-12). They realized that intermarriage would create cultural divisions and weaken their religious identity as a separate and "chosen" people. What makes this charge particularly outrageous is that priests and Levites, who should know the Law (compare Hos 4:6), are also participating in this "unfaithful" practice.

9:1. people list significance. The list of non-Israelite peoples names the standard population groups from the time of the conquest (that the Israelites had been charged with driving out) and mixes in some of those that had treated Israel poorly in the exodus period (Deut 23:3-6). It therefore reflects the time period of the law Ezra is citing rather than the postexilic period. A number of these people groups were no longer in existence in Ezra's time. The intent of the list is not, then, to target these particular peoples but to identify certain categories. In the postexilic context there were those who could be identified as needing to be driven out, as well as those who had set themselves up as enemies of the Jews. Any people identified in one of those categories would thereby be ineligible for intermarriage.

9:3. Ezra's response. Ezra's initial response to the charges of intermarriage are traditional grief rituals: tearing clothing and pulling hair. These practices were common throughout the ancient Near East and are found depicted in Egyptian tomb paintings and in literature (Ugaritic Tale of Aqhat). For more information on these and other mourning practices see comment on Esther 4:1.

9:10-12. the offense of exogamy. Although the prohibition against exogamy, marriage outside the designated group, comes primarily from Deuteronomy 7:1-5, the citation here is actually a synthesis of several passages from Leviticus and Deuteronomy. It was common among ancient Near Eastern societies to marry inside one's clan (endogamy), or to make a marriage alliance with another friendly group. Cultural attitudes discouraging exogamy can be seen as early as the Sumerians. The myth The Marriage of Martu describes the Bedouin people as barbarians who eat raw meat and do not bury their dead—a group with whom no civilized people should intermarry. The Israelites had been commanded to marry within their "spiritual" clan (i.e., the worshipers of the Lord). In this time period, however, the issues went beyond spiritual homogeneity. Election and covenant issues made landownership theologically significant. Intermarriage was one of the ways that land tenure could be jeopardized and, with it, covenant benefits. The Elephantine texts (Jewish texts less than fifty years removed from Ezra and Nehemiah) show how land became redistributed and lost to a family through foreign women marrying into Jewish families and becoming enfranchised. Marriage with peoples of the land would culturally contaminate the Israelites, weakening their religious identity as a people set apart by God and violating the terms of the covenant that allowed them to "eat the good things of the land" (Deut 6:11).

10:1-44

The Solution to the Problem of Intermarriage

10:3. divorce in the Persian period. There is no specific requirement in Jewish law that a man is to divorce his foreign wife. According to Deuteronomic legislation (Deut 7:1-5), this sort of union was not supposed to occur in the first place. What is known of divorce in the Persian period comes from the Jewish documents from Elephantine. Marriage contracts often included stipulations concerning the disposition of the dowry, bride price, property and children in the event of a divorce. Divorce appears to have been common and uncomplicated, with economic implications being of greatest concern. At Elephantine no reason for the divorce had to be offered.

10:8. forfeiture of property, expelled from assembly. A three-day period is sufficient for all citizens to make their way to Jerusalem to answer for the practice of mixed marriage. Forfeiture of property to the temple (seen also in the apocryphal 1 Esdras 9:4) and expulsion from the assembly are complementary punishments, since membership in the assembly entitled a citizen to property (note the death sentence in 2 Chron 15:13). The crime is considered a violation of the covenant and a sign of disloyalty to the community. As early as

Hammurabi's Code sexual crimes could lead to the sentence of exile. In both cases the crime involved inappropriate sexual activity and a violation of societal norms.

10:9. chronology. This event occurs on the twentieth of Kislev (the ninth month) during the third week in December in the year 458 B.C., just over four months since his arrival. The heavy rains and cold in Jerusalem at that time of the year would have certainly discomforted the assemblage. Their trembling and the high emotions associated with the dissolution of their marriages were simply compounded by the weather.

10:13. rainy season. October through February is the cold and rainy season in Judah and Jerusalem. The word used here often describes torrential rains. It would not be unusual for temperatures to be in the forties at this time of year. It is possible that holding an assembly in an open square during the rainy season of late December (the nineteenth) might dampen spirits enough that the men would be willing to compromise and accept Ezra's solution to the marriage issue. However, the discomfort of the cold and the rain might also have raised tempers, especially if the men had to stand there very long. Referring the matter to a commission at least would get them out of the elements.

10:16-17. chronology. A ten-day delay was needed to assemble the commission. They began work on the first day of the tenth month (Tebeth) and continued until the first day of the first month (Nisan). Thus their task required them to make inquiries from late December until late March (March 27, 457 B.C.; about seventy-five days).

10:16-17. what is being investigated. At issue is whether the wives of 110 individuals were in fact non-Israelites. There certainly must have been numerous ambiguities concerning questions of ancestry and regarding which groups the new legal rulings referred to. The list of those questioned includes priests, Levites, singers, gatekeepers and persons not associated with the temple community. Since many of these men were influential, it may be assumed that the commission had to handle their task diplomatically. Each must have been carefully questioned. The matter of any children by these marriages was determined, since this also affected inheritance patterns within the community. Then each was required to take an oath (see 1 Chron 29:24) to put aside their wives and disown their children by these foreign women. In addition, it would be determined what the appropriate guilt offering should be (see Lev 5:14-26).

NEHEMIAH

1:1-11

Nehemiah's Prayer Concerning His Mission

1:1. Nehemiah. Nehemiah held the important position of cupbearer to the king of Persia in the mid-fifth century B.C. during the reign of Artaxerxes I (465-424 B.C.). A revolt broke out in Egypt in 460 B.C. that took five years to put down. Megabyzus, a satrap north of Mesopotamia, also rebelled in 448 B.C. Thus this was a turbulent period in the life of the empire. Because of this, it can be surmised that the Persians were willing to ally themselves with a number of the minority groups within the empire, such as the Jews. It is thus plausible that Jews such as Nehemiah held high positions within the empire in the middle of the fifth century B.C.

1:1. Kislev. Kislev was the postexilic Hebrew month name corresponding to our mid-November to mid-December. The Jews apparently followed the Babylonian monthly calendar after their deportation to Babylon in the late sixth century B.C. and continued to employ this system into the Persian period.

1:1. chronology. It is not certain what the "twentieth year" refers to. It may refer to the twentieth year of Nehemiah at Susa. More likely is the idea that the twentieth year refers to the reign of Artaxerxes I (r. 465-424 B.C.), and his name was simply omitted (see Neh 2:1). If this is the case, then the twentieth year was 445 B.C.

1:1. citadel of Susa. The citadel of Susa was the winter residence of the Persian kings. It was set apart from the remainder of the city of Susa, an area that had an ancient past. Susa had been inhabited since at least the fourth millennium B.C. Later, Susa was an Elamite stronghold until it was captured by the Medes and Persians in the seventh century B.C. The ten-acre citadel is located on an elevated area on the northern point of the site, the Apadana. The palace was built by Darius and used by several of his successors. Excavation of the palace has identified many of its features, including the audience hall, where the Persian kings held court. It was a square building over 350 feet on each side featuring seventy-two stone columns each estimated at sixty-five to eighty feet tall. Greater Susa, located about 225 miles east of Babylon, was built on three hills overlooking the Shaur River. The diamond-shaped mound is about two and a quarter miles in circumference, covering nearly 250 acres. An additional twenty acres comprises the merchant quarter across the valley to the east.

1:2-3. condition of Jerusalem. Jerusalem still lay in ruins from its destruction by Nebuchadnezzar II 140 years earlier. A city that had its walls and gates broken down was entirely vulnerable to outside aggression. The book of Ezra describes an earlier aborted attempt to restore the walls during the reign of Artaxerxes I (c. 458 B.C.). Thus it is apparent that the individuals were describing this most recent endeavor which failed. Some have suggested Persian action against Jerusalem during the reign of Xerxes, but the evidence is scant, though fighting between the Persians and Greeks in the southern Levant is attested.

1:4. Nehemiah's response. The response of Nehemiah was in fact typical of Jews who were confronted with tragedy (see Ezra 9:3-5). Mourning was often accompanied with the shaving of the head and beard. Fasting was often added to prayer so the individual could concentrate wholly on the issue at hand, at the expense of physical needs.

1:4. "God of heaven" in Zoroastrianism. The term "God of heaven" was well-known in the Persian empire and had become part of the religious language of the Jews. The term is also found in the Jewish correspondence in texts from Elephantine in Egypt dating to the fifth century B.C. The origin of the term can be traced to Zoroaster, an Iranian holy man who probably lived in the late second millennium B.C., although his exact dates are not known and remain controversial. Zoroastrianism had become the religion of the Persian kings by the time of Darius I (r. 521-486 B.C.). The Zoroastrians worshiped the "God of heaven," known as Ahura Mazda, an eternal being with moral designs. They also acknowledged the existence of an evil deity who was the exact counterpart to Ahura Mazda and equal to him in power. Nehemiah, however, does not hesitate to attribute this familiar title to Yahweh.

1:11. cupbearer. The cupbearer in the ancient Near Eastern court held a very important position. He had direct access to the king and thus had great influence. Texts and reliefs describe cupbearers in Assyrian and Persian courts. The cupbearer was in close proximity to the king's harem and thus was often a eunuch, although there is no evidence that this was the case with Nehemiah. Later sources identify the cupbearer as the wine taster. In addition he was the bearer of the signet ring and was chief financial officer.

2:1-10
Nehemiah Sent on a Mission

2:1. Nisan. The Hebrew month of Nisan corresponds to our mid-March to mid-April. Nisan brought early rains as well as the barley and flax harvests. Nisan was a month name borrowed from the Babylonians during the Jewish captivity. Abib had been the previous name of the month.

2:1. Artaxerxes. Three Persian kings were named Artaxerxes. The one mentioned in Nehemiah is most likely the successor of Xerxes I, Artaxerxes I (r. 465-424 B.C.). Outside of Scripture, little is known of him. The Greek historian Herodotus described a taxation list and some poor economic policies that occurred during this king's reign. The Greek city-states, fresh from their victories against the Persians at Salamis and Plataea (480-479 B.C.), used every occasion to undermine Persian authority in the Near East. Thus Artaxerxes endured two revolts during his reign (see the note on Neh 1:1). He was, however, able to rule for forty years.

2:1. responsibilities of courtiers in king's presence. In Persian reliefs courtiers are sometimes portrayed with their hands shielding their mouths so as not to offend the king by breathing on him. Whether this represents health consciousness (unlikely), the prevalence of bad breath or simply extreme deference is unknown. As a result, however, facial expressions would be somewhat masked. It would have been expected that the joy of being in the king's service would be reflected on every face.

2:5. rebuilding of city where fathers are buried. Family ties were of supreme importance in most ancient Near Eastern cultures. The living inhabitants of a family were required to pay strict attention to the preservation of the remains of family members who had passed on. In the ancient cultures this entailed performing ritual acts to ensure the maintenance of the dead. In Israel the bones of the dead were preserved. It was apparently thought that they did have a conscious existence after death. Joseph implored his family to return his bones to Canaan when they left Egypt, and Nehemiah was concerned about maintaining the tombs of his fathers.

2:6. queen sitting beside king. There are numerous examples in ancient Near Eastern iconography of the queen seated next to the king, usually upon her own throne. Many have argued that queens had an unusually powerful influence at the Persian court in this period, based upon the writings of the Greek historian Herodotus. Artaxerxes' wife was Damaspia, but there is a possibility that the queen's throne was occupied by the queen mother, Amestris, known to be a strong personality (see the comment on Esther 5:3), who was still taking an active role as late as 449 and perhaps was still alive at this time.

2:6. length of journey (distance and time). Nehemiah most likely took a long overland route from Susa to Jerusalem on the Persian Royal Road into northern Mesopotamia and west into Syro-Palestine. The distance was about nine hundred miles and would have taken about four months. That is the length of time it took Ezra to make the journey (see comment on Ezra 7:1).

2:7. governors of Trans-Euphrates. The term used here for "governors" can either refer to a district governor of a small province or a satrap, a major regional governor of the Persian empire. The empire was organized into a large number of compact satrapies that were highly efficient and often somewhat autonomous. The Trans-Euphrates governors ruled the area due north of Mesopotamia in the region of Armenia and Georgia.

2:7. letters of safe passage. Since Nehemiah's purpose was political, he may have anticipated hostility from the local Persian officials. He also may have been concerned because of the unrest that existed in various parts of the empire (see comment on Neh 1:1). Aramaic documents from the fifth century include such a letter. Its main function is to instruct regional officials to provide the travelers with provisions from the king's stores.

2:8. keeper of the king's forest. The keeper of the king's forest had a Hebrew name (Asaph). The forest was probably in Lebanon (which the Persians had overtaken in the mid-sixth century B.C.), although some areas in the coastal plain of Palestine may have served in this capacity. Greek historians such as Xenophon and Diodorus mention local parks under the care of officials of the Persian government.

2:8. use of timber/intended construction. The timber was requested for clearly specified uses: (1) the gates of a citadel, the forerunner of the Antonia fortress, built on the north side of the second temple by Herod the Great; (2) the reconstruction of the city wall (though the walls were built of stone and mud brick, timbers were used for stabilization and for gateways); and (3) for Nehemiah's own residence (as governor). Though mud brick and stone were the most common materials for residence construction, cedar would be used for interior paneling.

2:10. Sanballat. Sanballat the Horonite was governor of Samaria. He is attested in Aramaic papyri from Elephantine in Egypt, which also mentions two of his sons. Papyri from Wadi Daliyeh give a sequence of Samarian governors, three of whom were named Sanballat. As his sons had names with the theophoric element of Yah, Sanballat may have been a worshiper of Yahweh (although see Neh 13:28). The term Horonite is not clear, although it may simply mean a person who came from one of the towns with the element "Horon" in it. Sanballat opposed Nehemiah because Jerusalem and Judah had previously been under his jurisdiction, though it is unclear whether Judah was part of his province or that he had been given administrative oversight of the Judean district.

2:10. Tobiah. Tobiah was an Ammonite and thus was of foreign origin. He may have been an ancestor to the important Tobiad family from Jordan in later generations. Though it is not expressly stated, he may have been governor of Ammon, as his grandson (also Tobiah) of the third century was.

2:11-20
Nehemiah's Night Inspection

2:13-15. topography of fifth-century Jerusalem. It has been very difficult to locate the places mentioned in these verses. The walls and gates inspected by Nehemiah on the north and west sides no longer exist, or are buried under Herod's temple platform. The King's Pool on the eastern side is probably to be identified with the Pool of Siloam. The valley referred to here is most likely the Kidron Valley. Excavations have shown a strewn mass of stones, which are at least like the ones that blocked Nehemiah's path. Nehemiah had evidently chosen to abandon the eastern slope of the town and to build the new city wall there. Thus the city was certainly smaller than in preexilic times. It is estimated that the circumference of the city at this time was about one and a half miles, enclosing perhaps eighty or ninety acres.

2:16. groups referred to. The *officials* were likely representatives of the Persian empire, either those who had come with Nehemiah or those who had local jurisdiction. The term *Jews* referred to the citizenry at large. The *priests* took on a major role in the life of the Jerusalem community after the exile, with an increasing political role. The *nobles* refers to the heads of the

important families in the area, perhaps the equivalent to what are called elders in earlier literature.

2:19. Geshem. Geshem the Arab is known from extrabiblical sources. There is a Geshem in Libyanite and Aramaic inscriptions who is known as the king of Kedar. The name is also found in a later inscription at Beth Shearim, as well as on a silver vessel dedicated by his son Qainu to the goddess Han-'Ilat found at Tell el-Mashkuta in the Egyptian Delta. The Arabs had recently settled in the Negev and Transjordan regions (see Neh 2:10).

3:1-32
Building Assignments

3:1-32. assigning sections. In Assyrian times the building of walls was assigned out by sections to various groups of laborers. When Sargon built his capital at Khorsabad, the wall was assigned in sections to workers from the various provinces of the empire.

3:1. Sheep Gate. The Sheep Gate (other times called the Benjamin Gate) north of the temple mount, exits from the area of the Bethesda Pool (known in this period as the Sheep Pool) into the Kidron Valley. It is toward the northern side of the east wall and would have led to the Jericho road.

3:1. tower of the hundred and tower of Hananel. These two towers were positioned on the northwest side of the city near the Temple Mount. This is about the same location as the Antonia fortress in Herod's Jerusalem.

3:3. Fish Gate. The Fish Gate (otherwise known as the Ephraim Gate) led out of the city toward the northwest. This would be one of the routes one would take to the coastal plain.

3:3. gate structure. The text mentions four parts of the gate: the doors, the beams, the bolts and the bar. Two gate doors were generally set into stone sockets buried just under the ground. The beams flanked the gate on either side. They were made of wood and joined to the wall. The bars slid across the gates and the end fit into holes or brackets in the beam. These bars could be locked in place by a series of small wooden dowels that slipped into holes on a block mounted on the gate. One could therefore not exit the city without a key once the gate was locked.

3:6. Jeshanah Gate. Sometimes called the Old Gate, this gate is generally located just south of the Fish Gate. Some would identify this as the Mishneh Gate that opened into the western quarter of the city.

3:8. goldsmith and perfume-maker. In an-

cient cities certain quarters were occupied by
the members of particular guilds. Craft guilds
often were made up of families that had developed their own techniques and trade secrets, which would be practiced and passed
on from generation to generation.

3:8. Broad Wall. Excavators on the western
hill in Jerusalem have uncovered an unusually
thick wall (over twenty feet thick) from this
period that extends toward the west from the
western wall of the Temple Mount. Repairs
were not made to the Broad Wall itself for it
seems that the western hill was not occupied
during this time.

3:9. ruler of a half district. The familiar Assyrian title *rab pilkani*, "head of the district," offers the best understanding of the terminology used only in this context. Unfortunately,
little is known of the details of the administrative districting of the region.

3:11. Tower of the Ovens. Most interpreters
associate this with the bakers' district, which
was situated in this part of town so as to be
near the palace and temple complex (see Jer
37:21).

3:13. Valley Gate. The Valley Gate is in the
western wall along the slope of the City of
David leading into the Tyropoeon Valley.
What is believed to be this gate was identified
in Crowfoot's excavations in 1926-27. It is approximately twelve feet wide.

3:13. Zanoah. This is a town in the Shephelah
region about fifteen miles west-southwest of
Jerusalem.

3:14. Dung Gate. The Dung Gate is at the
southern tip of the city of David, a little over
five hundred yards south of the Valley Gate. It
opens into the Valley of Hinnom and the road
to the spring at En Rogel and is to be differentiated from the Dung Gate in the present con-
figuration of the city (near the southwest
corner of the Temple Mount, dating to the Ottoman period).

3:14. district of Beth Hakkerem. Beth Hakkerem is modern Ramat Rachel, just outside of
Jerusalem.

3:15. Fountain Gate. Located at the southeastern side of the city, this gate is only a few hundred yards from the Dung Gate and probably
gave access to the Pool of Siloam where the
Gihon Spring was channeled. Such a gate was
excavated in the 1920s.

3:15. district of Mizpah. Mizpah is identified
as Tell en-Nasbeh about eight miles north of
Jerusalem.

**3:15. wall of the Pool of Siloam and the
King's Garden.** This pool is generally thought
to refer to a canal that channeled the waters of
the Gihon Spring for irrigation along the east-

ern flank of Jerusalem. It was located at the
southern end of the city and provided water
for the King's Garden, at the juncture of the
Kidron and Hinnom Valleys.

3:15. steps from city of David. These steps
were located at the southern end of the city to
ease the steep ascent from the Kidron Valley.
Remains of an ancient staircase have been
found in this area.

3:16. half district of Beth Zur. Beth Zur was
the southern extremity of the province. It is located about four miles north of Hebron.

3:16. tombs of David. The place often identified to tourists as David's tomb on present-
day Mount Zion is a late tradition. The only
monumental tombs from the first temple period are in the modern village of Silwan across
the Kidron Valley from David's Jerusalem.
These are from Iron Age II but are not royal
tombs. The Judahite kings from Rehoboam to
Ahaz were buried in the City of David (except
for some notable exceptions). Later kings were
either buried in the "garden of Uzziah" (Manasseh and Amon) or in their own tomb (Josiah). The burial places of Hezekiah and the
successors of Josiah are not mentioned. The
site of the royal burials in the City of David
has not been determined with certainty.

3:16. artificial pool. This was a separate pool
from that referred to in the last verse but was
in the same vicinity.

3:16. house of the heroes. This most likely refers to the barracks used by the elite troops,
represented early by David's mighty men (see
comment on 2 Sam 23:8).

3:17. half district of Keilah. Keilah is located
nearly between Zanoah (v. 13) and Beth Zur
(v. 16), twenty miles southwest of Jerusalem.

3:25. description. The palace area was just
south of the temple mount. The tower at the
corner of the palace complex was skirted by
the city wall, and this angle is most likely the
one being referred to.

3:26. Ophel. The Hill of Ophel is identified as
the section between the Temple Mount and
the southern ridge known as the City of David. Apparently it featured fortifications that
surrounded the temple-palace complex. Some
believe that there was a citadel located here
that was itself designated "the Ophel."

3:26. Water Gate. This gate was across the
ridge from the Valley Gate and opened to the
east, leading to the Gihon Spring and the
Kidron Valley.

3:27. wall of Ophel. The wall of Ophel extended from the Ophel to the southwest along
the Kidron Valley to the Water Gate. In earlier
times this portion of the wall had been positioned partway down the slope, but Nehemi-

ah repositioned it at the crest of the slope. Portions of this wall have been found in the excavations in the City of David.

3:28. Horse Gate. This gate led from the temple complex east down into the Kidron Valley.

3:29. East Gate. Some associate this with what is now commonly called the Golden Gate on the east side of the temple complex. Beneath the current Golden Gate the arch of an older gate has been observed.

3:31. Inspection Gate. Little is known about this gate, which is sometimes called the Muster Gate. Most would identify it as a gate in the wall of the temple complex rather than in the city wall itself.

3:31. room above the corner. This is generally associated with the northeast corner of the city. It most likely functioned as a watchtower.

3:32. Sheep Gate. See comment on 3:1.

3:32. goldsmiths and merchants. One of the important merchant centers of the city was located by the gates on the north, so it is logical that these groups be assigned this section.

4:1-23
Enemy Opposition

4:1. Sanballat. See comment on 2:10.

4:2. army of Samaria. Though not a military colony, the governor of Samaria had an army to aid the Persian king. However, it is not certain whether these troops were Persian garrison troops or a local militia.

4:2. sacrifices. Typically major construction projects were dedicated with sacrificial rituals. Foundation sacrifices are well known in the ancient Near East.

4:2. bring stones back to life. This phrase may refer to the ancient Near Eastern idea that stones blackened with fire were cursed and could not be reused as building material. The Israelites do not have the time to quarry fresh stone, and the burnt limestone from the previous walls would be too unstable and fragile to reuse.

4:3. Tobiah. See comment on Nehemiah 2:10.

4:18. man who sounded trumpet. Throughout the biblical period trumpets were used for signaling in religious, civil and military contexts. This text speaks of the ram's horn (shofar) that is used for signaling all the way back at Mount Sinai (Ex 19:13). For more information on signaling, see comments on Numbers 31:6 and Joshua 6:4-5.

5:1-19
A Ruling to Aid the Poor

5:3-5. nature of the complaint. Because of the work of reconstructing Jerusalem, these people were not able to produce enough grain to stay alive. They had to buy grain but did not have enough funds, causing them to mortgage their property (fields, vineyards and houses). Furthermore, the Persian kings evidently took over a real estate tax that had been imposed by the Chaldeans. Darius I (r. 521-486 B.C.) levied a tax on the crops yielded in fields. Often both in Israel and elsewhere in the ancient Near East, parents sold their children into slavery to enable them to meet their material needs, hoping to redeem them at a later date (see comment on Ex 21:2-6).

5:7. usury. Usury in its purest sense was the charging of interest on a loan. An individual was forbidden to charge a fellow Israelite interest on a loan (see comments on Ex 22:25; Lev 25:38; and Deut 15:1-11). It was permissible, however, to charge a foreigner interest. Interest is mentioned as being permissible in the Babylonian Code of Hammurabi (eighteenth century B.C.). However, these were commercial loans, and there was no counterpart in Israel. An Israelite loan was considered charity and was done to help a needy fellow countryman, not to help a merchant build up his business.

5:11. solution. Any land that had been seized because the individuals had been unable to repay a debt was now to be returned without any conditions. It was a common practice in the ancient Near East to take over one's property (including children) if that person could not repay a debt. It appears that interest had also been raised in this case and was returned to the debtors.

5:14. time period of Nehemiah's governorship. Nehemiah was appointed governor from 445 to 433 B.C. This was his first term as governor. Some believe a second term followed some time later (see comment on 13:6-7). There is no extrabiblical information concerning Nehemiah or his term as governor.

5:14. food allotted to governor. Like a satrap, a Persian governor had the right to collect taxes from his subjects for his own treasury, not just for the Crown. Monies collected in this way paid for local projects and supported the administration. Food and drink went to the governor and his household. Elamite texts from this period discovered at Persepolis (Treasury Texts) reflect this practice as they document outlays from the royal treasury.

5:15. forty shekels. While the previous governors referred to may have been Judean, it is possible that the reference is to non-Jewish governors appointed by the satraps of the region. The only other governor mentioned in the biblical text is Zerubbabel seventy years earlier. It is unclear in the text whether the forty shekels was an annual amount paid by each citizen or the daily amount used to support the administration. In either case it is a large amount. Storage jars have been found in excavations that are thought to have been used by the Persian governors as a tax-gathering apparatus. Stamp impressions are also believed by some to preserve the names of governors of this period.

5:18. daily provision. The meal provisions for the 150 Jewish officials were likely part of their salary. Like other governors, Nehemiah was required to entertain regularly for both domestic officials and foreign dignitaries. Because of the great cost of this, it is all the more amazing that he did not collect taxes for his personal treasury.

6:1-19

Conspiracy Against Nehemiah and the Completion of the Wall

6:2. Plain of Otto. The Plain of Otto (or Ono) is about twenty-seven miles northwest of Jerusalem. During the Persian period, it was either at the northernmost border of the province of Judah or in neutral territory between the provinces of Ashdod and Samaria. At any rate, it was dangerous territory in which to meet one's enemies.

6:7. prophetic proclamation of kingship. Though there is little known about the prophetic offices in postexilic times, prophets played a role as "kingmakers" in earlier periods. The northern kingdom, Israel, had come into being by means of a prophetic pronouncement (1 Kings 11:29-39), and each of the major dynasties (Jeroboam, Baasha, Omri, Jehu) rose and fell in accordance with prophetic pronouncement. In the ancient Near East priests often play significant political roles, but no prophets from the ancient Near East are known to have played the same role as these Israelite kingmakers. Nonetheless, throughout the ancient world it was believed that prophets not only proclaimed the message of deity but in the process unleashed the divine action. One can understand why rumors of prophetic proclamations might incite insurrection or impose doom.

6:15. time of completion. Although the Jewish historian Josephus (A.D. 37-100) claims the walls were built in two years and four months, the biblical text does say it took a mere fifty-two days to complete the work. There are some parallels in antiquity for such

a feat. For example, Thucydides claims that a wall around the city of Athens was built in one month (fifth century B.C.). Since Jerusalem was small (archaeologists consider that the circuit of the wall in this time was merely one and a half miles), only the eastern wall was built from the foundation (as the other walls were refurbished), and archaeologists claim that the work was not one of a high standard, it is not unreasonable to assume that the task was completed in such a short time.

7:1-73

Family Records

7:2. commander of the citadel. The Persians employed numerous military commanders of garrisons throughout their empire. Though often staffed with Persian troops rather than local militia, they were under the command of the governor or his appointees.

7:65. eating restrictions. This restriction is repeated in Ezra 2:63. Those priests with uncertain genealogies were restricted from eating from the "most holy things" (see Lev 2:3; 7:21-36), food that priests are as their portion after the cultic rites. The Urim and Thummim were oracular devices (see comment on Ex 28:30) that would be used to inquire of God as to the credentials of those who claimed priestly ancestry.

7:70. a thousand drachmas of gold. Gold drachmas were either the Persian daric, the Median shekel or the Greek drachma (which was in more common use). Darics were not coined until the time of Darius. Darics were about 8.4 grams, so one thousand of them would equal about eighteen and a half pounds. The shekel was equal to the daric, while the Attic drachma was the equivalent of half a daric.

7:72. twenty thousand drachmas of gold, two thousand minas of silver. In gross weight this represents about 370 pounds of gold and 2220 pounds of silver (a mina was equal to sixty shekels). To compare this to the amounts used for Solomon's temple, see the comments on 1 Chronicles 22:14. A number of silver coins have been found in archaeological excavations that were minted at or near Jerusalem during the Persian period. These were struck with the inscription *yhd* or Yehud (Judah). They depicted the head of Pallas Athena, with an owl (the insignia of Athens) on the back side. The craftsmanship was clearly inferior to the Greek drachma. The coins had only a fractional value of silver and thus were worth less than counterparts found along the coast at Tyre and Sidon.

8:1-18

The Reading of the Law

8:1. chronology. It is presumed that the Israelites gathered together in the year that Nehemiah arrived, 445 B.C. Ezra would have already been there for thirteen years. The seventh month is Tishri (spans September-October), the beginning of the civil new year and the month that Yom Kippur and the Feast of Tabernacles are celebrated.

8:1. Water Gate. The Water Gate (see Neh 3:26) was near the Gihon Spring and thus afforded access to the water source. It has been argued that the gate referred to a preexilic wall that was not rebuilt by Nehemiah. It is not known whether this gate was included in the new wall or was east of it. In any case, Ezra did not read the Torah in or near the temple.

8:1. scribe. In Persian and general Mesopotamian usage, the position was that of a local commissioner charged with maintaining law and order, but a much broader scope is observable in the ancient world. Scribes would have been trained in reading of the various languages in use at the time, in the production of texts (whether copying, receiving dictation or composing), in the knowledge of traditional literature (canonical and noncanonical), in the range of international literature (particularly wisdom literature) and in the interpretation of literature (perhaps including legal literature or ritual literature). Scribes in Israel were, therefore, experts in the Law of Moses. One of their primary duties was to study the Scriptures. They became paramount in Jewish life in the postexilic period. They may have been organized into families and guilds (see 1 Chron 2:55). Later they were originators of the synagogue service. Many scribes were also priests and/or community leaders, as Ezra was. They were guardians of culture and tradition. Persian interest in this is shown in Darius's commissioning of an Egyptian high priest to reorganize the scribal school and temple practice of Sais. It is likely that scribes had the most significant role in the canonization process of the Old Testament.

8:1. Book of the Law of Moses. The Book of the Law of Moses contained, if not the entirety, at least a large proportion of the first five books of our Old Testament (Genesis—Deuteronomy).

8:3. public reading of state documents. Because of the lack of accessibility of written materials in the ancient Near East, the public reading of state documents by a scribe or herald was a very common occurrence. Letters from Kalhu in Assyria feature an Assyrian official reading a pronouncement in front of the people of Babylon.

8:4. reading platform. The platform referred to here can be compared to the platform Solomon used at the dedication of the first temple (2 Chron 6:13). The term used here has the root meaning of tower, emphasizing the height of the structure, so everyone could view Ezra as he read.

8:5. books or scrolls? Although the Hebrew word is translated as "book," Ezra certainly read from a scroll. Folded pages in the form of a modern book were not in existence until the second century A.D. and did not fully replace the scroll until some two centuries later.

8:5. stand up for reading. Standing up was a sign of respect in the Old Testament (see Judg 3:20; Job 29:8; Ezek 2:1).

8:6. worshiped. The response to the reading of the Scriptures was one of worship. The raising of the hands showed the people's dependence on God (see Ezra 9:5; Ps 28:2; 134:2). Prostration demonstrated their humility before God and his word. Prostrating oneself before a superior was a common occurrence throughout the Near East. The princes in the Akkadian letters from Amarna in Egypt symbolically prostrate themselves before Pharaoh.

8:7-8. interpretation of religious documents. The thirteen people mentioned in verse 7 were Levites who were responsible for the interpretation of the Law (2 Chron 17:7-9). They also translated the text, presumably from preexilic Hebrew into Aramaic, the common language of Palestine by the fifth century B.C. It also is possible that the word "translate" means that the Levites "broke down" the text, or in other words translated or interpreted the text paragraph by paragraph. Akkadian documents have various terms for commentaries on documents as well as attesting an oral commentary tradition. These commentaries are connected to canonical literature such as the omens of *Enuma Anu Enlil* as well as to legal traditions.

8:10. food. We are not told the specific type of feast the Israelites had when they were sent to their homes. It was certainly a feast of thanksgiving, since they were required to give a portion to their neighbors. Eating of the "fat," or choicest portions, was a common occurrence (see Lev 3; 2 Sam 6:19; 1 Chron 12:40-41; 29:22; 2 Chron 7:8-10; 30:21-26).

8:14-17. celebration of the Feast of Booths. For information on the feast see comments on Exodus 23:16; Leviticus 23:33-36, 39-43; and Deuteronomy 16:13-15. The Feast of Booths was normally celebrated on the fifteenth day of the seventh month. The uniqueness of the celebration appears to have to do with the combination of traditions. Leviticus 23:40 instructs the celebrants to gather branches, and verse 42 tells them to live in booths. But Leviticus does not specify the building of booths, nor does it require pilgrimage to Jerusalem. Deuteronomy 16:15 designates the festival as one of the three pilgrimage feasts but says nothing about gathering branches or living in booths. Ezra's ruling combines these traditions so that the people are gathering branches and building booths in which to live in Jerusalem for the time of the feast.

8:16. Water Gate and Gate of Ephraim. For the Water Gate see the note on verse 1. The Ephraim Gate was part of the preexilic wall (see comment on 2 Chron 25:23) and was located about six hundred feet from the Corner Gate. This gate may have opened in the direction of Ephraim to the northwest. However, there is no mention of this gate in the list in Nehemiah 3.

9:1-38
Confession of Sins

9:1. chronology. The fasting occurred a few days after the celebration of the Feast of Booths, in the seventh month of 445 B.C. If it started on the fifteenth as prescribed in the Law, it would have continued through the twenty-second. In that case it would be odd that there is no mention of the Day of Atonement, which is supposed to be observed on the tenth day of the seventh month. Verse 13, however, suggests that the festivities began on the second day and therefore would have lasted until the ninth. Perhaps the Day of Atonement was also slightly out of time and is represented in this fast, though no reference is made to the rituals of Leviticus 16.

9:1. occasion for fast. Fasting is little attested in the ancient Near East outside the Bible. It generally occurs in the context of mourning. In the Old Testament the religious use of fasting is often in connection with making a request before God. The principle is that the importance of the request causes an individual to be so concerned about his or her spiritual condition that physical necessities fade into the background. In this sense the act of fasting is designed as a process leading to purification and humbling oneself before God (Ps 69:10). As indicated in the following prayer, the Jews are here concerned about their own sins and the sins of their forefathers that have violated the covenant. This has become evident in the reading of the law. Their request is to be delivered from foreign rule.

9:1. sackcloth. Sackcloth was a typical sign of mourning and repentance in the Bible. It was a coarse cloth, normally of black goat's hair. It was usually worn next to the skin as a band or a kilt tied around the waist. The symbolic significance of the wearing of sackcloth can be found among the Assyrians, Moabites, Phoenicians and Arameans.

9:6. you alone are Yahweh. This is a typical biblical admission of the absolute uniqueness of God (see comment on Deut 6:4). The uniqueness is expressed particularly in relation to creation and the covenant.

9:6. creator deities in Persian period. The Persians (or at least the Persian state) were primarily Zoroastrian during the period of Nehemiah. They believed that the god representing the power of good, Ahura Mazda, by his spirit created the world perfectly good. However, an equally powerful deity existed, Angra Mainyu, who brought forth evil and ignorance, thus perverting the creation of Ahura Mazda. However, by way of foreknowledge, Ahura Mazda made his creation to combat this evil god, paving the way for the restoration of the world to its original pure state.

9:6. multitudes of heaven. The "(starry) host" early in the verse and the "multitudes of heaven" near the end of the verse translate the same Hebrew term. The term can refer either to the stars or the angelic host, both of which were objects of reverence (and often indistinguishable since the stars were manifestations of gods) in the surrounding cultures. In Zoroastrianism, Ahura Mazda created all the other gods (*yazatas*), but he was, in some ways, dependent on them and offered sacrifices to them.

9:7-37. recitation of history in prayer. The reciting of Israel's history in prayers or hymns is a common occurrence in the Bible (e.g., Ps 78; 105; 135; 136). In this regard the Israelites were unique. Their neighbors referred to the New Year in prayers but did not refer to either creation or past historical events.

9:20. Spirit to instruct them. Because of the phrase "your good Spirit," a common appellation for the Zoroastrian god, Ahura Mazda, some have argued for a Persian influence upon Judaism. However, the differentiation between the Spirit of the Lord and an evil spirit was used long before any contact between the two peoples (see 1 Sam 16:14; 1 Kings 22:23-24). Additionally, in the Persian period the Israelites were not shy about adopting titles familiar from Zoroastrianism and attaching them instead to Yahweh (see comment on 1:4). Such reuse of familiar divine titles can be observed as early as Abraham (see comments on Gen 14:17-24).

9:36. slaves to the Persian king? The Jews, like all other people groups of the Persian empire, were subjects of the Persian king and were required to pay taxes. In virtually all ancient Near Eastern monarchies all inhabitants were considered slaves (or subjects) to the king. However, the monarch himself was a slave to the national deity (Ashur in Assyria, Marduk in Babylon).

9:38. seals. Seals were very commonly used throughout the ancient Near East from Egypt to Iran from the fourth millennium B.C. onward. Literally thousands of seals have been found in archaeological excavations. They were used as a mark of authenticity and prestige, to witness a document or to prevent anyone from entering doors or opening other receptacles. The most common form of seal in Mesopotamia was the cylinder seal, but Israelites favored stamp seals. Most seals were engraved by a skilled seal-cutter, using a variety of materials. Hundreds of Hebrew seals have been found, as well as over one thousand jar handles with seal impressions.

10:1-39
Decision of the People

10:30. endogamy clause. The legal background for this clause is found in Ezra 9:1-2. Since the Law of the Pentateuch, Israelites had been forbidden to take foreign wives (see comment on Deut 7:3). The Israelites had intermingled with the nations about them and thus had been contaminated by their religious practices. It was common among ancient Near Eastern societies to marry inside one's clan (endogamy) or to make a marriage alliance with another friendly group. The Israelites were thus encouraged to marry within their "spiritual" clan (i.e., the worshipers of the Lord). In this time period, however, the issues went beyond spiritual homogeneity. Election and covenant issues made landownership theologically significant. Intermarriage was one of the ways that land tenure could be jeopardized and, with it, covenant benefits. The Elephantine texts (Jewish texts less than fifty years removed from Ezra and Nehemiah) show how land became redistributed and lost to a family through foreign women marrying into Jewish families and becoming enfranchised.

10:31. Sabbath regulations. Sabbath regulations prohibited Israelites from engaging in their vocations on the seventh day. At first this would have included mostly farming and herding activity. As Israel developed a merchant economy in the monarchy period, the prohibition had been applied to engaging in the vocation of trade, that is, in the selling of merchandise. In this postexilic period the question arose whether buying of merchandise from those not prohibited from selling it (foreign merchants) was permitted on the Sabbath. It could be argued that buying is not the exercise of one's vocation. Nevertheless, the community leaders extended the Sabbath prohibitions to apply to selling as well as buying.

10:31. seventh year regulations. The "seventh" year described here is likely the sabbatical year described in Exodus 23:10-11 and Deuteronomy 15:1-3 (on which see comments). It is speculated that Nehemiah was combining the two and perhaps even regulating their observance so that everyone was practicing the two together at the same time. This would certainly have made the law more enforceable.

10:32-33. temple tax. Originally there was no annual tax levied for the upkeep of the temple. Exodus 30:13 prescribes one-half of a shekel to be paid to the temple at the time of a census, but that is a different matter. Though the Persian kings Darius I and Artaxerxes I had promised to assist the building of the temple (see Ezra 6:9-10; 7:21-24), they had not endowed its operation budget (though Ezra 7:21-22 may refer to some ongoing aid). Coinage had become the economic standard during the reigns of Darius and Xerxes. The development of a cash-based economy during this period required cash support for the operations of the temple. The third of a shekel mentioned here was probably due to an adjustment made to adapt to the monetary system used in the Persian empire. At this time the basic coin of the Persian empire, the daric, weighed 8.4 grams and was equated to the Babylonian shekel. The Aramaic *zuz* was one-half of that and equivalent to the Greek drachma. The standard Israelite shekel, however, had long been 11.4 grams (as was the Assyrian shekel), but there was also a royal shekel ("heavy" shekel in Ugaritic terminology), which is represented in archaeological finds as weighing 12.5 to 12.8 grams. Therefore a *zuz*, at 4.2 grams, could be roughly equated to one-third of the traditional royal shekel.

10:34. wood provision. In the monarchy period the temple had sufficient staff to gather the wood that was necessary. Cutting wood was one of the jobs assigned to the Gibeonites in Joshua 9:27. In this period, however, the temple is significantly understaffed, so an alternate plan is necessary for the provision of the wood.

10:35. firstfruits commitment. The general religious principle involved in offering the "firstfruit" (animal, vegetable or human) to the gods is based on the promotion of fertility. From earliest times, the assumption is made that the gods create life in its various forms and that they expect to receive as their due offering the first of the harvest or the firstfruit of the womb. Israelite religion tempered this by allowing for the redemption of some animals and all human firstborn males (Ex 13:11-13; Num 18:14-15). The giving of the firstfruits could also take on a political character. The Assyrian annals of Sennacherib (705-681 B.C.) contain his command that conquered peoples pay their firstfruit offerings of sheep, wine and dates to the gods of Assyria. In Israel the firstfruits of the harvest were traditionally part of the support of the priests. Numbers 18:12-13 specifies grain, wine and oil. Here fruit trees are added to the list.

10:36. firstborn commitment. Since human children and unclean animals were redeemed, this practice provided for some "cash flow" for the temple operations. For more information on the laws concerning the firstborn see comment on Exodus 13:1-3.

10:37. offerings to priests and Levites. Whether or not the worshiper ate a portion of the sacrifice, a number of the sacrifices provided an opportunity for the priests to eat. This was also true in Babylonian practice, according to which the king, the priest and other temple personnel received portions of the sacrifices. As early as Sumerian texts it was considered a grievous crime to eat that which had been set apart as holy. Most peoples in other ancient Near Eastern religious traditions were required to maintain temples in much the same way. The food was to be "consumed" by the god(s) but, of course, was instead eaten by the temple personnel. For more information on tithing see comment on Numbers 18:31-32.

11:1-36
Populating Jerusalem

11:1-2. why would people not want to live in Jerusalem? The mere fact that lots were cast implies that some were forced to live in Jerusalem. Lot casting was considered in the ancient Near Eastern and Mediterranean world as a way of allowing God (or the gods) to determine the fate of a certain situation. Thus the people who were chosen to go considered it a divine mandate (for more information about the casting of lots see comments on Josh 7:14-18 and Jonah 1:7-10). Since Jerusalem had been devastated and was the point of great contention between the Jews and neighboring

peoples, it was not an attractive nor a safe place in which to live in the fifth century B.C. Additionally, it can be understood that people would not be anxious to abandon their farms and jeopardize their landholdings.

11:23. singers under the king's orders. The king referred to here is most likely the Persian king Artaxerxes I, who was interested in the continuation of the cultic practices (see Ezra 4:8-10; 7:21-24). Most ancient Near Eastern kings from the third millennium B.C. onward employed professional singers in their courts. For instance, Zimri-Lim of Mari (c. 1780-1760 B.C.) had a large retinue of singers connected to his court. For singers in Israel see comment on 2 Chronicles 29:27-30.

11:24. the king's agent. There is evidence in the sources dealing with the Persian empire of high-level emissaries who represented the king in the various satrapies. They occasionally appear in the Persian court to make appeals on behalf of the satrap, and they report to the king about activities in the region and advise him on local matters.

11:25-36. territorial settlements. All of the names of the cities in the list appear in Joshua 15, except for Dibon, Jeshua and Meconah. The list shows that the Jews lived in a comparatively large area. The Judah list focuses on the Negev and the Shephelah, while the Benjamin list covers the central hills and the coastal plain. This may offer the parameters of the Persian province.

12:1-26
List of Priests and Levites

12:8. in charge of songs of thanksgiving. There is a detailed account of the organization of the Levitical choir and orchestra by David in 1 Chronicles 15:16-24. However, few other descriptions of the music of the court are given. There may have been an equal number of males and females in the choir (see Ezra 2:65). Some have argued that the choir actually chanted rather than sang. Apart from this passage we have no evidence of the responsibilities of the person in charge of the songs of thanksgiving. Musicians are counted among temple personnel in Neo-Assyrian inscriptions and included both male and female singers. A chief singer is mentioned in one text from Nimrud.

12:24. instructions of David. The only instructions for worship associated with David are those found throughout 1-2 Chronicles (e.g., see 1 Chron 15—16; 23—29).

12:25. gatekeepers who guarded the storerooms at gates. For a discussion of the function of the gatekeepers see comment on 1 Chronicles 9:22-27.

12:27-47
Dedication of the Walls

12:27. cymbals, harps and lyres. For information concerning musical instruments see the comments on 2 Chronicles 5:12 and 29:25. The terminology used for musical instruments in Israel has close parallels with terms used at Ugarit.

12:28-29. surrounding villages. The guild villages are all in close proximity to Jerusalem: Netophah, southeast of Jerusalem, Geba and Azmaveth, two Benjaminite cities six miles north of Jerusalem. Beth Gilgal was likely a longer term for Gilgal near Jericho.

12:30. purifying gates and wall. It is unclear what is meant by the purification of the gates and wall, as it is an unprecedented idea in the Bible. The term used here normally applies to objects used in rituals or to places where rituals were performed, though houses that have mildew needed to be purified (see comments on Lev 14:34-53). If the former is in mind, it may reflect an idea of the sanctity of Jerusalem as a holy city. If the latter, it seeks to remedy the uncleanness brought on at the time the walls were destroyed (specifically by corpse contamination or idolatrous practices performed in the gates or on the walls, or generally from their moral corruption; see Jer 13:27). The purification ritual is not described here. The walls may have been sprinkled, a concept that was practiced with the cleansing of private houses.

12:31-37. placement of first choir. The processions appear to have begun in the vicinity of the Valley Gate on the west side of the city. This first choir procession walked southward (counterclockwise) on the top of the wall to the Dung Gate at the southern tip of the city. They then proceeded north along the eastern flank to the Water Gate directly east across the narrow saddle of the ridge from the Valley Gate. They thus made the circuit of the southern half of the city, the old City of David.

12:38-39. placement of second choir. Another procession followed Nehemiah clockwise from the west to the north and east. They also began around the Valley Gate and did the circuit of the northwest end of the city. The gates and towers are mentioned in Nehemiah 3, while the Ephraim Gate is mentioned in Nehemiah 8:16. The Guard Gate is mentioned only here in Scripture and is generally considered the meeting point of the two groups by the temple complex (the first group arriving from the Water Gate, the second from the Sheep Gate). Each

group traveled about two-thirds of a mile on the walls. That distance on the modern ramparts is from the Jaffa Gate to Herod's Gate, which takes about thirty minutes to walk.

13:1-31
Other Reforms

13:1-3. exclusion of foreigners from worship. The law referred to here is Deuteronomy 23:3-6, concerning the exclusion of Ammonites and Moabites from worship. The law was thus interpreted in a wider sense to include any foreigner in the community who did not worship the God of Israel. The Ammonite reference was especially relevant, since Tobiah's Ammonite ancestry was well known (see Neh 2:10).

13:4-5. provisions for Tobiah. For information on Tobiah, see comment on 2:10 (see also 6:17-19). The Persian king, Cambyses, is similarly reported to have purged foreigners from the temple complex at Neith in Egypt.

13:6-7. details of Nehemiah's two terms as governor. Since this section deals with other matters, we are told little of the details of Nehemiah's terms as governor of Judah. Nehemiah was absent from Jerusalem for an undetermined period of time. Since he had to ask permission to return, it probably was not the intention of Artaxerxes I to have him return for a second term of office. The text does not say nor imply that he returned in the same capacity of governor. It is possible he returned specifically because of the aforementioned circumstances concerning Tobiah.

13:16. men from Tyre. The men of Tyre were famous Phoenician merchants (see Ezek 27:12-36; 28:16) who traded throughout the entire Mediterranean world. Ancient economists had concluded that it was not enough to have caravans traveling the cities and towns of the region. They went the next step of establishing merchant colonies in the large trading centers as an ongoing outlet for their merchandise. There was evidently a colony of Tyrians in Jerusalem who had been permitted to operate outside the parameters of Jewish law. See the comment on 10:31.

13:24. language of Ashdod, language of Judah. Though Ashdod had been a Philistine city in preexilic times, it is not known what language was spoken here during this period. They would have spoken either a dialect of Aramaic, the diplomatic and trade language of the Persian empire, or some generic Canaanite dialect. The "language of Judah" refers to biblical Hebrew (see comment on 2 Chron 32:18).

13:28. Sanballat. See comment on Nehemiah 2:10.

ESTHER

1:1-22

Vashti Deposed

1:1. Xerxes. Xerxes, the Greek name for the king the Hebrew text refers to as Ahasuerus, ruled Persia from 486 to 465 B.C. His father was Darius the Great, and his mother was Atossa, the daughter of Cyrus. He inherited an extensive empire from his father but was unable to expand its borders during his reign despite several attempts. His policies toward religious groups changed dramatically from the tolerance that had characterized Cyrus and Darius. His own religion, like that of his father, was Zoroastrianism. He was more sensitive to religion as a basis for rebellion and was known to have destroyed many temples in an effort to curb nationalism. The lack of new conquests also created economic tensions that had not previously existed. The wars with Greece, rather than supplying booty and tribute to the treasuries and expanding trade opportunities, became a drain on the economy. There are over twenty inscriptions associated with Xerxes, the most important known as the Daiva Inscription. For more information see comment on Ezra 4:6.

1:1. 127 provinces. The primary administrative geographical division in the Persian empire was the satrapy. The number of these varied between twenty and thirty-one, so the text is not referring to satrapies. It is likely a reference to smaller administrative districts or to the people groups who constituted the empire.

1:1. India to Cush. The territory of the Persian empire extended from the Indus Valley in northwest India, across the Near East and into northern Africa, including Egypt, Libya and Cush (modern Sudan). In the northwest it included Thrace, the Scythians and all of Asia Minor, and ranged east across Armenia, Urartu and Bactria.

1:2. citadel of Susa. The ten-acre citadel is lo-

cated on an elevated area on the northern point of the site, the Apadana. The palace was built by Darius and used by several of his successors. Excavation of the palace has identified many of its features, including the audience hall, where the Persian kings held court. It was a square building over 350 feet on each side, featuring seventy-two stone columns each estimated at sixty-five to eighty feet tall. Greater Susa, located about 225 miles east of Babylon, was built on three hills overlooking the Shaur River. It had long been the capital of ancient Elam. The diamond-shaped mound is about two and a quarter miles in circumference, covering nearly 250 acres. An additional twenty acres comprises the merchant quarter across the valley to the east. Susa served as the capital for the Persian kings only in the winter months. Since temperatures soared to as high as 140 degrees in the summer the court moved north to Ecbatana.

1:3. chronology. Xerxes came to the throne upon the death of his father in November of 486. The third year of his reign was therefore March 483 to March 482 B.C. The main events that are known from this period are the two revolts in Babylon, a minor one in 484 and a more significant one in August 482.

1:3. officials on guest list. It was common for kings to sponsor lavish parties. Assyrian king Ashurnasirpal once claimed to have entertained nearly seventy thousand for a ten-day extravaganza. The guest list details people from all over Assyria in addition to foreign dignitaries, people from the capital city (Kalah) and palace dependents. Persian banquets were known to host up to fifteen thousand guests. The guests in Esther include the aristocracy of Media and Persia, the courtiers who were ranking officials in the administration, the military brass and perhaps the provincial governors.

1:4. six-month display. Verse 5 speaks of another banquet, one for the citadel staff. The

---

HERODOTUS

Herodotus was a Greek historian who lived in the fifth century B.C. He is best known for his *Histories* (written about 445 B.C.), which document the history of the Persian Wars against the Greeks, including the battles at Marathon, Thermopylae and Salamis. As a contemporary of the events, he provides valuable information concerning the history and culture of both Greece and Persia during this period. Though he is considered too willing to accept the validity of rumors, his work is valuable both for its reports on events and its descriptions (for instance, of the city of Babylon). Above all, Herodotus is valued as a great storyteller. Though his stories can at times be contradictory, he is considered an important chronicler of events, places and practices. There are numerous places in the book of Esther where comparison can be made with the information contained in Herodotus. These comparisons sometimes clarify what is found in the book, while at other times they can bring confusion.

citadel was a residence only for the king's household and administration, but the wording here suggests that lower ranking officials who served in the citadel were also included. The six-month display of the treasury stretches between the two banquets. The practice of showing off the royal treasury is also seen in Israel (Is 39:2).

1:5. enclosed garden of king's palace. The enclosed garden is connected to the *bitan* (NIV: "palace"), which is a technical term from the Akkadian, *bitanu*, a separate building in the palace complex. The *bitanu* in Esarhaddon's palace complex measured 150 by 50 feet. It is understood as a gazebo-style pavilion reserved for royal use. This building was often surrounded by a private garden planted with fruit trees and shade trees, with watercourses, pools and paths—more like a park. Its arboretum often contained many exotic trees and plants. Such gardens have been excavated at Pasargadae, Cyrus the Great's capital city.

1:6. garden decor. The main area for the banquet was a large colonnaded courtyard outside the pavilion paved with mosaics. In the classical world mosaics were very popular. The stone was not artificially colored, but rather stones of different shades were imported from wherever they could be found to give color to the mosaic. The earliest mosaic floors were made from colored pebbles laid out in geometric designs. Only later did they begin cutting the stone into cubes (tessellation) and forming them into pictures. The earliest examples of mosaics in the Near East date to the eighth century B.C. (Gordion in Asia Minor), though the art of inlay was known as early as the third millennium (as in the royal standard of Ur). A number of the words used in the description of the garden furnishings are obscure, but the extravagance was clearly spectacular. The fabrics are the best available and colored with the most expensive dyes (see comment on Num 4:6). The variety of vessels used to serve the wine (not goblets for drinking as in the NIV) was typical of Persian elegance.

1:6. marble. Some translations call this alabaster. Marble had to be imported from Greece and is not evident in the ancient world until its introduction into Phoenicia in the Persian period. Marble capitals (the decorative tops of pillars) are not attested archaeologically in the Near East until the first or second century A.D. Oriental alabaster was a calcium carbonate-like marble, unlike European alabaster, which is gypsum. It was used for fine vessels throughout the region during the biblical period, as well as for columns in architecture. In Sennacherib's "palace without rival" mostly white limestone was used, though he had some access to alabaster.

1:7-8. drinking protocol. The alleged protocol for these gala affairs was that when the king drank, everyone drank. In contrast, here the guests were not obliged to follow that guideline. They were not required to follow the king's lead by drinking every time he did, and there was an "open bar" policy that allowed them to drink freely. Examples of beautifully crafted golden drinking cups have been found dating to this period. One famous one features a winged lion whose hindquarters flare up into a goblet shape.

1:9. Vashti. Vashti is never mentioned in Herodotus, nor is she known from contemporary Persian records. Her name is a typical Persian name, but no further information is available. In Herodotus's account, Xerxes' wife is named Amestris. She is the mother of Artaxerxes, the successor of Xerxes, who was born about 483. Ctesias records several examples of the cruel power she exercised as queen mother during the reign of Artaxerxes, as well as her death in 424. Some linguists believe that Vashti and Amestris are the respective Hebrew and Greek attempts at rendering the same Persian name.

1:9. separate banquet for women. It is known that Persian queens had considerable estates and were well provisioned. On the other hand, there is no documentation for the women eating separately from the men or banquets that are just for one group or the other.

1:9. Xerxes' harem. Xerxes followed a policy of monogamy, but that did not eliminate his harem. Though he had only one wife at a time, his harem consisted of over 360 concubines. His many affairs were likewise well documented and were the cause of much court intrigue.

1:10. high in spirits. Herodotus reports that the Persians typically made important decisions while drunk and then validated them once they were sober.

1:10. seven eunuchs. Eunuchs were highly valued in government service in many varied roles. The great demand for eunuchs led to young boys being included in the tribute paid to Persia so that they could be castrated and trained for government service. They had no families to distract them from their service. They were often entrusted with the care and supervision of the royal harem. Having been castrated, they posed no threat to the women of the harem and could not engender children by the harem women who might be mistaken for royal heirs. They would be less likely to become involved in conspiracies, because they would have no heirs to put on the throne. Assyria, Urartu and Media had all made use of eunuchs in government offices prior to the Persian period. Four of the names in this list have been attested in Elamite documents and can therefore be considered authentic names of the period. Herodotus names the chief eunuch of Xerxes Hermotimus. Herodotus describes the men surrounding Xerxes as cringing, fawning leeches who tell the king only what they think he wants to hear.

1:11. display her beauty. One need not think that Vashti was asked to do anything immodest or morally compromising (as early rabbinic interpretation assumed). In some eastern societies, the harem was carefully sequestered and the law prohibited anyone from looking on the faces of the royal women. Persian women of this period went about in closed carriages so as not to be exposed to the gaze of the general public. If this is the case, as Josephus reported it was, Xerxes would be requesting Vashti to do something beneath her station and demeaning to her royal personage. Exposing her to the gaze of the entire citadel population would be a far greater humiliation than not bowing to an honored official, but would be a similar violation of protocol.

1:13-14. consulting experts in matters of law. Herodotus reports that the Persian kings had a panel of judges with lifetime appointments whom the king relied upon for interpretations of the law. Xenophon likewise confirms this panel of seven principal advisors.

1:19. laws of the Medes and the Persians. No concept of "laws of the Medes and Persians that cannot be changed" has been documented outside the books of Daniel and Esther. Nonetheless, a tradition at least as early as the time of Hammurabi (eighteenth century B.C.) recognized that a judge could not change a decision that had been made. In this sense, we may be dealing with a ruling rather than a law. Greek sources conflict with one another, as Herodotus indicates significant freedom on the part of Persian kings to change their minds, while Diodorus Siculus cites an instance where Darius III could not. Certainly no lower official could countermand the decrees of the Persian king, and the king himself may have thought it humiliating to go back and reconsider something he had already decreed. The royal code of honor would have made it out of the question for the king to rescind an order.

1:19. Vashti's punishment. The punishment decreed for Vashti is not execution or divorce. She was simply demoted within the harem so that she would have no chance of an official presence in Xerxes court. This would effectively strip her of power and prestige, and remove her from a position where she could hope to receive favors from the king.

1:20. circulation of dispatches. The Persian Empire was renowned for its communication system—similar to that used by the Pony Express in the American West over two millennia later. Herodotus describes the system as featuring stations for every day of the journey with a man and a horse for each day. He even comments that neither snow, rain, heat or darkness deters them from their task.

2:1-18
Esther Becomes Queen

2:1. time interval. The gathering referred to in chapter one is generally assumed to involve planning for the Greek campaign. Herodotus mentions such a conference at which Xerxes makes a stirring speech urging action against the Greeks. The campaign was launched in the spring of 481, Xerxes' fifth year. For over two years he was engaged in the west, as the Greeks and Persians fought in the Battles of Thermopylae (August 28, 480), Salamis (Sept 22, 480), Plataea and Mykale (August 479). In the fall of 480 Xerxes left Greece but wintered in Sardis on the west coast of Asia Minor. He did not return to Susa until the fall of 479, about the seventh month of his seventh year. Perhaps it was during his winter in Sardis that he began to miss Vashti and put the plan into action to replace her.

2:3. beauty search. This practice is only documented in the time of the Sasanian king, Chosroes II (about A.D. 600), when each satrap was commanded to seek out beautiful girls to be sent up to the king.

2:3. harem life. Life in the royal harem clearly had its advantages and disadvantages. While the women enjoyed every sort of material comfort and were indulged and pampered in many ways, they had no recourse for intimate relationship with a husband. Their opportunities to be intimate with the king would have been rare and would offer no companionship. Undoubtedly they found companions among the other women of the harem or even occasionally with the eunuchs entrusted with the care of the harem. But the special relationship found with a husband, raising children within a family setting—these pleasures were denied them.

2:5. Benjaminite son of Kish. This is a familiar pedigree—King Saul had also been a Benjaminite son of Kish, and Shimei is known as a relative of Saul's in the time of David (2 Sam

16:5). It is difficult to know whether the Kish and Shimei referred to here are actually the characters from the books of Samuel or just ironically share the same names. Given the extensive use of irony throughout the book of Esther, the latter would not be out of place. For further intriguing connections see the comment on 3:1.

2:6. chronological perspective. Chapter 2 is taking place in 479/478 B.C. The exile of Jehoiachin under Nebuchadnezzar took place in 597 B.C., about 120 years earlier. For this reason it is logical to assume that it was one of the listed ancestors who had been taken captive in 597 rather than Mordecai himself.

2:9. special food. This simply indicates that Esther was put on a regulated diet provided through the palace kitchens.

2:12. nature of beauty treatments. One common suggestion is that a process was used in which the woman was daily exposed to the smoke of burning spices so that both her clothing and her skin would absorb the aroma. Archaeologists have discover many cosmetic burners that they believe were used in this way. While this would suit the details given in the passage, the actual practice is not attested until modern times. Ointments were used to moisturize the skin, which easily became dry in the arid climate of the Near East. Myrrh was imported from southern Arabia (modern Somalia and Yemen), where it was manufactured from the resin collected from *commiphora* bushes when they were tapped.

2:14. concubines. Concubines were girls who came to a marriage without a dowry. They had not been taken into the harem in connection with political alliances with other countries nor for associations to be made between the crown and a wealthy family. As concubines they would continue to be supported as a member of the royal household but would be unlikely to enjoy any of the king's attention in the future (see comment on 2:3).

2:16. chronological placement. Xerxes had returned from his stay in Sardis (in connection with the Greek campaign) by the seventh month of his seventh year (see comment on 2:1). Esther was summoned in the tenth month of that same year. This would be January-February 478. Herodotus gives little information concerning Xerxes after the Greek campaign ends, so there is no detailed record of the events of this period.

2:17. Esther in Persian records. There are no contemporary records from either Persian inscriptions or Greek historians that mention Esther or any of the events in which she was involved.

2:19-23
Mordecai Reports a Conspiracy

2:19. king's gate. Excavations at Susa have identified a monumental gatehouse about one hundred yards east of the main palace. The passageway through the gate was about fifty feet long. Four towers graced the outside of the structure, and four pillars (about forty feet high) decorated the 12,000-square-foot chamber through which the passageway entered the palace complex. An inscription ordered by Xerxes at the gate identifies it as having been built by his father Darius.

2:23. hanged on a gallows. "Gallows" is somewhat interpretive since the Hebrew text vaguely indicates a wooden object. From what is known of Persian practice, this likely does not refer to the actual means of execution. Instead, it is generally agreed that this reflects the practice of impaling the corpse of the executed victim on a pointed stake in public view. This practice is known in Persia, in, for example, Amestris's execution of Inaros (leader of a Libyan revolt) during the reign of her son, Artaxerxes. The victim was thus denied proper burial, as the birds and insects devoured the remains. Hanging is unattested as a form of execution in the ancient world. If a form of execution is intended here, it would most likely be crucifixion (as interpreted by the Septuagint), which is identified by Herodotus as a Persian practice. But it must be noted that for Herodotus even crucifixion could be something done to a corpse.

2:23. royal annals. Royal annals were kept throughout the ancient Near East, with most examples coming from mid-second millennium Hittite kings and from ninth- to sixth-century Assyria and Babylon. The annals could be represented by annalistic royal inscriptions that give detailed accounts of military campaigns. In addition there are court chronicles that give information of important events in each year. As of yet no annals from Achaemenid Persia have been discovered.

3:1-15
Haman's Plot

3:1. Haman the Agagite. Just as Mordecai was identified in such a way as to evoke memories of King Saul (see comment on 2:5), Haman is now introduced in a way that associates him with Saul's ancient protagonist, Agag, king of the Amalekites (see 1 Sam 15:7-9, 32-33).

3:1. Haman's office. Though no title is given to Haman in the text of Esther, those who study the book often title him the vizier. In

Persian reliefs the high-ranking official pictured in the king's presence is designated the *hazarapatish* (often translated "chiliarch") and holds the king's weapons. This officer commanded the royal guard and determined who could or could not get in to see the king. Another important official in the Persian court was designated the "King's Eye." Xenophon reports that this office observed the peoples of the provinces and reported what he saw.

3:2. homage protocol. Herodotus reports that the Persians of equal rank greeted one another with a kiss on the mouth. Someone of slightly lower status would greet a superior with a kiss on the cheeks. If there was a great difference in their status, prostration was the required protocol. Mordecai's refusal is unlikely to concern inhibitions about worship, for there is no suggestion that Mordecai had trouble prostrating himself before the king. The Israelites were known to show deference through this sort of obeisance. Though obeisance could be an act of worship, that was because it was a way of showing reverence and respect. There was no inferred deification here. More likely is that Mordecai was not willing to acknowledge the wide difference in status between himself and Haman that the act would have implied.

3:7. chronology. The twelfth year of Xerxes is 474 B.C., so Esther has been queen for about four years. The month of Nisan begins in our March. The month of Adar was the twelfth month, beginning in February.

3:7. casting of the *pur*. *Pur(u)* is the Babylonian word for lots. Archaeologists have discovered an example of these clay cubes. The lot of Iahali, the vizier of Shalmaneser III (ninth century) measures about one inch per side. Though shaped like dice (which go back at least to the third millennium), this has an inscription (prayers for good luck) rather than dots. The purpose of the casting of lots is to determine which would be a favorable day for the type of action that Haman plans to undertake. One speculation concerning a way the month could be determined would be by casting the *pur* on a board that had each month's name written on it to see in which space it would land. Typically the same answer would have to come three consecutive throws in order to be considered valid.

3:8-9. Persian intolerance. The Persians are often considered by historians to be relatively tolerant. This assessment is supported mainly by the policy of Cyrus allowing exiled peoples to return and rebuild their temples. But it need not be assumed that an attitude of tolerance motivated this decision. There are economic, political and religious factors that would commend such a policy. It had now been sixty years since Cyrus's decree, and it had become obvious that tolerance did not eliminate revolt. In general in the ancient world, religious persecution, where it existed, had political or economic roots (perhaps today is no different). As Haman presents the problem, it is not a religious group or worship practice that needs to be eradicated, but an ethnic group with customs that preserve a nationalism whose fervor has brought it to the brink of revolt.

3:9. amount provided by Haman. Ten thousand talents of silver (according to the standard set by Darius) is about 333 tons. At current market value of roughly five dollars an ounce, this would be the equivalent of about $5.6 million. A more useful understanding, however, can be gained when we compare this amount to contemporary quantities. Herodotus reports the amounts of annual tribute paid by twenty provinces to Darius. The highest paying province, Assyria Babylonia, paid one thousand talents (thirty-three tons). The total tribute income from these twenty provinces is the equivalent of about thirteen thousand talents of silver (by the standards of Darius). This then is a significant amount that Haman feels is necessary to fund the extent of military activity he has in mind (the last phrase in v. 9 makes it clear that the money is offered for funding purposes). An even more interesting comparison can be made to the contribution offered by the Lydian, Pythius, to finance Xerxes' war effort in Greece. Pythius, reported in Herodotus to be the second wealthiest man in the world (after Xerxes), had a fortune valued at 16,400 talents of silver, which he placed entirely at Xerxes' disposal. For one final comparison, Thucydides reports that Athens, in its golden age, had a total reserve of 9,000 talents of silver (= 10,440 by the Persian standard).

3:10. signet ring. Current evidence suggests that the early Persian kings used cylinder seals for empire business and stamp seals or signet rings for personal business, though the latter were growing in usage through this period. A signet ring held the official seal of the king by which he authorized the business of the empire. Only a few of these have been found by archaeologists. The seals were typically made of chalcedony and featured pictures of the king doing heroic acts (like killing beasts) under the protection of the winged sun disk (representing Ahura Mazda). Many of the Persepolis fortification tablets contained stamp seal impressions.

3:11. keep the money. The phrase NIV translates "keep the money" actually says "the silver is yours" (as several commentaries observe) and suggests that Xerxes thus approved the expenditure (notice that 4:7 assumes the money has been transferred). It is unclear whether Haman is providing the funds from his personal fortune or from funds that he has access to. Each district had its own treasury and staff. If Haman was a provincial official, he may be transferring funds from his provincial treasury into the royal treasury, from which it was disbursed for the military expedition under the auspices of the crown. The Persepolis treasury texts illustrate the role of the treasurer, who assigns work groups and disburses funds for their rations.

3:12. chronology. Passover, that great celebration of deliverance of the Israelites, was celebrated on the fourteenth of Nisan. The edict was written on the thirteenth of Nisan, so it began to be distributed on the fourteenth. Thus, just as the Jews were celebrating deliverance from their great enemy of the past, the Egyptians, they were learning of a new plot from a new enemy.

3:13. nature of the decree. It is clear from verse nine that formal military action was intended (NIV: "for the men who carry out this business"; the same phrase is used in 9:3 for the ones who helped the Jews). Since each of the provinces provided troops for the Persian army, there were garrisons placed in each of the nations that made up the provinces. We do not need to assume that a decree went out to the general public encouraging and allowing anybody who wanted to kill Jews. Rather, all of the troops of every people, in every garrison, in every province were put on alert for concentrated military action on the given day. It is not necessarily confined to a "single" day. The Hebrew expression is best rendered "the same day" meaning that this was a coordinated action--all the provinces were acting at the same time.

4:1-17
Esther's Help Enlisted

4:1. torn clothes, sackcloth and ashes. The practice of putting dirt, dust or ashes on one's head was a typical sign of mourning throughout the Old Testament and into the New Testament period. It is a practice also known from Mesopotamia and Canaan. Many mourning rites function as a means for the living to identify with the dead. It is easy to see how dust on the head and torn clothes would be symbolic representations of burial and decay. Sackcloth is made of goat or camel hair and was coarse and uncomfortable. In many cases the sack-

cloth was only a loin covering. Persian mourning as recorded by Herodotus included tearing clothes, weeping and wailing.

4:2. limitations on going beyond king's gate. Herodotus identifies the king's gate as a place where supplicants stand and wail when they are victims of an injustice created by the system that they desire the king to rectify. It would be logical that there would be restrictions against such supplicants crowding into the palace complex, but no such law is known from ancient sources.

4:4. maids and eunuchs. These are the two categories of personal attendants for the queen. For more information on eunuchs see comment on 1:10.

4:11. limited access to king. It was a common necessity of proper court function that there must be limited access to the king, and Herodotus gives indications that the same was true of the Persian rulers. But the details concerning the death penalty and the gold scepter are not described. Many commentators have wondered why Esther could not have simply gone through proper channels to secure an audience with the king or perhaps even waited longer to see if she would be summoned (the set time was many months away). If, however, Haman holds the office of *hazarapatish* (see comment on 3:1), she would have to make arrangements through him and thereby jeopardize the whole plan.

4:11. gold scepter. Persian reliefs of kings in audience scenes depict them holding long scepters.

4:11. Esther's lack of access. Whereas one might think that the queen and chief wife of the king would have many opportunities to have a passing word with the king, such was not necessarily the case. The queen did not regularly share the king's bed, nor were their meals taken together. She had her own private quarters. While she could be invited to join the king in the audience chamber, she did not have unlimited access.

4:16. fasting. In the Old Testament the religious use of fasting is often in connection with making a request before God. The principle is that the importance of the request causes an individual to be so concerned about their spiritual condition that physical necessities fade into the background. In this sense the act of fasting is designed as a process leading to purification and humbling oneself before God (Ps 69:10).

5:1-14
Esther's Request and Haman's Plot

5:1. topography of palace. Since the king is on

his throne, this is undoubtedly the audience chamber. Despite the extensive excavations at Susa and at palaces at other Persian sites, the terminology used here is too vague to attach it to specific areas of the palace complex. See comment on 1:2 for what has been found of the palace complex at Susa.

5:3. Xerxes' granting of requests. Herodotus tells of two occasions when Xerxes made open-ended offers to grant requests and ended up regretting it. On the first occasion his offer was intended to win the favors of his intended mistress, Artaynte. Unfortunately for everyone she requested his beautiful robe that had been handwoven by his wife, Amestris. Amestris therefore discovered Xerxes' affair and sought revenge. She gained it when, on his birthday, she was granted a request and asked for Artaynte's mother (whom she believed to be behind the whole fiasco). She had the woman brutally mutilated, and this led the woman's husband, Xerxes' brother, to instigate a revolt. The offer of half the kingdom is known as early as Neo-Assyrian literature, when it is suggested that the Assyrian king would have given away half the kingdom for someone to cure his son's illness.

5:4. banquets in the Persian world. Banquets were popular among the Persian royalty and were sumptuous affairs. Herodotus describes a typical birthday banquet as featuring a whole cooked animal (ox, horse, ostrich, camel or donkey). Persians were especially fond of desserts and large quantities of wine. Musicians and attendants to care for every detail were present. Their feasts tended to be dignified rather than disorderly, and did not honor or encourage the cycle of gluttony and disgorging.

5:14. gallows. See comment on 2:23.

6:1-14

Haman Honors Mordecai

6:1. circumstance in Esther. In the book of Esther, circumstance is a powerful literary motif. While men such as Haman try to harness circumstance to their advantage through schemes and omens, the Jewish audience would have seen circumstance as being in the hands of God who works behind the scenes. Of interest, then, are the words that Herodotus places in the mouth of Artabanus, an adviser to Xerxes, on the threshold of what will become a disastrous Greek campaign: "Men are at the mercy of circumstance, which never bends to human will." Haman is about to learn the same lesson.

6:1. book of the chronicles. See comment on 2:23.

6:7. royal robe. The Persian king's robe is described by Xenophon as purple with gold embroidery. In Plutarch's *Themistocles*, Demaratus, the exiled king of Sparta (contemporary of Xerxes), requests as his gift to ride through Sardis wearing the crown of the Persian kings. Plutarch also reports that Artaxerxes once honored a request for his royal robe but qualified the gift with the command that it not be worn. Xerxes had a famous robe featured in one of Herodotus's stories as a gift begrudgingly and fatefully given to his lover (see comment on 5:3).

6:8. royal crest on the horse. Persian reliefs at Persepolis depict a horse with a crest perched between its ears.

7:1-10

Haman's Fall

7:7. palace garden. The banquet was probably being held in the same location as the banquet in chapter 1 (see comment on 1:5).

7:8. couch where Esther reclined. Persian style was to recline on couches while eating. Haman, in his desperation, had violated strict protocol about approaching the person of the queen. To be found on the same couch on which any member of the harem was reclining had the direst consequences. In eleventh-century Assyria, no one could approach within seven paces of a member of the harem.

7:8. covered face. Greeks and Romans typically covered the head of criminals condemned to death, but if that were the case here we would expect the word "head" instead of "face." In an Assyrian elegy covering the face is seen as a treatment of the dead. Since the hanging is generally considered to be a treatment of the corpse rather than a means of execution (see comment on 2:23), this face covering can be presumed to indicate Haman has died. The king does not issue a death sentence.

8:1-17

Deliverance for the Jews

8:1. Haman's estate given to Esther. Herodotus gives examples of confiscation of the property of those executed by order of the crown. That Xerxes would have been likely to grant Esther such property is demonstrated by another example from Herodotus. After Artaynte had asked for the cloak that Amestris had woven for Xerxes (see comment on 5:3), the king had offered her whole cities, vast amounts of gold and even her own personal army in an attempt to get the cloak back.

8:1. Mordecai in Persian records. There is a Persian official, Marduka, identified in a tablet from Borsippa, who is sometimes equated with Mordecai by commentators. Marduka is an accountant who lived during the last days of Darius and the early days of Xerxes. The name occurs frequently on the Elamite Persepolis tablets dating between 505 and 499 B.C. and belongs to several different individuals. Whether any of these individuals represents a Mordecai before his elevation cannot be determined. There are no sources that refer to him in the elevated position in which the book places him.

8:2. signet ring. See comment on 3:10.

8:9. chronology. Sivan 23 fell in the month of June 474 B.C., seventy days after the issuing of the edict.

8:9-10. Comments on the provinces and the extent of the empire can be found in 1:1. For comment on the signet ring see 3:10. For the courier service see comment on 1:20.

8:11. strategy of decree. Since the previous edict could not simply be revoked, the strategy was to offset the first by the second. The first had removed the protection of the empire from the Jews and had provided the financing for military action against them. The second edict allowed the Jews to form their own militia groups and, in effect, withdrew the royal protection (though not the funding) from those who had been hired against the Jews. Royal support was neutralized so that action against the enemies of the Jews would not be construed as rebellion against the crown. This puts Haman's crew in the same situation as the Jews, making them targets that could be attacked without fear of reprisals from the government.

8:15. Mordecai's garments. The colors and materials of Mordecai's regalia identified him with nobility and high political station. The royal colors could only be worn by those closely associated with the king. The gold "crown" does not designate rule but favor. So Herodotus reports that Xerxes rewards a ship master whose advice had saved the ship from sinking with a gold crown. It is gold, so it is not just a turban. But since this type of headgear is generally bound on, a coronet worn on the forehead is most likely.

8:17. became Jews. This word occurs only here in the Bible and has been interpreted in a number of different ways. The non-Jewish population could "become Jews" by conversion, by claim ("made themselves out to be Jews" because of the potential benefits) or by association ("sided with the Jews"). The last would explain the upcoming victory of the

Jews, as they would have had many willing participants in their militia groups.

9:1-17
Victory for the Jews

9:1. chronology. This is now late February or early March of the year 473 B.C.

9:1-10. enemies of the Jews. The enemies of the Jews are those who are still engaged in Haman's plot against them. They are groups of mercenaries or garrison troops who had been organized by Haman and funded by him for this military action. Verses 7-10 suggest that Haman's sons had carried through with the plot of their father. Herodotus tells how during the reign of Darius a high-ranking official and close associate of the king was judged to be involved in a revolt. As a result most of his family was executed. Additionally Herodotus tells the fascinating story of how two magi attempted to seize the throne after the death of Cambyses and were assassinated by Darius and seven other conspirators. The day turned into a public outrage against all the magi, in which the general populace became involved in killing every magus they could lay hands on. Herodotus even reports that the anniversary of the day became an important holiday in the Persian calendar.

9:18-32
Establishment of Purim

9:18-32. Purim. Though this passage gives account of the origins of the celebration of Purim, the evidence for the celebration's being customary does not come until much later. The apocryphal book of 2 Maccabees (15:36) contains the earliest reference to the festival outside of Esther. There the thirteenth of Adar is identified as the day before Mordecai's day. In the first century A.D. Josephus called the holiday *phrouraios,* and soon after that, the Mishnah uses the term Purim.

9:24-26. *pur.* See comment on 3:7.

10:1-3
Mordecai

10:2. book of the annals of the kings of Media and Persia. See comment on 2:23.

10:3. Mordecai's position. Though identified as second to the king, no official position is named for Mordecai. Positions that may be significant enough to designate the official second to the king are discussed in relation to the position of Haman in the comment on 3:1.

POETIC &
WISDOM
LITERATURE

Introduction

A modern reader acquainted with the book of Psalms would sense some resemblance when reading certain Egyptian or Babylonian material. The attributes that deity is praised for, the issues that induce prayer, the personal and corporate concerns, and even the turn of phrase would ring a chord of familiarity. In any of the ancient Near Eastern societies the gods were considered responsible for maintaining justice and were concerned about justice in the human realm. This was frequently the subject of praise and the basis for petition. Additionally, all peoples shared the plight of humanity and wanted relief from common ills of sickness, oppression, abandonment and life's trials.

Hymns and Prayers
Despite the surface-level similarities, deep-seated differences in the worldviews of Israel and her neighbors can be discerned from this literature. When requests for deliverance and rescue, or mercy and grace, are made, certain assumptions are exposed about how the divine world works and how it interacts with the human world. Both the Israelites and their neighbors believed that they suffered because of deity's inattention. In the ancient world at large it would have been typical to believe that the deity was inattentive because he or she had been offended. Since ethical behavior played a much less significant role in how they understood their responsibilities to deity, the assumption would usually have been that the deity had become offended at not receiving the appropriate attention from the afflicted individual. The worshiper would have little hope of discerning what ritual might

have been omitted or what had caused the offense. The only option was to try to relieve the god's anger rather than specifically redressing the offense. Thus the individual would willingly concede guilt (for who knows what) and direct the prayers, incantations and rituals toward appeasement (soothing the heart of the deity) to try to regain the attentive care and protection of deity.

The Israelites were less convinced that Yahweh's inattention was due to his anger. They readily confessed that they were sometimes mystified as to why he didn't come to their aid. As individuals they were usually not willing to concede guilt but focused their prayers on pleas for vindication. They needed vindication because their suffering would naturally lead others to conclude that God was punishing them for some sin. God's answer to their prayer would demonstrate that he was not angry with them and that they had not committed some grave offense. When they committed offense, it was recognized as concerning ethical failure rather than ritual omission. They expected God's grace to emerge from who he was; they did not expect to be able to induce it by means of gifts and flattery or to conjure it out by magical rites.

Despite these fundamental differences, there is much in the ancient Near Eastern literature that can lend understanding to the biblical psalms. Many biblical metaphors come out of the cultural setting of the time. The imagery of God as, for instance, a shepherd, a rock or a shield will find ready parallels in the literature of Mesopotamia. Phrases such as the "desire of one's heart," being "raised from the pit" or using the winds as messengers have precedents that help explain what Israelites would have meant by them.

There are scores of compositions from all parts of the ancient world that fall into the general category of address to deity. Sumerian, Akkadian and Egyptian literature all have numerous representatives. There is very little hymnic material in Ugaritic or Hittite. In addition to praise hymns, there is an extensive incantation literature in Mesopotamia. These include *ershemmas*, psalms intended to appease an angry deity; *ershaḫungas*, laments concerning sorrow or calamity; *shuillas*, prayers of petition; *shigus* and *dingirshadibbas*, prayer of penitence; and *shurpu*, prayers of purification, just to name a few of the more prominent categories. Egyptian hymns date primarily to the second millennium and are full of descriptive praise. They are grandiose, optimistic and confident, with little trace of lament or petition (with notable exceptions in the Nineteenth-Dynasty texts of Deir el-Medina and Papyrus Anastasi II).

Wisdom Literature

A modern dictionary definition of wisdom would include words such as common sense, prudence, discernment, judgment, insight and understanding. Any reading of the biblical wisdom literature would indicate that these same components would be associated with Israelite wisdom. But we would be mistaken if we thought that wisdom in the ancient world was restricted even to areas such as knowledge, intelligence, education or maturity. Instead, wisdom reflected a much broader concern to understand the place of human beings in the cosmos. It is probably best understood as the ability to bring order out of chaos or to perceive order in the midst of chaos. The wisdom of deity (whether Israelite or otherwise) was reflected in bringing order out of chaos by organizing, maintaining, sustaining and operating the cosmos. That is why there is such a prominent creation theme in wisdom literature. Wisdom includes understanding the natural world and the human world; society and civilization; the commoner and the king; the world of the gods and the world of nations. Human beings are faced with the challenge of achieving wisdom as they bring order out of chaos in their own world and perceive the order that God has built into the cosmos. This includes ethics and etiquette; philosophy and psychology; and understanding how the world works (science) and how the human heart works (establishing justice).

Egyptian thought is most linked to the order that comes in establishing truth and justice. The term *ma'at* encompasses this aspect of natural, social and political propriety. Mesopotamian literature shows a great concern for understanding the order that can be achieved through the reading of omens, the recitation of incantations and the performance of rituals. This wisdom is the skill that is expressed by the term *nemequ*. Many of the proverbial sayings found in Mesopotamia are connected to omen series and can be classified as omen-wisdom. Omens made observations (often from natural phenomena) and drew conclusions (often about destiny or future happenings). Wisdom likewise makes observations (often about behavior) and draws conclusions (often about inevitable results). Old Testament wisdom literature insists that only the fear of the Lord (as the beginning of wisdom) can bring order out of the chaos of life. Additionally, however, the rituals of the temple were also a means by which order was maintained.

The materials from the ancient Near East include proverbial sayings, admonitions and instructions, and philosophical debate in the form of dialogues, monologues and fables. These deal with many of the same subjects as the Israelite wisdom literature, including, notably, several examples in which a sufferer is exploring the reasons for his suffering.

The problem under discussion that ties all of these "righteous sufferer" works together is theodicy—the justice of deity. Tension is created between divine justice and human suffering based on a belief in what is termed the retribution principle. Simply stated, this principle affirms that the righteous will prosper and the wicked will suffer. If an apparently righteous person is suffering and the retribution principle is accepted, then doubt is cast on God's justice. This tension was not as strongly felt outside of Israel because there was not as strong a belief in the ethical qualities of deity. Furthermore, in a polytheistic setting an individual's behavior might please one deity but offend another. Human suffering for no apparent reason or doubts concerning the existence of divine justice understandably undermined the ability to affirm an ordered world. When life is going wrong, one feels surrounded by chaos rather than order. Mesopotamian wisdom literature typically resolved the problem by objecting that there really was no such thing as a righteous sufferer. They were also willing to accept that the gods were inscrutable.

Instruction literature is most prominent in Egypt, where over a dozen compositions range over more than two thousand years (early third millennium to late first millennium). These compositions demonstrate that Israelite wisdom literature such as that found in Proverbs was part of an international genre (just as the book of Kings claims, 1 Kings 4:30). Ancient Near Eastern instruction literature includes short, pithy statements like those found in Proverbs 10—29, as well as longer admonitions like Proverbs 1—9. The closest parallel is found in comparing the *Instruction of Amenemope* (about 1200 B.C.) to Proverbs 22:17—24:22, where there are quite a few similar phrases and topics.

The treatise of Ecclesiastes has been related to a subcategory known as "pessimism literature" and exemplified by the Akkadian Dialogue of Pessimism and by the Egyptian Songs of the Harper and *The Dispute Between a Man and His Ba*. These all display a tongue-in-cheek cynicism about life. The Dialogue of Pessimism portrays a conversation between a master and his slave in which the master states his intention to embark on various different enterprises. Each suggestion is met with the slave's affirmation of the benefits of the proposed course of action. In each case the master then changes his mind and decides not to carry out his plans. The slave then replies with an affirmation of this decision as well, citing all the disadvantages the action would have incurred. The topics include going to the palace, eating, hunting, settling down with a family, leading a revolution, loving a woman, offering sacrifice, setting up a creditor business and serving public charity. The piece ends as the master finally asks the slave about a suggested course of action. He responds, "To have my neck and your neck broken and to be thrown into the river is good." The basis of this type of literature is to make the point that it is not simple to find meaning and purpose for life and its pursuits. Drawing order out of chaos is rarely accomplished to one's satisfaction.

The Song of Songs is also often included in the wisdom literature. This categorization can be supported by the realization that the book uses love poetry to illustrate a wisdom teaching (8:6-7). Other examples of the love poetry genre are known in the Sumerian mythological literature concerning Dumuzi in the third millennium, but the closest parallels are found in a group of Egyptian love songs from the period of the Judges (Egyptian Nineteenth and Twentieth Dynasties, 1300-1150 B.C.). These love songs were typically performed at festivals and share many of the features found in Song of Songs. They lack, however, the wisdom teaching that the biblical book considers crucial: romance, love and sex can also be forces of chaos that need to be brought under the umbrella of order.

It is evident in all of the above that as God included poetic and wisdom genres in his revelation to Israel, he did not design new literary styles to use or new issues to address. Instead he used that which was very familiar to any resident of the ancient Near East. He met his people where they were and communicated in clear and powerful ways. Increasing our knowledge of ancient Near Eastern culture and literature can therefore only enhance our understanding of the Bible.

JOB

1:1—2:13

Trials of Job

1:1. Uz. The location of the land of Uz is not precisely known. It may have been a general term for the Near East. A southern location is implied in Lamentations 4:21, where the daughter of Edom lives in the land of Uz. However, in Jeremiah 25:20-21 Uz is associated with Philistia, Edom and Moab.

1:3. size of herds. The size of Job's herds was enormous. Aristotle claims that the Arabs had as many as three thousand camels, the same number listed here. The numbers can be compared to the three thousand sheep and one thousand goats of Nabal (1 Sam 25:2). Third-millennium texts record temple flocks of about fourteen thousand sheep, but personal flocks were usually much smaller. In the ancient Near East sedentary herds would generally not exceed three hundred animals. Transhumant herds (practicing controlled migration) would range from two to five hundred. Nomadic herds would be the largest, numbering in the tens of thousands. The ratio of small animals to large in Job's herd is fairly typical. Most numbers that are available in ancient sources are connected with Assyrian tribute lists that give little indication of what personal holdings would be.

1:3. people of the East. The "people of the East" (literally, "sons of the east") in Semitic languages usually refers to the inhabitants of the region east of Byblos where seminomadic Semites lived. This is how the term is used in the Egyptian Story of Sinuhe from the early second millennium B.C. In Genesis 29:1 the term refers to Arameans living along the northern Euphrates River, in Isaiah 11:14 to the Edomites, Moabites and Ammonites, and in Judges 6:3 to the Midianites. In sum, the "people of the East" appears to be a general term like "Uz."

1:5. purification after feasts. Purification usually provides for an individual to enter sacred space or to participate in ritual activities. In Israel there were levels of purity required for remaining "in the camp" and for entering the sacred enclosure or temple precinct. Job is ritually fastidious as he seeks to maintain a level of purity for his family at all times. Like Balaam in Numbers 23, Job presided over the sacrifices as the patriarch of his family, without a priest. Balaam was obliged to offer one bull, one ram and seven male lambs (Num 29:36). It is possible that the purification involved washing and changing of clothes (Gen 35:2 and Ex 19:10).

1:5. cursing God in heart. The term for "cursed" is literally "blessed," a euphemism found elsewhere in Scripture (e.g., Job 1:11; 2:5, 9; 1 Kings 21:10, 13). The term often means "to despise, esteem lightly." Thus, instead of actually cursing God, Job's children may have neglected or disregarded God. The term can refer to anything from treating with disrespect to outright repudiation.

1:6. angels (sons of God). In the ancient Near East the "sons of the gods" were lesser members of the pantheon. In both Mesopotamian and Ugaritic texts there are glimpses of the meetings of the gods and their divine court. In Israel the sons of God are angels, who, like the sons of the gods, station themselves before God at the divine court. Micaiah ben Imlah had a vision of God holding court with his subordinates (1 Kings 22:19-23). The sons of God are also called "gods" in Psalm 82:1, 6.

1:6. Satan. It is important to note that the term here, *satan* (literally, "the accuser"), is preceded in Hebrew by the definite article ("the"). Thus, in the context of Job it appears to describe a function rather than serving as a proper name. Though the individual functioning as an adversary to Job here may well be the one who later bears the name Satan, that cannot be concluded with certainty. The Hebrew word *satan* is used to describe an adversary and can be used of human beings or supernatural beings. Even the angel of the Lord can exercise this function (Num 22:22). The term does not clearly take on the role of a personal name until the intertestamental period (specifically the second century B.C.). Those who serve as adversaries are generally in the role of monitoring or challenging God's policies and decisions. It is not clear whether Satan was one of the sons of God (NIV's "angels").

1:6. role of accuser. The term *satan* refers to one who acts like a prosecuting attorney. The same term is used for a political foe who attempts to overthrow the king (e.g., 2 Sam 19:22). It also refers to one who brings charges against another in court (Ps 109:6; Zech 3:1-2). In Persia and Assyria similar secret agents toured the empire, attempting to discern the allegiance of particular groups and individuals, and then bringing charges in court.

1:15. Sabeans. There are three groups of Sabeans in Scripture. One group is from Sheba, modern Yemen, an area that was highly urbanized and had achieved a complex degree of civilization by this period (1 Kings 10). Many inscriptions have been found from the Sabeans in this area. There are also Sabeans in Ethiopia (Is 43:3). In Job 6:19 the Sabeans are equated with Tema in north Arabia, and are probably identified with the Saba of the Assyrian inscriptions of Tiglath-Pileser III and Sargon II in the late eighth century B.C. These Sabeans are most likely the ones mentioned here in Job 1.

1:16. fire of God. Lightning is described here as the "fire of God." During the contest between Yahweh and Baal in 1 Kings 18:38, the lightning is called the "fire of the LORD" (also see 2 Kings 1:12; Job 20:26; Num 11:1-3; 16:35; and 26:10). Storm gods are typically pictured with lightning bolts clutched in the hand.

1:17. Chaldeans. The Chaldeans are known from Assyrian annals as early as the time of Ashurnasirpal II (r. 884-859 B.C.). They appear to have been a seminomadic group that had settled in Babylonia and was successful in controlling the area in the late eighth century B.C. Moreover, they succeeded the Assyrians as the great empire builders of the Near East in the late seventh century B.C. The height of their power came during the reign of Nebuchadnezzar II (r. 605-562 B.C.), the destroyer of Jerusalem.

2:7. painful sores. In Ugaritic this term refers to fever rather than sores. In Hebrew the term has usually denoted a variety of skin diseases (see comment on Lev 13:2). In Ugaritic texts the disease strikes the loins and leaves the victim prostrate. It is not certain which skin disease is depicted here in Job 2. Pathology in the ancient Near East was always considered in the light of supernatural cause and effect. Either hostile demons or gods angry at the violation of some taboo were considered responsible. Categories of disease are classified by symptoms rather than by cause, so diagnosis is often difficult if not impossible.

2:8. broken pottery. Broken pottery (Greek, *ostraca*) has been found in great abundance in archaeological excavations throughout the Near East. Such broken pottery was often "recycled" or put to some use. It is not clear in this context whether the ostraca were used to scratch the skin for relief or to scrape the body as a sign of grief. In most cases in Scripture ostraca are used for the latter purpose. In Mesopotamia and in the Ugaritic tale of Aqhat the "mound of potshards" appears to have been a name for the abode of the dead. In the Baal epic, when El mourns for Baal he puts dirt on his head and scrapes his skin with a stone.

2:8. sitting among the ashes. The ashes mentioned here were most likely found on a "dunghill" or town dump outside the city limits, where dung from the town was periodically burned. Mourners in the Near East went to sit amidst the dung ash heap and lacerate themselves. Priam, the father of Hector in the *Iliad*, rolled himself in the dung of the city ash heap.

2:11. lands of Job's friends. Classical (Pliny the Younger) and early church scholars (Eusebius and Jerome) associate Teman with Nabataean territory near the city of Petra in present day Jordan. Cuneiform sources identify a Suhu as a site along the Middle Euphrates south of the Habur River. However, Shuah was the son of Abraham and Keturah, and an uncle of Sheba and Dedan, thus implying a southern locale for the Shuhite. Nevertheless its location is not certain. The Naamathite is possibly identified with Jebel el Na'amaeh in northwest Arabia, although that is not certain.

2:12. mourning practices. In ancient Israel tearing one's garments and sprinkling dust on one's head were considered signs of mourning. They are also known from Mesopotamia and Canaan. Many mourning rites function as a means for the living to identify with the dead. It is easy to see how dust on the head and torn clothes would be symbolic representations of burial and decay.

3:1-26
Job's Lament

3:3-6. cursed and unlucky days. Day lists in Mesopotamia identify evil days in the month (days 7, 14, 19, 21 and 28). These were inauspicious days in which the person was encouraged not to engage in business activities, to build a house or to marry. It was even forbidden to eat fish and leeks on the seventh day of the seventh month. In addition, Mesopotamian omen lists describe days in which it was improper for a man and woman to engage in sexual relations, for a woman to give birth and for people to engage in a variety of other social activities. Furthermore, certain events that occurred caused a day to be unlucky (e.g., the birth of an anomaly or the death of a king). In the *Myth of Erra and Ishum* the governor of the city that is being destroyed is portrayed as expressing to his mother a wish that he had been stillborn or obstructed in the womb so that he would not have been born to this destiny.

3:8. rousing Leviathan. Leviathan appears in the Bible as a sea monster representing the forces of chaos who is defeated by God (Ps 74:14; Is 27:1). This text requests the services of a skilled magician who would even be able to rouse a dormant Leviathan by an incantation. The description of Leviathan has similarities with Babylonian and Ugaritic sea monsters who threaten the existence of creation (see comment on 41:1).

3:9. morning stars. The morning stars here are Venus and Mercury, which should have remained "dark." These planets were considered the forerunners of each day.

3:13-19. afterlife concept. The Israelite concept of afterlife was very similar to that of their neighbors in Ugarit and Mesopotamia. However, death is not usually described as a place of rest as it is here in Job. Death (Hebrew, *sheol*) is a precise place where the dead eat dust and drink dirty water. According to the Akkadian epic of the *Descent of Ishtar*, there are bars and gates keeping the dead in. Sheol is also a place of darkness where there is no light, only silence. The dead cannot praise God in their condition. For more information see sidebar in Isaiah 14.

4:1—5:27

First Speech of Eliphaz

4:9. destructive breath of God. Here in Job the breath of God represents the wind of the desert that destroys vegetation (Hos 13:15 and Is 40:7). Normally it refers to God's dynamic activity (see Gen 2:7).

4:13-15. spirit bringing dreams. The theme of God causing a heavy sleep to fall on a person in order for them to receive a dream recurs throughout Scripture. For example, God caused a heavy sleep on Abraham during the covenant ceremony (Gen 15:12-21). This also occurred with deities in Mesopotamia. Dagan (biblical Dagon) often spoke to temple worshipers at Mari and Terqa in northeast Syria through the use of dreams. These worshipers often stayed overnight to sleep in the temple, hoping to receive a dream. In the Gilgamesh Epic a zephyr passes by that brings sleep and gives a dream. In Mesopotamian thinking, Zaqiqu was the god of dreams, and his name is from the word that denotes a spirit. This spirit or breeze passes through the cracks in doors to come to people at night. Both the *Odyssey* and the *Iliad* attest the same idea.

4:18. charging angels with error. Second Peter also describes the punishment of rebellious angels, but clear evidence of such a belief in the Old Testament is not available. In Ugaritic myths, subordinates to the gods (specifically,

---

RETRIBUTION PRINCIPLE

Verses seven and eight articulate what is referred to as the retribution principle. In its most basic form it contends that the righteous will prosper and the wicked will suffer. On a national level this principle is built into the covenant, with its potential blessings and threat of curses. On the individual level it had been determined that this was necessary in order for God to maintain justice. Since the Israelites had only the vaguest concept of the afterlife and no revelation concerning judgment or reward in the afterlife, God's justice could only be accomplished in this life. Most Israelites believed that if God were to be considered just, rewards and punishments in this life would have to be proportional to the righteousness or wickedness of the individual. These beliefs had also then led most Israelites to believe that if someone was prospering, it must be a reward for righteousness, and if someone was suffering, it must be a punishment for wickedness. The greater the suffering, the greater the wickedness must be. Babylonian and Assyrian writers of magical texts describe this same principle of retribution. But since they were not completely convinced of the justice of the gods, it was not as big a theological issue in Mesopotamia. In the book of Job this principle is turned on its head, because Job, the apparent epitome of righteousness, is suffering every possible disaster. All of the characters in the book believe in the retribution principle. This is the basis on which Job's friends accuse him, and it is the reasoning by which Job questions the justice of God. It is even the logic by which the satan can feel so confident about his accusation. He uses the retribution principle to create the tension for his accusation against God. If God operates by the retribution principle, the satan argues, then he will prevent the development of true righteousness, because people will behave righteously only to gain the reward. On the other hand, if God does not operate by the retribution principle, then people like Job will conclude that God is unjust. The satan's case can be won if Job relents to the pressure of his friends. They want him to appease God by simply confessing to anything and everything, regardless of whether he considers himself to be faultless or not. In this way he can rejoin the ranks of the righteous and regain his prosperity. This is the integrity that Job refuses to compromise—he is not a righteous man simply for the gain. He is interested in being exonerated, not just in regaining his prosperity. His integrity is a vote of confidence for God, because it insists that to God, righteousness is more important than appeasement. The book resolves the problem by suggesting that the retribution principle does not constitute a guarantee or a promise, but that God delights in rewarding righteousness and takes seriously the need to punish the wicked. God's justice cannot be evaluated, because no one has sufficient information to call him to account. Instead people can believe that he is just because they are convinced that he is wise (the thrust of God's discourses).

divine slave girls) are often found to be disobedient and untrustworthy. To add to the difficulty, the term translated "error" occurs only here in the Old Testament, and its meaning is uncertain.

4:19. houses of clay. "House" is used as a figure for the body in the apocryphal work Wisdom of Solomon 9:15, in 2 Corinthians 5:1 and in 2 Peter 1:14, but the idea of the spirit inhabiting the body is unknown elsewhere in the Old Testament. Clay and dust signify the weakness of the human body and human mortality.

5:1. holy ones. The term "holy ones", which designates servants or angels, occurs elsewhere in Scripture (Hos 11:12; Zech 14:5; Dan 4:10, 14, 20; 7:13; and Ps 89:7). They are holy because of their closeness to God, not because of any inherent purity.

6:1—7:21
First Speech of Job

6:2. anguish and misery on scales. Balance scales were used by merchants to quantify objects by weight. Job desires here that his misfortune be weighed against the largest thing that he knows, the sand of the seas, which often represents an immeasurable amount or massive weight.

6:4. Almighty (Shaddai). Shaddai ("almighty") is occasionally an epithet of God (Gen 17:1). Here Shaddai functions as a reverser of fortunes, similar to Resheph, the god of plague and war in the Canaanite pantheon, who spread diseases by shooting victims with bow and arrow.

6:15-17. wadis. The wadis of Palestine are similar to overflowing rivers in the rainy season. However, they have little or no water during the summer season, precisely the time when water is most needed.

6:19. caravans of Tema. Tema (modern Teima) was an important oasis and trade center in northwestern Arabia, two hundred miles south of Damascus. Tema is also listed as a son of Ishmael (Gen 25:13-15).

6:19. merchants of Sheba. Sheba was an important trade center in southwestern Arabia. See the note on Job 1:15.

7:1. hard service, hired man. The term for "hard service" was used of military service and occasionally corvee labor, such as that which Solomon exacted for laborers to cut down trees in Phoenicia (1 Kings 5:13-14). The hired man also was used both for military service (Jer 46:21) and domestic service (Ex 25:40). They were considered to be poor and were obliged to be paid daily (Lev 19:13). In

the Babylonian creation epic, humankind was created specifically to do the menial tasks that the gods were unwilling to do (build the god's houses and provide food for the gods).

7:6. weaver's shuttle. Some of the language needs clarification here. The word NIV translates "weaver's shuttle" is elsewhere always rendered "loom." The adjective they translate "swift" has the basic meaning of "light" or even "insubstantial." Finally, the word translated "hope" also means thread (e.g., Rahab's scarlet thread in Josh 2:18). On the horizontal looms of the day, four stakes were driven into the ground in a rectangular pattern. The threads that would make up the warp of the fabric were tied at regular intervals to sticks on both ends, and the sticks were then used to stretch out the threads between the stakes. When the ends of each stick were braced behind the stakes, the threads would be stretched horizontal to the ground, taut for weaving. A shuttle would then be tied to the thread that was to be woven in as the woof of the fabric, with a bar being used to separate alternating threads of the warp to allow the shuttle with the woof thread to pass through. Once the woof thread was in place, the pin would be used to tighten that row against the previous rows. When the fabric was complete, the warp threads would be cut from the loom, leaving only remnants of threads tied to sticks. The following translation picks up the imagery: "My days are more insubstantial than a loom in that they come to an end with no hope/thread."

7:8. the "eye." In Egyptian mythology the sky god Horus had one eye injured in a battle with Seth. The sun is seen as his good eye and the moon as his injured eye. Thus day and night the eye of Horus looks down on the world of men.

7:9-10. afterlife concept. Here the emphasis is on the finality of death. For more information about concepts of afterlife, see comment on 3:13-19.

7:12. sea monster under guard. In ancient Near Eastern traditions the sea or the monsters that inhabited it represented the forces of chaos that had to be defeated and contained so that order could be brought to the world. Marduk, the divine champion in the Babylonian creation myth, took hold of Tiamat and put her under a vault, where a bar was pulled down and guards were posted. Yamm, the sea monster in Ugaritic mythology, was taken captive by Baal and placed under guard. This sort of imagery is also used in poetic sections of the Old Testament (Ps 74:13; 89:9-10; 104:7-9).

7:14. frightened with dreams. Nightmares

were traditionally seen in the ancient Near East and the classical world as coming from a demonic or malevolent divine agent. There are also references to demonic terrors of the night in the writings of the classical authors Ovid and Plutarch. Here in Job 7:14, however, the agent is God. In the Babylonian story of the man who is suffering without knowing why *(Ludlul bel Nemeqi)*, the sufferer also reports being plagued by fearful omens and terrifying dreams.

7:15-16. preference for death in ancient Near Eastern wisdom literature. The unique Mesopotamian Dialogue of Pessimism is a satirical discussion between a master and his slave. At the end of the discussion, the master asks what is good, and the slave responds by saying that both he and his master should have their necks broken and then they should be thrown into the river. However, the cynical context for these statements does not allow us to argue that suffering Mesopotamians preferred death to life.

7:20. watcher of men. In ancient Near Eastern usage the divine watcher is usually serving a positive role of protection. Perhaps the closest parallel would be found in the occasional reference to the seven ancient sages as watchers. This is also usually true of Yahweh's protective watching over Israel (Deut 32:10; Ps 12:7; 25:20; 31:23; 40:11; 61:7). In this case, Job sees God as a scrutinizer rather than a preserver of human beings.

8:1-22

First Speech of Bildad

8:6-7. retribution principle. See the sidebar in chapter 3.

8:8-10. importance of traditional instruction from ancient Near East wisdom. Along with other passages in Scripture (Job 15:18; Deut 4:32; and the apocryphal Ecclus 8:9), a great deal of wisdom literature from Mesopotamia (e.g., the Babylonian Theodicy, "I Will Praise the Lord of Wisdom" and various Sumerian proverbs) contends that wisdom from the ancients is significant. In Mesopotamian tradition the bearers of wisdom are the seven sages of old, known as the *apkallu*, who brought wisdom and the crafts of civilization to humankind. This tradition is represented in the works of Berossus by his statement that the sum total of revealed knowledge was given by the antediluvian sages.

8:11-12. papyrus analogy. Papyrus was not only used in Egypt but also in Palestine. Ugaritic texts describe papyrus coming from the marshlands of Lake Samak. It was used for a variety of things, including baskets, mats and parchment for writing. Papyrus grows to a great height, sometimes over ten feet. But its luxuriance quickly dissipates if the water source dries up.

9:1—10:22

Second Speech of Job

9:2. no one righteous before God. The Sumerian wisdom text titled *Man and His God* states that "never was a sinless child born to his mother." This was no concept of original sin however, as this thought echoes the Sumerian idea that the gods had incorporated evil into human civilization from the outset.

9:5-9. cosmic control by deity in ancient Near East. The last half of verse 4 along with verse 8 make it clear that the context for these comments is the cosmic conflict of the divine warrior. The cosmic conflict motif depicts the principal deity overcoming cosmic forces (usually forces of chaos like death or sea) to bring order to the cosmos. In the ancient Near East these forces are usually personified as gods, but this passage preserves a certain ambiguity on that count. Here Yahweh overcomes mountains (v. 5), terrorizes the netherworld (v. 6; the Hebrew word translated "earth" at times means netherworld, and the verbs here convey shuddering in horror, not earthquake), extinguishes the sun (v. 7; probably by eclipse), locks the stars in their sequence of appearance (v. 7), stretches out the heavens (v. 8; with corpse of defeated enemy as in *Enuma Elish*?), vanquishes the sea (v. 8) and forms the constellations (v. 9).

9:6. pillars of the earth. Pillars are sometimes thought to represent boundaries. Solomon's temple featured two free-standing pillars on the portico, which may have served as a boundary to the holy place. The tabernacle used pillars from which the partitions were hung to create a boundary for the courtyard. Even when the pillars supported something (as in the Philistine temple that Samson tumbled), archaeological information suggests that they stood as boundaries to porticos or courtyards. In Babylon, boundary markers known as *kudurru*s were pillar-shaped, but the connection may be incidental. Ancient Near Eastern literature has no parallel for the earth being supported by pillars. The only other reference in the Old Testament is Psalm 75:3, which could be interpreted as maintaining boundaries of distinction. In Job 26:11 the heavens have pillars, but this comment also occurs in the discussion of boundaries (v. 10). It is more likely that cosmic boundaries of the earth would be those between the living and the dead. The word translated "earth" in this verse sometimes refers to the netherworld. In Akkadian literature, the boundaries of the netherworld are represented by gates.

9:7. seals the stars. The word "light" (NIV) does not occur in the Hebrew, which says, "He affixes a seal around the stars." This would suggest that Yahweh is the one who dictates the sequence of their appearances and the paths they will follow. In Mesopotamian astronomy (Mul-Apin series) the thirty-six principal stars were divided into three segments known as the paths of Anu, Enlil and Ea. These fixed stellar paths occupied the northern, southern and equatorial bands of the sky. In the omen series known as *Enuma Anu Enlil* the gods Anu, Enlil and Ea established the positions, locations and paths of the stars. In *Enuma Elish* Marduk sets up the stations of the stars. In Mesopotamian understanding the stars were engraved on the Jasper surface of the middle heavens, and the entire surface moved. All of these examples give explanation to the verb "to seal" used here in the text, since that which is fixed or inscribed is sealed.

9:8. treads on waves. The term "waves" is more likely denoting the "back" of something. This is how the same Hebrew word is used in Deuteronomy 33:29, where the backs of the enemy are trampled. In the Baal myths, Yam, "Sea," is one of Baal's main opponents. Since *Yam* is also the Hebrew word for Sea in this verse, treading on its back would be an appropriate image of subjugation. Egyptian iconography pictures the pharaoh using the defeated enemies as his footstool. Just as treading on the back expresses defeat of an enemy, stretching out the heavens evokes the imagery of Marduk using the corpse of the defeated enemy, Tiamat, to form the heavens. Both of these reflect back on verse 4: "Who has resisted him and come out unscathed?"

9:9. constellations. Textual evidence from Babylonia, including the "Venus tablet" of Ammisaduqa (c. 1650 B.C.), indicates that astronomical studies were conducted with skill and precision. Although astrology was also prevalent in late Egyptian periods and in Persian period Mesopotamia, it seems that this divinatory activity, interpreting omens (see Is 47:13), is only an extension of the work of a true science. There are records of the movement of the planets, placement of the major fixed stars and constellations, as well as descriptions of the phases of the moon and solar and lunar eclipses. Given the widespread knowledge of the stars and the planets in both

Mesopotamian and Egyptian cultures, it would have been necessary for the biblical writers and prophets to attribute these celestial bodies to Yahweh's creation. Mesopotamian constellations included: animal figures such as a goat (=Lyra) and snake (=Hydra); objects such as an arrow (=Sirius) and a wagon (=Big Dipper); and characters such as Anu (=Orion). The most popular of the constellations was Pleiades, often portrayed on seals even in Palestine and Syria. Neo-Assyrian texts preserve sketches of stars in constellations. A prayer to the gods of the night from about 1700 B.C. invokes the constellations by name calling on them to give answers to the diviner seeking an omen. The first constellation mentioned in this verse is uncertain. Leo and Ursa Major are the two prime candidates.

9:9. constellations of the south. In Mesopotamian literature the southern band of the sky is referred to as the path of Ea. But the text here refers to the "chambers" of the south, which may or may not refer to constellations.

9:13. Rahab and cohorts. Rahab is described as one of the sea monsters slain by God (Job 26:12, Ps 89:11, Is 51:9). In both the Babylonian and Ugaritic myths of creation, the champion deity (Marduk in Babylon and Baal in Ugarit) fights and slays a sea monster and its cohorts in a manner similar to that of Yahweh. In other contexts, Rahab is symbolically used as a designation for Egypt (Is 30:7; Ps 87:4). The name Rahab has not yet been found in extra-biblical sources.

9:17. crush with storm. Some interpreters have argued (with support of an ancient version) that the Hebrew word for "storm" is actually "hair" since one is not necessarily "crushed" with a storm. It would thus read "for a hair, He crushes me," meaning, that God crushes Job for a hair (or for little or no reason). Against this is the fact that the verb need not be so specific as "crushed," but refers to dealing someone a potentially mortal blow (same verb as that used twice in Gen 3:15). The reference to storm would also fit better in the cosmic context.

9:26. boats of papyrus. There are artistic representations from Egypt showing that they used papyrus reeds for the construction of some of their boats. This is stated explicitly by the classical author Pliny in his *Natural History.* Isaiah 18:1-2 refers to these reed vessels which were considered to be very light and swift but very fragile.

9:30. soap, washing soda. The terms used here are soapwort, derived from the plant Leontopetalon, and lye, and alkaline solution, two of the strongest cleaners known to the Israelites.

Since the cleaning of the body was normally done by covering the skin with oil which was then rubbed off, the use of these powerful detergents was an extreme measure.

9:31. slime pit. Although the term for slime pit usually designates the abode of the dead in Israel (Job 17:14, 23:22; 28) and the ancient Near East, here the term refers to a cesspool.

9:33. arbitrator in the ancient Near East judicial system. Sumerian texts often describe an individual's personal god who pleaded the person's cause before the high council of the gods. He was in fact his advocate. Moreover, the judicial system in Mesopotamia was very sophisticated. A judge often arbitrated between two parties that were contesting movable and immovable property (e.g., inheritance, location and dimensions of land, and the sale price of property). The Egyptian *Instruction of Amenemope* advises "Do not say, 'Find me a protector, for one who hates me has injured me.' Indeed, you do not know the plans of god" (translation of M. Lichtheim).

10:15. full of shame. Given the belief in the retribution principle (see sidebar in chap. 3), shame would be the natural result of suffering. Suffering would proclaim to all around that the victim was being punished by God. The more dramatic the change of fortunes and the more serious the suffering, the greater the sin was supposed to be. Job therefore would have been judged a vile person based on the circumstantial evidence, thus leading to public humiliation.

10:18. wish to have never been born. In the *Myth of Erra and Ishum* the governor of the city that is being destroyed is portrayed as expressing to his mother a wish that he had been stillborn or obstructed in the womb so that he would not have been born to this destiny.

10:21-22. land of deepest night. Five Hebrew words are used here to describe darkness in the land of "deepest night," Sheol, the abode of the dead. This place was considered darker than the dead of night on earth. The netherworld in the ancient Near East is typically considered a place of darkness (Akkadian "house of darkness") where there is no light.

11:1-20
First Speech of Zophar

11:13. stretch out hands. Stretching out one's hands as a common gesture of prayer was a typical form in ancient Near Eastern iconography. The individual raised the hands with the palms outwards but close together and at face level. It was considered a gesture of humility.

12:1—14:22
Third Speech of Job

12:24. leaders deprived of reason. There were many examples in the ancient world of kings who became victims of their own quests for glory. Whether individual quests such as Gilgamesh's search for immortality that took him to the ends of the earth; religious (economic?) quests such as Nabonidus' thirteen-year self-imposed exile in Teima; or military quests such as Persia's disastrous attempt to expand into the western Mediterranean, these were fed by colossal megalomania and characterized by insatiable self-indulgence.

13:4. physicians methods in the ancient Near East. There were two types of medical technicians in Mesopotamia: a magician who cured the patient by means of incantations (usually to expel evil demons), and a doctor who usually used herbs and drugs. The doctor was normally subservient to the magician, who directed the former by means of the incantations. The functions of the two were not exactly distinct; the magician often used drugs in his cures, and the doctor often used incantations.

13:12. proverbs of ashes. Ashes were mixed with water to form soot that was used for a writing substance. It was used only in the most informal and temporary situations. Much like chalk today, it was easily erased or obliterated. One would certainly not want to record memorable truths for all time using ashes. Job suggests that the legacy of his friends' wisdom is nothing but chalk graffiti.

13:12. defenses of clay. The uncertain meaning of the word translated "defenses" creates several possibilities here. If "defenses" is part of the metaphor, and a city's defenses are referred to, then the clay is that used to make mud brick. In Mesopotamia the clay bricks were baked resulting in a very durable material. In other regions, including Israel, sun-dried brick was a significantly inferior building material, and city walls of mud brick would not withstand attack. A second possibility is that "defenses" refers to verbal defenses, that is, the rhetoric of the friends. In this case the clay might refer to a clay tablet that could be written on but then wiped clean, continuing the theme of how vacuous their arguments were.

13:27. marks on the soles of feet. The exact symbolism of this phrase has escaped commentators. Some suggest the prisoner's feet were marked or branded in some way so that he would be successfully tracked, but there is no evidence of such a practice.

14:5. number of man's days decreed. The idea

that man's days were numbered is known elsewhere in Scripture (Ps 39:4). However, the idea here is probably not that any particular lifespan was predetermined but that any lifespan was a comparatively insignificant period of time. In the Gilgamesh Epic Gilgamesh tells Enkidu that the gods live forever, but man's days are numbered and nothing they achieve is of any substance.

14:10-13. afterlife concept/Sheol. See comment on 3:13-19.

14:13-14. resurrection in ancient Near East. There are several different concepts of afterlife that are evidenced in the ancient Near East. The most fundamental concept is continued existence in a gravelike netherworld where there is no differentiation in the treatment of the righteous and wicked. The Israelites called this place Sheol, and they believed that it allowed for no interaction with God. In Canaan and Mesopotamia there were netherworld deities who governed this realm. In Egypt the netherworld existence was more congenial for those who passed the judgment and entered its confines. Those who were not approved were devoured. None of these concepts include the idea of resurrection out of the netherworld. In general, the only awakening that took place in the ancient worldview was the calling up of spirits of the dead (which was not permanent and not a bodily presence) or the awakening of the fertility gods of nature cycles. These died annually when the agricultural cycle came to an end, and "wintered" in the netherworld. Then they were ritually awakened in the spring. None of this bears any resemblance to a theological doctrine of resurrection. Likewise not comparable are the occasional revivifications (when an individual is restored to life) or the indications of national return to life (Ezekiel's dry bones). A fully developed doctrine of resurrection in the modern sense includes six elements: (1) individual, not national; (2) material, not spiritual; (3) universal, not isolated; (4) outside of the netherworld; (5) permanent immortality; and (6) distinctions drawn between righteous and wicked. Zoroastrianism appears to have all of these elements, but the nature of the sources makes it difficult to determine how early the Persians developed these concepts (For further discussion see comment on Is 26:19).

14:17. sealed in a bag. Important items (such as papyrus documents) were often put in a bag and sealed, usually with clay, and thus were made inaccessible to unauthorized persons. Thousands of clay sealings have been found throughout Mesopotamia and elsewhere in the Near East. In Mesopotamia,

however, clay sealings and bags (or jars) were not used for documents. Important clay tablets were sealed by a clay envelope that actually summarized the contents of the document inside.

15:1-35
Second Speech of Eliphaz

15:7. first man equated with wise man. In Israelite tradition the first man, Adam, was made, not born, and was never equated with a tradition of wisdom. In the Mesopotamian tradition, Adapa, sometimes considered the first man, was given as a model for mankind by Ea, the god of wisdom. Adapa was given wisdom but not, however, eternal life. When offered eternal life by Anu, the king of the gods, Adapa was tricked into refusing it. Thus, all of mankind was now resigned to a fate without eternal life and that instead now included death and disease. Adapa was considered first in a line of seven sages who passed the arts of civilization on to mankind. It is unlikely, however, that a specific tradition is being referred to in this verse.

15:27-28. connection between fat and prosperity. Fat was equated with health and wealth in Israel because only those who were wealthy and prosperous had the resources to overeat and the leisure to grow fat. Thus obesity was a sign of God's blessing and favor.

15:33. vine stripped of unripe grapes. This is speaking not of an unhealthy vine but of one that has its young (sour) grapes stripped off before they can ripen.

15:33. olive tree shedding blossoms. Although the olive tree brings forth a great amount of blossoms, most of them are shed and do not come to full maturity. Thus, the wicked's designs, like the sour grapes and olive tree blossoms, will not come to full maturity.

16:1-16
Fourth Speech of Job

16:9. ruthless gods. Belligerent deities would not have been unusual in the religious worldview of the ancient Near East. In a polytheistic system the gods were not considered to be friendly, forthright or predictable. Examples would include the Mesopotamian god Ea telling his "favorite" Adapa that the food he would be offered was "bread of death" when in reality it would have procured eternal life for him. In the Gilgamesh Epic, Ea advises deceiving the people into thinking that blessings cannot rain down on them unless Utnapishtim leaves in his boat. After they send him off they are rained on in a totally unexpected way as the flood comes and destroys them. Around 1200 the Libyans complain that the gods gave them initial success against Egypt with the intent to eventually destroy them. In Egypt the mortuary texts (Pyramid texts and Coffin texts) are targeted against hostile deities. Many examples exist of both of the gods as well as practitioners of magic casting an evil eye on someone.

16:15. sackcloth. Sackcloth was worn by those in sorrow over a catastrophe or the death of a loved one. It was the most conventional sign of mourning in the ancient Near East. The clothing itself was most likely a large piece of cloth, probably in the shape of a sack of grain, or a smaller cloth worn around the midsection. The reference here in Job is the only occasion in Scripture where sackcloth is stitched, although this is probably a metaphorical reference to Job stitching it permanently to his skin (i.e., he will be in mourning for the remainder of his life).

17:3. pledge/security. The making and receiving of pledges was common in Scripture (see comments on Ex 21:2-6; 22:6-7, Deut 24:10-15) and in the ancient Near East. However there are proverbs warning people not to make pledges without collateral (Prov 6:1; 11:15; 17:18; 22:26). The pledge was a piece of property (garment, ring or even a child) which the individual gave to his creditor as a guarantee that he would repay his debt.

17:16. gates of death. Sheol was believed to be like an earthly city in that it contained houses and even a city wall (primarily to keep its inhabitants in Sheol). In the *Descent of Ishtar* the netherworld has a gate complex with seven gates and gatekeepers at each one to control access.

18:1-21
Second Speech of Bildad

18:13. death's firstborn. The prevailing opinion is that Job is describing a deadly disease. Ugaritic texts describe a deity named Death (Mot), who was the ruler of the underworld, although there is no mention of his first-born. A logical choice would be Resheph, the god of plague, sometimes equated with the Mesopotamian ruler of the netherworld, Nergal. Unfortunately no indication is given of Resheph's ancestry.

18:14. king of terrors. Mot was the king of terrors in Ugaritic mythology. Terrors were most likely the demonic host commissioned by Mot to inflict the living. Demonic hosts in both Mesopotamia and Greece were considered to be terrors to the living.

18:15. burning sulfur. Burning sulfur (brimstone) is found in regions with volcanic activity (e.g., the Dead Sea area). When it burns it forms the noxious sulfur dioxide gas. The term is often associated with God's wrath (see comments on Is 30:33 and Ezek 38:22). The land affected by burning sulfur was infertile (see comment on Deut 29:23).

19:1-29
Fifth Speech of Job

19:20. skin of my teeth. Some have thought there is an irony here, in that the teeth, like the nails, are a part of the body that is not covered by skin. Alternatively, others have considered it a reference to the gums, meaning that all his teeth have fallen out.

19:24. iron tool on lead. It has been assumed that this is describing an iron stylus that incised letters, which were filled in by lead. The Behistun inscription of Darius I of Persia in Iran appears to have been inlaid with lead. Moreover, lead tablets were used by the Hittites, as well as the Greeks and Romans.

20:1-29
Second Speech of Zophar

20:8. dream flies away. "Flying away" can be used for death (Ps 90:10). Other texts describe enemies as phantoms in dreams (Ps 73:20 and Is 29:7). In Mesopotamian thinking, dreams were brought from the gods by the deity Zaqiqu, whose name is derived from a word meaning spirit or breath.

20:24. iron weapon/bronze tipped arrow. Iron and bronze together were considered symbols of strength (Job 40:18). The word for weapon is a general term referring to anything that would be found in an armory (both defensive and offensive; see representative list in Ezek 39:9). An iron weapon would therefore refer to a lethal weapon. It may be significant, however, that the Ugaritic cognate refers more specifically to a dart. "Bronze tipped arrow" is the NIV's interpretation of "bronzed bow." The effectiveness of a bow depends on its flexibility. One would not therefore expect a bow to be made of bronze. Bronze models of bows have been found that have been dedicated display pieces, but no operational bows with bronze ornamentation have been discovered.

21:1-34
Sixth Speech of Job

21:12. tambourine, harp and flute. These are

all typical musical instruments of the time and are attested in ancient Near Eastern texts, reliefs and paintings as early as the third millennium B.C. The "harp" is hand held and consists of a few strings with a frame made of wood. The tambourine has been identified in archaeological reliefs as the tambour, a small drum (leather stretched over a hoop) that would not have the tinny rattle sound of modern tambourines. The instrument translated as flute is likely a double pipe made of either bronze or reed.

22:1-30
Third Speech of Eliphaz

22:2. man's benefit to God. In Mesopotamia mankind was considered to have been created for the express purpose of serving the gods and doing the menial tasks that they were unwilling to do. Thus, the gods were dependent on mankind for the upkeep of their houses (i.e., temples), for their daily nourishment and for their clothing needs. The statues of the gods were literally dressed daily, and food offerings were presented on a daily basis.

22:6. security. A creditor was allowed to accept something for security that the debtor selected, except for a tool that he used in his work (see Deut 24:6, 10-11). If it was a cloak, it had to be returned to the debtor at evening, as protection from the cold (Ex 22:26-27, Deut 24:12-13).

22:14. vaulted heavens. A Babylonian hymn to the sun god, Shamash, extols him as the one in the circle of heaven who is the director of people. The Hebrew word NIV translates as "vaulted" is the same word that is translated "circle" in Isaiah 40:22 (see comment there). The Akkadian term used in this and similar contexts suggests a circular but flat shape, a disk rather than a sphere for the shape of both the heavens and the earth. There is some textual evidence that suggests the heavens were viewed as a dome, but more information would be needed to arrive at that conclusion. Israel, having no revelation otherwise, shares this ancient view.

22:24. gold from Ophir. Gold from Ophir is mentioned in an eighth century inscription from Tell Qasile. The precise location of Ophir is unknown. The fact that it was shipped in at Ezion Geber suggests an Arabian location, though sites in India and East Africa have been considered.

23:1—24:25
Seventh Speech of Job

23:10. come forth as gold. The analogy here is that of the process of the purification of gold. Gold is refined or purified by means of a process called cupellation. The gold is placed in a crucible with lead and melted. As air is blown across the surface of the molten mixture, the impurities are absorbed as dross and the purified metal remains. Like the gold that comes forth from the purifying process, Job will have his honor restored after his own "purifying process" (i.e., his troubles).

24:2. moving boundary stones. Unlawfully moving a boundary stone (i.e., property marker) was considered a terrible crime (Deut 19:14; Prov 23:10). The purpose of the stones was to protect family property (usually land). In Mesopotamia the boundary stones were inscribed with a description of the property lines and a terrific curse that was leveled against the criminal who transgressed the stone. These curses were usually a description of diseases directed toward the offender's body. Ironically, they have taught us much about the Mesopotamian understanding of disease.

24:9. infant seized for debt. In Mesopotamia infants were sometimes given as surety for a debt or simply seized by the creditors when the debtor could not repay their debt. However, the creditors are considered to have been unlawful in this case. Also see the comment on Job 17:3.

24:11. olives among the terraces. It is possible that the term used here (shur) refers to terrace walls that allowed the olive trees to grow on hillsides. Other interpreters believe the term refers to the equipment used for processing olive oil. The twenty-two olive oil factories in the caves of Maresha provide details of the process by which olive oil was made. The initial crushing of the fruit was done in a stone basin by means of a lens-shaped rock on its edge that was rolled over the olives. In the second stage reed baskets full of pulp were put into presses hollowed out of the rock where weights suspended from beams would be used to extract the remaining oil. One of the Akkadian words for reed basket is shuru.

24:11. winepresses. The final stage of winemaking is mentioned here, as the grapes were tread by foot into the winepress, which emptied the juice into vats. Winepresses have been found by archaeologists in Palestine. They were usually square or circular pits cut out of rock or dug out of the ground, sealed with plaster or lined with rocks. The grapes were placed in the pit and then trampled on. The juice then flowed from a channel into a lower vessel (wine vat) which collected the grape juice and functioned as a fermenting container.

24:17. terrors of darkness. The use of "king of terrors" in 18:14 and the context of the term in Ezek 27:36 and 28:19 suggest that "terrors" can be used as a reference to the spirits of the dead, those who have been consigned to the netherworld.

25:1-6

Third Speech of Bildad

25:2. order in the heavens. The literal phrase is "He makes peace in His heights," that is, in the heavens. Most have argued that the writer is alluding to the primordial conflict (Job 9:13; 26:12-13) where God defeated Leviathan and other monsters. Both Baal (Ugarit) and Marduk (Babylon) made peace in the heavens after the defeat of their enemies. The NIV translation is not unrelated since the defeat of the chaos monsters is the means by which order was established in the cosmos.

25:5. stars not pure. There is no known tradition of personified or deified stars being guilty of some trespass or sin. The word "pure" can also carry the connotation of clear or clean, and probably here refers to the fact that the stars do not always shine clear and bright in the night sky but can be obscured or dimmed.

26:1—27:23

Eighth Speech of Job

26:6-11. cosmology. There was a triparite division of the cosmos: the heavens, the earth and the realm of the dead below the earth (Sheol and Abaddon in v. 6). This threefold cosmology was roughly similar to that known from Mesopotamia and somewhat like that in the texts from Ugarit. The picture of the universe described here was the common cosmological view of the ancient Near East. The sky was a circle (dome? See comment on 22:14) that arched over the disk of the earth, which sat on top of a primordial ocean. Under the primordial ocean was the netherworld, virtually a mirror image of the space above the earth. Thus, the entire universe was an enormous sphere, cut in the center by the earth.

26:6. Abaddon. The parallel to Sheol (NIV: death) suggests that this refers to a place rather than a person. The Hebrew root from which it is built confirms that it is a place of destruction. In 28:22 it is personified along with Death (Hebrew, *mot*), a well-known name for the Canaanite god of the netherworld. The Hebrew is adopted as a personal name in Revelation 9:11 where it is equated with the Greek Apollyon. In Greek mythology, Apollo is a god of plague and destruction. In Akkadian

the netherworld is referred to as the house of darkness but not as the place of destruction.

26:7. north. The Hebrew word *Zaphon* only comes to mean north because it refers to a mountain that was in the north (commonly identified with Mt. Casius, Jebel al'Aqra, in Syria, elev. 5807 ft.). Its function here is not as a direction but as the "sacred mountain" (Ps 48:1), the high heavens where the gods meet in assembly and, in Ugaritic literature, where Baal's house is.

26:7. spread out on nothing. It is the vast trackless waste of primordial waters that is described as the "nothing" on which the earth sits. Evidence for this is that the word describing what the north is spread out on (NIV: "empty space") is the same word that describes the watery cosmic chaos of Genesis 1.2 (NIV: "formless"). In Babylonian literature, Shamash is praised as the one who suspends from the heavens the circle of the lands. This was part of ancient perception of the cosmos rather than a covert allusion to modern scientific understanding. See comment on Psalm 24:2.

26:10. horizon as boundary. In the ancient Near Eastern worldview, the sun, moon, stars and clouds enter the sky through gates, and the horizon serves as the boundary where the gates are. So when the sun rose or set, it was passing through the gate on the horizon that passed into the netherworld. They believed that during the night the sun passed through the netherworld to arrive at the other side. Here this is described as the boundary between light and darkness.

26:11. pillars of heaven. See comment on 9:6.

26:12. churning sea. This description indicates a typical mythical scene in which the churning of the cosmic ocean disturbs the creatures (often sea monsters) who represent the forces of chaos and disorder. In *Enuma Elish* the sky god, Anu, creates the four winds that stir up the deep and its goddess, Tiamat. It is also reminiscent of Baal's defeat of Yam in Ugaritic mythology.

26:12. Rahab. Rahab is described as one of the sea monsters slain by God. In both the Babylonian and Ugaritic myths of creation the champion deity (Marduk in Babylon and Baal in Ugarit) fights and slays a sea monster and its cohorts in a manner similar to that of Yahweh. In other contexts Rahab is symbolically used as a designation for Egypt (Ps 87:4 and Is 30:7). The name Rahab has not yet been found in extrabiblical sources.

26:13. gliding serpent. This is most likely another allusion to the defeat of the sea monster and its allies. Marduk defeated Tiamat by means of a mighty wind and the use of a net to capture her. The fleeing or gliding serpent also appears in Isaiah 27:1 (see comment there).

27:18. watchman's hut. The hut built by a watchman was by nature flimsy, as it was used only on a temporary basis. Farmers put up temporary booths in the middle of their fields in order to guard the crops during harvest.

27:23. claps hand in derision. Gestures and body language take on different meanings in different cultures. In current Western society clapping hands can be used to show appreciation, to summon subordinates or children, to get someone's attention, to accompany music or to express frustration (one clap). There were also several functions in the ancient world. Clapping could be used in praise (Ps 47:1) or applause (2 Kings 11:12), or as a gesture of anger or derision (Num 24:10). Variations may exist in the precise movement involved: compare the different significations in Western culture of (1) striking the palms together parallel to the body on a horizontal plain (applause); (2) slapping the palms together in a roughly vertical movement (frustration); and (3) striking the palms together perpendicular to the body while alternating which hand is on top and which is on bottom (as if knocking the dust off).

28:1-28
Wisdom Hymn

28:1-11. mining in ancient Near East. Palestine, like Mesopotamia, was generally poor in mineral resources. There are numerous deposits of a poor quality of iron ore in Palestine, but few of high quality ore. The only major deposits of iron ore known in Palestine today are at Mugharat el-Wardeh in the Ajlun hills by the Jabbok River. Copper mining sites are mostly in Transjordan. While iron can be mined on the surface, copper mining requires shafts. Gold was mined in Nubia and South Arabia, while Turkey was mined for its silver. Evidence for the mining of ores comes from Egypt as early as the First Dynasty (c. 3000 B.C.). The method of metallurgy described here in Job can be seen on a number of Egyptian funerary wall reliefs from the New Kingdom (c. 1550-1050 B.C.). The underground mining that is described here (commonly called *pitting*) begins about 2000 B.C. in the ancient Near East. It involved digging vertical shafts at intervals in order to reach the horizontal ore-bearing strata. In Egypt they preferred open cut mining and sometimes dug horizontal shafts into the sides of mountains

or cliffs. By the middle of the second millennium they were doing more shaft mining. The copper and turquoise mines of Egypt in the Sinai have yielded much information of mining techniques and the profession.

28:5. fire. In ancient mines rock was broken up by a process called fire-setting in which the rock was heated by large fires and then doused with cold water mixed with vinegar (believed to enhance the cold).

28:6. sapphires (lapis lazuli). Sapphire (lapis lazuli) was a deep, dark blue stone found primarily in Iran. It has often been found in archaeological excavations in the Tigris-Euphrates region, especially in Mesopotamian royal graves. Lapis deposits were often veined with pyrites, perhaps the gold referred to here.

28:16-19. gems. The various gems were all of great value. The term for gold comes from an Egyptian word from where it was obtained, probably Nubia. The identity of the precious stone in verse 16 is not certain, some have suggested either onyx or carnelian. Glass was made in Egypt as early as the fourth millennium B.C., primarily for ornamentation (although glass vessels were not common in Palestine until the first century B.C.). The first gem in verse 18 has been considered coral, a red gem used for ornamentation. The word for crystal (*gabish*) is the origin of the term gypsum, and is used only here in Scripture. The gem in verse 18 is a type of ruby, while topaz designates yellow chrysolite.

28:20-28. source of wisdom in ancient Near East thinking. Wisdom in Mesopotamia was not considered an intellectual ability or as having moral content, but a specific skill, usually in cultic and magical rituals. The primary deity associated with wisdom was Enki (or Ea), who bestowed the cultic and ritual arts on mankind. Thus, the source of wisdom was Enki himself, though he is simply the most informed repository rather than the originator. Likewise Yahweh, in verses 23-27, is portrayed as one who knows where to find wisdom rather than as its originator or creator. If, however, wisdom is viewed as the ability to discern the inherent order in the created world, it can only be achieved through the one who established the order. Likewise, then, the sovereignty attributed to Marduk by the Babylonians allowed him to be addressed as the Lord of Wisdom.

29:1—31:40
Job's Discourse

29:6. path drenched with cream. The imagery here emphasizes the wealthy nature of Job.

His flocks produced such an abundance of curds (cream) that Job was able to wash his feet in them.

29:6. olive oil from rock. Olive trees, which were the main source of oil, were able to grow in rocky soil because they could thrive with minimal amounts of water. This meaning of the verse is affirmed through comparison with Deuteronomy 32:13.

29:7. seat of respect at the gate. The city gate in ancient Near Eastern cities was a broad, open area that also housed the town square, or marketplace. It was also where business was transacted and where judicial and other governmental proceedings took place. Thus, it was the most visible area in the town. As Job was a family head (i.e., elder), he took his "seat" (residence) at the city gate, emphasizing his distinct importance.

29:12. help for orphan and widow. See comments on Exodus 22:22-24.

29:20. glory fresh, born new. One's glory (literally liver) signified his innermost feelings. Job's fresh "liver" meant that he had a strong emotional stability, and felt content and happy. A bow could dry out and become brittle or could be overused and lose resilience. The bow often signified one's virility and physical vigor. Thus, Job was a "new man" with youthful strength.

30:4. salt herbs. Salt herbs, or saltwort, has been identified as *artiplex halimus*, an edible plant with a very sour taste. The Talmud says this plant was for the poor and those who were in danger of starving.

30:4. broom tree. The roots of the broom tree *(retana roetam)* were not edible, but were used for making charcoal (see Ps 120:4). It grows primarily in the desert regions of the Sinai and Dead Sea.

30:11. imagery of unstrung bow. An unstrung bow appears to signify Job's loss of strength. The term for bow here, however, is obscure and has been interpreted in different manners. It may also denote a tent cord, which if loosened would cause the entire tent to collapse. The imagery is clear; Job's body is frail and near death.

30:28. blackened. The term "blackened" appears to refer to Job's skin (although some argue it may refer to his garments). The term translated "blackened" is usually used for mourning, and that would make the best sense here. The same phrase is used in Psalm 38:6 where the NIV translates "mourning." Though it could refer to the black (goatskin) sackcloth, perhaps more likely is the black soot from the ashes that a mourner puts on their head. In verse 30 the blackened

(different word) skin is related to Job's disease.

31:1-40. legal parallels to Job. Job's renunciation of evil is similar in many respects to the negative confession from the Egyptian Book of the Dead. In this work an individual after death is presented before the judgment seat of Osiris where he recites a lengthy list of forty-two sins that he did not commit. The list includes lying, theft, murder, killing the sacred bull, eavesdropping, homosexuality, being disruptive, talking loud, being impatient and conjuring against a god, just to give a range of examples. Even more to the point, in a Hittite prayer to the Storm-god for relief from suffering, Kantuzilis declares his innocence of a list of items (breaking oaths, eating forbidden things, withholding sacrifices). This oath has clearly put Job in the position of defendant. A declaration of innocence was a common element in legal proceedings that were being appealed to a judge for a public hearing. Since it was often impossible to gather sufficient evidence in this type of court case, the swearing of an oath took on great significance. Up until this point Job has been distressed that God has been silent. By swearing to this oath of innocence, Job hopes to turn any continued silence to his advantage. If God ignores his oath it will be tacit admission of Job's innocence.

31:12. Abaddon/destruction. Along with Sheol, Abaddon is a name for the abode of the dead (see comment on 26:6), and is paralleled with the grave. The term literally means destruction. The term appears as Apollyon in Revelation 9:11, where it refers to the angel of the bottomless pit.

31:36. wearing indictment on shoulder. Wearing or carrying something on the shoulder caused the item to be considered important, and the bearer displayed it proudly (see Is 9:6; 22:22). Moreover, an item inscribed or bound on the hand, neck or forehead became a constant reminder for the wearer, and an advertisement to spectators (Prov 6:21; Ex 8:16; Deut 6:8; 11:18).

32:1—37:24
Elihu's Discourses

32:2. Buzite. Buz was the nephew of Abraham (Gen 22:20-21) and presumably the ancestor of this Aramean clan (Ram). Jeremiah mentions Buz along with Sheba and Dedan (Jer 9:25; 49:32). The annals of the Assyrian king Esarhaddon mention the geographic name Bazu, which has been identified on the island of Bahrein in the Persian Gulf.

32:19. bottled up wine/new wineskins. New wineskins are able to endure fermenting wine, since the skins expand along with the wine. If the wineskins are bottled up in this process, they are in danger of exploding, unless they are vented (Jer 20:9).

33:15-16. God speaking in dreams. See the comment on Job 4:13-15.

33:22. pit/messengers of death. Akkadian also has a word for the netherworld that is translated "pit" (*ḥashtu*). The terminology is drawn from the hole dug to serve as the grave. The identity of the messengers of death is not certain. In Mesopotamian literature there are several gods that are called the "death bringers." But the word "messengers" is not in the text here, and some interpreters have plausibly suggested "place of the dead" as a parallel to the pit.

35:10. songs in the night. Since troubles were associated with the night, songs in the night would be a welcome change whether individuals sang about their disappointments or expressed their confidence in God's presence. Alternatively, there are some Semitic cognates of the term translated "song" that mean strength or protection, and that would fit with some of the parallels in Hebrew (for instance, in Ex 15:2, where it would be "The LORD is my strength and protection").

36:14. male prostitutes. The male prostitutes described here are probably referring to a Canaanite fertility cult. For more information concerning cultic prostitution in general, see the comment on Deuteronomy 23:17-18. The term used here occurs in both feminine and masculine forms and refers, perhaps euphemistically, to ones who have been set apart for particular functions. This same term is used in Akkadian literature to refer to those who have been consecrated as functionaries serving at the shrines or temples. The prostitute was among those functionaries, as was the wet nurse and the midwife. It is unclear what other functions the males might have served. For more information see comment on 2 Kings 23:7.

36:27. water cycle. Though some modern interpreters have attempted to read this verse as a scientific description of the condensation-evaporation cycle, the context is clearly operating from a different perspective (see v. 32, where God fills his hands with lightning bolts that he throws like spears). The two verbs in this verse speak of a process of drawing out or refining (as precious metals would be drawn out in the refining process). It was believed in the ancient Near East that raindrops came from a heavenly stream or ocean, a great body of water that enveloped the earth, and from subterranean waters. Thus there were waters above and below the earth. It was these waters from which God is seen as drawing out raindrops.

37:2-4. storm gods. In Ugaritic myths the storm god Baal-Hadad struck terror in his enemies and caused them to flee by the power of his voice (also see Ps 29). The Akkadian equivalent, Adad, also thundered with his voice. Storm gods typically were pictured with lightning bolts clutched in the hand.

37:9. chamber of the tempest. It was believed that winds were stored in chambers in the heavens. The chambers were periodically emptied by God. The Canaanites and Babylonians attributed manifestations of storms to Adad, the storm and wind god. Similar (and more frequent) imagery describes Yahweh having storehouses of rain, hail and snow, which are set in motion by the wind, presumably instigated by his breath. The word translated storehouses can be used to refer to treasuries that would store precious objects, as well as royal weapons. Hail, snow, wind, thunder and lightning are often seen as the weapons that God uses to defeat his enemies. Likewise storehouses could serve for the storage of raw materials such as barley, dates, grain or tithes in general. In the same way God rations out the products from his storehouses as necessary. Cosmic storehouses are not common imagery in the ancient Near East.

37:13. rain as judgment of God. Storms were used by God for both blessing and judgment, depending on the situation. It brought much needed water for the crops to grow but could also come in destructive storms. In the ancient world the people believed that the weather was under total control of deity and was used to reward or punish. They did not view the world as operating by natural laws.

37:18. bronze mirror. Mirrors in antiquity were made out of bronze and were very hard and difficult to break. The imagery was appropriate to the sky on those dry, hot summer days when the heat of the sun reflected on the rock and dirt through the still, golden haze. Additionally in the ancient world it was believed that the sky was a solid dome or disk.

38:1—41:34

God's Discourses

38:1. God speaking out of storm. God often presented himself by means of a storm (2 Kings 2:11, Ezek 1:4) and he came in tempest to judge the nations. Storm gods in the ancient Near East (Baal-Hadad at Ugarit, Adad in Mesopotamia) also manifested themselves in this way. Yahweh is portrayed as master of the storm and controller of the winds, which can bring life as well as destruction. This type of figurative language demonstrating God's majesty is a common feature in ancient Near Eastern epic poetry. For example, in the Ugaritic epic of Baal and Anath, the god Baal is described as the "Rider of the Clouds" and his "voice" is the sound and fury of thunder and lightening. Similarly, in the Babylonian story of creation, *Enuma Elish*, the storm god Marduk defeats the primordial goddess of watery chaos, Tiamat, through his control of the winds and his use of the lightning. See comment on Zechariah 9:14.

38:4. God responding to challenge using rhetorical questions. In the *Erra Epic* Erra (=Nergal) challenges Marduk concerning his loss of divine dignity. Marduk's long answer gives explanation for his condition but then defends his sovereignty by posing a series of unanswerable "where" and "who" questions to Erra in order to demonstrate his wisdom and control.

38:4-6. earth's foundation, footings, cornerstone. In the ancient world the cosmos was viewed in terms of a temple, and the temple was understood to represent a microcosmos. Here the most important elements in building the temple are referred to in God's setting up of the cosmos. The foundation determined the size and orientation of the temple and so was laid out very carefully. It involved survey of the site but, more importantly, communication from the deity because of the importance of the orientation. The word translated "footings" is most often used for the sockets that held the pillars used in the tabernacle. The cornerstone or, better, the foundation brick is always significant in temple building and restoration. One of the most detailed temple building accounts in ancient Near Eastern literature describes Gudea's construction of a temple for Ningirsu around 2000 B.C. The ceremony concerning the premier brick shows its centrality to the building procedure.

38:5. measuring line in creation. The placement and orientation of a temple was considered extremely important (see the comment on Ex 26:1-36). This is also evidenced in temple building texts both mythological and historical in Mesopotamia. When Marduk is preparing to build his cosmic temple in *Enuma Elish*, he measures the Apsu (the area where the foundation of the temple will be laid). From Sumerian times through Assyrian and Babylonian periods, the possession of the measuring equipment is a sign of the divine

commission for the rebuilding project. It is through this equipment that the leader is given divine direction.

38:7. morning stars/angels. It was typical that the bringing in of the "premier brick" was accompanied by great celebration. The morning stars (usually planets such as Mars and Venus) were worshiped as divine beings in the ancient Near East, and were personified as part of the heavenly hosts in Israel. In the context of Job 38, these "stars" are parallel to the created angelic beings. A Ugaritic poem describes the birth of a number of astral deities.

38:8. sea from womb. In Mesopotamian thinking, the cosmic region from which the subterranean waters emerge is called the Apsu, and is located between the earth and the netherworld. In one incantation the mother of Apsu is the river goddess. The Babylonian creation myth recounts how Tiamat, the sea goddess, was the mother of all creation who was defeated by Marduk. Similarly, Baal in the Ugaritic creation myth defeated Yam, the sea god. The motif here in Job concerning the birth of the sea god is not known elsewhere. Some have concluded that Yahweh's restriction of the sea from the womb suggests that he did not have to defeat a rebellious sea threatening with chaos (as Marduk and Baal had done) but that it had always been under his control.

38:10. doors and bars of sea. Marduk, after having defeated Tiamat, created the seas and placed guards to keep back the waters. The Babylonian *Atrahasis Epic* refers to a bolt of the Sea in the possession of the god Ea (=Enki). Other texts speak of locks of the sea. One of the main tasks of the head of the pantheon was to keep the sea in check so that chaos would be restrained and order would prevail.

38:14. clay under seal. Stamp seals and cylinder seals were produced by engraving a pattern into clay or rock (see sidebar at Jer 32). A stamp seal pressed into wet clay brings shape, contour, design and meaning to that which has had no distinct or distinguishable features. The light of sunrise likewise brings topographical features into sharp relief.

38:17. gates of death. In the Mesopotamian epic of the Descent of Ishtar the goddess Ishtar had to traverse seven gates to arrive in the netherworld and then to return back to the land of the living. The Israelites also believed that death (Sheol) was held by gates.

38:19. abode of light. The question most likely concerns where each one goes when the other is present. In the ancient Near East the sun passed through the netherworld during the night or resided in sequestered chambers. The

Gilgamesh Epic refers to a place called the region of darkness. This is an area that is constantly in darkness along what is called the Path of the Sun.

38:22. storehouses of snow and hail. The Israelites believed that snow and hail, like rain, were collected in storehouses to be used when necessary (see comment on 37:9).

38:28-29. birth of nature. In the ancient Near East and Greece there is a strong tradition of theogony (birth of the gods as natural elements of the universe). The Babylonian epic of creation commences with the divine natural elements all generated from a watery mist (Tiamat). These natural elements in turn generated other divine natural forms. Similar imagery is found in Greece in Hesiod's *Theogony*. It is difficult to determine whether the verse here discounts this view or is just indicating Job's ignorance of the answer. Canaanite literature knew of Pidrya, daughter of mist, and Taliya, daughter of showers in the Ugaritic Epic of Baal. In Mesopotamian literature, dew is sometimes seen as coming from the stars. Shamash, the sun god, is seen as the one who provides dew, mist and ice.

38:31-32. constellations. The three constellations mentioned here (Pleiades, Orion and the Bear) are the same as mentioned in Job 9:9 (see comment there). The fourth constellation is not certain, but may be a term for the planets. The Babylonians were quite adept at charting the stars (cf. Is 47:13) and believed that the movements of the heavenly bodies influenced earthly affairs. Moreover, by charting their movements one was able to forecast the weather.

39:13-18. behavior of the ostrich. Engraved art from Israel starting about 1000 B.C. and continuing for several centuries portrays a deity flanked by ostriches. O. Keel believes these represent the numinous powers that survive in the wilderness under the control of a deity. It is not difficult to see why the peculiar habits of the ostrich have become the core of proverbs. They appear to be indifferent to their young in that when predators attack, the ostriches attempt to draw them away from the young by running off and leaving them reasonably camouflaged, lying flat on the ground. The eggs of an ostrich are indeed laid in the sand, but the danger of crushing them is not as great as it may seem. The shell is six times thicker than that of a chicken egg. The male shares the incubation responsibilities and undertakes the greater part of the chick's care after it is hatched. An adult ostrich can maintain a speed of fifty miles per hour for a half-mile or so. Ostriches were hunted by pharaohs (portrayed as the prey of Tutankhamun) who prized the plumes for fans. They became extinct in western Asia only in the twentieth century.

40:15-24. Behemoth. Since about the seventeenth century Behemoth has traditionally been identified with the hippopotamus, which flourished in Egypt and much of Africa. The monarchs of Egypt hunted this animal, as depicted on numerous wall reliefs. The hippopotamus plays a role in many Egyptian myths, where it often symbolized enemy powers against the throne. There was even an Egyptian festival where a hippopotamus was ritually slain, symbolic of pharaoh's enemies. The difficulty with this identification is that the description in the text is not particularly suitable to a hippopotamus (especially v. 17). Early intertestamental interpretation favors a mythical/supernatural identification (for instance, many would equate the beast and the dragon of Revelation to Behemoth and Leviathan). In Ugaritic literature the seven-headed dragon (see comment on 41:1 below) is paired with a creature identified as Arshu, also known as El's calf, Atik.

40:24. means of capture. The hippopotamus was considered in antiquity very difficult to capture. One tactic was to pierce the nose of the creature so that it was obliged to breathe through its mouth. It could then be killed by shooting a harpoon in the mouth's opening.

41:1. Leviathan. Leviathan has often been identified as a crocodile, which were found mostly in Egypt (where it symbolized kingly power and greatness) but also sparsely in Palestine. However, the multiple heads in Psalm 74:14 and the fiery breath here in verses 19-21 make the crocodile identification difficult. Alternatively Leviathan has been depicted as a sea monster (see Ps 74:14; Is 27:1). Support for this is found in Ugaritic texts which contain detailed descriptions of a chaos beast, representing the seas or watery anarchy, in the form of a many-headed, twisting sea serpent who is defeated by Baal. There is a close affinity between the description of Leviathan in Isaiah as a "coiling serpent" and the Ugaritic Baal epic, which speaks of how the storm god "smote Litan the twisting serpent." In both cases there is a sense of the god of order and fertility vanquishing a chaos monster. Several other passages in the Old Testament mention Leviathan, but most of them, like Psalm 74:14, speak in terms of God's creative act that establishes control over watery chaos (personified by the sea serpent). In Isaiah 27:1, however, that struggle between order and chaos occurs

at the end of time. It may be that the fall of
Satan, portrayed as a seven-headed dragon
in Revelation 12:3-9, also echoes the Ugaritic
image of Litan as "the tyrant with seven
heads." Biblically, Leviathan would therefore most easily fit into the category of "supernatural" creature (like cherubim) as
opposed to natural or purely mythological.
As such it may appear in extrabiblical mythology, as well as being symbolized by
something like a crocodile (as in Ezek 29:3,
though Leviathan is not specifically referred
to in that context).

41:18-21. flame-emitting creatures. Flame-emitting creatures were known from Ugaritic
myth of Baal against the sea (Yam). Yam's terrible messengers terrorized the divine assembly by their fiery appearance. In the
Gilgamesh Epic the guardian Huwawa is described by the phrase "his mouth is fire itself."

42:1-17

Job's Restoration

42:11. gifts. The Hebrew term here for "piece
of silver" (*qesita*) was an ancient unit used primarily in the Patriarchal age (Gen 33:19). One
hundred *qesita*s were required to buy a sizable
piece of real estate (see Josh 24:32), and thus
one *qesita* was a substantial gift. The gold ring
may have been a nose ring or earring worn
usually by the wealthy.

42:12. size of herds. Job now has double the
size of herds that he had at the beginning of
the story (see Job 1:3).

42:15. daughters inheriting along with sons.
Daughters normally inherited in ancient Israel
only when there was no son (see Num 26:33).
Thus the daughters inheriting along with sons
is unique in the Old Testament, although there
are parallels from the Aegean in the early first
millennium B.C. and from Ugarit.

PSALMS

COMMON CONCEPTS

Acrostics. "Acrostic" is a literary form in which the first letters of consecutive lines form a pattern.
In alphabetic acrostics the pattern is the alphabet (the first line begins with the first letter of the
alphabet, the second line with the second letter, etc.). Other forms of acrostic might spell out a
message or a name (for instance, the scribe who composed the work or the deity being honored).
There are a number of acrostics in the book of Psalms (9—10, 25, 34, 37, 111, 112, 119, 145). Psalm
119 is the most complex in that each letter of the Hebrew alphabet is represented by eight consecutive lines. All Hebrew acrostics in the Bible are alphabetic acrostics. The seven examples of acrostics in Mesopotamian literature are name/sentence acrostics (since Akkadian was syllabic, there
was no alphabet and, therefore, no alphabetic acrostics) and generally date to the first half of the
first millennium. Egyptian examples offer numerical sequences or complex messages that involve
both horizontal and vertical patterns. They are more dependent on puns to accomplish their stylistic objective. Acrostics depend on writing and therefore would not be composed orally. They are
intended to be read, not just heard, because of the importance of the visual element. This is especially clear in the Babylonian examples, where a variable sign needs to be read with one value in
the poem but a different value in the acrostic. Some of the Babylonian examples also contain a pattern in the last sign of each line. Another variation is found in those examples where the acrostic is
repeated each stanza.

Afterlife. Sheol is the Hebrew word for the netherworld. Though it may be considered an act of
judgment for a person to be consigned to Sheol from life, it is not in itself a place of judgment to be
contrasted with a heavenly destiny of rewards. The word is sometimes used as a synonym for
grave because the grave was the portal through which one entered the netherworld. Besides
"Sheol" the Psalms also frequently refer to "the pit." This type of terminology occurs as a variant
term for the netherworld as early as the Sumerian period. This is entirely logical given the understanding of the grave (a pit dug in the earth) as the entry to the netherworld. The Israelites
believed that the spirits of the dead continued to exist in this shadowy world. It was not a pleasant
existence, but it is never associated with the torment of hellfire in the Old Testament (the imagery
seen in Is 66:24 is not associated with Sheol). It is not clear that in Israelite thinking there were any
alternatives to Sheol. People who were spared from Sheol were spared from it by being kept alive
rather than by going somewhere else. There was at least a vague idea of somewhere else to go seen
in the examples of Enoch and Elijah, who avoided the grave and presumably did not go to Sheol.

But those texts are very unclear about what the other alternative was. Lacking specific revelation to the contrary, Israelite beliefs conformed generally to many of those current among their Canaanite and Mesopotamian neighbors.

A composite sketch of Mesopotamian beliefs would suggest that the dead needed to cross a desert, mountains and a river, and then descend through the seven gates of the netherworld. Though described in Mesopotamian literature as a place of darkness where the inhabitants were clothed in bird feathers and ate dust, kinder accounts were also current. The denizens of this shadow world also were sustained by the offerings presented by those who were still alive, and they enjoyed some light as the sun god passed through the netherworld when it was night in the land of the living so he could rise in the east again the next morning. The rulers of the netherworld, Nergal and Ereshkigal, were assisted by a group called the Anunnaki. Despite the depressing descriptions, no one wanted to be turned away from the gates because the alternative was to be a wandering spirit with no access to funerary offerings.

There are some expressions in Psalms that have often been interpreted as a reference to an afterlife in God's presence, though other explanations are possible. Some psalms speak in terms of awakening and seeing God's face (11:7; 17:15). In the context of Psalms this is an anticipation not of heaven but of an experience in the temple, as 27:4 and 63:3 make clear. This phrase occurs with the same meaning in Akkadian, where, for instance, Ashurbanipal longs to look at his god Ashur's face (in the temple) and bow before him. In a hymn to Ishtar it is said that the sick man who sees her face revives. In more general terms the Babylonian sufferer in *Ludlul Bel Nemeqi* says that he calls to his god, who does not show his face, yet he hopes that the morning will bring him good things. The psalmist also expects his deliverance to come when he awakes in the morning (139:18). A second expression concerns being redeemed from Sheol (49:15). This only means that the psalmist has been spared from death for the moment, not that he will go to heaven instead of Sheol (compare the wording and contexts in 18:16-19; 30:2-3). Again, comparable wording occurs in Mesopotamian literature, where Marduk is considered one who restores life from the grave (see comment on 30:3) or gives life to the dead. Gula, the goddess of healing, states that she can return the dead from the netherworld. These are expressions not of resurrection but of healing. For discussion of resurrection, see comment on Daniel 12:2.

Creation in Psalms. The praise of Yahweh as the Creator in Psalms is focused mainly on his ordering and maintenance of the cosmos. His control and his sovereignty are indicated as he shows his mastery of the heavens, clouds, sun, moon, stars, earth, seas, thunder and lightning. As in the rest of the ancient world, in Israel it is more important who is in charge than where things ultimately come from. Nevertheless, Yahweh is also seen as the originator of every part of the cosmos. This also extends to the inhabitants of the cosmos from people and down through the various species of animal life, no matter how obscure. The poetic language of the Psalms does not hesitate to adopt the imagery of the cosmos that is common to the worldview contained in the mythology and old-world science of the ancient Near East. Though today in our scientifically enlightened world, some would desire to find in the Psalms a scientific accuracy garbed (disguised) in poetic language, such an approach poses a methodological dilemma. The Israelite audience was familiar only with its own cultural perspectives. Since these were not informed by revelation (e.g., God had not told them that a round earth revolved around the sun and was held in orbit by gravity), they would have closely resembled those common in the ancient world. If this is so, then the words, images and ideas used in the text communicated to them what to them was reality, not just poetic language. Nevertheless, God's sovereign control of nature is the point.

Whether his control of the storm is depicted in the imagery of God armed with lightning bolts and riding on clouds or is understood in his control of high and low pressure systems and the jet stream, the point of his sovereignty remains unchanged. God did not inform them concerning the science of meteorology so that he could give them an "accurate" idea of his control of the weather. He used the understanding that they had. In the same way God did not inform them that the organ they actually used for thinking was the brain, not the heart or the kidneys, as the ancient world believed. Instead he affirmed his interest in their minds, using the understanding that they had of physiology. The ancient worldview concerning the cosmos is evident in many passages of the Old Testament. For a sampling see the comments in Genesis 1:6-8; Deuteronomy 32:22; Job 9:6, 7; 22:14; 26:7, 10; 36:27; 38:1-31; Psalms 8:3; 24:2; 104:1-35; Proverbs 3:19-20; and Isaiah 40:22. There is no instance in which the text supersedes the science of the day or assumes a more sophisticated view of science.

Lament. Laments may be personal statements of despair, such as that found in Psalm 22:1-21, dirges following the death of an important person (David's elegy for Saul in 2 Sam 1:17-27) or communal cries in times of crisis, such as Psalm 137. The most famous lament from ancient Mesopotamia is the *Lament over the Destruction of Ur,* which commemorates the capture of the city in 2004 B.C. by the Elamite king Kindattu. For more information on this latter category see the sidebar in the book of Lamentations. In the book of Psalms more than a third of the psalms are laments, mostly of an individual. The most common complaints concern sickness and oppression by enemies. There are a number of technical terms that describe the lament literature in Mesopotamia, and many of them are connected to incantations (that is, magical rites are being performed to try to rid the person of the problem). The petitions that accompany lament are very similar to those found in prayers from the ancient Near East. They include requests for guidance, protection, favor, attention from the deity, deliverance from crisis, intervention, reconciliation, healing and long life.

Praise. Praise psalms can be either individual or corporate. Over a third of the psalms in the book are praise psalms. Corporate psalms typically begin with an imperative call to praise (e.g., "shout to the LORD") and describe all the good things the Lord has done. Individual praise often begins with a proclamation of intent to praise (e.g., "I will praise you, O LORD") and declare what God has done in a particular situation in the psalmist's life. Mesopotamian and Egyptian hymns generally focus on descriptive praise, often moving from praise to petition. Examples of the proclamation format can be seen in the Mesopotamian wisdom composition *Ludlul Bel Nemeqi.* The title is the first line of the piece that is translated "I Will Praise the God of Wisdom." As in the individual praise psalms, this Mesopotamian worshiper of Marduk reports a problem that he had had and how his god brought him deliverance.

Private worship. How much of the worship connected to Psalms was associated with the annual festivals at the temple and the pilgrimages made to those festivals? How much of it was associated with sacrifices that were being made? A large percentage of the people who lived in Israel lived many miles from the temple. Only those who lived in close proximity to Jerusalem could visit there regularly (though there would be no reason to if one had no sacrifice that needed offering). The observant Israelite male might have traveled there three times each year as the law required (see comments on Ex 23:15-17), but there is little evidence in the text that such observance ever became commonplace in the Old Testament period. As a result many Israelites would perhaps only see the temple a few times in their life. Certainly, then, there must have been other contexts in which worship could take place. The synagogue is generally thought to be a postexilic invention at the earliest, and the high places throughout Israel were disapproved in the ideal world of biblical religious practice. Sabbath was not clearly designated as a day set aside for worship, though at the temple in Jerusalem, at least, there were worship activities that took place on that day. We know that Israel's worship centered around sacred space (the temple), sacred times (Sabbath, festivals), sacred rituals (sacrifice) and sacred words (prayers). Additionally we know that the focus of worship was preserving the holiness of God's presence, preserving the Law and the covenant, and recognition of who God was and what he had done. Nevertheless, we have very little idea of the routine of worship in the individual's life.

Retribution principle. In its most basic form the retribution principle contends that the righteous will prosper and the wicked will suffer. On a national level this principle is built into the covenant, with its potential blessings and threat of curses. On the individual level it had been inferred that this was necessary in order for God to maintain justice. Since the Israelites had only the vaguest concept of the afterlife, and no clear idea of judgment or reward in the afterlife, God's justice could only be accomplished in this life. The Israelites believed that if God were to be considered just, rewards and punishments in this life would be proportional to the righteousness or wickedness of the individual. These beliefs had also then led Israelites to believe that if someone was prospering, it must be a reward for righteousness; and if someone was suffering, it must be a punishment for wickedness. The greater the suffering, the greater the wickedness must be. Because of the retribution principle, suffering had become a source of shame. The authors of Babylonian and Assyrian magical texts describe this same principle of retribution, but since they were not completely convinced of the justice of the gods, it was not as big a theological issue in Mesopotamia.

Temple worship. The temple was not a structure designed for corporate worship. It was a structure to provide a place for God to dwell in the midst of his people. It had to be maintained in holiness and purity so that God's continuing presence could be vouchsafed. The priests existed to maintain that purity and to control access. The temple idea was not invented so that there would be a place to offer sacrifices. Rather, several of the sacrifices existed as a means of maintaining the temple. God's presence was the most important element to preserve. The most important acts of worship were those which recognized his holiness and worked to maintain the holiness of his sacred space. For this reason, words of worship often included acts of worship. Though corporate worship at times took place at the temple, it was not a place that was set up for worship to take place. It was designed to adequately house God, and consequently worship there was inevitable. The word most often used for worship in the Old Testament also means "service." In the ancient Near East most people saw worship as serving the needs of the gods by providing them with food (sacrifice), clothing (placed on the idols) and shelter (luxurious and ornate temples). The God of Israel did not have needs, but it was still appropriate to serve him, as, for instance, the priests and Levites did.

Festivals in the ancient world centered around cycles of nature (New Year's or fertility festivals), mythological events (enthronement of deity conquering chaos), agricultural events (harvest) or historical memorials (dedications or deliverances). They celebrated what deity had done and sought to perpetuate deity's action on their behalf. Often these elements were combined. They usually were celebrated at a holy place and therefore often required pilgrimage. The major religious festivals and holy days celebrated throughout the ancient Near East were for the most part agriculturally based. While daily offerings were made to the gods, there were "patron days" in specific towns and villages for locally honored deities as well as occasions when the national god(s) were processed from one town to another, "visiting" shrines and promoting the general fertility and well-being of the land. The single most important of the Mesopotamian festivals was the *Akitu* or New Year's celebration. The monarch assumed the role of the chief god, while the high priestess served as his consort and represented the chief goddess. Their performance of a series of intricate sacred rituals and sacrifices were designed to please the gods and thus insure a prosperous and fertile year ahead. During the year, based on a lunar calendar, New Moon festivals were celebrated, as were the events of the agricultural calendar (the coming of the rains or annual flood waters, plowing and harvesting). Some rituals grew out of the changing of the seasons, such as the mourning for the "dying god" Tammuz (or Dumuzi), who could only be released from the underworld through the tears of devotees (see Ezek 8:14). At these corporate festivals individuals were generally little more than spectators. It was not unusual for there to be festivals of one kind or another six or eight times during a month.
common metaphors for God

COMMON METAPHORS FOR GOD

In the ancient Near East it was a common practice to multiply names and titles for deity, sometimes using metaphors, other times just descriptive phrases. At the end of *Enuma Elish* the champion and new head of the pantheon, Marduk, is praised by having his fifty names declared. Some of the most intriguing, along with part of the description connected to them, include Namtilla, the one who gives life; Namru, the pure god who purifies the path; Agaku, who created human beings to set them free; Shazu, director of justice; and Agilima, who built the earth above the water. Below are a few of the common metaphors used as titles for Yahweh in Psalms.

Horn (18:2; 75:10; 89:17; 92:10; 112:9; 132:17; 148:14). This metaphor is only used for God in one place in the Psalms (18:2). In ancient Near Eastern iconography, rays or horns on the crowns of deities symbolize power. These are related to the divine glory (Akkadian, *melammu*) that emanated from the gods and especially from their heads or crowns. So, for instance, one text makes reference to the god Enlil "whose horns gleam like the rays of the sun." It was common in Mesopotamia for kings and gods to wear crowns featuring protruding or embossed horns. Sometimes the sets of horns were stacked one on another in tiers. The winged lion from Ashurnasirpal's palace has a conical crown on its human head with three pairs of tiered horns embossed on it. Both in the Bible and the ancient Near East, then, the awe-inspiring power of the deity could be invested in humans, particularly the king.

Judge. The judge had the responsibility of making decisions concerning legal cases that were brought before him. In the cultures of the ancient Near East the king represented the highest court of appeals from a human standpoint. In many cases, however, there was simply insufficient evidence to allow a human being to arrive at a confident decision. As a result, cases were often settled by deity, thus giving rise to the concept of deity as the judge who sees all the evidence and gives an informed and just decision. There were three significant mechanisms by which this system worked. First was the oath. An oath was taken in cases where physical evidence was unavailable or responsibility for loss was uncertain (Ex 22:10-13; Hammurabi). In this way God was solicited as a witness, and the person taking the oath laid himself open to divine justice. Second was the oracle. In this situation a priest would oversee a process by which the deity would be questioned concerning the innocence or guilt of the accused party. In the ancient Near East omens were generally used in oracular cases. An animal would be sacrificed and the entrails examined to determine what the deity's verdict was (favorable meant innocent; unfavorable meant guilty). In Israel the Urim and Thummim were used for this purpose. The third mechanism by which deity was involved was trial by ordeal. "Ordeal" describes a judicial situation in which the accused is placed in the hand of God using some mechanism, generally one that will put the accused in jeopardy. If the deity intervenes to protect the accused from harm, the verdict is innocent. Most trials by ordeal in the ancient Near East involved dangers such as water, fire or poison. When the accused was exposed to these threats they were in effect being assumed guilty until the deity declared otherwise by action on their behalf. In each of these situations, God was understood to be the judge who was rendering verdicts. Beyond these more formal contexts, deity was also understood as the judge in the sense that he maintained justice in society. This meant taking up the cause of the unfortunate, the poor, the vulnerable and the oppressed. In Ugaritic literature, Baal is sometimes given the title "Judge," but more frequently it is associated with Yamm ("sea"), who is regularly called "Judge River" (perhaps alluding to the river ordeal by which judgments were passed). In Akkadian literature the sun god Shamash is the god of justice and therefore frequently cast in the role of divine judge. In Egypt, Amon-Re, also the sun god, was seen as responsible for justice.

King. In the ancient Near East the role of king was attributed to the chief national god, the head of the pantheon. During the Old Testament period this included El or Baal for Canaanites, Marduk for Babylon, Chemosh for Moab, Milcom for Ammon, Ashur for Assyria, Dagon for Philistia, Ra for Egypt, Qos for Edom and Hadad for Aram. The rule of these gods in the divine realm was exercised over the other locally worshiped gods (as head of the divine assembly). In the human realm these gods would be closely identified with the human king as they were involved together in military exploits, building projects (especially temples) and maintaining justice in society. All of the areas that the human king was seen as responsible for, the divine king was ultimately responsible for. Military success meant that the rule of the deity was extended over other national deities whom he had conquered. Thus Sennacherib tried to intimidate Hezekiah by listing the gods that had fallen before him (see comment on 2 Chron 32:11). In the days of Ahab, Yahweh had to compete with Baal for kingship of Israel (see comment on 1 Kings 17:1). In the days of Samuel the people had lost faith in Yahweh's kingship and sought to replace him with a human king (see comment on 1 Sam 8:7). In Psalms, Yahweh is repeatedly proclaimed as king. Whether or not this is associated with a formal enthronement festival in Israel (see comment on Day of Yahweh in the sidebar in Joel), Yahweh's position as king recognizes his sovereignty over individual crises and the events that drive them, over national disasters, over the nations and their gods, and over the cosmos and its operation.

Redeemer. In Israelite society the redeemer's (go'el) role was fulfilled by a kinsman who helped recover the tribe's losses, whether those losses were human (in which case he hunted down the killer), judicial (in which case he assisted in lawsuits) or economic (in which case he recovered the property of a family member). He was a family member who protected the interests of the family when there had been some intrusion on the rights or holdings of the family. This is the term most frequently used in Psalms. A second term (pdh) refers in the legal sphere to freeing someone from standing claims against them or from obligations they have incurred. So redeeming the firstborn involved freeing him from obligation by paying an agreed price. In the Old Testament neither these words nor any of their synonyms refer to redeeming or saving someone eternally from their sins. Psalm 130:8 is the closest, but even that refers only to freeing from the obligations of punishment the nation had brought on itself. In both Ugaritic and Akkadian this verb is used with deity as the subject.

Rock (18:2, 31; 19:14; 28:1; 31:2; 42:9; 62:2; 71:3; 78:35; 89:26; 92:15; 94:22; 95:1; 144:1). There are two different Hebrew words that are used for this divine title, with no discernable difference in their usage. The title does not occur as such in the literature of the cultures surrounding Israel, but we know that it was used because it can be found as the theophoric element in Aramaic and Amorite personal names. A rock could be a foundation for a building, it could provide protection (to hide behind) or shade (to sit beside), and it could be impervious and unmovable. All of these qualities made it an apt metaphor for describing God.

Shepherd. In the ancient Near East both kings and gods were often portrayed as shepherds of their people. Just as the sheep were totally dependent on the shepherd for their care and protection, people depended on the king and the gods. Shamash, the Mesopotamian sun god and the god of justice, is praised as being the shepherd of all that is below. The Egyptian sun god, Amon, is described as a shepherd who brings his herds to pasture, thus providing food for his suffering people.

Shield (3:3; 5:12; 7:10; 18:2, 30; 28:7; 59:11; 84:11; 144:2). In battle the type of shield would be chosen to suit the type of combat one expected to encounter. If siege was being laid to defend city walls, one would want a body-length shield that would provide protection from arrows and sling stones raining down from the walls. In contrast, hand-to-hand combat in the open field would favor a small maneuverable shield that could be used to ward off thrusts by sword or spear. Nearly all of the examples in Psalms refer to the latter (all of the above except 5:12). The metaphor of deity as a shield is familiar from the ancient Near East in, for instance, a prophetic oracle given to the Assyrian king Esarhaddon, who is assured by the goddess Ishtar that she will be a shield for him. Ishtar, as the goddess of war, is referred to as "lady of the shield," and her planet, Venus, takes the Akkadian word for shield, *aritu*, as one of its names.

Stronghold/fortress (9:9; 18:2; 27:1; 31:2; 37:39; 43:2; 46:7; 48:3; 52:7; 59:9,16,17; 62:2, 6-8; 71:3; 91:2; 94:22; 144:2). There are three different Hebrew terms that are used in conveying this metaphor, with the occurrences divided fairly evenly. The range of meaning that they cover extends from naturally defensible locations like a rocky outcrop or a cave, to garrison forts, to fortified cities and even to fortified citadels within cities. In an Assyrian text the king is identified as a fortress to the people. There is no sign of this metaphor for deity in Egyptian or Akkadian literature.

Warrior. In the divine warrior motif, the deity is fighting the battles and defeating the deities of the enemy. In Assyria, Nergal is the king of battle, and Ishtar is viewed as a war goddess. The Canaanite Baal and the Babylonian Marduk are divine warriors. In this worldview human warfare is viewed simply as a representation of warfare among the gods. The stronger god would be victorious regardless of the strengths or weaknesses of the human combatants. Thunder and lightning were considered to regularly accompany the presence of a deity, often in a battle setting. From the Sumerian *Exaltation of Inanna*, to the Hittite myths about the storm god, to the Akkadian and Ugaritic mythologies, the gods are viewed as thundering in judgment against their enemies. Baal is depicted as grasping a handful of thunderbolts. In Psalms, Yahweh is sometimes portrayed as the divine warrior coming to the aid of the psalmist against his enemies. Additionally, however, he is depicted as doing battle against the forces of cosmic chaos. Ancient mythologies often portrayed gods in battle against chaos, resulting in the harnessing and organizing of the cosmos. Both Marduk (Babylonian) and Baal (Canaanite) subdue the sea, which is personified in their divine foe (Tiamat and Yamm respectively). The cosmic conflict motif depicts the principal deity overcoming cosmic forces (usually forces of chaos like Death or Sea) to bring order to the cosmos. In the ancient Near East these forces are usually personified as gods, but Psalms preserves a certain ambiguity on that count.

MUSICAL TERMS

As would be the case with any hymnal, the text of the book of Psalms also contains instructions on orchestration, which tune to use to perform a psalm, the appropriate tempo, as well as performance markings or rubrics such as pauses, breath marks and the use of crescendo and decrescendo modulations. In modern music much of this information is written in Italian or Latin. A musician or singer must learn these technical terms in order to perform the music properly. However, two thousand years from now the meaning of many of these terms may well be lost to memory. It is not surprising therefore to discover that we cannot translate and do not fully understand some of the technical terms that appear in the superscriptions of the Psalms.

Alamoth. Title of Psalm 46. This term only appears in Psalm 46, but it is also mentioned in 1 Chronicles 15:20, where temple musicians are to play their harps "according to Alamoth." By comparison with the Greek word *élumos*, which means small flute, this may refer either to a high-pitched voice or to playing on the upper register of the instrument.

Death of the Son. Title of Psalm 9. This is an incipit or set of cue words for a tune now lost. There is some difficulty translating *'alumot*. The LXX renders it "the strength of youth." The translation in the NIV is apparently based on connection with the Ugaritic god Mot, "death" (see Ps 48:14).

Do Not Destroy. Title of Psalms 57—59; 75. This is likely an incipit, the opening words of a text or song title (possibly based on Is 65:8). Accompanied by *miktam*, it may also serve as a shorthand means of forbidding the destruction or removal of an inscription or text.

Doe of the Morning. Title of Psalm 22. This short phrase is a cue given to the director of the psalm to perform it according to a popular tune, "The Doe of the Morning." It would be a common practice to set new words to an old, familiar tune. Some have suggested a tie to the Ugaritic god *šhr* and thus an ancient origin for the song.

Dove on Distant Oaks. Title of Psalm 56. The phrase is a cue for a song title and tune for the performance of this psalm. There is some uncertainty in whether to translate *'elim* as "doves" or "gods."

Flutes. Title of Psalm 5. It is suggested that the term translated "flutes" here (neḥilot) refers to "lamentation-pipes" such as those that are depicted in Egyptian art of professional mourners. Note also the instruments used by the ecstatic prophets in 1 Samuel 10:5, which may have been flutes. The phrase "to the flutes" may also be a cue for the tune of the psalm.

Gittith. Title of Psalms 8; 81; 84. Some interpreters tie this term to a musical instrument, possibly associated with the Philistine city of Gath. It is also possible that it is a cue word signifying a rhythm, a song or a dance patterned after the work of grape treaders in the winepress (Hebrew *gat*; see Is 16:10; Jer 25:30).

Higgaion. 9:16. This term may be an orchestration cue to the musicians. It has the meaning "utterance" or "musings" (see Is 16:7 for its use as "mourn") and thus may indicate a type of glissando or fluttering sound, perhaps by string accompaniment.

Jeduthun. Title of Psalms 39; 62; 77. Since this is the personal name of one of David's temple singers (1 Chron 25:1-6), it is possible that its appearance in three superscriptions is simply a reference to that person or possibly to a style of performance attributed to him. It may also be a cue to a tune associated with Jeduthun.

Lily of the Covenant. Title of Psalms 60; 80. This is a set of cue words or an incipit for a song title whose tune is now unknown. See also Psalms 45 and 69 and 2 Chronicles 4:5 for the use of this word for "lily."

Mahalath. Title of Psalm 53. Based on 1 Kings 1:40 this term probably refers to a type of flute or pipe used in celebratory processions. Since it can also be translated as "sickness" (1 Kings 8:37), it is possible that the instrument was used in healing rituals.

Mahalath Leannoth. Title of Psalm 88. The word *le'annoth* means "to afflict" and therefore may be added here to coincide with the theme of penitence in Psalm 88. Since this term may be a form of the Hebrew word *'anah*, "to chant" (Ex 15:21), its use along with Mahalath, "flute," could therefore be a reference to an antiphonal line of music for more than one instrument or alternating chanted and instrumental lines.

Maskil. Title of Psalms 32; 42; 44; 45; 47; 52—55; 74; 78; 88; 89; 142. Since it appears in so many psalms and has the meaning "to comprehend" (from Hebrew *sakal*), this may have been a general label for a set of didactic or penitential songs (see the possible connection to mourning in Amos 5:16-17). It may also refer to an "artfully crafted" song or argument, with uplifting words, exhorting the people to praise God (see 2 Chron 30:22).

Miktam. Title of Psalms 16; 56—60. This term always appears accompanied by "of David." The LXX translates the word *miktam* as *stelographia*, "inscription carved on a monument," and thus the word may represent formal declarations or an official song or ritual performance. It may also refer to a song or declaration that was both inscribed on stone and recited publicly in the temple.

Petition (Hazkir). Title of Psalms 38; 70. The root verb, *zakar*, appears in Leviticus 2:2 and Numbers 5:16 in reference to a cereal offering accompanied by frankincense. Similarly, in Isaiah 66:3 it refers to an offering of frankincense. Elsewhere it is used to refer to invoking God's name (Ex 20:21; Amos 6:10). Thus it may refer to a public ritual including both an offering and a petition for God's aid.

Prayer (Tephillah). Title of Psalms 17; 86; 90; 102; 142. This is a term for a psalm designed to call on the people or on a sinner to pray to God for forgiveness (see 1 Kings 8:38). The song takes the form of a lament, recognizing the right of God to chastise the people, and bids them to pray while wearing mourning clothes and engaging in fasting (Ps 35:13).

Psalm (Mizmor). Title of Psalms 47—51; 62—68; 76; 77; 80; 82—85; 87; 88; 91; 98; 100; 101; 108—110; 139—141; 143; 145. This technical term appears fifty-seven times in the superscriptions of Psalms and is accompanied by "of David" thirty-five times. Because of its relation to the Hebrew verb "to prune a grapevine" (Is 5:6), some commentators suggest it refers to a stringed instrument whose strings would be plucked in much the same manner as a vine is snipped by the thumbnail of a vinedresser. However, comparison with the Akkadian *zamaru*, "to sing," may point to *mizmor* simply being a generic term for a song or for a song accompanied by stringed instruments.

Selah. Psalms 3; 4; 7; 9; 20; 21; 24; 32; 39; 44; 46—50; 52; 54; 55; 57; 59—62; 66—68; 75—77; 81—85; 87—89; 140; 143. This is the most ubiquitous of the technical terms in Psalms. It appears seventy-one times in thirty-nine psalms and three times in Habakkuk 3, but never in a superscription. Since it is impossible to determine if the word's placement is original or is the result of editors or copyists, its exact purpose remains uncertain. Among the suggestions for its meaning is "interlude," indicating a break in the text or performance. It is also possible that it is a cue for the choir to repeat a litany or affirmation of a statement in the psalm or for a particular instrument, possibly a drum, to be beaten to keep the rhythm or emphasize a word.

Sheminith. Title of Psalms 6; 12. It is possible that this technical term can be translated as "eight-stringed instrument" and that the reference here is either to the use of this device or possibly to the use of the eighth string. This upper register would provide a high pitched sound, imitating the voices of female singers (see 1 Chron 15:21).

Shiggaion. Title of Psalm 7. Based on comparison with the Akkadian *šegu*, "to howl or lament," it is likely that this term (also found in Hab 3:1) is a label or indicator of a psalm of lament. The word in Hebrew means "to go astray" and in this context may refer either to the subject of the song or poem or perhaps to an exaggerated rhythm or enthusiastic chant.

Song (*Shir*). Titles of Psalms 46; 48; 65—68; 75; 76; 83; 87; 88; 91; 108. This is simply a generic term for "song," appearing many times in the Psalms and elsewhere (Ex 15:1; Num 21:17; Deut 31:19). It is placed both in the superscriptions and in the body of some psalms (69:30; 78:63) and is sometimes accompanied by *mizmor*. As such it must have had both a general as well as a technical meaning within the body of religious music, for instance in the title "Songs of Ascent" (Ps 120—134).

Songs of Ascent. Title of Psalms 120—134. Medieval and rabbinic tradition held that these fifteen psalms were to be sung on the fifteen steps leading up from the court of the women to the court of the Israelites in Jerusalem's postexilic temple. More likely, however, is the explanation that they were chanted or sung by religious pilgrims as they made their way up to Jerusalem or "Zion" during the three major religious festivals each year (see the comment on Ex 23:17).

Stringed Instruments. Title of Psalms 4; 6; 54; 55; 61; 67; 76. It is unclear whether a specific type of stringed instrument is indicated by this term, *neginot*, "to run over the strings." However, reference to the lyre played by David in 1 Samuel 16:16 and the string player in 2 Kings 3:15 and in the Egyptian Tale of Wenamon suggest this is a hand-held instrument (see also Is 23:16).

Tune of Lilies. Title of Psalms 45; 69. This is an incipit or set of cue words for a tune now unknown. It may also be an instruction to accompany the song with a lily-shaped instrument played with either six strings or six bells. It is possible the term for "lily" derives from the Akkadian *šuššu*, "a shock of," but that cannot be confirmed.

Wedding Song. Title of 45. Psalm 45 contains the celebration of an Israelite king's marriage to a princess from Tyre, possibly Ahab to Jezebel (1 Kings 16:31). It only appears here but may have been applied to documents solemnizing the marriage.

Psalms 1—41

Book One

1:5. standing in judgment. One who stands (arises up) in judgment or in the assembly is one who is given the floor or provided a forum in which to speak his or her piece. Usually the action applies to a witness (as in Deut 19:15 and Ps 27:12), but in Job 30:28 it describes Job as the plaintiff. In the Ugaritic Baal Cycle an accuser of some sort stands up and spits on Baal in the assembly of the gods (sons of El).

1:5. assembly of the righteous. The assembly is a formal judicial body, just as the assembly of the sons of El was in the previous entry. This phrase is similar to an idea in Psalm 82:1, where God functions in relation to a judicial council as cases are decided. In the heavenly realm there was a divine council that served this function (see comment on Is 40:13-14), but human courts also operated by means of an assembly (Josh 20:9).

2:6. deity installing king. The term to anoint or install has been found as a Ugaritic root in a mythological text. The office of king was a divine appointment in ancient Israel and other areas of the Near East. Sargon of Akkad (c. 2300 B.C.) claims to have been installed by Ishtar, while the Sumerian King List (compiled sometime after 2000 B.C.) claims that towns received their monarchs by divine appointment. This ideology continued into the Israelite period. Kings of Assyria and Babylon celebrated yearly enthronement festivals in which the chief deity was celebrated as king and the whole enthronement process for both god and king was reenacted. Mesopotamian kings saw themselves as established on the throne by means of a divine decree. In Egypt Horus installed the kings in a coronation ceremony that involved consecration and purification rites.

2:7. king as son of deity. In the ancient Near East kings were commonly understood as having a filial relationship to deity and were often considered to have been engendered by deity. Egyptian kingship was particularly strong on this point, since the kingship of the pharaoh was seen as derived from the divine realm. More particularly he was conceived as the son of Re, the sun god. In Ugaritic literature, Keret, king of Khubur, is identified as the son of El, the chief god of the Canaanites. Furthermore, iconographic evidence shows two princes suckling the breasts of the goddess Anat. Among the Aramean kings the designation was even included in their throne names (Ben-Hadad means son of Hadad). In Mesopotamia, from Gilgamesh in the mid-third millennium through kings such as Gudea, Hammurabi, Tukulti-Ninurta and Ashurbanipal, just to name a few, it was part of the royal prerogative to claim divine heritage. The Israelite kings, however, were sons of the deity on the basis of a covenant and not sons by nature (see Ps 89:26; 2 Sam 7:14).

2:9. iron scepter. The scepter was representative of kingship, and iron was symbolic of strength. Egyptian rulers as early as the Narmer palette are portrayed as striking enemies with a rod/scepter. Of particular interest is the fact that the evidence from the execration texts (see next entry) suggests that the pots were smashed with a mace.

2:9. dashed to pieces like pottery. Egyptian kings celebrated their rule by writing the names of their enemies on pots and symbolically smashing them. These are referred to as the execration texts. Assyrian kings likewise used the metaphor of smashed pottery to assert their supremacy over enemies.

4:6. light of God's face. The metaphor "light of God's face" is found in royal letters from the Egyptian city of Amarna and in Ugaritic correspondence. For example, "the face of the Sun (i.e., Pharaoh) shone brightly upon me" is a statement made by one of the Egyptian king's subordinates. Two small silver scrolls (about one inch long) have been found in the area known as Keteph Hinnom in Jerusalem. They were amulets in a burial cave from the sixth or seventh century B.C., and they contained the benediction from Numbers 6:25, which includes the request that the Lord "make his face shine upon you." At present they represent the oldest example of any text of Scripture. The concept of the shining face of the deity resulting in mercy is found in Mesopotamian documents and inscriptions from as early as the twelfth century B.C.

6:6. Israelite beds. The poetical metaphor of crying on one's bed is also found in Ugaritic literature: "His tears are poured forth like shekels upon the ground, like pieces-of-five upon the bed." Beds in ancient Israel were most likely like those represented iconographically in the Near East. They were in essence reclining couches and high beds. The poor probably slept on flat mats on the floor, while the average person used a cot.

7:13. flaming arrows. The Old Testament never uses the word for arrows to describe the flaming arrows used by human armies ("firebrands" of Prov 26:18). In Akkadian there are a few references to the use of flaming arrows that kings rain down on the enemy. These arrows were presumably dipped in a type of oil or pitch and set on fire. The arrows shot by Yahweh are usually considered to be bolts of lightning (see 2 Sam 22:15; Ps 77:17-18 for the two in parallel). Lightning would fit well with the concept of flaming arrows in that it is sometimes just called fire. In the divine warrior motif the deity is fighting the battles and defeating the deities of the enemy. In Assyria Nergal is the king of battle, and Ishtar is viewed as a war goddess raining down flames in war. The Canaanite Baal and the Babylonian Marduk are divine warriors. Thunder and lightning were considered to regularly accompany the presence of a deity, often in a battle setting. From the Sumerian *Exaltation of Inanna*, to the Hittite myths about the storm god, to the Akkadian and Ugaritic mythologies, the gods are viewed as thundering in judgment against their enemies. Baal is depicted as grasping a handful of thunderbolts. Thundering terminology is picked up in royal rhetoric as Hittite or Assyrian kings portray themselves as the instruments of the gods, thundering against those who have violated treaties or stood in the way of empire expansion.

8:3. heavens as work of fingers. In Akkadian literature the various levels of heaven are said to be made of various types of stone. The lower heavens were made of jasper, and Marduk, the chief god of Babylon, was reported to have drawn (etched) the constellations on them. This verb is used when pictures or reliefs are being made. In *Enuma Elish* Marduk draws the boundary lines for the year in the heavens. This refers to his setting the courses of the stars. The second half of verse three indicates that this psalm also has the heavenly bodies in mind. God elsewhere inscribes with his finger (Ex 31:18; Deut 9:10), but fingers can also be used parallel to hands with regard to handiwork (Is 2:8).

8:4-6. dignity of humankind. The status of the human race in Israelite thinking was very high when contrasted with the status people were given in Mesopotamian thinking (as seen in the Babylonian epic of creation). In the Mesopotamian view the gods had no plan to create people as an integral part of the world that they had set up for themselves. People were only brought into existence as a consequence of the gods becoming tired of working so hard to provide for themselves. Humans were made to be servants to deities, who had no interest in hard labor. In this way of thinking human dignity was achieved through the idea that the gods needed them. Here, instead, people rule over all other creatures.

9:12. avenger of blood. See the comment on Numbers 35:9-34 for a discussion of the responsibility of the family to avenge a death. It is possible that the title "avenger of blood" evolved out of the family obligation to engage in blood revenge when one of their clan members was slain. Such a process, while typical of tribal society, is extremely disruptive to the maintenance of order within an organized state. As a result the "avenger of blood" may have been appointed by the government to serve both the needs of the family and the state by apprehending the accused and then carrying out sentence if the verdict was murder. It is possible that a more general function is intended in this psalm, since it does not use the same technical term used in the Numbers passage. See the comments on Genesis 4:14-15 and 9:5-6.

9:13. gates of death. The netherworld, Sheol, was believed to be like an earthly city in that it contained houses and even a city wall (primarily to keep in its inhabitants). In the *Descent of Ishtar* the netherworld has a gate complex with seven gates and gatekeepers at each one to control access. In Egyptian iconography the gates of death are portrayed as gateways into the necropolis.

9:20. striking with terror. The dread of a deity as a divine warrior was often believed to precede a powerful, successful army into battle. Egyptian and Assyrian texts and reliefs portray the god as a winged disk terrifying the enemy before the arrival of their own armies. In the inscriptions of Thutmose III this terror is attributed to Amun-Re, and Hittite, Assyrian and Babylonian texts all have their divine warriors who strike terror into the hearts of the enemy. The concept of deity having an awesome, unapproachable appearance was not limited to Israelite theology, for in Mesopotamia the gods displayed their power through their *melammu*, their divine brilliance. The splendor or "glory" of God overwhelms the enemy. In the face of such divine magnificence, both the gods and the forces of other nations are utterly defeated and forced to submit to the supreme deity.

11:6. fiery coals and burning sulfur on the wicked. In Akkadian texts sulfur burnt on coals is a fumigating agent. The gods Ea and Enlil send down sulfur as a purifier that counteracts witchcraft. But it is not part of the divine warrior's arsenal for the judging of enemies. The terms here are reminiscent of, though not identical to, those used in the account of the destruction of Sodom and Gomorrah (see also Ezek 38:22).

11:7. seeing face of judge. Seeing the face of a judge or god was a metaphor in Mesopotamia and was equivalent to being on their "good side," because it referred to gaining access to their presence. It usually refers to a supplicant or plaintiff gaining an audience with a judge. If a judge or god turned his face toward you, you were looked on with favor.

12:6. clay furnace. The Hebrew term used for furnace is found only once in the Bible. Because of the mention of silver, the context implies that a clay crucible used for smelting purposes is being described. Crucibles appear in Egyptian wall paintings, and clay exemplars have been found by archaeologists.

12:6. seven purifications. Usually silver went through the refining process a few times to remove all of the dross. The imagery here is that if one is purified seven times (the number of completion in Hebrew), one is completely purified.

13:2. how long? This question occurs nearly twenty times in Psalms, usually in connection with a lament psalm. It is found also in Mesopotamia as the Sumerian *Lament over the Destruction of Sumer and Ur* asks, "How long will the enemy eye be cast upon my account?"

16:4. blood libations. Most libations in the ancient Near East were of beer, wine or water, though honey, oil and milk are also found. No evidence of blood libations has yet been found.

16:6. boundary lines. The imagery of God determining boundaries is also found in Deuteronomy 32:8, where God made boundaries for the nations. In Mesopotamian land-sale contracts the boundary lines were usually clearly delineated. Furthermore, the Kassites of Late Bronze Age Babylonia used boundary stones (Akkadian, *kudurru*) to mark property divisions. They had texts on them that included detailed curses for those who violated the boundaries. In an inheritance the property was divided among the heirs, and obviously certain portions of land would be more desirable and productive than others.

For common concepts, metaphors for God and musical terms, see pages 511-18.

16:8. positioned at the right hand. A fully armed warrior would hold his weapon in his right hand and his shield in his left. The person to the right of a king would have the privilege of defending him. For a king to put someone there would be an affirmation of trust and therefore an honor. In contrast, when the Lord takes up his position at someone's right hand, as here, he is in a position to offer defense with his shield (see Ps 109:31). The metaphor transitions easily from the battlefield to the courtroom. Akkadian usually juxtaposes right and left in parallel lines, but there are occasions where deity is said to walk at the right side of a person in battle.

16:10. not abandoned to the grave. In the context this refers to not allowing someone to be put to death at the hand of malicious enemies. The psalmist will not be consigned to Sheol; he will not see decay because his life will be spared (see Ps 30:2-3). An early Sumerian text recounts the tale of an individual who is facing capital punishment for the crimes of which he is accused. Instead, however, he finds himself snatched from the jaws of destruction and praises the goddess Nungal for his deliverance.

17:8. apple of eye. Literally the term is "the little one of the daughter of your eye." This idiomatic expression is also found in Deuteronomy 32:10. The pupil or apple of the eye is the most sensitive part of the body and thus the part needing the most protection.

17:8. shadow of wings. The metaphor of taking refuge under the wings of deity is found also in other psalms (36:8; 57:2; 61:4; 91:4) and is consistently related to issues of care and protection connected with the covenant. The metaphor is also known from other ancient Near Eastern cultures, particularly Egyptian, where even disembodied wings represent protection. Deities with wings are often portrayed overshadowing the king. Likewise an ivory from Arslan Tash dated to the eighth century shows characters in human form with wings protecting a figure in the center.

10.4. cords of death/grave. Noose snares were commonly used by hunters in the ancient Near East. In this metaphor, death or Sheol is the hunter. For many cultures in the ancient Near East, Sheol, the abode of the grave (i.e., underworld) was a very real place where individuals led an amorphous existence, eating clay and dust, and hoping that their descendants would take care of their needs. There were gates and gatekeepers to keep the dead inside, and thus it was called "the land of no return." This description can be found in the second-millennium B.C. Akkadian epic *The Descent of Ishtar.* Apparently the Hebrew view of the grave was not unlike this, although there is no elaborate description of it in the Old Testament.

18:8 smoke from nostrils, fire from mouth. This imagery is not found elsewhere in the ancient Near East. The closest example is in *Enuma Elish,* where it is said of Marduk that when his lips moved, fire blazed forth. Though Yahweh could not be portrayed in any form (animal or otherwise), poetic description of Yahweh by means of animal imagery in order to highlight certain attributes was legitimate (lion/leopard in Hos 13:7; flying birds in Is 31:5; bear in Lam 3:10; wild ox in Num 24:8 [all translations but NIV]).

18:9. dark clouds under feet. The term for "dark clouds" has been found in the Ugaritic epic of Baal and Anath, where the god Baal is described as the "rider of the clouds" and his "voice" as the sound and fury of thunder and lightning.

18:10. mounted cherubim and flew. In Syro-Palestine iconography deities are often portrayed standing on the backs of wild creatures (usually bulls). An Assyrian relief from Maltaya pictures seven gods, each standing on the back of a different animal. Most intriguing is an Assyrian relief that pictures a storm god replete with weapons, riding the back of a composite creature with a lion's body, an eagle's wings and a bull's head. In the Old Testament Yahweh is described as enthroned on the cherubim in the Holy of Holies in the temple (see comment on 1 Sam 4:3-4), and in Ezekiel's throne vision (chaps. 1, 10) Yahweh is transported on a mobile chariot-throne borne by composite creatures.

18:12-15. weapons of divine warrior. Yahweh's arrows are usually considered to be bolts of lightning. In the divine warrior motif, the deity fights the battles and defeats the deities of the enemy. In Assyria, Nergal is the King of Battle, and Ishtar is viewed as a war goddess. The latter rains down flames in war. The Canaanite Baal and the Babylonian Marduk are divine warriors.

Thunder and lightning were considered to regularly accompany the presence of a deity in the ancient Near East, particularly in a battle setting. From the Sumerian *Exaltation of Inanna* to the Hittite myths about the Storm God to the Akkadian and Ugaritic mythologies, the gods are viewed as thundering in judgment against their enemies. Baal is depicted as grasping a handful of thunderbolts. Thundering terminology is also picked up in royal rhetoric as Hittite or Assyrian kings portray themselves as the instruments of the gods, thundering against those who have violated treaties or stood in the way of empire expansion.

18:16. deep waters. When the Babylonian god Marduk brings restoration he is praised for taking hold of the individual and drawing him out of the waters of the Hubur River. This is the river that flows at the gates of the netherworld, and being drawn from its waters indicates being saved from death at the last moment. This imagery continues into Greek mythology with the famous River Styx and even finds its way into Christian literature as indicated by the river of death that flows in front of the golden city in *Pilgrim's Progress*.

18:28. keeping lamp burning. Lamps were often used metaphorically in Israel to symbolize life and prosperity. They were often placed in tombs for this reason. The expression "his lamp" is used often in Scripture to symbolize life. As an eternal flame is a symbol of endurance and remembrance, the reign of a descendant of David in Jerusalem provides a link to God's promise to David's dynasty (2 Sam 7:8-16). Similar uses of the word in Ugaritic and Akkadian are tied to perpetuation of rule or divine presence. Assyrian king Tiglath-Pileser III is referred to as the light of all humankind. An Old Babylonian idiom expresses a family having no descendants by the image of its brazier going out. Alternatively, in the superstitious world of the ancient Near East there were demons lurking everywhere who especially favored the dark. One of the ways that gods were figuratively seen as providing protection was by imparting continuous light, suggested by phrases such as "the lamp of the gods" in texts from Ugarit. The Canaanite god Sapash was given the attribute of "divine lamp." In Mesopotamia, Lamashtu was a particularly feared demon. The god Nushku was represented by fire, and his lit lamp held the feared demons at bay. Here the psalmist may be referring to the lamp lit on his behalf. Yahweh is the lamp by the side of the psalmist warding off danger.

18:33. feet of deer. The term used here refers to one of the species of deer known throughout the ancient Near East. It is often discussed with other caprids such as the Nubian ibex, mountain sheep and gazelles. All of these caprids are known for their sure-footedness on treacherous paths. As early as Sumerian literature (e.g., *Dumuzi's Dream*) this type of metaphor is used for swift sure-footedness.

18:34. bow of bronze. If this expression reflects an actual weapon, it may either indicate a wooden bow decorated with bronze or bronze-tipped arrows. On the other hand, it may simply be a poetic way of denoting the strength of the warrior's bow. The bow was a symbol of royal strength in both Assyria and Egypt, as well as one of the weapons of the gods. In the latter regard the sun disk is portrayed as drawing a bow that, as the weapon of the sun god, could be understood to be bronze. An Assyrian relief from about the time of David portrays the sun god, Ashur, delivering what the connected inscription calls a magnificent bow into the hands of the king.

19:1-4. nature revealing God. In the Egyptian *Papyrus Insinger* (a composition from the intertestamental period), it is observed that the hidden work of a god is made known on earth day by day. For the next twenty lines he describes many of the aspects of the operation of nature that have been created by the god and presumably are involved in this revelation. These works of creation included light and darkness; day, month and year; summer and winter; constellations; the birth process; sleep; and the succession of generations.

19:5. bridegroom pavilion. The chamber of a bridegroom was the specially prepared room in which the marriage was consummated. The use in Joel 2:16 suggests this in its parallelism. It has this meaning in early rabbinic Judaism, but after the destruction of the temple in 70 A.D. it takes on a reference to the pavilion in which the formal wedding ceremony was conducted.

19:6. ancient perceptions of sun's journey. In many ancient Near Eastern cultures it was assumed that the sun ran a daily course through the heavens. Mesopotamian texts refer to the gates of the heavens where the sun enters and exits. In these texts all of the heavenly bodies have paths or courses that they follow, represented as bands across the sky. Egyptian materials also offer these concepts in both text and iconography. The sun god is portrayed as riding in his barque across the skies between entry and exit spots on either horizon.

19:7. Law and sun. In the ancient world the sun god was usually the god of justice. For the psalmist, then, it is natural to move from the relationship of Yahweh and the sun to Yahweh's provision for justice through the law. Much of the imagery used to describe the law can also be found related to sun gods in the ancient world.

19:8. light to the eyes. Light to the eyes refers

to life and therefore, in one sense, is given to all (Prov 29:13). The law, however, is able to bring extended life to those who follow its commands. When the light goes from the eyes, death is near (13:3; 38:10).

19:10. pure gold. The imagery of "pure gold" is known from other ancient Near Eastern cultures. For example, a number of inscriptions on doors at a Ptolemaic period Egyptian temple at Edfu read, "Everyone who enters by this door, beware of entering in impurity, for God loves purity more than millions of possessions, more than hundreds of thousands of fine gold." The word translated "pure gold" is somewhat obscure (it is a single word, not a noun with an adjective). It could refer to a particular grade or to a particular variety, for instance, red gold or white gold.

19:10. date honey compared to bee honey. Honey represents a natural resource, in most occurrences the syrup of the date rather than bees' honey. Since sugar was not available, honey was the most commonly used sweetener. There is no evidence of bee domestication in Israel, though the Hittites had accomplished that and used bee honey in their sacrifices (as did the Canaanites). In the Bible honey occurs in lists with other agricultural products (see 2 Chron 31:5). It is possible that the reference to honey in the third line of the verse is date honey, but the last line of the verse is clearly referring to bee honey since the honeycomb is mentioned.

19:12. unwitting sin. The belief in the ancient world was that the gods had many more regulations, requirements and restrictions than were known to people. In a "Prayer to Every God" an Assyrian worshiper goes through an elaborate listing of possible offenses (the forbidden thing I have eaten, I do not know; the prohibited place on which I have set foot, I do not know) asking that his unwitting sins be pardoned, claiming that the offense was committed in ignorance. Additionally the penitential prayers from Mesopotamia known as *shigu* prayers contain frequent reference to being absolved of unknown sins. Egyptians were also concerned as reflected in a late demotic wisdom piece *(Papyrus Insinger)*, where the author begs forgiveness for unwitting sin.

20:5. banners. Banners were used by the Israelites and others, including the Assyrians, as standards of warfare (Song 6:4) and as an assembly of tribes (Num 2:2). In the Egyptian army the divisions were named for various gods (e.g., the division of Amun, division of Seth), and the standards would identify the division by means of some representation of the god. Holding high the banners was evi-

dently a sign of victory. Banners are described in significant detail in the texts from Qumran.

21:8. right hand seizing foes. In its attempt to be colorful, the NIV has unfortunately distorted the picture of this verse. The verb ("to find") used in both lines of the verse describes attacking the enemy with a weapon, not apprehending him. Most soldiers were right-handed, so one would not seize the foe with the right hand—that is where the weapon would be held. The right hand, then, is used for offense, and it will "find" its mark. A hymn to Shamash says that the god's weapon will make straight for the wicked man and there will be none to save him. In Egyptian reliefs and paintings (also Ugarit) the king often strikes a pose with his weapon upraised in his right hand, while his left hand lays hold of the enemy. This verse is only describing part of that picture because the lines are parallel, not contrasting. Both lines describe what the right hand does.

21:9. fiery furnace. God is pictured as a fiery furnace that destroys everything that is put into it. The writer is probably referring to the large ovens used to bake bricks and to smelt metals. For more information about furnaces see comment on Daniel 3:6.

22:12. bulls of Bashan. Bashan was a very fertile region east of the Jordan River, well known for its sheep and plump cattle. In this prime cattle-grazing area, one could find pampered cattle being raised for the market, as well as a breed of ferocious undomesticated cattle that roamed free. Legal texts demonstrate that goring oxen were a danger, and that they could even occasionally be found wandering the streets.

22:13. lions. It is known that lions were captured and kept in cages so that they could be released for hunting. In Assyrian texts oath-breakers were put into cages of wild animals set up in the city square to be publicly devoured. More relevant to this passage, in seventh-century Assyrian literature the lions' pit occurs as a metaphor for vicious and antagonistic courtiers of the king. In one piece of Babylonian wisdom literature Marduk metaphorically closes (muzzles) the mouth of the lion (the oppressor) to put an end to his devouring tactics.

22:14. bones "out of joint." "Out of joint" is somewhat interpretive here; the Hebrew reads "scattered about" (comparable verb form only occurs in three places: Job 4:11; 41:17; Ps 92:9), as when a predatory pack has devoured a victim and each member of the pack carries off its share. Some of the cultures of the ancient Near East practiced secondary burial: the body would be laid out (in a cave, for instance) until the flesh decomposed, and then the bones would be buried in the final resting place. Even if a body was devoured, proper burial could be carried out if the bones could be retrieved. So Ashurbanipal speaks of punishing his enemies by taking their bones out of Babylon and scattering them around outside the city. He also boasts of opening the graves of past kings of his enemies and carting off their bones "to inflict unrest upon their ghosts." For more information see comment on 53:5.

22:16. dogs. Dogs are equated with evildoers in this passage. Though in the Near East they were domesticated at a very early date in the Neolithic period, they still lived as scavengers, often roaming in packs on the outskirts of town (Ps 59:6, 14) and scavenging in town itself (1 Kings 14:11). For these reasons the term *dog* is often one of derision and contempt in the Bible. However, this may not have been the case throughout the entire Near East. A large Persian period dog cemetery (in an apparent noncultic context) of over seven hundred burial pits has been uncovered at Ashkelon. Dogs were revered in Zoroastrian Persia but were not, however, buried in cemeteries. Dogs (and puppies in particular) played a major role in elimination and purification rituals in Anatolia and Mesopotamia. Many cult functionaries in Hittite Anatolia and Phoenicia (who were condemned in Israel) were called "dogs." Finally, canines in Mesopotamia were considered to have healing qualities. In fact, Ninkarrak, the goddess of healing in Mesopotamia, was often represented by a dog figurine. See comment on 1 Kings 21:19.

22:16. description of hands and feet. The understanding of the description of the hands and feet here has been problematic. The Hebrew verb, traditionally translated as "pierced," occurs only here and can only be translated that way if it is emended. As it stands it indicates that the psalmist's hands and feet are "like a lion," which some commentators have interpreted to mean that the psalmist's hands and feet were trussed up on a stick as a captured lion would be. Unfortunately, despite all the lion-hunting scenes that are preserved and described, no lion is shown being transported this way. If a verb is desirable here, a suitable candidate must be found among the related Semitic languages. The most likely one is similar to Akkadian and Syriac cognates that have the meaning "shrink or shrivel." Akkadian medical texts speak of a symptom in which the hands and feet are shrunken. Matthew 27 is of no help because it does not refer to this line.

22:18. casting lots for clothing. Although the Roman soldiers had the right to the clothes of the convicted criminal (as the soldiers gambling by means of lots for Jesus' tunic), there is no evidence of this for soldiers supervising an execution in the Old Testament period. Nevertheless, in this period we do know that booty was sometimes divided by lot, so it is not difficult to understand a person's clothing being divided that way on his demise. It should be noted, however, that the psalm does not indicate that those casting lots for the clothing were the executioners. Inheritance procedures often used lots to divide the property among the heirs. A Mesopotamian lament indicates this as the person on his deathbed bemoans the fact that his valuables are already being divided up before he is dead.

23:2. needs of sheep. Sheep in the Levant grazed on the fertile grass produced by rain. In the summer and autumn they fed on weeds and stubble left over from harvest. Like camels sheep can go long periods of time without water and then drink as much as nine liters. In contrast to goats, who are quite independent, sheep depend on the shepherd to find pasture and water for them. Shepherds also provide shelter, medication and aid in birthing. In sum, they are virtually helpless without the shepherd. In an Old Babylonian text King Ammiditana claims that the god Ea gave him the wisdom to shepherd his people. He continues the metaphor by saying that he provides them with fine pastures and watering places, and makes them lie down in safe pastures.

23:4 use of rod and staff. The rod was a club worn at the belt, while the staff was a walking implement that doubled as a weapon in time of need (1 Sam 17:35) and guided and controlled the sheep. These were traditional tools of the shepherd, as is shown already in a cylinder seal inscription of the third millennium.

23:5. anointing with oil. Banqueters in the ancient world were often treated by a generous host to fine oils that would be used to anoint their foreheads. This provided not only a glistening sheen to their countenance but also would have added a fragrance to their persons and the room. For example, an Assyrian text from Esarhaddon's reign describes how

---

For common concepts, metaphors for God and musical terms, see pages 511-18.

he "drenched the foreheads" of his guests at a royal banquet with "choicest oils." Oil preserved the complexion in the hot Middle Eastern climate. Both the Egyptian Song of the Harper and the Mesopotamian Epic of Gilgamesh describe individuals clothed in fine linen and with myrrh on their head.

23:6. dwelling in house of the Lord. The house of the Lord is used as a term for the temple but never for the heavenly dwelling place of God (very clear in 27:4). The term "forever" could be confusing in this regard, but the Hebrew says only "for length of days," that is, for extended periods (Lam 5:20). If the translation "dwell" (following the Septuagint) is correct, then it would suggest a priestly office for the psalmist, for priests were the only inhabitants of the temple precinct. If instead we should follow the Hebrew text by translating "I will return to the house of the Lord," we would find here the anticipation of enjoying many future opportunities to worship at the temple ("time and again"). The Babylonian king Neriglissar expresses to his god that he wants to be where he is forever. Another text requests, "May I stand before you forever in worship and devotion." A Hymn to Marduk requests that the worshiper may stand before the deity forever in prayer, supplication and entreaty. In the third millennium B.C. Sumerian worshipers tried to accomplish this objective by placing statuettes of themselves in the posture of prayer in the temple. In this way they would be continuously represented in the temple.

24:2. earth founded on seas. In the Babylonian perception of the cosmos the earth's foundation is on what is called the *apsu*. This is a primordial watery region that is under the jurisdiction of the very important deity Enki/Ea. From the standpoint of physical geography it represents the water table that surfaces, for example, in marshes and springs as well as being associated with the sweet water cosmic seas and rivers. In *Enuma Elish* one of Marduk's names, Agilima, identifies him as the one who built the earth above the water and established the upper regions.

24:4. lifting up soul to idol. This expression means to "nurse an appetite" for something. The word translated "soul" here refers, physiologically, to the throat, and thereby the meaning arrives at appetite or desire. In a number of contexts the same expression is used with God as the object (Ps 25:1; 86:4; 143:8). The term for idol here is related to the word for emptiness or vanity. Other writers use the term "no-gods" for idols (e.g., Jer 5:7).

24:7. gates and ancient doors. In a Hymn to Shamash, the Babylonian sun god, various parts of the temple are said to rejoice over Shamash, including the gateways and entrances. A Nabonidus text refers to the gates of the temple being open wide for Shamash to enter. These would occur in the context of regular processions of the statue of the deity into his temple. If the "head" of the gates refers to an architectural feature, it would most likely be the beam or projection across the top of the gates that served as a cornice. This was a common feature in Egyptian and Mesopotamian architecture, and the Akkadian word for it, *kululu*, also refers to a headdress or turban. The idea that these would be lifted off the posts of the gates to allow something large to pass through is ingenious but not persuasive in that the usual design of gates would not have unencumbered cornices that could be so easily moved. The alternative, that the lifting of the heads is metaphorical, seems more likely. In Ugaritic literature the gods lower their heads when they are being humbled, and they raise up their heads when they have reason to rejoice.

27:4. dwelling in the house of the Lord. See comment on 23:6.

29:1. comparison to Ugaritic hymn. This psalm has more connections to Ugaritic literature than any other psalm. A commonly cited scholarly view goes so far as to claim that this psalm was originally a Phoenician/Canaanite hymn that was modified and adapted into the Hebrew religious corpus. It is claimed that all three of the places named are in Syria (vv. 6-8) and that the psalm features terms, concepts and even grammatical structures that are more familiar from Ugaritic than from the Old Testament. However, though there are sufficient parallels and similarities to identify Canaanite-like elements in the psalm, there is as yet no evidence of a Canaanite original. All of the elements that have been identified as Canaanite in nature also occur in other clearly Israelite settings, so they only show the general similarities that existed between Israelite and Canaanite language and culture. It is possible that the psalmist is using this psalm to attach to Yahweh many of the Baal functions but not to argue against Baal so much as to elevate Yahweh and proclaim his glory. On the other hand, it would present no problem if the psalmist did choose to pattern his composition after a Canaanite original so that praise was transferred from Baal to Yahweh.

29:1. mighty ones. In Canaanite mythology the "mighty ones" or "sons of god" were lesser gods who were subordinate to El, the king of the gods. In the Old Testament the phrase refers to angels who gathered in Yahweh's heavenly court (see Ps 89:7; 103:20; 147:1; 1 Kings 22:19; Is 6:2; Job 1:6; 2:1).

29:3. thundering voice. Ancient Near Eastern literature is full of references to storm gods whose voices are heard in thunder. These include Baal in Ugaritic and Amarna texts and Adad in Akkadian texts. It is also common in descriptions of Yahweh (see comment on 7:13).

29:5-6. cedars break, mountains skip. In the Ugaritic tale concerning the building of Baal's palace his enthronement is preceded by his voice thundering forth with the result that the high places of the earth leap or quake. A few lines later he is described holding a cedar in his right hand as a weapon. Similarly, in a hymn to Marduk his thundering voice is said to make the earth quake. His word is a deluge that sweeps away lotus trees. The Hebrew verb translated "skip" is often thought to describe a frolicking or gamboling type of motion but is more likely the undulating appearance of a flock of sheep or goats moving along a path (see comment on 2 Sam 6:14-21). This would be an appropriate image to describe the heaving of the earth in an earthquake.

29:6. Sirion. Sirion is equated with Mount Hermon (see comment on Deut 3:9) and is poetically synonymous with Lebanon. Sirion may appear in parallelism with Lebanon in Ugaritic texts, but this is not clear. They are clearly used in parallel in the Gilgamesh Epic as they are broken up during the battle waged against Huwawa by Gilgamesh and Enkidu. They occur as well in other Akkadian literature, showing that they are used not exclusively in Canaanite literature but throughout the ancient Near East.

29:8. desert of Kadesh. The desert or steppe of Kadesh is also mentioned in a Ugaritic text and is presumably in Lebanon in the vicinity of the city of Kadesh near the Orontes River. Alternatively, it could be a reference to Kadesh Barnea in the south, where the Israelites spent much of their time during the forty-year wilderness period.

29:10. enthroned on the flood. A sculptured scene from the temple of Shamash on a tablet from the Neo-Babylonian king Nabu-Apal-Idinna shows Shamash, the sun god, residing on a throne under a cosmic mountain and a number of wavy lines that are considered to represent the cosmic ocean. The scene is remarkably like Yahweh sitting enthroned over

the flood (or better, the celestial sea, see comment on 104:3) in this verse. In this regard, it may be of interest that in Akkadian the word for deluge can also refer to a chaos monster. More prominently in Akkadian literature, the deluge is seen as a weapon of the gods and is sometimes even used in descriptive titles of kings and gods. The deluge can precede the warrior and can be put on by the god going into battle. Shamshi-Adad V refers to the god Ninurta as the exalted lord who rides on the deluge. In contrast to the Hebrew *tehom*, which represents the cosmic waters on the earth, this word, *mabbul*, represents the cosmic waters in the heavens where rain comes from. In Genesis 6—8 it is the *mabbul* that comes on the earth in Noah's time.

30:3. brought up from Sheol, spared from pit. In the Babylonian composition titled *Ludlul Bel Nemeqi* the god Marduk is reported as bringing restoration to one of his followers who has been suffering for unknown reasons: "The Lord took hold of me, the Lord set me on my feet, the Lord gave me life, he rescued me [from the pit,] he summoned me from destruction, [...] he pulled me from the *Hubur* river, [...]. He took my hand" (from W. G. Lambert, *Babylonian Wisdom Literature*, 59).

33:2. harp, lyre. These are both typical musical instruments of the time and are attested in ancient Near Eastern texts, reliefs and paintings as early as the third millennium B.C. There is still some disagreement among authorities as to which of the Hebrew words in this passage ought to be translated "harp" and which one as "lyre." The one the NIV translates "lyre" is here identified as a ten-stringed instrument, while the one translated "harp" is thought to have had fewer strings. Both are hand-held with frames made of wood. A musical text has been discovered at Ugarit that sheds light on Late Bronze Age music. This text has the chords to be played on a lyre accompanying a Hurrian cult hymn.

35:2. shield and buckler. The "shield and buckler" represent the two extremes in personal defensive equipment. Respectively they refer to a small, round shield and a large, full-length body shield; the latter most likely carried by an aide. In the same way spear and javelin (v. 3) represent the full range of offensive weaponry. The Hebrew root (*sgr*) translated "javelin" occurs nowhere else as a weapon in the Old Testament. Herodotus refers to a Scythian double axe (*sagaris*), and the Dead Sea Scrolls use the root for the handle of a

---

For common concepts, metaphors for God and musical terms, see pages 511-18.

lance. In the latter case the text simply speaks of two uses for the same piece of equipment. The long wooden handle can be used to parry and deliver blows as a staff, while the pointed end is used for the finishing blow. There are numerous depictions of these and other Iron Age I-II pieces of military equipment on wall reliefs at the Assyrian cities of Nineveh and Kalah (Nimrud).

36:7. shadow of wings. See the comment on Psalm 17:8. The Canaanite goddess Anat is shown with outstretched wings on an ivory footboard from Ugarit.

36:8. river of delights. Since the word translated "delights" has the same root letters as Eden, there is possibly a reference to the waters flowing out of paradise in this phrase. The association between ancient Near Eastern temples and spring waters is well attested. In fact some temples in Mesopotamia, Egypt and the Ugaritic myth of Baal were considered to have been founded on springs (likened to the primeval waters), which sometimes flowed from the building itself. This would explain the parallel between God's house in the first part of the verse and these rivers (see Ezek 47).

36:9. fountain of life. In many other places the fuller expression "spring of living waters" is used (as in Jer 2:13). Living water refers to flowing spring water (in contrast to collected runoff or rainwater). This is most likely the divine source of life in this world (also see Prov 10:11; 13:14). Certainly in the ancient Near East the gods are considered to be the source of life, but the metaphor of a fountain is not attested.

37:4. desires of heart. In Akkadian texts this phrase is used to refer to the reception of a favorable omen concerning either intended activities or needs such as illness or oppression from which one seeks deliverance. One text reports that when the individual prayed to the gods, he was granted his desire. If the Israelite concept has any similarity, the desire referred to here is not just any desire but particularly the desire that concerns the psalmist in this prayer (which is articulated in v. 6; see Ps 20:4, where the context is a request for one's plans for relieving distress to succeed).

Psalms 42—72

Book Two

42:title. sons of Korah. The superscriptions of Psalms 42; 44—49; 84—85; and 87—88 contain the phrase "sons of Korah." The Korahites are first listed in Numbers 26:58 among the chief Levitical families. In the description of the temple bureaucracy in 1 Chronicles 24—26 the Korahites are listed as "gatekeepers" (1 Chron 26:1). Their association with praising the Lord in 2 Chronicles 20:19 may also be the basis for their mention in the Psalms and as a part of cultic psalmody.

42:1. deer/soul. A number of engraved seals from Judah during the eighth and seventh centuries feature a doe wandering around (seeking water?). O. Keel suggests that this artistic motif's popularity is connected to the metaphor used in this psalm.

42:2. soul. Within the Hebrew Old Testament the word translated as "soul" is *nephesh*. It refers to the "self" or to "a living being" (see Gen 2:7) but not to the "immortal soul" of the New Testament writings. So there is no intimation of the *nephesh* surviving after one's death. The word is related to Akkadian *napašu*, which refers to the neck or throat and by extension to breath. There is no differentiation in the Hebrew usage between the body and the life principle, and therefore in passages like 1 Kings 19:4 *nephesh* is used to mean "life." The body's energy or life force can be drained by a "pouring out of the soul" (1 Sam 1:15; Ps 42:5), as it is in this lament. In Egyptian thinking the *ba* is the animate vital force and is portrayed as a human-headed bird. It is separated from the body at death and is considered immortal. Its place is in heaven rather than in the netherworld to which the body is consigned. Egyptian literature preserves a composition entitled *Dispute Between a Man and His Ba*, which is a discussion of the feasibility of suicide. In contrast, the *ka* is more like the shadow of what is left of the person after he has died. It inhabits the funerary statue and receives the offerings to the dead, and is therefore more like the spirit of the dead. In Mesopotamia this spirit is called the *etemmu*; it receives offerings and must be appeased. It is often associated with a ghost. The other element of one's being in Mesopotamia is called a *zaqiqu* and appears to be closest to the soul. Like the *etemmu* it also survives death, but little else is written about it. In Israelite terminology the spirit of the dead was called *elohim*, as shown when the term is used to refer to Samuel's spirit (1 Sam 28:13).

42:4. festival processions. Although such processions are seldom mentioned, this probably refers to the festal celebration described in Psalm 68:24 in which a procession led by priests and accompanied by singers, string players and other musicians makes its way to the entrance of the Jerusalem temple. Psalm 118:27 also refers to a festal procession in which the participants carry branches in hand, dancing up "to the horns of the altar" (see comment there).

42:6. Hermon. The geographical perspective of the psalmist seems to begin with a very general term, "the land of Jordan," and then gradually becomes more specific with reference to "the heights of Hermon." The Anti-Lebanon range is usually considered the northern border of Israelite control (Josh 11:17), and Mount Hermon, the highest peak, is over nine thousand feet above sea level. Archaeologists have uncovered the remains of more than twenty temples on the slopes of Hermon. This may be due to its prominence and the association of high places with the worship of gods in the ancient world.

42:6. Mount Mizar. The exact location of this place is unknown. The name means "the little hill," and therefore it may refer to a specific peak in the Hermon range. However, this would depend on the geographical perspective and poetic intent of the writer. It is quite possible that the psalmist is referring to Mount Hermon as "little" in terms of its sacredness in comparison to Yahweh's holy hill, Zion (Ps 43:3).

44:title. sons of Korah. See the comment on Psalm 42:title.

44:2-8. divine warrior. See the comment in the sidebar on common concepts in Psalms for more information.

44:20. forgetting the name. A deity's name is often associated with that god's power and essential being (see Ex 3:13-14; Is 9:6). In Jeremiah 23:27 the false prophets plan to remove God's name from the people's memory so they will be enticed to follow Baal. For more information see comment on Deuteronomy 12:5. Failure to invoke the name of Yahweh as their God is a violation of the covenant and cause for God to punish the people (1 Sam 12:9).

44:20. spread hands. The position described here is one of prayer or supplication. It is also mentioned in Ezra 9:5 and in Psalm 88:9. For a full discussion see comment on 2 Chronicles 6:13.

45:title. sons of Korah. See comment on Psalm 42:title.

45:1. verses for king. Psalms directed to the king rather than to the deity are common in the ancient Near East, but this is one of the few examples in the book of Psalms. Like the Egyptian marriage stele of Rameses II, the marriage portrayed in this psalm is the result of military strength—it represents a political alliance that is desirable because of the king's military victories.

45:1. bards. Scribes and sages were the official storytellers of the kings of the ancient Near East. Their command of the traditions and their association with the royal bureaucracy made it appropriate that they perform songs and stories that remind the people of the king's role to feed and protect the land as God's political agent. Thus during the New Year's festival in Babylon, the *Enuma Elish* creation epic was recounted, representatives from other cities came to give their homage to the king, and sacred procession wound their way through the streets of the city to the great temple of Marduk, the patron god of Babylon. When Nehemiah the scribe performs a covenant renewal ceremony, he reads the people the Law, reminding them of their sacred story (Neh 8:1-13).

45:7. anointing with oil of joy. Middle Assyrian Laws feature the bride being anointed by the father of the bridegroom as part of the wedding ceremony, but in this psalm the anointing is part of the kingship (rather than the wedding) section and represents God anointing the king to his position (for more information see comment on 1 Sam 10:1).

45:8. fragrant robes. This psalm contains language and detail suitable for a marriage anthem or the anointing of a king (Ps 133:2). In the ancient Near East these two were combined in the sacred marriage ritual described in Ur III, which involved a magnificently robed king processing to the temple, portraying himself as the god as he participated in a marriage/fertility ritual. It seems likely that the robes of the participants would be oiled and dusted with fragrant herbs and perfumes. For discussion of these substances see the comments on Song of Songs 1:3 and Proverbs 7:17.

45:8. ivory palaces. For the lavish use of ivory to decorate furniture and wall panels see comments on 1 Kings 22:39 and Amos 3:15; 6:4. The wealth of a nation might well be displayed in the king's palace—a sign of power and prestige for the state.

45:8. string music. This translation is based on an emendation of the Hebrew text from *minni* to a plural noun *minnim*, based on a similar usage of the word in Psalm 150:4. It is not clear what sort of instrument this refers to except as a generic term for strings.

45:9. gold of Ophir. See the comments on 1 Kings 22:48 and Isaiah 13:12 for this choicest quality gold.

For common concepts, metaphors for God and musical terms, see pages 511-18.

45:12. gift. Letters from Mari record how the king of Mari sought to contract a marriage with the daughter of the king of Aleppo. From this correspondence it is clear that the year-long negotiations were considered as finalized when the wedding gift arrived at the palace of Mari and was deemed acceptable by the king.

45:12. daughter of Tyre. While it is possible that a particular daughter of the king of Tyre is mentioned here, it is more likely that the expression is a euphemism for the inhabitants of this Phoenician port city. Similar expressions exist, such as "daughter of Zion" (Ps 9:14) and "daughter of Babylon" (Ps 137:8). Since the Phoenicians had become quite wealthy as a result of their control over the carrying trade in the Mediterranean Sea, gifts from Tyre were expected to be lavish, exotic and expensive. Note here the parallel with "men of wealth."

45:13. gold threads. Clothing was a status marker in the ancient world. The princess bride in this psalm is dressed in the richest garments. Like the young bride in Ezekiel 16:10-13, she wears elaborately embroidered robes, probably dyed with Phoenician purple. Adding to the majesty of her ensemble is gold stitching. It would have been impossible to create a durable thread made from gold, but gold dust could have been encrusted into the thread and the garment to give it this added touch of wealth. Exodus 39:3 explains the process by which gold was worked into each thread used to weave the garment.

46:title. sons of Korah. See comment on 42:title.

46:9. wars cease. Just as Yahweh functions as the divine warrior to aid the Israelites in battle (see the comment on Josh 3:17), the God of the covenant is also the source of peace and prosperity. This theme of world peace is one of the hoped for aspects of the restoration of the nation in prophetic and apocalyptic literature. As Isaiah 2:4 notes, God will settle all disputes between nations, and "they will beat their . . . spears into pruning hooks." Similarly, Ezekiel states that one of the means Yahweh will use to insure that "the nations know that I am the Lord" will be to create an age when weapons of war can be used for fuel (Ezek 39:7-9).

47:title. sons of Korah. See comment on 42:title.

47:5-8. enthronement in ancient Near East. One of the most important ceremonies in the ancient Near East was the ritual of enthronement of a king and the investiture of that person with his symbols of office. This can be seen in the investment of Marduk with his royal insignia in the *Enuma Elish* creation epic.

He was named king and then given his scepter, throne, robes and weapons by the other gods. This ritual was mirrored in the coronation practice in Assyria in which all court officials surrendered the symbols of office, resigning so that the king could decide whether to reappoint them to their duties. In Mesopotamia enthronement was also tied into the majesty and power of the gods since it was believed that "kingship descended from on high." For instance, in the prologue to Hammurabi's code of laws the king of Babylon states that the gods called him by name and installed him to carry out their commands on earth, including the restoration of cities, purification of sacred rites, and to "establish truth and justice as the declaration of the land." During the Babylonian New Year's festival (*Akitu*), the grant of power to the king had to be reinvested in his person, so an enthronement ritual was reenacted. Many scholars assume that Israel used psalms like this one in their own enthronement festival (for Yahweh and his king), but no positive proof has yet come forth to confirm that hypothesis.

48:title. sons of Korah. See comment on 42:title.

48:1. holy mountain. The book of Psalms repeatedly refers to Mount Zion as Yahweh's "holy hill" or holy mountain (Ps 2:6; 3:4; 15:1; 43:3; 99:9). However, it should be understood that this place ascribes its importance and sanctity entirely from God's presence there. Other sacred mountains are associated with the gods: Baal with Mount Zaphon, and Marduk and others with the artificial mountains, the ziggurat temples of Mesopotamia.

48:2. heights of Zaphon. This refers to Mount Casius (Jebel el-Aqra, elev. 5807 feet), twenty-five or thirty miles northeast of Ugarit, the mountain associated with the dwelling place of Baal (see the comment on Is 14:13). In Ugaritic literature Mount Zaphon is considered to be the mountain of the gods where the divine assembly meets. In the announcements of Baal's messengers Mount Zaphon is praised as beautiful and a hill of victory. In the context of this psalm it may be serving either as a direction, north, or as a reference to the temple at Dan, technically on Mount Hermon at the northern boundary of Israel. However, it is also possible that in this psalm Yahweh is seen as a universal God who will replace all other gods in their sacred locales, with Zion becoming what Zaphon had once been considered, the seat of God.

48:7. ships of Tarshish. See the comments on 2 Chronicles 9:21 and Isaiah 23:1.

48:9. worship within temple. Unlike the kings

who fled away at the sight of God's power (48:4-7), the Israelite pilgrims gain great comfort from the majesty of God's presence at Zion because that is where their deliverance comes from. The use of *ḥesed* (NIV: "unfailing love"), the legal term employed in connection with the covenant, indicates a sense of fulfillment on their part and is the basis for their fervent worship. "Within" in this case may be simply entrance into Jerusalem (Mount Zion) or into the Temple Mount complex, since pilgrims would not be allowed access to the inner precincts of the temple itself.

48:12-13. towers, ramparts and citadels in a fortified city. The basic architecture of a fortified city functioned as its defense system and also served as a form of monumental display of the physical power of the state. Towers were placed at regular intervals within the wall system and dominated each gate. The ramparts, ranging as high as forty feet (as at Tell Dan) were set between the towers, often in an offset-inset pattern that provided more angles for archery and other missiles dropped or thrown by the defenders. Within the city a citadel would be constructed as the strong point in case the city walls were breached. Since it was usually constructed at a high elevation, the citadel tower could also serve as a link in the signal fire system used to communicate between cities (see the comments on Is 32:14 and Neh 3:26 for the Hill of Ophel in Jerusalem). For further discussion of towers and wall systems as city defenses, see the comment on Isaiah 2:15. For discussion of fortified gateways, see the comment on Isaiah 54:12.

49:title. sons of Korah. See comment on 42:title.

49:4. proverb. The term translated here as "proverb" is *mashal.* It has a wide range of meanings: "allegory" (Ezek 17:2), "poem" (Num 21:27), "oracle" (Num 23:7). In this case, as in Proverbs 10:1, it refers to an "instruction" from God to the people, warning the Israelites specifically but relying on the universality of a wisdom theme so that "all peoples" can be addressed, not just the Israelites. It may also be compared to the "dark saying" in Habakkuk 2:6 in which the Assyrian aggressors are taunted with the loss of their ill-gotten wealth.

49:4. wisdom accompanied by harp. The measured parallelism of the verse would be aided in its rhythm by the strumming of a harp or zither. This might be compared to the musician employed by Elisha when he spoke

an oracle (2 Kings 3:15). A similar occurrence also appears in the Egyptian *Tale of Wenamon* where a musician and a prophet are paired. Certainly words of praise were chanted or sung to the sound of lyre and harp (Ps 92:1-3). It would be natural for minstrels and story tellers to recite the mighty acts of God and of Israel's heroes to the sound of music (Judg 5:11).

49:14. death will feed on them. In the Ugaritic Baal epic the image of death, the god Mot, is of a ravening monster whose open mouth consumes the living: "The dust of the grave devours its pray. Death eats whatever it wants with both hands." Job (24:19) describes a similar picture of Sheol, the underworld, which "snatches away those who have sinned." Job 18:2-13 also contains this description of death devouring the limbs of the wicked. Proverbs 1:12 describes the grave as a mouth that swallows its victims, and this same concept is echoed in the epic of Baal and Anath where the god of death, Mot, is said to "devour its prey," eating them "with both hands."

49:15. Israelite hope. Like the people of Mesopotamia, with whom they shared a number of religious and social ideas, the Israelites did not have a widespread understanding of resurrection from the dead, a last judgment or an afterlife of reward or punishment. This only becomes evident in Judaism in the postexilic period, as exemplified by Daniel 12:2. Thus in this context the psalmist is contrasting the fate of the psalmist's enemies, for whom there will be no escape from the grave, and the psalmist's own hope of redemption by Yahweh. It is unlikely that the writer is referring, as some have suggested, to escape from death altogether in the manner of Enoch (Gen 5:24) or Elijah (2 Kings 2:11). The NIV's inclusion of the phrase "to himself" is totally interpretive, not being found in the Hebrew text. The concept of God "taking" a person as a reference to saving his life can be seen clearly in Psalm 18:16-17, where the NIV translates the same phrase as "took hold of me." See the comments on afterlife in the sidebar on common concepts in Psalms.

50:title. Asaph. This may be an abbreviation for the "sons of Asaph" and thus a reference to one of the temple choirs or their repertoire of music. In Ezra 2:41 the singers who returned to Palestine with Ezra were "descendants of Asaph." According to the list of temple musicians in 1 Chronicles 6:39, Asaph was appointed by David to serve in the Jeru-

---

For common concepts, metaphors for God and musical terms, see pages 511-18.

salem temple as Heman's associate.

50:1-4. sun god as judge imagery. There is a drawing at the top of the seven-foot-high diorite pillar containing a copy of Hammurabi's law code. It depicts the Babylonian sun god Shamash seated on his throne with Hammurabi standing before him. In the prologue that follows, the king accepts the responsibility "to make justice prevail in the land" and "to rise like Shamash over all humankind." He becomes the god's judicial representative for the Babylonian empire. Shamash's role as divine judge is also found in Akkadian prayers for forgiveness. The Egyptian *Hymn to the Aten,* composed for the court of Pharaoh Akhenaten in the fourteenth century B.C., contains creation imagery very similar to that in this psalm. This is especially the case with regard to a sense of order and universality: "Your glory shines high above the land; your rays enrich the land you have created." See the comment on God as judge in the sidebar on common concepts in Psalms.

50:8-15. ideology of sacrifice. A proper understanding of the purpose of sacrifice is outlined in this psalm. This is intended to serve as a contrasting ideology to the sacrificial practices of Israel's neighbors. Two points are emphasized here. First, God does not need to be sustained with food like the gods of Mesopotamia and Egypt (as in the Gilgamesh flood epic, where the gods flock like starving flies to Utnapishtim's sacrifice). Second, and perhaps more important, is that the Israelites have an obligation to God to make "thank offerings" as a sign of their acknowledgment of the covenant. It is the failure of the people to differentiate between ritual and the knowledge of God that is so often condemned by the prophets (1 Sam 15:22; Hos 6:6). Micah in particular parodies these ineffectual offerings and notes that all God requires of Israel is "to act justly and love mercy" (Mic 6:8).

50:21. god like people. God accuses the people of forgetting that the deity is not "just like them," willing to look the other way when evil occurs or even able to approve of their sinful actions. This ultimate form of anthropomorphizing God is a terrible crime deserving of rebuke and punishment. Divine silence is not to be considered a sign of weakness or of disinterest. Jeremiah in his "temple sermon" (Jer 7:9-11) makes similar accusations, noting that the people of Judah seem to believe they can commit any sin and then come to the temple and proclaim, "We are safe." He declares that God is watching them and is not blind to their deeds. The Old Testament begins its story by relating how people wanted to become like God and thereby fell into sin. Having failed in their attempt, human history becomes the story of people remolding God in their own image. The gods of Mesopotamia and Egypt are described as acting much like humans—engaging in unthinking acts of violence (the Gilgamesh and Atrahasis flood stories) or tricking humans out of a potential reward (Adapa)—but they still have superhuman powers and must be treated with official respect. The psalmist and wisdom writers raise Yahweh above the level of any other god to an ideal of moral and just behavior far beyond anything attainable by god or human (see Job 42:2-6).

51:1-2. mechanism for removing sins. In the ancient Near East it was not sins that were removed but the deity who was appeased. The individual only became aware of sin when he or she experienced circumstances considered the punishment of deity. The goal then became to relieve the anger of the deity (whether such anger was believed to be justified or not). When they asked for sins to be removed ("strip off my misdeeds like a garment"), they meant that the deity should be willing to overlook their sin, put away wrath and restore his favor. The rituals that accompanied this sort of approach to deity were meant to purify the individual and pacify the deity. The ritual did not remove sin; it only enabled the individual to hope that the deity would offer absolution from the sin. In Israel we should think in terms not of sins being eternally removed but of the sacrifices cleansing away the desecration of God's presence caused by sin (see comment on Lev 1:4, "atonement"). The rituals paved the way for forgiveness (see comment on Lev 4:13-32). This psalm is not talking about that process (v. 16). Only God's gracious act would remove a sin from the record books. It is understood that the penitent can only ask, not demand, absolution of sins (see Ps 32:10). What is asked for is a display of God's compassionate mercy based on the supplicant's trust and the covenantal promise to Israel. God's favor may then "blot out" sin in much the same way that a parchment scroll is scraped clean or a clay tablet is either washed clean (see Num 5:23) or broken. This metaphor is mentioned in a Babylonian ritual text, where it states that a king may order that "the tablet of my sins be broken," thereby canceling or commuting debt or criminal charges. Similarly, in Hammurabi's Code an illegal contract for the purchase of a soldier's land may be cancelled by breaking the cuneiform tablet. Mesopotamian literature contains references both to tablets recording evil deeds (in the *Shurpu* texts) and those recording good deeds.

51:3. knowledge of offense. In the ancient Near East individuals typically claimed that they were mystified concerning what they could possibly have done to offend deity. There were several factors that contributed to this ignorance. First, the gods of the ancient Near East had offered no permanent revelation of themselves that might be used as a guide. Second, polytheism posed a problem in that a deed that pleased one god might potentially offend another. Third, the gods were not characterized as acting consistently from one day to the next, thus making it difficult to assess one's standing. Finally, offenses often took the form of neglecting rituals that the individual was not even aware of. As a result, in Babylonian penitential literature *(shigus)* for instance, the offender sometimes simply accepts blame for all sorts of sin, hoping in the process to confess to whatever has offended the deity. Yet at other times he lists offenses and asserts that he is well aware of his sins. In the Hittite *Prayers of Mursilis* confession of one's guilt is the step toward reconciliation with his lord. In Israel the Law was clear enough and offenses could be clearly identified.

51:4. against deity only. If David is identifying Yahweh alone as the one sinned against, whom is he ruling out? Certainly he has wronged Bathsheba and Uriah. It is important to notice that in the context the issue concerns who has a right to pass judgment and carry out sentence (second half of v. 4). In Israel the family of the murder victim had a right to blood vengeance, and there were always political enemies who would be happy to stylize themselves as the arm of God's justice against a wayward king. Perhaps by this statement David is limiting his acknowledgment of culpability, so that only Yahweh has the right of punishment.

51:5. conceived and born in sin. As is so often the case when speaking to God, the penitent draws the contrast between divine perfection and inherent human weakness (see Job 4:17; Ps 130:3; Jer 17:9). The same point is made in a nineteenth-dynasty Egyptian prayer to Amon that confesses that it is "normal" for humans to do wrong just as it is "normal" for the god to be merciful. It should be emphasized in this context that the act of conception was not considered sinful. Sexual activity, including intercourse, pregnancy and childbirth, all rendered the participants ritually unclean (see Lev 15:16-33), but within marriage this was never declared to be sinful. Statements such as those in Job 15:14 and Isaiah 6:5 simply define humans as unclean by nature in relation to God's absolute purity. Although this psalm has been used by some commentators to bolster the doctrine of "original sin," it seems a more appropriate interpretation to see it as part of the general confession of the penitent. In Mesopotamian incantations the sentiment is expressed that there is no one who has not sinned—everyone who exists is sinful. An admonition to confess the sinfulness of the human state appears in the Egyptian teachings of Amenemope, "Say not: 'I have no wrongdoing.'" The Israelites would have agreed with that theology in that they would have acknowledged a general inclination to sin that was characteristic of all people. They did not go the next step of Christian theology by seeing Adam's sin imputed to people.

51:6. internalization as divine expectation. Based on the birth image in the previous verse and a similar phrase in Job 38:36, it is likely that E. Dalglish is correct in his interpretation of this verse as referring to obtaining knowledge while still within the womb (the mother's "innermost part"). The penitent is acknowledging that his sin is not to be excused for lack of knowledge. He is aware, even from the womb, of what is right behavior, and he has failed to obey what he knows to be lawful (see v. 3). A similar image of prenatal learning is found in the Egyptian *Hymn to the Aten*. The writer repeatedly praises the god for supplying all that is necessary for human survival, even within the womb. To counter human nature's tendency to disobey, Egyptian religious thought is filled with the need to internalize *ma'at*, "truth." It is described as the bread that sustains humans (as in the royal annals of Queen Hatshepsut).

51:7. hyssop. This dwarf bush, *Origanum syriacum* (majoram), grows wild among the rocks in Palestine. The aromatic fragrance emitted by its blue or reddish flowers and leaves may be the origin of its presumed medicinal value. In the biblical text, however, it is associated with rituals of purification, as in the ceremony associated with the cleansing of a leper in Leviticus 14:4-6. They also are employed in the ritual sacrifice of the red heifer (Num 19:6) and in the marking of Israelite doorframes during the Passover (Ex 12:22).

51:7. white = purity. As noted in Isaiah 1:18,

For common concepts, metaphors for God and musical terms, see pages 511-18.

in the biblical tradition white is identified with purity or joy. Dark colors, especially black, are used to signify mourning or lamentation—both of which are associated with states of impurity (see Ps 35:13; Zech 3:3-5). In an Assyrian prayer the king calls on his god to "whiten" and thus free his heart from his sin of blasphemy. In Akkadian the verb "to brighten" overlaps with the verb "to make white." In one Babylonian magical text the petitioner requests that he might "become as pure as heaven, as cleansed as the earth, and as bright as the center of heaven."

51:10. pure heart. Having acknowledged his sinful condition from his birth, the penitent now asks God, the only power able to grant his request, to purify his "heart" (the seat of the intellect in Hebrew tradition). A Sumerian prayer of repentance also pleads for divine mercy from the gods and transformation of "the sin I have done . . . into goodness." This is similar to the petition in the *Lament over the Destruction of Ur,* which calls on the goddess Nanna to insure that "every evil heart of its people be pure before thee!" The concept of regeneration or redirection is also found in Ezekiel's oracle of a restored nation, in which God promises to "give you a new heart" (Ezek 36:26).

51:11. removing holy spirit. While God's spirit occurs many times in the text, only in Isaiah 63:10-14 is the expression "holy spirit" used synonymously with Yahweh's presence. To have that presence removed or to be excluded from communion with God is the ultimate punishment imaginable. On a national scale it would be the end of the covenant relationship and the total destruction of the people (Jer 23:39; compare Hosea's third child "Not My People" in Hos 1:9). For a reigning monarch, who is God's representative, being cut off from Yahweh's voice or presence would be the signal that his dynasty has been rejected and will come to an end (see the comments concerning Saul's plight in 1 Sam 16:14; 28:6). The petitioner in the Sumerian "Prayer to Every God" also pleads that the god "not cast thy servant down," presumably away from divine favor, because of his transgressions.

51:16. no delight in sacrifice. Like Jeremiah's direct attacks on what he considered a totally corrupt cultic system in Jerusalem (Jer 6:20; 7:4; 31:31-35), the psalmist denies the value of animal sacrifice without an ethical dimension to sustain it. The Egyptian *Instruction of Merikare* contains this same sentiment: "More acceptable is the character of one upright of heart than the ox of the evildoer." They share Samuel's (1 Sam 15:22) and Hosea's (Hos 6:6)

argument that God prefers a devout worshiper's heart and prayers, not his or her ritual pantomime (see comments on 1 Sam 15:22; Is 1:16-17; and Jer 7:9). This is also noted in Babylonian wisdom literature, where the pious are encouraged to pay daily homage "with sacrifice, prayer and appropriate incense-offering." But most important is to "feel solicitude of heart" toward their god.

52:2-4. evil tongue. The tongue in this expression is synonymous with the person. Similar examples of this metaphor can be found in the Assyrian *Words of Ahiqar,* where the "tongue of the ruler" is equated with his sovereign power. The charge made in this psalm is that the deceitful choose to speak and do evil (compare Prov 12:17), a complaint also registered in the Middle Egyptian *Dispute over Suicide.*

53:5. scattering bones. One common image of utter defeat and hopelessness is the battlefield covered with the scattered, bleached bones of the slain. The Assyrian annals of Shalmaneser III report the destruction of their foes, with "pillars of skulls" erected and battle sites covered with corpses. Ezekiel 37 uses this as the basis of his oracle of restoration. Jeremiah 8:1-2 prophesies the violation of the tombs of false priests and unfaithful kings, with their bones scattered about "like refuse lying on the ground." See also the comment on 22:14.

54:1. plea for vindication. Based on the premise of the retribution principle (see comment in the sidebar on common concepts in Psalms), a person who was suffering was believed to be receiving punishment from God. Since God was considered to be just, then the punishment would have been deserved. The psalmist's troubles would therefore be taken as evidence of his sinfulness. Vindication of the psalmist would then come when God intervened to turn the tables and punish his enemies. Such action from God would proclaim his innocence and show that he had not lost God's favor. In this sense God is his only hope. The eloquent peasant of Egyptian wisdom literature also calls on his god-king, Pharaoh, as his "last hope" and "only judge."

54:6. freewill offering. See the comment on Numbers 15:1-31 for the general elements of the Israelite sacrificial system. A "freewill" offering is a nonobligatory sacrifice, made in thanks or to fulfill a vow (see the comment on Lev 22:17-30). It may be offered at the altar with the intention of partaking in a communal meal with God or as a whole burnt offering. For the role of this offering in Psalms see comment on 50:8-15.

55:14. throng at house of God. Israelites were

instructed to attend the annual pilgrimage festivals and bring their sacrifices to the temple in Jerusalem (see the comments on Ex 23:17 and Deut 16:16). A sense of fellowship was created as large groups of people and close friends joined in this unified (LXX uses *en homonoia*, "in unity," in translating this verse) religious journey, physically demonstrating their commitment to the covenant. The psalmist here seems extremely distressed that someone who had shared this pilgrimage could betray him.

55:15. alive to the grave. The judgment sought by the psalmist on his enemies is an untimely death. Like the rebellious Levite Korah and his followers (Num 16:31-35), they are to be swallowed up by the earth without any further opportunity to commit mischief. The parallel here to "by surprise" clarifies that going alive to the grave does not mean they will not die. Rather a sudden death is requested. The image of death as an open mouth swallowing the unaware is found in the Ugaritic Baal epic, where the god of the underworld, Mot, is described as a "pool luring the wild oxen," which "eats whatever it wants with both hands."

55:21. speech/heart. An Akkadian proverb draws the same distinction, observing that a man may speak friendly words with his lips but have a heart full of murder. The incantation series *Shurpu* speaks of one whose speech is straightforward but whose heart is devious.

56:8. scroll/record. Like the journal of remembrance kept for future justice's sake in Daniel 7:10 and Malachi 3:16 (see comments on both), the psalmist refers to a record that God has kept of his misery during his life's wanderings. This written repository is compared to saving the sufferer's tears in a bottle or skin bag. In both cases the imperative form is used to show how important this record is so that only the deserving remain in God's "book of life" (see Ps 69:28).

57:1. shadow of your wings. It is possible that the psalmist is playing off the metaphor of God as a protective eagle sheltering its young with outstretched wings found in the "Song of Moses" in Deuteronomy 32:10-11. This image of eagles' wings is a common metaphor for God's covenantal saving acts (see Ex 19:4). This reference may also be a reflection of the wings of the cherubim on the ark of the covenant (1 Sam 4:4; 1 Kings 6:23-28) or the winged seraphs said to surround Yahweh in

Isaiah's call narrative (Is 6:2). The metaphor of taking refuge under the wings of deity is found also in other psalms (36:7; 61:4; 91:4) and is consistently related to issues of care and protection connected to the covenant. The metaphor is also known from other ancient Near Eastern cultures, particularly Egyptian, where even disembodied wings represent protection. Deities with wings are often portrayed overshadowing the king. Likewise an ivory from Arslan Tash dated to the eighth century shows characters in human form with wings protecting a figure in the center.

57:4. enemies as lions. Though in seventh-century Assyrian literature the lions' pit occurs as a metaphor for vicious and antagonistic courtiers of the king, the combination with weapons here opens up another possibility. Ugaritic sources refer to an archery division that marches under the standard of the lion-goddess. The psalmist could also be alluding to a group of mercenaries going by that standard.

57:8. harp and lyre. Praise accompanied by both harp and "ten-stringed lyre" is also found in Psalm 33:2 (see comment there). In Psalm 98:5-6 the harp is paired with trumpets and the ram's horn to sharpen the enthusiasm of the psalmist's celebration and possibly to engender a prophetic utterance (see Elisha in 2 Kings 3:15). A similar joyous anticipation of the dawn is found in the Egyptian *Hymn to the Aten*, in which "the two lands of Egypt rejoice" at daybreak when the sun disk rises over the horizon.

58:4. cobra with stopped ears. The metaphor is an attempt to equate the fool/wicked, who will not listen, with a cobra (a term found in both Egyptian and Ugaritic) who pays no attention to the snake charmer. Both cause pain and suffering by their unreasonable behavior. Although snakes do not have hands to cover their ears (an internal organ), the issue here has to do with unnatural, perverse actions. Along this line, the Egyptian *Instruction of Ankhsheshonqy* notes that there is no point in trying to instruct a fool, who will not listen and will hate you for attempting to teach him something. Similarly, the *Instruction of Amenemope* cautions that the words of fools are more dangerous than storm winds.

58:5. snake charmer. The profession of snake charmer must have involved an intimate knowledge of the serpent's behavior pattern. One admonition that could well have come from this stock in trade is found in the *Instruc-*

tion of Ankhsheshonqy, stating that a well-fed snake will not strike. The charmer may have also used magical incantations in addition to music or some physical props to control the serpents in their act. Snakes were greatly feared in the ancient world as magical beings as well as for their venom. Both Egyptian and Mesopotamian literatures contain examples of incantations against serpents and their bites. The word translated "charmed" here should not evoke cartoonlike images of swaying serpents hypnotized by pipe-playing swamis. Alternatively it may refer to snakes against which the incantations are ineffective. Akkadian texts also speak of snakes that are "unconjurable."

58:6-11. imprecations compared to incantations. This psalm is known as an "imprecatory" psalm because it calls down curses (imprecations) on the enemy. In the ancient Near East such curses were enhanced or activated by magical rituals and spells, but this sort of practice would have been unacceptable in the biblical system. Imprecatory psalms can be best understood against the background of the retribution principle (see discussion in the sidebar on common concepts in Psalms). Since God's justice was seen as requiring punishment proportional to the seriousness of the sin, the psalmist is calling down the curses that would be appropriate if justice were to be maintained. These are the same magnitude of curses that God pronounces on his enemies (see Is 13:15-16). The forceful language of this passage contains aspects of an East Semitic curse formula that relies on the deity to carry out vengeance on the enemy nations. An example of this type of indirect curse is found in the vassal treaties of the Assyrian king Esarhaddon as he calls on a host of gods to do the treaty-breaker harm. It is also employed, in the addition of ritual acts of execration, in the Aramaic Sefire inscription: "Just as this bow and these arrows are broken, so may Inurta and Hadad break the bow of Mati'el and the bow of his nobles." The psalmist indirectly curses by imprecation, calling on God to "laugh at them" in their puny efforts to menace Israel. He does not employ magical incantations or execration rituals against them but instead relies on God to render these peoples impotent—breaking their power and their weapons of destruction (see Jer 49:35; 51:56; Ezek 39:3).

59:title. incident. It seems most likely that the event mentioned in the superscription comes from the time prior to David's accession to the throne, when he was an outlaw and continually harassed by Saul's men. For examples of

this type of continuous surveillance and pursuit see 1 Samuel 19:11 and the narrative in 1 Samuel 24.

60:title. incident. The editors of the book of Psalms sometimes attempt to link historical events from the life of David with the subject of a psalm. In this case the reference is to David's campaign against the Arameans and Edomites (see the comments on 2 Sam 8:3-14).

60:3. wine that makes one stagger. The power of God's wrath against the people is compared to a potent cup of wine, which makes them stagger in a drunken/impotent manner (see Is 51:17, 22 and the comment on Is 28:7). This cup may be compared with the cup of bitterness drunk by the suspected adulteress in Numbers 5:16-22 and with the cup of salvation in Psalm 116:13. See comment on 75:8.

60:4. banner. Battle flags and standards were used by the military as signaling devices and rallying points for the army or were hung from city walls (see Jer 4:6). Their colors and insignia designated their allegiance and would in many cases have included a symbol of the god(s) who were expected to participate in the battle along with the human forces (see Jer 50:2). The Assyrian army of Shalmaneser III traveled with its "standards" attached to the royal chariot. When camp was made, they were erected near the royal pavilion and became the focal point for sacrifice and acts of devotion to the gods.

60:6. parceling Shechem. Since the covenant promise had always included God's grant of land to the Israelites, it would be within Yahweh's right to parcel out Shechem (Tell Balata, forty miles north of Jerusalem) as a prize of war to those who were true to the covenant. Perhaps because of its proximity to two nearby peaks, Mount Gerizim and Mount Ebal, it has had a long history as a sacred site. Shechem is known from many ancient sources, including the Egyptian records of Sen-Usert III (nineteenth century B.C.) and the El Amarna tablets (fourteenth century B.C.). Nearly continuous occupation is evidenced through the second and first millennia, demonstrating the importance of this strategic city on the highway network running north from Egypt through Beersheba and Jerusalem and on to Damascus. It was Abram's first stop in Canaan. Jacob purchased land near the city in Genesis 33:18-20, and thus it is connected to the origins of granting the Promised Land to the Israelites. The fertile soil in this area promoted agriculture as well as good grazing.

60:6. Valley of Succoth. The city of Succoth is located east of the Jordan River near the point where it connects with the Jabbok River, an area known as the Ghor Abu Obeideh. This is a fertile region which like Shechem has a connection with the Jacob narrative (Gen 33:17) and could thus represent the total area of the Promised Land within the covenant agreement. A number of archaeologists have identified it with the site of Tell Deir 'Alla, based on Egyptian records (the Stele of Shishak) and cultural remains dating from the Chalcolithic to Iron Age II. The name, which means "booths," would be appropriate for the temporary housing of this region's mixed population of pastoral nomads and miners (evidence of smelting has been found in Iron I levels). It is located in the valley just west of the highlands of Gilead as the land comes down to the Jordan.

60:7. Gilead, Manasseh. The Transjordanian region of Gilead, roughly lying between the Yarmuk River in the north and the Arnon River in the south, was given in the distribution after the conquest to the tribes of Gad (see the comment on Josh 13:24-29) and to Manasseh (see the comment on Josh 13:30-31). For the general distribution of the tribal settlements in this region, see the comment on Numbers 32:34-42.

60:7. Ephraim, Judah as helmet and scepter. In this metaphorical portrayal of Yahweh as the divine warrior, the two kingdoms of Israel (Ephraim) and Judah serve as helmet and staff of office respectively. A similar image is found in Zechariah 9:13, where Judah is God's bow and Ephraim his arrow. The term translated "helmet" is not used elsewhere as a reference to armor or headgear. The Hebrew text refers to "a fortress for my head" or perhaps "my chief fortress." The scepter is now often identified as a ceremonial engraved mace, which kings are sometimes portrayed holding in their hands as a symbol of office. It is referred to elsewhere in Genesis 49:10 and Numbers 21:18.

60:8. Moab as washbasin. This may be a reference to Moab's proximity to the Dead Sea, but it certainly denotes the subjugation of that nation by Yahweh (repeated in Ps 108:9). They are forced into servanthood, being placed in a position where they must wash the feet of their master (compare Jn 13:5). The container referred to here is usually used for cooking but is a multipurpose pot/basin that comes in various sizes. Washbasins were typically used for ritual washing or ritual bathing, and occur in lists of fine gifts in the Amarna tablets. The imagery here is obscure.

60:8. sandal to Edom. Sandals were the ordinary footwear in the ancient Near East, but they were also a symbolic item of clothing. This may have been due to the fact that land was purchased based on whatever size triangle of land the buyer could walk off in an hour, a day, a week or a month (1 Kings 21:16-17). Land was surveyed in triangles, and a benchmark was constructed of fieldstones to serve as a boundary marker (Deut 19:14). Since they walked off the land in sandals, the sandals became the moveable title to that land. Casting a sandal was a symbolic, legal gesture employed in those situations where a levir refused to accept his responsibility to a widow. She in turn then removed his sandal, the symbol of ownership and inheritance, and cast it at him. This signified his loss of inheritance rights to the lands of his relative (see Deut 25:9 and Ruth 4:7-8). Land transfers in the Nuzi texts also involved replacing the old owner's foot on the land with that of the new owner. In this verse God aggressively casts a sandal onto Edom as a gesture of conquest or the assumption of ownership of that nation's lands.

60:9. fortified city/Edom. Since the "fortified city" is parallel to Edom, one is inclined to think of the major fortified city in Edom. This would be Bozrah, whose name is built from the same root as the word used here for fortified city. Bozrah was the capital of ancient Edom and is to be identified with Buseirah in the northern region of the country. It guards a portion of the king's highway and is fairly close to the copper mines found five miles to the southwest at Wadi Dana. Excavations demonstrate seventh- or sixth-century levels from the most heavily fortified and largest settlement in the area.

61:4. shelter in wings. See comment on 57:1.

61:8. king fulfilling vows. Kings in the ancient Near East owed obligations to the god(s) who were the source of their power. For instance, at Mari the kings were required to make annual sacrifices to gods all over their kingdom, to rebuild their temples and to insure that the priestly community was receiving its due income. In addition, special vows were taken to insure good crops, a victory in war (see Judg 11:30-31; 1 Sam 14:24) or to obtain an heir. An example of this latter effort is found in the Ugaritic epic of Keret, in which the king goes to the sanctuary of Asherah and makes a vow to give the goddess "double the bride price in silver" of a royal wife if he is al-

---

For common concepts, metaphors for God and musical terms, see pages 511-18.

lowed to marry the princess Hurriya.

62:9. highborn. As in Psalm 4:2, this term, *benê 'ish*, functions as both a euphemism for the wealthy and powerful as well as a generic term for all men of influence. Both Egyptian and Babylonian contain similar expressions for this class of individuals. For example, Babylonian texts regularly make the distinction between "a gentleman" and an "ungentlemanly person."

63:1. soul/body and ancient anthropology. As noted in the comment on Psalm 42:2 on the concept of "soul" in the ancient Near East, the cultures of the Mesopotamians and Israelites did not differentiate between soul and body. Both represented the individual being, not a separate spirit or entity. In Egypt, however, the life force, *ka*, contained the essence of animated life as well as the sustenance to maintain living beings. After death the Egyptian's "soul" or *ba* manifested that life essence and was often depicted in tomb paintings as birds with human faces. The ability to differentiate between the living being and his soul is found in the Middle Egyptian wisdom piece titled *The Dispute Between a Man and His Ba*. In this document a man argues with his soul. In his despair the man states that the troubles of life demand that he commit suicide. This angers the *ba* and it threatens to leave him, a threat that the man takes very seriously since it would mean that he would not be resurrected into the afterlife.

63:7. shadow of wings. See comment on 57:1.

65:4. living in the temple courts. While the temple complex was primarily the realm of the priestly order, it was the desire of every member of the covenant community to "dwell" in God's presence (see Ps 84:2 and 96:8). The importance of the temple precinct as the place where God dwelt can be found in its use for prayer and in judicial proceedings when someone comes to take an oath "before a god" (see Hammurabi's Code). In this psalm the concept of being the "chosen" is emphasized, along with the closeness of Yahweh's promise and power. For more information see comment on 23:6.

65:7. stilling the seas. This phrase relates to Yahweh's creative power over watery chaos (as in Gen 1:2-10 and Ps 93:3). It is quite likely that the Israelite psalmist is also drawing on the terminology of the religious epics of Mesopotamia (the *Enuma Elish* creation story in which Marduk defeats Tiamat, the goddess of the primeval waters) and of Ugarit. In the latter, Baal has a monumental struggle with Yamm, the god of the sea. The use of this cosmic battle motif in other psalms (73:14;

89:9-10) is another indication of how the Israelite writers employed the religious drama of other cultures but used it as a way of demonstrating the supremacy of Yahweh over all other gods. See comment on 107:29.

65:12. grasslands of the desert. In this image of fertility even in the wilderness, the psalmist describes grasslands flourishing in the desert. During the rainy season the desert does support a growth of annuals and wild flowers in addition to the stunted scrubs, such as the white saxaul *(Haloxylon persicum)*. These cling to the salty and sandy soils along the wadi beds and upper slopes where more moisture falls or collects.

66:10. refined like silver. See the comments on Proverbs 17:3 and 25:4.

67:1. make his face shine. The appearance of the deity in Israelite and Mesopotamian traditions is a shining light that in many cases is a physical danger to humans (see the comments on Ex 16:10-11 and 33:18-23). In this case the image is benevolent, with God's manifest power providing comfort and reassurance. Similarly in the Ur III coronation hymn of Ur-Nammu (c. 2000 B.C.) the monarch receives his right to rule when Enlil looks upon him "with his shining forehead." See comment on 80:3.

68:4. rides on the clouds. In Ugaritic epic literature the storm god Baal is regularly referred to as the "rider of the clouds." References can be found in both the Baal and Anat cycle and in the story of the hero Aqhat. This image of power over the winds and weather comes into the Psalms as another example of how the stories from other cultures have been restructured to demonstrate Yahweh's universal control over nature and nations (see Ps 104:3; Jer 4:13). It also serves as a polemic against belief in any other god who might be thought to provide the fertility God promises in the covenant.

68:6. lonely in families. The Egyptian *Tale of the Eloquent Peasant* provides a model for this set of responsibilities to the weak. The king in this Middle Kingdom wisdom piece is called the father to the orphan and the "mother to the motherless." In this psalm Yahweh is the compassionate lawgiver who insures that orphans, widows and the stranger (translated here "the lonely" or "the desolate") are cared for as if they were members of an Israelite clan (see the comments on Deut 24:17-18 and 24:19-22 for laws dealing with justice for the vulnerable). Ecclesiastes 4:8-9 also examines the plight of the one who is isolated, lonely and neglected.

68:6. freeing prisoners. In the ancient Near

East the freeing of prisoners (from debtors' prison) as an act of justice often occurred in the first or second year of a new king's reign (and then periodically after that). For example, the Old Babylonian period king Ammisaduqa (seventeenth century B.C.) cancelled economic debts on behalf of Shamash. Thus the "jubilee" in this case was primarily concerning those in debt (for either financial or legal reasons) and for the freeing of debt-slaves. Unlike the case in Israel, this Babylonian edict was entirely at the whim of the monarch and there is no evidence that it was divinely sanctioned. For an example of this as being accomplished by an ideal king see comment on 11:1. Historically, a proclamation of freedom is recorded by the last king of Judah, Zedekiah (Jer 34:8-10). For these and other characteristics of a just king's reign, see comment on 49:9-10.

68:13. gilded dove. There is no clear consensus on the meaning attached to dove "sheathed with silver" and gold. Some consider it a reference to the battle standards of the fleeing kings, which were topped by a dove, the symbol of the Canaanite goddess Astarte. Others see it as a reference to Israel (see other bird images in Ps 74:19; Hos 7:11). Tate's suggestion of doves, perhaps adorned with colored cloth, being used as a signal of victory seems plausible.

68:14. Zalmon. Because of the parallel in verse 15 with Bashan, it is unlikely that Mount Zalmon in this psalm is the same as the mountain mentioned in Judges 9:48 near Shechem. The name means "dark" or "black" and could refer to a peak shrouded in clouds. It would also require more elevation in order to serve as a snow-covered eminence.

68:15. mountains of Bashan. The Bashan region, northeast of the Galilee, is a fertile plateau about two thousand feet in elevation. It is surrounded by extinct volcanic peaks and rolling hills with sufficient forestland to complement its cattle-raising economy (see Is 3:13 and Amos 4:1-3). The rugged mountains mentioned here probably refer to the hard-to-climb basaltic hills in this area.

68:18. ascending leading captives. Like the victorious Saul in 1 Samuel 15:7-15, the triumphant Yahweh is accompanied by a procession of prisoners, loot and tribute payments. A similar image can be found in the Assyrian annals of Sennacherib, who claims to have taken over two hundred thousand prisoners from Judah, along with their animals and other booty. The major deities of the ancient Near East were associated with high places, so for Yahweh to "ascend" would be to return to his holy mountain (see Jer 31:12), just as Baal uses Mount Zaphon as his divine base of operations in the Ugaritic and Canaanite traditions.

68:23. feet washed in the blood of enemies. The poetic language attached to battle reports can at times be rather grisly. This is certainly the case with this phrase (also used in Ps 58:10). The similar image of wading through the blood of one's enemies is also found in the Ugaritic epic of Baal and Anath. There the goddess gleefully slaughtered whole armies and "waded knee-deep in the warriors' blood."

68:24. procession into the sanctuary. The New Year's festival (Akitu) in ancient Babylon included a procession in which the image of the god Marduk was paraded along a "sacred highway" through the streets of the city. The god was guided by the king ("taken by the hand") up to the Esagila temple, where the image resided during the year. It was not the normal practice for this sort of procession to take place in Jerusalem, since Yahweh could not be represented by an image. However, the ark of the covenant, which functioned as an icon of God's power and presence, was brought into the city by King David and placed within the tabernacle (see 2 Sam 6), and this may be celebrated in this psalm.

68:25. musicians in procession. The appointment of temple musicians is found in 1 Chronicles 15:16-22. It was their task to accompany the singing of hymns of thanksgiving with stringed instruments and cymbals (see Ps 42:4). Egyptian tomb paintings contain images of singers, dancers and musicians in procession, much as they are described in this text.

68:30. beast among the reeds imagery. The most likely choices for this beast are the hippopotamus and the crocodile. Both were major hazards along the shores of the Nile River in Egypt. The tomb paintings from Beni Hasan include a number of scenes in which fishermen work while a crocodile lurks in the reeds nearby or papyrus boats are being used to hunt this dangerous amphibian. Politically, the reference is most likely to Egypt.

68:31. Egypt and Cush. Since there have been Cushite dynasties that have ruled Egypt, it is not unusual to find Egypt and Cush used in parallel here. It is possible that the bringing of tribute from this southern region of Ethiopia is keyed to God's power, which can command

---

For common concepts, metaphors for God and musical terms, see pages 511-18.

homage from the ends of the earth (cf. Is 18:7).

68:33. rides the ancient skies. See comment on 68:4.

69:10. fasting. See comment on Judges 20:26.

69:11. sackcloth. See comment on 1 Kings 20:31.

69:19. scorn for the sufferer. The Israelites believed that if God is to be considered just, rewards and punishments in this life must be proportional to the righteousness or wickedness of the individual. These beliefs had also led them to believe that if someone was prospering, it must be a reward for righteousness, and if someone was suffering, it must be a punishment for wickedness. The greater the suffering, the greater the wickedness must be. Because of the retribution principle (see comment in the sidebar on common concepts in Psalms), suffering had become a source of shame. Since the supplicant is without friends or comforters, he turns to God, who "knows" his suffering and will not scorn his pleas for help (cf. Lam 1:2, 7, 9). This feeling of despair is echoed in the "Babylonian Theodicy" (c 1000 B.C.) that pictures a world turned upside down in which the sufferer states he must "bow down before the dregs of society, who treat me with contempt."

69:21. gall in food. In some contexts this word refers to poison (e.g., snake venom in Deut 32:33), whereas on other occasions it refers to something bitter. This would match the parallel with vinegar. In the former it could lead to almost certain death, while in the latter it may be understood as some kind of sedative. Presumably the fast of mourning would be broken with food brought to the sufferer by comforters (2 Sam 3:35). In this case, however, instead of comfort and nourishment the mourner receives just the opposite—poison (compare Amos's charge that justice has been transformed into poison in Amos 6:12).

69:21. vinegar. The bitter, worthless vintage offered to the sufferer is like that described in Isaiah's "song of the vineyard" (Is 5:2). Equally repugnant is the metaphor for a "nation without sense" in Deuteronomy 32:28-33, in which the people are compared to "grapes filled with poison" and bitterness, whose wine has become "the venom of serpents."

69:28. blotted out of book of life. In a Sumerian hymn to Nungal the goddess discusses her justice as she punishes the wicked and brings mercy to those who deserve it. She claims to hold the tablets of life in her hands, on which she writes the names of the just. See comment on Malachi 3:16.

69:31. horns and hoofs. Devout worship and praise of Yahweh please God much more than rituals and sacrifices (compare similar statements in 1 Sam 15:22 and Hos 6:6). Reference to horns and hoofs indicates a full-grown bull (compare Micah 6:6), an expensive sacrificial animal, which is ritually pure according to the holiness code (see Lev 11:3-8).

71:7. portent. The use of the Hebrew term *mopet* is indicative of an extraordinary event that serves as a sign of God's power, and in this case judgment or punishment (compare the curses in Deut 28:45-46). This technical term appears often in the narrative of the plagues in Egypt (Ex 7:3; 11:9) and is used to signal a coming event (1 Kings 13:3, 5).

72:1. coronation hymns in ancient Near East. There is a good deal of evidence to indicate that in the civilizations of ancient Mesopotamia the kingship was viewed as a gift from the gods. The prologue to Hammurabi's Code contains a statement that the king has been proclaimed "the shepherd" by the god Enlil, and that it is his task to "cause justice to prevail in the land." During the *Akitu* New Year's festival, the king was reinvested with his powers of office. This would have included a great procession and mass celebration. The Ur III texts from about 2000 B.C. contain hymns composed for these occasions, celebrating the coronation of King Ur-Nammu. These compositions contain a set of statements that chronicle the stages of the investiture ritual, including the "pressing of the holy scepter" into the king's hand. These verses are to be sung by or for the king proclaiming his god-given duties as lawgiver and the constructor of canals that bring fertility to the land. There is an answering litany by the priests containing the king's titles and affirming him as "king of Ur."

72:8. extent of reign. In order to indicate that God has granted this king universal rule, the psalmist employs images that are also used in the Karatepe inscription of the Luwian king Azitiwada (730-710 B.C.). Just as the psalmist refers to "rule from sea to sea," these annals proclaim that the king has extended his rule "from sunrise to sunset." Akkadian texts also feature a king boasting that all of the human race submitted to him, from the Upper Sea to the Lower Sea.

72:9. desert tribes. This text is generally emended from the Hebrew *siyyim*, "desert dweller" to *sarayw*, "his foes." If the original reading is retained, then it could relate back to the use of Cush (the desert region of Ethiopia) in Psalm 68:31 as a geographic term for the "ends of the earth" and thus follow the coronation promise in 72:8.

72:10. Tarshish, Sheba, Seba. In order to indicate the extent of the king's power rulers from throughout the world are said to come to him with gifts. Thus Tarshish, associated with the islands and nations in the western Mediterranean, represents all points to the west (see the comment on Is 23:1). Sheba is identified with southern Arabia (Yemen) and the Sabaean kingdom (see the comment on Is 60:6). Seba's location is still disputed, although some place it in Ethiopia or along the northwest Arabian incense road (see Is 43:3).

72:12-14. king's job. It is standard in ancient Near Eastern literature to portray the king as lawgiver (Prov 29:14) and defender of the weak (an attribute of God in Ps 35:10). The Egyptian *Tale of the Eloquent Peasant* states that the king's duty is to "father the orphan." The coronation hymn of the Ur III king Ur-Nammu is described as the "sustainer of Ur." The prologue of his law code tells how the gods gave Hammurabi of Babylon the task of "promot[ing] the welfare of the people" and "caus[ing] justice to prevail in the land" so that "the strong might not oppress the weak."

Psalms 73—89
Book Three

73:24. take me into glory. The NIV's inclusion of the word "into" is totally interpretive, not being found in the Hebrew text. The concept of God "taking" a person as a reference to saving his life can be seen clearly in Psalm 18:16-17, where the NIV translates the same phrase as "took hold of me." The word "glory" is never used in Hebrew as a synonym for heaven and here refers to an "honorable" resolution to the psalmist's crisis. His difficulties have brought him shame because suffering was considered a sign of sin and God's displeasure (see comments on retribution principle and on afterlife in the sidebar on common concepts in Psalms).

74:4. standards. Standards or statues of the deity were usually carried to symbolize the presence of the gods. Assyrian kings of the ninth and eighth centuries regularly refer to the divine standard that goes before them. Banners were used by the Israelites and others, including the Assyrians, as standards of warfare. In the Egyptian army the divisions were named for various gods (e.g., the division of Amun, division of Seth), and the standards would identify the division by means of

some representation of the god. Battle flags and standards were used by the military as signaling devices and rallying points for the army or were hung from city walls (see Jer 4:6). Their colors and insignia designated their allegiance and would in many cases have included a symbol of the god(s) who were expected to participate in the battle along with the human forces (see Jer 50:2). The Assyrian army of Shalmaneser III traveled with its "standards" attached to the royal chariot. When camp was made, they were erected near the royal pavilion and became the focal point for sacrifice and acts of devotion to the gods.

74:6. carved paneling. It is difficult to determine whether this refers to carved panels in the temple or to engravings on some of the bronze or gold pieces connected to the temple. What is clear is that the intricate artwork that embellished this temple (like many others in the ancient world) was being ruthlessly destroyed.

74:13. split sea. There is nothing in this psalm to suggest that reference is being made to the dividing of the Red Sea. The context concerns instead the cosmic battle with the sea that is referred to many times in Psalms. The verb used here is used only here in this form, making precision somewhat difficult. If splitting is intended, it may be parallel to Marduk's splitting of Tiamat ("sea") that is recounted in *Enuma Elish*. Others have translated it as a reference to the churning of the sea that sometimes precedes such battles (see comments on Dan 7:2, 3).

74:14. Leviathan. Leviathan has often been identified as a crocodile, which were found mostly in Egypt (where it symbolized kingly power and greatness), but also sparsely in Palestine. However, the multiple heads here and the fiery breath in Job 41:19-21 make the crocodile identification difficult. Alternatively, Leviathan has been depicted as a sea monster (see Is 27:1). Support for this is found in Ugaritic texts, which contain detailed descriptions of a chaos beast, representing the seas or watery anarchy, in the form of a many-headed, twisting sea serpent who is defeated by Baal. There is a close affinity between the description of Leviathan in Isaiah as a "coiling serpent" and the Ugaritic Baal epic, which speaks of how the storm god "smote Litan the twisting serpent," which is described as having seven heads. In both cases there is a sense of the god of order and fertility vanquishing a chaos monster. In Akkadian literature there is

---

For common concepts, metaphors for God and musical terms, see pages 511-18.

a creature named *bashmu* that is described as having six tongues and seven mouths. In one text *bashmu* is named alongside other fabulous creatures including one with two heads and one with seven heads. The latter is also pictured on a cylinder seal. This seal shows four of the heads hanging limp while the battle continues with the remaining three. Several other passages in the Old Testament mention Leviathan, but most of them speak in terms of God's creative act that establishes control over watery chaos (personified by the sea serpent). In Isaiah 27:1, however, that struggle between order and chaos occurs at the end of time. It may be that the fall of Satan, portrayed as a seven-headed dragon in Revelation 12:3-9, also echoes the Ugaritic image of Litan as "the tyrant with seven heads." Biblically, Leviathan would therefore most easily fit into the category of "supernatural" creature (like cherubim) as opposed to natural or purely mythological. As such it may appear in extrabiblical mythology, as well as being symbolized by something like a crocodile (as in Ezek 29:3, though Leviathan is not specifically referred to in that context).

75:3. pillars of the earth. Pillars typically represent boundaries. Solomon's temple featured two free-standing pillars on the portico, serving as a boundary to the holy place. The tabernacle used pillars from which the partitions were hung to create a boundary for the courtyard. Even when the pillars supported something (as in the Philistine temple that Samson tumbled), archaeological information suggests they stood as boundaries to porticos or courtyards. In Babylon boundary markers known as *kudurru*s were pillar shaped. Ancient Near Eastern literature has no parallel for the earth being supported by pillars. In Job 26:11 the heavens have pillars, but this comment also occurs in the discussion of boundaries (v. 10). It is more likely that cosmic boundaries of the earth would be those between the living and the dead. The word translated "earth" in this verse sometimes refers to the netherworld. In Akkadian literature the boundaries of the netherworld are represented by gates.

75:8. cup of judgment, spiced wine. The image of wine as a cup of punishment is found often in the Old Testament (Jer 49:12; 51:17; Hab 2:15-16). It is especially clear from Isaiah 51:17 that the cup results in drunkenness (staggering), not death. Those forced to drink this cup lose all control of themselves and all ability to defend themselves (vv. 22-23). They become senseless. During the Hellenistic period wine was often mixed with water so that a greater quantity could be consumed and conversation could continue throughout the meal. However, in earlier periods blended or mixed wine, a more potent intoxicant, was common; it had to be consumed with more moderation (see Judg 9:13; Prov 9:2). In Mesopotamia, where wine was less common until the time of the Assyrian empire, wine was served on special occasions. Sometimes only grape syrup would be available, mixed with honey to create a liqueur.

75:10. horns of the righteous and wicked. See the comment on "horn" in the sidebar on common metaphors in Psalms.

78:2. parables. The term translated here as "parable" is *mashal*. It has a wide range of meanings: "allegory" (Ezek 17:2), "poem" (Num 21:27), "oracle" (Num 23:7). In this case, as in Proverbs 10:1, it refers to an "instruction" from God to the people warning the Israelites specifically but relying on the universality of a wisdom theme so that "all peoples" can be addressed, not just the Israelites. It may also be compared to the dark saying in Habakkuk 2:6 in which the Assyrian aggressors are taunted with the loss of their ill-gotten wealth.

78:9. defeat of Ephraim. There are not enough details given to identify the battle that is being referred to here. Ephraim is often used as a title for the entire northern kingdom of Israel. This could refer to something fairly early in Israelite history such as the defeat to the Philistines that brought about the loss of the ark. This would be supported by the fact that the listing of problems ends with that incident (vv. 60-64). Alternatively, others would go as far into history as the fall of the northern kingdom to the Assyrians in 722.

78:12. Zoan. Zoan refers to the Egyptian city of Dja'net, which the Greeks called Tanis. It became the capital city of the delta region in the Twenty-First Dynasty (twelfth century). It is in the area where the Israelites were settled in Egypt at the time of Moses.

78:14. fire and cloud. This is a reference to the pillar of cloud and fire that accompanied the Israelites in the wilderness. For more information see comment on Exodus 13:21-22.

78:15. water from rock. For information about this incident see comments on Exodus 17 and Numbers 20.

78:24. manna. For information about manna see comment on Exodus 16:4-9.

78:27. quail. For information about quail see comments on Exodus 16.

78:44-51. plagues. For discussion of the plagues see comments on Exodus 7—11.

78:60. abandoned Shiloh. Shiloh (modern Khirbit Seilun), in the heart of the Ephraimite hills, was the site where Israel convened sacred assemblies before using Jerusalem. Excavations have exposed extensive architecture by the eleventh century B.C. The site lasted throughout the Iron Age, but the sacred structures served as an example of a sanctuary that had come under God's judgment. It is thought to have been overrun by the Philistines in the aftermath of the victory at the Battle of Aphek (1 Sam 4).

78:61. Ark into captivity. For more information in this incident see 1 Sam 4—6 and the comments there.

79:1. historical context. The only time in the Old Testament period in which the temple was defiled and the city of Jerusalem destroyed was in the fall of the city to Babylon in 587 B.C.

79:2. dead as food to birds and beasts. In the Gilgamesh Epic the guardian of the cedar forest, Huwawa, tells Gilgamesh that he should have given his flesh to be eaten by birds of prey and scavengers. For more information see comment on exposure of the corpse in 1 Kings 16:4.

79:5. how long? This question occurs nearly twenty times in Psalms, usually in connection with a lament psalm. It is found also in Mesopotamia as the Sumerian *Lament over the Destruction of Sumer and Ur* asks, "How long will the enemy eye be cast upon my account?"

80:1. enthroned between cherubim. The cherubim are associated with the ark of the covenant, which they were either mounted on or flanked. They appear in ancient art with some regularity, flanking the thrones of kings and deities. The combination of cherubim as throne guardians, chests as footstools and statements in contexts like this one concerning Yahweh being enthroned on the cherubim supports the concept of the ark as representing the invisible throne of Yahweh. In Egyptian festivals the images of the gods were often carried in procession on portable barques. Paintings portray these as boxes about the size of the ark carried on poles and decorated with or flanked by guardian creatures. Biblical descriptions as well as archaeological discoveries (including some fine ivory pieces from Nimrud in Mesopotamia, Arslan Tash in Syria and Samaria in Israel) suggest that the cherubim are composite creatures (having features of a number of different creatures, like the Egyptian sphinx), often four-legged animal bodies with wings.

80:3. face shine upon us. The metaphor "light

of God's face" is found in royal letters from the Egyptian city of Amarna and in Ugaritic correspondence. For example, "and the face of the Sun (i.e., Pharaoh) shone brightly upon me" is a statement made by one of the Egyptian king's subordinates. Two small silver scrolls (about one inch long) have been found in the area known as Keteph Hinnom in Jerusalem. They were amulets in a burial cave from the sixth or seventh century B.C., and they contained the benediction from Numbers 6:25, which includes the request that the Lord "make his face shine upon you." At present they represent the oldest example of any text of Scripture. The concept of the shining face of the deity resulting in mercy is found in Mesopotamian documents and inscriptions from as early as the twelfth century B.C.

80:5. bread of tears. The word translated "bread" here can also be used more generally to refer to food. Akkadian texts use the same metaphor, as they contain statements like "for bread I ate bitter tears" or "weeping is my nourishment."

80:11. Sea, River. Given the geographical description it is likely that these are references to the Mediterranean Sea and the Euphrates River.

80:13. boars. Pigs were domesticated very early, but the wild variety continued to thrive in the Near East and are represented in Egyptian and Mesopotamian art.

81:2. tambourine, harp, lyre. See comment on 150:3-5.

81:3. ram's horn at New Moon. Keyed to their use of a lunar calendar, ancient Israel marked the first day of the month, with its "new moon" phase, as a festival day (every twenty-nine or thirty days). As on the Sabbath, all work was to cease (see Amos 8:5), and there were sacrifices to be made (Num 28:11-15). In the monarchy period the king became a prominent figure in these celebrations (see Ezek 45:17). The festival continued to be observed in the postexilic period as well (Ezra 3:5; Neh 10:33). New Moon festivals were also prominent in Mesopotamia from late in the third millennium down to the Neo-Babylonian period in the middle of the first millennium B.C. In light of the parallel with the full moon, however, it is likely that this line refers not to any New Moon celebration but to the Feast of Tabernacles (see next comment).

81:3. feast day at Full Moon. The only pilgrimage feast that potentially spans the New Moon and Full Moon is the Feast of Taber-

---

For common concepts, metaphors for God and musical terms, see pages 511-18.

nacles. The description in Numbers 29 includes instructions for both days, including the sounding of horns.

81:7. thundercloud, Meribah. There was thunder at Sinai, but it is hard to see how that was an act of rescue, and Meribah preceded it. It is therefore more likely that the thundercloud is seen as the weapon of the divine warrior, Yahweh, who delivered Israel from Egypt (same term used as in Is 29:6). Meribah is where Yahweh gave water from the rock (see comments on Ex 17).

81:16. honey from rock. While most honey spoken of in the Old Testament is the syrup from the date palm, mention of the rock here suggests bees' honey from honeycombs in the rocks.

82:1 assembly judging among gods. In the ancient Near East the major decisions were all made in the divine council. There the gods would consult with one another and share their information and opinions. The familiar picture of a heavenly throne surrounded by the divine assembly is well known from the Ugaritic texts (most notably the epic of Keret), though this Canaanite council is made up of the gods of the pantheon. Examples occur also in the tenth-century building inscription of Yehimilk from Byblos and the Karatepe stele of Azitawadda. In the Akkadian *Enuma Elish* it is the assembly of the gods that appoints Marduk as their head. Fifty gods made up this assembly, with seven in the inner council. In Israelite belief the gods were replaced by angels or spirits—the sons of God or the heavenly host.

82:5. foundations of the earth. In the Babylonian perception of the cosmos, the earth's foundation is on what is called the *apsu*. This is a primordial watery region under the jurisdiction of the very important deity Enki/Ea. From the standpoint of physical geography, it represents the water table that surfaces, for example, in marshes and springs, as well as being associated with the sweet water cosmic seas and rivers. In *Enumu Elish* one of Marduk's names, Agilima, identifies him as the one who built the earth above the water and established the upper regions. For further information see the comments on Job 38:4-6 and on creation in the sidebar on common concepts in Psalms.

82:6. gods/sons of the Most High. See comment on 82:1.

83:6-8. members of the alliance. The first seven peoples/nations mentioned are all located just to the east and south of Judah. The most uncertain is Gebal, which is the name usually used for Byblos on the far northern Mediterra-

nean coast. An alternative location, however, is found near Petra, which suits this context better. Philistia and Tyre are traditional enemies to the west and north respectively. The mention of Assyria as the formidable member of the alliance suggests a situation somewhere between the mid-ninth century and the end of the eighth century. The mid-ninth century presence in the west was focused in the north, so the eighth-century conflicts are more likely. Judah took the brunt of Assyrian invasions during the times of Sargon and his son, Sennacherib. In the context of Sennacherib's siege of Jerusalem, the Assyrian inscriptions report that the kings of Tyre, Byblos, Ashdod (Philistia), Ammon, Moab and Edom had already submitted before Sennacherib came against Jerusalem. This may have been enough to identify them as co-conspirators. In contrast to attempting to identify a historical situation behind the psalm, the alternative is that this is simply a list of Israel's traditional enemies.

83:9. Midian, Sisera/Jabin. This is a reference to two battles during the Judges period when there was divine intervention on behalf of Israel. For the defeat of Midian at the hands of Gideon, see the comments on Judges 6—8. For Deborah and Barak's victory over King Jabin and his commander, Sisera, see the comments on Judges 4.

83:10. Endor. Endor is not mentioned in the account of these battles in Judges, but it is in the vicinity of both of them. The eastern end of the Valley of Jezreel is about ten miles wide from north to south. The north end is blocked off by Mount Tabor, while the south end is blocked off by Mount Gilboa. The ten-mile stretch between the two is broken into two passes by the smaller Hill of Moreh. Endor is located in the middle of the northern pass, between the Hill of Moreh, where the Battle of Midian took place, and Mount Tabor, where Deborah and Barak mustered their troops.

83:11. kings. The four kings mentioned here are the ones who led the forces of the Midianites against Gideon and the Israelites. Their defeat and execution are recorded in Judges 8.

84:title. sons of Korah. See comment on 42:title.

84:1-2. yearning for dwelling place. The temple, the dwelling place of deity, was a place where one enjoyed favor and blessing. The verb used here is similar to the English idiom of "missing" someone or something. It carries a bit of nostalgia; one longs for the return of a fondly remembered circumstance or situation. Here the pilgrim misses being around the temple.

84:4. dwelling in the Lord's house. In Israel

the priests were the only ones who dwelt within the temple precinct. Throughout the ancient Near East it was considered a privilege to be constantly in the deity's presence. The Babylonian king Neriglissar expressed to his god that he longed to be where he was forever. Another text requests, "May I stand before you forever in worship and devotion." A hymn to Marduk requests that the worshiper may stand before the deity forever in prayer, supplication and entreaty. In the third millennium B.C. Sumerian worshipers tried to accomplish this objective by placing statuettes of themselves in the posture of prayer in the temple. In this way they would be continuously represented in the temple.

84:6. Valley of Baca. If this is a reference to a geographical location, it is obscure. The word *Baca* means "weeping," but this would likewise be difficult to understand. The alternative suggestion is that the word describes a tree, specifically the balsam (see comment on 2 Sam 5:24). None of these help locate the valley or identify its significance.

84:10. doorkeeper in temple. One of the most important tasks assigned to priestly personnel was controlling access to the temple precinct, the inner circle of the "sacred compass" (on this concept see comments on Lev 16:2 and Num 18:1-7). Defiling the sanctuary with impurity required a purification offering ("sin" offering, see comment on Lev 4:1-3) and could bring punishment on the individual as well as the people. The gatekeepers had to prevent unqualified intrusion. There were also many valuable items in the temple precinct. Gold and silver were plentiful and a temptation to the unscrupulous individual who may not have feared divine retribution for trespass or theft of temple property. These valuables also had to be guarded. Misappropriation of that which was sacred required a reparation offering ("guilt" offering, see comment on Lev 5:14-16). The gatekeepers were charged with guarding against these offenses. For the psalmist, however, the gatekeeper was one of those privileged people who had the opportunity to be continuously in proximity to God's presence.

84:11. sun connection. The relationship between sun and shield is that they both offer protection. For the shield that is obvious, but we would not necessarily think of the sun in those terms. Nonetheless Assyrian kings use the metaphor of their protection spreading over the land like the rays of the sun.

85:title. sons of Korah. See comment on 42:title.

87:4. Rahab. Rahab is described as one of the sea monsters slain by God (see Job 26:12; Ps 89:10; Is 51:9). In both the Babylonian and the Ugaritic creation myths the champion deity (Marduk in Babylon and Baal in Ugarit) fights and slays a sea monster and its cohorts in a manner similar to that of Yahweh. In other contexts, as here, Rahab is symbolically used as a designation for Egypt (Is 30:7). The name Rahab has not yet been found in extrabiblical sources.

87:4. list of nations. No historical situation needs to be sought here, because the text is simply listing some of the nations that will be counted among those who acknowledge Yahweh. This list includes the great powers, Egypt (Rahab) and Babylon, the near neighbors, Philistia (southwest) and Tyre (northwest), and the distant nation (Cush or Nubia, south of Egypt).

87:6. register of peoples. In the ancient world royal estate cities typically housed the administration (composed largely of relatives of the king), and their citizens enjoyed certain privileges, including exemption from taxation, corvée labor, military duty and imprisonment, as well as being beneficiaries of the most beautiful and elaborate building projects. Such privileges *(kidinnutu)* were enjoyed by Babylonian cities such as Nippur, Sippar and Borsippa, based on their status as religious centers rather than as political capitals. Political capitals such as Nineveh and Babylon also were endowed with similar status. It is presumed that records would be kept to identify those who enjoyed such privileges. In this verse the psalmist alludes to the privileged status of those born in Zion.

88:title. sons of Korah. See comment on 42:title.

88:title. Heman the Ezrahite. Along with Ethan (in Ps 89), Heman is listed as one of the famous wise men of Solomon's time (1 Kings 4:31) and was appointed one of the Levitical musicians during the time of David (1 Chron 15:17, 19).

88:3. dread of death. This psalm is full of the dread of death as the psalmist laments his condition as one who is doomed to die. This is reminiscent of Gilgamesh in the Gilgamesh Epic, who responds to his own dread of death by going on a quest for immortality. Gilgamesh's actions are motivated by the death of his close friend Enkidu in the same way

---

For common concepts, metaphors for God and musical terms, see pages 511-18.

that the psalmist despairs over the loss of his close friend (vv. 8, 18).

89:title. Ethan the Ezrahite. This name occurs among the sages of the time of Solomon (1 Kings 4:31) and perhaps among the Levitical musicians during the time of David (1 Chron 15:17, 19). Nothing else is known about him.

89:7. council of the holy ones. In the ancient Near East the major decisions were all made in the divine council. There the gods would consult with one another and share their information and opinions. The familiar picture of a heavenly throne surrounded by the divine assembly is well known from the Ugaritic texts (most notably the epic of Keret), though this Canaanite council is made up of the gods of the pantheon. Examples occur also in the tenth-century building inscription of Yehimilk from Byblos and the Karatepe stele of Azitawadda. In the Akkadian *Enuma Elish* it is the assembly of the gods that appoints Marduk as their head. Fifty gods made up this assembly with seven in the inner council. In Israelite belief the gods were replaced by angels or spirits—the sons of God or the heavenly host.

89:9. rule over the surging sea. In the Bible as well as in the ancient Near East the sea represents chaos and disorder, as do the sea monsters that live there. The obvious physical struggle between the sea and the land as well as the fierce, seemingly unstoppable energy displayed by the savage sea gave rise to cosmic myths in the ancient Near East. The *Enuma Elish* creation epic from Babylon describes how Marduk vanquishes Tiamat while this goddess of watery chaos is in the form of a dragon. Much of the cycle of stories about Baal in Ugaritic legend involves Baal's struggle against his rival Yamm, the god of the sea. Similarly, the Ugaritic epic has both Anat and Baal claim to have conquered Litan, the seven-headed dragon, and thus gained mastery over the seas. Rule over the sea then concerns Yahweh's sovereign control over the chaotic forces that were thought to constantly threaten the cosmos. That rule is expressed by the calming of the sea (see comments on 65:7 and 107:29).

89:10. Rahab. Rahab is described as one of the sea monsters slain by God (see Job 26:12 and Is 51:9). In both the Babylonian and the Ugaritic myths of creation the champion deity (Marduk in Babylon and Baal in Ugarit) fights and slays a sea monster and its cohorts in a manner similar to that of Yahweh. In other contexts, Rahab is symbolically used as a designation for Egypt (Is 30:7 and Ps 87:4). The name Rahab has not yet been found in extra-biblical sources.

89:12. created north and south. The determination of directions in the ancient world was an uncertain science. The North Star was about twelve degrees south of true north during this period, so paths of stars and constellations were used. In everyday determinations fixed topographical points were used as indicators. In Mesopotamia the east wind was known as the mountain wind because of the mountains to the east. In Israelite terminology north was sometimes, as here, referred to as Zaphon, the name of a mountain in Syria (see comment on Is 48:2).

89:12. Tabor and Hermon. These are the two most prominent mountains in Israel. Mount Hermon (elev. 9,232 feet in the Anti-Lebanon Range) is at the northern boundary of the land and is often snowcapped. Mount Tabor is at the northeastern end of the Valley of Jezreel. Even though at 1,929 feet it has a much lower elevation than Hermon, it stands in stark isolation as it rises out of the plain. If these two mountains are supposed to be parallel to the north and south of the first line, the author must be located in the Galilee region.

89:14. righteousness and justice as foundation of throne. The idea of righteousness and justice as the most fundamental obligation of the king is expressed throughout the ancient Near East. It is graphically portrayed in Egyptian art, where the symbol of Maat (the deity associated with justice and truth) is the pedestal on which the throne sits.

89:18. king as shield. See comment on "shield" in the sidebar on common metaphors for God.

89:20. anointed with sacred oil. Anointing a king was common practice in some parts of the ancient Near East. Among the Egyptians and Hittites, anointing was believed to protect a person from the power of netherworld deities. Much of the evidence comes from Hittite sources describing enthronement ceremonies. There is no evidence of kings being anointed in Mesopotamia. In Egypt the pharaoh was not anointed, but he anointed his officials and his vassals. His anointing of them established their subordinate relationship to him and indicated the pharaoh's protection on that individual. In the Amarna texts there is reference to a king of Nuhasse (in modern Syria) being anointed by the pharaoh. This model would fit the idea of David being anointed as a vassal to God. In 2 Samuel 2:4 it is the people who anoint David. This anointing suggests some sort of contractual agreement between David and the people he will govern. In Nuzi individuals entering a business agreement anointed one another with oil, and in Egypt oil anointment was used in wedding ceremonies. For information on royal coronations see comment on 1 Samuel 11:15. The spices which were to be used for anointing purposes were myrrh, cinnamon, cane and cassia (see recipe in Ex 30:23-25). Oil symbolizes the gifts of God to the people and the responsibilities now laid on their leaders through this ceremony. In Israelite practice anointing was a sign of election and often closely related to endowment by the Spirit. Additionally, throughout the ancient world anointing symbolized an advance of a person's legal status. Both concepts of protection and change of status may correlate to the king's anointing, for it would offer him protection on the throne and identify him with the divine realm.

89:24. horn. See the comment on "horn" in the sidebar on common metaphors for God.

89:35-37. royal line lasting forever like sun and moon. In a blessing on the Assyrian king Ashurbanipal one of his courtiers prays that his kingship may be as firmly established as the moon and the sun in the sky. In the Levant the inscription of Azitawadda claims that the name of this king will endure forever like the names of the sun and moon. Another blessing on an Assyrian king says, "Just as heaven and earth last forever, may the name of the king, my lord, last forever in Assyria" (CAD Q:123). This thought is echoed in a hymn to the god Sin, where the deity is petitioned to make the reign of Sargon (eighth-century Assyrian king) last as long as heaven and earth, and his throne firm over the four quarters of the earth. Finally, Ashurbanipal requests of the god Ea that he grant him long life, good health and happiness, and that he make the foundation of his throne secure and as firm as the heaven and netherworld.

Psalms 90—106

Book Four

90:10. life expectancy. Joseph died at the age of 110, considered the ideal age for an Egyptian. Examination of mummies has demonstrated that the average life expectancy in Egypt was between forty and fifty. The Egyptian *Papyrus Insinger* details that ten years are spent in childhood and ten more learning a trade. The writer accounts for ten more in storing up possessions and another ten in gaining wisdom. He thus concludes that two-thirds of one's years are lost to him (suggesting a normal life expectancy of sixty) yet contends that the godly man will still have sixty years remaining of the days assigned by Thoth, making a round one hundred.

See comments on Deuteronomy 31:2 and Isaiah 40:6-7.

91:1. rest in shadow. The shadow offers protection and is usually referred to as the shadow of his wings. See comment on 17:8.

91:3. fowler's snare. The very familiar image of fowlers trapping birds in nets and snares may be the origin of this common metaphor (see Josh 23:13; Ps 69:22; Is 8:14). There are numerous examples of this activity from Egyptian tomb paintings, and it also provides the basis for the Sumerian *Stele of the Vultures* (see the comment on Ezek 12:13). There were a number of different techniques used to snare birds. Although hunters might simply use a sling, throwing stick (as in the Beni Hasan tomb painting) or a bow to take down individual fowl, the majority of instances in the biblical text and in ancient art depict large flocks of birds being captured in nets or cages. For instance, the tomb of Ka-Gemmi at Saqqarah (Sixth-Dynasty Egypt) portrays the fowler using a net. Apparently some fowlers also used decoys in their snares to attract the birds along with bait food (attested in Ecclus 11:30).

91:11. guardian angels. In the ancient Near East it was deities rather than angels who served as guardians. Mesopotamians believed that personal gods or family gods offered special care and protection that the great cosmic or national deities would not be bothered with. The Akkadian texts also speak of guardians of well-being and health, as well as guardian spirits. These spirits were assigned to an individual by the deity, just as here. The protection that was expected in the ancient Near East was against demonic powers, who were believed to be the cause of illness and trouble. Related to that was the danger of magical spells and hexes that could be pronounced against someone. The Israelites certainly believed in the reality of the demon world, and many Israelites would not have successfully divorced their thinking from the magical perspectives of their neighbors. Nevertheless, the psalmist does not typically understand the problems he faces in those terms. This is the only place in the Old Testament where there is any reference to guardian angels.

92:title. Sabbath liturgy. This is the only psalm that is designated for the Sabbath. There is little indication in the Old Testament of any special worship ceremonies on the Sabbath. It has been suggested that this psalm ac-

---

companied the daily offerings on the Sabbath.

92:3. ten-stringed lyre. This is a typical musical instrument of the time and is attested in ancient Near Eastern texts, reliefs and paintings as early as the third millennium B.C. The lyre is differentiated from the harp by the number of strings. Both are hand-held with frames made of wood. A musical text has been discovered at Ugarit that sheds light on Late Bronze Age music. This text has the chords to be played on a lyre accompanying a Hurrian cult hymn.

92:10. exalting the horn. See the comment on "horn" in the sidebar on common metaphors for God.

92:10. fine oils. Banquet guests in the ancient world were often treated by a generous host to fine oils to anoint their foreheads. This provided not only a glistening sheen to their countenance but also would have added a fragrance to their persons and the room. For example, an Assyrian text from Esarhaddon's reign describes how he "drenched the foreheads" of his guests at a royal banquet with "choicest oils." Oil preserved the complexion in the hot Middle Eastern climate. Both the Egyptian *Song of the Harper* and the Mesopotamian Gilgamesh Epic describe individuals clothed in fine linen and with myrrh on their head.

93:3-4. comparison to seas. In the Bible as well as in the ancient Near East, the sea represents chaos and disorder, as do the sea monsters that live there. The obvious physical struggle between the sea and the land as well as the fierce, seemingly unstoppable energy displayed by the savage sea gave rise to cosmic myths in the ancient Near East. The *Enuma Elish* creation epic from Babylon describes how Marduk vanquished Tiamat while this goddess of watery chaos was in the form of a dragon. Much of the cycle of stories about Baal in Ugaritic legend involve Baal's struggle against his rival Yamm, the god of the sea. Similarly, the Ugaritic epic has both Anat and Baal claim to have conquered Litan, the seven-headed dragon, and thus gained mastery over the seas.

95:8. Meribah/Massah. These are the terms applied to Rephidim near Sinai to describe the quarrelsome nature of the people. God responded by bringing water from the rock. For more information on the incident see the comments on Exodus 16—17.

97:2. surrounded by clouds. The image of a rampant God storming through the heavens in a cloud chariot is a common one (Ps 68:4; 104:3; Jer 4:13). Such descriptions of storm theophany may be found in the texts that speak of the Ugaritic god Baal. In both the Aqhat epic and in the Baal and Anat cycle of stories, Baal is referred to as the "rider of the clouds." Baal's attributes, commanding the storms, unleashing the lightning and rushing to war as a divine warrior, even appear in the Egyptian El Amarna texts. The characteristics of Yahweh as Creator, giver of fertility and divine warrior share a great deal in common with these earlier epics. One of the ways that Yahweh presents himself to the Israelites as the sole divine power is by assuming the titles and powers of the other ancient Near Eastern gods.

98:1. holy arm. The image of an outstretched or mighty hand or arm is common in Egyptian inscriptions to describe the power of pharaoh. It is used throughout the exodus narratives to describe God's power over pharaoh. In the fourteenth-century B.C. Amarna letters, Abdi-Heba, the governor of Jerusalem, refers to "the strong arm of the king" as the basis for his government appointment. Similarly, the Eighteenth-Dynasty hymn to Osiris equates his growing to majority with the phrase "when his arm was strong," and Haremhab's hymn to Thoth describes the moon god as guiding the divine bark through the sky with "arms outstretched."

98:5-6. worship with instruments. See comment on 150:3-5.

98:8. personification of nature. It is not unusual for the Bible to personify the forces of nature, but they do not embody them with personality as was done in the rest of the ancient Near East. In Mesopotamia, Canaan and Egypt the forces of nature were manifestations of individual deities, who had jurisdiction over that realm of nature and were integrated into it.

98:9. equity. The term here is comparable to that used in Mesopotamia for the declaration of release from debts. In the ancient Near East the freeing of prisoners (from debtors' prison) as an act of justice often occurred in the first or second year of a new king's reign (and then periodically after that). For example, the Old Babylonian king Ammisaduqa (seventeenth century B.C.) cancelled economic debts on behalf of Shamash. One of the ways to bring justice was to bring relief to those who were suffering under debt (usually of no fault of their own).

99:1. enthroned between the cherubim. The cherubim are associated with the ark of the covenant, which they were either mounted on or flanked. They appear in ancient art with some regularity, flanking the thrones of kings and deities. The combination of cherubim as throne guardians, chests as footstools and statements in contexts like this one concerning Yahweh being enthroned on the cherubim supports the concept of the ark as representing the invisible throne of Yahweh. In Egyptian festivals the images of the gods were often carried in procession on portable barques. Paintings portray these as boxes about the size of the ark carried on poles and decorated with or flanked by guardian creatures. Biblical descriptions as well as archaeological discoveries (including some fine ivory pieces from Nimrud in Mesopotamia, Arslan Tash in Syria and Samaria in Israel) suggest the cherubim are composite creatures (having features of a number of different creatures, like the Egyptian sphinx), often four-legged animal bodies with wings.

99:5. worship at footstool. First of all, it must be recognized that the ark of the covenant was considered the footstool of God's invisible throne (see comment on Ex 25:10-22). Second, the footstool must be understood to be an integral part of the throne, representing the closest accessibility to the king. Third, the imagery of the footstool has significance because it is used to express the king's subordination of his foes (see comment on Ps 110:1). Finally, worshiping at the footstool is another way of expressing the reverence that is shown by prostrating oneself at the feet of God or king. On the black stela of Shalmaneser III, the Israelite king Jehu is portrayed kissing the ground before the Assyrian king. In *Enuma Elish* the tribunal of gods kisses the feet of Marduk after he has put down the rebellion and established himself as head of the pantheon. This was the common act of submission offered to kings and gods. Taking hold of the feet was a gesture of self-abasement and entreaty. This gesture occurs in a wide range of Akkadian literature as fugitives or supplicants take hold of the king's feet to demonstrate their submission or surrender and make their petitions.

103:12. east and west. In an Egyptian hymn to Amun-Re the deity is praised for his judgment of the guilty. As a result of the god's discernment the guilty are assigned to the east and the righteous to the west.

103:20-21. mighty ones, heavenly hosts. The "host of heaven" in the ancient Near East referred to the assembly of the gods, many of whom were represented by celestial bodies (whether planets or stars). The Bible sometimes uses the phrase to refer to the illegitimate worship of these deities (see comment on Deut 4:19). On other occasions, the phrase

is used for Yahweh's angelic council (see comment on 2 Chron 18:18). A third type of usage treats the term as a reference to rebel angels (perhaps in Is 24:21; commonly in the intertestamental literature). Finally, it can refer simply to the stars, with no personalities behind them (Is 40:26). In the ancient Near East the major decisions were all made in the divine council. There the gods would consult with one another and share their information and opinions. The familiar picture of a heavenly throne surrounded by the divine assembly is well known from the Ugaritic texts (most notably the epic of Keret), though this Canaanite council is made up of the gods of the pantheon. Examples occur also in the tenth-century building inscription of Yehimilk from Byblos and the Karatepe stele of Azitawadda. In the Akkadian *Enuma Elish* it is the assembly of the gods that appoints Marduk as their head. Fifty gods made up this assembly with seven in the inner council. In Israelite belief the gods were replaced by angels or spirits—the sons of God or the heavenly host. Yahweh is often portrayed as the "Lord of Hosts"—the commander of the heavenly armies.

104:1-35. comparison to *Hymn to the Aten.* There is a famous composition of the Egyptian king Akhenaten dating to the fourteenth century B.C. that has a number of similarities to Psalm 104, mostly in wording and content. The hymn praises the god Aten, a sun god, for all of his care over creation. One could find some of the same motifs and analogies in other hymns to other sun gods. Once the psalmist determined to use solar motifs in a hymn to Yahweh, it was inevitable that parallels would occur. Sun worship was one of the syncretistic deviations that characterized preexilic Israel (see comments on 2 Kings 23:11 and Ezek 8:16), and adoption of sun motifs (both literary and iconographic) has been attested (in Old Testament see also Ps 84:11; Hab 3:4; Mal 4:2). Nevertheless, there is nothing syncretistic in the beliefs expressed by this psalm. It is only the imagining of Yahweh in solar terms that brings out the similarities.

104:2. garment of light. In Egyptian worship of Aten the sun disk itself was considered to be the deity. As a result the imagery of wrapping oneself in light would have been particularly appropriate to Atenism but not to the worship of other sun deities. Nevertheless, this phrase is not used in the Aten hymn. Akkadian literature speaks of celestial gods wearing the garment of heaven, but this refers

---

For common concepts, metaphors for God and musical terms, see pages 511-18.

to clouds. Another passage may be more relevant in which Marduk is clothed by another deity with radiance.

104:3. beams of upper chambers. In the ancient world there were several levels of heavens, and they were understood as having floors, walls and roofs (see comment on Ex 24:10). In Mesopotamian texts *(Enuma Elish)* the waters of the heavens were made from one half of Tiamat's body when Marduk defeated her and set up the cosmos. These waters are identified with the highest level of the heavens, Anu's heaven (Anu was the ancient chief deity, before Enlil or Marduk). If this imagery is being used, Yahweh is seen as inhabiting the highest heavens, the beams being the roof beams of the upper story of his cella. In the Mesopotamian texts the cella of the chief god (Marduk) is in the middle heavens, but the description of Anu's abode in the highest heavens likewise presupposes a cella.

104:3. cosmos as temple. The psalmist's attempt to express God's complete control over all creation includes a multistoried or many-chambered sanctuary or palace in the heavens (cf. Ps 78:69; Is 66:1). In the biblical and ancient Near Eastern view the cosmos was a temple and the temple was a microcosmos. The cosmos can therefore be described in architectural terms as a temple would be.

104:3. riding the clouds. The image of a rampant God storming through the heavens in a cloud chariot is a common one (Ps 68:4; Jer 4:13). Such descriptions of storm theophany may be found in the texts that speak of the Ugaritic god Baal. In both the Aqhat epic and in the Baal and Anat cycle of stories, Baal is referred to as the "rider of the clouds." Baal's attributes, commanding the storms, unleashing the lightning and rushing to war as a divine warrior, even appear in the Egyptian El Amarna texts. The characteristics of Yahweh as Creator, giver of fertility and divine warrior share a great deal in common with these earlier epics. One of the ways that Yahweh presents himself to the Israelites as the sole divine power is by assuming the titles and powers of the other ancient Near Eastern gods.

104:4. winds, flames as messengers. In both *Enuma Elish* and the *Tale of Anzu* the winds carry the news of the victory by the hero deity over the chaos monster. In the former, the north wind carries the blood of Tiamat as tidings of her demise; in the latter, the feathers of the defeated Anzu are carried on the wind to Enlil. Flames of fire can refer to the destructiveness of God's wrath (as can winds for that matter).

104:6-9. watery chaos. This does not refer to the flood but to the initial creation narrative where the dry land emerged as all of the waters were assigned their places. The defeat of the forces of chaos, personified in the primordial sea, was one of the most common elements of ancient Near Eastern cosmology (Baal defeating Yamm in Ugaritic texts; Marduk defeating Tiamat in *Enuma Elish*).

104:9. boundary for waters. Marduk, after having defeated Tiamat, created the seas and placed guards to keep back the waters. The Babylonian *Atrahasis Epic* refers to a bolt of the sea in the possession of the god Ea (Enki). Other texts speak of locks of the sea. One of the main tasks of the head of the pantheon was to keep the sea in check so that chaos would be restrained and order would prevail. One of the earliest reflections of this motif is found in the *Myth of Ninurta and Azag*, where Ninurta builds a stone wall to contain the waters.

104:19. moon marking seasons. In contrast to the sun, which marks days by its rising and setting, the phases of the moon marked the months, which are linked to the seasons. By early in the first millennium the ancients were well aware of the difference between the solar cycle (365+ days) and the lunar cycle (354+ days). They also had a growing awareness of calendrical reckoning by the sequence of stars and constellations rising and setting. The moon remained the main determiner of months and seasons, though supplementary months were added every three years to readjust the months to the solar cycle. If only lunar calculations were used, the months would gradually drift away from their festivals that marked the planting and harvest times (which, of course, were determined by the sun).

104:26. Leviathan. See comment on 74:14.

104:28. open hand. In the Egyptian reliefs showing the worship of Aten, the deified sun disk is portrayed with numerous arms reaching from it, each one with a hand at the end of it symbolizing the giving of blessings and favor.

104:32. volcanic activity in the Near East. People in the ancient Near East were aware of the phenomenon of volcanoes but had little chance to observe them. Both Mesopotamia and Egypt are river cultures, with few mountains nearby, let alone active volcanoes. Ararat is one of the active volcanoes in the Fertile Crescent (but it has not had an eruption in historic time). Additionally there are several in Syria and quite a few along the southern rim of Turkey. Most significantly, the Aegean features half a dozen volcano sites, including at least one that had an eruption during the Old Testament period (Santorini, 1650 B.C.).

105:13-15. patriarchal wanderings. Abraham left Ur of the Chaldees in either northern or southern Mesopotamia (see comment on Gen 11:28) and traveled to Canaan. He had incidents in Gerar and Egypt. Jacob traveled to Paddan Aram in northern Mesopotamia and back again to Canaan. Joseph and his whole family journeyed to Egypt and sojourned there. God's care for them was evident in each of their lives.

105:18. shackles and irons. The shackles around the ankles chaining the feet together are clear enough. Since the other instrument goes around the neck, it must be an iron collar. These were at times used to link prisoners together. Assyrian inscriptions from the ninth and eighth centuries depict captives being transported or laboring with wooden yokes around their necks.

105:23. land of Ham. This is an alternate name for Egypt, where some of the descendants of Ham, the son of Noah, settled.

105:29-36. plagues. For discussion of the plagues see comments on Exodus 7—11.

105:39. cloud. This is a reference to the pillar of cloud and fire that accompanied the Israelites in the wilderness. For more information see comment on Exodus 13:21-22.

105:40-41. quail, manna, water. For information concerning these miraculous acts of provision see comments on Exodus 16—17.

106:7. Red Sea. For more information see comments on Exodus 14—15.

106:15. wasting disease. See Numbers 11:33. There is no information available on the nature of this disease. See comment on Numbers 25:8.

106:17. Dathan and Abiram. See comments on latter part of Numbers 16.

106:19. Horeb. Horeb is another name for Mount Sinai and is most likely located in the southern section of the Sinai peninsula. For more detailed discussion see comment on Exodus 19:1-2.

106:19-20. calf/bull. See comments on Exodus 32.

106:28. Baal of Peor. This is a reference to the incident in which the Israelites got involved with the women of Moab. See Numbers 25 and the comments there.

106:33. Moses' rash words. Moses' offense took place during the second incident where

water came forth from the rock. See Numbers 20 and the comments there.

106:37. sacrificed to demons. This word for demon is used elsewhere in the Old Testament only in Deuteronomy 32:17, but it is a well-known type of spirit/demon in Mesopotamia, where the term (*shedu*) describes a protective guardian mostly concerned with the individual's health and welfare. It is not the name of a deity but a category of being (like cherub would be in the Old Testament). A *shedu* could destroy one's health just as easily as it could protect it, so sacrifices to keep it placated were advisable. They are depicted as winged creatures (similar to the cherub, see comments on Gen 3:24 and Ex 25:18-20), but they do not have idols (as the gods have idols) by which they are worshiped (see comment on Deut 4 for how this worked). For information concerning child sacrifice see comments on Genesis 22:1 and Leviticus 18:21.

106:38. idols of Canaan. Gods of the Canaanites included El, Baal (Hadad), Dagon and Anat.

Psalms 107—150

Book Five

107:10. exiles in prisons. While most of those who had been deported to Babylon would not have been imprisoned, there would have been some political prisoners. Pits were used as prisons in most of the ancient Near East. The modern idea of a prison where prisoners were to be reformed into good citizens was foreign to the ancient world. Those in debt, criminals awaiting trial and political prisoners were held in confinement of one sort or another.

107:16. gates of bronze, bars of iron. The Greek historian Herodotus described Babylon as having "one hundred gates in the circuit of the wall, all of bronze with bronze uprights and lintels." Large bronze gates have been excavated at the Assyrian period site of Balawat, giving a glimpse of what the Babylonian walls may have been like. Gates were locked by means of a bar slid across the gateway, and iron would obviously be the most difficult to break (see comment on Deut 33:25).

107:18. gates of death. Sheol was believed to be like an earthly city in that it contained houses and even a city wall (primarily to keep in its inhabitants). In the *Descent of Ishtar* the netherworld has a gate complex with seven gates and gatekeepers at each one to control access.

107:23-30. storms on the sea. The Babylonian

hymn to Shamash also has a section in which Shamash is seen as rescuing merchants (and their goods) from storms at sea. But it does not speak of Shamash either sending the waves or stilling the storm, only of watching over the traveler and saving his life.

107:29. stilling the storm. The sea was the most powerful image of uncontrolled chaos known to the ancient world. In the chaos combat motif featured in the mythologies as well as in the Old Testament, the forces of cosmic chaos were most frequently represented in the sea. Creation is sometimes spoken of as overcoming those forces and bringing order and control to the cosmos. In this context it is not the primordial past that is under discussion but Yahweh's ability to (again) bring the sea under control and restore order for these merchants. This idea of transforming cosmic acts into the historical realm occurs also in incidents like the Israelite crossing of the Red Sea, when the sea was harnessed and controlled by Yahweh to do his bidding. It should not be missed that this was a significant element in Jesus' calming of the sea as well.

107:33-35. world upside down. In the world-upside-down motif, all that is considered most consistent and reliable is jeopardized. The concept can be applied to the cosmic realm (sun growing dark), the natural realm (mountains being leveled), the political realm (empires overthrown), the social realm (poor becoming rich) and the animal realm (lion and lamb together). It is often used in prophetic literature in connection with the Day of the Lord and coming judgment. The Babylonian epic of Irra is roughly similar in that it describes a reversal of Marduk's creation of order out of the original primeval chaos.

108:2. awaken the dawn. Dawn (*šahar*) was often personified in the Old Testament and is known from Phoenician and Ugaritic inscriptions, as well as being referred to at Emar. In Akkadian dawn is personified under the name Sheru. There are no references to any of these roles in the mythology nor to rituals intended to awaken the dawn.

108:7. Shechem, Valley of Succoth. The site of Shechem has been identified with Tell Balatah, east of modern Nablus and thirty-five miles north of Jerusalem. Perhaps because of its proximity to two nearby peaks, Mount Gerizim and Mount Ebal, it has had a long history as a sacred site. Shechem is known from many ancient sources, including the Egyptian records of Sen-Usert III (nineteenth century B.C.) and the El Amarna tablets (fourteenth century B.C.). Nearly continuous occupation is evidenced through the second and first mil-

lennia, demonstrating the importance of this strategic city on the highway network running north from Egypt through Beersheba, Jerusalem and on to Damascus. It was Abram's first stop in Canaan. The fertile soil in this area promoted agriculture as well as good grazing. Succoth is situated east of the Jordan River near its confluence with the Jabbok River (Judg 8:5). A number of archaeologists have identified it with the site of Tell Deir 'Alla, based on Egyptian records (the stele of Shishak) and cultural remains dating from the Chalcolithic to Iron Age II. The name, which means "booths," would be appropriate for the temporary housing of this region's mixed population of pastoral nomads and miners (evidence of smelting has been found in Iron I levels). It is located in the valley just west of the highlands of Gilead as the land comes down to the Jordan.

108:8. helmet, scepter. The term translated "helmet" is not used elsewhere as a reference to armor or headgear. It only occurs in the parallel Psalm 60:7. The Hebrew text refers to "a fortress for my head" or perhaps "my chief fortress." The scepter is now often identified as a ceremonial engraved mace that kings are sometimes portrayed holding in their hands as a symbol of office. It is referred to elsewhere in Genesis 49:10 and Numbers 21:18.

108:9. Moab as washbasin. The container referred to here is usually used for cooking but is a multipurpose pot/basin that comes in various sizes. Washbasins were typically used for ritual washing or ritual bathing and occur in lists of fine gifts in the Amarna tablets. The imagery here is obscure.

108:9. sandal tossed on Edom. Sandals were the ordinary footwear in the ancient Near East, but they were also a symbolic item of clothing. This may have been due to the fact that land was purchased based on whatever size triangle of land one could walk off in an hour, a day, a week or a month (1 Kings 21:16-17). Land was surveyed in triangles, and a benchmark was constructed of fieldstones to serve as a boundary marker (Deut 19:14). Since they walked off the land in sandals, the sandals became the moveable title to that land. By removing the sandals of her guardian a widow removed his authorization to administer the land of her household. Land transfers in the Nuzi texts also involved replacing the old owner's foot on the land with that of the new owner.

108:10. fortified city. Since the "fortified city" is parallel to Edom, one is inclined to think of the major fortified city in Edom. This would be Bozrah, which name is built from the same root as the word used here for fortified city. Bozrah was the capital of ancient Edom and is to be identified with Buseirah in the northern region of the country. It guards a portion of the king's highway and is fairly close to the copper mines found five miles to the southwest at Wadi Dana. Excavations demonstrate seventh- and sixth-century levels from the most heavily fortified and largest settlement in the area.

108:11. God going out with armies. In the divine warrior motif, the deity fights the battles and defeats the deities of the enemy. In Assyria Nergal is the king of battle, and Ishtar is viewed also as a war goddess. The Canaanite Baal and the Babylonian Marduk are divine warriors. In most situations prayers would be made and omens asked to assure the god's presence. Standards or statues of the deity were usually carried to symbolize their presence. Assyrian kings of the ninth and eighth centuries regularly referred to the divine standard that went before them. The ark, as Yahweh's standard, represented the Lord as clearing the way before the Israelites and leading the armies into Canaan. This concept is not very different from the Assyrian belief that the gods empowered the weapons of the king and fought before him or at his side. Nearly every army in the ancient Near East included priests and diviners (as seen in the Mari texts), prophets (2 Kings 3) and portable sacred objects (Assyrian annals of Shalmaneser III [858-824 B.C.]). In this way the god(s) could be consulted on the battlefield or invoked to lead the soldiers to victory. The psalmist here is invoking God's aid against their enemies in battle.

108:13. trampling enemies. Egyptian kings in the early third millennium B.C. are depicted as trampling over the corpses of defeated enemies. For instance, Narmer, possibly the one who unified Egypt, is seen with a mace smashing enemies and stepping over them. Likewise, the Sumerian kings from Lagash are depicted as marching over the dead bodies of their enemies. The tradition of trampling on one's enemies continued on into the first millennium in Assyria and Babylonia.

109:6-15. relationship between imprecations and hex/spell. This psalm is known as an "imprecatory" psalm because it calls down curses (imprecations) on the enemy. In the ancient Near East such curses were enhanced or activated by magical rituals and spells, but this sort of practice would have been unac-

ceptable in the biblical system. Imprecatory psalms can be best understood against the background of the retribution principle (see discussion in the sidebar on common concepts). Since God's justice was seen as requiring punishment proportional to the seriousness of the sin, the psalmist is calling down the curses that would be appropriate if justice were to be maintained. These are the same magnitude of curses that God pronounces on his enemies (see Is 13:15-16). The forceful language of this passage contains aspects of an East Semitic curse formula that relies on the deity to carry out vengeance on the enemy nations. An example of this type of indirect curse is found in the vassal treaties of the Assyrian king Esarhaddon as he calls on a host of gods to do the treaty breaker harm. It is also employed, with the addition of ritual acts of execration, in the Aramaic Sefire inscription: "Just as this bow and these arrows are broken, so may Inurta and Hadad break the bow of Mati'el and the bow of his nobles." The psalmist indirectly curses by imprecation, calling on God to "laugh at them" in their puny efforts to menace Israel. He does not employ magical incantations or execration rituals against them but instead relies on God to render these peoples impotent—breaking their power and their weapons of destruction (see Jer 49:35; 51:56; Ezek 39:3).

109:7. prayers condemning. From the context it could be concluded that this refers to a petitionary prayer in a courtroom situation. Such prayers could be accompanied by oaths of innocence (such as Job's in Job 31). If the party were not truly innocent, such an oath would be a basis for divine punishment.

109:24. fasting. Fasting is little attested in the ancient Near East outside of the Bible. It generally occurs in the context of mourning. In the Old Testament the religious use of fasting is often in connection with making a request before God. Presumably the principle is that the importance of the request causes an individual to be so concerned about his or her spiritual condition that physical necessities fade into the background. In this sense the act of fasting is designed as a process leading to purification and the humbling of oneself before God (Ps 69:10).

110:1. seat at the right hand. A fully armed warrior would hold his weapon in his right hand and his shield in his left. The person to the right of a king would have the privilege of defending him. For a king to put someone

---

For common concepts, metaphors for God and musical terms, see pages 511-18.

there would be an affirmation of trust and therefore an honor. In contrast, when the Lord takes up his position at someone's right hand, as in Psalm 109:31, he is in a position to offer defense with his shield. A statue of Pharaoh Horemhab (fourteenth century B.C.) portrays him seated at the right hand of the god Horus.

110:1. enemies a footstool. The Assyrian king Tukulti-Ninurta I (thirteenth century) "puts his foot on the neck of" individual conquered kings as well as (symbolically) on that of conquered lands, clarifying that they have thus become his footstool. This is graphically depicted in a tomb painting from the fifteenth century B.C. showing Thutmose IV seated on the lap of his mother (?) with his feet resting on a box that is filled with enemies laid out in a pile. For further information see comment on 108:13.

110:4. priestly order of Melchizedek. Melchizedek was the priest-king of Jerusalem in the time of Abraham (see comments in Gen 14). As a result Jerusalem had a history of a king exercising some of the prerogatives of priestly office. For evidence of this being practiced in David's family see comment on 2 Samuel 8:18. It was not unusual in the ancient world for the king to hold office as the highest ranking priest as well (compare the American president as the commander in chief of the armed forces; or the sovereign of England as the titular head of the Church of England).

114:2. Judah as sanctuary. This reflects a temple-as-state imagery. God's throne was in the temple just as the king's throne was in his palace. God and king reigned over the country from their respective thrones. This concept goes all the way back into earliest recorded history, as the temples served as the earliest administrative centers for the state. In this way it can be seen that the two lines of this verse are parallel in that the sanctuary is the central feature in the "dominion" (kingdom).

114:4. mountains skipping. In the Ugaritic tale concerning the building of Baal's palace, his enthronement is preceded by his voice thundering forth, with the result that the high places of the earth leap or quake. Similarly in a hymn to Marduk his thundering voice makes the earth quake. The Hebrew verb translated "skip" is often thought to describe a frolicking or gamboling type of motion but is more likely the undulating appearance of a flock of sheep or goats moving along a path (see comment on 2 Sam 6:14-21). This would be an appropriate image to describe the heaving of the earth in an earthquake.

115:4-7. idol ideology. Idols came in a variety of shapes and sizes in the ancient Near East. They were typically carved of wood and overlaid with hammered out sheets of silver or gold. Basically human in appearance (except those from Egypt which combined human and animal characteristics), they had distinctive, even formalized, poses, clothing and hairstyles. Images of deity in the ancient Near East were where the deity became present in a special way, to the extent that the cult statue became the god (when the god so favored his worshipers), even though it was not the only manifestation of the god. Rituals were performed to bring the god to life in its idol. As a result of this linkage, spells, incantations and other magical acts could be performed on the image in order to threaten, bind or compel the deity. In contrast, other rites related to the image were intended to aid the deity or care for the deity. The idols then represented a worldview and concept of deity that was not consistent with how Yahweh had revealed himself. The idol was not the deity, but the deity was thought to inhabit the image and manifest its presence and will through the image. Archaeologists have found very few of the life-sized images that the texts describe, but there are renderings of them that allow accurate knowledge of details. The images of deities in Mesopotamia were fed, dressed and even washed daily. Food sacrifices were brought to the deity on a daily basis (which were no doubt eaten by the temple technicians). Other attendants were required to dress and undress the statue, and still others were employed to wash the statue and transport it in times of celebration.

116:13. cup of salvation. The connection in this context to the payment of vows in the temple suggests that a libation is being poured out as testimony is given of God's goodness and protection. Libations were a common form of thanksgiving in the ancient world, as depicted on Egyptian, Phoenician and Mesopotamian reliefs. The libation represents the deliverance (salvation) afforded by deity and also accomplishes deliverance from the vow.

116:14. fulfilling vows. Vows are voluntary, conditional agreements that were common in most of the cultures of the ancient Near East, including the Hittite, Ugaritic, Mesopotamian and, less often, Egyptian. In the ancient world the most common context for a vow was when a request was being made to deity. The condition would typically involve God's provision or protection, while that which was vowed was usually a gift to deity. The gift would most frequently take the form of a sacrifice, but other types of gifts to the sanctuary or priests would be options. Fulfillment of a vow could usually be accomplished at the sanctuary and was a public act. In Ugaritic literature King Keret makes a vow in requesting a wife who could produce offspring. In return he offered gold and silver corresponding to his bride's weight.

118:22. stone rejected by builders. Israelite Iron Age architectural design made increasing use of cut-stone masonry over the rough boulders and rubble construction of earlier periods. In order to provide stability and to bind two adjoining walls together, a finely shaped block of stone was inserted that became the cornerstone. It would have been a larger stone than those normally used, and its insertion often required special effort or rituals. Its large, smooth surface was a natural place for inscribing religious slogans, the name of the architect or king responsible and the date of construction. It is possible that the cornerstone could also serve as the foundation stone. For information on the latter see the next entry and comments on Ezra 3:3 and 3:10.

118:22. capstone. The cornerstone or, better, the foundation brick is always significant in temple building and restoration. One of the most detailed temple-building accounts in ancient Near Eastern literature describes Gudea's construction of a temple for Ningirsu around 2000 B.C. The ceremony concerning the premier brick shows its centrality to the building procedure.

118:27. festal procession. To represent the abundance and lushness of the land, Israelites were instructed to celebrate the Feast of Tabernacles, waving branches and decorating their booths with fruit (citron) as well as leaves and branches from willow and palm trees. The festal occasion probably included dancing and processions carrying bundles of the leafy branches. In this way the people acknowledged the abundance provided by God and communally celebrated the visible fulfillment of the covenant. Ancient Near Eastern texts also describe the itineraries of priestly processions. These differed in that they took the images of gods, along with their various divine accoutrements, from one town to another within a kingdom. This allowed the god to visit shrines, make inspection tours of facilities owned by the principal temple community and participate in annual festivals outside the capital. These sacred processions paraded the images and symbols of the gods through the city streets to their shrines, where sacrifices, sacred dancing and other cultic activities would take place.

119:1. acrostic. The divisions every eight verses that are marked in most translations represent the consecutive letters of the Hebrew alphabet. Each verse in the set of eight begins with the same Hebrew letter. This is known as an acrostic. For more information on acrostics see the sidebar on common concepts.

119:72. thousands of pieces of silver and gold. This is a way for the psalmist to express a fortune. A common wage would have been about ten shekels of silver a year.

119:83. wineskin in the smoke. Though the skin bag referred to here once carried wine (1 Sam 16:20), it is not the vessel used for fermenting the wine but that used for carrying various liquids (for example, milk in Judg 4:19). The Akkadian cognate *(nadu)* is used for a waterskin (often of sheep hide), and the Gibeonites may well have used these bags for that purpose (Josh 9:4, 13). The word translated "smoke" is also unusual and could possibly refer to ash rather than smoke. In Genesis 19:28 it fills the air after the destruction of Sodom and Gomorrah and is said to come out of a furnace. In Psalm 148:8 it is paired with snow in a series of destructive forces of nature (in which case it would refer to the ash from a volcano, see 104:32). Snow and ash (different word) are also compared in Psalm 147:16. Here in Psalm 119 the metaphor that would fit the context is one of waiting with no apparent response. Placing a skin sack in ash would reflect a situation where low-level heat was required over a sustained period of time, such as in the production of yogurt. Though ghee was the more common dairy product (see comment on Is 7:15), yogurt was known in antiquity.

120:4. burning coals of the broom tree. The trunk of the broom tree provided hard wood that made excellent charcoal.

120:5. Meshech, Kedar. Meshech, a central Anatolian kingdom, was conquered by Sargon II of Assyria and invaded by the Cimmerians from southern Russia. It is thought that they were incorporated under Lydian control after the conclusion of the Cimmerian wars. They were known to the Assyrians as Mushku and to Herodotus as the Moschi. At the end of the eighth century the king of Mushku was Mita, known to the Greeks as Midas, the king with the golden touch. His tomb has been identified at Gordion and excavated. Kedar, the second son of Ishmael (Gen 25:13), was the name of a tribe that flourished from the eighth to the fourth centuries B.C. The tribe is known from Assyrian and Late Babylonian texts as Qadar. The personal names of the Kedarites appear to have been related to the southern branch of the Semitic languages. These tribal peoples were based in the Arabian peninsula and often made their way into the Levant via the Sinai. They worked as sheep breeders and caravaneers at least as late as the Hellenistic period. Since these places are in opposite directions from Israel, they are probably paired as representatives of remote and barbaric places.

121:1. help in hills. The NIV properly captures the idiom that sees the hills (mountains) as a place where one would need help. As a pilgrim the psalmist is intimidated by the mountains (because of the rigor of the treacherous walk and the dangers that may lurk there in the form of robbers or wild beasts) and seeks divine protection on his journey.

121:3-4. sleeping. In Mesopotamian literature a sleeping god is one who is unresponsive to the prayers of the person who is calling out for help. Enlil is said to be awake even when he appears to be asleep. In a Babylonian prayer the worshiper wonders how long the deity is going to sleep.

121:6. harm from sun and moon. Anyone who has traveled in the Middle East knows the threat of dehydration and sunstroke. Many of the roads to Jerusalem exposed the traveler to oppressive heat. Just as too much exposure to the sun could be dangerous, it was believed in the ancient world that too much exposure to the moon could pose a health threat. Medical diagnostic texts from first-millennium Babylonia and Assyria identify several conditions as a result of the "hand of Sin" (Sin was the moon god), including one in which the patient grinds his teeth and his hands and feet tremble, and another that has all the symptoms of epilepsy. English words like "moonstruck" and "lunatic" show that such belief persisted into relatively recent times.

122:5. thrones for judgment. As the highest judicial authority in the land, the king periodically held audience to hear cases that were being appealed. A throne was set up precisely for this purpose, either in an audience hall in the palace complex or at the main gate of the city. In the excavations at Dan just such an area has been uncovered at the entrance to the gate, where the king would have sat on a canopied throne in order to pass judgment.

124:7. fowler's snare. The very familiar image of fowlers trapping birds in nets and snares may be the origin of this common metaphor

(see Josh 23:13; Ps 69:22; Is 8:14). There are numerous examples of this activity from Egyptian tomb paintings, and it also provides the basis for the Sumerian *Stele of the Vultures* (see the comment on Ezek 12:13). There were a number of different techniques used to snare birds. Although hunters might simply use a sling, throwing stick (as in the Beni Hasan tomb painting) or a bow to take down individual fowl, the majority of instances in the biblical text and in ancient art depict large flocks of birds being captured in nets or cages. For instance, the tomb of Ka-Gemmi at Saqqarah (Sixth-Dynasty Egypt) portrays the fowler using a net. Apparently some fowlers also used decoys in their snares to attract the birds along with bait food (attested in Ecclus 11:30).

126:4. streams in the Negev. The wadis of Palestine are similar to overflowing rivers in the rainy season. However, they have little or no water during the summer season, precisely the time when water is most needed. In the arid desert region south of Jerusalem the periodic flooding of these wadis brought relief and life.

129:6. grass on the roof. The uppermost roof on the common dwelling places in Israel would have been constructed of beams laid across the walls intertwined with reeds and grasses. The whole roof would then be plastered with mud to fill in the gaps and make them somewhat watertight. Any lingering seeds in the grass or mud might briefly sprout but would quickly die for lack of roots.

132:6. Ephrathah, Jaar. Ephrathah is identified in several passages as the home territory of David (Ruth 4:11; Mic 5:2). The "fields of Jaar" are generally considered to be Kiriath Jearim, where the ark stayed for twenty years. See comment on 1 Samuel 6:21.

132:7. worship at footstool. First of all, it must be recognized that the ark of the covenant was considered the footstool of God's invisible throne (see comment on Ex 25:10-22). Second, the footstool must be understood to be an integral part of the throne, representing the closest accessibility to the king. Third, the imagery of the footstool has significance because it is used to express the king's subordination of his foes (see comment on Ps 110:1). Finally, worshiping at the footstool is another way of expressing the reverence that is shown by prostrating oneself at the feet of God or king. On the black stela of Shalmaneser III the Israelite king Jehu is portrayed kissing the ground before the Assyrian king. In *Enuma Elish* the tribunal of gods kisses the feet of Marduk after he has put down the rebellion and established himself as head of the pantheon. This was the common act of submission offered to kings and gods. Taking hold of the feet was a gesture of self-abasement and entreaty. This gesture occurs in a wide range of Akkadian literature as fugitives or supplicants take hold of the king's feet to demonstrate their submission or surrender and make their petitions.

132:17. horn for David. See comment on "horn" in the sidebar on common metaphors.

132:17. lamp for anointed one. See comment on 18:28.

133:2. oil on the head. Banquet guests in the ancient world were often treated by a generous host to fine oils for anointing their foreheads. This provided not only a glistening sheen to their countenance but also would have added a fragrance to their persons and the room. For example, an Assyrian text from Esarhaddon's reign describes how he "drenched the foreheads" of his guests at a royal banquet with "choicest oils." Oil preserved the complexion in the hot Middle Eastern climate. Both the Egyptian *Song of the Harper* and the Mesopotamian Gilgamesh Epic describe individuals clothed in fine linen and with myrrh on their head. Anointment of priests used the finest oil and would symbolize the gifts of God to the people and the responsibilities now laid on their leaders through this ceremony. In Israelite practice anointing was a sign of election and often closely related to endowment by the Spirit. See the comment on Leviticus 8:1-9.

133:3. dew of Hermon. The word translated "dew" is also used of light rain or drizzle. Hermon obviously got plenty of moisture because of the streams that flowed from it, a symbol of its life and prosperity. Zion is here seen as the beneficiary of the same abundance.

134:1. night service in the temple. The verb that the NIV translates "minister" has to do with taking up one's post or station. This need not refer to a ritual service of some sort but simply to those priestly personnel who were assigned guard duty at night. The temple was guarded twenty-four hours a day so that neither its sanctity would be violated nor its valuables stolen. Even such "mundane" duty gave one the opportunity of worship. On the other hand, night rituals cannot be entirely ruled out. Night rituals would have been common in the ancient Near East, but there the worship of the moon god and astral deities was of central significance. In one Assyrian prayer to the moon god that was recited in

conjunction with the New Moon celebration, the worshiper speaks of spreading out a pure incense offering of the night. Interestingly, the Assyrian hymn is a *shuilla,* a "lifting of the hand" composition.

135:7. clouds from ends of earth. In the Sumerian composition titled *Enki and the World Order,* Ishkur, the weather god, opens the gates of heaven. This was the way Mesopotamians understood where clouds came from. In Mesopotamian cosmology the "ends of the earth" refers to the horizon. This is where the gates of heaven are located because the sun is seen as setting there as it goes through the gates of heaven.

135:7. wind storehouses. The Canaanites and Babylonians attributed manifestations of storms to Adad, the storm and wind god. However, Jeremiah claimed that Yahweh was solely responsible for atmospheric phenomena. He used the imagery of Yahweh having storehouses of rain, hail and snow, which are set in motion by the wind, presumably instigated by his breath (also see Deut 28:12; Ps 33:7; Job 38:22). The word translated "storehouses" can be used to refer to treasuries that would store precious objects, as well as royal weapons. Hail, snow, wind, thunder and lightning are often seen as the weapons that God uses to defeat his enemies. Likewise storehouses could serve for the storage of raw materials such as barley, dates, grain or tithes in general. In the same way God rations out the products from his storehouses as necessary. Cosmic storehouses are not common imagery in the ancient Near East.

135:11. Sihon and Og. These battles are initially recorded in Numbers 21. Sihon is only known from the biblical records, and archaeology has little to offer regarding his capital city or his kingdom. There is also no extrabiblical information from historical sources or archaeology to shed light on Og.

135:15-17. idol ideology. See comment on 115:4-7.

136:6. earth spread on waters. In the Babylonian perception of the cosmos, the earth's foundation is on what is called the *apsu.* This is a primordial watery region that is under the jurisdiction of the very important deity Enki/ Ea. From the standpoint of physical geography it represents the water table that surfaces, for example, in marshes and springs as well as being associated with the sweet water cosmic seas and rivers. In *Enuma Elish* one of Mar-

---

For common concepts, metaphors for God and musical terms, see pages 511-18.

duk's names, Agilima, identifies him as the one who built the earth above the water and established the upper regions. For further information see the comment on creation in Psalms in the sidebar on common concepts.

136:19-20. Sihon and Og. See comment on 135:11.

137:2. poplars. A poplar is a willow-type tree that grows best by streams or rivers (such as the Tigris or Euphrates in Babylon). The Euphrates poplar was native to the region and had low-hanging branches and limbs. For information on harps see comment on 33:2.

137:7. Edomites' action. The principal theme of the book of Obadiah is an indictment of Edom for its crimes against Judah. This nation, located south and east of the Dead Sea, has a mixed tradition among the Israelites. Much like the relationship between Jacob and Esau, the traditional founders of each nation, Edom is at times seen as a friend and ally (Deut 2:2-6; 2 Kings 3:9) and on other occasions as a deadly enemy (Num 20:14-21; Amos 1:11-15). During the period of the Neo-Assyrian empire and the Neo-Babylonian empire (734-586), Edom had been a vassal state. Most likely Obadiah's complaint against Edom, as well as that of the psalmist, relates to the participation of that nation in the final destruction of Jerusalem and the exile of its people by Nebuchadnezzar of Babylon in 587/6 B.C. Unfortunately, however, records are unclear concerning the precise role that Edom played.

139:2-4. divine omniscience in the ancient Near East. It is not unusual in the ancient world for it to be implied that gods or kings know everything or that there are no limits to their knowledge. So Nabonidus claims to be wise, knowing everything and seeing hidden things (see even 2 Sam 14:19). But in most cases this is little more than patronization. While there is no reason to see this psalm in that light, it should be recognized that the context is judicial rather than dealing in theological abstraction. Yahweh is being addressed as the judge who is in possession of all the information for judging the psalmist's case wisely and fairly. In a hymn to Gula her spouse is praised as one who "examines the heights of heaven, who investigates the bottom of the netherworld" (Foster). Shamash is praised as one who (as the sun god) sees all the lands, but it goes further as he is said to know their intentions and see their footprints. It is more common for the gods to be attributed boundless wisdom.

139:8-12. divine omnipresence in the ancient Near East. It is difficult to distinguish "having access to every place" from "being simulta-

neously in all places." The former is all that is demanded from the words of the psalmist and is likewise the norm in the ancient Near East. Since the sun god is usually the god of justice, and there is nowhere his light does not shine, he sees all. Even the netherworld was known because the sun was believed to traverse the netherworld during the night as he moved from the western horizon to the east to rise again. As a result the divine judge would again have all the information needed. Nothing could have been done secretly. There is no concept in the ancient Near East of deity being in every place simultaneously in the way that omnipresence is construed in Christian theology.

139:8. heights and depths. This contrast expresses the extent of God's jurisdiction. In one of the Amarna letters Tagi, a local ruler, acknowledges the pharaoh's control by stating: "Should we go up into the sky, or should we go down into the netherworld, our head is in your hand" (Moran). Similarly a hymn to Shamash affirms that no one "goes down into the depths" without Shamash.

139:9. wings of the dawn. This verse may be adopting solar terminology (rising with the dawn = east, setting in the far side of the sea = west), but "dawn" is more often equated with the "morning star." It is not unusual for the heavenly bodies (or the gods that are associated with them) to be portrayed with wings, but the phrase "wings of the dawn" does not occur in Akkadian.

139:13. deity making in the womb. There is an Egyptian parallel to the idea of the deity knowing an individual before birth. The god Amun knew Pianki (an Egyptian monarch of the Twenty-Fifth Dynasty in the eighth century B.C.) while he "was in the belly of his mother," where he knew he was to be the ruler of Egypt. In the Gilgamesh Epic, Gilgamesh's role as king was said to be destined for him "when his umbilical cord was severed." Personal gods are praised as the "producer of my progeny." Nebuchadnezzar praises Marduk as the one who created him. In the *Atrahasis Epic* the goddess Mami is identified as the womb, the creatrix of humankind. In Sumerian literature the goddess Ninhursag (Nintur) is responsible for the birth process from conception through gestation and delivery, and even serves as midwife. In Egypt Khnum (a creator god portrayed as a potter) is described in his fashioning of people. He knots the flow of blood to the bones and is said to knit the bones from the start. It is clear then that the psalmist is not introducing new theological concepts but using stock phrases familiar in the ancient world.

139:16. written in book. In a *Hymn to Nabu* the sufferer laments, "My life is spent, O account-keeper of the universe" (Foster). An Old Babylonian letter says that a favorable destiny was decreed for the writer of the letter ever since he was in his mother's womb. In contrast, the Hittite prayer of Kantuzilis wonders how the god could have ordained his sickness (and impending death?) from his mother's womb. For information on the similar book of life, see comments on Jeremiah 17:13 and Malachi 3:16.

140:10. burning coals punishment. Calling down burning coals onto someone is found in Esarhaddon's vassal treaties as a punishment for breaking the treaty. Other texts describe deities raining down fire or fiery stones on their enemies. This is a punishment from God, not from other people.

140:10. thrown into fire punishment. Burning was used as a form of execution as early as the Hammurabi laws. In fifth-century Persia (during the reign of Darius II, son of Artaxerxes), and in the second century (2 Macc 13:4-8), there are examples of execution by pushing into a bin of ashes.

141:7. bones scattered at mouth of grave. Some of the cultures of the ancient Near East practiced secondary burial: the body would be laid out (in a cave, for instance) until the flesh decomposed, then the bones would be buried in the final resting place. Even if a body was devoured, proper burial could be carried out if the bones could be retrieved. So Ashurbanipal speaks of punishment of his enemies by taking their bones out of Babylon and scattering them around outside the city. He also boasts of opening the graves of past kings of his enemies and carting off their bones "to inflict unrest upon their ghosts."

142:title. in cave. During the time that David was fleeing from Saul, he spent a lot of time in caves (1 Sam 22—26). The Judean wilderness, where David spent his fugitive years, has abundant caves scattered throughout the region.

143:10. leading on level ground. The roads of the ancient Near East were for the most part unpaved (except for a few roads in the Late Assyrian period). Although unpaved, those which were intended for wheeled transport (called "wagon roads" in the Nuzi texts) had to be staked out, leveled and consistently maintained. However, very few texts describe

the construction and maintenance of these roads. Roads for heavy transport were somewhat rare and were primarily along the trade routes. Thus, a vassal king complained to the king of Mari that he had to arrive at the Syrian capital by a roundabout route along a major highway. Assyrian kings rarely boasted of their road constructions, as it appeared to be the duty of the local populations. In a treaty text Esarhaddon commands that when his son succeeds him the vassal must submit to him and "smooth his way in every respect." In a hymn to the goddess Gula the deity says that she makes straight the path of one who seeks her ways.

144:6-7. rescued from waters. See comments on 18:16 and 30:3.

144:9. ten-stringed lyre. This is a typical musical instrument of the time and is attested in ancient Near Eastern texts, reliefs and paintings as early as the third millennium B.C. The lyre is differentiated from the harp by the number of strings. Both are hand-held with frames made of wood. A musical text has been discovered at Ugarit that sheds light on Late Bronze Age music. This text has the chords to be played on a lyre accompanying a Hurrian cult hymn.

144:12. pillars carved for palace. Palaces in the ancient world featured open courtyards, audience halls and garden pavilions that all used pillars, both structurally and decoratively. Caryatids (pillars in the shape of human statues) are unattested in Israel, which would have had little statuary due to the ban on images. Caryatids of a sort are evidenced in Egypt, where, for instance, mortuary temples featured pillars that had half-figures attached to them. The word used here, however, appears to have something to do with corners (used elsewhere only in Zech 9:15). In Israel pillars would have featured the fine, detailed sculpture that represented the height of their skills.

147:4. names of the stars. Mesopotamian constellations included animal figures such as a goat (Lyra) and snake (Hydra); objects such as an arrow (Sirius) and a wagon (Big Dipper); and characters such as Anu (Orion). The most popular of the constellations was Pleiades, often portrayed on seals even in Palestine and Syria. Neo-Assyrian texts preserve sketches of stars in constellations. For further information see the comment on 8:3.

148:7. great creatures of the ocean. In the Babylonian *Hymn to Shamash*, the sun god is

---

For common concepts, metaphors for God and musical terms, see pages 511-18.

said to receive praise and reverence even from the worst groups. Included in the list are the fearsome monsters of the sea. The hymn thus suggests that there is a total submission of all creatures to Shamash, just as the Genesis creation texts shows all creatures created by, and therefore submitted to, Yahweh. The *Labbu Myth* records the creation of the sea viper, whose length was sixty leagues.

148:14. raised up a horn. See the comment on "horn" in the sidebar on common metaphors for God.

149:3. dancing. Much of the dancing that is attested in the ancient world takes place in cultic contexts, though both Mesopotamian and Egyptian sources frequently depict dancers involved in entertainment. The dancing connected to festivals would probably resemble folk dancing of today, featuring the coordinated movements of a group of dancers. At other times the dances could more resemble ballet, where a scene or a drama is acted out. Single dancers usually performed either whirling, squatting, leaping, hopping type dances, or acrobatics approximating a modern gymnast's routine. Dancers sometimes performed scantily clad or in the nude. In cultic contexts the participating officials (i.e., priests and administration) at times danced, not just the professionals. In one Hittite ritual this specifically included the queen.

149:3. tambourine and harp. See comment on 150:3-5.

149:6. double-edged sword. This is literally a sword of two mouths. In the Late Bronze Age (Joshua's time), the standard sword was curved like a sickle with the sharp edge on the outside of the curve. This shape is considered responsible for the development of the idiom "the mouth of the sword" (for instance in Josh 6:21). It is possible that the idiom was retained even when the shape of the sword evolved, and a two-edged sword could be referred to as "two-mouthed" despite the loss of the shape that determined the idiom. Others, trying to retain the association between language and physical shape, have suggested a double-sided axe, though in that case the word translated "sword" here would have to be understood more broadly as blade, a difficult (though not impossible) extension.

149:8. fetters and shackles. Though the terms used here are not the typical ones, it is likely that the former were wrist cuffs chaining the hands together, while the latter went around the ankles chaining the feet together (as is clear in 105:18). Iron was used for these as early as the eighth-century Assyrians.

150:3-5. musical instruments. Musical instruments were among the first inventions of early humans. In Egypt the earliest end-blown flutes date to the fourth millennium B.C. A number of harps and lyres as well as a pair of silver flutes were found in the royal cemetery at Ur dating to the mid-third millennium. Flutes made of bone or pottery date back at least to the fourth millennium. Musical instruments provide entertainment as well as background rhythm for dances and ritual performances, such as processions or cultic dramas. Other than simple percussion instruments (drums and rattles), the most common instruments used in the ancient Near East were harps and lyres. Examples have been found in excavated tombs and painted on the walls of temples and palaces. They are described in literature as a means of soothing the spirit, invoking the gods to speak, or providing the cadence for a marching army. Musicians had their own guilds and were highly respected. These are all typical musical instruments of the time and are attested in ancient Near Eastern texts, reliefs and paintings as early as the third millennium B.C. There is still some disagreement among authorities as to which of the Hebrew words in this passage ought to be translated "harp" and which one as "lyre." The one the NIV translates "lyre" is a ten-stringed instrument, while the one translated "harp" is thought to have had fewer strings. Both are hand-held with frames made of wood. The tambourine has been identified in archaeological reliefs as the tambour, a small drum (leather stretched over a hoop) that would not have the tinny rattle sound of modern tambourines. The instrument translated as flute is likely a double pipe made of either bronze or reed. Cymbals are made of bronze and are in the percussion group, so the only remaining question concerns their size.

PROVERBS

1:1—9:18
Wisdom Exhortations

1:1. sages in the ancient Near East. The tradition of sages who expound on the wisdom of ancient cultures is a longstanding one in the ancient Near East. The manner employed in such wisdom pieces as the *Teaching of Ptah-Hotep* and the *Instruction of Amenemope* suggests that there were wisdom schools in ancient Egypt and Mesopotamia. The "sage" functioned as the students' "father," conveying the substance of the culture's store of wisdom and standing as a source upon which to draw precedents. The *Words of Ahiqar* from eighth-century Assyria may indicate that some of these sages also were attached in some way to the palace bureaucracy, perhaps as members of the scribal class. The "words" of the sages included essays on personal deportment and etiquette in a variety of social situations. Their sayings also include short statements giving advice on political and diplomatic affairs. In this way they transmitted a form of cultural memory as well as a sense of their society's basic values.

1:1. Solomon as a sage. According to 1 Kings

3:7-12 Solomon asked for and received a "wise and discerning heart" to better rule his people. The tradition of Solomon as a wise king thus carries over in the superscription to the book of Proverbs. The many areas of his wisdom are detailed in 1 Kings 4:30-33 (see comments on those verses).

1:6. wisdom categories. This verse lists three of the many types of wisdom writings. The proverb or *mashal* is an aphorism, a short statement often consisting of contrasting parallel lines. It is generally moral-laden and always didactic in character. Parables are extended contrast pieces that in narrative form both tell a story and require the audience to see a double or hidden meaning (see the first two comments in 2 Sam 12:1-10). Although there are no riddles in the book of Proverbs, they were apparently common enough as a form of intellectual game (see comment on Samson's riddle in Judg 14:12-14). The term used for riddle in Proverbs 1:6 only appears in Proverbs and comes from a root that is usually translated as "scornful" or "cynical." This may be an attempt to downgrade riddles as true wisdom sayings. A longer form of wisdom literature is found in Ecclesiastes, which includes both

---

PROVERBS ECHOED IN ANCIENT NEAR EAST

Several pieces of Egyptian and Mesopotamian wisdom literature contain parallels (linguistic, stylistic and content) with the book of Proverbs. From ancient Egypt this includes (in chronological order) the *Teaching of Ptah-Hotep* (c. 2500 B.C.), the *Tale of the Eloquent Peasant* (c. 2000 B.C.), the *Instruction of Amenemope* (c. 1200 B.C.) and the *Instruction of Ankhsheshonqy* (c. 200 B.C.). There are also some echoes in the *Memphite Theology of Creation* (c. 2200 B.C.) and the *Dispute over Suicide* (c. 2000 B.C.). Similar proverbial sayings may also be found in the Assyrian *Words of Ahiqar* (c. 700 B.C.) and in the Ugaritic epics of *Baal and Anat* and of *Aqhat* (c. 1400 B.C.). Most of the similarities between these pieces of wisdom literature can be attributed to the universality of wisdom sayings and the very common practice of borrowing phrases, imagery, proverbs or even entire parables or stories. Here are some examples:

☐ Proverbs 1:12 describes the grave as a mouth that swallows its victims, and this same imagery is echoed in the epic of Baal and Anath, where the god of death, Mot, is said to "devour its prey," eating them "with both hands."

☐ Proverbs 6:23-29 and 7:24-27 both admonish the wise son to conquer his lust for women who will bring him to disaster in much the same way that Ptah-Hotep cautions that one should "stay away from the women of the house" and "keep your mind on business."

☐ Proverbs 16:8 and 21:9 provide examples of the "better than" saying that is also found in the *Instruction of Ankhsheshonqy*, "Better to dwell in your own house than in someone else's mansion," and in the *Instruction of Amenemope*, "Better is a single loaf and a happy heart than all the riches in the world and sorrow."

☐ The progression pattern found in Proverbs 6:16-19, "There are six things the LORD hates, seven that are detestable to him," is also used by Ahiqar, "two kinds of people are a delight, a third pleases Shamash."

☐ The model wife described in Proverbs 31:27-31 is also extolled by Ptah-Hotep, as is the son who is willing to listen carefully to his father (see Prov 2:1-5).

☐ The "Sayings of the Wise" that appear in Proverbs 21:17—24:22 find a structural model in the *Instruction of Amenemope*. Both contain a general introduction followed by thirty chapters of very similar advice on a variety of topics. For instance, both *Amenemope* and Proverbs 22:22 forbid the exploitation of the poor and weak, and both the Egyptian sage and Proverbs 23:10 counsel not to move or topple a field's boundary stone lest "your conscience destroy you."

a group of sayings as well as a set of reflections on the ironies of life. The largest category of all in the Hebrew Bible is the philosophical discourses of the book of Job. Using the common theme of suffering, Job and his friends examine and even test their understanding of why pain and suffering comes to the righteous.

1:8. instruction of the son. The call to listen to the instructions of one's parents stands as a corollary to the law requiring children to honor their father and mother (Ex 20:12). Thus the wisdom of mothers, who generally served as a child's first teacher, is equated with that of fathers. The saying also contrasts with similar statements in the *Teaching of Ptah-Hotep* and the *Words of Ahiqar* that only mention a son attending to the words of his "father." "Son" may also be understand in each of these cases as the one who receives the saying and does not always require blood relation. Students would have memorized the sayings and analogies of their teachers, but the wise would have been those who learned to apply what they had learned (see Hos 14:9). The omission of daughters reflects the reality that royal sons were generally educated, while royal daughters typically were not.

1:9. garland and chain. The words of the father and mother, which embody the wisdom of the society, can become a decorative wreath for the son's head and a chain or necklace of office. Just as a champion is adorned with a garland of victory and a newly appointed official is given the chain and vestments of his office, so too is the attentive son assured of prosperity and a stable life (see Prov 4:1-6). As Ptah-Hotep says, "The wise follow their teacher's advice [and] consequently their projects do not fail." In Egyptian literature Maat, the goddess associated with wisdom, truth and justice, provides a garland of victory to the gods and is depicted as being worn as a chain around the neck of various officials.

2:18. paths to the spirits of the dead. Ancient Near Eastern literature has several examples of the types of offers reflected here. In the Gilgamesh Epic the goddess Ishtar, impressed with the prowess displayed by Gilgamesh when he defeated the dread Huwawa, offers to make him her husband. Despite the many benefits she cites, Gilgamesh details the life in the netherworld that is the inevitable result of her seduction. Likewise, in the Ugaritic *Tale of Aqhat*, the goddess Anat offers Aqhat gold, silver and eternal life in exchange for his marvelous bow. Like Gilgamesh, Aqhat sees the lie and expounds on the inevitability of death. An affair with an adulteress is mentioned in several wisdom pieces as one of the surest ways to an early death (*Ankhsheshonqy* says, "A man who makes love to a married woman will be executed on her threshold"; see also Prov 6:25-26). The dangers involved are also reminiscent of the fate of the Sumerian goddess Ishtar's consort, Tammuz, who was forced to live half the year in the underworld as ransom for her release from the nether regions. The shadowy world where the spirits dwelt was an extremely undesirable place.

HOW PROVERBS WERE USED

As is the case in modern conversations, proverbs in ancient times functioned as a colloquial means of getting a point across. Then as now they were considered ancient wisdom that must be considered seriously (see 1 Sam 24:13). So when the proverb "A penny saved is a penny earned" is quoted today, the speaker is advocating the wisdom of personal thrift. In the same way, when Ezekiel quotes the proverb "Like mother, like daughter" (Ezek 16:44), he is condemning Jerusalem for following in the evil foot steps of her "mother" Samaria (compare Jer 3:6-11 for this theme, but using "sisters" as the kinship term). Ezekiel also used proverbs to signal a change in policy or fortunes. For example in Ezekiel 18:2-3, the prophet quotes a proverb that on its surface simply acknowledges the well-known fact that a person who sees another person eat something sour will experience a similar reaction. In Israel, however, the proverb had been used to indicate the legal idea of corporate responsibility in which a son was held responsible for the sins of his father (see Ex 20:5). Now, however, Ezekiel states no person will be punished for anyone's sins but his or her own, and thus the proverb "shall no more be used by you in Israel."

Naturally, a proverb is only as useful as the context in which it is spoken. Thus the writer of Proverbs notes that "like a lame man's legs that hang limp is a proverb in the mouth of a fool" (Prov 26:7). This is a common saying in other wisdom literature. For instance, the *Instruction of Ankhsheshonqy* warns that "fools cannot tell teaching from insult," and the *Instruction of Amenemope* states that one should not "take counsel with fools," since their words "blow like a storm" and are without substance. It is clear then that proverbs were not simply phrases to be memorized that anyone could understand. Their instruction needed to be unpacked and expounded by a wise teacher. It is like a curriculum that assumes the presence of a teacher to accomplish its aims.

According to the Gilgamesh Epic, the "House of Dust" contained no light, the dead were "clothed like birds," and "dust [was] their fare and clay their food." Still, it seems that the spirits could be consulted by the living (see 1 Sam 28:11-15).

3:3. bound around neck. See the comment on Deuteronomy 6:8 for the use of amulets to serve as a reminder of the Law and a form of protection against evil. The use of the covenantal term *ḥesed* for "love" in this verse may also be compared to its use in Jeremiah 31:3, in which God "draws" the nation to him with "loving-kindness."

3:3. tablet of the heart. It is conceivable that the writer is referring to a practice of wearing a small clay tablet as an amulet (compare Judah's cord and seal in Gen 38:18). However, the parallel with Jeremiah 31:33 makes it more likely that the writer is referring to an internalization of God's law with God writing "it on their hearts."

3:6. make paths straight. In a treaty text Esarhaddon commands that when his son succeeds him, the vassal must submit to him and "smooth his way in every respect." In a hymn to the goddess Gula the deity says that she makes straight the path of one who seeks her ways.

3:15. rubies as most precious gem. While both rubies and sapphires are forms of the mineral corundum, which consists primarily of aluminum oxide, rubies are much rarer and therefore considered that much more precious. The Egyptian sage Ptah-Hotep also compares true wisdom with rare gems (emeralds), adding weight to such analogies. Diamonds were not known in the ancient world.

3:18. tree of life. The theme of the tree of life is common in ancient Near Eastern epic and art. In the Gilgamesh Epic there is a plant called "old man becomes young" that grows at the bottom of the cosmic river. Stylized trees often figure prominently in ancient Near Eastern art and on seals from both Mesopotamia and Canaan. These have often been interpreted as depicting a tree of life, but more support from the literature would be necessary to confirm such interpretations. The tree is transformed in Proverbs into an image of wisdom. As in Proverbs 11:30, wisdom, embodied in the metaphor of the "tree of life," provides the key to a fuller and more enriching life. The idea of "embracing" wisdom holds sexual connotations found in several places in Proverbs (8:17; 18:22) and may be compared to the woman of worth in 31:10 and contrasted with "Dame Folly" or the "strange woman" (9:13-18 and

5:3-14, respectively). The sense of fertility and contentment inherent to both a good marriage and a flowering tree is thus promoted as a desirable goal.

3:19-20. language of old world cosmology. As in Psalm 104:2-9, Proverbs details Yahweh as the lord of creation, a sort of "divine architect," who shapes the cosmos like a well-ordered building (compare Job 38:4-7). The extra dimension is added in these verses of God personified as "Wisdom" (see Ps 104:24 and Jer 10:12). If a deity's "desire" may be equated with wisdom, then the Egyptian *Hymn to the Aten* expresses a similar concept, saying, "You have created the world according to your desire, while you were yet alone!" According the sages, the creative act, in order to fully demonstrate God's presence and concern, is followed by an ongoing and sustaining of the structures of the heavens and the earth. The "deeps" is the Hebrew word *tehom*, which refers to the primordial cosmic ocean. In the Babylonian creation epic, *Enuma Elish*, the goddess representing this cosmic ocean, Tiamat, is divided in half by Marduk to make the waters above and the waters below.

4:9. garland/crown. The image of a marriage feast is given substance with the bestowing of the tradition symbols of union by the bride (wisdom) on her protégé (groom). In this case the marriage symbolism of the crown of splendor (see Is 61:10) could be compared with the fragrant bridal garments in Song of Songs 4:11. In the metaphorical sense it could also be paralleled with Isaiah 28:5, where God becomes a "glorious crown, a beautiful wreath" for the Israelites.

4:23. heart as wellspring of life. It is a common tradition in the ancient Near East for the heart to be the seat of the intellect (see Prov 14:33) and the source of stability for one who would adhere to a just and wise life (see Solomon's request in 1 Kings 3:5-9). In Egyptian religious thought the heart (*ib*) is distinguished from the soul (*ba*) and is considered the very essence of a person's being. It is the heart that is weighed in the balance of truth when a deceased individual is examined by the gods Anubis and Thoth. The Book of the Dead provides spells to protect and strengthen the heart as preparation for this ordeal.

5:3. adultery in the ancient Near East. Having sexual relations with another man's wife was punishable by death in both the biblical and the ancient Near Eastern codes. The Egyptian *Tale of Two Brothers* calls it a "great crime" that is not to be considered by an honest man or woman. This was an attack on a man's household, stealing his rights to procreate and endangering the orderly transmission of his estate to his heirs (see comment on Ex 20:14). The act itself defiles both participants (Lev 18:20). Since it is not only an attack on the sanctity of the household but also a source of general contamination, adultery serves as a reason for God to expel the people from the land (Lev 18:24-25). The Egyptian *Instruction of Any* (mid-second millennium) has a paragraph that advises to beware of the strange woman away from her husband who is seeking to ensnare.

6:1. securities and pledges. The expression used here and paralleled in 11:15 and 17:18 shows an aversion to some common business practices, including charging interest on loans and standing surety for debts. The Laws of Eshnunna and Hammurabi's Code both describe in great detail the rules applied to these business transactions and the consequences of forfeiture. The weight that debt bears on an individual is graphically portrayed in the Assyrian sage Ahiqar's statement, "I have hauled sand, and carried salt, but nothing is heavier than debt." Proverbs thus provides the admonition to pay one's own debts, not burden others with interest on loans, and not become a creditor who may in turn lose everything based on bad loans (see Prov 22:26-27).

6:6. ant behavior. Examination of the creatures of nature provides both good and bad examples of behavior. The ant is proclaimed the paragon of hard work and foresightedness (compare Prov 30:25), storing food against the future. Yet another aspect of their character is noted in a letter from the El Amarna archive, stating that the ant, despite its small size, is willing to defend itself when provoked.

6:21. bound on the heart, fastened around the neck. This introductory statement, like that in 3:1-3 and 7:1-3, combines the importance of the wisdom statements with a physical object as a perpetual reminder. Thus the "Shema" statement of Deuteronomy 6:6-9 is to be tied "as symbols on your hands" and bound "on your foreheads." See the comment on Deuteronomy 6:8 for the use of a warding amulet, worn around the neck, near the heart, to protect the bearer from evil.

7:3. bind on fingers. See comments on 3:3 and 6:21.

7:8, 12. corner. Babylonian texts speak of small open-air shrines or niches on street corners or courtyards. One text says that there were 180 of them in the city of Babylon to the goddess Ishtar. These shrines featured a raised structure with an altar on the top and seem to have been frequented primarily by women. In this sense, the word "corner" may refer to what is basically a cultic niche.

7:13. brazen face. Compare the stance and attitude of the "brazen prostitute" in Ezekiel 16:30. The Hebrew term translated here as "brazen" is more often rendered as "strong" or "fierce" (see Deut 8:23), but it can also take on the connotation of "impudent" as in Ecclesiastes 8:1. This latter translation fits the context of the adulteress who lies in wait for her victims and confidently invites them into her perfumed chambers. It also can be compared to the wife in Hammurabi's Code who is "not circumspect" and "disparages her husband."

7:16. colored linens from Egypt. One of the most important trade items produced in Egypt was linen (see Ezek 27:7). Royal and personal texts contain mention of its production from flax thread and its use as a medium of exchange or barter. One Eleventh Dynasty text (First Intermediate Period) describes how a farmer used cloth woven from flax harvested on his land to pay rent. Colored cloth, adding an additional step to the manufacturing process, would have been costly and in the case of the adulteress was used as both a sign of wealth and a brightly colored enticement to enter her chamber.

7:17. perfumed bed. Like her linen coverings the adulteress uses foreign fragrances to transform her bedchamber into an exotic and desirable trap. Perfumes (like myrrh, frankincense and aloes—see Song 3:6; 4:14) traveled to Palestine by caravan from India and the Arabian desert and up the Red Sea coast. Perfume jars have been excavated at many sites in the Near East. Manufacture and rendering of spices and perfumes are depicted on Egyptian tomb paintings, but much of the details of these ancient processes have been lost.

7:23. arrow piercing liver. Egyptian tomb paintings often depict the noble deceased hunting in the marshlands. Beaters frighten the fowl to break from cover, and in their terror a hail of arrows from the hunters unexpectedly meets them. The unsuspecting character of the adulteress's victim suggests this same attitude of preoccupation or obliviousness to the real danger he faces. The liver was considered among the most vital organs, so is mentioned as the target here.

8:11. rubies as most precious gem. See comment on 3:15.

8:22-29. wisdom as preceding cosmos. Just as the Gospel of John begins with the statement "In the beginning was the Word," here the author(s) of Proverbs makes the claim that wisdom was the first of God's creations, existing alongside God from the dawn of time. Throughout the creation of everything else in the universe, wisdom is present. Like the Egyptian *Maat*, which is described as escorting the creator sun god Re, wisdom appears to be Yahweh's messenger, the oldest of created beings. It is possible that there are also some connections between this view of wisdom and the Babylonian creation myth or the Ugaritic depiction of El, but they cannot be clearly established.

8:30. wisdom as craftsman. R. Murphy has correctly connected this verse with the use of "I am" in Exodus 3:14 as a reference to God the Creator. If the role of wisdom is to serve with God as a "master craftsman" or the spirit of creativity, then this is an apt parallel with the image found in Proverbs 3:19. If, on the other hand, wisdom is "a little child" (some translations prefer this to "craftsman") playing at God's feet, there is still a sense of "delight" in being in God's presence and sharing in the thrill of emergent creation at a time when there are no other cares. Maat in Egyptian texts is also referred to as a "child of the gods," whose play delights them. There are also numerous examples of craftsmanlike creative acts, such as Marduk's shaping of humans in the Babylonian epic *Enuma Elish* and the depiction of the contest between Nintu-Mami and Ea-Enki to create humans from clay in the Babylonian *Atrahasis Epic*. In Egyptian creation texts from Memphis, the creator deity, Ptah, is portrayed as the craftsman engaged in the creative work. Beyond this, Akkadian literature speaks of the seven great "craftsmen" who are the ancient sages who came just after the flood and brought wisdom to the early kings.

9:1. seven pillars of wisdom's house. There have been many theories suggested for wisdom's seven-pillared dwelling. They include the firmaments of heaven, the planets, the days of creation, the books of the law and the seven sages of ancient Mesopotamia. In addition, the Ugaritic epic of Baal and Anat contains a reference to the dwelling place of the high god El. He is said to abide in "the seven chambers of wisdom, the eight halls of judgment." Murphy's suggestion that the book of Proverbs and its chapters comprise Dame Wisdom's house is also attractive. In the Sumerian lament over Eridu, Eanna the temple of Enki (the god of wisdom) is described as having seven niches and seven fires.

9:3. significance of highest point in the city. Wisdom calls at the city gate in 8:3 as the place for making public proclamations. But the "highest point" is usually equated with the temple or the palace that typically occupies the acropolis of a site. The sense of a call to study, wisdom and righteousness is also found in Isaiah 2:2, where the Lord's temple in Jerusalem serves as the high point that draws worshipers and "all nations" to that place (see also Mic 4:1). The good tidings that are to be proclaimed to the returning exiles in Isaiah 40:9 are also to be shouted from a "high mountain."

PROVERBS AS GENERALIZED TRUTH

While there is a universality to wisdom in the book of Proverbs, many of these sayings represent the collective common sense of the ancient Near East and its cultures during that time period. However, it should also be understood that statements like "keep my commands and you will live" (Prov 7:2) and "the LORD does not let the righteous go hungry" (10:3) are not explicit promises or universal truths. The values expressed in the biblical world do not necessarily translate perfectly into our modern age. In addition, there is the physical reality of poverty, need and want that is not an indicator of a lack of righteousness but merely an expression of economic problems, mental defect and social ills.

So what is recognized as true of modern proverbs should also be understood as characteristic of ancient proverbs (biblical or otherwise). They do not represent absolute truth but true perspectives on life's circumstances. "April showers bring May flowers" is not a promise or a guarantee. Crime sometimes *does* pay. This quality of proverbs is demonstrated for biblical proverbs in the fact that opposite solutions can be offered to the same problem. Proverbs 26:4 advises not to answer a fool according to his folly, while the very next verse urges answering a fool according to his folly. The fact is that there are situations in which verse 4 would be appropriate as well as situations in which verse 5 would be appropriate. The advice to be followed is often dependent on the situation, and a wise person will know which course to choose. Our own modern proverbs show a similar tendency in "contradictory" proverbs, such as "He who hesitates is lost" but "Look before you leap." Or "Birds of a feather flock together" but "Opposites attract."

10:1—22:16

Proverbs of Solomon

10:6. retribution principle. The comparison between the wise person and the fool is a common theme in the wisdom literature of the ancient Near East. One task of wisdom is to reassure the people that evil or foolish behavior will not be rewarded. Thus in the Egyptian teachings of Ptah-Hotep (c. twenty-fifth century B.C.) the sage expresses the proper attitude about work: "The wise rise early to start to work, but fools rise early to worry about all there is to do." The ability to make one's way in society without causing undue harm or distress is described in a saying by the Egyptian sage Amenemope (c. eleventh century B.C.): "More dangerous are the words of fools than storm winds on open water." Another Egyptian teacher, Ankhsheshonqy (c. eighth century B.C.), notes that "a wise man seeks friends, and a fool seeks enemies." In each of these statements the wisdom tradition makes it clear that there is a retribution principle operating in the universe that balances the harm caused by unthinking words and actions with the healing words and actions of the wise or righteous person. For general discussion of the retribution principle see the sidebars in Job 4 and on common concepts in Psalms, and the introduction to the poetic and wisdom literature.

10:10. winks maliciously. The word "maliciously" is interpretive here, and the other occurrences of this phrase include both eyes, so winking is unlikely. An alternative is suggested by the Akkadian omen-wisdom that contains a series of omens related to the eyes. One of them asserts that if a person closes his eyes, he will speak falsehood. It is uncertain whether this refers to frequent blinking or to squinting the eyes shut while talking. This same concept is expressed in 16:30.

10:11. fountain of life. As the Egyptian sage Amenemope states, abundant life is to be found in wise action and speech, but "fools who talk publicly in the temple are like a tree planted indoors" that withers and dies for lack of light and is burned or cast away as trash. On the other hand, "the wise who are reserved are like a tree planted in a garden," which bears sweet fruit, provides shade and flourishes "in the garden forever."

11:1. cheating in the marketplace. The practice of using "dishonest scales" was a temptation for shopkeepers and bankers. Within the civil authority of the state, the Babylonian Law Code of Hammurabi attempted to curtail this illegal practice by threatening forfeiture of an investment by a corrupt banker. In the realm of wisdom admonition, however, people are encouraged to strive for proper behavior. Thus the "eloquent peasant" of Egyptian wisdom literature advises the king and his officials of a dangerous situation in which "those authorized to give full measures short their people." The assumption is that the king will see the wisdom of eliminating such harmful practices. See the comments on Amos 8:5-6 for discussion of dishonest business practices in eighth century Israel.

11:15. securities and pledges. See comment on 6:1.

11:30. tree of life. See comment on 3:18.

13:12. tree of life. See comment on 3:18.

13:24. child discipline in the ancient world. There was a real concern in ancient legal (see Sumerian law code and Ex 20:12) and wisdom writings to teach children to honor and obey their parents. For instance, the Assyrian sage Ahiqar makes the familiar statement that to "spare the rod is to spoil the child." He also notes the persons "who do not honor their parents' name are cursed for their evil by Shamash, the god of justice." The parents' responsibility for their children is also a concern. It is clearly pointed out in the Egyptian *Instruction of Ankhsheshonqy:* "The children of fools wander in the streets, but the children of the wise are at their parents' sides" (compare the legal injunction regarding the prodigal son in Deut 21:18-21).

14:19. bowing down at the gates. In this instance "gates" refers to the household gates of the righteous, not the city gates (compare the obeisance of the king's servants at the king's gate in Esther 3:2). In that sense, therefore, the parallelism of the verse indicates that the evildoers will be forced to show subservience to the righteous, becoming their servants. A similar case in which due respect is granted by those who had previously taken no notice of their "new masters" is found in Moses' prediction in Exodus 11:8 that the Egyptian officials would "bow down before me."

15:4. tree of life. See comment on Proverbs 3:18.

15:25. widow's boundaries. Removal of a boundary marker was considered a covenant violation since the land was part of the people's inheritance (see Deut 19:14). In Babylonian ritual texts one explanation given for an illness is violation of the taboo against setting up a false boundary stone. The Egyptian Book of the Dead includes a disclaimer by the petitioner of moving a neighbor's boundary marker. To add to the nature of the crime, the widow lived without the normal legal protection of her husband and could have been easily preyed on. Thus the proverb speaks against infringing her rights. A parallel to this injunction is found in the teachings of Amenemope: "Do not poach on the widow's field."

16:10. king as oracle. The words of a king carry more weight than those of an average citizen. This becomes a major responsibility for monarchs, for as Ahiqar notes, the words of rulers "are two-edged swords." Few if any may challenge the words of a king, and thus as the spokesman for the nation and the god(s), the ruler must not infringe of the rights of the people or allow injustice to occur. As the eloquent peasant says to his pharaoh: "You are my lord, my last hope, my only judge."

16:11. weights and measures. See comment on 11:1. Note also the statement in the Egyptian Book of the Dead where the soul about to be judged by the gods of the afterlife includes in his "oath of clearance" that he has "not used false weights for scales."

16:33. lots. See the comment on 1 Samuel 14:40-43 for the use of lot casting as a means of decision-making. It is a form of divination in which the assumption is that God will determine the cast and thus provide the answer (usually yes or no) to the question that is posed.

17:3. refining precious metals. Gold and silver may be refined in a graphite crucible. Gold melts at a temperature of 1,945.4 degrees Fahrenheit and sterling silver at 1,640 degrees Fahrenheit. An additional 338 degrees is necessary to allow the metal to be poured without freezing and not so hot that a destructive crystalline structure forms or alloys are dissipated before the metal cools. It is also important to avoid oxygen infiltration as much as possible during the melting process so that the structure of the metal will not become porous. The refining process requires expertise and an intimate knowledge of the tools and metals involved. As such it is an apt metaphor for God's testing of the heart (compare the "weighing of the heart" in the judgment of the soul in Egyptian religious tradition).

17:18. securities and pledges. See comment on 6:1.

18:18. casting lots to settle disputes. See comments on 1 Samuel 14:40-43 and Joshua 7:14-18 for the use of lots to determine the truth of a situation. On the one hand lots were used when a random decision was needed (as we might draw straws or flip a coin). On the other hand, despite that, it was believed that God controlled the cast (see 16:33).

19:12. king as lion. Akkadian literature as early as the third millennium B.C. described a king (Sargon) as roaring like a lion.

20:8. role of the king. The traditional role of the king was to dispense justice from his throne of office (compare comment on 2 Sam 15:2-6, where problems are created when King David fails in this responsibility, with comment on Solomon's role as a wise king in 1 Kings 3:16-28). Although the statement is made repeatedly in the teachings of Amenemope that justice "is a gift of the gods," the assumption is made that the king, as the gods' representative, voices their wishes on earth. Thus Ahiqar, the Assyrian sage, can state that "the tongue of the ruler is gentle, but it can break a dragon's bones."

20:16. security for wayward woman. The law regarding taking a garment in pledge for a debt is found in Exodus 22:26-27 and Deuteronomy 24:10-13 (see comments there). Its abuse is mentioned in Amos 2:8 and the Yavneh Yam inscription. Both of those are directed toward how one is to treat his neighbor. This proverb deals with those whose reputation is either unknown or questionable. It stands as an admonition to the creditor not to be foolishly lenient and thus risk losing the investment (compare Prov 27:13).

20:23. weights and scales. See comment on 11:1.

20:26. threshing wheel. See comment on Isaiah 28:28 for a description of the threshing sledge with attached wheels (or rollers). This type of sledge (*'ôpan 'agalah*), minus the stones and metal teeth found on the *morag* (platform sledge), would not have damaged the grain so severely and thus would have left the job of separating the chaff from the grain to the winnowing process.

21:2. weighing the heart. In Egyptian religious tradition the dead had to face a final judgment before the gods. Thoth, the scribal god, recorded the responses of the examined, while the dead person's heart was weighed in a scale against a feather symbolizing Truth. If the answers were correct, and the heart did not overbalance the feather, then the soul could enter the realm of Osiris and live forever. Failure meant extinction, since a demonlike god, Sebek, in the shape of a crocodile consumed the soul. The Pyramid Texts and the Book of the Dead contained spells and a list of the proper responses to be given during this "final examination." Israelite thought took over the imagery of this idea, portraying

God as weighing the "heart," the seat of the intellect and thus the decision-maker, to determine a person's capacity for good or evil (see Eccles 3:17; Jer 20:12).

21:9. corner of a roof. The "better" sayings provide a contrast or extreme that is preferable to contact with evil or with the disagreeable. The corner of a roof or a cramped attic chamber (see 1 Kings 17:19) would be an uncomfortable perch, but its dangers or inaccessibility might protect the sufferer from an even more unpleasant contact with a nagging wife (see Prov 21:19; 25:24). The teachings of Amenemope also use this type of saying: "Better is a single loaf and a happy heart than all the riches in the world and sorrow."

22:16—24:34
Sayings of the Wise

22:20. thirty sayings. A portion of the book of Proverbs (22:17—24:22) seems to imitate, at least in part, the literary structure of the Egyptian *Instruction of Amenemope*. Both contain a general introduction that is followed by thirty chapters or units of very similar advice on proper behavior. There is some dispute among scholars on the identification of the thirty units within the biblical text, since there are breaks in the sections that may indicate unrelated segments (see "my son" diversions at 23:15, 19 and 26). Also arguing against the connection is the fact that the NIV had to slightly emend the text to arrive at thirty units and had to provide the noun sayings so that there would be something that there were thirty of. Beyond this difficulty is the fact that the thirty sections in Proverbs would each be only a few verses long (four to six lines), while the thirty chapters in Amenemope average twelve to sixteen lines in length. The closest parallels between Amenemope and Proverbs come to an end at 23:11, and the remaining units have close ties to other pieces of wisdom literature, including the teachings of Ahiqar. This may indicate that the biblical writer or wisdom school had a general familiarity with Amenemope and other wisdom literature, but also a measure of literary independence.

22:26. pledge and securities. See comment on 6:1.

22:28. boundary stone. Plots of land in the ancient Near East were marked with boundary stones at each corner. It was common in Mesopotamia for these stones or *kudurrus* to contain an inscription cursing anyone who dared to remove or shift the marker. God symbols were also carved into the stones as a sign of the landowner's divine patron. Several pieces of ancient wisdom and legal materials contain injunctions against tampering with boundary stones, including the Egyptian Book of the Dead, the teachings of Amenemope, and Deuteronomy 19:14 (see the comment on Prov 15:25).

23:10. fields of the fatherless. There is a general admonition in Israelite law not to take advantage of the poor and powerless, such as widows and orphans (Ex 22:22; Deut 27:19). However, such abuse did occur. For instance, Micah 2:2 charges evildoers with seizing fields and defrauding their fellow Israelites of their inheritance. Concern for dependents of prisoners of war or their widows can also be found in the Middle Assyrian Laws, where the government can be petitioned to provide for the needs of these people.

23:13-14. child discipline. The discipline of children, including corporal punishment, was considered wise and essential to the child's welfare. The Aramaic proverbs of Ahiqar include almost identical lines to those found here. "Do not withhold your son from the rod, or you will not be able to save him. If I strike you, my son, you will not die, but if I allow you to follow your heart [you will not live]."

23:21. gluttony. Gluttony was often condemned in Egyptian wisdom literature. Closest to this verse is the instruction found in *Papyrus Insinger:* "Do not be a glutton lest you become the companion of poverty."

23:30. bowls of mixed wine. The alcoholic potency of the wine, normally mixed with water, is enhanced with the addition of honey or pepper to create a type of "spiced wine." As in Proverbs 20:1 the fool is the one who overindulges in wine. Drunkenness runs counter to the wisdom tradition. For instance, the Greek custom of the "symposium," or drinking party, regulated the amount of wine consumed so that rational discourse was possible and a general atmosphere was maintained in which the celebrants could freely release their cares and display their talents in song and poetry. See comment on Ecclesiastes 9:7.

23:31. wine when it is red. It is not clear whether there is some fascination with the color red that is a further inducement to overindulge in strong drink (as is suggested by the Septuagint reading here) or whether there is a translation problem at this point. The sparkling nature of wine may indicate a particularly potent vintage that is smooth to the palate (see Song 7:9) or may be related to a term for wine in the Ugaritic Baal epic. The Egyptian *Instruction of Any* likewise includes warnings against drunkenness as leading to careless speech, bodily harm, rejection by friends and loss of senses.

24:13. honey and honey from the comb. The wisdom writer here follows a tradition found in both Psalm 19:10 and Ezekiel 3:3 in which God's words/laws are equated with wisdom and are therefore to be desired. In most Old Testament texts honey represents a natural resource, probably the syrup of the date rather than bees' honey. There is no evidence of bee domestication in Israel, though the Hittites had accomplished that and used bee honey in their sacrifices (as did the Canaanites). In the Bible honey occurs in lists with other agricultural products (see 2 Chron 31:5). Here the reference to the honeycomb differentiates the product as bees' honey. Note also that honey from the comb would be the freshest and tastiest kind. Akkadian texts also use honey figuratively as they speak of praise being sweeter than honey or wine.

25:1—29:27
Proverbs of Solomon Gathered by Hezekiah's Men

25:1. Hezekiah's men. Who these councilors or scribal officials might be is uncertain. Several advisers to King Hezekiah of Judah are mentioned in 2 Kings 18:18, but there is no way to equate them with the recorders of the "proverbs of Solomon." National crisis, however, is a time for reflection, and perhaps Hezekiah attempted to gain God's favor by having traditional wisdom sayings recorded and disseminated (compare the teachings of Ahiqar, a guide to proper behavior, which were presented to the king of Assyria as a means of his returning to royal favor). Certainly the text suggests that Hezekiah had court-sponsored sages who gathered and compiled wisdom sayings.

25:4. refinement of silver. For silver to be shaped into jewelry or decorative design it must be purified of the iron oxide that naturally occurs within the ore, or it will corrode or become too brittle when cool. Care must also be taken that no foreign matter be alloyed with the silver during the smelting process. This requires a temperature of 1,640 degrees Fahrenheit for sterling silver (containing 7.5 parts of copper alloy) and a graphite crucible. Proper refining of the metal thus forms a parallel with a king who attempts to purge his court of evil by removing disloyal and foolish advisers. The eloquent peasant of Egyptian wisdom also admonishes the pharaoh to be just, "a ruler without greed" and "a destroyer of lies."

25:11. apples of gold in silver settings. As in 15:23 a well-turned phrase or a wisdom statement is said to be of great value. The writer here uses the metaphor of a finely worked piece of jewelry whose craftsman has been able to balance a golden piece of fruit amidst an intricately designed silver setting. The delicacy of this decorative device draws the eye, just as a clever saying touches the mind. Some have suggested that the fruit named here is an apricot rather than an apple, but it makes no difference to the imagery.

25:13. snow at harvest. According to the work calendar outlined in the Gezer Almanac (late tenth-century Hebrew inscription), harvest activity occurred in the spring and in the mid and late summer months. Thus the dream of a cool breeze or even snow may well have been on the mind of workers laboring in the hot sun. An alternate interprets "snow" as water melted from snow and therefore cool and refreshing. Others have seen a reference to carefully packaged ice and snow being brought from the mountains. Either way this serves as an apt metaphor for the relief brought by a long-awaited messenger whose news refreshes and soothes the mind (the teachings of Ptah-Hotep likewise express the value of a messenger's words).

25:20. vinegar on soda. This verse has textual problems too numerous and complex to discuss here, and there is a disagreement in the ancient translations (LXX, Syriac) over its details. Vinegar is an acidic product, while soda is a base. Combining them would immediately produce a very noticeable chemical reaction. Taking away a coat on a cold day would likewise bring an extreme reaction (shivering with cold). Historically, singing to someone who was depressed also brought an extreme reaction when Saul tried to kill David.

25:22. heap burning coals on his head. The *Instruction of Amenemope* also advises the wise person to shame fools or their enemies by pulling them out of deep water and by feeding them one's bread until they are so full that they are ashamed. Similarly, the precepts and admonitions in Babylonian wisdom literature states that the wise man should not "return evil to the man who disputes with you" and should in fact "smile on your adversary." This is surely the direction this proverb goes, but the metaphor of heaping burning coals on the head remains elusive. Suggestions offering cultural explanations have included the following: (1) there is an Egyptian ritual (mentioned in a late demotic text from the third century B.C.) in which a man apparently gave public evidence of his penitence by carrying a pan of burning charcoal on his head when he went to ask forgiveness of the one he had offended; (2) in the Middle Assyrian laws there is an example of a punishment in which hot asphalt was poured on the offender's head. Both of these have difficulties. The first is in a late text and the action referred to has been variously interpreted. The second is hot tar, not coals, and is a punishment much like tarring (and feathering) in more recent history. Paul quotes this proverb in Romans 12:20.

25:23. north wind. In Israel a north wind does not bring rain but fair weather. It is therefore suggested that this proverb had its origin in Egypt where the north wind does bring the rain off the Mediterranean (five to ten inches per year in the delta).

25:24. corner of a roof. See comment on 21:9.

26:1. weather cycles in Palestine. Snow never occurs in the summer in Palestine, and rain is an extremely rare event during the harvests of spring and summer. The Mediterranean climate of Syro-Palestine brings rain and cooler temperature (below freezing in the higher elevations as at Jerusalem) during the winter months (October to February), and the remainder of the year is dry, with only an occasional freak shower. Thus this statement is like many in ancient wisdom literature (*Amenemope* and *Ankhsheshonqy*) in which the fool is described as "unteachable" and dishonorable. As Ahiqar notes, there is no point is sending the bedouin to sea, for it is not his natural habitat.

26:16. seven. R. Clifford has suggested that this is a reference to the tamed seven sages who brought civilization and wisdom to the world in Mesopotamian lore. The seven *apkallu* came before the flood, and their counterparts, the seven *ummanu*, came after the flood. This is possible, but one would expect a definite article (*the* seven) if it were the case.

26:23. pottery and glaze. While a glaze may be applied to pottery as decoration, it may also hide flaws and thus cheat the one who purchases the pot. Similarly, a silver dross or covering made of adulterated, oxidized metal may initially look good but will quickly tarnish or flake off. Thus the fervent or "burning" lips (see 16:27) of a scoundrel may attempt to cover his hatred and malice with deceitful words.

26:24. lips/heart. An Akkadian proverb draws the same distinction, observing that a man may speak friendly words with his lips but have a heart full of murder. The incantation series *Shurpu* speaks of one whose speech is straightforward but whose heart is devious.

27:9. perfume and incense. Various pungent scents were part of the Israelite's everyday life. To cover some of the more offensive smells, to enhance one's sexual attractiveness

(Esther 2:12; Song 1:13; see the thirteenth-century B.C. Egyptian love songs) and to serve as an offering to God (see comment on Ex 30:34-38), perfumes were concocted and incense burnt. Among the most common were frankincense, myrrh, saffron and mixtures of cinnamon, cassia and olive oil. Such a pleasant fragrance is an apt parallel with a friend's wise advice.

27:13. securities and pledges. See comment on 6:1.

27:21. refining precious metals. See comment on 17:3.

28:8. exorbitant interest rates. The law forbade charging interest on money or commodities loaned to fellow Israelites (see comment on Ex 22:25). It was lawful to charge interest in transactions with non-Israelites (Deut 23:20), and there is ample evidence of interest rates as high as 20 percent in Hammurabi's Code (see the comment on Ex 22:25). Usury as a means of building one's own fortune was considered inappropriate for Israelites, since loans were designed to aid one's fellow, not to take advantage of his financial difficulties (see comment on Neh 5:7).

30:1—31:9
Sayings of Agur and Lemuel's Mother

30:25. ants. See comment on 6:6.

30:26. coneys. The Syrian hyrax or rock badger is an ungulate mammal that lives in rocky cliff faces and inaccessible rocky climes. As a result it finds its protection in its isolated existence (see Ps 104:18). In addition, the ingenuity it takes to live in seemingly uninhabitable places points up the adaptability and resourcefulness of this creature.

30:27. locusts. See comments on Amos 4:9 and Joel 1:4-7 for the destructive power of the locust. The fact that their swarms move en masse without a clear leader makes their strength even more ominous to behold.

30:28. lizard. The ability of lizards to scurry along the ground (Lev 11:29) into the most secure places, including the royal palace, may make them the envy of some humans who wish for such exalted residences. There is also a sense here that despite the fact that they lack natural defenses and can be captured by hand, lizards make the most of what abilities they do have to succeed.

31:4-7. drunkenness in ancient world. The brewing of various types of beer and the fermenting of wine from dates and grapes is known in Mesopotamia and Egypt from protoliterate times (c. 4000 B.C.). Banqueting scenes are common in Assyrian art and depict parties of men and women eating from tables stacked high with food and drinking from cups and through straws. The Babylonian creation epic, *Enuma Elish*, describes how the gods banqueted, making "the sweet liquor flow through their drinking tubes" (a necessity since the lees of the beverage were so thick). A Sumerian hymn to the goddess Ninkasi celebrates the brewing process and gives thanks for the beverage that slakes the thirst and gushes forth in abundance like the Tigris and Euphrates. The ills of drunkenness are found in Psalm 69:12 and Proverbs 20:1 and in the drunken parties portrayed in Daniel 5:1-4 and Esther 1:3-8, and were also well recognized across the ancient Near East. Egyptian wisdom literature warns against intoxication with its accompanying lack of control and the resulting social rejection. There is evidence from the Mari texts of intoxication being viewed as a favorable condition for receiving divine oracles.

31:10-31
Noble Wife

31:10. rubies as most precious gem. See comment on 3:15.

31:13. selection of wool and flax. The idealized wife in this extended proverb has the ability to wisely choose the best grades of wool and flax for her weaving (note the prohibition against weaving wool and linen together in Deut 22:11). Flax was grown for its seeds and its fibers, and could be used to make clothing, belts and lamp wicks. Wool and flax are also paired in Hosea 2:9, along with grain and wine, as the gifts that God, Israel's husband, gives as part of the covenantal promise (also listed in Hammurabi's Code and the Middle Assyrian laws as part of a husband's responsibility to his wife).

31:16-24. business enterprises for women. Hammurabi's Code contains several laws regulating the activities of Babylonian women who operate inns or taverns. However, this may not be construed in the same light as having the ability to buy a field or sell finely dyed

and woven garments as a professional seamstress. The idealized picture of the "perfect wife" in this proverb goes beyond anything that the biblical text elsewhere suggests was open to women. Ordinarily they did not have the legal standing to purchase land, although they certainly worked hard with their families to cultivate it and deal with its produce. The one industry mentioned in ancient Near Eastern texts that was open to female enterprise was weaving, and this may be the model for all the other activities.

31:19. distaff and spindle. The terms translated as distaff and spindle only appear here. However, the context suggests that the translation is appropriate and that these are simply technical terms related to the task of spinning and weaving. There is a sense of intense activity performed by a determined woman willing to "gird up her loins" (i.e., pull up her sleeves) and produce large quantities of woven goods for both her family and for merchants to sell for her.

31:21. scarlet. See the comments on Exodus 25:4 and 25:5 for discussion of the various dyes used to color fabrics, especially linen. A red or purple dye would have been expensive and reserved for the wealthy.

31:22. fine linen and purple. A sheet of fine linen would have been a valuable and desirable commodity, to be used as a bed covering or cut into smaller pieces for garments (see Judg 14:12-13 and Is 3:23). A purple dye made from the glandular fluid of sea mollusks would have been quite expensive and in this context is a symbol of how prosperous the ideal wife makes her household.

31:23. elders at the city gate. The traditional place for the city elders to gather to do business (see Lot in Sodom's gate in Gen 19:1) and to hear legal arguments was at the city gate (see Ruth 4:1-4). Old Babylonian records note the legal role of the elders in judging land disputes, hearing the taking of oaths and serving as witnesses to various transactions (see Jer 32:12).

ECCLESIASTES

1:1. "son" of David. The term "son" can signify either a political relationship or kinship (any male descendant can be called a son). In this

context it associates the Teacher with one of David's royal descendants, Solomon being the most obvious candidate that comes to mind.

1:2. meaningless. As early as Sumerian literature and throughout the traditions of the ancient Near East the meaninglessness of existence, and particularly of the human plight, had been recognized: from the days of old there has been vanity (wind).

1:9. nothing new under the sun. From Assyrian royal inscriptions it appears that the kings were constantly seeking out accomplishments so they could boast they had done something that had never been done or achieved before. The king could thereby include himself among the "creators" or "founders"—ones who had established precedents. Such accomplishments included quest or conquest; building of a road, palace, temple or city; or the introduction of a new technique or celebration.

1:13. role of the sage. Sages seem to have comprised a different guild from the scribes, though their exact function and nature is obscure. They were certainly teachers, but whether they had formal training or taught formally is unknown. Sages were known in other ancient Near Eastern cultures and were sometimes counselors to royalty. For more information see comment on Proverbs 1:1.

2:5. gardens and parks. Palaces were often surrounded by a private garden planted with fruit trees and shade trees, with watercourses, pools and paths—more like a park. The arboretum often contained many exotic trees and plants. Such gardens have been excavated at Pasargadae, Cyrus the Great's capital city.

2:6. irrigation systems. Mesha of Moab (ninth century B.C.) also claims in his list of achievements to have built reservoirs for water in the king's house. The Jewish historian Josephus claims in his *Jewish War* that the King's Pool in Jerusalem was built by Solomon.

2:7. slavery in Israel. There were individuals in Israel who were deprived of at least part of their freedom and who could be bought and sold. The most common term for slave in Torah was *'ebed*. This term, however, was vague (similar to its Akkadian counterpart, *wardu*), since it was used for anyone in a subordinate position to someone of a higher rank; it was thus a term for general dependence. It has often been translated as "servant." Even patriarchs and monarchs were servants of God, and all the inhabitants of both Israel and Judah were servants or subjects of the king, including the members of the royal family. David was at one time a slave (vassal) of the Philistine king Achish, and Ahaz of Judah was servant to the Assyrian king Tiglath-Pileser III. A chief source of slavery was prisoners of war, who were sold as slaves. However, in the Mosaic Law an Israelite could not be forced to do the work of a slave. The only way an Israelite could be reduced to servitude was because of his or her own poverty or if he or she had been given over as security for a relative's poverty. This slavery ended once the debt was paid. There is very little mentioned about the number of domestic servants and slaves in ancient Israel. For example, a census taken after the exile (fifth century B.C.) recorded over seven thousand slaves, as compared to over forty thousand free persons. A well-off family probably owned one or more domestic servants. Although a slave was considered property, he or she was also considered human and thus had certain rights. The slave was considered a part of the family, as evidenced by the requirement of circumcision. Although there was no predominance of slave labor in agriculture, the artisan trades or any branch of the economy, there appears to have been some employment of state slavery during the period of the monarchy (c. 1000-586 B.C.). David set the population to work making bricks, while Solomon used "slaves" to work in the mines at Arabah, in the factories at Ezion Geber and in the work of the royal palace and temple. Most of these slaves were Canaanites and not Israelites.

2:8. singers. Musicians were usually retained for the ruler's entertainment or for cultic ceremonies. Since both male and female singers are included here, the latter is more likely. Mesopotamia and Egypt had long histories of both popular and religious music that must have been known to the Israelites. Ancient Egyptian tomb paintings demonstrate the postures of dancers as well as a wide variety of musical instruments. Court musicians, both male and female, are attested at many royal courts throughout the ancient Near East. They are attested in texts (including, for instance, Uruk and Mari) in the Tigris-Euphrates Valley, Hittite Anatolia and Egypt. They were included among permanent palace personnel, as rations lists demonstrate.

2:8. harem. The term here is usually considered a designation for concubines, but the word occurs only here and is obscure. Certainly the taking of concubines was a normal pattern of behavior for kings. Others have suggested that the word should be translated "treasure chests."

3:5. scattering and gathering stones. Stones were cleared away from a field so that the farmer could use it for agricultural purposes (see Is 5:2). One threw stones into an enemy's field so that it could not produce yield (2 Kings 3:19, 25; Is 5:2).

3:16. corruption of the judiciary. The writer bemoans the fact that what had previously been justice has become wickedness. In other words, the normal course of the world has been overturned, a common theme in Mesopotamian literature, especially in the literary piece called the Babylonian Job. For more information see comments on Isaiah 5:23.

4:12. cord of three strands. This phrase was evidently well known in the ancient Near East. In the Sumerian story of *Gilgamesh and the Land of the Living* Gilgamesh encourages Enkidu as they anxiously anticipate their battle with the fearsome Huwawa. He suggests that the two of them can defend one another and so they will succeed.

5:1. options in the temple. Ancient Near Eastern literature offers similar cautions. The Egyptian *Instruction for Merikare* commends the character of someone who is upright in heart over the sacrifice of an evil person. An inscription from Ugarit comments on the actions of a fool who rushes to offer prayers to appease his god even though he has no sense of guilt. The options mentioned in the text contrast the direction of communication. The sacrifice of the fool usually accompanies a petition to the deity for favor or the granting of a request. What one listens to in the temple would typically be an oracle in which the deity can express favor or disfavor. The Egyptian *Teaching of Ptah-Hotep* spends nearly fifty lines extolling the virtues of one who hears over the foolishness of one who speaks rashly.

5:2. swearing of oaths. This verse most likely refers to the swearing of oaths, for rash oaths were known to be a problem. The swearing of an oath was considered a very serious matter in ancient Israel. An oath was always sworn in the name of a god. This placed a heavy responsibility on the one who swore such an oath to carry out its stipulations, since he would be liable to divine as well as human retribution if he did not. Oaths were used in legal proceedings and for political treaties and covenants. Client kings and dominant kings alike were required to abide by their oaths to support each other.

5:3. dreams. Dreams in the ancient world were thought to offer information from the divine realm and were therefore taken very seriously. Some dreams given to prophets and kings were considered a means of divine revelation. Most dreams, however, the ordinary dreams of common people, were believed to contain omens that communicated information about what the gods were doing. Those that were revelation usually identified the deity and often involved the deity. The dreams that were omens usually made no reference to deity. Dreams were often filled with symbolism necessitating an interpreter, though at times the symbols were reasonably self-evident. The information that came through dreams was not believed to be irreversible, but a dream could be a cause for concern, if not alarm. This verse would then best be read, "As a dream is accompanied by many worries, so a fool's speech comes with many words."

5:4. vows. Information concerning vows can be found in most of the cultures of the ancient Near East, including the Hittite, Ugaritic, Mesopotamian and, less often, Egyptian. Vows were voluntary agreements made with deity. The vows would typically be conditional and accompany a petition made to deity. They were cultic commitments to God in which the worshiper promised to undertake a certain action if God answered his or her request. Artifacts used as votive offerings have been found at various archaeological sites in the Levant. Moreover, votive stelae from Phoenicia and literature (prayers and thanksgiving texts) from Mesopotamia, Egypt and Anatolia show evidence of vow-making. For more information see comment on 1 Samuel 1:11.

5:6. temple messenger. Scholars are not certain as to who this temple messenger was, as there is no other biblical reference to the office. From this verse we can assume there was a temple official whose job was to make sure that worshipers had fulfilled their vows. Similar functionaries may have been referred to on Phoenician inscriptions.

5:8. corrupt bureaucracy. The king in the ancient Near East was required to protect the legal rights of his people. The royal bureaucracy was thus responsible for justice and righteousness. Too often, however, reality was much harsher. By the time everyone (local officials all the way up to the temple and palace) got their share of the farmer's crop (in the form of produce taxation), bare subsistence was all that was possible.

5:17. eating in darkness. If one works in the fields from sunup till sundown, then both breakfast and supper are eaten in the dark. Thus those who desire wealth will not have fulfillment.

6:3. importance of proper burial. In Mesopotamia those who had not been properly buried were condemned to wander the earth aimlessly as spirits and to bother the living. This idea is implied in the horror observed in biblical texts concerning individuals who died in a violent manner without proper burial. Most ancient peoples believed that proper, timely burial affected the quality of the afterlife. See the comment on 1 Kings 16:4. In the Gilgamesh Epic Enkidu, having returned from the netherworld, reports to Gilgamesh that the one who died unburied has no rest and that the one who had no living relatives to take care of him could only eat what was thrown into the street. A Babylonian curse relates burial to the uniting of the spirit of the dead with loved ones. We know that even Israelites believed that proper burial affected one's afterlife, because they, like their neighbors, buried their loved ones with the provisions that would serve them in the afterlife most often pottery vessels (filled with food) and jewelry (to ward off evil), with tools and personal items sometimes added.

6:6. all go to the same place. In Israelite understanding (reflected also in many of the surrounding cultures) the choices were not heaven or hell but life or death. This verse is talking about human destiny, and therefore the place where all went was Sheol, the abode of the dead. For more information about afterlife beliefs see the comments on Job 3:13-19 and the sidebar on Isaiah 14.

7:1. fine perfume. Banqueters in the ancient world were often treated by a generous host to fine oils that would be used to anoint their foreheads. This provided not only a glistening sheen to their countenance but also would have added a fragrance to their persons and the room. For example, an Assyrian text from Esarhaddon's reign describes how he "drenched the foreheads" of his guests at a royal banquet with "choicest oils."

7:6. crackling thorns under the pot. The thin wood of thorn bushes produces a lot of noise that draws attention as it bursts quickly into flame. In reality, however, it makes very poor firewood and gives off no lasting heat.

7:7. bribery in Israel. Gift-giving was common in ancient Israel. Sacrifices and other offerings were considered gifts to God. Gift-giving between individuals was also important, although in some cases gifts were considered improper (because of the motive of the giver), causing the gift to be considered a bribe. It is in this context that the Israelites were commanded not to take gifts (i.e., bribes) since they "blind the wise" (see comment on Ex 23:8). As evidenced by the preface to the Code of Hammurabi (c. 1750 B.C.) and the statements made by the eloquent peasant in Egyptian wisdom literature (c. 2100 B.C.), the standard of behavior for those in authority was to protect the rights of the poor and weak in society. An efficiently administered state in the ancient Near East depended on the reli-

ability of the law and its enforcement. To this end every organized state created a bureaucracy of judges and local officials to deal with civil and criminal cases. It was their task to hear testimony, investigate charges, evaluate evidence and execute judgment (detailed in the Middle Assyrian Laws and the Code of Hammurabi). The temptation for judges and government officials to accept bribes is found in every time and place. In the ancient Near East taking bribes became almost institutionally accepted in bureaucratic situations, as competing parties attempted to outmaneuver each other. However, at least on the ideal level, arguments and penalties were imposed to eliminate or at least lessen this problem. Thus Hammurabi's Code 5 placed harsh penalties on any judge who altered one of his decisions (presumably because of a bribe), including stiff fines and permanent removal from the bench.

7:12. money as shelter. The word the NIV translates "shelter" is the word usually rendered "shade." It is a metaphor for the protection and comfort that come with relief from the hot sun. This may have been a well-known proverb, but it has not been found elsewhere. Presumably the shadow of money, like wisdom, is the protection that money affords the individual.

7:13. straighten what is crooked. In the ancient Near East the pious were constantly baffled concerning what the gods were doing and why they were doing it. In a Sumerian hymn to Enlil the poet says, "Your immensely clever deeds are dismaying, their meaning is a twisted thread that cannot be separated" (ANET, 575).

8:2. courtier's conduct. Advice concerning how to conduct oneself as a courtier is expected in wisdom literature, since its primary function was training future palace functionaries. The Egyptian *Teaching of Ptah-Hotep* addresses many of its paragraphs to people in various leadership capacities. The *Instruction of Ankhsheshonqy* advises in much the same way as this section of Ecclesiastes: "Do not make a judgment in which you are wrong" (16:17); "Do not hasten when you speak before your master" (17:10). The advice to the courtier described here is also similar to that in the *Words of Ahiqar,* a counselor at the Assyrian court in the seventh century B.C.

8:11-12. criminal punishment in Israel. Israel shared a common legal tradition with the rest of the ancient Near East concerning criminal punishment. The most common penalties in the Bible were stoning, death by fire and mutilation. Ancient Near Eastern sources (e.g., the

Code of Hammurabi and the Middle Assyrian Laws) occasionally mention the methods of punishment, which included drowning, mutilation and impalement. Imprisonment was not used as a punishment for crime, though there were debtors' prisons and political prisoners. Additionally, prisons would be used to detain those awaiting trial.

9:5, 10. no reward. The term "reward" here probably refers to the benefits of life, in which the dead cannot partake. They cannot enjoy any of those things that are considered blessings in this life. Beyond that, this also indicates the Israelite belief that there was no heavenly reward for a life of faith or good works. They believed that God's justice was carried out in this life rather than in the afterlife.

9:7-10. eat, drink and be merry. The Greek philosopher Epicurus was not the first to commend this approach to life. Even Gilgamesh was advised to let his belly be full, make merry day and night, and let his garments be clean and fresh and his body be bathed. He was urged to take delight in his children and wife. In Egyptian literature the *Harper's Song* from the first half of the second millennium advise a life of rejoicing and pursuing pleasure. This includes anointing the head and dressing in fine clothes.

9:7. wine. There were a number of different types of wine in ancient Israel. The most common form of wine was from the *Vitus vinifera L.* grape. It was typically red (Gen 49:11-12; Prov 23:31; white wine is mentioned only in rabbinic sources). The Old Testament mentions the existence of a "sweet wine," probably produced by exposing the grapes to the sun for at least three days before treading. Vinegar (i.e., sour wine) was used for seasoning and for its medicinal value. The most common mixture was wine diluted with water, although spices were also mixed with this beverage. As in the rest of the Near East wine was not the most common beverage but was used for special occasions, including feasts, coronations and weddings. There were certain biblical restrictions to the drinking of wine that were primarily of a cultic (e.g., Lev 10:9) and dedicatory nature (i.e., Nazirite vow). Wine was also used in the Israelite cult (e.g., drink offerings). Wine was apparently an important commercial item, as Solomon provided wine to Hiram of Tyre in exchange for the building of the temple (2 Chron 2:10, 15).

9:8. clothed in white. Scholars have understood the color white to symbolize purity, festivity or elevated social status. In both Egypt (Story of Sinuhe) and Mesopotamia (Epic of Gilgamesh) clean or bright garments conveyed a sense of well-being. Moreover, the hot Middle Eastern climate favors the wearing of white clothes to reflect the heat.

9:8. anointed head. Oil preserved the complexion in the hot Middle Eastern climate. Both the Egyptian *Song of the Harper* and the Mesopotamian Epic of Gilgamesh describe individuals clothed in fine linen and with myrrh on their head.

9:11. concept of fate. Fate, an impersonal force, controlled the destiny of things. Enki, the god of wisdom, wore a sorcerer's hat, showing that he attempted to control and predict fate, much like a human sorcerer. Fate was written on tablets, and those who controlled them controlled the destiny of the universe. If they were in the wrong hands, there was chaos in the world. In one myth a bird deity (Anzu) stole the tablets of fate, which caused quite a stir within the divine community until he was killed. The Israelite concept of fate or chance was different than in Mesopotamia. Instead of viewing something as a random happening (Fate), they would consider it simply an unexpected event (serendipity). "Time" and "chance" are presented here not as two separate contingencies but as a single factor. A "well-timed coincidence" can occur in any situation and alter what would have been considered an assured outcome.

9:12. hunting/fishing. Although Ishmael and Esau were known as hunters, hunting was not a typical vocation in Israel except in time of hunger or to get rid of the wild animals that caused danger to flocks. In both Assyria and Egypt, however, there are numerous wall reliefs depicting royal hunting scenes. Hunting is also implied for Solomon's court (1 Kings 4:23). This vocation was known well enough in Israel to be the basis for some metaphors. Fishing, like hunting, is not mentioned as a recreational activity in ancient Israel. The book of Job describes fishing by spear or harpoon (41:7) or by hook (41:1-2; Is 19:8). Like hunting, fishing was often the basis of metaphors, primarily as a figure of God's judgment on individuals or nations.

10:1. flies in the perfume. This little phrase is somewhat like the modern "one bad apple ruins the whole barrel." Something as insignificant as flies will ruin even the best perfume by making it so disgusting that the whole container will have to be discarded.

10:2. right and left. While there is no doubt that the right side was considered the place of honor and the most protected position, there is no indication that there was anything negative or inherently weak or evil connected to the left side, either in the ancient Near East or in Israel. It was secondary in honor and an unexpected direction from which to attack. The fool chose the path of vulnerability and lower status.

10:8-9. dangers of stated activities. (1) Digging a pit was an activity designed to catch a large animal. With that purpose in mind, the pit was disguised, making it possible that one could stumble into it oneself. (2) When a stone wall was dismantled, or when a breach was made in a wall for a gate, a farmer could unwittingly disturb a snake who had taken up residence among the cool stones. (3) The quarrying of rocks referred to here is probably not that done by professionals, because the other activities are all normal agrarian activities. The verb is used for quarrying but is also used in more general contexts that deal with uprooting or taking something out. Alternatively then, this line could refer to a farmer clearing stones from his field. Injury could come from dropped rocks, hernias or scraped arms. (4) Finally, the dangers inherent in splitting logs are easily recognizable. The axhead could fly off the handle or glance off the wood, resulting in serious injury.

10:11. snake charming. Snakes were greatly feared in the ancient world as magical beings as well as for their venom. Snake charming was a skill known throughout the ancient Near East. Snake charmers appear to be represented on Egyptian scarab-amulets (see comment on Ex 7:11-12). Both Egyptian and Mesopotamian literature contains examples of incantations against serpents and their bites. The word translated "charmed" here should not evoke images of swaying serpents hypnotized by pipe-playing swamis. Instead the reference is to snakes against which the incantations are ineffective. Akkadian texts also speak of snakes that are "unconjurable."

10:20. birds as tattlers. Stories of "little birds" who told secrets are found in Aristophanes' *The Birds*, a classical Greek comedy, and in the Hittite tale of Elkuliirsa. The proverbs of Ahiqar assert that a word is like a bird and that one who releases it lacks sense.

11:1. bread on waters. This proverb has been found in the Egyptian source the *Instruction of Ankhsheshonqy* ("do a good deed and throw it in the river; when it dries up you shall find it") and in Arabic proverbs. If Ecclesiastes follows the route of Ankhsheshonqy, it suggests that a spontaneous good deed carries no guarantees of reciprocity but that "what goes around, comes around."

11:2. giving of portions. The giving of portions generally assumes a situation in which goods or assets are being distributed (not just invested). This could be in the context of inheritance or generosity.

12:1-8. effects of old age. One line of interpretation sees a physiological allusion in each of these lines:

verse 2: sight dimmed, depressed
verse 3: trembling hands, stooping posture, losing teeth, cataracts
verse 4: loss of hearing, awakening early
verse 5: increased fears, gray/white hair, slow movements, decreased sexual drive
verse 6: weakened spinal cord, deteriorated mental powers; loss of bladder control; heart failure
verse 7: death

Some of these connections go back to the Targums (Jewish interpretive translations into Aramaic dating to as early as the first century A.D.), but the connections are difficult to substantiate since many of them are not attested elsewhere. So, for instance, to see the "golden bowl" as a reference to the brain would be unlikely, since in the ancient world they were unaware of the function of the brain. Could the silver cord be the aorta and the golden bowl the heart? The fact that no one can say shows the speculative nature of the whole line of interpretation. The Egyptian *Teaching of Ptah-Hotep* from the Middle Kingdom (first half of second millennium B.C.) opens with a dozen lines describing the effects of old age (such as eyes dim, ears go deaf, bones ache, memory and discernment gone), but it speaks in straightforward terms rather than using metaphors.

12:3. keepers of the house. The "keepers of the house" could be male servants, common as house slaves throughout the ancient Near East, who often were people in authority (like Joseph in Potiphar's house).

12:3. grinders. The grinders are female servants or prisoners who perform the daily work of grinding grain to provide bread for the entire estate. Grinding grain into flour was usually done with millstones and was the job of the lowest members of society. One of the basic "appliances" of any ancient household would have been the handmill (called a saddle quern) with two stones for grinding (see comment on Judg 9:53). Larger milling houses often served as prison workhouses in Mesopotamia, but each prisoner still used a handmill for grinding. Grinding houses would include prisoners of war, criminals and those who had defaulted on their debts.

12:3. looking through windows. There is a familiar motif of a woman looking out the window that is beautifully represented in ivory carvings found at Nimrud, Samaria and Ar-slan Tash (in which the woman is adorned with an Egyptian wig). In literature the woman is gazing into the distance awaiting news of a husband or son who has gone to war (see comment on Judg 5:28). This is possibly the basis of the metaphor used here.

12:4. sounds of activity. The doors being shut are double doors and therefore must refer to the city gate where all the bustle of activity takes place. Neither the city noise nor the laborers' noise (from the mill) is now heard. These sounds died out at the end of the day.

12:5. almond tree. The white blossoms of the almond tree apparently represent the white hair of old age. The almond tree was the first tree to bloom in late January-early February, rising to a height of fifteen to thirty feet. The almond flower is white with shades of pink, ripening with almonds about ten weeks later.

Other ancient metaphors for old age include white gypsum on a black mountain.

12:6. silver cord/golden bowl. The word for bowl here also is found in Zechariah 4:2-3, where it is a bowl that holds the wicks of candles. Some have assumed that the silver cord holds the expensive golden bowl, which, if severed, would cause the bowl to be smashed. This symbolizes the aging process and death. Josephus describes a golden lamp hung on a golden chain at the Jewish temple at Leontopolis in Egypt.

12:6. pitcher at spring/wheel at well. Both items are associated with a well or cistern. The wheel has been thought to represent the pulley, which lifts the jar out of the well, though these devices were not widely used. Alternatively, the word translated "wheel" (*galgal*) may refer to a cooking pot, based on a similar term in Akkadian (*gulgullu*, which, perhaps not coincidentally, also means "skull").

SONG OF SONGS

1:2. kiss. A kiss on the lips was used as a passionate expression throughout the Near East, though Egyptians in the early periods often touched noses instead.

1:3. perfumes. A number of oil- and resin-based perfumes were employed to scent the body and burnt as incense. Among these were myrrh, frankincense and bdellium (see Is 60:6; Jer 6:20). Saffron, calamus and aloes were imported from India, cinnamon from Sri Lanka and nard from Nepal. For other biblical usage see the incense recipe in the comment on Exodus 30:34-38 and the perfumes mentioned in the comments on Proverbs 7:17 and 27:9.

1:5. Kedar. The Kedar were among the most powerful of the northern Arabian bedouin tribal groups in the period between the eighth and fourth centuries B.C. They are mentioned in the Assyrian and Neo-Babylonian annals and are tied to the genealogy of Ishmael in Genesis 25:13 (see the comments on Gen 25:12-16; Is 21:16 and 42:11). Their tents consisted of animal skins or woven fabric stretched over poles to form a three-sided pavilion. The black color would have come from the use of black goat hair (see the comment on Ex 26:7-13).

1:7. veiled woman. Although this reference is uncertain, it may hinge on the differences

in costuming required in various social settings. According to the Middle Assyrian Laws, the wives, widows and unmarried daughters of citizens were required to wear a veil when out in public (note how Rebekah veils herself prior to meeting Isaac in Gen 24:65). In the house or in a setting where only family members or servants were present (such as her husband's sheepfold) the veil would be unnecessary. Note also the veil worn by Tamar in Genesis 38:14-15. This may indicate the use of the veil in Canaanite context as a sign of sacred prostitution or possibly by harlots working among the shepherds.

1:9. mare among Pharaoh's chariots. A tactic of battle attested in Egyptian literature was to release a mare in the vicinity of the chariots so that the stallions pulling the chariots would become distracted and confused. The word "harnessed" (NIV) does not occur in the Hebrew text.

1:11. earrings of gold studded with silver. As in Proverbs 25:11 the biblical writer uses the image of a finely crafted piece of precious jewelry to demonstrate devotion and affection. In this case the earrings probably had pendants of silver or studs embedded in the gold setting (see comment on Is 3:18-23).

1:13. sachet of myrrh. Myrrh bushes grow in

the arid region just north of the coastal mountains of Yemen and Oman in the rain shadow of the southwest monsoon. The reddish myrrh resin, extracted by gashing the thorny stems and exposing the inner bark, appears as juicy drupes. It was crushed for use in making perfume or as a medicinal ingredient. Its natural fragrance, somewhat like turpentine, was long-lasting enough to be placed in a sachet to enhance sexual pleasure or serve as an aromatic mask to the odors often present in ancient homes. Pouches worn around the neck containing various elements were worn as amulets in Egypt.

1:14. henna blossoms. Henna is a flowering shrub, *Lawsonia inermis L.*, with fragrant white blossoms. It grows in many areas of the Middle East, and has been discovered in the tomb of the pharaoh Tutankhamen. The leaves and twigs produce a red, yellow or orange dye that can be used to color the hair and other parts of the body. Their fragrance is similar to roses.

1:14. En Gedi. This is an oasis located thirty-five miles southeast of Jerusalem and nestled within a ravine on the western shore of the Dead Sea. The name means "spring of the young goat," and the excavation of the fourth-millennium temple within its precincts attests the antiquity of its refreshing character. In this metaphor the peculiar location of the oasis between the ridges of the surrounding hills makes it an apt parallel to the sachet of myrrh and the bouquet of henna blossoms between the "beloved's" breasts.

1:15. eyes are doves. Doves figure prominently on seals and other iconography as a symbol of lovemaking or seduction. They are sometimes understood as messengers of love. In this case the eyes are seen as having seductive power.

2:1. rose of Sharon. While the exact flower referred to here is unknown, the use of the Hebrew word *shushan* for "lily" in this verse indicates a plant with six petals. A likely choice, therefore, would be the polyanthus narcissus, which grows in the hills and moist valleys of the Sharon Plain. It flowers during the winter and has white petals and an orange cup or corona enhancing the beauty of each cluster. Narcissi have been found as offerings in Hellenistic tombs in Egypt.

2:4. banner over me is love. The translation of *degel* as "banner" is uncertain. Both Murphy and Fox make reference to an Akkadian cognate, *diglu*, "glance" or "intent," and Fox chooses to translate "his intent towards me was love." In either case, setting a standard as a symbol of possession or making an intent to carry out an action arrives at the same conclusion, to make love to the beloved (see Jer 2:33).

2:5. raisins/apples as aphrodisiac. The woman asks for raisins and apples as a cure restorative for her "love sickness" (similar to the lovesick male in Chester Beatty's love songs from Egypt). It can only be cured by the return of her lover. It is possible that the raisins are associated with the raisin cakes mentioned in association with the worship of the goddess Ishtar (see the comment on Jer 7:18). Apples also were understood as aphrodisiacs in Assyrian incantations.

2:7. gazelles and does. Gazelles and does are often portrayed as the companions of the god-

SEXUAL METAPHOR

The explicit nature of portions of the Song of Songs may be a bit shocking to some readers. However, metaphorical erotic literature was not uncommon in the ancient Near East, as is seen especially in Egyptian Love Songs. Fertility was a major issue for the people of these cultures, since their lives revolved and relied upon the harvest. Most of their religious festivals and holidays centered on the agricultural calendar, and it was an easy step to employ these images of plowing, seeding, cultivation and harvest to human relations. As a result, the sexual metaphors that appear in the text express the high emotions of a loving couple, who find it difficult to be separated and who in sometimes flamboyant terms describe each other's merits and beauty. It would be impossible in the light of their passion to speak in anything other than sensuous and intimate terms.

There is a celebration of life here, both in the natural world and amongst humans. So when the "beloved" speaks of her lover as being graceful as a gazelle, leaping over hills (2:17) and thus demonstrating his energy and athletic skills, it is easy to enter into her passionate realm. He equates her with all that is beautiful, "a mare among Pharaoh's chariots" (1:19), with eyes like doves (1:15; 4:1) and lips a "scarlet ribbon" (4:3). She in turn describes him as a fragrant sachet of myrrh worn around her neck and close to her heart (1:13-14). Such comparison masks the thorns of everyday life and for a time restores a sense of the idyllic essence of Eden.

Most English translations disguise some of the most blatant erotic imagery with euphemism and metaphor, as is appropriate considering the poetic nature of the literature and the need to preserve a certain propriety for a general audience.

dess of love in ancient Near Eastern art.

2:9. peering through the lattice motif. The finely carved ivories found in excavations of the Iron Age levels at Samaria and Nimrud include the motif of "the woman in the window." Some associate this with the Phoenician goddess Astarte, who was identified with a cult of sacred prostitution (see the adulteress's spying through the lattice in Prov 7:6). In this case, however, it is the impatient man who periodically glances through the screen to see when his lover will be ready to admit him.

2:13. early figs. The word used for fig here, *paggâ,* does not appear elsewhere in the Bible, but there are Aramaic and Arabic cognates which refer to the first unripe fruit to appear on a fig tree. Ordinarily the fig tree has two crops a year. The first ripens in June and the second in August or September (see Jer 24:3; Hos 9:10).

2:15. foxes. In the Egyptian love poetry foxes represent sexually aggressive men, rather like the term "wolf" in American idiom.

2:16. lilies. Some translators consider the lilies mentioned here to be lotus flowers, which were symbols of sensuality and fertility in Egypt and Canaan.

3:2. motif of searching through the city. See the comment on Jeremiah 5:1 comparing Jeremiah to the Greek philosopher Diogenes in his search through a city for an "honest man." The motif of searching a city is also found in Ezekiel's vision of the executioners and the scribe in Ezekiel 9. There is an intensity in this verse that is tied to the desperation and anxiousness of the woman for her lover, which even draws her into a potentially dangerous search. Ordinarily an honorable woman would not be out on the streets alone (compare the adulteress in Prov 7:6-20). Mythological literature also depicts the search of the consort for her lover. In Canaanite mythology Anat goes seeking for Baal; in Egyptian literature Isis goes on a quest for Osiris.

3:4. mother's house. As is the case in Genesis 24:28 in the story of Rebekah and in Ruth 1:8 when Naomi instructs her daughters-in-law to return to their "mother's house," in this instance the term "mother's house" is indicative of both a spatial and a social realm. The *bêt 'em* in each of these texts is to be equated with the *bêt 'ab,* or "father's house." While most texts, perhaps due to the legal issues of inheritance and landownership, employ "father's house" (see Gen 38:11; Lev 22:13), the importance of females within the household with respect to procreation as well as management of its affairs (see Prov 31:10-31) made these terms of equal social value within Israelite culture.

3:6. merchant spices. Merchant caravans brought quantities of incense, both frankincense and myrrh, from the desert regions of southern Arabia and Somalia. These expensive items not only provide a cloud of fragrance for the procession described here but also enhance the sexual desirability of the woman. The Egyptian love songs repeatedly refer to "myrrh-anointed beauty" and other aromas as sexual intoxicants.

3:9. wooden carriage. The lovers compare their bower to the royal canopy of King Solomon, constructed from the finest wood from Lebanon and decorated with gold and silver. The term translated "carriage" here has had many interpretations based on Egyptian, Aramaic and Greek cognates. Ideas range from a litter or sedan chair to a throne room or "magnificent building." Fox's idea of a covered pavilion in a garden (see Esther 1:6) or a garden kiosk such as those in Mesopotamian texts and Egyptian tomb paintings is a likely suggestion.

3:11. crowned by mother at wedding. Wedding garlands were worn by the couple as they processed to their nuptial ceremony (Is 61:10; compare the Persian king placing a crown on Esther's head when he makes her his queen in Esther 2:17). There is no evidence elsewhere in the text of a mother crowning her son as king, although given the theme of Solomon's wise reign it may be a reference to the "crown of splendor" that Dame Wisdom places on the head of her chosen (Prov 4:9). The mother held the position of priority in the family concerning all matters of the heart.

4:1-7. description of lover's body. As Keel points out, for the most part the descriptions focus on dynamic powers rather than shapes. So the eyes are not shaped like doves but act like doves (see comment on 1:15).

4:3. temples as halves of pomegranate. Rather than "halves" of a pomegranate, Keel plausibly suggests slit of the pomegranate revealing the tender red fruit. This would fit well with the parallel of the lips earlier in the verse. If that is the case, the word translated "temples" should be translated as "cheeks."

4:4. tower of David. According to the fashion described in the Egyptian love songs and depicted in art (bust of Nefertiti) a long neck was a characteristic of a beautiful woman. Thus a comparison with a tall, well-built tower is quite apt (see 7:4 and comparison with an "ivory tower"). However, the structure itself is unknown to archaeologists, and it is unclear whether it stood in Jerusalem or some other city. More important than the shape, however, was the fact that a tower represented the pride and glory of a city. This is the imagery also used for the neck in the Bible (for instance, Ps 75:5).

4:4. shields hung on tower. The metaphor of a woman's adorned neck continues by comparing the shields used to decorate the structure (compare 1 Kings 10:16-17) with the necklaces and strings of jewels worn by wealthy or beloved women (see Prov 1:9; Song 1:10; Ezek 16:11). In his "Lament for Tyre" Ezekiel describes how shields were hung on the city walls to add to its beauty (Ezek 27:10-11).

4:8. crest of Amana. Now the lover calls his beloved to join him from her inaccessible heights and distant lands. This is a metaphor of his desire for her presence rather than her actual geographic location. The Amana is one of the peaks of the Anti-Lebanon Range, near the source of the Amanus River.

4:8. Senir/Hermon. These are alternate names for the same peak, Mount Hermon (see comment on Deut 3:9). Assyrian records mention Senir within the Lebanon range, in northern Transjordan. The song here simply uses this metaphorically inaccessible region as synonymous with the lover's feeling of isolation when separated from his beloved.

4:8. lions and leopards. These wild animals are often the companions of goddesses, particularly Ishtar, the Mesopotamian goddess of love. Keel says that the motif stretches from Neolithic art all the way into the classical Greek and Roman period.

4:12. gardens. Gardens were places of delight and refreshment and therefore served easily as a metaphor for the beloved. Sumerian literature used the metaphor to describe the lover's partner as a well-stocked garden, and Akkadian proverbs describe a woman as a garden of delight. In Egyptian love songs the woman describes herself as a field planted with all sorts of plants.

4:13-14. spices. As is commonly the case in the Egyptian love songs, the beloved woman's beauty and desirability is compared to fragrant fruits, trees and spices (see the comments on Prov 7:17 and 27:9). The exaggeration of the number and variety of exotic plants listed here may simply be a reflection of a "lover's flattery." Nine types of spices are listed, and three actually grow in Israel (balsam, henna, saffron). The crimson saffron crocus produces such minute quantities of spice that over four thousand flowers are needed to produce an ounce. Frankincense, aloes and spikenard were imported from Arabia, India, Nepal and China, and thus were extremely expensive. Spikenard is obtained from camel grass in the deserts of Arabia and North Africa, but is also referred to as "pure nard" (see

Mk 14:3). It is made from the flowers of a plant growing on the slopes of the Himalayas (thirteen thousand feet in elevation) and was considered an aphrodisiac. Myrrh, cinnamon and sweet cane/calamus were also imported. Calamus comes from an aromatic grass found in India, which today is used to produce citronella oils.

5:7. treatment by guards. It is possible that the watchmen considered an unaccompanied, young female out at night a harlot. They take away her veil or light scarf (see Is 3:18, 23), perhaps in line with the Middle Assyrian law that permits only "mothers of households, widows and other free women" to wear a veil in public. The woman may have launched into her search so quickly that she is only half dressed, like the lovesick woman in the Egyptian love songs.

5:15. pillars of marble. Now it is the woman's turn to describe her lover in flamboyant terms. Her comparisons of his legs with a pair of finely carved marble pillars set on golden bases is similar to the description Ben Sira uses for a woman's shapely legs and feet (Ecclus 26:18). A similar portrayal of perfect physical symmetry can be found in the description of the Babylonian god Marduk in the *Enuma Elish* creation epic.

6:4. Tirzah. Although the capital of the northern kingdom of Israel was moved from Tirzah (Tell el-Far'ah) during Omri's reign, that does not mean it was totally abandoned. It is possible the writer here wishes to avoid comparisons between Jerusalem and Samaria, political rivals, so Tirzah could be a substitute. The name also serves as a pun, based on the Hebrew root *rṣh*, "pleasing" or "beauty." This allows the lover to intensify his statement that she is as "beautiful as Tirzah."

6:8. harem. A royal harem consists of (1) women who are designated as "queens" and whose sons are automatically in the line of succession; (2) concubines who have a lesser status and whose sons may not inherit without the direct command of the king; and (3) maidens who may be either women who have not yet been presented formally to the king (see Esther 2:8-14) or those who have not yet borne children. In this case the man boasts that his beloved is more beautiful that any number (sixty plus eighty equals infinity) of women in the king's harem.

6:11. nut trees. While pistachios and pine nuts were common in ancient Palestine, there were no naturally occurring "nuts" such as walnuts (*Juglans regia* L.). The term *'egoz*, which only appears in this verse in the Bible, has been translated as "walnut," and that suggests that the tree may have been introduced in Palestine from its natural habitat in Persia and India prior to the Hellenistic period.

6:13. Shulammite. Since a definite article precedes this name, it is probably an epithet, such as "perfect one," not a personal name. The name may be based on a feminine form of the name Solomon, or possibly there is a connection with the Mesopotamian goddess Shulmanitu or Sala. It is unlikely that the name refers to an inhabitant of Shunem, since the woman is so closely associated with Jerusalem in the songs.

6:13. dance of Mahanaim. No specific dance has been associated with Mahanaim, a site in Transjordan on the Jabbok River (see 2 Sam 2:9). The name means "two camps," and thus some have interpreted the reference to mean a dance in which the men and women separate and dance in lines opposite each other. Dance is often associated with the celebration of a victory (1 Sam 18:6-7) and as an expression of joy (Ex 15:20; Judg 11:34).

7:2. blended wine. During the Hellenistic period wine was often mixed with water so that a greater quantity could be consumed and conversation could continue throughout the meal. However, in earlier periods blended or mixed wine was drunk. This was a more potent intoxicant and thus had to be consumed with more moderation (see Judg 9:13; Prov 9:2). In Mesopotamia, where wine was less common until the time of the Assyrian empire, wine was served on special occasions. Sometimes only grape syrup would be available, mixed with honey to create a liqueur.

7:4. ivory tower. See the comment on 4:4 for a comparison between a woman's shapely neck and a tall structure.

7:4. pools of Heshbon. Since pools of water reflect the light, they serve as an excellent metaphor for the beloved's dazzling eyes. Excavations at Heshbon, ten miles north of Madaba in Transjordan, have uncovered a large eighth-century B.C. cistern or reservoir that could be the basis for this image. The long, dry months of summer would have required the storage of water in cisterns, and these pools of water would have been beautiful indeed to the inhabitants of the city as they saw light sparkle off the water.

7:4. gate of Bath Rabbim. This place name has not been located, although one may presume that it was the entrance to the city reservoir. There may also be a pun on the meaning of the phrase, "daughter of many," based on the similar sounding title *bat nadib,* "nobleman's daughter," thereby granting the beloved an honorable title.

7:4. tower of Lebanon. A tall mountain, such as Mount Hermon in southern Lebanon, may be meant here. However, Fox's suggestion of a play on *L'bonah,* "frankincense," with the place name Lebanon is attractive. Thus the woman's nose is fragrant and as desirable as a tall pile of this expensive incense.

7:13. mandrakes. The fruit of the mandrake is also mentioned in the Egyptian love songs as an aphrodisiac. Rachel quickly moves to obtain a mandrake when her sister Leah's son Reuben finds it in a field (see the comment on Gen 30:14-15). The plant has broad leaves with purple flowers with a strong fragrance and small yellow fruit.

8:2. spiced wine. See the comment on blended wine in 7:2. In some cases wine was made from fruit juices such as the pomegranate. Egyptian sources record the use of palm sap, date syrup and figs to make wines. The sweet flavor of such beverages is paralleled here with the sweetness of a kiss (1:2; 5:16).

8:6. seal metaphor. The metaphor reflects the intimacy of the constant and close contact represented by a seal ring (see Jer 22:24) or a cylinder seal worn around the neck as an amulet and thus near the heart (see comment on Gen 38:18, 25). One of the Cairo love songs (Group B, known as the "seven wishes") contains a phrase that is comparable: "If only I were her little seal ring, the keeper of her finger!"

8:11. Baal Hamon. This place name has not been identified and only appears in this verse. A similar name, Belamon, appears in Judith 8:3, but this may only be a coincidence. The name may have been chosen simply because it means "the possessor of wealth" and thus becomes synonymous with the fruitful nature of the vineyard and by extension of Solomon's harem containing a thousand women.

8:14. spice-laden mountains. These mountains are to be equated with the "hills of ether" (NIV: "rugged hills") mentioned in 2:17. The invitation in both cases is for the young man to come to the fragrant pleasures offered by the young woman, symbolized by the mountains or hills. The image is similar to that of Ishtar's divine lover Tammuz, who as a shepherd "springs over the hills."

PROPHETIC
LITERATURE

Introduction

Since as Christians we believe that there is only one God, and since we understand that prophecy contains messages from that God, we are often inclined to think that prophecy in the Bible is a unique phenomenon. While we may be justified in thinking that any prophecy outside the Bible is fraudulent, the fact remains that biblical prophecy is part of a long tradition of prophecy in the ancient Near East. Even the Bible makes this fact known to us in the narratives about Balaam and the prophets of Baal sponsored by Ahab and Jezebel.

Divination can refer to any process that seeks to gain messages from beyond the human realm. In the ancient world divination took many different forms (see comments in Deut 18), but most of them were illegal for use in Israel because they assumed a low view of deity. Prophecy was a form of divination that was practiced legally by the Israelites. It was not mantic divination that required knowledge and training in specialized literature (e.g., spells or omen texts) or the use of magical rituals but instead was premised on direct inspiration by the deity. Texts that speak of prophets and present the messages of prophets are scattered throughout ancient Near Eastern literature. In some of these the prophets use other forms of divination in order to receive their messages.

The most prominent corpus of prophetic messages is found in about fifty letters preserved on tablets found in the royal archives of the town of Mari. These date to early in the second millennium B.C. (contemporary with the events of Genesis). The letters report to the king prophecies that were brought to the attention of local officials. The prophecies come from various deities and instruct the king in military matters and other issues of government policy. Occasionally they call for certain rituals to be performed.

A second corpus of nearly thirty oracles comes from the Neo-Assyrian period (seventh century). The primary deity is Ishtar of Arbela, and the prophecies typically forecast victory and prosperity for the king in his various undertakings. Some of the oracles are collected on large tablets that served as archive copies, while others are smaller texts concerning single oracles. The oracles are fairly brief, ranging from a sentence to a paragraph or two at the most.

In Egyptian literature there are no texts claiming to represent oracles from deity, but works such as the *Admonitions of Ipuwer* and the *Visions of Neferti* (both thought to date to the early second millennium) do contain observations concerning the chaotic state of society and warnings of coming judgment. They also at times refer to a coming restoration of order. These compositions therefore include the same types of messages that can be found in Israel's prophetic literature. Despite this similarity, there is no observable prophetic institution in Egypt like that found in the rest of the ancient Near East. The most obvious reason for this difference is that in Egypt deity was incarnate in the person of the pharaoh. There was therefore no need for a mouthpiece speaking for deity—deity was in their midst.

The prophetic oracles that are known from the ancient Near East are similar to an early phase of Israelite prophecy. The writing prophets of Israel have been designated as the "classical prophets," and the earliest of these appear at the beginning of the eighth century. Prior to that time prophets such as Nathan, Elijah, Elisha and many others are mentioned in the historical literature, but no collections of their oracles are known. They are referred to as the "preclassical prophets." These preclassical prophets show the most similarity to the prophets known from the ancient world. Their messages are directed to the king and concern public policy or other issues of national significance. In that sense these prophets serve as official or, more frequently, unofficial advisors to the king. In contrast, the classical prophets often address the people as they offer their social and spiritual commentary. Though their messages include the pronouncement of blessing or rebuke, it is now directed toward society as a whole. As a result, the writing prophets express warnings concerning captivity, destruction and exile that are new to this period and to the prophetic institution.

Prophets were often identified as madmen—a consequence of the fact that it was not unusual for them to receive their messages while entranced. One of the titles used for prophets in Akkadian literature is *muḫḫu*, which is usually translated "ecstatic." Nevertheless, prophets were taken very seriously. The very act of speaking their word was considered determinative in bringing their message to reality. This was true regardless of the social standing of the prophet. Some prophets were part of the temple personnel or on the king's council of advisors. But it was not at all unusual for the prophet to be a layperson or a commoner. In Babylon or Assyria the word of the prophet would be subject to confirmation. This was accomplished by using divination procedures. The question would be posed as to whether or not the message was to be received favorably, and the divination priest would look for the answer to be "written on" the entrails of the sacrificed animal.

It is clear that all of the cultures of the ancient world believed that the gods communicated through select individuals. In most of the ancient Near East the prophets appear to have been supportive of imperial ideology. In Israel they more often represented a counterculture movement. As such the prophets tended to cluster around periods of great turmoil. During the preclassical period the prophets Moses, Deborah, Samuel, Elijah and Elisha all served during troubled times. During the classical period prophetic activity surrounds three key periods:

1. the Assyrian crisis that brought the fall of the northern kingdom and the siege of Jerusalem (760-700: Amos, Hosea, Micah, Isaiah)

2. the Babylonian crisis that brought the fall of Assyria and the fall of Judah and Jerusalem (650-580: Habakkuk, Zephaniah, Nahum, Jeremiah, Ezekiel)

3. the postexilic period with its Persian rule and identity crisis (530-480: Haggai, Zechariah, Joel, Obadiah, Malachi; Daniel could be counted among these, although he served during the exile)

The oracles of the writing prophets can be divided into four general categories. *Indictment oracles* notified the people of what they had done wrong. *Judgment oracles* described God's intended response to their offenses. *Instruction oracles* (which are relatively scarce until the postexilic period) told the people what they needed to do and how they needed to act and think. *Aftermath oracles* informed the people about God's plans after the judgment has come. All but the last occur also in ancient Near Eastern prophecies, but in the ancient Near East these prophecies were never collected, "published" and canonized as they were in Israel.

ISAIAH

1:1-31

Indictment of Rebellion

1:1. chronology. In 6:1 the commissioning of Isaiah is placed in the year King Uzziah died, about 739 B.C. Here it is indicated that his prophetic ministry continued into the time of Hezekiah, at least until after the siege of Jerusalem by Sennacherib in 701. This was a tumultuous half-century that witnessed the rise and dominance of the Neo-Assyrian empire, which was eventually responsible for the northern kingdom invasion, the fall of Samaria and massive destruction in Judah. Isaiah's commission coincided with the beginning of this renewed Assyrian threat (for details of the Assyrian threat in the previous century see comments on 1 Kings 22:1 and 2 Kings 9:14), as Tiglath-Pileser III conducted his first western campaign in 740-738. This campaign targeted Arpad in northern Syria but resulted in tribute being paid by some of the southern states such as Damascus, Tyre, Sidon and Samaria.

1:2. addressing heaven and earth. In other ancient Near Eastern literature the gods would be called as witnesses to an important event. Here the Lord is issuing a formal indictment against Israel, and the nondeified cosmos is called as witness. In one Hittite treaty, after a long list of divine witnesses, the mountains, the rivers, the sea, the Euphrates, heaven and earth, the winds and the clouds are also listed. In the covenant God made with Israel (see comment on Deut 4:26) heaven and earth had been called as witnesses, so it is appropriate here that they be called on to hear the indictment detailing the violation of that covenant.

1:4. accusations of national sin. The *Myth of Erra and Ishum* (eighth-century Babylon) speaks of the destruction of cities that was justified because the people abandoned justice and righteousness, committed atrocities and plotted wicked schemes. Nevertheless, explanations of famous city destructions in the ancient world are generally seen as a result of divine abandonment. The abandonment was usually blamed on either the violations the king had committed or simply on the idea that fate had decreed it.

1:7. fields stripped, laid waste. The devastation of the land was a natural consequence of invasion. Invading armies often lacked an adequate supply line and therefore expected to live off the land they were invading. What they didn't use for their own purposes they destroyed. Not only were the crops burned, but the trampling of the land often crippled the agricultural cycle for several seasons afterward. Sometimes people who were being attacked would even burn their own crops so that the enemy would not have the use of the food they had worked so hard to grow. The elements included in this threat of divine destruction are typical. A well-known section of the *Myth of Erra and Ishum* describes Erra's destructive intentions as including devastating cities and making them a wilderness; destroying mountains, cattle and produce; wiping out the population; putting a fool on the throne; bringing a plague of wild beasts; and leveling the royal palace.

1:8. daughter of Zion. Zion is the name for the mountain on which Jerusalem is situated and represents that cosmic location from which the Lord conquers and reigns. It is therefore also associated with the Davidic covenant and kingship ordained by God. The daughter of Zion would then be the city itself.

1:8. nature of comparison. Small huts were built in fields so that watchmen could stand guard over the fruit that was ready to be harvested. At the end of the harvest these huts would be abandoned and left desolate in a field stripped bare of its produce. So Jerusalem is portrayed as vacant and deserted with nothing left to protect.

1:9. nature of comparison. In the Sodom and Gomorrah account in Genesis 19 these cities are not destroyed by invading armies, but that is not the nature of the comparison here. The totality of the destruction as God's judgment is the emphasis of the text. Once the connection is suggested, verse 10 goes the next step by suggesting that the degree of wickedness is likewise comparable. A just God would be expected to bring comparable judgment for comparable crimes.

1:11. burnt offerings. Burnt offerings usually accompany petition. Many in the ancient world viewed sacrifice as providing food for the gods. If one had a special request to set before the gods, it was judged proper protocol to provide a meal. In Israel even though the burnt offerings were associated with petitions, the "meal for the gods" mentality had been theoretically discarded. As Isaiah and other prophets demonstrate, however, the revised view had not taken hold very firmly and there were frequent lapses into the popular syncretism. The problem with the "feeding the gods" mentality was that it presupposed that God had needs that worshipers could meet and therefore procure his favor.

1:12. trampling of courts. Temples in the ancient world were considered sacred spaces that were protected by closely monitored, restricted access. Admission to the general public was granted only when a sacrifice needed to be offered and then only to the outer court. Entrance to sacred space for anything but holy purpose would be sacrilegious trespassing.

1:13. incense. In the ancient world incense was valued as an accompaniment to sacrifice. Its sweet scent effectively masked any of the unpleasant odors resulting from the performance of the rituals. It was expensive (see comment on Lev 2:1) but was believed to be favored by the gods.

1:13. New Moons and Sabbaths. Keyed to its use of a lunar calendar, ancient Israel marked the first day of the month, with its "new moon" phase, as a festival day (every twenty-nine or thirty days). As on the Sabbath all work was to cease (see Amos 8:5), and there were sacrifices to be made (see comments on Num 28:11-15). The festival continued to be observed in the postexilic period (Ezra 3:5; Neh 10:33). New Moon festivals were also prominent in Mesopotamia from late in the third millennium down to the Neo-Babylonian period in the middle of the first millennium B.C.

1:13. convocations, assemblies, appointed feasts. There were three major festivals that featured pilgrimage gatherings in Jerusalem and several others that would have included more local gatherings. Religious festivals offered frequent opportunity for celebrations, communal meals and social gatherings. What had been designed as a means to praise and honor God, however, was not bringing any pleasure to him.

1:15. spreading hands in prayer. In 2 Chronicles 6:12 Solomon is described as standing with his arms upraised and palms opened upward as he addresses the assembly and prays a dedicatory prayer for the temple. The incantation prayers of Mesopotamian sources, such as that to Ishtar, imply prostration of the supplicant as well as a ritual of raising the hands. Hittite sources suggest similar postures and gestures. Akkadian literature features a form of incantation called the *Shuilla* ("raising of the hand"). For more information see comment on 2 Kings 5:11.

1:15. deities ignoring prayers. The motif of the frustrated supplicant is well known in ancient literature. As an example, in the "Prayer

to Every God" found in Ashurbanipal's library at Nineveh, the supplicant goes through a sequence of asking forgiveness for every offense he can imagine, from every deity. He then laments that despite his contrition no deity is willing to take him by the hand or stand by his side—no one hears him. Taking the standpoint of deity, the *Lament over the Destruction of Ur* reports that Anu and Enlil had determined not to heed the petitions for deliverance but were determined to carry out their plans for destruction.

1:16-17. ethical dimension of religion. Doing justice would be a basic requirement that any god would have for any people. In fact the instruction given here could not be more formulaic. These are considered the responsibilities that any civilized society would have. Establishing justice and defending the vulnerable are the hallmarks of a successful king. The only difference between Israel and the rest of the ancient world in this area would concern how these responsibilities related to spiritual obligations. In the ancient Near East the gods had the responsibility of maintaining justice. Part of that came to them for pragmatic reasons: oppressed people would be inclined to bother the gods with their continuous (annoying?) requests for relief. More foundationally they believed that justice was built into the fabric of the cosmos and its laws were under the guardianship of the gods. The difference in the Israelite worldview was that in their belief, justice was built into the very character of God and was an attribute, not just a stewardship. Mesopotamians had the spiritual obligation to please the gods. This was accomplished primarily by rituals but also by not rocking the boat of civilization. Israelites had the spiritual obligation to be Godlike. This was accomplished by ethical behavior and personal holiness. Mesopotamians would have viewed the washing in physical terms accomplished through ritual. Israelites were to accomplish it in spiritual terms through repentance and reformation.

1:18. nature of comparison. The dyes mentioned here are of the most durable and striking type, creating the most noticeable and permanent stains. There is nowhere in the Old Testament or in the ancient Near Eastern literature where red is specifically symbolic of sin, though white is symbolic of purity.

1:22. silver and dross. In the ancient world silver was extracted and assayed through a process called cupellation. In the initial smelting process silver was extracted from lead ores (galena) containing less than 1 percent silver in a given sample. The lead was melted in shallow vessels made of porous substances such as bone ash or clay. A bellows was then used to blow air across the molten lead, producing lead oxide (litharge). Some of the lead oxide was absorbed by the bone ash, while some could be skimmed off the surface. Ideally the silver would remain. Unfortunately this process had many potential problems. If the temperature was too high or if the sample contained other metals (copper or tin were common), the cupellation would be unsuccessful. In this situation, when the litharge was skimmed off, rather than resulting in silver extraction what remained was tainted silver mixed with other metals and therefore unusable. This unusable product is perhaps what is referred to in the translation as "dross." Another possibility is that the text refers to the assaying process. This involved heating a sample of silver together with large amounts of lead in order to draw off the impurities. One of the possible results of the assaying process was that the quantity of lead would be insufficient to draw off the impurities, rendering the silver useless. Rather than being purified, then, the silver would be in worse shape than before the process. Perhaps this process is envisioned by the text, and the silver becomes this useless junk. The assaying process can be repeated and may eventually succeed (see v. 25).

1:22. choice wine. Many consider the beverage referred to here to be beer rather than wine because of the related term in Akkadian. The most common variety of beer was made from barley malt, but other types were made from emmer or even dates. There were many varieties of wine, and some were valued more highly than others. The library of Ashurbanipal contained a text that named the ten best wines (pure wine from Izalla was considered the best).

1:23. orphans and widows in courts. A major aspect of Israelite legal tradition involved making provision for groups classified as weak or poor: widows, orphans and the resident alien (see Ex 22:22; Deut 10:18-19; 24:17-21). Concern for the needy is evident in Mesopotamian legal collections as early as the mid-third millennium and generally addresses protection of rights and guarantee of justice in the courts. Based on very early statements in the prologues of the Ur-Nammu Code and the Code of Hammurabi it is clear that kings considered it part of their role as "wise rulers" to protect the rights of the poor, the widow and the orphan. Similarly, in the Egyptian *Tale of the Eloquent Peasant* the plaintiff begins by identifying his judge as "the father of the orphan, the husband of the widow." This reflects a concern throughout the ancient Near East that the vulnerable classes be provided for.

1:25. nature of imagery. For identification of dross see comment on 1:22.

1:26. judges/counselors. Since this section has to do with justice in society and in the court system, the judges here are most likely judicial functionaries rather than the deliverers of the Judges period. This would also be supported by the parallel term "counselors," which is never used to describe the deliverers in the book of Judges. The counselors were responsible for helping the king to formulate and carry out policies. The judges were responsible for helping the king to formulate and enforce law. National policy and the justice system are under indictment here.

1:29. sacred oaks and gardens. Gardens in the ancient Near East were often parks of fruit and shade trees, arboretums serving as outdoor shrines or providing comfortable surroundings for sacred enclosures. Sacred trees played a significant role in popular religion of the day. These popular beliefs would have viewed stone and tree as potential divine dwellings. In Canaanite religion they were believed to be symbols of fertility (see Deut 12:2; Jer 3:9; Hos 4:13), though there is very little in the archaeological or literary remains of the Canaanites that would clarify the role of sacred trees. Excavations at Late Bronze Kition have uncovered a temple that featured a sacred grove with sixty tree pits.

2:1-5

Jerusalem in Days to Come

2:2. mountain of the temple. Topographically, Jerusalem is elevated above its surroundings, so that one always had to climb up to the city. Additionally, the temple is located on the highest ground in the city, so one goes up to the temple from other locations in the city. This oracle uses these topographical data to proclaim the future political elevation of the city. The Weidner Chronicle declares that the city of Babylon should be elevated and exalted in all lands. In addition, Assyrian building inscriptions often talk about elevating the temple by restoring it and increasing its height. In Babylonian literature the Marduk Prophecy (from several centuries before Isaiah) announces the future elevation of Babylon with the temple doubled in height. That text also mentions returning the scattered ones (by which it means the statues of the gods that have been disenfranchised from their temples). It continues by describing a period of peace, justice and prosperity, including the dismantling of fortresses. This general language of city restoration and elevation is therefore familiar in the rhetoric of the ancient Near East.

2:2. all nations coming. Texts as early as 2000 B.C. speak of the universal appeal that will characterize a new temple. Gudea speaks of the temple he is building to Ningirsu as attracting people from distant and foreign lands who will gather together to honor the deity. Temples are where oracles are given to decide legal disputes and to inquire of the deity regarding courses of action that should be taken. It is not unusual for foreign people, even kings, to travel great distances to consult a deity. The Persian king Cambyses, for instance, received an oracle from the famous Egyptian shrine of Leto in Buto.

2:4. swords into plowshares. Rather than "plowshares" that turn over the dirt as they plow, this may refer to the metal tip of the plow that breaks up the earth and scratches out a furrow. This tip is about seven inches long. However, this same Hebrew word is used in 2 Kings 6:5, where it appears to refer to some sort of ax. Since the sword is "broken up," it is possible that the resulting product is metal shards that could then be put to various uses.

2:4. spears into pruning hooks. Pruning hooks are the small knives used to remove leaves and new shoots from the grapevines. Archaeological samples found are simply thin, short pieces of metal with a curved hook at the end sharpened on the inside edge as a sickle would be. The shape is reminiscent of the tangtype spearheads that had been popular during the Bronze Age.

2:6-22

The Coming Day of the Lord

2:6. superstitions, divination. The ancient worldview was heavily encumbered with superstitions of all sorts. For centuries omens that identified many occurrences or circumstances as favorable or unfavorable had been observed and recorded. The disposition of the gods toward an individual could only be assessed by the good or bad things that happened to him or her. Demonic forces were believed to be abroad and active, so prophylactic and apotropaic rituals were pursued to combat them. Spells and curses were cast by experts in magic, and the spirits of the dead were believed to wander the earth. Divination was the science of being able to interpret the

omens and formulate incantations that would be effective in dispelling the powers that threatened them. For more information see comments on Deuteronomy 18.

2:7. full of horses and chariots. Assyrian chariots were large, carrying four men and being pulled by four horses. The chariotry corps and cavalry represented the cutting edge of military technology. Vast economic resources were required to import the animals, build the chariots and train the horsemen and charioteers (for an indication of the expense see 1 Kings 10:29). Assyrian military supremacy was dependent on the horses, and even the kings worried about the supply of horses and gathering the necessary fodder to care for the horses. Careful census figures were kept of the types of horses available, and horses were often collected in tribute or captured in raids. Reliefs show great care taken with the horses, and the army on campaign traveled with principal mounts as well as remounts for the cavalry.

2:8. idols. Idols came in a variety of shapes and sizes in the ancient Near East. They were typically carved of wood and overlaid with hammered-out sheets of silver or gold and then clothed in the finest attire. Basically human in appearance (except those from Egypt, which combined human and animal characteristics), they had distinctive, even formalized, poses, clothing and hairstyles. Images of deity in the ancient Near East were where the deity became present in a special way to the extent that the cult statue became the god (when the god so favored his worshipers), even though it was not the only manifestation of the god. Rituals were performed to bring the god to life in its idol. As a result of this linkage, spells, incantations and other magical acts could be performed on the image in order to threaten, bind or compel the deity. In contrast other rites related to the image were intended to aid the deity or care for the deity. The idols then represent a worldview, a concept of deity that was not consistent with how Yahweh had revealed himself. The idol was not the deity, but the deity was thought to inhabit the image and manifest its presence and will through the image. Archaeologists have found very few of the life-sized images that the texts describe, but there are renderings of them that allow accurate knowledge of details.

2:10. splendor of the majesty of deity. In the ancient world a bright or flaming aura surrounding deity is the norm. In Egyptian literature it is depicted as the winged sun disk accompanied by storm clouds. Akkadian uses the term *melammu* to describe this visible representation of the glory of deity. It is especially evident in the divine warrior motif where the deity unveils his glory as he fights for his people (for more information on the divine warrior see comments on Ex 15:3; Josh 3:17; 6:21-24; 10:11; 1 Sam 4:3-4; 7:10). Akkadian literature occasionally evidences the same connection as here, when the word for fear or dread is associated with the *melammu*.

2:12. Day of the Lord. See sidebar at Joel 2.

2:13. cedars of Lebanon, oaks of Bashan. These two types of tree were valued for their size, beauty, strength and durability. They would be used in the building projects (such as gates and palaces) that were the sources of pride for nations and in which they would put their trust.

2:15. towers and walls. Walls of this period were solid (in contrast to the casemate walls of the previous age) and could be made of mud brick, fieldstone or ashlar hewn stone. While towers and walls were features of fortified cities, there were also many garrison fortresses built along trade routes and borders. In Israel both the fortresses and towers were rectangular. Examples at Kadesh Barnea and Horvat Uza measure between twenty and twenty-five thousand square feet. Since city walls have not been preserved to their original height, it is difficult to say how high they were. A width of fifteen to twenty feet was common, and judging from their massive foundations and the length of ladders used for scaling the walls, a height of thirty to forty feet would not be unusual. The walls at Lachish were about fifty feet high. Assyrian inscriptions usually give the height in courses of brick. The wall of Sennacherib's Nineveh is said to have been constructed of 180 courses of brick (sixty to seventy feet?). At the time of Isaiah Sargon's capital city at Khorsabad had a wall nearly one hundred feet thick with 150 towers circling the 750-acre city.

2:16. ships. Trade by means of seagoing vessels was already taking place in the first half of the third millennium B.C. By mid-second millennium a fleet of ships from Ugarit numbered 150. Excavations of a sunken merchant ship (off the coast of Uluburun, Turkey) from the period give a good idea of the variety of items being shipped. Trading ships of the first millennium were single-masted with a crow's nest and could feature either one or two banks of oars. A typical length would be about fifty feet, though larger ones are known.

2:19. effects of theophany. In the ancient Near East the trembling of the earth is an indication of the divine involvement in battle. Addition-

ally, the dread of a deity as a divine warrior was often believed to precede a powerful, successful army into battle. Egyptian texts attribute this terror to Amun-Re in the inscriptions of Thutmose III, and Hittite, Assyrian and Babylonian texts all have their divine warriors who strike terror into the hearts of the enemy.

2:20-21. rodents and bats, flight to caves. A Sumerian Hymn of Enheduanna to the goddess Inanna from the third millennium depicts the gods fluttering away like bats to their caves from the goddess's terrible presence. This suggests the possibility that in these verses it is the idols being carried to caves and crags by the rodents (the flight of men has already been reported in v. 19). Just as men have fled from before the glory of the Lord, so do the idols, but, incapable of moving on their own, they are transported by the lowliest creatures.

3:1—4:1
Judgment on Jerusalem and Its Women

3:1. reality of siege. Siege warfare was designed to isolate a city and create a blockade that would eventually force a surrender. With the enemy camped around the city, the fields could not be harvested for their food supply. No one could get in to bring in food, so the people in the city had to live on whatever had been stockpiled in the city. If the water source for the city was a well or spring outside the city walls, the siege would be short, for the cisterns would quickly run dry. Jerusalem had a water supply that could be accessed from inside the city walls (see comment on 2 Chron 32:3). Support is typically viewed in terms of human leaders. The "resources" to survive a siege would be found in capable leadership that could keep morale high and successfully manage food rationing.

3:2-3. classes of leadership. The list of leadership resources here is fairly extensive, covering the military, clan leadership, religious personnel (both legitimate and illegitimate) and political advisors.

3:5. status of the elderly. In Israelite society the oldest active male was the head of the household. He typically represented the family in the community and made the decisions for the family. As a result the senior members of the family usually commanded a high degree of respect and honor.

3:6. cloak of leadership. The cloak was a basic piece of clothing that even the poor were expected to own. It was considered essential enough that it was forbidden to keep overnight a man's cloak taken in pledge (see comment on Ex 22:26-27). Though this passage may suggest that the situation had gotten so bad that hardly anyone had cloaks (and therefore possession of one distinguished a person), there is also something special about a king's cloak. In Assyrian texts of this period the cloak of the king figured prominently in certain rituals, particularly the substitute king ritual. When there were omens suggesting that the king's life was in danger, a substitute king would be designated, who would take the king's place by being garbed in his cloak and generally suffer the consequences. While there is no suggestion of a substitute king ritual here, there may have been an important function for the cloak.

3:16. ornaments on ankles. Ankle bracelets were solid rings usually made of bronze. The word is also used of the irons used to hobble camels. Some burials of the Iron Age evidence arm and ankle rings still on the body.

3:17. sores and baldness. The translation "bring sores" is very uncertain. Another possibility is that it is another expression for inflicting baldness. While many translations suggest the shaving of the entire head, the forehead seems to be specifically indicated by the Hebrew word. In Mesopotamia shaving off half the hair was used as a punishment intended to bring public humiliation. Additionally, a particular style of haircut was used to designate a slave.

3:18-23. ancient finery. The NIV's "head bands" (v. 18) have now been identified as sun ornaments, while the crescent necklaces are moon ornaments. Many of the terms used admit of various interpretations. For instance, "perfume bottles" (v. 20) is highly interpretive, and though perfume bottles have been found by archaeologists, they could hardly have been worn as jewelry. Others have suggested some sort of amulet to parallel the next term. Information about jewelry in the ancient world comes from a number of different sources. Some literary works make reference to the wearing of various ornaments. Other written sources include inventories (such as one found at Mari) and lists of gifts or tribute. The pieces that are referred to can sometimes be matched up with pictorial representations in reliefs and paintings or with archaeological finds. But many words cannot confidently be matched with objects.

4:1. offer of the seven women. It is to be presumed that these women have lost their husbands and sons, and are therefore left socially defenseless even though they are not without

means. This was a common aftermath of war. It was contractually and legally the husband's responsibility to provide food and clothing. These women are not looking for financial provision and would certainly be willing to bypass the usual conventions of bride price. Their need for familial association may simply stem from social mandates or, in the worst cases, may reflect the desire for a household for children that have been conceived through rape by enemy soldiers.

4:2-6
Future Glory

4:5-6. imagery. The cloud of smoke and fire is reminiscent of the pillar that offered the Israelites guidance and protection in the wilderness. In the ancient world a bright or flaming aura surrounding deity is the norm. In Egyptian literature it is depicted as the winged sun disk accompanied by storm clouds. Akkadian uses the term *melammu* to describe this visible representation of the glory of deity, which in turn is enshrouded in smoke or cloud. In Canaanite mythology it has been suggested the *melammu* concept is expressed by the word '*anan*, the same Hebrew word here translated "cloud," but the occurrences are too few and obscure for confidence. In any case, the pillar here would then be one beacon; smoke being visible in the daytime, while the inner flame it covered would glow through at night.

5:1-7
Parable of the Vineyard

5:1-2. parables and allegories in the ancient Near East. There is continued discussion about whether this should be categorized as a parable or an allegory, the distinction being how broad a comparison is intended by the tale. Parables are known from ancient Near Eastern literature as early as the Sumerian period, and a few are available from the Neo-Assyrian period. The metaphor of a city as an unproductive plant is known from the *Myth of Erra and Ishum* (copies date to the eighth century), in which Marduk laments Babylon. He says that he filled it with seeds like a pine cone, but no fruit came from it, and he planted it like an orchard but never tasted its fruit. For more information see the comment on Ezekiel 17:1.

5:1-6. vineyard preparation and upkeep. Grapes were among the basic staple products of the ancient Near East and therefore the care necessary for a vineyard was well known. In the rocky and hilly terrain of Israel special care had to be taken to preserve the soil and the moisture necessary to produce good fruit. As the rocks were cleared from the hillside, the stones were used to create terraces to level the ground. This would prevent water drainage and soil erosion. More stones were used to build huts and watchtowers that would be used to protect the crop when it neared harvest time. Constant hoeing between the rows of vine was necessary to prevent weeds from springing up and sapping off the water supply in the soil. Various irrigation techniques were used to assure sufficient groundwater. If the ground did not have adequate moisture or if the vines were not pruned back, the resulting crop would be small and sour. Finally, some of the stones were also used for winepresses and cisterns on the site so that the grapes could be processed without risking damage during transportation.

5:8-30
Woe to Israel

5:8. oppressive real estate development. Expansion of real estate holdings in the ancient world was usually at someone else's expense. Bad harvests over several seasons could necessitate giving up ownership over property in order to pay off or work off debt. In Israel this was a theological as well as an economic crisis. Since God had given them the land as a benefit of the covenant, each family considered its landholdings as its little share in the covenant. Therefore, what otherwise would be a financial tragedy (often with an oppressive dimension) also served to deprive family members of their part in the covenant. For more information see comments on Leviticus 25. Additionally, the decision-making body in any community was comprised of landowners. The individual who obtained all the land rights in the community would have the power to do whatever he wanted.

5:10. normal levels of production. A vineyard would typically be expected to yield at least one thousand gallons of wine per acre. Harvests of grain in irrigated areas across the ancient Near East yielded a normal seed to crop ratio of about one to ten (though higher yields are attested in the literature). Therefore a homer of seed would usually be expected to yield ten homers of grain. Here the ratio is reversed as ten to one (an ephah is about one-tenth of a homer). The yields represented here, then, are meager fractions of that normally expected.

5:12. musical instruments. These are all typical musical instruments of the time and are attested in ancient Near Eastern texts, reliefs and paintings as early as the third millennium B.C. There is still some disagreement among authorities as to which of the Hebrew words in this passage ought to be translated "harp" and which one as "lyre." The one the NIV translates "lyre" is a ten-stringed instrument, while the one translated "harp" is thought to have had fewer strings. Both are hand-held with frames made of wood. The tambourine has been identified in archaeological reliefs as the tambour, a small drum (leather stretched over a hoop) that would not have the tinny rattle sound of modern tambourines. The instrument translated as flute is likely a double pipe made of either bronze or reed.

5:14. grave. The grave was understood as the doorway to the netherworld (Hebrew *sheol*). As the entryway it was considered part of Sheol, so the context must determine whether an author is referring to the place of burial or the world of departed spirits. Sheol was not a pleasant place. There were no possessions, memory, knowledge or joy. It was not viewed as a place where judgment or punishment took place, though it was considered an act of God's judgment to be sent there rather than remaining alive. Subsequently it is inaccurate to translate Sheol as "hell," for the latter is by definition a place of punishment. The Israelite understanding of the netherworld was more similar to the concepts found in Mesopotamia than to those found in Egypt. For more information see comment on 14:9. The idea of Sheol swallowing or devouring the wicked is paralleled in the Egyptian Book of the Dead. As the heart of the individual is weighed, the composite chaos monster with crocodile head stands by expectantly, prepared to devour those who fail the test.

5:22. alcoholic beverage. A wide variety of alcoholic beverages was available in the ancient world. Wine (from honey, dates or grapes) and beer were the most common. What is classed today as "hard liquor" (requiring a distillation process) was not yet known. The two terms used in this verse may refer respectively to grape wine and date wine, but it is difficult to be certain. The mixing that is mentioned here involves mixing in herbs, spices or oils.

5:23. judges bribed in ancient Near East. As evidenced by the preface to the Code of Hammurabi (c. 1750 B.C.) and the statements made by the eloquent peasant in Egyptian wisdom literature (c. 2100 B.C.), the standard for behavior by those in authority is to protect the rights of the poor and weak in society. True justice (see Lev 19:15) is expected of kings, officials and local magistrates. In fact the world turned upside down theme found in the book of Judges and in prophetic literature (1:23) describes a society in which "laws are enacted, but ignored" (for example in the Egyptian *Visions of Neferti* [c. 1900 B.C.]). An efficiently administered state in the ancient Near East depends on the reliability of the law and its enforcement. To this end every organized state creates a bureaucracy of judges and local officials to deal with civil and criminal cases. It is their task to hear testimony, investigate charges made, evaluate evidence and execute judgment (detailed in the Middle Assyrian Laws and the Code of Hammurabi). There are some cases, however, that require the attention of the king (see 2 Sam 15:2-4) and appeals are occasionally forwarded on to that highest magistrate (as in the Mari texts). The temptation for judges and government officials to accept bribes is found in every time and place (see Prov 6:35; Mic 7:3). Taking bribes becomes almost institutionally accepted in bureaucratic situations as competing parties attempt to outmaneuver each other (see Ezra 4:4-5; Mic 3:11). However, at least on the ideal level, arguments and penalties are imposed to eliminate or at least lessen this problem. Thus Hammurabi's Code 5 places harsh penalties on any judge who alters one of his decisions (presumably because of a bribe), including stiff fines and permanent removal from the bench. Exodus 23:8 forbids the taking of bribes and the perversion of justice as an offense against God, the weak and innocent, and the entire community (see Amos 5:12).

5:26. banner, whistling. The banner, or standard, was used as a means of calling out an army of a particular territory or indicating the place where a muster was taking place or a camp was located. It often featured an insignia of the tribe or division. The word translated "whistle" can also refer to a hiss. For the significance here see the comment on 7:18.

5:27. significance of belt and sandal thong. Neo-Assyrian military uniform consisted of a knee-length kilt fastened by a broad leather belt. Many of the infantry went barefoot, but the cavalry was equipped with knee-high soft leather boots held on by long crisscrossed thongs.

5:28. bows, arrows, horses' hooves, chariots. Horses were not shod by the Assyrians, so horses with hard hooves were the more desirable, especially for the rocky terrain of Syro-Palestine. The (composite) bow was the main offensive weapon of the Assyrian army. Arrowheads were made of various materials including bone, horn and various metals.

Chariots could accommodate four people and had heavy six or eight spoke wheels.

5:29. lion behavior. The lion would typically roar as a warning in a territorial confrontation. The growl is appropriate to the seizing of prey. Both images are reflected here.

6:1-13
The Throne Vision and Isaiah's Commissioning

6:1. chronology. Uzziah is generally supposed to have died in 739. This is a critical juncture in history. In 740-738 Assyrian king Tiglath-Pileser III made his first campaign into the west. This is the beginning of a serious military threat that will eventually bring about the downfall of the northern kingdom, Israel, the destruction of the capital city of Samaria (along with many other cities of Israel and Judah) and the deportation of large segments of the population. The Assyrians are on the brink of establishing the empire that will dominate the ancient Near East for over a century. For more information on Uzziah's reign see comments on 2 Chronicles 26.

6:1. throne. The central Holy of Holies was viewed as the throne room of the Lord, so it is logical that the vision is set in the temple complex. The ark is portrayed as the footstool of his throne, and the cherubim typically flank the throne. This is, of course, the invisible throne of the invisible deity. For more information on thrones see comments on 2 Chronicles 3:10-13; 9:17-19.

6:1. train of robe filling temple. The word translated "train" elsewhere (and probably here) refers to the hem. It is the richly decorated and distinctive border around the high priestly robe (see comments on Ex 28:31-35). The hem was used as a mark of identity for people of rank such as priests and kings. In ancient Near Eastern iconography deities were also portrayed with such garments. The edge of the cloth was embroidered, and a fringe of three- or four-inch-long tassels trimmed the skirt by the ankles. The huge size of deity is common in the ancient Near East. For instance, at the Syrian temple in 'Ain Dara footprints more than three feet long are carved into the stone slabs leading into the entrance hall.

6:2. seraphs. This is the only place in Scripture where a supernatural creature is designated as a seraph. The serpents that plagued the Israelites in the wilderness, however, also go by that designation, and Isaiah twice refers to flying serpents (NIV: "darting" 14:29; 30:6). Since supernatural creatures are often portrayed as composite (see comment on Gen 3:24), there is therefore good reason to think of the seraphs as winged serpents. Since the Hebrew root *sarap* is usually associated with "burning," there is also good reason to associate these creatures with fire. Ancient Near Eastern literature offers some support for these portrayals. Fiery serpents are well known in Egyptian art and literature. There the serpent, or uraeus, is a symbol of royalty and authority. It adorns the crown of Pharaoh and sometimes is pictured with wings (usually either two or four). It is not unusual for them to have hands, feet or faces. Serpents in an upright position with wings also decorate the throne of Tutankhamen. Many seals decorated with winged uraei have been found in excavations in Palestine dating to this period, so we know that the Israelites were familiar with this motif. Examples of six-winged creatures are not so widely attested. A relief from Tell Halaf, however, from approximately this period portrays a human-shaped figure with six wings.

6:4. effects of seraph calls. In Akkadian texts as well as in Amos 9:1 the shaking of doorposts or thresholds indicates the beginning of demolition. If this was the case, the smoke could be the result of destructive forces at work. The cries of the seraphs, however, are not easily taken as warning of imminent destruction (a consequence of God's holiness being compromised?). It is probably better to see smoke and trembling doorways as accompanying the theophany. This same word for smoke is used in 4:5.

6:7. purification of lips. Mesopotamian rituals often feature the purification of lips as symbolic of the purification of the person. It is viewed as a prerequisite, especially for diviner priests, before they may appear before the divine council and report what they have witnessed.

6:7. atonement. Translations have struggled with this term (for instance, some render it "forgiven"). For information on the ritual concept see the comment on Leviticus 1:4. The same verb occurs in Akkadian ritual literature referring to "wiping" away ritual impurity and is used specifically in the purification of the mouth. In one Old Babylonian prayer the diviner wipes his mouth with resin in preparation for appearing before the assembly of the gods. In Babylonian incantation texts fire is commonly seen as a purifying element. One incantation series is titled *Shurpu* ("burning") and is concerned with removing ritual offense or uncleanness.

6:8. us. The familiar picture of a heavenly throne surrounded by the heavenly council is well known from the Ugaritic texts (most notably the Epic of Keret), though this Canaanite council is made up of the gods of the pantheon. Examples occur also in the tenth century building inscription of Yehimilk from Byblos and the Karatepe stele of Azitawadda. In the Akkadian *Enuma Elish* it is the assembly of the gods that appoints Marduk as their head. Fifty gods made up this assembly with seven in the inner council. In Israelite belief the gods were replaced by angels or spirits—the sons of God or the heavenly host.

6:9-10. role of the prophet. The description of eyes and ears that do not function as they should or a heart that is hard or heavy matches that which occurs elsewhere in medical texts or in contexts of fear. In 1 Samuel 25 Nabal suffers some sort of paralysis, stroke or heart attack, and his heart becomes as stone. In a Babylonian wisdom hymn a sufferer describes his fear-induced paralysis as resulting in eyes that do not see and ears that do not hear. It is difficult to know whether the paralysis that meets Isaiah's messages comes from spiritual sickness or from fear. The prophet's role was to deliver the message regardless of whether there was any response or not. If the message did not result in response, it would at least establish clearly the people's guilt.

7:1-25
Immanuel

7:1. chronology. The chronology of the reigns of Jotham, Ahaz and Hezekiah is very complex. Nevertheless, the invasion referred to in this verse can be fairly confidently dated to 735. By 734 Tiglath-Pileser III had begun responding to the problems here in the west, and the coalition would not have felt at liberty to take such aggressive action.

7:1. political situation. Assyrian king Tiglath-Pileser III was occupied with Urartu and Media between 737 and 735. During this time the western states were working to put together a coalition that might resist Assyrian incursions. Rezin (see next entry) had most likely played a major role in bringing Pekah to the throne of Samaria (see comments on Pekah in 2 Kings 15). It is suspected that the attack against Jerusalem was related to Ahaz's pro-Assyrian (or at least neutral) position. The siege was intended to result in replacing Ahaz with an anti-Assyrian representative on the throne, who would then join in the coalition.

7:1. Rezin. Known to the Assyrians as Raqianu, which most likely represented the Aramaic name Radyan, Rezin ruled in Damascus from at least 738 (when he is named as paying tribute to Tiglath-Pileser III) to the fall of Damascus in 732.

7:3. location. Hezekiah's tunnel had not yet been constructed at this time. Water was conducted from the Gihon spring (in the Kidron Valley on the east side of the city) toward the south through an aqueduct that brought the water to a reservoir at the southwestern tip of the city. This aqueduct is known as the Siloam Channel and in biblical times went by the name Shiloah (see 8:6). Presumably the waters of the reservoir (Pool of Siloam) would have been periodically released into an area below this to provide water for laundering. The road to the Washerman's Field would likely have traveled through the Kidron Valley. This would be a good place to find Ahaz if he were inspecting the water supply of the city to see how it could be secured for use inside the city in the eventuality of a siege.

7:6. son of Tabeel. Though nothing is known historically of this individual, the name Tabeel is Aramaic and thus suggests someone in the royal household (likely of Davidic lineage) whose mother was perhaps a princess from the area of Aram. Such an individual would be more likely to be a sympathizer with Aramean causes. Another possibility that has been suggested is that this is a reference to Tubail (=Ethbaal) the king of Tyre, who also had paid tribute to Tiglath-Pileser in 738.

7:8. chronology. From 735, the date of these events, sixty-five years would stretch to 670 B.C. This has seemed strange to some interpreters since Ephraim suffered significant territorial reduction in 733, and Samaria was destroyed and the people deported by 721. Esarhaddon was near the end of his reign in 670. He had successfully invaded Egypt in 671 and had a number of other campaigns to the west during this time period. So far, however, there is no indication of deportations into or out of Israel during his reign.

7:11. divine sign. There are a number of cases of signs being given from deity in the Old Testament. The most similar examples are found in 1 Samuel 2:34 and 2 Kings 19:29. In these instances the sign relates to the beginning of the fulfillment of the prophecy. Signs given by deity in the larger ancient Near Eastern context would typically be connected to omens. Behind the omens was the belief that there was an interconnectedness that stretched across all boundaries. The omens were related to historical events the way that symptoms are related to the onset of disease. Historical events were therefore considered to be related to corresponding happenings or phenomena in the natural world. For example, the gods wrote

their signs in the heavens or on the kidneys or liver of sacrificed animals. These signs would not only portend coming events but would be thought of as part of those events.

7:11. depths and heights. Babylonian texts also speak of the range of signs (omens) in heaven and on earth, as their diviners tried to make use of all possible sources of information concerning what the gods were up to.

7:14. portentous names. Names were generally believed to be related to the character and destiny of the individual. In Egypt throne names were given (usually five of them) that embodied the claims, hopes and dreams of Pharaoh. Babies were sometimes named to reflect on a situation at the time of their birth (Gen 29—30; 1 Sam 4:21).

7:15. curds and honey. "Curds" would be better understood as a butter type product, since Proverbs 30:33 shows that it is produced by churning, not by coagulation or fermentation. In Assyrian and Babylonian texts the word used here in the Hebrew text is identified as a product called "ghee"—a refined form of butterfat—that is sweet and does not spoil as easily as other dairy products. It is the liquid produced when butter from cow's milk is melted, boiled and strained. In the Mesopotamian texts this product is most frequently paired up with honey in a variety of texts including ritual texts, medical texts and descriptions of food products. It was one of many products that were used for libation offerings for the gods. Honey is often a reference to the syrup from dates or figs. Bee honey was available when found, but bees were not yet domesticated for honey production. Honey and ghee were nourishing products that traveled well and would suit the needs of someone living off the land rather than farming the land. They were mixed together and used as a condiment on either confectionery date cakes or the more common wheat cakes.

7:16. fate of two kings. The land of Pekah was the northern kingdom of Israel. In 733 the Assyrians greatly reduced the territory of Israel, leaving only the capital, Samaria, and its environs. The remainder of the country was annexed and over thirteen thousand people were deported. Pekah himself was killed in a conspiracy led by Hoshea, his successor, and backed by the Assyrians (as indicated in Tiglath-Pileser's inscriptions). The pro-Assyrian Hoshea paid tribute to Tiglath-Pileser and accepted vassal status. He would reign until the final overthrow of the northern kingdom in 721—a likely time to consider the boy referred to in this verse as knowing good and evil (about age thirteen). The land of Rezin was

Aram, with its capital city, Damascus. The Aramean state was annexed by Assyria in 732, Damascus was overthrown and Rezin was executed.

7:17. Neo-Assyrian empire. The Neo-Assyrian empire was inaugurated soon after Tiglath-Pileser III's accession to the throne in 745. It was not to be overthrown until 612, when Nineveh fell to the alliance of the Medes and Babylonians. Though significant deterioration can be seen as early as 630, this still represents over a century of domination over a large expanse of the Near East. For a decade or so this even included Egypt. The major Assyrian kings, Tiglath-Pileser III, Shalmaneser V, Sargon II, Sennacherib, Esarhaddon and Ashurbanipal, are known from the biblical text as well as from many documents recovered from the period, including royal annals and chronicles from several of them. The empire expanded in all four directions: absorbing Urartu to the north, the Medes to the east, Babylonia and Elam to the south and Syro-Palestine to the west. At its height it included all or part of the modern countries of Iran, Iraq, Turkey, Syria, Lebanon, Jordan, Israel and Egypt. Assyria's reputation as a militaristic regime is supported by extensive documentation and stands as its historical legacy. Its strategy of psychological warfare included terrifying rhetoric, brutal destructions and carefully chosen examples of cruel torture. Its expansion was fueled by the potential for economic gain, which would come through the plunder, tribute and tariffs that would result from control of trade and the trade routes. For Assyrian activity in this period see comments on 1:1; 6:1; and 7:1.

7:18. flies and bees imagery. The word translated "whistle" can also refer to a hiss. Part of the lore of beekeeping maintained that a swarm could be lured out of its hive to another location by a whistling sound. Attacking armies are compared to flies and bees in Homer's *Iliad* as well.

7:19. imagery. This verse simply continues the imagery of bees by listing the places where bees are naturally inclined to make their hives.

7:20. shaving captives. In Assyrian nomenclature "barber" could be used as a divine title. Here the function is attributed to Yahweh. While many translations suggest the shaving of the entire head, the forehead seems to be specifically indicated by the Hebrew word. In Mesopotamia shaving off half the hair was used as a punishment intended to bring public humiliation. Additionally, a particular style of haircut was used to designate a slave. Most

commentators believe that "the hair of your legs" is a euphemism for pubic hair.

7:23. value of vines. It is difficult to determine whether the text makes reference to a thousand vines that would be bought or sold for a shekel each (an exorbitant price), or, more reasonably, to a vineyard housing a thousand vines whose annual produce would bring a thousand shekels. The latter understanding would find support in Song of Songs 8:11.

7:24-25. farmland to pasture. Cattle and flocks could be devastating to agricultural land. Their movements would trample the soil, and their grazing would defoliate it, eventually leading to massive erosion of the topsoil and depletion of water sources.

8:1-10
Assyrian Invasion

8:1. scroll. If the writing instrument used is an engraving tool (see next entry), the material must be something that requires etching or incision—usually suggesting stone or clay that will be baked. The word used to describe the writing material is used only one other time in the Old Testament, Isaiah 3:23, where the NIV translates "mirrors" in the middle of a list of clothing. Akkadian texts list cylinder seals (worn around the neck) among other items of women's garments. These were worn as amulets to ward off demonic forces. They were inscribed with the name of the individual and often with artistic decoration as well. In Israel stamp seals were typically used, so there is no indication of what the word for cylinder seal would be, though cylinder seals have been found in Syro-Palestine and were well known there. Since cylinder seals were engraved with the name of the individual, and here an official document is being engraved with the name of an individual (including the preposition, not represented in the NIV's translation, that typically precedes the name on stamp seals as well as on Aramaic cylinder seals), it is possible that a cylinder seal is being made here, though the Hebrew word cannot be identified with any confidence (there is no known West Semitic technical term for cylinder seal). In the Neo-Assyrian period large cylinder seals (one, for instance, that is seven and one-half inches long) were used for seals of the gods. All of this information would fit well with the usage in 3:23 and with Isaiah's emphasis on significant names. Assyrian dream texts show an interesting relationship between a seal being given in a dream and information about a future offspring. One line says that if someone in his dream gives him an

inscribed seal, he will have a "name" or a son.
8:1. ordinary pen. The term for this tool is
used only one other time in the Old Testament, Exodus 32:4, where it is used in the
manufacture of the golden calf. It is therefore
assumed to be some sort of drill or chisel. Exodus 32:16 uses the verbal root related to this
noun to describe the inscription of the Ten
Commandments on the tablets. Cylinder seal
artisans used drills, including a "fine drill."
The word translated "ordinary" here, when
modifying a person, refers to humanity's fragile mortality. Perhaps here the use of a fragile
drill is intended to suggest high-quality workmanship.
8:1-2. document. The presence of witnesses
suggests an official document being drawn
up. While some have suggested a marriage
contract (because of v. 3), given the prominence of designating a name, something referring to a birth or naming appears more likely.
8:3. prophetess. The title "prophetess" is never used simply to designate the wife of a
prophet but consistently for a female prophet.
While we need not doubt that this prophetess
was Isaiah's wife, she must also be regarded
as a woman who functioned prophetically in
her own right. Prophetesses, though somewhat rare, are known from Mesopotamia. The
Mari texts from Syria in the early second millennium B.C. give evidence of both males and
females in this position. Women are also
known to have spoken out as prophetesses
during the reign of Esarhaddon of Assyria.
The females appeared to have served in the
same role as the male prophets.
8:3. portentous names. See comment on 7:14.
8:4. plundering of Damascus and Samaria.
Certainly the wealth of Damascus was carried
off at the fall of the city in 732. It is more difficult to determine when one might consider
the plundering of Samaria to have taken
place. Second Kings 17:3 reports that Hoshea
paid tribute to Shalmaneser, but this is not reported as a plundering of Samaria. It is more
likely that the plundering should be associated with the fall of Samaria in 721.
8:6. waters of Shiloah. Hezekiah's tunnel had
not yet been constructed at this time. Water
was conducted from the Gihon Spring (in the
Kidron Valley on the east side of the city) toward the south through an aqueduct that
brought the water to a reservoir at the southwestern tip of the city. This aqueduct is
known as the Siloam Channel and in biblical
times went by the name Shiloah.
8:6. Rezin. See comment on 7:1.
8:7. flood waters overflowing its channels.
This common metaphor is known as early as

the Cuthean Legend of Naram-Sin (beginning
of second millennium), in which the invading
foe is likened to a flood, a deluge that overflowed the banks of the canals and destroyed
cities.
8:8. Judah's treatment by Tiglath-Pileser.
Tiglath-Pileser's records do not record any action taken against Judah in the campaigns of
734-732. Either that record is not preserved or
verse eight offers a longer view of the eventual
Assyrian invasion of Judah by Sargon and especially Sennacherib. The longer view is to be
preferred, since the people of Judah would not
have been "rejoicing over Rezin" (v. 6) until after the 732 campaign when Damascus was destroyed.
8:9-10. threat against the nations. Though
many interpreters have attributed these
words to Judah, it is more likely the threat of
the Assyrians. It was a common strategy for
the Assyrians to claim that the deities of their
rebellious vassals had abandoned them because they had broken the oaths that had secured their loyalty to the Assyrians. Examples exist as early as Tukulti-Ninurta and
as late as Esarhaddon.

8:11-22
Response to the Prophetic Message
8:14. imagery. Sanctuary and rock imagery go
together in Psalms as well (such as Ps 18:1-2).
The temple provided sanctuary for people in
trouble, and it was built on a foundation rock.
In spiritual imagery they would also then
speak of God as their foundation rock. The
trap and snare are used for hunting birds and
small animals, though the latter more likely
refers to a throwing stick, perhaps like a boomerang.
8:16. sealed documents in ancient world.
Scrolls could be sealed either by tying a string
around them and sealing the knot with clay or
by placing them in a jar and sealing the cover.
The clay or the seal around the lid would be
impressed with the owner's seal. Mesopotamia used cylinder seals, Egypt used scarab
seals, and Syro-Palestine used stamp seals.
Tablets would be sealed inside a clay envelope, which would be impressed with the
owner's seal. The seals were intended to ensure the integrity of the contents. They
warned against tampering and, if intact, attested to the authenticity of the document. For
more information see Nehemiah 9:38.
8:19. consultation of the dead. Because of the
well-developed ancestor cult pervading much
of the ancient Near East (evident, for instance,
in the emphasis on the role of the male heir to

care for the father's shrine in Ugaritic documents), the dead were considered to have some power to affect the living. It was believed that if libations were poured out on behalf of the dead ancestors, their spirits would then offer protection and help to those still living. In Babylon the disembodied spirit *(utukki)* or the ghost *(eṭemmu)* could become very dangerous if not cared for and often were the objects of incantations. Proper care for the dead would begin with proper burial and would continue with ongoing gifts and honor of the memory and name of the deceased. The firstborn was responsible for maintaining this ancestor worship and therefore inherited the family gods (often images of deceased ancestors). Such care would have been based on a belief, as seen in Saul's consultation of the witch of Endor, that the spirits of the dead could communicate and had information on the future that could be of use to the living. These spirits were consulted through the efforts of priests, mediums and necromancers. This could be a dangerous practice, since some spirits were considered demons and could cause great harm. While it is difficult to totally reconstruct Israelite beliefs about deceased ancestors and the afterlife, it seems clear that prior to the exile there existed a cult of the dead or ancestral worship. This is evidenced by archaeological remains: (1) standing stones *(maṣṣebot);* (2) channels cut into tombs for the deposit of food and drink offering for the dead (see Deut 26:14; Ps 106:28); and (3) the importance placed on family tombs (see the ancestral tomb for Abraham and his descendants at Hebron) and mourning rituals performed at these tombs (see Is 57:7-8; Jer 16:5-7). The local and family ancestral cults were condemned by the prophets and the law.

9:1-7
Future Hope

9:1. treatment of Zebulun and Naphtali. The tribes of Zebulun and Naphtali were among those hardest hit by the Assyrians in the 733 campaign (see 2 Kings 15:29, supported in the inscriptions of Tiglath-Pileser). Their tribal territories comprised most of what became the Assyrian province of Magiddu (see next entry).

9:1. three regions. When Assyria came west in 733 to punish the northern kingdom of Israel for its participation in anti-Assyrian activities, one of the results was the reduction of their territory. All but the Ephraim hills was annexed as Assyrian territory. This territory was set up in three administrative districts referred to in the Assyrian records as Du'ru, Magiddu and Gal'aza. These are reflected in the three regions mentioned by Isaiah. Galilee of the Gentiles is the Magiddu (Megiddo) province (from the Valley of Jezreel north to the Litani River); the way of the sea is the Du'ru (Dor) province (the coastal plains from Joppa to Haifa); and along the Jordan is the Gal'aza (Gilead) province (Transjordan from the Dead Sea to the Sea of Galilee). Recent excavations in Dor have demonstrated a significant Assyrian presence at this time.

9:2. light of hope and deliverance. In Mesopotamian texts it is logically the sun god, Shamash, who provides light. He is praised for setting right the darkness and providing light for humankind. As a king who reigns justly, Hammurabi claims that he provides light for the lands of Sumer and Akkad.

9:4. Midian's defeat. The Midianite oppression in the middle of the Judges period had been some five hundred years earlier, but it still stood as the most outstanding example of God's ability to bring deliverance against overwhelming odds. It is clear that the reference is to that particular defeat of Midian because of the more specific reference in 10:26.

9:4. yoke imagery. Prophetic speech often refers to the burden of political domination as a yoke. In the Amarna letters the rulers of the Canaanite city-states speak to Pharaoh of how they willingly placed themselves in the yoke to serve Egypt faithfully. Akkadian wisdom literature indicates that bearing a god's yoke is desirable because of the fringe benefits. In the *Atrahasis Epic* the gods find the yoke of Enlil unbearable and rebel. Assyrian inscriptions describe their conquest of other lands as imposing the yoke of the god Ashur on the people, and rebellion was portrayed as throwing off the yoke. Needless to say, the prophet is using an image familiar throughout the ancient Near East.

9:5. warrior's boot. The word for boot occurs only here in the Old Testament but is equivalent to one of the common Akkadian terms for sandal or shoe. In the Assyrian army many of the infantry went barefoot, but the cavalry was equipped with knee-high soft leather boots held on by long crisscrossed thongs. Officers also were equipped with boots. Boots would be among the most common plunder stripped from the slain.

9:5. garment rolled in blood. In Assyria it was common rhetoric to speak of cities and countrysides dyed red with the blood of enemies and of the army marching through the blood of their enemies. In Ugaritic literature the war goddess Anat is described in battle as plunging her knees into the blood of the guards and her skirts in the gore of warriors. Paintings at Til-Barsip show Assyrians in red uniforms, and classical sources describe soldiers of this period as wearing red or purple tunics. Though there is no parallel to rolling garments in blood, there is one Assyrian text that speaks of dipping weapons in blood.

9:6. portent of the birth of an heir to the throne. In the ancient Near East the birth of an heir to the throne was a momentous occasion. An example can be seen in the Egyptian Myth of the Birth of the Pharaoh. Framed as a prophetic oracle from the god Amon, Hatshepsut's birth is announced with a proclamation of all that she will accomplish. Her name is decreed, and she enjoys the protection and blessing of the god. Even though this text represents Hatshepsut's contrived attempt to legitimate her claim to the throne, it illustrates the type of proclamation that would not be out of place in a birth ceremony.

9:6. throne names and titulary in the ancient Near East. It was common in the ancient world for the king ascending to the throne to take a throne name for himself. We should not imagine that the name Sargon, which means "The King Is Legitimate," just happened to be the given name of an individual who became king. But beyond that was the matter of titulary, titles that accredited the king with various qualities and accomplishments. In Egypt it was a formal, time-honored practice to bestow a titulary of five names on a pharaoh ascending to the throne as part of the accession ceremony. These were an expression of the Egyptian beliefs in the deity of the pharaoh. Perhaps even more intriguing is the titulary of Niqmepa, king of Ugarit (mid-second millennium) which includes titles such as Lord of Justice, Master of the Royal House, King Who Protects and King Who Builds.

9:6. sentence names in the ancient Near East. Most names in the ancient world make statements. That is, they are self-contained sentences. Many of the statements are about a deity. One can easily recognize the deity name in names such as *Ashur*banipal, *Nebu*chadnezzar, or *Ra*meses. Anyone even casually familiar with the Bible has noticed how many Israelite names end in -iah or -el, or start with Jeho- or El-. All of these represent Israel's God. This type of name is called a theophoric name, and it affirms the nature of the deity, proclaims the attributes of the deity or requests the blessing of the deity. One way to interpret the titulary of this verse is to understand it as reflecting important theophoric affirmations: The Di-

vine Warrior Is a Supernatural Planner, The Sovereign of Time Is a Prince of Peace (note: the word "is" is not used in such constructions, as all names demonstrate).

9:6. compound names in the ancient Near East. The name Maher-Shalal-Hash-Baz in 8:1 is a compound name comprised of two parallel statements. Since 9:6 proposes this child's name (singular) rather than his names (plural; NIV translates around this), an attractive option is to consider this also to be just one (long and complex) compound theophoric name. Though such compound names are not the norm in the ancient Near East, Isaiah is not presenting these as common. Assyrian use of compound names can be observed in the names Tiglath-Pileser III gives to the palaces and the gates he built in Calah. The latter are named "Gates of Justice Which Give the Correct Judgment for the Ruler of the Four Quarters,Which Offer the Yield of the Mountains and the Seas, Which Admit the Produce of Mankind Before the King Their Master."

9:7. concept of coming king with ideal reign. In a work titled the Marduk Prophecy (from about 1100 B.C.) a king is "prophesied" who will rebuild temples and reestablish prerogatives for Babylon. His reign is characterized by reform, stability and prosperity. His favor with deity will open the gate of heaven permanently. Peace and justice will result from the deity's rule through this ideal king. Though the Marduk Prophecy may well have been written as propaganda for the king, who desired it to be understood as applying to himself, it demonstrates that the rhetoric used in Isaiah would have been familiar as a way to describe a future ideal kingdom.

9:8-21
Judgment Against Israel

9:10. bricks to dressed stone, figs to cedars. Sun-dried mud brick was a common building material in Palestine. It was inexpensive, readily available and reasonably sturdy. Sycamore (fig) was one of the most common trees in the region. A rapid growing tree, its shrub-like character and soft wood made it less than ideal for posts and beams, but it was used nonetheless. The contrast of carefully dressed stone and imported hardwood cedar suggests luxury and permanence.

9:11. enemies of Rezin. The most notable enemies of Rezin are the Assyrians, and they are the ones from whom the judgment comes.

9:12. Arameans and Philistines. Arameans and Philistines were the other two major targets of the Assyrians in the 734-732 campaigns. It would be awkward, though not impossible, to view them as being devoured along with Israel by the enemies of Rezin. Since Rezin is the king of the Arameans, it is difficult to see them as comprising his enemies. The other possibility is that captured Philistines and Arameans had been pressed into service in the ranks of the Assyrian army as it moved against Israel. There is ample evidence of this practice during the time of Tiglath-Pileser.

9:14. palm branch and reed. The text does not refer to the date palm tree being cut off but to the frondlike branches that grow out of the top of the trunk. The head and the tail, being inseparable, are known to both go the same direction. The frond and reed are the same as they will bend in whatever direction the wind is blowing. They have no ability to act independently.

9:20. cannibalism. It is uncertain whether this text refers to cannibalism or not. Nevertheless, cannibalism is a standard element of curses in Assyrian treaties of the seventh century. It was the last resort in times of impending starvation. This level of desperation could occur in times of severe famine (as illustrated in the *Atrahasis Epic*) or could be the result of siege (as during Ashurbanipal's siege of Babylon, about 650 B.C.) when the food supply had become depleted, as anticipated in the treaty texts. Siege warfare was common in the ancient world, so this may not have been as rare an occasion as might be presumed.

10:1-34
Woes on Judah and Assyria

10:1. oppressive laws in the ancient Near East. Reference is made here not to creating a justice system but to issuing decrees or regulations regarding specific issues. In the political climate that existed in Isaiah's time one of the special issues that had to be addressed was the raising of funds with which to pay tribute. This was generally accomplished through special tax levies, though there were always exemptions granted to either classes of people or cities that had been given sacred status. Other possible issues include the manumission of debt slaves or the disposition of property in forfeiture. Usually the claim of unjust laws was made against a ruler by his successor. The Reform Text of Uruinimgina identified oppressive practices of former days that he put a stop to. Ur-Nammu claims that he did not "impose orders" but eliminated violence and cries for justice.

10:2. orphans and widows as victims. Based on the statements in the prologues of the Ur-Nammu Code and the Code of Hammurabi, it is clear that kings considered it part of their role as "wise rulers" to protect the rights of the poor, the widow and the orphan. Similarly, in the Egyptian *Tale of the Eloquent Peasant*, the plaintiff began by identifying his judge as "the father of the orphan, the husband of the widow." Individual statutes (seen in several Middle Assyrian laws) protected a widow's right to remarry and provided for her when her husband was taken prisoner and presumed dead. In this way the vulnerable classes were provided for throughout the ancient Near East.

10:9. list of cities. The first two cities represent northern Syria, with the southern city (Calno) treated as the northern one (Carchemish) had been. The second pair represents middle Syria, again with the southern one (Hamath) having been treated like the northern one (Arpad). The third pair represents southern Syria and Palestine, with the southern city (Samaria) having been treated like the northern one (Damascus). This presents a geographical rather than a chronological sequence. This leads to a final north-south sequence, with Jerusalem juxtaposed to Samaria in verse 11.

10:9. Calno. Also known as Calneh or, in the Assyrian texts, Kullani, this city was subjugated by the Assyrians in 738. The site has not been positively identified as yet, but it is in the vicinity of Arpad, in a territory known as Unqi in Assyrian texts. It was considered a significant victory by Tiglath-Pileser in that he included a relief in the Calah annals that depicts the gods of the city being carried away captive and the king bowed in submission with Tiglath-Pileser's foot on his neck. Kullani was identified as the principal target of the 738 campaign.

10:9. Carchemish. Carchemish was likely one of the allies of Urartu under Sarduri in the 743 coalition against Assyria. Carchemish did not actively oppose Tiglath-Pileser in the 738 coalition, rather its ruler, Pisiri, is listed among those that paid tribute in that year. It was not annexed until 717. The city was located on the west bank of the Euphrates, just inside modern Turkey, and was about fifty miles northeast of Arpad.

10:9. Hamath. After Arpad and its coalition collapsed in 740, another coalition was put together, including many of the cities of southern Syria. Hamath was among them and paid tribute when the coalition was broken up by Tiglath-Pileser in 738. Hamath (modern Hama, almost 100 miles south of Aleppo and about 130 miles north of Damascus) is located on the Orontes River.

10:9. Arpad. Arpad (modern Tel Rifaat), about twenty miles north of Aleppo in northern Syria, was one of the first in the west to take a stand against Tiglath-Pileser and feel the result of his determination. In 743 Mati'el king of Arpad formed a coalition with the Urartian king Sarduri and his allies to try to keep the Assyrians out of northern Syria. Tiglath-Pileser broke up the coalition in 743 but took three more years to finally subdue and annex Arpad in 740.

10:9. Samaria and Damascus. These were, of course, subjugated in the campaigns of 733-732 as Tiglath-Pileser extended his control farther and farther south.

10:10. images that excelled. There is no distinction made in this speech between the religious practices of Israel and Judah on the one hand and the other cities of the west. There is no adjective expressed in this verse, but only implied by the syntax. The idols of the nations are therefore identified as exceeding the idols of Jerusalem and Samaria. If the NIV is correct, the comparison may concern how ornately they were manufactured or clothed. The NASB prefers "greater," suggesting perhaps that they were capable of more impressive shows of strength. A third possibility could refer to the greater number of idols in the other cities. One of the grandest moments in the conquest of a city was when the idols were led out subdued and captive.

10:11. images and idols in Israel. Israelite religion was ideally supposed to be aniconic (no images). In actual practice, though, this was not the case. Isaiah as well as most other preexilic prophets indicted the people for their use of idols. For Ahaz's employment of idols see 2 Chronicles 28:2. This textual portrayal is not as well supported by the archaeological record as might be expected. The absence of idols dating to the monarchy, however, may be due to the diligence in destruction by reformers such as Hezekiah and Josiah, and the thoroughness of plunderers such as the Assyrian and Babylonian kings.

10:13-14. claims of royal inscriptions. The arrogant claims put in the mouth of the Assyrian king by Isaiah is not at all exaggerated. The royal inscriptions of these kings are extreme in the claims they arrogate to the king. Tiglath-Pileser declares himself beloved of the gods, light of all his people and shepherd of humankind, who subdued many kings, despoiled cities and imposed tribute. He claimed that he considered his enemies mere

ghosts. One of his predecessors, Ashurnasirpal, shows a great propensity for proliferate titles, often including more than two dozen. Among them are included ferocious dragon, marvelous shepherd, holy creature, martial sovereign, fearless in battle, trampler of enemies, merciless hero and mighty floodtide who has no opponent and who by his lordly conflict has brought under one authority ferocious and merciless kings from east to west (excerpts from Grayson, *Assyrian Royal Inscriptions 2*).

10:16-19. judgment on Assyria. Though the Assyrian king fashioned himself as the light of all his people, Yahweh, the Light of Israel, was going to outshine him. The Assyrian kings boasted of their destructions of fields and orchards, and of their incineration of cities— now they will suffer a similar fate. The armies that were the power and pride of these kings were to be decimated by disease (epidemics were a constant threat to army camps) if the army is referred to here (see next comment). A devastation of the Assyrian army did take place outside the walls of Jerusalem in 701, though not through consumption (NIV: "wasting disease"; see 2 Kings 19:35). The overthrow of Assyria was not accomplished until about eighty-five years later as the Medes and Babylonians conquered Ashur and Nineveh.

10:16. wasting disease. There is little reason to accept the NIV translation of "sturdy warriors" in this verse (it nowhere else refers to soldiers or army). The word refers to that which is rich or luxuriant and in Daniel 11:24 applies to territory. Preference here would be for the idea that God would make the lushest regions of Assyria unproductive.

10:22-23. divine decree of destruction. The divine decree that a city should be destroyed is a familiar motif in the ancient Near East. As early as the Sumerian Laments the divine council decreed the destruction of the city of Ur. There, however, it is lamented that there is no explanation for Enlil's decree. In the Marduk Prophecy the god decrees his own removal to Hatti. The Weidner Chronicle reports that Marduk decreed the destruction of the city of Babylon at the hands of the Gutians. In this piece it was for the offenses of Naram-Sin. Ishtar became angry and stirred up an enemy against her city of Uruk in the *Myth of Erra and Ishum*. Though there is not always a reason that could be cited as "righteous," the concept presented here is very familiar.

10:24. Egyptian role. Egypt had little involvement in the affairs of Syro-Palestine during the reign of Tiglath-Pileser III, since this was a time of division and competing claims between Egypt, Nubia to the south and Libya to the west. A single incident reports that Hanun king of Gaza fled to Egypt for protection when Tiglath-Pileser came against his city in 734. It was not until the accession of Shalmaneser V to the throne of Assyria in 727 that Hoshea of Israel was emboldened to approach the Egyptians for help (see comment on 2 Kings 17:4). The reference to Egypt here is to the time of the exodus.

10:26. rock of Oreb. This is a reference to the Lord's deliverance of Israel under Gideon against all odds. The Midianite ruler Oreb was killed at the (unlocated) rock of Oreb in Judges 7:25.

10:27. yoke imagery. See comment on 9:4.

10:28-32. itinerary. The twelve cities mentioned here cut a path from the north directly toward Jerusalem. This is not the itinerary followed by Sennacherib when he came against Jerusalem in 701. In that campaign he cut off all the cities of the Shephelah southwest of Jerusalem, Lachish being the last, and so approached Jerusalem from that side. Aiath is usually identified with Ai, about ten miles north of Jerusalem. Migron is thought to be the Wadi Swenit that forms a deep pass between Micmash and Geba (see comment on 1 Sam 14:2). As the army camps at Geba, there is uncertainty which of the three roads out of Geba will be used. One road goes west to Ramah (under two miles); one goes southwest to Gibeah (about three and a half miles); and a third goes south to Anathoth (about four miles). The Anathoth road would lead by Gallim (uncertain location) and then south of Anathoth would pass through Laishah to Nob. Nob is believed to have been located on what is now called Mount Scopus, overlooking the city of Jerusalem from the northwest. Mademah and Gebim remain unidentified.

10:34. Lebanon. See comment on 2:13.

11:1-16
The Future Davidic King and His Kingdom

11:1. oracle of a future ideal ruler. See comment on 9:7. Texts from both Egypt and Mesopotamia predict kings coming to power who will be successful in bringing peace, justice and prosperity, though these are usually written after the king is on the throne as a means of legitimating his rule. Such an oracle in the time of Ashurbanipal includes the hungry being fed, the naked being clothed and prisoners being set free. Tiglath-Pileser III is described as the shoot or scion of the city of Baltil (=Assur) who brings justice to his people.

11:2. endowment with divine spirit in the ancient Near East. In the Judges period the Spirit of the Lord endowed an individual with central authority that only the Lord possessed (see comment on Judg 6:34-35). The role of the king represented a more permanent central authority and likewise relied on empowerment by the Lord. The king was an agent of deity and a heavenly functionary just as judges and prophets were. The Spirit is able to give the positive attributes of courage, charisma, insight, wisdom and confidence. In Mesopotamia the king was seen as being endowed with the *melammu* of the gods (the visible representation of the glory of deity). It designated him as the divine representative and indicated that his reign was legitimate and approved by the gods. In Assyrian inscriptions it is pictured hovering over the king. An additional correlation may be found in the Akkadian term *bashtu*. It refers generally to a sense of dignity and is often bestowed by the gods, but it also is personified as a protective spirit. It provides various attributes, as here, and gives authority to its recipient.

11:3-4. judge's challenge. The foremost responsibility of a king in the ancient world was to establish justice, and therefore the rhetoric of kings throughout the inscriptional material proclaims their success in that endeavor. The wisdom of a king was assessed by the brilliance of his insight into complex cases, and his suitability for the throne was evaluated by his commitment to provide for the vulnerable classes of society. The ability to resolve difficult cases was believed to be divinely endowed (compare Solomon; see comments on 1 Kings 3:16-28 and 2 Chron 1:12) and therefore was not dependent solely on the evidence that could be presented in court (see Prov 16:10).

11:5. belt/sash. The same word is used in both lines of this verse, but one item is a wrap around the thighs, while the other winds between the thighs. These are the most basic articles of clothing, and without them an individual would be naked.

11:6-8. animal behavior to convey utopian conditions. From Sumerian times the myth called *Enki and Ninhursag* describes a utopian situation in which the lion does not kill and the wolf does not snatch the lamb. Other utopian works describe an absence of predators (no snake, scorpion, lion or wolf in the account in *Enmerkar and the Lord of Aratta*).

11:10. banner. The banner, or standard, was used as a means of calling out an army of a particular territory or indicating the place where a muster was taking place or a camp was located. It often featured an insignia of the tribe or division. In the Egyptian army the divisions were named for various gods (e.g., the division of Amun, division of Seth) and the banners would identify the division by means of some representation of the god.

11:11. places of exile. The places named here are not necessarily intended to represent locations of known exile for Israelites. Rather they are equivalent to the four quarters of the earth referred to in the next verse. Assyria is mentioned first as the actual location of exiles but also as a representative of the northeastern area. Egypt, to the southwest, is identified in three segments up the Nile, including the kingdom of Nubia (NIV: Cush). Elam and Babylonia represent the southeast extremes, while Hamath represents the regions to the north. Finally, the "islands" is a way of representing the areas furthest west.

11:12. four quarters. It was typical in the ancient world to refer to four regions of the inhabited world. Akkadian literature speaks of kings ruling the four quarters, most likely making reference to the most distant coasts or extremities in the four major directions. In this sense it is referring to not four slices of the geographical pie but four edges, thereby including everything in between.

11:14. near neighbors. As the previous verses had focused on a universal perspective, this verse addresses the near neighbors on the east, west and south.

11:15. gulf of the Egyptian Sea. This is the only occurrence in the Bible of a body of water called the Egyptian Sea and is therefore difficult to place with any certainty. Most commentators identify it with the Gulf of Suez.

11:15. Euphrates in seven streams. In Mesopotamia the water supply was regulated for irrigation use by separating and diverting sluice channels from canals that drew water off from the river system. As water was diverted, the various channels slowed the flow of the water.

12:1-6

Song of Victory

12:1-6. victory songs. The concept of an angry God who has now concluded the just punishment of the nation will be repeated later in Isaiah (40:1-2). The call to praise God's name is found in many Psalms, including 22:22-25 and 116:12-13. This theodicy of divine wrath followed by restoration of fortunes is also found in the Moabite inscription of Mesha. There the king notes how their god Chemosh allowed them to be conquered for a time but had eventually chosen to give them victories

over their enemies. Similarly, the Assyrian annals of Esarhaddon, Shalmaneser I and Tukulti-Ninurta I praise their triumphant god Ashur, who has "universal sovereignty" and has given them authority to subjugate all nations.

13:1-22

Oracle Against Babylon

13:1. oracles against foreign nations. See comment on Jeremiah 46:1.

13:1. Babylon in Isaiah's time. At the time that Isaiah functioned as a prophet (second half of the eighth century B.C.), the Neo-Assyrian empire, under the Sargonid rulers, Sargon II and Sennacherib, was the most powerful political network the world had ever seen. It stretched across the Near East and would eventually even include Egypt for a short time. During this period Babylonia and its Chaldean rulers were subjugated, just like all other nation states by the Assyrians. However, they, like the Medes in western Iran, periodically tested the Assyrian hegemony with revolts or by attempting to subvert Assyria's allies and vassal states. Particularly troublesome was Merodach-Baladan, who ousted the Assyrian rulers of Babylon on at least two occasions. Finally, in 689 B.C. Sennacherib sacked the city and assumed the title of king of Babylon. Shortly after 660, as the Assyrian empire began to crumble, Babylonia and Media combined to put even greater pressure on the last of the great Assyrian kings, Ashurbanipal. His death in 627 marked the end of Assyrian world power and the emergence of Nebuchadnezzar and the Neo-Babylonian empire.

13:10. constellations. The constellations, according to the Mesopotamian creation epic *Enuma Elish*, were the divine assembly of the great god Marduk, placed there to oversee the forces of nature and help him manage creation. Since it was assumed that movements of heavenly bodies were omens for events that would occur on earth, astronomic observations were constantly made and recorded (such as the collection in *Enuma Anu Enlil*). Eventually this was also applied to the preparing of individual horoscopes in Mesopotamia, Egypt and Greece. In this way lucky and unlucky days could be determined by consulting the guild of magicians and astrologers. Mesopotamian constellations included animal figures such as a goat (Lyra) and snake (Hydra); objects such as an arrow (Sirius) and a wagon (Big Dipper); and characters such as Anu (Orion). The most popular of the constellations was Pleiades, often portrayed on seals even in Palestine and Syria. Neo-Assyrian texts preserve sketches of stars in constellations.

13:10. darkened stars, sun and moon. By declaring that on the "day of Yahweh" the heavens and all of its celestial bodies would be damped out, Isaiah claims that the glory of Yahweh will outshine and mask the brilliance of all other supposed gods (compare the language of Ps 104:19-22, in which Yahweh is said to control the moon and sun). Since Assyria and Egypt both worshiped the sun god (Shamash and Amun respectively) as their primary deity and the moon god Sin was of great importance in Babylonia, the prophet targets these gods and these arrogant enemy nations. Such portents of darkness, as in the Deir 'Alla inscription of Balaam, generally forecast a time of great disaster, but Isaiah's message is one of triumph in which "lesser lights" are extinguished to better illumine Yahweh.

13:12. gold of Ophir. The particular purity of the gold of Ophir is the measure for the cleansing of humanity by Yahweh's intervention. The actual location of Ophir is still unknown, although Arabian and East African (Zimbabwe or Somalia) sites are favored (1 Kings 9:28). An eighth-century B.C. inscription from Tell Qasile mentions the gold of Ophir, and it further supports the idea that the name Ophir had become synonymous with purity.

13:13. heavens and earth trembling. Isaiah uses language similar to that which is used in the "storm god" theophany common in the Ugaritic Baal Epic cycle. The divine warrior manifests himself by convulsions of nature, strong winds and a booming within the heavens that nearly tear the very fabric of earth apart. A similar example is found in David's song of praise in 2 Samuel 22:8-16 (see comment there).

13:17. Medes. Median tribes and kings begin to appear in Assyrian texts in the late ninth century B.C., especially in connection with the acquisition of horses and in gaining control of trade routes through the Zagros Mountains. Tiglath-Pileser III and Sargon II each invaded the area several times, exacting tribute and deporting portions of the population (2 Kings 17:6). The Medes inhabited the region of central western Iran with their capital at Ecbatana. The Iranian kingdom of Elam ruled the area to the south. They do not appear to be a unified people until the seventh century, when their king Cyaxares combined forces with Nebuchadnezzar and the Chaldeans of Babylon to attack and destroy Nineveh (612 B.C.). Subsequently the Medes were con-

quered or absorbed into the Achaemenid empire by Cyrus II in 550 B.C. (Esther 1:3).

13:17. no interest in silver or gold. As the Assyrian annals of Sennacherib attest, it was possible for a city to ransom itself during a siege for a high price (2 Kings 18:13-16). However, the reputation of the Medes is that they were such fierce warriors that they could not be bribed or bought off once they had begun a campaign (see Zeph 1:18).

13:19. overthrow of Babylon. Despite the fact that Assyria is the source of Israel's destruction in Isaiah's time, that empire is seen as "the rod of God's anger" (Is 10:5), although assurance is given that its time of judgment will eventually come (14:25). Thus the elimination of the short-lived Chaldean monarchy of Merodach-Baladan provides an initial example within the larger picture of "the day of Yahweh" that will ultimately usher in a new age. The Bit Yakin tribe of the Chaldeans, who had previously inhabited the area south of Babylonia, established their rule over Babylon in 722 B.C. First Sargon II and then Sennacherib moved against them, but a final resolution of what came to be a series of revolts and counterrevolts did not occur until 689, when Sennacherib razed the city and many of its monumental buildings. The ruins of the city broke the Chaldeans for a century, and the memory as well as the sight of the destruction might well have been compared to the fate of Sodom and Gomorrah. Yet the involvement of the Medes suggests that the final destiny of Babylon provided the ultimate fulfillment of this prophecy as the Medes and Persians overran the city in 539.

13:20. fate of Babylon. The description of utter devastation and its perpetual emptiness follows a pattern of city lament found in the Sumerian Laments for Ur (c. 2000 B.C.). In a similar example of a woe oracle the Egyptian *Visions of Neferti* describes the end of the Old Kingdom, leaving the people without direction, the canals dry and Egypt open to invasion by Asiatics and desert herders. Babylon's ultimate demise came not at the hands of a destructive enemy but through gradual deterioration as the course of the Euphrates shifted and left the fabled city an isolated and abandoned wilderness.

14:3-23

Taunt Against the King of Babylon

14:4. taunt song. This song uses the metric pattern of a dirge but parodies the genre by mocking rather than eulogizing the dead.

14:8. woodsman. The forests of Lebanon were

considered a treasury by kings of the ancient world. The timber from the cedar trees was essential for temples and palaces. Kings boasted of having extended their conquests to these forests and of cutting trees from it. Nebuchadnezzar calls it the forest of Marduk, and the Gilgamesh Epic portrays the cedar forests as divine property guarded by the fearsome Huwawa. Invading them and taking their resources was the greatest adventure of all. Isaiah 37:24 and Ezekiel 31 portray a similar concept.

14:9-11. dead kings. In the ancient world it was believed that spirits of the dead were quite capable of returning to haunt the living. The status or power one enjoyed in life was often transferred into the netherworld existence, perhaps with the thought that the spirit would be content to remain. In the description here in Isaiah, however, it is not the return of the spirit that is the concern. The king of Babylon is portrayed stripped of all of his power and grandeur. In Canaanite mythology the god Mot is the ruler of the netherworld and is portrayed with royal characteristics. But it is Baal who descends into the netherworld to become the leader of all the fallen heroes and honored ancestors. In Ugaritic literature these are called the *Rapiuma*, the same word that the NIV translates as "spirits of the departed" in verse 9.

14:12. morning star. The Hebrew word behind this translation, *helel*, is not used anywhere else in the Old Testament. Many interpreters, ancient and modern, see it as a designation of Venus, the morning star. It is this interpreta-

tion that was behind the early Greek translation of the term, as well as the Latin Vulgate's *luciferos* (shining one, i.e., Venus). Most modern interpreters believe that Isaiah is using a well-known mythological tale as an analogy to the failure and consequences of the king of Babylon's rebellion and arrogance, but no known literature matches the details of Helel's rebellion.

14:12. son of dawn. Dawn (*shahar*) was often personified in the Old Testament and was a known deity in Phoenician and Ugaritic inscriptions.

14:13. rebellion in heaven in the ancient Near East. Some have seen some similarity between the story of Helel and a Ugaritic tale concerning the god Athtar. In Baal's absence, Athtar attempted to sit on his throne (rule in his place) but found he was not up to the task and subsequently took his place in the netherworld. Though Athtar's name may have a similar meaning to Helel, he is not the son of Shahar (as Helel is described), nor is he thrown down from his attempt to sit on Baal's throne. Neither is the attempt itself an act of rebellion. The theme of revolt against the gods is, nevertheless, a familiar one. One of the best examples from ancient literature is the *Myth of Anzu*, where a lion/bird creature attempts to steal the Tablet of Destinies by which the gods governed the world. Anzu decides to take supremacy of the world and the gods by stealing the tablet from the chief god, Enlil. He utters a series of "I will" statements just as the king does here: "I myself will take the gods' Tablet of Destinies. The responsibilities of the

---

AFTERLIFE BELIEFS IN ISRAEL AND THE ANCIENT NEAR EAST

Sheol is the Hebrew word for the netherworld. Though it might have been considered an act of judgment for a person to be consigned to Sheol from life, it was not in itself a place of judgment to be contrasted to the reward of a heavenly destiny. The word was sometimes used as a synonym for "grave" because the grave was the portal through which one entered the netherworld. The Israelites believed that the spirits of the dead continued to exist in this shadowy world. They were not thought to have a pleasant existence, but Sheol is never associated with the torment of hellfire in the Old Testament (the imagery seen in Is 66:24 is not associated with Sheol). It is not clear that there were any alternatives to Sheol. People who were spared from Sheol were spared from it by being kept alive rather than by going somewhere else. There was at least a vague idea of somewhere else to go seen in the examples of Enoch and Elijah, who avoided the grave and presumably did not go to Sheol. But those texts are very unclear about what the other alternative was. In the absence of specific revelation to the contrary, Israelite beliefs conformed generally to those current among their Canaanite and Mesopotamian neighbors.

In Mesopotamian beliefs the dead needed to cross a desert, mountains and a river, and then descend through the seven gates of the netherworld. Though described in Mesopotamian literature as a place where there is darkness and the inhabitants are clothed in bird feathers and eat dust, kinder accounts were also available. The denizens of this shadow world were believed to be sustained by the offerings presented by those who were still alive. They enjoyed some light as the sun god passed through the netherworld when it was night in the land of the living so he could rise in the east again the next morning. The rulers of the netherworld, Nergal and Ereshkigal, were assisted by a group called the Anunnaki. Despite these depressing descriptions, no one wanted to be turned away from the gates because the alternative was to be a wandering spirit with no access to funerary offerings.

gods I will seize for myself. I will establish myself on the throne and wield the decrees. I will take command over all the Igigi-gods." Boastful arrogance was typical of the antagonist in this type of account.

14:13. stars of God. The word used for God here is El. While this is sometimes used to refer to Israel's God in the Bible, it is also known as the name of the chief god in the Canaanite pantheon. In the Old Testament the word "stars" occasionally refers to angels of the heavenly court (Job 38:7), while in Ugaritic and Mesopotamian texts it would describe astral deities.

14:13. mount of assembly. Since the gods of Canaanite mythology were believed to live on the mountain heights (see next entry), it is understandable that their place of assembly was also located on an elevated place. In fact, El is portrayed as convening the divine assembly of the pantheon on the heights of Zaphon. Though the term "mount of assembly" has not been found, the council of the assembly is said to meet on the mount of El.

14:13. sacred mountain. Ancient Near Eastern thought, not unlike that familiar from Greek mythology, visualized a mountain height as the dwelling place of deity. There would have been little difference in their minds between the tops of mountains and the heavens. Baal's home was purported in Ugaritic literature to be Mount Zaphon (commonly identified with Mount Casius, Jebel al'Aqra, in Syria, elev. 5807 feet). The Hebrew word *zaphon* means "north" and is translated here by the NIV "sacred mountain" (see Ps 48:2).

14:14. Most High *(Elyon).* In the Old Testament the term *Elyon* is normally a title for Yahweh. However, since it also occurs as a divine title (and perhaps even as a divine name) in other literature from the ancient Near East (Ugaritic, Aramaic and Phoenician), its use in a context such as this can be ambiguous. It is best known outside the Bible as a title for Baal in the Ugaritic texts.

14:15. brought to the pit. In a Sumerian myth that shares some material with the *Anzu Myth* (see comment on 14:13), the god Ninurta overcomes the creature Anzu but ambitiously wants to gain power himself. When Enki discovers his scheme, Ninurta is thrown into a pit, and Enki chides him as a bragging upstart who recklessly tried to seize power that did not belong to him.

14:19. cast out of tomb. The mythological metaphor in verses 12-15 separates the response in the netherworld (vv. 9-11) from the response on earth in verses 16-17. Since the mutilated corpse of the enemy leader was often exposed by being displayed in a public place (see comment on 1 Sam 31:10), people would pass by and stare. The phrase used here, better rendered "cast out, without a tomb," indicates that the king will be deprived of proper burial. This represented a final humiliation and a desecration, for most ancient peoples believed that proper, timely burial affected the quality of the afterlife. See comment on 1 Kings 16:4. In the Gilgamesh Epic, Enkidu, back from the netherworld, reported to Gilgamesh that the one who died unburied had no rest and that the one who had no living relatives to take care of him could only eat what was thrown into the street. A Babylonian curse relates burial to the uniting of the spirit of the dead with loved ones. We know that even Israelites believed that proper burial affected one's afterlife, because they, like their neighbors, buried their loved ones with the provisions that would serve them in the afterlife; most often pottery vessels (filled with food) and jewelry (to ward off evil), with tools and personal items sometimes added.

14:19. fate of the slain. Alternatives to the corpse being put on public display would include the ignominious end of being piled in a heap of the slain or of being trampled and unrecognizable. The reference to "stones of the pit" is obscure.

14:20. never be mentioned. The mentioning of the name of the dead was one way of giving honor to them (examples in Gen 48:16; Ruth 4:14). Alternatively this phrase could refer to the name being either invoked or renowned. In any case, the idea is clearly that this king will not enjoy a prominent place in history.

14:24-27
Oracle Against Assyria

14:25. Assyria. The judgment pronounced against Assyria again appears to refer to the destruction of Sennacherib's army outside Jerusalem in 701 (see comment on 10:16-19).

14:26-27. plans of deity. Though there were fixed decrees that the gods superintended, the idea that a deity had a plan that stretched across time and space was not easily maintained in the polytheism of the ancient world. The gods were not immune to the changes of time, nor was any deity's jurisdiction universal. These would greatly limit the ability of a god, even of a powerful head of pantheon such as Ashur or Marduk, to sustain a plan such as that claimed by Yahweh here and elsewhere in Isaiah. Nevertheless, Assyrian kings do claim that it was in the plan of the gods that their throne was established, their conquests made and their empires expanded. But often these divine plans were seen to be made on a short-term schedule. The gods were believed to meet each New Year's to make their plans for the year. Their decrees would be recorded on the tablets of fate to be enacted throughout the year. Divination was typically used when people wanted to find out more about those plans.

14:28-32
Oracle Against Philistia

14:28. chronology. The chronology of this period is very complicated and it is not easy to determine the year of Ahaz's death. Some chronological systems overlap Ahaz and his son Hezekiah in a coregency, with Hezekiah being the lead ruler (due perhaps to the strength of the anti-Assyrian contingent in the administration). His death may have come as early as 726 or as late as 715. The earlier one is supported by the synchronism of 2 Kings 17:1.
14:29. Philistines in eighth century. Philistia had been under the control of Judah during the reign of Uzziah, which took up the whole first half of the eighth century. It regained its independence during the reign of Ahaz and became the aggressor. With the rise of the Neo-Assyrian empire, Philistia came under attack just as the rest of the nations did. Tiglath-Pileser targeted Gaza in his campaign of 734, and the cities of Philistia thus became tribute-paying vassals. When Sargon came to the throne, the Philistines attempted to break free of Assyria, but in 720 Philistia again came under attack and Gaza renewed its loyalty. In 712 Sargon again had to come west to subdue the revolt led by Ashdod. Ekron and Gath were also targeted at this time. Sennacherib's 701 campaign brought changes on the thrones of several of the Philistine cities, but only Ekron needed to be besieged. Through most of the eighth and seventh centuries the Philistines shared the fate of their neighbors in Judah.
14:31-32. fate of Philistia. Eventually the Philistines were defeated and deported by Nebuchadnezzar just as the Judeans were. The five cities retained some degree of prominence, but by the Persian period the people had been gradually assimilated into the general mix of the empire population.

15:1—16:14
Oracle Against Moab

15:1. Moab in eighth century. Like many of the small Syro-Palestinian states during the eighth century B.C., Moab was dominated by Assyrian hegemony over the region. Several Assyrian texts list Moabite kings paying tribute or being implicated in the periodic revolts by coalitions of these small nations (Ashdod revolt of 713 recorded in a prism from Sargon II's reign). Since Isaiah is probably speaking during the early reign of Hezekiah, the destruction of Moabite cities is probably due to incursions by desert tribes rather than the Assyrians. It seems clear from Sennacherib's annals that Moab attempted to ingratiate herself during the 701 campaign that saw much of Judah devastated and Jerusalem besieged. As a result Israelite prophets (Amos 2:1-5 and Jer 48) generally list Moab as an enemy nation.
15:1-4. cities. Those cities listed as destroyed or damaged are all in the northern sector of Moab: Kir (Kir Hareseth in 16:7) is on the upper portion of the Wadi el-Kerak and serves as the capital of the district of Ar; Nebo and Medeba both are located just east of the northern end of the Dead Sea and about twenty miles north of Dibon. Also attacked were Heshbon and Elealeh, located northeast of Nebo. The more southern cities of Dibon (twenty miles north of Kir) and Jahaz were apparently not directly affected by the raiders but were in fear of future incursions.
15:2-3. mourning practices. Communal and individual laments throughout the ancient Near East included weeping, the shaving of heads and beards, wearing sackcloth and lying on the ground or rolling about. These are all illustrative of grief as well as a temporary (usually seven-day) identification with the dead. See the comments on Micah 1:8 and 1:16 for discussion of these practices and extrabiblical evidence from Ugaritic and Assyrian texts.
15:5. flight itinerary. The key to the line of flight for the Moabite fugitives is Zoar since none of the other sites mentioned can be identified (only mentioned elsewhere in the parallel text in Jer 48:3, 5, 34). According to Genesis 14:2-3 Zoar is one of the cities of the plain. Speculation on its exact location, however, places it near Mount Nebo (Deut 32:1-3), near the northern tip of the Dead Sea, as well as in the area at the southern end of the Dead Sea. Considering the apparent focus of the attack in Isaiah 15:1-4 around Kir and Nebo, it seems that a southern site for Zoar and these other cities would be more appropriate for a flight to safety towards Edom.
15:6. waters of Nimrim. Following the same reasoning regarding a flight south by the Moabite fugitives, it seems best to identify Nimrim (Jer 48:34) with the Wadi en-Numeirah,

which flows west into the southern end of the Dead Sea. There is also a nearby site, Numeirah, which may have been associated with the water source and served as a Moabite outpost.

15:7. ravine of the poplars. Assuming a southern route for the fugitives, this poplar-lined ravine would be the Wadi el-Hesa (Zered River), which marks the border between Moab and Edom. This wide valley (up to four miles across) runs for thirty-five miles and concludes at the southeast end of the Dead Sea (Num 21:12).

15:8. Eglaim. Isaiah's oracle would indicate a southern location for this site, but no exact identification has been made. Among the possibilities are Eusebius's listing of Agallim, just south of Rabbah, and Aharoni's suggestion of Mazra', a site east of the Lisan Peninsula.

15:8. Beer Elim. This site has not been positively identified. Some scholars speculate that it is to be equated with Beer of Numbers 21:16, but the large number of place names which begin with Beer, "well," makes such an identification problematic. Following the line of thought used on other sites in this oracle, one would expect it to be a southern site near the Dead Sea, possibly in the vicinity of el-Kerak.

15:9. Dimon's waters. Because of its proximity to the Wadi Ibn Hammad on the Moabite plateau, Dimon has been identified with Khirbet Dimneh, about two and a half miles northwest of Rabbah. Surface survey has not revealed Iron Age pottery, but no excavations have been undertaken at the site.

16:1. lambs as tributes. Much of the Moabite plateau is suitable for grazing herds of sheep and goats (Num 32:4). Since this would have been a major part of their economy, it would make a suitable form of tribute (2 Kings 3:4). Assyrian annals often list huge quantities of precious metals, slaves and luxury goods as tribute payments (more likely war booty). However, in the normal course of taxing subject people, sheep would better serve the daily needs of officials (Ashurnasirpal II lists a thousand cattle and ten thousand sheep paid by the frightened ruler of Hattina).

16:1. Sela. This word, meaning "rock," appears only a few times as a place name. The best known usage is in 2 Kings 14:7, referring to an Edomite fortress that was conquered by Amaziah of Judah and is identified with either Petra or modern Sela', two miles northwest of Buseira. The site mentioned in Isaiah's oracle has not been identified. It is unlikely to be the same as the Edomite site because all of the other places mentioned in this text stop short of entering Edom.

16:2. fords of the Arnon. The Valley of the Arnon is in places three miles across and is a major barrier to traffic north and south. The fords refer to the point where the north-south highway crosses the wadi at Dibon (as in Mesha's mention of this in the Moabite Stone). This would a natural crossing point for the Moabite fugitives as well as an extremely strategic site (compare the military importance of fords in Judg 12:5; Jer 51:32).

16:7-9. cities. Recapping the area of devastation, the oracle describes the physical and economic ruin of the northern section of Moab. This includes the tableland cities of Heshbon and Kir Hareseth (Kir; see 15:1-4), and Jazer (Khirbet Gazzir, at the northern end of the Dead Sea). Both Sibmah and Elealeh are listed as part of the Heshbon district and were at one time part of Reuben's allotment (Num 32:3, 37; Josh 13:19). Sibmah's location is uncertain, while Elealeh is generally identified with Khirbet el-'Al, just over a mile northeast of Tell Hesban.

16:14. Moab's fate. While no exact historical event can be suggested for the prophet's oracle against Moab, it is conceivable that raids by desert tribes or perhaps the backlash of an Assyrian army as it passed through the region is the basis for this destruction.

17:1-14
Oracle Against Damascus

17:1. Damascus. The Syro-Ephraimitic War (see comments on 7:1), which raged during the middle 730s, ended with the Assyrian king Tiglath-Pileser III invading Syria and Israel and devastating both of these rebellious states (734-732). The Syrian kingdom, ruled from Damascus by Rezin (see 7:1-9), had been Israel's principal political and economic rival. He had meddled in Israel and Judah's internal affairs and had encroached on their territories for over a decade. It seems apparent, however, that Rezin overstepped his bounds in leading an anti-Assyrian coalition. Assyria did not welcome a rival "Greater Syria," and the destruction of Damascus in 732, as recorded in the Assyrian Annals, was massive, leaving hundreds of sites looking "like hills over which the flood had swept." This widespread destruction also included both the reduction of much of the city of Damascus to rubble as well as the redistribution of its territories in Syria as well as in Transjordan and the Galilee.

17:2. Aroer. The Assyrian campaign through Transjordan would have naturally included the capture of the strategic fortress site of Aroer on the Arnon ('Ara'ir, three miles southeast of Dibon and two and a half miles east of the King's Highway). It guarded the passage through the valley of the Arnon and controlled the border between Moab and Ammon. It is possible that an earlier site for the city was located at Tel Esdar (one and a half miles north) and the name was moved to 'Ara'ir after its destruction in the eighth century.

17:3. fate of Damascus. Tiglath-Pileser III's Annals describe how he completely destroyed the sixteen districts and most of the cities of Aram in 732, deported portions of the population and gave charge of most of the cities and territories of Syria to other, more loyal vassals (the list includes 591 towns destroyed). Damascus was badly damaged but survived the experience to become the capital of a newly constituted Assyrian province. Subsequently Damascus joined yet another anti-Assyrian coalition, led by the Syrian state of Hamath, in 720. This rebellion was crushed by Sargon II in 720, and thereafter Damascus is ruled by Assyrian governors until 609. The city only regained its independence temporarily until the Neo-Babylonian empire absorbed it in 604.

17:5. imagery of reaper. The process of reaping, as depicted in Egyptian tomb paintings, involved the reaper grabbing the stalks of grain in his left hand while cutting them with a sickle in his right hand (Ps 129:7). In this way he was already prepared to tie together the stalks into a bundle that could be transported to a threshing floor. What little remained from this cutting would be gathered by gleaners (Ruth 2:3, 7).

17:5. Valley of Rephaim. This valley and its farms extend southwest of Jerusalem. It provided much of the food for the inhabitants of the city and must have also been heavily gleaned by the poor. A drought or a siege of the city would have put a major strain on the food supply, creating the image found in Isaiah's oracle. The Ein Yael Project has extensively surveyed the archaeological remains of the agricultural activity in this valley. It has shown the widespread use of terracing, an indication of the need to utilize as much of the land as possible to feed the growing population of Jerusalem and its vicinity.

17:6. olive gleaning. Like the grain harvesters, the workers who beat the branches of the olive trees to gather the fruit were told to leave a portion for "the alien, the fatherless and the widow" (Deut 24:20). Their long sticks brought most of the fruit to the ground, but that in the uppermost branches was to be left (Is 24:13). This provides an excellent image of a remnant who will survive to restore the covenantal relationship with Yahweh.

17:8. Asherah poles. See the comments on Deuteronomy 7:1-26 and Judges 2:13 for discussion of these cultic symbols of the fertility goddess of the Canaanites.

17:8. incense altars. Archaeological excavations have demonstrated a wide variety of incense altars throughout the ancient Near East. They range from large, elaborate stands containing intricate decoration (see the Taanach stand) to simple pedestals used in domestic worship as well as to fumigate houses, covering odors and repelling insects. While there is a long history of burning incense in Israelite worship (Ex 30:7-8; Num 16:46-48), it also has close associations with the gods of other peoples as well as magic (Is 65:3; Jer 19:13).

18:1-7
Oracle Against Cush

18:1. land of whirring wings. It is possible that this is a reference to the multitude of insects that infest the Nile Valley (Deut 28:42 contains a similar use of the Hebrew word). However, given the context of "envoys" on the waterways, this more likely refers to the many swift boats made of bundled papyrus that sped their way up and down the Nile.

18:1. rivers of Cush. Cush can refer to several different places in the Old Testament, though it most frequently is the designation for the area translations usually render "Ethiopia." This is misleading, for the area Cush refers to is not modern Ethiopia (Abyssinia), but the area along the Nile just south of Egypt, ancient Nubia (in modern Sudan). The boundary between Egypt and Nubia in ancient times was usually either at the first or second cataract of the Nile. It is unlikely that Nubia ever extended much beyond the sixth cataract at Khartoum. The period from 730 to 715 was one of flux in this area. During the Third Intermediate Period the Twenty-Fifth Dynasty was beginning to emerge, headed by Ethiopian monarchs Pianchia and his successor Shabaka. They remained for a time in the kingdom of Cush but were moving to gain control over all of Egypt and unite the country under their rule. This required battling the native Egyptian kings who held the Delta region, holding off threats from Libya to the west and negotiating mutual defense treaties with the expanding Assyrian empire to the east.

18:2. envoys by papyrus boats. Certainly there would have been a great deal of diplomatic activity during this period. There is some question, however, who is sending these envoys and to whom they are being sent. Given the desire of the Ethiopian dynasts to gain full control over Lower Egypt and the Delta, they may well be sending messengers to Assyria seeking assistance or at least a recognition of their legitimacy to rule in Egypt (see the vision of good relations between Egypt and Assyria in 19:23-25). The use of papyrus boats on the Nile rather than the larger barque associated with nobles and troop carriers suggests some stealth was necessary. The light rafts made of papyrus could easily navigate the rapids along the Nile or could be carried past dangerous or highly populated sections.

18:2. tall and smooth-skinned. Although it seems clear that Ethiopia is sending diplomatic overtures to Assyria, they would not be making the entire trip in papyrus boats. These light crafts would only be suitable for the Nile. Since the Assyrians were neither tall nor smooth-skinned (we have many representations of short, bearded men in Assyrian reliefs), then the envoys may also be spreading the word to the Ethiopian people to join in the effort to unite Egypt. Herodotus's picture of the Ethiopians as the tallest of the Africans would fit this reconstruction.

18:2. strange speech. Despite the translation found here, the Hebrew form is a duplicated adjective (*qaw-qaw*), which means "mighty." The onomatopoeic sound could characterize the rhythmic cadence of a marching army, and the resultant fear might arise from the blended or garbled voices of this host.

18:2. land divided by rivers. This is an apt description of Mesopotamia, the "Land of Two Rivers," the Tigris and Euphrates. However, since the envoys of the Ethiopian pharaoh Shabaka, at least initially, are being sent throughout Egypt, the "rivers" in this case may well be the tributaries and canals linked to the Nile River.

18:5. imagery from grape harvest. It is the wise farmer who knows the correct times of the year to cultivate and prune his vines to insure maximum yield. The grapevines first bloom in May, and the fruit will begin to ripen by August. There are two calculated prunings: (1) as noted in the Gezer Calendar, in the fall before the vines become dormant, the unproductive bunches from the previous year are removed, and (2) once the grapes appear, excess leaves and tendrils are cut away to encourage greater yield and even ripening. Yahweh will thus bide his time until the appropriate moment to make his pruning of nations on earth.

18:6. judgment by animals. The cuttings from the grape vines were often used for fuel (Ezek 15:2-4), but in this example they are left as food and nesting for birds and other animals.

The pruned cuttings, like the shattered nations, become little more than scattered sticks, incidentally useful through the coming seasons, but no threat to Yahweh or to Judah.

19:1-25
Oracle Against Egypt

19:1. Egypt in eighth century. Egypt is a divided nation during much of the eighth century. The nominal rule of Sheshonq's successors at Tanis was virtually ignored by the dynasts at Thebes and the patchwork of kings and chiefs in the Delta. The rising threat to Egypt represented by the expansion of Assyria under Tiglath-Pileser III after 745 may have fueled the emergence of the Cushite kings Piankhy and Shabaka. Their efforts to unite all Egypt were stalled for about twenty years by the rulers of Sais, who had managed to merge all of the northern nomes under their leadership. The Saite success was aided by increased trade with the Philistines and the rest of the Levant. It was probably to the Saite king Tefnakhte that many of the Assyrian border states (Philistia, Israel, Transjordan) looked for aid in their attempts to rebel. Finally, in 712 the Sudanese king Shabaka conquered all of Lower Egypt and once again united the country under the single rule of the Twenty-Fifth Dynasty.

19:1. cloud as chariot. The image of a rampant God storming through the heavens in a cloud chariot is a common one (Ps 68:4; 104:3; Jer 4:13). Such descriptions of storm theophany may be found in the texts that speak of the Ugaritic god Baal. In both the Aqhat Epic and the Baal and Anat cycle of stories, Baal is referred to as the "Rider of the Clouds." Baal's attributes, commanding the storms, unleashing the lightning and rushing to war as a Divine Warrior, even appear in the Egyptian El Amarna texts. The characteristics of Yahweh as Creator, Fertility God and Divine Warrior share a great deal in common with the characteristics of the gods in these earlier epics. One of the ways that Yahweh presents himself as the sole divine power for the Israelites is by assuming the titles and powers of the other ancient Near Eastern gods.

19:1. idols trembling. The gods/idols and the people of Egypt are paralleled here in their awe of Yahweh's command over all of nature and every creature and nation. The anthropomorphic image of "trembling" idols is comparable to the fear of the Mesopotamian gods who through their collective efforts created the flood (Gilgamesh Epic and the *Atrahasis Epic*). They were overwhelmed by the ferocity of the forces they had unleashed and are described as cowering like whipped curs behind a wall. Yahweh's magisterial entrance into Egypt may be compared to the derision of idols in Psalm 96:4-5 and Isaiah's general attitude toward nations that are "full of idols" but lack real divine power (Is 2:8; 10:10-11; 31:7).

19:3. consultation of idols and the dead. Following his similar description of Egyptian divination in 8:19, Isaiah derides that nation for its useless dependence on idols and mediums (see, however, the comments on 1 Sam 28:7-11). There is a great deal of information on the use of magic in ancient Egypt by priests and professional practitioners. They used herbs, chants, ritual performances and bloodletting to cure illnesses, exorcise demons, curse enemy nations and their leaders, and influence the gods. A portion of these magic texts was designed to speed the journey of the spirits of the dead through the process of judgment and on to a blessed afterlife. It was assumed that these spirits could also be consulted on a variety of matters. A number of "letters to the dead" soliciting information have been recovered.

19:4. fate of Egypt. An immediate threat to the native Egyptian rulers was the Ethiopian king Shabaka. His Nubian kingdom eventually conquered the Egyptian Delta states in 716 B.C., and that would fit the time period. It is also possible that Isaiah is referring to Assyria. The Delta kings had joined the Philistine revolt lead by Gaza against Assyria and Sargon II in 720. It could easily be surmised that Assyria would eventually wish to conquer Egypt and add it to the empire. Both Tiglath-Pileser III and Sargon II made treaties with Arab tribes along the Sinai and Philistine borders to keep a check on Egypt. Tensions continued to grow between the nations until in 663 Ashurbanipal successfully marched south through the Nile Valley and sacked Thebes.

19:5-7. Egypt's dependence on the Nile. Like the riverine system in Mesopotamia, Egyptian agriculture and commerce was completely dependent on the Nile River system. They were fortunate in that the Nile was a fairly predictable and manageable river. Its inundations occurred on a regular schedule (carefully recorded by scribes and kept in official repositories). Failure of the Nile's flood would mean poor harvests and the destruction of its industries (especially flax). The Nile's banks could be cut with canals and irrigation channels to expand the size of fields and the movement of light shipping. In addition, the controlled flooding of the Nile brought a rich silt to Egyptian fields, insuring abundant crops and

lessening the need for fertilizing or crop rotation. Travel was also based on movement up and down the Nile. There was constant, heavy barge traffic carrying grain and other raw materials, manufactured goods and building stones. Royal messengers, bureaucrats and priests from the many temple communities sailed the Nile, visiting and supervising fields and the collection of taxes. In fact the very size of Egypt's domain was made possible because troops could quickly move from one end of the kingdom to the other.

19:9. flax and linen industry. The warm and humid climate in Egypt necessitated light clothing styles. Flax, cultivated since Neolithic times, was one answer to this need. It provided both food (seeds and linseed oil) as well as a fiber that could be woven into linen cloth. In Egypt flax was tightly planted (to increase height and prevent branching) in late October and harvested at a height of three feet in April or May. Such a field would be quite susceptible to hail storms (Ex 9:23-25). Younger plants were pulled up by the roots to produce fine linen, while older plants were used for ropes and belts. The stems were first soaked in tanks of stagnant water (retting) and then dried before the fibers were separated (Josh 2:6). The dried stems were beaten and the fibers combed out for spinning, with the longer threads being used for clothing and the shorter (tow) set aside as lamp wicks (1:31). There were several grades of linen produced. The best set was aside for the pharaoh, the nobility and the priests. Any interruption in production would have had a ripple effect, destroying the livelihood of countless workers in the fields and factories.

19:11. officials of Zoan. The highest ranking members of the pharaoh's court and of the priesthood were representatives of the noble families of Egypt. Those associated with Zoan, located in the upper Delta just twenty-nine miles south of the Mediterranean coast, considered themselves the direct descendants of the most ancient noble clans in the country. Their impotence to deal with this crisis underscores the lack of importance such lineage actually possessed. Zoan had become the capital of Egypt at the beginning of the Twenty-First Dynasty (1176-931 B.C.), the same period as the development of the Israelite monarchy. Memories of official court dealings between Jerusalem and Zoan may form the basis for this reference, since the Egyptian capital was moved to Sais and Napata after 873 B.C.

19:11. disciple of the ancient kings. Because it had such a long, virtually uninterrupted history, Egyptian officials faced with a crisis or an unexplained omen would chant ancient prayers and magical incantations (such as those found in the execration texts). Or they would consult the records of previous administrations and the instructions of model officials. The cultural memories, recorded on papyrus for generations, had great authority, and the descendants of these earlier officials took great pride in being the inheritors of such wisdom (including the twenty-fifth-century B.C. *Teaching of Ptah-Hotep* and the twenty-second century B.C. *Instruction of Merikare*). However, this attitude also could prevent creative or innovative decision-making. Isaiah ridicules these men who pride themselves in wisdom but fail to understand how to deal with present crises (compare 43:8-9).

19:13. leaders of Memphis. Prior to 715 B.C. the Delta region of Egypt was ruled by at least four rival pharaohs. The area was divided into the Tanis region (eastern delta), the region of Leontopolis (central delta) and the Saite region (western delta). There were also many petty kingdoms claiming independence and a portion of Egypt's ancient legacy. Mention here of Memphis (Hebrew reads Noph) simply ties Egypt's administrative chaos to the ancient capital city. This contrasts the irony of current anarchy with past greatness. Only after the Nubian Twenty-Fifth Dynasty arises under Shabaka will Egypt once again be united under a single ruler.

19:15. palm branch or reed. See the comment on 9:14 for this contrasting metaphor. The leaders of Egypt are so confused that they cannot tell the difference between heads or tails or the powerful (for whom palm branches are waved) or the weak, who bow like reeds before the great (58:5).

19:18. five cities. It is impossible to identify these cities based on any historical event. Jeremiah 44:1 does mention four (Migdol, Tahpanhes, Noph and Pathros) in which Israelites are dwelling, but that may have no relation to this verse. Certainly there is evidence from the time of Solomon onward (Elephantine colony, Leontopolis) of an Israelite presence in Egypt (diplomatic and commercial). What seems most important to the statement is the very idea of Yahweh worship in Egypt and perhaps even in a major city associated with an Egyptian god.

19:18. language of Canaan. Normally when a foreign community is established in a nation, it is expected that they will speak the language of that country, except among themselves. It would be difficult to do business or engage in diplomatic activity otherwise. Thus

for the Israelite languages of Hebrew or Aramaic to be spoken in Egypt would be unusual. Most likely this refers to the study of the sacred writings of the Yahwists and prayer raised to Yahweh. This suggests, as do verses 19-21, a conversion of Egyptians to Yahwism.

19:18. city of destruction. The meaning of this phrase is uncertain. The various sources do not agree on whether the original text read *heres*, "destruction," or *heres*, "sun." The Septuagint adds another reading, *'ir haṣṣedeq*, "city of righteousness." If "city of the sun" is meant, that could refer to Heliopolis, the city of the sun god Re. If this is one of the cities where Hebrew will be spoken, then a major religious revolution would be at hand.

20:1-6
Ashdod, Egypt and Cush

20:1. Sargon's campaign against Ashdod. This is one of those rare instances where the biblical account of the Ashdod revolt of 713-711 B.C., the Assyrian records, and the archaeological remains all corroborate one another. The Philistine city revolted at the instigation of King Azuri, perhaps with the expectation of Egyptian support. The Assyrian Annals charge him with refusing to pay tribute and fomenting rebellion among his neighbors. The Assyrian emperor Sargon II responded with a swift campaign that quickly suppressed any hopes for independence. He placed Azuri's younger brother, Ahimeti, on the throne, who in turn was almost immediately deposed by a usurper named Yamani. Sargon sent another expedition in 712, and Yamani fled to Egypt. An Assyrian commissioner was then appointed to manage Ashdod for the empire. Excavations in stratum 8 of the city have revealed a number of mass graves under the floors. Several fragments of an Assyrian monumental stele were also found. They come from a copy of the one erected in Khorsabad, listing Sargon's conquests, including Ashdod.

20:2. Isaiah's role play. The enacted prophecy employed by Isaiah was startling. This older man (who had been called to be a prophet thirty years before, in 742 B.C.) is commanded by God to strip himself naked and parade before the people in that shameful state. His purpose is to graphically demonstrate to them their ultimate fate if they choose to join the Ashdod revolt. They too will be stripped naked and taken away as slaves (compare Mic 1:8; Nahum 3:5). Since style and quality of clothing was a status marker in the ancient world, criminals were also displayed naked as a sign of their loss of social status (Middle Assyrian Laws).

20:3. role of Egypt and Cush in Ashdod campaign. The Assyrian records (Sargon's Nimrud Prism) mention the establishment of a Mediterranean harbor jointly held by Egypt and Assyria. Such cooperation may have been forced on Egypt because of Assyrian control of Cyprus and their pacification of Arab tribes along the Sinai border. The Delta kings, fearing further incursions, attempted to take some of this pressure off by supporting first the revolt of Hanno of Gaza and then that of Aziru of Ashdod. Because of this clandestine support, the usurper Yamani fled to the Delta at the approach of Sargon II's army in 712. However, the people there refused to harbor him or give him any further military aid. Yamani then attempted to gain help from the Nubian dynast Shabaka. This was to no avail; Shabaka was more interested in conquering the Delta kingdoms and did not want to raise Assyrian ire. Thus Yamani was delivered to the Assyrians in chains as a peace offering. Sargon's annals record this as a sign of how far word of his "awe-inspiring glamour" had spread.

20:4. treatment of captives. Prisoners of war were considered spoils to be divided among the conquerors. They would become slaves, and it was necessary to immediately break their spirit and at the same time use them as a means of shaming their home countries or cities. Assyrian annals include lists of captives among the other items taken by to Ashur or in some cases impaled as an example to other rebels. Egyptian royal tomb paintings often depict lines of prisoners, bound together by the neck, marching into captivity. While these figures are not completely naked, they have been stripped of all valuables and insignias of rank (see comment on 2 Sam 10:3).

21:1-10

Oracle Against Sealand

21:1. Desert by the Sea. The Hebrew here might better be translated "wilderness by the sea" or "swampland." Either would fit the southern portion of Mesopotamia, an area of marshes and quagmire as one gets closer to the Persian Gulf. At issue is concern for the capture of Babylon by the Assyrians in 703 B.C. and the expulsion of the Babylonian leader Merodach-Baladan. The anti-Assyrian party within Hezekiah's court had hoped that Babylon would be able to successfully challenge Assyria and thus give the outlying provinces like Judah an opportunity to gain their independence. These hopes were dashed with the resurgence

of Assyrian power under Sennacherib. Thus the oracle of woe reflects that disappointment.

21:2. role of Elam and Media. While verse 9 makes it clear that Babylon is the city to be attacked, it is less clear what role Elam and Media would play in these events. Both of these Iranian peoples from east of Tigris had been helpful to Merodach-Baladan when he had established himself in Babylon in 720, and after Sargon II ousted him, he fled to Elam in 710. It is possible that the prophet is urging Elam and Media to once again help Merodach-Baladan against their common enemy, Assyria. However, the chaotic conditions of the time, with attendant looting and betrayal, could see a shifting of earlier alliances. In any case Elam ceased to be a factor in Near Eastern politics after 680, and that may be the result of the growth of Median power as well as pressure from Assyria.

21:5. set tables, spread rugs. The apparent banquet scene portrayed here might suggest that Babylon was unprepared for the attack that would capture the city. It may also refer to preparations for battle (as Anat in the Ugaritic Epic set up bleachers and tables so her warriors could watch as she slaughtered her enemies) or possibly a sketching out of Babylon's defenses or her various districts prior to a siege.

21:5. oil shields. The practice of oiling shields in preparation for battle may be based on the desire to make the leather more flexible and less brittle (2 Sam 1:21). Classical sources (Aristophanes' *Acharnians* and Virgil's *Aeneid*) suggest an oiled shield was more flexible and could shed a blow. The shine from a freshly oiled leather shield might also be helpful in blinding an opponent.

21:7. chariotry in eighth century. The Assyrians used chariot corps, divided into squadrons of fifty, as the heart of their army's campaign forces. They held two, three or four men crews, with one man serving as driver and the others as archers or shield bearers. In earlier periods (Ashurnasirpal) a third horse was attached to the side of the chariot, to be detached if one of the others was injured or the charioteer needed to escape a crippled vehicle. Depictions of chariots in Assyrian reliefs demonstrate that they initially had medium-sized wheels with six spokes, and a single pole extended from the front to hitch a team of two horses. Later, during the reign of Shalmaneser III, the chariots were heavier, with huge eight-spoke wheels. Sennacherib also added an additional team of horses to help pull these heavier chariots.

21:7. cavalry in eighth century. Most of what we know about the use of cavalry in the eighth century comes from depictions on Assyrian reliefs. They show that in areas such as hilly or wooded country where chariots were ineffective, the armies in the ancient Near East employed cavalry. Some of these men were equipped with bows, while other served as lancers, carrying a long spear. These latter forces would be used as shock troops, charging along with chariots against a massed enemy, driving wedges in their ranks so the Assyrian infantry could follow into the breaches (see 1 Kings 20:21). Cavalry archers often fought in pairs, with one using his bow while the other carried a shield to protect his companion (see 2 Kings 9:25). Riders were also used to carry messages on the battlefield and to report events to nearby fortresses and cities (see Ben-Hadad's escape with covering cavalry in 1 Kings 20:20).

21:9. fall of Babylon. At the death of Sargon II in 705, Merodach-Baladan once again set himself up as the ruler of Babylon. This signaled yet another series of revolts throughout the Assyrian empire (among them the Anatolian provinces of Que, Tabal and Hilakku). Sennacherib's annals describe how he systematically subjugated each rebellious region. Babylonia and Elam were dealt with first because of their proximity to the heart of the Assyrian empire. Fighting took place at Kish and then within the marshlands of southern Mesopotamia when Merodach-Baladan fled Babylon. Still the Babylonian leader was able to maintain control over a portion of the south and cause Sennacherib continual problems, despite Assyrian attempts to conciliate the Chaldean people. Babylon was finally besieged in 689, and when the walls were breached the Assyrians slaughtered the population and destroyed the wall systems, the temples and every house within the city. They even dug canals to channel water from the Euphrates through the city to wash away foundations and brickwork.

21:9. shattered images. Sennacherib's annals contain graphic accounts of the capture of Babylon in 689. In their frenzy of destruction the Assyrian soldiers had no respect for the gods of their enemy, smashing Babylon's sacred images and crushing many of them into tiny fragments. In the midst of this destruction, however, the soldiers managed to rescue two statues of their own national gods, Adad and Shala, which had been captured 480 years earlier by the Babylonian king Marduk-Nadin-Ahe.

21:11-12
Oracle Against Edom

21:11. Dumah. This is an oasis town in north central Saudi Arabia near the southern end of the Wadi Sirhan. Its association with the Kedarite confederacy of Bedouin tribes of that region (Gen 25:13) may explain the place name's tie to Edom. There may also be a pun expressed here in the Hebrew of this word (*duma*), which means "silence," and Edom.

21:11. Seir. This portion of the territory of Edom included the wooded area which stretched from the Transjordanian plateau south to the Wadi al-'Arabah, perhaps including Petra (see Judg 5:4). The term appears in fourteenth-century Egyptian texts listing the names of peoples and cities as the "country of Seir-nomads."

21:11. Edom in eighth century. During the eighth century Edom was struggling to maintain its independence. The country was weakened by Judah's interest in expanding into the region: Amaziah (801-787 B.C.) staged a raid at the turn of the century (see 2 Kings 14:7), and his successor, Uzziah, rebuilt the port of Elath on the Gulf of Aqaba (2 Kings 14:22). A further sign of their weakness was Edom's payment of tribute to the Assyrian king Adad-Nirari III (809-782 B.C.). When the Syro-Ephraimitic war caused turmoil in Judah in the 730s, the Edomites regained Elath (2 Kings 16:6). However, they were forced into vassalage by Tiglath-Pileser III after 732 B.C. and became a link in the Assyrian empire's trade route south from Damascus to the Aqaba, the King's Highway. Assyrian tribute lists also demonstrate that for the rest of the century Edom remained loyal to the empire, giving little or no support to the other rebellious Palestinian vassals.

21:13-17
Oracle Against Arabia

21:13. Arabia. Comprising territories claimed by various Bedouin tribal groups, Arabia was an area that Assyrian kings listed as a part of their empire but never truly controlled. The Arab tribes occupied the region between the southern Negev and the north central portion of the Arabian Peninsula. This could suggest a translation in this passage of "wasteland" rather than Arabia, paralleling it with "swampland" in 21:1. Some Arab groups engaged in caravan trade, transporting frankincense and myrrh, slaves and dyes to both Egypt and Mesopotamia. The number of raids mentioned in various ancient texts also attest to their occasional occupation as predators on the caravan routes. Arabs appear in the records of Shalmaneser III dealing with the alliance formed against him at the Battle of Qarqar in 853 B.C. They continue to appear in Assyrian records down to the reign of Ashurbanipal at the end of the seventh century. It is also noted in the annals of Sargon II that some Arabs were forced to resettle in Palestine after the fall of Samaria in 722 B.C.

21:13. Dedanites. The Dedanite tribes used Khuraybah (modern al-'Ula) in northwest Arabia as their base of operations. Excavations had uncovered an extensive group of small satellite villages in the nearby valley of Wadi al-Qura. They operated as caravaneers with contacts in Syria, Phoenicia and Palestine. During the seventh century they may have been part of Edom's sphere of influence and subject to Assyria's control.

21:14. Tema. Based on its mention in Assyrian and Aramaic inscriptions, Tema has long been identified with the oasis city of Tayma, located on the western border of the North Arabian Desert. It lies at the crossroads of three major trade routes of the "incense road" from South Arabia to Syria, Mesopotamia and eastern Arabia. The riches of Tema were tapped by the emerging Mesopotamian empires of the first millennium B.C. The Assyrian king Tiglath-Pileser III lists the city as one of those paying tribute in 734 B.C. Along with Dedan, Tema served as a major urban center for its region during the seventh and sixth centuries. The Chaldean monarch Nabonidus made it his headquarters for ten years (553-543) as he attempted to gain control over the incense trade.

21:16. Kedar. Assyrian and Neo-Babylonian texts refer to these North Arabian tribes as *Qidr* or *Qadr*. Tied to the Ishmaelites in Genesis 25:13, the Kedarites functioned as sheep breeders and caravaneers at least as late as the Hellenistic period. Their mention in this verse along with Tema may refer to Nabonidus's expedition to conquer the area in 553 B.C. There is clear evidence of ties between Kedar and Tema in Babylonian economic texts.

22:1-25
Oracle Against Jerusalem

22:1. Valley of Vision. Based on 22:5, this is probably a reference to Jerusalem and perhaps to the Hinnom Valley (see its use in Jer 7:31-34 for divination rituals). Isaiah rebukes a people who have sought guidance from other gods and thus, despite their physical location on Mount Zion, have no true vision of events.

22:1. going up on roofs. This may also be a reference to divination or false worship. There is ample evidence in the prophetic books of Israelites burning incense on the roofs of their houses (Jer 19:13; Zeph 1:5). This may also refer to the symbolic "roofs" of incense stands like the one excavated at Megiddo. It is shaped like a house, with cornices around the top and contained charred remains on top. The first alternative would be supported by the ancient Near Eastern evidence. Offerings on a rooftop occur in narrative both in Mesopotamia (Gilgamesh) and in Ugarit (Keret).

22:2-3. historical context. These events occur during the 701 B.C. campaign of Sennacherib (see comments on 2 Kings 18:1—20:21). The Assyrian king led a huge army of mercenaries and conscripts from throughout his empire. During the course of the invasion of Palestine, they will, according to Sennacherib's annals, "lay siege to forty-six fortified cities, walled forts, and countless villages." King Hezekiah was bottled up in Jerusalem "like a bird in a cage." Any of his officials who attempted to escape were captured, and many were executed. The strategic western border citadel at Lachish was captured and burned. Archaeological evidence of a mass grave indicates that its garrison was massacred, and Assyrian reliefs from the palace in Nineveh depict prisoners being taken into exile. Sennacherib claims to have taken 200,150 prisoners of war—an inflated figure so large that there would have been virtually no one left in Judah. Both the biblical account and the Assyrian records agree there was widespread destruction, but the invaders eventually withdrew after Hezekiah paid a huge sum as tribute and ransom for the city of Jerusalem (2 Kings 18:13-16).

22:6. Elam. See the comment on 21:2. Sennacherib regularly conscripted levees of soldiers from subject and allied peoples. Although Elam has previously supported the Babylonians and opposed Assyria, in this 701 campaign it seems clear that they have supplied a contingent of bowmen for Sennacherib's host.

22:6. Kir. There is no consensus on the exact location of the country of Kir. Because of its association with the Arameans in Amos 9:7, several attempts have been made to place it either in northern Syria or in the western desert (west of the Euphrates). Its mention here with Elam also suggests proximity to that country east of the Tigris River.

22:8. palace of the forest. See the comment on 1 Kings 7:1-12 for this storehouse within the palace complex. The people hope to draw on the arsenal it contained to defend themselves against the Assyrian invaders.

22:9. storing water in lower pool. Based on the comment in 2 Kings 20:20 and the discovery of the Siloam Tunnel inscription, it seems clear that Hezekiah constructed a water tunnel over eighteen hundred feet long from inside the walls of Jerusalem to the Gihon Spring in the Kidron Valley. In this way he was able to insure a safe and continuous water supply for Jerusalem during the Assyrian siege. The "lower pool" was one of two reservoirs used to hold and channel water (see 7:3). It was designed to provide irrigation flow to the terraced areas along the slope of the Kidron Valley, and it eventually drained into the Pool of Shelah, modern Birket el-Hamra.

22:9-11. building in Jerusalem in preparation for siege. The defenses of Jerusalem had to be repaired and strengthened in anticipation of Assyrian efforts to take the city. There was also a need to balance the demands for more housing by the people of Judah who had fled to Jerusalem for protection and the all-important defense of the city. As a result the area between the city's dual wall system was cleared of all temporary shelters to provide a "killing ground" should the Assyrians penetrate the outer defenses. This area was also partially flooded to make it more difficult to transverse and to add to the city's water supply.

22:15. royal steward. The position of "royal steward" may have evolved from a relatively insignificant post into that of a chamberlain, who was in charge of all of the affairs of the palace in Uzziah's time. There is precedent for this title in Ugaritic and Phoenician texts, and it would be comparable to the position of vizier in the Egyptian court. It has been argued that the steward in question here is Shebna, mentioned as a scribe or secretary in 2 Kings 18:18. The possibility exists that Shebna was addressed by various titles during his career, depending on his current assignment. One would expect, however, that as royal steward he would have been the preeminent adviser and facilitator for the king. If he was referred to by a lesser title in Hezekiah's reign, then it may be surmised that he had been demoted.

22:16. rock-hewn tomb. The valleys and slopes around Jerusalem contain a large number of tombs hewn from the native limestone cliffs. Among them on the slope of Silwan is a tomb containing a partial inscription and the title *'asher 'al habbayit*, the same phrase used in verse 15 to describe the position once held by Shebna. The lack of a name in this inscription makes it impossible to tie it conclusively to Shebna. Isaiah's rebuke of this official is based on the extravagance of constructing an indi-

vidual tomb rather than utilizing a communal cave or hewn mortuary chamber within the confines of his family holdings. These more traditional tombs included shelves for internment of the bodies and lamp niches, as well as a recessed pit for disposal of bones when the shelves were needed for fresh burials. Only the very wealthy could afford to carve an individual chamber, perhaps incorporating Phoenician or Egyptian design (pyramids or elaborate facades).

22:20. Eliakim on seal. The name of this official, which means "May El establish," has been found on seal impressions from Tell Beit Mirsim, Beth Shemesh, and Ramat Rahel. He served as *'asher 'al habbayit*, royal steward, under King Hezekiah (see 2 Kings 18:18; 19:2; Is 36:3), and therefore would have been expected to affix his official seal to many documents. The seal impression containing the name Eliakim appears on a large collection of jar handles dating to Hezekiah's reign. The Iron Age Lachish stratum 3, dated to 701 B.C., is the most important of the sites where these handles have been found. It is likely that Eliakim's seal appears on these jars as a part of his regular duties, managing palace stores and distributing oil and wine to royal fortress sites like Lachish.

22:22. key to house of David. The relatively tiny locks used to secure our doors today require a very small key. However, in the biblical period locks were quite large and required a correspondingly large and heavy bronze or iron key (see Judg 3:25; 1 Chron 9:27). When Eliakim is given this key, its size and probably its elaborate decoration would serve as a visible symbol of his authority to lock and unlock the rooms and gates of the palace in Jerusalem. This is also known as one of the functions of the Egyptian vizier.

22:23-25. imagery. The apparently domestic images portrayed here, a tent peg in firm ground or pegs driven into mud-brick walls to hold up shelves or to hang kitchen ware, function as part of a ritual of installation for Eliakim. The origins of such images probably go back to the village culture of ancient Israel, and their basic familiarity gave them the authority that compares to Jeremiah's commissioning: "to uproot and tear down, to destroy and overthrow, to build and to plant" (Jer 1:10). One of the most well-known installation ceremonies in ancient literature is Marduk's installation as the chief Babylonian deity in *Enuma Elish*. There it is proclaimed that his command cannot be changed and that the limits he sets (for the gods) will be inviolable.

23:1-18

Oracle Against Tyre

23:1. Tyre in eighth century. The eighth century B.C. was a time of commercial and political expansion for the Phoenicians. A colonial empire was established, with Carthage as the principal city in the western Mediterranean (founded by Dido about 814 B.C.). The degree to which the Phoenicians of the island city of Tyre and of Sidon operated freely depended in this period on the extent of Assyrian influence over them. Adadnirari III (810-783) received tribute from them, but no significant Assyrian pressure was applied until the reign of Tiglath-Pileser III (744-727). The Assyrian king skillfully played on the fear of Tyre's expanding commercial empire to gain alliances with the city-states on Cyprus. He also forced Tyre to pay a huge amount annually (evidence of which is found in Assyrian tribute lists) to save themselves from military invasion. The wealth of Tyre was legendary (see Ezek 28:4-5; Zech 9:3), and in order to defend it Tyre's king Lulli forced the Cypriot states to submit to him. This brought on a five-year siege of Tyre by Shalmaneser V (726-722) and his successor Sargon II (721-705). Some attempts were made by Lulli to negotiate an end of the hostilities since the Assyrians occupied all of the Tyrian mainland. However, when he again revolted at the time of Sennacherib's accession, the Assyrians forced Lulli to flee to Cyprus and installed Ittobaal over the Sidonian kingdom.

23:1. Tyre in the seventh century. Tyre and Sidon continued to vacillate in their allegiance to Assyria throughout the seventh century. In response to the Phoenician alliance with the Ethiopian Tirhakah of the Egyptian Twenty-Fifth Dynasty, Assyrian armies repeatedly invaded the coastal region around Tyre and Sidon, devastating towns and villages and placing increasing pressure on the port cities to submit to Assyrian rule. Finally in 677 B.C. Esarhaddon utterly destroyed Sidon, parading the head of its ruler, Abdimilkutte, in Nineveh. Severe diplomatic restrictions were placed on Baal I of Tyre in an effort to prevent him from aiding the Egyptians. Ashurbanipal (667-627) also records dealing with anti-Assyrian rulers in Syro-Palestine. After crushing the Egyptians and destroying their capital at Thebes in 663 B.C., Ashurbanipal installed a native Egyptian, Psammeticus I, as ruler of Lower Egypt. He then brought his army back up the coast to punish Baal I and the Phoenicians. He completely stripped Tyre of its autonomy, transforming all of Phoenicia into an Assyrian province and taking full control of the shipping trade that had been the basis of Phoenician wealth and independence. However, after Ashurbanipal's death Tyre regained its supremacy in Mediterranean trade.

23:1. ships of Tarshish. The tonnage required for a merchant ship to make a profit and be seaworthy enough to ply the waters of either the Mediterranean or the Red Sea required skillful building practices. Since the "ships of Tarshish" are often mentioned in relation to trade mission (see 1 Kings 22:48; 2 Chron 9:21), there must have been a particular type of ship involved. It is possible that they were constructed in Tarshish, but it may be that they were named for their ability to sail as far as Tarshish in the western Mediterranean. Assyrian reliefs and the bronze gate covers of Shalmaneser III from Balawat depict these ships being used for military transport as well as carrying cargoes of tribute taken from their many vassals. A relief found in the palace at Nineveh depicts Lulli of Sidon's flight to Cyprus. Among the ships in his fleet are tub-by-looking merchantmen with a row of shields along the hull and two levels of oarsmen on either side to aid the ship's movement when the sails were becalmed. Ships like this with two rows of oarsmen were called biremes.

23:2. merchants of Sidon. The silence of the usually boisterous and wealthy Sidonian merchants may be based on the extension of Assyrian hegemony over the area starting in the mid-eighth century, cutting off some of their profits. Or it refers to the growing pressure placed on that area by Sennacherib (after 701) and ending in 677 with the destruction of the city of Sidon by Esarhaddon. A new Assyrian city was built over its ruins by levies from throughout the Assyrian sphere of influence and named Kar-Esarhaddon.

23:3. grain of Shihor. Phoenician merchants transported items from throughout the Mediterranean. Grain from Shihor, possibly Egyptian *p̄ shhr*, where Shihor would be translated "pool of Horus." It represents the fertile harvests of Egypt, shipped up the Nile and on to the coast by way of either the Wadi el-Arish (Brook of Egypt in 1 Kings 8:65) or the Pelusiac arm of the Nile. The stream may also parallel a portion of the "Way of Horus" that connected Palestine and Egypt.

23:3. economic role of Tyre. Standing out from the coast approximately six hundred yards from the mainland, the island city of Tyre and its harbor were secure from anything but a sustained siege. The waters were also deep enough to allow for heavily laden ships to approach and offload their cargoes. Dedicated to commercial activity, Tyre was supplied with food and other essentials by its sister city of Ushu. Tyrian fleets established colonies, including some on Cyprus and the North African city of Carthage, around the Mediterranean to draw on the resources of these areas, especially metals, and to funnel goods back and forth between the eastern and western Mediterranean. Archaeological evidence from throughout this region of Phoenician metalwork and pottery indicates the extent and longevity of trade relations. Their principal exports were cedar wood, fabrics and dyes, and glasswork. The economic partnership between Solomon and Hiram I (969-936) that extended Phoenician and Israelite interests south to Somalia may have been only one such venture. The expansion of Assyrian hegemony over the Levantine coast forced Tyre and Sidon into cooperating with the Mesopotamian power. Efforts to revolt or withhold tribute payments resulted in invasion and curtailment of economic activity. However, the Assyrians also needed Tyrian expertise and access to the sea, so it is likely business continued virtually uninterrupted despite occasional hostilities.

23:4. fortress of the sea. Tyre was originally founded around 2750 B.C. on a sandstone reef about six hundred yards off the coast of southern Lebanon. Its occupied area was enlarged in the tenth century when Hiram I used fill to connect the older city with a nearby reef. To approaching sailors it must have looked like a city floating on the sea. No army was successful in capturing the city until the time of Alexander of Macedon, who built a causeway from the mainland in 332 B.C. However, Tyre was not totally self-sufficient. Its vulnerability was shown when its sister city of Ushu was captured by the Assyrians. As a result a vassal treaty was signed in the time of Esarhaddon that reflected Tyre's capitulation to the extent of even having an Assyrian official present whenever the king read diplomatic correspondence.

23:5. report from Tyre. The exact time period or event described here is unclear. It could be referring to any number of events that would have dismayed the Egyptians, representing the cessation of trade and the elimination of an important political ally. Possible occasions include the Assyrian incursion into Phoenicia by Sennacherib in 701 and the destruction of Sidon in 677 by Esarhaddon. Some commentators also suggest the much later period when Sidon was conquered by the Persian king Artaxerxes III (343 B.C.) or even Alexander's capture of Tyre in 332. Such a late date, however,

requires either a prophetic vision of an event long after Isaiah's time or the removal of this passage completely from its Isaianic context, making it a later editor's gloss.

23:6. Tarshish. The ambiguity in biblical and extrabiblical sources only indicates that Tarshish is to be found to the west of Israel. This would allow for identification with Carthage in North Africa and sites on the southeastern coast of Spain, including Tartessos. There is even some support for identifying it with Ezion-Geber in the Gulf of Aqaba. After his defeat of the Egyptians in 677, Esarhaddon claims in his annals to have sovereignty over Cyprus, Greece and Tarshish, in other words the entire Phoenician commercial empire.

23:10. Tyre's harbor. Tyre's original site was built on two large reefs approximately six hundred yards offshore. Since the island had limited living space, multistoried houses were closely packed together (based on scenes in the Assyrian reliefs). A port existed on each side of the island to accommodate the large number of ships that were constantly arriving and departing. The natural harbor existed on the north end and was protected by a sea wall and roadstead, sheltered by a chain of smaller islands. An artificial harbor was also constructed at the southern end of the island. This southeastern area was eventually transformed after Alexander of Macedon constructed a ramp to connect the city with the mainland and further silting created a broader peninsula. Excavations are difficult since a modern city still occupies much of the site of ancient Tyre.

23:11. Phoenicia. The Hebrew text here actually reads "Canaan." The choice to translate "Phoenicia" helps the reader stay focused on Tyre's destruction. However, that destruction is (1) based on the Canaanite culture of the Phoenicians that is condemned by Yahweh and (2) exemplified here by Yahweh stretching out his hand over the sea to demonstrate that this friendly resource of the Phoenician traders will not save them. This terminology is reminiscent of the motif of the contest between Baal and Yamm in the Ugaritic epics where the sea god is defeated.

23:12. Cyprus. Cyprus lies just seventy-six miles off the Syrian coast. It served as a place of refuge for Phoenician kings (Lulli of Tyre escapes to Cyprus under pressure from Sargon II's Assyrian armies). This oracle discounts it as a safe haven. If the Phoenicians lose control of Tyre and Sidon, their merchant fleet will become orphans. Their cargoes may either rot or be turned over to the Assyrians.

23:13. Babylon punished by Assyrians. See the

comments on 13:1 and 13:19 for the historical background of Sennacherib's capture of Babylon in 689 B.C. and the exile of the Babylonian leader Merodach-Baladan. In this passage the destruction of southern Mesopotamia's major city is cited as an example of Tyre's ultimate fate at the hands of the Assyrians.

23:13. siege towers. Assyrian reliefs from the palace at Nineveh and the annals of several kings depict a number of different types of siege engines. One of the most common was the siege tower, which was rolled up as close as possible to a city's walls. From its heights archers could target enemy soldiers, and assault bridges could be extended onto the ramparts. At the base of the tower, protected from the rain of stones, hot oil and arrows, engineers and sappers could work to undermine the walls or employ battering rams (see 29:3; Ezek 21:22).

23:15. Tyre's seventy years. There are several instances in the prophets where seventy years became a term of exile or punishment (Jer 25:12; Dan 9:2; Zech 1:12). There is also a sense of completion in this number, suggesting that Tyre and the Phoenicians are in God's hands and will not be allowed to prosper again until divine judgment is fulfilled. In fact, for much of the seventh century Tyre was dormant as a succession of strong Assyrian rulers controlled both the city and its commercial activities. There was a brief resurgence after the destruction of Nineveh in 612, but the city was then besieged for thirteen years by the Babylonian ruler Nebuchadnezzar, severely limiting its contacts with the mainland. The Persians exercised control over the Phoenician ports as well, with Artaxerxes III burning Sidon in 345 after it had joined an Egyptian-inspired revolt. Tyre's destruction by Alexander of Macedon in 332 followed a seven-month siege and effectively ended the independence of the city.

23:15-16. song of the prostitute. The pitiful condition of Tyre after Yahweh's judgment of the city is compared to an aged prostitute who must now walk the streets singing to advertise her profession and attract customers who are no longer willing to come to her door. The tune and coupleted lyrics were probably part of the raucous culture of Mediterranean seaports that catered to sailors on leave.

24:1-23

Judgment of the Day of the Lord

24:1-13. description of city's desolation. The litany of destruction found in this city lament

parallels the style contained in the Sumerian *Lament over the Destruction of Ur* as well as in other ancient Near Eastern expressions of grief over fallen cities. Comparisons include the descriptions of utter desolation, the fact that no person of any rank has been spared, and the failure of nature to provide what had previously nurtured the people. The Sumerian lament speaks of devastating winds, drought, famine and bodies piled in the streets unburied. The twentieth-century B.C. Egyptian *Visions of Neferti* also depicts a land laid bare and cursed by the disappearance of the sun and the drying up the life-sustaining canals. The prophecies of Balaam (found at Deir 'Alla and dating to 700 B.C.) describe angry gods who "lock up the heavens," turning every creature into a scavenger and forcing even princes to wear rags and priests to "smell of sweat."

24:18. floodgates. See the comment on Genesis 7:11 for this metaphorical expression describing the cataclysmic effects of flood waters raining down from heaven and bursting from the waters of the underworld. The scene is one of utter destruction.

24:22. prisoners in a dungeon. The apocalyptic character of this passage makes it more likely that the author is describing the imprisonment of other powers (angels) who have attempted to rival God's power, rather than earthly kings. Certainly the pattern in much of the Old Testament is for kings to be executed (see Judg 8:21; 1 Sam 15:33) or forced to negotiate terms of surrender (2 Sam 10:19). Mesopotamian texts from Mari describe the "imprisoning" of sacred images as does the Cyrus Cylinder from Persians records. The idea of holding prisoners for long periods beneath the earth is eventually developed in the apocalyptic visions of Revelation 19:20—20:15 and in *Enoch* 18:16.

25:1-12

Victory Banquet

25:6. banquet hosted by the gods. Banquets hosted by the gods were most common in coronation settings—when a deity was ceremonially ascending the seat of his domain of power. This is the case when El calls the Rephaim (see comment on 14:9-11) to a banquet to honor Baal. Marduk's enthronement also includes a banquet. Though these banquets were for the gods, the people would join in the feasting when the enthronement was celebrated annually.

25:7-8. destruction of the shroud and swallowing of death. In the Old Testament, death is occasionally personified (Hos 13:14), but in Ugaritic mythology, Mot ("death") is a deity of the netherworld who is an enemy of Baal. Since Baal is a fertility god, his defeat of Mot is a cyclic symbol of life returning to the world each spring. Mot is often pictured as one who swallows his prey. Rituals that target Mot are intended to put an end to his destructive activities. Here it is Yahweh who swallows death (Mot) and the setting is political (nations) not agricultural. It is the ruthless, devouring empire that threatens death to the nations who are being destroyed, so that the death masks are removed from those who have been so close to extinction.

26:1-21
Judah's Song

26:19. resurrection in the ancient Near East. Concepts of afterlife are most clearly defined in Egyptian texts. The Book of the Dead provides a guide for dealing with the questions asked of each soul on entering the nether regions. Mummification, the construction of tombs, the rich grave goods and the priestly and family cult that supplied food and drink for the dead through eternity all testify to elaborate preparations for a life beyond this one. Even in this rich afterlife doctrine, however, resurrection is reflected in the belief that the righteous dead can be resuscitated in the afterlife. Mesopotamian concepts are more pessimistic. Gilgamesh, the hero who crosses the "sea of death" and seeks out the flood hero Utnapishtim, is told by the barmaid/goddess Siduri that humans are fated to die from their conception. She advises a life filled with personal enjoyment and accomplishment, since there is no joy in death. Job echoes this opinion when he says (7:9) that "he who goes down to the grave does not return." Only in Daniel 12:2 does the Old Testament clearly refer to bodily resurrection. Thus this passage, like Ezekiel 37:4-14, may speak only of God's ability to reawaken a dead nation, to revive a covenantal community. There may be some Egyptian influence here, however, in the use of "dew" as the expression of God's power. Egyptian texts describe the dew as the "tears of Horus and Thoth," containing the power of resurrection. Dew is the only moisture available to keep plants alive during the long, dry months of summer and thus is an appropriate symbol of resurrection (for further discussion see comment on Dan 12:2).

27:1-13
Israel Gathered

27:1. gliding serpent, coiling serpent. This same description occurs in the Ugaritic Baal Cycle as one of the supernatural opponents of Baal: "When you killed Litan [Leviathan], the fleeing serpent, annihilated the twisty serpent, the potentate with seven heads" ("fleeing" is the same word as NIV's "gliding"; "twisty" is the same word as NIV's "coiling"). For seven heads see comment on Psalm 74:14.'s

27:1. Leviathan. Ugaritic and Canaanite myths contain detailed descriptions of a chaos beast representing the seas or watery anarchy in the form of a many-headed, twisting sea serpent. There is a close affinity between the description of Leviathan in Isaiah as a "coiling serpent" and the Ugaritic Baal Epic, which speaks of how the storm god "smote Litan the twisting serpent." In both cases there is a sense of the God of order and fertility vanquishing a chaos monster. Several other passages in the Old Testament mention Leviathan, but most of them, like Psalm 74:14 and Job 41:1-34, speak in terms of God's creative act that established control over watery chaos (personified by the sea serpent). In 27:1, however, that struggle between order and chaos occurs at the end of time. It may be that the fall of Satan, portrayed as a seven-headed dragon in Revelation 12:3-9, also echoes the Ugaritic image of Litan as "the tyrant with seven heads."

27:1. monster of the sea. The obvious physical struggle between the sea and the land as well as the fierce, seemingly unstoppable energy displayed by the savage sea gave rise to cosmic myths in the ancient Near East. The *Enuma Elish* creation epic from Babylon describes how Marduk vanquished Tiamat when this goddess of watery chaos was in the form of a dragon. Much of the cycle of stories about Baal in Ugaritic legend involve Baal's struggle against his rival Yamm, the god of the sea. Similarly, the Ugaritic Epic has both Anat and Baal claim to have conquered Litan, the seven-headed dragon, and thus gained mastery over the seas. In Psalm 104:26 Yahweh is said to play with Leviathan, and in Job 41:1-11 God challenges Job to show his control over Leviathan as God does. Although the text is not explicit here about whether the monster represented a nation or city, it could be a reference to Egypt or Tyre, both of which had connections with the sea.

27:9. chalk stones. Limestone is crushed to produce a chalky substance that can be used for mortar, as a liming agent in cesspits and to seal stone walls with a type of "whitewash." For altars to be crushed in this manner is to completely extinguish their sacred nature. Isaiah in this passage describes the reform measures of Hezekiah in 2 Kings 18:4 and prophesies the religious reforms of Josiah in 2 Kings 23:12.

27:9. Asherah poles. See the comment on Deuteronomy 7:5 for a description of these sacred objects associated with the Canaanite goddess and her cult.

27:9. incense altars. The term in Hebrew may refer to the small incense altars, usually shaped like houses, that continually burnt frankincense or some similar spice to honor the gods of Canaan. It has also been suggested that the word used here, *hammamim,* is a term for "standing stones," another monumental cult object of the Canaanites (see comment on Deut 7:5).

27:12. threshing imagery. There is an artful double meaning to the word in this passage for a "flowing stream *[shibbolet].*" Isaiah is speaking of Yahweh gathering all of the people from the area between the "stream of Egypt" (the Wadi el-Arish) and the Euphrates. However, this is coupled with the other meaning for *shibbolet,* "ears of grain." Thus the image of grain gathered to the threshing floor where the stalks and kernels of grain are separated becomes clear.

27:12. territory from Euphrates to wadi of Egypt. One traditional way of speaking of the full extent of the scattering of the exiles is to say from the Euphrates River in Mesopotamia to the Wadi el-Arish, which forms the boundary with Egypt (see Gen 15:18; 2 Kings 24:7). See the comment on 1 Kings 4:21 in which this geographic range is used for the limits of Solomon's kingdom. Mention of the wadi of Egypt is found in the Assyrian annals of Tiglath-Pileser III (744-727 B.C.). This is the limit of Assyrian expansion until Ashurbanipal finally conquers Thebes in 663 B.C.

27:13. great trumpet. Perhaps because of their use for signaling in battle (as in the reliefs from eighth-century Carchemish depicting military musicians), the blast of a trumpet became a common image used in eschatological and apocalyptic literature as a signal for the end time (see Zech 9:14 and Rev 8:6-12). Here it awakens the exiles to the moment when they will return from Assyrian exile and from the places in Egypt where they have fled for refuge.

28:1-29
Woe Oracle Against Ephraim

28:1. wreath. The garland worn by revelers is usually a sign of joy and happiness (see Prov 4:9; Is 61:10). In this instance, however, the wreath will quickly fade as the party turns sour and drunkenness presages the destruction of the city of Samaria by the Assyrians in 722 B.C.

28:2. characteristics of theophany. A theophany is an appearance by a divine being to a human. To indicate the power of the deity, this encounter generally includes such things as smoke and fire, mighty winds and storms, and earthquakes (see comments on Josh 10:11 and 1 Kings 19:11-13). The manifestation of God's presence, of course, is done for a purpose, usually to call a leader or prophet to service or to carry out judgment on an enemy nation (Hab 3:13) or the wicked (Ps 94:1-3). Theophanies also are common in the Ugaritic epic (Anat and Keret both receive divine visits), and in Mesopotamian texts they often occur in dreams, either to priests or to kings.

28:7. drunkenness in ancient world. The brewing of various types of beer and the fermenting of wine from dates and grapes is known in Mesopotamia and Egypt from protoliterate times (c. 4000 B.C.). Banqueting scenes are common in Assyrian art; they depict parties of men and women eating from tables stacked high with food and drinking from cups and through straws. The Babylonian creation epic *Enuma Elish* describes how the gods banqueted, making "the sweet liquor flow through their drinking tubes" (a necessity since the lees of the beverage were so thick). A Sumerian hymn to the goddess Ninkasi celebrates the brewing process and gives thanks for the beverage that slakes the thirst and gushes forth in abundance like the Tigris and Euphrates. The ills of drunkenness are found in Psalm 69:12, Proverbs 20:1, and in the drunken parties portrayed in Esther 1:3-8 and Daniel 5:1-4, and were also well recognized across the ancient Near East. Egyptian wisdom literature warns against intoxication with its accompanying lack of control and the resulting social rejection. There is evidence from the Mari texts of intoxication being viewed as a favorable condition for receiving divine oracles.

28:15. covenant with death. It is tempting to see in this passage a treaty or act of submission to the Canaanite god Mot ("death") or to the Egyptian god of the dead Osiris (see 30:1-2). Both would then represent political alliances made with various Syro-Palestinian nations or with Egypt against the Assyrians. The prophet warns the Israelites, however, that this is folly and a sign of their wicked nature (see Job 8:5-21). As the Mesopotamian hero Gilgamesh learned, no human, except in rare individual cases (Enoch, Elijah, Utnapishtim) escapes death (Job 30:23).

28:16. architectural function of cornerstone.
Israelite Iron Age architectural design made
increasing use of cut-stone masonry over the
rough boulders and rubble construction of
earlier periods. In order to provide stability
and to bind two adjoining walls together, a
finely shaped block of stone was inserted that
became the cornerstone. It would have been a
larger stone than those normally used, and its
insertion often required special effort or rituals. Its large, smooth surface was a natural
place for inscribing religious slogans, the
name of the architect or king responsible and
the date of construction. It is possible that the
cornerstone could also serve as the foundation
stone. For information on the latter see comments on Ezra 3:3 and 3:10.

28:21. Mount Perazim. Known as Baal Perazim in 2 Samuel 5:18-20, it commands the
heights above the Valley of Rephaim (Josh
15:8). Although its exact location is unknown,
the text suggests that it is just northwest of
Bethlehem, near Jerusalem.

28:21. Valley of Gibeon. The site of Gibeon
(el-Jib) is located six miles northwest of Jerusalem. It is best known for its association with
Joshua's treaty with the Gibeonites (Josh
9:3-10:15) and for his driving a Canaanite
army from Gibeon to the Beth Horon Valley
(Josh 10:9-11). In this case, however, Yahweh
will reverse his role of Divine Warrior and allow the Israelites to be defeated in this place
of former victory.

28:25. sowing strategy. Two sowing strategies
are employed here. Black cumin, a condiment,
and cumin, a spice and a source of oil, were
broadcast by hand. This was done in the freshly plowed furrows after the first rains. Wheat,
barley and spelt had to be handled more carefully to avoid mixing the seed. It seems likely
that the Israelites used a seed drill to push
holes into the furrows as oxen pulled the plow
through the fields. A man following kept the
hollow shaft of the drill filled with seed,
which dropped into the ready-made spots.
The action of the plow then covered the seed.
Representations of the seed drill in action are
found in Kassite and Assyrian art.

28:27. threshing caraway and cumin. The
seeds of these two grains were too fragile to
use the larger threshing instruments. Using a
rod would accomplish the threshing process
without damaging the seeds.

28:28. sequence of grain production. No
bread can be made if the farmer performs only
one of his tasks. Therefore it is necessary to
bring the harvested grain to the threshing
floor, where it can be crushed under the feet of
the oxen (Deut 25:4) and further processed by

running a threshing sledge over it. The
wheel-thresher mentioned here was a common wooden device with two or more rows of
wheels affixed. Once the grain had been separated from the stalks, it had to be winnowed,
sieved and then given to the women to be
crushed on grinding stones to make the fine
flour used for baking.

29:1-24
Woe Oracle Against Jerusalem

29:1. Ariel. This is a descriptive term for the
city of Jerusalem. The name itself refers to the
"altar hearth of El" (translated this way at the
end of v. 2; see also Ezek 43:15). The present
oracle tells of a city that will be destroyed like
the sacrifices brought to the altar.

29:1. cycle of festivals. See the comments on
Exodus 23:15-16 and Deuteronomy 16:9-17 for
descriptions of the Feast of Unleavened Bread,
Feast of Harvest and the Feast of Ingathering
that served as the major agricultural festivals
of the Israelite calendar. The Gezer calendar, a
tenth-century B.C. schoolboy exercise on a
small limestone tablet, also provides the
breakdown of the year according to planting,
harvesting and feasting.

29:2. altar hearth. The hearth was the uppermost block of the altar, on which the sacrifice
would be burnt (Lev 6:9) and from which the
horns projected on each corner (1 Kings 2:28).
In Ezekiel 43:15 the hearth of the altar in the
vision of the reconstructed Jerusalem temple
is described as being eighteen feet square.

29:3. siege works and towers. See the comment on 23:13 for a description of siege towers
erected by an army attacking a walled city. Assyrian reliefs depict these moving towers as
well as engineers tunneling to undermine
walls, battering rams being employed on
walls and city gates, and siege ramps built to
facilitate the movement of towers (Jer 32:24).
Siege camps also would have been established
to house the army and to prevent the city
dwellers from escaping (see 2 Kings 25:1; Jer
52:4). One of the most striking examples still
in existence is the remains of the first-century
A.D. Roman camps and enveloping wall
around the Jewish fortress of Masada.

29:6. characteristics of theophany. See the
comment on 28:2.

29:10. covering heads of seers. Closing the
eyes and covering the head are most likely images of death here, as they are parallel to the
deep sleep of the first line. Both phrases, however, are used only here and are therefore difficult to decipher.

29:11. sealed in scroll. Official documents

were written on scrolls of papyrus or vellum and then, when stored or dispatched by messenger, were rolled up and sealed with string and an affixed seal (see 1 Kings 21:8; Jer 32:10-11). The seal, either a ring or signet, was impressed into either wax or a lump of clay known as a bulla (Job 38:14). Archaeologists have found many of these clay bullae with the names of Israelite officials.

29:17. Lebanon. Using the same image of nature reversed that is found in 32:15, the prophet describes how the mountains of Lebanon, known from the Gilgamesh Epic and the Egyptian Tale of Wenamon for their stands of cedar forest, will become a fertile field. The fields of Carmel will become forest land. The sense is of the fulfillment of the covenant and a magnification of fertility that will restore Israel's fortunes.

30:1-33
Woe Oracle Against Stubborn Disobedience

30:1. alliance. See the comment on 28:15 and its warning against making a "covenant with death," referring to political dealings with the Egyptians.

30:2. Egypt's role. During Hezekiah's reign the Nubian-based Egyptian Twenty-Fifth Dynasty and Pharaoh Shabaka continuously attempted to foment revolt among the Syro-Palestinian peoples against Assyria. Sennacherib's account of his 701 B.C. campaign against an Egyptian army takes him as far as Eltekeh, just about one hundred miles from Egypt's border. In Josiah's time it was Pharaoh Psammeticus I who took advantage of the growing weakness of Assyria at the end of the reign of Ashurbanipal (d. 627 B.C.). He too hoped to expand Egyptian influence but was stymied by the rising power in Babylon.

30:4. Zoan, Hanes. Isaiah emphasizes the futility of Hezekiah's diplomatic overtures to Egypt. He says that despite having ambassadors travel to the Egyptian capital at Zoan (Tanis in the upper Delta, just twenty-nine miles south of the Mediterranean) and to Hanes (Heracleopolis Magna, forty-five miles south of Cairo on the west bank of the Nile), their mission will be in vain. Hanes was an important regional capital under both the Twenty-Fifth Dynasty ruler Shabaka as well as during the Twenty-Sixth Dynasty reign of Psammaticus I (663-609). It would have been necessary for Hezekiah to send representatives to meet with the Egyptian leaders in both of these important cities in order to initiate treaty alliances or plan strategies against Assyria.

30:6. animals of the Negev. The dangers of travel through the difficult terrain of the arid Negev are magnified by reference to wild beasts that assault the unwary. The remains of carnivores such as lions and leopards appear in excavations from the Chalcolithic to the Iron Age. Poisonous snakes, including the adder and the cobra, are also known in the area. The Assyrian king Esarhaddon's annals describe a "flying serpent" that plagued his campaign (see Num 21:8; Is 14:29).

30:6. caravan from the Negev. The caravan described here is most likely that of Hezekiah's ambassadors. The route they took avoided the normal coastal highway that was blocked by Assyria during Sennacherib's reign. Instead they traveled south to Aqaba and across the Sinai to Egypt. What they carried with them may have included the sort of goods that would have been expected to induce Egypt to become involved: frankincense, resins for cosmetics and embalming, ingots of copper or iron, indigo, ivory and lapis lazuli.

30:7. Rahab. Although not mentioned in any known text outside the Bible, Rahab is comparable to the chaos monster Leviathan, which also takes the form of a twisting serpent (Job 26:12-13; see the comment on Is 27:1). Rahab is also used synonymously for Egypt. For instance, in Psalm 87:4 the major nations are listed as subject to the power of Yahweh. Rahab, Egypt's metaphorical name, is paired here with Babylon in terms of importance. The further sign of Rahab's dual character may be found in 51:9-11, a passage that refers to Yahweh's destruction of the monster (see Ps 89:10) as well as how God "dried up the sea," a clear reference to the exodus tradition and the defeat of Egypt. In 30:7 the prophet taunts an impotent Egypt/Rahab's ability to help Israel or stop Assyria.

30:8. tablet, scroll. While the mention of both tablet and scroll may simply be parallelism, writing down a prophecy on both a clay tablet (or possibly an ostracon) and a scroll may be a sign of the coming destruction. For instance, in the first-century pseudepigraphal *Life of Adam and Eve*, Eve instructs her son Seth to write down her "testament of the fall" on both stone and clay tablets to insure some record would survive either flood or fire. This charge to write is also found in 8:1, Jeremiah 30:2 and Habakkuk 2:2. Like the spoken word, the process of writing enacts the prophecy, and it also holds it secure for later generations to see.

30:10. manipulated prophets. It is a common charge by Yahweh that the Israelites have either ignored the prophets or told them to prophesy only pleasant words and visions (see Jer 7:25-26;

Amos 2:12). Throughout the ancient world it was believed that prophets not only proclaimed the message of deity but in the process unleashed the divine action. It is no wonder then that there would be some attempt to control a negatively disposed prophet. In Assyrian king Esarhaddon's instructions to his vassals he requires that they report any improper or negative statements that may be made by anyone, specifically naming prophets, ecstatics and dream interpreters. One can perhaps understand why people would be inclined to discourage a prophet whose very words might impose doom.

30:13-14. basis of imagery. Given the extensive use of mud-brick architecture throughout the ancient Near East, this must have been a common occurrence. Egyptian tomb paintings as models depict the process from gathering clay, water and straw to shaping the bricks in molds (see Ex 5:7-8). As the bricks weathered, they eroded and lost stability. If the bricks were only sun-dried and not fire-hardened in a kiln, then they were subject to crumbling under the weight of a high wall. This would often first be manifested in cracks and bulges, and eventually the entire structure would come down in an avalanche of masonry (see 9:10). To guard against faulty construction and increase the life of the brick walls, Hammurabi's Code provided strict punishments for careless contractors.

30:22. defiling idols. There could be no more defiling substance than menstrual blood (Lev 15:19-23) and, for the people, no more defiling object than an idol (Deut 4:15-19). Here then, the idols, usually among the most precious objects in the culture, will be treated as the most disgusting piece of trash.

30:24. fodder and mash spread with fork and shovel. Because of the people's return to covenant obedience, even their draft animals will share in the abundance provided by God. Fodder for animals normally consisted of the remains of the chaff left by the threshing process. A common term for fodder means "small pieces of straw," which might be mixed with barley. Here, however, the stock are fed chickpeas that had been specially prepared for them using a wooden shovel and winnowing fork. Both of these implements helped separate the grain from the chaff and were used to create heaps.

30:28. sieve of destruction. The two types of sieves used by Israelite farmers gave them different results. The *kebara* (Amos 9:9) had large holes that caught stones and other large objects as the worker shifted it back and forth. The sieve in this passage, the *napa*, had smaller holes and was meant to separate out the smaller items from the grain through a swift up-and-down motion. This makes an excellent

metaphor for God's act of judgment.

30:30. characteristics of theophany. See the comment on 28:2.

30:33. Topheth. This instance is the only case in the Hebrew Bible where this word is used as a noun, meaning "crematory" or "pyre." God's wrath is to literally burn up the Assyrian king in much the same way that sacrifices were made in the cult site in the Valley of Hinnom near Jerusalem to the god Molech (2 Kings 23:10). In fact, the Assyrian king Sin-Shar-Ishkun died in the flames of his palace when the city of Nineveh was destroyed in 612 B.C.

30:33. burning sulfur. Finely ground sulfur can increase the intensity and brightness of a fire. It may be this property that has made it a symbol of God's wrath, as in the case of Sodom. In this image of Assyria's funeral pyre it magnifies the power of God to punish the enemy nation. Mixed with salt, sulfur could also rob the soil of fertility, again a sign of God's extreme displeasure.

31:1-9
Woe Oracle Against Political Alliances

31:1. role of Egypt. See the comment on 30:2.

31:8. fate of Assyria. The ultimate fate of Assyria is its annihilation as a nation by a coalition of states headed by the Chaldeans of Babylon and the Medes. The Babylonian Chronicle describes how Nineveh falls to an allied army led by Nabopolassar of Babylon and the Median ruler Cyaxares in 612. The final battle at Carchemish in 605 demonstrated the ability of the Babylonian leader Nebuchadnezzar to totally demoralize the formerly invincible Assyrian shock troops and their Egyptian allies. Thus the hand of Yahweh and the loss of strong Assyrian leadership after the death of Ashurbanipal in 627 spelled elimination of that people's influence from the ancient Near East.

32:1-8
The Coming King

32:1-5. visions of better times. These verses form a reversal of the conditions faced by Isaiah in his call narrative in 6:9-10. What changes Israel's fortunes is the rise of a righteous king who enforces the law and maintains order. Statements such as these are part of the wisdom tradition of the ancient Near East that includes works from Egypt and Mesopotamia on the "just king." Among them is the Egyptian *Tale of the Eloquent Peasant*, who describes a righteous king as one who is "father to the orphan" and "mother to the motherless." Similarly, the eighth-century Egyptian sage Ankhsheshonqy states that "blessed is a city with a just ruler."

32:9-20
Oracle Against the Women of Jerusalem

32:11. sackcloth around waist. One of the rituals associated with mourning and supplication is to wear sackcloth (Gen 37:34; 1 Kings 20:31-32). Pictorial representation of this practice is found on the sarcophagus of the Phoenician king Ahiram (c. 1000 B.C.), which depicts two mourning women as well as other figures performing symbolic acts associated with the passage of the deceased.

32:14. citadel and watchtower. The Lachish Letters, which date to the early sixth century and the invasion of Judah by Nebuchadnezzar, describe signal fires that are lit in towers in each of the important border towns. The writer of this passage may be referring to these signal/defensive towers, or it is possible that the word for citadel (*'ophel*) refers to a portion of Jerusalem where a specific watchtower stood (see comment on Neh 3:26).

33:1-24
Woe Oracle Against Those on Whom the King Will Take Vengeance

33:4. locusts. The image of locusts as a ravaging horde stripping the land of its harvest and wealth is more fully developed in Joel 1:4-12 and Amos 7:1-2. See also the comment on Deuteronomy 28:42. The irony in the Isaiah passage is that the former destroyer, Assyria, is now to be picked over even more thoroughly than were its victims.

33:9. Lebanon, Sharon, Bashan, Carmel. The shattering of nature's normal function, coupled with a gloomy recital of areas known for their fertility, once again reflects God's displeasure at work (see 24:4-7; comment on 24:1-13). The itinerary runs generally north to south: from the lush forests of Lebanon and the wine country of the Beqa' Valley (Ps 72:16; Hos 14:7), south to the fertile plain of Sharon on the coastal plain (Song 2:1), east of the Galilee to the Bashan plateau and its excellent grazing areas (Ps 22:12), and then south again to the Carmel range also known for its herding (1 Sam 25:2; Jer 50:19).

33:18. officials. Every government requires bureaucrats to conduct its business. In this vision of the future when God's king will reign once again, the people think back to the "bad old days" when their lives and fortunes were strained by the activities of men who recorded tax assessments, counted out the tribute payments and determined ("counted towers") how many soldiers would be needed to man the Assyrian garrisons (for which they had to provide troops). The Mari texts contain a number of letters sent to local officials from provincial governors and the king, instructing them to perform these tasks. The harshness of punishments threatened against the officials for failure to collect taxes or draft workers and soldiers assured that they would in turn be a "terror" to the people they oppressed.

33:19. foreign language. The Assyrian tax collectors, some of whom may have come from various parts of the empire, spoke Aramaic, while the majority of Israelites spoke only Hebrew (see 36:11). They may also have had strange-sounding accents, which added to the sense of foreign control and oppression for the people of Judah (see Jer 5:15 for the same reaction under Babylonian rule).

33:22. role of lawgiver. One of the attributes that all kings claim is "lawgiver." For instance, as early as the end of the third millennium Sumerian king Urukagina of Lagash and the Neo-Sumerian king Ur-Nammu pledge in their royal inscriptions "not to hand over the widow and orphan to the powerful." In the same vein the eighteenth-century B.C. prologue to Hammurabi's law code contains a statement that the gods appointed him "to cause justice to prevail in the land" so that "the strong might not oppress the weak." The similarity of wording in these texts, plus the language in 2 Samuel 8:15 in which David is described as "doing what was just and right for all his people," suggests a common ancient Near Eastern tradition of the "just king." However, when the monarch fails to perform this essential task, God steps in to restore order and justice (see Ezek 34:7-16).

33:23. boat metaphor. A similar metaphor is known from an Assyrian elegy about a woman who died in childbirth. She is described as a boat that is adrift with its mooring rope cut and the seat where the oarsman would sit broken.

34:1-17
Oracle of Judgment Against the Nations

34:4. imagery of disappearing stars. Always in command of all creation, Yahweh shows mastery over the heavens and celestial bodies, causing their brightness to be snuffed out in a reversal of creation. Prominent astral motifs in the Mesopotamian religion included the idea that the gods were given stations within the heavens and "their astral likenesses" marked the zones of the calendrical year (for instance, in the Babylonian *Enuma Elish* creation epic). In the celestial omens the disappearing of a star or planet always suggested that the related deity had suffered defeat in battle. Astral deities were considered among the most prominent and powerful of the gods. The dissolving of the stars and the fall of the starry host are therefore related. Both the natural manifestation as well as the deity connected to it are overcome in this act of judgment. Additionally, dream omens in Mesopotamia hold that the observation of stars falling is a bad omen. In the destruction described in *Erra and Ishum,* Erra says that he will make planets shed their splendor and will wrench stars from the sky.

34:4. sky rolled like a scroll. More often the heavens are compared to a canopy (40:22) or a tent (Ps 104:2) spread over the earth. This image in Isaiah of the whole panorama of the sky being rolled up like a parchment scroll is unique in the Hebrew Bible (see the New Testament parallel in Rev 6:14). Additionally, the three major Babylonian gods are not represented by stars but by the sky itself. Anu is the sky god, and the horizon is divided into three paths (connected to Anu, Enlil and Ea). Therefore, rolling up the sky is an act of judgment against the three main deities of the ancient world.

34:5. role of Edom. Since the larger passage here (see vv. 1-4) is concerned with God's punishment of the nations, it may be that the description of Edom as a sacrificial victim is simply a example of what will happen to them all (compare 63:1-6). Certainly Edom serves in many cases as Israel's prototype "enemy" (see Obad 5-9; Mal 1:2-4). The lack of a specific act by Edom in the late eighth-early seventh century against Jerusalem (although see 2 Chron 21:8-10) has convinced many scholars that this passage is a reference to Edom's role as Babylon's ally in 587 B.C. (see Ezek 35:2-15).

34:6. Bozrah. This is the capital of ancient Edom and is to be identified with Buseirah in the northern region of the country. It guards a portion of the King's Highway and is fairly close to the copper mines found five miles to the southwest at Wadi Dana. Excavations demonstrate seventh to sixth century levels from the most heavily fortified and largest settlement in the area.

34:9. pitch and sulfur. Although often mentioned as a sealant material for boats (see Gen

9:14; Ex 2:3), boiling pitch appears in Old Babylonian texts as a form of punishment. Coupled with the foul smell of burning sulfur, both materials being available in the region of the Dead Sea, they could easily be associated with God's wrath (see Gen 19:24).

34:11. owls and ravens. The symbol for utter destruction here is that birds best known as inhabiting and scavenging desolate places (Job 38:41; Ps 102:6) have settled in the ruins of towns (see Is 13:22). One parallel to this picture is found in the Egyptian *Visions of Neferti* (c. 2000 B.C.), which describes an Egypt so weak that a "strange bird will make its nest near the people" and "desert herds will drink from the Nile."

34:13-15. jackals, hyenas, falcons. Isaiah's vision of Edom's desolation concludes with a land left to scavengers and phantoms (see Jer 9:11). It is easy to imagine the cry of jackals and hyenas would sound demonic in origin to people who are already in fear of their lives (Mic 1:8). Some commentators read Lilith, the Mesopotamian female night demon (v. 14), as one of the creatures inhabiting this nightmare world.

35:1-10
Restoration

35:2. Carmel and Sharon. With the elimination of Edom, regions north of that land are freed from oppression and are restored to fertility and prosperity. These include Carmel and Sharon (see the comment on 33:6, where this is reversed), the area along the northern coastal plain of Israel. Even the desertlike portions of the Arabah (within the Jordan Rift Valley; Jer 17:6) will become rich and abundant with life, like these normally fertile areas.

35:7. jackals/papyrus contrast. Jackals are creatures of the steppe and desert regions, ranging over a barren landscape (Mal 1:3). In Isaiah's vision of a garden replacing what once had been wilderness, these haunts for wild predators will be transformed into wetlands like those in the Huleh Valley (see 43:20). The marshy area will remain moist year round, allowing for the growth of grasses and papyrus plants (see Job 8:11-13 and Is 19:5-6).

36:1—37:38
Sennacherib's Siege of Jerusalem

See comments on 2 Kings 18—19 and 2 Chronicles 32.

38:1-8
Hezekiah's Illness

See comments on 2 Kings 20.

38:9-20

Hezekiah's Prayer

38:9. Hezekiah's letter. A thanksgiving psalm
such as this pertaining to a situation that
threatened the life of the king would typically
be inscribed on a stone stele. An example of
this is found in the inscription of Sin-Iddinam,
who was king over the town of Larsa in the
nineteenth century B.C. In a letter to the god
Nin-Isina (known as a healer) the king presents his piety, benevolence and effectiveness
as reasons why the god should extend healing
mercy, which is granted.

38:11. seeing the Lord. Hezekiah does not
view "seeing the Lord" as an afterlife experience. Seeing the Lord involved worshiping in
the temple and enjoying the Lord's favor.
Verses 18-19 continue to make it clear that the
king anticipated no positive afterlife experience. See comment on 14:9 for more information about Israelite beliefs concerning afterlife.

38:12. metaphors. The shepherd moved frequently from place to place and therefore
could break camp quickly. The weaver
working on a horizontal loom had the
threads and material stretched on bars between stakes. When it had to be moved, the
bars could simply be pulled off the stakes
and rolled up (see comment on Judg
16:13-14). When the weaver finished a piece
of cloth, the threads connecting the material
to the loom had to be cut. The weaving of
Hezekiah's life had been completed, and he
was now to be cut loose from the land of the
living. Life or history as a fabric being woven is known from Greek mythology but
has not been identified in ancient Near Eastern literature.

38:20. play my songs. The king's involvement
in psalm composition is particularly well
known in connection with David but neither
began nor ended with him. As early as the end
of the third millennium, Shulgi king of Ur was
famous for his hymns offering prayers for the
health and welfare of the king. As late as the
Roman period, Nero was a patron of the arts
and considered himself a first-rate composer.
The ideal king was a wise king, and music
was one of the realms of wisdom.

40:1-31

Comfort in God's Sovereignty and Transcendence

**40:3-4. building roads in the ancient Near
East.** The roads of the ancient Near East were
for the most part unpaved (except for a few
roads in the Late Assyrian Period). Although

unpaved, those intended for wheeled transport (called "wagon roads" in the Nuzi texts)
had to be staked out, leveled and consistently
maintained. However, very few texts describe
the construction and maintenance of these
roads. Roads for heavy transport were somewhat rare and were primarily along the trade
routes. Thus, a vassal king complained to the
king of Mari that he had to arrive at the Syrian
capital by a roundabout route along a major
highway. Assyrian kings rarely boasted of
their road constructions as it appeared to be
the duty of the local populations. In a treaty
text Esarhaddon commands that when his son
succeeds him the vassal must submit to him
and "smooth his way in every respect."

**40:3-9. voice in the wilderness, bringer of tid-
ings.** Messengers were well known in the ancient Near Eastern world. They played an
essential role as the bearers of political and
civic news to the inhabitants of a city. Virtually every town had a "crier" who announced
important news to the inhabitants. Foreign invaders often sent a herald to a town to discuss
terms with those remaining in the city. An example similar to the Rabshakeh's visit to
Jerusalem is when the Assyrians sent a herald
to Babylon to discuss terms during a seventh-
century attack in southern Mesopotamia.

40:6-7. human mortality. The awareness of
fleeting human mortality is not exclusive to
ancient Israel. According to the Mesopotamian Epic of Gilgamesh, the gods decreed mortality for humans, while immortality was left
only to the gods themselves. Nonetheless, the
Sumerian king Gilgamesh went on many adventures to gain immortality. He first attempted to gain a type of immortality through
procreation, by making a name for himself
through the vanquishing of nonhuman foes,
and then by searching for Utnapishtim, the
hero of the flood, who had been granted immortality by the gods. Though Gilgamesh was
successful in finding the flood hero and even
located the "plant of life," he unselfishly
wanted to bring the plant back home with him
to his city (Uruk), so that all of the citizens
could partake of the plant. Alas, it was stolen
by a snake, and Gilgamesh returned home
empty-handed. However, the reader was reminded that Gilgamesh had built the walls of
Uruk, which still stood, and thus had gained a
form of immortality. Thus the epic was in part
an explanation for something that every Mesopotamian person knew: life was short and in
death one was confined to a dreary existence
in the netherworld.

**40:8. what stands forever in ancient Near
East.** The concept of "forever" in the ancient

Near East connotated continuous and permanent time rather than endless time. Mesopotamian kings hoped that their names would be established "forever." Kings gave property to individuals and their families "forever" (i.e., in perpetuity). According to the Epic of Gilgamesh, only the gods' days were "forever" (continuous), while human days were "numbered." The concept of a word standing forever is paralleled in the fixing of destinies. In the Gilgamesh Epic Enkidu uses a curse to "fix the destiny" of Shamhat forever. Assyrian inscriptions also refer to gods whose orders cannot be changed and whose words are valid forever. In *Enuma Elish* the rebel leader Kingu and Marduk each have their destiny fixed so that their command will not be changed and their word will be eternal.

40:10. reward on return of king from battle. The terms for reward and payment were probably technical words for tribute and booty brought home by victorious warriors and kings from battle. The Assyrian kings made specific reference to the large booty received from conquered peoples. For instance, Sennacherib constructed a Lachish Room in his palace at Nineveh to house all of the booty collected from the destruction of this Judahite fortress city in 701 B.C. The return home from successful battle was an opportunity for the distribution of rewards to those who were favorites of the king.

40:11. king as shepherd. The ideology of the king as a shepherd to his people is found with Lugalzagessi of Sumer as early as c. 2450 B.C. The contemporary king Urukagina of Lagash claimed that the god Ningirsu owned his state and that the king had been chosen as a "shepherd" to administer the city on behalf of the gods and the people. For the most part this ideology continued in the ancient Near East into the period of the Israelite monarchy.

40:12. ordering of cosmos. It was the job of the chief deity to bring order to the cosmos. In *Enuma Elish* (the Babylonian creation epic) the deity Marduk, after having defeated the goddess Tiamat, "crossed the heavens and surveyed the regions; he squared Apsu's quarter, the abode of Nudimmud, and measured the dimensions of Apsu." He continued to organize the constellations, the divine astral images and other heavenly bodies.

40:13-14. council of the gods in the ancient Near East. In the ancient Near East the major decisions were all made in the divine council. There the gods would consult with one another and share their information and opinions. In the Babylonian creation epic Apsu and Tiamat, the gods from whom spawned all living creatures, had as their trusted advisor

Mummu, who often rebuked them. When the high council of gods assembled to determine how to attack Tiamat, they drank themselves into a stupor and subsequently chose Marduk as their king, accepting his harsh demands of absolute rule. Isaiah insists that Yahweh has no advisors nor does he work within an assembly of gods (though a divine council of sorts was believed to be operative; see comments on Ex 20:3 and 2 Chron 18:18).

40:15. dust on the scales. The dust of the earth was used to express abasement, smallness and insignificance in the Old Testament. In this passage the dust of the nations makes no significant difference in the scales. The Babylonians took no notice of a little dust on the scales when meat or fruit were being weighed.

40:16. wood and wildlife of Lebanon. The Israelites considered that the land with the greatest forests and most varied animal life was Lebanon. In addition to supplying lumber for the temple of Solomon, the cedars of Lebanon provided sacred barges for Egypt and ships for Tyre. Moreover, the Assyrians exacted a tribute of timber from Lebanon for temple building.

40:19. manufacture of idols. Images in the ancient Near East were either cast or carved. Wooden idols were manufactured by a sculptor who stretched a line over the wood to measure the length and width of the image. He then drew an outline of the idol with his stylus, chiseled out the rough spots and put all of the body parts in the right proportion. Here, however, the reference is clearly to cast images. These would have been anywhere from four to ten inches high. The mold would be created by coating wax figurines with clay, then melting out the wax and baking the clay. The bronze would then be poured into the mold through a spout on the bottom of the feet, which would later serve as a peg to attach the idol to a wooden base. The cast would then be overlaid with gold or silver foil using a small hammer to affix it to the edges provided for that purpose. Grooves were also designed on the cast so that gold or silver wires (NIV: "chains") could be squeezed into them. Then a solid wood was chosen for a base. Recent suggestions have identified the wood as sissoo, a wood similar to teak, native to India. Literally thousands of idols throughout the Near East have been uncovered by archaeologists.

40:22. circle of the earth. The picture of the universe described here is the common cosmological view of the ancient Near East. The sky was a dome that arched over the disk of the earth, which sat on top of a primeval ocean. Under the ocean was the netherworld, virtually a mirror image of the space above the earth. Thus, the entire universe was an enormous sphere, cut in the center by the earth. Nevertheless, here it is the earth itself that is described as circular. In Babylonian literature Shamash is praised as the one who suspends from the heavens the circle of the lands. Likewise, in a prayer to Shamash and Adad Adad causes it to rain on the circle of the earth. The circle simply reflects the curvature of the horizon (thus, disk-shaped) rather than a sphere (for which Hebrew uses another word). In the ancient world the earth was consistently regarded as being circular.

40:26. creator gods. There are many creation traditions throughout the ancient Near East. Not many of them, however, speak of the creation of the heavens or the stars. In the prologue to a Sumerian astrological treatise the three great gods An, Enlil and Enki, are credited with setting up the heavens and the astral gods and decreeing their courses. Marduk in the Babylonian creation epic is given the power of creation by the assembly of the gods, and he tests it by destroying and recreating a constellation. After defeating Tiamat, he sets up the positions of the great gods and establishes the constellations.

40:26. names of the starry host. In the Babylonian creation epic Marduk constructed stations for the gods in the heavens and fixed their astral likenesses (i.e., heavenly bodies) as images for them. Thus, although he did not actually name the stars, he appointed a deity for a respective star.

40:27-28. gods being unaware or tired. In the ancient world the gods were viewed as having human weaknesses and often were inattentive or simply unaware of events that were taking place. One result of this was that the pantheon of gods were constantly outwitting or tricking each other. For example, when Enlil brought on the flood to destroy humankind, Enki outwitted him by saving a remnant of humans. However, Enki may have been tricked when he advised the human Adapa to reject the "bread of death" while in the presence of Anu, the high god. Anu subsequently gave Adapa the "bread of life," which was apparently unexpected by Enki. The gods were not indefatigable. They were in constant need of food, drink and shelter. In fact, humans were created to do the hard labor the gods preferred not to do.

41:1-29

God's Help for His Servant Israel

41:1. islands. The islands or coastlands are a reference to the far-off reaches of the Mediterranean. The word describes any place that was reached by sea travel.

41:7. smith's craft. See comment on 40:19. In this verse the craftsman is the one who prepares the mold and creates the cast figurine. The goldsmith attaches the plating and inlay. Then the hammer is used to planish (smooth out) and burnish (shine) the overlay. The last step is difficult to translate because it is full of technical terms, but it appears to refer to the fitting of the tenon (peg) into the hole in the wooden base.

41:11-12. similarity to ancient Near Eastern prophetic oracles. Prophetic oracles were not unique to Israel. They were a common theme in certain periods in Mesopotamia. The largest corpus of prophetic oracles is found at the city of Mari on the Middle Euphrates (c. 1800 B.C.). For the most part these oracles are on a mundane plain, placing divine demands (usually of a very material nature) before the king and his advisors. They are also often concerned with the well-being of the king. Closer to the time of Isaiah, the Assyrian kings Esarhaddon and Ashurbanipal received oracles concerning the king's responsibility to shepherd his people and to act justly. Like the verses here in Isaiah, they often promise victory over enemies. In one prophecy to Esarhaddon, Ishtar states that his enemies will roll before his feet "like ripe apples."

41:15. threshing sledge. The threshing sledge was a heavy wooden sledge with stone or iron teeth. It was used to separate the grain from the chaff before the winnowing process.

41:16. winnowing. The process of winnowing was usually carried out on hilltops, where the wind carried away the chaff and allowed the grain to fall to the ground. The grain was tossed into the air with wooden shovels or fans. There are numerous depictions of winnowing on funerary wall reliefs from Egypt.

41:19. reforestation. The reforestation of depleted areas was done only on a minor scale in the ancient world. The Assyrian kings planted many "gardens" in their chief cities, including hundreds of trees, but this cannot be considered full-fledged reforestation.

41:25. parallel between north and rising sun. There is no contradiction here, as both statements here concern Cyrus of Persia, who was from the east but descended on "the rulers" (Babylon) from the north, conquering Armenia and northern Mesopotamia first. The same Cyrus is said to have come from the east (41:2).

42:1-25

The Servant of the Lord Who Will Bring Judgment

42:5. creator of heavens, earth and people. The creator gods of the ancient Near East were more limited in their range of creation. Often the cosmic elements are generated by procreation of the gods, though a creator deity may have oversight in some versions. Especially in Mesopotamian traditions, people are created by a separate deity. Egyptian traditions have more of a tendency to consolidate creative activity in one deity.

42:9. proclaiming past and future. The gods of the ancient Near East were not necessarily able to predict the future. The future was in the hands of Fate, an impersonal force that controlled the destiny of things. Enki, the god of wisdom, wore a sorcerer's hat, showing that he attempted to control and predict fate, much like a human sorcerer. Fate was written on tablets, and those who controlled the tablets controlled the destiny of the universe. If they were in the wrong hands, there was chaos in the world. In one myth a bird deity (Anzu) stole the tablets of fate, which caused quite a stir within the divine community until he was killed. At any rate it was not in the god's nature to predict the future, but rather it was a concept they desired to control.

42:11. Kedar and Sela. Kedar was a nomadic Arab tribe living in northern Arabia between Edom and Babylonia, while Sela was an Edomite capital, possibly located at the later site of Petra. They both represent remote areas of the desert and mountains who are invited to worship Yahweh.

42:13. divine warrior. In the divine warrior motif the deity is fighting the battles and defeating the deities of the enemy. In Assyria Nergal is the king of battle, and Ishtar is viewed as a war goddess. The Canaanite Baal and the Babylonian Marduk are divine warriors. This is not to be viewed as "holy war" because in the ancient Near East there was no other kind of war. In most situations prayers would be made and omens asked to assure the god's presence. Standards or statues of the deity were usually carried to symbolize their presence. Assyrian kings of the ninth and eighth centuries regularly refer to the divine standard that goes before them. The Assyrians believed that the gods empowered the weapons of the king and fought before him or at his side.

42:22. parallel between pits and prisons. When prisons were far off or not available, pits were often used to hold prisoners for a temporary period of time. In fact, prisons were primarily for detention of individuals awaiting trial or for political reasons, both in Israel and Babylonia.

43:1-28

God's Mercy on Israel

43:3. Egypt, Cush, Seba. The Persians successfully invaded Egypt and gained control of Cush (Nubia) during the reign of Cyrus's successor, Cambyses. Seba's location is disputed.

43:14. Babylonians as fugitives in ships. This passage is describing the defeat and capture of Babylon (i.e., Chaldeans) by Cyrus. Though not found in other sources, apparently the Chaldeans unsuccessfully attempted to escape the conquest by traveling in their own ships by sailing on the Euphrates to the Persian Gulf.

43:15. deity as king. Many of the polities in the ancient Near East considered the god as the true king of the land; the earthly ruler was merely a viceroy to the god. For example, the Assyrian kings were regents for the god Ashur. Marduk was king at Babylon, as was Baal in many Canaanite states. Even in ancient Sumer, Enlil was king of the gods. In fact, kingship itself was described in Sumerian as "Enlilship" (Enlilutu).

43:24. calamus. Calamus (botanically known as *acorus calamus*) was used in the manufacture of incense. It is a strongly aromatic cane that grew in the swamps of Syria and was imported from India to the west.

43:24. fat. The fat parts of the animal were also to be included in the sacrifice. Neither fat nor blood was to be eaten. Blood was drained and then sprinkled on the altar. The fat was always burned on the altar as part of the essentials of sacrifice. For more information see comment on Leviticus 3:4.

44:1-5

Servant Israel

44:2. Jeshurun. Jeshurun was an endearing name for Israel (see Deut 32:15; 33:5, 26). The meaning of the name is somewhat obscure, but some think it is derived from a Hebrew root meaning "upright."

44:5. writing on hand. The writing on the hand probably refers to the mark of a master on the hand of a slave (see 49:16). Slave markings were common throughout the Near East. For example, in many periods in Mesopotamia the slave was required to be "marked" by shaving half of the hair on his head. The marking on the hand by tattoo or brand also signifies ownership. Generally it was the owner's name that was incised on the right hand. Hundreds of jar handles have been found in Israel from the Iron Age that are inscribed *l'mlk,* "belonging to the king."

44:6-20

Worthless Idols

44:10-14. blacksmith and carpenter in manufacture of images. See the notes on Isaiah 40:19 and 41:7. In the eighth-century copies of the Epic of Erra and Ishum, Marduk speaks of the manufacture of his image. It starts with the wood of a sacred tree with its top brushing heaven and its roots in the netherworld. The roles of the skilled carpenter and the metalworker using millstones are featured, and the craftsmen are praised for their skills.

44:17-18. how images are "brought to life." The ancients did not believe that the idol was the deity itself but a representation of the deity. However, they did believe that the god's spirit came to inhabit the image, and thus they prayed to the image as if it were the god itself. The gods of ancient Egypt were consecrated with a ritual called the Opening of the Mouth. Life was symbolically imparted to them in much the same way that the Opening of the Mouth gave life to a mummy. There was an Opening of the Mouth ritual in Mesopotamia as well. This was a rite that was performed to purify and introduce into the temple the divine image. The same ritual was repeated when the image came into contact with impurity or impure individuals.

44:21-28

Redemption of Israel

44:24. alone created. The fact that the Bible portrays Yahweh as having no pantheon means that all divine activity is carried out by him. This is in contrast to many of the traditions of the ancient Near East, where various deities were involved with different aspects of creation. Another common belief in the ancient Near Eastern creation traditions is that cosmic elements came into being through the birth of the gods associated with those elements, rather than by a creative act of a deity. This concept of creation through procreation maintains that cosmogony (the origins of the cosmos) is related to theogony (the origins of the gods). Such a concept is rejected in this text. Yahweh has no consort, and therefore neither he nor the cosmos is the result of procreation, nor does he carry out his creative activity by means of procreation. (There have

been some inscriptions found in Palestine that imply that some Israelites believed that Yahweh had Asherah, a Canaanite goddess, as his consort. These texts are in direct contradiction to the writings of the Old Testament.)

44:25. diviners made fools. This verse connects to the previous one in that the omens consulted by the Assyrian and Babylonian diviners were drawn from heaven and earth. In fact, major prognostications had to be confirmed by omens from both realms. Yahweh's creation of those realms indicates his control of any signs being given. Prophets were supposed to be giving messages from deity, and diviners were presumably using their arts to determine what the gods were up to by reading the omens in heaven and earth. These professionals therefore offered a constant flow of theoretically divine insight concerning the course of political events. When Yahweh's plans brought about completely unanticipated events, those who were respected as wise men were shown to be farces.

44:28. Cyrus's background. Cyrus was born about 590 B.C. in the modern Iranian province of Fars. Virtually nothing is known of him until he came to the throne of Persia in 559 B.C., except for a few legends concerning his childhood written down by Herodotus, the Greek historian.

44:28. foundation of temple. All ancient Near Eastern temples were built with foundations. The building of temples in Mesopotamia was accompanied by certain ceremonies that are not fully understood. A series of items was deposited in the foundations of the buildings. This is known from building inscriptions and ritual texts, as well as actual foundation deposits found by archaeologists. Deposits included peg- or nail-shaped objects, animal sacrifices, cones, cylinders and tablets. One of the primary purposes of the foundation deposit was to memorialize the building of the edifice (for more information see comments on Ezra 3:3 and 3:10).

45:1-25

God's Restoration of Israel

45:1. Cyrus's accomplishments. Cyrus of Persia was one of the greatest conquerors in world history. He inherited the throne of Persia from his father, Cambyses I, in 559. In 556 the Babylonian king Nabonidus, motivated by a dream, abandoned the treaty that his country had maintained with the Medes for over half a century and made a treaty with Cyrus. This gave Cyrus the freedom to move against the Medes (ruled by his grandfather Astyges) whom he conquered in 550. The new Medo-Persian Empire was thus formed, with control over the entirety of Iran. By 546 he defeated the Anatolian kingdom of Lydia and Ionia. For the next five years he consolidated his control over the tribes in northeastern Iran. All of this success paved the way for his crowning achievement, the conquest of Babylon in 539 B.C. The whole of the Near East (excluding Egypt) was under the control of the Persians when Cyrus was killed in battle in 530.

45:2. gates of bronze, bars of iron. The Greek historian Herodotus described Babylon as having "one hundred gates in the circuit of the wall, all of bronze with bronze uprights and lintels." Large bronze gates have been excavated at the Assyrian period site of Balawat, giving a glimpse of what the Babylonian walls may have been like. Gates were locked by means of a bar slid across the gateway, and iron would obviously be the most difficult to break (see comment on Deut 33:25).

45:4. religion of Cyrus. Cyrus most certainly was not a worshiper of Yahweh. In his inscriptions his polytheism is evident. In one case he requests that all the gods pray for him to Nabu and to Marduk his lord, whom he claims to worship. Other indications suggest that Cyrus was a Zoroastrian (a religion based on the teachings of Zarathustra, an Iranian holy man who lived sometime in the early first millennium B.C.). Zoroastrianism flourished during the Achaemenid empire in Iran (for more information see comment on Ezra 1:2). Though there is no concrete evidence for Zoroastrianism until the reigns of Darius I and his successor Xerxes I, the names of Cyrus's children show Zoroastrian influence, and he is known to have set up a fire stand (important in Zoroastrian worship) for the king's daily ritual.

45:13. Cyrus's policy of return and rebuilding. Judah was not the only land that benefited from Cyrus's policy of returning exiles to their place of origin and rebuilding the major cities of a ruined area. For example, he claimed to have restored Marduk to his rightful position as the god of Babylon. He claimed to have restored many other people groups to their homelands (including displaced Babylonians) and restored their temples and other public buildings (for more information see comment on Ezra 1:2-4). Many Babylonian structures were rebuilt during Cyrus's reign.

45:14. Egypt, Cush, Sabeans. A major canal was built in the Red Sea by the Persians during the reign of Darius I that linked the Nile cultures of Egypt and Cush with Arabia (Sabeans). This facilitated the flow of shipping between the two continents. Also see the note on 43:3.

46:1-13
Yahweh's Superiority to the Gods of Babylon

46:1. Bel. Bel was not a proper name in Babylonia but was the Akkadian equivalent of "lord" (Hebrew, *Ba'al*). The Sumerian deity Enlil of Nippur was called "lord," a title also given to Marduk the god of Babylon in later periods. Bel in this context is most certainly a name for Marduk. Marduk was the chief god of Babylon, its patron deity and the head of the pantheon. The Babylonian creation epic, *Enuma Elish,* is actually a myth recounting his elevation to that position, believed to have taken place at the end of the second millennium. He was considered to be the son of one of the members of the most august ancient triad, Enki, the patron of Eridu. Though we often see Baal in the Bible as the principal rival of Yahweh, no deity in the first millennium had the political clout that was connected to Marduk. His principal shrine was the temple Esagila ("temple with the exalted head") in Babylon, which was connected to the famous ziggurat, Etemenanki ("foundation of heaven and earth").

46:1. Nebo. Nebo (Akkadian, Nabu) was the god of Borsippa, a city near Babylon. He was the god of wisdom and the patron deity of scribes and the son of Marduk. His prominence in the Neo-Babylonian period is demonstrated by the fact that most of the kings' names make statements about Nabu (e.g., Nebuchadnezzar, Nabonidus). He was already prominent in Isaiah's time, as is demonstrated by the fact that Sargon made his shrine the most prominent one in his new capital, the citadel called Dur-Sharruken (=Khorsabad). An eighth-century inscription urges worshipers to trust in Nabu and not in any other god.

46:1-2. idols taken captive. Babylonian festivals were frequently occasions for the idols of the gods to be brought out in grand processions. But this passage does not refer to a victory parade. There are many examples of images of Mesopotamian deities taken captive during battle. Marduk the god of Babylon was taken captive and removed from Babylon on a number of occasions. The Hittites in 1595 B.C., Tukulti-Ninurta I of Assyria (r. 1244-1208 B.C.) and Sennacherib (r. 705-681 B.C.) all plundered Babylon and took the Marduk statue, which was eventually returned in all three cases.

46:6. use of silver and gold in image manu-

facture. See the notes on 40:19 and 41:7.

46:7. treatment and use of idols. The images of deities in Mesopotamia were fed, dressed and even washed daily. Food sacrifices were brought to the deity on a daily basis (and no doubt eaten by the temple technicians). Other attendants were required to dress and undress the statue, and still others were employed to wash the statue and transport it in times of celebration.

46:10. deity with purpose. The gods of the ancient Near East were not capable of controlling the destiny of the world without help. In Mesopotamia there existed the "tablets of destiny," texts which contained the destinies of all things (including the gods) in the universe. Whoever controlled these tablets controlled fate. Occasionally these tablets came into the "wrong hands," and chaos ensued. Some gods, including Enki, wore sorcerer's hats, showing that they had the ability to control and predict the future, but only by way of spells and incantations. Conversely, Yahweh controlled all things without resort to superficial means of tablets or spells (see comment on 14:26-27).

47:1-15
Babylon's Disaster

47:1. virgin daughter of Babylon. The biblical writers, like their cuneiform counterparts, often depicted cities as feminine in nature. The term "virgin daughter" was addressed to a community that faced disaster. In the ancient Near East no one was considered a more helpless victim of war than the unmarried girl. Defeat often meant the loss of an intended husband as well as the loss of virginity at the hands of the marauding victors. The *Lamentation over the Destruction of Ur*, an early-second-millennium B.C. Sumerian literary text, describes the fall of the city Ur in such a manner.

47:2. grinding as lowly occupation. Grinding grain at the flour mill was one of the most menial of tasks, often done by slave girls in both Egypt and Mesopotamia (see comments on Ex 11:4 and Judg 16:21).

47:2. veil. In most ancient Near Eastern cultures a married woman was partially veiled in public, and this was the mark of her marital status. This is found in the Middle Assyrian Laws. Slaves or concubines could not afford veiling, and in any case they did not have the legal right to be veiled.

47:2. wading through streams. Bridges were virtually nonexistent in the ancient world, so streams and rivers were waded across at fords. A slave had to cross a stream on foot, in contrast to a rich person who was carried over in a carriage or in a chair carried by servants.

47:5. daughter of the Babylonians. This terminology is used in Akkadian literature to refer to female inhabitants of a region, city or people. Here it is a reference to the personified city of Babylon, a usage not observed in extant Babylonian literature.

47:8. "I am, and there is none beside me." The use of "I am" would have immediately struck a chord for this Israelite audience (see Ex 3:14). There was no claim too arrogant for these kings to make for themselves. An Assyrian king of the ninth century, Ashurnasirpal, had a list of eleven "I am" titles for himself.

47:9. sorceries and spells. Babylonia was famous in the ancient world for its magic and divinatory practices. Literally thousands of texts have been uncovered, dealing with a multitude of subjects, including incantations that help alleviate the pain of a toothache, help a baby that is stuck in the womb and help a mother who is barren. It appears that the common person hired an incantation priest for even the most mundane problem. The priest then came and recited a spell to exorcise a problematic demon or other divine irritant. How much more did they resort to incantation priests to practice their art for the avoidance of disasters that were either portended or threatened. Incantations were intended to magically bind the supernatural powers that posed a threat.

47:11. ways of avoiding portended calamities. There are thousands of omen texts in which the Babylonians attempted to predict and control future events. The common person hired an omen priest before he or she made any important decision. The priest then recited the proper omen, which told the individual what to expect in the event of a certain action. The omens were related to historical events the way that symptoms are related to the onset of disease. Thus the individual who was fearful of a portended calamity avoided it by not participating in a particular activity that was harmful. For example, there were certain days in which a husband and wife were not to engage in sexual relations, since these days portended disaster (including death). In other instances, the individual would hire an incantation priest to utter a spell or incantation that would neutralize the dreaded event. Best known are the *namburbu* avoidance rituals in which ritual acts were used in conjunction with formalized prayers to the gods. Such procedures could not be sought if there had been no indication of impending danger.

47:13. astrologers and stargazers. A form of

fortunetelling in Mesopotamia that rivaled divination was astrology. In the Late Assyrian Period (c. 900-612 B.C.) reports were regularly made to the king about the appearance of the moon and planets, with comments about what these things foretold. The Babylonians appeared to have invented the twelve signs of the zodiac about 500 B.C., roughly the same time as Cyrus of Persia. For more information see comments on Isaiah 2:6; Deuteronomy 18; Joshua 10:12-13; 2 Kings 23:4.

48:1-22
Announcement of the End of Captivity

48:10. silver refining. Silver in the ancient world was refined by a process in which it was melted in order to rid it of base components. Silversmiths, as well as goldsmiths, used blowpipes to ventilate their furnaces and cast their products with the aid of steatite or clay molds. For more information see comment on 1:22.

48:13. heavens and earth. See comments on 40:12 and 42:5.

48:14. Cyrus's campaign against Babylon. Cyrus began a propaganda campaign against Nabonidus king of Babylon, an action attested in later Babylonian sources. The Persian king advanced against Babylon in 539 B.C. and fought a victorious battle at Opis, about fifty miles north-northeast of Babylon on the Tigris in early October. On the eleventh of October, Sippar (thirty-five miles north of Babylon) fell. On October 13 the Persian army marched into Babylon peacefully, welcomed by the local populace. Cyrus himself entered the city on October 30 and was proclaimed its liberator.

49:1-26
The Servant Brings Deliverance and Restoration

49:1-7. kings with divinely ordained tasks of deliverance. Although kings in the ancient Near East were given responsibilities by the gods, they generally perceived themselves as having been ordained to conquer rather than to deliver. Cyrus of Persia was seen by the priests of Marduk and the city of Babylon as a savior from an oppressive regime. In the prologue to his laws Hammurabi claims himself to be the one who gathers the scattered people of the city of Isin and gives shelter to the people of the city of Malgium.

49:2. mouth as sword imagery. The sword imagery is also used for the prophet's word (see Jer 23:29) and God's word in the New Testament (e.g., Gal 6:17). Since the sword was an offensive weapon, the implication is that the word is in some sense aggressive. One of the Hebrew words for mouth *(peh)* also signified the term edge, as in "edge of the sword." Thus there may be a play on words in this verse.

49:9-10. characteristics of restoration. In Assyrian literature the just reign of a king is characterized by prosperity, diligent worship, rejoicing, freeing prisoners, healing of sickness, anointing with oil, and providing food and clothing for the needy. Similar elements are projected for Yahweh's restoration of his people and become part of the messianic profile.

49:11. building of highways. See the comment on 40:3.

49:12. Aswan (Sinim). Sinim was the city on the First Cataract of the Nile, the ancient boundary of Egypt and Nubia to the south. The site was later known in Greek sources as Elephantine and is the modern city of Aswan.

49:16. engraved on palms. The meaning of this imagery is that Jerusalem will be cut into (or tattooed, although this was forbidden; see Lev 19:28) the flesh of God and thus will be on his mind permanently. See comment on 44:5.

49:18. ornaments of a bride. The Israelite bride sometimes wore embroidered garments, jewels, a special girdle and a veil. In this passage the bride wears an ornamental waistband. There are scores of texts from Mesopotamia that describe the exchange of gifts between two families for the purpose of marriage, but little is said of the attire of the bride or of the ceremony itself.

49:26. imagery. "Eat on their own flesh" and "be drunk on their own blood" are most likely metaphors meaning they are reduced to the last extremity (see comment on 9:20).

50:1-11
Sin and Punishment

50:1. children sold to creditors. When one took out a loan or mortgage in the ancient Near East, the security took the form of a pledge of a personal item. Where there was no security to forfeit, debtors or their family members could be sold into slavery. For example, the Middle Assyrian Laws regulate the pledge of children to pay off debts. Of course, the extended family took great pains to make sure that family members stayed within the family structure. See comment on Exodus 21:2-6.

51:1-23
God's Deliverance of His People

51:6. end of heavens and earth. This is not an

apocalyptic verse concerning the end of the earth. The writer intends on emphasizing the permanence of God's salvation, which is even more permanent than the creation itself. In the ancient Near East the universe (or rather, matter) was an uncreated entity. In the Babylonian creation epic matter had apparently always existed and was later formed by Marduk into the heavens, the earth and the netherworld. There is no discussion concerning the end of the material world.

51:9. Rahab. Although not mentioned in any known text outside the Bible, Rahab is comparable to the chaos monster Leviathan, which also takes the form of a twisting serpent (Job 26:12-13; see the comment on 27:1). Rahab is also used synonymously for Egypt. For instance, in Psalm 87:4 the major nations are listed as subject to the power of Yahweh. Rahab, Egypt's metaphorical name, is paired here with Babylon in terms of importance. See comment on 30:7.

51:14. prisoners set free from dungeons. While most of those who had been deported to Babylon would not have been imprisoned, there would have been some political prisoners. Pits were used as prisons in most of the ancient Near East. The modern idea of a prison as a place where prisoners are to be reformed into good citizens would have been foreign to the ancient world. Those in debt, criminals awaiting trial and political prisoners were held in confinement of one sort or another.

51:18. imagery of sons caring for elderly parents. In Mesopotamia as well as Israel the eldest son received a larger inheritance than the rest of the children for the purpose of caring for the parents in their old age. The imagery here shows Jerusalem as a mother without any children to take care of her in her old age.

51:20. head of the street. Some cities in the ancient Near East show evidence of intense city planning. The norm, however, especially in the smaller towns, was a very haphazard approach in which there were few real streets but only passageways or open areas on which no homes were built. The "head of the street" refers to a corner or intersection. Most cities and towns featured blocks of housing tracts filled with random alleyways and dead ends with no intersecting routes. The intersections would occur when one emerged into an open square.

51:23. walking over captives. Egyptian kings in the early third millennium B.C. are depicted as trampling over the corpses of defeated enemies. For instance, Narmer, possibly the one who unified Egypt, is seen with a mace

smashing enemies and stepping over them. Likewise, the Sumerian kings from Lagash are depicted as marching over the dead bodies of their enemies. The tradition of trampling over one's enemies continued on into the first millennium in Assyria and Babylonia.

51:1-12
Captive Zion Set Free

52:11. vessels of the Lord. The vessels of the Lord were temple vessels that were transported to Babylon during the conquests of Jerusalem (for specific vessels see comments on 2 Chron 4). They were returned to Jerusalem during the Persian period. In the palace of Sennacherib at Nineveh there were numerous artifacts from the Judean fortress city of Lachish.

52:13—53:12
The Suffering Servant

52:14. battered king. During the Babylonian Akitu festival (at the New Year), the king was required to "take the hand of Bel" (Marduk) and proclaim his innocence as a righteous monarch. On the fifth day of the eleven-day festival the king was taken before the high priest, who stripped the monarch of his royal insignias (mace, loop and scepter) and struck him on the cheeks. The priest then dragged the king by his ears and forced him to bow to the ground before Marduk, again proclaiming his innocence.

53:4-10. substitutionary rites in the ancient Near East. The rite of the substitute king was used in Assyria when evil omens (especially an eclipse) suggested the life of the king was in danger. It is attested primarily in the reign of Esarhaddon in the early seventh century but had been practiced for over a thousand years. It worked on the principle that evil could be transferred from one individual to another. When the dangerous period was to occur, the king was replaced by a substitute on whom the evil fate could fall. In some cases this substitute was someone considered of no significance and was perhaps even mentally or physically impaired. He was then exalted to high status and office for as long as one hundred days, though often a shorter period. During this time the real king was kept in relative isolation (a virtual exile) and participated in numerous purification rituals. Meanwhile the substitute was going through the motions of being king and sitting on the throne. He was portrayed as the shepherd (a common title for Mesopotamian kings), but one could understand that he was simply a sheep about to be slaughtered. At the end of the period the substitute was put to death so that the evident design of the gods would be accomplished. The omens had suggested that it was the will of the gods to crush him. As one text puts it, he died to save the king and the crown prince. He was given a rich state funeral and an offering was made and exorcism rituals performed (including washings and sprinklings) so that the omens would be cancelled and the days of the king could be prolonged.

53:4. healing of diseases. The Ugaritic myth of the struggle of Baal and Mot contains the story of the Rapiuma (saviors or healers), led by Baal, who had risen from the dead. These venerated ancestors were believed to intervene on behalf of the living. They healed mortals' diseases, helped in matters of fertility and protected them against the evils of society. The Rapiuma, however, did not take the infirmities of the mortals on themselves.

53:7. sheep silent before shearers. Ancient Near Eastern texts often describe the shearing of sheep, who underwent their lot in silence. Shearing was done annually in the spring, using shears, which were invented about 1000 B.C. An individual could shear twenty to thirty sheep a day.

53:10. guilt offering. The reparation offering was traditionally termed the guilt offering. Though the term that is used is often appropriately translated as guilt, the term serves a more technical function within the sacrificial system. This offering is designed to address a particular category of offense—a breach of faith or an act of sacrilege. Breach of faith would appropriately describe the violation of a covenant, while sacrilege refers generally to desecration of sacred areas or objects. See comment on Leviticus 5:14-16. In this context, Israel's violation of the covenant would be the most likely cause for a guilt offering to be required.

54:1-17
The End of God's Anger

54:2. enlarging tents. Zion is seen here with the patriarchal image of the tent. As a mother who has been blessed with many children, Zion will need a spacious tent. The tents were made of hand-woven, three-feet-wide strips of dark goats' hair. When more family members needed to be accommodated, additional strips could be sown on. The cords that stretched from center poles to corner poles would have to be longer and the stakes made

of stronger, thicker wood in order to hold the weight.

54:4. shame of youth, reproach of widowhood. The metaphor here is clarified in verse 6. A woman who was unable to bear children in the ancient world was believed to be under the punishment of deity, incapable of serving the function for which she was married and therefore liable to be rejected and abandoned by her husband. The word translated "youth" here refers to one who has not borne a child. Her shame is her barrenness. She is a widow because her husband has abandoned her (as most marriage contracts allowed) and therefore is the object of reproach with little hope of remarrying. She is thus stripped of short-term support by a husband and the support in her old age that could be expected from children.

54:11. stones of turquoise, foundations of sapphires. An alternate translation of the word rendered "turquoise" is antimony, which was used for a mortar, especially for mosaics. The word here translated "sapphire" is generally considered to be lapis lazuli, a beautiful blue stone that was highly valued in the ancient world. The procession way to the famous Ishtar gate in Babylon was lined with intricate patterns with the background made by blue glazed bricks that gave the appearance of lapis. In a work referred to as the Uruk Prophecy, it is said that a future king will build the gates of Uruk of lapis lazuli.

54:12. gate description. The description of the approach in verse 11 leads to discussion of the gateway. The word translated "battlements" is actually "suns" and most likely refers to the round, burnished shields used as crenellations along the top of the towers that flanked the gate. These are visible along the entire wall in Sennacherib's portrayal of the fortifications at Lachish (see also Ps 84:11 for the association of sun and shield). NIV's "ruby" is a guess here, and others support jasper. The word is used only here and in Ezekiel 27:16, where it is listed among exports from Aram. Red burnished copper was popular for gates and would be plausible for these sunlike shields. The stonework of the gate area features some sort of sparkling stone. The word translated "walls" is a technical term for low walls that lined the inside passage of the gateway (see Ezek 40:12). They are described here as being made of "desirable stone"—high-quality stonework, perhaps with mosaics.

54:17. invincibility. Since the Assyrian attack in 701 B.C. there had been a tradition in Judah that Jerusalem was invincible from attacks from invaders. This idea was trampled by the Babylonian conquest and destruction of the city (605-586 B.C.). Now Isaiah states that in the future the city will be absolutely invincible.

55:1-13
Call to Seek the Lord

55:8-9. distinctions drawn between the ways of gods and mortals. In the ancient Near East there was considerable continuity between the divine and human realms. There was a hierarchy of divinity. For example, the Mesopotamian pantheon had a council of seven gods at the top of the hierarchy, followed by numerous other gods, descending to personal gods, angels, demons, heroes (humans who had attained a semidivine status) and lastly humans. Even the highest gods resembled humans in their character and behavior, and were subject to many of the same laws and limitations as their human counterparts. They were not elevated above the natural world nor transcendent in the way that Yahweh was understood to be. Instead they were part of the natural order. Nevertheless, statements such as those made here are also made in Mesopotamian literature. Wisdom literature considers the ways of the gods unknowable. In *Enuma Elish* the proclamation of Marduk's fifty names serves as a delineation of his ways.

55:11. word will not return empty. The claim of sovereignty represented in orders and commands that cannot be countermanded and are effective without exception is made for the gods of the ancient Near East as well. As early as the Sumerian myth *Lugal-e*, Ninurta is praised as one whose orders are not changed and whose decisions are truthfully carried out.

55:13. reforestation. See comment on 41:19.

56:1—57:21
Justice and Judgment

56:2. keeping Sabbath. The Sabbath observation has no known parallel in any of the cultures of the ancient Near East and is distinctive in that it is independent of any of the patterns or rhythms of nature. A similar term was used in Babylonian texts for a full moon day when the king officiated at rites of reconciliation with deity, but it was not a work-free day and had little in common with the Israelite Sabbath. There were particular days of the month in Mesopotamia that were considered unlucky and were often seven days apart (that is, the seventh day of the month, the fourteenth day of the month, etc.). Israel's Sabbath was not celebrated on certain

days of the month; it was simply observed every seventh day. During the Babylonian captivity, the Sabbath became the most conspicuous marker showing membership in the community of Yahweh worshipers. It thus became one of the central themes in postexilic Judaism (including during the time of Jesus).

56:4-5. eunuchs in temple service. This Hebrew term can at times refer simply to a court official, but it later came to refer specifically to eunuchs. Eunuchs were highly valued in government service in many varied roles during the Neo-Assyrian and Neo-Babylonian periods. The great demand for eunuchs led to young boys being included in the tribute paid to Persia so that they could be castrated and trained for government service. They had no families to distract them from their service. They were often entrusted with the care and supervision of the royal harem since they posed no threat to the women of the harem and could not engender children by the harem women who might be mistaken for royal heirs. They would be less likely to become involved in conspiracies because they would have no heirs to put on the throne. Assyria, Urartu and Media had all made use of eunuchs in government offices. Eunuchs (or, better, castrated ones) had originally been forbidden in the Israelite community (Deut 23:1). The context in Isaiah 56:5 makes it clear that these officials cannot have children, yet the Lord provides for them.

56:9. beasts as punishment. Wild beasts were a constant source of fear for city dwellers throughout the ancient Near East. Of course, in this passage wild beasts are a metaphor for human "beasts" who plunder and pillage city dwellers. In Assyrian texts and reliefs of this period the kings are seen hunting lions to symbolically rid the city of the scourge of wild beasts. In one case it has been suggested that the killing of eighteen lions represents the eighteen gates of Nineveh and the roads leading out of them.

56:10-11. dogs in Israelite society. Dogs in the ancient Near East lived as scavengers. They often roamed in packs on the outskirts of the city (sometimes in the city) and wherever they found refuse (Ps 59:6, 14). They were often the source of a biting insult (2 Sam 3:8). However, dogs were also often associated with healing and were used in rites of purification and exorcisms, and as offerings in both Mesopotamia and Anatolia. The term *dog* was used for certain cultic functionaries in Israel (Deut 23:19), Phoenicia and Anatolia. Some have thought that these "dogs" were prostitutes. Strangely enough a dog cemetery with over seven hundred shallow burial pits has been uncovered at Ashkelon in Philistia during the Persian period. There is no evidence of any cultic activity (although dogs were revered by the Persian Zoroastrians).

57:1. death for righteous a reward rather than a punishment. This verse implies that there has been a complete overturning in society, since the righteous perish. A number of Babylonian wisdom texts discuss this theme. For example, the Babylonian Theodicy (a text similar to the biblical book of Job) complains that the just man suffers from all kinds of injustice, while the evil man is free to do his evil activities. The writer also complains that his personal god has done nothing to alleviate the problem. This verse offers the explanation that the righteous are not being *punished* with death but rather are being spared from evil times.

57:2. afterlife of peace and rest. The line is obscure but the sense is that the death of the righteous brings them into a peaceful state. This does not offer a hope of heaven but an escape from turmoil. Even Sheol is to be preferred to the wicked state of affairs on earth.

57:3. sorceress. Sorcery and adultery together point to polytheistic fertility rites. In Mesopotamia sorcery was usually forbidden, however. The Mesopotamians as well as Hittites made a distinction between black (malevolent) magic, performed by a sorcerer/sorceress, and white (benevolent) magic, performed by a legitimate exorcist. Sorcery was punishable by death in the Middle Assyrian Laws. It involved the use of potions, figurines and curses designed to bring death, disease or bad luck to the victim. The Egyptians do not appear to have made a distinction between black and white magic. The few Ugaritic, Aramaic and Phoenician magical texts show that those people appear to have viewed magic and sorcery in a similar way to their Mesopotamian counterparts.

57:5. lust among oaks. Gardens in the ancient Near East were often parks of fruit and shade trees, arboretums serving as outdoor shrines or providing comfortable surroundings for sacred enclosures. Sacred trees played a significant role in the popular religion of the day. These popular beliefs would have viewed stone and tree as potential divine dwellings. In Canaanite religion they are believed to be symbols of fertility (see Deut 12:2; Jer 3:9; Hos 4:13), though there is very little in the archaeological or literary remains of the Canaanites that would clarify the role of sacred trees. It is likely no coincidence that the word for oaks (*'elim*) can also mean "gods." The Canaanite fertility goddess was Asherah, and these trees

(or wooden poles) were her cult symbol. A cult stand from Taanach pictures a sacred tree flanked by lions, as the goddess Asherah is usually pictured. The fertility of the earth was symbolized by the fertile union of humans, cynically described here by Isaiah as "lust among the oaks."

57:5. child sacrifice. The biblical writers attributed child sacrifice to the Phoenician worshipers of Molech (see comments on Lev 18:21 and 2 Chron 28:3). Archaeological discoveries at Carthage (a Phoenician site in north Africa) give evidence of child sacrifice, as hundreds of urns containing the charred remains of infants have been found. Commemorative stelae describe the role of the children as sacrificial victims, referred to in Punic as *mlk* (i.e., Molech) offerings. Outside of Scripture, however, the evidence in Syro-Palestine for child sacrifice is scant. There is a possible reference from the ninth century B.C. from Tell Halaf and from penalty clauses in Late Assyrian juridical contracts.

57:6. smooth stones of ravines. The ravines or wadis were the place where child sacrifices took place, the most notorious being the Hinnom Valley on the west side of Jerusalem. These wadis were the preferred burial place in Israel and therefore also served as the logical choice for the rituals used in the worship of the dead. If "smooth stones" is the correct translation, the text may refer to the rock-cut tombs that were found in these wadis and were so identified with them that the word for wadi can also take the meaning of tomb or grave. An alternate suggestion is based on the identification of this same root (translated "smooth stones") with a root meaning "to die, perish" in a number of Semitic languages closely related to Hebrew. This would then be a reference to the dead who had been buried in the wadis and had become the objects of worship. The cult of the dead is referred to in the latter part of the verse.

57:6. drink offerings, grain offerings. Because of a well-developed ancestor cult that pervaded much of the ancient Near East (evident, for instance, in the emphasis on the role of the male heir to care for the father's shrine in Ugaritic documents), the dead were considered to have some power to affect the living. It was believed that if libations were poured out on behalf of the dead ancestors, their spirits would then offer protection and help to those still living. In Babylon the disembodied spirit (*utukki*) or the ghost (*etemmu*) could become very dangerous if not cared for and often was the object of incantations. Proper care for the dead would begin with proper burial and would continue with ongoing gifts and honor of the memory and name of the deceased. The firstborn was responsible for maintaining this ancestor worship and therefore inherited the family gods (often images of deceased ancestors). Such care would have been based on a belief, as seen in Saul's consultation of the witch of Endor, that the spirits of the dead could communicate and had information on the future that could be of use to the living. These spirits were consulted through the efforts of priests, mediums and necromancers. This could be a dangerous practice since some spirits were considered demons and could cause great harm. While it is difficult to totally reconstruct Israelite beliefs about deceased ancestors and the afterlife, it seems clear that prior to the exile there existed a cult of the dead or ancestral worship. This is evidenced by archaeological remains: (1) standing stones (*maṣṣebot*), (2) channels cut into tombs for the deposit of food and drink offering for the dead (see Deut 26:14; Ps 106:28) and (3) family tombs (note the importance of the ancestral tomb for Abraham and his descendants at Hebron) and mourning rituals performed at these tombs (see Jer 16:5-7). The local and family ancestral cults were condemned by the prophets and the law.

57:7. bed on a hill. The bed on a hill is a probable reference to the Canaanite high places (cf. Jer 2:20) where cultic fornication was committed. Its double meaning of "a place to lie down" also brings out the image of death and the grave.

57:8. fertility symbols. There is no clear indication as to what these symbols were. They may have been symbols of the household gods (fertility figurines?) or phallic symbols of fertility. This latter is likely because the last line of the verse also refers to male genitalia (NIV: "nakedness"). The Israelites also had a memorial behind their door, consisting of a metal container with a portion of Scripture inside (Deut 6:9; 11:20).

57:8. cultic prostitution. Much of the so-called sacred prostitution in the ancient Near East may have been an occasional prostitution for the payment of a vow (see comment on Deut 23:17-18). The texts that describe cultic prostitution from either Canaanite or Mesopotamian sources are ambiguous at best. One can conclude that prostitution was occasionally organized by the temple estates. The Old Testament has ample evidence of feasts that led to sexual excesses, but this does not mean that cultic prostitution was institutionalized in these regions.

57:9. Molech. The Old Testament describes Molech as a Canaanite deity to whom children

were brought for sacrifice. There is literary evidence from the ancient Near East as early as the third millennium B.C. of a god Malik or Milki\u who was worshiped at Ebla and Mari in Syria. He was also worshiped in Assyria and Babylonia, as well as Ugarit (where he was known as *Mlk*). From these texts it appears that Molech was a netherworld deity involved in the cult of dead ancestors. The term Molech is probably related to the Semitic root denoting "king." See the comment on Isaiah 57:6 for the idea that Molech was involved in child sacrifice in Phoenician North Africa (see comment on Lev 18:21).

57:9. olive oil and perfumes. It is not certain what the olive oil and perfumes were used for. The olive oil may have been offerings, while the perfumes were to kindle incense offering. Another suggestion is that they were used to anoint the children that were being offered to Molech.

57:9. ambassadors/descended to Sheol. These ambassadors are those who practice necromancy, the consultation of the dead on behalf of the living. The ambassadors probably went to the shrines where the powers of the netherworld (Sheol) were venerated in order to seek their will by oracular means. Molech was the god of the netherworld.

57:13. collection of idols. In Ugaritic literature the term that occurs here is used to make reference to deceased spirits.

57:14. building highways. See comment on 40:3.

58:1-14
Fasting and Sabbath

58:2. seeking information by oracles. Oracular divination was employed throughout Mesopotamia, Anatolia and Egypt from 2000 B.C. onward to communicate with their deities. Intuitive divination involved oracles, prophecies and dreams. The Mari letters describe the relationship of Dagan to his worshipers, who spoke by way of oracles, dreams, ecstatic possession and oral command. He gave messages to both male and female prophets, as well as commoners. For example, a certain woman named Yanana claimed that Dagan came to her in a dream saying that only Zimri-Lim (the Mariote king) was able to save a kidnapped girl who had been traveling with her.

58:3-7. fasting. Fasting is little attested in the ancient Near East outside the Bible. It generally occurs in the context of mourning. In the Old Testament the religious use of fasting is often in connection with making a request before God. The principle is that the importance of the request causes an individual to be so concerned about his or her spiritual condition that physical necessities fade into the background. In this sense the act of fasting is designed as a process leading to purification and humbling oneself before God (Ps 69:10; 102:4). It is not an end in itself, but rather it is the disciplined training in preparation for an important event.

58:9. pointing the finger. In the ancient world pointing the finger was involved in a formal accusation (as in Hammurabi's laws). The omen literature attaches to the gesture the power of a curse. Here it is indicative of malevolent slander.

58:12. rebuilding ancient ruins. Many ancient cities were rebuilt after having been destroyed. For instance, Babylon was plundered by the Assyrians at least three times; by Tukulti-Ninurta I in the thirteenth century B.C., by Sennacherib in 689 B.C. and by Ashurbanipal in 648 B.C. Each time the ruins of Babylon were rebuilt, often making the city more splendid than before.

58:13. significance of Sabbath. According to later rabbinic writings, the Sabbath in the postexilic period took on the idea of laying aside the day to worship God. The Sabbath became one of the primary means of showing loyalty to God and his statutes. In a Babylonian wisdom hymn the worshiper claims that the day of worshiping the god was a pleasure to him and that it was a delight and joy to make music to honor the deity.

58:13. Sabbath in the ancient Near East. The Sabbath observation has no known parallel in any of the cultures of the ancient Near East and is distinctive in that it is independent of any of the patterns or rhythms of nature. That is, it was not celebrated on certain days of the month and was not linked to the cycles of the moon or to any other cycle of nature; it was simply observed every seventh day. Though Mesopotamians did not divide time into seven-day periods, there were particular days of the month that they considered unlucky and that were often seven days apart (that is, the seventh day of the month, the fourteenth day of the month, etc.). In addition a similar term was used in Babylonian texts as a full moon day when the king officiated at rites of reconciliation with deity, but it was not a work-free day and has little in common with the Israelite Sabbath. The biblical legislation does not require rest as much as it stipulates cessation, interrupting the normal activities of one's occupation.

58:14. riding on the heights. Cities were typically built on hills because of their natural defensi-

bility, and armies chose hills as strategic points of control. The metaphor of treading on the heights is therefore one that speaks of victory and security. As Israel rides the heights, its God rides the clouds. The image of a rampant God storming through the heavens in a cloud chariot is a common one (Ps 68:4; 104:3; Jer 4:13). Such descriptions of storm theophany may also be found in the texts that speak of the Ugaritic god Baal. In both the Aqhat epic and in the Baal and Anat cycle of stories, Baal is referred to as the "Rider of the Clouds." Baal's attributes, commanding the storms, unleashing the lightning and rushing to war as a divine warrior, even appear in the Egyptian El Amarna texts.

59:1-21
Yahweh as Redeemer

59:17. warrior's raiment. Yahweh is here again taking the role of the divine warrior and girding himself for battle. In the divine warrior motif the deity is fighting the battles and defeating the deities of the enemy. In Assyria Nergal is the king of battle, and Ishtar is viewed as a war goddess. The Canaanite Baal and the Babylonian Marduk are both divine warriors. When Marduk prepares for battle with Tiamat in *Enuma Elish,* he is equipped mostly with weapons for attack rather than the defensive gear referred to here. But he is said to be clothed with a cloak of awesome armor and crowned with a terrible radiance. Stone sculptures of the gods doing battle sometimes portray them with breastplate and helmet, but often they have only weapons.

60:1-22
Zion's Glory

60:6. camels from Midian and Ephah. Camels were freight carriers for merchants; thus those who had many camels were considered wealthy. Midian was a nomadic Arabian tribe that had had dealings with Israel from Mosaic times. Ephah is mentioned only two other times in Scripture (Gen 25:4; 1 Chron 1:33) and is associated with Midian, possibly a clan of that tribe. It is also mentioned in the Assyrian annals of Tiglath-Pileser III.

60:6. Sheba. The kingdom of Sheba was a great trading center in southwestern Arabia that exported precious stones, gold and incense. This kingdom is known as Saba in native sources and in the Assyrian annals. It had a very advanced urban civilization in the first millennium B.C. For more information see 2 Chronicles 9:1.

60:7. Kedar. Kedar was a nomadic Arabian

tribe. They were also mentioned in Assyrian and Neo-Babylonian texts. The tribe is mentioned in a text from Tell el-Maskhuta, in apocryphal writings, and even by the Latin writer Pliny the Elder.

60:7. Nebaioth. The Nebaioth were a nomadic tribe also found in the annals of the Assyrian king Ashurbanipal. They are also mentioned in the Taymanite inscriptions, dated to the sixth century B.C. They may have been a precursor to the Nabataeans, an Arabian tribe known in Hellenistic and Roman times.

60:9. ships of Tarshish. The ships of Tarshish were large heavy vessels built for long voyages with high tonnage. Tarshish was thought to have been a Phoenician colony in Spain.

60:13. glory of Lebanon. The "glory" of Lebanon was its cedar forests (see 35:2), but other types of lumber were also exported.

60:16. nursing imagery. The Egyptian kings are often shown in iconographic portraits as being nursed by the gods. For example, the female monarch Hatshepsut is shown suckling at the breasts of Hathor, the bovine goddess of women, dance, drunkenness, sexuality and the dead. She was usually depicted as a woman with the horns of a cow. The image represents being given the finest of care and personal attention.

60:19-20. obsolescence of sun and moon. Both the sun and the moon were important deities in the Babylonian pantheon. The sun god was Shamash, god of justice, and the son of the moon god. As the god of justice, Shamash gave Hammurabi, the Babylonian lawgiver, the authority to make laws. Sin, the moon god, was the lord of the calendar and the god of vegetation. His consort was Ningal, the mother of Shamash. Though his main centers were at Ur and Harran, he played a fundamental role in Babylon during the period of the last Babylonian king, Nabonidus. Since these gods were so central in the religious system of the ancient world, there is no suggestion in other texts that they would become obsolete or cease to function.

61:1-11

Yahweh's Blessings

61:1. freeing prisoners as act of justice. In the ancient Near East the freeing of prisoners (from debtors' prison) as an act of justice often occurred in the first or second year of a new king's reign (and then periodically after that). For example, the Old Babylonian king Ammisaduqa (seventeenth century B.C.) cancelled economic debts on behalf of Shamash. Thus the "jubilee" in this case was primarily concerning those in debt (for either financial or le-

gal reasons) and for the freeing of debt-slaves. Unlike that of Israel this Babylonian edict was entirely at the whim of the monarch, and there is no evidence that it was divinely sanctioned. For an example of this as being accomplished by an ideal king, see comment on 11:1. Historically a proclamation of freedom is recorded by the last king of Judah, Zedekiah (Jer 34:8-10). For these and other characteristics of a just king's reign see comment on 49:9-10.

61:4. rebuilding ancient ruins. See comment on 58:12.

61:10. adorning of bridegroom and bride. The evidence for clothing and grooming in Western Asia relies heavily on iconographic images. It appears that in ancient Israel both the bride and the bridegroom wore ceremonial clothing. The Babylonian and Israelite brides sometimes wore embroidered garments (Ps 45:13-14), a special girdle (Joel 2:32) and a veil (Gen 24:65). Here the groom wears a "garland." The type of special festive clothing probably depended on the economic status of the marriage partners.

62:1-12

Zion's Elevation

62:10. building roads in the ancient Near East. See comment on 40:3.

62:10. banner for the nations. Banners in ancient Israel were used for marking tribes. They appear to have been used most often in military contexts, either to rally troops together or to identify regiments of troops. In this, Israel was most certainly imitating its neighbors. The Assyrians used standards to identify particular regiments of troops.

62:11. reward for return of king from battle. See comment on 40:10.

63:1-19

Judgment on Edom, Loyalty to Israel

63:1. Edom, Bozrah. See comment on 34:5-6.

63:3-6. divine warrior. In the divine warrior motif the deity is fighting the battles and defeating the deities of the enemy. In Assyria Nergal is the king of battle, and Ishtar is viewed as a war goddess. The Canaanite Baal and the Babylonian Marduk are divine warriors (for more information on the divine warrior see comments on Ex 15:3; Josh 3:17; 6:21-24; 10:11; 1 Sam 4:3-4; 7:10). In Assyria it was common rhetoric to speak of cities and countrysides dyed red with the blood of enemies and the army marching through the blood of their enemies. Isaiah 9:5 refers to a practice of warriors rolling their garments in blood. In *Enuma Elish,* after Marduk has defeated Tiamat and her general Kingu, he tramples the battle filth of his enemies, including the lower part of Tiamat's corpse.

64:1-12

Prayer for Yahweh's Deliverance

64:4. difference between Yahweh and other gods. Yahweh was distinct from other gods in the ancient Near East in a number of ways. Most fundamentally Yahweh was transcendent, meaning that he was not subject to or locked within the material universe. This is in stark contrast to the gods of Mesopotamia, who inhabited the material world. He was an only God, without consort or pantheon, unlike the gods of other nations, who shared in a multiplicity of power. The specific issue in this verse is the willingness of God to act on behalf of his faithful followers. The key here is that which motivates Yahweh to action. He does not have to be bribed or coerced into action. In the ancient polytheistic beliefs faithfulness to a deity was expressed in the gifts that were given—gifts that were intended to provide care for the deity (e.g., food). If these gifts did not motivate the kindness or action of the gods, then magical rituals could be used to bind the god or force the sort of action that was desired. See comment on 1 Samuel 15:23.

65:1-25

New Heavens and New Earth

65:3. sacrifices in gardens. Gardens in the ancient Near East were often parks of fruit and shade trees, arboretums serving as outdoor shrines or providing comfortable surroundings for sacred enclosures. Sacred trees played a significant role in popular religion of the day. These popular beliefs would have viewed stone and tree as potential divine dwellings. In Canaanite religion they are believed to be symbols of fertility (see Deut 12:2; Jer 3:9; Hos 4:13), though there is very little in the archaeological or literary remains of the Canaanites that would clarify the role of sacred trees. Excavations at Late Bronze Kition have uncovered a temple that featured a sacred grove with sixty tree pits. These gardens were likely the sacred groves of the Canaanite fertility cult of Asherah.

65:3. brick altars. Most incense altars were made of limestone. This has led to the very plausible suggestion that the word NIV translates "brick" can also mean "incense altars" (as it does in the inscription on a fifth-century limestone altar from Lachish). These were common features on the high places where illegitimate worship took place. Alternatively, there were Babylonian rituals directed toward celestial deities that included sacrifices made on bricks.

65:4. night vigils in graveyards. Many individuals who practiced necromancy (contacting the spirits of the dead, see comment on 57:6) in the ancient Near East spent the night in the graveyards, waiting for communication from the dead. This is similar to incubation rituals (see comments on 1 Sam 3:3 and 2 Chron 1:7-12).

65:4. eating pig meat. Assyrian wisdom literature calls the pig unholy, unfit for the temple and an abomination to the gods. There is also one dream text in which eating pork is a bad omen. Yet it is clear that pork was a regular part of the diet in Mesopotamia. Some Hittite rituals require the sacrifice of a pig. Milgrom observes, however, that in such rituals the pig is not put on the altar as food for the god but absorbs impurity and then is burned or buried as an offering to underworld deities. Likewise in Mesopotamia it was offered as a sacrifice to demons. There is evidence in Egypt of pigs used for food, and Herodotus claims they were used for sacrifice there as well. Egyptian sources speak of herds of swine being kept on temple property, and they were often included in donations to the temples. The pig was especially sacred to the god Seth. Most evidence for the sacrifice of pigs, however, comes from Greece and Rome, there also mostly to gods of the underworld. In urban settings pigs, along with dogs, often scavenged in the streets, making them additionally repulsive. The attitude toward the pig in Israel is very clear here in Isaiah, showing close connection to worship of the dead. It is very possible then that sacrificing a pig was synonymous with sacrificing to demons or the dead.

65:10. Sharon. Sharon was a coastal plain verging on the Judean hill country in the east and the Mediterranean Sea on the west. The valley was known for its beauty, desolation and pastureland. It was about thirty-two miles in length and was on average eleven miles in width.

65:10. Valley of Achor. The Valley of Achor was probably located on Judah's northern border and is identified with the modern El Buqe'ah, a small plain in the northern Judean wilderness in the vicinity of Jericho. Three Iron Age settlements have been uncovered in El Buqe'ah.

65:11. Fortune/Destiny. The proper (divine?) names used here, Gad (NIV: "Fortune") and

Meni (NIV: "Destiny"), are obscure. Gad is attested in Canaanite and Phoenician texts and is considered a good luck deity. Meni may have something to do with portion, and therefore some have thought that it may have had something to do with fate or fortune. It may have been the same as the Arabian goddess Manat mentioned in the Qu'ran. In the Babylonian pantheon the god Namtar ("Destiny") was the vizier of the netherworld. Fate was also at times personified and deified.

65:17-25. utopian visions. Although there is nothing else quite like the utopian visions found in the Bible, there are apocalyptic (futuristic, prophetic) visions found in Akkadian literature of the second and first millennia B.C. The Akkadian texts are pseudo-prophetic, that is, they were predictions composed after the event in question. They appear to have been written to justify a particular event that had taken place or institution that had been created. A typical phrase used is "a prince will arise." The prince is usually anonymous but easily discernible. In one of these, the Marduk Prophecy, Marduk projects a king who will arise and "draw the plans of heaven and earth" in the shrine Ekursagil. He will gather the scattered peoples, bring prosperity to the land and show compassion to the people, and society will function properly. Beyond this, however, in 66:1 it is clear that the heavens and the earth, the cosmos, is God's temple. The creating of new heavens and a new earth may then be equated to the making of new sanctuaries or renewing sanctuaries in the ancient Near East. This was a very common activity. The New Jerusalem is the new capital city, which also represents God's chosen dwelling place. Similarly Marduk orders that the new holy city of the gods, Babylon, will be rebuilt.

66:1-24

Peace Like a River

66:1. house for deity. In the Ugaritic Baal Cycle Baal wants to build a house for himself so that he will have a resting place. Likewise Ningirsu makes a request that Gudea build a house for his repose. The former is more pertinent here because Baal is building the house for himself, just as Yahweh has done. In *Enuma Elish,* after Marduk has defeated the enemy Tiamat, he proclaims that he will make a house for himself, which he names Babylon, that will serve as a resting place for the gods. At the end of tablet five a somewhat broken section relates this to Marduk's creating of the

earth and his authority over it.

66:3. breaking dog's neck. The dog was not a sacrificial animal in Israel, although it was used in this manner in Hittite Anatolia.

66:3. pig's blood. Pigs and dogs figured prominently in the rituals of the Hittites in Anatolia in the Late Bronze Age. When confronted with a ritual impurity, the Hittites often slaughtered a pig (usually by cutting it in half). Pigs and dogs were particularly prominent in worship of chthonic deities (those having to do with the netherworld or the fertility of the land). For more information see comments on 56:10-11 and 65:4. Some have suggested that the treatment of the pig in this type of ritual may have been one reason why the pig was considered unclean.

66:15. fire, chariots, whirlwind. In the ancient Near Eastern imagery major deities are at times accompanied by charioteers. There is a deity known as Rakib-El, who is the charioteer of the Canaanite god El. In Akkadian literature Bunene, the advisor to the sun god Shamash, is designated the charioteer. The charioteer would be responsible for transporting the deity, especially into battle. In Israelite religious belief Yahweh is sometimes portrayed or manifested in ways familiar to ancient Near Eastern thought. For instance, in Elijah's contest with the Baal prophets, Yahweh is shown to be a God who controls fertility and responds with fire, and figurative language often associates him with the sun (Ps 84:11). Here his portrayal may share elements with Hadad, the storm god who is accompanied by a charioteer. These similarities suggest the possibility that familiar imagery was being used to clarify the involvement of deity in this unprecedented event.

66:17. rituals in gardens. See comment on 65:3.

66:17. eating flesh of pigs and rats. This is another description of foreign rites, probably of Canaanite origin (see comment on Lev 11:7). There is no extrabiblical evidence illuminating this custom. The word translated "rat" here can refer to a wide variety of small rodents.

66:19. Tarshish. Tarshish represented the farthest land across the sea to the west. See comment on 23:1.

66:19. Libyans. Here Libya is a translation of "Put," but in Nahum 3:9 the two are different entities. Ancient Libya was mostly along the coast west of Alexandria but included the long expanse of desert west of the Nile Valley. Put is more difficult. The most likely conclusion is that Put is an alternative name for Libya and that together they refer to the area to the west of ancient Egypt represented by the modern state of Libya. This was the most distant land across land to the southwest.

66:19. Lydians. Lud was probably the area of Lydia in west central Turkey. The Lydians spoke an Anatolian language similar to Hittite. They carved out a large empire in Turkey during the sixth century B.C. but were defeated and conquered by Cyrus of Persia. This was the most distant land across land to the northwest.

66:19. Tubal. Tubal was probably an area south of the Black Sea. It is mentioned in the Assyrian annals as Tabal and in the *Histories* of Herodotus as Tiberanoi. It represented the most distant land to the northeast.

66:19. Greece. *Javan* probably represents the Greek name Ionia, the Greek region of the western coast of Turkey and the Aegean islands. Ionian Greeks settled this area just before the first millennium B.C. There is evidence of contact between them and the Assyrians by the eighth century B.C. Classical Greek literature (e.g., Homer) and philosophy appear to have begun in Ionia.

JEREMIAH

1:1-19

Jeremiah's Call

1:1. Anathoth. The precise location of Anathoth, a priestly city in Benjamin, has long been debated. It was either located on the high mound of Ras el-Kharrubeh just south of the village of Anata or in the valley adjacent to Anata (the Jewish historian Josephus identified Anathoth with Anata). The most recent idea is that Ras el-Kharrubeh was initially Anathoth, but the city relocated to Anata after the Babylonian exile of the late sixth century B.C. The archaeological record appears to confirm this. The city is first mentioned as the home of some of the bodyguards of David, and later Abiathar the priest was exiled there. According to Isaiah 10:30 the city was on the route of the Assyrian invasion of Palestine, but it was not destroyed.

1:2. chronology. Jeremiah's ministry began in the thirteenth year of Josiah's reign (c. 627 B.C.) and continued until the eleventh year of Zedekiah and the second deportation (c. 587 B.C.). He was apparently active for a few years after the exile (see 42—44). The initial year was a significant one in that it was just one year after the beginning of Josiah's reform activity and one year before Babylon's declaration of independence from Assyria. Both the political world and the religious world were about to see dramatic changes.

1:2. Josiah. During the early years of Jeremiah's ministry Josiah was king of Judah (640-609 B.C.). The Book of the Law (an unidentified portion of Scripture) was found early in his reign, after which Josiah enacted many religious and cultural reforms. He may have seized this opportunity because of a catastrophic civil war in Assyria (c. 631-626 B.C.). When the Assyrian empire began to collapse a decade later, Josiah sided against their Egyptian allies and was either killed in battle or murdered at Megiddo in 609 B.C.

1:3. Jehoiakim. Jehoiakim was placed on the throne of Judah by the Egyptians, who had rushed into the vulnerable area of Palestine after the end of the Assyrian empire (c. 608 B.C.). His given name was Eliakim, but the Egyptians changed it to Jehoiakim. He was a vassal to Egypt until 605 when the Babylonians under Nebuchadnezzar II defeated Egypt at Carchemish and subsequently took control of the Levant. Because of the Babylonian setback on the border of Egypt four years later, Jehoiakim rebelled against them and once again sided with Egypt. However, Jehoiakim suffered reprisal when the Babylonians captured Jerusalem in 598/7, and he was either killed or deported (the Jewish historian Josephus states that Nebuchadnezzar killed him in Jerusalem).

1:3. chronology. Jeremiah continued his ministry until the eleventh year of Zedekiah (c. 587 B.C.).

1:3. exile. Jeremiah was evidently active after the second deportation in 587 B.C. (see 42—44). The Babylonians exiled the leading citizens of the land. Excavations in the Shephelah, Negev and Judean desert show signs of the Babylonian destruction. Babylonian sources describe the siege of Jerusalem and the deportation of many prisoners to Babylon.

1:5. ancient Near Eastern examples of deity knowing and electing before birth. There is an Egyptian parallel to the idea of the deity knowing an individual before birth. The god Amon knew Pianki (an Egyptian monarch of the Twenty-Fifth Dynasty in the eighth century B.C.) while he "was in the belly of his mother," where he knew he was to be the ruler of Egypt. In the Gilgamesh Epic, Gilgamesh's role as king was said to be destined for him "when his umbilical cord was severed."

1:5. prophet to the nations. The term translated "nations," when used in the plural, usually signifies foreign nations. Thus there were no limits to the scope of Jeremiah's prophetic ministry. His messages were not only to Judah but also to the nations who would be potential allies, as well as those who would be enemies.

1:9. hand on mouth as commissioning in ancient Near East. Royal mouth purification rites in Egypt show the idea of preparing the mouth for utterance. Mesopotamian rituals often featured the purification of lips as symbolic of the purification of the person. It is viewed as a prerequisite, especially for diviner priests, before they may appear before the divine council and report back on what they have witnessed. In contrast Yahweh put words in the mouth of his prophet, with no ritual purification.

1:11. almond tree. The almond tree reached a height of fifteen to thirty feet. It was the first tree to bloom in late January/early February. The almond flower is white with shades of pink, ripening with almonds about ten weeks later.

1:14-15. northern kingdoms. This is either a reference to Babylon or Scythia or an echo of a future where all nations come up against Jerusalem (see Ezek 38—39; Joel 3; Zech 12—14). The north was often a symbol of dark powers, such as the Philistines, Assyrians and Arameans. Enemies often had little choice but to come at Jerusalem from the north, because of the way the major routes went. As early as 627, there was little evidence that Babylon had the ability to launch an invasion in the Levant. The Scythians, however, did invade western Asia at this time, according to the Greek historian Herodotus.

1:15. thrones in gateway. The gateway was the usual site for a king to publicly perform his duties. It could have been used for ceremonial or diplomatic occasions or legal proceedings. The Ugaritic Epic of Aqhat describes King Danil sitting in the gate area judging the cases of widows and orphans. A conquering king would take his seat on this public throne in the gateway in order to pass judgment on a city and its leaders. Recent excavations at Tel Dan have revealed what appears to be a stone platform set inside the gate area, which once

was canopied and may have held a throne.

1:16. purpose of burning incense. Incense was a mixture of spices that made a pleasant fragrance when burned. Offerings of incense were common throughout the Near East and Israel. They were used in conjunction with sacrifice (see comment on 44:18). One of the more luxurious spices was frankincense (a white gum resin) which came from Sheba in south Arabia. Excavations have produced a large variety of incense altars throughout Israel, including two at Arad and ten at Miqne/Ekron.

1:18. iron pillar metaphor/bronze wall metaphor. Iron and bronze were symbolic of strength in many biblical passages (see comment on Is 45:2). Bronze gates built by the Assyrians have been found at Balawat. They were a decorative feature on strong walls. Thutmose III of Egypt described himself as a wall of iron and bronze for Egypt, meaning that he was like an impregnable fortress city.

2:1—3:5

Israel's Abandonment of God

2:8. prophesied by Baal, following idols. Despite the reforms of Hezekiah and Josiah, the people of Judah often reverted back to religious syncretism, performing the rituals and worshiping the deities of Canaan. The prophets who were associated with this syncretism would offer messages from Baal in his name and would ask for oracles before the idols of Baal.

2:10. coasts of Kittim. Kittim is mentioned in the table of nations (Gen 10) as a descendent of Javan (Greek, Ionia), who is associated with the Aegean and eastern Mediterranean. Kittim is probably the Hebrew term for Kition, near modern Lanarca on the south central coast of Cyprus, but most likely referred to the whole island. It was a Bronze Age site. In the period of Jeremiah, the term Kittim most likely denoted Greece or in general a faraway place. Ostraca from Arad in the seventh century B.C. mention individuals from Kittim who have Greek names. These were probably Cypriot traders.

2:10. Kedar. Kedar, the second son of Ishmael (Gen 25:13), was the name of an Ishmaelite tribe that flourished from the eighth to the fourth centuries B.C. The tribe is known from Assyrian and Late Babylonian texts as Qadar. The personal names of the Kedarites appear to have been related to the southern branch of the Semitic languages. These tribal peoples were based in the Arabian peninsula and often made their way into the Levant via the Sinai. The Kedarites inhabited the eastern wilderness, while the Kittim inhabited the western reaches of the sea.

2:11. nations changing gods in the Near East. Because of the infiltration of foreign elements, many nations added gods to their pantheon. Moreover, the names of gods endured slight alterations as time went on. But the concept of a nation exchanging its god(s) for others was a foreign idea in the ancient Near East. The verb possibly carries the idea of "barter" in which case it does not refer to simply a change but to trading for something of greater value.

2:13. broken cisterns. Cisterns were often built in hills made of limestone. An individual had to plaster the inside with lime plaster and direct rainwater into it. But these cisterns often developed cracks, and water would seep out, with the farmer losing a life-giving commodity.

2:15. lion metaphor. This probably represents the Assyrians who, like lions, devoured cities and lands. Any number of Assyrian military campaigns are being alluded to here. The Assyrians had winged human-headed lions at the gates of many of their cities.

2:15. burned towns. This refers to specific campaigns of a number of Assyrian rulers who came into the Levant, including Tiglath-Pileser III (745-727 B.C.), Shalmaneser V (727-722 B.C.), Sargon II (721-705 B.C.), Sennacherib (705-681 B.C.) and Esarhaddon (681-668 B.C.). Since the Assyrians had no intention of occupying these towns, their practice was to burn them in order to warn against the cost of noncooperation.

2:16. Memphis. Memphis was the residence of the early Egyptian kings. Many Judeans (as well as Phoenicians, according to Herodotus) fled there during the Babylonian invasion of 587 B.C. It is identified with the modern site of Mitrahineh, about fifteen miles south of Cairo, on the west bank of the Nile. The city had been in decline since about 1000 B.C. However, it was restored by the Twenty-Fifth Dynasty and became the primary residence of the Egyptian kings in the seventh century B.C. It was most likely also the residence of the kings of the Twenty-Sixth Dynasty. For more information see comment on 46:19.

2:16. Tahpanhes. Tahpanhes was an outpost in the eastern Delta region of the Nile, bordering the Sinai. It was known as Daphne by the Greeks, who inhabited the outpost as mercenaries by the seventh century B.C. The Greek historian Herodotus states that Daphne was one of three outposts set up by the Egyptians to stop the Assyrian invasion. The Jews in flight from the Babylonians may have stopped

there in the early sixth century B.C.

2:16. shaved head. A shaved head in the ancient Near East usually (but not always) denoted a slave or a subordinate. However, the Hebrew term used here "to shave" is problematic and there is little agreement on its meaning.

2:18. Shihor. Shihor is probably the Hebrew name for "waters of Horus," the falcon deity of Egypt. Although it was probably a body of water in the northeast Delta region of the Nile, its location is uncertain. Some have associated it with the Brook of Egypt, the first body of water seen traveling south into Egypt from Palestine.

2:18. the River. In Scripture the Euphrates River is often referred to as the River.

2:20. high hill and spreading tree as place of prostitution. Part of the fertility rites of local Canaanite sanctuaries were carried out on hilltops in connection with various sorts of trees (including oaks, poplars and terebinths). The sexual rituals dedicated to gods of fertility are also mentioned in Hosea 4:13. Asherah is pictured in Israelite iconography as a stylized tree.

2:22. soda, soap. The term translated "soda" refers to a sodium carbonate byproduct, most likely imported from Egypt. Soap was made from the ashes of a local plant.

2:23. Baals. The employment of the plural Baals refers to the many cult centers of Baal in Canaanite practice. In other words, there was a Baal for each city (e.g., Tyre, Sidon and Gad). A number of place names in the Old Testament contain the element Baal (e.g., Baal-Zephon and Baal-Peor). It is presumed that they mean "Baal of Peor," or "Baal of Zephon." Baal, which means "lord," occurs as a divine name as early as the eighteenth century B.C. in Amorite personal names from Mari. Some would offer examples as early as the late third millennium. By the fourteenth century the title was used by Egyptians to refer to the storm god. The name is also evident in texts from Alalakh, Amarna and Ugarit as the personal name of the storm god Adad. Baal was a fertility deity and was a dying (winter) and rising (spring) god. In the mythology of Ugarit he is pictured in combat with Yamm (the sea) and Mot (death). His consorts are Anat and Astarte.

2:23-24. camel/donkey metaphor. Young female camels are not at all reliable creatures and nervously wander around in a disorderly fashion. The female donkey, when in heat, becomes almost violent and chases after the male donkey, just as Israel, like the wild female donkey, chases after the Baals.

2:27. wood-father, stone mother. In this case the tree was an image of Asherah, a female deity, and the male symbol is that which "gave me birth." Thus the Israelites are completely confused as to their worship. It is difficult to determine whether the text is referring generally to polytheistic worship or specifically to fertility symbols.

2:28. as many gods as towns. The various pantheons of most ancient Near Eastern peoples included hundreds and sometimes even thousands of deities. Jeremiah is claiming that the Judeans are no different from their polytheistic counterparts. It was also common practice for towns to have patron deities, so that gods could multiply as towns developed.

2:32. jewelry. The term for jewelry here is translated elsewhere as "jewels," but here it probably denotes the bridal attire or a specific item that was unique to the bride. See comment on Ezekiel 16:11-12 for description of the ornaments.

2:36. disappointed by Egypt and Assyria. It is not certain whether Jeremiah is referring to specific events or to these nations in general. By at least 732 B.C. both Judah and Israel entered into a vassal relationship with Assyria. However, in the end Assyria did not protect its vassals but destroyed them, as they did to Israel in 721 B.C. and to Judah in 701 B.C. Egypt, however, had been unable to protect its vassals against the power of Assyria or other West Asiatic kingdoms. In the end then, neither kingdom provided the safety or security that Judah was looking for.

2:37. hands on head. The "hands on the head" gesture was a sign of grief in the ancient Near East. It has been illustrated by the mourning female figures on the Phoenician sarcophagus of Ahiram, thirteenth-century king of Byblos. The Egyptian Tale of Two Brothers also describes this gesture as an indication of mourning.

3:1. divorce legislation. There are numerous texts from both Mesopotamia and Egypt that describe divorce legislation. Although the laws were usually in favor of men, in both cultures women were allowed, under certain stipulations, to obtain a divorce. Jeremiah in this context is referring to the one specific piece of divorce legislation in the Old Testament, Deuteronomy 24:1-4, which states that a man may not remarry his ex-wife if she has been married to another man in the interim. Thus, the answer to Jeremiah's query is no, a man may not remarry her.

3:3. spring rains. The two kinds of rains described here are the showers, which usually fell in March, and the late rains of spring,

normally falling in April.

3:6—4:4
Faithless Israel Called to Return

3:6. worship practices. See comment on 2:20.

3:8. certificate of divorce. Divorce certificates were well known in the ancient Near East. In fact, even a royal certificate of divorce written on a clay tablet from Ugarit in the Late Bronze Age has been found. Scores of texts describing divorce legislation have been found in cuneiform texts from Mesopotamia and in papyri from Egypt.

3:9. adultery with stone and wood. Committing adultery with stone and wood refers to the "spiritual adultery" of following after the Asherim (the sacred trees, i.e., wood) and the Baals (stone).

4:4. metaphor of heart circumcision. Circumcision was not unique to Israel, as iconographic evidence has been found in Egypt. But the meaning behind it was unique, as it was a sign that the people of Israel belonged to Yahweh. Regular circumcision symbolically put the organ of generation under the control of Yahweh as a reminder of his covenant promise to make Israel a great nation. The concept of circumcision of the heart symbolically put the organ of the will under the control of Yahweh as a recognition of the obligation to the law.

4:5-31
Enemy from the North

4:5. major fortified cities of Judah. According to Sennacherib, king of Assyria (r. 705-681 B.C.), Judah had forty-six strong cities (i.e., walled towns), which he had overrun, and countless small cities or villages. There were thus a number of cities with major defensive systems. The defensive system at Lachish, one of the primary fortresses in Judah, has been extensively excavated in this century. It contained two layers of city walls and strong towers.

4:6. nature of signal. The blowing of the horn announced a state of emergency (see Amos 3:6). On hearing it citizens who lived in villages or were out farming fled into the confines of the walled city. In this case the trumpet was blown throughout the entire land because of a national emergency.

4:6. army from north. see comment on 1:14-15.

4:8. sackcloth. Sackcloth was a black coarse linen garment (usually goat's wool) worn by mourners in time of sorrow (death of a loved one) or great disaster. It was also used by Palestinian shepherds because it was cheap and durable.

4:11. wind to winnow or cleanse. The hot wind from the desert was most likely the sirocco, a wind that was too strong for winnowing the grain on the threshing floor, as it carried away both the grain and the chaff. The metaphor is thus clear; God's judgment will be like the hot wind, engulfing both the good and the bad. The word translated "cleanse" here is used in the Dead Sea Scrolls to refer to the separating of the grain and most likely has that connection here as well.

4:15. announcement from Dan. The city of Dan (modern Tel el-Qadi) was at the northern limit of Israel. Excavations have shown that it was a substantial city during the time of Jeremiah. This city would have noticed the northern invaders first. Thus a messenger from Dan would run southward, "causing all Israel to hear" the bad report.

4:15. hills of Ephraim. From Dan the invader descends the Golan Heights until reaching the hills of Ephraim, the mountainous region in the center of the former northern kingdom, reaching from Shechem to Bethel.

4:23-26. world upside-down motif. Jeremiah has taken his imagery from the creation account in Genesis 1:2. He describes in poetic imagery the reversion of creation back to its chaotic stage before God had done his work. The Babylonian *Myth of Erra and Ishum* is roughly similar in that it describes a reversal of Marduk's creation of order out of the original primeval chaos. In the world upside-down motif all that is considered most consistent and reliable is jeopardized. The concept can be applied to the cosmic realm (sun growing dark), the natural realm (mountains being leveled), the political realm (empires overthrown), the social realm (poor becoming rich) or the animal realm (lion and lamb together). It is often used in prophetic literature in connection with the Day of the Lord and coming judgment.

4:28. heavens growing dark (eclipse). In this poetic imagery the earth is personified (as are many inanimate objects in Hebrew) as if it is in mourning and "turning black" or "growing dark." It is not necessary to assume that Jeremiah is attempting to describe a heavenly phenomena, such as an eclipse, though that could be described in similar terms.

4:30. dressing in scarlet/eye paint. Scarlet clothing represented the most exquisite finery for a woman. The dye for this color was made from the eggs of an insect that were collected from oak leaves. The eye paint (antimony) was used (and is still used in the modern Middle East) to make the eyes look larger and thus enhance one's beauty. Neither of these were specifically associated with prostitutes but were simply used when a woman wished to be her most attractive.

5:1-31

Israel's Falsehood

5:1. comparison to Diogenes. Somewhat like Diogenes, the Greek Cynic philosopher of the fourth century B.C., the people of Judah are asked to traverse the city and search for an honest (or in this case, a just) man. The comparison to Diogenes ends, as the Judeans are searching for someone that acts justly and is faithful to Yahweh. Diogenes was looking for someone who conformed to his secular idea of justice, an idea not necessarily attached to a deity.

5:6. how common were predator attacks? Lions and other predators were much more common in the Middle East than they are today. An attack by a predator was not considered a rare or surprising occurrence. Thus the Judeans would have been well acquainted with this metaphor.

5:8. stallion metaphor. Stallions were known for their powerful sexual proclivity and mindless obedience to their instincts. In much the same way the people of Judah pursued their promiscuity, whether that was their spiritual adultery or their participation in the sexual aspects of the fertility cult.

5:12-13. prophets proclaiming peace. Certainly a prophet who offered the people the hope of peace, security and resolution of the problem would be popular. Denial is the path of least resistance. There would likewise be no shortage of prophets who saw personal gain in supporting the desires of the throne on these matters and were therefore willing to represent the best interests of the king and whatever propaganda he desired to circulate. The literal term for these prophets is that they "will become wind": in other words, they will be like old windbags whose words do not have any value.

5:24. autumn and spring rains. The autumn and spring rains were simply called the "former and latter" rains. Israel has a rainy season (winter months) and a dry season (summer months). The rainy season begins with the autumn rains ("early rains," October-November) and ends with the spring rains ("latter rains," early April). These are important for what they contribute to the overall moisture levels in the earth and for softening the ground for plowing. Baal was considered the lord over nature who controlled the rains in the Canaanite cults of Palestine. However, Jeremiah argues that it is Yahweh who should be worshiped as the giver of rains in their proper season.

6:1-30
Siege of Jerusalem by the Army from the North

6:1. Tekoa. Tekoa (Khirbit Tequa) was a town in the highlands of Judah ten miles south of Jerusalem on the border of arable land and desert. A refugee from Jerusalem was able to reach the city within one day.

6:1. Beth Hakkerem. Beth Hakkerem was associated with Tekoa and Bethlehem, but its precise location is uncertain. The early church father Jerome stated that it could be seen from Bethlehem, and thus it has been tentatively identified with 'Ain Karim, four miles west of Jerusalem, or Ramath Rahel, two and a half miles south of Jerusalem, which would have been ideal for a signal location.

6:6. siege ramps. The ancients were notorious for their inability to conduct siege warfare. The construction of a siege ramp was a useful tool but very precarious, as the city defenders made every attempt to thwart its progress. It was normally made as a sloping ramp, built with a foundation of trees and large stones and mixed with earth and other elements at hand. Numerous wall reliefs from Assyria depict Assyrian siege ramps employed throughout the Near East. Moreover, remains of an Assyrian siege ramp have been uncovered at the Judean city of Lachish (for more information see comment on 32:24), where the Assyrians were successful in capturing and destroying the fortress city.

6:20. incense from Sheba. One of the more luxurious spices used for incense was frankincense (a white gum resin) which came from Sheba in south Arabia, a center of the spice trade. Incense accompanied sacrificial offerings (see comment on Lev 2:1).

6:20. sweet calamus. Sweet calamus (or aromatic spice cane) most likely originated from India. It was among the ingredients listed in the anointing oil in Exodus 30:23. It was a marsh plant that was used as a tonic and stimulant. It is not to be confused with sugar cane, which spread east after the Old Testament period.

6:23. cavalry units in seventh century. Chariot and cavalry warfare in the seventh century B.C. were primarily used as shock weapons. However, with the reforms of Tiglath-Pileser III of Assyria (r. 745-727 B.C.), horses and chariots also played the role of light artillery, as arrows were shot from the horse-drawn chariots. Later a heavier chariot with four men appeared with Ashurbanipal (r. 668-627 B.C.). Cavalry (exclusive of chariotry) was developed in Urartu (biblical Ararat), which furnished up to a thousand specialized units to the Assyrian army by the time of Sargon II (r. 721-705 B.C.). Stud farms were created in various points of the empire, especially in Syria and in the Assyrian capitals. This cavalry tradition was inherited in its entirety by the Chaldeans in the late seventh century B.C. For more information see comment on Habakkuk 1:8.

6:26. rolling in ashes. Rolling or groveling in the dust or sprinkling ashes on oneself was a sign of mourning in the ancient Near East.

6:27. metal assayers. The assayer/refiner here was a metallurgist whose duty was to assess the quality of the ore. It was then refined by stripping it of its impure elements. However, if there were a great deal of impurities in the metal, the item was totally discarded.

6:28. bronze, iron metaphor. In the ancient world silver was extracted and assayed through a process called cupellation. In the initial smelting process silver was extracted from lead ores (galena) containing less than 1 percent silver in a given sample. The lead was melted in shallow vessels made of porous substances such as bone ash or clay. A bellows was then used to blow air across the molten lead producing lead oxide (litharge). Some of the lead oxide was absorbed by the bone ash, while some could be skimmed off the surface. Ideally the silver would remain. Unfortunately this process had many potential problems. If the temperature was too high, or if the sample contained other metals (iron, copper or tin were common), the cupellation would be unsuccessful. In this situation, when the litharge was skimmed off, rather than resulting in silver extraction, what remained was tainted silver mixed with other metals and therefore unusable. This unusable product is perhaps what is referred to in the translation as "dross." Another possibility is that the text refers to the assaying process. This involved heating a sample of silver together with large amounts of lead in order to draw off the impurities. One of the possible results of the assaying process was that the quantity of lead would be insufficient to draw off the impurities rendering the silver useless. Rather than being purified, then, the silver would be in worse shape than before the process. Perhaps this process is envisioned by the text, and the silver becomes this useless junk.

7:1-29

Sermon in the Temple Court

7:2. proclamations at the temple gate. Proclamations were typically made at public places where a lot of traffic could be expected. Gateways were hubs of activity in the ancient city. The temple gateway would receive all the traffic of those doing business at the temple, including anyone who was bringing a sacrifice. This is the target audience for Jeremiah's proclamation.

7:2. nature of worship. The two terms in Hebrew that are used for worship signify "service" and "prostration" (reverence). The latter is used here and usually represents an act of humility, often associated with petition. The temple was primarily a state sanctuary and thus was part of the royal estate. The temple was the "house of God" and was his residence. It was not intended as a place of corporate worship, and worshipers were admitted into the temple courts but not into the temple itself. Sacrificial rituals were done in the courts and elsewhere. Though there are many texts describing temples in the ancient Near East, none describe in any detail the nature of the individual's worship within the walls of the temple. We know that worshipers were given dreams by the deity (e.g., at Mari) when viewing its image, but actual entry into the temple must have been rare.

7:4. temple ideology. The people in this context had come to believe that the temple was so important to God that the people were also secure. In the ancient Near East the entire city was considered protected by the city deity. In these terms Jerusalem was considered inviolable because of housing the temple and thereby God. This was certainly enhanced by the salvation of Jerusalem during the reign of Hezekiah a century earlier. In a similar way temples in ancient Western Asia were described as the "house of god." The most righteous of kings was the one who kept the god's house in order and did constant rebuilding on it. The god dwelt in the temple, just as the king and people dwelt in their own houses. The temple had to be kept up in much the same way the image of the deity had to be fed and clothed daily. These were the needs of the gods. The deity "needed" a house, so it was believed that he would protect that house and the city that provided for his housing. The Israelites, thinking too much like their neighbors, had come to think the same way about their God and his temple, converting it to a protective talisman.

7:6. vulnerable people in ancient Near East- ern law. Mosaic Law had a profound concern for human welfare, especially for historical reasons. Since the Israelites had been slaves in Egypt, they were to be sensitive to the needs of slaves, widows, orphans and other vulnerable people. There are numerous legal texts in Mesopotamia concerning dealings with unfortunates such as widows, orphans and foundlings. However, these texts usually dealt with their legal rights (or lack thereof) and not with their care. For example, widows in the Neo-Babylonian period were under the legal protection of their father, brother or brother-in-law. Those who were financially independent after their husband's death were not legally considered widows, however, and thus were not in need of a protective ward. For more information see comment on Exodus 22:22-24.

7:9. ethics and religious responsibility. The religions practiced by Israel's neighbors would have expected ethical behavior from people but perhaps with a slightly different logic behind it. In Babylon, for instance, Shamash the sun god was the god of justice. Shamash was responsible for insuring that justice was maintained in the world because justice was a part of the order that was the fabric of the cosmos. In much the same way, a shop proprietor might require honesty from his employees because he knows that will contribute to the success of his business. He himself may not be honest at all. In Israel it was not the smooth operation of the cosmos that motivated Yahweh to insist on moral behavior. The law grew out of his character, and the holiness that he required was a reflection of him.

7:10. house bearing the name. The temple is where God chose to set his name or in other words, where he laid his legal claim and thus was his personal property. The temple in the ancient Near East was considered the private residence of the deity and thus his private property. The king was merely the caretaker of the building and responsible for its upkeep.

7:10. temple as providing sanctuary. In Mesopotamia and Israel the temple provided sanctuary because the deity resided there and thus the worshiper had greater access to the god's protection. Unlike in ancient Greece, however, there was no special law of sanctuary for an individual just because they were in the confines of the temple property.

7:12. Shiloh. Shiloh (modern Khirbit Seilun), in the heart of the Ephraimite hills, was the site where Israel convened sacred assemblies before using Jerusalem. Excavations have exposed extensive architecture by the eleventh century B.C. The site lasted throughout the

Iron Age, but the sacred structures were most likely in ruins by Jeremiah's time. It is thought to have been overrun by the Philistines in the aftermath of the victory at the Battle of Aphek (1 Sam 4).

7:18. cakes for the Queen of Heaven. The term for cakes described here is a loanword from Akkadian. The Babylonians used sweetened cakes in the cult of the goddess Ishtar. It is possible that the Queen of Heaven here is Ishtar as well, but some evidence points to an unnamed mother-goddess or to Asherah. The cakes were baked directly on the embers of the fire and not in an oven. As described in this passage, the entire family took part in the cult rituals. Offering cakes to deities was very common in Babylonia. Forty-seven molds for cakes representing a goddess (some female-shaped, some star-shaped) were found in an early second millennium B.C. royal kitchen at Mari in northeast Syria.

7:18. drink offerings. Drink offerings were common in Israel, but the phrase used here, "pour out libations," normally refers to offerings that are described elsewhere as offered to other gods on the roofs of houses (see comment on 32:29), suggesting astral worship.

7:20. anger against beasts, trees, produce. The parallel between "man and beast" is common in Scripture (for instance, Ex 8:13-14). However, the addition of trees and produce is not seen elsewhere. When Enlil, the king of the gods in Mesopotamia, brought on the flood, it was leashed on all flesh indiscriminately. The Babylonian *Myth of Erra and Ishum* also describes devastation that took both humans and animals. On the other hand, warfare tactics often targeted the produce and the trees. Trees were chopped down for the needs of the besieging army or simply as punitive deforestation. Produce was used to supply the army, trampled underfoot or intentionally destroyed in order to cripple the economy.

7:21. eating the meat of burnt offerings. Since the burnt offering was entirely consumed on the altar, it was supposedly unavailable as food for worshipers. However, since God had no intention of listening to the petitions that accompanied the burnt offering, they might just as well have eaten the meat themselves.

7:29. cutting off hair and throwing it away. The cutting of the hair was normally a gesture of mourning. However, the object of the verb here is often used for the consecration of priests and Nazirites, who took a vow not to cut their hair. Thus, Yahweh is ironically commanding the people to cut their consecrated

hair, for their vows will accomplish nothing.

7:30—8:3
Death in the Hinnom Valley

7:31. high places of Topheth in the valley of Hinnom. "Topheth" was the cultic installation where children were offered to the god Molech. The word is thought to signify the hearth where the child was placed. The Hebrew term has parallel terms in both Ugaritic and Aramaic with the meaning "furnace or fireplace." Scholars have thought that Topheth was at the edge of the valley of Ben Hinnom before connecting with the Kidron Valley. The valley of Ben Hinnom has been identified with Wadi er-Rahabi southwest of the City of David. Many consider Molech to have been a netherworld deity whose rituals had Canaanite origins and focused on dead ancestors. An eighth-century B.C. Phoenician inscription speaks of sacrifices made to Molech before battle by the Cilicians and their enemies. The name Molech appears to be related to the Hebrew term *mlk* ("to rule"). Sacrifices to Molech were done at the installation of Baal, which may mean that the term was an epithet of Baal himself, as well as other deities (32:35).

7:31. burn sons and daughters in the fire. Evidence for this practice outside of Scripture is rare indeed. Assyrian legal texts describe a penalty clause as "he will burn his son to Sin (a lunar deity) and his daughter to Belet-seri." Also see the comment on 2 Chronicles 28:3.

8:2. exposure of bones. Bones in tombs were considered sacred. The bridge between life and death in the ancient Near East was different from ours. Individuals were understood to have a consciousness after death as long as their bodies (i.e., bones) still existed and had been buried properly. Often the desecration of graves was not merely to retrieve treasure but to disturb the bones of the dead. Ashurbanipal, king of Assyria, attacked the Elamite capital of Susa and carried off the bones of the dead with the purpose of "imposing restlessness upon their spirits and depriving them of food offerings and libations." Cults of the dead abounded throughout the Near East. In Israel the bodies of the dead were also treated carefully; disturbing tombs was looked on with horror. One is reminded that both Jacob and Joseph desired that their bones be taken to the Promised Land when the Israelites returned there.

8:2. astral worship. The "host of heaven" (NIV: "stars") was the celestial army that was made up of the planets and stars that were inhabited by divine spirits who were in control of human destiny. The Babylonians were experts in the discipline of astral divination, attempting to predict and control fate by the use of omina by examining the stars. Modern astrology has its roots in Babylonia of the Hellenistic period (after 331 B.C.), centuries after Jeremiah. Israelite stamp seals of the seventh century show that astral symbols for deity were very popular in this period. For more information see comments on Deuteronomy 4:19; 17:3; 2 Kings 23:4; 2 Chronicles 33:5.

8:4—9:26
Punishment Coming

8:7. bird migration metaphor. Though the exact identification of the birds mentioned here is uncertain, it is clear that they obey Yahweh's will (by migrating to the right place at the right time), while his children do not.

8:14. poisoned water metaphor. It was crucial for a city under siege to have access to a protected water supply. If the supply was poisoned, the city became literally defenseless and was obliged to surrender to its attackers. This then is a metaphor for shortening the siege.

8:16. Dan as direction of attack. See the comment on 4:15.

8:17. snakes in Palestine. The snakes here are most likely a metaphor for the Chaldean army. The snakes described in Scripture appear to have been of the poisonous variety, although no particular species can be determined. Isaiah 11:8 describes the "hole of the asp," and commentators have suggested that the cobra is being described, since they typically live in holes. Other poisonous snakes were probably the carpet viper (known for its striking without provocation) and the desert viper.

8:17. charmed vipers. Snakes were greatly feared in the ancient world as magical beings as well as for their venom. Both Egyptian and Mesopotamian literatures contain examples of incantations against serpents and their bites. The word translated "charmed" here should not evoke cartoonlike images of swaying serpents hypnotized by pipe-playing swamis. Instead the reference is to snakes against which the incantations are ineffective. Akkadian texts also speak of snakes that are "unconjurable."

8:20. connection between seasons and deliverance. Since the time when grains and fruits were gathered was over, and the season of growth and ripening was over, there was nothing in the granaries. This is describing a time of famine; because of invading armies there was no opportunity to harvest, and the prospect was a winter without food.

8:22. balm of Gilead. Although balm is associated with Gilead, there is no evidence for a balm-producing tree or shrub ever having grown there, although the boundaries of Gilead were never well defined. There are two possibilities: either the reference is to something other than balm (see comment on 46:11), or Gilead was the importer of balm rather than the producer of it. The King's Highway, the main trade route in the region, passed through Gilead, and balm was a primary commodity of trade. Spice caravans from the east followed that route, and no doubt balm was traded there (see Gen 37:25). Balm was probably the resin of the storax tree, obtained by an incision on the bark of the tree. It was believed to have had medicinal qualities. Josephus claimed that En-Gedi near the Dead Sea was a major center for the cultivation of perfume-producing plants (including balm), a fact confirmed by archaeologists, who have discovered at Tel Goren at En-Gedi on the west shore of the Dead Sea something that appears to be a balm installation.

9:15. bitter food. The term here for bitter food is wormwood (the name for several plants of the genus *Artemisia*), a low shrub with very bitter leaves and fruit used in folk medicine, primarily for intestinal problems. It is eaten by goats and camels, and today Bedouin dry the leaves to make a strong aromatic tea. The term wormwood in Scripture is used figuratively for bitterness and sorrow.

9:17-20. trained mourners. This is the only reference in Scripture to professional mourning women, although it was a widespread custom throughout the ancient Near East. Professional mourners (women in virtually every case) are depicted on numerous wall reliefs in Egyptian tomb paintings. They are also often mentioned in Mesopotamia and in Syria as lamenting for not only the human dead but for the dying and rising gods (e.g., Dumuzi or Tammuz). The custom was also prevalent in the eastern Mediterranean, notably in classical Greece, and continues in some parts of the Middle East today.

9:26. circumcised heart. See comment on 4:4.

10:1-25
Contrast Between the Lord and the Idols

10:2. celestial omens. The celestial gods (sun god, moon god and Venus particularly; in

Babylonia, Shamash, Sin and Ishtar respectively) were primary in most ancient religions. Controlling calendar and time, seasons and weather, they were viewed as the most powerful of gods. They provided signs by which omens were read, and they looked down on all. By the end of the second millennium, a major compilation of celestial omens, the seventy tablets of the work known as *Enuma Anu Enlil,* had been compiled and was consulted for nearly a thousand years. There were many constellations recognized by the Mesopotamian astrologers (many, though not all, the same we recognize today, transmitted through the Greeks), but the Zodiac was not yet known.

10:3-4. manufacture of idols. See comments on Isaiah 40:19; 41:7; 44:10-14.

10:5. ancient Near Eastern beliefs about and treatment of idols. Idols came in a variety of shapes and sizes in the ancient Near East. They were typically carved of wood and overlaid with hammered-out sheets of silver or gold. Basically human in appearance (except those from Egypt, which combined human and animal characteristics), they had distinctive, even formalized, poses, clothing and hairstyles. Images of deity in the ancient Near East were where the deity became present in a special way, to the extent that the cult statue became the god (when the god so favored his worshipers), even though it was not the only manifestation of the god. Rituals were performed to bring the god to life in its idol. As a result of this linkage, spells, incantations and other magical acts could be performed on the image in order to threaten, bind or compel the deity. In contrast, other rites related to the image were intended to aid the deity or care for the deity. The idols then represent a worldview, a concept of deity that was not consistent with how Yahweh had revealed himself. The idol was not the deity, but the deity was thought to inhabit the image and manifest its presence and will through the image. Archaeologists have found very few of the life-sized images that the texts describe, but there are renderings of them that allow accurate knowledge of details. The images of deities in Mesopotamia were fed, dressed and even washed daily. Food sacrifices were brought to the deity on a daily basis (and were no doubt eaten by the temple technicians). Other attendants were required to dress and undress the statue, and still others were employed to wash the statue and transport it in times of celebration.

10:5. impotence of idols. The word translated "scarecrow" occurs only here in the Old Testament. This was as close to an image that Israel was allowed to make. Thus, the "sacred" idols

are diminished to the status of scarecrows, no more powerful than palm fronds twisted around a pole. They certainly inspired no fear.

10:9. silver from Tarshish, gold from Uphaz. Although Uphaz was known for its gold (Dan 10:5), its precise location is not known. An Aramaic targum locates it at Ophir, a source of gold in southern Arabia. Uphaz also may be an adjective meaning "pure." There are a number of references to Tarshish in the context of precious stones. These references appear to connect Tarshish with Ezion Geber in the Red Sea area, which correlates Uphaz with Ophir. In other passages, however, Tarshish clearly denotes a western location.

10:9. dressing idols in blue and purple. Ancient color words are difficult to interpret. These terms indicate shades of blue/purple and were colors of royalty and divinity (for more detail see comment on Num 4:6). Many images in the ancient Near East were gold or gold-plated and clothed in these colors.

10:12-13. creator God/cosmic God. This description of Israel's God portrays him both as a creator deity and a cosmic deity. He established order in the cosmos, and he maintains order in his governance of the operation of the cosmos. These two areas of operation did not often coexist in one deity in the ancient world. Marduk, the chief deity of Babylon, however, did have thunder and rain connections as well as being the creator god.

10:13. wind from storehouses. The Canaanites and Babylonians attributed manifestations of storms to Adad, the storm and wind god. However, Jeremiah claimed that Yahweh was solely responsible for atmospheric phenomena. He used the imagery of Yahweh having storehouses of rain, hail and snow, which are set in motion by the wind, presumably instigated by his breath (also see Deut 28:12; Job 38:22; and Ps 33:7). The word translated "storehouses" can be used to refer to treasuries that would store precious objects as well as royal weapons. Hail, snow, wind, thunder and lightning were often seen as the weapons that God uses to defeat his enemies. Likewise storehouses could serve for the storage of raw materials such as barley, dates, grain or tithes in general. In the same way God rations out the products from his storehouses as necessary. Cosmic storehouses are not common imagery in the ancient Near East.

11:1-17

Conspiracy Against the Covenant

11:4. iron-smelting furnace. In the ancient world they did not use a blast furnace such as is used today to produce cast iron. Iron has a melting point of 1537 degrees centigrade, a temperature that could not be consistently achieved by ancient technology. But once the iron is heated beyond 1100 degrees centigrade, it takes a spongy, semisolid form that can be forged. The furnace was usually fueled by charcoal to provide the carbon necessary for the chemical process. The strength of the steel is dependent on the amount of carbon it is able to absorb. The lower the temperature, the more often the process has to be repeated in order to get rid of enough slag to achieve a usable product. While a furnace can certainly be a metaphor of oppression, the fire of the smelting furnace is not destructive but constructive. It is the furnace that transforms the malleable ore to the durable iron product. The Egypt experience transformed Israel into the covenant people of God.

11:5. land flowing with milk and honey. The phrase "flowing with milk and honey" was a common cliché in Scripture designating the fertility of an area. The Canaanites described the land in ritual texts in a similar manner, as did the Egyptian literary text of Sinuhe (early second millennium B.C.) from Egypt. For more information see comment on Exodus 3:7-10.

11:13. as many Baal idols as streets. The phrase is emphasizing the large amount of Baal idols in Jerusalem. A typical city in the ancient Near East had dozens of street corners in residential districts. The text does not imply that each street corner had a Baal image. Nevertheless, Babylonian texts speak of small open-air shrines or niches on street corners or courtyards. One text says that in the city of Babylon there were 180 of them dedicated to the goddess Ishtar. These shrines featured a raised structure with an altar on the top and seem to have been frequented primarily by women.

11:15. consecrated meat. Much of the meat that was consumed in Israel was connected to the sacrificial system and was therefore eaten in specified areas in the temple. Consecrated meat would refer to meat that was used under such circumstances. The irony here is that even as they sit in the temple precincts and partake of a sacral meal, they discuss their wickedness in the table conversation.

11:16. storm as judgment of god. The storm god imagery has already been used several times in the book. God's storm of judgment is accompanied by lightning that ignites the tree that stands for Israel. For more information see comment on 1 Samuel 7:10.

11:18-23
Conspiracy Against Jeremiah

11:21. Anathoth. See comment on 1:1.

11:21. prophesying as a capital crime. Elsewhere in Scripture those who prophesied falsely were legally put to death. Prophecy was a vocation employed throughout the ancient Near East, but capital punishment for false prophecy is known primarily from Israel. Nevertheless the men of Anathoth have not suggested that Jeremiah's prophecies are false. Their threats seek simply to silence him. Speaking a prophecy was a means of effectuating it (just as writing it down was; see comment on 36:23), so they believe that by silencing him (by either threat or murder), they can prevent the disasters he is announcing from taking place.

12:1-17
Jeremiah's Lament and God's Response

12:4. basis of cynical thinking. In the ancient Near East disaster struck when the deity became angry and removed his protection. The people would then be subject to all sorts of problems, many believed to be demonically perpetrated. In Deuteronomy 32:20 God says that he will respond to Israel's wickedness by hiding his face. He would then "see what their end will be"— that is, how well they would fare without his blessing and protection. Here in Jeremiah, God has hidden his face (evident from the drought and famine), but the evildoers are convinced that God will not "see their end" (same phrase as in Deuteronomy) because they are determined to survive on their own

12:5. Jordan thickets. The thickets (literally, "height") of the Jordan is a term that refers to the area where the Jordan River overflows to its junglelike thicket of reeds, bushes and trees, which often became a den for lions. It was a dangerous place and difficult to navigate.

12:9. speckled bird of prey. This word is used only in this context, and many consider it to refer not to a bird at all but to a hyena who is surrounded by birds of prey. This is supported by the Septuagint reading as well as by usage in related Semitic languages, but the text remains difficult.

13:1-14
Belts and Wineskins

13:1. identification of garment. There were two different depictions of the loincloth. One is a Canaanite depiction of a wrapped cloth that did not pass between the legs, while the other is in an Egyptian depiction of Syrians, where the garment is composed of narrow strips of overlapping cloth that did not pass between the legs. Some of these garments were made of leather, but others were made of linen, as this one was.

13:4. Perath. Perath is a term often used for the Euphrates River, which is over 350 miles north of Anathoth, which would make for two very long round trips! Others have suggested it refers to the Wadi Pharah (symbolically called Perath?), some four miles northeast of Anathoth (referred to in Josh 18:23).

13:12. wineskins filled with wine. This has been a notoriously difficult phrase to interpret. It is possible that Jeremiah is quoting a current proverb about everything having its use; wineskins fulfill their purpose by being filled with wine in much the same way that a hat fulfills its purpose by being on a head. Jeremiah is likely making an ironic statement with a simple proverb, similar to Isaiah 28:23-29.

13:15—14:12
Judgment: Captivity, Drought, Famine

13:18. queen mother. The queen mother was an official title in ancient Israel. It was an office with high rank and official prerogatives, especially when the monarch was a minor (and the queen's husband, the former king, had died). She did not just have influence over her son the king but had great authority of her own. Athaliah was able to seize the power of the throne (2 Kings 11). Since the queen mother had an official position in the kingdom, the writer of the books of Kings mentioned her in nearly every case in conjunction with her son. She was probably afforded rank on the accession of her son as king. There are general parallels in Hittite and Ugaritic texts concerning the office of queen mother. There is no direct evidence of the office in the northern kingdom of Israel. For more information see comment on 1 Kings 2:19. The queen mother mentioned here is most likely Nehushta, the mother of Jehoiachin who sat on the throne briefly in 597 until he was carried off captive to Babylon.

13:18. crowns. The royal crown in Judah was probably a golden diadem worn over a turban (see Ps 21:3; Ezek 21:26). Kings in Egypt wore an elaborate variety of crowns, while kings in Assyria usually wore a truncated conical cap

with embroidery or precious stones, and Babylonian kings wore a curved cap that came to a point.

13:19. cities in the Negev. The term *Negev* normally referred to the large desert area south of Judah. In this context, however, it likely denotes the portion of southern Judah dotted with towns and garrisons running from Bethlehem to Beersheba, with Hebron in the middle. It is unclear to what extent these cities came under attack by Babylon in 597, but the ostraca from Arad suggest that Edom posed a threat to them.

13:23. Ethiopian, leopard. In the Egyptian *Instruction of Ankhsheshonqy* a similar saying ("There is no Nubian who leaves his skin") occurs in a sequence of results that are inconceivable (e.g., "There is no fool who finds profit"). In the Aramaic *Words of Ahiqar* there is a conversation between a leopard and a goat in which the former offers the latter his coat so that the goat can be warm. The goat replies that the leopard only wants to take his skin away, an exchange of coats.

13:26. skirts covering face. This does not describe women being carried away into captivity but enemy soldiers ranging through the town, raping and pillaging. Judah is here portrayed metaphorically as suffering a similar fate.

14:12. fasting. Fasting was total abstention from food for a temporary period of time. The Day of Atonement was the only national fasting day listed in Scripture, although public fasting was called at special times, especially in the postexilic period. Individuals fasted in times of mourning and penitence. Fasting is little attested in the ancient Near East outside of the Bible. When it does occur, it is usually in the context of mourning. In the Old Testament the religious use of fasting is often in connection with making a request before God. The principle is that the importance of the request causes an individual to be so concerned about his or her spiritual condition that physical necessities fade into the background. In this sense the act of fasting is designed as a process leading to purification and humbling oneself before God (Ps 69:10). In connection with repentance the Israelites would fast in order to remove any sin or other obstacle that may have led to their subjection.

14:13—15:21
False Hopes and Only Hope

14:22. Israelite meteorology. Like most people from the ancient Near East the Israelites viewed seasonal climate as coming from the four winds derived from the four corners of the earth. God not only controlled the winds but created them. The north wind was associated with cold conditions, dispersing rain and snow. The south wind was at times the bringer of the sirocco. The east wind brought a dry wind from the wilderness. The west wind came in from the Mediterranean Sea and was described as the "father of rain." It is clear in this verse that the common Israelite would have thought it absolutely ridiculous to imagine that the skies rained all by themselves. Weather did not happen independent of deity.

15:4. actions of Manasseh. Second Kings 21:3-7 and 2 Chronicles 33:3-7 describe Manasseh's wicked acts, which included astral worship and Baal altars even within the temple itself. He was considered to have done the most to combine the worship of Yahweh with Canaanite cultic ritual. Though he later repented (2 Chron 33:12), his sins were so great that their consequences were not to be overturned by God.

15:7. winnowing at the gate. After grain has been threshed, it is winnowed with the winnowing-fork, with the remainder of the chaff removed with the winnowing shovel. This activity did not take place at city gates but on threshing floors out in open countryside. Here, however, winnowing is a metaphor for judgment (since winnowing separated the good from the bad), and judgment did take place in the gate areas. This verse could refer to the decisions of a conqueror made at the city gates determining who would be put to death, who would be deported and who would remain. Alternatively, the term translated "land" is sometimes a reference to the netherworld. In this case the imagery would still be of the judgment of God at the gate of the netherworld consigning people to death.

15:8. destroyer. Noon was considered the most secure time of the day and thus the time for surprise attacks. The destroyer here represents the Chaldean army, which is being prepared by God to attack his people. This is not the same word as used for the destroying angel in the Passover (Ex 12:23), but it is used of the military operations conducted by the Lord in 47:4 and 51:55.

15:20. wall of bronze metaphor. Bronze gates built by the Assyrians have been found at Balawat. They were decorative features on strong walls. Thutmose III of Egypt described himself as a wall of iron and bronze for Egypt, meaning that he was like an impregnable fortress city.

16:1—17:18

Disaster Approaching

16:4. no burial. Burial was a mandatory duty in ancient Israel. To be left unburied, vulnerable to the elements and beasts, was the worst curse imaginable. Furthermore, as there was no clear distinction between body and soul in the Hebrew mentality, death was not regarded as the separation of those two elements. Thus one who had no burial was still thought to be conscious (in some form) of his fate. In the ancient Near East those who were left unburied were restless until a proper burial had been performed.

16:5. funeral meal. The Hebrew term for funeral meal is used only here and in Amos 6:7, although it is well known in many other Semitic traditions. Extrabiblical information concerning the funeral meal have been found in Ugaritic texts, Aramaic texts from Elephantine (Egypt) and inscriptions in Punic, Nabataean and Palmyrene. In these examples the funeral meal was often held in a banquet hall with an excess of drinking and inappropriate behavior. The context in Amos 6:7 suggests the same type of atmosphere. Whatever the Israelite custom, Jeremiah was forbidden to participate (as he was forbidden to attend marriage ceremonies).

16:6. mourning rites. The rites mentioned here were both forbidden in Israelite tradition (see comments on Lev 19:28 and Deut 14:1). Slashing oneself is also mentioned in 5:7 in the context of Baal worship.

16:20. idols not gods. See comments on 10:5.

17:1. engraved tablets. The iron-engraving tool referred to here is used for etching permanent inscriptions on stone, while the flint (emery-stone) was used in engraving gems. Their hearts are here portrayed as an extremely hard writing material.

17:1. inscribed altar horns. The horns of the altar were protrusions fixed on the four corners of the altar. Though they functioned to provide a means to secure the wood and animals on the altar, they were also where the blood of the animal was dabbed to purify the altar from defilement. The imagery suggests that the sins of Judah will be permanently inscribed there, with the result that sacrifices cannot expunge them.

17:2. Asherah poles and spreading trees. See comment on 2:20.

17:3. high places. See comment on 1 Samuel 9:12.

17:6. salt land. The presence of salt in the land was a curse. There are a number of texts from Mesopotamia that describe a progressive salinity in the soil of southern Iraq in the third and second millennia. When it reached a certain point of salinity, the land was unable to be used for agriculture and was thus abandoned, sometimes for a period of centuries.

17:11. partridge behavior. The partridge lays her eggs in shallow nests on open ground. Though the eggs are therefore vulnerable to predators or to accidents, the bird lays many eggs, and both the male and female brood over them. The analogy here of laying eggs it does not hatch thus refers to hopes and plans that never come to fruition. There is no evidence that partridges hatch the young of other birds, as the NIV translation suggests.

17:13. written in the dust. This problematic passage either has the idea of a name that is written in the dust, which will disappear quickly, or a name written in the earth (or underworld). This word is not one of those usually translated "dust," but it is the same word used in 15:7, where it could mean either land or netherworld. The latter would make the best sense of the context. To have one's name written in the netherworld would mean being consigned to death. To be written in heaven's ledgers meant that one was destined for continuing life. To be blotted out from that book of life and to have one's name recorded in the ledgers of the netherworld meant doom. Psalm 88:4 expresses the same concept using different terminology.

17:13. deity as spring of living water. "Living" water refers to running water in contrast to the stagnant or contaminated water that gathers in cisterns or pools.

17:19-27

The Sabbath

17:19. gate of the people. The "gate of the people" (literally, "the gate of the sons of the people") is otherwise unknown. The gate seems to have been in the north wall of the city, where the kings left and entered the city.

17:19. number of gates in Jerusalem. There were numerous inner and outer gates in Jerusalem during the period of the divided monarchy. There were at least six outer gates and numerous gates that protected the temple and palatial enclosures. The gates were the areas where public proclamations would normally be made.

17:22-24. carrying a load. In Isaiah 46:1-2 the "burden" is made up of images that are carried around in procession, but Nehemiah 13:15 uses the same word to refer to agricultural products being brought in on the Sabbath by merchants. Either one could be referred to here.

18:1—19:15

The Lesson of the Potter and the Pot

18:2. potter's house. The potter's house, or workshop, needed to be near the clay sources and where water was available. It needed space for the potter's wheel, a space for treading, a kiln, a field for storing vessels and a dump for those discarded items. Once the pot was fired there was painting to be done. The typical hand-turned wheel was made of two pieces of stone. The upper stone had a cone-shaped protrusion on the bottom that fit into a corresponding recess in the top of the bottom stone and served as a pivot.

18:3-4. shaping a vessel on the wheel. There were two kinds of potter's wheel, a slow or hand-turned wheel (or a tournette), and the fast or kick wheel, which was rotated by foot. The potter shaped the clay vessel by hand on the smaller revolving stone that was on top. The lower stone provided the momentum and quickened the turning. The potter rotated the lower disk with his foot. This created a centrifugal force on the clay, which was shaped by the potter's hands as he exerted force to shape it against its own force.

18:13. Virgin Israel. The term translated "virgin" here refers to a woman who is still legally under her father's supervision. Comparable to such a girl who betrays her father's trust and honor is Israel's unfaithfulness to Yahweh, often described in the Old Testament as "playing the harlot." In Ugaritic texts this same word is used as a title for Baal's sister, "Virgin Anat," whose behavior is less than commendable and is thought by some to be promiscuous (though the evidence is not as strong as previously thought).

18:14. snow of Lebanon. The snow of Lebanon probably refers to the highest mountains of Lebanon (e.g., Qurnat as-Sawda), where snow does not leave until late August. At any rate, many of the high peaks are snowcapped for the better part of the year.

18:15. roads not built up. A paved road was one that was built up. Paving was an expensive undertaking. In Babylon dirt and gravel were used to build up the roadbed. Then bricks were laid in asphalt to form a foundation. Finally, limestone slabs were laid on top, and the crevices were filled with asphalt. This process was only affordable on the most prominent streets in a city. Excavated examples occur in Palestine as early as the Middle Bronze Period. Cobblestone streets using pebbles and pottery shards set in clay were the norm. Sometimes they were coated with a lime plaster. There is no evidence of paved country roads during this period. Even an unpaved road, however, could be built up with dirt so that water flowed off it to the sides. The alternative was a road that had simply been traveled often enough to cut a path. These were etched into the terrain and tended to gather water and become mud holes.

18:20. digging a pit. Pits were dug in the ancient Near Eastern world for a variety of reasons. A great number of pits found in archaeological excavations were for storage of ceramics, burying rubbish or, less often, to create a makeshift prison for criminals. The terminology here is borrowed from hunting and trapping practices, where pits and snares were used.

19:1. type of pottery. The type of pottery here is described as a "flask," a word used twice in Jeremiah 19 and in 1 Kings 14:3 (where it is a container for honey) for storing liquids. Its Hebrew name, *baqbuq*, suggests the sound made by a wide-bellied bottle with a narrow neck. Because of the narrow neck, it could not be mended. This type of vessel was used throughout Palestine in the Iron Age.

19:2. Valley of Ben Hinnom. The Valley of Ben Hinnom was on the south side of Jerusalem and joined the Kidron Valley at the southeast corner of the city. It became infamous for Baal worship because of the acts of Ahaz and Manasseh. Josiah defiled the region in order to prevent future idolatrous acts.

19:2. Potsherd Gate. The location of the Potsherd Gate, mentioned only here in Scripture, is unknown. It may have been the same as the Dung Gate (known from various passages in Nehemiah), as both dung and pottery were among the items of trash thrown into the Valley of Ben Hinnom. If the Potsherd Gate was adjacent to the valley, it was on the southeastern side of Jerusalem.

19:5. burning sons and daughters. See comment on 7:31.

19:9. cannibalism in the ancient Near East. Cannibalism existed in the ancient Near East during times of famine or siege. The cities of Samaria (2 Kings 6:24-31) and Jerusalem (Lam 4:10, and later during the war with Rome, according to Josephus) both experienced cannibalism. Furthermore, "eating the flesh of one's children" was a typical curse form in Mesopotamia. There are sparse references in Mesopotamian sources concerning cannibalism for the same purposes mentioned in Scripture (dire famine conditions, city under siege).

19:10-11. smashed as pots. This imagery is known as far back as Sumerian times. The *La-ment over the Destruction of Sumer and Ur* states that the people of Ur were smashed as if they were clay pots.

19:13. burning incense to astral gods. Sacrifice to pagan astral gods was often done on the roofs of houses (see 2 Kings 23:12; Zeph 1:5). Ninsun, the mother of Gilgamesh in the Mesopotamian Epic of Gilgamesh, ascended the roof to offer incense to Shamash, the sun god. The same ritual is described in the Keret Epic from Ugarit. (Also see the comment on 8:2).

20:1-18
Confrontation and Imprisonment

20:2. stocks at the Upper Gate. The meaning of the term translated as "stocks" is not certain. It also occurs in Jeremiah 29:26 and 2 Chronicles 16:10 ("house of stocks"). It was most likely a device that confined the body in a stooped position or perhaps simply a dungeon or guardhouse. At any rate, it is clear that Jeremiah was incarcerated.

20:11. divine warrior. The idea that God fought as a partner in battle was a common theme in the ancient Near East. Victories were attributed to deities in both Egypt and Mesopotamia. The encounter was initiated by the deity itself, who then fought alongside the monarch (see comment on 1 Sam 4:3-7). In Egypt regiments were named after the god under whose standard they fought. In Canaan the divine warrior was identified as one who devastated nature. However, it was recognized by these societies that the gods also participated through the use of individual agents who had been commissioned to do the god's bidding in battle.

20:12. kidneys as seat of intelligence. The NIV's "heart and mind" translates the Hebrew "kidneys and heart." In the ancient world a number of human organs were held to have psychical functions, including the kidneys, which were seen to be the center of the affections and hidden motives. The kidneys could be troubled (Job 19:27; Ps 73:21), be "tested" by God (Jer 11:20) and rejoice (Prov 23:16). The kidneys also instructed (Ps 16:7), a concept known from Ugaritic texts. Akkadian texts tend to connect these abstract notions to the liver rather than the kidneys.

20:14-18. cursing one's birth. In the *Myth of Erra and Ishum* the governor of the city that is being destroyed is portrayed as expressing to his mother a wish that he had been stillborn or obstructed in the womb so that he would not have been born to this destiny.

21:1-14

God's Pronouncement of Judgment on Zedekiah

21:2. Nebuchadnezzar's attack of Jerusalem. In 589 Zedekiah had decided to withhold tribute, relying on the new, anti-Babylonian Egyptian pharaoh, Hophra, for support against the Babylonians. On January 15, 588 (by the Tishri calendar, 587 by the Nisan calendar) Nebuchadnezzar's troops arrived at Jerusalem and blockaded the city, while eliminating any potential sources of aid, including the Egyptians (see comment on 34:21). Other fortified cities were destroyed, and then full siege of Jerusalem began as the Babylonians worked toward creating a breach in the northern walls. The wall was breached in mid-August of 586.

21:7. devastations of siege. The hardships of the siege were significant. The whole idea of siege is to drive the inhabitants to the extremities of hunger and thirst so that they capitulate without a fight. Famine in this case is not an environmental condition but the results of the siege when food supplies have been exhausted. Overcrowded conditions tax the infrastructure of the city, and when water becomes scarce, people will drink even water that has been contaminated. As a result illness often reaches epidemic proportions during siege.

21:7. Zedekiah's eventual fate. See the note on 32:4. It appears that Zedekiah died in captivity after being handed over to Nebuchadnezzar.

21:14. forests of Jerusalem. Rather than referring to the adjacent woods, the term "forest" is an expression used in connection with the royal palace (see comment on 1 Kings 7:1-12) because of the large amounts of cedar used in its construction.

22:1-30

The Fate of Kings

22:5-6. making the palace a ruin. In the *Myth of Erra and Ishum* the destruction of towns and the royal palace is treated in similar terms. Erra expresses his intention to allow wild beasts from the mountains and the countryside to enter the city and devastate the public areas. He specifically states that he will make the palace a ruin.

22:6. Gilead and the summit of Lebanon. Gilead was on the east side of the Jordan River. The northern limits of Gilead were vague, and the east was bounded by desert. The summit of Lebanon refers to its forests (also see

Zech 10:10). Both Gilead and Lebanon were known for the lush productivity of their forests.

22:10. exiled king. The exiled king mentioned here was probably Shallum, the fourth son of Josiah, who succeeded his father in 609/8 B.C. He took the throne name of Jehoahaz. After he had been king of Judah for three months, he was then exiled to Egypt by Necho II, where he later died. He was condemned by the writer(s) of Kings as a wicked ruler.

22:13. forced labor for palace building. This may be a reference to a rebuilding and enlargement of Solomon's palace by Jehoiakim or to another palace altogether. At Ramat Rahel a number of structures have been found that possibly date to the time of Jehoiakim, together with a large collection of stamped jar handles bearing the phrase "belonging to the king." Since the king needed to pay a heavy tribute to Egypt, he may have engaged in the forced labor project. Forced labor without compensation is reminiscent of practices during Solomon's time (see comment on 1 Kings 11:28) and of practices periodically observed in both Egypt and Babylonia. It is a form of taxation.

22:14. cedar paneling. Cedar paneling was considered the most luxurious and expensive material that could be used. It was used almost exclusively in palaces and temples. Wall painting is not widely attested in Israelite excavations but is well known in the larger Near Eastern context. Frescoes such as the coronation scene at Mari attest to the preference for red and orange in interior decoration. This characteristic is also referred to in the wall decorations in Ezekiel 23:14.

22:18. Jehoiakim. See comment on 1:3.

22:20. Lebanon, Bashan, Abarim. These are three mountainous areas; Lebanon was in the north, Bashan in Transjordan in the northeast, and Abarim in Moab to the southeast. Whether these mountains represent places for mourning, homes of allies or centers for natural resources is uncertain.

22:24. signet ring. The term "signet" probably refers to a seal, which could have been either a cylinder seal worn with a cord around the neck or a stamp seal embedded in a ring, as found here. The former was very common in Mesopotamia, while the latter was used in Israel. Thousands of cylinder seals and stamp seals have been found in Mesopotamia and Syro-Palestine, respectively. They were a sign of authority, identification and ownership. By pulling off the signet ring (i.e., Jehoiachin), Yahweh was effectively rejecting his kingship.

22:25. Jehoiachin's fate. Jehoiachin was only

on the throne for three months before he was forced to surrender to Nebuchadnezzar. He was taken into exile in Babylon, where he spent the rest of his life (see 2 Kings 25:27-30). He is mentioned on a rations list from Babylon, confirming the biblical information that he was fed at the king's table.

23:1-8
The Branch

23:5. branch as royal heir. The term "branch" appears in the messianic passages such as Zechariah 3:8 and 6:12, where it is attributed to Zerubbabel. Most consider it a technical term referring to the rightful heir of an established dynastic line—in Israel, a future Davidic king who would restore the monarchy. Similarly, an early third-century B.C. Phoenician votive inscription honoring Melqart that has been found in Cyprus refers to a legitimate "branch" of the Ptolemaic dynasty of Egypt. The Dead Sea Scrolls from Qumran do not use the term in a messianic sense, but the kingship sense does occur in Ugaritic and Assyrian texts. For instance, Tiglath-Pileser III is described as the shoot or scion of the city of Baltil (Assur), who brings justice to his people. The statement that he will do what is right and just in the land also finds a parallel in the reform declarations commonly made by Babylonian kings. Zedekiah issued such a proclamation in 588 (see comment on 34:8-11).

23:9-40
False Prophets

23:13. prophesying by Baal. Baal prophets had found support in Samaria as early as the middle of the ninth dynasty (Ahab and Jezebel). Two centuries have passed, and though the dynasty of Ahab had been wiped out, syncretism had never fully departed from the north. When the northern kingdom fell in 721, the Assyrian deportation policy had brought foreigners in to mix with the population that remained of the northern kingdom of Israel. Second Kings 17:24-34 describes the resulting syncretism that plagued the area. Undoubtedly these prophets were spreading false hopes that Baal, a fertility god, could break the drought (v. 10) and restore the land's productivity.

23:18. standing in the council of the Lord. The council of the Lord was probably the assembly of beings who stood in his heavenly court, similar to the council of holy ones of Psalm 89:7. Deities from other cultures in the ancient world were assumed to have divine

councils where various gods and goddesses assembled to conduct their business. Prophets were often viewed as being privy to this assembly's actions (as in 2 Chron 18:18). For more information see the comments on Isaiah 6:8; 40:13-14.

23:19. storm of the Lord. See comment on 11:16.

23:23. God nearby, far away. Yahweh is affirming both his transcendence (above and beyond the created world) and his immanence (integrally involved in the created world) in this passage. Moreover, he is affirming his omnipresence, as no one can be hidden from him, and he is aware of everything, no matter how remote or obscure. In the broader religious spectrum of this time period a shift had taken place from seeing deities associated with the sun, aloof and removed, to deities associated with the stars and planets, who were seen as more approachable and involved. Another possibility is that "near and far" may combine the aspects of a locally involved patron deity and a powerful cosmic deity. Few gods in the ancient world would have been believed to fit this profile.

23:25. dreams as form of revelation. Dreams were one of the standard means for receiving messages from a god in the ancient Near East (see Jacob in Gen 28:12; Joseph in Gen 37:5-11; Nebuchadnezzar in Dan 2, 4). They appear in Old Babylonian omen texts, along with the reports of the examination of sheep livers, anomalies in the weather and birth of animals, and other presumed signs of the divine will. Among the most famous is the dream of Gudea of Lagash (c. 2150 B.C.), who was commanded in a dream to build a temple by a figure reminiscent of the apocalyptic figures in Daniel's dreams and Ezekiel's call narrative (Dan 7; Ezek 1:25-28). The royal correspondence from Mari (c. 1750 B.C.) contains around twenty prophetic utterances involving dreams, always from nonprofessional personnel. These portents were taken quite seriously and studied. The professional priesthood in both Mesopotamia and Egypt included instruction in the interpretation of dreams and other omens (see the comment on Dan 2:4).

24:1-10
Good Figs, Bad Figs

24:1. circumstances of Jehoiachin's exile. See the comments on 22:5 and on 2 Kings 24:12.

24:1. Nebuchadnezzar. Nebuchadnezzar II (r. 605-562 B.C.) was the second of the Chaldean kingdom centered at Babylon which ruled the ancient Near East for nearly a century. He was the son of Nabopolassar, a Chaldean who declared independence from Assyria in 626 B.C. In his long reign of forty-three years Nebuchadnezzar pacified Egypt (though he was unsuccessful in conquering it) and literally rebuilt Babylon. In fact, most of the city of Babylon that was uncovered by modern excavators dates from Nebuchadnezzar's reign. The Chaldean kingdom was primarily his creation, and it crumbled only a generation after his death. This great king was remembered in many cultural traditions, including sources from Greece (who knew him as a great builder) and Israel (not only the biblical material, but later rabbinic sources).

24:2. early ripening figs. The branches on fig trees from the previous year bore early fruit in late May/early June, even before the new leaves sprouted. The new branches brought forth figs at least three months later.

25:1-38
Seventy Years of God's Wrath

25:1. chronology. The fourth year of Jehoiakim and the first year of Nebuchadnezzar II of Babylon has been synchronized as 604 B.C. The Babylonian king had just defeated the Egyptians at Carchemish and prepared to make Judah its vassal.

25:9. Nebuchadnezzar as Yahweh's servant. The kings of nations who came against Israel are often described as servants of God, in that they are carrying out the will of Yahweh. Since Yahweh is unconquerable, any conqueror is doing his bidding as his rod of punishment. It does not mean that the Babylonian king was a worshiper of Yahweh. Cyrus is described in a similar manner, though there is no evidence that he worshiped Yahweh (Is 44:28—45:1). In ancient Near Eastern treaties the vassal became the servant of the suzerain, and his armies became the suzerain's to command. They were at the disposal of the overlord and did his will.

25:10. millstones and light of the lamp. The cessation of the most familiar daily activities left nothing but an eerie stillness, with no food production and a fearful and terrifying darkness.

25:11. seventy-year period. Though the expression "seventy years" could denote generally an individual's life span, as it does in a statement of Esarhaddon of Assyria, it can also make reference to a specific span of time. The period of seventy years was approximately from the destruction of the temple in 587 B.C. to its rededication in about 515 B.C. It also represents the time that elapsed from the initial subjugation of Israel under Nebuchadnezzar in 605 to the return from exile by Cyrus's decree in 535.

25:12. seventy-year exile. When Esarhaddon of Assyria discusses his father Sennacherib's destruction of Babylon, he views it as Marduk's judgment of his own city. Marduk's anger with the people of Babylon led him to decree a seventy-year exile of himself from the city. Esarhaddon rebuilds the city only a decade after its destruction and announces that Marduk reduced the exile to only eleven years. Little is known of Palestine during the exile and partial reoccupation of the land. The deportation followed the destruction of Jerusalem in 586 B.C. Only the leading citizens went into exile. Signs of destruction have been found throughout Judea, but not everything was destroyed. The peasants continued their life in the area, and some even worshiped amid the ruins of the temple (see 41:4-5). Judah became a Babylonian province, with headquarters at Mizpah, north of Jerusalem.

25:15. wine of wrath. The image of wine as a cup of punishment is found often in the Old Testament (Ps 11:6; 75:8; Jer 49:12; 51:17; Hab 2:15-16). It is especially clear from Isaiah 51:17 that the cup results in drunkenness (staggering) and not death. Those forced to drink this cup lose all control of themselves and all ability to defend themselves (v. 27). They become senseless.

25:19-26. geographical coverage. The geographical context of these areas is quite wide. From Egypt in Northeast Africa, Jeremiah lists the kings of Uz (probably the Negev), the Philistine cities along the coast, the Transjordanian states (Edom, Moab, Ammon) and back to the coastal regions in the north (Phoenicia). The coastlands beyond the sea refer to Cyprus and other islands. Jeremiah then traverses south across northern Arabia (Dedan, Tema and Buz; Akkadian Bazu in Arabia). He skips Mesopotamia (the land of Babylon) and travels to southwest Iran (Elam and Media). He then summarizes by adding "all the kings of the earth." The specific areas mentioned were all terrorized by Nebuchadnezzar.

25:26. Sheshach and the use of cryptograms. Sheshach is an "atbash" for Babylon. The atbash was a code in which the letters of a name counted from the beginning of the Hebrew alphabet are exchanged for letters counted from the end (see also the comment on 51:1). In English A would be represented by Z, B by Y, and so on. In the previous passage Elam becomes Zimki in Hebrew, and Babylon *(bbl)* becomes Sheshach *(shshk)*. The atbash was used to disguise the identity of the adversary. There is no atbash in Akkadian, since cuneiform uses syllables, not an alphabet.

25:30. shouts of those who tread grapes. The shout mentioned here is used both for those who tread grapes and for those who fight in battle. Yahweh's roar is like the shout of those who tread grapes. Treading grapes marked the end of the harvest season and was used as an opportunity for community celebration before the onset of winter. It was characterized by a tumult of rejoicing, sometimes heightened by overindulgence in the wine being produced.

25:34-38. shepherd/leader metaphor. The metaphor of national leaders as shepherds over their people (sheep) is a very common one in the ancient Near East. It portrayed the ruler's responsibility and authority. Just as a sheep owner would call his shepherds to account for their sheep, so deity held kings accountable for the welfare of their people. Here it is no longer the sheep who are being slaughtered but the shepherds.

26:1-24
Death Sentence for Jeremiah

26:1. chronology. The phrasing used here refers technically to what is termed the accession year. This was the initial portion of the year between when a king first came to the throne and the new year, when his first year officially began. The period of the accession year of Jehoiakim was about from September 609 B.C. to April 608 B.C.

26:6. Shiloh. See comment on 7:12.

26:8-9. prophecy as treason. Throughout the ancient world it was believed that prophets not only proclaimed the message of deity but in the process unleashed the divine action. In Assyrian king Esarhaddon's instructions to his vassals, he requires that they report any improper or negative statements that may be made by anyone, specifically naming prophets, ecstatics and dream interpreters. One can perhaps understand why a king would be inclined to imprison a prophet whose very words might incite insurrection or impose doom.

26:10. topography of Jerusalem. Jerusalem is situated on a limestone plateau about eight hundred meters above sea level in the central hill country of Judea, on the border of the desert. It consists of two main ridges surrounded by the Hinnom and Kidron Valleys, and the small depression of the Tyropoeon. The eastern ridge included the original city of David and the temple complex. The latter is on the northern and highest section of the ridge, thus one had to go up from the palace to the temple. The New Gate is also mentioned in 36:10, but its exact location is unknown. Speculation usually places it on the south side of the court as a passage between the temple precinct and the royal palace just to the south.

26:18. chronology. Hezekiah ruled a century earlier at the end of the eighth century. Here it is evident that prophetic messages were recorded and remembered.

27:1-22
Under the Yoke of Babylon

27:1. chronology. There is a major problem in this verse because the Hebrew text identifies the setting as the accession year of Jehoiakim yet in the following verses identifies the king as Zedekiah. Most interpreters think that this phrase has been misplaced here from 26:1. The chronological notation should instead read the fourth year of Zedekiah, 594 (see 28:1).

27:2. yoke construction. The yokes used for draft animals consisted of a wooden frame that sat across the top of the necks with pegs fitting through holes on either side of the neck. Under the neck the pegs were connected with straps. Yokes were used for certain human tasks as well as on plow animals. Assyrian inscriptions from the ninth and eighth century depict captives being transported or laboring in such yokes. Bars on either side of the neck are clearly visible. For more information concerning yoke imagery see comment on Nahum 1:13.

27:3. occasion for gathering of envoys. The envoys from Edom, Moab, Ammon, Tyre and Sidon all conspired to revolt against Babylon in 594 B.C. The meeting was probably in response to a domestic rebellion in Babylon against Nebuchadnezzar in December 595 and January 594, which is described in one of the Babylonian Chronicles.

27:6. subjection of wild animals. Just as the yoke symbolized the subjection of domesticated animals, the prophecy goes on to suggest that wild animals will likewise come under the domesticating hand of the Lord. There are numerous depictions on wall reliefs of Assyrian kings hunting wild animals, such as lions and other large carnivores. The domestication of wild animals was also at times included in utopian visions of a kingdom controlled and at peace (see comment on Is 11:6-8).

27:7. survey of Neo-Babylonian empire. The Neo-Babylonian empire was founded by Nebuchadnezzar II's father, Nabopolassar, a Chaldean who freed himself from Assyrian rule in 626 B.C. The founder reigned until 605 B.C. and thus contributed to the end of Assyria. He oversaw the great victory of the Babylonians over Egypt at Carchemish, causing most of Western Asia to fall into the hands of the Babylonians. Nebuchadnezzar inherited this powerful state in 605 B.C., becoming its most famous king. He literally rebuilt the city of Babylon and solidified Babylonian control throughout the Near East and even attacked Egypt (although unsuccessfully). His long reign lasted until 562 B.C. He was briefly succeeded by three descendants, who reigned a total of six years. The last king of the dynasty was Nabonidus, who had apparently been a high official during Nebuchadnezzar's reign. He reigned until 539 B.C. when Babylon was captured by the Medo-Persians under Cyrus the Great. Although Nabonidus is not mentioned in Scripture, his son Belshazzar figures prominently in the book of Daniel as king. Since Nabonidus abandoned Babylon and lived in Arabia for about ten years, Belshazzar took the place of his father for that time.

27:8-11. prophets advising submission. Though the biblical prophets counseled submission, such advice is unattested in ancient Near Eastern prophetic texts. Kings in the ancient world generally had high opinions of themselves, and prophets had a reputation for telling kings what they wanted to hear. If there was submission to be advised, it was submission to a god through certain rituals, not political submission. In contrast, there were diviners who might advise against one political action or another on the premise that the omens were not favorable for a particular action at a particular time.

27:9. categories of professional. Five categories of experts are identified here. The prophets received messages from deity and passed them on. Diviners read omens, most of which came from the examination of the entrails of sacrificial animals (see comment on Deut 18:11). Dreams were believed to be an important form of revelation throughout the Near East. Interpreters used a variety of academic resources (see comment on Dan 2:4). The medium was one who made contact with the dead and offered advice from them. The last category, the sorcerer, was one who specialized in spells and incantations. In seventh-century letters to Assyrian kings the five principal classes of scholarly experts serving the king were astrologer/scribe, diviner, exorcist, physician and chanter of lamentations.

27:16. articles from the Lord's house. The articles here probably refer to all types of movable objects in the temple, including vessels and utensils. Nebuchadnezzar carried off many of the temple treasures in the first capture of Jerusalem in 597 B.C., but there were still some accessories that were carried off eleven years later. For more information see comments on Daniel 1:2 and 5:2. For description of the articles see the various comments in 2 Chronicles 4.

27:19. pillars. The bronze pillars (see comment on 1 Kings 7:15-22) were just outside the forecourt situated in the courtyard of the temple. They were given names (Jachin and Boaz), and evidently the king stood by one of them on special occasions (2 Kings 11:14; 23:3).

27:19. sea. The molten sea (see comment on 2 Chron 4:2-5) was a very large bronze basin over fifteen feet in diameter and over seven feet high. It rested on the backs of twelve bronze oxen, arranged in threes, with each group of threes facing in different directions. The vessel held about ten thousand gallons and was for ritual washing.

27:19. movable stands. The movable stands were ten smaller bowls used for washing sacrificial animals. These were supported by decorated stands mounted on four mobile bronze wheels. Each basin had the capacity of two hundred gallons. Archaeologists have found a bronze stand that would have held just such a basin dating from the twelfth century B.C. The stand had wheels and was decorated with winged composite creatures (see 1 Kings 7:29).

27:20. Jehoiachin's exile. See the note on 2 Kings 24:12. A Babylonian administrative text describes tribute from Iakukinu (Jeconiah, or Jehoiachin) to Nebuchadnezzar.

27:22. sacred things taken into exile and brought back. Jerusalem was not the only temple in the ancient world that had its articles carried off and returned at a later date. For example, the statue of Marduk was plundered from Babylon on a number of occasions (e.g., by the Hittites in 1595 B.C., by Tukulti-Ninurta I of Assyria, c. 1235 B.C., and by Sennacherib in 689 B.C.). Eventually the statue of the deity was returned to its original place in Babylon.

28:1-17
Hananiah and the Yoke

28:1. chronology. Given the time necessary for King Zedekiah to organize his government (see 27:3; 51:59) after the capture of Jerusalem in 597 by Nebuchadnezzar, it seems most likely that the reading of "in the fourth year" is correct. This would date the event to 594-593 B.C. The proximity to the meeting of ambassadors to plan a response to the revolt against

Babylon in December 595 also argues for this date.

28:1. Gibeon. See the comment on Joshua 9:3. Like Anathoth, Gibeon (el-Jib) is located in Benjamin (six miles northwest of Jerusalem), making it likely that Hananiah and Jeremiah were acquainted prior to this incident.

28:10. breaking the yoke. Some commentators think it more probable that it is the pegs that hold the yoke in place on either side of the neck that are being broken, rather than the crossbar (for yoke construction see comment on 27:2). This would make sense of the choice of terms used throughout the passage.

28:13. contrast between wooden and iron yoke. It is likely again that it is the yoke pegs that are visualized as made from iron. Clearly a wooden yoke could be broken, providing a dramatic gesture of release from oppression. However, iron could not be broken so easily.

28:14. subjection of wild animals. See the comment on 27:6.

29:1-32
Letter to the Elders of the Exiles

29:1. letter to exiles. Evidence of correspondence between Jerusalem and the exiles taken away in 597 is found in this letter, presumably delivered by a Babylonian messenger or a merchant traveling to Mesopotamia. There is ample precedent for the transport of both private and official correspondence throughout the Old Testament period. The Lachish Letters represent the type of internal communication employed in the kingdom of Judah during the Assyrian invasion of 701. For evidence that this letter was received and respected see Daniel 9.

29:2. queen mother. The queen mother in Judah apparently had a high status and was both an influence on her son the king as well as a power in her own right (see comment on 1 Kings 2:19 and the need to remove her from power in Asa's time in 1 Kings 15:13). In this case we know that Jehoiachin's mother was named Nehushta (see 2 Kings 24:8; Jer 13:18) and that she was also stripped of her crown and attendant power when they were taken together into exile.

29:2. exile of craftsmen and artisans. In choosing persons to take as hostages in the exile of 597, Nebuchadnezzar naturally took members of the royal family and their advisers among the nobility and priesthood. Craftsmen (see 10:3) and skilled artisans might have been useful to the king's ambitious building plans, but they also represented the relatively wealthy middle class of Judah. Most impor-

tantly, the skills of craftsmen and artisans were generally passed on through families, generation to generation, and often comprised trade secrets. The Babylonians would desire to preserve these and benefit from them. This same respect for the guilds is seen in Utnapishtim's inclusion of artisans in his ark in the Gilgamesh flood story.

29:10. seventy-year period. There are a number of different ways that the seventy-year period can be calculated. The capital city of Assyria, Nineveh, fell in 612. In 605 the Babylonians gained nominal control of all Syria-Palestine. Twice the Babylonian armies came against Jerusalem and went away with exiles, 597 and at the destruction of Jerusalem and the temple in 586. Any of these four can be identified as starting points. On the other end, Babylon fell in 539, and the first return of deportees took place in 538. The temple was rebuilt in 515. While it is therefore not difficult to put together a scenario that involves a literal seventy years, it should also be recognized that seventy is often a symbolic number representing a period of divine judgment. When Babylon was destroyed in the seventh century by Sennacherib, it was said that Marduk, the god of Babylon, had decreed seventy years as the period that it would lay in ruins. Sennacherib's son, Esarhaddon, however, used a trick of interpretation to reduce the number to eleven and had the city rebuilt.

29:26. stocks and neck irons. The word used for "stocks" here only appears twice elsewhere (2 Chron 16:10 and Jer 20:2), and in neither case is its meaning clear. Some have suggested a narrow or low prison cell, but the addition of "neck irons" in this passage suggests a restraining device of some sort in which the prophet could be held and displayed in a humiliating and uncomfortable stance (see Jeremiah's complaint in 20:7-8). Further identification will have to await future discoveries.

30:1-24
Oracle of Restoration

30:2. books. The book of Jeremiah is one of the few prophetic works in the Bible that makes explicit mention of writing down the words of Yahweh to the prophet. Jeremiah was aided in this task by Baruch, a professional scribe (see 36:2-4). In this passage the word translated as "book" is a general term for a written document, and in that time period it meant a scroll. Papyrus scrolls were in use in Egypt from the third millennium, and the climate of Egypt has allowed for the preservation and recovery of numerous documents. In Mesopotamia, where clay tablets had long been the favored medium, scrolls are attested beginning in the Neo-Assyrian period (eighth century). Israelites were probably using scrolls during most of the Old Testament period, but little evidence has been recovered prior to the second century Dead Sea Scrolls (of these, over 90 percent are parchment). The oldest example is a few lines of a letter dated to the seventh century B.C. found in the caves at Wadi Murabba'at. An average papyrus scroll would contain about twenty pages of papyrus sheets glued together. The resulting scroll would be about fifteen feet long and about one foot tall. Parchment (using animal skins) was much less in use during the Old Testament period but was known.

30:14. situation with allies. Jehoiakim of Judah had been put on the throne by the Egyptians in 609 and remained loyal to them until Nebuchadnezzar's domination made that impossible. After the fall of Ashkelon to Nebuchadnezzar in 604, Jehoiakim paid tribute to Babylon for a few years. But when Nebuchadnezzar failed in his attempted invasion of Egypt in 601, Jehoiakim again sided with Egypt and stopped sending the yearly tribute east. Thus in 597 when Nebuchadnezzar undertook his punitive raid against Jerusalem, Egypt was the principle ally on whom Judah relied. Later that year Nebuchadnezzar put Zedekiah on the throne. He almost immediately began meeting with a coalition of the small western states to stand together against Nebuchadnezzar (see comment on 27:3). In 595 a new pharaoh, Psammeticus II, took the throne of Egypt. He enjoyed an early military success against the Nubians in the south, and one papyrus reports that his success was celebrated with a victory tour in Palestine. Therefore, though Egypt was not the instigator of the alliance, there was cause to expect their support against Babylon. It is uncertain which nations were actually part of the alliance when it finally took shape. As it turned out, Egypt's army was routed in their confrontation with the Babylonians in 588 (see 37:5-7), and it would appear, based on Psalm 137:7, that allies such as the Edomites threw their support to Babylon when it became clear that Jerusalem was about to fall. Only Ammon and Tyre of the western states became objects of Nebuchadnezzar's wrath.

30:23. storm of the Lord. The poetic style of these verses resembles that found in the Sumerian *Lament over the Destruction of Ur* (c. 2000 B.C.). Both there and here devastation is ascribed to a storm or a blistering wind. In one strophe of the Sumerian text the wind "blows through the gate of the city" like an invading army, while in another the author despairs over "the day of the storm fated for me." Nearer the time of Jeremiah a first-millennium lamentation titled He Is a Storm, At the Healing portrays the anger of the gods in the form of a storm sweeping over the nations. This is one of over three dozen compositions identified as *balag* lamentations that make frequent use of the storm metaphor. The original function of these lamentations was to appease a deity whose temple had been or was being razed. For more information on the elements of a storm accompanying divine activity see comment on 1 Kings 19:11-13.

31:1-40

New Covenant

31:4. Virgin Israel. See comment on 18:13.

31:8. gathered from ends of earth. This is similar language to Isaiah 11:11, where Israel is gathered from the four edges of the earth. Akkadian literature speaks of kings ruling the four quarters, most likely making reference to the most distant coasts or extremities in the four major directions. Rather than referring to four slices of the geographical pie, "the ends or edges of the earth" refers to the farthest points, thereby including everything in between.

31:9. led beside running wadis. In a land where rainfall is seasonal (basically from October to February), the wadis (stream beds) are often dry. This makes them useful as pathways (for instance the Wadi Kelt that runs between Jericho to Jerusalem), but the image of them bearing water brings to mind other examples of refreshing, even miraculous, water in the wilderness (Num 20:1-13) as well as the covenantal promise of fertility (for this theme, see the comment on Deut 8:7). As he did in the wilderness, God will provide for them as he brings them back to the land.

31:10. coastlands. See 2:10 for the use of this term for coastlands and islands. There it refers to Phoenicia, Cyprus and the Greek Islands. In this context it is a generic term for faraway lands or the ends of the earth.

31:12. grain, new wine, oil. The basic staples of life in the Mediterranean world are grain (wheat or barley), the products of the vineyard and olive oil (Hos 2:5, 8). They are the physical expression of fertility in the covenant with Yahweh. In the ancient law codes of Mesopotamia, a husband's obligation to his wife or concubine is defined in terms of his providing her with barley, oil and clothing (Code of

Lipit-Ishtar, Laws of Eshnunna, Hammurabi's Code).

31:15. Ramah. This site is most likely to be identified with er-Ram, three miles north of Jerusalem. The name itself means "height" and thus is applied to many towns in Palestine since such a place would be easier to defend. Jeremiah's reference to lamentation here may be based on the use of the site as a staging area for shipment of exiles to Babylonia after the fall of Jerusalem in 587 (see 40:1). The tie to Rachel is probably based on the proximity of Ramah to Zelzah, the site of Rachel's tomb (see comment on 1 Sam 10:2).

31:21. road signs and guideposts in ancient world. While there is no mention of formal road markers prior to the Roman period, Jeremiah's injunction to the departing exiles to mark their way with piles of stones or cairns suggests that this was not a new practice. Otherwise roads were distinguished by landmarks (*ittu* in the Gilgamesh Epic and the Enuma Elish) or by their destination (King's Highway in Num 20:17).

31:21. Virgin Israel. See comment on 18:13.

31:23. sacred mountain. Ancient Near Eastern thought, not unlike that familiar from Greek mythology, visualized a mountain height as the dwelling place of deity (see comment on Is 14:13). Since Jerusalem, the dwelling place of God, was on an elevated area, it is referred to as God's holy mountain.

31:33. written on the heart. Extispicy is the practice whereby diviners pose a question to deity and seek the answer by examining the entrails of sacrificed animals. When extispicy was being performed, the incantation priests asked the deity to write his revelation on the exta (entrails) of the sacrificed animal so that his will or instruction could be understood. Another frequent diviner's prayer was to place the truth in the exta. Both the verbs of this verse (*put*, write) and the nouns ("mind" = entrails, specifically intestines; heart) are the same words as are used in extispicy omens in Akkadian literature. But if Jeremiah is using the language and concepts of omens, it is only as a convenient bridge to his message. God's decrees and will are going to be made known through the careful examination of the heart of his people. Akkadian also uses the nouns (heart and mind) parallel to one another in reference to the center of reason and emotion.

31:36. cosmic decrees. In Mesopotamia the Tablets of Destiny contained the decrees that were the foundation for all that happened on earth. The people took omens seriously because they believed that these decrees were mirrored in the heavenly bodies, in the behav-

ior of animals and even in the entrails of animals. The assumption is that a divine decree is binding for all time. For instance, in the Babylonian creation epic *Enuma Elish* the gods proclaim that Marduk's "word shall not be challenged" and his "decree shall not be altered." Similarly, the wisdom sayings of the Egyptian Amenemope about justice state that "judgment belongs to the divine assembly, verdicts are sealed by divine decree." In the Ugaritic epic of Baal the goddess Anat, in her attempt to flatter the chief god El, tells him that his "decrees are wise" and his "wisdom endures forever." Occasionally a text will refer to a god's decree as "evil," as in the Atrahasis flood story, but still these commands are carried out because of the lordship the ancient gods are said to have over creation. For information concerning the reigns of kings related to the endurance of the cosmos, see comment on Psalm 89:35-37.

31:37. unknowns of the cosmos. While Yahweh is capable of measuring the heavens (see comment on Is 40:12) and is intimately familiar with the foundations of the earth, these are beyond the reach of any human endeavor. The various creation epics from Mesopotamia (Atrahasis, *Enuma Elish*) describe the establishment of the heavens and the earth, the ordering of the universe and the charges given to each god to regulate his/her sphere of influence. Thus the knowledge of the heavens and the nether regions belongs only to the divine. There is no instance in which any human succeeds in quests to gain such knowledge (the heroes Gilgamesh and Adapa come the closest, but they are also limited by their mortality). The mysteries and prerogatives of election are exclusive to Yahweh, just as much as the mysteries and prerogatives of the cosmos are.

31:38. Tower of Hananel to the Corner Gate. See the comments on Nehemiah 3:1 and 2 Chronicles 25:23. The reference is most likely to the western part of the north wall where the Babylonian armies are believed to have breached the fortifications and entered the city. The north side of the city was the most vulnerable because there were steep valleys to deal with on the other sides.

31:39. Gareb and Goah. The exact locations of these two hills near Jerusalem are unknown. They function as part of a restored Jerusalem in Jeremiah's vision. Gareb is generally identified with the southwest hill of the city, west of the Tyropoeon Valley and north of the Hinnom Valley (today called Mount Zion). If this is correct, Goah would be south or east of Gareb.

31:40. topography of Jerusalem. In this vision

of the restoration of Jerusalem's holy precincts Jeremiah refers to several adjacent areas. First is the Hinnom Valley (Wadi er-Rababi, west of Jerusalem), the site of Baal worship and human sacrifice. The Kidron Valley lies to the southeast of the city. Terracing of hillsides to provide space for vineyards and olive trees is common throughout Palestine. Naturally agricultural areas would not have been inside the city walls, but their importance to the city would have led them to be described as part of the city's resources. The Horse Gate was located on the east side of Jerusalem near the northern end of the Kidron Valley (see comment on Neh 3:28).

32:1-44
Jeremiah's Land Purchase

32:1. chronology. There were two different systems for reckoning a king's reign in use by Israel and her neighbors. One counted years from Nisan to Nisan (Nisan is March/April) in accordance with the religious calendar, while the other counted years from Tishri to Tishri (September/October) in accordance with the civil calendar. If the Israelite calendar began in the spring, Zedekiah's tenth year would extend from March 588 to March 587. The Babylonian king Nebuchadnezzar's eighteenth regnal year extended from March 587 to March 586 (it is known that they used the Nisan system). For this and other reasons a case has been made that Israel used the Tishri system at this time, in which case Zedekiah's tenth would overlap Nebuchadnezzar's eighteenth by six months. There are problems with either scheme, and at this point the difficulties cannot easily be resolved.

32:2. siege of Jerusalem. The events described here relate to the more detailed description of the siege of Jerusalem in 37—38 (with the siege probably starting on January 15, 588; alternatively, January 5, 587). There was a brief respite in the intensity of the siege when the Babylonian forces had to be partially withdrawn to deal with an approaching Egyptian army (37:5). One of the Lachish Letters mentions negotiations between a Judean official and Egypt. This may have prompted a preemptive strike by the Egyptians in hopes of preventing a Babylonian invasion of their territory. Once that allied contingent had been effectively repulsed, Nebuchadnezzar was able to concentrate all of his attention on Jerusalem.

32:4. Zedekiah's fate. See the comments on 39:4-7. Jeremiah's prophecy of Zedekiah's fate contains an ironic note since it describes an "eye to eye" confrontation with the Babylo-

nian king. As punishment for his rebellion, Zedekiah will be forced to watch his sons executed, and then he will be blinded. This idea of the danger of close contact with the king parallels similar expressions of fear and danger in the theophanic appearances of God (see Jacob's reaction in Gen 28:16-17 and Isaiah's startled cry in Is 6:5). The Assyrian Annals of Sennacherib contain a similar example of the king's manifest "glory." In this inscription from a previous siege of Jerusalem, it states that Hezekiah "was overwhelmed by my [Sennacherib's] terror-inspiring splendor."

32:7. land redemption. In Israelite tradition the ownership of land is tied to membership in the covenantal community (see Nabal's rejection of Ahab's attempt to purchase his vineyard in 1 Kings 21:3). When Jeremiah's relative is forced to sell the property, the prophet has the obligation of "redeeming" the field so that it will remain within the extended family of his clan (see Lev 25:25-31). There is no clear indication why Hanamel felt compelled to sell the land. It may be that he simply wished to escape the Babylonian invasion and take away something with which to start over. Or, this may be a reflection of his heavy debts in a time when it would have been difficult to bring crops to market.

32:8. courtyard of the guard. Jeremiah was confined, in protective custody, within an area of the king's palace known as the courtyard of the guard (see Jer 37:21). Presumably, he would have been quartered with members of the royal guard. This was much more comfortable accommodations than the "vaulted prison" in Jeremiah 37:15-16 and the empty cistern in 38:6.

32:9. seventeen shekels of silver for land. With 11.4 grams per shekel, this would make the price of Hanamel's field about 194 grams or less than half a pound of silver. This would be the equivalent of about a year and a half of income for the regular laborer. Considering the immanent danger of Babylonian occupation of the entire area, it would seem that land prices would be depressed. However, with no other example to compare, and no idea of the size of the field, it is not possible to say whether this was a fair price.

32:10. deeds. Real estate transactions are found on some of the earliest Mesopotamian clay tablets. These documents, recording the stipulations of purchase and sale, were placed in a clay envelope that also had the details of the transaction written on it. Hammurabi's Code also contains restrictions on the sale of feudatory holdings since they are simply deeded temporarily to soldiers. For other examples of land deeds, see Genesis 23:16-18 and 33:19.

32:10. weighing silver in the scales. Standard commercial procedure would have required that the purchase price be publicly weighed out before witnesses to insure the satisfaction of both parties (see Gen 23:16; Is 46:6). This was necessary since coined money, with standardized weight and value, would not be commonly circulated until the late sixth century.

32:11. sealed and unsealed copies. The Elephantine papyri contain land deeds similar to the one drawn up by Jeremiah and Baruch. The practice of making two copies on a single piece of papyrus or parchment allowed for one to remain open and available for public inspection. The other half, containing the same inscription, served as an archival record to prevent alteration of the stipulations of the transaction. It would have been rolled up and sealed with the names of the witnesses inscribed on it.

32:12. legal agreements in courtyard. Business was often transacted in places like the city gate, where the elders of the city sat (Ruth 4:1; Prov 31:23). The addition of the notation that Jeremiah signed and sealed his deed for the purchase of Hanamel's field before witnesses and "all the Jews sitting in the courtyard of the guard" may be an attempt to mark that place as a suitable place of legal transaction. It may also be related to the charge made against Jeremiah in 37:12-15 that he was attempting to desert the city. He answered that he had only planned to view his newly acquired field, but the captain of the guard, who should have been witness to the transaction, refused to listen and imprisoned him.

32:14. deed sealed in clay jar. Given the un-certain future for Jerusalem, Jeremiah wanted to do everything he could to preserve his deed for the future. Placing the document in a sealed clay jar is similar to what the first-century A.D. inhabitants of Qumran did to store the Dead Sea Scrolls in the face of Roman occupation of their settlement.

32:17-20. connection between creator, judge, and planner. The flow from one area to another in Jeremiah's prayer demonstrates the integrated view of deity that was common in Israel and the ancient world. The role of deity was seen in terms of bringing order out of chaos. In the primeval past this had been accomplished on the cosmic scale through the creation and ordering of the universe. Whether chaos was viewed as monsters that needed to be subdued or the formless void that need to be filled and made functional, the role of deity as creator brought order to the cosmos. On a day-by-day basis, this role was accomplished in society by establishing justice. The chaos of anarchy had to be overcome in the life of the individual, the family, the community and the country. Third, God in his capacity as planner has brought order to the direction of history. As the future unfolds under his guidance, meaning and purpose are brought to what often appear to be random and jumbled sequences of events.

32:21. terror of theophany of divine warrior. The terror in this case is that which is imposed on Israel's enemies (see the comment on Ex 15:13-16). The splendor or "glory" of God overwhelms the enemy. In Mesopotamian texts, the might of the gods is referred to with the term *melammu*, "terrifying radiance and splendor." It is the gods who infuse the kings of Assyria and Babylonia with the knowledge of warfare, give them strength to overcome

---

SEALS AND BULLAE

Seals are small oval stones (sometimes semiprecious) engraved with names or designs to identify the owner. They were stamped onto clay or wax as a signature. The lump of clay or wax is called a bulla. Official and legal documents were sealed to indicate their authenticity. Thousands of seals and bullae have been found by archaeologists, most dating from the eighth to the sixth centuries B.C. These stamp seals were popular in Israel, in contrast to the cylinder seals that were used in Mesopotamia (see comments on Is 8:1 and 8:16). The seals were often engraved with the owner's name and either his father's name or his position. Seals of many periods feature a decoration of some sort. There are many names on these seals that are known from the Bible, but most of the seals do not refer to the person in the Bible, just to someone of the same name. There are, however, about a dozen biblical personages who are named on seals or bullae. This list includes kings such as Jeroboam II, Uzziah, Jotham, Pekah, Ahaz, Hezekiah and perhaps Jehoahaz and Manasseh. Another seal names a Jezebel who may well be the queen who was Elijah's nemesis. Other high officials include Eliakim (Is 22:20), Baruch (in this passage), Jerahmeel (Jer 36:26), Gedaliah (40:5), Jaazaniah (40:8) and perhaps Pelatiah (Ezek 11:1, 13). The seal of Baalis, the sixth-century Ammonite king (see 40:14), has also been found. The greatest significance of the seals is in their ability to help trace the popular beliefs from one period to the next, since the images represented in the art and the divine names used in the personal names both offer authentic data concerning that which was of most importance to the people.

the enemy "like a clashing flood" (Sargon II) or "the onslaught of a storm" (Sennacherib). In the face of such divine magnificence, both the gods and the forces of other nations are utterly defeated and forced to submit to the supreme deity.

32:22. milk and honey. See comment on Numbers 13:27.

32:24. siege ramps. Evidence for the use of siege ramps in the mid-first millennium includes archaeology, reliefs and textual material. The ramp built by the Assyrians for the siege of Lachish in 701 is still visible today. It is estimated that its construction required about twenty-five thousand tons of soil and stone and would have taken a thousand workers three to four weeks to build. Sennacherib's depiction of the siege likewise shows the ramp being used for the battering rams and siege machines. Literary references include Tiglath-Pileser III's description of the artificial mounds and siege works that he used to conquer cities. For more information see comment on 6:6.

32:29. burning incense on roofs. See the comment on Isaiah 22:1 for information on incense altars. Rooftop offerings are predictably made to celestial deities and are attested in Mesopotamia (Gilgamesh's mother in the Gilgamesh Epic) and in Ugarit (Keret).

32:34-35. apostate practices. This litany of offenses relates to the apostasy of Ahaz and Manasseh as traced in the books of Kings and Chronicles. For details see the comments on 2 Chronicles 28 and 33. See the comment on Deuteronomy 12:2-3 for discussion of outdoor shrines. See the comment on Deuteronomy 18:10 for the practice of child sacrifice associated with the god Molech. See the comment on 1 Kings 11:5, 7 for discussion of Molech/Milcom, an Ammonite deity also mentioned in the Old Babylonian Mari texts. Phoenician texts also mention the sacrifice of children to Molech.

33:1-26

Coming Restoration

33:4. tearing down buildings to be used against siege ramps. The Hebrew in this passage is difficult and may be based on technical terms referring to the construction of battlements during the siege of Jerusalem. During time of siege, residences along the wall (common or royal) were commandeered for military use. Some would be used for headquarters or army barracks; some would be dismantled or scavenged for building materials to strengthen the fortifications; some

would be used for makeshift hospitals and morgues; some would be torn down to make room for additional towers, ramparts or a counter-ramp. In Lachish the evidence remains of a counter-ramp that was built inside the walls of the city to strengthen the wall against the ramp the Assyrians constructed outside the city. Archaeological excavations on the eastern slope of Jerusalem, overlooking the Kidron Valley, have uncovered huge masses of masonry that may have been the evidence of the Babylonian attack and the demolishing of private homes that once stood there on terraces. But if this is referred to here, it is difficult to understand what verse 5 is referring to when it says they will be filled with corpses.

33:15. Branch. See comment on 23:5.

34:1-22

Proclamation of Release

34:1. chronology. A more detailed chronology for the beginning of the siege of Jerusalem appears in 2 Kings 25:1 and Jeremiah 52:4, the ninth year of Zedekiah's reign and the tenth day of the tenth month (January 588). The events described in Jeremiah 34:1-7 most likely took place in early spring 588, prior to the Egyptian invasion that briefly lifted the siege.

34:5. funeral fire. These funeral rites were quite elaborate and included the burning of spices as well as a general lamentation and internment in the family tomb. The fire does not imply cremation of the body or an attempt to mask the odors associated with a diseased body, but rather was an expensive display of the king's wealth. The practice is well known among Assyrian kings, where it was used as an apotropaic ritual.

34:7. Lachish and Azekah. These two Judean fortresses guarded the Shephelah border and were the last remaining towns to fall to the invading Babylonians. Dominating the Shephelah and western Judah, Lachish served as the center point of the defensive line of the kings of Judah. Located midway between Jerusalem and the Philistine city states, Lachish guarded the major roads from the coast inland. Its site, Tell ed-Duweir, shows evidence of occupation from the Chalcolithic Period, with massive construction of city defenses and an impressive city gate in the Middle Bronze II (as a major Canaanite city) and Iron II (as the western bastion established after the division of the kingdoms; 2 Chron 11:5-10). Despite its commanding position (a tell 150 feet high), the city fell after a siege by the Assyrian king Sennacherib in 701 B.C. (Annals of

Sennacherib; for more information see 2 Chron 32:9). Graphic evidence of the ferocity of this siege are found in Assyrian reliefs from the royal palace at Nineveh depicting the events and the remains of a massive siege ramp on the southwest corner of the tell. A mass burial, with approximately fifteen hundred bodies, may also be a result of the fall of the city. The city was rebuilt toward the end of the seventh century, but it never regained the importance it had in Assyrian times. Written records of the Babylonian siege in Jeremiah's time exist in the form of twenty-one ostraca letters that were discovered in a guardroom in the city gate (see next entry). Azekah (Tell Zakariya), stood eleven miles north of Lachish and eighteen miles southwest of Jerusalem. It is only a one-acre site overlooking the Elah Valley, but since it is about thirteen hundred feet above sea level, it has strategic value as a mountain stronghold (mentioned in the Assyrian records of Sargon II). The Lachish Letters mention when Azekah's signal fire went out— a very ominous sign for both Lachish and Jerusalem.

34:7. Lachish Letters. The Lachish Letters consist of twenty-one inscribed pieces of broken pottery (ostraca—only twelve of which are actually letters), found at Tell ed-Duweir in British excavations led by J. L. Starkey between 1932 and 1938. The letters were written in a cursive form of Hebrew with a reed pen and a soot-based black ink. They were found in the remains of the city's guardroom and may have been copies of letters sent to Jerusalem by the commander of the garrison during the invasion of Judah by Nebuchadnezzar in 589-587. The letters reflect the breakdown in military discipline during this time of emergency and describe the negotiation with Egypt to reinforce Judah and the desperate situation of the defenders as they note the extinguishing of the signal fires from neighboring Azekah.

34:8-11. proclamation of release. Zedekiah's extraordinary proclamation to release all Hebrew debt slaves comes in the period after the beginning of the Babylonian siege of Jerusalem (January 588) and before the Egyptian invasion of Palestine that temporarily ended the siege (summer 588). It is unclear whether the release was simply a way to add to the number of available defenders for the city or was associated in some way with the slave legislation found in Exodus 21:2-6, Leviticus 25:39-55 and Deuteronomy 15:2-3. In the ancient Near East the freeing of prisoners (from debtors' prison) as an act of justice often occurred in the first or second year of a new king's reign

(and then periodically after that). For example, the Old Babylonian period king Ammisaduqa (seventeenth century B.C.) cancelled economic debts on behalf of Shamash. Thus, the "jubilee" in this case was primarily on behalf of those in debt (for either financial or legal reasons) and debt-slaves. Unlike that of Israel, this Babylonian edict was entirely at the whim of the monarch, and there is no evidence that it was divinely sanctioned.

34:14. sabbatical year release. See the comments on Exodus 21:2-6; Leviticus 25:39-55; and Deuteronomy 15:2-3. Each of these passages deal with the matter of releasing slaves either in the seventh year or during the Jubilee year.

34:18. cutting a calf in two. The ritual of severing an animal body as part of a covenant-making ceremony is found only here and in Genesis 15:9-10 (see the comment on this passage). Ancient Near Eastern parallels from the Old Babylonian Mari letters and the eighth-century Aramaic text of the Sefire Treaty between Abban and Yarimlim both describe cutting an animal in two. The symbolic aspect of this type of sacrifice is to provide a graphic picture of what would happen to the covenant-breaker. When the landowners of Judah took back their debt slaves after the Egyptian invasion had temporarily lifted the siege of Jerusalem, they broke their solemn oath to Yahweh and laid themselves open to horrendous punishment.

34:21. Babylonian withdrawal. The Egyptian pharaoh Psammeticus II had spent much of his reign attempting to regain the territory in Phoenicia and Palestine that Nebuchadnezzar had taken away from his predecessor Necho II. Judah relied heavily on Egyptian promises of aid in return for rebellion against the Babylonians (as noted in the Lachish Letters). Their hopes and the hopes of the Judean exiles were seemingly answered when Pharaoh Apries (who had succeeded to the throne in 589) finally invaded southern Palestine in early summer 588 (see Ezek 30:20-26). This, plus an Egyptian fleet that sailed to Tyre and quickly took control there (mentioned by the Greek historian Herodotus), forced Nebuchadnezzar to withdraw from Jerusalem. The Egyptians, however, were quickly defeated (possibly near Gaza), and the siege resumed by late summer 588.

35:1-19

The Example of the Recabites

35:2. Recabites. This clan associated with the Kenites (1 Chron 2:55) took on a special distinction as a result of the founding of a nomadic order or guild of craftsmen by a ninth-century member, Jehonadab (or Jonadab) son of Recab (2 Kings 10:15-23). Over two centuries later the clansmen told Jeremiah that they lived according to their "father's" rule a nomadic existence, never planting a crop, cultivating a vineyard or tasting wine.

35:6-10. lifestyle of Recabites. What we know about the Recabites is found only in this passage. They claim to follow the command of their founder, Jonadab son of Rechab, who instructed their community to live a nomadic existence, dwelling in tents. They were not to build houses, cultivate fields or drink wine. Frick's evaluation of this group removes them from the realm of religious fundamentalists who have rejected the corrupt religion of the cities of Judah. Instead, he sees them as itinerant craftsmen, doing metal work and repairing chariots and weaponry. This is based in part on Ugaritic and Aramaic texts that associate the name Recab with chariot makers or chariot drivers (see Jehu's invitation to Jonadab in 2 Kings 10:15). By maintaining an independent life on the fringes of settlements, the Recabites were free to move to where employment was available and did not have to be troubled by local jurisdictions or taxes. Their refusal to drink wine may be a defensive measure designed to prevent guild secrets from being disclosed by a drunk member. Their loyalty to the rules of their founder stands in stark contrast to the broken covenant in Zedekiah's time.

35:11. Aramean army. The magnitude of the danger to Judah's inhabitants is found in the Recabites' acceptance of refuge in Jerusalem and the inclusion of an Aramean army in the coalition of Nebuchadnezzar's forces. These events actually occur during the reign of Jehoiakim, and the Recabites are speaking to Jeremiah during the first siege of Jerusalem in 600-597. The Babylonian Chronicle lists a series of campaigns by Nebuchadnezzar into Syria and Palestine between 601 and 598. As a result of these military forays, legions of vassal troops would have been added to the Babylonian ranks. Though we are most familiar with the Arameans connected to the Aramean state north of Israel, there were also eastern Arameans, a Semitic-speaking people who inhabited much of the Tigris-Euphrates Valley. They often appear alongside the Chaldeans. It appears that the Chaldeans were more of an urban based group, while the Arameans were seminomadic.

36:1-32
Burning the Scroll

36:1. chronology. The fourth year of king Jehoiakim was 605-604 (using the Tishri calendar, see comment on 32:1). Nebuchadnezzar's first full regnal year had begun in the spring of 604 (See comments on Daniel 1:1-2). Though Jehoiakim was pro-Egyptian, it is considered likely that he had paid tribute to Nebuchadnezzar in Syria in early 604. The dictation of the scroll probably takes place at the end of Jehoiakim's fourth year (August-September 604), because it is not read until the fifth year (v. 9). Toward the end of 604, Nebuchadnezzar traveled down the coast of Palestine and captured the Philistine city of Ashkelon. There was a massive destruction of the city and a significant deportation. Nebuchadnezzar's march into the south was an occasion for much fear in Judah.

36:2. scroll. The Hebrew in this case suggests a technical term for a special or finer quality scroll, suitable for official use by a government scribe. Such a medium for writing would only be used for the most important proclamations of the king. For more information on scrolls see comment on 30:2.

36:4. scribe taking dictation. The public nature of Jeremiah's dictated oracle required that a careful copy be made, and Baruch's skills as a professional scribe are therefore employed. Many Egyptian tomb paintings as well as the *Teachings of Khety* attest to the importance of scribes to ancient society. Scribes, of course, could be used by anyone, but archaeological evidence (seal impressions containing his name) strongly suggests that Baruch is a royal scribe.

36:6. day of fasting. Baruch is instructed to read the dictated scroll on a fast day when a large crowd would be gathered in Jerusalem. A "fast day," other than the one associated with the Day of Atonement, was not a part of the regular religious calendar but instead was called in the face of some emergency that required the full religious energies of the people. This was likely based on the arrival of Babylonian forces in Palestine (December 604).

36:9. chronology. The ninth month of the fifth year was November-December 604. In December 604, the Babylonian army marched down the Philistine coast and captured the city of Ashkelon. The likelihood that this enemy "from the north" would then turn east toward Jerusalem would be plausible occasion for the fast day on which Baruch was to read the dictated scroll. Nebuchadnezzar returned to Babylon January/February 603.

36:10. topography. The temple of the monarchy period featured three stories of side chambers surrounding the temple on three sides. It can be assumed that Gemariah's chamber was one of these. Little description is offered in the Old Testament of the courts of the temple. It is likely that the upper court referred to here should be considered the same as the "inner" court of 1 Kings 6:36, the area surrounding the temple itself. This is the highest elevation in the temple precinct. The New Gate is also mentioned in Jeremiah 26:10, but its exact location is unknown. Speculation usually places it on the south side of the court as a passage between the temple precinct and the royal palace just to the south.

36:12. secretary's room. The king's audience chamber must have been offset by small rooms where groups could meet to discuss official business or share information. One sign of authority as a king's advisor or scribe would be to have one of these rooms designated as his "office." It seems likely that Jehoiakim's advisers gathered in "Elishama, the secretary's room" prior to taking Jeremiah's scroll to the king because this was their regular meeting place.

36:16. obligation to report prophetic message to king. According to the eighteenth-century Mari texts, it was a strict obligation of any royal adviser or official to report prophetic speech to the king. Several of these documents report warnings by prophets, in one case of a possible revolt, in another to offer a sacrifice, while yet another cautions the king against going on campaign. The emphatic nature of the Hebrew in this verse reinforces the urgency associated with such startling warnings. These officials are frightened by the message, but they also know how important it is to apprise the king of the potential danger in Jeremiah's oracle.

36:18. ink. The composition of the ink used by scribes in the ancient Near East varied somewhat, although they all contained a carbon base. In Egypt, it was common to combine a gum mixture with lampblack. Chemical analysis of the ink used to write the Lachish Letters shows that iron ink was created by mixing the carbon with oak galls and olive oil.

36:22. firepot. Since this event occurred in December, it would have been necessary for the king to have several braziers burning in his audience chamber. It was therefore not surprising that one was near at hand for warmth and perhaps to burn a fumigating incense. It is possible this was actually a permanent hearth within his "winter apartment," but the narrative seems to suggest a portable brazier into which the scrap of scroll could be dramatically dropped.

36:23. written in columns. The word used for "column" in this verse is usually translated as "door." This may suggest that the sheets of the scroll are hinged together or perhaps only that the size of each sheet is approximately the same as that of hinged writing tablets. These tablets, usually wood covered with beeswax, have been found in ancient shipwrecks as well as in a Neo-Assyrian context (the latter being sixteen ivory boards found at the bottom of a well in Nimrud).

36:23. scribe's knife. It is conceivable that Jehoiakim borrowed the scribe's penknife to cut the scroll or that he simply ordered the scribe to do this task. However, if this is a parchment scroll, it would have been easier to cut the leather hinges binding the portions of the scroll together. Parchment would also be slow to burn and would leave a foul odor. If this was a papyrus scroll, the text could have more easily been shredded and burned.

36:23. cutting and burning as means of nullifying. In a sense, by cutting and burning Jeremiah's scroll the king is performing an execration ritual. Early in the second millennium the Egyptians had the practice of writing down the names of cities to be attacked on clay bowls or figurines and, after reciting appropriate spells, smashing them. The writing down of a prophecy like Jeremiah had done was a means of effectuating it (just as speaking it would be). By burning the scroll Jehoiakim hopes to undo or take away the effect of the pronouncement.

36:30. exposure of corpse. What is combined in this phrase is the physical act of dishonoring a corpse by leaving it unburied as well as the divine pronouncement that Jehoiakim's family will be denied the right to rule Judah. A similar curse was laid on Jeroboam by the prophet Ahijah in 1 Kings 14:10-11 and on Ahab by Elijah in 1 Kings 21:21-24. In a later period the Jews of Elephantine cursed their regional governor, Vidranga, who had ordered the destruction of their temple. They prayed to God to allow his corpse to be eaten by dogs, having been exposed to the elements instead of being given proper burial. On the importance of proper burial see comment on 1 Kings 16:4.

37:1-21

Jeremiah Imprisoned

37:1. chronology. Jehoiachin succeeded his father Jehoiakim during the Babylonian siege of

Jerusalem in December 598. His reign only lasted until the city was taken three months later. At that point, his uncle Mattaniah (see 2 Kings 24:17) was placed on the throne by the victorious Nebuchadnezzar and renamed Zedekiah.

37:5-8. Egyptian troop movements. During the siege of Jerusalem in 588, the Egyptian pharaoh Apries dispatched an army into Palestine. This required the Babylonians to temporarily lift their siege (see the comments on Jer 32:2 and 34:21). This action by the Egyptians may be based on treaty commitments made between Zedekiah and Psammeticus II when that pharaoh made a brief visit to Palestine in 592 (based on the Rylands IX papyrus). No actual treaty document exists, and it is not clear whether Zedekiah personally met with the pharaoh or whether (according to the Lachish Letters) a Judean delegation was sent to Egypt. References in Herodotus indicate that the Egyptian troops were more concerned with re-establishing their control over the Phoenician ports of Tyre and Sidon, and there is no indication of a battle with the Babylonians in Palestine before their withdrawal to Egypt.

37:13. Benjamin Gate. Of the many gates of Jerusalem, the Benjamin Gate opened to the northeast and would have been the most convenient for Jeremiah to use when he wished to visit Anathoth. Its importance and the amount of traffic going through this gate are attested in Jeremiah 17:19 and the fact that King Zedekiah used it as a seat of office in Jeremiah 38:7.

37:15. prisons. In the ancient Near East, prisons were used for temporary detention, usually pending a final judgment or prior to execution of sentence. For instance, Mesopotamian practice included imprisonment in a holding cell in a temple (Nungal Hymn) or under house arrest (Mari letters). The fact that Jeremiah is imprisoned in the house of Jonathan the secretary suggests that formal prisons were also uncommon in monarchic Jerusalem. Prisons are seldom mentioned in biblical literature. Only Joseph is described (Gen 39:20) as being held with other prisoners in a detention facility. The prophet Micaiah is imprisoned in an unspecified location pending judgment on whether his prophecies against Ahab came true (1 Kings 22:27). Other examples of imprisonment include work houses, such as that in which the blinded Samson was forced to grind grain (Judg 16:21).

37:16. vaulted cell in a dungeon. Since Jeremiah was accused of attempting to defect to the enemy, it may be presumed that his cell was in an undesirable portion of the house of Jonathan the secretary. Quite likely the architecture of a house built near a gate area or the temple complex would include some small alcoves among the ceiling vaults. These cramped spaces would probably have been too small for a man to stand erect and might well have been poorly ventilated.

37:21. courtyard of the guard. See the comment on Jeremiah 32:8 for this minimum-security area where Jeremiah was next confined.

37:21. street of the bakers. Several references in the prophets suggest that the city of Jerusalem had market and manufacturing districts (see Is 7:3—fullers; Jer 18:2—potters). Similar establishments are mentioned in the Egyptian *Teachings of Khety,* which describe a weaver's shop where workers were confined to an airless room all day. The courtyard of the guard was located near the palace (Jer 32:2), and thus the street of the bakers must have been near by.

38:1-13
Imprisoned in a Cistern

38:6. imprisoned in a cistern. A staging area for troops would have had a cistern to store rainwater during the dry months. Since this stage of the siege of Jerusalem took place during the normally rainy winter months of 588-587, the fact that a narrow-necked limestone cistern was available as a prison and was empty of water attests to the larger population in the city and the desperate situation they faced. The quagmire at the bottom of the cistern, however, would have prevented Jeremiah from resting and would have been extremely unhealthy. Since the king was afraid to execute Jeremiah, he may have been relying on disease or malnutrition to rid him of the prophet (see Ps 79:11).

38:7. Cushite official in the palace. Since Ebed-Melech had a Hebrew name (meaning "servant of the king"), it is likely that he was either an Ethiopian slave or a freedman who had come into royal service. The easy manner in which he confronted Jeremiah's guards and King Zedekiah as he sat in judgment in the city gate suggests both familiarity with the king and that his counsel was held in high esteem. The designation "eunuch" may indicate either his capacity as a royal official and/or his physical condition (see comment on Is 56:4-5).

38:7. king sitting at the Benjamin Gate. There is ample biblical and archaeological evidence available for kings having regularly sat in judgment at the city gate. For example, the

Iron Age gate area at Tell Dan contains a raised platform with stone pedestals for a canopy that served as a place of justice. Absalom argued against his father David's political ability when he charged that the king was not sitting at the gate hearing the cases of his people (2 Sam 15:2-6).

38:14-28
Audience with Zedekiah

38:14. third entrance to the temple. This "third" entrance to the temple is only mentioned in this text. However, since Zedekiah wished a very private audience with Jeremiah, no more secure place could be found than the king's personal entrance to the temple precincts.

38:23. wives and children brought out. When a city fell and a king was taken, his family and his administration were taken also. It was a fearful time, for prospects included, at best, exile and captivity, and at worst, rape, torture and death. Less is known about Babylonian treatment of captives than about the Assyrian practices.

39:1-18
Fall of Jerusalem

39:1-2. chronology. The siege of Jerusalem began in January 588 and ended as the wall was breached on July 18, 586, and the temple destroyed in mid-August of the same year. See comments on 2 Kings 25:1-12.

39:3. seats in the middle gate. The place where the Babylonian officers took their place after the walls of Jerusalem were breached is only attested in this passage. Recent archaeological excavations by Avigad in the Jewish Quarter of the Old City have revealed a portion of the northern wall and a gate area that shows signs of attack and burning. Others believe it should be identified with the Fish Gate in Nehemiah 3:3.

39:4. Zedekiah's flight. Realizing that the city had fallen, Zedekiah and his court took flight through a southern gate (the Babylonian attack was targeting the north wall; see comment on 31:38), located near the "king's garden." This royal estate was probably an orchard watered by the springs of the Kidron Valley (see Neh 3:15). The reference to the two walls may be the section of wall reconstructed by Hezekiah when he bolstered the city's defenses against the Assyrian threat (see 2 Chron 32:5).

39:5. Jericho on way to Arabah. The Arabah refers to the Jordan Valley, where Zedekiah

hopes to cross at the fords of the Jordan by Jericho and escape to Moab or Ammon to find asylum. The road from Jerusalem to Jericho plains is about fifteen miles, a steep descent through barren rocky hills. There are no places to hide, no alternate routes and no defensible fortress on the way—the king is simply counting on a head start to help him escape the country. He nearly made it—he was within a few miles of the river when the Babylonians overtook him.

39:5. Riblah in Hamath. The site of Riblah is located on a large plain in Syria. It was then being used by Nebuchadnezzar as the headquarters for his army. The modern city of Ribleh is located on the Orontes River just south of Lake Homs (see comment on 2 Kings 23:33). Necho II had used the same site as his staging area during the Battle of Carchemish. Hamath refers to both the Syrian city of Hamath as well as the district, which includes the entire area of the Orontes Valley.

39:7. blinding captured kings. See the comment on 2 Kings 25:7. The Assyrian vassal treaty between Ashur-Nirari V and Matti-Ilu of Arpad includes the curse that the one who breaks the treaty will have his eyes torn out. The Assyrian king Esarhaddon boasted of depriving his enemies of ear, nose and eye. Other examples of the use of blinding as a punishment for rebellion can be found in Samson's fate (Judg 16:21) and in the Ammonite threat to blind the right eye of every man in Jabesh-Gilead (1 Sam 11:2).

39:7. bronze shackles. There is evidence from the Assyrian bas-reliefs in Ashurbanipal's palace of prisoners being shackled together as they are herded off to captivity. As early as Tiglath-Pileser III, iron fetters began to be used, and certainly this would be expected in the Neo-Babylonian period. There is no reason to think, however, that bronze shackles did not continue to be used as well.

39:9. Babylonian policy of deportation. The Neo-Babylonians continued the policy of deporting rebellious populations that was first employed by the Assyrian kings Ashurnasirpal II and Tiglath-Pileser III. This was both a political and an economic ploy. It was designed to hold a portion of the people as hostages while a native dynast continued to rule the vassal state. Thus, in 597 Zedekiah had been placed on the throne of Jerusalem while Jehoiachin, much of the royal family, high-ranking priests, nobles and artisans had been taken back to Mesopotamia. Even after Zedekiah's revolt and the fall of Jerusalem, Nebuchadnezzar attempted to maintain native Judean rule through the appointment of Gedaliah. However, his assassination resulted in a Babylonian governor being installed. It should be noted that only a portion of the population was ever deported. The Babylonians still wanted to derive revenue from Judah, and thus land was redistributed to the landless poor with the expectation that the economy of the region could be restored.

39:10. gift of vineyards to poor. Not all of the people of Judah were deported after the fall of Jerusalem in 586. Many of the people, like Jeremiah, had actually been pro-Babylonian or at least anti-Jerusalem in their sentiments (compare Micah's condemnation of Jerusalem in Hezekiah's time—Mic 3:8-12). By redistributing the land that had belonged to persons now exiled, the Babylonians created friendships with the landless poor and also laid the foundation for the agricultural and economic restoration of a land that had been devastated by years of warfare.

40:1-6

Jeremiah Given Freedom

40:1 imperial guard While Nebuzaradan's honorific literally means "chief butler," this is clearly a traditional job title. It had evolved into a position as the commander of a contingent directly under imperial orders. He and the company of soldiers in his charge were given specific tasks (see Jer 39:10, where he is in charge of the deportation of prisoners, and 2 Kings 25:8-11, in which his company destroyed the Jerusalem temple). Delicate tasks, such as the release of Jeremiah from the prisoner-of-war camp at Ramah after the fall of Jerusalem were also part of this extraordinary official's duties.

40:1. Ramah. See the comment on Jeremiah 31:15. This site just north of Jerusalem was being used as a staging area for the deportation of prisoners from Judah.

40:5. Gedaliah. After the fall of Jerusalem in 586 and the arrest of Zedekiah, Nebuchadnezzar installed Gedaliah, son of Ahikam, of the important but non-Davidic house of Shaphan, as governor of Judah. During approximately one to two months of work, he began the restoration of the country's economy from his new administrative center at Mizpah (see 2 Kings 25:22-26). A seal impression bearing the name Gedaliah has been found at Lachish, suggesting that this man had some administrative experience. It is also possible that he was "Master of the Palace" under Zedekiah, a post fitting him for his Babylonian appointment. His efforts at getting a harvest in did encourage some of the refugees to return to

Judah (Jer 40:12), but this was cut short when he was assassinated by Ishmael, son of Nethaniah, who was a member of the royal house and did not want a precedent set of non-Davidic rule.

40:6. Mizpah. After the destruction of Jerusalem and most of the southern Judean cities, Gedaliah was forced to place his administrative capital in the border fortress of Mizpah. The most widely accepted location for this site is Tell en-Nasbeh, eight miles north of Jerusalem on the border with Israel. Archaeological excavations reveal Iron Age fortifications at Tell en-Nasbeh and no destruction level from this period, both suggesting the suitability for immediate use by a newly appointed royal governor. There is also a significant architectural change in the Babylonian period evidencing the change from fortress to government center.

40:7—41:18

Assassination of Gedaliah

40:11-12. refugees in ancient Near East. The nearly continuous periods of warfare in the ancient Near East from the eighth to the sixth centuries created many refugees. While this could include whole families, many times unattached males slipped away, perhaps to form guerilla bands (like those commanded by Jephthah and David in earlier periods) or to blend into the wadis and isolated caves, waiting for the invaders to leave. The less fortunate are depicted on the walls of the palace in the Assyrian capital of Nineveh. These reliefs show some of the refugees from the destroyed city of Lachish (principally women and children), riding in and walking beside wagons containing their few salvaged belongings. Both Assyrian and Babylonian annals contain accounts of the number of prisoners taken from the sacked cities of Syro-Palestine, but one may presume that many others fled before the armies, hiding in the hills, crossing the Jordan River into Moab or joining Bedouin groups.

40:14. Baalis. This Ammonite king may have been supporting the Davidic family's claim to the Jerusalem throne, or he may have simply been an anti-Babylonian monarch who wished to further destabilize Gedaliah's fledgling government. He appears nowhere else in the Bible, but a recently recovered seal impression may provide extrabiblical evident of his reign. This seal, which dates to around 600 B.C., was found at Tell el-'Umeiri, just south of Amman, Jordan. The inscription contains the names Baal-yasha, "Baal saves" and Milkom'or,

"Milkom is light." Recently the seal of Baalis has also been found.

41:1. chronology. Although some commentators suggest that Gedaliah's administration lasted as many as five years, most consider his assassination to have taken place in 586, just one month after the destruction of the temple. The seventh month would have been the time of the Feast of Booths, when many pilgrims would have been on the road, masking the group led by Ishmael.

41:5. shaved beards. See the comments on Leviticus 19:28; Isaiah 7:20; and Esther 4:1 for these common mourning practices and their prohibition. Clearly, popular practice, especially during this period after the destruction of Jerusalem, still included shaving the beard, but there is little attestation of this practice in the extrabiblical texts.

41:5. bringing sacrifices to a destroyed sanctuary. With Jerusalem and its temple destroyed, it seems curious that pilgrims would be on their way to make sacrifices there. Considering the places from which these pilgrims are coming (Shechem, Shiloh and Samaria), all of which have been cultic and political centers, their journey may have overtones of an attempted restoration of Jerusalem. It may be that they even were planning to perform cultic rituals to purify the destroyed temple and thus restore its usefulness (compare the restoration by Josiah in 2 Chron 34:8 and see comment there). Considering the number of destroyed shrines throughout the ancient Near East, there must have been prescribed rituals designed to cleanse them and prepare them to be used once again. Evidence of this is found in the Assyrian annals of Esarhaddon that describe how Marduk allowed Babylon and its temples to be destroyed and restored.

41:9. historical reference. Since Mizpah was not destroyed by the Babylonians, its architectural remains from that period are more intact than those of most other sites. They include large-roomed houses and possibly a small palace indicating Gedaliah's administrative center. There have also been a number of rock-cut cisterns uncovered, one of which may be the one referred to here as having been constructed by King Asa three hundred years earlier (see comment on 2 Chron 16:6). At that time the king of Judah received help from Ben-Hadad of Syria in his war against Israel's King Baasha. A portion of the looted building materials taken from Baasha's fortress at Ramah was used to fortify Mizpah.

41:10-12. distance and directions. If the party is trying to get to Ammonite territory, Gibeon is in the wrong direction. From Mizpah travelers would usually go a couple of miles north to Bethel or a couple of miles south to Ramah to connect to a major road heading east to Jericho and the Jordan. One could only surmise that perhaps when they reached Ramah they found they were being pursued from the north, or perhaps they were even confronted by Johanan's party cutting off the eastern road. Such circumstances might explain their decision to head west toward Gibeon rather than continue east. Gibeon (el-Jib, six miles northwest of Jerusalem) was about three miles southwest of Mizpah.

41:17. Geruth Kimham. This site near Bethlehem is probably the traditional holding of Kimham (2 Sam 19:37). Royal pensioners such as this man generally received a plot of land in exchange for their service (a practice also found in the Mari texts). Geruth is a word unknown elsewhere in the text and may mean "fief" or "land holding."

42:1-22
The Egypt Decision

42:10. God grieving over punishment he sent. In the *Myth of Erra and Ishum,* Marduk abandons his shrine in Babylon to allow Erra, a destructive god, to bring judgment on the people of the city. When the destruction has been carried out, Marduk is full of grief for the city of his dwelling. Yahweh's grief is over the destruction that Jerusalem brought on herself, not second thoughts wishing that he had not acted the way that he did. There is much that is different between the Israelite and Babylonian material, but the motif of a deity grieving over destruction that he himself has brought or allowed is an element common to both. In earlier Sumerian literature, a similar motif is reflected when deities abandon a city for which the divine council has decreed destruction.

43:1-13
Flight to Egypt

43:7. Jewish settlements in Egypt. The flight of Judean refugees to Tahpanes after the assassination of Gedaliah simply swelled the existing Israelite population in Egypt. Isaiah 11:11, dating to the Assyrian period, mentions remnants of the Israelites in both Upper and Lower Egypt. Jeremiah himself addresses Judean settlements in Lower Egypt at Migdol and Memphis (44:1 and 46:14) and in Pathros in Upper Egypt. Papyri found at some of these sites contain obviously Jewish names. The best known of the Jewish communities in

Egypt was that at the island military colony of Elephantine, founded prior to 525, and mentioned in Josephus's "Letter to Aristeas" as the home of mercenary troops in the employ of Pharaoh Psammeticus I. Letters and legal documents from Elephantine speak of a transplanted culture attempting to maintain traditional customs in the face of some hostility by the local Egyptian government and populace. For instance, a small temple was constructed there, but it was subsequently destroyed. Among the letters are communications with the returned Jewish community in Jerusalem during the time of Nehemiah.

43:7. Tahpanhes. This Egyptian fortress is located in the eastern Delta region as it borders on the Sinai. It has been identified with Tell ed-Defenna, with its earliest substantial occupation coming in the seventh century, when Psammeticus I placed a garrison of Greek mercenaries there. Its proximity to the major road leading to Syro-Palestine makes it a likely spot for Judean refugees to find sanctuary.

43:9. Pharaoh's palace in Tahpanhes. Excavations at Tell ed-Defenna are centered on a large rectangular building that dates to the Saite period (seventh-sixth centuries B.C.) and probably served as a governor's residence/administrative center. It is possible that this is the building referred to as "Pharaoh's palace," since all bureaucrats were extensions of royal power. The burial of the large stones at this point could easily symbolize a change of rulers, as the prophet lays the foundation in a clay-brick courtyard (the Hebrew word used occurs only here, and the translation is based on a related word appearing in 2 Sam 12:31 and Nah 3:14).

43:10. royal canopy. For King Nebuchadnezzar to sit in state, it would be necessary to construct a temporary throne, covered by a canopy. The latter served to shelter the king from the sun and also functioned as a symbol of his universal rule (compare God's glory manifested by a canopy of smoke and cloud in Is 4:5).

43:11-12. Babylonian invasion of Egypt. It was inevitable that Nebuchadnezzar would eventually invade and attempt to conquer Egypt. The Medes had united the territory east of the Tigris, effectively cutting Babylon off from direct trade with the east, and the Egyptians, with their Phoenician allies, were constantly causing political and commercial problems in the west and along the Arabian trade routes. An extended (thirteen years according to the fourth-century Greek historian Menander) siege bottled up Tyre and devastated much of Phoenicia (584-571). A fragmentary portion of

Nebuchadnezzar's annals from his thirty-seventh year, Herodotus and Ezekiel 29:19-21 refer to the invasion of Egypt in 568, but no details are given other than victories over desert tribes. It is likely that some Babylonian garrisons were installed in the fortresses of the Sinai following this campaign.

43:13. temple of the sun. Jeremiah applies the Hebrew place name "Beth-Shemesh" (NIV: "temple of the sun") to designate the Egyptian city of Heliopolis in this instance. The usual name applied to this city located near Cairo is On (Gen 41:45), but the prophet apparently wishes to emphasize the worship of the sun god Amon-Re at this site.

43:13. sacred pillars. The Hebrew term used here refers to pillars or standing stones erected to commemorate an event, mark the concluding of a covenant agreement or the entrance to a sanctuary, or as an image of a god (see Gen 28:18-22; Ex 31:49-32; 1 Kings 14:23). In the Egyptian context, these free standing monumental stones are usually termed obelisks, and they were commonly erected to commemorate major victories or the dedication of a temple. For example, the procession way leading up to the temple of Amon-Re in Heliopolis was lined with two rows of obelisks.

44:1-30

Judgment in Egypt

44:1. geographical territory. Jeremiah's message to the Israelite settlements in Egypt encompasses the general area around Tahpanhes in the Delta region, including Migdol (located about twenty miles to the northeast; see Ex 14:2 and Num 33:7) and Memphis. Pathros (NIV: "Upper Egypt"), is a place name referring to the area south of the Delta in Upper Egypt between Memphis and Aswan. Assyrian inscriptions use similar terminology, and Egyptian terminology supports the identification. Excavations at a site now being identified with Migdol reveal Saite period pottery and a fortress whose walls stretch over six hundred feet on either side.

44:15. upper and lower Egypt. The geographical area where Judean refugees had established settlements are spoken of in general terms with this reference. They were primarily situated in the Delta and were not scattered throughout the full length of Egyptian territory. Since the Nile flows north, Upper Egypt is the southern portion. Lower Egypt, the north, includes the Delta region and extends to the region of Memphis.

44:17. Queen of Heaven. See comment on 7:18.

44:18. incense and drink offerings. Incense was valued in the ancient world as an accompaniment to sacrifice. Its sweet scent effectively masked any of the unpleasant odors resulting from the performance of the rituals. It was expensive (see comment on Lev 2:1) but was believed to be favored by the gods. In Mesopotamia, incense was used for dedicatory and propitiatory offerings. The people believed that the incense helped transport prayers to the deity, who would then inhale the incense (for more information see comment on Ex 30:7-8). Pouring out libation offerings is common throughout Mesopotamian history, including offerings of water, wine and blood (compare David's action in 2 Sam 23:16). Assyrian art stylized libation offerings into various classes depending on the type of liquid and where and on what it was poured.

44:19. cakes in her image. It is likely that the use of offering cakes shaped in the goddess's image is a practice borrowed from Mesopotamia. The Hebrew word *kawwanim* is a loan word from Akkadian *kamanu,* a type of sweet cake associated with the cult of Ishtar. They were baked in ashes and often were sweetened with honey or figs. The ritual texts describing *eshsheshu* festivals in Mesopotamian cities mention both meat and cake offerings.

44:30. Hophra's demise. As in Isaiah 7 the prophet Jeremiah offers a sign of God's intentions to a disobedient people. Hophra (known in Greek in Herodotus as Apries) was the fourth king of the Twenty-Sixth Dynasty, succeeding Psammeticus II in 589. He did send a relief army into Palestine during Nebuchadnezzar's siege of Jerusalem, but it quickly withdrew (see Jer 37:5). His naval expedition flanking the Babylonian land forces was partially successful, with Cyprus being conquered. After the fall of Jerusalem, Hophra provided for refugees to settle in the Egyptian Delta region. His eventual end came as a result of his overreliance on mercenary troops and his inability to control the Greek colony at Cyrene. Both Herodotus and a fragmentary stele from the period report that he was killed in a coup carried out by his successor, Amasis, around 570.

45:1-5

Rebuke to Baruch

45:1. chronology. The fourth year of Jehoiakim's reign would have been 605/604 B.C. It was the year in which Nebuchadnezzar defeated the Assyrians at Carchemish. At that point Jehoiakim is still a vassal of the Egyptians, but his political masters are soon to change. See comment on 36:1.

46:1-28

Oracle Against Egypt

46:1. oracles against foreign nations. There is a distinct literary genre within prophetic literature known as oracles against foreign nations. They are found in Isaiah 14—21, 23 and Ezekiel 25—30, Jeremiah 46—51, Amos 1—2, Zephaniah 2 and the books of Obadiah and Nahum. Although they are all condemnations of Israel's enemies, taunting them, their rulers and their gods, each is a distinct unit, free to accomplish its mission without being constrained to follow a set structure or outline. Because these oracles appear in chapter 25 in the Septuagint version of Jeremiah, it is often suggested that they were a distinct unit that circulated as an independent body of literature before being added to the book of Jeremiah. In most cases the oracles were not delivered to the countries they targeted, because their intended audience was Israel. There are short examples of the genre as early as the Mari texts. In one prophecy, the god Dagan delivers a message to Zimri-Lim, king of Mari, concerning his enemy Babylon: "O Babylon, what are you trying to do? I will gather you up in a net."

46:2. Necho. Ruling from 609 to 595 B.C., Necho II was a member of the Egyptian Twenty-Sixth Dynasty. As Assyrian influence waned, this pharaoh expanded his commercial dealing with Palestine and captured the former Philistine city of Gaza (see Jer 47:1-7). The Babylonian Chronicle describes how he took advantage of the mortally wounded Assyrian nation, allying himself with them just prior to the 605 Battle of Carchemish. His expedition to that northern Syrian battlefield to help Ashuruballit took him through Palestine. He defeated Judah's king Josiah in 609 at the Battle of Megiddo and subsequently claimed all the territory he had traversed going north (see comments on 2 Kings 23:33; 2 Chron 35:20; Dan 1:1-2). After the Assyrian defeat at Carchemish, the Babylonian Chronicle details how the Egyptian army was overtaken and utterly destroyed. Babylon extended its sovereignty over Judah in 604, confining the Egyptians to their own territory for the rest of Necho's reign.

46:2. Battle of Carchemish. After the destruction of Nineveh in 612 by a combined Babylonian and Median army lead by Nabopolassar, the last Assyrian dynast, Ashuruballit II, moved his capital to Haran. This stronghold was then captured in 610. Ashuruballit was able to secure an alliance with Necho II of Egypt and continued to claim territory along the Upper Euphrates for the next several years. However, it was only the remnants of the once "invincible" Assyrian army that were defeated at the Battle of Carchemish in 605. The victory was achieved under the leadership of the crown prince, Nebuchadnezzar. Carchemish may be considered a major turning point in ancient Near Eastern history. It signals the final collapse of the largest empire to that time and set the stage for an even larger Persian empire that will succeed the short Neo-Babylonian period. While Egypt gained some temporary claim to Palestine and Phoenicia, Nebuchadnezzar's Babylonian armies quickly followed up the Carchemish campaign by establishing their hold over all of Syro-Palestine by 604.

46:3. large and small shields. Because most ancient Near Eastern warriors were not heavily armored, it was necessary to supply them with shields that would deflect arrows as well as the thrust of sword or dagger (see the equipment for Asa's army in 2 Chron 14:8). The small shield (*magen*) served as a buckler, either held in the left hand or attached to the left arm. Its maneuverability aided hand-to-hand combat. The larger shield (*ṣinna*), which might be either oblong or a figure eight, made from heavier material—either metal, leather or wood—was designed to withstand thrown spears or arrows. However, it was cumbersome and might be difficult to carry into close combat. Some warriors were aided by a shield bearer (see 1 Sam 17:7).

46:4. use of cavalry in seventh century Egypt. Since Egyptian art does not depict cavalry and no mention is made of cavalry in Egyptian texts from the period of the Battle of Carchemish, it is probably fair to say that this feature had not become an important part of the Egyptian army during this era. However, the Medes and Babylonians had been using horsemen as messengers, scouts and mounted warriors (archers as well as shock troops) for at least two centuries prior to Carchemish. For example, a tenth-century relief from the Syro-Hittite site of Tell Halaf depicts horse-men in battle dress. The mobility afforded cavalry, as opposed to the heavier chariots, would have given the Babylonians an edge in battle and in communications on the field. Jeremiah's remarks may then be as ironic as those of the Rabshakeh, who had offered Hezekiah two thousand horses if he had men to ride them (2 Kings 18:23). It is possible that the prophet is taunting an Egyptian army for its lack of men to "mount their steeds."

46:9. Cush, Put and Libya. The Egyptian army included contingents of mercenary and allied troops that evoke past political events in Egyptian history. The list included in this verse, and the order in which each name appears, can be compared to the list of the sons of Ham in Genesis 10:6. A Cushite dynasty ruled Egypt from 711 until 593 B.C. Its recent glory thus gives it prominence of place in the list. Put and Libya are synonymous and represent a much earlier foreign domination of Egypt during the Twenty-Second and Twenty-Third Dynasties (950-720 B.C.). Ionian Greek mercenaries were also part of the Egyptian host. A Greek shield is among the artifacts unearthed at the site of the Battle of Carchemish.

46:11. balm of Gilead. As part of Jeremiah's taunting of the defeated Egyptian forces, he suggests they salve their wounds with the medicinal balm of Gilead, though he gives them no hope of relief. The Hebrew word *ṣori*, based on the Septuagint Greek translation, *rhetine*, "pine resin," is apparently a healing salve made from this resin and mixed with olive oil. It is a product of the upper Galilee and Transjordan region and is referred to by the ancient Greek botanist Theophrastus (see Jer 8:22; 51:8). It remains a matter of dispute which tree or shrub was the source of the resin.

46:13. Nebuchadnezzar's invasion of Egypt. See comment on 43:11-12.

46:14. geographical territory. See comment on 44:1.

46:18. comparison to Tabor and Carmel. Perhaps playing on Egyptian art, which always depicted the pharaoh as much larger than all other men, the prophet now predicts the coming of one (Nebuchadnezzar) whose height and power is to be compared to the mountain peaks (Tabor—1800 feet; Mt. Carmel—1700 feet). This could also be a reference to the route of flight taken by the Egyptians. Mount Tabor is at the eastern end of the Valley of Jezreel, and Mount Carmel forms part of the range of hills that lead south down the Palestinian coast.

46:19. destruction of Memphis. During the seventh and sixth centuries B.C., Memphis (Hebrew: Noph, fifteen miles south of modern Cairo) was the cultural and political capital of Egypt. During the Assyrian period (674 B.C.), Esarhaddon had been successful in capturing Memphis (see comment on 2 Kings 19:9), but that was well before Jeremiah's time. Nebuchadnezzar had moved against Egypt in 601 but had not successfully invaded their territory. The Babylonian forces were repulsed at the Egyptian stronghold of Migdol on the Gaza road and forced to retreat. There is some evidence of Nebuchadnezzar undertaking a second invasion, in his thirty-seventh year (568), but there is no information concerning what success he might have had or whether Memphis was involved. Memphis was captured by the Persian king, Cambyses, in 525, and the pharaoh, Psammeticus II, was taken captive.

46:20. gadfly metaphor. This insect occurs only in this passage, so any identification can only be made with the information provided by the context. With Egypt cast as a heifer in this metaphor, it is easy to see the applicability of the attacking Babylonians as the gadfly or some comparable stinging insect.

46:22. hissing serpent metaphor. The Hebrew text speaks of the snake's "voice" rather than mentioning hissing specifically. Nonetheless, one can imagine a snake hissing its warning at a would-be attacker. The snake is an important part of Egyptian religion and a symbol of royal authority.

46:22. axes, cutting down trees. Destruction by a conqueror often included cutting down trees or orchards (see comment on 2 Kings 19:28). In addition conquest at times had the objective of gaining access to natural resources (see comment on Is 14:8), though, of course, Egypt was not known for its forests.

46:25. Amon of Thebes. The Greek name "Thebes" referred to the city the Egyptians called Waset, about 325 miles south of Memphis. The great temple of Karnak at Thebes was dedicated to Amon-Re, the chief god of Egypt's pantheon beginning with the pharaohs of the Eighteenth Dynasty (sixteenth and fifteenth centuries). Associated with the wind or the "breath of life," Amon was combined with the sun god Re as his worship encompassed all of Egypt. This god's prominence increased as the fortunes of Egypt's empire expanded. As a result, he was credited with being the creator god and his city of Thebes as the site of creation. Thebes had been sacked by Ashurbanipal's Assyrian army in 663 B.C., and much of its wealth had been plundered. Like Memphis, it was also raided by Cambyses in 525.

47:1-7

Oracle Against the Philistines

47:1. Egyptian attack of Gaza. Nebuchadnezzar began his move toward invading Egypt in early 601. However, the investing of Palestine, including the acceptance of Jehoiakim's pledge of loyalty to Babylonian rule, required some delays that prevented any direct move against Egyptian territory until November of that year. Perhaps the king hoped to make as easy a conquest of Egypt as had Ashurbanipal in 663. Since that time, however, the Saite pharaohs of the Twenty-Sixth Dynasty had concentrated much of their efforts and wealth on building several lines of defense along the Gaza road as well as further south. This was designed to prevent an army from making either a direct march along the Sinai's Mediterranean coast or inland across the desert. When, according to Herodotus, Nebuchadnezzar's army was defeated at the Egyptian fortress of Migdol on the eastern branch of the Nile Delta, Necho II's forces pursued him north and captured Gaza. They held it for two years until Nebuchadnezzar once again campaigned in Palestine.

47:4. Philistine situation at end of seventh century. The Philistine city states had been subject to Assyrian rule for much of the seventh century. Ekron, for instance, served as a major olive oil manufacturing and distribution site, bolstering Assyrian fortunes in the region. With the demise of the Assyrians after the death of Ashurbanipal in 627, the Egyptian pharaohs Psammeticus I and Necho II moved into Philistia. Excavations at Ashkelon have revealed evidence (bronze statuettes of Egyptian deities, bronze weights, pottery) of an Egyptian enclave in this Philistine seaport city. Their sway only lasted a couple of decades until Nebuchadnezzar's fall 604 campaign. The Babylonian Chronicle describes a November-December drive to capture Ashkelon signaling a "scorched-earth" policy that eventually totally devastated Judah and Philistia, and was followed by the deportation of a large portion of their population. The Babylonians were primarily concerned with Egypt and did not want to have to deal with establishing a bureaucracy and presence in Philistia as the Assyrians had.

47:4. Philistine relations to Tyre and Sidon. While there may have been some political ties between Philistia and Phoenicia, most of their relations were based on trade and mutual economic interests. The Phoenician seaports of Tyre and Sidon sent their ships throughout the Mediterranean Sea. Their cargoes of "fine ware," ingots of metal and amphoras of oil and wine came from ports in Ionia, Greece and Cyprus. The Philistines, especially Ashkelon and Ashdod, served as one of the markets for these products as well as distributors to customers in Egypt, Arabia and Palestine. The Egyptians also exploited the Phoenician seaports (see the comments on Jer 37:5-8), competing with Nebuchadnezzar for them. The competition eventually leaves Philistia in ruins and Tyre and Sidon in Babylonian hands.

47:4. coasts of Caphtor. This place of origin for the Philistines is most often identified with the island of Crete. The name *kftyw* appears in Egyptian, Ugaritic, Greek and Akkadian texts. While some attempts have been made to equate this with Cyprus, archaeological and geographical indications favor Crete.

47:7. attack on Ashkelon. The Babylonian Chronicle, although a fragmentary account, boasts that Nebuchadnezzar's Babylonian army attacked Ashkelon in the month of Kislev (November-December). This was unusual since it was during the rainy season, a time when most armies do not attempt major campaigns (compare 2 Sam 11:1). The Chronicle notes that not only were the walls were breached and the city taken, but the soldiers burned and leveled the inner city as well, transforming the "city into a mound and heaps of ruin." Modern excavators have found ample evidence of this destruction in every part of the city. Among the artifacts are piles of smashed pottery, skeletal remains showing traumatic injuries, charred grain and collapsed houses.

48:1-47
Oracle Against Moab

48:1. Moabite situation at end of seventh century. Like Philistia, Moab was a vassal state of the Assyrians during the seventh century B.C. Assyrian texts list four Moabite kings who paid tribute down to the reign of Ashurbanipal. Herodotus notes that the Transjordanian kingdoms of Moab and Ammon then fell under the sway of the Babylonians shortly after the fall of Jerusalem. This was a further step by Nebuchadnezzar to exclude the Egyptians from Syro-Palestine and to control the important caravan route through Transjordan. The Egyptians had had a long history of economic and political activity in Moab, dating back to the reign of Thutmose III (c. 1479-1425) and reflected in the eighth-century Shihan Stele, depicting the god Chemosh wearing an Egyptian-style kilt.

48:1. Nebo and Kiriathaim. The site of the town of Nebo, identified with Khirbet el-Mekhayyat just over a mile from the highest peak of Mount Nebo, is mentioned in the Moabite Stele of King Mesha as a Moabite settlement and thus appropriate to this oracle. Mesha claims in his victory stele to have built

Kiriathaim. Its exact location is still unsettled, although several sites have been suggested.

48:2. Heshbon. See the comment on Deuteronomy 2:26 for this Moabite city.

48:3. Horonaim. The strategic location of sites along the King's Highway that transverses the Moabite Plateau must have been a necessity for the Moabite rulers. The Mesha Stele mentions Horonaim as one of these important posts. It was probably located near the modern city of Kathrabba, on the southwestern portion of the plateau—with a clear view of both the Dead Sea valley and the King's Highway.

48:5. Luhith. Extrabiblical source material, including a Nabataean inscription from Madeba and a contract written in Hebrew dating to the Bar Kochba revolt (A.D. 132-135), indicates that Luhith was located in the southwestern section of the Moabite Plateau. There is a Roman road at this point that leads off the plateau and descends to the southern end of the Dead Sea. Surface surveys of pottery suggest occupation during the Iron Age and later at several sites southwest of Kerak and near the modern town of Kathrabba.

48:7. Chemosh. See the comment on Judges 11:24 for this principal deity of the Moabites. A dedicatory stele depicting Chemosh and dating to the ninth or eighth century B.C. has been found at Shihan. As this god is described in the Moabite inscription of Mesha, this meter-tall stele portrays Chemosh as a divine warrior, holding a spear and standing ready to defend the Moabite people.

48:8. valley and plateau, topography in Moab. The Moabite Plateau runs approximately sixty miles north-south as its ragged edge borders the Dead Sea valley on the west and the Arabian desert on the southwest. It then extends about fifteen miles east and west, with an elevation of about three thousand feet. Cutting through this plateau east to west is the Wadi el-Mujib, which has been created by the Arnon River. The southern border is marked by another deep canyon, the Wadi el-Hesa (Zered River). There is an extension of the plateau, known as the "tableland of Medeba" to the north that is more accessible since it does not contain the deep canyons demarking the south.

48:9. salting Moab. See the comment on Judges 9:45 when Abimelech salted the ground of the destroyed city of Shechem. The Annals of the Assyrian king Tiglath-Pileser I record how captured the enemy stronghold of Hunusa and sowed salt over its ruins while pronouncing a curse on anyone who dared to rebuild the town (compare Josh 6:26). The translation of Hebrew *sits* as "salt" is based on a Ugaritic parallel.

48:11. wine dregs. After the grapes have been trod, the resulting juice was poured into large storage jars (9 ¾ gallons), which were sealed with clay, leaving only a small vent hole to bleed off the fermentation gases. The fermentation process was allowed to continue for forty days, as the wine lay with its dregs or lees. Jeremiah's metaphor here relates to the fact that the Moabites had never suffered deportation and so their "processing" was not complete.

48:11-12. pouring from jar to jar. In order to complete the wine-making process, the fermented grape juice must be poured from its original jars into fresh ones. This also involved straining out the dregs so that the fermentation could be completed and the flavor of the wine could age in the underground storage cellars, where a constant 65 degrees Fahrenheit could be maintained. Wine cellars of this type have been discovered at Gibeon and Tell Qasileh. Finally, portions of the wine would be poured into smaller jars for immediate transport and consumption.

48:13. trusting in Bethel. It is likely that this reference is to the Northwest Semitic deity Bethel, attested in personal names and texts for over a thousand years, including the vassal treaties of Esarhaddon (c. 675 B.C.) and at the sixth century B.C. Jewish military colony of Elephantine. The comparison between Chemosh and Bethel adds weight to this being a citation of that god's name. However, it also provides a dual reference to Jeroboam's sanctuary at the city of Bethel (see 1 Kings 13:26-33; Amos 7:13).

48:15-16. invasion of Moab. The only source currently available for a Babylonian invasion of Moab is Josephus. He notes that five years after the destruction of Jerusalem, in the twenty-third year of Nebuchadnezzar's reign (582/ 581), the Babylonian king campaigned in Transjordan, subjecting both Moab and Ammon to his rule. Since hardly any of the Babylonian Chronicles are preserved beyond 594, this cannot be confirmed at this time.

48:18. Dibon. See comment on Numbers 21:30. This city north of the Arnon Gorge was the Moabite capital during the ninth century reign of Mesha.

48:19. Aroer. See the comment on Deuteronomy 2:36-37 for this city located southeast of Dibon and right on the lip the Arnon Gorge.

48:20. Arnon. See the comment on Deuteronomy 2:24 for this deep river valley that bisects Moab east-west.

48:21-24. towns of Moab. The tableland towns mentioned for destruction include unidentified sites (Holon) and some that are uncertain. Jahzah (most likely Khirbet Medeiniyeh, on the eastern edge of the Moabite Plateau), Beth Meon (Ma'in, four miles southwest of Medeba), Kerioth (possibly Khirbet Aleiyan, northeast of Dibon), Dibon, Kiriathaim (possibly el-Qereiyat, five miles northwest of Dibon), Beth Diblathaim (possibly Khirbet Libb, eight miles north of Dibon), Bozrah (possibly Umm el-'Amed, east of Heshbon) are all mentioned in the Mesha inscription. Beth Gamul only appears in this text and may be identified with Khirbet el-Jemeil, eight miles east of Dibon.

48:25. horn. In Mesopotamia the crowns of gods and kings often featured horns as a sign of their power and authority, particularly as it relates to ferocity in war. This would explain why the word horn is often synonymous with strength. Another explanation is that here the word means "bow." This is based on one of the materials used to construct the composite bow (described in the Ugaritic epic of Aqhat) and the phrase "to break the bow" found in Jeremiah 49:35 and Hosea 1:5. There is possible support for this usage in Greek and Egyptian literature.

48:28. dove behavior. The flight of the Moabites from danger is compared to the nesting habits of rock doves. These birds relied on placing their nests in fairly inaccessible cliff faces and the crevices along the sides of gorges like the Arnon to protect their young. The shade afforded would also aid the young birds until their plumage was complete.

48:31. Kir Hareseth. Identified with modern Kerak (seventeen miles south of the Arnon and eleven miles east of the Dead Sea), this was a major Moabite site. It guarded a portion of the King's Highway as well as caravans traveling east and west across the Moabite Plateau.

48:32. Jazer and Sibmah. See comment on Numbers 21:32 for Jazer. Sibmah has not been positively identified, although Khirbet Qarn el Qibsh and Bet Baal Meon have been suggested. It must have been within the region commanded by Heshbon and was apparently known for its vineyards (see Is 16:8-13).

48:34. cites of Moab. For Heshbon see comment on Numbers 21:25-28. For Jahaz see comment on Numbers 21:23. For Horonaim see comment on Jeremiah 48:3. Elealeh is located one and a half miles northeast of Tell Hesban at Khirbet el-'Al. Eglath Shelishiyah has not been identified (see Is 15:5). Zoar (possibly Safi, on the south bank of the Wadi Zered) is the most southern point in this oracle and would be near the Dead Sea. The waters of Nimrim are usually identified with the

Wadi en-Numeirah, a stream that flows into the Dead Sea at its southern end.

48:37. mourning practices. Each of the actions described here are common mourning practices in the ancient Near East. See the comments on Leviticus 10:6-7; Isaiah 15:2-3; 32:11; and Jeremiah 41:5 for further discussion of these rituals and clothing styles.

48:40. eagle metaphor. This is an image of an attacking bird of prey (Babylon), either an eagle or a vulture. The "swoop" is not an easy glide, but an all-out plunge to sweep up the prey (in this case Moab) and carry it away (compare Ezek 17:3-4).

48:41. Kerioth. This Moabite town is mentioned in the Mesha Inscription as well as in the oracle in Amos 2:2. Its exact location still has not been determined, although some possibilities are el-Qereiyat and Khirbet Aleiyan, both in the Moabite tableland.

48:45. Heshbon, Sihon. For Heshbon see the comment on Numbers 21:25-28, and for Sihon see the comment on Numbers 21:24-30. Since Sihon was an Amorite king of the Moab region and his capital was at Heshbon, the reference here must be to the territory he once ruled.

49:1-6
Oracle Against Ammon

49:1. Ammonite situation at end of seventh century. Although the Ammonite kingdom, centered around the capital at Rabbah, was to come under the control of the Babylonians, there is no record of a general exile of its people (v. 3). Inscriptional evidence from Tell el-'Umeiri and Heshbon shows that the Ammonite language continued to be used into the Persian period. There is also a continuity of architecture, with no major destruction levels and the existence of administrative facilities that show continuous use. In addition, there was no disruption in the Iron II style pottery produced even during the Persian period.

49:1. Molech. See comment on 1 Kings 11:5, 7 for this Ammonite god, written Milcom in the Hebrew, not Molech. Coming as it does from the word for "king," the name probably refers to this god as the head of the Ammonite pantheon. He is most often associated with child sacrifice but in this verse refers to the Ammonite takeover of territory once controlled by the Israelite tribe of Gad.

49:1. territory of Gad. See the comment on Numbers 32:34-42 for the extent of Gad's settlements in Transjordan. They are principally in Gilead and Bashan.

49:2. Rabbah. The capital city of the Ammon-

ite kingdom was located at Jebel Qal'a. It presently is in the middle of the modern city of Amman but has been surveyed and partially excavated. Occupation at the site and in its vicinity goes back to Paleolithic times. Although it was occasionally subjected to Israelite rule (see 2 Sam 12:26-31), during the sixth century, the Ammonites attempted to expand their rule northward after the destruction of Jerusalem.

49:3. connection of Heshbon, Ai and Rabbah. The connection between Ammon and Moab in this oracle is clear: both kingdoms and their capital cities are put on notice of coming destruction. However, the mention of Ai seems out of place. The city of Ai (usually identified with et-Tell) is located near Bethel in Israel and has no direct relation to Heshbon or Rabbah. It is possible, since this city name means "the ruin," that another Ai is the subject of Jeremiah's warning.

49:7-22
Oracle Against Edom

49:7. Edomite situation at end of seventh century. Edom had become an Assyrian vassal state in the reign of Tiglath-Pileser III and continued under Assyrian rule until the death of Ashurbanipal a century later. It is likely that the Edomites submitted themselves to Nebuchadnezzar's rule in 605 B.C. Although some Judean refugees may have found shelter in Edom, they apparently remained passive as Jerusalem was destroyed (see Ps 137:7 and Obad 11). The Babylonian campaign against Ammon and Moab in 594 seems not to have affected Edom. It is likely that they remained unscathed until the time of Nabonidus's campaign in 552.

49:7. Teman. This is a geographical name synonymous with Edom (Obad 9) or with the northern section of that southern Transjordanian kingdom, with its capital at Bozrah (see Amos 1:12). It is likely that the nation of Edom originated in this region and eventually was able to expand to the south (see Ezek 25:13).

49:7. wisdom tradition in Teman. See the comment on Obadiah 8. While various types of wisdom are ascribed to ancient peoples, it is possible that that of the Edomites originated in their ability to adapt to their rugged physical environment (see the comment on Obad 3) or their facility in dealing with the caravaneers that regularly passed through their land.

49:8. Dedan. This northwest Arabian oasis (modern al-'Ula) served as a major caravan stop during the sixth century B.C. Although it is mentioned in conjunction with Teman in Ezekiel 25:13, there is no clear evidence of Edom's control of territory that far south. However, inscriptional and pottery evidence do indicate that continual commercial activity, resident merchants and possible political ties may have existed. It is also possible that Edom and the Arabs were being mentioned collectively by the prophets (see Is 21:13).

49:13. Bozrah. Located just west of the King's Highway as well as by the western trade route to the Wadi Arabah, Bozrah (modern Buseirah) served as Edom's capital. Excavations confirm that there was no destruction during Nebuchadnezzar's reign, when Edom was able to stay out of the conflicts that destroyed Jerusalem. There is evidence, however, of a cultural transition after 550, due to Nabonidus's campaign and the shift to Persian rule.

49:23-27
Oracle Against Damascus

49:23. Damascene situation at end of seventh century. Following the collapse of the Assyrian empire, it may be assumed that Aram (Syria, of which Damascus was the capital) regained temporary independence. However, like all the other small states, it then would have had to submit to Babylonian rule after 605. There is no extrabiblical evidence concerning the role or status of Damascus or Aram during the subsequent period, and no large scale excavations have been possible in the modern city. The fact that only Syrian cities are mentioned in this oracle suggests that the nation had been fragmented and that contingents of troops from these sites have raised the prophet's and Yahweh's ire against them.

49:23. Hamath and Arpad. The site of Hamath is in central Syria on the Orontes River, about 130 miles north of Damascus. It has a long history, going back to the third millennium Ebla texts, as a commercial and administrative center. Arpad (Tell Rifaat), was a regional center in northern Syria, and like Hamath had a history of influence until the Assyrian conquest. Both sites are mentioned often in the Assyrian Annals, but their power and intermittent revolts were quenched by the end of the eighth century. For more information see comments on Isaiah 10:9.

49:27. fortresses of Ben-Hadad. As is the case with Omri for the kingdom of Israel (Mesha Inscription and Assyrian Annals) and David for the United Kingdom and later for Judah (Hazael Inscription from Tell Dan), Ben-Hadad's name is associated with the ruling house of Aram. No king bearing that name actually ruled during the seventh or eighth centuries. However, it was traditional to continue to use the founding ruler's name when referring to the nation or its resources.

49:28-33
Oracle Against Kedar and Hazor

49:28. Kedar. The Kedar are one of the north Arabian tribal groups. The name appears in Assyrian and Neo-Babylonian texts suggesting that this was a particularly powerful group. The reference here may be to Nebuchadnezzar's campaign into Arabia in 599-598 and may in fact refer as much to the geographical limit of his army's march as it does to the people they had to deal with.

49:28. Hazor. This refers to the country of the *ḥaṣerim* rather than to the city of Hazor in the upper Galilee region. The desert tribesmen, perhaps associated with those mentioned as inhabitants of the Negev in Joshua 15:23-25, would have been among the targets of Nebuchadnezzar's campaign to pacify and incorporate the northern Arabian area.

49:33. jackals. It is quite common, especially in Jeremiah (see 9:11; 10:33), for desolate or uninhabited places to be referred to as the lair of jackals (see Ps 44:19; Is 34:13). These scavengers would only frequent the desert wastes. What is particularly telling in this verse is that Nebuchadnezzar's campaign will transform these already desolate desert regions into totally uninhabitable places. Similar descriptions occur both in Egypt in the visions of Neferti, and in Mesopotamia, in the Sumerian *Lament over the Destruction of Ur.*

49:34-39
Oracle Against Elam

49:34. Elamite situation at end of seventh century. Occupying much of the Iranian Plateau east of the Tigris River, the Elamite kings allied themselves with the Babylonians for much of the seventh century, as they both fought the Assyrians. The Babylonian Chronicle details many examples of their help, starting with the reign of Merodach-Baladan. Ashurbanipal's annals describe the capture of the Elamite capital of Susa in 640, the systematic pillaging of its treasures and the seizure of their gods. The anger of the Assyrians is seen in the treatment of the Elamite king's body. It was preserved in salt and brought to Nineveh, where it was cremated and the ashes were scattered to the winds. Despite Assyrian hostility, another Elamite dynasty was established after the death of Ashurbanipal and continued to rule in Susa until the merging of their territory with that of the Medes and Persians under Cyrus in the mid-sixth century. This latter situation was facilitated by Nabopolassar's alliance with the Medes prior to the Battle of Carchemish and a resulting deemphasizing of former ties with Elam.

50:1—51:64
Oracle Against Babylon

50:2. fall of Babylon. Jeremiah's predicted fall of Babylon did not actually occur until 539, when Cyrus the Persian king captured the city. Herodotus records that the Persians diverted the waters of the Euphrates and thus entered the Babylon by means of one of its many water channels. Even then the city was not destroyed or looted, since Cyrus was assisted in its capture by disaffected priests of the chief god Marduk and other Babylonian citizens who had become dissatisfied with Nabonidus's rule. (The Cyrus Cylinder preserves the Persian version of these events; see comments on Is 45:1; 48:14.) Since Jeremiah makes no direct mention of Cyrus in his oracle, it may be assumed that this material was written and edited prior to the actual fall of Babylon. He had certainly called for the destruction of the Babylonians and the return of the exiles on other occasions (see Jer 27:7; 29:10). It is therefore appropriate that in this current set of oracles against the nations that Babylon's demise be targeted as the greatest achievement of Yahweh and the greatest good for the people of Judah.

50:2. Bel and Marduk. The title Bel was applied to the supreme god of the Akkadian pantheon, which until the beginning of the second millennium B.C. was Enlil (the patron of the city of Nippur). After the emergence of Babylon as the chief city of Mesopotamia, the title was transferred to its patron deity, Marduk. Evidence of this succession to divine supremacy can be seen in Marduk's prominent place in the Babylonian creation epic *Enuma Elish* and in the prologue to the Code of Hammurabi. In both instances, Marduk is said to have achieved the rank of chief god through his combative powers and the will of the other gods. The name Bel Marduk then continues to be used by the Assyrians and the Neo-Babylonians, and his New Year's festival is the celebration of the renewal of fertility and life (see comment on Is 46:1). Even the Persian king Cyrus looked at his own accession to power and the capture of the city of Babylon as having been achieved through the assistance of Bel Marduk. Connections in the northwest Semitic pantheon with Bel are to be found in the name Baal, also translated as "lord."

50:9. alliance from the north. This is a piece of irony that harks back to Jeremiah's call narrative (Jer 1:14-15), where Babylon was the threat from the north that was destined to overwhelm Jerusalem. Now, in this oracle predicting Babylon's demise, they in turn are to be destroyed by an alliance of forces from the north. In fact this came in the form of the alliance between the Medes and the Persians that had been shaped over a period of twenty years by Cyrus.

50:19. geographical designations. The restoration of the exiles to Israel includes a resumption of their basic economic activities, herding and farming, and a restoration of the covenant promise of fertility within the promised land. Bashan and Carmel are both known for their grazing, while the hill country of Ephraim held rich vineyards and fields, and Gilead served as both a farming area and pastureland. The range of these place names fully encompasses the boundaries of the northern kingdom of Israel.

50:21. Merathaim. The term employed here by Jeremiah is a play on words for Babylon or Babylonia. It is based on an Akkadian term, *marratum,* which is used for the marshy area in southern Mesopotamia where the Tigris-Euphrates delta merges with the salt waters of the Persian Gulf. Thus this Akkadian word that actually means "bitter" fits well with the prophet's oracle of doom against a people who had made the Israelites bitter and now faced rebellion and bitterness themselves.

50:21. Pekod. Again, Jeremiah is using an Akkadian term as a synonym for Babylon. Among the Aramean tribal groups inhabiting Babylonia was one named the Puqudu. The prophet references this tie while employing a pun on the Hebrew word for "punish," *paqad.* It is possible that Jeremiah's choice of the Puqudu, who dwelt principally in the Sealands of southern Mesopotamia and east of the Tigris River, is a further taunt of a once powerful state that has become fragmented and subject to the rebellions of tribal groups within its domain.

50:38. idols going mad with terror. The theme of taunting worthless idols is found elsewhere in the prophets (see Is 40:18-20; Hos 8:4). However, personifying them to the extent of giving them emotions like fear and madness is less common (see Is 19:1). It may be that Jeremiah is drawing on allusions in the Gilgamesh flood epic, where the gods who were responsible for creating the flood waters became frightened by them and "cowered like dogs crouched against the outer wall."

50:39. history of Babylon after 539. After the capture of Babylon by Cyrus of Persia in 539, the city's native dynasty headed by Nabonidus and his son Belshazzar was eradicated and a Persian administrator was appointed to rule there. Economic texts from the year of the takeover indicate little disruption of trade or normal activity, as the Persians made a smooth transition. Each successive Persian king included among his titles "King of Babylon" and used the city as one of their official residences (according to Xenophon). However, there were periodic revolts in Babylonia that had to be quelled (522-521 and again in 482-481). Fearing future uprisings, Xerxes removed the eighteen-foot golden statue of Marduk and destroyed the Esagila temple. The final insult came when the city was merged with the province of Assyria for political purposes. When Alexander seized the Middle East from Persian rule, Babylon was thrown open to the young conqueror and restoration of the Esagila Temple commenced. The city fared poorly under Alexander's successors. Seleucus had a new city, Seleucia on the Tigris, built north of Babylon. This new city competed with Babylon and in 275 B.C. was declared the royal city. The population of Babylon was forcibly removed to Seleucia, and Babylon became no more than an archaic sacred site. By the first century B.C., its desolation was complete.

50:43. Nabonidus in 540-539. Fearing the approach of the Persians, Nabonidus had returned to Babylon from his Arabian capital at Tema in 543. He gathered the images of the gods from his empire (reported on the Cyrus Cylinder) and for the first time in ten years conducted the New Year's festival honoring the god Marduk. According to his own Chronicles, Nabonidus also restored the temple of his personal god Sin. However, his long absence from the city and the neglect of its priesthood and gods by Nabonidus and his coregent Belshazzar had taken a serious toll. He could not prevent the fall of the city of Babylon. Cyrus advanced against Babylon in 539 B.C. and fought a victorious battle at Opis, about fifty miles north-northeast of Babylon on the Tigris in early October. On the eleventh of October, Sippar (thirty-five miles north of Babylon) surrendered, apparently without a battle. On October 13 the city of Babylon submitted, and the Persian army marched into Babylon peacefully. Persian reports claim that they were welcomed by the local populace and that when Cyrus himself entered the city on October 30, he was proclaimed its liberator. This, however, is standard conqueror's rhetoric and may obscure other facts. Classical sources suggest that after the city was captured, the king was taken away as a hostage and died in Persia.

51:1. Leb Kamai cryptogram. The phrase used here is a form of cryptogram known as an atbash. This literary device exchanges the letters of the intended word with corresponding letters counted from the other end of the alphabet (another example occurs in Jer 25:25-26, where Babylon, *bbl*, is replaced by Sheshak, *shshk*). In English this would require replacing A with Z, B with Y, C with X, etc. Thus New York might be referred to as New Blip. In this passage the name Chaldea is masked by using the consonants *lbqmy* (Leb Kamai) for *ksdym* (Caldea). Possibly this was done because of the dangers involved in speaking the name of the enemy, but more likely it is a form of taunting.

51:8. Balm as medicinal ointment. See the comments on 8:22 and 46:11. Akkadian prescription texts exist that take note of symptoms and provide a list of herbs to be used and instructions on how to administer them. The healing balms or resins Jeremiah refers to, however, may be a taunt of these medicines and a reference to God's healing power.

51:11. Medes. During the eighth and seventh centuries, the Median tribes began to organize as a result of their conflict with the Assyrian empire. Eventually, they were able to form an identifiable kingdom in northwestern Iran. The kingdom of Media, led by their king Cyaxares, then allied itself with the Neo-Babylonians to eliminate the Assyrian empire's last hold on Mesopotamia. This alliance allowed the Medes to expand their territory significantly. The Babylonian Chronicle and Herodotus record most of what is known about the conflict between the Medes and the Persians. It seems to have begun with a revolt by Cyrus against his lord, Astyages, king of Media. Once Cyrus had conquered the Median king in 550, he then was able to take advantage of Media's gains to create a much larger empire for the Persians almost immediately.

51:17. no breath in images. See comment on 10:14. Just as Isaiah taunts those who trust in images made my human hands of wood, gold or silver (see comment on Is 44:17-18), Jeremiah ridicules them as lifeless frauds. This is just the reverse of the Israelite God, whose breath brings humans to life and restores the nation from the "dry bones" of Ezekiel 37:5-10. Mesopotamian rituals to activate a cult image include the mouth-washing ritual, a reenactment of the birth of the deity and the use of holy water to open the mouth and eyes and allow the statue to move, but nothing that is intended explicitly to give it breath.

51:27. Ararat. The geographic region referred to here is Urartu, a large area in eastern Asia Minor near Lake Van. It united into a kingdom starting in the ninth and continued to appear in Assyrian and Babylonian records until the sixth centuries. Its conflicts with the Assyrians were the result of Urartian attempts to expand to the southwest and enlarge its trading contacts as far as the Mediterranean. During most of the early period of the kingdom the Urartians built many cities, and their manufactured goods were transported as far away as Greece. They were finally overwhelmed by the coalition of Medes and Scythians in a campaign in 585 that swept through their territory. Subsequently their territory was added to the Persian empire.

51:27. Minni. This nation, summoned by Yahweh to punish Babylon, is the Manneans, who lived in the region just south of Lake Urmia in the northern part of western Asia. These people were caught between the territorial and economic ambitions of Urartu and Assyria. Assyrian texts mention them from the early eighth century onward. Because they were allied with Assyria at the time of the Battle of Carchemish in 605, their territory was given to the Medes and was eventually absorbed into the Persian empire.

51:27. Ashkenaz. The Ashkenaz are mentioned as the Ishkuza in the Assyrian Annals of Sargon II and thereafter, and are referred to by Herodotus as the Scythians. They occupied the region around the Black and Caspian Seas in northwestern Iran starting in the eighth century. These horse-riding pastoralists may be the most likely of the three nations to be a real threat to Babylon in the sixth century. They are mentioned in Babylonian and Persian texts as fierce, even savage, fighters, who occasionally allied themselves with the major powers but also raided them quite often. The excavation of their graves shows widespread contact with Near Eastern and Greek sources as well as a native art style known as "animal style."

51:28. Medes. See comment on 51:11.

51:32. river crossings seized. Military objectives always include control of the fords of streams and rivers (see Judg 3:28; 12:5). In this way, communication links are cut and armies can no longer take the most direct route and are prevented from flanking an enemy force. One of the major fords across the Tigris came under the control of the Persians when they took the city of Opis a few weeks before Babylon fell. They took Sippar on the Euphrates just a few days later. By the possession of these two cities the Persians could effectively cut off any supplies coming down either the Tigris or Euphrates. It would have been extremely demoralizing to the Babylonians to hear that they were becoming increasingly isolated from

their allies as well as the towns and villages that supplied their food and raw materials. This report might well be compared to the progressively negative reports chronicled in the Lachish Letters during Nebuchadnezzar's 598 campaign in Judah.

51:32. marshes on fire. In addition to the wall systems, towers and other typical defensive installations, Babylon was also protected by a number of ditches and pools, designed to slow or stop enemy advance to the city. Within these pools or bordering them were canebrakes. If these were set on fire, they would have added to the sense of peril for the city's inhabitants, and the smoke would have masked enemy movements and intensified the breathing difficulties of people downwind. The fires would also have flushed out any sentries or advance troops that the Babylonians might have stationed along these water obstructions.

51:41. Sheshach. See comment on 25:26 for this cryptogram.

51:44. Bel. See comment on 50:2 for this divine title.

51:58. walls leveled, gates on fire. The main defenses of an ancient city were the walls and fortified gate area. Babylon had a defensive system consisting of two walls surrounding the city. The inner wall was twenty-one feet thick, while the outer wall was over twelve feet thick. Excavations have been unable to reveal evidence of the gates in the outer wall, but there were nine massive gates built into the inner wall, each with the name of a god. The Ishtar gate has been excavated and restored, and is now in the Berlin Museum. It is decorated with lions and dragons, and gives some idea of the grandeur of the ancient city. These walls and gates were constructed of a combination of stone and mud brick. However, in the gates there would have been rooms that required the use of timber as beams and scaffolding for the movement of troops. When submitted to fire, the stone would weaken and collapse (see Judg 9:42-49). With the walls breached and systematically leveled, and the gates in ruins, the physical and symbolic power of the city would evaporate. In the Persian conquest, however, the city was taken without a fight as the Babylonians submitted peacefully to the Persian army (see comment on 50:43).

52:1-34

The Fall of Jerusalem

52:1-27. the fall of Jerusalem. See comments on 2 Kings 25:1-26.

52:31-34. Jehoiachin. See comments on 2 Kings 25:27-30.

LAMENTATIONS

1:1-22
Despair and Distress: First Acrostic Lament

1:1. acrostics. "Acrostic" is a literary form in which the first letter in consecutive lines form a pattern. In alphabetic acrostics the pattern is the alphabet (the first line begins with the first letter of the alphabet, the second line with the second letter, etc). Other forms of acrostic might spell out a message or a name (for instance of the scribe who composed the work or of the deity being honored). There are a number of acrostics in the book of Psalms. Psalm 119 is the most complex in that each letter of the Hebrew alphabet is represented by eight consecutive lines. All Hebrew acrostics in the Bible are alphabetic acrostics. In Lamentations the first four chapters are all alphabetic acrostics. In chapters one and two each verse begins with the appropriate letter and contains three lines. In chapter three there are three lines that start with each letter. In chapter four each verse starts with the appropriate letter and contains two lines. Chapter five has the appropriate number of verses for an acrostic but does not contain one. The seven examples of acrostics in Mesopotamian literature are name/sentence acrostics (since Akkadian was syllabic, there was no alphabet and therefore no alphabetic acrostics) and generally date to the first half of the first millennium. Egyptian examples offer numerical sequences or complex messages that involve both horizontal and vertical patterns. They are more dependent on puns to accomplish their stylistic objective. Acrostics depend on writing and therefore would not be composed orally. They are intended to be read, not

just heard, because of the importance of the visual element. This is especially clear in the Babylonian examples, where a variable sign needs to be read with one value in the poem but with a different value in the acrostic. Some of the Babylonian examples also contain a pattern in the last sign of each line. Another variation is found in those examples where the acrostic is repeated each stanza.

1:3. chronology. Although Judah's deportations had begun a decade earlier, the event that is the focus of the book is the destruction of the temple and the city of Jerusalem, along with the general deportation and exile that occurred in 586 B.C.

1:4. pilgrimage feasts. There were three pilgrimage festivals in the Israelite calendar: the Feast of Unleavened Bread, the Feast of Weeks and the Feast of Tabernacles. Under normal circumstances the roads would be filled with pilgrims traveling to Jerusalem during those times. They were occasions for joy and celebration. In troubled times, few would have taken the risk, and now there was no city or temple to come to.

1:10. pagans in sanctuary. There were very strict regulations about non-Israelites gaining access to the temple courts (see Deut 23). Only priests had any access to the sanctuary, and that was limited. The care taken to preserve the sanctity of God's dwelling place had been frustrated in desecration.

2:1-22
Yahweh's Anger: Second Acrostic Lament

2:1. footstool. The footstool of God's throne

LAMENTS OVER FALLEN CITIES IN THE ANCIENT WORLD

As the fall of Jerusalem became a pivotal point in the history, theology and literature of Israel, the fall of Ur (to an army from the east) at the end of the Ur III Dynasty (about the year 2000) served in the ancient Near East as an illustration of the divine abandonment of a city, resulting in its destruction. The lamentations that memorialize the weeping and the theological reflection on those two great falls are preserved in their respective literatures. Two separate works lament the fall of Ur (known as *The Lament over the Destruction of Ur* and *The Lament over the Destruction of Sumer and Ur*). Other city laments exist for Nippur, Uruk, Eridu and Ekimar (though the last three of these are fragmentary). These date to the twentieth century B.C. Unlike the biblical Lamentations, each of the ancient Near Eastern works includes a decision of the gods to restore the city. Literarily they played a role in the attempts to legitimize a new dynasty.

The major theme of these works is that the gods have abandoned the city, thus exposing it to destruction at the hands of the enemy. In poetic detail the distress of the population is described--loss of land and homes, death of loved ones, exile and captivity. This despair is reflected in the wondering questions of why they have been treated in this way by the gods and how long their condition will persist. When explanations are offered, the fall of the city is not blamed on offense but simply reflects the fact that change and the shifting of political power is inevitable.

was the cherished ark of the covenant (see comment on 1 Chron 28:2). As the most sacred relic of their faith, it was considered that which Yahweh would most jealously protect. If even that held no sway, nothing would be guarded from his anger.

2:3. horn. Horns symbolized strength, but they also represented leadership. The latter would fit better with the end of verse 2. It was common in Mesopotamia for kings and gods to wear crowns featuring horns. Sometimes the sets of horns were stacked one upon another in tiers. The winged lion from Ashurnasirpal's palace has a conical crown on its human head with three pairs of tiered horns embossed on it. In the Sumerian *Lament over the Destruction of Sumer and Ur* the description of the dismantling of the deity's throne includes the line "Its mighty cows with shining horns were captured, their horns were cut off."

2:8. measuring line of destruction. The measuring line was used to determine the area of landholdings, where boundaries were drawn, and what territory belonged to which landholder (private or city), but none of these explain the connection to the walls and ramparts in this verse. From the use of this metaphor in 2 Kings 21:13 and Isaiah 34:11, it can be assumed that it represents a typical action connected with military conquest. A besieging army would not have the leisure to do such measuring during the battle, so this must refer to the demolition phase. It was rare for city walls to be totally demolished, and from Nehemiah we know that Jerusalem's wall was not totally demolished. However, many sections of wall could have suffered damage due to siege machines, battering rams and sapping operations. Plumb lines would have been used to help determine segments of wall that were no longer stable, and the measuring line would have been used to delineate how much of which sections would need to come down.

2:9. gates and bars. In the Sumerian laments it is the gates and bars of the temple that are thrown down as part of the desecration of the temple. Here it is the city's gates and bars. For further discussion of the functions of bars in the gate structure see comment on Judges 16:3.

2:15. clapping hands. Gestures and body language take on different meanings in different cultures. In current Western society, clapping hands can be used to show appreciation, to summon subordinates or children, to get someone's attention, to accompany music or to express frustration (one clap). There were also several functions in the ancient world.

Clapping could be used in praise (Ps 47:1) or applause (2 Kings 11:12), but in these verses a different verb is used. The verb used here designates a gesture of anger or derision (Num 24:10; Job 27:23). Variations may exist in the precise movement involved: compare the different significations in Western culture of (1) striking the palms together parallel to the body on a horizontal plain (applause); (2) slapping the palms together in a roughly vertical movement (frustration); and (3) striking the palms together perpendicular to the body while alternating which hand is on top and which is on bottom (as if knocking the dust off). It is unclear precisely what motion is conveyed here.

2:19. heart poured out like water. Their oppressors clap their hands (*spq kappayim*, v. 15), but here Israel is encouraged to pour out like water (*shpk kammayim*) their hearts. Pouring out water is an act of worship (libation).

2:20. cannibalism. Cannibalism is a standard element of curses in Assyrian treaties of the seventh century. It was the last resort in times of impending starvation. This level of desperation could occur in times of severe famine (as illustrated in the *Atrahasis Epic*) or could be the result of siege (as during Ashurbanipal's siege of Babylon, about 650 B.C.) when the food supply had become depleted, as anticipated in the treaty texts. Siege warfare was common in the ancient world, so this may not have been as rare an occasion as might be presumed.

3:1-66
Hope in God's Faithfulness: Third Acrostic Lament

3:15. bitter herbs and gall. Gall (wormwood) is a bitter-tasting shrub used for medicinal purposes and also occasionally to brew a strong tea. The word translated "bitter herbs" occurs only elsewhere in the Passover passages. It is related to an Akkadian word for lettuce, but since the noun is simply drawn from a word for "bitter" there are numerous other possibilities.

3:16. teeth broken with gravel. The second phrase would suggest that the teeth were broken by shoving the face hard into the gravel rather than forcing someone to chew gravel.

4:1-22
Sin's Results: Fourth Acrostic Lament

4:3. ostriches. There is still controversy over whether "ostrich" is the proper translation of this Hebrew word. Ostriches occur in hunting scenes in Egyptian paintings as well as on cylinder seals, and inhabited many of the regions of the ancient Near East. The alternative translation preferred by some is "eagle-owl." The ostrich identification would correspond with the inattention to the young attributed to the ostrich (different word) in Job 39:16. Casual observation could make the ostrich appear heartless since it lays its eggs in the sand and often leaves the nest to hunt for food.

4:5. delicacies. With the rarity of this word, it must provisionally be concluded that it refers not to a specific food or dish but generally to the delicacies of any sort that would have graced the royal table.

4:5. nurtured in purple. Again the allusion is to royalty, as the color of the garment indicates. Blue/Purple dye was very expensive (see comment on Num 4:6 and Esther 8:15), and its use was restricted to the ceremonial garments of only the highest ranking civil and religious leaders.

4:10. cannibalism. See comment on 2:20.

4:17. expected help from allies. In 597 when Nebuchadnezzar undertook his punitive raid against Jerusalem, Egypt was the principle ally on whom Judah relied. Later that year, Nebuchadnezzar put Zedekiah on the throne. He almost immediately began meeting with a coalition of the small western states to stand together against Nebuchadnezzar (see comment on Jer 27:3). In 595 a new pharaoh, Psammeticus II, took the throne of Egypt. He enjoyed an early military success against the Nubians in the south, and one papyrus reports that his success was celebrated with a victory tour in Palestine. There was cause to expect his support against Babylon. It is uncertain which nations were actually part of the alliance when it finally took shape. As it turned out, Egypt's army was routed in its confrontation with the Babylonians in 588 (see Jer 37:5-7), and it would appear, based on Psalm 137:7, that allies such as the Edomites threw their support to Babylon when it became clear that Jerusalem was about to fall.

4:21. Edom's role. Edom had become an Assyrian vassal state in the reign of Tiglath-Pileser III and continued under this rule until the death of Ashurbanipal a century later. It is likely that they submitted themselves to Nebuchadnezzar's rule in 605. Although some Judean refugees may have found shelter in Edom, the Edomites apparently remained passive as Jerusalem was destroyed (see Ps 137:7 and Obad 11). The Babylonian campaign against Ammon and Moab in 594 seems not to have affected Edom. It is likely that they remained unscathed until the time of Nabon-

idus's campaign in 552.

4:21. Uz. Uz, the homeland of Job, is identified with Edom and northwest Arabia in Esau's genealogy (Gen 36:28).

5:1-22
Joy Is Gone: Nonacrostic Lament

5:6. Egypt and Assyria. From the beginning of the seventh century, Judah had been under Assyrian control. Manasseh was a loyal vassal for most of his fifty-five years. During the time of Josiah, Judah experienced a glimpse of independence as the mantle was shifting from Assyria to Babylon. During that interim, Egypt began to exercise more control in the region. Jehoiakim, son of Josiah, had been put on the throne by the Egyptians in 609 and remained loyal to them until Nebuchadnezzar's domination made that impossible. After the fall of Ashkelon to Nebuchadnezzar in 604 Jehoiakim paid tribute to Babylon for a few years. But when Nebuchadnezzar failed in his attempted invasion of Egypt in 601, Jehoiakim again sided with Egypt and stopped sending the yearly tribute east. Thus in 597 when Nebuchadnezzar undertook his punitive raid against Jerusalem, Egypt was the principal ally on whom Judah relied. It can fairly be said then that Judah had been totally dependent on Egypt and Assyria—and that goes back a century or more.

5:12. princes hung by their hands. The Hebrew text is ambiguous regarding whether the princes are hung "at the hands of the enemy" or are hung "suspended from their own hands." There is no precedent for the latter. Hanging implies execution and was generally used after the execution had taken place. Victims were usually hung by being impaled. The practice was most commonly used on rebellion leaders or members of the royal house (1 Sam 31:10). The practice of impaling the bodies of their defeated enemies was commonly used by armies in the ancient Near East. For instance, the Assyrians considered it a psychological ploy and a terror tactic (as depicted on the walls of their royal palaces). See also the comment on Esther 2:23.

5:13. toiling at millstones. Grinding grain into flour was usually done with millstones and was the job of the lowest members of society. One of the basic "appliances" of any ancient household would have been the handmill (called a saddle quern) with two stones for grinding: a lower stone with a concave surface and a loaf-shaped upper stone. The daily chore of grinding grain into flour involved sliding the upper stone over the grain spread on the lower stone. Larger milling houses often served as prison workhouses in Mesopotamia, but each prisoner still used a handmill for grinding. The large rotary mill that could be powered by donkey or slave labor was not invented until after the Old Testament period. The palace at Ebla had a room containing sixteen handmills inferred to be a place where prisoners ground grain. Grinding houses would include prisoners of war, criminals and those who had defaulted on their debts.

5:13. loads of wood. Wood was a constant necessity for keeping the fires of the kitchens supplied. Palace, temple and the upper class employed the services of slave labor to man the system. Even children were capable of helping transport and distribute the wood.

5:16. crown. Crowns are worn by royalty as a symbol of their status and authority. As a result the word was extended to refer to the abstract concept of the dignity and honor that are the natural accompaniment of status and authority. In this passage the reference is not to an actual crown that Israel wore but to the dignity and honor.

EZEKIEL

1:1-28

The Chariot Throne Vision

1:1-2. chronology. The fifth year of Jehoiachin's reign would have been the year 593 B.C., at the end of the month of July (the fourth month). This chronology takes into account Jehoiachin's accession to Judah's throne during the siege of Jerusalem, which according to the Babylonian Chronicle began in November/December 598. There has been a great deal of speculation regarding the meaning of "in the thirtieth year," because 593 is not the thirtieth year of anything. A common suggestion is that this simply refers to Ezekiel's own birth date and qualifies him to speak on these matters since he has officially reached the age required for admission into the working priesthood (Num 4:30).

1:1. Kebar River. Rather than being an actual river, the Kebar was a canal that diverged from the Euphrates River north of Babylon and continued for sixty miles southeast until it rejoined the Euphrates near Erech. The network of irrigation and transport canals was known as the "waters of Babylon" (Ps 137:1). It served as a means of extending the arable land of southern Mesopotamia and provided water to small settlements along its course (see comment on 3:15).

1:1. apocalyptic visions. Apocalyptic literature is characterized by visions filled with the imagery associated with God's manifold powers as creator. A divine messenger usually interprets the message that is conveyed to the prophet (see Rev 1:1-3). There are some pieces of Akkadian literature that show prototypes of some of the characteristics of biblical apocalyptic, but nothing that is very close (for closest connection see sidebar on Akkadian apocalypses at Dan 11). Apocalyptic literature is most recognizable in its use of rich symbolism that draws heavily on mythological motifs. In prophetic literature the symbols are rarely interpreted. Often the visions themselves do not symbolically represent a foretold happening but serve as occasions for a message concerning what God is going to do. Most scholars now consider Ezekiel's prophetic visions as being influential on later apocalyptic literature (see Dan 7—12 and Zech 8—14). For instance, his vision of God enthroned in a shining chariot has been incorporated into Daniel 10:5-6 and the pseudepigraphal 1 Enoch 14:18.

1:2. Jehoiachin's exile. Along with most of the royal court and many of the influential or wealthy members of Judean society, Jehoiachin was taken into exile when Jerusalem fell to Nebuchadnezzar's army in 597 (see 2 Kings 24:8-17). Babylonian ration lists include mention of quantities of oil being supplied to the "king of Judah" along with other high-ranking prisoners of war and dependents of the royal household. Eventually, in 561 B.C., during the reign of Nebuchadnezzar's successor, Amel-Marduk (the biblical Evil-Merodach), Jehoiachin was freed from his imprisonment (probably house arrest) and allowed the freedom of the king's court (see 2 Kings 25:27-30). He died in exile, bringing an official end to the Judean monarchy.

1:3. exilic community. The exilic community, of which Ezekiel was a member, was a relatively small group in 593 B.C.—perhaps ten thousand persons. However, looking at Nebuchadnezzar's list of deportees in 2 Kings 24:14-16, it would appear that they comprised the military, political and religious leaders as well as craftsmen who could be employed in the Babylonian king's numerous building projects. The trained soldiers were also probably pressed into service in the Babylonian army. It was only after 587 that a large portion of Judah's population joined their fellows in Mesopotamia. This policy of deporting hostages and large segments of a rebellious nation was widely used by both the Assyrians and the Babylonians. The Babylonian practice of settling the exiles in self-contained villages is demonstrated in texts from Nippur. While it was a traumatic event for the people of Judah, they were encouraged to settle into their new situation (see Jer 29:4-23). Textual evidence from the Persian period (fifth century B.C. Murashu texts) suggests that they followed this advice, starting businesses, working farms and creating an identity for themselves in exile.

1:4. elements of theophany. A theophany consists of a manifestation of God's presence to a human (see the classic example in the Sinai theophany of Moses in Ex 3). This may occur in person, although God's person is never actually described in any detail, and there is always a great sense of dread on the part of the human involved (see Gen 28:16-17; 32:24-30). Fear is generated by the power evidenced in God's "glory" (*kabod*), a divine attribute also found in Mesopotamian epics (there called *melammu*). The purpose of a theophany is often to call a human to serve the deity. Thus Elijah, although already serving Yahweh as a prophet, is called to greater tasks during his meeting with God on Mount Horeb (1 Kings 19). The major prophets each have a theophany that marks the beginning of their ministry. For instance, Isaiah's vision (Is 6) encompasses the Jerusalem temple and harks back to Moses' experience, and Jeremiah's call narrative has coronation overtones (Jer 1). In Ezekiel's case the appearance of God is described as overwhelming and mysterious. There are symbols of God's power implicit in the divine chariot, the accompanying creatures and the dominance of all of nature's forces. Naturally, once chosen, prophets must ultimately accept their mission, although they generally try to provide excuses.

1:5. winged, upright creatures as throne guardians in ancient Near East. There are numerous examples from ancient Near Eastern art of winged creatures with human faces, especially from the Assyrian palaces and temples of Nimrud and Nineveh, but most of these are quadrupeds. Among these are the massive guardian figures uncovered in the remains of the Nimrud palace of the Assyrian king Sennacherib. One is a winged bull with a human head, and the other has the body of a lion with a human face. Ashurnasirpal's palace at Kalhu contains figures of this type strategically placed at the entrance to palaces and temples and in throne rooms. Their huge size (eight feet high) was designed to intimidate all who entered. Syro-Phoenician art contains similar images of winged sphinxes (lion's body, eagle's wings and human head). Upright (biped) composites are less attested. Four-winged, eagle-headed human figures are portrayed in the Ninurta temple at Nimrud. Achaemenid Persian iconography depicts upright creatures that have four wings, human heads and bull legs and hooves.

1:6, 10. four-faced creatures. There does not seem to be any exact Near Eastern parallels to these multifaced creatures. Though eagle, bull and lion faces are all common on composite creatures (in fact, these are the only beasts so featured in Mesopotamian art), there are few examples of multiple faces on the same creature. One example exists that has a lion head with a human head perched on top of it. Only the far-removed Roman god Janus provides an attenuated model, with one face looking forward and one backward. The purpose of these creatures is also multifaceted. By being able to look in all four directions, the creatures serve the same function as the wheels of the chariot (v. 17), which could travel in any of the four directions. Both represent the power of the deity to be present anyway and to be aware of all events on earth. In addition, the animal bodies represented here (lion, eagle, bull/ox) all have parallels in Near Eastern art, and each symbolizes specific powers or attributes that signify the omnipotence of God: the lion indicates strength (2 Sam 1:23); the eagle indicates speed and gracefulness (Is 40:31); the ox indicates fertility (Ps 106:19-20).

1:15-18. wheel technology. Naturally a chariot with wheels facing all four directions could not travel effectively in any direction. However, the purpose of the image is found in its symbolic value of attention to all of the corners of the world—God's omnipresence. In addition, the chariot is actually upheld on the outstretched wings of God's four-faced creatures and flies through the air. There is, however, a sense of motion implicit in having the wheels in place. This is based on a comparison with the winged-bull figures that guarded entranceways in Assyrian palaces. Many of them have a fifth leg to suggest that though the figure is frozen in the relief, it is actually dynamic and in motion. Assyrian art also provides examples of wheeled chariots with high rims and multiple spokes that may be the origin of this image in Ezekiel. The wheels sometimes feature thick rims made up of concentric bands, as well as spokes. The depiction of a "wheel within a wheel" may thus represent greater stability for the chariot, as multiple axles and tires do for modern trucks. The description of "eyes" within the wheels finds its explanation in Babylonian terminology where the word "eyes" is used for oval gems. Semiprecious stones were embedded in the rims to sparkle and dazzle onlookers.

1:22. expanse over the heads. Above the heads of the four creatures is a platform sparkling like crystal or ice. Ancient Near Eastern glyptic art and sculpture contain images of winged creatures holding up a pillar, a throne or a platform. For instance, in the seventh-century Assyrian palace at Nineveh, miniature sphinxes served as column bases. Similarly, a twelfth-century Phoenician wheeled cult stand depicts a human-faced, lion-bodied, winged figure. Its wings and head appear to be holding up one side of the stand. More significantly, first-millennium Mesopotamian texts speak of three levels of the heavens, each of which feature pavements of different colored stone. The lower heavens are said to have a platform of jasper, usually associated with a glassy, translucent or opaque appearance. In these texts the pavement of the middle heavens is lapis lazuli (see comment on Ex 24:10) and holds up the dais of the god Bel (Marduk).

1:26. throne chariot. Since the gods in the ancient Near East often participated in processions, there were vehicles used for their transport. Engraved cylinder seals from the end of the third millennium show a deity standing in a four-wheeled chariot/cart drawn by a composite quadruped with a lion's head and wings. Assyrian reliefs show wheeled thrones for both kings and gods that also feature poles for bearers to use to carry the throne.

1:26-28. appearance of throne and figure. The dazzling character of this vision can only be compared to a rainbow or a fiery visage. This would be in keeping with the Mesopotamian concept of *melammu* ("clothed with power") as it regularly appears in the description of Mesopotamian gods (for instance, Marduk in the *Enuma Elish* creation story). In Mesopotamian texts of this general period, a platform in the middle heavens made of lapis lazuli (a better interpretation of the word translated sapphire in v. 26) supports a cella and dais of Bel. The cella is said to shine with the appearance of glass and crystal. The description of the elements of this vision conform to the conventions of the motifs familiar in Mesopotamia.

2:1—3:15
Ezekiel's Call

2:6. briers, thorns and scorpions. Call narratives for prophets generally follow a set pattern. When the chosen prophet makes excuses and shows apprehension, God provides reassurances (see Jer 1:7-8). In Ezekiel's case the use of unusual terms (these particular words translated briers and thorns appear only in Ezekiel) is somewhat confusing. However, what may be implied is that God is building a protective wall around the prophet made of stinging thorns. It has been plausibly suggested that "scorpion" here refers to a type of bush rather than the stinging creature.

3:1-3. eating a scroll. The imagery associated with Ezekiel eating the scroll presented to him by God is part of his call narrative and his acceptance of his mission. The words on the scroll must be internalized. They are also empowering in much the same way that God's touching Jeremiah's mouth empowered him to speak his prophecies (Jer 1:9). There are no direct ancient Near Eastern parallels. It is possible that consuming a piece of parchment or papyrus with an incantation or the name of a god was part of the ritual practices of either Egypt or Mesopotamia. The term *asakku*, meaning "set aside for the gods" or taboo, is used in the Mari texts and other Old Babylonian texts in reference to not "consuming" what belongs to the gods.

3:9. imagery of hard forehead. Comparison with Akkadian usage of the same term suggests that Ezekiel's forehead is being compared with the hardest of stones. It is unlikely to be a diamond since there is no attestation of diamonds in the ancient Near East for another century after Ezekiel.

3:14. transported by the spirit. In Hebrew the word for spirit can also mean wind. As early as Sumerian usage the word for wind/spirit was also used in connection with dreams and visions. The god of dreams was named "the winds." In Akkadian the name of the god who brought dreams was Zaqiqu, which is derived from the word for wind/spirit. Additionally, in a dream or vision, it was believed that the "spirit" of the person arises and may move around. In later literature the pseudepigraphal book of *1 Enoch* describes the antediluvian patriarch being transported by angels to the garden of Eden, where he served as a "watcher" of the doings of humanity and recorded them in a book.

3:15. Tel Abib. Technically, the name Tel Abib (Babylonian *til abubi*) means a place created by the flotsam and jetsam of a flood. A "tell" is the term used for any ruined city site. Thus the exiled families of Judah might have been set in a place that had been destroyed, either by war or flood, and expected to rebuild it and bring the Nippur area on the canal Kebar back into production. There is also an excellent dual meaning, since the people of Judah had been swept here by the tide of Babylonia's military victory.

3:16-27
Ezekiel the Watchman

3:22-26. results of Yahweh's hand (mute). Some have suggested physical ailments, from aphasia to schizophrenia, as the cause of Ezekiel's problems. Several commentators have also suggested either a conscious decision on Ezekiel's part to limit his role as mediator between the people and God, or a divine restriction on his speech (either one being divinely imposed). Ezekiel's experience is comparable to that described in Akkadian incantation texts, which speak of being "touched by a god" and struck dumb. This material would have been familiar to the prophet and provided him with an excellent parallel to the nature of his prophetic state rather than a physical diagnosis. The sense of paralysis (cf. 4:8) and the inability to speak were well-known symptoms of supernatural overpowerment in the ancient world. Incantations sought to impose such conditions, and demonic oppression was characterized by them. In one piece of Babylonian wisdom literature *(Ludlul Bel Nemeqi)*, an individual who cannot understand why he is suffering describes his condition as including his lips being struck dumb and his arms and legs being stiff and paralyzed. His suffering is all attributed to the "heavy hand of Marduk."

4:1—5:17
Sign-Act Prophecies of Coming Destruction

4:1. sign acts. In the Mari texts from over a millennium earlier than Ezekiel, prophets were already using symbolic actions and wordplays as a medium for their prophetic message. In one instance a prophet devoured a raw lamb to announce an imminent danger that could devour the land. Forms of street theater are employed by Isaiah (Is 20—traveling naked) and Jeremiah (Jer 19—execration ritual following a procession) to engage their audience and demonstrate through their actions how serious the threat is to the people.

4:1. clay tablets used for maps. While it is rare to find a clay tablet that contains a map image, there is a Kassite period (fifteenth century B.C.) map of the city of Nippur. It shows canals radiating from the Euphrates River and suggests that these water channels into neighborhoods divided the city. The map shows two parallel lines and indicates three gates and the city walls. Temples and storehouses also are marked on the drawing. A world map was found near the site of Sippar dating to the seventh century B.C. A river surrounds the circular disk of the world, and mountains are drawn at the top of the image. Babylon, Assyria and other cities, regions and nations are identified on the map.

4:2. siege strategies. All of the strategies described here are typical of Assyrian and Babylonian siege engines and techniques. They are often depicted on palace walls in Nineveh and Babylon. See the comments on Jeremiah 6:6 and Isaiah 29:2 for siege works and ramps. Battering rams are sometimes attached to portable towers that are wheeled up to city walls or gates. The glacis, a slope built diagonally against the wall, was constructed to prevent effective use of the ram. Camps were erected all around a city to prevent the escape of the inhabitants. One of the most graphic examples of this still in existence is the remains of the Roman camps built all around the fortress of Masada during the revolt of A.D. 70.

4:3. function of iron pans. The Israelites baked their bread and prepared grain offerings on griddles laid over an open fire or placed into an earthen oven. The rich would have been able to afford copper or iron griddles, while the poor would have used ceramic disks.

4:3. symbolism of iron wall. Iron in earlier periods was counted among the precious metals. Although more commonly used in the sixth century B.C., it still would have been considered a prized object because of its strength and durability. Since Ezekiel is directing the symbolic siege, he must represent God. The iron wall is then understood to be the barrier between God and the people of Jerusalem. It signals that they may expect no help in the coming siege from the Divine Warrior Yahweh.

4:9. ingredients of bread. The items listed

here from which Ezekiel is to make his loaf of bread include some common grains (durum wheat, barley and emmer wheat). These grains were part of the diet of all the peoples of the ancient Near East, and there are cognate words in Akkadian and Ugaritic for each of them. Millet is a summer grain. The unusual items in this recipe are beans and lentils. While these vegetables were used for soups and occasionally ground up and mixed with wheat to make a crude bread, that would have been unusual. D. Block suggests plausibly that Ezekiel's mixture is symbolic of a siege bread made from whatever could be scraped from the bottom of all of the food bins.

4:10. amount of food. The fact that Ezekiel's food has to be weighed out and eaten at a particular time signals that this is the hard rationing that would have been necessary during a siege. Twenty shekels would be equivalent to eight ounces of food. That amount of calories would keep him alive, but it would also significantly weaken him. The weakness of a starvation diet mirrors conditions in Jerusalem.

4:11. amount of water. Water rationing would also be necessary during the siege, since the people would be dependent on the supply in cisterns (see the comment on Jer 38:6) and the pool deriving from the Siloam tunnel. Ezekiel's ration is one-sixth of a hin or two-thirds of a quart per day. The extremely hot conditions during the summer and fall of 588 would have severely taxed the besieged people of Jerusalem. Such a small water ration would have further contributed to their misery.

4:12, 15. fuel for fire. The typical fuel in areas like Mesopotamia and Palestine was dried animal dung or cakes made from the waste pulp of crushed olives. Trees were too precious to be cut for cooking and warming. Ezekiel, however, is horrified when God commands him to cook using human dung, an unclean substance that must be buried away from human habitation (Deut 23:12-14). He was a priest and this act would defile him; he simply cannot bring himself to obey. Thus God compromises by allowing him to cook over animal dung.

5:1. sword as razor. A sword would have been an awkward instrument to shave the beard and head. Though "sword" is the usual translation of this Hebrew word, it can be used for other sharp implements, including axes, daggers and chisels (cf. 26:9 and Josh 5:2). In Ugaritic, an implement described by this word is used to carve roast meat. A general-purpose translation like "blade" would be preferable. The choice of this word may have been dictated by the desired reference to the use of the sword by the Babylonians to shame and conquer Jerusalem.

5:2. use of hair in offerings. Cutting or shaving the hair is most often associated with rituals of mourning (see comment on Is 15:2). However, when a Nazirite vow has been completed, the law commands that the hair that has been dedicated during the period of the vow is to be cut and placed as a sacrifice in the fire (Num 6:18). In ancient thinking, hair (along with blood) was one of the main representatives of a person's life essence. As such it was often an ingredient in sympathetic magic. This is evident, for instance, in the practice of sending along a lock of the presumed prophet's hair when the prophecies were sent to the king of Mari. The hair would be used in divination to determine whether the prophet's message would be accepted as valid.

5:10. cannibalism. One of the terrible results of a long siege of a walled city was food shortage. It sometimes became so severe that the inhabitants of the city resorted to cannibalism (see comment on 2 Kings 6:29). For instance, the Assyrian annals of Ashurbanipal describe his siege of Babylon 650-648 B.C. and the desperation of the starving people who were reduced to cannibalism. There are also a number of Mesopotamian treaties that contain a curse that calls for the violator of the treaty to feed on his own family or his own people (as in the Ashurnirari V's treaty with Mati'ilu of Arpad). Biblical versions of this type of curse can be found in Leviticus 26:29 and Deuteronomy 28:53-57.

5:17. famine and wild beasts. These two punishments are related only as part of a typical group of punishments that deity is inclined to send (two more, plague and bloodshed, occur in the second half of the verse). As early as the Gilgamesh Epic in Mesopotamia, the god Ea had reprimanded Enlil for not sending lions to ravage the people rather than using something as dramatic as a flood. The gods used wild beasts along with disease, drought and famine to reduce the human population. A common threat connected to negative omens in the Assyrian period was that lions and wolves would rage through the land. In like manner, devastation by wild animals was one of the curses invoked for treaty violation (see also Deut 32:24).

6:1—7:27
Prophecies of Judgment Against Israel

6:3. high places. See the comment on 1 Samuel 9:12 for these local places of worship often associated with Canaanite or false religious practices.

6:5. bones scattered around altars. There are three significances that combine to give this action meaning. The first concerns the exposure of the corpses of the dead. For the importance of proper burial, see the comments on Joshua 8:29 and 1 Kings 16:4. The second concerns desecration of the holy sites. In Israelite thinking, contact with the dead rendered someone or something unclean. Sacred sites could therefore be permanently contaminated if they were made repositories for that which was unclean (see comment on 2 Kings 10:27). The third significance concerns assigning responsibility for the fate of the Israelites who have perished. Their death is on the heads of these idols and altars that did nothing to save them. For yet one more significance, see the comment on verse 13.

6:11. body language. Gestures and body language take on different meanings in different cultures. In current Western society, clapping hands can be used to show appreciation, to summon subordinates or children, to get someone's attention, to accompany music or to express frustration (one clap). There were also several functions in the ancient world. Clapping could be used in praise (Ps 47:1) or applause (2 Kings 11:12), or as a gesture of anger or derision (Num 24:10; Job 27:23). Variations may exist in the precise movement involved: compare the different significations in western culture of (1) striking the palms together parallel to the body on a horizontal plain (applause); (2) slapping the palms together in a roughly vertical movement (frustration); and (3) striking the palms together perpendicular to the body while alternating which hand is on top and which is on bottom (as if knocking the dust off). Ezekiel is instructed by God to perform a series of symbolic gestures (clapping, stomping his foot and uttering an exclamation) that display God's wrath. Stomping one's foot is often a sign of frustration or anger, as in the Ugaritic Epic of Aqhat. In that tale the hero refuses to give his bow to the goddess Anat, telling her hunting weapons are for men. She is so angry that she violently stamps her foot and goes off in a rush to seek revenge from the gods. The exclamation (NIV: "Alas") that is used indicates that someone will get what's coming to them ("you'll be sorry!"), reinforcing this scene of impending divine punishment.

6:13. slain around altars (provided no sanctu-ary). False altars can offer no right of sanctuary. Just as God scoffs at those who put their trust in other gods as if in a rock of "refuge," (Deut 32:37), now Yahweh denies them the safety ordinarily extended to those who approach or grab hold of the altar (compare 1 Kings 1:50-51).

6:13. spreading tree and leafy oak. The degree to which idolatry has spread is emphasized in this reference to cultic shrines beneath the branches of every spreading oak (see the comment on Deut 12:2-3 on Canaanite "outdoor shrines"). Hosea 4:13 also uses this image of hilltop and leafy glade as places of idol worship.

6:14. desert to Diblah. The geographic range here, like the more familiar "from Dan to Beersheba," expresses God's ability to punish the Israelites from one end to the other of their territory. The desert refers to the wilderness around Beersheba. Diblah appears in the Septuagint and is a variant of Riblah, which was in the land of Syro-Hamath just south of Kadesh (2 Kings 23:33). Its mention here may refer to the city's use by Nebuchadnezzar. It was the headquarters for his army's campaign during his siege of Jerusalem in 588-586 B.C.

7:2. four corners. The idea of the whole earth is implied by this reference to the "four corners" of the land. A similar expression is found in Malachi 1:11 and the royal Phoenician inscription of Azitiwadda (730-710 B.C.) from Karatepe. These texts express universal rule and power by referring to the land "from sunrise to sunset." The Assyrian annals of Shalmaneser III state that the "totality of the countries" have been placed in his hands. The phrase used here and elsewhere in Assyrian texts, as in Ezekiel, refers to the four corners of the earth as the king's domain.

7:13. seller will not recover land. The extent of the doom pronounced upon the nation is such that even the Jubilee year will not be celebrated (see the comment on Lev 25:8-55). Ordinarily, property that had been sold to satisfy debts could be redeemed during the Jubilee, thereby restoring the grants of lands that were first made after the conquest (the Code of Hammurabi contain similar clauses regarding redemption of land). Now the "divine lease" has been revoked, and there will be no economic advantage for buyer or seller in the age of destruction to come.

7:18. sackcloth. Sackcloth, one of the traditional signs of mourning and repentance, was made of goat or camel hair and was coarse and uncomfortable. In many cases the sackcloth was only a loin covering. This custom not only set a person aside with a mark of separation from normal life, but as the sackcloth chaffed the skin, it also served as a continual reminder of the pain of loss.

7:18. shaved heads. Although this practice is condemned in Deuteronomy 14:1 (perhaps as part of the ancestor cult—see the comment on Deut 14:1-2), shaving the head as a sign of mourning was very common (see Job 1:20 and Jer 48:37). It also occurs as part of the purification ritual for the diseased (Lev 14:8-9) and in the law of the Nazirite (Num 6:9). In Mesopotamia shaving off half the hair was used as a punishment intended to bring public humiliation.

7:23. chains. Captives are usually depicted in Egyptian and Mesopotamian art bound in chains. This is the case in a relief found in the Ramesseum at Thebes picturing Asiatic, Ethiopian and central African captives being paraded before Rameses II. A similar scene of captive Canaanite and Philistine prisoners is carved into the wall of the mortuary temple of Rameses III at Medinet Habu.

7:24. sanctuaries desecrated. Mention of the desecration of the temple in Jerusalem (Ps 74:7) and of Josiah's systematic destruction of the high places throughout his domain and at Bethel (2 Kings 24:8-15) indicates that sanctuaries were not safe from the hand of avenging or crusading rulers. Ancient texts from Old Babylonian Mari and the Persian period Cyrus Cylinder describe the destruction of temples and the taking of sacred images as "hostages." In Ezekiel's vision the false altars and shrines erected by the Israelites will now be swept away and destroyed by an avenging God.

7:26. vision, law, counsel as means of deliverance. The prophetic vision offered a message from God that might at times bring encouragement or hope of deliverance. The priest's instruction here is possibly ritual instruction intended to point the way toward appeasing divine wrath. The counsel of the elders was believed to be a channel for divine wisdom leading to proper decisions. In a time of upheaval and destruction, the land is left without direction from God or regarding God. All of the traditional means of providing guidance are lost or ineffective (see these groups of counselors in Jer 26:7-17). Just as the *Visions of Neferti*, a twentieth-century B.C. Egyptian seer, describe how "officials no longer administer the land" and "those who could speak have been expelled," now Judah faces a future without the counsel needed to plan and make decisions (compare Saul's dilemma in 1 Sam 28:6).

8:1—11:25

Transported to Jerusalem in a Vision

8:1. chronology. Fourteen months after his initial vision calling him to serve as a prophet, Ezekiel now experiences a new vision that will dramatically demonstrate the decadence of Jerusalem's religious state. Based on the calendar used for Ezekiel 1:1, the date of this vision would be September 17-18, 592 B.C.

8:2. figure of metal and fire. A divine apparition that confronts Ezekiel is similar in its brilliance to the one in his call narrative (Ezek 1:26-27). In both instances he uses qualifiers and the combination of blinding fire and shining metal or electrum. It is the magnificence of God's or a divine messenger's glory that is being conveyed here. This follows the pattern of the dangerous nature of contact with the divine found throughout ancient Near Eastern literature (see the comment on Ezek 1:26-28).

8:3. transported in visions. Since Ezekiel will not physically leave the exile, it is necessary for him to be transported in a vision to Jerusalem, where he can witness the city's abominations. There is little in the literature of the ancient Near East to provide information on visions or visionary experiences. In one interesting text, *A Vision of the Netherworld* (seventh century), an Assyrian prince sees Nergal, king of the netherworld, seated on his throne, with lightning flashing from him. The text does not say how the prince was transported, but it does mention that he is dragged by his hair to Nergal. A parallel to spiritual transport might be found in the Mesopotamian hero Adapa's appearance before the divine assembly. His patron god, Ea, causes him to "take the road to heaven," and Adapa has the opportunity to gaze from that vantagepoint "from the horizon of heaven to the zenith of heaven."

8:3-16. temple complex topography. The rectangular temple structure (facing east) is surrounded by a walled inner courtyard. Outside of this wall is the outer courtyard. The wall is lined with chambers used for various purposes. Ezekiel first is set down in his vision outside the north gate leading from the outer courtyard into the inner court. From this outer courtyard, Ezekiel could look through the gate at the altar that dominated the inner courtyard. The gates leading into the temple precincts were added after Solomon's original construction of the temple (2 Kings 15:35). The hole near the gateway (v. 7) area may have led into one of those chambers lining the courtyard wall, perhaps a storage room that had been transformed into a shrine where the seventy elders stood in their own separate niches and worshiped idolatrous images. The next scene (v. 14) is outside a gate in the same wall further to the west, where women would be allowed. Then at verse 16 Ezekiel is led into the inner court of the temple where he will view a further abomination in the area between the porch of the temple and the altar.

8:5. idol of jealousy. The image of Asherah that Manasseh set up in the temple complex is referred to in a similar way (2 Chron 33:7, 15). Though this should not be considered the same image, it could easily be another Asherah. This is further suggested by the fact that the word used for "image" here is an unusual one that is thought to be a loan word from Phoenician or Canaanite. According to the second commandment of the Decalogue, any image that was the object of worship would provoke Yahweh's jealousy.

8:10. wall decorations as objects of worship. The text specifies these as images carved in relief on the walls. This art form was well known in Assyria and Babylon. Verse 12 additionally suggests that each of the seventy was worshiping in front of a separate niche where an image was engraved. The fact that these carvings were of animals suggests some connection to Egyptian mortuary practices. Animals were not typically the objects of worship in Canaanite or Mesopotamian practice. But the Egyptians used apotropaic rituals to ward off various creatures from the tombs of their ancestors, and incense was used throughout the ancient Near East in apotropaic contexts. The decoration of the walls of houses in Mesopotamia with images of ants and cockroaches may also have been apotropaic.

8:14. mourning for Tammuz. Like other fertility-oriented "dying gods," the Sumerian demigod Tammuz spent part of the year in the underworld (representing the dry, unproductive seasons) and then came back to life during the time of rains, planting and harvesting. The Mesopotamian ritual that formed part of his worship begged the gods to restore Tammuz and the land's fertility. It included a series of laments (based on those initiated in the epic story by his wife Inanna and his mother and sister). The women who performed these laments would wail and shed tears (a symbolic gesture of the need for rain). The fact that Ezekiel describes women performing this ritual before the gates of the temple in Jerusalem may reflect either the adoption of this fertility god as a substitute for Yahweh or wailing for Yahweh as a dying and rising fertility god using Tammuz lamentation liturgy. This adds a Mesopotamian heresy to the Canaanite- and Egyptian-style heresies in the two previous scenes.

8:16. sun worship. Evidence of official sun worship in ancient Israel seems to be tied primarily to the reign of Manasseh. The horses and chariots of the sun that he set up were destroyed by Josiah when he attempted to cleanse the temple complex of foreign religious influence (see comment on 2 Kings 23:11). Place names such as Beth Shemesh, Ein Shemesh and Mount Heres (Josh 15:7; Judg 1:35) also attest to the popularity of sun worship. Perhaps it is not coincidental that the chapter is dated to the time of the autumn equinox when the sun would be at the angle to shine directly into the temple at sunrise. While Egypt, Canaan and Mesopotamia all had sun gods (Amun-Re, Shemesh and Shamash respectively), it is more likely that this is syncretistic worship of Yahweh as a sun god. This would complete the series of scenes that portrayed Canaanite worship (v. 5), Egyptian worship (v. 10-11), Mesopotamian worship (v. 14) and syncretistic worship of Yahweh (v.16).

8:17. branch to the nose. There is an Akkadian expression *(laban appi)* that refers to a gesture of humility used to come contritely before deity with a petition. When this act is portrayed in art, the worshiper has his hand positioned in front of his nose and mouth, and is sometimes shown with a short cylindrical object in his hand. From the Sumerian tale called *Gilgamesh in the Land of the Living* there is some evidence that what is held is a small branch cut off a living tree. This would suggest that in Ezekiel the people are putting on a show of humility. It must be admitted, however, that these connections are very hazy and the significance may lie somewhere else entirely.

9:2. six slaughterers. While there is an obvious parallel between this vision of divinely directed executioners and the "Destroyer" in the Passover narrative (Ex 12:23), the motif of seven destroyers is best exemplified in the eighth-century Neo-Babylonian *Myth of Erra and Ishum.* In this ancient poem the god Anu begets seven deities (Sebitti, associated with Pleiades) and gives them to Erra to serve "as his fierce weapons." These merciless beings spare no one, killing all in their directed path and thus functioning as the tools of chaos and violence. The poem, like Ezekiel's vision, provides a religious explanation for the destruction and humiliation of a major city (Babylon), but here there are only six rather than seven, the seventh having been replaced by a scribe (see next entry).

9:2. record-keeper. The motif of a divine

record-keeper is found in the Gilgamesh Epic where Belet-Seri kneels before Ereshkigal (the queen of the underworld in Akkadian belief) and reads out the names of mortals who will die. But the scribal writing kit carried by the man here would evoke the image of Nabu, the god of scribes and scribe of the gods. Nabu was one of the most popular Babylonian gods of the period, as is demonstrated by his appearance in many of the names (e.g., Nebuchadnezzar). He is the one who keeps the accounts on the tablet of life, just as the scribal personage here in Ezekiel is doing.

9:2. writing kit. The ancient scribe typically carried a writing case that would serve as a palette when he was writing and also stored his pens and containers of ink (usually both black and red ink). In this passage, the term used for the writing kit included an Egyptian loan word (*qeset*) that identified it as a particular style of palette, with slots for the pens and two hollowed-out places to store ink. These palettes appear in numerous Egyptian tomb paintings. The pen was a rush or reed cut to a point that could serve as brush or point depending on the shape of the letter being drawn. Ink was made from a mixture of carbon and gum. Red ink had iron oxide added to produce the color needed for rubrics or the lines on the scroll. Completing his kit would be a knife to sharpen his pens (Jer 36:23).

9:2. bronze altar. The bronze altar was part of the furnishings of the original temple complex created by Solomon (see comment on 2 Chron 4:1). It had sat in front of the temple "between the new altar and the temple," and had then been moved to the north side to make room for the idolatrous altar erected by Ahaz (2 Kings 16:14).

9:3. glory of the Lord above the cherubim. There is an association between God's "glory" and the ark of the covenant as early as the Samuel narratives (see comment on 1 Sam 4:3-4). In Ezekiel God's presence is tied to the "glory"—a physical manifestation that also plays on the image presented of the ark of God enthroned between the wings of the cherubim (for the iconography of the ark, see comment on Ex 25:10-22).

9:4. marks on the forehead. The action of the scribe conjures up several parallels. The mark is the Hebrew letter *taw,* the last letter of the Hebrew alphabet, which was used as a signature in some periods of Israelite history (Job 31:35). In the script used during Old Testament times it was either an X shape or a + shape. It may represent God's ownership of the remnant of the people who deserved to survive the coming destruction (a sentiment also expressed in the Egyptian *Visions of Neferti).* Jewish tradition continued to employ this sign as a mark of the righteous from the Dead Sea Scrolls, through the intertestamental period and into rabbinic traditions. Certainly, marking those who will survive God's wrath is comparable to the blood on the doorpost during the Exodus event (Ex 12:11). The same mark used in Ezekiel was early associated with the blood mark on the doorposts at Passover, but its resemblance to a cross made that connection unpopular among the rabbis in the post-Christian era.

10:1. throne of sapphire (lapis lazuli). The mention of God's throne is a reiteration of 1:26. At least since Roman times, based on the writings of Pliny, *sapphire* has actually denoted lapis lazuli. It remained common until the end of the medieval period to employ the term *sapphire* when referring to the deep blue of lapis lazuli. The word *sapphire* comes from the Sanskrit and was borrowed into Latin. Lapis lazuli, a combination of minerals including felspathoid, sodalite and lazurite, comes from the mountains of Afghanistan. It is a brittle stone and has been used for jewelry, in mosaics and to decorate furniture. Its sparkling character, a desirable quality for decorative purposes, is the result of pyrite fragments blended with the stone. In Akkadian texts this stone was commonly associated with the dwelling place of the high god.

10:1. cherubim. See the comment on Exodus 25:18-20 and 26:1-6 for the decorative appearance of cherubim in the tabernacle and on the lid of the ark of the covenant. In the Jerusalem temple two cherubim were made from olivewood and overlaid with gold (see 1 Kings 6:23-28). The significance of the iconography in each of these instances is to be found in the idea of God's presence being upheld on the wings of the cherubim. The close association of God and the cherubim may be related to the image of Canaanite and Mesopotamian gods riding or standing on the backs of animals (i.e., Baal astride a bull). It should also be noted that the winged beasts of Assyrian art may have also had some influence on the biblical depiction of the cherubim (see the comment on Ezek 1:5). In chapter 1 these creatures were not identified as cherubim, but here they are placed in that category. This is logical since cherubim were most commonly portrayed as the guardians of divine property or presence.

10:2. wheels. See comment on 1:15-18.

10:4. radiance of the glory of the Lord. See the comments on Ezekiel 1:4 and 1:26-28 for discussion of the *kabod* or "glory" of God and how it compares to the concept of *melammu,* "divine brilliance," that appears in Mesopotamian literature. For a comparison with Egyptian and Akkadian religious texts dealing with the radiance of the gods and the danger to humans who see this divine light, see the comments on Exodus 13:21-22 and 33:18-23.

10:9. chrysolite. As in 1:15 the semiprecious stone mentioned is *tarshish*. Most interpreters identify it as either beryl or topaz, both of which would have reflected the light and provided the sense of translucent brilliance in this text.

10:12. full of eyes. See comment on 1:15-18 for the discussion of the wheels "full of eyes."

10:14. four faces. See comment on 1:6.

10:15. Kebar River. See comment on 1:1.

10:18. importance of the threshold. Entranceways have great symbolic significance in the biblical world. They serve as a place of judgment (Deut 22:20-21) as well as a legal site where acts of submission and worship may take place (1 Sam 5:4; Ezek 46:1-2). They also mark the point of entry and exit from a private home or, as in Ezekiel, from the realm of sacred space to the secular world.

10:19. east gate. This would be the gate of the outer court of the temple. While the temple complex had an east-west orientation, it is unclear how closely tied to this sacred precincts were the buildings and courtyards of the royal palace. It is possible that the gate Ezekiel is referring to in this case is one of those that connected temple and palace. If this is the case, then its significance is heightened as Yahweh prepares to abandon both the religious community and the secular authorities to their fate.

11:1. leaders. All of these names appear on seals from this period, but with the exception of Pelatiah, it is unlikely that the seals should be related to the individuals named in this verse. The Pelatiah seal possibly refers to this individual, but there can be no certainty. For more about seals and persons named on them, see the sidebar in Jeremiah 32.

11:3, 7, 11. metaphor of cooking pot and meat. Ezekiel refutes the claims of Jerusalem's new rulers that they have created a safe haven in the city for the people. He turns this around, transforming the pot (Jerusalem) from a tightly sealed storage jar into a cooking pot in which the people (see Mic 3:3) and their false rulers will be broiled over the flame of Yahweh's anger (compare Ezek 22:18-22).

11:18. images and idols. See the comments on images in 8:5 and 8:10.

11:19. heart of stone. The concept of a heart of stone would have had a couple of associations in the ancient world, mostly from Egypt. First

of all, in Egyptian beliefs it was the heart that was weighed in judgment to determine whether or not the afterlife could be attained. If it was weighed down with guilt and sin, the results could be disastrous (see comment on Ex 8:11). A heart of stone would be a heavy heart. More important is the imagery connected to the mummification process. From New Kingdom times on, the heart was removed from the mummy and placed in a canopic jar, as the other important organs were. This was done because the Egyptians believed that the heart might betray the individual when he came to judgment and thereby jeopardize the afterlife. The heart was replaced with a stone carved in the shape of a dung beetle. In Egypt this insect was the symbol of eternal life. By transplanting it inside the mummy in place of the heart, they believed they were securing the renewal of the person's life and vitality. In contrast, Yahweh is going to bring his people back to life by returning to them hearts of flesh that will not betray them. The imagery of an unhardened heart would be apt in that verses 17-20 suggest a new exodus and a new covenant.

11:23. mountain east of the city. The mount to the east of the temple complex would be the Mount of Olives. From here one can look down on the temple mount and the city. From a vantagepoint in Jerusalem, this would be the limit of how far one could look to the east. Whether the implication is that God is going to sit outside the city and watch (compare Jon 4:5), or whether it is from here that he returns to heaven (it is the traditional site of the ascension of Christ as well, though New Testament support is slight).

12:1-28

Prophecy of the Exile

12:5. digging through the wall. As depicted in Assyrian reliefs, a number of different measures were used to breach the defenses of a city under siege. Among these was undermining or drilling through the city walls. Ezekiel, since he was digging from the outside of his wall inward, therefore took on the role of the Babylonians, who were working, at God's command, to break through into the city.

12:6. covering the face. There were occasions when the face was covered in mourning or shame, but those use a different verb than the one used here. It is likely that covering the face here symbolizes the fate of the king he is representing (vv. 12-13).

12:6. sign to Israel. Ezekiel's enacted prophecy provided God's sign of the coming destruction of Jerusalem and the exile of the people. By performing this set of actions, Ezekiel became the message. Sign-acts often go even further, as the prophet's life itself becomes a sign (see Is 8:18; Jer 16:2; Hos 1).

12:10. prince in Jerusalem. At the time Ezekiel was speaking, Zedekiah was the ruler of Jerusalem. He was the third son of Josiah to sit on the throne, although his power to rule was strictly curtailed and under the supervision of Nebuchadnezzar (see 2 Kings 24:15-17). The fact that Ezekiel refers to Zedekiah as "prince" (Hebrew *nasi'*) instead of as king (Hebrew *melek*) is an indication that he does not consider him the true successor of David.

12:13. net, snare. The image of God snaring his enemies in a net is a common one in ancient Near Eastern art. Among the most graphic is the Stele of the Vultures, which depicts the Sumerian god Ningirsu holding a net of woven reeds in his left hand. Imprisoned within the net are the soldiers of Umma who had attacked Eannatum, the king of Lagash. Egyptian art from the reign of Necho II portrays the pharaoh gathering his foes in a gigantic net (see Hab 1:14-15).

12:13. land of Chaldeans. The Chaldeans are first mentioned in Mesopotamian sources in the ninth century B.C. Although related ethnically to the other Aramean tribes of southern Babylonia, they had a distinct tribal structure. As the Assyrian empire began to weaken, Chaldean leaders, including Nabopolassar and Nebuchadnezzar, eventually gained their independence and established the Neo-Babylonian dynasty after 625 B.C. The areas that they controlled and within which they settled the exiles from Judah ranged from all of southern Mesopotamia to the region west of Haran on the upper reaches of the Euphrates River.

12:13. will not see it, there he will die. This statement was fulfilled in the blinding of King Zedekiah after the capture of Jerusalem by Nebuchadnezzar's troops. Although he would be taken into the exile and would spend the rest of his life a prisoner, Zedekiah's eyes were destroyed after he was forced to witness the execution of his children (see 2 Kings 25:7). The practice of gouging out a prisoner's eyes appears in the Assyrian Annals of Ashurnasirpal II in the ninth century and those of Sargon II in the eighth century. This was simply one of several terror tactics employed to frighten and humiliate their enemies.

12:18. anxious eating and drinking. Since eating and drinking are the most basic activities of daily life, the mood at the table often re-

flects current conditions. At the Passover, the Israelites were to eat their meal "in haste" as a reflection of their readiness to leave. Here the anxiety betrays the threat they are living under.

12:24. flattering divinations. The task of the diviner was to determine the will of a god or gods through various ritualized actions—the examination of sheep entrails, consultation with the dead (1 Sam 28:8) or the study of the astrological configurations. All of these practices were forbidden by Israelite law (see the comment on Deut 18:10-13) because of their association with false gods and false religions. Naturally, a diviner would wish to please his paying clients and thus might be inclined to flatter or seduce them with his manner and statements (compare Prov 26:24-26). Such desirable predictions were out of place and to be considered similar to those condemned by Jeremiah (see Jer 27:9-10).

13:1-23

False Prophets

13:10. flimsy wall covered with whitewash. Ezekiel uses an analogy similar to that in Jeremiah 6:14 and 8:11. In both prophets reality is covered up and people delude themselves into believing that a wound is not serious or a wall is sturdy. It reflects the tendency to hide structural problems with cosmetic solutions. Mesopotamian law codes also deal with unscrupulous builders and homeowners who neglect repairs or attempt to hide unsafe workmanship (see both the Laws of Eshnunna and Hammurabi's Code).

13:11. God's destructive forces. The flimsy walls, held together by layers of plaster, cannot withstand the forces of nature unleashed by God. As in Isaiah 28:2 and 30:30, rain with accompanying high winds and destructive hailstones was to be considered God's voice, thundering out an answer and indictment on Judah. A similar image is found in the Sumerian *Lament over the Destruction of Ur*. In this recitation of misery, the poet describes how the god Enlil withheld the gentle winds that bring the rains needed for their crops. In their place were the desert winds (sirocco) that evaporated all the moisture from the ground and raging storm winds that collapsed buildings and whistled alarmingly through the gates of abandoned cities.

13:14. foundation laid bare. God's wrath is so strong that the symbolic wall constructed of deceptive prophecy is to be totally razed to its bare foundations. Its foundation will be seen for what it is: self-interest and self-advancement rather than the word of God. Foundations usually consisted of a few courses of stone laid in trenches.

13:18. sewing magic charms on wrists. The practice described here is a bit uncertain since the Hebrew term *kesatot* only appears in this chapter (vv. 18 and 20). It is possible that it is related to the Akkadian *kasitu*, "binding magic." Babylonian incantation texts describe how persons wishing to bind others to their will made bands that they wore on their arms or wrists, empowering them with an oath. Perhaps these false female prophets were employing something similar, or perhaps Ezekiel was simply comparing their influence to a practice known to him from Babylonia.

13:18. various length veils. Again, an Akkadian word, possibly *sapaḫu* ("to loosen"), may be the basis for the item mentioned here. If it is a parallel to the wristbands previously mentioned, then the "veil" might have been worn around the neck as another magic device to bind people to the woman's will. Certainly, a form of "attachment" is intended. Whatever paraphernalia are referred to in this verse, it is generally accepted that it indicates the presence of a familiar type of witchcraft that attempts to control its victims.

14:1-23
Judgment Against Idolatry

14:1-3. elders coming to inquire. The elders served as the authorities for the exiles. They came to Ezekiel as supplicants seeking counsel and an oracle. The gesture of sitting before him (at his feet) indicates his role as teacher and spokesperson for God. There is some question whether they sincerely accepted his authority or were simply curious about what he could offer as a word of God.

14:14. Noah, Daniel, Job. While Noah and Job are easily identified as righteous sages of antiquity, it has seemed unlikely to many interpreters that Ezekiel would place a contemporary prophet, Daniel, in this group. This chapter, however, likely dates from the late 590s. By that time Daniel had been in Babylon for almost fifteen years and would have been in his late twenties or early thirties. His success had come early (see comment on Dan 2:1), so he had been in a high position in the court for a decade. Nevertheless, Daniel does not mesh easily with the profile of the other two. First, both of them are non-Israelites. Noah lived during the flood and prior to Abraham. Job was from Uz, usually located around Edom. A Babylonian wisdom docu-

ment that contains arguments on suffering similar to those in the book of Job suggests a long tradition for his character. Seeking a highly reputed character from antiquity, some interpreters have considered it possible that the Daniel mentioned here refers to Danil, the wise king of ancient Ugarit who was the father of the hero Aqhat. Like Deborah (Judg 4:5), Danil sat beneath a tree hearing the cases of his people, dispensing justice to widows and orphans. Since he is not associated with Yahweh worship, however, it would be difficult to envision Ezekiel giving Danil such an elevated status. As in the case of the marking of the innocents in Ezekiel 9, these three great wise men, known for their individual righteousness, could only save themselves during the coming catastrophe. The implication that a certain number of righteous persons is necessary to save a city from God's wrath (see Gen 18:23-32; Jer 5:1) is thus set aside in the face of Judah's violations of the covenant.

14:15. wild beasts as judgment. In the passage from verses 15-20, God posits a variety of means to punish the people of Judah for their crimes and thus cleanse the land of its impurity. With respect to using wild beasts as the instrument of God's wrath, see the comment on 5:17.

15:1-8
Analogy of the Vine

15:2-7. vine parables and metaphors. Like Isaiah in the "Song of the Vineyard" (Is 5:1-7), Ezekiel uses the vine as a metaphor for Judah (see also Ezek 17:5-10). In each case the uselessness of the vine versus a branch or a tree well rooted is the justification for its destruction. A similar image appears in an Egyptian wisdom piece, the *Instruction of Amenemope*. There too a plant that serves as the metaphor for fools who speak without thinking is uprooted, burned and destroyed because it soon withers and has no value once uprooted. The metaphor of a city as an unproductive plant is known from the *Myth of Erra and Ishum* (known copies date to the eighth century) in which Marduk laments Babylon. He says that he filled it with seeds like a pine cone, but no fruit came from it, and he planted it like an orchard but never tasted its fruit.

16:1-63
Analogy of the Discarded Woman

16:3. ancestry in land of Canaanites. Biblical references to Jerusalem describe it originally as a Jebusite city (Josh 18:28). David captured it and transformed it into the Israelite capital (2 Sam 5:6-10). Mention of Jerusalem is also found in nineteenth- and eighteen-century B.C. execration documents from Egypt and the fourteenth-century El Amarna texts. By making this identification, Ezekiel attempts to set aside the people's pride in Jerusalem as their city as God begins to lay out the indictment against Judah.

16:3. father an Amorite, mother a Hittite. This passage operates on two levels. First, it is correct to tie Jerusalem, at least the Jebusite city, to Amorite and North Syrian Hittite political origins. This is established by its mention in the El Amarna texts. However, on a symbolic level, in confronting Jerusalem with its mixed ancestry (tying it to three of the seven major inhabitant groups of Canaan listed in Ex 3:8), God identifies the place and the people as utterly corrupt. When the land was conquered, it was the responsibility of the Israelites to purify it of its idolatrous traditions (Deut 7:1-5), but instead the people became just like the nations they were supposed to displace.

16:4. treatment of a newborn. All of the actions described here would ordinarily be those of the midwife. She would cut and tie off the umbilical cord, rinse the placenta off the newborn, clean the baby's skin with salt water and finally wrap it in a blanket. The child would then be presented to the parents to be named. However, in this case the child is not accepted as a member of the household and instead is abandoned in a field, where its fate is left up to God. In the ancient world the role of the midwife in preparing the birthing room and caring for the newborn is often attributed to deity, especially in metaphors. In a segment of the Babylonian *Atrahasis Epic* the fertility goddess Mami is the midwife of the gods who brings humanity into being. In the Egyptian *Hymn to the Aten,* the sun god presides as midwife over the lands of Egypt each morning. The midwife rituals involved provide for the physical needs of the child as well as making a symbolic transference from the realm of the womb to the living world.

16:5. child exposure. Both classical and ancient Near Eastern sources make mention of infanticide. Graphic evidence of this from the Roman-Byzantine period has been found in recent excavations at Ashkelon, where the remains of a hundred infants who had been disposed of in a sewer drain were uncovered. Infanticide was usually employed to get rid of female or malformed children. This was done as a means of either population control or economic necessity, since many villages were barely able to feed and care for healthy chil-

dren and adults. The fact that the infant's parents "cast it out" into a field has legal implications as well. They are renouncing all legal claims to the child and leaving it up to God and/or another person to "adopt" and thus save the child's life. Among the examples of this practice are Moses' exposure in the Nile (though this was not total abandonment; his sister was instructed to watch and see what would happen; Ex 2:1-10) and the birth legend of Sargon of Akkad.

16:8. covering nakedness with corner of garment. This is a legal and symbolic gesture by the husband that he intends to provide for the needs of his wife. It is further confirmed by the taking of an oath *(berît).* Another example of the practice is Boaz's expansive covering of Ruth on the threshing floor when he agrees to serve as her advocate before the village elders (Ruth 3:9).

16:9. ointments. As part of the marriage ritual, a "day of bathing" and anointing occurred that symbolized the transference of care of the young woman from her parents to her husband. Old Babylonian documents attest to this ceremony, and it may also be at the heart of a Middle Assyrian law in which a man pours oil over the head of a woman who is about to become a part of his household. This gesture stands in stark contrast to the lack of care given the infant child in Ezekiel 16:4.

16:10. embroidered dress. Among the bridal gifts is embroidered cloth for her gown. Only the finest cloth was embroidered, and it was considered a prize in war (Judg 5:30) as well as a luxury item suitable for trade with other countries (Ezek 27:16). On a more practical level, both Hammurabi's Code and the Lipit Ishtar Code from Mesopotamia list oil, grain and clothing as the items that husbands are required to supply their wives.

16:10. leather sandals. Ordinary sandals were made from woven fibrous material, secured with leather thongs (Is 5:27). For footwear to be entirely made of leather would be a luxury and a signifier of both wealth and power. Fine leather sandals are represented on Shalmaneser III's Black Obelisk panels (ninth century B.C.) and on wall paintings from the time of the Assyrian king Sargon II (721-705 B.C.).

16:11-12. jewelry. The full array of jewelry provided by the husband consists of many of the types of jewelry regularly used to adorn a woman's body and head (compare the more complete list in Is 3:18-23). Like the bride gifts for Rebekah (Gen 24:22), there are arm bracelets, possibly with animal heads at each end. The necklace may have been a strand of beads or linked metal rings similar to those in Assyrian reliefs or the Nimrud ivories depicting royal Assyrian women. The nose ring again follow the style of Rebekah's adornment (Gen 24:22), and the earrings were probably ovoid loops inserted into pieced ears. Most striking of all is the golden crown or tiara that completes the ensemble of a ruler's wife and has parallels in both Egyptian and Assyrian art.

16:13. fine foods. Just as Yahweh has provided the Israelites with food throughout their history, now, in this marriage metaphor, Yahweh as the bridegroom and husband provides Jerusalem the bride and wife with the very best quality flour, honey and olive oil. These staples are listed in the Mesopotamian law codes as the items due a wife for her daily maintenance. In this case, however, special provision is made to insure that she receives the very best with which to make her bread—something that will then serve as a charge against her when she offers these items to other gods (Ezek 16:19).

16:15. prostitution in the ancient world. In ancient Mesopotamia a distinction can be drawn between commercial prostitution and "sacral sexual service" (as G. Lerner terms it). The term *harimtu* is used for both in cuneiform texts (for instance it is a *harimtu* who "civilizes" Enkidu in the Gilgamesh Epic), but there is a difference in social status as well as purpose. The sacral sexual service provided at the temple was tied into the sacred marriage ritual that insured fertility for the land. There were various levels of priestesses, from the high priestess, who represented the goddess Ishtar/Inanna and was said to be "visited" by the god Marduk each night, to cloistered female orders and more public figures like the *naditu*, who could own property, conduct business and even marry. The fact that commercial prostitution occurred near temples is based on the same considerations that brought prostitutes to frequent taverns and the city gate—high traffic areas mean more customers. Both temple sacral servants and prostitutes accepted payment, but the former were expected to dedicate these offerings to the gods. What is particularly incongruous about the bride Jerusalem is that she is said to pay her lovers for their favors, an obvious reference to idolatry and the rejection of the covenant with Yahweh. For further discussion see comment on Deuteronomy 23:17-18.

16:16. garments used to make high places. Once again the double meaning in the text refers both to the high places (*bamôt*) where idolatrous worship took place as well as to the gaudily decorated beds of prostitutes on raised platforms. Similarly, Isaiah 57:7 describes making one's bed on a lofty hill where sacrifice is made to idols. Proverbs 7:16-17 warns that the harlot's bed is covered with enticingly colorful and expensive garments (compare Ezek 23:17)—choice colored linens like those that God had given to the bride Jerusalem in Ezekiel 16:10.

16:17. male idols. Mesopotamian sacred texts contain exact descriptions for fashioning an image of the god. There were additional rituals, including the "opening of the mouth" ceremony, which animated the image so that it could serve as a repository of the god's power and presence. Since this is specifically a male idol in Ezekiel, it is possible that an exact replica of a god is meant (usually featuring a crown or raised spear). However, it is also possible that a bull (compare the golden calf in Ex 32:2-4) or a phallic symbol was created. Using precious metals to create an idol is also found in the story of Micah in Judges 17:4-5.

16:20. human sacrifice. For previous discussion of child sacrifice to Molech, see the comments on Leviticus 18:21 and Deuteronomy 18:10. In this instance, children, the gift of Yahweh as part of the covenantal agreement, are being "fed" to the gods who have become Jerusalem's "lovers." This follows the line of reasoning that had begun with creating the image, dressing and anointing it, and then providing it with meals. All of these rituals have Mesopotamian counterparts in descriptions of their temple service, where two meals a day were served to the images of the gods. It was more specifically Phoenician and Canaanite practice, however, to offer children as sacrifices to the gods.

16:24. built a mound. To demonstrate her desire to play the role of the prostitute, Jerusalem constructed mounds (Hebrew *geb*) in prominent places. These may have been stylized representations of the harlot's bed (see Prov 7:16-17) that served as the prostitute's "shingle," advertising her presence and her profession.

16:24-25. shrine in every square. The term employed here, *ramâ*, is not the usual one for shrine. It appears elsewhere as a platform (1 Sam 22:6), and like *geb*, may have simply been the symbol used to advertise the presence of a prostitute in that place. The fact that it is constructed in a public square simply makes good business sense. The woman would have wanted as high a traffic flow as possible in order to insure her commercial success. Taking it back to the metaphor of Jerusalem's idolatry recalls the multiple altars and shrines erected by Solomon for the gods of his foreign wives (1 Kings 11:4-8). For shrines on every street corner see the comment on 2 Chronicles 28:24.

16:27. territory reduction. When the treaty obligations of an ally or vassal are not fulfilled, it is the prerogative of the overlord to take punitive action. For instance, when Hezekiah of Judah refused to pay his annual tribute to the Assyrian king, Sennacherib, the latter states in his Annals that Hezekiah's territory was reduced and given to other vassal kings to administer. In this passage, a double meaning is expressed in the use of the word *hoq* for "territory." It usually refers to a regular allotment of food (Prov 30:8), but here in a covenant context it connotes that portion which the nation assumes belongs to it but is in fact a gift of God.

16:26-29. Egypt, Assyria, Babylonia. As Ezekiel expounds on the theme of the evil that comes from foreign entanglements, he cites, in chronological order, countries that have seduced Judah away from Yahweh. These alliances have subsequently brought ruin upon the nation. It was Egypt's political meddling that the Rabshakeh (NIV: "field commander") chided Hezekiah about in Isaiah 36:6. More recently, Zedekiah's apparent alliance with Psammeticus II had brought Nebuchadnezzar's armies to besiege Jerusalem (see the comment on Jer 37:5-8). The Assyrians had imposed vassalage on Judah, but Ahaz had freely submitted himself, providing even more political and social assistance to the Assyrian cause (see 2 Kings 16:3-9). Finally, in Ezekiel's time the king of Judah continued the long-standing relationship with the Chaldeans that had begun in Hezekiah's time with the envoys of Merodach-Baladan (2 Kings 20:12-19). The reference to a "land of merchants" may be Ezekiel's astute judgment that Judah once again was simply a pawn in the economic and political game of the Near Eastern superpowers.

16:36. children's blood. This is a reiteration of the charge made in verse 20 that Jerusalem has sacrificed her children on the altars to other gods. As is noted in Psalm 106:38-39, not only is this considered an abomination, but it also would be considered the shedding of "innocent blood," one of the worst possible sins (see 2 Kings 21:16; Jer 26:15).

16:45. father an Amorite, mother a Hittite. See the comment on Ezekiel 16:3. Ezekiel's reference is not only to these Canaanite peoples but also to the intermarriage that must have taken place over the centuries between them and the Israelites.

16:46. Samaria and Sodom. The warning is quite clear here. Both Samaria, the capital of the northern kingdom of Israel, and Sodom were destroyed, having been judged corrupt by God (see Gen 19:12-25 and 2 Kings 17:5-18). The reference to Samaria as the older or "big" sister may refer to its relative importance as the capital of ten tribes. It was constructed by Omri (1 Kings 16:24) in the ninth century and thus was much "younger" than even David's Jerusalem. God may have chosen Sodom simply because of the tradition of its destruction (Amos 4:11). As a city, it probably predated Jerusalem's founding, but it was probably smaller in terms of size, given the ease with which it is said to have been captured in Genesis 14:8-11.

16:57. Edom and Philistia. Given the apparent alliance between the Edomites and the Chaldeans at the time of Jerusalem's siege (see Ps 137:7), they would be in a position to gloat over or even loot Judah once the Babylonians had conquered the capital (see the comment on Jer 49:7). Philistia during the seventh century vacillated between antagonism and alliance with the Babylonians. Ashkelon, for instance, was sacked and burned by Nebuchadnezzar in 604 B.C. In any case, Jerusalem's capture in 597 and destruction in 587 would have been the basis upon which other states could chide the people of Jerusalem, considering that city to be the new Sodom and evidence of God's righteous anger against a corrupt and disobedient nation.

17:1-24
Eagles and the Vine

17:1. allegories and parables in ancient world. It was a common rhetorical device in ancient storytelling to use allegories and parables to make a point or create an image that would be more understandable or expressive to the audience. This is especially true in ancient wisdom literature and in prophetic texts. For instance, in the twentieth-century B.C. Egyptian *Dispute Between a Man and His Ba* a despondent man's soul tells him a parable about death and its unpredictability. Another Egyptian text, the *Instruction of Ankhsheshonqy* (eighth century B.C.), uses a vacant house and an unmarried woman as allegories for waste. The Egyptian Love Songs (thirteenth century B.C.) are filled with allegories comparing the various attributes of a beautiful woman to a lush marsh, a lotus bud and mandrake blossoms. In the prophetic visions of the Egyptian sage Neferti (twentieth century B.C.), he describes the invasion of Egypt as marked by the nest of a "strange bird" in the marsh and the appearance of desert herds drinking from the Nile. The images conjured up by these short tales and wordplays enhance enjoyment and drive home the author's point.

17:3. animal and tree fables. Among the most popular types of fables were those in which an animal talks (see the comment on Num 22:28-31) or trees have a conversation or perform some action (see comment on Judg 9:8). There are several examples of this in ancient Near Eastern literature. For example, there is a dialogue between a thorn bush and a pomegranate tree in the Assyrian *Words of Ahiqar* (eighth century B.C.) over their relative merits. In the thirteenth-century Egyptian *Tale of Two Brothers* his cows warn the younger brother, Anubis, that his jealous brother Bata planned to kill him.

17:4. land of merchants. See Ezekiel 16:29 for the previous reference to the "land of merchants" as equivalent to Babylonia. King Jehoiachin, perhaps the "topmost shoot" in this allegory, had been taken into exile in 597 along with his royal court. Babylonian ration lists show that they were held under house arrest in the city of Nippur.

17:4. city of traders. Although the Phoenicians are more often associated with trade, their role was actually more as "middlemen," while the bankers and merchants who supplied the goods for transport were based in the cities of Mesopotamia (see Is 23:8). It was the Chaldean commercial empire that had, through the military efforts of the king, been able to absorb all aspects of business into their control. This is a theme that is found in many Mesopotamian annals in which a king makes an expedition "to the sea" and gains control of the "Cedars of Lebanon."

17:6-7. vine parables. See the comment on Ezekiel 15:2-7. The initial efforts of the gardener to care for his vine, planting it near abundant water in fertile soil, are rewarded by lush growth. However, at the appearance of the second eagle, the vine seems to reject the gardener's attentions and loses its purpose. It sends out tendrils toward the second bird as if seeking another, unnecessary, water source. This failure to respond as expected makes the parable similar to the "Song of the Vineyard" in Isaiah 5:1-7.

17:12. deportation of king and nobles. The interpretation of the parable of the eagle and the vine is the taking of Jehoiachin and his royal court as hostages by Nebuchadnezzar after the city of Jerusalem was captured in 597 B.C. (2 Kings 24:6-17). Like the well-cultivated vine, Jehoiachin is treated with dignity, and the ration lists from Nebuchadnezzar's official

records prove that he was well fed. If the model of Daniel and his three friends could be used here, it seems likely that Jehoiachin and his advisers were being assimilated into Babylonian culture so that they could eventually be restored to Jerusalem to serve as the king's loyal administrators (Dan 1:3-5).

17:13. member of royal family. After capturing Jerusalem in 597 B.C., the Babylonian Chronicle records that Nebuchadnezzar took King Jehoiachin, son of Jehoiakim, as his hostage. Nebuchadnezzar then installed Jehoiachin's uncle, the third son of Josiah, on the throne of Judah. His name was originally Mattaniah, but the Babylonian king renamed him Zedekiah as a gesture demonstrating his puppet status (2 Kings 24:17).

17:15. Zedekiah's rebellion and deal with Egypt. Despite the example of 597 and the deportation of Jehoiachin, Zedekiah entertained ideas of rebellion against the Babylonians. He met with envoys from Edom, Moab, Ammon, Tyre and Sidon early in his reign (Jer 27:3) and apparently had dealings with Pharaoh Psammeticus II (see the comment on Jer 34:21). See the comment on Jeremiah 37:5-8 for discussion of the troop movements of the Egyptians. Pharaoh Apries made at least a brief response to Zedekiah's plea for help, but it did not prevent the fall of Jerusalem.

17:17. ramps and siege works. Although the portion of the Babylonian Chronicle that has survived does not contain a description of the siege of Jerusalem (see 2 Kings 25:1), a similar operation is described in Sennacherib's Assyrian Annals from 701 B.C. It may be assumed that plans were laid for a long siege, since a great deal of time-consuming labor went into the construction of ramps and towers. See the comments on Jeremiah 6:6 and Ezekiel 4:2 for discussion of siege technology.

17:18. oath and covenant. Zedekiah's fate is attributed to his failure to honor his oath or treaty obligations. Treaties between nations typically contained a list of curses that will be inflicted on the party that violates the covenant between them. These treaties were signed under oath to the respective deities. That way, if the treaty were violated, it would become the responsibility of the country's own god(s) to punish the oath-breaker.

17:22. planting a cedar sprig. Just as the great eagle first plucked the topmost shoot from the cedar in verse 4, now Yahweh (identified as the eagle) will take a tender sprig and plant it on a high mountain. Following this line of reasoning, the Davidic house will be allowed to continue through the line of Jehoiachin. Similar horticultural metaphors for the revival of the Davidic House are found in Isaiah 11:1 and Jeremiah 23:5.

17:23. cosmic tree where animals find shelter. The concept of the cosmic tree or the "one tree" is common to many peoples and traditions. It stands as a representation of beauty and fertility, drawing its sustenance from the waters of the earth and providing shelter and food to all creatures that shelter under its bows. In ancient Near Eastern sources its symmetry and stability provide a check against death and a promise of the continuance of existence. Thus in Assyrian art is found a stylized tree of life that may have represented the role of the king to care for his people (see comment on Dan 4:10-12).

18:1-32
Responsibility for Sin

18:5-9. negative confession from the Book of the Dead. Since the soul or *ka* of the dead Egyptian was to be examined by Osiris, the god of the underworld, a primer to prepare a person for this "final exam" was created, entitled the Book of the Dead. Its form, often painted on or carved into tomb walls, has its origins in early dynastic periods (2500 B.C.), and it continued to be refined at least until 500 B.C. One of the most popular sections was a declaration of innocence in the form of a negative confession. Examples include "I have not sinned against my neighbors" and "I have not mistreated cattle." A similar document appears in Job 31.

18:6. eating at mountain shrines. Presumably this is a charge of idolatry at local high places *(bamôt)*. However, there is no parallel from biblical or ancient Near Eastern law to help illumine this practice. It might be compared to the giving of Jerusalem's children as food to the gods in 16:20 and to the charge that the people of Judah are willing to "worship on every high hill" throughout the land. A similar condemnation of the use of hilltop shrines can be found in Hosea 4:13.

18:6. idols of the house of Israel. It would appear that Ezekiel is using a stock phrase coined during the late monarchy or perhaps during the exile to refer to the extreme impurity associated with idol worship. His language is intentionally vulgar and characterizes the idols in the crudest possible way—they are best likened to feces or stools of excrement.

18:8. usury in ancient Near East. Consistent with biblical law, Ezekiel considers the practice of charging interest on a loan an unrighteous act. See the comment on Exodus 22:25

for further explanation of money lending practices in the ancient Near East and the comment on Deuteronomy 15:1-11 for discussion of the financial systems that existed in these areas of the ancient world.

18:20. individual responsibility in the ancient Near East. While the social structure of the ancient Near East was primarily oriented toward the group (tribe, clan, family), there is a strand of individual responsibility that appears in literary and philosophical works. Among the examples of this is a statement in the Gilgamesh Epic. The Mesopotamian god Ea berates the chief god Enlil for bringing on the great flood without just cause: "On the sinner impose his sin, on the transgressor impose his transgression."

18:31. new heart, new spirit. See comment on 11:19.

19:1-14
Lament over the Princes of Israel

19:1. laments in ancient Near East. Laments may be personal statements of despair, such as that found in Psalm 22:1-21, dirges following the death of an important person (David's elegy for Saul in 2 Sam 1:17—27) or communal cries in times of crisis, such as Psalm 137. The most famous lament from ancient Mesopotamia is the *Lament over the Destruction of Ur,* which commemorates the capture of the city in 2004 B.C. by the Elamite king Kindattu. It contains eleven stanzas, each describing a facet of the city's demise and the end of the ruling dynasty (compare Lam 2:9). Subsequently the work would have been employed prior to and during the rebuilding of the city's walls and public buildings. For more information see the sidebar in the book of Lamentations.

19:1-9. lion hunting, lion symbolism. Because of the many references in Israelite (Is 5:29; Nah 2:11-12), Egyptian and Assyrian texts to the royal associations of lions, it is not surprising to find Ezekiel employing this image. There are numerous examples of lion hunting. It was a royal sport as well as a necessity when a beast became a man-eater (as on the ninth-century Assyrian plaque of Ashurnasirpal II depicting a Nubian being devoured) or a threat to villages (as in one Mari text, where a pit was used to trap the animal). The symbolism in this "lament" refers to two of the last kings of Judah (most likely Jehoahaz and Jehoiakim). This is probably a play on Jacob's blessing of his son Judah in Genesis 49:8-12, in which he refers to him as a "lion cub."

19:10-14. vineyard analogy. There is a strong parallel between this symbol in Ezekiel and the "Song of the Vineyard" in Isaiah 5:1-7. In both instances God's wrath against the vineyard is the result of failed expectations. Neither plant performed its proper role. Isaiah's vineyard produced "bad fruit," while Ezekiel's vineyard grew "high above the thick foliage," but there is little mention of fruit. All of its energy had gone to extending its branches farther and farther, a symbol for the hubris of the nation of Judah and her kings (Jehoiachin and Zedekiah). The fate is the same for these vineyards. They both become wastelands, dried by the winds, broken down with no root or branch remaining. Ezekiel in this way provides the basis for a lament over the end of the nation's independence and the setting aside of God's covenant with the House of David. See the comment on Ezekiel 15:2-7.

20:1-49
Indictment, Judgment and Restoration

20:1. chronology. Based on the year in which Jehoiachin and his court were taken into Babylonian exile, this date formula would correlate to August 15, 591 B.C. It is possible that it could refer to 593 if one were counting from the beginning of the year when Jehoiachin became king in Jerusalem.

20:1. inquiring through a prophet. Oracles were sought in troubled times. In Babylonian religious practice the occurrence of an omen might lead someone to go to a prophet or priest to ask for an interpretation. At other times a historical event would have made it desirable to have a word from God. It may be that the elders hoped to demonstrate their trust in Yahweh by this act. However, there is also evidence in Jeremiah of representatives of the king (Jer 21:1-2) seeking out the prophet and virtually ordering him to speak an oracle of salvation for Jerusalem. There is no indication in the text of what may have motivated this visit to the prophet. Since the speech of Ezekiel goes back to the wilderness situation and makes frequent reference to Israel's early history with Egypt, it may well be a potential agreement between Egypt's pharaoh, Psammeticus II, and Judean king Zedekiah that prompted concern among the elders. It is believed that Psammeticus made overtures to Zedekiah in 592.

20:5. swearing with uplifted hand. There are many references in the Bible to taking an oath by raising up a hand to heaven (see Deut 32:40; Dan 12:7). Ezekiel uses the phrase ten times, with God being the one to take an oath by raising the hand. Among the extrabiblical

examples of this gesture are Mari texts that refer to "touching the throat" and an eighth-century Aramaic inscription of Panammu I in which an accused person is commanded to take an oath and lift both hands up to god.

20:6. milk and honey. This description goes back to Exodus narratives and refers to the bounty of the Promised Land for a pastoral lifestyle, but not necessarily in terms of agriculture. Milk is the product of herds, while honey represents a natural resource, probably the syrup of the date rather than bees' honey. Egyptian texts as early as the Story of Sinuhe describe the land of Canaan as rich in natural resources as well as in cultivated produce.

20:12. Sabbaths as a sign. While the individual's sign of participation in the covenant was circumcision, the sign of Israel's corporate participation in the covenant was the keeping of the Sabbath. Like circumcision, the keeping of the Sabbath was a continuous obligation required of each generation. Unlike circumcision, it was not an individual's one-time act but an attitude to be consistently maintained and periodically expressed in action. Instead of repeating the reasoning of the ten commandments—the Sabbath was to be celebrated as a commemoration of God's creation—the Sabbaths (the plural perhaps signifying all of the sacred holidays of Israel) are here cited to remind the people that they are the chosen. No other people have received this sign, and thus, with the laws, they become both gift and insignia of membership in the covenant community as established in Exodus 31:13.

20:25. statutes and laws that were not good. The Hebrew terms used here are extremely important to a proper understanding of Ezekiel's controversial statement. This is not a reference to the Law given at Sinai, and the word "Torah" is not used. The word NIV translates as "statutes" is the same word that in verse 24 is translated "decrees," except that there it is feminine (as usual) rather than masculine (as here). The word NIV translates "laws" is the word for God's judicial decisions. The consequence of Israel's unfaithfulness, then, was that God decreed events that were not in their favor, and he made judicial decisions that threatened their survival. This resulted in God's use of forces that devastated Israel, such as war, famine, plague and foreign armies.

20:26. sacrifice of firstborn. Following Ezekiel's theme of the indisputable power of God to command creation, the decree to sacrifice the firstborn here plays off of the statement in Exodus 13:2 that all firstborns, human and animal, belong to God. This is demonstrated by the tenth plague in Egypt (Ex 13:14-16) but is mitigated or "redeemed" through sacrifice (Ex 34:20) and by the sacrificial act of circumcision (Gen 17:9-14; Ex 22:29). Within Phoenician and Canaanite religion, however, the sacrifice of the firstborn is a common practice (see the comment on "passing children through fire" as part of Molech worship in Deut 18:10). Closer to Ezekiel's time, kings Ahaz and Manasseh are both accused of child sacrifice (2 Kings 16:3; 21:6). Since these men as descendants of David and participants in the "everlasting covenant" with Yahweh (2 Sam 23:5) were the guardians of the Law and the enforcers of divine and civil decree, their detestable actions in this regard could easily fit the image of "bad laws" in Ezekiel 20:25.

20:28-29. illicit worship. Ezekiel continues to contrast God's adherence to the covenant promise of "land and children" with the Israelites misuse of these gifts. Each of the four worship practices listed here, with the possible exception of offering libations, reflects activities associated with Yahweh worship. However, they are described as illicit because they clearly are aimed at "feeding" other gods, a regular aspect of Mesopotamian and Canaanite religion. Instead of making offerings that create a "pleasing aroma" (see Gen 8:21) and demonstrate proper action toward God, this food and drink is tied to the belief that the gods require regular meals (seen in the famished gods in the Gilgamesh flood epic). See the comments on Ezekiel 6:13 for other condemnations of idolatrous worship practices and the use of high places and sacred groves.

20:32. serving wood and stone. The prophets regularly taunt other nations as well as the Israelites for serving gods made of metal, wood and stone (see Jer 51:17-18; Hos 8:4). Archaeologists have discovered stone molds in which molten metals were poured to mass-produce idols. The assumption is that these images then took on the presence of the gods they represented through rituals such as the "opening of the mouth" incantation found in Babylonian religious texts.

20:46. forest of the southland. The term for south or southland used here is *Negev*, usually associated with the desert region to the south of Judah. In this case, Ezekiel seems to simply be using it as a direction marker (see Ezek 40:2; 46:9 for other examples of this). Since the area of the Negev is unforested, the suggestion that the "forest" mentioned here is Jerusalem makes good sense.

21:1-32

Yahweh's Sword: Babylon

21:3. enemy armies as divine punishment. As early as the end of the third millennium, the invasion of armies is interpreted as the intentional actions of a patron deity who has been angered by the behavior of the people (the Gutian invasion that brought an end to the empire of Agade in the *Curse of Agade*). In Mesopotamia this traditional theology is represented also in Cyrus's rhetoric concerning the overthrow of the Babylonians because of Marduk's displeasure with Nabonidus.

21:18-20. roads to Rabbah and Jerusalem. The movements of the Babylonian army are discussed in this command to draw a map in the sand. Ezekiel traces the troop movements to a crossroads, most likely Damascus, and from there the decision has to be made on whether to divide the army into two groups or proceed together. If the omens suggest it, they will travel south on the King's Highway (Num 20:17) to the Ammonite capital city of Rabbah (twenty-three miles east of the Jordan River). Given other portents, they may turn west through the Golan region north of the Sea of Galilee. The army may travel south to Beth Shan, then west through the Valley of Jezreel to Megiddo and then south along the coastal highway. Or they may take a more direct route south along the Jordan River to Jericho before turning west into the Judean Hill Country to besiege Jerusalem.

21:21. travel omens. Given the gravity of the situation, Nebuchadnezzar's decision to seek guidance from the gods is easily understood. Standing at the crossroads, a significant spot for divine action (see Jer 6:16), he employs various means of divination, casting lots to determine which enemy city (Rabbah or Jerusalem) should be attacked first. Each technique is designed to determine the god's will. One remarkable parallel appears in a Mari text in which an inquiry is made to determine which of three routes should be taken.

21:21. arrow omens and liver omens. Nebuchadnezzar employs belomancy, shaking up a group of arrows and then choosing one. He also consults the images of the household gods that he has brought with the army. The text here refers to *teraphim*, which are now considered to be images of the ancestors rather than images of deities (see comment on Gen 31:19). Finally, he has his diviner priests examine a sheep liver (hepatoscopy). This practice was so common that clay models of the livers were created as teaching tools by apprentice priests.

21:22. battering rams, ramps and siege works. See the comment on Ezekiel 4:2 for the use of these engines and methods of siege warfare.

21:26. king's headgear. Based on descriptions in Mesopotamian texts and artistic renderings on Assyrian palace walls, it seems that the "crown" of a king was in fact more like a turban. A cloth was wound around the head several times, and it in turn was encrusted with jewels and golden ornaments and elaborately embroidered with symbols of the king's majesty. Ezekiel, in calling for Zedekiah to remove his headgear, is commanding the king to relinquish his primary symbol of power because he no longer deserves to wear it.

21:28. Ammonites. Like Judah, Ammon had been engaging in anti-Babylonian activities, probably at the urging of the Egyptians. The omen mentioned in 21:20 directed Nebuchadnezzar to attack Jerusalem first instead of the Ammonite capital of Rabbah, modern Jebel Qal'a. It presently is in the middle of the modern city of Amman but has been surveyed and partially excavated. Occupation at the site and in its vicinity goes back to Paleolithic times. Although it was occasionally subjected to Israelite rule (see 2 Sam 12:26-31), the Ammonites attempted to expand their rule northward after the destruction of Jerusalem. Josephus notes that five years after the destruction of Jerusalem, in the twenty-third year of Nebuchadnezzar's reign (582/581 B.C.), the Babylonian king campaigned in Transjordan, subjecting both Moab and Ammon to his rule. Since hardly any of the Babylonian Chronicles are preserved beyond 594, this cannot be confirmed at this time.

22:1-31
Indictment Against Jerusalem

22:6-12. list of crimes. The bill of indictment read by Ezekiel condemns the people of Judah and their leaders for a set of crimes that violate the basic elements of the Holiness Code in Leviticus 18—20. These range from failure to honor one's parents to profaning the Sabbath and exhibiting various lewd behaviors. Lists such as this are also found in Jeremiah's temple sermon (Jer 7:6-11) and in Amos's oracle against the nation of Israel (Amos 2:6-12). This theme of moral and religious corruption also is found in the twentieth-century B.C. Egyptian *Dispute Between a Man and His Ba*, which charges that "everyone is a thief, there is no love among neighbors . . . everyone chooses evil." Many similar offenses also occur in the listing in Babylonian absolution rituals *(shurpu).*

22:18. dross in the furnace. In the smelting process, silver is separated from lead and other alloyed metals (copper, tin and iron) through a two-stage process. During the second stage, after all vestiges of sulfur have been removed, the silver is liquefied, while the lead dross floats on the surface and can be skimmed off. Ezekiel's metaphor suggests a further purification of Judah is necessary (the exilic experience) so that the dross of its lawless, covenant-breaking nature can be removed by God's hot wrath (see Mal 3:1-4). See comment on Jeremiah 6:28.

22:20. metallurgy. The refining process continues with God placing several metals, including the silver that represents Judah, into the furnace. Divine breath is used instead of bellows to increase the oxygen level and thus the heat of the fire. The fact that the blacksmith does not always use bellows can be seen in an Egyptian painting depicting a metalworker blowing air through a pipe into a furnace. While each metal is in the furnace, it, like the exiles, exists in an intermediate state, being transformed, purified or alloyed with another metal. The furnace here and elsewhere is thus a crucible of social and religious change designed to be God's vehicle to purify a wayward nation. For more information about furnaces of this period see comment on Daniel 3:6.

22:28. false visions and lying divinations. As in his previous condemnation of the false prophets (Ezek 13:6-9), Ezekiel charges them with fabricating visions and divinatory revelations for their own purposes. Jeremiah makes the same indictment of prophets who prophesy lies in Yahweh's name (Jer 29:8-9). See the comment on Ezekiel 13:10 for another example of prophets "whitewashing" the truth with their false statements. Babylonian *baru* priests were in charge of reading omens, but they could be shamed or dismissed for making a false prediction. Failures, however, could also be blamed on failure to follow proper ritual procedures.

23:1-49
Lewd Sisters

23:3. prostitution in the ancient Near East. See the comment on Ezekiel 16:15 for discussion of prostitution in the ancient world. The comment on Deuteronomy 23:17-18 provides a fuller description of cultic prostitution. Ezekiel's references, however, are to the idolatry of Israel and Judah, as they took "lovers" (i.e., other gods) in Egypt and from the Assyrians (compare Hosea's marriage metaphor with his wife Gomer in Hos 1-3).

23:3-5. Egypt and Assyria historical references. The political jockeying for power between Egypt and Assyria meant that both Israel and Judah had to maintain contacts with these superpowers. The flirtations that Ezekiel condemned were reflections of the political accommodations forced on the smaller states. There were numerous contacts between Israel, Judah and the pharaohs of the Twenty-Fifth Dynasty in Egypt, including diplomatic exchanges and possible alliances (such as the one that temporarily brought Egyptian troops to the aid of besieged Jerusalem in 597). Evidence of Israel's ties with Assyria can be found in the portrayal of Jehu bowing before Shalmaneser III on the Black Obelisk and an inscription from the annals of Tiglath-Pileser III in which Menahem pays tribute. Judah also had to submit to Assyrian power, as in Ahaz's cry for help during the Syro-Ephraimitic War (2 Kings 16:7-9) and Hezekiah's ransoming of Jerusalem from Sennacherib's army (2 Kings 18:13-16). Additionally, most of Manasseh's fifty-plus years of reign were spent in submission to Assyrian overlords.

23:6. clothed in blue. Archaeological evidence has demonstrated that the murex snail was collected in great quantities off the coast of Phoenicia as a source of a prized purple dye (see Ezek 27:7). Since large numbers of snails were necessary to extract enough dye from their hypobranchial glands to make it a commercial enterprise, the cost of the dye would have been high (for more information see comment on Num 4:6). Thus the fact that these military officers were clothed in blue suggests both high rank and wealth.

23:6. mounted horsemen. Cavalry units were employed by the armies of Assyria and Babylonia (mentioned in the ninth-century Assyrian annals of Tukulti-Ninurta II). However, the Hebrew term used here is more suggestive of charioteers because of its parallel Akkadian word (Heb. *parašim* and Akk. *Parašsannu*). Note the contribution of King Ahab's two thousand chariots to the force that met the Assyrian king Shalmaneser III at the Battle of Qarqar in 853 B.C.

23:14. men portrayed on a wall. One of the standard means of decorating the walls of Mesopotamian palace gates and walls was with the figures of soldiers, kings and symbolic beasts (such as the dragons on the Ishtar Gate in Babylon). For instance, the Assyrian palace in Nineveh has preserved scenes of siege warfare, hunting and royal and divine figures. Much of what we know about the appearance and clothing of the soldiers and military techniques and weapons come from these reliefs. Although much of the paint has now worn away, it is evident that these figures were once brightly colored, in some cases larger than life, and undoubtedly intimidating to subject peoples. Such power by association might have also been enticing to the leaders of Judah, as Ezekiel suggests.

23:14-15. Chaldean dress. It is unfortunate that most of the wall paintings and reliefs are either Assyrian or Persian, thereby leaving us less informed on the details of Babylonian dress. Working from the drawings we do have, these men must have been clothed in embroidered and ornamented belts (see Is 5:27). Babylonian soldiers are portrayed with caps or headbands with long tassels at the ends.

23:15. chariot officers. Assyrian and Babylonian chariots generally carried three men: a driver, the commander who wielded bow and spear, and a shield bearer, who also handed weapons to the commander as needed. The Akkadian term for this individual was *salsu*, and this may be a cognate for the Hebrew *šališim* used here (the Hebrew root makes it likely that there is some connection to "three"). An alternative suggestion has been that the term refers to an officer of the third rank.

23:15. Chaldea. Babylon during the sixth century was ruled by a non-native dynasty of Chaldeans. They had first appeared in the ninth century in the areas south of Babylonia. While their tribal structure was similar to that of the neighboring Arameans, they were a distinct group. By the time of Ezekiel, to name a person a Chaldean (*kasdim*) was to acknowledge that person's high social status.

23:23. Pekod, Shoa and Koa. While these ethnic names refer to Babylonian allies inhabiting the Trans-Tigris region, they also have a chilling meaning: "Punishment, War Cry and Shriek." Pekod is an Aramean tribe (see Jer 50:21) mentioned in Tiglath-Pileser III's annals. Shoa probably refers to the Suti, prominent as a difficult tribe to manage for the Amorite kings of Mari. Koa is presently unknown, although some equate them with the Guti.

23:24. armor and equipment. Charioteers, as portrayed in Assyrian reliefs, wore pointed helmets or turbans and chain mail over their upper torso, and were protected by round shields. Infantry, while not as heavily armored due to the need for greater flexibility and speed, carried large round shields. Their clothing was girded with a cross belt and they protected their heads with conical-shaped helmets. Each warrior fought with spears, swords, axes or maces (see the list for Uzziah's infantry in 2 Chron 26:14).

23:25. face disfigurement. While it was not uncommon for conquerors to disfigure some of their captives, it is also possible that the marriage metaphor is extended here to the punishment for the unfaithful Oholibah/Jerusalem. Ezekiel may have been familiar with the Middle Assyrian Law Code or some similar legislation regarding the husband's rights to punish his wife. According to these Assyrian laws, the husband may cut off his wife's nose and mutilate the adulterer's face and turn him into a eunuch.

23:37. child sacrifice as food. On this charge of human sacrifice, see the comment on Ezekiel 16:20.

23:38. defiling sanctuary. Child sacrifice, the shedding of innocent blood, had defiled the hands of the people of Jerusalem and yet they have the temerity make these offerings to other gods and then enter Yahweh's sanctuary (compare Jer 7:9-11). Sanctuary defilement was a very serious charge. It brought jeopardy to the individual and the city (since they risked destruction by an offended deity), but more significantly, it could drive the deity away. By bringing their impurity there they have defiled God's holiness, making it impossible for the divine presence to remain (see Ezek 10).

23:38. desecrated sabbaths. See the comment on Ezekiel 20:12 on the significance of the sabbaths as a sign of the covenant relationship. Just as the violation of the temple's sacred space could result in the loss of God's presence, the violation of sacred times could jeopardize the equilibrium that God's presence maintained. The temple was the place for God to take up his repose. It was a place of perfect equilibrium. The sabbath of the people was set aside for them to mirror this equilibrium in their lives and reflect on the source of this equilibrium. To fail to keep the sabbath was to threaten to undo the equilibrium and move toward chaos. Desecration of these holy days and events violates the heart of the covenant agreement and, as with any treaty in the ancient Near East, makes the penalty or curse clause operative.

23:40. painted eyes. Women throughout the ancient Near East regularly enlarged and darkened their eyes with a mixture compounded of olive oil mixed with malachite (green) or galena (black; see comment on 2 Kings 9:30). Babylonian sources mention eye paint that included stibnite, antimony trisulphide. Decorated palettes were used to grind the ore and mix it for application. These palettes have been found at many Iron II sites in Israel, including Megiddo.

23:41. elegant couch. The adulteress Jerusalem is portrayed in much the same light as the prostitute in Proverbs 7:10-23. Both seduce their lovers with an inviting couch, incense and persuasive words. Prior to the Hellenistic period, all references to the couch are associated with a sleeping chamber (see 2 Sam 4:7; Ps 6:6), not the banqueting room.

23:41. incense and oil on table. As part of the anticipated sexual activity, the adulteress Jerusalem has perfumed her bedchamber with incense (see Song 1:3; 4:10) and has sweet-smelling oils at hand for anointing her hair and bodies (Esther 2:12). Similar images are found in the Egyptian love songs discovered by archaeologists in the Karnak temple complex in Luxor.

23:42. Sabeans. Whether the text refers to the Arabian tribal group known as the Sabeans (see Job 1:14-15; Joel 3:8), or to drunk leaders of small nomadic tribes, the point is to highlight the indignity of an adulteress whose lovers are ruffians and foreigners.

24:1-27
The Cooking Pot

24:1. chronology. Basing his dating scheme on the accession year for Zedekiah (596 B.C.), then the date for the beginning of siege of Jerusalem by Nebuchadnezzar's army would be January 5, 587 B.C. (the tenth day of the tenth month [Tebet] of Zedekiah's ninth year; alternatively, this has been reckoned at January 15, 588).

24:3. cooking pot. The pot is usually a wide-mouthed ceramic jar, though here it is made of copper (v. 11). When manufactured for temple use, the vessel would be made of silver or gold. Available in various sizes, they could be used over a fire if placed on a platform or tripod of stones as in the narrative in 2 Kings 4:38. For the use of a cooking pot as part of a prophetic oracle, see Jeremiah's "boiling pot" in Jeremiah 1:13.

24:6. pot and the lots. Ezekiel probably describes the contents of the pot (choice pieces of meat, v. 4), rather than the pot itself, as tainted or diseased. The casting of the lot would be done to decide which pieces would be reserved for special use (perhaps to be gifts to the temple). But in this analogy, though they were choice pieces of meat, they had gone bad and were not eligible for holy use.

24:7. pouring out blood. Because blood was the essence of life, it was not to be consumed by the Israelites. See comments on Deuteronomy 12:16 and Leviticus 17:11,12. Here, however, the issue is not the consumption of blood, but the exposure of blood. When the blood of an animal was shed and poured out, it was to be covered with earth (Lev 17:13). Exposed blood would "cry out" for vengeance (Gen 37:26).

24:10. spices. In recipes from eighteenth-century B.C. Babylonia, seasonings for meat dishes and stews included salt as well as onions, leeks, mint and garlic. In these ancient preparations, the cooks added distinctive flavor with anise, coriander, cumin and dill. Given the metaphorical nature of this meal, the well-cooked meat may even refer to bodies being prepared for burial with spices.

24:10. charring bones. The meat is cooked so thoroughly that it easily comes off the bones. The bones then are broken so that the marrow will mix with the other ingredients and add flavor to the broth. Once this has been poured off, what remains is a virtually useless mass of carbonized bits. For easy disposal they will be burnt so completely that they literally fall apart and can be scattered over the refuge heap (compare Ezek 22:15). A thorough job of purification or destruction could be drawn from this metaphor.

24:17. acts of mourning. For other examples of mourning practices, see the comments on Leviticus 19:28 and Deuteronomy 14:1-2. Like Jeremiah (Jer 16:5-7), Ezekiel is commanded not to engage in the usual expressions of mourning. In fact, he is told to put on a festive turban and wear his sandals as if nothing unusual had happened.

25:1-7
Oracle Concerning Ammon

25:1. oracles against foreign nations. See comment on Jeremiah 46:1.

25:2. Ammonites in early sixth century. Although Ammon felt free to taunt Jerusalem over its siege and destruction (see Ezek 21:28), Nebuchadnezzar did eventually turn his forces against this Transjordanian kingdom. According to Herodotus, the campaign against Ammon occurred in 582 B.C. and resulted in widespread devastation of the area. Whether there was a significant deportation of its population has now come into question because of the discovery of seal impressions dating to the Persian period. They indicate a continuity of the Ammonite culture and political existence as late as the fourth century B.C. See the comment on Jeremiah 49:2.

25:4. people of the East. As in Jeremiah 49:28, this nomadic group is associated with the peoples of the Midianite desert region (see Judg 6:3). Their caravans carried goods from the various states of Transjordanian and Palestine, and they were a target of invading armies (Is 11:14). In this case, however, these tribal people will now inhabit the lands of the Ammonites. This is reminiscent of the Egyptian *Visions of Neferti,* which also mentions "desert herders" settling in formerly populated areas.

25:4. fruit and milk. The standard benediction is that one should enjoy the fruit of one's own labors/vineyards (Ps 128:2; Is 3:10). In this case, however, what has been worked for will become the property of invaders (compare Ezek 23:29). Both agricultural and herding products will be confiscated and the full range of the economy shattered.

25:5. Rabbah. See comments on Jeremiah 49:2 and Ezekiel 21:18-20.

25:8-11
Oracle Concerning Moab

25:8. Moab in the early sixth century. Moab was among the states represented at Zedekiah's strategy meeting in 597 B.C. (Jer 27:3). Although it apparently survived and served as a place of refuge for Judeans fleeing Nebuchadnezzar's destruction of Jerusalem in 587, its role as a potential troublemaker in the region was not forgotten. Josephus records a later campaign by the Babylonian king in 582-581 to reduce both Ammon and Moab. There is not sufficient evidence to demonstrate how effective this campaign actually was, but, like Ammon, the nation of Moab probably survived to become a part of the Persian empire at the end of the sixth century.

25:9. towns. Each of these towns were part of Moab's western line of defense. Beth Jeshimoth (Tell 'Azeimeh) lies in the Shittim Valley north of the Dead Sea. Baal Meon, mentioned in the Mesha Stele, is generally identified with Khirbet Ma'in, four miles southwest of Madaba and thirteen miles southeast of Beth Jeshimoth. Kiriathaim is also listed in the Mesha Stele and presumably is located on the Moabite Plateau (Josh 13:19). It has been identified with several sites, including el-Qereiyat and Jalul, but there is no consensus on its location.

25:12-14
Oracle Concerning Edom

25:12. Edom in the early sixth century. Edom apparently stayed neutral or pro-Babylonian (Ps 137:7) during the conflicts that led to the destruction of Jerusalem. Jeremiah 40:11 indicates that Edom did accept Judean refugees after 587 B.C. Nebuchadnezzar apparently did not extend his Transjordanian campaign of 582 as far as Edom, but his successor, Nabonidus recorded in his Chronicle a siege of the Edomite city of Bozrah in 552 B.C. Archaeological excavations at Buseira and at Tell el-Kheleifeh indicate destruction levels during this period followed by a quick rebuilding and a resumption of economic activity along the southern range of the King's Highway.

25:13. Teman and Dedan. For descriptions of these cities see comments on Jeremiah 49:7 and 49:8.

25:15-17

Oracle Concerning Philistia

25:15. Philistia in the early sixth century. The omission of the cities of Philistia from the list of states represented at Zedekiah's meeting in 597 (Jer 27:3) suggests that this area was firmly in the control of the Babylonians at that time. This region had been badly weakened by the late-seventh-century campaigns of Pharaoh Psammeticus I as Assyrian control waned there (see Jer 25:20; Zeph 2:4). The sons of the king of Ashkelon are recorded in Babylonian ration lists dating to 592, indicating their hostage status. When the Philistine states joined in the Judean revolt of 588, Nebuchadnezzar deported them and apparently settled them near Nippur. By the Persian period, little of the indigenous Philistine population remained in Philistia.

25:16. Kerethites. Ezekiel creates a poetic parallelism between Philistines and Kerethites, while it is still unclear whether these two peoples are actually related ethnically or historically. The Kerethites are most often associated with the island of Crete, and it would appear these people became mercenaries shortly after their migration to the southern coast of Palestine near Gaza (see 1 Sam 30:14; 2 Sam 8:18).

26:1—28:19

Lament and Oracles Concerning Tyre

26:3. Tyre in the early sixth century. After Egypt's defeat in 605 B.C., Tyre was the main foe of Babylon in western Asia. It was the leading city in Phoenicia and renowned for its maritime trade. Standing out from the coast approximately six hundred yards from the mainland, the island city of Tyre and its harbor were secure from anything but a sustained siege. The waters were also deep enough to allow for heavily laden ships to approach and offload their cargoes. Dedicated to commercial activity, Tyre was supplied with food and other essentials by its sister city of Ushu. Tyrian fleets established colonies around the Mediterranean, including those on Cyprus and the North African city of Carthage, to draw on the resources of these areas, especially metals, and to funnel goods back and forth between the eastern and western Mediterranean. Throughout this region there is archaeological evidence of Phoenician metalwork and pottery, indicating the extent and longevity of trade relations. The principal exports were cedar wood, fabrics and dyes, and glasswork. According to Josephus, Tyre and its king, Ethbaal III, were involved in numerous coalitions and conspiracies against the Babylonians.

26:7. Nebuchadnezzar's siege of Tyre. According to Josephus the Babylonian siege of Tyre lasted thirteen years (c. 586-573 B.C.). A Babylonian text claims that Nebuchadnezzar was present during the siege. Apparently the long siege ended with a treaty stipulating that the Tyrian royal house was to be deported to Babylon. Although the king of Tyre was allowed to stay, he was under the control of a Babylonian commissioner. Tyre's power was effectively exhausted by the long siege.

26:8. siege works and ramps. The writer has an intimate knowledge of siege warfare. One constructed siege mounds and ramps up against the city wall of the city to be besieged. There is plentiful evidence of siege ramps on Assyrian wall reliefs, and a siege ramp has been uncovered at the city of Lachish that was used by the Assyrians in their successful conquest of the Judean fortress. Tyre was especially difficult to conquer because much of the city was on an island near the coast.

26:8. raising shields. A roof of shields was constructed over the battering ram to protect the attackers when the ram was brought up to the city walls.

26:9. battering rams. Battering rams were often depicted by the Assyrians as large wooden wheeled machines used to break apart the city gates.

26:10. Babylonian use of cavalry and chariotry. The Chaldeans were renown for their use of cavalry and chariotry, inheriting the use of both from the Assyrians (see comment on Jer 6:23). The Assyrians often depicted horse-drawn chariots in the midst of battle on wall reliefs.

26:11. strong pillars. The strong pillars are probably a symbolic expression signifying the end of resistance. However, Herodotus mentioned emerald and gold pillars that adorned the Heracles (Melqart) temple at Tyre. Assyrian wall reliefs depict two external pillars on a Tyre temple.

27:3. Tyre's merchant city status. Tyre had two major sea ports, a natural harbor to the north and an artificial one to the south. By this time, Tyre served as a middleman for the Mediterranean world, transferring products to and from distant ports for at least half a millennium.

27:5. pine trees from Senir. The type of the tree mentioned is probably of the juniper variety, the eastern savin. According to Deuteronomy 3:9, Mount Senir was the Amorite name for Mount Hermon in the southern portion of the Anti-Lebanon range east of the Baka Valley. The Assyrians called it Saniru.

27:5-7. shipbuilding materials. The shipbuilding materials listed here were of the highest quality in the eastern Mediterranean. Pine and fir were preferred by the Egyptians for masts and yards. The hardwood oars lining both sides of the Phoenician biremes (ships with two racks of oarpullers on each side) were of the most durable wood. Inlaid ivory came from Kittion on the island of Cyprus. Variegated linens from Egypt were in high demand throughout the region. The dyes used for the awnings were the most expensive.

27:7. Elishah. The location of the islands of Elishah is uncertain. Elishah was a son of Javan (Gen 10:4). The name was applied to a Tyrian colony famous for its dyes. Elishah is probably the Alashiya of the Amarna tablets, usually designated as Cyprus. Seven Amarna tablets mention a king of Alashiya, who wrote letters to the Egyptian monarchs in the thirteenth century B.C.

27:8. Sidon and Arvad. Sidon and Arvad were Phoenician cities that lay on the Mediterranean coast north of Tyre. Arvad was about 110 miles north, while Sidon was about 25. They appear at this time to have been subordinate to Tyre. Both cities were often mentioned in the Amarna letters and Assyrian annals.

27:9. Gebal. Like Sidon and Arvad, Gebal (or Byblos) was a Phoenician city on the Mediterranean coast north of Tyre, about sixty miles away. It was apparently in a subordinate position to its southern neighbor. Byblos was a trading partner with Egypt in the third millennium B.C. and figured prominently in the Amarna texts and Assyrian annals.

27:10. Persia, Lydia, Put. In listing Persia, Lydia and Put, Ezekiel was signifying the peoples living at the outermost parts of the known world. Persia was in western Iran and Lydia in central Turkey, while Put may re-

ferred to the Libyans west of Egypt.

27:11. Arvad, Helech, Gammad. The city of Arvad has already been encountered in verse 8. *Helech* (Hebrew, "your army") is unattested elsewhere in the Old Testament as a toponym. It has, however, been associated with Hilakku (Cilicia in southeastern Turkey) in the Assyrian annals. The location of Gammad is uncertain, but it may be equated with Qumidi in the Amarna tablets, possibly north of Tyre on the Mediterranean coast.

27:12. Tarshish. Tarshish was associated with metal industries. The annals of the Assyrian king Esarhaddon associate a place called Tarsisi with Cyprus and other islands. There was also a Tartessus mentioned in classical sources as a Phoenician colony in western Spain.

27:13. Greece, Tubal, Meschech. Javan (or Ionians) was the biblical designation for the Greek world. Tubal (Taballu) was the Assyrian designation for a central Anatolian kingdom. Like Tubal, Meschech (Mushku) was listed as a central Anatolian kingdom in the Assyrian annals. Both Anatolian states had bad relations with Assyria.

27:14. Beth Togarmah. Beth Togarmah was most likely the capital city of Kammanu, a central Anatolian kingdom. It was known in Hittite sources as Tegaramara, and in Assyrian sources as Til-Garimmu.

27:15. Rhodes. The mention of Rhodes here is problematic in the earliest manuscripts of the Old Testament. Others read Danuna, a region north of Tyre mentioned in the Amarna letters.

27:16. Aram. Aram refers to the Syrian hinterland from Upper Mesopotamia in the north to Damascus in the south.

27:17. Minnith. Minnith was an Ammonite region in the Transjordan mentioned in Judges 11:33. Eusebius, the fourth-century A.D. church historian, identified it with the town Maanith, four miles from Heshbon.

27:18. Helbon, Zahar. Helbon is identified with the Assyrian Hilbinu, modern Helbun, ten miles north of Damascus. Zahar (or Sahar) was probably the wilderness of es-Sahra northwest of Damascus.

27:19. Greeks from Uzal. Uzal is probably equated with Izalla, a site in the Anatolian foothills of Cilicia. Greeks (or Ionians) may have had a relationship with the town, but this is otherwise unattested.

27:19. Cassia and Calamus. The city of Damascus traded in *qiddu* (probably cassia), a costly perfume native to east Asia. Calamus was an aromatic grass used in perfume, cosmetics, flavoring and medicine. This particular type of calamus probably came from India.

27:20. Dedan. Dedan was a central Arabian oasis where Tyre received its special riding gear. It is identified with the modern site of al-Ula, which is situated on the frankincense road from Yemen to Palestine.

27:20. saddle blankets. The term here translated as "saddle blankets" is probably derived from an Akkadian root referring to "a covering for a horse."

27:21. Kedar. See comment on Isaiah 42:11.

27:22. Sheba and Raamah. For Sheba, see comment on Isaiah 60:6. Raamah is mentioned in the Old Testament only in conjunction with Sheba. It may be associated with Rgmt (the vowels of the ancient name are not certain), a city in the district of Najran in central Arabia.

27:23. Haran, Canneh, Eden, Sheba, Ashur, Kilmad. All these areas were to the north and east of Tyre. Haran was situated on the Balikh River in Upper Mesopotamia. Canneh is probably Assyrian Kannu, the location of which is unknown. Eden is Bit Adini, an Aramean state west of the Balikh River in Syria. Ashur was the name of the old capital city of Assyria, as well as the name of the primary god of Assyria. Kilmad is otherwise unknown.

27:24. merchandise. The merchandise listed here is very rare and exotic. Many of the words are *hapax legomena*, that is, words that occur only here in Scripture. Cognates with Akkadian have helped somewhat in shedding light on their meaning. The "choice garments" are specially crafted garments of some type. They are accompanied by expensive blue-purple and embroidered cloaks. They are followed by a coat or mantle, woolen garments, and a multicolored coat.

27:25. ships of Tarshish. Although verse 12 denotes a specific region for Tarshish (i.e., Spain), the designation "ships of Tarshish" seems to imply a Phoenician provenance similar to what is found in Isaiah 23:1-18. Thus they may have been ships bound for Tarshish.

28:2. ruler of Tyre. The king of Tyre at this time was Ethbaal III, although nothing in this oracle is known to be specifically about him. The text claims that the prince is claiming equality with the patron deity of Tyre, Melqart, a fact unattested in extrabiblical literature.

28:3. Daniel. Some perceive this person to be a famous extrabiblical character known from the Ugaritic Epic of Keret. But the Ugaritic Danil was not particularly known for great wisdom. The biblical Daniel was probably well known to Ezekiel because of his exceptional gifts. For more information see the comment on 14:14.

28:12. lament. There are numerous laments or funeral dirges in the Old Testament and in ancient Near Eastern literature. They are often directed towards cities or nations, but there are also laments concerning the death of individuals. In this case the "lament" is a sarcastic piece of mocking literature. See comment on 19:1.

28:12. seal of perfection. Assyrian royal epithets included the titles "perfect man" and "perfect king." The term was also used in divine attributes. Here the king is likened to a finely carved stamp seal (see sidebar in Jer 32). These were often made from semiprecious stones and served both as a mark of identity and a protective amulet.

28:13. list of precious stones. In Exodus 28:17-20 and 39:10-13 the high priest's breastplate contains twelve precious stones, many of which are repeated here. A gem-studded garment would be a very clear indication of his grandeur, but there is no indication here that a breastplate is intended. Kings sometimes wore gem-encrusted headbands. Jeweled pectorals or breastplates are known from the ancient world as well. The identification of a number of these gemstones is problematic. Thus modern translations have not agreed on the nature of the nine gems. Carnelian is preferable to ruby; topaz is possibly the yellow-green olivine called peridot; the third is not diamond (NASB) or emerald (NIV), but it is a hard stone of some sort; the fourth is likely a yellow stone (D. Block suggests Spanish gold topaz); for the fifth, onyx is normal and probable; the sixth is commonly regarded as some sort of jasper; the seventh is lapis lazuli (with the NIV note); the eighth is very uncertain; and the last is believed by most to be emerald.

28:14. cherub. The term *cherub(im)* occurs over ninety times in the Old Testament in reference to heavenly creatures. They appear to be winged beings but are greatly varied. There are examples of cherubim with many faces, bovine faces, aquiline faces and human faces. They are described in a way to correspond to various forms of composite beasts depicted in ancient Near Eastern art, especially in Assyria. Because of their composite animal and human features, they were apt symbols of divine presence, both in Israel and in surrounding regions. Here it is undoubtedly a reference to the guardian of the tree of life in Genesis 3:24 (see comment there). Likening the prince of Tyre to a cherub suggests that he was entrusted with the stewardship of divine property. The natural resources of this region, especially the cedar forests, were often considered the property of the gods in Mesopotamian sources (for instance, the Gilgamesh Epic). Artifacts also support the picture presented here. Cherubim are frequently depicted on the carved ivories of this period, and at times the king is portrayed as a cherub. The carvings can be jewel-studded, and decorations feature flowers and mountains. For more information on cherubim, see comments on 10:1 and Exodus 25:18-20.

28:14. holy mountain. The concept of holy mountains was common in the ancient world. Ancient Near Eastern thought, not unlike that familiar from Greek mythology, visualized a mountain height as the dwelling place of deity. There would have been little difference in their minds between the tops of mountains and the heavens. Baal's home was purported in Ugaritic literature to be Mount Zaphon. In Israelite terms the two most significant sacred mountains were Mount Sinai and the Temple Mount in Jerusalem. While there is no parallel in ancient Near Eastern thinking suggesting a paradise on a mountain, the garden of Eden functions as a paradise largely because it is the place of God's presence, a cosmic Holy of Holies. The holy mountain is then very appropriate as a parallel to Eden, for both concern God's presence. In Ezekiel 31:16 the forests of Lebanon and the garden of Eden are again associated.

28:14. fiery stones. There are numerous connections possible for understanding the "fiery stones." In the realm of iconography they are represented as the decorative ornamentation on some of the ivory pieces (see comment on "cherubim" above). In mythology, it should be noted that there is a palace of fused gemstones described in Ugaritic texts. In legend, Gilgamesh encounters on his journeys a grove where the trees and bushes are full of precious stones. Any of these could offer a context for the picture given here by the text.

28:16-17. Satan connection. From early on in church history there has been an interpretive tradition understanding this passage as an account of the fall of Satan. Though this same type of interpretation in Isaiah 14 was fervently denied by well-respected exegetes such as John Calvin (who bluntly ridiculed it), it has persisted into modern times. From a background standpoint, it must be noted that Satan is never portrayed as either being a cherub or being with the cherub in the garden in any passage of Scripture. Furthermore, Israel's understanding of Satan was far more limited than that found in the New Testament. Even in Job, Satan is not a personal name but a function (see comment on Job 1:6). "Satan" does not become identified as the personal name of the chief of demons until about the

second century B.C., and he does not take up his position as the source and cause of all evil until the unfolding of Christian doctrine. Consequently, the Israelites could not have understood this passage in this way, and no New Testament passage offers a basis for departing from the Israelite understanding of it. In the context, it is a metaphorical description of the high stewardship entrusted to the prince of Tyre (as significant as the cherub's role in the garden). Rather than treating this sacred trust with reverence and awe, he exploited it to his own benefit—as if the cherub of the garden had opened a roadside fruit stand. He was therefore discharged from his position, relieved of his trust and publicly humiliated.

28:18. desecrated sanctuaries. In Ezekiel, the temple of Israel is desecrated when it is despoiled by the Babylonians (Ezek 7:21-22). Something can also be "desecrated" by failing to treat it as holy. Since it is unlikely that Ezekiel would consider the sanctuaries of Tyre as holy, it is more likely that in this passage the prince is charged with pillaging sanctuary treasuries or misappropriating temple funds.

28:20-26
Oracle Concerning Sidon

28:21. Sidon in the early sixth century. The great trading city of Sidon had been defeated by the Assyrian king Sennacherib in 701 B.C., who deposed Luli for joining an anti-Assyrian coalition. Under Abdimilikutti, Sidon again revolted against Esarhaddon of Assyria in 677 B.C. The city was destroyed to its foundations and its king was beheaded. The Assyrians rebuilt the city and named it Kar-Asarhaddon, and it became the center of Assyria's administration of the area. In Jeremiah 27:3 envoys from Sidon were included in the conspirators that met in Jerusalem in 594. A few years later Sidon was forced to submit to Nebuchadnezzar of Babylon, and many of its people were deported. There is no account of the details, but some Sidonian exiles are known from the city of Uruk in Babylonia in this period. Herodotus reports that in 588 the Egyptians fought against Sidon in an attempt to gain control of the Phoenician coast, but it is likely that Sidon was already a Babylonian vassal at this time.

29:1—32:32
Oracles and Laments Concerning Egypt

29:1. chronology. Though compared to the date given in 24:1 this appears to be one year later, it has often been concluded by commentators that the notation in 24:1 was made in accordance with an nonaccession year system rather than an accession year system (see comments on 24:1; Jer 26:1; and Dan 2:1). If this is so, this oracle was given only two days after the siege of Jerusalem began. This is more likely, because the Egyptian response to the siege took place that first summer.

29:2. Egypt in the early sixth century. In the early sixth century B.C. Egypt was under the Saite or Twenty-Sixth dynasty. With the fall of Assyria, Egypt attempted to control the Levant as it had done in previous centuries. However, Nebuchadnezzar of Babylon was able to fill the power vacuum in the area, decisively defeating Egypt at the Battle of Carchemish in 605 B.C. The Egyptian pharaoh Psammeticus II (595-589) had spent much of his reign attempting to regain the territory in Phoenicia and Palestine that Nebuchadnezzar had taken away from Necho II (610-596) at Carchemish. Apries (Hophra) came to the throne in 589. During the early summer of the first year of the siege of Jerusalem, he dispatched an army into Palestine. This required the Babylonians to temporarily lift their siege. This, plus an Egyptian fleet that sailed to Tyre and quickly took control there (mentioned by the Greek historian Herodotus), forced Nebuchadnezzar to withdraw from Jerusalem. The Egyptians, however, were quickly defeated (possibly near Gaza) and the siege resumed by late summer.

29:3. identity of pharaoh. The reigning monarch in Egypt at this time was Apries (Hophra), who ruled 589-570 B.C. However, Ezekiel is most likely addressing the office of pharaoh in general, rather than any particular monarch.

29:3. monster among the streams. For the metaphor of Egypt as a monster of chaos see comment on Isaiah 30:7. More concretely, the word used here could easily be used in reference to a crocodile. There are probably elements of both intended here.

29:4. fish metaphor. The Greek historian Herodotus described the procedure of catching crocodiles in the Nile. The hunter baited a hook with pork, letting it float in the middle of the river. On the banks of the river, the hunter began to beat a live pig. Upon hearing the cries of the pig, the crocodile went after the sound, meeting the pork, which it swallowed. In the meantime the hunter pulled the line, which included the hook and crocodile.

29:6. staff of reed metaphor. Whether used as a cane or a crutch, the reed will only collapse and cause physical damage rather than offering reliable support. The Assyrians claimed the same about Pharaoh in Isaiah 36:6. The prominence of reeds in Egypt made this a very apt metaphor for depending on Egypt. More specifically, the pharaoh held several scepters that represented his power and office. The *was* scepter was forked at the bottom, and the top handle was carved in the shape of a dog's head. The *heqa* scepter was shaped like a shepherd's crook. Though these were generally not made of reed, tomb discoveries have confirmed that at least in one instance a reed staff was included among the staffs of Pharaoh.

29:10. Migdol to Aswan. Migdol ("tower") was the name of several military stations in Egypt's northeastern frontier. Although we cannot be certain just which one is mentioned here, the term marks the northeastern border of Egypt. Syene (modern Aswan) was just north of the first cataract of the Nile, the traditional southern border of Egypt (the border of Cush/Nubia). Thus, Migdol to Aswan was the entire length of Egypt.

29:11-12. forty-year desolation and exile. Forty years was the period in which one generation flourished and died off. Thus it was a period of temporary national punishment. In a Moabite inscription, Mesha of Moab claimed that Israel occupied his land for forty years. There is some evidence of Nebuchadnezzar undertaking an invasion of Egypt in his thirty-seventh year (568), but there is no information concerning what success he might have had or whether there was any deportation of the population. Memphis was captured by the Persian king Cambyses in 525, and Pharaoh Psammeticus II was taken captive. Egypt then came under Persian control through most of the Achaemenid empire, with a brief period of revolt and independence around 460.

29:14. Upper Egypt. Upper Egypt (or the land of Pathros) designated all of Egypt south of Memphis. An ancient Egyptian tradition asserted that the nation had originated in the south in Upper Egypt. Esarhaddon of Assyria claimed to be the king of Musur (north Egypt) and Paturisi (Pathros).

29:14-15. lowly and weak kingdom. The term "lowly and weak kingdom" appears to denote that Egypt will be relegated to vassal status. Although we are not told to whom the nation will be subject, the historical record is clear enough. Conquered by Cambyses in 525, Egypt became a Persian vassal for the next two centuries.

29:17. chronology. The date is April 26, 571, one or two years after the end of the siege of Tyre.

29:18. Nebuchadnezzar's siege of Tyre. See comment on 26:7.

29:18. head rubbed bare, shoulder raw. Nebuchadnezzar's soldiers will have bare heads and raw shoulders because of the burdens put upon them in order to throw up earthworks to attack the city of Tyre. The siege ramps used to build a slope up to the walls required tons of dirt. Additionally, there was an attempt to build a causeway out to the island portion of the city. Dirt would have been carried in baskets on the head and on the shoulder.

29:18. no reward. Soldiers usually received booty in the form of persons, animals and possessions. However, Tyre was able to get an exemption from destruction by yielding to Babylon. Thus there was no pillaging of the city.

29:19. Nebuchadnezzar and Egypt. It was inevitable that Nebuchadnezzar would eventually have to invade and attempt to conquer Egypt. The Medes had united the territory east of the Tigris, effectively cutting Babylon off from direct trade with the east, and the Egyptians, with their Phoenician allies, were constantly causing political and commercial problems in the west and along the Arabian trade routes. An extended (thirteen-year according to the fourth-century Greek historian Menander) siege bottled up Tyre and devastated much of Phoenicia (584-571). A fragmentary portion of Nebuchadnezzar's annals from his thirty-seventh year, Herodotus and Ezekiel 29:19-21 refer to the invasion of Egypt in 568, but no details are given other than victories over desert tribes. It is likely that some Babylonian garrisons were installed in the fortresses of the Sinai following this campaign.

29:21. horn metaphor. The horns of an animal were considered tokens of their power and thus were a figure of strength. Many of the deities of Mesopotamia were depicted with horns. Thus, making a horn to sprout signifies a return of Israel's power. Additionally, it must be noted that the crowns of kings also often featured horns, and a horn could therefore refer more specifically to a king (see comment on Dan 7:7).

30:4. Egypt connected to Cush. Cush, the neighboring country to the south of Egypt, known as Nubia, had had relations with its northern neighbor since the beginning of recorded history. Egypt had a dominant trading relationship with Cush for many centuries and occasionally conquered the area. By the mid-eighth century, however, the Cushites had been successful in conquering Egypt, and they ruled the land for nearly a century.

30:5. geography. The first three areas listed (Cush, Put and Lud) are also mentioned in

Ezekiel 27:10. Cush (Nubia) was adjacent to Egypt on the south; Put (Libya) was adjacent to the west. Lydia was to the north across the Mediterranean and was a frequent ally of Egyptians against various enemies to the east. Arabia could refer to the Arabian peninsula to the southeast, but it would be unusual for this Hebrew word to be used that way. It is more frequently used to refer to a mixed assortment of ethnic groups. It is known that the Egyptians during this period used mercenaries from throughout western Asia and the eastern Mediterranean. Kub (NIV: Libya) is an unknown area probably also within modern Libya. The "land of the covenant" is a reference to soldiers of an unnamed country, probably Judah, which had a military relationship with Egypt at this time and probably supplied mercenaries, as did all of these other lands. Jeremiah is aware of a Jewish settlement in Egypt (see comment on Jer 44:1).

30:6. Migdol to Aswan. See comment on 29:10.

30:9. messengers to Cush in ships. The term here for "ships" (an Egyptian loan word) refers to military boats rather than reed boats or merchant ships. Nubia felt that having Egypt as a buffer zone offered a certain amount of protection from any of the powers from the east that would arise. Though the Egyptian pharaoh Psammeticus II campaigned against Nubia in 593, it is not attack from Egypt that is threatened in this passage. The Persian king Cambyses invaded Nubia in 525, and from that time it was counted as part of the empire. Nubians served as mercenaries in the Persian army.

30:10-11. Nebuchadnezzar and Egypt. See comment on 29:19.

30:12. sell land. In the ancient world the concept of selling something did not emphasize "getting money" as it might in today's economy. Rather the emphasis was on the transfer of ownership. In Akkadian the word for sell is also the word for give. Ruth 4:3-5 shows that flexibility in the Hebrew term used here as well. As a result, it is not pertinent to ask what Yahweh is receiving in return. That is not the issue. He is transferring possession of the land from Egypt to Babylon.

30:13. images of Memphis. Memphis was the royal residence during this period and the center of the cult of the god Ptah. It was the city in which kings were enthroned. Ptah was one of the few deities that did not have an animal head. He was a creator deity and patron of the craft guilds.

30:14. Pathros. This is a reference to Upper Egypt; see comment on 29:14.

30:14. Zoan. Zoan (Hellenized as Tanis) was a town in the eastern Nile Delta, an important administrative center in the eighth and seventh centuries B.C.

30:14. Thebes. Thebes (or No-Amon in Egyptian) was the main city of Upper Egypt and had been the capital of the nation for centuries during the New Kingdom. It was surrounded by a spectacular array of monumental sacred precincts.

30:15. Pelusium. Sin was an important fortress town in the northeast frontier of the Delta region usually identified with Pelusium. It held a strategic position in Egypt's defense against invaders from Western Asia.

30:17. Heliopolis. Aven (Hellenized as Heliopolis, "city of the sun god") was at the apex of the Nile Delta region, just north of the city of Cairo. It normally appears in Hebrew as On (see Gen 41:45, 50).

30:17. Bubastis. Pi-Beset (Hellenized as Bubastis) was a town in the Nile Delta region. It is modern Tell Basta, located thirty-five miles south of Cairo on the Tanitic branch of the Nile. It was the residence of Sheshonq (Shishak), a powerful monarch of the Twenty-Second Dynasty in the tenth century B.C.

30:18. Tahpanhes. Tahpanhes was an outpost in the eastern Delta region of the Nile, bordering the Sinai. It was later known as Daphne by the Greeks, who inhabited the outpost as mercenaries by the seventh century B.C. The Greek historian Herodotus states that Daphne was one of three outposts set up by the Egyptians to stop the Assyrian invasion. The Israelites in flight from the Babylonians may have stopped there in the early sixth century B.C.

30:20. chronology. The date is April 29, 587 B.C., just a few months after the date given in 29:1. The Egyptian interference is imminent, but Ezekiel warns that nothing will come of it.

30:21. the arm of Pharaoh. In Scripture the arm is the symbol of aggressive power, and thus the breaking of the arm signifies that the individual in question has been rendered impotent (see Ps 10:15; 37:17). The image of an outstretched or mighty hand or arm is common in Egyptian inscriptions to describe the power of Pharaoh. It is used throughout the Exodus narratives to describe God's power over Pharaoh. In the fourteenth-century B.C. Amarna letters, Abdi-Heba, the governor of Jerusalem, refers to "the strong arm of the king" as the basis for his government appointment. Similarly, the Eighteenth-Dynasty Hymn to Osiris equates his growing to majority with the phrase "when his arm was strong," and Haremhab's Hymn to Thoth describes the moon god as guiding the divine

bark through the sky with "arms outstretched."

30:23. scattering Egyptians. See comment on 29:11-12.

31:1. chronology. The date is June 21, 587 B.C., nearly two months after the date mentioned in Ezekiel 30:20. Since there is no firm information concerning the date of the Egyptian interference, it is difficult to relate this oracle to the timing of the event.

31:2. identity of Pharaoh. As in 29:3 Ezekiel is probably addressing the office of pharaoh in general. Hophra was the reigning monarch in 587 B.C. (see the note on 29:3).

31:3-17. extent, duration and power of Assyria. The power of the Assyrian state waxed and waned for nearly three centuries (c. 900-612 B.C.). At its height its geographic range was enormous, ranging from Iran in the east to central Egypt, central Anatolia and Cyprus in the west. It covered much of the Arabian desert in the south and ranged as far north as modern Armenia. In Ezekiel's time it had passed off the scene rather recently (about twenty years earlier), so it served as a perfect image of a long-standing superpower that had crumbled to nothing.

31:3-14. tree metaphor. The tree used for the metaphor here is the cedar, a well-known ancient Near Eastern symbol of majesty. It was used for the construction of many important palaces and temples. Egyptian, Assyrian and Babylonian kings all recount how they cut down the cedars of Lebanon in order to construct their mighty edifices. The myth of a cosmic tree is also found in Mesopotamian contexts. Its roots are fed by the great subterranean ocean, and its top merges with the clouds, so that it binds together the heavens, the earth and the netherworld. The Sumerian account of the Epic of Gilgamesh has a motif of a great tree offering shelter to animals. The Sumerian goddess Inanna discovered the sacred cosmic tree on the banks of the Euphrates and transplanted it into her sacred garden at Uruk (biblical Erech), where it attracted the mythical Anzu (a bird deity), a snake and Lilith (an evil demon). In the *Myth of Erra and Ishum,* Marduk speaks of the *meshu* tree whose roots reach down through the oceans to the netherworld and whose top is above the heavens. In Assyrian contexts the motif of a sacred tree is also well known. Some have called it a tree of life, and some also associate it with this world tree. It is often flanked by animals or by human or divine figures. A winged disk is typically centrally located over the top of the tree. The king is represented as the human personification of this tree. The tree is thought to represent the divine world order, but textual discussion of it is lacking. As is often the case in Ezekiel, this mythical motif is transformed to a political image.

31:8-9. garden of God. The garden of God in Ezekiel is identified as Eden. Here, however, it is not invoking the image of a utopian home from which humans have been driven. Unlike the paradise motif in the Bible, the Mesopotamian garden of the gods was the beautiful protected property of the gods that humans trespassed at their peril. Such was the cedar forest to which Gilgamesh and his companion Enkidu gained access when they defeated the divinely appointed guardian of the forest, Huwawa. These gardens, like the royal gardens of this period, were wooded parks featuring beautiful and exotic trees. This description is also appropriate for the biblical Eden.

31:12. Assyria's fall. The Assyrian empire was at its height in the early seventh century B.C., as it was successful in conquering Egypt. However, a great civil war in 652-648 B.C. showed the inherent weakness of the huge state. After the devastation of the civil war Assyria quickly weakened. By the end of Ashurbanipal's reign (either 631 or 627 B.C.) all economic and other textual sources disappear from Nineveh, the Assyrian capital. By 626 B.C. the Chaldeans of Babylonia had declared their independence. Within fourteen years all of the major Assyrian cities had been destroyed, the monarchy had fled to Harran in Syria, and the army was in chaos. The Assyrians may have participated in the Battle of Carchemish against Nebuchadnezzar, but they were never heard from again. Thus in the forty or so years after the great civil war, Assyria had been consigned to oblivion.

31:16. comparison of Eden to Lebanon. This comparison draws together the biblical motif of Eden as the protected property of Yahweh and the Mesopotamian motif of the cedar forest as the protected property of the gods. See comment on 31:8-9.

31:18. uncircumcised. There is evidence that Egypt's priests and kings endured some form of circumcision. In general, the Israelites disdained the uncircumcised, and possibly the Egyptian royalty felt the same way. Contempt of the uncircumcised appears in both the Egyptian and Israelite practice of cutting off the uncircumcised penises of enemies.

32:1. chronology. The date is March 3, 585 B.C., a few months after the report of the fall of Jerusalem had reached Ezekiel.

32:2. monster in the seas. The monster in this case is not located in the Nile River but "in the seas." This reference is probably to the cosmic

monsters destroyed by God (see Is 51:9-10; Ps 74:13). In the Bible as well as in the ancient Near East, the sea represents chaos and disorder, as do the sea monsters that live there. The obvious physical struggle between the sea and the land as well as the fierce, seemingly unstoppable energy displayed by the savage sea gave rise to cosmic myths in the ancient Near East. The *Enuma Elish* creation epic from Babylon describes how Marduk vanquished Tiamat while this goddess of watery chaos was in the form of a dragon. Much of the cycle of stories about Baal in Ugaritic legend involves Baal's struggle against his rival Yamm, the god of the sea. Similarly, the Ugaritic epic has both Anat and Baal claim to have conquered Litan, the seven-headed dragon, and thus gained mastery over the seas. In Psalm 104:26, Yahweh is said to play with Leviathan, and in Job 41:1-11, God challenges Job to show his control over Leviathan as God does. The kingdoms represented by these beasts are therefore associated with the forces of chaos that bring disorder to God's world and need to be overcome (see comments on Dan 7).

32:2. lion/monster. The parallel between lion and monster (dragon) seems strange to us but was not at all unusual in Ezekiel's world. The famous Ishtar Gate in Babylon and the procession way leading up to it used glazed bricks to create alternating images of lions and dragons. Additionally, in the mythological traditions of Mesopotamia a composite creature that combined lion and dragon features was common. This is especially true of Labbu in the Labbu Myth. From as early as the beginning of the second millennium, kings used lion and dragon in parallel to describe themselves.

32:2. churning, muddying waters. This description indicates a typical mythical scene in which the churning of the cosmic ocean disturbs the creatures (often sea monsters) who represent the forces of chaos and disorder. In *Enuma Elish* the sky god, Anu, creates the four winds that stir up the deep and its goddess, Tiamat. Here it is the monster who churns up the sea with the threat that chaos will bring disorder to the world.

32:3. capture with net. In both the Erra Epic and *Enuma Elish* the creature representing the forces of chaos (Anzu and Tiamat respectively) is captured in a net.

32:4. huge carcass devoured by birds and beasts. In the Labbu Myth, Labbu is described as a monster fifty miles long and a mile wide.

32:6. drenched with blood. In the Labbu Myth the blood of the slain monster is said to flow for three years and three months.

32:7-8. cosmic effects. These cosmic effects reflect the world-upside-down motif that is well known in the ancient world (see comment on Jer 4:23-26). It additionally strikes at the heart of the Egyptian religion, which featured the sun god most prominently.

32:11. sword of the king of Babylon. See comment on 29:19.

32:14. streams flowing like oil. The muddy waters have settled at the bottom of the river and have given way to clear, smoothly flowing rivers that run like oil. Similar phraseology ("heavens raining down oil") is found in the Ugaritic Baal texts, but there, as elsewhere in the Bible, it is an image of prosperity. In the contrast presented here, flowing like oil means that it is undisturbed, and it is undisturbed because the land is desolate.

32:17. chronology. The date is March 17, 585 B.C., two weeks later than the date mentioned in 32:1.

32:21-22. Assyria with her dead in Sheol. The nations listed in 22-30 all suffered significant devastation. Ezekiel probably has in mind the final defeat and destruction of the Assyrian empire at the end of the sixth century B.C. Her armies were probably finally destroyed at the battle of Carchemish, where Egypt (and probably Assyria) was decisively defeated by Nebuchadnezzar of Babylon. Thus, the imagery sees that the final end of Assyria is in Sheol, the abode of the dead.

32:24. Elam. Elam was an important state in southwestern Iran (modern Khuzistan). Its main city was Susa, which had a very ancient history and is mentioned in Sumerian and proto-Elamite records from the outset of the third millennium B.C. Elam was devastated by the Assyrians in the late seventh century B.C. It was invaded by Nebuchadnezzar in 596 and was taken over by the Medo-Persians later in the sixth century B.C.

32:26 Meschech and Tubal. At the end of the eighth century, these two Anatolian kingdoms were ravaged by internal warfare, conquered by Sargon II of Assyria and invaded by the Cimmerians from southern Russia. Unfortunately, little of their history survives from the seventh and early sixth centuries. It is thought that they were incorporated under Lydian control after the conclusion of the Cimmerian wars. In the spring of 585 the Lydians are at war with the Medes (see chronology in v. 1 above and comment on 38:1). They are mentioned again in the Persian period as separate ethnic identities. They are known to the Assyrians as Mushku (central Anatolia) and Tabal (eastern Anatolia), and to Herodotus as the Moschi and Tibarenoi (subject states of the

Persian empire). At the end of the eighth century the king of Mushku was Mita, known to the Greeks as Midas, the king with the golden touch. His tomb has been identified at Gordion and excavated.

32:29. Edom. Edom was a Semitic-speaking neighbor of Judah, south and east of the Dead Sea. In the eighth century B.C. Edom fell under the control of the Assyrians, as noted in the annals of Tiglath-Pileser III (r. 745-727 B.C.), and continued under their rule until the death of Ashurbanipal a century later. During that time the Edomites were often conscripted into the Assyrian armies and thus figure often in the annals. During the Babylonian period Edom evidently sided with the great empire, although there are no extrabiblical records to verifying this. It is likely that they submitted themselves to Nebuchadnezzar's rule in 605 B.C. Although some Judean refugees may have found shelter in Edom, it apparently remained passive as Jerusalem was destroyed (see Ps 137:7 and Obad 11). The Babylonian campaign against Ammon and Moab in 594 seems not to have affected Edom. It is likely that they remained unscathed until the time of Nabonidus's campaign in 552 B.C.

32:30. princes of the north. The princes of the north are most likely Aramean rulers or sheiks. There were a number of hostile Aramean kingdoms north of Israel/Judah, the largest centered in Damascus.

32:30. Sidonians. See the comment on 28:21.

33:1-20

Ezekiel's Role as a Watchman

33:2-6. role of watchman. The watchman stood at the place in the city where he would have the most strategic view of the surroundings and watched for any approaching enemy army. He reported either by word of mouth or by trumpet. His task was simply to sound the alarm of the approaching enemy. He was absolved of responsibility if the city dwellers refused to heed his call. The watchman is found throughout the ancient Near East. The spiritual sense used here is not found in the ancient Near East but is picked up (probably from Ezekiel) in the Dead Sea Scrolls sectarian documents, where the leader of the community is on the lookout for the judgment of God.

33:3. trumpet signal. The trumpet here is the ram's horn, which had a limited musical range. The term (Hebrew, *shopar*) is likely be related to Akkadian *shappar*, which is in turn a loan word from Sumerian denoting a wild goat or ibex. It was significant not only for its use in war (to proclaim victory, announce the disbanding of the army and call troops to arms) but also for the cultic rites of Israel (see Ps 81:4 and Lev 25:9). In fact, it is the most frequently named musical instrument in the Old Testament. For more information see comment on Joshua 6:4-5.

33:7. prophet as watchman. Ezekiel's portrayal of himself as prophetic watchman is similar to the charge given to Isaiah (21:6-9) and Jeremiah (6:17). Though no similar label has been found attached to prophets in the ancient Near East, the concept is familiar enough. The prophets were expected to warn the king of impending situations (in military or cultic realms) that might jeopardize his person or the stability of his kingdom.

33:15. pledge for loan. Pledges for loans were customary throughout the ancient Near East. Thousands of loan contracts uncovered from Mesopotamia show that it was quite an ordinary procedure. For example, at Terqa in Middle Bronze Age Syria, a certain Puzurum made a loan at the local temple of the sun god Shamash. He retained one-half of a cuneiform contract, while the temple (functioning in this case as a bank) retained the other. Thus the two halves functioned as a receipt. When Puzurum paid off the loan, the temple returned to him the remaining portion of the contract. The return of a pledge by a repentant wicked person suggests that an oppressive debt situation was resolved with the debt being forgiven.

33:21-33
Jerusalem's Fate

33:21. chronology. The date is January 19, 585 B.C. It is about five months after the fall of Jerusalem. Most commentaries agree that this is not a fugitive or even a refugee, but one of the survivors who has been brought captive to Babylon with the first wave of exiles from the destruction.

33:25. eating meat with blood. The phrase literally is "eating over blood." Leviticus 19:26 associates this with banned forms of divination. Medieval rabbinical texts identified this with a practice of the Sabians, a north Arabian sect that had a communal meal in which humans ate meat whose blood was poured on the ground to attract spirit beings. Similar practices were done throughout the entire Near East. The land of Israel was understood theologically as the camp that surrounded the temple. The violations listed are the sort that would result in the person being sent outside the camp.

33:27. wild animals as punishment. Wild beasts were a constant source of fear for city dwellers throughout the ancient Near East. In Assyrian texts and reliefs of this period the kings are seen hunting lions to symbolically rid the city of the scourge of wild beasts. It has been suggested that the killing of eighteen lions represents the eighteen gates of Nineveh and the roads leading out of them. See comment on 5:17.

33:32. love songs for entertainment. Love (or erotic) songs had long been sources of entertainment for city dwellers. The itinerant singer of songs traveled from town to town, entertaining the people. Many of these songs were written down in the cuneiform record. For example, portions of the Epic of Gilgamesh may well have been sung to the city dwellers in Sumer in much the same way that Homer's *Iliad* and *Odyssey* were sung by traveling poets before being written down centuries later. Love songs are connected to Ritual Marriage texts (the Tammuz liturgy) in Sumerian times and were popular in Egypt during the second half of the second millennium (Eighteenth and Nineteenth Dynasties). It is a severe indictment that the people have reduced the role of the messenger of God to mere entertainment.

34:1-31
Oracle to the Shepherds

34:3. perquisites of leaders. The three staple byproducts of sheep and goats (goats' milk/curds, sheep's wool, meat) are used here to extend the metaphor of the leaders gleaning all the benefits but not fulfilling their responsibilities. Royal and priestly administrations were of necessity supported by the population through taxations of various sorts, but it was expected that the population would in turn benefit rather than be exploited.

34:3-4. shepherd tasks. As the previous metaphor concerned the privileges of the shepherd, attention now turns to the neglected responsibilities. The metaphor goes beyond the normal responsibilities of making sure that the sheep were protected and fed. Instead it focuses on the remedial duties, caring for the sick and finding the lost. These would equate to the need for kings to bring about justice for alienated and disenfranchised people (such as the widow and orphan).

34:7-16. shepherd/king metaphor in ancient Near East. The ideology of the king as a shepherd to his people is found with Lugalzagessi of Sumer as early as around 2450 B.C. The contemporary king Urukagina of Lagash claimed that the god Ningirsu owned his state and that the king had been chosen as a shepherd to administer the city on behalf of the gods and the people. Gods responsible for maintaining justice (Shamash in Mesopotamia, Amun in Egypt) are likewise represented in this way. This ideology continued in the ancient Near East into the monarchy period, occurring in reference to Ashurbanipal of Assyria (seventh century) and Nebuchadnezzar (sixth century).

35:1-15
Oracle Concerning Edom

35:2. Mount Seir. Mount Seir was the ancient name of the mountainous region south of the Dead Sea on both sides of the Rift Valley running south to the Gulf of Aqaba. The name Seir is found in the Amarna texts from Egypt in the fourteenth century B.C. According to Scripture the mountains of Seir were occupied first by the Horites (Deut 2:12, 22), who were later displaced by the Edomites. Seir became synonymous with the entire country of Edom. **35:5. Edom's role in fall of Jerusalem.** This verse addresses the long-standing dissension between Edom and Israel. We are told elsewhere in Scripture that the Edomites cheered when Nebuchadnezzar II destroyed Jerusalem (e.g., Ps 137; Joel 3:19; Obad 1-14). This is the only text that implies that they played an active role in the conquest.

36:1-38
Oracle of Restoration

36:5. Edom's conduct. See comment on 35:5.
36:25. sprinkled with clean water. While sprinkling with water for purification was a part of the ritual ablutions used by the priests, the term "clean water" is not used anywhere else in the Old Testament.
36:26. metaphors. The heart was considered the seat of the mind and its will, or inclinations. For more information concerning a heart of stone or a heavy heart see comments on 11:19; Isaiah 6:9-10; and Exodus 8:11.

37:1-28
Valley of Dry Bones

37:1. transported in visions. See comment on 8:3.
37:2. valley full of bones. The large amount of bones described here implies that this was the scene of a major catastrophe. The depiction of a large number of corpses that had been denied a proper burial is reminiscent of many battle scenes and descriptions of battle scenes

found in the earliest periods of Mesopotamian and Egyptian history. Furthermore, the Assyrian annals describe the destruction of their enemies in similar terms. A typical ancient Near Eastern curse has the corpse of the cursed victim exposed to the elements.
37:12-13. resurrection in ancient Near East. The concept of resurrection was known in some parts of the ancient Near East. The Egyptians believed that some of the deceased rose as stars and took their place in the heavens. However, in general the only awakening that was part of the ancient worldview was the calling up of spirits of the dead (which is not permanent and not a bodily presence) or the awakening of the fertility gods of nature cycles. These died annually when the agricultural cycle came to an end and "wintered" in the netherworld. Then they were ritually awakened in the spring. None of this bears any resemblance to a theological doctrine of resurrection. Occasional revivifications or indications of national return to life as found in this passage are not representative of a doctrine of resurrection. See comment on Isaiah 26:19. Some have suggested that there is a greater likelihood that Ezekiel is transported east this time. Zoroastrian practice was to leave bodies unburied with the hope that they would someday be reassembled and revived. A drawback to this is that the spread of Persian culture and ideas dates to some decades after Ezekiel, and Zoroastrianism does not take hold in the Persian empire until the end of the sixth century.
38:15-16. writing on wood. It is likely, since this wood is being written on, that Ezekiel is using two wooden tablets. It was a common practice to use wooden boards coated with a beeswax concoction for the writing of messages that were formal but did not need to be archived and preserved.

38:1—39:29
Gog and Magog

38:2. Gog. The identification of Gog has perplexed commentators for centuries. The most likely explanation is that the name is a derivative of Gyges, who was a Lydian king mentioned in Assyrian and Greek sources. In the former he is called Gugu and he rules over *mat Gugu*, which is Akkadian for the "land of Gugu." His reign, however, is fifty or more years prior to the time of Ezekiel, so some have argued that the name became a dynastic title used by his royal descendants. The king of Lydia at the time of Ezekiel is Alyattes. There is no evidence that Lydia ever threatened Judah, but the Lydians were involved in a serious war against Cyaxares and the Medes in 585. Gog looks similar to the names Agag and Og, two famous enemies of Israel.

38:2. Magog. Magog is likely a Hebrew form of Akkadian Mat Gugu, "the land of Gog," which Josephus identified as Lydia in western Anatolia.

38:2. Meschech and Tubal. At the end of the eighth century, these two Anatolian kingdoms were ravaged by internal warfare, conquered by Sargon II of Assyria and invaded by the Cimmerians from southern Russia. Unfortunately, little of their history survives from the seventh and early sixth centuries. It is thought that they were incorporated under Lydian control after the conclusion of the Cimmerian wars. In the spring of 585 the Lydians were at war with the Medes. They are mentioned again in the Persian period as separate ethnic identities. They are known to the Assyrians as Mushku (central Anatolia) and Tabal (eastern Anatolia), and to Herodotus as the Moschi and Tibarenoi (subject states of the Persian empire). At the end of the eighth century the king of Mushku was Mita, known to the Greeks as Midas, the king with the golden touch. His tomb has been identified at Gordion and excavated.

38:4. hooks in your jaws. The Assyrians typically put hooks in the jaws of defeated enemies, either for the purposes of humiliation or to deport them to other lands. This practice is often described in their annals and graphically depicted in their wall reliefs. Esarhaddon is depicted on a stele from Zinjirli in Syria as leading Baal of Tyre and Tirhakah of Egypt by a rope tied to a ring through their lips. Ashurbanipal claims to have pierced the cheeks of Uate' (king of Ishmael) with a sharp-edged tool and put a ring in his jaw.

38:4. large and small shields. These were body shields and hand shields respectively. See comment on 23:24.

38:5. Persia, Cush and Put. See comment on 27:10.

38:6. Gomer. Gomer has been equated with the Gimirrai of the Assyrian annals and the Cimmerians of Greek sources. In Homer's *Odyssey* they lived on the north shore of the Black Sea. They attacked the kingdom of Urartu from the north and caused problems for the Assyrians in the eighth century. Sargon died in battle against them in Tubal. They appear to have been driven through the Caucasus mountains into Anatolia according to Herodotus. They came to be involved with the Anatolian kingdom of Lydia in the seventh century B.C. They overran the Phrygians and sacked the capital at Gordion, the royal seat of

the famous King Midas, in 676. In 644 they overthrew Sardis, the capital of the Lydian state. This was when Gyges met his death. During Ezekiel's time the Cimmerians had been driven out of Lydia by Alyattes. They later came under the control of the Medes.

38:6. Beth Togarmah. Beth Togarmah was most likely the capital city of Kammanu, a central Anatolian kingdom. It was known in Hittite sources as Tegaramara and in Assyrian sources as Til-Garimmu.

38:11. unwalled villages. The unwalled villages (mentioned here and in Zech 2:8 and Esther 9:19) have normally been defined as rural settlements without walls, bars or gates, in contrast to fortified cities. They were defenseless and vulnerable.

38:13. Sheba and Dedan. The kingdom of Sheba was a great trading center in southwestern Arabia that exported precious stones, gold and incense. This kingdom is known as Saba in native sources and in the Assyrian annals. It had a very advanced urban civilization in the first millennium B.C. For more information see 2 Chronicles 9:1. Dedan was a central Arabian oasis where Tyre received its special riding gear. It is identified with the modern site of al-Ula, which is situated on the frankincense road from Yemen to Palestine.

38:13. merchants of Tarshish. In this context the merchants of Tarshish appear to represent merchant peoples who did their trade on the overland routes across the Arabian Desert to Sheba and Dedan, and on to the Mediterranean Sea.

38:14. Gog. See comment on 38:2

38:19. earthquakes in Israel. This appears to be a cosmic earthquake, similar to ones described in Exodus 19; Judges 5:4-5; Isaiah 30:27-28; Habakkuk 3:3-7; and Psalms 68:8-9 and 114 (see comment on 1 Sam 14:15). This type of imagery is also found in the annals of Esarhaddon of Assyria. The Levant was prone to earthquakes, but Israel is on the edge of the zone that has its center in Anatolia. The well-known historical quakes occurred in 760 and 31 B.C. In the Christian era the region has averaged about one major quake per century.

38:22. hailstones and burning sulfur. The occurrence of hailstones as divine judgment in conquest accounts is not unique. In a letter to his god (Ashur), Sargon of Assyria reports that in his campaign against Urartu (714 B.C.) the god Adad stormed against his enemies with "stones from heaven" and so annihilated them. This battle included a coalition that fled through the passes and valleys pursued by Sargon, with the enemy king hiding at last in the clefts of his mountain. Burning sulfur ("brimstone") is a yellow crystalline substance that ignites in air, often found in volcanic regions. It has no connection with hailstones except they were both calamities that would befall the area.

39:1. Gog. See comment on 38:1.

39:4. food to the birds and wild animals. To be left unburied, vulnerable to the elements and beasts, was the worst curse imaginable. Furthermore, as there was no clear distinction between body and soul in the Hebrew mentality, death was not regarded as the separation of those two elements. Thus one who had no burial was still believed to be conscious (in some form) of his fate. In the ancient Near East those who were left unburied were thought restless until a proper burial had been performed.

39:6. Magog. See comment on 38:2.

39:9. weapons used for fuel. Passages that speak of the destruction of weapons of war usually focus on using them for practical and beneficial purposes. The wooden parts could be burned in place of firewood as here (this sometimes extended even to the clothing, as in Is 9:5), and the metal parts could be recycled into agricultural use (Is 2:4 and Mic 4:3).

39:11. burial place. The burial place (*'oberim*) has defied an absolute identification. Scholars have identified it as the "Valley of Travelers" or, based upon an Ugaritic parallel, "those who have passed on." The latter makes more sense. Gog has desired to be identified with the great kings of old, and now he is, since they are all dead. Ugaritic texts refer to a group called the Rephaim, who are beings of the netherworld (see comment on Is 14:9-11).

40:1—48:35
Restored Temple and Land

40:1. tenth day of the first month. The time of the year is described as the "head of the year," similar to an Akkadian equivalent. The present vision is thus dated to 10 Nisan in the twenty-fifth year of the exile or April 28, 573 B.C. In the Israelite calendar this was the beginning of Passover activities. The lamb was to be chosen on this day and slaughtered on the fourteenth.

40:3. linen cord and measuring rod. The linen cord may be similar to the measuring line that was used in Zechariah 2:5 to measure the city. It appears that it was used for extremely long distances. The measuring rod was for short distances. Some have argued that the stele of Ur-Nammu of the Sumerian city of Ur shows a similar representation.

40:5. long cubit, length of rod. The normal cubit (six handbreadths) has been estimated at 17.6 inches and the long cubit here at about 20.5 inches. The rod mentioned by Ezekiel was about six cubits or ten feet long.

40:6. significance of east gate. The east gate was the gate through which Yahweh's glory would make its entry (Ezek 43:1-5). God's glory had left the temple through the same gate (10:19). Since temples tended to be oriented toward the east, this would be the most important gate.

40:7-16. gate architecture. The size and design of the gateway show its great importance in the temple complex. The jambs were decorated with palm fronds, presumably similar to those in the Solomonic temple (1 Kings 6:29-36). These types of fortified installations were built for military and not religious purposes. Later in Ezekiel we are told that the gates were to be manned by the Levites, who guarded the sacred places in the temple. The overall design of the gatehouse is typical of a number of preexilic Palestinian city gates from Megiddo, Hazor and Gezer. While these gates are typical of city gates, they are much more extensive than would be usually found with temples.

40:7-16. measurements compared to archaeologically known gates. This structure is clearly a guardhouse and measures fifty by twenty-five cubits (eighty-six by forty-three feet). It compares to the guardrooms of Solomon's temple (1 Kings 14:28), although their size is not mentioned. Of nearly twenty Iron Age gate systems excavated in Israel, this would be larger than most. The gates at Dan, Megiddo and Lachish were between eighty and one hundred feet wide (compared to the forty-three feet of this gate). But they are larger than most, and the average runs closer to the width of the gate described here. The depth of this gate, however (eighty-six feet), is on the large size. One of the deepest excavated gates is at Lachish, which is nearly eighty-two feet. The descriptions and measurements of the chambers are comparable to Iron Age gates.

40:17-19. outer court description and size. With the addition of information from Ezekiel 42:6 the outer court had a group of rooms that may have been used by worshipers as eating and meeting places during the periods of religious events. The rooms were pillared porticos. The number of rooms and their size is not given. The area did contain a raised pavement of about one hundred cubits. The term for pavement is a rare word. In Esther 1:6 the term represents a mosaic floor inlaid with precious stones.

40:20-27. north and south gate dimensions and description compared to east gate. The north and south gates have the same features as the east gate: recesses, jambs, niches, a vestibule and palm decorations. The measurements of the three gates are also identical.

40:26. palm tree decorations. The palm tree decorations were not only artistically beautiful but were reminiscent of the Solomonic temple (1 Kings 6:29-36). These types of decorations were common in Iron Age Palestine, particularly in connection with temple facades.

40:28-37. inner court gates (and absence of west gates). The inner court gates were mirror images of the outer gates. The inner courtyard backs up to the wall on the western side, with a structure between the wall and the back of the temple. That is why there were no western gates.

40:39. offerings. For discussion of the various types of offerings, see the comments in the early chapters of Leviticus.

40:43. function of double pronged hooks. The double-pronged hooks on the walls have traditionally been interpreted as being used to hang utensils. A more recent interpretation argues that they were niches or ledges for the storage of the utensils, much like what is described in the Temple Scroll (30:13).

40:47. inner court size. The inner court was a perfect square, one hundred cubits, or about 170 feet, on each side. This is about two-thirds of an acre.

41:1. outer sanctuary description and size. The outer sanctuary shows vague Babylonian influences and specific parallels to the older city gates of Megiddo, Hazor and Gezer, structures which may have been built by Solomon (1 Kings 9:15). For example, the north gate at Megiddo had in the passageway of the gate the identical three gate recesses described in Ezekiel. Here in 41:1 is described the great hall, the room between the vestibule and the Holy of Holies. Numerous Mesopotamian temples were constructed with this model (see comments on Ex 26 and 1 Kings 7).

41:5-11. architectural design. Ezekiel describes here the auxiliary structures of the temple. There are a number of technical architectural expressions discussed in this section, many of which have uncertain meanings. Much of the description, however, is reminiscent of that found in 1 Kings 6:5-8 concerning the Solomonic temple. Although Ezekiel sketches the auxiliary structures around the temple, he does not describe their function, nor does the author of 1 Kings. Similar single and multistoried rooms from Egyptian reli-

gious centers imply that they were used as storehouses for temple treasures. For example, temples built by Merenptah and Rameses II (thirteenth century B.C.) had storage spaces three to four times larger than the temple itself. This was also common in Mesopotamia.

41:13-14. dimensions compared to Solomon's temple. Both the Solomonic temple and the temple of Ezekiel consisted of three rooms. The dimensions of the holy room and the great hall in both temples are identical.

41:15. identification of second building and galleries. The identification and function of the second building mentioned here is primarily determined by understanding the obscure term used for "galleries" or "ledges." These galleries appeared on the outside of the structure. They either came in threes or were three levels. They could be seen from both the inner and outer courts. Some have concluded that these functioned as galleries or walkways (or both).

41:16. narrow windows. The narrow windows were probably set high in the walls above the level of the annex rooms, similar to Solomon's temple (1 Kings 6:29-35). They correspond to the triple rabbeted design in the "Lady at the Window" carving found at the Assyrian site of Nimrud, dating to the early first millennium B.C.

41:17-20. palm and cherub imagery. The palm and cherub imagery is clearly reminiscent of the Solomonic temple (1 Kings 29-36). However, these cherubim have only a human and a lion head, unlike the four for the Solomonic temple. These were no longer free-standing structures but were carved into the walls, which is most likely why there were fewer heads. The figures were flanked by the palm imagery, a common motif on ivories and other art forms. The same imagery is seen on ivory carvings from Arslan Tash in first millennium B.C. Syria and on a scene painted on storage jars from Iron Age Kuntillet 'Arjud in Palestine.

42:13-14. provision of priest's rooms in temple. Though little is known of priest's rooms in the Solomonic temple, they were well known in Babylonia. The *bit pirishti* was a room in the Babylonian temple complex in which the priestly vestments and the costly garments of the statues of deities were stored.

42:14. holy garments. The Babylonian *bit pirishti* was associated with the wardrobe of the priests, at least during the Seleucid era (after 330 B.C.). These vestments were highly valued because of the gold and silver objects used to decorate the garments. Goldsmiths received official permission to enter into these rooms in order to work on the vestments of the priests and the divine images.

43:3. Kebar River. See comment on 1:1.

43:7. lifeless idols of kings. These "lifeless idols" are probably not corpses but refer to a pagan cult of the dead, similar to that of Leviticus 26:30. Ezekiel probably had in mind a veneration of the spirits of Israel's royal ancestors, much like a cult of the royal dead at Ugarit. Whether the kings were considered deified at either place is not clear.

43:8. thresholds and doorposts. The statement here in verse 8 corresponds with the description of the Solomonic temple in 1 Kings 6—7. The original temple was built as one element of the entire Solomonic palace complex. Only a wall separated the temple and palace, and they bordered "threshold to threshold, and doorpost to doorpost."

43:13. long cubit. See comment on 40:5.

43:13-17. altar architecture. Although the technical vocabulary for the altar is similar to that found in Akkadian, the altar of Ezekiel is most similar to the Solomonic Temple (2 Chron 4:1; 1 Kings 2:28). The length of the sides is similar in both cases, while horns were a common motif in altars in the Levant. Though the altar is large, it is not as large as Solomon's and is comparable to those uncovered by archaeologists.

43:19. family of Zadok. Zadok was the representative of Aaron's line who served as high priest during the reigns of David and Solomon. In the postexilic community the sons of Zadok had the altar duties reserved for them, while the Levites had less significant duties than before. The Zadokites held the high priesthood until the time of the Greek ruler Antiochus IV (175-163 B.C.). In fact, some have supposed that the Dead Sea community may have been formed in response to the end of the Zadokite priesthood.

43:24. salt. The reference here is to a "covenant of salt" (see comments on Lev 2:13 and Num 18:19). The preservative qualities of salt made it a symbol of the permanence of the covenant relationship. Thus, the addition of salt was a reminder of God's covenant.

43:25-26. seven-day dedication. In the ancient Near East generally and in Israel particularly, seven-day installation and dedication services were the norm.

44:1-2. east gate permanently shut. The Sacred Gate of the city of Babylon was the gate through which the procession of Marduk (the primary god of the city) and other deities passed and returned again. Like the east gate described by Ezekiel, the Sacred Gate was apparently opened for the deity to pass through

and was shut at all other times.

44:3. prince. The prince in this context is a religious figure who is responsible for eating his sacrificial meals before the Lord in the sacred gate. Earlier in Ezekiel the term was used for a Davidic figure (e.g., 34:24; 37:25). Here he has no royal or political role to play, only a role inside the temple precincts. He has no access through the east gate that is reserved for divine use; he only has an act to perform there. It is clear that he is not serving a priestly function, for he is not allowed to actually step inside the inner court.

44:3. portico of the gateway. The prince was able to enter the gate structure through the portico (or vestibule) of the gateway, meaning that he had already come into the courtyard through another gate and entered the eastern gateway from the inside. He stood by the post of the gate, which enabled him to see the cultic activity of the priests.

44:8. others in charge. Foreigners had been recruited for temple service probably as temple guards perhaps since the time of Manasseh and Amon. Furthermore, Neo-Babylonian and Phoenician records appear to affirm the probability of the installation of foreigners in this type of temple service.

44:14. duties of the temple. The duty of guarding the gates of the house implies more than just the temple but the entire temple complex. The Levites were also responsible for caring for the temple and grounds, and supervised activities on the temple grounds. For more information on the importance of this task see the comment on 1 Chronicles 9:22-27.

44:17. linen, not wool. One possible reason for the prohibition of wool may be a practical one. Wool was more likely to cause one to sweat. Since many bodily excretions caused defilement, steps needed to be taken to prevent their occurrence in the temple complex. This appears also to be the case in Egypt, where, according to Herodotus and the Roman writer Lucian, linen was used in the material for priestly garments. Herodotus adds that the Egyptian priests were constantly washing their linen garments.

44:19. sacred rooms. See comment on 42:14.

44:20. hair regulations. Shaving the head bald or letting the hair grow very long was most likely forbidden because of the pagan customs associating it with Canaanite cults of the dead. The taboo has its inspiration in Leviticus 21:5 (see comment there).

44:21. wine prohibition. This prohibition has its parallel in Leviticus 10:9. Though ritualized intoxication was well known, for example, from the Babylonian creation epic, *Enuma*

Elish, it is most likely that the prohibition was to make sure that the priest had control of his faculties (see comment on Is 28:7).

44:22. marriage regulations. The explicit prohibition concerning the priest and marriage comes from Leviticus 21:7, 10-14 (see comments there). There, it appears that the concern was for maintaining the purity of the priestly line, although Ezekiel does not mention the reason for the prohibition.

44:29-30. priest's portions. Although these verses provide the physical sustenance for the priests, there is more. The priests were actually invited to eat Yahweh's food. For more information see comments on Numbers 18:12-19. They were also authorized to eat the *herem* or "every irredeemable devoted thing." These items were evidently those designated for any use, except that which was prescribed for the cult.

45:1. concept of sacred district. The sacred district was land reserved for use by the God of the temple area. Ezekiel portrays the land as a gift that was returned to the divine benefactor. As early as the early fourth millennium B.C., the city of Uruk in southern Mesopotamia had sacred districts in the center of its town. In ancient Mesopotamia either the sacred districts were separated by retaining walls for the structure, or a large citadel wall surrounded the entire sacred precinct. Access to sacred precincts was limited, and strict standards were maintained regarding who could enter and on what occasions. This is a continuation of the sacred compass idea that was established in Israel when the tabernacle was set up in the wilderness period (see comments on Lev 10:10 and Num 18:1-7).

45:2-6. dimensions of sacred district. The larger consecrated area was about eight miles long and six and a half miles wide, an area of over 50 square miles. This could be compared to the approximately 620 square miles of the entire district of Yehud under Persian rule. One half of this area was reserved for the priests and sanctuary, which was in the center of this area. One other area, eight miles by more than three miles, was reserved for the city, which was most likely Jerusalem, although the name is not given. If this design were superimposed on the land of Israel, it would encompass a large central segment of the tribal allotment of Judah. The territorial scheme shows the relative importance of the officials of the state, depending upon their placement near the center where there was the closest access to God.

45:7. prince. See comment on 44:3.

45:10. accurate scales. In an economy that did not have standardized weights and measures, traders were often tempted to cheat by falsifying the balances and measurements, often by using improper weights and false bottoms and other ways to alter the sizes of vessels.

45:10-12. measures. The two-armed balance scales were used to weigh out goods in Israel. The ephah was a dry standard used in measuring grain and equaled about half a bushel. The bath was a liquid measure of about six gallons. It was used for the measure of oil, wine and water. Both an ephah and a bath are one-tenth of a homer.

45:17. prince's contributions. Here the prince is seen in a royal role. Typically in the ancient Near East the king was the one who provided the sacrifices for the festival rituals. This can be observed in biblical texts as well as in the nations surrounding Israel. At the large public festivals the general population often played the role of audience, while the leaders of the people (court and temple) took center stage. The pageantry could be grandiose, and the largesse of the king was made evident.

45:18-20. inaugural festival. The ritual described here has all the earmarks of a purification ceremony to dedicate the new sanctuary. These were typically seven-day affairs that ensured that the holy place and holy objects were ready for use. It marked the beginning of the operation of the sanctuary.

45:21-25. new Passover. In Ezekiel's formulation, Passover takes on a different look than the traditional observance established in Exodus 11—12. Originally it had been established as a family-oriented festival in which the head of the household served a priestly role and the home was the location of the festivities. The related Feast of Unleavened Bread had gradually merged with Passover, as is indicated here as well. In the Passover celebrations carried out by Hezekiah (2 Chron 30) and Josiah (2 Chron 35), there was a more national and centralized aspect to the observance, but that is even more the case here in Ezekiel.

46:1. New Moon significance. Keyed to their use of a lunar calendar, ancient Israel marked the first day of the month, with its "new moon" phase, as a festival day (every twenty-nine or thirty days). As on the Sabbath, all work was to cease (see Amos 8:5), and there were sacrifices to be made (Num 28:11-15). In the monarchy period the king became a prominent figure in these celebrations. The festival continued to be observed in the postexilic period (Ezra 3:5; Neh 10:33). New Moon festivals were also prominent in Mesopotamia from late in the third millennium down to the Neo-Babylonian period in the middle of the first millennium B.C. The cult of the moon was widespread throughout the ancient Near East, and the moon deities figured prominently in mythological texts. Although the Israelites were forbidden to worship any heavenly bodies (including the lunar cult: e.g., Deut 23:5, and Jer 8:2), they were allowed to celebrate the first of the month with trumpets and burnt offerings.

46:2. prince's entrance. See comment on 44:3.

46:3. worship on the sabbath at the gateway. This is one of the few explicit references in the Old Testament to worship on the sabbath, which is usually only spoken of in terms of prohibited activities. Many of Israel's festivals featured "holy convocations," but such are never mandated for the Sabbath. Here it is also interesting to note that the temple is the focal point for this Sabbath worship. Temples served as gathering places when public sacred rituals were being performed (at events designated as holy convocations). One must be careful not to associate too closely our worship in church on Sunday with Israel's acts of worship at the temple on the Sabbath. The differences are both profuse and profound.

46:9. entrance and exit by opposite gates. This prohibition appears to simply regulate the congestion on occasions of great crowds in the temple and ensuring the orderly flow of people. The temple area is to represent the epitome of orderliness, including even the traffic pattern. Anything that is uncontrolled or reflects confusion has no place.

46:19-24. kitchens for offering preparation. A good number of temples in the ancient Near East were attached to kitchens. These have been found at Ur, Tell Asmar and Terqa in Mesopotamia, and at Karnak in Egypt. Many of the kitchen complexes were larger than the temple it serviced. Second Chronicles 35:11-13 implies the existence of kitchens associated with the Solomonic temple.

47:1. water flowing out of temple. The association between ancient Near Eastern temples and spring waters is well attested. In fact, some temples in Mesopotamia, Egypt and in the Ugaritic myth of Baal were considered to have been founded upon springs (likened to the primeval waters), which sometimes flowed from the building itself. Thus, the symbolic cosmic mountain (temple) stood upon the symbolic primeval waters (spring).

47:8. sea water becoming fresh. The seawater in the Dead Sea becoming fresh is a miraculous transformation. The Dead Sea is 1,296 feet below sea level, the lowest point on earth. The high mineral content of the Dead Sea is a result of the fact that it has no outlet. Waters flow in through a number of sources carrying their various minerals at a rate of seven million tons per day. Then the water evaporates, leaving the minerals behind. Total salinity is 26-35 percent (compared to 18 percent for the Great Salt Lake in Utah and 3.5 percent for the average ocean salinity).

47:15-17. north border. Although the north border is described in great detail, none of the place names can be identified with any certainty. Thus, it is not possible to draw any boundary lines for Israel's northern frontier. There are, however, some affinities with the list in Numbers 34:7-9, a border that coincided with the northern limits of the land of Canaan, which was the name of the Egyptian controlled area of Syro-Palestine. Ezekiel uses general terms here to describe a territory rather than a boundary line.

47:18. east border. Like Numbers 34:10-12 Ezekiel excludes in his description of the east border the Transjordanian regions that had been occupied by Gad, Reuben, and one-half of Manasseh. Thus, the main border was the Jordan River running south from the Sea of Galilee until the Dead Sea.

47:19. south border. The southern border begins at Tamar, the final point of the eastern boundary, to Mount Halak to Meribah Kadesh, or Kadesh Barnea (modern 'Ain el-Qudeirat), a fertile oasis on the southern border of the desert of Zin. From there, the border line follows the Wadi of Egypt (not the Nile), which drained the northern Sinai Desert and formed a natural boundary between Egypt and Palestine.

47:20. west border. The western border, as in Numbers 34:6, is the Mediterranean Sea.

48:1-7. tribal allotments compared to historical. Israel's tribal allotments here in Ezekiel follow the premonarchical order of excluding the Levites and cutting the tribe of Joseph in half (Ephraim and Manasseh) in order to keep the number of allotments of twelve. However, they show little concern for historical realities. As with Ezekiel 47 the territory east of the Jordan is overlooked. Further, the east-west boundaries run in contrast to the natural physical landscape, which is defined by north-south lines. The tribal allotments are identical to one another in size and also respect the traditional genealogical relationships among the tribes, discriminating between the descendants of Jacob's wives and handmaidens. Judah and Benjamin, however, retain their close proximity to the sanctuary.

48:9-14. size of allotment for priests and Levites. The portion of land for the Levites has become smaller, showing their decline in importance. Both the Zadokite and Levitical priests receive identical plots of about eight by three-plus miles.

48:15-20. size of allotment for the people. The city is given walled space of about one and a half miles square. It is flanked on either side by open rectangular spaces of about five square miles each.

48:21-22. prince's allotment. The prince's land lies on either side of the central square. The width of both is twenty-five thousand cubits (about eight miles), and the land is considered separate from the public and the Levites.

48:23-28. remaining tribal allotments compared to historical. See comment on 48:1-7.

48:31. gates named after tribes. In cities of the ancient world such as Babylon the gates were often named after the gods. It was not unusual, however, for gates to be named for where they led to. This was the more common practice in Israel.

DANIEL

1:1-21

Daniel and His Friends Arrive at Nebuchadnezzar's Court

1:1. Nebuchadnezzar. Nebuchadnezzar II (r. 605-562 B.C.) was the second ruler of the Chaldean kingdom centered at Babylon that ruled the ancient Near East for nearly a century. He was the son of Nabopolassar, a Chaldean who declared independence from Assyria in 626 B.C. In his forty-three-year reign, Nebuchadnezzar pacified Egypt (though he was unsuccessful in conquering it) and literally rebuilt Babylon. In fact, most of the city of Babylon that has been uncovered by modern excavators dates from Nebuchadnezzar's reign. Thus the Chaldean kingdom was primarily his creation, and it crumbled only a generation after his death. This great king was remembered in many cultural traditions, including sources from Greece (who knew him as a great builder), and Israel (not only the biblical material, but later rabbinic sources).

1:1-2. chronology. The third year of Jehoiakim was 606-605 B.C. (calculating on a Tishri calendar, see comment on Jer 32:1, and an accession year system, see comment on 2:1). At this point Nebuchadnezzar is still crown prince conducting campaigns for his father, Nabopolassar, who dies in mid-August this same year. Early in the summer of 605, Nebuchadnezzar, along with his allies, the Medes, conquered the last bastion of Assyrian strength at Carchemish. The Babylonians and the Medes then proceeded to divide up the Assyrian empire between them. Nebuchadnezzar staked a claim to Syria and set up his base at Riblah (see comment on 2 Kings 23:33), where he began to collect tribute from his new subjects.

Judah fell within the territory allotted to the Babylonians, and Nebuchadnezzar was back in the area at the end of 604. There is no record of any direct siege of Jerusalem by the Babylonians until 597, but the language in this verse is general enough to admit a number of possibilities.

1:1-2. Jehoiakim. Jehoiakim was a son of Josiah who was put on the throne by the Egyptian pharaoh, Necho, as he attempted to exercise control over Syria-Palestine. When Josiah was killed in battle, the people had enthroned his son, Jehoahaz, who represented an anti-Egyptian faction. This situation lasted for three months (while Necho was busy at Haran). Then Necho deposed Jehoahaz and sent him off as a captive to Egypt. Pro-Egyptian Jehoiakim was then placed on the throne with the expectation that he would be a loyal Egyptian vassal. The situation changed dramatically when Nebuchadnezzar gained control of the region following the fall of Carchemish. Jehoiakim played the role of reluctant Babylonian vassal for several years, but after Nebuchadnezzar's failure to invade Egypt in 601, he again broke with Babylon and sought the support of Egypt in his rebellion. This disloyalty eventually proved fatal and led to the Babylonian siege of Jerusalem in 597 (see comment on 2 Kings 24:10-11).

1:2. articles from the temple. These articles would have been attractive booty not only because they were made of precious metals, but because they had been dedicated to the God Yahweh for use in the rituals of the temple. Power was demonstrated over the deity by taking those things that were most significant to him. For descriptions of some of these articles see comments in 2 Chronicles 4.

1:2. carried off to temple. As we know from

references in the Mari texts as well as the Cyrus Cylinder, sacred objects, including idols and the many types of vessels used in worship, were taken hostage when a people was conquered. A way of demonstrating the power of one's own god over the gods of conquered peoples was to desecrate their sacred objects or place them in a position of submission.

1:2. his god. Marduk was the chief god of Babylon, its patron deity and the head of the pantheon. The Babylonian creation epic, *Enuma Elish*, is actually a myth recounting his elevation to that position, believed to have taken place at the end of the second millennium. He was considered to be the son of one of the members of the most august ancient triad, Enki, the patron of Eridu. Though we often see Baal in the Bible as the principal rival of Yahweh, no deity in the first millennium had the political clout that was connected to Marduk. His renowned temple, Esagila, along with its ziggurat, Etemenanki, were the most dominant buildings in the beautiful city of Babylon.

1:3. Ashpenaz's office. The title translated "chief of the court officials" is also assigned to one of the three representatives of Sennacherib who are sent to confront Hezekiah (see comment on 2 Kings 18:17). The Hebrew term translated "court official" sometimes refers to eunuchs (see comment on Is 56:4-5), though it is difficult to tell when it is that specific.

1:4-5. serving in king's palace. The training the young men were scheduled to receive was intended to prepare them for royal service. As courtiers, they might serve as scribes, advisors, sages, diplomats, provincial governors or attendants to members of the royal household. In seventh-century letters to Assyrian kings the five principal classes of scholarly experts serving the king are mentioned as being astrologer/scribe, diviner, exorcist (this term is used to describe those compared to Daniel and his friends in v. 20), physician and chanter of lamentations. It would not be unusual for an individual to be trained in a number of these disciplines. Training foreigners for these positions was expected to result in the assimilation of the best and brightest of the next generation. Their skills would then benefit the Babylonians rather than their enemies.

1:4. language of Babylonians (Chaldeans). The traditional language of Babylon was Akkadian, a complex and ancient language written by means of a cuneiform script (using a stylus to make wedge-shaped characters), in which each symbol represented a syllable. Much of the canonical literature of the Babylonians was written in Akkadian. Scholars

therefore had to receive training in that language. Additionally, there were numerous dialects of Akkadian, though perhaps many of the ancient documents had been reworked into the current dialect. The reigning dynasty, however, was not native Babylonian, but ethnically Chaldean (see comment on Is 13:19). Their language and the diplomatic language of the time was Aramaic. This used an alphabetic script similar to that used by Hebrew. The widespread use of Aramaic in the world of this time makes it possible that Daniel and his friends already had some fluency in it. Alternatively, it is possible that in referring to the language of the Chaldeans, the text is not speaking of the ethnic Chaldeans but the priestly guild of diviners who, at some point, had become known as the Chaldeans. In the book of Daniel the term is used both ways (ethnic group and professional guild).

1:4. literature of Babylonians (Chaldeans). It is difficult to be certain whether the training involved a wide range of literature, as scribal training and general education would, or whether the training focused on the specialized literature used by the diviners. The diviners' principal literature was embodied in the omen texts. The credentials listed for various scholars indicates that they have mastered the omen series. This literature represented over a millennium of observations of various phenomena along with the favorable or unfavorable events they portended. In addition there are instruction manuals and correspondence in which the reports of these specialists are given to the king. Some of the recorded omens, such as dreams or astronomical observations, are simply observed and preserved in writing. Other times some mechanism might be used to generate the omen (divination by means of the entrails of sacrificed animals) or a human medium may be involved. The omens themselves began to be collected as early as the Old Babylonian period (early second millennium) and were generally presented in an "if-then" form. The exorcists (see comment on 1:20), with whom Daniel appears to be classified and compared, had their special literature as well. These professionals specialized in recognizing the danger of various portents (astronomical happenings, dreams, birth anomalies) and providing the rituals to protect against them. The literature of this defensive magic is represented in the *namburbu* texts.

1:5. rations from king's table. There were many individuals who were given the right to receive rations from the king's table. The classification does not suggest enjoying the privilege of cozy, intimate soirees with the king, but simply that they were made dependents of the state. Those who received such rations in the Neo-Babylonian period included certain ranking members of the administration, craftsmen, artisans (native or foreign), diplomats, businessmen and entertainers, as well as political refugees and members of royal families who had been deported to, or were being held hostage in, Babylon. Depending on their status, these individuals could receive barley and oil rations or much more luxurious fare. Clothing and housing could also be included in their maintenance.

1:5. royal food. The term *(patbag)* used here (and throughout the chapter) is known in Persian and is thought to be a loan word. It refers to food portions sent by the king to friends of the crown. There is no reason to think of it as a meat dish. When later Greeks referred to descriptions of this fare in the Persian literature they had available to them, it is identified as a baked bread product made of barley and wheat, accompanied by wine.

1:5. three-year training. The normal training period for a scribe was three years. In the literature available from the Old Babylonian period, training included the language and literature areas mentioned above as well as mathematics and music. It is probable that the training period for a diviner was longer, but precise indications in the literature are lacking.

1:7. new names. To change someone's name is to exercise authority over them and their destiny. Foreign rulers showed this propensity throughout the biblical period. Since assimilation was ostensibly one of the objectives of the whole procedure in which Daniel was involved, a Babylonian name would be appropriate. Likewise, since names often made statements about deity, Babylonian names would impose at least a subtle level of acknowledgment of the Babylonian gods on the young men.

1:8. defilement from royal food. There have been extensive discussions and a variety of suggestions regarding the reasons why Daniel and his friends refused the king's food. Most work on the assumption that the contrast is between meat and vegetables (see comments on 1:5 and 1:12 for the problems). It is true that sharing the king's food implied some level of allegiance to the king, but that would hold no matter what the young men ate. Jewish dietary laws (kosher) would likely have rendered meat unclean, but improper storage or preparation could render other food unclean as well. Furthermore, the Jewish dietary laws

did not prohibit wine. The finest meats were undoubtedly supplied to the palace from the temples, where they had been offered before idols (and the wine poured out in libations before the gods), but any food could easily have come through the same route. The decision certainly has nothing to do with vegetarianism or avoidance of rich foods for nutritional purposes (see 10:3). There are numerous examples in intertestamental literature of Jews seeing the necessity of refraining from the food served by Gentiles (Tobit, Judith, Jubilees). It is not so much something in the food that defiles as much as it is the total program of assimilation. At this point the Babylonian government is exercising control over every aspect of their lives. They have little means to resist the forces of assimilation that are controlling them. They seize on one of the few areas where they can still exercise choice as an opportunity to preserve their distinct identity.

1:12. vegetables. The word used here generally refers to the seeds used for animal feed, fodder or planting. In neither Akkadian nor Hebrew is it used to describe human food. But the text does not suggest that they are being provided with a restaurant-style prepared and served meal. As explained above (1:5), to eat from the king's table meant only that they were provided rations at the expense of the royal budget. Military rations, for example, consisted of measured amounts of grain that the soldiers then used to prepare their meals. Cereal grains could be ground, mashed and cooked in water to produce a porridge. This could therefore involve the same amount of ration as referred to in 1:5 but prepared by themselves rather than in the king's kitchens.

1:17. visions and dreams. Dreams were believed to have importance for revealing the work of the gods as early as the third millennium B.C. They were considered to be communications brought from the gods by a spirit messenger. In Akkadian this messenger was named Zaqiqu. Sometimes information was sought through dreams (see comment on 2 Chron 1:7-12).

1:20. magicians and enchanters. The first term used here refers to Egyptian dream interpreters. It is the same word used in Genesis 41:8 and Exodus 7:11. The Babylonians were known to include Egyptian dream interpreters among their court advisors. The second term refers to the Mesopotamian specialist in exorcism: defending against threatening messages in the omens or in dreams. The latter's skills include identifying the threatening sign, determining a course of action to avert the evil, and performing apotropaic rituals and reciting incantations to turn aside the danger. Sickness was often included in the group of threatening signs, so the exorcist was counted among the "health care professionals" of Babylonian society. The use of the two terms clarifies that Daniel's skills exceeded those of the foreign specialists as well as the native practitioners.

1:21. first year of Cyrus. This is most likely a reference to the first year of Cyrus' reign over Babylon, which began in October 539 B.C. This would mean that Daniel's tenure of service extended over a sixty-five-year period.

2:1-49
A Troubling Dream

2:1. chronology. In Babylonian reckoning, from the time the king took the throne until New Year's Day (in Nisan, March-April) was counted as an "accession year." His first year began with the start of the first full year. Nebuchadnezzar came to the throne on September 6, 605. His first year was from spring 604 to spring 603. The dream of this chapter, then, would have taken place sometime between spring 603 and spring 602. The Babylonian Chronicle for this year is broken in crucial places but is sufficient to show that Nebuchadnezzar faced some significant military challenges. His fourth year brought the famous, though unsuccessful, attempt to invade Egypt.

2:1. assortment of advisors. Akkadian literature refers to this general class of experts as *ummanu mudu*, masters of esoteric knowledge. The first two terms are the same as those used in 1:20. The third term is used in the Old Testament as a general term for the practice of magic and for practitioners labeled "sorcerers." In Babylonian usage the term refers specifically to those who cast spells. The fourth term, "astrologers," is the word usually rendered "Chaldeans" and here refers to the priestly guild of diviners. In later times they specialized in astrology.

2:1. dreams that trouble. See comment on 1:17. Since dreams were considered to be messages from the gods, they often caused concern, if not alarm. The very nature of the king's dream would have suggested that the news was not good news. He feels the type of apprehension that an employee feels being called in to the boss's office when reorganization is taking place in the company.

2:4. Aramaic. It is normal that the experts would address the king in Aramaic, because that was the language of the realm. From this point in the text through the end of chapter seven, the book of Daniel is in Aramaic rather than Hebrew. The two languages use the same letters, so the page in the original languages would look no different to the English reader.

2:4. dream interpretation. Dream interpretations were usually carried out by experts who had been trained in the available dream literature. More information is available from Mesopotamia than from Egypt. Both the Egyptians and the Babylonians compiled what we call dream books. They contained sample dreams along with the key to their interpretation. Since dreams often depended on symbolism, the interpreter would have had to have access to these documents that preserved the empirical data concerning past dreams and interpretations. Typically, however, it was only the central theme of the dream that was significant for interpretation, rather than all the details. Interpretation of dreams included identifying the meaning of the symbols in the dream, declaring its meaning, consequences and the timing of the events it addresses, and composing an appropriate response to the dream. The response could include apotropaic rituals to defend against the portents or actions that the king should take.

2:5-9. the king's demand. If the king had forgotten the dream, he would not want to admit it, because forgetting a dream was a bad omen indicating that his god was angry with him. Furthermore, such forgetfulness would logically result in the request that the gods send the dream again. Important dreams were often repeated two or three times (notice that v. 1 suggests more than one dream by the use of the plural). An alternative is that Nebuchadnezzar felt that the dream was so ominous that it could too easily be used as a mechanism for subversion against the throne. Divine utterances had long served the purposes of conspirators and usurpers (see 2 Kings 8:8-15 and comment on 2 Kings 9:6-10). He sought evidence that the interpretation represented the gods' message rather than human agenda by requiring that the gods reveal the dream to the interpreter.

2:11. the wise men's claim. It was believed that the gods communicated through dreams, and the experts believed that the gods would reveal to them the interpretation of the dreams through their use of the resources available to them. There was nothing in their resources that would enable them to discern what the dream was. There was no precedent for the gods revealing that sort of information.

2:12. annihilation of the wise men. The annihilation of entire groups suspected of conspiracy or incompetence is all too familiar in the ancient world. Herodotus records a couple of instances during the Persian period. One involves the magi, one of whom had actually usurped the throne, being executed by Darius I. A second is the execution by Xerxes of the engineers who had built a bridge that collapsed in a storm. A biblical example occurs during the reign of Saul, who almost wiped out the priesthood when he suspected them of collusion with David (1 Sam 22:13-19).

2:14. commander of the king's guard. This is the official title of an important functionary whose duties were sometimes unsavory. When Jerusalem fell at the hands of the Babylonians, the commander in charge of methodically destroying and dismantling the city and disposing of captives either by execution or deportation carried this title. It is similar to the title held by Potiphar in Genesis 37:36. The terminology suggests something like "chief cook," but like some of our government titles (such as "party whip") the office must be understood by examining its function, not its title.

2:19. "God of heaven." This became a popular title for deity in the sixth century. In Persian documents it was commonly used for Ahura Mazda, the chief deity of Zoroastrianism (see comments on Ezra 1:2 and Neh 1:4). The Israelites also found it a usable title for their God, Yahweh.

2:31. statue in a dream. The Egyptian pharaoh Merenptah (thirteenth century B.C.) reports seeing a huge image of the god Ptah in a dream. The god gave him permission to go to war against the Libyans. In a dream reported during the reign of Ashurbanipal, an inscription on the base of a statue of the god, Sin, forecast the failure of the rebellion in Babylon.

2:32. statues of mixed elements. Statues of mixed elements were not uncommon. Since the images of the gods were generally clothed, more care and expense was afforded to the portions that would show. So, for instance, in a mid-second millennium Hittite prayer a promise is made to supply a life-sized statue of the king with head, hands and feet of gold, the rest of silver. Another example of how various metals could be used is the small bronze calf figurine found at Ashkelon. After the body was cast in bronze, forged copper was used for some of the extremities, and the whole image was overlaid with silver. Numerous second-millennium divine images have been uncovered that are likewise made of bronze and covered with gold or silver. Even small figurines were often not cast in one piece but made in parts and joined together with tenons or rivets. Most of the features in

the dream are realistic, not surreal. The head is the most important part of the image and would logically have gold plating over the bronze cast. Parts of the arms and chest would at times be visible, thus silver overlay would be appropriate. The torso would need no overlay attached to the bronze, since it was always covered. Iron was not yet being cast at this period, though one Egyptian papyrus mentions iron statues (probably wrought iron). The only way of actually mixing clay with iron would be if the clay were being used as a flux, but the word used in the text for the clay favors baked clay. One suggestion has been that the iron feet would have featured terra cotta inlays. Statuary from both the Neo-Babylonian and Persian periods is nearly nonexistent, and no major divine images from first-millennium Mesopotamia have been recovered. The Assyrian king Esarhaddon boasted of a statue that he had made of himself of silver, gold and copper that was to be placed before the gods to present petitions on his behalf.

2:34-35. rock not cut by human hands. The only incidence of anything even vaguely similar to this appears in the Gilgamesh Epic. Gilgamesh reports a dream about the coming of Enkidu in which Enkidu is represented as a meteor that lands at Gilgamesh's feet. But here there is no destruction by means of the rock.

2:36-40. four kingdoms. The kingdoms are not identified in the text except for the equation that Nebuchadnezzar is the head of gold. Some have suggested a sequence of Babylon, Media, (Medo-)Persian, Greek, while others prefer Babylon, (Medo-)Persian, Greek, Roman. Most of the evidence that would point to one scheme over another comes from Daniel 7 and is examined there.

2:36-40. four-kingdom patterns. The idea of presenting history in terms of four empires or ages has several parallels in ancient and classical literature. In Akkadian literature the *Dynastic Prophecy* (Seleucid period, third century B.C.?) refers to four successive kingdoms (Assyrian, Babylonian, Persian, Greek) in a very broken text. The *Sibylline Oracles* (whose source dates to the second century B.C.) contain a four-empire scheme (Assyrians, Medes, Persians, Macedonians; a number of examples in the Roman period add Rome to the list to make five empires). The fifth-century A.D. Roman author Servius says that Sibyl portrayed the ages by comparing them to metals, but no such comparison is preserved in currently known Sibylline Oracles. The characterization of ages by metals has been thought to correspond to the Zoroastrian representation of four periods of human history. Zoroastrian Avestan texts identify ages (not empires), sometimes as branches on a tree respectively of gold, silver, steel and iron-mixed (an obscure designation). The texts in which this material is recorded are late but preserve material that some believe date back to the second or third century B.C. Perhaps the most significant comparison of ages to metals is found in the early Greek author Hesiod (*Works and Days*, eighth century B.C.), who identifies five ages, four of which are represented by metals (gold, silver, bronze and iron).

2:44. kingdom enduring forever. In a work known as the *Uruk Prophecy* from the twelfth century B.C., there are four kings who arise and do poorly, followed by a king who will restore the statue of Ishtar to Uruk from Babylon. The prophecy says that his son will succeed him and that his kingdom will be established forever (an alternative interpretation dates it to the seventh century and identifies the son as Nebuchadnezzar).

2:46. Nebuchadnezzar's treatment of Daniel. The verb NIV translates "presented" is usually used in Hebrew for pouring out libations. But neither the (grain) offering nor the incense that are mentioned here can be poured out in libations. The text here, however, continues to be in Aramaic, in which the verb means "to provide." This makes Nebuchadnezzar's treatment of Daniel a bit more understandable, as he provides Daniel with the materials with which Daniel can make an appropriate offering to his God.

2:47. revealer of mysteries. The role as a "revealer of mysteries" is highlighted here as Daniel has exceeded what could normally be accomplished by the wise men of Babylon. The gods were believed to have revealed themselves when omens (such as dreams) were given, and they were believed to offer revelation of the interpretation of the omens through the interpretive wisdom they provided to the sage as he used the resources and literature at his disposal. But Daniel had received the additional revelation of the contents of the dream, enhancing his reputation.

2:48. ruler over province of Babylon. The empire was divided into provinces, or satrapies, of which Babylon was one. Daniel is exalted to high office in the province, but that vague description finds definition in the next statement that clarifies the nature of this high office: he is made prefect over the wise men. This is more likely ranking within his guild rather than a administrative position in the civil government.

3:1-30

The Fiery Furnace

3:1. image of what. The image is never positively identified as the image of a deity, though verse 28 could easily suggest it. If the image were a divine image, it would be odd for the name of the deity not to be given and even more unusual for it to be set up in an open area rather than associated with a temple. Part of the care of the gods was to house and feed them, and such maintenance could not easily be kept up in an open location. If it is not the image of a god, it becomes more difficult to understand the three friends' refusal to participate (for an understanding of the thrust of the second commandment see comment on Ex 20:4). The other main alternative is to see it as an image of the king. But there was no prohibition against bowing down before kings as an act of respect. Additionally, images of kings during the Assyrian and Babylonian periods were usually made to be put in temples to stand before the deity requesting the well-being of the king. Typically, then, they represented the king to the god, not to the people.

Perhaps the best alternative is to understand the event in the context of the Assyrian practice of erecting stelae or statues (often in inaccessible places) that commemorated their rulers. While these were intended to exalt the king, the reliefs on the Balawat gates demonstrate that offerings were made before these representations. In the scene portrayed on the gates the king himself is present, but the offerings are made to the stele. In this way the king is given the honors that are generally given to the gods, but by personally distancing himself he avoids making himself equal to the gods. Such rituals were used as occasions for provincial territories to take a loyalty oath. This would make sense here in light of the suggestion in the dream of Daniel 2 that the Babylonian kingdom would have a limited time of rule. In Assyrian practice the weapon of Ashur (perhaps even a battle standard) was set up for ceremonies in which vassal kings entered into loyalty oaths. Failure to participate would suggest insubordination, whereas participation would signify the acceptance of the deity's (and king's) sovereignty. The three friends are not being asked to worship a deity, but they are being asked to participate in rituals that honor the king in ways similar to how the gods were treated, even though the king is not being viewed as a deity. Daniel's absence could be explained easily by the occasion's setting in only a single province.

3:1. dimensions. Herodotus describes two large statues in Marduk's temple in Babylon, both of solid gold. One is Bel seated on a golden throne. The image and the golden table next to it were reported to have used twenty-two tons of gold. The second is described as the statue of a man. Herodotus says it is fifteen feet high, though other accounts put it at eighteen feet. The Persian king, Xerxes, melted it down in 482 B.C., and the resulting bullion weighed eight hundred pounds. The Colossus at Rhodes was reported to be just over one hundred feet tall, so a ninety-foot-tall statue is not out of the realm of possibility, though it is also possible that the ninety feet includes a pedestal. The unusual thing is that the width is only ten percent of the height. The width of a properly proportioned human figure would normally be about twenty-five percent of the height. If this statue is human shaped and nine feet wide, we would expect the statue to be thirty-five or forty feet tall. This would then require a pedestal of fifty-plus feet. Even so, imagine the instability of something ten stories tall and only nine feet wide.

3:1. Dura. There are several towns named Der, and Dura (=walled area) is a common element in place names (e.g., Dur-Kurashu, Dur-Sharruken, Dur-Kurigalzu, Dur-Katlimmu). It is therefore impossible at present to locate this plain with certainty (the reference is as unclear as talking about a place named "San" in California).

3:2. occasion. As mentioned in 3:1, it is likely that the occasion for this gathering was the taking of a loyalty oath. A century earlier it is known that Assyrian king Ashurbanipal gathered his chief officials together in Babylon to take a loyalty oath. A letter has been preserved from one of the officials who was out of town and therefore made arrangements to take the oath in the presence of the palace overseer. The letter specifically mentions that when he took the oath he was surrounded by the images of the gods.

3:2. attendees. The list of officials includes two Semitic titles (prefect, governor), with the remaining five being Persian titles. The list appears to be in rank order. The first three terms are well enough known, the first being a Persian term borrowed into Aramaic as early as the sixth century for the ruler of the province. The next two are good Semitic terms for the next two levels of subordinates. The last four are Persian loan words whose translation is very tentative.

3:5. musical instruments. The names of several of these instruments are Greek, but there had been enough contact with Greece by the sixth century that this is not unusual. Nebuchadnezzar was known to make use of foreign musicians, as shown in the rations lists. These lists also attest to the presence of some Greeks in Babylon. The first two instruments are wind instruments. Judging by the word used for the horn, it is an animal's horn rather than a metal trumpet. The flute is of the variety that is played by blowing through the end. The next three in the list are stringed instruments. Two of them have names borrowed from Greek, and the middle one occurs as a foreign word in Greek. The first is known from Homer's writings (eighth century B.C.) and is a type of lyre. There were a wide variety of lyres in the ancient world, but no early attestations of the zither or dulcimer. The second in the list is probably a harp, and the third is most likely a different style of lyre. The last is the most difficult. Suggestions have ranged from bagpipes to double flute to percussion. It is a Greek loan word into Aramaic, and it happens also to come into English as "symphony."

3:6. furnace. Furnaces were used for baking pottery or bricks for construction projects, as well as for metalwork (forging, smelting and casting). There is not a lot of information about furnaces in the ancient Near East, but many early furnaces were enclosed and domed with side doors for ventilation. They were built of clay or brick, though the inside chamber was often lined with specially selected types of stone. It is logical to assume that the furnace was in this location serving a purpose (perhaps in the manufacture of the image) rather than having been set up to use as an instrument of punishment. There is little in the ancient literature to suggest that furnaces were specifically used for punishment. One possible exception is from around 1800 B.C., when Rim-Sin ruled that someone who had pushed a slave into a kiln should have one of his slaves thrown into a furnace. In general, however, burning was used as a form of execution as early as the Hammurabi Code. In fifth-century Persia (during the reign of Darius II, son of Artaxerxes), and in the second century (2 Macc 13:4-8), there are examples of execution by pushing into a bin of ashes.

3:19. seven times hotter. Blast air from a bellows was usually used to raise the temperature in the furnace. "Seven times hotter" is just an expression. Depending on what the furnace was being used for, the temperature would be maintained at between nine hundred and eleven hundred degrees centigrade. With their technology they were not able to exceed fifteen hundred degrees centigrade.

3:25. son of the gods. This phrase comes from Nebuchadnezzar's lips, so we do not expect him to be representing any deep insight or sophisticated theology. The phrase "son of the gods" represents a common Semitic expression for identifying a supernatural being.

4:1-37
The King's Illness

4:1-2. royal proclamations. A proclamation such as this would typically be recorded on a stele and set up in a prominent place. Sometimes copies would be made to be circulated, as was done with Darius' Behistun Inscription. Many of the elements of this proclamation are common to royal inscriptions or to Aramaic letters, though it is unusual for a king to be so vulnerable as here.

4:10-12. world tree. The concept of the cosmic tree in the center of the world is a common motif in the ancient Near East. It is also used in Ezekiel 31. The roots of the tree are fed by the great subterranean ocean, and its top merges with the clouds, thus binding together the heavens, the earth and the netherworld. In the *Myth of Erra and Ishum* Marduk speaks of the *meshu* tree whose roots reach down through the oceans to the netherworld and whose top is above the heavens. In the Sumerian epic *Lugalbanda and Enmerkar* the "eagle-tree" has a similar role. In Assyrian contexts the motif of a sacred tree is also well known. Some have called it a tree of life, and some also associate it with this world tree. It is often flanked by animals or by human or divine figures. A winged disk is typically centrally located over the top of the tree. The king is represented as the human personification of this tree. The tree is thought to represent the divine world order, but textual discussion of it is lacking.

4:13. watchers. The watchers are a well-known class of supernatural being in a wide range of the intertestamental literature, especially the books of *Enoch*, as well as in the Dead Sea Scrolls. Though the term is often used in that literature in reference to fallen angels, it is not limited to that group. There is so far no attestation of the term being used in this specialized way prior to the third century B.C., but the Mesopotamians did recognize a variety of protecting spirits and demons. Perhaps the closest parallel would be found in the occasional references to the seven ancient sages as watchers. Additionally, they are sometimes portrayed as caretakers of the sacred tree, so they would fit well in this context.

4:15. binding a stump. It is difficult to determine whether it is a part of the tree that is bound with iron, or whether it is the king. If it is the tree, the text indicates that its taproot should be bound (not the stump). While trees are sometimes gilded with metal bands in ancient Mesopotamia, there is no case of treating a stump that way, much less a taproot.

4:15. dew of heaven. In Babylonian texts, dew was considered to come down from the stars of heaven and was sometimes seen as the mechanism by which the stars brought either sickness or healing.

4:16. seven times. It should not be assumed that the condition lasts for seven years. The Aramaic word "times" is interesting here. The cognate in Akkadian means "specified periods" and can refer to stages of a disease or to periodic sequences. When omens occurred, they often had a set time over which their effects could take place. Some "times" such as phases of the moon, or favorable days, might occur monthly. Others occur annually. Still others, such as equinoxes or solstices, occur a couple of times a year. Many possibilities exist here.

4:16. the king's malady. See comment on 4:33.

4:28. royal palace of Babylon. Nebuchadnezzar's building projects in Babylon were magnificent. The Euphrates was channeled into a number of canals that passed through the city. His palace, on the north side of the city near the Ishtar Gate, was luxuriously appointed with all the finest materials. The palace gardens were terraced and gained international reputation, eventually being named one of the seven wonders of the ancient world. It was a parklike enclosure with an arboretum of exotic trees. Additional building projects included the temples and the streets.

4:33. Nebuchadnezzar's condition. Interpreters seeking illnesses to which these symptoms might apply have identified conditions such as lycanthropy, a depressive illness in which the patient thinks of himself as a beast. But the characteristics also coincide with the typical description of primitive or primordial man, who lacks good sense (compare NIV: "sanity" vv. 34, 36) and has an animal-like nature and habits (v. 16). In older myths this condition is characteristic of precivilized man. It later is applied to Enkidu, the uncivilized creature of the Gilgamesh Epic. It is then used of those who are driven away from civilization after their city has been destroyed. From the early texts about the Sumerian adventurer Lugalbanda to the late texts concerning the Assyrian courtier Ahiqar, individuals are also described as having developed some of these characteristics while cut off from society. As a result, it is possible that at least some of Nebuchadnezzar's symptoms describe not a psychological illness but exile from civilization (only food gathered wild, no home, no personal hygiene). A fragmentary cuneiform text suggests the possibility that Nebuchadnezzar had some problem that caused him to become disengaged from his responsibilities for a time, during which his son, Amel-Marduk, was perhaps in control. But the text is too uncertain to draw any firm conclusions.

4:34. Prayer of Nabonidus. One of the documents found at Qumran (4Q242 or 4QPrNab) is entitled The Prayer of Nabonidus. In this piece it is the last king of Babylon, Nabonidus, rather than his more famous predecessor, Nebuchadnezzar, who is afflicted. Similarities include the seven-year illness and restoration by a Jewish diviner (unnamed). A dream is involved and worship of the correct deity is the result. The scroll preserves no mention of comparison to a beast, though some interpreters have reconstructed a line to include such a reference. The scroll connects the seven-year illness with Nabonidus's well known stay in Teima.

5:1-31

Belshazzar's Feast

5:1. Belshazzar. Belshazzar was the son and coregent of Nabonidus, the last king of Babylon. Nabonidus spent ten years in Teima while his son was carrying out all the royal duties in Babylon. A number of documents have been found that mention him by name. About thirty years have passed since the last chapter. Nebuchadnezzar died in 562, and the banquet of this chapter takes place in October 539.

5:1. the banquet. The banquet is taking place in mid-October (15 Tashritu) 539. In the past few days the Persians have taken the city of Opis (fifty miles north on the Tigris) in a bloody battle and then crossed over to the Euphrates, where the city of Sippar surrendered without a fight on the fourteenth of Tashritu. It is likely that Babylon has received word of these events and that Belshazzar knows that the Persian army is on the march toward Babylon. Nabonidus had been with the army at Opis and fled when the city fell. When he was captured, it was in Babylon, but the texts are unclear about when he arrived. Berossus (third-century B.C. Chaldean historian, quoted by Josephus) claims that he was trapped in the city of Borsippa (about seventeen miles south of Babylon). In light of all of this, it appears that the banquet represents one final gathering before the momentous events that are about to transpire. Herodotus refers to a festival celebration that was taking place when the city fell. There is no reason to think, however, that the banquet reflects Belshazzar's pessimism about the outcome. Babylon was a defensible city, and they believed their gods to be strong.

5:2. vessels from Jerusalem. See comment on 1:2. Everyone in the ancient world understood the significance of sacred vessels. The fact that these had not been melted down suggests that they had been preserved because of their sacred character. Since the god of Babylon was seen as the conqueror, the things that belonged to the "conquered" gods would have been taken as booty into the temple of Marduk. Perhaps the use of the vessels was a way of calling to remembrance the god's previous victories (see comment on 5:4).

5:2. relation to Nebuchadnezzar. Belshazzar was known to be the son of Nabonidus, the last king of Babylon, with whom he was coregent. Nabonidus has no firmly established relationship to Nebuchadnezzar. As early as Herodotus (fifth century B.C., see sidebar at Esther 1), Nebuchadnezzar and Nabonidus had the same name (Labynetos) and were at times confused. Additionally, however, in the ancient world, successive monarchs were often identified as sons of famous predecessors even when there was no dynastic or genealogical connections. So, for instance, on the black obelisk of Shalmaneser III, Jehu, king of Israel, is identified as "son of Omri," even though he had been responsible for wiping out the line of Omri and was no relation (a fact probably well known to the Assyrians).

5:4. praised the gods. Belshazzar and his administration are well aware that the empire hangs by a thread and that the next several days will be of utmost significance. They are hoping that their gods will bring victory for them as they had in the days of Nebuchadnezzar's great conquests. To that end they are "toasting the gods" and celebrating their past victories. It is also possible, though not explicitly stated, that libations were poured out to the gods from these vessels. They are not only making their supplications to Marduk, the patron of Babylon, but to the gods of other cities of the region whose images had been gathered into Babylon during these troubled times.

5:5. the hand. A lifeless, detached hand would have suggested a defeated enemy. Casualty counts were made by cutting off the right hands of all of the dead (recall the broken-off hands of Dagan in 1 Sam 5:3-4). By drinking from the vessels the Babylonians were recalling the defeat of Yahweh (perhaps along with other gods and nations), but this is no lifeless, severed hand of a dead god at all. It is quite animated and has a message to give. The effect might be similar if the head of a decapitated victim began to speak.

5:5. location of the writing. The statement that the writing was on the plaster wall near the lampstand is a curious detail since one might have expected plaster all around the room, which would be illuminated by many lampstands. The excavation of the throne room in Babylon can offer some explanation. It was a 170-by-55-foot hall entered through three spacious courtyards that led from the entrance just inside the Ishtar Gate. Some of the wall space was covered with blue enameled brick, while other parts were plaster. The word used for lampstand is an unusual one and may be a Persian loan word. As such it likely represents a distinct, singular lampstand, perhaps of a special type.

5:7. rewards offered. The purple clothing was made using expensive dye (see comment on Num 4:6 and Esther 8:15) and was worn only by royalty. The gold chain would have been an insignia of office. These are seen as royal gifts in Herodotus, where Cambyses sends them to the Ethiopian king. Being made third in the kingdom may be intended to rank Daniel only behind Belshazzar and his father, Nabonidus.

5:8. could not read the writing. Though some have suggested that the inscription was written in an obscure language (such as Old Persian cuneiform), there is no indication in the text that it is written in anything other than the native Aramaic. Aramaic, like Hebrew, is written without vowels and at times without word divisions, yielding מנאתקלפרס *(mnʾtqlprs)*. Confusion over where to make the word divisions and which vowels to supply was sufficient to undermine their confidence in reading the words and offering an interpretation. In another case of an inscribed and perhaps cryptic message, the seventh-century Lydian king Gyges saw the name "Ashurbanipal" written out in a dream that was accompanied by a voice urging him to battle against the Cimmerians.

5:10. queen mother. Nabonidus's mother, Adad-Guppi, was a very influential person and the quintessential queen mother. Her 104 years, however, had come to a close about 546, so she was no longer alive at this time. Nabonidus's wife, Belshazzar's mother, identified by Herodotus as Nitocris, is more likely referred to here.

5:25-28. the inscription. The words can be tak-

en as verbs for weighing and assessing, or as nouns for the various weights that are used with the balance scales that were the ancient cash registers—necessary at every place of business. Archaeologists have discovered many such weights, sometimes inscribed with these Aramaic labels. Scales and weights were also used to depict divine evaluation and judgment (as in the Egyptian Book of the Dead). Daniel appears to have used both noun and verb forms in his interpretation. Wordplay was a common means used to interpret omens in this period. An example of this is Nabonidus's interpretation of a lunar eclipse as a directive to install his daughter as a priestess.

5:27. scales. A. Wolters has pointed out that the imagery of the scales may also find an astronomical connection to the constellation Libra, represented in Babylonian astronomy as scales. Babylon fell on the sixteenth of Tashritu (September-October), October 12 or 13, 539, so the banquet took place the evening of Tashritu 15/October 11 or 12. The Babylonians traditionally related the month of Tashritu to the constellation Libra, and the annual rising of Libra was associated in the manuals with the fifteenth of that month. This would have been well known to the astrologers of Babylon's court, specialists in celestial divination, who were counted among the wise men. This would have importance since the Babylonians often sought linkage between classes of omens to confirm a message.

5:30. fall of Babylon. There are several ancient traditions concerning the fall of Babylon represented in Persian and Greek sources. Herodotus (see sidebar on Esther 1) tells of a siege of Babylon by the Persians that ended when Cyrus diverted the Euphrates and sent a company inside the wall where the river had flowed through. Cyrus's account in the Cyrus Cylinder reports that Marduk allowed him to enter Babylon without a battle, where he was received as a liberator. The *Chronicle of Nabonidus*, a pro-Persian contemporary account, offers a similar view.

6:1-28

Daniel and the Lions

6:1. Darius the Mede. There is no known historical character named Darius prior to Darius the Great, who is too late to fit in here. Since Cyrus became ruler when Babylon fell, some have identified Darius the Mede and Cyrus as one and the same (see 6:28). Others suggest that Darius is an alternate name (or a throne name) for Ugbaru, the commander who led the Persian army into Babylon. He was governor of the Gutium and thus could easily be connected with the Medes (though he died just three weeks after the fall of Babylon). One named Gubaru was appointed the governor of Babylon and is also named by some as a candidate. There is reason to question that anyone but Cyrus could be called the king (v. 6), and he was about sixty-two when Babylon fell. But Cyrus was a Persian, not a Mede, and was the son of Cambyses (not Ahasuerus, see 9:1). Further information will need to become available before a firm identification can be made.

6:1. 120 satraps. The primary administrative geographical division in the Persian empire was the satrapy. The number of these varied between twenty and thirty-one, so the text must be referring to lower-level administrative governors (for whom this term is used in Greek historical sources).

6:7. the king's edict. Persian kings were not at all inclined toward self-deification. Furthermore, the gods were considered too important to be ignored. Even in the traditional Iranian religion, prayer three times a day was the norm, and Zoroastrianism increased it to five. Alternatively, it is likely that Darius was persuaded to issue the decree to address some religious/political problem without ever intending to prohibit what Daniel (and most of the population of the empire) was doing. Herodotus describes Persian ritual by reporting that no altar nor fire is used. Most importantly, he says that when the offering is made, the worshiper is not permitted to pray for anything personal but can only invoke blessings on the king or community.

6:7,17. lions' den. It is known that lions were captured and kept in cages so that they could be released for hunting, but there are no examples in currently known Persian literature that feature the punishment of being thrown into a den of lions. In earlier Assyrian texts, oath-breakers were put into cages of wild animals set up in the city square to be publicly devoured. Additionally, in seventh-century Assyrian literature, the lions' pit occurs as a metaphor for vicious and antagonistic courtiers of the king. In one piece of Babylonian wisdom literature, Marduk metaphorically closes (muzzles) the mouth of the lion (the oppressor) to put an end to his devouring tactics.

6:8. laws of the Medes and Persians. No concept of "laws of the Medes and Persians that cannot be changed" has been documented outside of the books of Daniel and Esther. Nonetheless, a tradition at least as early as the time of Hammurabi (eighteenth century B.C.)

recognized that a judge could not change a decision that had been made. In this sense we may be dealing with a ruling rather than a law. Greek sources conflict with one another, as Herodotus indicates significant freedom on the part of Persian kings to change their minds, while Diodorus Siculus cites an instance where Darius III could not. Certainly no lower official could countermand the decrees of the Persian king, and the king himself may have thought it humiliating to go back and reconsider something he had already decreed. Royal code of honor would have made it out of the question for the king to rescind an order.

6:10. prayer three times a day toward Jerusalem. Prayer toward Jerusalem had been established practice as early as the building of the temple by Solomon (1 Kings 8:35). The frequency of prayer in Israelite practice had not been established in law. Neither the Old Testament nor the Dead Sea Scrolls show any norms other than the pattern established by the morning and evening sacrifice regularly offered in the temple. As mentioned in the comment on 6:7, normal Persian practice called for three or five daily prayers.

6:17. signet ring. Current evidence suggests that the early Persian kings used cylinder seals for empire business and stamp seals or signet rings for personal business, though the latter were growing in usage through this period. A signet ring held the official seal of the king by which he authorized the business of the empire. Only a few of these have been found by archaeologists. The seals were typically made of chalcedony and featured pictures of the king doing heroic acts (like killing beasts) under the protection of the winged sun disk (representing Ahura Mazda). Many of the Persepolis fortification tablets contained stamp seal impressions.

6:19-23. innocence by ordeal. "Ordeal" describes a judicial situation in which the accused is placed in the hand of God using some mechanism, generally one that will put the accused in jeopardy. If the deity intervenes to protect the accused from harm, the verdict is innocent. Most trials by ordeal in the ancient Near East involved dangers such as water, fire or poison. When the accused was exposed to these threats, he or she was in effect being assumed guilty until the deity declared otherwise.

6:24. wives and children included in punishment. This is more severe than any of the legislation found in the legal collections in Mesopotamia. In the Old Testament when the family is included in the punishment, it usually reflects that the family line is being wiped out. This extends the punishment beyond life to legacy (see comment on Josh 7:25). Herodotus tells how during the reign of Darius, a high-ranking official and close associate of the king was judged to be involved in a revolt. As a result most of his family was executed.

6:28. Darius/Cyrus. For those who identify these two as the same, the translation "the reign of Darius, that is, the reign of Cyrus the Persian" is acceptable (see comment on 6:1).

7:1-28
Vision of the Four Beasts

7:1. chronology. This vision takes place before the events of both chapters five and six. It is difficult to tell what the first year of Belshazzar was. It should not be equated with the first year of his father, Nabonidus (556), but more likely with the beginning of his coregency when Nabonidus set up his royal residency in Teima (552). It is unknown, however, whether Belshazzar was immediately made coregent. The Nabonidus Chronicle first notes Belshazzar's coregency in Nabonidus's seventh year (549), but the Chronicles for years four, five and half of six are not available. It is in Nabonidus's sixth year, 550, that the empire succession takes shape as Cyrus defeats the Medes and the Medo-Persian empire is formed. As a tangential note of interest, a dream text of Nabonidus is preserved from *his* first year, in which it was foretold that Cyrus would conquer the Medes.

7:2. winds of heaven on the great sea. This description indicates a typical mythical scene in which the churning of the cosmic ocean disturbs the creatures (often sea monsters) who represent the forces of chaos and disorder. In *Enuma Elish* the sky god, Anu, creates the four winds that stir up the deep and its goddess, Tiamat. There, as here, it is a disruptive wind bringing unrest.

7:3. beasts with odd characteristics. In the Babylonian omen series called *Shumma Izbu*, with which Daniel would have been well acquainted from his training, various birth abnormalities are recorded along with what sort of event they forecast. Several of the descriptions of the beasts in Daniel's visions can also be found in the *Shumma Izbu* series. Some of the common elements in the descriptions include the creature being raised up on one side and having multiple heads or multiple horns. Most of the observations of abnormalities were made of domesticated species, a large proportion being sheep and goats. Some of the abnormalities are described by compari-

son to various wild beasts. There are examples of sheep giving birth to lambs that (in some way) resemble a wolf, a fox, a tiger, a lion, a bear or a leopard. In this chapter, Daniel is not observing these abnormalities in reality but in a dream, thus combining two important omen mechanisms (dreams and odd births). The dream books often feature ominological information (celestial or extispicy omens) viewed in dreams and carrying the same significance as if they were viewed in reality. Being familiar with both literatures, Daniel would have been inclined to interpret the dream along the lines suggested in the *izbu* omens. The omen interpretations often concerned political events such as "the prince will take the land of his enemy." Nevertheless, Daniel's dream goes well beyond the *izbu* omens. The descriptions suggest that he does see fearsome chaos beasts rather than simply sheep or goats with odd characteristics. Additionally, many of the features of Daniel's beasts are neither found nor expected in *izbu* omens, like wings and iron teeth. For this reason it is also important to understand the nature of some of the mythological imagery that pertains to the dream.

7:3. beast imagery. A number of different mythological sources offer similarities to the beast imagery used by Daniel. A seventh-century Akkadian piece called *A Vision of the Netherworld* includes fifteen divine beings in the form of various hybrid beasts. Following that, Nergal, king of the netherworld, is seen seated on his throne, and identifies himself as the son of the king of the gods. There are many significant differences between this vision and Daniel's, but the similarities in imagery are helpful background.

7:3. out of the sea. In the Bible as well as in the ancient Near East, the sea represents chaos and disorder, as do the sea monsters that live there. The obvious physical struggle between the sea and the land as well as the fierce, seemingly unstoppable energy displayed by the savage sea gave rise to cosmic myths in the ancient Near East. The *Enuma Elish* creation epic from Babylon describes how Marduk vanquished Tiamat, goddess of watery chaos, while she was in the form of a dragon. Much of the cycle of stories about Baal in Ugaritic legend involve Baal's struggle against his rival Yamm, the god of the sea. Similarly, the Ugaritic epic has both Anat and Baal claim to have conquered Litan, the seven-headed dragon, and thus gained mastery over the seas. In Psalm 104:26 Yahweh is said to play with Leviathan, and in Job 41:1-11 God challenges Job to show the same control over

Leviathan that God has. The kingdoms represented by these beasts are therefore associated with the forces of chaos that bring disorder to God's world and need to be overcome.

7:4. symbol of lion with wings. Winged figures are common in the art and sculpture of Mesopotamia. The winged bulls and winged lions, both with human heads, flanked thrones and entryways in Assyria, Babylon and Persia. Winged human figures (wearing headdresses with horns) are known as early as the eighth century and stood guard at Cyrus's palace in Pasargadae. Winged creatures also figure in dreams. Herodotus reports a dream that Cyrus had just a few days before his death, in which he saw Darius (then a young man) with wings that overshadowed Asia and Europe. In the *Anzu Myth* (see next entry), Anzu is defeated by having his wings plucked. This motif is also significant in the story of Etana, who helps an eagle whose wings have been plucked.

7:7. the fourth beast. In the *Anzu Myth* a composite creature (Anzu) steals the Tablet of Destinies, which comprised a sort of constitution of the cosmos. The goddess Mami is called forth, who created all the gods, the most ancient of deities. She is asked to send her son, Ninurta, to battle Anzu. The god Ninurta defeats the monster and recovers the tablet. Ninurta (who is also known for his defeat of other beasts such as the bull-man in the sea, the six-headed ram and the seven-headed serpent), is then granted dominion and glory. There are certainly many differences with Daniel 7, and there should be no thought that the *Anzu Myth* figures prominently here. Those who would have been familiar with the *Anzu Myth*, however, would likely have seen echoes of it in this vision. The tale has roots as early as the beginning of the second millennium but is principally known from mid-first millennium Babylonian texts. One ninth-century relief inscription from Nimrud pictures Ninurta fighting a beast with lion's legs but standing upright on eagle's feet. It is feathered and has two wings, lion paws for hands with sharp, extended claws, a gaping mouth with fierce teeth and two horns. It is thought to be a depiction of Anzu.

7:7. ten horns. It was common in Mesopotamia for kings and gods to wear crowns featuring protruding or embossed horns. Sometimes the sets of horns were stacked one upon another in tiers. The winged lion from Ashurnasirpal's palace has a conical crown on its human head with three pairs of tiered horns embossed on it. Another interesting connection is that in *Enuma Elish* Tiamat is the fear-

some beast that the hero of the gods has to defeat. To help her she creates eleven monsters that must also be defeated. Here also the fourth beast is associated with eleven horns (the ten plus the little horn).

7:9. Ancient of Days. In Canaanite mythology the head of the pantheon is El, an aged deity addressed by the title "father of years." In the Mesopotamian *Anzu Myth* the ancient one is a goddess, Mami, whose son defeats the monster (Anzu) and is granted dominion.

7:9. throne with wheels. A wheeled throne flaming with fire is also described in Ezekiel's throne vision (Ezek 1, 10). The prototypes of wheeled thrones go back to the end of the third millennium as pictured on cylinder seals. These were simply chariots or carts used for processions for the image of the deity. Some seal impressions even picture composite creatures drawing the vehicle. Continued use of thrones with wheels can be seen in reliefs down into the ninth and eighth centuries.

7:10. books opened. Every royal court in the ancient world kept records of day-to-day activities and detailed accounts of the events that transpired. The actions of the beast/king would have been logged, and that record is now brought out to provide evidence as he is brought before the divine court for judgment.

7:13-14. son of man. The phrase "son of man" is simply a common Semitic expression to describe someone or something as human or, at least, humanlike. In Israelite theology, Yahweh is the high God and also is portrayed as the rider on the clouds. In Canaanite mythology, the roles described here are filled by the god El, the high god of great age (see comment on 7:9) and his son, Baal, the rider on the clouds. In one of the Baal myths, Yamm, who represents the chaos of the sea, is defeated, and Baal is declared king and granted everlasting dominion. In the cosmic conflict myths of Mesopotamia (such as *Enuma Elish* or the *Anzu Myth*) a deity (Marduk and Ninurta respectively) defeats the threatening chaos and regains authority and dominion for the gods and for himself. Daniel has been trained in such literature, and his revelations build on that familiarity, though the common motifs are entirely repackaged. Intertestamental literature such as the book of *1 Enoch* as well as New Testament and early Christian literature identifies the son of man with the Messiah.

7:16. one standing there. Interpreting angels were present in Ezekiel and Zechariah, and are common in apocalyptic literature from the Old Testament period on. No such figure is known in Mesopotamian literature.

7:17. the four kingdoms. For information on

the four-kingdom pattern in ancient literature, see comment on 2:36-40. The identification of the four kingdoms has occasioned much controversy. The text offers no interpretation of any of the characteristics of the dream beasts, except that the horns are kings. It is difficult to know whether the characteristics (e.g., three ribs in the mouth) symbolize historical events or whether they serve another purpose, such as offering omen insight (see comment on 7:3). Alternatively, they may serve only to give flavor to the imagery. If they do represent historical realities, still only speculation can suggest associations. Are the three ribs in the mouth of the second beast representative of Lydia, Babylon and Egypt, the three major conquests of the Medo-Persian empire? Or are they the Urartians, Manneans and Scythians conquered by the Medes (Jer 51:27-29)? Are the four heads and wings of the third beast the four generals who divided Alexander's empire among them? Or are they the four kings of Persia alluded to in Daniel 11:2? Are the ten horns of the fourth beast a kingdom still future? Or are they the ten independent states that Alexander's empire becomes by the end of the third century B.C.? The text does not answer these questions, nor can background information resolve them.

7:18. saints. The text refers to "holy ones" who are not only the eventual recipients of the kingdom (vv. 18, 22, 27) but also the victims of the oppression (vv. 21, 25). While many interpreters think this refers to godly people, the term is most frequently used to describe supernatural beings (this is also true in the use of the equivalent term in Ugaritic and Aramaic, as well as in the Dead Sea Scrolls literature). This would receive further support since it is the host of heaven that is under assault in the related vision of next chapter (8:10).

7:24. the ten kings. At least on this point the text makes it clear that the ten horns represent ten kingdoms/kings. The ten kingdoms that spring from Alexander's empire are Ptolemaic Egypt, Seleucia, Macedon, Pergamum, Pontus, Bithynia, Cappadocia, Armenia, Parthia and Bactria. Yet others believe that the ten are successors to the Roman empire and as such, may be still future.

7:25. change set times and laws. In Mesopotamian thinking the times and laws are governed by the cosmic decrees embodied in the Tablet of Destinies. They are normally entrusted to either the assembly of the gods or to the head of the pantheon. In a number of ancient tales they are misappropriated. In *Enuma Elish* Kingu, Tiamat's sidekick, has them. In the

Anzu Myth (see comment on 7:7) a monster (Anzu) stole them and threatened to wield them, thus putting everything in the cosmos in jeopardy.

7:25. time, times and half a time. The word "time" used here is the same as that used in 4:16 (see comment there). The word "times" is simply a plural and does not necessarily suggest two times. The Babylonians were very sophisticated mathematicians, and early on the gods had been represented numerically (Sin = 30; Ishtar = 15). Furthermore, the gods, with their numerical valuations and planetary associations, figured in the astronomical terminology by which the cyclic movements in the heavens were used in calendrical calculations. All of these factors make it very difficult to unpack the significance of this phrase.

8:1-27
Vision of the Goat and the Ram

8:1. chronology. Determination of what year this refers to shares the same difficulties as mentioned in the comment on 7:1. Belshazzar's third year is likely either 550 or 547. In the vision of chapter seven, only one empire (Babylon) was identified by name. Now, two years later, two more empires are named.

8:2. geography. The Ulai Canal is in the vicinity of Susa, the capital of the territory of Elam, some two hundred miles from Babylon. The city will later become the royal residence of the Achaemenid kings of Persia, so it is a suitable locale for the vision. The canal is an artificial one on the north side of the city that was closely associated with Susa both in cuneiform and classical sources. Daniel could have actually made the journey, but it is more likely that he is transported in a vision as Ezekiel sometimes experiences.

8:3. ram as astral sign of Persia. In later literature (first several centuries A.D.), the signs of the zodiac are associated with countries, and the ram is associated with Persia. There is no evidence, however, that such an association was made as early as the book of Daniel. The concept of the zodiac has its origin in the intertestamental period.

8:9. small horn. This appears to be a reference to the Seleucid king, Antiochus IV Epiphanes, whose activities in the second century will be detailed in the next several entries.

8:9. Beautiful Land. From 11:16, 41, it is clear that this is a reference to the land of Israel. Antiochus III marched east against Parthia, Armenia and Bactria from 212 to 205, and in 200 gained control of Palestine at the Battle of Panium. Both he and his son, Antiochus IV, were frustrated in their attempts to gain control of Egypt (to the south). Antiochus IV also had campaigns to the east (against Armenia and Elam) and was well known for his actions against Judah and Jerusalem (see comments on below and on 11:21-39).

8:10. starry host overthrown. The host of heaven in the ancient Near East referred to the assembly of the gods, many of whom were represented by celestial bodies (whether planets or stars). The Bible sometimes uses the phrase to refer to the illegitimate worship of these deities (see comment on Deut 4:19). On other occasions, the phrase is used for Yahweh's angelic council (see comment on 2 Chron 18:18). A third type of usage treats the term as a reference to rebel angels (perhaps in Is 24:21; commonly in the intertestamental literature). Finally, it can refer simply to the stars with no personalities behind them (Is 40:26). In the destruction described in *Erra and Ishum*, Erra says that he will make planets shed their splendor and will wrench stars from the sky. Here the starry host represents one side in the cosmic battle and falls temporarily victim to the evil horn, thus suggesting they are some of God's minions.

8:11. daily sacrifice. The daily sacrifice was a burnt offering occurring every morning and evening (see comments on Ex 29:38 and Num 28:1-8). It represented the most basic maintenance of the sanctuary and was foundational for preserving the presence of Yahweh in their midst.

8:14. 2,300 evenings and mornings until reconsecration. If 2,300 sacrifices will be missed, and two are offered each day, 1,150 days will pass (roughly three years and two months). Antiochus IV Epiphanes instituted sacrifices to his gods in the temple on the twenty-fifth of Kislev (December) in the year 167 B.C., but he had put a stop to the Jewish rituals some time earlier that year (reported in 1 Macc 1:44-51), and the exact date of the proclamation and its enforcement is not known. The rededication of the temple in the aftermath of the Maccabean revolt took place three years to the day after the desecration on the twenty-fifth of Kislev, 164.

8:16. Gabriel. This is the first reference to the name of an angel in the Bible. The only other angel named in the Bible is Michael (see 10:13). In intertestamental literature (*1 Enoch*) Gabriel is in charge of Paradise. In the War Scroll from Qumran he is one of the archangels who surround the throne of God. He is the one who brings the message to Mary of the impending birth of Jesus (Luke 1:19). Angels not only delivered messages from deity,

but they explained those messages and answered questions concerning them. Thus Gabriel is seen here as one who can interpret the vision. In the ancient world's polytheistic context, the messengers of the gods were generally gods themselves (of lower rank). In Mesopotamia we find individuals such as Nuska and Kakka, while Hermes serves the function in Greek mythology. In a dream of Nabonidus a young man appears to offer an interpretation of a celestial omen that has been observed.

8:22. the kingdoms. The king represented by the large horn is undisputed: Alexander the Great, whose Greek army swept away the Persian Empire between 335 and 331 B.C. When Alexander died suddenly in 323 at the age of 33, the two who could claim ancestral rights to the kingdom (his illegitimate half brother, Philip Arrideus, and the son of Alexander and Roxane, Alexander IV, born two months after his father's death) were installed as figureheads while the operation of the kingdom was entrusted to three experienced officers, Antipater (viceroy of Macedon), Perdiccas (head of the armies) and Craterus (in charge of the treasury and advisor to Arrideus). By 321 these three regents had sufficiently antagonized one another that a battle was instigated by a fourth player, Ptolemy, who had been given a position of authority in Egypt. Craterus was killed in battle, and Perdiccas was assassinated in a mutiny by several of his generals, one of whom was Seleucus. Meanwhile Antipater took the lead and placed a friend, Antigonus, in Perdiccas's position. In 319 Antipater died an old man, and despite his appointment of another, within two years his son, Cassander, had gained control of Macedonia and most of the territory of Greece. In the summer of 317, those opposing Cassander executed Philip Arrideus. Alexander IV and his mother Roxane were placed under house arrest and effectively deposed, though they were not executed until 310. The three who ruled were now Cassander in the west, Ptolemy in Egypt and Antigonus in the east. As Antigonus sought to solidify his control of the east, he attempted to dominate Seleucus (now governor of Babylon), who in 315 exposed Antigonus's schemes for power to the other leaders, Ptolemy, Cassander and Lysimachus (governor of Thrace). Battles continued to be fought until 311 when Antigonus parleyed for peace with Ptolemy, Cassander and Lysimachus, leaving Seleucus isolated but in control of Babylonia. By 309 Ptolemy decided to move against Antigonus but pushed too far and ended up in 306 under the attack of Antigonus and his son, Demetrius. Antigonus's invasion of

Egypt failed, and in 305 Ptolemy, along with Cassander, Seleucus and Lysimachus (most likely to be identified as the four horns), declared themselves the successor kings to Alexander. Yet it was still four more years until Antigonus was killed in the Battle of Ipsus, 301. Cassander died only three years later (298), and Demetrius continued to cause trouble, but the division of the empire into four parts represents the fallout of this twenty-year succession struggle.

8:25. stern-faced king. The description in verse 23-25 pertains to Antiochus IV Epiphanes, who reigned from 175 to 164 B.C. His wisdom was corrupted for use in hypocrisy, intrigue, double-crossing and treachery. For summary of his actions see comments on 11:21-39.

8:26. seal up the vision. See comment on 12:4.

9:1-27
Seventy-Sevens

9:1. chronology. Assuming Darius the Mede's reign coincides with that of Cyrus, his first year would be 539. Again, the timing is significant as a major change of empires is in process (see comment on 7:1).

9:2. Jeremiah's prophecy. In 597 the prophet Jeremiah wrote a letter to the exiles (Jer 29) informing them that the length of the exile would be seventy years. This is most likely the subject of Daniel's interest as he ponders whether the time might be right for the return.

9:3. fasting, sackcloth and ashes. In the Old Testament the religious use of fasting is often in connection with making a request before God. The principle is that the importance of the request causes an individual to be so concerned about his or her spiritual condition that physical necessities fade into the background. In this sense the act of fasting is designed as a process leading to purification and humbling oneself before God (Ps 69:10). The practice of putting dirt, dust or ashes on one's head was a typical sign of mourning throughout the Old Testament and into the New Testament period. It is a practice also known from Mesopotamia and Canaan. Many mourning rites originated as a means for the living to identify with the dead. It is easy to see how dust on the head and torn clothes would be symbolic representations of burial and decay. Sackcloth was made of goat or camel hair and was coarse and uncomfortable. In many cases the sackcloth was only a loin covering.

9:17-18. desolation of city and sanctuary. The city of Jerusalem had been destroyed by the Babylonians in 586 and was little more than a desolate ruin. Fifty years had come and gone since the temple had been dismantled and razed.

9:21. Gabriel. See comment on 8:16.

9:21. swift flight. In Isaiah 6 the creatures called seraphim fly, and in Zechariah 5 there is a vision of women with wings who fly, but this is the only occasion when a being identified as an angel flies. Though other supernatural creatures (the ones listed earlier, as well as cherubim) are portrayed with wings, angels (messengers) are not, despite the artistic renditions of the past fifteen hundred years. In Mesopotamian art protective genies are portrayed with wings, as are a variety of demons. In intertestamental literature the earliest reference to flying angels is in 1 Enoch 61:1 (though cherubim and seraphim are by then included in the category). The Hebrew construction used is a complex one, and many commentators have concluded (with good cause) that the text expresses weariness ($y'p$) rather than flight ($'wp$).

9:21. time of the evening sacrifice. From the Israelite perspective the day ended about six o'clock in the evening (rather than our midnight). As a result the evening sacrifice was offered late in the afternoon, between three and four o'clock.

9:24. seventy sevens. A period of seven years was the sabbatical year cycle (see especially Lev 26:34-35 and the reference to it in 2 Chron 36:21). Seven sabbatical year cycles constituted a Jubilee cycle, at the end of which slaves were set free and land was returned to its proper owner (Lev 25). Seventy sabbatical cycles equal ten Jubilee cycles. The first Jubilee cycle is distinguished here (seven sevens in v. 25), and the last sabbatical cycle is distinguished (the seventieth week). It is clear, then, that these numbers are laden with theological significance that give them a schematic appearance. In Mesopotamia the numbers seven and seventy represent a full measure of time. Schematic usage of the term "weeks" can be seen in Jewish literature in the book of 1 Enoch (in the Apocalypse of Weeks), and the period of seventy weeks is also found at Qumran. The schematic use of time has been referred to as "chronography," which is to be differentiated from "chronology."

9:24. seal up vision and prophecy. See comment on 12:4. Sealing concerns authentication. The authentication of Jeremiah's prophecy and Daniel's vision will only be accomplished when the designated period of time passes.

9:24. anoint the most holy. The consecration ceremony that involves anointing and purification of the Holy of Holies in Exodus 29 (especially vv. 36-37) is sufficient background for understanding this statement. The desecration of the holy place requires its purification. Assyrian temple inscriptions also refer to the anointing of a temple that is to be repaired and restored by a future prince.

9:25. word to restore and rebuild. The NIV translates this as "decree," but in its note indicates that it is a "word"—and this usually refers to a prophetic oracle, not a royal decree. In fact the same combination of verb and noun ("word going out") has just been used in verse 23. This identification of the "word" is even more likely in light of the fact that Daniel is reflecting on the writing of Jeremiah, who proclaimed the prophetic oracle concerning return and restoration in his letter to the exiles (see comment on 9:2). Notice especially Jeremiah 29:10. The "going forth" of this word would then be dated to sometime between 597 and 594.

9:25-26. anointed one. It is important to note that the noun here is indefinite, thus *a* messiah (*an* anointed one, as in the NIV note), rather than *the* Messiah. The prophetic literature had not yet adopted this term as a technical term for the ideal, future Davidic king (besides this chapter, the term is used only in the prophets in Is 45:1, referring to Cyrus, and Hab 3:13, in a generic way). Priests and kings were both anointed to their tasks in Israel. Some have maintained that the two references to anointed individuals require two different anointed individuals, one after the first cycle of forty-nine years (plausibly Cyrus, since he has already been given anointed status in the prophets, though leaders of the return such as Zerubbabel or Joshua would not be impossible); the second to be cut off before the last week. This view is favored by the Hebrew punctuation that suggests a period should be placed between the two numbers (as reflected in the RSV) rather than after the sixty-two sevens. It was forty-nine years between the fall of Jerusalem (586) and the decree of Cyrus (538).

9:25. streets and a trench. "Streets" refers to the city squares and plazas that are the major features of city planning. This is where the public functions of the city take place, from government to merchant activities. "Trench" can only refer to the dry moat that was a common element of a city's defenses. The combination indicates that Jerusalem will again be a place of security and prosperity, providing all of the civic functions of a smoothly operating urban center.

9:26. anointed one cut off. The most common identification of the cut off anointed one is Onias III, the high priest murdered by Antio-

chus Epiphanes in 171 (referred to in 11:22). Many find this an irresistible option because it initiated a seven-year period of persecution in Jerusalem that included the desecration of the temple in 167.

9:27. abomination of desolation. The consistent use of the noun translated "desolation" (*shmm,* see also 8:13) is quite intentional. The Syrian Baal Shamem ("Lord of Heaven") was the deity whose worship was instituted in the temple on the altar of sacrifice by the Syrian citizens who were brought into Jerusalem by Antiochus and his military commander, Apollonius. Antiochus worshiped this deity as Olympian Zeus. This desecration perpetrated by Antiochus served as a prototype for all future desecrations. Even in the sixth century, however, this concept had precedent. In a work called *The Verse Account of Nabonidus* the priests of Marduk list the offenses of Nabonidus that purportedly led Marduk to dethrone him in favor of the Persian king Cyrus. Among the accusations are that he built an abomination, a work of unholiness (a statue of the god Nanna placed in the temple of Marduk), and ordered an end to the most important rituals.

10:1-21

The Final Vision

10:1. chronology. The third year of Cyrus's rule in Babylon was 537/536. This is very close to the time when the first wave of Jews are returning from captivity and beginning the rebuilding of the temple (recorded in the first chapter of Ezra). Verse 4 indicates that the vision took place on the twenty-fourth day of the first month (Nisan). This would be in early April. The celebration of Passover and the Feast of Unleavened Bread (14-21 Nisan) would have come and gone during Daniel's three weeks of preparation.

10:1. Cyrus. Cyrus of Persia was one of the greatest conquerors in world history. He inherited the throne of Persia from his father, Cambyses I, in 559. In 556 the Babylonian king, Nabonidus, motivated by a dream, abandoned the treaty that his country had maintained with the Medes for over half a century and made a treaty with Cyrus. This gave Cyrus the freedom to move against the Medes (ruled by his grandfather, Astyages), whom he conquered in 550. The new Medo-Persian empire was thus formed, with control over the entirety of Iran. By 546 he defeated the Anatolian kingdom of Lydia and Ionia. For the next five years he consolidated his control over the tribes in northeastern Iran.

All of this paved the way for his crowning achievement, the conquest of Babylon in 539 B.C. The whole of the Near East (excluding Egypt) was under control of the Persians when Cyrus was killed in battle in 530. For more information see comments in Ezra 1.

10:3. choice food. In extrabiblical Jewish apocalyptic literature, fasting is often essential preparation for receiving a vision. Daniel is not undertaking a total fast but abstaining from pastry, meat and wine—thus returning to a more spartan diet. It should be noted that while this verse does not use the same terminology as the text at 1:5, it is now clear that Daniel had not made a lifelong commitment to bland food.

10:3. lotions. In the absence of showers and deodorants, personal grooming involved the use of perfumed oils. Inattention to such amenities was characteristic of mourning (2 Sam 12:20; 14:2).

10:5-6. description. White linen is the typical clothing for priests as well as for supernatural operatives (Ezek 9-10). The gold waistband is lavishly impressive, but most of the description focuses on the physical features of the man (usually identified as Gabriel). The five features described ([1] body/chrysolite; [2] face/lightning; [3] eyes/torches; [4] limbs/bronze; [5] voice/multitude) can also be found in the descriptions of the creatures that bear the chariot throne in Ezekiel 1. The general appearance of the vehicle is compared to a torch and lightning, the wheels by which the creatures stand are compared to chrysolite, and the legs of the creatures are like burnished bronze. All of the same Hebrew terms are used. In Ezekiel 1 the sound of the creatures' wings was like an army, whereas the angel in Daniel has a voice that sounds like a multitude. Daniel is clear, however, that his visitor had the appearance of a man rather than the composite beasts seen by Ezekiel. In the Babylonian wisdom composition entitled *Ludlul Bel Nemeqi* the sufferer, after a long period of suffering and mourning, has a dream in which he sees an impressive young man (both in physique and attire) standing over him, resulting in his body being numbed. The individual's message is not preserved, but it is generally assumed that it had to do with approaching deliverance.

10:13. prince of the Persian kingdom. The context demands that this antagonist be considered a supernatural being rather than a royal human individual. The literature from Qumran also uses the title "prince" as a reference to chief angels. There is no clearer evidence than this chapter on the biblical concept

that conflicts in human history are paralleled by conflicts in the supernatural realm. Indications of this concept are already evident in the concept of the divine warrior (see comments on 1 Sam 5:2; 17:37; 17:45-47). Just as the Israelites had a divine assembly filled with angels instead of gods, so they eventually exchanged the concept of national patron deities for a concept of supernatural creatures who represented the interests of a nation. This reflects the ongoing process of emptying the heavens of competing deities while retaining a supernaturalist view of reality.

10:13. Michael. As indicated with the name Gabriel (see comment on 8:16), there are no names given for angels in earlier literature. Michael becomes a much more familiar figure in the Qumran literature and in the intertestamental literature, primarily the book of *Enoch*. He is considered the guardian of the people of Israel.

10:20. Persia, Greece. As in chapter 8, reference is made here to the sequence of empires in which the Greek empire of Alexander will supersede the Persian empire.

10:21. Book of Truth. This book has been compared to the Babylonian Tablet of Destinies, which was considered to contain and dictate the course of history and the cosmos (see comment on 7:25). This not only fits with the nature of the material that is revealed in chapter 11, but it accords with the introduction to that material in 11:2, where the information is specifically categorized as "the truth."

11:1-45
Kings of North and South

11:2. four Persian kings. Cyrus is already king when this is taking place, so he would not be counted among the four. His immediate successors were Cambyses, Smerdis (Bardiya/ Gaumata), Darius, Xerxes and Artaxerxes. Seven more kings followed in the royal line before Alexander the Great brought about the fall of the empire. The last was Darius III. Xerxes was arguably the richest of the kings and was the one who was most involved with battles against the Greeks. This spans about seventy years of Persian history.

11:3. mighty king. The mighty king is none other than Alexander the Great. The text skips about 130 years from the end of Xerxes' reign to 336, when Alexander took the throne of Macedon. Within five years his military prowess had toppled the Persian empire and ushered in the Greek.

11:4. division to four winds. Alexander died in 323, and a twenty-year struggle for succession ensued that eventually led to a four-way division of the empire (see comment on 8:22). Two of those divisions were in the Aegean region (Cassander had Greece and Macedonia; Lysimachus had Thrace), while the other two divided up the Near East (Ptolemy had Egypt and Palestine; Seleucus had Syria, Mesopotamia and Persia). The Ptolemaic line is going to represented by "the king of the South," while the Seleucid line will be represented by "the king of the North."

11:5. Ptolemy I Soter (305-285). The text will now focus on the two kingdoms (Ptolemaic Egypt and Seleucia) that flanked Palestine. Ptolemy was a power broker and instigator during much of the twenty-year succession struggle (playing a significant role as early as 321), but Seleucus emerged as the stronger party with the largest kingdom. Ptolemy's military action in 321 broke up the original group that had assumed power after Alexander's death. One of his few failures came in 309, when he attempted to move against Antigonus (Seleucus's predecessor). By 306 it was clear that he had overextended himself, and he had to fall back and regroup. Still in 306 he was able to declare himself king of Egypt.

11:5. Seleucus I Nicator (312-280). After Alexander died, Perdiccas became head of the armies, and Seleucus was one of his generals. He was among the group that assassinated Perdiccas. Seleucus briefly gained control of Babylon, but was forced to flee when Perdiccas's successor, Antigonus, moved against him in 316. He then served as a general for Ptolemy from 316 to 312. They fought together against Antigonus at the Battle of Gaza. After Antigonus's defeat at Gaza, Seleucus regained control of Babylon, which became the center of his power. Verses four and five cover the period from Alexander's death through the

reigns of the first kings of the two empires, about forty years.

11:6. failed alliance of Ptolemies and Seleucids (246). The text now moves forward about forty years. These years had witnessed the first and second Syrian wars (274-271; 260-253), mostly over the control of the trade routes, ports and natural resources of Syria. In the aftermath of the second war there was interest in peace, and the text now focuses on this pivotal moment in history. About 252, Ptolemy II Philadelphus (285-246) sent his daughter, Berenice, with her entourage to marry the Seleucid king, Antiochus II Theos (261-246), and thereby to establish an alliance between their kingdoms. The alliance would give Ptolemy control of Syria and Antiochus control of Asia Minor. The fragile relationship held for a couple of years, and Berenice had a child, but a former wife of Antiochus, Laodice, whose sons had been cut off from succession, allegedly poisoned Antiochus and consequently had Berenice and her son (along with many from her entourage) murdered. Ptolemy II also had died in that year. Needless to say, the alliance crumbled and the next fifty years are full of tumultuous warfare between the two kingdoms.

11:7. Ptolemy III Euergetes (246-221). Upon hearing of the death of Antiochus, Berenice summoned her brother (who had acceded to the throne in Egypt) to intervene in Syria in order to support her son's claims to the throne. He was unable to secure control of Syria before the murder of his nephew and sister. In 245 (Third Syrian War) he pressed his invasion of Seleucia and successfully attacked the Syrian capitals of Antioch (on the Orontes) and Seleucia (this is Seleucia Pieria in Syria) and took much plunder. The cities were quickly recovered by Seleucus II after Ptolemy re-

---

AKKADIAN APOCALYPSES

In Akkadian literature there are a few pieces (dating from the twelfth century to the third or fourth century) that have been labeled apocalypses (the Marduk Prophecy, the Shulgi Prophecy, the Uruk Prophecy, the Dynastic Prophecy, and Text A). It has been demonstrated that there is a literary relationship between some of these works and the (astrological) omen texts, thereby placing them in Daniel's area of specialty. One prominent feature of these is that they ostensibly predict a series of unnamed kings who will arise, summarizing a couple of their deeds. Often these deeds are of a negative sort and the intention of the literature is to condemn those kings. Invariably the sequence ends with a king who will arise and set things right (the Dynastic Prophecy may be an exception, but the end is so fragmentary that it is difficult to be certain). These have been recognized as pieces of propaganda composed during the reign of the last king listed, who is using this genre to indict his predecessors and legitimate his own reign. As such they could be called "pseudoprophecies," because their "predictions" in actuality occur after the fact. Chapter 11 of Daniel undeniably shares some common characteristics with this genre as it presents a sequence of unnamed kings and a summary of some of the events of their reign. Daniel, however, has no king at the end of the sequence to promote. The opposite is true, as the last, Antiochus Epiphanes, is the worst of the lot. As throughout the book, then, Daniel uses a recognized motif but totally repackages it for his own distinctive use. For more information on apocalyptic literature in general see the sidebar at Zechariah 1.

turned to Egypt.

11:9. Seleucus II Callinicus (246-226). Laodice's son, Seleucus II, emerged the beneficiary of all of the treachery and intrigue of his mother. In 243 he attempted to gain control of southern Syria and Palestine. Not only was he unsuccessful, but the momentum turned against him and he ended up losing territory.

11:10. Seleucus III (226-223). For the last fifteen years of his reign, Seleucus II was engaged in an ongoing struggle with his brother, Antiochus Hierax. Both died about the same time, and Seleucus III came to the throne. Verse ten telescopes the events of the next ten years. Seleucus III was killed in a campaign against Pergamum in Asia Minor. He was succeeded by his brother, Antiochus III, who began mustering troops for the Fourth Syrian War (221-217) against Ptolemy IV.

11:10. Antiochus III the Great (223-187). The next nine verses are occupied with the deeds of Antiochus III and cover about thirty years. His reign is considered significant for the text of Daniel because he is responsible for taking Palestine out of Ptolemaic control and incorporating it into the Seleucid kingdom, ending a century of Ptolemaic rule over Israel. This began in 218, when he successfully penetrated Galilee and Samaria.

11:11. Ptolemy IV Philopator (221-203). For most of the years of the Fourth Syrian War, Ptolemy IV had little success militarily against Antiochus the Great and only forestalled his progress south through repeated diplomatic initiatives. Many of Antiochus's successes were carried out with the help of traitors rather than through military power or genius. In fact his lackadaisical tactics allowed Ptolemy to gather, train and field a significant armed force by 217.

11:11-13. Fourth and Fifth Syrian Wars. In 217 Ptolemy IV engaged Antiochus III at the Battle of Raphia for what would turn out to be the climactic battle of the Fourth Syrian War. Raphia was a traditional dividing line between Palestine and Egypt, about twenty miles southwest of Gaza on the Mediterranean coast. Antiochus claimed an army of seventy thousand, but even with the superior size of his armies he was beaten badly by the Egyptians. This victory restored Syro-Palestine to the control of the Ptolemies. This status was maintained until the death of Ptolemy IV in 204. The suspicious circumstances of the death of Ptolemy IV (still in his thirties) brought his six-year-old son, Ptolemy V Epiphanes (204-180), to the throne of Egypt. Antiochus took the opportunity of conflict over who was in charge to initiate the Fifth

Syrian War (202-200), allied with Philip V of Macedon.

11:14-16. Antiochus III's occupation of Palestine. The Battle of Gaza in 201 gained Antiochus temporary control of Palestine, but he was pushed back again by Egyptian forces under the command of Scopas. In the next year, however, at the Battle of Panion (at one of the sources of the Jordan; the New Testament Caesarea Philippi, modern Banias), Antiochus defeated the Egyptians and took control of Palestine from them for the last time. At the same time, the Romans were getting a foothold in Greece in the Second Macedonian War.

11:14. violent men. The book of 3 Maccabees records a visit of Ptolemy IV to Jerusalem after the Battle of Raphia in which he was treated very badly when he wished to enter the temple. There is a question concerning the historicity of the account. There were pro-Seleucid (led by Onias II, the high priest) and pro-Ptolemaic factions (from the powerful Tobiad family, competitors for the office of high priest) within Judea at this period. Sources do not provide enough information to determine which party might be alluded to in this verse.

11:17-19. Antiochus III's defeat by Rome, Scipio (191, 190). The increasing Roman control in Greece was established by a peace accord in 196. The Greeks who were unhappy with this new state of affairs made contact with Antiochus, urging him to come to their aid. By this time, Antiochus, anticipating that he would need to neutralize Egypt, had entered a marriage alliance, sending his daughter, Cleopatra, to be Ptolemy V's bride. He expected her to also be a useful spy, but in this he was disappointed as her loyalties turned to her new husband. Nevertheless, he made his move toward Greece in 192. Constantly shifting alliances eventually worked against him, and he lost a large portion of his ten thousand troops at Thermopylae in 191. Antiochus then resorted to sea battle to try to keep the Romans out of Asia Minor but was again unsuccessful. By 190 the larger Seleucid army of seventy-thousand men had arrived to reinforce Antiochus's positions. Roman troops under Scipio were only half this strength when the forces met at Magnesia (about fifty miles north of Ephesus). Yet due to lack of training and tactical errors on the part of the Seleucid army, Antiochus was defeated and much of his army slaughtered. The terms of surrender were humiliating, devastating and accepted without argument.

11:20. Seleucus IV Philopator (187-175). This son of Antiochus III had a relatively peaceful reign and appeared to have maintained favorable relations with Jerusalem. The exception alluded to in this verse was when he dispatched one of his chief officials, Heliodorus, to Jerusalem to seize funds that were reported to be either in excess of what was needed or hoarded by anti-Seleucid factions. Before the high priest, Onias III, could get to Antioch to appeal the decision and offer explanation, Seleucus was assassinated in a plot carried out by Heliodorus, with Antiochus IV suspected by historians of complicity.

11:21. Antiochus IV Epiphanes (175-164). Antiochus IV, the brother of Seleucus, had been in Rome as a political hostage and was just returning (he had got as far as Athens) when the assassination of his brother took place. His goals included converting Jerusalem into a center for Greek culture and helping the Jews to make the transition to becoming Greek citizens with Greek ways. The intrigues that he became involved in were many, but certainly the main one concerning Jerusalem was how he handled the high priesthood (see next entry). The text calls him contemptible, and indeed he was. His title "Epiphanes" means "god manifest"—but the people preferred "Epimanes"—"madman." While he was certainly a member of the royal line, the throne should have gone to Seleucus's son, Demetrius (who instead was taking Antiochus's place as hostage in Rome). Another intrigue concerned the throne. He set up a coregency with his nephew (a minor), who a few years later was murdered.

11:22. prince of the covenant. Onias III was detained by Antiochus, and in the interim Jason, his brother, conspired to usurp his position. He paid a considerable sum to Antiochus and offered to be cooperative in the Hellenization of Judea (promotion of Greek culture at the expense of Jewish practices). Three years later Menelaus, with the probable support of the Tobiads, paid a larger sum and, the precedent having been established, was awarded the office over Jason. According to 2 Maccabees, Onias was murdered about 171. Many identify him as the prince of the covenant referred to in this verse, but others attach that title to Ptolemy VI (see below). The overwhelming army in some way represents the opponents to Antiochus's reign. This could include internal political opponents, Jewish antagonists or foreign opposition such as that which develops in Egypt.

11:25. First Egyptian War, 169. Antiochus's dreams of adding Egypt to his kingdom were finally acted on in 169. His invasion was prompted by Egypt's growing animosity and may even have been in response to Egypt's

military action, since the first encounter (November 170) was between Pelusium and Gaza. Nonetheless, Antiochus succeeded in capturing the city of Memphis and securing the surrender of Ptolemy VI.

11:26-28. Ptolemy VI Philometor (181-146). Ptolemy VI was young when he came to the throne and was aided by two officials, Eulaeus and Lenaeus, who stirred up antagonism against Syria. The humiliation of Ptolemy in the First Egyptian War is thought to have been the result of bad advice given by his two advisors with the intention of undermining him.

11:27. unsuccessful siege of Alexandria. After his successful siege of Memphis, the citizens of Alexandria defied him by making Ptolemy's younger brother king. Antiochus took immediate steps to break their revolt but was unable to take the city. As soon as he had returned to Syria, Ptolemy VI disavowed any loyalty to Antiochus and his coregency with his brother was reinstated.

11:28. action against the holy covenant. Roman, Greek and Jewish sources differ with regards to the details at this point. There is no question that on his return from Egypt, Antiochus raided the temple treasury, most likely to secure additional funds for his continuing military activities. The sources disagree about whether this incident took place after the First Egyptian War (September 169) or after the Second.

11:29-30. Second Egyptian War, 168. In the spring of 168 Antiochus again had to besiege Memphis, and he did so successfully, taking control of lower Egypt. As he again prepared to lay siege against a weakened Alexandria, he actually had himself crowned king of Egypt. But there was a difference this time. Egypt had appealed to Rome for help, and their ships arrived as he approached Alexandria. Roman consul Gaius Popillius Laenas met him by the walls of Alexandria and commanded Antiochus to leave Egypt. When Antiochus replied that he had to consult with his advisors, the Roman consul drew a circle in the dirt around the king and insisted that he give his answer before stepping out of the circle. A humiliated Antiochus conceded to Roman authority and straggled toward home looking for a way to vent his misery. This was probably in July 168.

11:30. fury against the holy covenant. There was a rumor in Jerusalem that Antiochus had been killed in battle. Jason, who had been ousted as high priest, took the opportunity to lead a rebellion against Menelaus, who at this time was high priest (see comment on 11:22). When Antiochus heard of trouble, he may have come himself to Jerusalem to put down the rebellion. In the process tens of thousands of Jews were massacred, and the temple was looted (Menelaus apparently cooperating in the plundering). Another report (perhaps of a subsequent action) says that Apollonius with a contingent of soldiers was sent by Antiochus to subjugate the riotous citizens of Jerusalem. According to the books of Maccabees this was accomplished through pretending to be peaceful but then slaughtering many. This may be a separate occasion, and the relationship of these events to those reported in the comment on 11:28 are difficult to determine. It is probably at this time that a citadel (the Akra) of Syrian soldiers was set up at the edge of the Temple Mount.

11:31. desecration of sanctuary. According to the book of Maccabees, an individual named Geron was sent by Antiochus to dismantle Jewish religious practice. It is possible that the Syrian military contingent, seeking accommodation for their own worship practice, was partially responsible for some of the changes described in the temple. In December 167 a systematic program of instituting Greek religious practices at the expense of Jewish ones began in earnest. The sacrificial system and the Sabbath and festival observances were halted. Worship sites were set up around the country and circumcision was forbidden. The temple was consecrated to Zeus and became a center of polytheism and prostitution.

11:31. abomination of desolation. This is usually taken as an idol of Olympian Zeus that was set up in the temple. Antiochus had identified this favorite god of his with the Syrian Baal Shamem, the chief deity of the Syrian portion of the population (see comment on 9:27).

11:32. flattery of covenant breakers. There were many Jews who favored the Hellenization process and therefore, if promised personal benefit, would gladly side with the new policies. Foremost among these was Menelaus, the high priest, who was totally dependent on Antiochus for his lucrative office.

11:32-35. Judas Maccabeus. In contrast, many of the Jews fought vigorously against the Hellenization of Judea—with many suffering martyrs' deaths. The major organized revolt was led by the Hasmonean family, initiated by its patriarch, Mattathias, a priest. In early 166 when Antiochus's envoy came to their town to enforce the new regulations, Mattathias and his five sons, John, Simon, Judas, Eleazar and Jonathan, responded with armed force and killed him. The family then fled the town and the rebellion was begun. With Judas as the

military commander, they began seizing control of small towns, intending thereby to cut off all the roads to Jerusalem. This created an effective blockade that eventuated in the retaking of Jerusalem and the purifying of the temple in December 164, exactly three years after the desecration, but Daniel 11 does not report this event. There is continued controversy over whether in this section the Maccabeans are referred to favorably or unfavorably.

11:36-39. If Antiochus IV is still in sight in these verses, they offer a general description of the difficult period surrounding the desecration. References to Antiochus's arrogance, his lavish support of some temples and his redistribution of land to those who support him are easily recognized as characteristic of this period.

11:37. the gods. Antiochus's Seleucid predecessors had elevated the god Apollo, while the Ptolemies had shown preference for Adonis (possibly referred to here as the one desired by women). Antiochus neglects them (though by no means rejects them) in favor of Olympian Zeus. The fact that he designated himself as God Manifest on his coins is sufficient to explain the comment in this verse.

11:38. god of fortresses. The fortress referred to here is usually considered to be the Akra, the garrison for Syrian soldiers that was adjoined to the Temple Mount.

11:40-45. final battle. There is no known historical sequence corresponding to that which is laid out in these verses. Antiochus IV was killed in battle in Persia in December 164. Many interpreters of Daniel consider this section (perhaps starting as early as v. 36) to contain a reference to a much more distant future.

12:1-13
Hope for the End

12:1. Michael. See comment on 10:13.

12:1. the book. This appears to be a reference to the book of life. In Exodus 32:32-34 Moses is willing to be blotted out of the book, an action that would result in his death. Yahweh replies that the one who sins is wiped out from the book. The metaphor is of a ledger that contains a list of the living. This is comparable to the book that contains the names of those destined for death that Enkidu sees in his dream of the netherworld. When someone's sins mandate judgment, their name is blotted out, thus leading to their death. This draws a connection between the book of life and the book of judgment (see comment on 7:10). Here the book still pertains to continued life, because those recorded will be delivered from the persecution. It is not yet conceived of as a book of eternal life.

12:2. resurrection in the ancient Near East. There are several different concepts of afterlife that are evidenced in the ancient Near East. The most fundamental concept is continued existence in a gravelike netherworld where there is no differentiation in the treatment of the righteous and wicked. The Israelites called this place Sheol (see comments on Is 14:9), and they believed that it allowed for no interaction with God. In Canaan and Mesopotamia netherworld deities governed this realm. In Egypt the netherworld existence is more congenial for those who pass the judgment and enter its confines. Those who are not approved are devoured. None of these concepts include the idea of resurrection out of the netherworld. In general, in the ancient worldview the only awakening that took place was the calling up of spirits of the dead (which was not permanent and not a bodily presence) or the awakening of the fertility gods of nature cycles. These died annually when the agricultural cycle came to an end and "wintered" in the netherworld. Then they were ritually awakened in the spring. None of this bears any resemblance to a theological doctrine of resurrection. Likewise not comparable are the occasional revivifications (when an individual is restored to life) or the indications of national return to life (Ezekiel's dry bones). A fully developed doctrine of resurrection in the modern sense includes six elements: (1) it is individual, not national; (2) it is material, not spiritual; (3) it is universal, not isolated; (4) it takes place outside the netherworld; (5) it leads to permanent immortality; and (6) it involves distinctions between the righteous and the wicked. Zoroastrianism appears to have all of these elements, but the nature of the sources makes it difficult to determine how early the Persians developed these concepts (for further discussion see comment on Is

26:19).

12:3. shining like the stars. Stars and angels are associated by the fact that both are referred to as the host of heaven (see comment on 8:10). Contemporary Greek thinking and intertestamental apocalyptic literature indicated that the righteous become stars or angels. Daniel only speaks of comparison, not identification.

12:4. seal the words. Already in the eighth century Assyrian texts of an esoteric nature were being preserved. The scribal notations (called colophons) at the ends of such works indicated that they contained secret lore to be shared only with those who were initiates. Scrolls could be sealed either by tying a string around them and sealing the knot with clay, or by placing them in a jar and sealing the cover. The clay or the seal around the lid would be impressed with the owner's seal. Mesopotamia used cylinder seals, Egypt used scarab seals, and Syria-Palestine used stamp seals. Tablets would be sealed inside a clay envelope, which would be impressed with the owner's seal. The seals were intended to vouchsafe the integrity of the contents. They warned against tampering and, if intact, attested to the authenticity of the document. For more information see Nehemiah 9:38.

12:7. time, times, half a time. See comment on 7:25.

12:11-12. 1,290/1,335 days. A lunar calendar was in use through most of the ancient world that resulted in years of 354 days. It had long been recognized that the solar year was 365 days, so periodic adjustments were made by adding months of a determined number of days. Greek practice used standardized thirty-day months that were also regularly adjusted to the solar cycle. Twelve hundred and ninety days is three years and seven months of thirty-day months

HOSEA

1:1-11
Hosea's Family

1:1. chronology. Hosea's prophecies span the eighth century, from the beginning of Uzziah's reign in Judah to the completion of Hezekiah's. The only king of Israel in this

superscription is Jeroboam II, who roughly covers the first half of that century. Most of Hosea's message deals primarily with events in the chaotic period after Jeroboam's death when there are a whole succession of weak and ineffective kings just prior to the Assyrian conquest of Israel and the destruction of Samaria in 721 B.C.

1:2. divine command to take wife. Marriage by divine command is a metaphor for Israel's covenant with Yahweh. Ezekiel demonstrated this in his oracle of the "foundling child" (Israel) who eventually became Yahweh's unfaithful wife (Ezek 16:1-43). An extrabiblical example of a marriage commanded by a god is found in the Hittite Annals of Hattusilis, many centuries before Hosea. Hattusilis declared that the goddess Ishtar appeared to him in a dream and instructed him to take Puduhepa, a daughter of Ishtar's priest, as his wife. This divine endorsement would have silenced any critics of this match and given the wife a right to participate in cultic as well as royal activities.

1:4. Jehu's massacre at Jezreel. Elisha had originally sanctioned the political revolution that brought Jehu to the throne (see 2 Kings 9:6-10). The speech made by the "son of the prophet" who anoints Jehu calls on him to avenge the blood of slain prophets by exterminating Ahab's entire house, including his wife Jezebel. Jehu does this, first killing King Joram in battle (2 Kings 9:24) as well as King Ahaziah of Judah (2 Kings 9:27). After marching on the city of Jezreel, he calls on the populace to choose sides, and Jezebel is thrown from a balcony to her death (2 Kings 9:32-33). A general purge of Ahab's "house," which is a euphemism for his political supporters and government officials, then takes place. At Jehu's orders the terrified officials in Jezreel behead seventy "sons of the house of Ahab" (2 Kings 10:6-8). The next day Jehu publicly denied any responsibility for the deaths of these seventy men and used this as a pretext to have all of the officials executed (2 Kings 10:9-11). It is this mass bloodletting, which swept away the dynasty and supporters of Ahab, that is the basis for the symbolic name for Hosea's first son. The name thereby becomes a reminder to the current ruler, a descendant of Jehu, that his dynasty will be held accountable for Jehu's murderous activities. It may also be forecasting a similar bloody end to that dynasty in the face of Syrian encroachment and the expansion of Assyrian hegemony in the region.

1:5. Valley of Jezreel. This extremely fertile (the name means "God sows") and strategic valley allows for movement east and west through the hill country of northern Samaria and the lower Galilee from Beth Shan on the east to Acco on the Mediterranean coast. Omri and Ahab had established a second capital at Jezreel because of its strategic and economic importance. Naturally the valley also became the battleground for armies that wished to control the region. A number of famous battles were fought here, the first of which is recorded in the annals of Pharaoh Thutmose III (1504-1450). For more information see comment on Judges 6:33.

2:1-23

Israel as Wife and Mother

2:3. stripped naked and turned out. Several documents, including wills found in the town of Nuzi, refer to this type of treatment of a wife who abandons her husband to live with another man. It is typically the children who perform this legal act. It is intended to humiliate and perhaps served as an instrument of divorce, though in cases where the husband has already died, it is related to property rights.

2:5, 8. staple products and fertility. Both Hammurabi's Code and the Middle Assyrian Law Code contain lists of items that a husband must by law supply his wife for her daily maintenance. These include grain, oil, wool and clothing. These staples formed the basis of the economy of the ancient Near East and were the symbols of fertility granted to the people by God (see Jer 31:12). Thus within the marriage metaphor employed by Hosea, the providing of these items represented God's fulfillment of the covenant agreement. However, Israel's choice is to take "lovers" (other gods), worship them and give them presents of gold and silver instead of acknowledging Yahweh's gifts (compare Ezek 16:13-19). Israel credited the fertility gods such as Baal for the provision of these needs.

2:8. Israel's Baal worship. Agricultural villages, whose produce fed themselves and the urban centers like Jerusalem, dominated the world of ancient Israel. The Mediterranean climate brought rain only during the winter and early spring months (October—April), and a drought meant that their fragile hold on life was severely threatened. It is no wonder, therefore, that the Canaanite storm god Baal was so pervasive a figure in ancient worship as well as in the ancient religious texts from Ugarit and Phoenicia. Rain meant life, fertility, economic prosperity and power for those blessed by it. The task for the Israelite prophets thus became an effort to demonstrate that Yahweh was the provider of fertility, including rainfall, and that Baal was a false god (see Jer 2:8; 23:13). More often than not, however, local villagers chose to combine Yahweh and Baal worship in order to maximize their chances of a good harvest (see Judg 2:11; 6:25-32). Similarly, the kings of Israel, like Ahab, in making diplomatic marriages, accepted the introduction of Baal and Asherah alongside Yahweh in the official worship centers (see 1 Kings 16:31-33). Only after the exile would Baal worship be supplanted by faithful Yahweh-only worship among the Israelites.

2:11. festival functions and Baal. The syncretistic religious practices of the Israelites are exposed here as they revel (part of the metaphor of Gomer's unfaithful behavior) in worship of Baal during the harvest and new moon festivals (see the similar list of cultic celebrations in Ezek 45:17). Passover, the Feast of Booths and the Feast of Weeks were the annual celebrations marking the agricultural year (see the comments on Ex 12:19 and 23:15-16 for a description of these festivals). The New Moon festivities seemed to be tied to the sabbaths in the sense that family celebrations occurred (see 1 Sam 20:5), and there was a cessation of work (see Amos 8:5). There was no distinction drawn between the gifts of Yahweh and the supposed gifts of the Canaanite god of fertility and rain, Baal. As a result, the true provider of their bounty would now withdraw his largesse so that the Israelites could see their error.

2:12. vine and fig payment from lovers. The Egyptian love songs of Papyrus Harris 500 mention the giving of a jug of sweet mandrake wine as a lover's present. Such gifts would have been common as an expression of endearment or affection, but the term for pay here is the one used to mean the fee of a prostitute rather than the offering to a lover. This draws the metaphor of Israel/Gomer's infidelity back into focus. The use of vines and fig trees also strikes at another source of wealth and festivity in ancient Israel. There could be no celebration without these important products that were harvested in August and September. God's threat to turn the place into a wilderness is similar to that expressed in Isaiah 5:6.

2:12. punishment by wild animals. The eighth-century Aramaic inscription from Deir'Alla that contains the prophecy of Balaam and the twentieth-century Egyptian *Visions of Neferti* both describe an abandoned land in which strange and ravenous animals forage for food. Ravaging wild beasts were considered one of the typical scourges that deity would send as punishment. As early as the Gilgamesh Epic in Mesopotamia (c. 2000) the god Ea had reprimanded Enlil for not sending lions to ravage the people rather than using something as dramatic as a flood. The gods used wild beasts along with disease, drought and famine to reduce the human population. A common threat connected to negative

omens in the Assyrian period was that lions and wolves would rage through the land. In like manner devastation by wild animals was one of the curses invoked for treaty violation. The image here is one of chaos when civilization falls apart. See the comment on Deuteronomy 32:23-25 for another example of God cursing the land and its produce.

2:13. incense to Baal. Given the large number of small incense altars discovered by archaeologists, such as those from Lachish and Tel-Miqne/Ekron, it is apparent that burning incense as an offering to Yahweh or other gods was common in individual homes as well as in official cultic settings (see Is 17:8; Jer 19:13). The Israelites had been commanded to burn incense before Yahweh's altar (Ex 30:7-8), but that proper form of worship was corrupted when the offering was made to Baal instead. Incense was typically used to accompany petition.

2:15. Valley of Achor. When Achan violated the *herem* during the capture of Jericho, he and his entire family were stoned to death in what came to be known as the Valley of Achor (Josh 7:25-26). The site is located on Judah's northern tribal border (Josh 15:7), modern El Buquê'ah. Hosea's mention of the "Valley of Trouble" is an attempt to demonstrate that if even such an ill-fated place can be transformed, then so can Gomer/Israel's relationship with Hosea/Yahweh.

3:1-5
Hosea Reclaims His Wife

3:1. sacred raisin cakes. See the comment on Jeremiah 44:19 for the offering of sweet cakes (made from figs or dates) to the gods of Mesopotamia. There is some uncertainty in translating the Hebrew word here. Some commentators suggest that jars of wine are meant rather than compressed cakes of grapes or raisins. In either case it is the produce of the grape harvest that is being used as an offering.

3:2. purchase price details. Given the value of the barley added to the fifteen shekels of silver, one estimate would make Hosea's total outlay approximately thirty shekels. This amount is equal to the amount due as compensation for the loss of a slave in Exodus 21:32. Since Gomer's situation is unclear, it is not possible to make a definite determination of why Hosea would pay out this amount. Based on Middle Assyrian Law, however, he may be redeeming her from a legal situation from which she could not extricate herself (such as paying a debt she owed).

3:4. sacrifice or sacred stones. See the comments on Exodus 23:24 and Deuteronomy 7:5 for the use of sacred stones and Asherah poles as part of Canaanite worship and Israel's idolatrous practices. Sacred stones did serve as a legitimate part of Yahweh worship, at least through the time of the divided monarchy (see Is 19:19). In the time of destruction to come, however, these cultic symbols as well as the kings will receive no word or support from Yahweh (see Deut 16:22).

3:4. ephod or idol. Sacrifice and sacred stones represent means of worshiping the deity; ephod and idol refer to means of consulting the deity. An ephod was part of the priestly wardrobe (see comment on Ex 28:6-14) and in both Egypt and Mesopotamia was reserved for clothing images of deity and for high-ranking priests. See the comment on Exodus 28:6-14 for a description of the appearance and use of the ephod as a device for divining God's will. People who wanted to ask information of deity would come (pay their fee) and receive an answer (through the mediation of the specialists. The teraphim idols referred to here (see comment on Gen 31:19) were among the tools or surrogates for consulting the gods in the ancient Near East. As with the pillars and sacrifices, however, God would not provide these diviners with any answers.

4:1-19
Indictment of Israel's Unfaithfulness

4:10, 14. prostitution. In ancient Mesopotamia a distinction can be drawn between commercial prostitution and sexual service for the temple. The term *harimtu* is used for both in cuneiform texts (for instance it is a *harimtu* who "civilizes" Enkidu in the Gilgamesh Epic), but there is a difference in social status as well as purpose. The sacral sexual service provided at the temple was tied into the sacred marriage ritual that insured fertility for the land. There were various levels of priestesses, from the high priestess who represented the goddess Ishtar/Inanna and was said to be "visited" by the god Marduk each night, to cloistered female orders and more public figures like the *naditu*, who could own property, conduct business and even marry. The fact that commercial prostitution occurred near temples was based on the same considerations that brought prostitutes to frequent taverns and the city gate—high traffic areas meant more customers. Both temple sacral servants and prostitutes accepted payment, but the former were expected to dedicate these offerings to the gods. Additionally a distinction

could be made between "sacred" prostitution and "cultic" prostitution. In "sacred" prostitution, as just mentioned, the proceeds go to the temple. It was quite possible for prostitutes to be employed by temples as a means of raising funds without their having any official status as priestesses. In "cultic" prostitution, the intent was to insure fertility through sexual ritual. We must also differentiate between occasional sacred/cultic prostitution (as in Gen 38) and professional sacred/cultic prostitution (as in 2 Kings 23:7). The evidence for cultic prostitution in ancient Israel or elsewhere in the ancient Near East is not conclusive. Canaanite texts list prostitutes among the temple personnel, and Akkadian literature attests those who were dedicated for life to serve the temple in this way. Furthermore, since women often did not have personal assets, sometimes the only way of earning money by which to pay a vow appeared to be prostitution. The injunction against bringing the wages of a prostitute to the temple may, however, be a reaction against practices like that of the Ishtar temple in the Neo-Babylonian period to hire out female members of their community as prostitutes.

4:11. old wine, new wine. The terms used for wine in this instance are in parallel, but they represent different degrees of fermentation. In the Ugaritic Tale of Aqhat (VI:7-8) the same terms are used in parallel, but the text is very broken and offers no further information. The sense of the phrase is to demonstrate how overindulgence in drinking wine befuddles the mind. These people's minds are clouded by their false religious practices as those of drunkards are by their wine (see comment on Is 28:7).

4:12. wooden idol. Although it is possible that Hosea is referring to the practice of rhabdomancy (divining the will of the gods by casting rods or wands; see the comment on Ezek 21:21 for a variety of forms of divination), this is more likely a reference to sacred groves or Asherah poles (see Ex 34:13). Idols were often carved from wood (see Jer 10:3-5; Hab 2:18-19), and this practice was so common in Mesopotamia that Sumerian texts refer to certain types of wood as the "flesh of the gods."

4:13. worship on mountains. High places and mountaintops have long been associated with divine worship (see the comment on 1 Sam 9:12). For instance, some of the most important events in Israelite history are associated with mountains (Moses at Mount Sinai; Elijah at Mount Carmel). Likewise, Mount Zaphon was identified as the home or seat of power for the Canaanite gods Baal and El in the Ugaritic epics. Since the Israelites seemed so prone to blending Yahweh worship with that of other gods, Hosea condemned the sacrificial activities at these outdoor shrines (just as they are condemned in Deut 12:2-3), seeing them as breeding grounds for corrupting succeeding generations.

4:13. sacred trees. From earliest times, trees have served as landmarks and have been associated with popular justice and religious activity (see the comment on Gen 35:4). Among the references to sacred or significant trees are Deborah's palm in Judges 4:5 and the tree under which the Ugaritic king Danil heard the cases of his people. These individual trees or sacred groves were also associated with the worship of Asherah (see the comment on Deut 12:3), and as such were a trap for the Israelites. Asherah is pictured in Israelite iconography as a stylized tree.

4:15. Gilgal. The exact location of this site near Jericho has yet to be determined (see Josh 4:19). Among the most likely suggestions, based on Iron Age deposits uncovered in survey work, are sites near Khirbet el-Mefjir, a little over a mile northeast of Jericho. Its name, meaning "ring of stones," suggests its importance as a cultic center. Both Amos (4:4; 5:5) and Hosea (9:15; 12:11) condemn Gilgal for the religious transgressions and inappropriate sacrifices made there. The nature of these religious activities is not spelled out, but it may be presumed that they involved the worship of gods other than Yahweh.

4:15. Beth Aven. Although it is not possible to determine whether Hosea himself was a Levite, his knowledge of wisdom themes and priestly matters at least suggests close ties with a Levite family. This may explain his ridicule of the royal sanctuary at Bethel and this pun on the place name (see Amos 5:5). He refers to the Ephraimite city of Bethel ("house of God") as Beth Aven ("house of wickedness"), pronouncing it an illegitimate place of worship and a source of evil within Israelite society (compare his usage in 5:8).

5:1-15
Continued Indictment

5:1. snare and net. The very familiar image of fowlers trapping birds in nets and snares may be the origin of this common metaphor (see Josh 23:13; Ps 69:22; Is 8:14). There are numerous examples of this activity from Egyptian tomb paintings, and it also provides the basis for the Sumerian Stele of the Vultures (see the comment on Ezek 12:13).

5:7. New Moons. While Hosea may be referring once again to the New Moon festivals that had become corrupted by Baal worship (see Hos 2:11), the term used here can simply mean the arrival of a new phase of month in the cycle of the year. It is therefore possible that the prophet is denouncing in general terms the continuous (cycle to cycle) self-destructiveness of the Israelites.

5:8. Gibeah, Ramah, Beth Aven. There is an allusion here to a military confrontation between the northern and southern kingdoms (Ephraim and Judah) concerning the border between the two. The reference to the three cities in Benjamin (Gibeah = Jeba'; Ramah = Er-Ram; Beth Aven = Khirbet el-'Askar) suggests either that they are being invaded by Ephraim (perhaps the beginning of an attack on Jerusalem) or that their men are being called to battle by Judah (perhaps to invade Ephraim). Each of these sites guards the northern track to Judah's capital. The alarm being raised is most likely associated with a phase of the Syro-Ephraimitic War of the 730s (see comments on 2 Chron 28:5 and Is 7:1).

5:10. moving boundary stones. See the comment on Deuteronomy 19:14 for discussion of this crime.

5:13. Ephraim turned to Assyria. The destructive effects of the Syro-Ephraimitic War will leave both Israel (Ephraim) and Judah exhausted and even more vulnerable to the political hegemony of the Assyrians. Realizing that their status as vassals was deteriorating, two Israelite kings— Menahem in 738 (2 Kings 15:19-20) and Hoshea in 732—were forced to pay large sums to keep the Assyrians from further ravaging their country. The Assyrian Annals of Tiglath-Pileser III record these tribute payments, along with those of many other small nations being economically drained by the empire's need for funds.

6:1—7:16
Turning Away from Repentance and Restoration

6:3. winter rains, spring rains. Based on the Mediterranean climate of the Middle East, Israel receives its rains twice during the year. The "winter" rains fall from December to February. As noted in the tenth-century Gezer calendar, this moisture softens the earth and prepares it for plowing and sowing of wheat, barley and oats. The "spring" rains come during March and April and provide the life-giving water needed for the sowing of millet and vegetable crops. It is the timing of these rains that makes the difference between a good harvest and famine. Tying Yahweh to the rains supersedes Baal's role as the rain and fertility god, and tying him to the sun supersedes the sun gods who were often associated with justice.

6:7. Adam. Since the end of the verse suggests a place ("there") and since there is a parallel to Gilead, most modern commentators assume this refers to a city rather than the first man. This site is generally identified with Tell ed-Damiyeh in Transjordan just south of the Jabbok River and north of the Wadi Far'ah, at a point that dominates the fords of the Jordan River. It is mentioned as one of the cities captured by Pharaoh Shishak during his tenth-century campaign into the region.

6:8-9. violence at Gilead and Shechem. The event chronicled here may be Pekah's rebellion against the Israelite king Pekahiah in 736 (2 Kings 15:25). Apparently the fighting began at Adam with the aid of a group of Gileadites and spread west along the Wadi Far'ah road into Israel as far as the city of Shechem. Apparently Pekah's supporters were aided by priests from Bethel in their efforts to eliminate the king's officials.

7:4-8. baking metaphors. In the light of the tumultuous nature of Israel's political scene in the 730s, these baking metaphors are quite apt. The oven depicted here was made of clay and was cylindrical in shape. Examples of this device have been excavated at Taanach and Megiddo. It may have been embedded into the floor or lay on it. The domed roof had a large hole covered by a door through which the baker would first add fuel (wood, dried grass, dung or cakes made from olive residue). Flames would escape through the hole until a hot bed of coals remained. The heat would be captured as the door was closed and would remain for many hours (enough for the bread to be kneaded and allowed to rise). Then the baker would place the slightly raised flat bread on the inner walls of the oven or amongst the coals. The metaphor plays on these mundane tasks and well-known images. The rebel forces of Pekah fiercely "flamed" within the oven of Israel's political affairs and destroyed Pekahiah's regime in 735. The resentment caused by this action smoldered like an oven holding its heat and waiting to burn those in charge. Then in 732 Hoshea assassinated Pekah and immediately reversed Israel's political alliances (2 Kings 15:30), shifting to Assyria for help and then three years later once again seeking an Egyptian alliance (see Hos 7:11). This muddled policy left Israel "half-baked," like a loaf left on the wall of the oven that had never been turned. It was burnt on one side and doughy on the other.

7:11. dove behavior. The vacillating political policy of the kings of Israel is compared to the gullibility (see Prov 14:15 for this applied to fools) of doves, who are an easy prey for the fowler's net. In addition, the dove's lack of concern over lost chicks may be compared to Israel's political amnesia with regard to Assyrian policies (see Hos 5:13).

7:11. Egypt/Assyria. Throughout much of his brief reign, Pekah practiced an anti-Assyrian policy and sought aid from the Egyptians. This had led to the campaign of Tiglath-Pileser III described in 2 Kings 15:29 that resulted in the capture of much of the Galilee region and a deportation of Israelites to Assyria (see the comment on 2 Kings 15:25-31). Once Hoshea had come to the throne, he initially had to pay tribute to the Assyrians, but then sent envoys to Egypt (see the comment on 2 Kings 17:4). Such duplicity enraged the Assyrian king Shalmaneser V, and he besieged Samaria for three years. His successor, Sargon II, then took the city in 721 and deported much of the Israelite population (see the comment on 2 Kings 17:6).

7:12. bird hunting. There were a number of different techniques used to snare birds. Although hunters might simply use a sling, throwing stick (as in the Beni Hasan tomb painting) or a bow to take down individual fowl, the majority of instances in the biblical text and in ancient art depict large flocks of birds being captured in nets or cages. For instance, the tomb of Ka-Gemmi at Saqqarah (Sixth Dynasty Egypt) portrays the fowler using a net. Apparently some fowlers also used decoys in their snares to attract the birds along with bait food (attested in Ecclus 11:30). Clearly, Israel's kings have been snared in the net of political ambitions cast by both of the ancient super powers, Egypt and Assyria.

7:16. faulty bow. The composite bow, made from a combination of wood, horn and animal tendons (indicated in the Ugaritic Tale of Aqhat), was subject to changes in weather and humidity. If it was not kept in a case, it could loose its strength and be described as unreliable or slack (see Ps 78:57). The Assyrian wisdom sayings of Ahiqar speak of the arrows of the wicked being turned back on them, and this may also be part of Hosea's condemnation of the Israel's leaders (see Ps 64:2-7).

8:1-14

Continued Indictment

8:1. trumpet signals. As in Hosea 5:8, the sounding of the trumpet or ram's horn is a signal of approaching danger. This would have set the people in motion, driving their animals into the protection of city walls (see Amos 3.6). For more information concerning trumpet signals see comments on Numbers 31:6 and Joshua 6:4-5.

8:1. eagle (vulture). Hosea employs an image of a bird of prey swooping down on its victim. It seems most likely that he is referring to Assyria, once again being used as a tool of God's wrath. The hunting eagle or vulture would have been a familiar sight, and they were often used in Near Eastern epic and myth (as in the Ugaritic Tale of Aqhat and the Akkadian myth of Etana; see comment on Deut 32:11).

8:5-6. calf idol. There is ample evidence of the association of Baal worship with bovine cult images or pictures of bulls (such as the zoomorphic depiction from Tell el-Asch'ari). See the comments on 1 Kings 12:28-30 for a full discussion of King Jeroboam's attempts to create his own shrines at Dan and Bethel as rivals to Jerusalem, with golden calves serving as representations of God's throne. Hosea now condemns the golden calves placed in these shrines as a source of false worship and a reflection of the syncretism of Baal and Yahweh worship in Israel. By Hosea's time only Bethel remained, since Tiglath-Pileser III had conquered Dan in 733 and presumably destroyed the shrine there.

8:6. calf of Samaria. The use of Samaria instead of Bethel as the site of the calf is a euphemism for all of Israel (see Hos 10:5). It was common practice in the Assyrian Annals to refer to an entire province by listing the name of its capital city (see 2 Kings 23:19).

8:14. palaces. The Hebrew term *hêkal*, perhaps a cognate of Akkadian *ekallu* (from Sumerian E.GAL), "big house," may mean either temple or palace. At least during Jeroboam II's early reign there was an effort to build fortified cities and monumental buildings in Samaria and other major cities (see 2 Chron 26:9-10 for similar construction in Judah). Efforts such as these can be taken as a symbol of royal power and thus worthy of Hosea's charge that they had "forgotten" God (see Deut 32:15-18).

9:1—10:15

Judgment on Israel

9:1. prostitute at threshing floor. One of the essential installations within the farming areas of Israel was the threshing floor. Harvested grain was brought here for processing and distribution (see Ruth 3:2, 7). It would also be the likely site for public gatherings (see the confrontation in 1 Kings 22:10) and for harvest celebrations (Deut 16:13). However, Israel is enjoined to rejoice no longer since the people have demonstrated their infidelity by expressing their faith in Baal's ability to provide their abundance (see Hos 2:7-8). Apparently common prostitutes as well as cult prostitutes frequented the areas where harvest and shearing festivals took place (see the comment on Gen 38:15-23). Thus Israel plays the prostitute amidst the grain, taking her hire from those gods she credited with the harvest rather than acknowledging Yahweh's role.

9:4. bread of mourners. A house in mourning, having had contact with the dead, was considered unclean for seven days and had to be ritually purified in order to resume normal social and religious activity (see the comment on Num 19:11). During the period of their impurity, all their food, by extension, was equally contaminated. While it could be used to nourish their bodies, these meals were joyless and none of the food was to be offered as a sacrifice to God (see Jer 16:7; Ezek 24:17). This is how Hosea characterizes life in the coming exile.

9:6. Memphis. During much of Egypt's history, Memphis (modern Mitrahineh) served as the capital of Lower Egypt. It was located about thirteen miles south of modern Cairo on the west bank of the Nile River.

9:7. prophet a maniac. There was sometimes a very fine line drawn between a person invested with the Spirit of God (1 Sam 9:6) and one considered to simply be insane (see 1 Sam 21:13-15; 2 Kings 9:11). In this case, however, Hosea's enemies attempt to discredit him by claiming his prophecies are actually just the ravings of a madman (compare the similar charges made in Amos 7:10 and Jer 29:25-28).

9:9. days of Gibeah. For a description of the heinous events that took place at Gibeah see the comments on Judges 19:12-14 and 19:25. Clearly this story was well known in Hosea's day, since he merely has to mention the name of the city to raise the specter of lawless and scandalous behavior.

9:10. fruit metaphors. There is a sense of unexpected pleasure to be found in grapes growing in the desert or ripe figs in the early part of the summer. Evidence of "grape cairns" in the Negeb indicate that viticulture is possible here and the small bunches are said to be particularly sweet. This is also the case of the small figs that ripen in May-June. They are considered such a delicacy that they are to be eaten immediately after picking (see Is 28:4; Nahum 3:12).

9:10. Baal Peor. See the comments on Numbers 25:1-18 for the incident at Baal Peor when the Israelite men were tempted into idolatry by the women of Moab near Shittim.

9:13. children to the slayer. It is possible that this is an allusion to the political turmoil in which the leaders of Israel have embroiled the people and thus laid their families open to the rampaging Assyrian armies (see the comment on Hos 7:11). The Sumerian *Lament over the Destruction of Ur* describes similar events during times of siege when parents abandon their children. Another possibility is that the "slayer of children" is a demon. Among the Babylonian demons was Pashittu, who was considered a baby snatcher. This would be another way of referring to child exposure. For more information on child exposure, see comment on Ezekiel 16:5.

9:15. wickedness in Gilgal. See the comment on Hosea 4:15. While Hosea's condemnation may be based on events during the conquest period or at the time of Saul's inauguration as king (1 Sam 11:12-15), it is also possible that he is referring to a contemporary event that is not recorded elsewhere and is now unknown.

10:1. sacred stones. See comment on 3:4.

10:4. poisonous weeds. The Hebrew term *rosh* may be in this instance the veined henbane (*Hyoscyamus reticulatus*), which occurs in plowed fields, especially those near steppe and desert regions. It grows to a height of two feet, with hairy foliage and a yellowish, pink-veined flower. Another candidate is the Syrian scabious (*Cephalaria syriaca*), which has poisonous seeds. Shallow planting actually helps spread these plants, since only the stalks are cut while their deep roots lie untouched (see Job 31:40).

10:5. Samaria, Beth Aven. See comment on 4:15.

10:11. threshing, plowing metaphor. It may be that young oxen were first trained to accept the yoke by putting them to work on the threshing floor. This relatively simple task, during which they had the opportunity of the reward of grazing (Deut 25:4), made them more docile (see Jer 50:11). Once they had achieved the stage when direction was easy, then a sledge could be added that would get the animals used to pulling a load (2 Sam 24:22). This in turn prepared them for the more disciplined task of plowing a furrow in a virgin field (1 Kings 19:19; Jer 4:3). In like manner, God chooses to use the docile and strong Israel to fulfill the divine plan.

10:14. Shalman at Beth Arbel. This event is unknown to modern historians. Hosea uses it as the measure of total destruction in much the same way that Jeremiah directs the people's attention to Shiloh (Jer 7:12-14; 26:6).

There have been several suggestions made on the name Shalman, including either Shalmaneser III, who may have campaigned as far as Israel during his 841 excursion against the Syrian capital of Damascus, or Shalmaneser V, who besieged Samaria in 722. Another possibility is the ancient Moabite king Salmanu, who is listed as one of the petty monarchs paying tribute to the Assyrian king Tiglath-Pileser III in the mid-eighth century. The mention of Moabite raiding parties in Israel in 2 Kings 13:20 may bolster this identification. As for Beth Arbel, the site of this horrendous destruction, it has been identified with Irbid, near the Decapolis city of Pella and just across the Jordan River from Beth Shan.

11:1-11
God's Historical Love for Israel

11:6. bars of gates. Two gate doors were generally set into stone sockets buried just under the ground. The posts flanked the gate on either side. They were made of wood and joined to the wall. The Iron Age outer gate excavated at Tell en-Nasebeh has slots in the stone beside the gate, where bars would have been placed. They would lock the gates by sliding the bars into sockets in the wall.

11:8. Admah and Zeboiim. These two cities, neither of which have been positively identified by archaeologists, are traditionally tied to Sodom and Gomorrah as sites of utter destruction and evidence of God's judgment (see comment on Gen 19:1). These cities are generally located in the Jordan Valley southeast of the Dead Sea. Among the more prominent sites discovered in this area are the Early Bronze cities of Bab edh Dra' and Numeira.

12:1-14
Continued Indictment

12:1. Assyria treaty. Like his predecessor Menahem, Hoshea was initially forced to pay tribute to the Assyrian king Tiglath-Pileser III. The Assyrian Annals even boast that when Hoshea assassinated Pekah to take the throne of Israel that the Assyrian king "placed Hoshea as king over them." It also notes that Hoshea paid "ten talents of gold [and] a thousand (?) talents of silver" as tribute, probably to confirm his position as king in 732.

12:1. oil tribute to Egypt. Shortly after Hoshea had accepted the role of Assyrian vassal king in Israel, he then shifted his allegiance by sending a large quantity of olive oil (one of Israel's major forms of wealth) to Egypt. This would have been a valuable commodity, especially in Egypt where olives were not grown. Playing to both superpowers and their factions, however, would soon draw Assyrian ire and lead in 722 to the invasion of Israel by Shalmaneser V.

12:4. struggled with angel. See several comments on Jacob's wrestling match with an angel in Genesis 32 (though the term for angel is clearly used here, it does not occur in Gen 32). Hosea recounts the patriarch's reputation for ambition and deceit. It is clear that the prophet believes Jacob overstepped the bounds that humans are supposed to have when dealing with God. This theme of placing limits on human behavior can also be seen in the story of Adapa, an ancient Sumerian hero and priest of the god Ea. He is brought before the divine assembly because he had had the effrontery to break the wing of the south wind and thus cause a drought.

12:7. dishonest scales. This same charge is made against unscrupulous merchants in Amos 8:5. The word translated "merchant" is the Hebrew word "Canaan," which at least evokes the idea of Canaanite influence. The indictment seems to be based on the idea that Israel and its economic community have been corrupted by the immoral practices of its neighbors. In an economy that did not have standardized weights and measures, traders were often tempted to cheat by falsifying the balances and measurements, often by using improper weights and false bottoms and other ways to alter the sizes of vessels.

12:10. prophets' parables. One of the ways that the prophet is able to convey God's message is through the use of analogies or comparative stories. The parable thus can provide a dual meaning, using scenes or images from everyday life and then providing an interpretation of God's will or judgment. For examples of this, see the comment on Isaiah 5:1-2 and Nathan's parable of the ewe lamb in the comment on 2 Samuel 12:2-4.

12:11. Gilead, Gilgal. For Gilead's association with Pekah's revolt see comment on 6:8-9. For an cultic activities at Gilgal see comment on 4:15.

12:11. altars as stone piles on plowed land. The piles of stones haphazardly scattered on the plowed fields could offer a picture of altars that have been knocked down. But since it is in the middle of an indictment, the context might rather lead to the picture of altars as numerous as piles of stones in a plowed field. There is additionally a play on words here in that the Hebrew word translated "piles" is *gallim*, sounding similar to elements in both city names.

12:12. Jacob's flight. Hosea returns to a theme he first used at the beginning of chapter 12, drawing on the traditions about Jacob and using them to parallel the nation of Israel's coming plight and possible redemption. So, just as the unscrupulous Jacob was forced to flee from Palestine to Haran to escape Esau's wrath (see the comments on Gen 27—28), now Israel will once again be forced to "live in tents" (Hos 12:19). The new life and family Jacob/Israel finds in Aram, however, led him back to Palestine and served as the origin of the Israelite people.

13:1-16
God's Anger

13:2. idol manufacture skills. See the comments on Judges 17:3; Isaiah 40:19; 44:17-18 for discussion of the manufacturing techniques employed in the creation of idols in the ancient Near East. The acquisition and use of the skills necessary to fashion these images is simply a further example, according to Hosea, of Israel's intent to syncretize or corrupt its worship with false gods.

13:2. kiss calf idols. On the black stele of Shalmaneser III the Israelite king Jehu is portrayed kissing the ground before the Assyrian king. In *Enuma Elish* the tribunal of gods kisses the feet of Marduk after he has put down the rebellion and established himself as head of the pantheon. This was the common act of submission offered to kings and gods. Likewise the kissing of the idol involved kissing its feet in an act of homage, submission and allegiance. In the Mari letters the governor of Terqa, Kibri-Dagan, advises Zimri-Lim, king of Mari, to come to Terqa to kiss the feet of the statue of the god Dagan.

13:3. chaff on threshing floor. Once again Hosea uses a series of images that would easily conjure up pictures in his audience's minds—scenes from everyday life. Among them is the threshing floor where farmers bring their grain to be crushed under the feet of the oxen or by a threshing sledge (see the comment on Hos 10:11). The worthless residue that remained on the surface of this installation would swirl about as the winds blew it about. This illustration, combined with the morning mist and wisps of smoke, speaks of the short-term aspects of life—an apt comparison between the eternity of Yahweh and the ephemeral character of other gods and their idols.

13:7. leopard. The idea of the leopard as a silent, stalking hunter fits God's role as the destroyer of the unprepared and the unvigilant Israel (see Jer 5:6). The cunning leopard appears in wisdom literature as well. For instance, there is a short fable about the leopard in the Assyrian *Words of Ahiqar*. In it the leopard attempts to trick a goat by offering to lend the goat his coat to shelter itself from the cold. The goat escapes and calls back that the leopard was merely hoping for its hide. Leopards still inhabit some regions of Israel (En Gedi) but in antiquity were not as common as lions.

13:16. gruesome punishments. Hosea forecasts that the warfare to come will destroy the town and villages of the Israelites, and not even women and children will be spared from the rampaging army as it pillages and rapes. It would appear that this phrase is a standard description of warfare's devastation. Ninth-century Assyrian conquest accounts speak of burning the young boys and girls. The practice of ripping open pregnant women is mentioned very rarely. It is a practice attributed to Assyrian king Tiglath-Pileser I (about 1100) in a hymn praising his conquests. It is also referred to in passing in a Neo-Babylonian lament.

14:1-9
Offer of Hope

14:5-6. plant metaphors. Yahweh's relationship with Israel is likened to dew that provides the only moisture available to flowers and trees during the dry months of summer (see Is 26:19). The lily is not common in Palestine today, though it can be found in some areas. There is dispute whether it was more common in antiquity or not. In addition, God's life-giving essence insures the fertility and virility of the nation so that it continues to grow and expand, like the massive root system of the olive tree. Comparison is also made to the great cedars of Lebanon—considered the most useful of the large growth trees in the ancient Near East. It was prized for its lumber (1 Kings 6:9-10), a source for construction and a symbol of wealth in Mesopotamian literature, including the Gilgamesh Epic and the annals of many kings from the Sumerians through the Assyrians.

JOEL

1:1-12
Locust Invasion

1:2. address to elders. The fact that elders are addressed here has led many interpreters to infer that there was no king at this time. Some have therefore dated the book to the middle of the ninth century, when Judah was ruled by wicked queen Athaliah (see comments on 2 Chron 22—22), and the righteous of the land would have refused to recognize the legitimacy of her reign. The problem with this view is that the book of Joel clearly represents classical prophecy, which did not begin until the eighth century (see comment on 2 Kings 14:27). If the address to elders indeed does suggest there was no king, it is likely that the book should be dated to the postexilic period. This is further supported by 3:3, which speaks of the dispersion in the past tense. Nonetheless, the dating of the book is very controversial and complicated.

1:4. locust swarms. Locusts were all too common in the ancient Near East and were notorious for the devastation and havoc they brought. The locusts breed in the region of the Sudan. Their migration would strike in February or March and would follow the prevailing winds either to Egypt or Palestine. A locust will consume its own weight each day. Locust swarms have been known to cover as many as four hundred square miles, and even one square mile could teem with over 100 million insects. If the locusts laid their eggs before being blown out to sea, the problem would recur in cycles. A single female laying her eggs in June could potentially result in eighteen million offspring within four months.

1:4. locust terms. Since locusts were very familiar to the agricultural economy of the Near East, the various languages are full of precise vocabulary. The four different terms in this verse (nine terms in the entire Old Testament) pale beside the eighteen terms known from Akkadian. Interpreters are divided on whether these four words refer to four different stages of development in the life cycle of the locust ([1] larval stage: black, hopping, wingless; [2] black and yellow with wings and jaws; [3] yellow and fully developed; [4] sexually mature adult), or whether they refer to different species (*gregaria* and *solitaria*).

1:6. locust metaphors. It is not uncommon in ancient Near Eastern literature for armies to be pictured as locusts. Such metaphors are found in Sumerian texts such as the curse of Akkad, in Ugaritic in the Tale of Aqhat, in Nineteenth-Dynasty Egyptian texts, and in Neo-Assyrian texts. Here it is the other way around as the locust swarm is metaphorically described as an invading army (as becomes clear in 2:4-5). The comparison to a lion is common in ancient Near Eastern literature because of the coloring of the locust and the shape of its face and mouth.

1:7. vine and fig. Locusts do not favor the trees mentioned here, so they only attack them when everything else is gone. This is an indication of the extent of the damage. Additionally, the vine and fig are signs of security and prosperity, so their devastation is symbolic of the mood among the population. The idyllic image of peace and prosperity in the ancient Near East was to be able to sit under one's own vine and fig tree. Egyptian tomb paintings, Assyrian reliefs and the biblical writers commonly use the phrase to refer to a people who control their own lives, without foreign interference, and are able to cultivate the land which the gods/God has given to them (1 Kings 4:25; Is 36:16). The vine and fig provided some shade as well as fruit, and enjoying them indicated some long-term prospects as each took several years to become productive.

1:7. stripping of bark. Locusts are known not only to devour plant life but also to break off branches and strip off bark. If there is significant damage to the bark the tree may not survive, and even if it does, the healing process will greatly reduce its fruitfulness.

1:8. virgin metaphor. The word translated "virgin" here refers to a woman who has not yet officially left the house of her father. She may have a "husband" by contract if the bride price has been paid, even if the marriage has not yet been consummated. The metaphor here then refers to the mourning of a woman who had been betrothed and very close to marriage when she lost her husband.

1:9. offerings cut off. An Assyrian hymn from the time of Sargon II (end of the eighth century) asks the deity (Nanaya) to bring an end to a locust plague. Like Joel, the prayer mentions several categories of locusts and laments that they are cutting off the offerings of the gods.

1:10-12. impact of army invasion on agriculture. The ecological destruction could cripple the economy for years. Sometimes fields would be so damaged as to have greatly reduced fertility. The destruction of trees would have even more devastating effects on the ecological balance. Not only would shade and wood supply be lost, but topsoil erosion would increase and the loss of forestation's contribution to the environment would accelerate the development of wasteland conditions. Some fruit trees (such as the date palm) take twenty years of growth before they become productive. Agricultural devastation and deforestation were typical tactics of invading armies seeking to punish those they conquered and as an attempt to hasten their surrender. The Assyrian records and reliefs detail punitive measures that include felling trees, devastating meadowlands and destroying canal systems used for irrigation.

DAY OF YAHWEH

Each year in Mesopotamia (often twice a year) there was an enthronement festival for the king of the gods. During the course of this *akitu* festival, the deity determined the destiny of his subjects and reestablished order, as he had done long ago when he defeated the forces of chaos. In fact, the creation account *Enuma Elish* that recounts Marduk's defeat of Tiamat and his elevation to the head of the pantheon was read during the course of the festival. Though the texts never refer to the *akitu* festival as the "Day of Marduk" there are some similarities. The Day of Yahweh refers to the occasion on which Yahweh will ascend to his throne with the purpose of binding chaos and bringing justice to the world order. The destinies of his subjects will be determined as the righteous are rewarded and the wicked suffer the consequences of their rebellion and sin. For Israel there is no firm evidence that this was represented in a regular ritual, but it is rather reflected in a historical expectation. As is often the case, then, to the extent that there is a connection, Israel appears to have historicized that which elsewhere is in the realm of myth and ritual. The Day of the Lord also has elements of theophany, usually connected with the divine warrior who defeats the disruptive powers (see comment on 1 Sam 4:3-7). Such theophanies often are accompanied by cosmic effects (see comment on 1 Kings 19:11-13). The cosmic effects often depict a world upside down (see comment on Jer 4:23-26). The Day of Yahweh was a momentous day, and these are the kinds of occurrences that characteristically accompany momentous days. All of this helps our understanding of the Day of Yahweh by showing us that Israelite thinking and the prophets' communication intersected with a wide spectrum of ideas current in the culture. The originality in the Israelite literature is not that whole new matrices are being created but that known ideas are being combined and applied in unique ways.

1:13-20

Call to Repentance

1:13. sackcloth. Sackcloth is made of goat or camel hair, and was coarse and uncomfortable. In many cases the sackcloth was only a loin covering. The sarcophagus of Ahiram depicts mourning women with what is likely sackcloth wrapped around their hips over their skirts.

1:14. holy fast. Fasting is little attested in the ancient Near East outside of the Bible. It generally occurs in the context of mourning. In the Old Testament the religious use of fasting is often in connection with making a request before God. The principle is that the importance of the request causes an individual to be so concerned about his or her spiritual condition that physical necessities fade into the background. In this sense the act of fasting is designed as a process leading to purification and humbling oneself before God (Ps 69:10). In connection with the call to repentance, Joel calls for a fast in order to remove any sin or other obstacle that may have led to the devastation they have suffered.

1:14. sacred assembly. Sacred assemblies were occasions for corporate worship. They often accompanied regular annual festivals but could be called for in times of need. In this context it appears to be a convocation of the elders and perhaps involved some decision-making as well as ritual acts.

2:1-27

Locust Army and Repentance

2:17. between the temple porch and the altar. The area between the porch and the altar is a place of limited access. Only the priest would have reason to proceed beyond the altar toward the temple. But it was also used to stage important public acts. In Ezekiel 8:16 this is the area where syncretistic sun worship was being carried out by twenty-five men. In 2 Chronicles 24:21 this is the area in which the prophet Zechariah, son of Jehoiada, was stoned to death (see Mt 23:35).

2:20. northern army. The north was often a symbol of dark powers. Enemies often had little choice but to come at Jerusalem from the north because of the way the major routes went.

2:20. eastern and western sea. The eastern sea would be the Dead Sea that served as a border on the east side of the land. The boundary on the west side was the Mediterranean.

2:23. autumn and spring rains. Israel has a rainy season (winter months) and a dry season (summer months). The rainy season begins with the autumn rains ("early rains," October-November) and ends with the spring rains ("latter rains," early April). These are important for what they contribute to the overall moisture levels in the earth and for softening the ground for plowing. Grain is harvested in the spring (barley in May, wheat in June), and the summer months (July and August) are for threshing and winnowing. Grapes are harvested in the fall, while the olive harvest stretches into the winter.

2:28-32

The Day of the Lord

2:28. pouring out of the Spirit resulting in prophecy, dreams and visions. In Israelite practice anointing was a sign of election and often closely related to endowment by the Spirit. Therefore one could speak of being anointed with the Spirit, or the Spirit being poured out. In Mesopotamia the king was seen as being endowed with the *melammu* of the gods (the visible representation of the glory of deity). In Hebrew the word for spirit can also mean wind. In the ancient Near East the word for wind/spirit was used in connection with dreams and visions as early as Sumerian times. The god of dreams was named "the winds." In Akkadian the name of the god who brought dreams was Zaqiqu, which is derived from the word for wind/spirit. Thus there is a long tradition of association between spirit and revelation through dreams and visions that often leads to prophecy.

2:30. blood, fire, billows of smoke. These are the normal accompaniment of the horrors of war. Blood flows in the streets, houses burn, and smoke rises from the city that can be seen for miles. These are the signs of crisis and judgment on earth just as the next verse speaks of the signs of crisis and judgment in the heavens.

2:31. sun dark, moon to blood. This is the description of solar and lunar eclipses. In a solar eclipse the sun is darkened as the moon passes between it and the earth. This can only occur at the phase of the new moon. In a lunar eclipse the moon is obscured by the earth passing between the sun and the moon. In a total lunar eclipse the moment of the most complete interference results in all but the red spectrum of light being blocked so that the moon glows with an eerie red-orange color rather than being blackened. This can occur only in the full moon phase.

2:31. eclipses in the ancient Near East. In Neo-Assyrian times, eclipses represented the most powerful and deadly omens, being considered the "prime revealer." They were the most frequent cause for the substitute king ritual being invoked (see comment on Is 53:4-10). The nature of the threat they signified was judged by the precise time of their occurrence, the position in the sky at the time of the eclipse and the direction from which the eclipse took place. The combination of signs in heaven and on earth would bring further confirmation of the sign and would suggest a more drastic consequence.

3:1-21
God's Judgment and Blessing
3:2. Valley of Jehoshaphat. There is no valley with this name known in Israel from the Bible or from other sources, or even from tradition. The alternatives are (1) that reference is being made to a valley that had something to do with the ninth-century king of Judah by the name of Jehoshaphat (the only mention of a valley in his account is in 2 Kings 3); or (2) that the valley's name accords with what takes place there (the name Jehoshaphat means "Yahweh judges"). If the latter is the case, as many commentators have concluded, the location would likely be one of the valleys surrounding Jerusalem.

3:3. slave trade. One of the most lucrative aspects of warfare and border raiding was the slave trade. Captives were sold to dealers, who would transport them far from their homeland. The actual number of such persons does not compare to the huge numbers of slaves found in Greek and Roman cities. The slave trade existed from earliest times in the ancient Near East. Slaves were generally war captives or persons taken in raids. Traders often accepted slaves, which they transported to new areas and sold. These persons seldom obtained their freedom. The vast majority of persons who ended up on the slave block were either sold to the slavers by their own families or were prisoners of war.

3:4. Tyre, Sidon, Philistia as oppressors. These coastal regions of the eastern Mediterranean provided the ports through which sea trade passed. From the next few verses one might infer that these cities acted as middlemen for handling captives (in this case from Judah) who were to be sold as slaves. A certain percentage of those taken in battle may have been considered not worth the trouble or expense of deporting. A quick solution was to pass them on to slave traders, who would handle all the details.

3:6. Greeks. The Hebrew term used here, "Ja-

van," was probably the Greek name Ionia, the Greek region of the western coast of Turkey and the Aegean islands. Ionian Greeks settled this area just before the first millennium B.C. There is evidence of contact between them and the Assyrians by the eighth century B.C.

3:8. Sabeans. There are three groups of Sabeans in Scripture. One group is from Sheba, present-day Yemen, an area which was highly urbanized and had achieved a complex degree of civilization by this period (1 Kings 10). Many inscriptions have been found from the Sabeans in this area. There are also Sabeans in Ethiopia (Is 43:3). In Job 6:19 the Sabeans are equated with Tema in north Arabia and are probably identified with the Saba of the Assyrian inscriptions of Tiglath-Pileser III and Sargon II in the late eighth century. It is difficult to determine which is referred to here, though most commentators favor the first option.

3:10. conversion of metals. Rather than "plowshares" that turn over the dirt as they plow, this may refer to the metal tip of the plow that breaks up the earth and scratches out a furrow. This tip is about seven inches long. However, this same Hebrew word is used in 2 Kings 6:5, where it appears to refer to some sort of axe. Pruning hooks are the small knives used to remove leaves and new shoots from the grapevines. Archaeological samples found are simply thin, short pieces of metal with a curved hook at the end sharpened on the inside edge, as a sickle would be. The shape is reminiscent of the tang type spearheads that had been popular during the Bronze Age. These farm implements could be melted down in time of war and reforged for weapons.

3:15. sun, moon and stars darkened. By declaring that on the day of Yahweh the heavens and all of its celestial bodies would be damped out, Isaiah had claimed that the glory of Yahweh would outshine and mask the brilliance of all other supposed gods (Is 13:10; see also the language of Ps 104:19-22, in which Yahweh controls the moon and sun). Since Assyria and Egypt both worshiped the sun god (Shamash and Amon respectively) as their primary deity, and the moon god Sin was of great importance in Babylonia, the prophet targets these gods and these arrogant enemy nations. Such portents of darkness, as in the Deir 'Alla inscription of Balaam, generally forecast a time of great disaster.

3:18. hills flowing with milk. This parallel of wine with milk is unique. The well-known combination of milk and honey is one way to speak of the potential of the region to support a herding economy (see comment on Ex 3:7-10). The word used for wine here refers to freshly squeezed and newly fermented fruit juice. Amos 9:13 also pictures it flowing from the hills, which is logical since vineyards were often planted on the slopes of hills.

3:18. fountain flowing from temple. The association between ancient Near Eastern temples and spring waters is well attested. In fact, some temples in Mesopotamia, Egypt, and the Ugaritic myth of Baal were considered to have been founded upon springs (likened to the primeval waters), which sometimes flowed from the building itself. Thus the symbolic cosmic mountain (temple) stood upon the symbolic primeval waters (spring).

3:18. valley of acacias. Acacias typically grow in dry, wilderness conditions. The wadi that goes from the Valley of Kidron on the east side of Jerusalem to the Dead Sea is still characterized by its acacias, making that the logical choice.

3:19. Egypt and Edom as oppressors. Both of these nations were prominent enemies of Israel in both ancient times and in the events surrounding the exile. Edom had become an Assyrian vassal state in the reign of Tiglath-Pileser III and continued under their rule until the death of Ashurbanipal a century later. It is likely that they submitted themselves to Nebuchadnezzar's rule in 605. Although some Judean refugees may have found shelter in Edom, they apparently remained passive as Jerusalem was destroyed (see Ps 137:7 and Obad 11). Both countries are objects of judgment oracles in Jeremiah and Ezekiel.

AMOS

1:1—2:5
Judgment on the Nations

1:1. Tekoa. The farming village of Tekoa has been identified with Khirbet Tequ'a, about seven miles south of Jerusalem and five miles south of Bethlehem. Because of its location on the edge of arable land, its inhabitants presumably had to work very hard to maintain their existence as farmers and shepherds (see 2 Chron 20:20). For additional information on this small village in the Judean hill country see the comment on 2 Samuel 14:2.

1:1. earthquakes. Seismic activity in Syro-Palestine is a common occurrence. The region lies over the Jordan Rift, which stretches from Damascus to the Gulf of Aqabah, and is therefore subject to periodic shifts of the earth. There is evidence of a sizeable earthquake in the stratum 6 excavations at Hazor, dating to approximately 760 B.C. It is possible that this is the one referred to here, but additional corroborating evidence needs to be sought at other sites, especially Bethel and Samaria. The fact that this earthquake is used to date both Amos's prophetic activity and the reign of King Uzziah (see Zech 14:4-5) suggests that it must have been massive and therefore an event that would have stuck in the minds of the people. If Amos actually predicted the earthquake (as is suggested by Amos 9:1), then it would have authenticated his role as a true prophet of Yahweh.

1:1. chronology. The kings named in Amos's date formula provide a range of time for his prophetic mission. Uzziah of Judah and Jeroboam II of Israel ruled for most of the first half of the eighth century B.C. The earthquake cited here may be the same as that attested by excavations at Hazor (stratum 6) dating to approximately 760. Since Amos claims not to be a professional prophet, many interpreters believe that the oracles of this book would have covered a short span of time rather than stretching over several decades.

1:2. top of Carmel. Mount Carmel overlooked the Mediterranean from the northern coast of Israel. The sea breeze and an annual rainfall of twenty-eight inches made it one of the most flourishing sections of the country. In antiquity its lush slopes were covered with olive trees, vineyards and rich pastureland (see Jer 46:18). Amos and other prophets create a contrasting image with this area's normal fertility and the drought brought on by God's wrath. The prophet also provides a sense of the geographic extent of the disaster, spreading from Jerusalem in the south to Carmel in the north.

1:3. oracles against foreign nations. For this common theme in the prophets see the comment on Jeremiah 46:1.

1:3. Damascus in early eighth century. The eighth century began disastrously for the kingdom of Aram and its capital city of Damascus. The Assyrian king Adad-Nirari III successfully besieged Damascus in 796. Accord-ing to the Assyrian Annals the Syrian king Bir-Hadad (Mar'i in Assyrian) was forced into vassalage. He was also required to make a huge tribute payment, including twenty-three hundred talents of silver and five thousand talents of iron, to save the city. There is even some suggestion that the weakened Syrian monarchy and its territory were subject to the Israelite king Jeroboam II during the mid-eighth century (see 2 Kings 14:28).

1:3. threshing Gilead. The Assyrian Annals of Tiglath-Pileser III give a thorough description of how another nation was defeated and left as though it had been run over by a "threshing sledge." The event mentioned here by Amos may relate to the mid-ninth century invasion of Gilead and the Galilee region by the Syrian king Hazael (see 2 Kings 8:12 and the recently discovered Hazael inscription from Tel Dan). For other examples of the use of a threshing sledge, see the comments on Deuteronomy 25:4; 2 Samuel 24:22; and Isaiah 28:28.

1:4. house of Hazael. Because of his achievements in the ninth century (see 2 Kings 10:32-33), the royal dynasty of Aram/Syria became known as the "house of Hazael." This phrase appears in the annals of Tiglath-Pileser III (744-727 B.C.), who reigned a century later than Hazael. Thus Amos is not referring to a specific king but rather to the dynasty and by extension to the country of Aram itself.

1:4. fortresses of Ben-Hadad. See the comment on Jeremiah 49:27.

1:5. Valley of Aven. Because *aven* means "wickedness" or "idolatry" in Hebrew, it is quite likely that this is not a city site but rather a region where Baal was worshiped (compare Beth-Aven = Bethel in Hos 10:8). It is possible that the fertile Beqa' Valley is the target of the prophet's barb.

1:5. Beth Eden. Ninth-century Assyrian annals from the time of Ashurnasirpal II and Shalmaneser III both mention Beth Eden (Bit Adini) as a rebellious Aramean kingdom located about two hundred miles northeast of Palestine, between the Euphrates and the Balikh rivers. Since it was subjugated and renamed in the reign of Shalmaneser III, the appearance of Beth Eden in the eighth-century prophecies of Amos raises the question of whether this is the same place. However, Tiglath-Pileser III's annals continue to use Beth Eden for an area containing Syrian cities, and Amos may just be using that tradition geographic designation. The ruler at the time of Amos was Shamshi-Ilu.

1:5. Kir. See the comments on Isaiah 22:6 and Amos 9:7 for this site designated as the homeland of the Arameans. It is also mentioned in 2 Kings 16:9.

1:6. Gaza in early eighth century. Since Amos uses Gaza as the synonym for all of the Philistine city-states, it was presumably the most prominent at that time. Because of its alliances with the Arab tribes that controlled the trade routes south to Arabia, Gaza was a major commercial competitor of Judah during the reign of King Jehoram (see 2 Chron 21:16-17). After the Assyrians began to expand their influence into Syro-Palestine, however, the political situation became more complicated. Amaziah and Uzziah were able to defeat the Edomites and regain control over the major port on the Gulf of Aqabah (Elath) in the beginning decades of the century (see 2 Kings 14:7, 22). Uzziah also gained victories over the Philistine cities and the Arabs during this time (2 Chron 26:6-7). It is possible that Amos is reflecting on the enmity between Gaza and Judah in this oracle. In any case, the Assyrian Annals of Tiglath Pileser III (734 campaign against the Philistines) show that as the century wore on the city of Gaza was forced to pay heavy tribute and serve as an Assyrian vassal state.

1:6. selling captives. One of the most lucrative aspects of warfare and border raiding was the slave trade. Captives were easily sold to dealers, who would transport them far from their homeland (see Ezek 27:13; Joel 3:6-7). Note that Mesopotamian administrative texts as far back as pre-Sargonic times (early third millennium) contain ration lists describing persons "belonging to" or "attached to" households or establishments (weaving shops). The actual number of such persons, who are perhaps better described as serfs or service laborers, is not large. Certainly it does not compare to the huge numbers of slaves found in Greek and Roman cities.

1:8. Ashdod in early eighth century. The size of the lower city and its fortifications, built during the tenth century in the Solomonic style found at Gezer and Hazor, suggests prosperity for this Philistine city-state during the ninth and eighth centuries. Excavations in stratum 9 demonstrate that the huge city gate of Ashdod was partially destroyed around 760. This may be attributed to the campaign of Judah's king Uzziah against the Philistines (2 Chron 26:6-7). Prior to Assyrian control over Syro-Palestine, the smaller states of Philistia, Judah, Israel and Transjordan vied for control of trade routes and periodically staged military campaigns as a means of gaining political hegemony in the region. After 750, however, Assyria and Egypt will use these smaller states as part of their own political maneuvering.

1:8. Ashkelon in early eighth century. Like Ashdod, Ashkelon was one of the five major Philistine city-states (see the comments on Judg 1:18 and 14:19). Most of what we know of the site during the eighth century comes from Assyrian Annals and tribute lists. However, there is not much mention of Ashkelon until the time of Tiglath-Pileser III's 734 campaign. The exotic nature of some of the tribute paid by Ashkelon to the Assyrian ruler (including roles of papyrus and elephantine hides) suggests it had commercial links with Arabia and Egypt.

1:8. Ekron in early eighth century. The site of Ekron shrank in size during the first two centuries of the first millennium. This may be due to Israel's domination of Philistia starting in the reign of Solomon. Some new construction does take place in the eighth century, including a fortress tower, suggesting a resurgence during the period when Judah's king Hezekiah controlled the region (2 Kings 18:8). Excavations have not demonstrated any remarkable wealth or prosperity during the early eighth century, and it may be that its name in this oracle is simply part of the usual listing of Philistine cities (see Jer 25:20).

1:9. Tyre in early eighth century. During the first quarter of the eighth century, King Pygmalion ruled Tyre. This was a time of great prosperity for the Phoenicians, who controlled most of the commercial activity in the Mediterranean. They had just expanded their colonial presence by founding Carthage in North Africa in 815. Interestingly, the Assyrian tribute list of Adad-Nirari III from this period includes the king of Sidon, but not that of Tyre. Apparently Tyre, like a prosperous Israel (see Amos 3:15; 6:4), was able to avoid Assyrian entanglements for the time being.

1:11. Edom in early eighth century. After being added to David's kingdom (2 Sam 8:11-13), Edom eventually rebelled and gained its independence from Judah during the reign of Jehoram (2 Kings 8:20-22). Amaziah was able to recapture at least a portion of Edom's territory (2 Kings 14:7) at the battle of Sela (= es-Sela on Edom's northern border), and by the reign of the Israelite king Jeroboam II (789-749) border clashes and tension continued to exist between Edom and its neighbors.

1:12. Teman, Bozrah. See the comments on Jeremiah 49:7 and 49:13 respectively for these Edomite sites.

1:13. Ammon in early eighth century. Like Edom, the Transjordanian nation of Ammon periodically rebelled against Israelite rule (2 Chron 20:1) and during the eighth century was forced to pay tribute to Judah (in Uzziah's reign, see 2 Chron 26:8). The shift in political fortunes is evidenced in one Assyrian source that refers to Ammonite ambassadors coming to Calah (Nimrud) in the eighth century to present tribute. However, the first king of Ammon to be listed in the Assyrian texts is Shobi, son of Hahash (Tiglath-Pileser III's 733 list).

1:13. treatment of pregnant women. The practice of ripping open pregnant women is mentioned very rarely. It is attributed to Assyrian king Tiglath-Pileser I (about 1100) in a hymn praising his conquests. It is also referred to in passing in a Neo-Babylonian lament.

1:14. Rabbah. See the comment on Jeremiah 49:2 for this city, which served as Ammon's capital.

2:1. Moab in early eighth century. The mid-ninth-century Moabite inscription of Mesha is the only extrabiblical documentary evidence (compare 2 Kings 3:4-27) currently available about this Transjordanian nation prior to Tiglath-Pileser's campaign into the area in 734. The hostilities that may have existed between Moab and the nations of Judah and Israel can be speculated on, but there is no concrete evidence. The crime of desecrating the bones of the king of Edom may be an indicator of Edom's alliance with Judah. However, without a historical context within which to place the event, it remains a mystery.

2:1. burning bones. The outrageous nature of this act centers not only on defiling the graves of the kings of Edom, but also on the further step of burning their bones to make lime (see Is 33:12). In this way all honor and respect is removed from the bodies, and the Moabites could actually point to walls or houses that had been painted with the resulting lime mixture. On the exhumation of human remains see the comment on 2 Kings 23:16.

2:2. Kerioth. Also mentioned in the Mesha inscription as a city where the Moabite god Chemosh had a shrine, this Moabite city has been identified with el-Qereiyat and Khirbet Aleiyan (see Jer 48:41).

2:6-16

Sins of Israel

2:8. nature of irony. The great irony in Amos's charges against the rich is that they display their excesses before sacred altars in a shrine dedicated to God. It is possible that they were within their legal rights to seize a garment in default of debt or to purchase wine with funds that had been generated by fining the poor for some offense. However, Yahweh had said (Ex 22:25-26) that the outraged cries of the poor would be heard, "for I am compassionate." As in the case of the worker in the Yavneh Yam inscription, the creditor is to not only obey the law but also take into consideration what seizure of property will do to prevent the debtor from earning a living (see Hammurabi's Code, which forbids seizure of a debtor's ox).

2:9. destroyed Amorite. Israel is reminded of the deeds of the Divine Warrior. Prior to the beginning of the conquest, Yahweh had given the Israelites a victory over the Amorite kings Sihon and Og (see the comments on Num 21:21; 21:24-30). Subsequently, the name Amorites becomes synonymous with the inhabitants of Canaan (see Judg 1:34-36 and 7:14).

2:9. fruit above, roots below. Amos uses a literary device known as a merism—paired polar opposites—to depict the total destruction of the Amorites. This is a common practice in prophetic speech (see Is 37:31; Hos 9:6). It is also found in a Phoenician curse formula (fifth-century *Eshmun 'azor* inscription): "May they have no trunk below nor boughs above." **2:11. Nazirites.** See the comments on Numbers 6:1-21 for this special class of Israelites who impose on themselves an oath of purification.

3:1-15
Legal Case Against Israel

3:2. choosing family. The verb used in the Hebrew text is "know." The same idiom of a god knowing a family is used in Akkadian texts to describe the care that family gods provide for their worshipers.

3:4. lion behavior. During the hunt a lion will roar to freeze its prey with fear as the lion makes its rush. Following a successful hunt a lion may drag a portion of the kill back to its den to be eaten later. It may growl while lying there as a sign of pleasure at its success or as a warning to other predators to stay away. See similar examples of lion behavior in Isaiah 5:29 and Ezekiel 22:25.

3:5. bird hunting. See the comment on Hosea 7:12 for the details of ancient bird hunting with traps and snares. It has been persuasively set forth by S. Paul that the word NIV translates "snare" should be rendered "bait," thus establishing what everyone knows, that the bird must be lured into the trap.

3:9. mountains of Samaria. Although the city of Samaria was located on a single hill, it was surrounded by a group of hills that were actually higher than the capital city (see the comment on 1 Kings 16:24). If the prophet is talking about affording a vantage point from which to see the ultimate destruction of Samaria, then these hills would be appropriate.

ECONOMIC CHANGES AND SOCIAL CLASSES IN EIGHTH-CENTURY ISRAEL

In the light of the political changes that took place at the beginning of the eighth century (Assyrian expansion and the capture of Damascus), Israel was able to widen its economic interests and restore its hegemony over a greater area of the Transjordan. In addition, both Israel and Judah were ruled during the first half of the century by strong kings (Jeroboam II and Uzziah respectively) with long reigns. This made it easier to establish a comprehensive economic policy that concentrated on the mass production of export items such as grain, olive oil and wine. Large areas of the Shephelah and the lowland valleys had already been given over to wheat production (2 Chron 26:10). Now, in the eighth century, the elite were able to impose this economic policy on the small hill country farms and villages. As a result, previous agricultural strategies that attempted to distribute potential risks between herding and farming were overturned, and the land was given over to specific cash crops. The smaller holdings of the peasant farmers, overburdened with debts, were enclosed into large estates. This very efficient use of the land, however, eliminated the mixed crops that had formerly been grown in the village culture and more quickly exhausted the soil. Leaving fields fallow and grazing animals on harvested fields would have been eliminated or rigidly controlled. Under this new policy, an attempt was made to increase exports to the extent that there was a real hunger problem for the peasant class, while the nobility and merchant-class were able to indulge in the luxury goods supplied by their Phoenician trading partners. Thus in addition to facing rising prices at home on basic goods, such as wheat and barley, the impoverished peasant farmers now found themselves forced into debt servitude or day labor. Seeing them ground under the heel of exploiting employers and cheated by greedy merchants who sold them adulterated or inferior grain for their meals, it is no wonder that Amos harangued the rich for their lack of concern for the poor. In such an atmosphere of social injustice, agricultural specialization and economic speculation, the prophet reminds the Israelites of their covenant obligations. Like the "eloquent peasant" of twentieth-century B.C. Egypt, Amos warns them that corrupt judges and dishonest businessmen can expect no mercy from an angry God.

3:11. time between prophecy and fulfillment. Amos, speaking in the 760s, may have assumed that the Assyrians would ultimately serve as God's instrument to punish Israel, but he does not state this explicitly. In any case, Samaria and the nation of Israel will fall to the Assyrian armies of Sargon II in 722, and much of the population will be deported to other portions of the Assyrian empire.

3:12. shepherd's responsibility. The legal codes of ancient Mesopotamia (including the Sumerian Law Code, Hammurabi's Code and the Hittite Laws) each contained a clause designed to aid shepherds who have lost an animal to a lion or other predator. The shepherd gave his testimony and took an oath before the gods. Presumably, if there was any physical evidence to display, such as "a piece of an ear," then this would also have been brought forward. In that way the shepherd would be above suspicion of theft. The pieces he brought did not suggest survival but were proof of destruction.

3:12. beds/couches. In the midst of the coming destruction the homes of the rich merchants and nobles of Samaria will be looted. The fleeing refugees will only be able to carry away with them fragments of their wealth. Amos satirizes their plight as they scavenge portions (the headboard and footpiece) of their beds. The irony of this is found in Amos 6:4, where the prophet condemns the rich for luxuriating on the ivory inlaid beds and couches.

3:14. altars of Bethel. See the comments on 1 Kings 12:29-30 for the establishment of Jeroboam's royal sanctuaries at Dan and Bethel at the time of the division of the kingdom. Despite Bethel's association with the altars of the patriarchs Abraham and Jacob (Gen 12:8; 35:7), it served as a rival to Jerusalem in Amos's time, and thus its altars are now to be condemned as part of Israel's apostasy.

3:14. cutting off horns of altars. The horns on the altar represented the place of sanctuary (Ex 21:13-14) and they were also associated with absolution and atonement (Lev 16:18). Cutting off these horns removed the altar's special qualities, desecrated it and transformed it into nothing more than a damaged stone. Israel is thus deprived of any hope for asylum or expiation for their sins in the face of the coming destruction.

3:15. winter and summer houses. One of the signs of luxury displayed by the rich of Samaria was two residences. A summer residence in Samaria took advantage of the cooler climate of the central hill country of Israel, and a winter home, possibly in the warm Valley of Jezreel, allowed residents to escape the extremes of weather and temperature. There are a number of examples of kings being able to indulge in climatic migration from one official residence to another, including the eighth-century Aramean king of Sam'al, Barrakub, and Cyrus, the king of Persia.

3:15. ivory adornment. Excavations at the site of ancient Samaria have revealed fairly large quantities of ivory that had been used to decorate furniture and the walls of the Omride palace (see the comment on 1 Kings 22:39). There are both Egyptian and Phoenician/Syrian decorative styles employed, including representations of the god Horus, lotus blossoms and the "lady in the window" motif. The Iron Age ivories differ from those of the Late Bronze (best represented by those found at Megiddo) with the addition of glass paste and inlaid semiprecious stones. It is possible that some of these ivories were carved and decorated by native Israelite craftsmen, but more likely they are expensive imports.

4:1-13
Judgments with No Effect

4:1. cows of Bashan. Once again demonstrating his background as a herdsman, Amos uses the finely bred cattle of Bashan as a metaphor. These prize animals grazed on the lush grass available in this region in Transjordan on either side of the Yarmuk River (see Deut 32:14). Amos compares these fine cows to the self-indulgent wives of the nobility and wealthy merchants of Samaria. Neither these cows nor these women are capable of seeing beyond their own personal needs and desires (compare Is 3:16). The women, like totally self-absorbed grazing cows, cannot even imagine that people may be starving while they call for another cup of wine or another extravagant meal. It is difficult to say for sure whether the reference is to domesticated pampered cattle or to undomesticated ferocious cattle. Both could be found in Bashan and either picture can make sense of the analogy.

4:1. upper-class women. The prosperity that had come to Israel's merchant class and nobility during the first half of the eighth century B.C. is the direct result of the spreading Assyrian hegemony. In 802 the Assyrian king Adad-Nirari III captured the city of Damascus and effectively removed Syria from its position as chief political and economic rival of Israel. For a brief time, therefore, the city of Samaria and the rest of Israel enjoyed a period of peace and prosperity that brought wealth and allowed for amazing self-indulgence in luxury goods and new construction projects.

Amos targets the wives of these prosperous individuals, singling them out as a base cause for the oppression of the poor. The covenant had placed obligations on the Israelites to care for the less privileged, but what Amos sees are persons who do not count the human cost that pays for their high living.

4:2. hooks, fishhooks. The Hebrew here is very uncertain. An attractive suggestion has been made that the verse describes not what fish are caught with but what they are transported in (baskets and pots). This metaphor is known from the prophetic literature of Mari, where the king's enemies are portrayed as wriggling like fish in a basket. Fishing in Mesopotamian streams and rivers was done with woven baskets (sometimes made from thorn bushes). In fact there is no evidence of the use of fishhooks in Mesopotamia after 3000. Amos's metaphor of the capture of the Israelites after the siege of Samaria may be better translated as "fish baskets." If hooks are in view, however, it is possible that he is referring to the grappling hooks that were used during the siege and that might have been used to impale and drag prisoners.

4:3. Harmon. Since this word occurs only here, there have been a number of suggestions on its meaning. Some scholars consider it a place name and thus the place where the captives are exiles. Among the suggestions here are Mount Minni in Assyria (see Jer 51:27) or Hermel near Kadesh on the Orontes River. For those who emend the text, the translation of "dung heap" for *hadmon* (exchanging a single letter for one that looks similar) is the most likely since it is a suitable place for the disposal of the bodies of prisoners.

4:4. cult sites at Bethel and Gilgal. Bethel has a long history of cultic activity, ranging back to the construction of an altar there by Abraham (Gen 12:8) and Jacob's dream there (Gen 28:10-22). It took on an ominous quality for Amos when it was designated as one of the two major cultic centers by Jeroboam (1 Kings 12:29-30). Cultic activity at Gilgal appears in the conquest narrative when the Israelites cross the Jordan and Joshua raises a memorial to commemorate the event (Josh 4:19-20). It is possible that after the division of the kingdoms, Gilgal was seen as a northern worship site because of its association with Saul (see 1 Sam 11:15 and 15:21). Hosea also condemns this place as corrupt (Hos 4:15 and 9:15).

4:4. three-year tithes. The better reading of the Hebrew here would be "on the third day" or "every three days" (instead of every three years, see NIV note). It is possible that Amos is satirizing an aspect of the northern kingdom's

cultic practice. There is a possibility that free-will offerings and noncompulsory tithes (compare Gen 14:20) were given at the sanctuary shortly after arrival or were tied to some coming event or vow. To Amos, however, such frequency of offerings cannot replace true piety or obedience to the covenant.

4:9. blight and mildew. Farmers are only too aware of what the forces of nature can do to their crops. Here God attempts to get Israel's attention by destroying the harvest. First, the sirocco winds strip all of the moisture out of the air and the plant life. Then, too much rain falls and the crops turn yellowish-brown and wither in the fields. See the comment on curses in Deuteronomy 28:22.

4:9. locusts. Insects can also play havoc with growing crops as well as the leaves on olive and fig trees. For another example of locust swarms and their relation to God's anger see Joel 1:4-7. Akkadian Mari texts report that locusts descended on a town and another explains that the harvest could not be completed because of the swarm of insects. For information concerning the devastation caused by locusts see the comment on Exodus 10:1-20.

4:13. connection between wind and thoughts. In Hebrew the word translated "wind" is the word that is also often translated "spirit." It is not so much that the word had two different meanings but rather that in the ancient world they did not find it so easy to differentiate between wind and spirit. In Mesopotamian thought the gods gave revelation of their thoughts through dreams. The messenger who brought these dreams was named Zaqiqu. The common word *zaqiqu* refers to a ghost or a phantom. It derives from the verb *zaqu*, which refers to the blowing of the wind, or to the breath of a god.

5:1-27

Seeking the Lord

5:5. Bethel, Gilgal. See comment on 4:4.

5:5. shrine at Beersheba. The discovery of a large horned altar in the excavations of Tell es-Saba' dating to the Iron II period provides corroboration of cultic activity at this southern site. It is mentioned in the ancestral narratives (Gen 21:33) and is the site where Samuel's sons operated as judges (1 Sam 8:1-2). The destruction of shrines outside Jerusalem by King Hezekiah (Arad, Beersheba; 2 Kings 18:4) may be a reflection of Amos's condemnation of these sites.

5:8. Pleiades and Orion, constellations in ancient world. Textual evidence from Babylonia, including the "Venus tablet" of Ammisaduqa (c. 1650), indicates that astronomical studies were conducted with skill and precision. Although astrology was also prevalent in late Egyptian periods and in Persian period Mesopotamia, it seems that this divinatory activity, interpreting omens (see Is 47:13) is only an extension of the work of a true science. There are records of the movement of the planets, placement of the major fixed stars and constellations, as well as descriptions of the phases of the moon and solar and lunar eclipses. Given the widespread knowledge of the stars and the planets in both Mesopotamian and Egyptian cultures, it was important for the biblical writers and prophets to attribute these celestial bodies to Yahweh's creation (see Job 9:9). Mesopotamian constellations included animal figures such as a goat (Lyra) and snake (Hydra); objects such as an arrow (Sirius) and a wagon (Big Dipper); and characters such as Anu (Orion). The most popular of the constellations was Pleiades, often portrayed on seals even in Palestine and Syria. Neo-Assyrian texts preserve sketches of stars in constellations. A prayer to the gods of the night from about 1700 B.C. invokes the constellations by name, calling on them to give answers to the diviner seeking an omen.

5:11. stone mansions. This refers to houses using hewn stone (called "ashlar"), for many of the houses in Israel used rough fieldstones in construction. Often the foundation was stone while the superstructure was of sun-dried mud brick. Only the very wealthiest of the upper class would have been able to afford this carefully dressed masonry. The limestone used for this construction was quarried near Samaria. The curse used here is called a "futility curse" because it calls for their efforts and labor to become futile, and it can be compared to an inscription on a Babylonian boundary stone calling on the gods to see that anyone who builds a house on stolen land should have the house taken from them.

5:12. judicial bribes and oppression. One of Amos's principal themes is criticism of social injustice (see Ex 23:6-8; Deut 16:19; and Hammurabi's Code for laws against bribery). There is a long history of peasant or wisdom literature pleading for justice under the law and from kings and officials. For example, in a collection of Babylonian Wisdom sayings the "unscrupulous judge" is one who accepts a present "and yet lets justice miscarry." Similarly, the twenty-first century "eloquent peasant" in Egyptian literature charges that "lawmakers approve of robbery" and "the inspector condones corruption." The tenth-century Babylonian "Theodicy" decries people who "fill the storehouse of the oppressor with gold" while they "empty the larder of the beggar of its provisions."

5:20. day of the Lord. See sidebar at Joel 2.

5:21. religious feasts and assemblies. Amos's attack is addressed at the empty, mechanically celebrated *ḥagîm*, the technical term for the three major pilgrimage festivals (Feast of Unleavened Bread, Feast of Harvest and Feast of Ingathering—see the comments on Ex 23:15-16). Religious festivals offered frequent opportunity for celebrations, communal meals and social gatherings. What had been designed as a means to praise and honor God, however, was not bringing any pleasure to him.

5:23. music in worship. Mesopotamia and Egypt have long histories of both popular and religious music that also must have been known to the Israelites. Professional musicians, like the *kalu* harp-player so well attested in ancient texts from Old Babylonian Mari and Sumerian Uruk, may well have been the model for the Levitical musicians in the Jerusalem temple as well as the musicians in the northern shrines of Dan and Bethel. The types of instruments, liturgical chants, penitential prayers and laments, and hymns of praise created by these ancient civilizations set a standard of style and composition for the Near East. Ancient Egyptian tomb paintings demonstrate the postures of dancers as well as a wide variety of musical instruments. One example of the technical expertise employed in sacred music is found in the Psalms associated with the recitation of the creation story— Psalms 8, 19, 104 and 139. They contain both the literary as well as the musical elements (based on the superscription rubrics, choral markers and assonances in the text) needed for a proper performance of music during worship and the enactment of sacred drama.

5:26. shrine of the king. Because of a mistaken belief that the god Sikkuth was not introduced until after the Assyrian conquest (see 2 Kings 17:30), there has been an attempt to emend the Hebrew so that the text is read "shrine" or "abode" of the king. In fact, Amos's statement probably reflects the degree of cultural influence exercised by Aramean merchants and other travelers on the Israelites. Sikkuth or ^dSAG.KUD is associated with Ninurta in Ugaritic sources and specifically with the planet Saturn.

5:26. pedestal of idols. This translation is also an attempt to remove the name of an astral deity from the text with an emendation of the word *kiyyun*. The Mesopotamian star god, Saturn, occurs as *kajamanu* in Akkadian texts and has the meaning "the steady one," an apt title for the slow-moving orbit of the planet Saturn. The images of these astral deities were carried in procession on their festival days.

5:26. star of your god. Since both of the gods mentioned in this verse are associated with the planet Saturn, the phrase "star of your god" is actually a reference to the people's worship of astral deities. Sacred processions paraded the images and symbols of these gods through the city streets to their shrines, where sacrifices, sacred dancing and other cultic activities would take place. Amos, however, is satirizing these practices. Instead of simply describing what has been occurring, he now predicts a "final" procession, but this time the people carry these idols with them into exile (compare the carrying of burdensome idols in Is 46:1).

5:27. exile beyond Damascus. Since the Assyrians are never directly mentioned in Amos, it is unclear that this is what he meant when he spoke of the coming exile of the people of Israel. Using such an imprecise phrase as "beyond Damascus" is reminiscent of Jeremiah's threat "from the north" (Jer 1:14), and both simply indicate the direction of Mesopotamia as the source of the coming destruction.

6:1-14
Woe and Indictment Oracles

6:1. Mount Samaria. For Amos's parallelism to work most effectively, Mount Samaria would have to also contain a worship center just as Mount Zion does in Jerusalem. It is likely a reference to the acropolis section of the city where the temple and palace would be located. Considering Micah's condemnation of Samaria and its idols (Mic 1:6-7) and Isaiah's reference to "Samaria and her images" (Is 10:11), it seems likely that Israel's capital had a major shrine during the reign of Jeroboam II.

6:2. Calneh and Hamath. Although its exact location is still uncertain, Calneh, the capital of the ancient state of Unqi, was most likely situated in the Antioch plain, near Aleppo. Hamath (modern Hama, almost 100 miles south of Aleppo and about 130 miles north of Damascus) is located on the Orontes River. (for more information see the comments on Is 10:9). Though both suffered destruction at the hands of the Assyrians in 738, Israel was also paying tribute at that time too, so Amos cannot be that late. We know too little of the history of northern Syria in the decades preceding Amos to identify what else he may be referring to.

6:2. Gath. Gath has been tentatively identified as Tell es-Safi, five miles south of Tell Miqne/Ekron. Of the five major cities of the Philistines, it was the closest to Judah. There has been little excavation at the site, though it has been confirmed that there are Iron Age remains. The city was located by the Elah Valley, one of the principal passes from the coastal plain into the hill country surrounding Jerusalem. It was the target of an attack by Uzziah of Judah (referred to in 2 Chron 26:6) in the time of Amos.

6:4. beds inlaid with ivory. The idea of a bed made from some exotic or luxurious material is reminiscent of King Og's iron bed in Deuteronomy 3:11 (see also Solomon's ivory throne in 2 Chron 9:17-19). Sennacherib's Assyrian Annals mention that Judah's king Hezekiah included a couch inlaid with ivory among his tribute items. Ivory decor was very popular at this time for inlays in furniture and for wall panels. One of the principal sources of ivory was elephant tusks, which were imported from Aram (where Syrian elephants were not yet extinct at this time). Elephant hides and tusks, as well as live elephants, were at times included in tribute payments. Excavations at Ashurnasirpal's palace at Kalah produced some very fine ivory carvings decorating the walls. Over five hundred ivory fragments have also been found in the excavations at Samaria dating to the ninth and eighth centuries B.C. Many feature Egyptian and Phoenician artistic motifs.

6:4. choice lambs, fattened calves. For those who could afford it, the best quality meats came from specially bred sheep and cattle that were kept in stalls (see Mal 4:2) and fattened with barley prior to slaughter. Presumably, these ancient feed lots could command a higher price and were well known (see Jeremiah's metaphor for overfed mercenaries in Jer 46:21). Evidence of this breed of sheep (Akk. *kirru*) is found in Ur III economic texts dating to the twentieth-century B.C.

6:6. wine by the bowl. The term used for bowl here is one that is usually associated with cultic activity (see Ex 24:6-8; Num 7:13). That suggests that Amos is accusing them not only of drinking to excess in large bowls but perhaps also of profaning sacred objects. Note that archaeologists have found a number of golden drinking bowls in tombs at Nimrud dating to the late Assyrian period, some of which have the names of Assyrian queens engraved on their sides.

6:6. fine lotions. Banqueters in the ancient world were often treated by a generous host to fine oils that would be used to anoint their foreheads. This provided a glistening sheen to their countenance and also would have added a fragrance to their persons and the room. For example, an Assyrian text from Esarhaddon's reign describes how he "drenched the foreheads" of his guests at a royal banquet with "choicest oils." Since Amos may be condemning the people for misusing cultic vessels in this verse, he may also be taking them to task for using the oils that would otherwise have been used as part of cultic practice (see Ex 30:31-32).

6:7. feasting. The word translated "feasting" here is a technical term for a funeral meal (more like a festal memorial meal; thus the use of vessels and oils usually connected with cultic rites). The term occurs only here and Jeremiah 16:5, although it is well known in many other Semitic traditions. Extrabiblical references to the funeral meal have been found in Ugaritic texts, in Aramaic texts from Elephantine (Egypt) and in inscriptions in Punic, Nabatean and Palmyrene. All of the elements listed in these verses are connected with these feasts: meat and wine, music, anointing and lounging.

6:10. burning the bodies. The burning of bodies was not a common practice (but see comments on 1 Sam 31:12 and 2 Chron 16:14), and the spelling of the verb is unusual. This has led a number of interpreters to an alternative reading such that the text does not suggest burning the body but embalming it with spices for burial.

6:10. not mentioning the Lord's name. God's wrath is such that the population of the city of Samaria is to be reduced to a tenth, and the survivors will be so frightened by what Yahweh has done that they will be afraid to mention God's name lest the angry deity take any further notice of them. In that sense then, the command "Hush!" is a sort of warding spell (like "God forbid" in English) to prevent the incautious from invoking God (compare Ex 23:13 and Josh 23:7). Assyrian royal documents from the reign of Enlil-Nirari (1326-1317) provide some light here. In one text the king calls out, "May the god by no means speak!" when the death of a member of the royal family is announced at court. His intent may be to ask that the god not act (speak) against anyone else.

6:13. Lo Debar. This site, one of those captured by Jeroboam II during his Transjordanian campaign (2 Kings 14:25), is most often identified with Tell 'el-Hammeh, just north of the Jabbok River, in what would have been Ammonite territory. Amos parodies this victory by revocalizing the city name to *Lo-dabar*, which means "nothing." He mocks their false

pride in these flimsy accomplishments that are as nothing to God's victories.

6:13. Karnaim. This important site is located in Bashan at Tell es-Sa'ad, on a northern tributary of the Yarmuk River (see Gen 14:5 and 1 Macc 5:26). Tiglath-Pileser III made it the capital of the Assyrian province of Qarnina when he conquered the region in his 738-737 campaign.

6:14. Lebo Hamath to the Wadi Arabah. See the comment on 2 Kings 14:25 for King Jeroboam II's attempt to restore Israel's borders.

7:1-9

Punishment Alternatives

7:1. locusts. See comment on 4:9.

7:1. king's share. Although it is not mentioned elsewhere in the biblical text, this reference indicates that the king was entitled, as a form of tax, to a portion of the mown grass. This may have been a measure instituted to insure the king's chariot horses and cavalry had sufficient fodder. A reverse example of this is found in a land grant made by the Assyrian king Ashurbanipal to one of his officials. This decree exempted the official's new lands from being levied for straw, grain or a portion of his flocks.

7:7. plumb line. This traditional translation is no longer acceptable, based on the recognition that the Hebrew *'anak* is a cognate of the Akkadian *annaku*, meaning "tin." A plumb line would have a lead or iron weight attached in order to determine that a wall is perpendicular during construction. S. Paul suggests this stands for a tin wall, a symbol of how weak or fragile Israel's defenses are (compare the iron walls in Jer 1:18; Ezek 4:3). For now the exact meaning of this phrase remains uncertain.

7:10-17

Amaziah Confronts Amos

7:10. prophetic message as treason. Throughout the ancient world it was believed that prophets not only proclaimed the message of deity but in the process unleashed the divine action. In Assyrian king Esarhaddon's instructions to his vassals, he requires that they report any improper or negative statements made by anyone, specifically naming prophets, ecstatics and dream interpreters. It is no wonder, then, that a prophet negatively disposed toward a king had to be controlled lest he bring about all sorts of havoc. One can perhaps understand why a king would be inclined to imprison a prophet whose very words might incite insurrection or impose doom.

7:13. king's sanctuary. Bethel was one of the two royal sanctuaries established by King Jeroboam to serve as alternative worship centers for the people of the northern kingdom (1 Kings 12:26-30). Amaziah's post was a political appointment since the priesthood at Bethel was established by the crown rather than being attached to tribal lineage as the Levites were (1 Kings 12:32). Naturally his loyalties were to the king, and he was very offended by any criticism of either the king or the shrine at Bethel. The state temple was one in which the king himself participated in the ritual activities.

7:14. shepherd. No village in Judah's central hill country could afford to engage in a single economic activity. Every household would have had their small fields of wheat and barley, as well as a small vineyard, a few fig trees and olive trees on their land. In this way they could hope that at least some of their agricultural endeavors paid off. In like manner, a few sheep, goats and cattle would have served as an economic hedge. It would have been easy enough to allow them to graze on the hillsides, accompanied by a boy (see David's occupation in 1 Sam 16:11). A Mesopotamian parallel to this practice is found in the Akkadian word *naqidu*, a term used for a breeder of cattle, sheep and goats.

7:14. caring for sycamore figs. The sycamore figs (*Ficus sycomorus L.*) originated in east central Africa and spread to Egypt and the Near East by the Iron Age. The trees are capable of as many as six crops per year. Since the fruit is inferior to that of the common fig (*Ficus carica L.*), the poor principally consume it. Date gardens take up to twenty years to reach their full productive potential. They require much attention because they have to be pollinated by hand. The care of the sycamore fig requires that the fruit be gashed or pierced to encourage an increase in ethylene gas that speeds the ripening process. The knife used to gash the fruit is depicted in Egyptian tomb paintings in Thebes.

8:1-14

Ripe for Judgment

8:5. clash between economic and religious concerns. As Nehemiah discovered several centuries later in Persian-period Jerusalem, the desire of merchants to conduct business sometimes makes their compliance with religious law and Sabbath regulations a matter for complaint or even circumvention (see comment on Neh 10:31). There were religious festivals in surrounding cultures (see com-

ment on Ex 20:8-11), but only Israel was commanded to obey the sabbath law and cease all work (see comment on Ex 31:12-17). This restriction on trade caused friction and apparently contributed to corrupt business practices as a way of "making up" the losses.

8:5. cheating in the market. Certainly, Amos's complaints against Israelite merchants are not unique. For instance, the charge made against merchants that they use false balances is found in the Egyptian *Instruction of Amenemope* and in a clause in the Babylonian wisdom literature. Similarly, Hammurabi's Code contains a statement about bankers who "use a light scale to measure the grain or the silver that they lend and a heavy scale to measure the grain or the silver that they collect."

8:6. sweepings with the wheat. In their efforts to squeeze as much profit as possible from their holdings, grain merchants were cheating the poor by selling the "husks" of the wheat. A similar charge is made in the Egyptian *Tale of the Eloquent Peasant* against those who "substitute lesser for better goods." The word translated as "sweepings" occurs only here, but it is related to the word "to fall" and reflects the poorest quality or that which is left over.

8:8. rising like the Nile. There is a three-month inundation cycle in the flow of the Nile River (from August to October). The increase in volume is the result of monsoon rains in Ethiopia that swell the Nile and its tributaries. Although the height of the inundation is irregular, the Egyptians early in their history learned to make efficient use, through irrigation canals and other means, of whatever the rise of the Nile brought to them.

8:9. sun go down at noon. Since a lunar or solar eclipse was considered a portent of evil or the anger of the gods in the ancient Near East, there are many citations in the literature. Among them is the prediction by the prophet Balaam in the Deir 'Alla inscription that the divine assembly has decided to "bring darkness instead of light." Priests of the moon god Sin in Babylonian would wear torn garments and sing dirges during an eclipse, and there are numerous letters and omen texts in Babylonian and Assyrian records referring to eclipses. Many are written to kings either warning them of a coming eclipse or assuring the monarch that they will be kept informed of the likelihood of coming occurrences. For biblical examples see Joel 3:15 and Zechariah 14:6.

8:10. mourning practices. See comments on Genesis 37:34-35; Leviticus 19:28; and Deuteronomy 14:1-2.

8:12. sea to sea. In their staggering search for

water during the drought, the people will search from one end of the kingdom to the other. From "sea to sea" is used fairly often to distinguish east and west (from the Mediterranean in the west to the Dead Sea or Jordan River) by the biblical writers (see Ps 72:8; Zech 9:10). A similar expression occurs in the Karatepe inscription of the Aramean king Azitawada: "from sunrise to sunset" (see Is 45:6) for east to west or a sense of universality. Since it is combined here with "north to east," it is possible that it defines the southern latitudinal border of the northern kingdom.

8:12. north to east. The southern boundary has been defined in the previous line, and the western boundary is obvious. From Bethel one could still search to the Galilee region to the north, heading for places like Samaria or Dan, and to the east, whether Beth Shan or the Transjordan territory of Gilead.

8:14. shame/Ashima. While the uncertainty with this word has led to its being translated "shame," it seems most likely that it is a reference to the Syrian god Ashima (NIV note). This deity's title comes from the Aramaic for "the name" and thus is a shorthand for any number of the northwest Semitic gods and goddesses (Baal, Anat, Astarte). Although official introduction of the worship of Ashima does not occur until after 722, this does not preclude this god's being worshiped in Samaria before this time. Later evidence for worship of Ashima comes from the Elephantine letters.

8:14. god of Dan. Since Jeroboam I had instituted the worship of Yahweh at Dan by creating a royal sanctuary there (1 Kings 12:28-30), it is appropriate for Amos to refer to the god of Dan. He is probably also referring to the golden calf placed there by Jeroboam as a symbol of Yahweh and as a substitute for the ark of the covenant. Dan continued to have cultic significance for many centuries. Evidence of this is found in a late-third-century bilingual (Greek and Aramaic) inscription that contained the phrase "to the god who is in Dan."

8:14. god of Beersheba. Amos now completes his condemnation of false worship practices among the Israelites by a reference to the "way" of the "god" of Beersheba. "From Dan to Beersheba" is a common phrase for the full extent of the land (Judg 20:1; 1 Sam 3:20), and Amos uses it to demonstrate the universality of Israelite apostasy (see Amos 5:5).

9:1-15
Coming Destruction and Restoration

9:1. tops of the pillars. In order to describe

how complete the coming destruction will be, Amos again employs a merism. This time his range is from the top to the bottom of the shrine at Bethel, from the capital that decorates the top of the pillars to the doorjamb (see Zeph 2:14). It is possible to compare these earth tremors to Isaiah's call narrative (Is 6:4), but there it is just a reflection of God's magisterial presence. Ancient Near Eastern examples of similar destruction mention walls, gates, doors or doorjambs being smashed or demolished (including the Gilgamesh Epic and the inscription of Tukulti-Ninurta I).

9:2. grave/heaven contrast. Amos employs a merism contrasting the cosmic distances between heaven and the depths of Sheol (see Ps 139:8). The boasting of Mot in the Ugaritic *Hymn to Baal and Anat* also provides this contrast to the powers of the underworld or death to that of heaven and life. In the ancient world, heaven and the netherworld were not considered to be "spiritual" places outside of the cosmos. Rather, they represented the extreme ends of the cosmos.

9:3. top of Carmel. As part of this series of phrases warning the Israelites that they cannot hide from God's wrath, Amos uses the image of the highest point within their nation. Mount Carmel stands eighteen hundred feet above sea level and is a commanding presence, with dense forests and many caves that some might presume to be excellent hideouts (see the comment on Amos 1:2).

9:3. serpent in the bottom of the sea. From the mountaintop to the bottom of the ocean, there is no place to hide. Even at these depths, God can command the sea serpent to do his biding (compare Jon 1:17). The Israelites knew well the tradition of Yahweh subduing the great sea creatures (see comment on Ps 74:14 and 104:26). Similar contests of strength are found in the Babylonian creation epic, *Enuma Elish,* and the Egyptian hymn to the sun god, Ra, who must repulse the dragon Apophis repeatedly in order to complete his circuit across the skies. For more information see comments on Genesis 1:20; Exodus 7:1; and Isaiah 27:1.

9:6. cosmic temple. Amos's attempt to express God's complete control over all creation begins with a multistoried or many-chambered sanctuary or palace in the heavens (compare Ps 78:69; Is 66:1). These "upper chambers" bind together the vaults of heaven while at the same time rest upon the waters (see Ps 104:3). A precedent for these lofty chambers is found in the *Enuma Elish.* It contains a description of the building of the Esagila temple to Marduk in Babylon in which the gods "built a stage-tower as high as Apsu (waters above the heavens)." In the biblical and ancient Near Eastern view the cosmos was a temple and the temple was a microcosmos.

9:7. Cushites. See the comment on Numbers 12:1 for a description of these people from ancient Nubia in the Sudan south of Egypt.

9:7. Philistines from Caphtor. For a Philistine connection with Caphtor (Crete), see the comment on Jeremiah 47:4. Ezekiel 25:16 connects them with another of the Sea People groups, the Kerethites. See the comment on Deuteronomy 2:23 for their connection with the Avvites. The prophet uses the universalism theme to show God's concerns for all nations. The Philistines and Arameans, like the Israelites, had been brought to Palestine, but Israel's covenant relationship with Yahweh now required them to be singled out for punishment.

9:7. Arameans from Kir. Amos refers to Kir as the homeland of the Aramean tribes here, but 2 Kings 16:9 speaks of Kir as the place where the conquering Assyrians exiled the Arameans after King Rezin was executed. Isaiah 22:6 seems to support this latter reference since it speaks of Kir in relation to Elam, south and east of the Tigris River. Assyrian records from the reign of Tiglath-Pileser I (1115-1107) speak of the migration of these tribes into Assyria during the twelfth century. What Amos may be doing here and in 1.5 is to point out

that just as the Arameans had been sent back to their place of origin, God just as easily could dispatch the Israelites from the land of Canaan.

9:9. grain in a sieve. The work of processing harvested grain included crushing the stalks on the threshing floor with a sled, winnowing (see Jer 4:11) and finally using a sieve to separate the kernels of grain from small stones and other debris. The sieve mentioned here (*kebarah*) has large holes and works best when shaken sideways and in a circular motion. This ordinarily forces the debris to the sides and allows the kernels to fall to the ground where they can be collected (see Ecclus 27:4). The initial NIV translation of *seror* was later corrected from "kernel" to "pebble" to reflect the true action of the sieve.

9:12. remnant of Edom. Amos employs the phrase "the remnant of" two other times (1:8 for the Philistines and 5:15 for Joseph). In this case he may be referring to a portion of the territory of Edom rather than to all of it. King Uzziah had captured the Edomite port at Elath (2 Kings 14:22), and it has subsequently been lost again in the reign of Ahaz (2 Kings 16:6) to the Syrians and Edomites. In this eventual restoration of the Davidic kingdom, Amos may have this valuable port city in mind.

OBADIAH

1. Edom. The principal theme of the book of Obadiah is an indictment of Edom for its crimes against Judah. This nation, located south and east of the Dead Sea, has a mixed tradition among the Israelites. Much as Jacob and Esau, the traditional founders of the two nations, had an ambivalent relationship, so Edom is at times seen as a friend and ally (Deut 2:2-6; 2 Kings 3:9) and on other occasions as a deadly enemy (Num 20:14-21; Amos 1:11-15). During the period of the Neo-Assyrian empire and the Neo-Babylonian empire (734-586) Edom had been a vassal state. Most likely Obadiah's complaint against Edom relates to its participation in the final destruction of Jerusalem and the exile of its people by Nebuchadnezzar of Babylon in 587-586 B.C., but records are unclear concerning the precise role that Edom played.

1. envoy building coalition. When nations went to war in the ancient Near East, it was necessary to call on all covenant partners and vassal states to send troops and supplies for a combined effort. Messengers would be sent to call on them to honor their treaty commitments and conscript the specified number of soldiers (seen in 1 Sam 11:3-4 and the reciprocal defense pact found in the treaty between Pharaoh Rameses II and the Hittite king Hattusilis III). The Mari texts even describe the practice of sending envoys to the temple of a god to inform the deity of the military situation and call on his aid in the coming conflict.

3. topography of Edom. The region of Edom is a mountainous land, dominated by ridges that extend from the Zered River south to the Aqaba. The area is filled with mountain peaks rising as much as fifty-seven hundred feet above sea level, sharp crags, caves and clefts in which armies could hide. A number of Edomite cities were also located in these nearly inaccessible sites, such as Bosrah and the rocky peak known as Umm el-Biyara in Petra, which some identify with Sela.

5. significance of grapes. Edom was known for its fine mountain-side vineyards. The destruction of the country is likened to the double despoilings of thieves and gleaners. What the thieves or harvesters leave, the gleaners will take. All that will remain is the rotten and crushed fruit left on the ground.

6. Esau/Edom connection. The use of Esau interchangeably with Edom is based on the understanding of Esau as the ancestor of that nation in Genesis 36:31-39 (see Mal 1:2-3). There one finds a list of eight kings who reigned in Edom prior to the establishment of the Israelite monarchy.

6. hidden treasures. This phrase occurs only here in the Old Testament and cannot be adequately translated because of its unusual formation and the lack of additional use elsewhere to help supply a context. Similar words in Isaiah 45:3 and Jeremiah 49:10 provide the basis for the current translation. What is indicated by the text is the thoroughness of the plundering of Edom. Secret treasuries were known in the ancient world, but this was especially appropriate to Edom, where, because of the terrain, whole cities could be kept secret.

7. breaches of international etiquette. Treaties between nations, such as that between Egypt and the Hittite empire (Rameses II and Hattusilis III) or the Vassal Treaties of the seventh-century B.C. Assyrian king Esarhaddon, functioned as mutual defense pacts and required the signatories to provide arms, information and legal reciprocity. Edom is accused here of a total breach in these agreements: refugees have been forced back to their own borders without any relief; nonaggression clauses by covenant partners have been violated; and hospitality customs, in which eating a meal together is the basis of peace agreements (seen in Ps 41:9 and phrases in Mari and El Amarna texts referring to covenant meals), have been completely ignored. The breaking of treaty agreements when convenient or beneficial is well attested in the ancient world. Examples include Egypt's failure to supply needed troops to the Canaanite kings during the Amarna period and the Babylonian king, Nabonidus, breaking his treaty with the Medes in order to make one with the Persians, whom he considered a greater threat.

8. reputation of wisdom of Edom. The tradition of Edomite wisdom can be somewhat substantiated by the nation's association with Job (from Uz, which is considered by some to be in Edom) and with Job's friend Eliphaz the Temanite. Living on the fringe of the northern Arabian desert and benefitting from the caravan trade and accessible copper deposits, it may be that Edom was known for its business acumen or diplomatic shrewdness (see the parallel statement in Jer 49:7).

9. Teman. There is some difficulty in pinpointing the exact location of the tribal territory of Teman. Some scholars tie it to Bozrah, identified as its capital city after the eighth century B.C., and place Teman in the northern region of Edom. However, a number of others, using the references from the fourth-century A.D. historian Eusebius, locate Teman in the southern part of Edom and tie it to the ancient king Husham (Gen 36:34). The Kuntillet 'Ajrud inscriptions also mention "Yahweh of Teman" and suggest a southern location for this region. In this passage it is synonymous with the nation of Edom.

10. violence against Jacob. The fraternal relationship between Edom/Esau and Jacob/Judah is common in Obadiah (see comment on v. 6) and thus does not have to denote a treaty arrangement. This adds to the shock and shame of violence done against a neighbor with traditional kin ties. The word used here for violence has a range of meaning, from murder and rape to wickedness and bloodshed. In this instance it serves as a "shock term" to emphasize the degree of damage inflicted and the justification for Edom's punishment. The Neo-Assyrian annals make similar statements expressing anger and amazement when a treaty partner revolts and military reprisal becomes necessary.

11. casting lots for Jerusalem. The practice of casting lots as part of the divination process in Babylonia and Assyria is described in the comment on Urim and Thummim in Exodus 28:30. The greed with which the invaders look upon Jerusalem suggests visions of looting and great wealth that will result from the city's destruction (see Is 17:14). Armies regularly established criteria for the division of spoils (seen in the penalties imposed on officers in the Mari texts who fail to share this wealth with their soldiers). Casting lots may have been one method for distribution of goods and slaves, since it implied divine intervention.

16. drinking on the holy hill. Edom initially drank in celebration of Jerusalem's fall along with her allies. Ultimately, however, it will be Edom, along with the nations who have participated in Jerusalem's destruction, who will be forced to drink perpetually from Yahweh's "cup of wrath" (see Ps 75:8; Is 51:17; Jer 25:15-16).

19. territorial changes. What is envisioned here is both retribution against Israel's enemies and the reclamation of all of Israel's traditional territories. Thus the Negev, synonymous with the area around Beersheba and the lower portion of the Dead Sea, would take over the territory of Edom. The Shephelah, a narrow ridge of land between the coastal plain and the hill country, would expand into the Philistine city-states. Ephraim and Samaria, the region conquered by the Assyrians in 721, would be reclaimed by the people of Judah. And, finally, Gilead in Transjordan (stretching from the lower Galilee to the Arnon River) would once again be ruled by Benjamin (the tribal territory between Bethel and Jerusalem).

20. Zarephath. Located on the coastal highway between Tyre and Sidon in Phoenicia, Zarephath is depicted as the restored Israel's northern border. A commercial center specializing in the processing of purple dye and manufacture of ceramics, this town is mentioned in Egyptian records from the thirteenth century and is included in the list of cities that surrendered to the Assyrian king Sennacherib in 701 (see 1 Kings 17:9).

20. Sepharad. Possible locations for this site range from Spain to the Hesperides to western Media. These identifications are based on place names and some textual evidence from the Neo-Assyrian period. However, the most likely site for Sepharad is Sardis in western Asia Minor. This was the Lydian capital during the Persian period, and a bilingual inscription found there names the city in Aramaic with the same consonants as the Hebrew name in Obadiah. This would be a very far distance for exiles from Jerusalem to travel, but the implication in the text is that even the most distant would return to reclaim a portion of the land.

JONAH

1:1-17
Jonah's Flight

1:1. chronology. Jonah is known from 1 Kings 14:25 as a prophet in the time of Jeroboam II who reigned in the first half of the eighth century B.C. (see comments on 2 Kings 14).

1:2. Nineveh. Nineveh is modern Tell Kuyunjik located on the Tigris River some six hundred miles upriver from the Persian Gulf in north Iraq. In the eighth century Nineveh had not yet entered its period of glory. At the beginning of the seventh century Sennacherib made this ancient cult center for the goddess Ishtar the capital city and beautified and enlarged it to nearly two thousand acres. Archaeologists have successfully excavated Sennacherib's famous "palace without rival," which features wall reliefs depicting Sennacherib's siege of Lachish in Judah. The temple of Ishtar that had been maintained by kings as early as 2400 B.C. has also been identified. At the time of Jonah it was one of the major metropolitan areas in Assyria with a circumference of a bit less than three miles.

1:2. Assyria and Israel in the first half of the eighth century. Assyria had posed a significant threat to Israel in the ninth century. Israel had been part of the western coalition that opposed Shalmaneser III's attempts to expand into the Mediterranean region (see comment on 1 Kings 22:1). In 841 the Israelite king Jehu accepted Assyrian control and paid tribute (see comment on 2 Kings 10:34). In the intervening decades, however, Assyria had weakened considerably, and by the time of Jeroboam II many decades had passed with no antagonism from Assyria.

1:3. Tarshish. Tarshish was the farthest known geographical point. While its exact location is unknown, most believe it was in southern Spain, though some have favored Carthage in north Africa. We can be certain that it was a port in the western Mediterranean known for its trade in exports.

1:3. Joppa. Joppa is located just south of modern Tel Aviv on the Mediterranean. This harbor town is mentioned in Egyptian and Phoenician texts as well as texts from Canaan (the Amarna tablets). During the monarchy period it was often under the control of the Philistine city Ashkelon.

1:3. ship. Merchant ships were of various sizes and averaged a speed of two to four knots. In Solomon's day the ships going to Tarshish would not return for three years. A ship of this size would have had a crew of less than a dozen. Cargo typically consisted of grain, wine and olive oil.

1:3. fare. From the language used many have concluded that the fare Jonah paid hired the whole ship for his use. Whether or not this is the case, the fare would have been substantial.

1:5. each cried to his own god. Patron deities were rarely cosmic deities, so the sailors would not have thought that their personal or family gods had sent the storm. In the polytheistic context of the ancient world, one could generally identify divine activity with confidence, but it was another matter altogether to discover which god was acting and why. The sailors call out to their gods in the hope that one of their patron deities might be able to exert some influence on whichever god has become disturbed enough to send the storm. They are calling out for assistance, not in repentance. The more contacts made the better, so the captain awakes Jonah so that he could also call upon his patron deity.

1:7-10. lots. Although the casting of lots was sometimes used to allow the deity to communicate, in many instances they were considered more like flipping a coin or drawing straws. As a result the lots were not cast here to determine who was guilty, but to decide who would be first to volunteer information about themselves that might expose an offense against the gods. It is understandable that no one would be eager to go first. For the casting of lots, each individual brought an identifiable marker. The markers were placed in a container, which was shaken until one of the markers came out.

1:9. cosmic deity. Jonah's reply to their questions identifies only his ethnic association (Hebrew) and the God he serves. Most significant is his description of the Lord as a cosmic, creator deity—just the type of God who would be capable of sending such a storm.

1:10. he had already told them. He had told them earlier that he was fleeing from his God, but that had not concerned them—that was his problem and probably not all that uncommon. Their terror now increases as they realize that Jonah's flight from a cosmic deity has put them all in jeopardy of suffering the wrath of Jonah's god.

1:11-16. what shall we do? The sailors' next question concerns appeasement. In the religious thinking of the ancient world the people rarely thought in terms of repentance, because the motivations of the gods could not easily be discerned. Since the gods were neither moral nor consistent, their anger might be entirely

whimsical and their acts of punishment arbitrary or childish. Therefore worshipers sought to appease the gods' anger. Different gods might be appeased in different ways, so Jonah is consulted.

1:12. throw me into the sea. The men are reluctant to follow Jonah's advice because they believed that deities were protective of the lives of their worshipers. Putting Jonah to death by throwing him in might expose them to the retributive vengeance of Jonah's God.

1:16. offered sacrifice. When the sea grows calm, the men respond with worship. The sacrifice was most likely a grain offering, probably not burnt on a wooden ship but perhaps thrown into the sea. Alternatively (since all the cargo had been jettisoned) the text may refer to a sacrifice that was made on their return to dry land (there would be no point in continuing on to Tarshish).

1:16. made vows. Vows in the Old Testament and in the ancient world typically concerned sacrifice. For instance, the sailors may have vowed to offer a memorial sacrifice of some sort to Yahweh each year on the anniversary of this event. The vows acknowledged that the sailors had experienced an act of divine power. The text in no way suggests that they had abandoned their gods and accepted the monotheistic faith in Yahweh. Acknowledging the power of one god did not preclude the worship of others.

1:17. great fish. Jonah was swallowed by what the text designates a "large fish"—probably the most general description that could be offered. There is nothing to settle the question of whether it was technically fish or mammal, because Hebrew would use this term for any sea creature. Species identification is therefore impossible. Although studies could be done on gullet sizes of various species that regularly inhabit the Mediterranean, the text's insistence on the Lord's direct involvement suggests that we should not expect that there was anything regular or ordinary about the fish. In the beliefs of the ancient world, large sea creatures represented the forces of chaos that were overcome by the creator deity in the act of creation. Here, as always, Yahweh is portrayed as in complete control of the sea creatures—this one is simply doing his bidding.

2:1-10

Jonah's Prayer of Thanksgiving

2:1-6. Jonah's prayer. This prayer may have been a well-known hymn or a piece adapted from known material. The fish is not mentioned and the threat of the waters is a common metaphor in hymnic material. The sea was considered a threatening realm of chaos, and only death could be expected there. However intimidating the fish may have been, Jonah understood it as the Lord's deliverance.

2:7-10. Jonah's relationship to the Lord. God's presence was in the temple, so Jonah's prayer reaches him there. Though Jonah is aware of his disobedience, he still considers himself loyal to the Lord. He has not taken up idol worship.

2:9. Jonah's vow. The prayer does not specify what it is that Jonah has vowed, but most vows in the ancient world concerned rituals to be performed. Leviticus speaks of vow offerings in its description of the various sacrifices (see comments on Lev 3:1-5 and 27:2-13). With no further specification of the nature of the vow, it is likely that Jonah would fulfill his vow with a sacrifice of thanksgiving. There is no indication that he vowed to obey by going willingly to Nineveh. In a hymn to Shamash the sun god is identified as the one who saves those who are surrounded by mighty waves and accepts libations in return.

3:1-10

Jonah and the Ninevites

3:1-4. went to Nineveh. The journey to Nineveh from Joppa (where we assume the fish left Jonah) was about 550 miles. Caravans usually traveled twenty to twenty-five miles a day to make the trip in about a month.

3:3. large city. The size of Nineveh is expressed in terms of the time that it would take Jonah to carry out his assignment. He is not circling the circumference of the walls but going to all the public places in the city to make his proclamation. His itinerary would have included many of the dozen gate areas as well as several of the temple areas. There would have been certain times during the day when significant announcements could be made.

3:4. Jonah's message. Jonah's message is one of impending judgment, as is common for a prophet. We should not confuse a prophetic role with a missionary role. The prophet in the ancient world had the task of conveying whatever message God gave him for a particular audience. The missionary has the task of conveying God's message of salvation given to everyone. The prophet's message was rarely as pleasant as the missionary's. In Jonah's message there is no hint of a call to repentance or a call to put away their false gods. There is no instruction concerning what God wants of them nor indictment of their evil deeds. There

are no conditional offers made. The prophet in the ancient world did not come to deliver a comprehensive theology or to convert to a particular religious worldview. He came to deliver a message from God.

3:4. prophets in ancient Near East. Prophecy was well known in the ancient world, so this kind of situation would not be foreign to the Assyrians. There are a number of references to Assyrian prophets and their messages in documents from the time of Ashurbanipal about a century after Jonah. Prophets served as official or unofficial advisors to the king. In the prophecies preserved in the time of Ashurbanipal, the messages are consistently positive, affirming the king's actions, decisions and policies. Earlier examples from Mari in the eighteenth century B.C. were more often negative but still show the prophets as offering messages to the king.

3:5-10. believing prophecy. The Ninevites believed that Jonah's message was a message from a god who was likely to do as he threatened. That conclusion would have been reached by comparing Jonah's message to the message of the omens. Omens were observations made in the natural world that were believed to be related to what the gods were doing in the historical realm. One of the most common opportunities to observe omens was by examining the entrails of animals that were sacrificed daily. The configurations of organs such as the kidney or liver were believed to give favorable or unfavorable omens. Other omens were recorded from the behavior of animals, the flight of birds, the movements of the heavenly bodies and many other phenomena. If omens had been unfavorable for a few days or weeks prior to Jonah's proclamation, the people would have readily accepted the truth of his message. If sacrifices were offered and the entrails verified an impending doom, Jonah's word would be taken very seriously.

3:5. reception of foreigner's prophecy. It would not have mattered that Jonah was an outsider representing another country or another deity. The polytheistic beliefs of the ancient world allowed for hundreds of gods, any of whom might be capable of impacting their lives for good or ill. Foreign delegations would at times have included prophetic personnel so that the favor or disfavor of the major deities involved could be expressed concerning any negotiations. If the Ninevites' own divinations had supported Jonah's message, they would have had no reason to suspect treachery or hoax. The fact that he was a foreigner would have served as evidence of the truth of his message, for why would someone have traveled all this distance unless impelled by deity? Remember that Jonah did not ask them to change religions, nor did he seek to dethrone their national god.

3:5-10. response. The response of the Ninevites is both typical and atypical. It is atypical in that there is little evidence for fasting as a religious response in the practice of Assyrians or Babylonians. There are examples of the king donning sackcloth "as befitting a penitent sinner" (*Esarhaddon, Ashurbanipal*). The usual approach would be to try to appease deity by the performance of certain rituals (sacrifices, libations, etc.) or by incantations to prevent the deity from acting. It is therefore likely that the Ninevites were trying an Israelite approach to responding to divine anger. What is typical is that they were trying to appease the angered deity. They had no idea what had angered Yahweh, but any inquiry into Israelite religion would have revealed that their God was interested in justice and that repentance of injustice featured fasting and sackcloth, which did regularly accompany mourning. Their rituals (sackcloth and fasting) and their ethical reforms show that they took Jonah seriously but do not offer evidence of conversion. The polytheism of Assyria would have had no conception of monotheism, covenant or law. The only conversion known in this system was the shuffling of the gods in the pantheon. The Ninevites did not get rid of their idols, nor did they show any inclination to replace their gods with Yahweh of Israel. To recognize a god's power was not the same as to accept him as your one and only god.

3:6. arose from his throne. In Assyria when an omen or prophecy suggested the king was in danger, it was common for a substitute king to be appointed. This individual would sit on the royal throne and wear the royal robes. Meanwhile, the king would engage in acts of purification. Often, after an appropriate time, the substitute king would be killed. It was hoped that this would divert the danger from the king. In this text there is no mention of a substitute, but the king's actions might reflect that this procedure was being used.

3:8. beasts covered with sackcloth. The dressing of the animals in sackcloth (a coarse material made of goat's hair) further expresses the Ninevites' lack of understanding of Israel's God. Even animals might offend deity, so they must be included in the appeasement ritual.

4:1-11
The Object Lesson

4:1-4. Jonah's anger. Jonah is angry that the Lord has so easily capitulated to the pagan tactics of appeasement. He is embarrassed and theologically scandalized that Yahweh should offer compassion so readily, for this suggests that Yahweh can be bought. The Ninevites would view him no differently from their own gods.

4:5-9. vine and worm. The plant that brings Jonah shade is described by a general term usually associated with the gourd family. As with the fish, the terminology does not allow a more specific identification. The insect that destroys the gourd plant is most likely of the aphid variety.

4:8. scorching east wind. The east wind here would not be a *hamsin* (or sirocco) because then the sun would not be a factor. The east wind was a problem in Palestine because of the desert to the east, but for Nineveh an east wind would often result in rain. Here it is a particular type of east wind (NIV: "scorching"), but this word is used only here so it is difficult to understand precisely.

4:11. population of Nineveh. Assyrian scholars have estimated the population of Nineveh (city and surrounding countryside) when it was the capital city at about three hundred thousand, so the hundred and twenty thousand here for an earlier period is not implausible.

MICAH

1:1-16
Judgment Coming to Samaria and Jerusalem

1:1. Moresheth. Located approximately six miles northeast of Lachish in the Shephelah, Moresheth (Tell el-Judeideh, about twenty miles southwest of Jerusalem) would have been one of the suburbs of the Philistine city of Gath (Tell es-Safi). After the establishment

of David's kingdom, it served, along with Lachish, Adullam and Mareshah, as a fortified
center (2 Chron 11:8). All of these sites, along
with "countless" villages, were destroyed by
Sennacherib's Assyrian army in 701 B.C.

1:1. chronology. Since the editor gives us the
names of the kings of Judah who reigned during Micah's ministry as a prophet, we can date
this material to the last half of the eighth century. Micah's first oracle (Mic 1:2-7), which
deals with Israel's northern capital of Samaria,
would date to just prior to that city's destruction by the Assyrians in 722 B.C.

1:3. treading the high places of the earth. The
sense of majesty inherent to a theophany is
magnified here by the impression of Yahweh
"coming" from his "dwelling place." The
power implicit in "treading on" is used very
often of vanquishing enemies (Deut 33:29; Ps
108:13). However, in this case the image is of
God displaying control over creation, using
the earth's mountains as stepping stones
(Amos 4:13). A similar image is created of the
swift, mountain-hopping movements of the
divine messengers in the Ugaritic *Epic of Baal
and Anath.* Cities were typically built on hills
because of their natural defensibility, and
armies chose hills as strategic points of control. The metaphor of treading on the heights
therefore also speaks of victory and security.

1:5. Samaria. It was Omri who built Samaria
and established it as the capital of the northern kingdom, Israel, early in the ninth century.
About twelve miles west of the previous capital, Tirzah, the city is located at an important
crossroads with easy access to the Jezreel Valley to the north, Shechem to the southeast and
the coast to the west. It is near both major
north-south routes that run west of the Jordan. The excavations at the site have uncovered what is believed to be Omri's palace on
the acropolis as well as parts of the wall separating the acropolis from the lower city. The
wall was about five feet thick and built using
the finest masonry of the day (ashlar stones
set in a trench using headers and stretchers).
Ahab improved the fortifications by adding a
casemate wall over thirty feet thick.

1:6. the fall of Samaria. The Assyrian sources
describe the "ravaging" of Samaria (c. 724-721
B.C.), which may have denoted the entire land.
Some archaeological evidence for the destruction has been found at the Israelite city of
Shechem. This accords with the typical Assyrian strategy of wasting the territory of a particular state and then surrounding the main
city, which had now been cut off from its resources. Both Sennacherib and Nebuchadnezzar II used this policy against Jerusalem. The

three-year siege of Samaria shows that it was
heavily fortified, for the Assyrians were unmatched in siege warfare. The city fell in 722/
721. Although Shalmaneser III is given credit
for the conquest of Samaria in the Bible, his
successor Sargon II claimed the very same in
the Assyrian annals. Sargon also claims to
have rebuilt the city.

1:6. pouring stones into the valley. The force-
fulness of Yahweh's wrath against Samaria is
compared to the destructiveness of earthquakes. Since cities were typically built on
hills, the destruction of a city wall was accomplished by pulling down the stone walls into
the valley around.

1:7. temple gifts. Many temple gifts would
have been given in exchange for the services
of the sacred prostitutes (see comments on
Deut 23:17-18). These gifts could have been
silver or gold (which could, in turn, be used in
the manufacture of idols) or grain or animal
gifts. Alternatively, however, Micah, like Hosea (Hos 4:10-15), may simply be equating
idolatry with harlotry. Supporting the false
worship at the idolatrous temples would be
an act of unfaithfulness to Yahweh. The idols
which have been worshiped in this shrine are
to be destroyed along with their worshipers,
and the looting of the temple will provide its
conquerors with the wealth to continue their
devastating path.

1:8. barefoot and naked. There are a number
of mourning rituals employed in the ancient
Near East. Some require sacrifices, like those
attested in the Ebla tablets, and are part of the
royal cult of the dead. In other cases, constant
weeping and lamenting mark the acts of
mourners (as evidenced in the Ugaritic Epic of
Keret). When mourners tear (Lam 2:10) or
strip away their clothing and footwear (compare Isaiah's enacted prophecy in Is 20:2), they
are putting aside their former status, signifying defeat (compare the restriction against
mourning in Ezek 24:17). In this way they acknowledge, as Job does, that they came into
this world naked (Job 1:21).

1:8. jackal and owl. The choice of animal voices here are those often heard in the wilderness
and wastelands (Is 34:13; Jer 50:39; "prophecy
of Balaam" from Deir 'Alla). Both make a
piercing sound that would chill the soul and
hint of death (note the use of the jackal as an
image for the Egyptian god Anubis, whose responsibilities were for the dead and for
tombs).

1:10-15. itinerary. All of the sites listed in these
verses are in western Judah, in the hill region
known as the Shephelah. Sennacherib's report
of his campaign offers detailed information

about the Philistine battles, but little about the Shephelah. In the Philistine account, Eltekeh, Timnah and Ekron are named. This would mean the army was poised just a few miles north of Gath as it prepared to go into Judah. If Micah 1 represents a line of march, it would suggest that the Assyrians came south through Gath and took the road that passes a couple of miles west of Lachish (the most prominent fortress of the region), then circled around to the south in order to come at Lachish from the southeast. After Lachish, the route heads northeast toward Jerusalem, with only Mareshah out of order. What is suggested is widespread devastation throughout the Shephelah region. Archaeological surveys have identified a reduction in the number of occupied sites in the region from nearly three hundred in the early eighth century to less than fifty in the seventh century. The population was likewise reduced to less than fifteen percent of what it had been. Gath is probably located at Tell es-Safi. Many of the city names are used for word play unique to this text: Beth Ophrah (meaning "dust"), Shaphir ("horn"; site unknown, though speculated to be Tell 'Eitun), Beth Ezel ("standing place"; location unknown), Zaanan ("she comes out"; possibly the Zenan of the Lachish area in Josh 15:37) and Maroth ("bitter"; site unknown). Lachish is the most important of the cities in this itinerary and will be discussed separately. Moresheth Gath is Micah's home village and is probably to be identified with Tell el-Judeideh (see comment on 1:1). It is in the center of a ten-mile radius in which all of these sites appear to be located. The pun on its name suggests the flight of its citizens. Aczib (possibly Tel el-Beida, northeast of Lachish) is compared to a "failed stream," which here equates with a fortress that failed to serve the king's defensive line. Mareshah, northeast of Lachish, is punned with the word meaning "heir," suggesting a country without a future. Adullam (Tell esh-Sheik Madhkur) similarly lacks a future in the face of the enemy assault.

1:13. Lachish. Dominating the Shephelah and western Judah, Lachish served as the center point of the defensive line of the kings of Judah. Located midway between Jerusalem and the Philistine city states, Lachish guarded the major roads from the coast inland. Its site, Tell ed-Duweir, shows evidence of occupation from the Chalcolithic Period, with massive construction of city defenses and an impressive city gate in the Middle Bronze II (as a major Canaanite city) and Iron II (as the western bastion established after the division of the kingdoms; 2 Chron 11:5-10). Despite its com-

manding position (a tell 150 feet high), the city fell after a siege by the Assyrian king Sennacherib in 701 (Annals of Sennacherib; for more information see 2 Chron 32:9). Graphic evidence of the ferocity of this siege are found in Assyrian reliefs from the royal palace at Nineveh depicting the events and the remains of a massive siege ramp on the southwest corner of the tell. A mass burial, with approximately fifteen hundred bodies, may also be a result of the fall of the city. Written records of a later siege by the Babylonian king Nebuchadnezzar in 586 also exist in the form of twenty-one ostraca letters that were discovered in a guardroom in the city gate. They describe the desperate situation of the defenders as they take note of the extinguishing of the signal fires from neighboring towns.

1:16. shaved heads. There are several rituals associated with mourning, including tearing one's clothing, cutting oneself (see the comment on Lev 19:28), fasting (see the comment on 2 Sam 12:16) and casting dirt or ashes in one's hair (see the comment on 2 Sam 13:19). Shaving the hair also functions as a sign of mourning (Jer 41:5) as well as a part of purification rituals (Lev 14:8-9; Num 6:9). For instance, Assyrian priests were shaved at the time of their installation. Similarly a man portraying himself as a doctor in *The Poor Man of Nippur* (Sultantepe Tablets) shaves his head. This may be associated with purifying himself or because of the physician's repeated contact with the diseased and dying.

2:1-13
Injustice and False Prophecy

2:2. seized property. The acquisition of property by oppressing the poor and weak violates both the law against coveting as well as the injunction not to violate the covenantal division of the land to each Israelite household after the conquest. Despite these laws, the mounting debt of small landowners and the political power exercised by large landowners led to abuses (see comment on Is 5:8), which are mentioned in Egyptian wisdom literature (*Instruction of Amenemope*).

2:5. assembly of the Lord. See the comment on Deuteronomy 23:1-8 for this technical term for the group of men enfranchised to make decisions within the Israelite community and to serve in the military.

2:5. dividing the land by lot. When the father of a family died, the landholdings were divided among the sons by lot. The Eshnunna Laws, the Hammurabi Code and the Middle Assyrian Laws all make reference to this situation. Texts from Tell Sifr specifically mention dividing the estate by lot. Here Micah suggests that the one who has oppressively accumulated landholdings will have no one to pass them on to.

2:11. acceptance of optimistic prophets. In Assyria, prophets were expected to be supportive of the king and his policies. Israelite prophets tended to be more counterculture and more often than not were critical of the reigning kings. As Jeremiah 28:8-9 notes, the people are to be wary of "the prophet who prophesies peace." The role of prophets in ancient Israel is to provide reproof and warning to the people when they violate their covenant obligations. This differs from ancient Near Eastern prophets, such as those mentioned in the Mari texts, who generally concern themselves with cultic violations (failure to make a sacrifice or build a promised temple) or with matters of warfare.

3:1-12

Corrupt Leaders

3:2-3. cannibal analogy. The rapacious nature of the leaders and judges of Judah is compared to a cannibalistic feast in which the people fall victim to the economic knives and voracious appetite of these corrupt officials. The realistic aspects of preparing the flesh and cracking the bones for their marrow may well be based on the necessities of survival during famines or military sieges (see comment on 2 Kings 6:29).

3:5-7. unsuccessful prophets. A failed or unsuccessful prophet is one who no longer receives any communication from God (see the "famine" of God's words in Amos 8:11-12). This has been brought about by the greed of the prophets who sell their deceptive prophecies rather than speaking them freely in response to God's prompting. The commercialization of prophetic speech assures "peace" or prosperity for the merchants and the nobility who give the prophets "bread" and brings down threats of ruin, allegorized here as "war," on those who fail to bribe them. Micah, who was not a member of the prophetic guild, but, like Amos, simply a man chosen by God to speak (Amos 7:1-15), replaces their failed rituals and divinatory practices with the true word of God. Prophets of this period in Assyria were often in the employ of the royal court and were expected to support the legitimacy of the regime. We would use the expression that it was important for them to recognize which side their bread was buttered on.

3:12. plowed like a field. An area had to be totally cleared of debris in order to be plowed and planted. This metaphor demonstrates how completely the city and its foundations would be destroyed. The armies of Assyria will plow the city, returning it to its original state as cultivated land (compare Is 5:6). While this did not occur in his lifetime, Jeremiah takes up the oracle, and it is quoted by the elders at his trial (Jer 26:18), demonstrating that the predictions of the prophets were compiled and studied.

4:1—5:15

Days Near and Far

4:3. swords into plowshares. Rather than "plowshares" that turn over the dirt as they plow, this may refer to the metal tip of the plow that breaks up the earth and scratches out a furrow. This tip is about seven inches long. However, this same Hebrew word is used in 2 Kings 6:5, where it appears to refer to some sort of axe. Since the sword is "broken up," it is possible that the resulting product is metal shards that could be put to various uses.

4:4. own vine and fig. Vineyards and fig trees were the basic elements of the diet and economy of the village culture of ancient Israel, and their loss would devastate the people (Joel 1:6-7). The idyllic image of peace and prosperity in the ancient Near East is to be able to sit under one's own vine and fig tree. Egyptian tomb paintings, Assyrian reliefs and the biblical writers commonly use the phrase to refer to a people who control their own lives, without foreign interference, and are able to cultivate the land which the gods/God has given to them (1 Kings 4:25; Is 36:16). The vine and fig provided some shade as well as fruit, and enjoying them indicated some long-term prospects as each took several years to become productive.

4:8. watchtower/stronghold. Although Migdal Eder (NIV: "watchtower of the flock") is a place name elsewhere (Gen 35:21), it is paralleled in this context with Ophel, a section of the old city of David on the eastern hill of the city of Jerusalem. As such, both images are of a citadel or watchtower protecting the "flock" and serving as a rallying point from which God's eventual restoration of the nation and the people will occur (compare the opposite image in Is 32:14). If the term refers to an actual citadel tower, it could be the central tower of the Ophel (the citadel or the hill it was on) in Jerusalem (daughter of Zion).

4:10. Babylon. It would have been more logical in Micah's day if he had assigned Ashur or

Nineveh as the place of exile. But prophecy is not always logical. In Micah's time, the Neo-Assyrian empire, under the Sargonid rulers, Sargon II and Sennacherib, was the most powerful political network the world had ever seen. It stretched across the Near East and would eventually even include Egypt for a short time. The ravaging army of Sennacherib was responsible for destroying many towns and villages in Judah during his two invasions, and the Assyrian reliefs even depict captives being taken away from Lachish. During this period, Babylonia and its Chaldean rulers were subjected, just like all other nation states, by the Assyrians. However, they, like the Medes in western Iran, periodically tested the Assyrian hegemony with revolts or by attempting to subvert Assyria's allies and vassal states. Particularly troublesome was Merodach-Baladan, who ousted Assyrian rulers of Babylon on at least two occasions. Finally in 689 B.C. Sennacherib sacked the city and assumed the title of king of Babylon. Shortly after 660, as the Assyrian empire began to crumble, Babylonia and Media combined to put even greater pressure on the last of the great Assyrian kings, Ashurbanipal. His death in 627 marked the end of Assyrian world power and the emergence of Nebuchadnezzar and the Neo-Babylonian empire.

4:12. sheaves to the threshing floor. One of the principal agricultural installations in the village culture throughout the ancient Near East was the threshing floor. Sheaves of grain were brought to this central location, where they would be threshed and winnowed. Because of the importance of agriculture and fertility, the threshing floor was often a place of ritual importance. Threshing floors were large, flat, open areas and certainly could have been useful for other purposes besides threshing. It is no surprise, therefore, that it should double as an open-air facility when space constraints or the desire for public visibility rendered the palace facilities inadequate. Consequently it became a place of assembly where legal as well as business transactions could be finalized. In the Ugaritic Epic of Aqhat, the king, Danil, publicly judges cases at the threshing floor outside the gate of his city. It was a place where the good was separated from the bad.

4:13. horns of iron, hooves of bronze. Although there are no direct references to animals pulling a threshing sled in the biblical text (see, however, comment on 2 Sam 24:22), Micah is clearly describing standard operations at a threshing floor. Egyptian tomb paintings depict oxen and donkeys pulling a

sled weighted with pieces of flint and metal over the grain, and this custom is still followed by farmers in the Middle East. There is also some evidence for metal shoes being attached to the feet of these animals to more efficiently cut the stalks of grain.

5:1. strike on the cheek with a rod. To be struck on the cheek is generally considered a gesture of contempt (see 1 Kings 22:24; Job 16:10). Hammurabi's Code provides for a variety of punishments for the person who strike others on the cheek—from flogging and mutilation to stiff fines. Striking Judah's "judge" implies both the contempt of the nations as well as the impotence of Judah's ruler to respond. In the New Year festival *(akitu)* that was practiced in both Assyria and Babylon, the priest slapped the king on the cheek in a ritual that led to the king claiming he was innocent of injustice.

5:2. Bethlehem. The double place name Bethlehem Ephrathah reflects a tribal distinction within the Bethlehem community and also reinforces the tie to David's family (see comments on Ruth 1:1; 1 Sam 16:4; 17:12). Linking the future messianic king to the origins of David's household rather than to Jerusalem recalls how David was chosen directly by Yahweh as king and breaks with the hereditary succession pattern. This suggests the expectation of a new David.

5:2. ruler with origins from ancient times. Most of the Neo-Assyrian kings claimed that their kingship had been ordered by the gods from days of yore. Ashurbanipal claimed to have been created by Ashur and Ninlil and proclaimed king since the days of yore by Ashur and Sin, created for kingship in the womb of his mother.

5:5. Assyrian invasion. The Assyrians invaded Judah in 713 (though the major objective of the campaign was Philistia) and in 701 under Sennacherib. This text more likely discusses the latter invasion. For detailed information see the sidebar in 2 Chronicles 32. Shepherds usually refer to kings, so the seven/eight may refer to the coalition that is expected to be organized against the invasion. Sennacherib's inscriptions mention Sidon, Ashkelon and Ekron (with help from Egypt and Nubia) as being fought and conquered. Other city-states and territories submitted and paid tribute (Arvad and Byblos in the north, and Ashdod, Ammon, Moab and Edom in the south). It is unclear how many of these may have actually been part of the anti-Assyrian coalition.

5:6. land of Nimrod. Nimrod, the "mighty hunter before the LORD," only appears in Genesis 10:8-11 (see comment there), in the period before the flood. There he is identified as the founder of many Mesopotamian cities, including Babylon and Nineveh, so he appropriately represents any Mesopotamian empire.

5:12. witchcraft. Literally thousands of texts have been uncovered that deal with magic, including incantations that help alleviate the pain of a toothache, help a baby that is stuck in the womb and help a mother who was barren. It appears that the common person hired an incantation priest for even the most mundane problem. The priest then came and recited a spell to either exorcise a problematic demon or other divine irritant. Certainly then they would resort to incantation priests to try to avoid disasters that were either portended or threatened. Incantations were intended to magically bind the supernatural powers that posed a threat. Magical and divinatory practices were common in Mesopotamia and Egypt, where exorcists, diviners and magicians were fixtures at court, interpreting omens and performing rituals. In addition to these professional practitioners, there were sorcerers who performed malevolent forms of magic. The biblical text outlaws both, since their work invoked deities other than Yahweh and attempted to manipulate the divine.

5:13. sacred stones. Standing stones or *maṣṣebot* were apparently a common feature of Canaanite religion and also appear as memorials in a number Israelite covenantal contexts (see Ex 24:3-8; Josh 24:25-27). Their association with Asherah, Baal and other Canaanite deities are the basis for their being condemned as a rival and threat to Yahweh worship. Archaeologists have discovered sacred stones at Gezer, Shechem, Dan, Hazor and Arad. In the latter three cases they are clearly within a sacred precinct and part of the cultic practices at these sites. The Hazor stones include incised representations of upraised arms and a sun disk.

5:14. Asherah poles. Asherah can be either the name of a fertility goddess or the name of a cult object (as here). The goddess was popular in the religious deviations in Israel and was sometimes considered a consort of Yahweh. An indication of this belief is found in the inscriptions from Kuntillet Ajrud and Khirbet el-Qom. In Canaanite mythology she was the consort of the chief god, El. She appears in Mesopotamian literature as early as the eighteenth century, where she is consort of the Amorite god Amurru. The cult symbol may or may not have born a representation of the deity on it. The pole may represent an artificial tree, since Asherah is often associated with sacred groves. Sometimes the cult object can be

made or built, while on other occasions it is planted. We have little information of the function of these poles in ritual practice. The writer of Kings points to the veneration of Asherah poles as one of several reasons for Assyria's conquest of Israel (see comment on 2 Kings 17:10). The reforms of Hezekiah and Josiah both attempted to outlaw these images sacred to the Canaanite goddess Asherah.

6:1-16
God's Lawsuit

6:1-2. court case of covenant violation. Using treaty formulas and terminology from ancient Near Eastern treaties, such as that negotiated between Rameses II and Hattusilis III, the *rib*-pattern or covenant lawsuit is found in most of the Hebrew prophets (see Is 1:2-4; Jer 2:4-9). As in this case, all of creation is called to witness Israel's violation of the covenant with Yahweh (see comment on Is 1:2), and a judgment is declared justifying the punishment of God's covenant partner.

6:5. Balak/Balaam. The prophet calls to mind for his audience the famous incident when a foreign nation and a renowned seer are thwarted. Instead of the requested curse, a blessing is pronounced over Israel. In Numbers 22:6 Balaam is said to be a man whose blessings and curses are effective. He was from the region of upper Mesopotamia, near Carchemish, and had an international reputation as a true prophet. Balak was the king of Moab at the time of the Exodus. His interest in Balaam seems to be based on his ability to invoke blessings or curses—no matter which god he called upon. In 1967, a Dutch archaeological expedition, led by H. J. Franken, discovered some inscribed pieces of plaster at a site in Jordan known as Deir 'Allah. Apparently written in Aramaic, the fragments date to about 850 B.C., and they mention Balaam son of Beor, the same figure described as a "seer" in Numbers 22—24. Although the text is very fragmentary, with many breaks and uncertain words, it can be established that (1) Balaam was a seer, (2) he received a divine message during the night, and (3) his message was not what his neighbors expected to hear. Whether this text refers to the events described in the Bible is problematic, but it does establish a nonbiblical tradition, current just a century before Micah, of a prophet named Balaam.

6:5. Shittim to Gilgal. See the comments on Joshua 2:1 and 4:19. Shittim was Joshua's camp east of the Jordan River, and Gilgal was the place where the Israelites miraculously crossed the Jordan and established a base camp from which to begin the conquest. An abbreviated itinerary such as this is typical of Mesopotamian royal annals that include the list of cities along the victorious trek of the king.

6:6. year-old calves. Yearling animals would have been more valuable than newborn ones. Thus to offer a year-old calf as a burnt offering would be real financial sacrifice and would represent a major ritual of purification or initiation. At the heart of this practice, however, is a polemic against the formulaic religious rituals of Mesopotamia and Egypt in which the process transcends the meaning. The prophet tries to establish exactly what Yahweh requires and like Samuel (see comment on 1 Sam 15:22) determines it is obedience and love, not simply going through the motions of making sacrifices.

6:7. hyperbole. There is a steady escalation of the size and precious nature of the offerings listed by Micah. Only Solomon could offer thousands of sacrificial animals (1 Kings 8:63). Oil was used for libations (see comment on Lev 14:15). Human sacrifice was abhorred by the Israelites, seeing it as a statute of Canaanite and Phoenician religious practice (see comment on Gen 22:1-2). In fact, while Yahweh had a claim on the first-born son of every family, the Law required them to redeem the sons and substitute animal sacrifice (see comment on Num 3:12-13). God was not asking to be appeased through extravagant gifts. The most extravagant offering they could give him would be their obedience.

6:10. ill-gotten treasures. Micah condemns corrupt merchants who cheat their customers to enrich themselves. While these practices were to be condemned whenever they occurred, it would be particularly harmful during times of war when profiteers would take advantage of shortages to raise prices (2 Kings 6:25). This is also a theme developed by Amos (8:5-6) and Hosea (12:7-8). There are also a series of fair business practice laws in the Code of Hammurabi and the Laws of Eshnunna which set prices and establish standards of behavior.

6:10. short ephah. Just as Amos criticizes dishonest merchants who make the ephah "small" and the shekel "great" (Amos 8:5), Micah also cautions them against cheating their customers with a false measure of grain. The ephah and the hin were used as the primary dry and liquid measures and were equal to half a bushel or one gallon (Lev 19:36). One of the offenses listed in the *Shurpu* incantations was buying by a large measure and selling by a small one.

6:11. dishonest scales/false weights. A just society was one in which the government standardized and guaranteed honest weights and measures. The prologue to the law code of the Ur III king Ur-Nammu (c. 2100) includes a list of the measures he had taken to insure justice and truth throughout his realm. This included the standardization of all the copper and stone weights used in commerce. The Egyptian *Instruction of Amenemope* warns against tampering with scales or the weights used for buying and selling. In a Babylonian Hymn to Shamash, Shamash as the god of justice will punish the merchant who uses deceptive practices with regard to the scales or the weights. The fact that Micah complains of false weights indicates a lawless period without strong government or a concern for covenant obligation (see Prov 11:1; 20:23).

6:14-15. punishment. These curses of infertility and loss are similar in form to those found in the Egyptian execration texts and in coffin texts found in tombs. They represent Yahweh's justice against the covenant violations of Israel (see the set of curses in Deut 28:15-44). Several other prophets also use this form of "futility" curse (threatening lack of success in a course of action: Hos 4:10; Zeph 1:13).

6:16. statutes of Omri. Like the "sins of Jeroboam" that are so often invoked as the height of evil by a king (2 Kings 13:2, 11), the names of Omri and Ahab also serve as labels for monarchs guilty of idolatry (for the crimes of Ahab see comment on 1 Kings 18:4). The dynasty of Omri had come to an end with the death of Zechariah in 753 just a generation earlier than Micah.

7:1-20

From Ruin to Restoration

7:1. agriculture reference. According to the Gezer Almanac, an inscription dated to around 925 B.C., the gathering of summer fruit was the last harvest of the year, taking place in late August and September. This would be the second crop of figs (the first ripening in June), and this fruit would be dried for consumption through the winter months (see Is 16:9; Jer 48:32). Once it had been harvested and the gleaners had taken all that remained, no further fruit could be expected for many months.

7:2. hunting with a net. Fowling and fishing were the common man's form of hunting since they required only nets and traps. Egyptian tomb paintings depict hunting birds with a net (see Prov 1:17) and the antiquity of the net is to be found in the Sumerian word for hunting that is an ideogram in the shape of a net. Isaiah 51:20 describes using a net, possibly a corral of nets, to hunt antelopes that may have been driven into the trap by a line of beaters. It is truly a lawless time when every man is both hunter and hunted (see Ps 10:9).

7:14. geography. Bashan and Gilead are fertile regions lying east of the Jordan River. They had originally been part of the division of the land (see the comment on Josh 13:24-29 and 13:30-31 for Gad's and Manasseh's assignment) but were lost to Assyria during the eighth century. The expectation here is that in the day of Yahweh's triumph all the lost territories would be restored to Israel (see Jer 50:19).

7:17. snake licking dust. Just as the serpent was cursed in the garden of Eden to eat dust (see comment on Gen 3:14), the enemy nations will also be humbled (see Ps 72:9). Since foreign nations are often depicted as serpents (Is 14:29; Jer 8:17), this may be a further condemnation of the use of snakes as fertility symbols and deities in Mesopotamian and Egyptian religious art. In the Amarna texts, eating dirt or dust is a metaphor for suffering defeat.

7:19. treading sins underfoot. Yahweh's forgiveness of Israel allows a conquest of sin in much the same way that a monarch triumphs over his enemy, treading him underfoot or placing his foot on his neck (see comments on Jos 10:24; Ps 60:12). Similar images of the activities of "Divine Warrior" gods are found in Anat slaughtering her enemies in Ugaritic epic and the military exploits of the Babylonian god Marduk and the Hittite god Teshub.

NAHUM

1:1. Nineveh. This oracle against the Assyrian capital city of Nineveh most likely dates to the period between 663 B.C. (the date that the Egyptian city of Thebes is captured by the Assyrians—Nahum 3:8) and the fall of the city to a combined army of Babylonians and Medes in 612 B.C. Nineveh, on the east bank of the Tigris River (ancient Kuyunjik and modern Mosul), was about six hundred miles upriver from the Persian Gulf and just over 250 miles from Babylon. It functioned as one of the major cities of Assyria for much of its history—serving the Old Akkadian, Amorite and Mitanni dynasties prior to the establishment of the Middle Assyrian kingdom in the mid-fourteenth century B.C. At the height of this expanding empire's power, in the reign of Sennacherib (705-681 B.C.), it became Assyria's capital. Excavation of its palaces has revealed stone reliefs of the invasion and ransacking of Judah in 701. The library of its last great king, Ashurbanipal (668-627 B.C.) has provided scholars with copies of much of ancient Mesopotamia's literature and scientific works.

1:1. Assyrian history of this period. The last great Assyrian king, Ashurbanipal, ruled from 668 to at least 635, when it is believed that he abdicated. It appears that he does not die until 627. After his reign, Assyrian history becomes confused, and it is sometimes difficult to determine who is in charge, though the two main rulers were Ashur-Etil-Ilani and Sin-Shar-ra-Ishkun. During Ashurbanipal's reign, most of Syria-Palestine passively accepted Assyrian rule (though Tyre presented continual difficulties). Manasseh of Judah was, for the most part, a cooperative vassal. However, from 652 to 648 a rebellion was led by Ashurbanipal's brother, Shamash-Shum-Ukkin (appointed king of Babylon), who appears to have won the support of Manasseh (see comment on 2 Chron 33:11). Babylon's last revolt came in 626, when the Chaldean Nabopolassar declared himself king and established a dynastic line that became the Neo-Babylonian empire. These Babylonians, allied with the Medes, brought the fall of the Assyrian empire, starting with the overthrow of Ashur in 614, then Nineveh in 612, Haran in 610 and, finally, Carchemish in 605.

1:1. Elkoshite. The place or clan name Elkosh only appears in the book of Nahum. No exact location for Nahum's village has been established. Jerome places it in the Galilee (possibly el-Kauzeh or Capernaum) and somewhat later traditions locate it either near Nineveh or in Syria. None of these suggestions currently have sufficient evidence to make a positive identification.

1:2. jealous deity. The theme of Yahweh as a jealous god appears first in the Ten Commandments (Ex 20:5), is repeated in Joshua's covenant renewal oration following the conquest (Josh 24:19) and is reflected again in Ezekiel's vision of the "image of jealousy" (Ezek 8:5), which blocks his entrance into Jerusalem's temple. The word represents a determination to defend zealously and aggressively that which rightfully belongs to him from those who would lay claim to it. This attribute of God is designed to prevent either comparison with other gods or any subordination of Yahweh in worship or ritual to any other deities. Failure to acknowledge Yahweh's sole position is justification for vengeance.

1:3. whirlwind and storm. As in Habakkuk 3:10, Yahweh is portrayed as master of the storm and controller of the winds that can bring both life and destruction. This type of figurative language, demonstrating God's majesty, is also found in the theophany in Job 38:1 (also see comment on 1 Kings 19:11-13) and is a common feature in ancient Near Eastern epic poetry. For example, in the Ugaritic *Epic of Baal and Anath* the god Baal is described as the "Rider of the Clouds," and his "voice" is the sound and fury of thunder and lightening. Similarly, in the Babylonian story of creation, *Enuma Elish*, the storm god Marduk defeats the primordial goddess of watery chaos, Tiamat, through his control of the winds and his use of the lightning.

1:4. drying bodies of water. The image of God controlling the power of the rivers and seas is a common one in the ancient world (compare Jesus' stilling the waters of the Sea of Galilee in Mk 4:39). The most potent Old Testament example is the parting of the Red Sea. The Ugaritic cycle of Baal stories portrays the storm god in a monumental contest for supremacy with the god Yamm, the sea—an image whose origin may have sprung from observation of the stormy seas off the Mediterranean coast near Ugarit. Yahweh's "rebuking" the waters is also mentioned in Isaiah 50:2 and Psalm 104:7. In each passage the majesty of God over the forces of nature is made clear, as is the ability to impose drought on generally fertile areas.

1:4. Bashan and Carmel. Among the most lush and fertile areas within the region of Syria-Palestine was Bashan and the Carmel range of hills. This comprised the northern portion of the Transjordanian plateau, east of the Sea of Galilee, and the hill country extending northwest toward the Bay of Acco on the Mediterranean coast, just south of Lebanon. Both Carmel and Bashan were known for their pastures and cattle grazing. To see them transformed into blighted and drought-stricken

lands would have been a reversal of their traditional role as places blessed with richness and plenty. This type of prophetic speech is part of the "world turned upside down" theme found outside the Bible in the prophecies of Balaam (Deir 'Alla inscriptions) and the visions of Neferti (Old Kingdom Egypt).

1:5. effects of theophany. The thunderous effects of Yahweh's voice and presence resemble the earth-shattering shocks of an earthquake. However, the references to the hill country and the control over the forces of the storm suggest that this theophany is modeled after the frighteningly close thunder, lightning and strong winds characteristic of a mountain storm. A similar example of this imagery is found in Psalm 29:3-9, where "voice of the Lord" shatters the mighty cedars of Lebanon and makes "Lebanon skip like a calf." Ugaritic (Baal cycle) and Hittite myth *(Song of Ullikummis)* both describe the use of winds and lightning by the storm god in much the same frightening manner.

1:13. yoke and shackles. Prophetic speech often refers to the burden of political domination as a yoke or shackles. In the Amarna letters the rulers of the Canaanite city-states speak to Pharaoh of how they willingly placed themselves in the yoke to serve Egypt faithfully. Akkadian wisdom literature indicates that bearing a god's yoke is desirable because of the fringe benefits. In the *Atrahasis Epic* the gods find the yoke of Enlil unbearable and so rebel. Assyrian inscriptions describe their conquest of other lands as imposing the yoke of the god Ashur on the people, and rebellion was portrayed as throwing off the yoke. The prophet is thus using an image familiar throughout the ancient Near East.

1:14-15. history of Nineveh after its fall. According to the Babylonian Chronicle, Nineveh was destroyed by the combined Medean and Chaldean (Babylonian) army led by Nabopolassar (625-605 B.C.) in the spring of 612 B.C. after a three-month siege. Ritual and actual desecration of the site occurred with the carrying of its ashes back to Babylon. The reported inundation of the city (based on classical sources, Diodorus Siculus and Xenophon) would have probably involved the damming of the Khosr River which flowed between the two citadels of Nineveh on the east bank of the Tigris River (Kuyunjik and Nebi Yunus). The city never reached its former heights again, although it was rebuilt and there are Hellenistic, Parthian and Roman remains at the site.

1:14. Assyrian temples and gods. From the time of Shamshi-Adad I (c. 1813-1781 B.C.) the principal gods of Assyria's pantheon were the king of the gods, Ashur, and Ishtar, the goddess of love and war. Other gods included Ninurta (warfare and hunting), Adad (storm god), Sin (moon god) and Shamash (sun god), as well as many lesser deities, and each had a cult center and attendant priestly community. These temples were heavily subsidized by the grants made to them by the monarchy, based on the looting of neighboring countries during nearly continuous periods of warfare. Much of their rituals and religious festivals were borrowed from older Sumerian and Babylonian forms. Nearly every Assyrian royal annal describing military campaigns includes the statement "by the command of Ashur" as the justification for war. The "Banquet Stele" of Ashurnasirpal II's palace at Nimrud, which chronicles his military victories, makes it clear that the gods of Assyria were residents of his palace. Similarly, the text bands that decorated the walls of the palace of Sargon II at Khorsabad include the invitation for "Ashur, father of the gods, the great lord, and Ishtar, who dwell in Assyria" to take up residence there. Sennacherib moved the Assyrian capital to Nineveh and rebuilt the huge temple complex to the goddess Ishtar as part of his building campaign to create restored cult centers for the gods and a "palace without rival." It was normal procedure in the ancient world to destroy the images of the gods and desecrate the temples of defeated cities. The images would be toppled over and disfigured, with heads and limbs cut off.

1:15. Judah's history under Assyrian power. From around 734 B.C. until the fall of Nineveh in 612, Judah was a vassal state within the Assyrian empire. King Ahaz paid tribute to Tiglath-Pileser III and stayed out of the plots to gain independence that led to the destruction of the northern kingdom of Israel and the devastation of many of the other neighboring states. Hezekiah did attempt to assert some measure of independence (cleansing the temple, closing the local high places), but that led to an invasion of Judah by Sennacherib (see comments on 2 Kings 18), the destruction of many towns like Lachish, the deportation of some of the population and a siege of Jerusalem that impoverished the nation. The long reign of Manasseh (see comments on 2 Chron 33) was marked by a complete submission to Assyrian control. In addition to a wide range of stipulations designed to promote and demonstrate political loyalty, Esarhaddon's vassal treaties required respect for the god Ashur as king of the gods and as their own god. Manasseh's cooperation allowed for a period of peace and rebuilding, but represented a political and theological compromise that marked him, in the eyes of the biblical writers, as the worst of kings. It is only the political chaos following the death of Assyria's last great king, Ashurbanipal (see comment on 1:1), that allows Judah to temporarily assert its freedom under King Josiah.

2:3. soldiers wearing red. Not yet bloodied in battle, the red uniforms of the soldiers may indicate they are a professionally equipped and well-trained fighting unit (see the blue-clad soldiers in Ezek 23:6). In Greece the Spartans were known for wearing red tunics under their armor as an indicator of membership in their ranks and as a further effort to intimidate their opponents. In Assyria it was common rhetoric to speak of cities and countrysides dyed red with the blood of enemies, and the army marching through the blood of their enemies. Additionally, Isaiah 9:5 refers to a practice of warriors rolling their garments in blood. It would be logical, therefore, that armies would choose to wear red tunics to suggest that they were covered with the blood of their enemies. Paintings at Til-Barsip show red uniforms, and classical sources describe soldiers of this period as wearing red or purple tunics.

2:3. metal on chariots. Metal ornamentation of chariot bodies to strengthen them for plowing through ranks of infantry is attested in the Judges period, and examples of decorated chariots have been found in Assyrian reliefs and Egyptian tomb paintings.

2:5. protective shield. This word occurs only here in the Bible and is possibly a term borrowed from the Akkadian language used by the Assyrians and their besiegers. In Akkadian the term refers to a plug or something used to stop something up. Since the next verse speaks of manipulating the sluice gates in an attempt to bring about the collapse of the palace, a plug may have been used to block where the water would usually have flowed through the city walls after the river had been dammed up at the reservoir created by Sennacherib about two miles up the Khosr River.

2:6. river gates at Nineveh. Sennacherib had created an elaborate network of canals and sluice gates to control the waters of the Khosr River and to provide irrigation channels to the city of Nineveh and its surrounding farm land. Though the language of this section is difficult, one scenario would involve damming the river, then scrambling to the walls while the dam held in order to position some sort of plug where the water entered the city. When the gates were opened, the wall of water would rush at the walls and effect their collapse. The Babylonian Chronicle does not mention the use of flood waters as one of the methods of conquering the city, though classical sources do. Archaeological evidence at Nineveh suggests a great conflagration but gives no indication of flood damage.

2:6. palace of Nineveh. The "palace without rival," or the "Southwest Palace" as it is known today, was built by Sennacherib between 703 and 691 and consists of a huge complex of interconnected rooms and courts (estimated at 1635 by 786 feet, an area large enough to fit twenty-five football fields). Those areas closest to the throne room were decorated with carved limestone facades, massive statuary (winged bulls and fish-scaled giants), and intricate reliefs of military campaigns, while the outer courts, with their more utilitarian functions, were devoid of elaborate design or statues. The palace has been excavated over a period of 120 years, starting in the 1850s by A. H. Layard, and is still not completely uncovered. Its layout was dictated by the preexisting Ishtar temple and ziggurat on the highest point of Kuyunjik and by the Khosr and Tigris Rivers to the southeast and west.

2:11-12. lion metaphor. The iconography of the Assyrian gods depicts Ishtar, the patron goddess of Nineveh, as accompanied by a lion, and the sun god Shamash is often portrayed as a winged lion. Assyrian kings, like Esarhaddon (680-669), described themselves like lions in their rage and fierceness in battle. Here, however, the lions who had so proudly taken whatever they wanted for themselves and their cubs are cowering and no longer in command. In this way the prophet throws one of Assyria's favorite metaphors back in its face as a taunt.

3:4. offenses of Nineveh. The actual events behind the crimes of Nineveh mentioned here are unknown. However, this harlotry and sorcery are both well-known metaphors used to depict a city or nation that victimizes others, for both witch and prostitute exert their power over the weak, vulnerable or unwary. Other instances of this seductive harlot image include Babylon in Revelation 18:3 and Jerusalem in Ezekiel 16:15-22 and 23:2-8. There may also be a reference here to Ishtar, the patron goddess of Nineveh, whose rituals and sacred stories often contained explicit sexual activity. It may actually be referring to the web of political intrigue created by the Assyrians as they expanded their control over much of the ancient Near East. The taunting of Hezekiah by Sennacherib's representative, the Rabshek-

ah (Is 36), includes reference to the maneuvering for power by Egypt and Assyria (Is 36:4-6), while the smaller states were drawn into treaties and vassalage that impoverished and destroyed them. Certainly the economic exploitation of the natural resources of Syro-Palestine by the Assyrians would also fit Nahum's list of charges against Nineveh (see Rev 18:14-17).

3:7. no one to comfort. One scholar (Becking), noticing the similarity between a number of the judgment pronouncements in Nahum and the curses in vassal treaties, recognized in this line the Assyrian curse that the dead would have no one to care for their spirit by pouring out libations.

3:8. Thebes. As he taunts Nineveh, Nahum reminds them that another heavily fortified city, Thebes (known as "No Amon" to the Greeks and thus named in the Hebrew), had not been able to withstand the Assyrian armies of Ashurbanipal in 663. The Kushite ruler, Tantamani, had taken control of Thebes and Memphis in 664, drawing a response from the Assyrians, who supported the current northern regime of Necho (whom Tantamani executed). Under the Assyrian onslaught, Tantamani briefly made a stand at Thebes before abandoning it to the invaders and fleeing to Napata. Thebes, located about 325 miles south of Memphis (which is about 15 miles south of Cairo) on the east bank of the Nile River, had, like Nineveh, an elaborate system of moats and other defenses that gave the illusion of invulnerability. Also like Nineveh, it was a sacred city, dedicated to the god Amon and containing the magnificent temples of the Karnak complex.

3:9. Cush, Egypt, Put, Libya as allies. At the time that Thebes was conquered by the Assyrians, it and Egypt was being ruled by a Cushite (Nubian) dynasty (Twenty-Fifth Dynasty). The capital of Nubia was Napata (between the third and fourth cataract of the Nile, eight hundred miles south of Thebes, in modern Sudan). Ancient Libya was mostly along the coast west of Alexandria but included the long expanse of desert west of the Nile Valley. Put is more difficult. The most likely conclusion is that Put is an alternate name for Libya and that together they refer to the area to the west of ancient Egypt represented by the modern state of Libya.

3:10. lots cast for nobles. As the leaders of Egypt were forced to surrender, they were distributed as slaves among the Assyrian commanders along with the rest of the loot. Provision for the division of spoils, including the casting of lots, is also found in Homer's *Il-*

iad, the Mari texts and Joel 3:3.

3:14. preparation for siege. Fortifications for cities in the ancient Near East consisted of earthen ramparts, a sloping glacis, towered gates and walls (sometimes twenty-five to thirty feet thick) constructed on a stone foundation and made of sun-baked mud bricks. However, wind and rain eroded these walls, and they had to be constantly repaired. Thousands of bricks were needed and countless hours were spent making them. Many royal annals and inscriptions mention the repair or construction of city walls as a major accomplishment, and this would have been even more important in anticipation of a siege. Nineveh's city walls, constructed by Sennacherib, ranged approximately seven and a half miles in circumference. It was also necessary to insure an adequate water supply during a siege. Nineveh's water came mainly from the river and the system of aqueducts connected to it, but that supply could be compromised by the enemy outside the walls. The drawing of water here would refer to the activity of filling huge cisterns within the city.

3:15-17. locust metaphor. Swarms of locust have periodically plagued the Near East throughout its history. They originate in desert and steppe regions as unwinged grasshoppers, and as their population grows they transform themselves into winged locusts whose numbers can literally blot out the sun as they eat, mate and infest the area with huge quantities of their young (see comment on Ex 10:1-20).

3:17. guards and officials. Nahum is using well-known Assyrian titles here referring to courtiers and scribes (probably a more general title for administrative officials). Records of the period show that some of the administration led by Ashur-Uballit II managed to flee west to Haran when the fall of Nineveh was imminent.

3:18. identity of king of Assyria. Since the date of the book of Nahum is uncertain, it is not possible to determine which king of Assyria is referred to in this final oracle. Most scholars would say that the earliest date would be shortly after the capture of Thebes in 663 and the terminus date would be the actual fall of Nineveh in 612. It may be Nahum was written as encouragement to the people of Judah to revolt as the Assyrian empire began to break apart after Ashurbanipal's death in 627. The reference may alternatively be to Sin-Shar-Ishkun, who was the Assyrian king when Nineveh fell.

HABAKKUK

1:1-11
First Complaint and Response

1:2-4. complaints about social injustice. Although Habakkuk is speaking to the people of Judah in the late seventh century B.C., his statements regarding social injustice are quite similar to those made by Amos to the northern kingdom of Israel in the eighth century. Both prophets condemn the self-indulgent and corrupt leaders of their time (see the sidebar on Amos 2:6-8 dealing with economic and social conditions in the eighth century and the comment on Amos 5:12 on the corrupt justice system). Accusations of social injustice are standard fare in Egyptian wisdom literature. The writers attempt to hold the leadership of the nation to a very high standard, and they feel it is essential for the survival of their culture that corruption be exposed and dealt with by the highest powers. Thus in the period of the Middle Kingdom (2050-1800) a *Dispute over Suicide* was composed to expose those social ills that had nearly destroyed Egyptian society during the just completed First Intermediate Period (2258-2050). The man who asks for the release of death through suicide complains that "everyone is a thief," "hearts are covetous," and "crimes outrage no one." Also during this time of instability, the *Tale of the Eloquent Peasant* speaks of the need for Egypt's administrators to check the actions of lawmakers who "approve of robbery" and inspectors who "condone corruption." He calls on judges not to accept bribes or to countenance perjury. In the ancient Near East justice was the most basic and necessary characteristic of society. It was the job of the king to maintain justice. To an even greater extent, the covenant required of Israel that justice be strictly maintained on both a personal and societal level.

1:6. chronology. If Habakkuk's prophecy is

to be understood as utterly amazing and unbelievable (1:5), it must have been given before Babylon was sweeping across the earth. It therefore seems necessary to conclude that the book should be dated prior to the Battle of Carchemish in 605. Otherwise, Habakkuk's prediction of Yahweh's "raising up the Babylonians" would have been anticlimatic. The Babylonians only became a significant threat to Judah after 605, and by 597 they had already captured Jerusalem and taken King Jehoiachin as a hostage (see the comments on 2 Kings 24:10-14). Babylon became an independent state in 625 and began its expansionist activities by 620. It is impossible to offer more precision for dating the oracles of Habakkuk.

1:6. Babylonians (Chaldeans). The Chaldeans are first mentioned in Mesopotamian sources in the ninth century B.C. Although related ethnically to the other Aramean tribes of southern Babylonia, they had a distinct tribal structure. As the Assyrian empire began to weaken, Chaldean leaders, including Nabopolassar and Nebuchadnezzar, eventually gained their independence and established the Neo-Babylonian dynasty after 625. Nebuchadnezzar inherited this powerful state in 605, becoming its most famous king. He literally rebuilt the city of Babylon, solidified Babylonian control throughout the Near East and even attacked Egypt (although unsuccessfully). His long reign lasted until 562. He was briefly succeeded by three descendents who reigned a total of six years. The last king of the dynasty of Nabonidus, who had apparently been a high official during Nebuchadnezzar's reign. He reigned until 539, when Babylon was captured by the Medo-Persians under Cyrus the Great.

1:8. Babylonian cavalry. Given the description here of swiftly moving cavalry, it seems most likely that these are spear-carrying horsemen rather than mounted archers. Assyrian reliefs from the palace of Sennacherib at Nineveh show how effectively these mounted soldiers could traverse hills and woodlands. Their sudden appearance would have terrified local villagers. In open country the chariot corps functioned as mounted infantry and archery platforms, serving as a frontal assault force, while the infantry followed them. Mounted bowmen and spear carriers, fighting in pairs for protection, stood on the flanks to protect the army from being taken in the rear and also to bar the escape of enemy soldiers.

1:10. earthen ramps. See comments on Isaiah 29:2 and Jeremiah 32:24; 33:4 for discussion of the use of earthen ramps in siege warfare.

1:12—2:20
Second Complaint and Response

1:12. rock. The metaphor comparing deity to a rock focuses primarily on the issues of protection and shelter. A large rock could provide shade, and caves were sometimes found in rocky areas. This is not a metaphor common in the river cultures of Egypt or Mesopotamia, with their abundance of alluvial plains (see the sidebar on metaphors at the beginning of Psalms). It is possible that the term is more than a metaphor because it appears in personal names in the same place as a divine name would normally appear (for example, Elijah means "Yahweh is my God," so by comparison Elizur [Num 1:5] would mean "Zur [Rock] is my God"). It also occurs in the Amorite and Aramaic personal names from Syria in the position of a divine name.

1:15-16. fishing equipment. At least in royal inscriptions and art, fishing was done with woven baskets rather than individual hooks (see the comments on Ezek 12:13 and Amos 4:2). Naturally, in these instances the point is political, depicting the strength of a ruler who can trap his enemies like fish or birds (see the comment on Hos 5:1) in a net.

2:2. herald running with tablets. The idea of running with a message suggests its urgency or importance. What is unclear is whether the "one who reads the message" is a herald (with NIV) whose task is to run from location to location reading aloud his proclamation, or whether it refers to anyone who reads the message. In the former case the inscribed tablets would be entrusted to a professional. In the latter the inscription would be set up in a public place, and as individuals read it, they would run off to spread the news. Preference lies with the former, since the text here speaks of tablets. Publicly posted inscriptions would usually be on stelae. Professional messengers were a common fixture in royal courts such as those at ancient Mari and Babylon. They were needed as "runners" to carry their lord's commands (see also Jer 36:4 and Baruch's mission as Jeremiah's scribe and messenger).

2:17. Lebanon. According to his royal annals, Nebuchadnezzar ordered his army to construct a road "for the transport of the cedars" of Lebanon. He describes how they "cut through steep mountains, split rocks, [and] opened passages" to build this commercial logging road. This was done in the name of freeing the land of its foreign enemies. However, these trees actually were used to build his palace and to enhance the temple of Marduk in Babylon. It may be assumed that the workers also hunted the mountainous areas of Lebanon for the food they needed to supplement their own stores.

2:18. image teaching lies. The uselessness of worshiping or consulting idols is once again declared here (see Is 46:7 and Hos 4:12 for other examples). Isaiah applied the phrase used here to a false prophet (Is 9:15), but Habakkuk is referring to the priests who manipulate people by "making the idol speak" or pronounce an oracle. The Babylonian *baru* priests functioned as diviners, interpreting omens, signs and performing rituals that were designed to solicit an answer from the gods.

2:19. bringing wood, stone to life. See the comment on Isaiah 44:17-18. The ritual of "opening the mouth" was employed in Babylon to transform a wooden image, decorated with gold and precious jewels, into the physical embodiment of the god. The incantations of the priests proclaimed to the god, "From this time forth you shall go before your father Ea." Ceremonial processions then take place, the mouth of the image is washed repeatedly (fourteen times in all), and food and drink are presented. After a evening of sacrifices the priest opens the eyes of the image with a wand of tamarisk, and then the "god" is enthroned within the temple and dressed with the insignia of office.

3:1-19

Habakkuk's Prayer

3:1. shigionoth. This verse serves as a superscription to the third chapter and functions in the much the same way that superscriptions or rubrics do in the Psalms. *Shigionoth* appears in the singular form in Psalm 7:1. Presumably it refers to a particular kind of song. If a linguistic connection can be made with Akkadian *shigu*, it possibly refers to a lament. However, its exact meaning is still unknown. For this and other musical terms, see the side bar on musical terms in Psalms.

3:2-19. Habakkuk's psalm and mythology. As can be seen frequently in Isaiah and Ezekiel, the prophets often make use of familiar mythological imagery in order to convey their message. Two of the ways that this can take place are (1) history can be told using mythological motifs; and (2) mythological tales can utilized with historical elements substituted in. The first is illustrated when the exodus and, especially, the crossing of the Red Sea are told using the mythological motif of divine combat with the sea (see comment on Ex 15:3). The

second can be seen in Isaiah 27 or Ezekiel 32, where familiar myths are turned into oracles against real nations in real historical contexts. Habakkuk uses both of these techniques as he interweaves elements from Babylonian and Canaanite mythology into this hymn. The general flow of this chapter shows some similarity to the Babylonian *Enuma Elish*. Marduk's praise is sung, he acquires weapons (similar list), he rides on the storm with assistants by his side, and the enemy is split open and crushed. This sequence is not unique to *Enuma Elish* but shows the intention of Habakkuk to adopt these well-known motifs and transform them to new use.

3:3. Teman. See the comments on Obadiah 9 and Jeremiah 49:7 for this site that is mentioned in the Kuntillet 'Ajrud inscription and either may be a city or a portion of the country of Edom.

3:3. Mount Paran. The area or "wilderness" of Paran is generally considered to be a region south of Palestine, but there is a difference of opinion on whether it lies westward into the Sinai peninsula or to the east of the Arabah in the vicinity of Teman (see the comments Num 10:12 and Deut 33:2).

3:3. sun metaphor. Hymns to the Babylonian sun god, Shamash, use similar terminology. One incantation refers to Shamash shining forth and filling the lands with his heavenly splendor. Yahweh is occasionally praised in terms that are also used in sun worship and in some periods was probably misconstrued as a sun god (see comment on 2 Kings 23:11). Official evidence of sun worship in ancient Israel seems to be tied primarily to the reign of Manasseh. The horses and chariots of the sun that he set up are destroyed by Josiah as he attempts to cleanse the temple complex of foreign religious influence (see comment on 2 Kings 23:11). Place names such as Beth Shemesh, Ein Shemesh, and Mount Heres (Josh 15:7; Judg 1:35) also attest to the popularity of sun worship.

3:4. rays in his hand. A typical pose of divine warrior storm gods in the ancient Near East is with bolts of lightning in an upraised hand.

3:5. plague, pestilence. The terms are personified here as associates of Yahweh in battle. The Hebrew word translated "pestilence," *resheph*, is the name of the Canaanite god of the plague. He is well known from Ugaritic, Phoenician (identified with Apollo) and Aramaic inscriptions. He is also associated with the Babylonian Nergal, who was connected with plague. In ancient Near Eastern mythology the gods going into battle are often accompanied by two associates.

3:7. tents of Cushan. This ethnic term, probably of a nomadic tribal group, appears nowhere else in the Bible. Since it appears in parallelism with Midian, it may be presumed that their territory was also in the southern steppe. They may in fact have been a subgroup of the Midianites.

3:7. dwellings of Midian. For Midian and the Midianites, see the comments on Exodus 2:15 and Numbers 22:4-7. Habakkuk here predicts the route of the divine warrior from his holy mountain to attack the Babylonians. Apparently this will startle but not harm the inhabitants of the southern regions.

3:8. conflict with rivers/sea. In Canaanite literature from Ugarit there is a lengthy myth devoted to the war between Baal and Yamm (Sea) and his associate Nahar (River), who represent the forces of chaos and destruction. Habakkuk indicates that Yahweh's anger was not directed against these mythological foes, but against the enemies of his people (v. 13).

3:9-11. cosmic effects of divine warrior. The idea of a divine warrior who leads his people into battle is well developed in the Israelite conquest narrative (see the comments on Josh

2:11 and 3:17). It also appears in the Moabite inscription of King Mesha and in the prophets (see the comment on Jer 32:21). A particularly spectacular example is found in the "Song of the War of Yahweh" in Isaiah 34 (see the comments on Is 34:4). It may be compared as well with a portion of the Ugaritic Baal epic in which that deity's approach is marked by the "withering of the heavens" and whose voice is described in the Aqhat legend as "double deep," a thundering exclamation that presages the rains. F. M. Cross cites an El Amarna text in which a subject prince, Abimilki of Tyre, refers to Pharaoh Akhenaten as the one "who utters his (battle) cry in the heavens, like Haddu so that the whole land shakes at his cry." A Mesopotamian lamentation of the first millennium uses terminology for divine judgment similar to Habakkuk when it speaks of the heavens rumbling, the earth shaking, the sun lying at the horizon, the moon stopping in the sky and evil storms sweeping through the land. For more specific information concerning the movements of the heavenly bodies connected to warfare see comments on Joshua 10:12-13.

ZEPHANIAH

1:1-13
Judgment Against Judah

1:1. chronology and pedigree. This superscription dates the book to the reign of Josiah (640-609 B.C.). Since Josiah came to the throne as a small boy, a regency made up of priests and court officials ruled Judah until 622 (see 2 Kings 22:1). Because there were several persons with the name Zephaniah in the period just prior to and during the exile, adding a short genealogy helped indicate which person was responsible for the oracles (compare a similar practice of attaching the prophet's name to a list of prophecies in the Mari texts and the Assyrian Annals of Esarhaddon).

1:4. Josiah's reform. The cultic abuses and idolatry described in this verse anticipate the actions taken by Josiah after 622 B.C. (see the comments on 2 Chron 34). When Josiah was able to effect his cleansing of the temple and elimination of foreign gods, idols and priests, he did it in the name of a restoration of the covenant's provisions (see 2 Kings 23:24-25). A similar reform had been carried out by

Hezekiah about eighty years earlier (2 Kings 18:4). In both instances the apparent weakness of the Assyrian monarchy contributed to attempts by small kingdoms like Judah to assert their political and religious independence.

1:5. worshiping starry host. Worship of the starry hosts refers to the celestial gods (sun god, moon god and Venus particularly; in Babylonia, Shamash, Sin and Ishtar respectively), who were primary in most ancient religions. Controlling calendar and time, seasons and weather, they were viewed as the most powerful of gods. They provided signs by which omens were read, and they looked down on all. By the end of the second millennium a major compilation of celestial omens, the seventy tablets of the work known as *Enuma Anu Enlil*, had been compiled and was consulted for nearly a thousand years. Stamp seals from Israel in this period show that astral deities were very popular. There were many constellations recognized by the Mesopotamian astrologers (many, though not all, the same we recognize today, transmitted through the Greeks), but the zodiac was not yet known. For more information see comment on 2 Chronicles 33:5.

1:5. Molech. See the comments on Leviticus 18:21 and Deuteronomy 18:10. Many consider Molech to have been a netherworld deity featuring rituals with Canaanite origins focusing on dead ancestors. An eighth-century B.C. Phoenician inscription speaks of sacrifices made to Molech before battle by the Cilicians and their enemies.

1:8. foreign clothes. Since Judah had been under foreign (Assyrian, Egyptian and Babylonian) domination for over a hundred years, it is not surprising that government officials and those who wished to curry favor with their overlords would adopt their clothing styles as well as other cultural traits. Neither Judean nor Babylonian dress of this period is well attested in the inscriptional materials, so detailed comparison is not possible. Differences could have included the articles of clothing that were worn or the style, material, weave or dyes that were used. A later example of the adoption of foreign styles is found in the Hellenistic period, when Jason, the high priest, forced the nobility of Jerusalem to wear a broad-brimmed hat associated with the Greek god Hermes (2 Macc 3:12).

1:9. stepping on threshold. The threshold was typically made of a single stone that spanned the doorway, raised slightly from the level of the floor. Sockets were cut into the outer edges of the threshold on which the gates or door swung. The height of the threshold would prevent the doors from swinging out. Entryways were often considered both sacred and vulnerable. Superstitious belief presumably held that stepping on the threshold would allow the demons that haunted the entryway to gain admission. Similar superstitions have continued in the Near East and the Far East from Syria to Iraq to China, but ancient information concerning this superstition is lacking.

1:10. Fish Gate. Jerusalem had many gates to serve its various quarters. The Fish Gate provided an entrance through the northern wall just to the west of the Tower of Hananel (Neh 12:38-39). Archaeological excavations confirm that it opened upon a ridge leading from the temple enclosure to the Benjamite plateau. Its name probably derives from the presence of a fish market established there by Tyrian merchants (see Neh 3:3).

1:10. New Quarter. This section of Jerusalem was created when Hezekiah built the first defensive wall around the western hills of the city (2 Chron 32:5). Manasseh apparently repaired these walls during his reign (2 Chron 33:14). Avigad's excavations have disclosed a seventh-century wall over 225 feet long and 24 feet thick. It may have surrounded the entire western hill, providing additional protection to the northern section of the city.

1:11. market district. As each district of Jerusalem is called upon in turn to lament, the Mortar or market district in the western section of the city takes up the wail. Based on the Hebrew word *maktesh* (bowl or mortar; see Prov 27:22), it was probably located in one of the folds or depressions within the Tyropoeon Valley and was enclosed within the city walls in the seventh century.

1:14—2:15
Day of the Lord Oracles Against Nations

1:14. Day of the Lord. See sidebar at Joel 2.

2:4. Philistine cities in late seventh century. After Sargon II's and Sennacherib's campaigns of the late eighth century and the capture and destruction of many of the Philistine cities, these sites were then rebuilt by the Assyrians, and several of them (particularly Timnah and Ekron) prospered as centers for olive oil production. Archaeological evidence has identified industrial districts where olive oil was processed and cloth was woven (based on large numbers of loom weights in these levels). There are indications of Egyptian presence in Philistia after the Assyrian empire collapsed (see comment on Ezek 25:15). These cities were then destroyed in 600 B.C. in the campaigns of the Babylonian ruler Nebuchadnezzar.

2:8-9. Moab and Ammon in late seventh century. Like all the small kingdoms in Syro-Palestine, Moab and Ammon were vassals of the Assyrians during the eighth and seventh centuries. Evidence of this is found in the mention of four Moabite kings in the Assyrian Annals (ranging from the time of Tiglath-Pileser III to Ashurbanipal). It can be expected that they gained some measure of independence toward the end of the seventh century as chaos reigned in Assyria (see the comment on Ezek 25:8). However, Josephus records that they were subjugated by the Babylonians shortly after the fall of Jerusalem (see the comment on Ezek 25:2).

2:12. Cushites in late seventh century. It is unclear what prompted this oracle against Ethiopia. The Cushites had not ruled Egypt since the supplanting of their dynasty in 664 by the Saite dynast Psammeticus I. While this native Egyptian pharaoh did ally himself with the Assyrians after 616, no specific event or campaign in Palestine is referenced in his or his successors' inscriptions prior to the 609 campaign of Necho II. There has been some suggestion that this reference to Cush should be understood in relation to Mesopotamia (as is possible in Gen 10:8), since it precedes the oracle on Assyria.

2:13. Assyria in late seventh century. After the death of Ashurbanipal in 627, the disputes among his heirs and potential successors so weakened the Assyrian empire that it swiftly fell apart. This collapse was hastened by two factors. First were the harsh administrative policies. The hatred generated against the Assyrians was further compounded by their use of extreme terror tactics in warfare (see the sidebar on the siege of Lachish in 2 Chron 32:9). The emergence of a Babylonian-Median coalition provided a match for Assyria's army, and by 612 the Assyrian capital at Nineveh had been captured and destroyed (see the comment on Is 13:1). The final step in completely eliminating all vestiges of Assyrian power came at the Battle of Carchemish in 605. Its empire fell to the Egyptians and Neo-Babylonians to divide (see the comment on Is 31:8).

3:1-20
Hope for Jerusalem

3:3. officials as lions. The prophet's analogy between Judah's officials and ravenous lions may be compared to the lament in Psalm 22:12-21, where the sufferer is threatened by roaring lions and calls out for rescue from their open mouths (see also Jer 2:30). In seventh-century Assyrian literature the lions' pit occurs as a metaphor for vicious and antagonistic courtiers of the king.

3:9. purifying lips. Mesopotamian rituals often featured the purification of lips as symbolic of the purification of the person. It was viewed as a prerequisite, especially for diviner priests, before they could appear before the divine council and report what they had witnessed.

3:10. rivers of Cush. As alluded to in 2:12 above, Cush can refer to several different places in the Old Testament, though it most frequently is the designation for the area translations usually render "Ethiopia." This is misleading, for the area Cush refers to is not modern Ethiopia (Abyssinia) but the area along the Nile just south of Egypt, ancient Nubia (in modern Sudan). The boundary between Egypt and Nubia in ancient times was usually either at the first or second cataract of the Nile. It is unlikely that Nubia ever extended much beyond the sixth cataract at Khartoum. This verse would then refer to the region of the Blue and White Niles in Upper Egypt. Alternatively, since no Israelites were known to have been scattered to the region of Nubia, this verse may refer to the rivers of Mesopotamia (see Gen 2:13).

HAGGAI

1:1-15
Call to Build the Temple

1:1. chronology. The use of a precise date to introduce a particular prophetic narrative is common in the postexilic writings. The monarch mentioned here is Darius I, who seized the throne of Persia on September 29, 522 B.C. This followed what had been almost seven months of trouble in the empire, beginning with the revolt by Gaumata on March 11 and his subsequent usurpation of the throne on July 1 of the same year, upon the death of Cambyses. Even after Darius secured the throne, revolts continued, as recorded on the famous Behistun Inscription. The date given in Haggai is August 29, 520.

1:1. Zerubbabel. Zerubbabel was the heir to the Davidic throne (grandson of Jehoiachin; see comment on 2 Kings 24) and served as governor of Judah under the Persian king Darius I. There was a significant amount of expectation surrounding him that had a messianic flavor to it. Undoubtedly some expected him to set up the promised kingdom and bring freedom from their slavery (to the Persians). While his duties were primarily secular, he is described in Ezra, along with the priest Joshua, as the force behind the rebuilding of the temple in Jerusalem. Governing under the auspices of the Persian king, he was responsible for maintaining law and order, and for the collection of taxes. Though Zerubbabel is the last Davidic heir to serve in the role of governor, archaeologists have found a seal of Shelomith (listed as a daughter of

Zerubbabel in 1 Chron 3:19), where she is designated as either a wife or an official of Elnathan, the governor who is thought to have succeeded Zerubbabel.

1:1. Joshua. Joshua was the high priest in the early postexilic period. His grandfather, Seraiah, had been executed by Nebuchadnezzar when Jerusalem fell to the Babylonians (2 Kings 25:18-21; note that Ezra is also from the line of Seraiah, see 7:1). Judah's heir to the throne, Zerubbabel, served as governor, but since Judah was still under Persian control, there were restrictions on the extent of his control (so as not to compete with the Persian king). Consequently, rule in the community was now divided between the governor and the high priest, giving the priest a more prominent role. Little is known about him except that he was one of the leaders who helped get the temple rebuilt. There are no contemporary extrabiblical references to him.

1:4. paneled houses. The term "paneled" can mean "covered," "roofed," or "paneled," but the point in any case is that it represents the finishing touches. Their homes were not "in process" but were fully appointed, while the temple remained a ruin. The term does not imply luxury or great expense, though paneling can be of that nature. Wood paneling was unusual in private residences, although Solomon's throne was "paneled" (1 Kings 7:7).

1:7. prophetic role in temple rebuilding. In the seventh century, Assyrian prophets offered encouragement to kings Esarhaddon and Ashurbanipal to rebuild the temples of particular deities. This message from the gods was considered essential for the kings to feel free to proceed with the building preparations. The deity who was to dwell in the temple was the only one who could authorize the undertaking.

1:15. chronology. The date here is about September 21, 520 B.C., three and one-half weeks after the first prophecy.

2:1-9
Temple Grandeur

2:1. chronology. This would have taken place on October 17, 520, about seven weeks after the first prophecy.

2:3-4. temple glory and God's presence. The main reason for all of the splendor built into a temple was to make it worthy of the deity's presence. Honor was bestowed by the wealth and luxury of the building and its furniture. Some would have even felt that this was necessary to induce the deity to make the temple his dwelling. Here Haggai deflates their fears

by assuring them that the Lord intends to inhabit the "less-than-glorious" house and will subsequently bring splendor to it.

2:10-23
Defilement and Blessing

2:10. chronology. The equivalent date is December 18, 520, over three and one-half months since the first prophecy.

2:12. transmission of purity. The "holy meat" consecrates anything it touches (e.g., the fold of a garment), but nothing that touches the fold of the garment would in turn be consecrated. The situation pictured here may have been quite common at this time. The altar had been rebuilt within a few years of the return (535), but the temple had not yet been built. This means that meat from the sacrifices could not be eaten in the regular temple precincts, as was the norm. Instead, the food would have to be transported to the eating place. The regulations governing the transfer of purity are not found in Scripture and so must have been part of Israelite oral tradition. The law in Leviticus 6:27 states that whoever touches the flesh of a sin offering will be consecrated, and when any of the blood splashes on a garment, that garment had to be washed.

2:13. transmission of impurity. Ritual defilement, however, was passed on by contact in a manner like a contagious disease (see comments on Lev 11:8; 22:3-9). In fact, contact with a corpse caused the highest degree of defilement. Those who were ceremonially unclean because of a corpse were not allowed to participate in organized worship (e.g., Num 9:6; see further the comment on Num 19:11) and often were sent away from the camp (Num 5:2). Thus, food touched by one who was defiled was contaminated.

2:17. blight, mildew and hail as divine punishment. The three punishments described here, blight, mildew and hail were all typical forms of divine correction in ancient Israel (see comment on Amos 4:9). Blight is derived from a Hebrew term signifying a scorching wind. The term usually refers to the hot east wind that blows across the land from the desert. The term "blight" refers to the debilitating effects of the wind, causing the withering and destruction of plants and grain. Mildew is a term that refers to a disease of grain caused by a fungus. It has been thought that it is often caused by drought and excessive rains. A third adverse weather condition is hail, which, if followed by a strong wind, will damage crops. Like the other terms, hail is often seen as divine judgment (see comment on Josh 10:11).

2:18. chronology. December 18, 520 (the same date mentioned in 2:10), is described here as the date of the founding of the Lord's temple. Thus the date of was great importance to Haggai.

2:23. signet ring. The term "signet" probably refers to a seal, which could have been either a cylinder seal worn with a cord around the neck or a stamp seal embedded in a ring, which is referred to here. The former was very common in Mesopotamia, while the latter was used in Israel. Thousands of cylinder seals and stamp seals have been found in Mesopotamia and Syro-Palestine respectively. They were a sign of authority, identification and ownership.

ZECHARIAH

1:1-6
Call to Repentance

1:1. chronology. Zechariah dates his oracles very precisely, as did his contemporary Haggai. His ministry began in November-December of the year 520 B.C., overlapping Haggai by one month.

1:1. Iddo. If several ancestors are mentioned in a genealogical note, the last one is usually someone of importance. In Nehemiah 12:4 an Iddo is mentioned among the priests who returned from exile with Zerubbabel in the first wave in 538. If this is the same Iddo, it indicates that Zechariah is of a prominent family with a priestly heritage.

1:7-17
First Vision: Myrtle Valley

1:7. chronology. This vision occurs several months after the initial oracle. It is dated to February 15, 519 B.C. Since the next chronological notation does not occur until after this sequence of visions, it should be considered as offering the framework for the visions, which give central attention to the rebuilding of the temple. It is likely not coincidence, then, that the vision occurs just one week prior to New Year's day, when temple building and restoration projects usually commenced in the ancient world. In addition, some scholars believe that Darius marched to Egypt in 519 to secure its renewed loyalty and that the preparations of the army for this march were a source of concern for the people of Judah. They could have felt very uncertain about what demands might be made on them and how they would be treated.

1:9. angel directing vision. Angels not only delivered messages from deity but explained those messages and answered questions concerning them. Thus Gabriel is seen in Daniel 8:16 as one who can interpret the vision. In the polytheistic context of the ancient world the messengers of the gods were generally gods themselves (of lower rank). In Mesopotamia

---

APOCALYPTIC LITERATURE

"Apocalyptic" is the name that has traditionally been given to a particular category (genre) of literature. Apocalyptic is defined by its characteristics. It has some traceable roots outside the Bible (see the sidebar on Akkadian apocalypses in Dan 11) but finds its earliest true members in Old Testament books such as Daniel and Zechariah. In the Bible it is intricately intertwined with prophetic literature. There are over a dozen Jewish apocalyptic works during the intertestamental period, the most prominent being 4 Ezra and the books of *Enoch*. The book of Revelation is the New Testament's contribution to the genre. Other Christian apocalypses began to appear on the heels of the New Testament, including works like the *Shepherd of Hermas*, the *Apocalypse of Peter* and the *Ascension of Isaiah*. The genre was a favorite of the Gnostics, whose literature contains numerous examples. Apocalypses feature a narrative framework and often portray an angelic interpreter or guide alongside the prophet. The angel may take the prophet on a tour of heavenly realms to convey certain realities and activities. Alternatively, he may unveil a future time of trouble and deliverance. This literature operates by means of a broad spectrum of symbols using significant numbers and mythological images. It draws heavily on both biblical and extrabiblical literature. It tends to schematize. When reading apocalyptic, there are a couple of important guidelines to keep in mind. First, each detail does not necessarily carry symbolic significance. Even the details that do carry symbolic significance may not be transparent to us and speculating accomplishes little. Second, it is important to remember that the apocalyptic vision is not the message itself but rather is the vehicle or occasion for the message. So, for instance, the message of the first vision of Zechariah (1:7-17) is *not* that there are going to be four horses of different colors in a myrtle grove. The message is laid out very clearly in verses 14-17. Apocalyptic is simply a medium.

we find individuals such as Nuska and Kakka, while the well-known Hermes serves the function in Greek mythology. In a dream of Nabonidus a young man appears to offer an interpretation of a celestial omen that has been observed.

1:10. sent throughout the earth. The Persians were well known for their mounted couriers, who traveled daily through the empire maintaining the most efficient communication system known in the ancient world. The myrtle trees evoke the image of palace gardens. Persian kings enjoyed the parks of trees that stood beside the audience halls and received visitors and reports there.

1:11. Persian peace. Just as royal couriers would be reporting to their superior that all was peace, so these angelic couriers bring their report to the angel of the Lord. The fact that Darius was now securely seated on the throne and smoldering revolts had been quenched would have been good news for the empire but bad news for the Jews. Their hopes for the restoration and reestablishment of a Davidic monarchy that had been excited at the prospect of the collapse of the Persian empire were now dashed. Additionally, if Darius's army is on the way to Egypt through Judah (see comment on 1:7), the horseman's report could offer assurance that there will be no trouble from the Persians as they pass through.

1:16. status of rebuilding. Ezra 3 reports work that had been done on the temple site prior to 520. Certainly the altar had been set up on its foundation and was operational, but the chronological note introducing the building of a foundation in Ezra 3:10 is not as clear as it could be (see comment on Ezra 3:8). It is not impossible that a foundation was laid a second time.

1:18-21
Second Vision: Horns and Craftsmen

1:18. four horns. It was common in Mesopotamia for kings and gods to wear crowns featuring either protruding or embossed horns. Sometimes the sets of horns were stacked one upon another in tiers. The winged lion from Ashurnasirpal's palace has a conical crown on its human head with three pairs of tiered horns embossed on it. It is difficult to determine what the significance of the four might be. Suggestions include the presentation of a four-empire scheme (see comment on Dan 7:17) or perhaps a reference to the four corners of the earth from where these enemies have

come (see comment on Ezek 7:2). Given the context of temple building, a persuasive suggestion is that the symbolism of the horns was evoked from the four horns of the altar. An altar had been set up on the temple site soon after the arrival of the returnees (see comment on 1:16) but probably would have had to be removed for the reconstruction work to take place.

1:20-21. craftsmen. Among the many categories of Babylonian temple personnel at the end of the sixth century was one designated "craftsmen" *(ummanu)*. A number of different guilds were included in this group (those who worked with materials such as wood, metal, leather, gold, cloth, stone and gems, as well as those who carried out tasks such as laundering). This same term was extended to serve as a title of royal advisors believed to be supernaturally endowed. Individuals of this title are also identified as the sages who composed famous pieces of literature. In short, this term referred to various experts in the employ of the palace and temple. The Erra Epic makes it clear that it was the *ummanu* who were responsible for crafting divine images. The Hebrew term used here can also refer to a wide range of guild workers, including those who craft images and serve the temples, but is never clearly extended to sages or royal administrative advisors. In the Canaanite pantheon the important deity Kothar-wa-Hasis is the craftsman of the gods. He makes the weapons of the gods and is responsible for building Baal's house. In the Egyptian pantheon, Ptah of Memphis is the craftsman deity, who was thereby considered a creator as well as the patron of artisans. If it is correct that these are the craftsmen who are dismantling the altar (see previous comment), then they are artisans in the employ of the temple carrying out a sacred and ceremonial task.

2:1-13
Third Vision: Measuring Line

2:2. measuring Jerusalem. The placement and orientation of a temple was considered extremely important (see the comment on Ex 26:1-36). This is also evidenced in temple building texts both mythological and historical in Mesopotamia. In *Enuma Elish* when Marduk is preparing to build his cosmic temple, he measures the Apsu (the area where the foundation of the temple will be laid). From Sumerian times through Assyrian and Babylonian periods the possession of the measuring equipment is a sign of the divine commission for the rebuilding project. It is through this equipment that the leader is given divine direction. Additionally this equipment was used to determine the exact location of previous temple foundations.

2:5. glory within. As early as Sumerian literature it can be observed that the presence of deity in a city represents the city's protection. For example, in the *Curse of Agade* the gods take their leave of the city and thereby make it vulnerable to its enemies.

2:6. land of the north. Especially in Jeremiah, the north was direction that the enemy was going to come from (see comment on Jer 1:14-15). Eventually it became clear that Babylon was that enemy from the north. Even though Babylon was located east of Jerusalem, all traffic flowed in an arc around the Syrian desert. Thus Babylonians would come into Judah from the north, and Israelites would go to Babylon from the north. Now Zechariah is urging them to flee from the lands of their captors.

2:6. four winds. In Mesopotamian thinking there were occasionally seven winds, but four was the more usual. The four were connected with compass points in accordance with the direction they blew from, just as they are today.

3:1-10 Joshua's Investiture

3:1. Satan. Here and in the book of Job the word *saṭan* appears with a definite article ("the"), which makes it clear that it is not being treated as a personal name. The Hebrew word *saṭan* is used to describe an adversary and can be used of human beings or supernatural beings. Even the angel of the Lord can exercise this function (Num 22:22). The term does not clearly take on the role of a personal name until the intertestamental period (specifically the second century B.C.). Though the individual functioning as an adversary to Joshua here may well be the one who later bears the name Satan, that cannot be concluded with certainty. Those who serve as adversaries are generally in the role of calling God's policies and decisions into accountability.

3:3. Joshua. Joshua is the high priest in the early postexilic period. His grandfather, Seraiah, had been executed by Nebuchadnezzar when Jerusalem fell to the Babylonians (2 Kings 25:18-21; note in 7:1 that Ezra is also identified as being from the line of Seraiah). Judah's heir to the throne, Zerubbabel, served as governor, but since Judah was still under Persian control, there were restrictions on the extent of his control (so as not to compete with the Persian king). Consequently, rule in the community was now divided between the governor and the high priest, giving the priest a more prominent role. Little is known about Joshua except that he was one of the leaders who helped get the temple rebuilt. There are no contemporary extrabiblical references to him.

3:4. those standing before him. The scene that includes an accuser and one standing in the dock evokes the imagery of a heavenly court. Such a concept had a long-standing tradition in both Israel and the ancient Near East. In the ancient Near East the major decisions were all made in the divine council. There the gods would consult with one another and share their information and opinions. The familiar picture of a heavenly throne surrounded by the heavenly council is well known from the Ugaritic texts (most notably the Epic of Keret), though this Canaanite council is made up of the gods of the pantheon. Examples occur also in the tenth-century building inscription of Yehimilk from Byblos and the Karatepe stele of Azitawadda. In the Akkadian *Enuma Elish* it is the assembly of the gods that appoints Marduk as their head. Fifty gods made up this assembly, with seven in the inner council. In Israelite belief the gods were replaced by angels or spirits—the sons of God or the heavenly host.

3:5. investiture. There is no mention in this section of the most notable items of the priest's regalia—no ephod, no breastplate, not even any linen—just the turban. This suggests that Joshua's priestly status is not the issue. In a relief of Ashurbanipal (seventh century) the king wears a special turban as he carries the foundation brick in a basket on his head. Alternatively, then, we could view Joshua being prepared for his role in the temple reconstruction.

3:8. branch. Most consider the word "branch" a technical term referring to a rightful heir of an established dynastic line—in Israel, a future Davidic king who would restore the monarchy. A similar usage has been found in a Phoenician votive inscription from Cyprus honoring Melqart that dates to the early third century B.C. There it refers to a legitimate "branch" of the Ptolemaic dynasty of Egypt. The Dead Sea Scrolls from Qumran do not use the term in a messianic sense, but the kingship sense does occur in Ugaritic and Assyrian texts. For instance, Tiglath-Pileser III is described as the shoot or scion of the city of Baltil (Ashur) who brings justice to his people.

3:9. seven eyes on the stone. It has generally been held that the seven "eyes" are seven facets. The problem is that gemstones were shaped but not faceted in the ancient world. Given the context, it is preferable to associate this stone with a new foundation stone for the temple (see the comment on 4:7). In Mesopotamia there are beads of precious stones given as gifts to the temple that are cut in the shape of eyes and engraved with the names of the donors. Assyrian and Babylonian kings included gemstones in the foundation deposits of temples. Nabopolassar reports spreading gold, silver and imported stones on foundations. Foundation stones were sometimes overlaid with precious metals and could therefore be encrusted with gems. If Zechariah reflects this practice, the seven "eyes" are being inlaid on the stone rather than engraved on it.

4:1-14

Lampstand and Olive Trees

4:1. angel directing the vision. See comment on 1:9.

4:2. description of lamp. This solid gold lamp consists of a pedestal on which a large bowl rests. Arranged around the rim of the large bowl are seven lamps. These lamps are small shallow bowls that hold the oil. Such bowl lamps are common throughout the biblical period, though they take varying shapes in different periods. Typically they feature a pinched area on the rim where a wick can be squeezed in with the bottom of it submerged in the oil. The wick will then draw oil up to burn. Each of the seven lamps here has seven pinched spouts around its rim, as attested in some excavated lamps. In this way the large lamp has forty-nine lights. The large bowl presumably contained oil that was somehow channeled to the seven smaller lamps. There are no excavated artifacts that bear a resemblance to the complex lamp described here. An alternative design that has a little more support from archaeology is that of the kernos. This type of vessel features a pottery ring (instead of a bowl) on which the seven lamps are mounted. Kernoi that were used as lamps have been found in Persian-period Palestine.

4:3. setting of the lamp. O. Keel has demonstrated that in the iconography represented on seals of the eighth and seventh centuries, the deity is often represented stylistically. Astral images usually represent the deity, most commonly the crescent moon with its horns facing upward. Both the shape and the fact that light is involved can easily parallel the lamp of this vision. Additionally, this symbol is flanked by worshipers, sometimes represented stylistically as trees, though often of the cypress variety.

It is not impossible that, as B. Halpern has suggested, the vision of the lampstand provides a description of that which will be inscribed on the foundation stone. The main advantage to this is that it draws together the seven eyes of the stone in 3:9 with the seven eyes representing the lamps in 4:10, since the lampstand and the stone would be one and the same.

4:6. Zerubbabel. Zerubbabel was the heir to the Davidic throne (grandson of Jehoiachin, see comments on 2 Kings 24) and served as governor of Judah under the Persian king Darius I. There was a significant amount of expectation surrounding him that had a messianic flavor to it. Undoubtedly some expected him to set up the promised kingdom and bring freedom from their slavery (to the Persians). While his duties were primarily secular, he is described in Ezra, along with the priest Joshua, as the force behind the rebuilding of the temple in Jerusalem. Governing under the auspices of the Persian king, he was responsible for maintaining law and order, and for the collection of taxes. Though Zerubbabel was the last Davidic heir to serve in the role of governor, archaeologists have found a seal of Shelomith (listed as a daughter of Zerubbabel in 1 Chron 3:19), on which she is designated as either a wife or an official of Elnathan, the governor who is thought to have succeeded Zerubbabel.

4:7. capstone. Rather than a capstone, this is more likely to be the foundation brick that is always significant in temple building and restoration. One of the most detailed temple-building accounts in ancient Near Eastern literature describes Gudea's construction of a temple for Ningirsu around 2000 B.C. The ceremony concerning the premier brick shows its centrality to the building procedure. In Neo-Assyrian texts, Esarhaddon personally brings out the old premier brick from the site of the temple so that restoration can begin. The reference to level ground here suggests that Zerubbabel is ceremoniously removing the premier brick from the prior temple to indicate that the restoration can begin.

4:9. Zerubbabel to complete the temple. In the *Autobiography of Adad-Guppi,* Adad-Guppi, the mother of King Nabonidus (just a few decades prior to Zechariah) is told in a dream that her son will construct the temple of the god Sin in Harran. He will complete the work and bring renewed glory to Harran and its patron deity.

4:10. plumb line. The Hebrew speaks only of a tin stone. Some temple restoration projects in the ancient world featured a tin bracelet used by the one who removed the premier stone (see the comment on 4:7 above). Tin was also occasionally used as a tablet for the foundation inscription.

4:10. seven eyes of the Lord. The seven "eyes" of the Lord are represented by the lamps. If the connections suggested between 3:9 and 4:3 above are correct, these seven "eyes" are also the same ones mentioned in 3:9 and are embedded in the foundation stone as part of the picture of the lampstand.

4:12. golden pipes. In the seals described in the comment on 4:3, there are also portrayed what Keel identifies as "tassels" extending from the crescent moon. In this vision they take the form of pipes conducting oil from the trees to the lamp.

4:14. significance of oil. The word used for oil in verses 12 and 14 refers to the raw material, unprocessed oil. This would not be used for anointing (NIV's "anointed" in the Hebrew is "sons of oil"). As a raw material it is often connected with prosperity, but it is difficult to know what connection that would have here. Given the context of laying the foundation of the temple, it may be important that the ceremonial laying of the foundation often featured mortar mixed with oil rather than water. If this connection is valid, it would again identify Joshua and Zerubbabel as the ones carrying out the building project. Sennacherib claims that he sprinkled a foundation with oil as if it were river water.

5:1-4
Flying Scroll

5:1. flying scroll. The description of the scroll as flying suggests that it is at least partially unrolled. Though in English we can speak of a flag flying as well as a creature flying, Hebrew usage is only in the latter category (though sparks and clouds are also said to "fly"). This is confirmed in verse 4, where the scroll is sent out and enters houses. There is no parallel to flying scrolls in extrabiblical literature.

5:2. dimensions compared. The dimensions of the scroll are the same as the portico area of Solomon's temple, but it is difficult to identify any significance to such a correlation. The thirty-foot-long scroll is not unusual for ancient scrolls, but the fifteen-foot width is extraordinary and out of proportion. Concern for proportionality has led some to consider the thirty-foot length as a reference to only the few columns that were visible in a partial unrolling of the scroll. It would be highly unusual to unroll the entire scroll. Conventional practice would be to unroll both sides of the

scroll simultaneously to move through the scroll, maintaining the visibility of just a few columns of text at a time. Having the open section thirty feet long would be more consistent with the giant size suggested by the fifteen-foot width. Since a column of writing on a scroll was typically about half as wide as the height of the scroll, probably two columns would be visible, with the still rolled portions on either side making up the remainder of the width.

5:3. curse on the scroll. The word used here for curse refers to the dire consequences called down on one who violates an oath, or to a public summons intended to collect information concerning a crime that has been committed (see Lev 5:1). Failure to reveal information that one has would implicate a person as an accomplice, subject to the same punishment as the perpetrator.

5:3. written on both sides. Though scrolls usually had writing on only one side, it is not without precedent for the writing to carry over onto the other side (see Ezek 2:10). Having said that, however, it is not at all clear that the text is referring to a scroll written on two sides. In almost every use of this idiom, the two sides are left and right, not front and back. If front and back were intended, the same idiom that is used in Ezekiel 2:10 would have been the logical choice. It is therefore more likely that two columns are exposed on the scroll (see comment on 5:2), with one addressing the punishment for theft and the other the punishment for swearing falsely.

5:3. thieves and oath breakers. The text suggests a connection between theft and oath breaking. What oath could be made that, if broken, would constitute theft? One possibility is that individuals had made pledges of funds to accomplish the building of the temple and were now reneging on their oaths. In that case they would be guilty of stealing (it had been pledged and, therefore, no longer belonged to them) and of oath breaking. The sanctions (represented in the scroll) are now going forth to ferret them out and bring the consequences down on them. The problem of investing in their own houses instead of the temple is referred to in Haggai 1:4; the accusation of theft for holding back that which has been pledged is seen to be a postexilic problem in Malachi 3:8-10.

5:4. curse entering a house and remaining in it. If, as suggested in the above comments, the offenders have reneged on their promised contributions to the temple, it is appropriate that their obstruction of the building of the Lord's house should result in the destruction of their own houses. It is another way of say-

ing that their unfaithfulness will come back to
haunt them in such a way that the punishment is suited to the offense.

5:5-11

Woman in the Basket

5:6. measuring basket. Special ceremonial
containers were used to transport the premier
stone as well as to house the foundation deposits. This container is described only by its
size, an ephah, which is generally considered
about two-thirds of a bushel. There is no indication as to what material it is made out of.
The container used for foundation deposits in
Mesopotamia is called a *quppu* and could be
either a wicker basket or a wooden chest.
Judging from what was placed in them, they
could be of varying sizes.

5:7. lead. Though the NIV interprets this as a
cover, the text refers to it in verse 7 as a "talent"
of lead (a particular weight, usually the shape of
a convex disk) and as a stone of lead in verse 8.
Temple foundation deposits often included metal pieces (gold, silver, iron, bronze, lead), sometimes small scraps, other times large blocks and
at times square convex tablets or bricks.

5:7. woman inside. The small size of the container has led to the conclusion that the woman
sitting inside refers to a figurine. The connection of this to temple building could be that figurines were often buried next to the foundation
deposit or beneath the door-pivot stone. Such
figurines could either indicate dedication to a

particular deity, or represent an apotropaic
(protective) deity. It is very tempting to see this
vision as entailing a foundation deposit box
taken from the ruins of the temple that contained a figurine and a piece of lead.

5:9. women with wings. In the Old Testament
angels are not female and are not portrayed
with wings (though in Dan 9:21 Gabriel perhaps comes in swift flight; but see comment
there). In Ugaritic literature Baal's sister, Anat,
is portrayed with wings. In Mesopotamian art
winged creatures are generally either protective genies or demons. The goddess Ishtar is
also occasionally portrayed with wings. Two
winged female genies are portrayed flanking a
stylized tree in a relief from the ninth century.

5:11. building a house for it. The pronoun "it"
is feminine, as are the woman and the ephah.
Since the second part of this verse makes reference to the container rather than to the
woman, the house is seen as being built for it
rather than for her. This would further confirm that the container should be identified as
a foundation deposit that will be set in place
in a temple there. The word "house" is often
used for a temple.

6:1-8

Four Chariots

6:1-5. charioteer messengers of deity. These
are called the four spirits, the same terms as
the four winds in 2:6. Psalm 104:4 refers to the
winds as the messengers of Yahweh, and that

SUMMARY OF THE TEMPLE-BUILDING CONNECTIONS TO ZECHARIAH'S VISIONS
The series of visions starts off with the affirmation that Yahweh still cares about his people despite the
secure standing of the Persian empire. The first vision indicates that his plan for the future is going to be
accomplished through the rebuilt temple. The second vision begins the process of preparing the site for
the rebuilding. The dismantling of the altar is envisioned as representing the terrifying of the nations. The
third vision continues the preparation by measuring the city (1:16 shows that measuring the city is part of
the preparation for building the temple). Measurements of the city served the purpose of determining the
placement of the temple. Such a process would not be productive in this case, however, because the city is
not going to have walls to calculate from. It would be highly unusual for a temple not to be protected by a
wall because of all the valuables stored there and the need to preserve the sanctity of the area. In a preamble to the fourth vision, Joshua is prepared to play his role; he is purified for the rituals surrounding the
premier stone and given the ceremonial cap on which the stone is carried. This foundation stone is ornamented with seven semiprecious stones that serve as seven lamps in the inscribed decoration. The
inscription on the stone is a typical scene of a lampstand (representing the temple and indirectly Yahweh,
who dwells there) flanked by stylized trees. Here they are olive trees that supply the oil to keep the lamp-
stand/temple going. Oil is also used to pour over the foundation and mix with the mortar for the placement of the ceremonial premier stone. In this vision, Zerubbabel is the one responsible for ceremonially
removing the previous premier stone so that the leveling of the site can take place. The fifth vision represents an attempt to call in the pledges that have been made for the funding of the building project. The
deadbeats are guilty of breaking their oaths and, in effect, of stealing because they have kept that which
had been pledged to the temple rebuilding fund. The sixth removes an idolatrous figurine that would
have been deposited in the foundations in a previous renovation. It is sent back to Babylon where it
belongs, and there a temple can be built for this foundation deposit. The sequence ends with the temple
serving its function as a base of operations from where Yahweh can carry out his military and political
plans.

is the function they are serving here. The horsemen in chapter 1 were comparable to the Persian courier service, but chariots were not used that way. It is unusual that a chariot should be used by a messenger, because it would only slow him down and tire his horses unnecessarily. In the ancient Near East a supernatural being in a chariot was usually transporting the deity rather than serving as a messenger (see comment on 2 Kings 2:11).

6:9-15
Joshua's Crown
6:11. high priest's crown. The crown referred to here is a circlet, and, though it is occasionally worn by royalty, it more often adorns a person who is being honored or celebrated. It can be made of precious metals, as it is here, but can also be made of flowers or greenery.

7:1-14
Fasting Question
7:1. chronology. The date equivalent is December 7, 518 B.C. This is nearly two years after the last date given in chapter 1 and the last date given in the book. There is no evident correspondence to any particular event in either the Jewish calendar or the activities of Darius that would give this date significance.
7:2. people of Bethel. The town of Bethel was about twelve miles north of Jerusalem and was on the northern fringe of the Persian province known as Yehud (Judah).
7:3. fast of the fifth month. Nebuchadnezzar's destruction of the temple had taken place in the fifth month (see 2 Kings 25:8). It is logical that a fast day had been established on that date. The delegation would undoubtedly wonder whether they should continue to observe a fast for the destruction of the temple now that it was being rebuilt. Zechariah responds by questioning whether the fast focused on a petition to rebuild the temple or on a petition that concerned repentance for the sins that had brought about the destruction.
7:5. fast of the seventh month. The only known event from the seventh month that could reasonably the occasion for a fast is the assassination of Gedaliah (Jer 41). He had been appointed governor of Jerusalem by Nebuchadnezzar after the fall of Jerusalem.
7:5. purpose of fasting. Fasting is little attested in the ancient Near East outside of the Bible. It generally occurs in the context of mourning. In the Old Testament the religious use of fasting is often in connection with making a request before God. The principle is that the importance of the request causes an individual to be so concerned about his or her spiritual condition that physical necessities fade into the background. In this sense the act of fasting is designed as a process leading to purification and humbling before God (Ps 69:10; 102:4). It is not an end in itself, but rather it is the disciplined training in preparation for an important event.

8:1-23
Oracles of Restoration
8:19. various fasts. The fasts of the fifth and seventh months have been identified in the comments on chapter 7. The other two also appear to be connected with the events surrounding the siege of Jerusalem. The fourth month represented the end of Davidic kings occupying the throne. It was in the fourth month that the last king of Judah, Zedekiah, secretly fled the city after a year and a half of siege. The tenth month had marked the beginning of the siege of Jerusalem by the Babylonian armies.
8:22. powerful nations seeking the Lord. This was already a theme in preexilic prophecy. See comment on Isaiah 2:2.
8:23. grasping the hem. Grasping the hem of the garment was a common phrase found in Ugaritic, Aramaic and Akkadian (languages related to biblical Hebrew). In Akkadian the phrase was "to seize the hem." In both Israel and Mesopotamia, grasping the hem of someone's garment was a gesture of supplication and submission. Saul's grasping of Samuel's skirt was a final plea for mercy. This is also the case in the Ugaritic Baal cycle, where Anat seizes the hem of Mot's garment to plead for her brother Baal.

9:1-17
Coming Judgment
9:1. Hadrach/Damascus. Hadrach is not known from any other biblical references but is familiar from Neo-Assyrian sources beginning in the mid-eighth century as the district of Hatarikka. It is located along the upper Orontes River between Aleppo and Hamath. It is the northernmost area of the Persian satrapy known as Abarnahara (land across the river) that dominated the region between the Orontes and the Euphrates. Damascus dominated the northeastern region of the satrapy between the Orontes and the Syrian desert. During this period it was a province, as was Hadrach.
9:2. Hamath in early fifth century. Hamath is

likewise a term that could refer to a region as well as a city. It was located about 130 miles north of Damascus along the Orontes. If it was a province during this time, as some suggest, its territory would most likely have been the area between the Orontes and the Mediterranean. Neither archaeological or literary sources provide much information for the sixth and fifth centuries.

9:2. Tyre and Sidon in the early fifth century. These cities represent the province(s) of Phoenicia between the Litani River and the Mediterranean. Though as port cities these two were important to the Persian military efforts in the west, there is little information about them during this period.

9:5-6. Philistine cities in early fifth century. The area of ancient Philistia was now identified as the province of Ashdod. Gaza served as the base for Persian military operations against Egypt, and Ashkelon was a prosperous port city. Excavations at Ashdod suggest a thriving town during the Persian period but historical documents give little information.

9:7. blood, forbidden food. This speaks of a change in Philistine diet such that they will conform to Jewish law. The Israelites were forbidden to eat meat without draining the blood (see comments on Lev 17:11-12, and there were regulations concerning animals that could or could not be eaten (see comments on Lev 11).

9:7. Ekron like Jebusites. The Jebusites were native to the region of Jerusalem at the time of the conquest of the land under Joshua. They continued to control Jerusalem for the centuries of the Judges period up to the conquest of Jerusalem by David. There are a few textual indications that they were absorbed into Israel rather than wiped out (see comment on 2 Sam 24:18). Ekron has been identified as Tell Miqne in the Sorek Valley, about twenty miles southwest of Jerusalem and fifteen miles from the Mediterranean. It features a forty-acre lower city, a ten-acre upper tell and a two-and-a-half-acre acropolis. Excavations since the early 1980s have given a good picture of this town. It was known for its production of olive oil and had over one hundred processing plants. An inscription found on the site in 1996 that dated to the seventh century B.C. provided the first example of the Philistine dialect of West Semitic using the Phoenician script. After Ekron's destruction by Nebuchadnezzar in 603, there was very little occupation of the site.

9:9. king riding donkey. It was common in the ancient Near East for a king to ride a mule (see comment on 1 Kings 1:33), but here the reference is to a common donkey. Although

Akkadian texts do evidence a king riding a donkey, it is by no means a royal mount. The word translated "colt" in the NIV refers to the same animal that is the mount for the sons of judges in Judges 10:3. Using a donkey for a mount is more likely to be connected to humility than to royalty.

9:10. battle bow. In Assyrian texts from the seventh century (Esarhaddon), a deity breaking the bow of the enemy is a way of describing conquest. In this passage the action appears to prevent future battle. In other biblical texts the same concept is expressed by the idea of beating swords into plowshares (see comment on Is 2:4).

9:10. sea to sea. Rather than referring to particular seas such as the Mediterranean and the Dead Sea, the universal tone of the passage suggests that reference is being made to cosmic seas that encompass all the inhabited lands.

9:10. River to ends of the earth. When "river" is used with a definite article, it is usually a name for the Euphrates. Here there is no definite article, suggesting a more abstract cosmic reference. In Akkadian literature the great cosmic river is known as *apsu* and would serve as a suitable contrast to the ends of the earth. "The ends of the earth" is used to refer to the most distant known places.

9:13. Greece in the early fifth century. The Hebrew term used here, "Javan," was probably the Greek name Ionia, the Greek region of the western coast of Turkey and the Aegean islands. Ionian Greeks settled this area just before the first millennium B.C. There is evidence of contact between them and the Assyrians by the eighth century B.C. By the time of Zechariah the Greeks have been involved in warfare with the Persians (see comment on Esther 2:1).

9:14. divine warrior. In the divine warrior motif the deity is fighting the battles and defeating the deities of the enemy. In Assyria Nergal is the king of battle, and Ishtar is viewed as a war goddess. The Canaanite Baal and the Babylonian Marduk are divine warriors. In this worldview human warfare is viewed simply as a representation of warfare among the gods. The stronger god would be victorious regardless of the strengths or weaknesses in the human combatants. Thunder and lightning were considered to regularly accompany the presence of a deity, especially in a battle setting. From the Sumerian *Exaltation of Inanna*, to the Hittite myths about the storm god, to the Akkadian and Ugaritic mythologies, the gods are viewed as thundering in judgment against their enemies. Baal is depicted as grasping a handful of thunderbolts. Thundering terminology is picked up in royal rhetoric as Hittite or Assyrian kings portray themselves as the instruments of the gods, thundering against those who have violated treaties or stood in the way of empire expansion.

9:15. bowl from sprinkling corners of altar. The horns of the altar were sprinkled with the blood of the sacrifices, so it was blood that filled these bowls. The comparison to the bowl therefore suggests massive bloodshed.

10:1—11:3
Deliverance of Judah from Oppressive Shepherds

10:1. Yahweh as fertility deity. There is a long history in the ancient Near East of particular worship being offered to the storm god who brought rain and fertility to the fields. Baal was that god in the Canaanite system. Israelites in the preexilic period had been inclined to attribute the fertility of the fields to Baal even while they gladly acknowledged Yahweh as their national God (see comment on Hos 2:1).

10:2. idols and diviners. The word translated "idols" is *teraphim,* which are not representations of the gods, but, most likely, of the ancestors (see comment on Gen 31:19). These images would most likely "speak" through omens or through the necromancers who professed skill in communicating with the spirits of the dead. Experts in divination not only interpreted dreams (see comments on Dan 1:17; 2:4), but also specialized in inducing revelatory dreams (see comment on 1 Sam 3:3).

10:3. leaders as shepherds. The ideology of the king as a shepherd to his people is applied to Lugalzagessi of Sumer as early as around 2450 B.C. The contemporary king Urukagina of Lagash claimed that the god Ningirsu owned his state and that the king had been chosen as a "shepherd" to administer the city on behalf of the gods and the people. Gods responsible for maintaining justice (Shamash in Mesopotamia, Amon in Egypt) are likewise represented in this way. This ideology continued in the ancient Near East into the monarchy period, occurring in reference to Ashurbanipal of Assyria (seventh century) and Nebuchadnezzar (sixth century).

10:4. cornerstone. Israelite Iron Age architectural design made increasing use of cut stone masonry over the rough boulders and rubble construction of earlier periods. In order to provide stability and to bind two adjoining walls together, a finely shaped block of stone was inserted that became the cornerstone. It would have been a larger stone than those normally used, and its insertion often required special effort or rituals. Its large, smooth surface was a natural place for inscribing religious slogans, the name of the architect or king responsible and the date of construction. It is possible that the cornerstone could also serve as the foundation stone.

10:4. tent peg. It could be said that the tent peg is to the tent what the cornerstone is to a building. Alternatively, there is an Old Assyrian inscription of Irishum that suggests that a peg is driven into the wall of a temple as a symbol of its completion. In such a case the foundation stone marks the beginning of the project, while the peg marks the end of it. The terms both came to be used metaphorically as that which is foundational (as in Is 22:23; Ezra 9:8). Such pegs were sometimes included in Mesopotamian foundation deposits.

10:10. places of exile. Although Assyria is the well-known site of exile for both the northern kingdom and groups from the southern kingdom (see comment on Is 22:2-3), it is evident that there were also colonies of Israelites that had either fled to Egypt or been taken to Egypt, perhaps as early as the eighth century but certainly by the seventh century (see comment on Jer 43:7).

10:10. Gilead and Lebanon. Referring to Gilead (tableland east of the Jordan) and Lebanon (Beqa Valley along the Litani River between the Lebanon and Anti-Lebanon mountain chains) for Israel would be like referring to Montana and Wyoming in the United States. Images would be evoked of wide open, sparsely inhabited spaces.

11:1-3. destruction of forests and pastures. Forestation and pasturage are valuable resources in this land that offers so little of them. Vast stretches of potentially productive land become trackless waste land when the greenery is destroyed. The modern state of Israel is reclaiming the land's productivity by reintroducing forestation into desolate areas. Ancient invaders strategically destroyed farmland, pasturage and forestation when seeking to cripple a nation long-term (see comment on 2 Kings 3:25).

11:4-17
Drama of Two Shepherds

11:4. flock marked for slaughter. The temple kept extensive herds that had been given as firstfruit offerings (and for other reasons) and were marked for slaughter in that they had been promised to the Lord. There would therefore be many shepherds in the employ of the temple to watch over these herds.

11:6. handing people over to neighbors. The Hebrew word for neighbor is very close to the Hebrew word for shepherd. The parallel with the word "king" in this verse has led some to conclude that the word "shepherd" was the original reading. Alternatively, there may just be a play on words here.

11:12. thirty pieces of silver. By verse 12 it is difficult to know whether Zechariah is still in his role as shepherd and is collecting shepherd wages, or whether he is collecting wages for his prophetic role (last line of v. 11). Information from the law codes in the second millennium B.C. indicates that a shepherd would normally make ten shekels in a year. On the other hand a prophet might expect to be paid well for his skills. The fact that a slave was worth thirty shekels is not helpful here, since Zechariah is not being bought as a slave. In Sumerian usage "thirty shekels worth" has an idiomatic meaning along the lines of "two bits" or "a plug nickel," meaning that something was virtually worthless. While this would fit the context here, the jump from Sumerian to postexilic Hebrew is a large one and cannot be relied upon.

11:13. thrown to the potter. Three possible explanations have been given here, and it is difficult to decide between them. First, it is likely that there was a pottery shop in the vicinity of the temple that served the temple's needs. But why would this money be thrown there? Second, the word for potter simply means "fashioner," so some have suggested that here it refers to a metalworker who is perhaps going to make a figurine out of the silver. This may offer an explanation of why the silver is thrown here, but it requires an unusual meaning to be applied to a fairly common noun. Third, it has been observed that the word rendered "potter" can, with very little change, be understood as "treasury." Some of the early translations take this route, and it can find some support in the New Testament as well (Mt 27:5-6, though Matthew also refers to the potter). Each interpretation has its difficulties, and no information from the ancient Near East can shed light on the actions of the prophet.

11:16. tearing off hoofs. Herds of sheep were rarely used for meat. The wool was far more valuable. A shepherd's main responsibility was to preserve the life and health of the sheep so as to vouchsafe their continued productivity. Eating the meat spoke of the short-sighted self-indulgence of undisciplined appetites rather than wise management of long-term resources. The tearing off of the hoofs may represent an attempt to persuade the owner that the sheep had been devoured by a wild animal so that the shepherd would not be held accountable. Alternatively, the shepherd may be seeking to sell the hoofs so as to get a small return.

12:1-14
Deliverance of Jerusalem

12:2. cup (bowl) of reeling. The expression "cup of reeling" is used elsewhere in Isaiah 51:17, 22, but here the text actually speaks of a bowl (*saph*) rather than a cup. It is possible that the author chose the word "bowl" in order to execute a wordplay. The Hebrew word *saph* also means "threshold." Just as the drink from a vessel could cause drunkenness and stumbling, a threshold could easily cause stumbling, because part of the threshold was raised above ground level. The threshold consisted of a large stone slab that featured sockets on each end into which the door pivots were fitted (though large gates would have separate sockets sunk in the ground). The door would close against the protruding threshold. This threshold slab could also be the immovable rock that is referred to in the next verse.

12:3. immovable rock. If the word translated "bowl" in the last verse is doing double duty as a reference to the threshold, then this would likely refer to the threshold slab. As an integral part of the gate structure, the threshold stone would probably be dislodged when the gates were destroyed. This would be a prime objective of a besieging army. Tearing down gates is mentioned in Neo-Babylonian texts, but the taking up of the threshold is not specifically referred to. A Sumerian lament over Eridu reports that the doorframe was ripped out. Akkadian texts describe the high grade of stone that is used and the function these slabs serve as a foundation for both gates and walls. When Sennacherib destroyed Babylon, he tore out the foundations of temples and walls and threw them into the canal. Temple thresholds were often inscribed with prayers for protection.

12:11. weeping of Hadad Rimmon. This name occurs nowhere else in the Old Testament, though each of the parts are known. Hadad was the name of the Canaanite storm god, the head of the Aramean pantheon, who was generally referred to by the title "Baal." A temple of Rimmon is referred to by Naaman in 2 Kings 5:18. Rimmon (or Ramman, "thunderer") is believed to be a title of this storm god Hadad. Though this association is confidently made, there has been no occurrence of this title outside the Bible. Though some interpreters have thought of mourning that took place at a location known as Hadad Rimmon, it is more likely that a reference is being made to a mourning festival or ritual connected to the deity Hadad Rimmon. When the expected rains did not come at their proper time, mourning for the storm god was one step taken to bring the rains needed for planting season.

12:11. plain of Megiddo. The plain of Megiddo is the Jezreel Valley. If mourning rites for a storm god are indicated here, the Jezreel Valley, the most fertile land in Israel, would be the likely site for the ritual. If Hadad Rimmon is a place in the Jezreel Valley, it may indicate the location of a devastating event. It was in the plain of Megiddo, for instance, that the promising and godly king Josiah lost his life attempting to stop the Egyptians from helping the floundering Assyrian empire in 609 B.C. (see comments on 2 Chron 35:20, 22). This loss was felt so deeply that a customary day of mourning was instituted (2 Chron 35:24-25).

12:12-13. historical significance of named clans. David and Levi are recognizable as the royal and priestly lines. Nathan and Shimei are more difficult in that there are numerous individuals in the Bible with those names. Since Nathan was one of the sons of David (2 Sam 5:14), and Shimei was one of the grandsons of Levi (Num 3:21), many see in these verses a reference to clans and subclans. Also of interest is the possibility that all of these clans had a relationship to Zerubbabel. He descended from David through Nathan and through Levi (Lk 3:29, 31), and Zerubbabel's brother is named Shimei (1 Chron 3:19).

13:1-9
Cleansing and Refining

13:4. prophet's garment of hair. The distinctive prophet's cloak was most likely made of animal skin and was hairy in appearance, though not all cloaks were so made. Very little is said about prophetic garb in the ancient Near East, so comparison is difficult. It may be of interest that Assyrian inscriptions beginning at this period portray a few individuals wearing lion-headed cloaks. These individuals seem to be involved in ritual activities (dance) and accompany deity. It is guessed that they may be exorcists.

13:6. wounds on prophet's body. Self-laceration is evident in 1 Kings 18:28 as part of a mourning ritual performed by the prophets of Baal. In the Ugaritic literature the gods are

portrayed as lacerating themselves when they hear of the death of Baal. Additionally an Akkadian wisdom text from Ugarit compares the blood-letting of mourning rites to that practiced by ecstatic prophets. Marks of self-flagellation would be indicative of practicing prophets.

14:1-21
The Lord Reigns

14:3. divine warrior. See comment on 9:14. The imagery of the deity standing on a mountain is well known in the ancient Near East (see comment on Mic 1:3), especially on cylinder seals. In these pictures the mountain is believed to represent the center of the earth.

14:4. Mount of Olives. The Mount of Olives is so named only here in the Old Testament. It is a ridge two and a half miles long running north and south just east across the Kidron Valley from Jerusalem.

14:4. splitting of Mount of Olives. In Akkadian literature leveling mountains is an act of destruction, but there is no reference to splitting mountains to provide for escape. The ascent up the Mount of Olives from the Kidron Valley is quite steep, so an east-west valley would certainly facilitate the refugees' flight.

14:5. Azel. There is no clear consensus regarding the location of Azel. In other verses it is only the name of a person in the genealogy of Saul. If the territory name is connected to the person, it would be located northwest of Jerusalem in the territory of Benjamin, but it is difficult to understand what is intended by having the valley extend there.

14:5. earthquake in Uzziah's days. Seismic activity in Syro-Palestine is a common occurrence. The region lies over the Jordan Rift, which stretches from Damascus to the Gulf of Aqabah, and is therefore subject to periodic shifts of the earth. There is evidence of a sizeable earthquake in the stratum 6 excavations at Hazor, dating to approximately 760. It is possible that this is the one referred to here, but additional corroborating evidence needs to be sought at other sites, especially Bethel and Samaria. The fact that this earthquake is used to date both Amos's prophetic activity and the reign of King Uzziah suggests that it must have been massive and therefore an event that would have stuck in the minds of the people.

14:7. cosmic effects. The cessation of markers of time signifies the most dramatic world-upside-down effect imaginable (see comment on Jer 4:23-26). It is accompanied by extensive topographical changes (vv. 8, 10) and by sweeping political developments (vv. 12-13), as well as by a redistribution of wealth (v. 14) and a reorientation of worship (v. 16).

14:8. Jerusalem as watershed with stream. "Living water" refers to flowing spring water (in contrast to collected runoff or rain water). In Jerusalem the source of water is the Gihon Spring on the southeastern flank of the city by the Kidron Valley. Although there are higher elevations south of Jerusalem (Bethlehem to Hebron), the land slopes away both in the west (through the Shephelah down to the Mediterranean coast) and in the east (down to Jericho, the Jordan Rift Valley and the Dead Sea). Many wadis in Israel contain water only during the rainy season (winter), but this verse speaks of a continuous flow. The Gihon Spring gushes daily throughout the year (see comment on 2 Sam 5:8).

14:10. Geba to Rimmon. Geba is located about five miles north of Jerusalem. It guards the Wadi Swenit near what was the northern border of the Persian province of Yehud. Rimmon is a little more difficult. There is a site known elsewhere as En-Rimmon on the southern end of the Shephelah (about ten miles north of Beersheba), but this would not have been in the territory of Yehud and appears too far south to be matched with Geba.

14:10. land like the Arabah. The term "Arabah" is capable of having both specific and general meanings. As a specific geographical designation it refers to the arid region around the Dead Sea and south to the Gulf of Aqaba. As a general topographical designation it refers to flat steppe land. The context of this verse demands the latter meaning.

14:10. Jerusalem topography. The Benjamin Gate (other times called the Sheep Gate), north of the Temple Mount, exits from the area of the Bethesda Pool (known in this period as the Sheep Pool) into the Kidron Valley. It is toward the northern side of the east wall (near the present day Lion's Gate) and would have led to the Jericho road. If First Gate is the name of a gate, it should probably be associated with the Old Gate (see comment on Neh 3:6). The Corner Gate is located on the northwest corner of the city's western expansion. It is in the vicinity of today's Jaffa Gate. The gates mentioned therefore span the city from east to west

along the northern walls. The Tower of Hananel was positioned on the northwest side of the city near the Temple Mount. This is about the same location as the Antonio Fortress in Herod's Jerusalem. Finally, the king's winepresses were probably in the area of the king's garden (see comment on Neh 3:15) at the southern end of the city. The winepresses combined with the Tower of Hananel span the city from north to south.

14:12. plague description. Among the most common treatments of prominent enemies in the ancient Near East were flaying the skin, putting out the eyes and cutting out the tongue. Here those are accomplished through "plague." These symptoms are unattested as connected to any particular plague in the ancient Near East.

14:16. feast of tabernacles as enthronement feast. Although an enthronement festival per se is unattested in Israelite practice, it is often assumed to have existed, and, if it did exist, it would most logically have been connected to the Feast of Tabernacles (see comments on 1 Kings 12:32-33 and Ezra 3:4). That would especially be significant in this context as the nations are expected to attend in order to acknowledge the kingship of Yahweh.

14:18. rain in Egypt. Egypt receives very little rain, and what it receives is not essential to its productivity. Agriculture in Egypt is dependent almost entirely on the annual flooding of the Nile.

14:20. bells of horses. When something is designated "Holy to the Lord" it is given sacred status as part of that which is purified for service within the sacred space of the temple precinct where Yahweh's presence dwelt. In Exodus 28:38 it was engraved on the golden plate worn by the high priest. Although priests wore bells on their garments (Ex 28:33), this is a different Hebrew word. The word used here may simply refer to metal disks that tinkled together.

14:20. cooking pots and sacred bowls. Sacred bowls would have been used for the most significant ritual activities such as transporting the blood of the sacrificed animals. Cooking pots, in contrast, were the most common of the temple vessels. Both could come in a variety of shapes and sizes.

MALACHI

1:3. Esau's mountains. "Esau's mountains" was most likely a designation for the hill country of Seir (Gen 36:8-9, 21), which was in the eastern Negev. The mountains of Seir are mentioned in Scripture (e.g., Gen 14:6, Deut 2:1). It was most likely a designation for the southern portion of the Edomite state, between the Wadi al-Ghuwayr and Ras en-Naqb.

1:4-5. Edom in the fifth century. Although Edom did not appear to join the rebellion against Babylonian rule in the sixth century B.C., the region appears to have been attacked by the last Babylonian monarch, Nabonidus. References in Obadiah, Jeremiah 49 and Ezekiel 25 refer to its destruction, but here in Malachi it implies that the territory was not as of yet abandoned by the Edomites. In the fifth century B.C., however, little is known of the fate of Edom. There appears to be some economic activity from Edom with the Levant and eastern Mediterranean, as well as evidence of new population groups in the area. The Qedarites appear to have belonged to the Syrian desert southeast of Damascus, raiding and migrating as far south as Moab and Edom. It is also possible that the Nabataeans, who conquered the area of Edom in the late third century B.C., may have begun to migrate north to this area from the Arabian desert.

1:8. offering defective animals. With the termination of funding from the Persian government (see comment on 3:10), various attempts were being made cut costs. Apparently one of them came in the form of relaxing the regulations concerning the animals that could be offered for sacrifices.

1:12. Lord's table. The phrase "the Lord's table" is found only here in the Old Testament. The term translated "table" is a common one used literally and figuratively to denote a table (e.g., Is 65:11). Tables were used in Ezekiel 40:39-43 at the gates of the inner court to slaughter sacrifices or for utensils. In the context of Malachi 1:12, the Lord's table appears to be synonymous with the altar, which has been defiled by the Israelites. It is figuratively described as a table because of the imagery of sacrifices being "food" for God. For discussion of this imagery see the comment on Leviticus 1:2.

2:5-7. role of postexilic priesthood. Over four thousand members of priestly and Levitical families returned to Palestine after the exile under the supervision of Zerubbabel and Joshua. Both groups engaged in a variety of activities, including the rebuilding of the walls of Jerusalem, instructing in the law and leading in the religious duties of the nation. However, the priestly cult must have deteriorated during this time (especially during Nehemiah's absence), since a foreigner (Tobiah the Ammonite) was allowed a room in the temple. In fact, the Levites had forsaken the temple for a time (Neh 13:10-11). Malachi 2 fits in this context, as the contemporary priesthood had abrogated its priestly responsibilities. The high priesthood continued to exist as an office, continuing in Zadok's line. The book of Zechariah indicates that many civil responsibilities exercised by the king or governor had been assigned to or simply absorbed by the priesthood so as to prevent the governor from competing with the authority of the Persian king.

2:11. marrying the daughter of a foreign god. Although the meaning is not entirely certain, the phrase "marrying the daughters of a foreign god" probably refers to mixed Jewish and non-Jewish marriages. The women who were married to Jewish men remained devoted to the service of their idols, and thus the Jews were brought into the family of foreign gods, making them liable to commit idolatry. These marriages were condemned by both Ezra and Nehemiah. For further information on the practice of endogamy (marrying within the group) see comment on Ezra 9:10-12.

2:14-16. marriage and divorce in fifth century. What is known of marriage and divorce in the Persian period comes from the Jewish documents from Elephantine. Marriage contracts often included stipulations concerning the disposition of the dowry, bride price, property and children in the event of a divorce. Divorce appears to have been common and uncomplicated with economic implications being of greatest concern. At Elephantine no reason for the divorce had to be offered.

3:1. preparatory role of the messenger. The idea of the preparation for the way of the Lord is also found in Isaiah 40:3. This concept probably comes from an ancient Near Eastern custom of sending messengers ahead of a visiting king to inform local inhabitants of his coming in order for them to pave the way (remove all obstacles) for the monarch.

3:2. launderer's soap. Launderer's soap was used to remove impurities and unclean elements from clothing and other items. The soap described here is the alkali that comes from the iceplant, which was found in Babylonia but not in Syro-Palestine. The term occurs elsewhere only in Jeremiah 2:22.

3:3. refiner and purifier of silver. In the ancient world silver was extracted and assayed through a process called cupellation. In the initial smelting process silver was extracted from lead ores (galena) containing less than 1 percent silver in a given sample. The lead was melted in shallow vessels made of porous substances such as bone ash or clay. A bellows was then used to blow air across the molten lead, producing lead oxide (litharge). Some of the lead oxide was absorbed by the bone ash, while some could be skimmed off the surface. Ideally, the silver would remain. Malachi might alternatively refer to the assaying process. This involved heating a sample of silver together with large amounts of lead in order to draw off the impurities.

3:5. sorcerers. The technical term here refers to those who were specialists in spells and incantations. These experts would have had familiarity with the literature for omens and dreams. They would have practiced sympathetic magic (based on the idea that there is an association between an object and that which it symbolizes; for example, that what is done to a person's picture will happen to the person) and would have used their arts to command the gods and spirits. Magic was the thread that held creation together. and it was used both defensively and offensively by its practitioners, human or divine.

3:8-10. tithes providing food. There is little difference in the ancient Near East between tithes and taxes. Both were exacted from villages as payment to the government and usually stored in temple complexes, from which the grain, oil and wine were then redistributed to maintain royal and religious officials. In collecting and redistributing the tithe, the distinction between sacred and secular is blurred. The tithe (literally, the "tenth part") mentioned here was a compulsory contribution for the maintenance of both the cult and the government of ancient Israel. It was also used among various other peoples in the ancient Near East, including the Phoenicians and Canaanites. Israel was commanded to tithe to God and to "eat before the Lord," probably a communal meal. It is unlikely that the one who is tithing is expected to eat the entire tithe. That would frustrate its purpose of providing for the priestly community and serving as a reserve for the destitute. The injunction probably has more to do with bringing the tithe (or its value in silver) to God's sanctuary in Jerusalem and thereby demonstrating devotion. See comment on Numbers 18:21-32 for further information.

3:10. shortfall in temple funds. The problem of appropriating for private use that which rightfully belonged to the temple was recognized early on in the ancient Near East. In a Sumerian prayer to Enki a worshiper denies that he has plundered the offerings of the deity. During the reign of Xerxes the funding of the temple by the Persian empire came to an end. This meant that there was a greater burden placed on the people to provide the support for all of the priests, the worship activities and the temple upkeep. This additional financial responsibility created what the people considered a hardship and led to rationalizations for cutting back temple spending.

3:16. scroll of remembrance. The expression "book of remembrance" is found only here in Scripture, although the idea of God having a book in which he recorded entries is found elsewhere (e.g., Ex 32:32; Ps 139:16; Is 4:3; 65:6; Ezek 13:9). Ancient Near Eastern kings often had a record written of the most important events in their reign (see comment on Esther 2:23). It was believed both in Israel and in the ancient Near East that deity kept books as well. In Exodus 32:32-34 Moses is willing to be blotted out of the book of life, an action that would result in his death. Yahweh replies that the one who sins is wiped out from the book. The metaphor is of a ledger that contains a list of the living. This is comparable to the book that contains the names of those destined for death that Enkidu sees in his dream of the netherworld. Mesopotamian literature contains references both to tablets recording evil deeds (in the *Shurpu* texts) and to tablets recording good deeds. See comment on Psalm 56:8.

4:2. sun of righteousness with healing in its wings. The sun of righteousness here is bringing justice. Throughout the ancient Near East solar deities are connected to justice. It is not unusual in the Old Testament for Yahweh's work to be depicted using this metaphor of solar terminology. "Healing in its wings" is a symbolic use of the wings of a bird with the rays of the sun. The wings denote protective care (hence the healing). An ancient Near Eastern motif in astral religions has the sun depicted as a winged disk. This is especially pervasive in the Persian period.

4:4. Horeb. Horeb was another name for Mount Sinai, the place where God revealed himself to Moses and gave him the Ten Commandments. Its precise location is uncertain, and there are at least four possible locations in the southern Sinai argued by scholars to be Mount Sinai: Jebel Musa, Ras es-safsafeh, Jebel Serbal and a mountain near al-Hrob. For discussion of the location see comment on Exodus 19:1-2.

GLOSSARY

Many terms that arise frequently in our discussions are explained in this glossary. To aid readers we have placed asterisks (*) throughout the text before terms that are found here. Not all terms will be found in exactly the same form here as in the text.

Adapa: a priest of the god Ea in the Sumerian city of Eridu. The story about him tells how he was tricked out of the opportunity to obtain immortality when he was advised not to eat divine food.

Ahiqar: an advisor to the Assyrian king Sennacherib (704-681 B.C.), who was exiled and wrote a set of teachings on "wise" and "foolish" men that parallels some of the saying in Proverbs.

Akkadian: term applied to Mesopotamian culture and language from about 2500 to 500 B.C.

Alalakh: a northern Syrian city in the southern part of the plain of Antioch that flourished in the early second millennium B.C. It produced numerous records that describe the politics and economy of the area, and it is mentioned in texts from Mari, Nuzi and the Hittite kingdom.

Amarna: see El-Amarna.

amulet: a carved ornament worn around the neck designed to ward off evil, cure disease or bring good luck to the owner.

Amorite/Amurru: a group of Semitic peoples who lived in an area west of Mesopotamia and including the Mediterranean seacoast during the second millennium B.C.

anachronism: a detail or word in a story that does not fit the time period of the story. Often anachronisms can be understood as clarifications or adjustments made to the text at a later time.

Anat: goddess of fertility and warfare, and principal consort of the god Baal in Canaanite and Ugaritic religion.

Anatolia: roughly equivalent to the area known in the New Testament as Asia Minor and today as Turkey. It was the home of the Hittites in the mid-second millennium.

annunciation: a birth announcement.

Apocrypha: books written in the Hellenistic period between the Testaments. These fourteen books were not part of the Jewish canon and are not included in the Protestant canon but are retained in the Catholic tradition.

apodictic law: a type of legal statement in the form of a command, without explanation.

apostasy: any action which allows or condones false worship.

apotropaic: an action taken or a symbol used to drive away evil.

Aqhat: the son of Danil. He is the hero of a Ugaritic epic in which he is portrayed as a mighty hunter and is murdered by the goddess Anat when he refuses to give her his bow. The story has parallels with the ancestral narratives and the book of Judges.

Aram: the northwestern half of Mesopotamia and the Mediterranean coast was the home of the Arameans in the late second and early first millennia B.C.

Asherah: Canaanite fertility goddess, consort of Baal, often associated with sacred groves or represented by sacred poles in the Bible.

Assyria: northern Mesopotamian area centered on the Tigris River. It has several periods of prominence, the most important being from 1000 to 612 B.C., when it conquered all of the Near East and produced a law code (Middle Assyrian Code) that parallels biblical law.

Astarte: a Canaanite and Phoenician goddess, consort of the god Baal, associated with fertility and known as the goddess of war.

Baal: Canaanite and Ugaritic god of storms and fertility.

Babylon: major Mesopotamian city located

at the closest conjunction of the Tigris and Euphrates Rivers, which dominated the history of that area during several periods.

Bronze Age: the era (divided into Early, Middle and Late periods) from approximately 3000 to 1200 B.C., characterized by bronze technology.

bulla: a clay stamp used to seal a papyrus document. The seal impression prevented tampering and also provided the name or the rank of the official who wrote the document.

casuistic law: a form of legal statement based on an "if-then" structure.

Chalcolithic Age: the era from 4300 to 3000 B.C., characterized by use of copper technology.

Chaldean: period of Mesopotamian history from approximately 700 to 540 B.C. and associated with the Neo-Babylonians and King Nebuchadnezzar.

Chemosh: Moabite national god, often associated with war.

circumcision: the religious ritual of removing the foreskin from the penis. It was employed by the Israelites to mark them as members of the covenant community.

cognate: languages that are part of the Semitic family and share vocabulary and numerous grammatical features with Hebrew. The principal cognate languages are Akkadian, Aramaic and Ugaritic. Among several other less significant cognates are Arabic, Moabite, Ammonite, Amorite, Ethiopic and Syriac. The literature written in these languages is referred to as cognate literature.

colophon: a statement or phrase placed at the end of a document, or a literary segment that may serve as a summary or simply as an end marker.

concubine: a secondary wife, who may have come to the marriage without a dowry and whose children may not inherit from their father unless he publicly declares them as his heirs.

corporate identity: a group is treated as a single unit. Reflected in a legal principle that rewards or punishes an entire household for the righteousness or the sins of the head of the household.

covenant: a contractual agreement associated in the Bible with the agreement between Yahweh and the Israelites that promises land and children in exchange for exclusive worship and obedience.

cult: the organization and activities of a religious group, including sacrifice and other rituals.

cuneiform: the wedge-shaped syllabic script invented by the Sumerians and used by every subsequent civilization in Mesopotamia until the coming of the Greeks.

demotic: a shorthand version, dating back to 700 B.C., of the Egyptian language known as hieratic, a more practical cursive script than its precursor, pictographic hieroglyphics.

divination: a process of determining the will of the god(s) through the examination of natural phenomena (cloud formations, the entrails of sheep) or by casting lots.

Dumuzi/Tammuz: a Mesopotamian god, consort of the goddess Ishtar, whose death and incarceration in the underworld represented the changes of the seasons.

Ea: Mesopotamian god of rivers and streams who figures in the flood story of the Gilgamesh Epic and in the Babylonian creation story, *Enuma Elish*.

Early Bronze Age: the era from approximately 3300 to 2300 B.C., characterized by the emergence of cities, the high civilization of Early Dynastic Egypt and Sumer, as well as bronze technology.

El: the high god in the Ugaritic pantheon and also a generic term for a god. It would be added to a place name (i.e., Bethel or El Elohe-Israel) to distinguish it as a place where a god has made his power manifest.

El Amarna: the capital of Pharaoh Akhenaten (fourteenth century B.C.) in which archaeologists have discovered hundreds of royal dispatches describing rather chaotic events in Canaan during this period.

Elam: country to the east of the Tigris River in modern Iran.

Elohim: one of the names for the Israelite god, generally translated as "God" in English but occasionally used for other gods or supernatural beings.

Emar: a Bronze Age city (Tell Meskene/Balis) located on the northern reaches of the Euphrates River in Syria. Texts found here from the Late Bronze period provide insights into daily life during the fourteenth through the twelfth centuries B.C.

Enlil: Mesopotamian storm god, the head of the divine assembly and instigator of the flood in the Gilgamesh Epic.

Enuma Elish: the Babylonian creation story.

Eshnunna: Mesopotamian city in the Diyala region east of modern Baghdad that produced a short-lived kingdom between 2100 and 2000 B.C. and a law code that contains some parallels to Hammurabi's Code and biblical law.

Etana: ancient Mesopotamian king, the subject of a legend in which he obtains a plant from heaven that provides fertility and thus is able to father a son to continue his rule. His flight to heaven is on the back of an eagle and thus he is depicted on ancient seals.

etiology: story that attempts to explain the origin of a name, a custom or a current reality, such as death or painful childbirth.

execration: a method of cursing an enemy by fashioning a doll or an incantation bowl containing the name of the accursed party.

exorcism: a ritual, including spells and incantations, designed to cast out or remove demons from persons or places.

fertility worship: a dominant religious practice in much of the ancient world. The principal gods were paired as male and female, and their rites were designed to insure plentiful rain, plant growth and bountiful harvests and herds. This worship could include sacrifices as well as sacred prostitution. In a society dominated by farming and herding, fertility is of utmost importance.

funerary: rituals and objects involved with the internment of the dead. Funerary rites were also part of a larger system of ancestor worship.

Gilgamesh: Sumerian king of Uruk who is the prototypical hero of Mesopotamian literature. His epic contains a quest for the secret of immortality and a flood story.

glyptic: a type of engraved art featured especially on seals where the design is engraved in reverse so that its impression on clay or wax will be embossed and upright.

Habiru: a term used in Mesopotamian texts for stateless persons.

Hammurabi: Babylonian king (1792-1750 B.C.) who compiled a law code containing a number of parallels with biblical law.

henotheism: a religion that acknowledges the existence of other gods but often insists on the supremacy of one's own god.

herem: "holy war" or the "ban" which requires the complete destruction of all persons, animals and property as a dedicatory sacrifice to Yahweh.

Herodotus: a Greek historian who lived in the fifth century B.C. He is best known for his *Histories* (ca. 445 B.C.), which document the history of the Persian Wars against the Greeks, such as the battles at Marathon, Thermopylae and Salamis.

Hesiod: a Greek philosopher from the eight century B.C. His major work was the *Theogony,* the earliest known Greek account of creation and the origins of the gods.

hieroglyphic: the pictographic, syllabic script developed by the ancient Egyptians.

Hittites: an Indo-European people who migrated into Anatolia after 2000 B.C. and created an empire that challenged Egypt for control of Syro-Palestine during the mid-second millennium. They also produced a law code with parallels to biblical law.

Hurrian: a non-Semitic people who created a kingdom in Mitanni, central Mesopotamia, during the mid-second millennium.

iconography: pictoral, rather than verbal, messages inscribed on ancient artifacts. These images include three-dimensional objects, reliefs, paintings, seals and even graffiti. As visuals, they are an important source of information that complement the textual data.

in situ: a term applied to the resting place or "find spot" of an artifact that has been uncovered and recorded by archaeologists.

Iron Age: the era in ancient Near Eastern history from 1200 to 300 B.C. characterized by the use of iron technology.

Ishtar: Mesopotamian goddess of love, the consort of Dumuzi, who appears in Gilgamesh's flood story.

Josephus: Jewish historian from the first century A.D. His two great works, *Antiquities of the Jews* and *Jewish Wars,* offer a detailed look at Jewish perspectives on their times and their history.

Kassites: a people originally from the mountainous region in northern Mesopotamia who conquered the Old Babylonian kingdom about 1595 B.C. and ruled in Babylon until 1157 B.C.

Keret: the king hero of a Ugaritic tale in which he receives instructions from the gods concerning how to acquire a wife and an heir to his throne. This family crisis is only one of a series that includes illness and rebellion by one of his sons.

Lagash: third-millennium Sumerian city-state (el-Hiba) containing several urban centers, which contested for control of the region with Ur, Uruk and Kish.

Larsa: early second-millennium Sumerian city, ten miles east of Uruk and twenty miles north of Ur.

Late Bronze Age: the chronological era from 1550 to 1200 B.C., which is marked by the Amarna age and New Kingdom in Egypt, the Hittite empire in Anatolia and the invasion of the Sea Peoples.

Levant: the area of the eastern Mediterranean. Also referred to as Syro-Palestine.

Lipit-Ishtar: king of the Ur III dynasty in Mesopotamia who produced a law code that parallels some aspects of biblical law.

Marduk: principal god of Babylon who defeats Tiamat in the creation story *Enuma Elish* and becomes the head of the divine assembly.

Mari: Mesopotamian city on the northern reaches of the Euphrates River that thrived from 2500 to 1700 B.C. and produced thousands of cuneiform documents describing political events, prophetic activity and the pastoral nomadic peoples of northern Syria.

Middle Bronze Age: the chronological era from 2300 to 1550 B.C., which includes the period of Israel's ancestors, the Old Babylonian period and Egyptian control of Syro-Palestine.

Mitanni: the kingdom of the Hurrians in central Mesopotamia during the mid-second millennium B.C.

monolatry: a situation where a person or group has determined to worship only one God regardless of whether other gods exist or not.

Nazirite: an Israelite (either male or female) who takes an oath to refrain from consuming any product of the grape, from coming in contact with the dead and from cutting his or her hair.

Nineveh: the capital of the Assyrian empire on the upper reaches of the Tigris River.

Nuzi: a Hurrian city of the sixteenth and fifteenth centuries B.C. that has provided family and business documents documenting marriage and inheritance customs similar to those in the ancestral stories.

Old Babylonian: a period of Mesopotamian history from 2025 to 1595 B.C. highlighted by the reign of Hammurabi (1792-1750 B.C.), who produced a law code and united all of the city-states under his rule.

oracle: a prophetic speech or a reading of divine will through the use of divination.

Osiris: the Egyptian god of the underworld.

pollution (uncleanness): ritual impurity is caused by contact with or consumption of polluted items, such as blood, and can only be removed through ritual acts designed to take away the person's impurity and transform him or her from an unclean to a clean state.

pseudepigraphic: literature produced under the persona of a respected and well-known individual. Old Testament pseudepigraphal works are attributed to people such as Enoch and Ezra, and date to the intertestamental period or later.

ritual acts: a prescribed set of actions taken for religious purposes, such as a sacrifice.

ritual prostitution: the practice of sexual acts as part of a religious ceremony, to promote fertility or to enrich a sanctuary.

Sea Peoples: a mixed group of peoples from throughout the Mediterranean area who served as mercenaries in the Egyptian and Hittite armies until about 1200 B.C. when they made a collective attack on the major civilizations of the Near East and disrupted them enough to allow for the emergence of new peoples in Canaan.

Sinuhe: an official of Pharaoh Amenemhat I (1991-1962 B.C.) who was exiled in Canaan for many years before being pardoned and allowed to return to Egypt. His story contains some parallels to that of the ancestors in Genesis as well as the story of Moses.

Sumer: the southernmost area of ancient Mesopotamia. It produced the first true civilization in that region about 3500 B.C., invented cuneiform script and created many of the myths that sustained religion for the next several millennia.

sympathetic magic: the ritualistic representation of reality in an object. A person's name, hair or blood may be used, or images may be made of the person or thing to be affected. The idea is for the person's essence to be linked or transferred to the representative object.

syncretism: the borrowing of cultural ideas, practices, and beliefs and combining them with one's own.

tell: an artificial hill that has been created by the successive layers of settlements on that site.

theophany: the appearance of God to a human being, as in the "burning bush."

theophoric: personal names that contain a reference to a named deity. Theophoric names such as Isaiah, Ezekiel, Jerubbaal and Nebuchadnezzar often make statements about the deity.

Thoth: the Egyptian moon god.

Tiamat: primordial Mesopotamian goddess of salt water, the consort of Apsu, god of fresh water. She is Marduk's opponent in the creation story *Enuma Elish.*

Ugarit: northern Syrian seaport city that controlled the Mediterranean carrying trade from approximately 1600 to 1200 B.C., when it was destroyed by the Sea Peoples. Several Ugaritic epic stories have been discovered that help illumine biblical stories from the ancestral and settlement periods. Ugaritic culture is thought to have approximated Canaanite culture.

Ur III: the period of Mesopotamian history from 2120 to 1800 B.C. founded by Ur-Nammu, centered in the city of Ur and characterized by a brief revival of Sumerian culture.

Ur-Nammu: Ur III king, father of Shulgi, who produced a law code that has some parallels with biblical law.

Uruk: third- and early second-millennium Sumerian city ruled by Gilgamesh.

Utnapishtim: hero of the flood story in the Gilgamesh Epic.

Wenamon: a priest of the Egyptian god Amon (c. 1100 B.C.), sent as an envoy to obtain logs for the royal barge from the rulers of Syria and the Phoenician coast. His mission was delayed by the weak stature of Egypt at that time and the chaotic political conditions following the invasion of the Sea Peoples.

Xenophon: Greek historian writing early in the fourth century B.C. His most famous historical work, *Anabasis,* focuses on the battle between Cyrus the Younger and Artaxerxes II.

Yahweh: one of the names for the Israelite God, sometimes anglicized as Jehovah and translated in English as "LORD."

Major Tablets of Old Testament Significance

NAME	NUMBER OF TABLETS	LANGUAGE	DIS-COVERER	LOCATION FOUND	DATE FOUND	SUBJECT	DATE OF ORIGIN	BIBLICAL SIGNIFI-CANCE
Ebla	17,000	Eblaite	Matthiae	Tell-Mardikh	1976	Royal archives containing many types of texts	24th c.	Provide historical background of Syria in late 3rd millennium
Atrahasis	3	Akkadian	Many found different parts	different parts in different sites	1889 to 1967	Account of creation, population growth and flood	1635 copy	Parallels to Genesis accounts
Mari	20,000	Akkadian (Old Babylonian)	Parrot	Tell-Hariri	1933	Royal archives of Zimri-Lim containing many types of texts	18th c.	Provide historical background of the period and largest collection of prophetic texts
Enuma Elish	7	Akkadian (Neo-Assyrian)	Layard	Nineveh (library of Ashurban-ipal)	1848-1876	Account of Marduk's ascension to the head of the pantheon	7th c. copy	Parallels to Genesis creation accounts
Gilga-mesh	12	Akkadian (Neo-Assyrian)	Rassam	Nineveh (library of Ashurban-ipal)	1853	The exploits of Gilga-mesh and Enkidu and the search for immor-tality	7th c. copy	Parallels to Genesis flood accounts
Boghaz-Köy	10,000	Hittite	Winckler	Boghaz-Köy	1906	Royal archives of Neo-Hittite Empire	16th c.	Hittite history and il-lustrations of inter-national treaties
Nuzi	4000	Hurrian dialect of Akkadian	Chiera and Speiser	Yorghun Tepe	1925 to 1941	Archive containing family records	15th c.	Source for contempo-rary cus-toms in mid-2nd millennium
Ugarit	1400	Ugaritic	Schaeffer	Ras Shamra	1929 to 1937	Royal archives of Ugarit	13th c.	Canaanite religion and literature
Amarna	380	Akkadian (W Semitic dialect)	Egyptian peasant	Tell el-Amarna	1887	Correspon-dence between Egypt and her vassals in Canaan	1370 to 1340	Reflects conditions in Palestine in the mid-2nd millen-nium
Baby-lonian Chron-icles	4	Akkadian (Neo-Babylo-nian)	Wiseman	Babylon	1956	Court re-cords of Neo-Babylonian Empire	626 to 594	Record of capture of Jerusalem in 597 and history of the period
Emar	800	Akkadian	Margueron	Tell-Meskene	1975	Royal Temple and family archives	13th c.	family cus-toms; religi-ous rituals
Alalakh	500	Akkadian	Woolley	Tell-Atchana	1939	Royal Temple archive; Statute of Idrimi	18th-17th c.	Treaties and contracts of-fer cultural background

Major Inscriptions of Old Testament Significance

NAME	LANGUAGE	DISCOVERER	LOCATION FOUND	DATE FOUND	SUBJECT	DATE OF ORIGIN (B.C.)	BIBLICAL SIGNIFI-CANCE
Beni Hasan Tomb Painting	Hiero-glyphic Egyptian	Newberry	Beni Hasan	1900	Tomb painting of Khnumhotep II	1920	Pictures Semites in Egypt
Laws of Hammurabi	Akkadian (Old Babylonian)	deMorgan	Susa	1901	Collection of Babylonian laws	1725	Illustrates ancient Near Eastern law
Merenptah Stela	Hiero-glyphic Egyptian	Petrie	Thebes	1896	Military accomplish-ments of Merenptah	1207	First men-tion of the name "Israel"
Sheshonq Inscription	Hiero-glyphic Egyptian		Karnak Temple	1825	Military accomplish-ments of Sheshonq	920	Confirma-tion of raid against Rehoboam
"House of David" Inscription	Aramaic	Biran	Dan	1993	Syrian con-quest of region	9th c.	Earliest men-tion of David in contempo-rary records
Mesha Inscription	Moabite	Klein	Dibon	1868	Military ac-complish-ments of Mesha of Moab	850	Moabite-Israelite relations in 9th century
Black Stela	Akkadian (Neo-Assyrian)	Layard	Nineveh	1845	Military accomplish-ments of Shalmaneser III	840	Picture Israelites paying tribute
Balaam Texts	Aramaic	Franken	Deir Alla (Succoth)	1967	Prophecy of Balaam about the displeas-ure of the di-vine council	8th c.	Connected to a famous seer known from the Bible
Silver Scrolls	Hebrew	Barkay	Hinnom Valley Tomb	1979	Amulet con-taining the text of Num 6:24-26	7th c.	Earliest copy of any portion of the Bible
Siloam Inscription	Hebrew	Peasant boy	Jerusalem	1880	Commemo-ration of the completion of Hezekiah's water tunnel	701	Contempo-rary example of Hebrew language
Sennach-erib Prism	Akkadian (Neo-Assyrian)	Taylor	Nineveh	1830	Military accomplish-ments of Sennacherib	686	Describes siege of Jerusalem
Lachish Ostraca	Hebrew	Starkey	Tell ed-Duweir	1935	18 letters from the captain of the fort of Lachish	588	Conditions during the final Baby-lonian siege
Cyrus Cylinder	Akkadian	Rassam	Babylon	1879	Decree of Cyrus allow-ing the re-building of temples	535	Illustrates the policy by which Judah also benefited

Legal Texts of the Ancient Near East

	NAME	CENTURY B.C.	DESCRIPTION
SUMERIAN	Reform of Uruinimgina (King of Lagash)	24th Early Dynastic III	Social reform
	Laws of Ur-Nammu (King of Ur)	21st (Ur III)	About 31 laws remain. Fragmented
	Laws of Lipit-Ishtar (King of Isin)	19th (Isin- Larsa)	Parts of 38 laws with prologue and epilogue: civil law only
AKKADIAN	Laws of Eshnunna	18th (Old Baby- lonian)	60 paragraphs civil and criminal law
	Laws of Hammurabi (King of Babylon)	18th (Old Baby- lonian)	282 laws remaining (35-40 erased) plus prologue and epilogue
	Middle Assyrian laws (Tiglath-Pileser I?)	12th (Middle Assyrian)	About 100 laws on 11 tablets civil and criminal law
HITTITE	Hittite laws (Murshilish I or Hattushilish I)	17th (Old Hittite)	About 200 laws civil and criminal law

Ancient Near Eastern Literature
Containing Parallels to the Old Testament

LITERARY WORK	LANGUAGE	DATE	OT BOOK	NATURE OF PARALLEL
Atrahasis Epic	Akkadian	~1635	Genesis	Creation, population growth and flood with ark
Enuma Elish	Akkadian	~1100	Genesis	Account of creation
Gilgamesh Epic	Sumerian Akkadian	~2000	Genesis	Account of the flood complete with ark and birds
Memphite Theology	Egyptian	~13th c.	Genesis	Creation by spoken word
Hammurabi's Laws	Akkadian	~1750	Exodus	Laws similar to those given at Sinai in form and content
Hymn to the Aten	Egyptian	~1375	Psalm 104	Wording used in motifs and analogies; subject matter
Ludlul bel Nemeqi	Akkadian	~13th c.	Job	Sufferer questions justice of deity
Babylonian Theodicy	Akkadian	~1000	Job	Dialogue between sufferer and friend concerning the justice of deity
Instruction of Amenemope	Egyptian	~1200	Proverbs 22:17—24:22	Vocabulary, imagery, subject matter, structure
Hittite Treaties (36)	Hittite	2nd m.	Deuteronomy; Joshua 24	Format and content
Lamentations over the fall of Sumerian Cities (5)	Sumerian	20th c.	Lamentations	Phrasing, imagery and subject matter
Egyptian Love Songs (54)	Egyptian	1300-1150	Song of Solomon	Content and literary categories employed
Mari Prophecy Texts (~50)	Akkadian	18th c.	Preclassical Prophecy	Addressed similar subjects (military undertakings and cultic activity)

Comparative Ancient Near Eastern Chronology 10,000-2100 B.C.

Anatolia/Syria	Mesopotamia		Palestine	Egypt
A **N** **C** **I** **E** **N** **T** **H** **A** **T** **T** **I**		10000 ———	Mesolithic: Natufian	
		8000 ———	Neolithic Pre-pottery	
	Jarmo	5000 ———		
	Hassuna Samarra Halaf		Neolithic Pottery Period	
		——— 4300	———	Predynastic Preiod:
	Ubaid (4300-3500)		Chalcolithic: Ghassulian	Fayyum A, Deir Tasa Badarian,
	South: North: Uruk Tepe (3500-3100) Gawra (3500-2900)	3300	———	Amratian Gerzean
	Pro-literate Jemdet Nasr (3100-2900)	3000	Early Bronze I	
		——— 2900	———	
	Early Dynastic I	2800		Protodynastic Period:
	————		Early Bronze II	Dynasties I and II (3000-2700)
		2700		
	Early Dynastic II			
	———	2600 ———		
	Early Dynastic III	2530	Early Bronze III	Old Kingdom Pyramid Age Dynasties III-V (2700-2350)
	———	2400		
	Akkadian Period	2300 ———		Dynasty VI (2350-2160)
	———		Early	
	Gutian Period: Dynasty of Lagash	2200	Bronze IV	First Intermediate Period (2160-2010)
	———	2100 ———		

Comparative Ancient Near Eastern Chronology 2100-332 B.C.

Anatolia/Syria	Mesopotamia		Palestine	Egypt
		——— 2100 ———		
	Ur III Dynasty		Middle	
		——— 2000	Bronze I	
	Isin-Larsa		Patriarchs	Middle Kingdom: Dynasties XI-XII (2106-1786)
		——— 1900 ———		
	Elam-Amorite Invasions		Middle Bronze	
		——— 1800	IIA sojourn	
Old Hittite Empire (1800-1600)	Old Babylonian Period:	1700		Second Intermediate Period: Hyksos (1786-1550)
	Age of Hammurabi		Middle Bronze IIB & C Sojourn	
		——— 1600		
		1500	Late Bronze I	
Mitanni-Hurrian Empire (1500-1350)			Exodus and Conquest	New Kingdom (1550-1069): Dynasty XVIII (1550-1295)
	Kassite Period	1400 ———		
Neo-Hittite Empire (1460-1200)		1300	Late Bronze II Judges to Deborah	
				Dynasty XIX Empire Age (1295-1186)
		——— 1200 ———		
Neo-Hittites of North Syria Through Eighth Century	Assyrian rise to power		Iron I	
		1100	Judges and United	
		1000	Monarchy	Dynasty XX (1186-1069)
		——— 900		Dynasty XXI (1069-945)
Syrian Strength till Fall of Damascus (732)	Assyrian Empire	800	Iron II Divided Monarchy	
		700		Late Period: Dynasties XXII-XXVI (945-525)
	Neo-Babylonian Empire	600		

PERSIAN CONTROL (539-332)

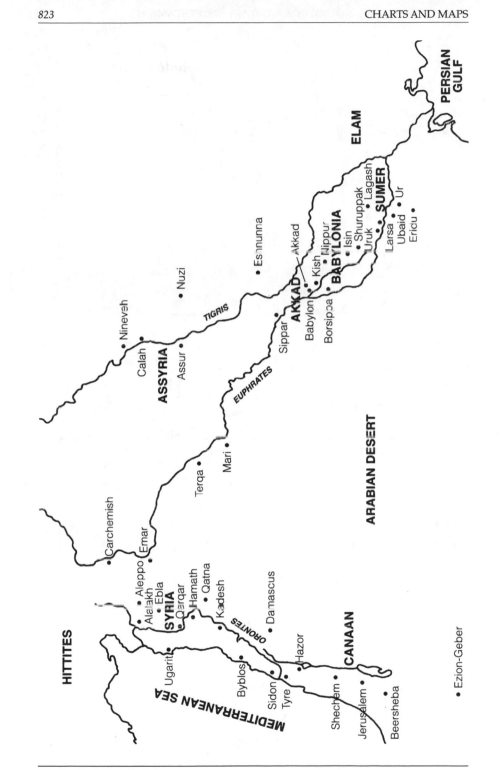

The Ancient Near East

Assyrian Empire c. 640 B.C.

Assyrian Empire c. 824 B.C.

Assyrian Empire

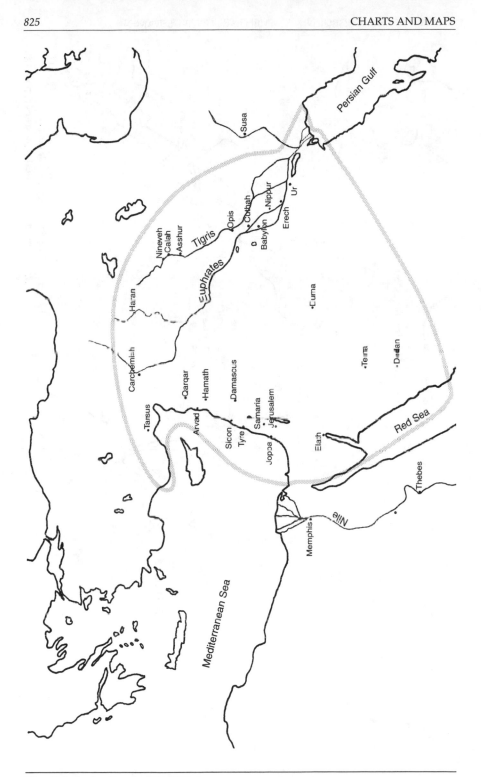

New Babylonian Empire 625-529 B.C.

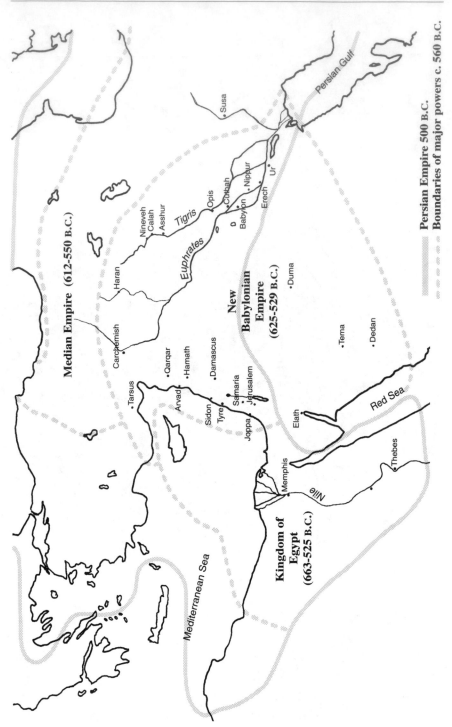

Persian Empire and Major Empires of the 6th Century B.C.

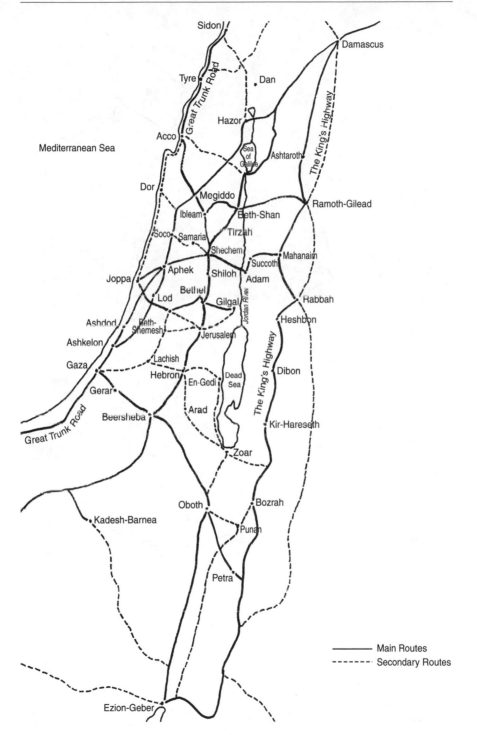

Roads of Palestine

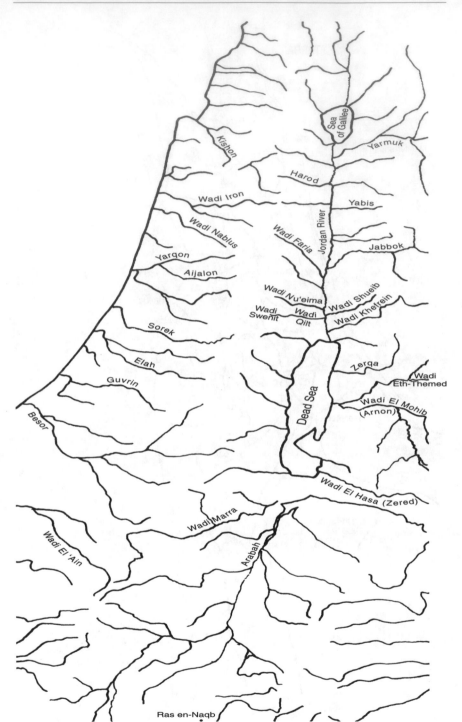

Rivers and Wadis of Palestine

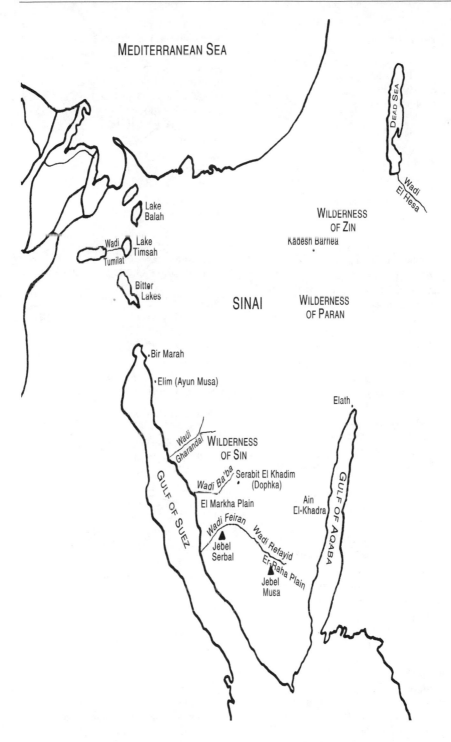

Rivers and Wadis of Egypt and Sinai

Topical Index

1. . . . in the Ancient Near East

afterlife beliefs, Is 14
arbitrator, Job 9:33
astral worship, Deut 4:19
blessings, Num 6:24-26
boundary lists, Josh 13:1
conquest narratives, Josh 10:16-43
consulting the dead, 1 Sam 28:8-11
cosmic control, Job 9:5-9
council of the gods, Is 40:13-14
creation of people, Gen 1:26-31
death, preference for, Job 7:15-16
dietary restrictions, Lev 11:2
divorce, Deut 22:29
drunkenness, Is 28:7
eclipses, Joel 2:31
election before birth, Jer 1:5
endowed with divine spirit, Is 11:2
festivals and holy days, Num 28:1-30
financial systems, Deut 15:1-11
firstfruit offering, Deut 26:1-15
foretelling by dreams, Deut 13:1-5
idols, Jer 10:5
incubation dreams, 1 Sam 3:3
individual responsibility, Ezek 18:20
judges bribed, Is 5:23
judicial structures, Deut 1:16
king chosen by deity, Deut 17:14-20
kingship, 1 Sam 8:6
laments, Lamentations sidebar; Ezek 19:1
life expectancy, Deut 31:2; Ps 90:10;
　Is 40:6-7
mining, Job 28:11
monotheism, Deut 6:4
omnipresence, divine, Ps 139:8-12
omniscience, divine, Ps 139:2-4
oppressive laws, Is 10:1
parables and allegories, Is 5:1-2
pathology, Deut 28:22

persuasive oration, 1 Sam 25:23-31
physicians' methods, Job 13:4
prophecy, Deut 18:14-22; Jonah 3:4
punishment, divine, Deut 32:23-25
refuge, cities of, Deut 19:2-3
refugees, Jer 40:11-12
resurrection, Is 26:19; Dan 12:2
road building, Is 40:3-4
sabbath, Is 58:13
sages, Prov 1:1
shepherd king, Ezek 34:7-16
slave laws, Ex 21:2-6
slave trade, Deut 24:7
spies, Josh 2:2
substitutionary rites, Is 53:4-10
temple ideology, 2 Chron 7:16
temple restoration, 2 Chron 24:4
tithing, Num 18:21-32
traditional instruction, Job 8:8-10
treaty curses and blessings, Deut 28:2-11
trial by ordeal, Num 5:23-24
usury, Ezek 18:8
verdict by omen, Deut 17:8-13
winged guardians, Ezek 1:5
wisdom, source of, Job 28:20-27

2. Material Culture

amulets, Deut 6:8
chariots, 2 Sam 8:4
fortifications, Is 2:15
gates and bars, Deut 3:5; Judg 16:3
grinding mill, Judg 16:21
house architecture, Josh 2:6; 6:1
iron, 1 Sam 13:19-20
loom weaving, Judg 16:13-14
metallurgy, Is 1:22
musical instruments, Gen 4:21; 1 Sam 10:5;
　2 Sam 6:5; 2 Chron 20:28; Ps 150; Dan 3:5
seals, Neh 9:38; Jer 32
shofar, Ex 19:13
siege ramps, Jer 6:6; 32:24
temple architecture, Judg 16:29
trumpets for signaling, Num 31:6; Josh
　6:4-5
writing, Ex 24:4

3. People Groups

Amalekites, Gen 36:12; Num 24:20
Ammonites, Deut 2:19
Amorites, Num 21:21; Deut 1:19
Arabians, Is 21:13

221.7
W239
c.2

LINCOLN CHRISTIAN COLLEGE AND SEMINARY

99799

3 4711 00153 7341